ESSENTIAL ROAD ATLAS
BRITAIN
AND NORTHERN IRELAND

Collins

Published by Collins
An imprint of HarperCollins Publishers
Westerhill Road, Bishopbriggs,
Glasgow G64 2QT

www.harpercollins.co.uk

Copyright © HarperCollins Publishers Ltd 2019
Collins® is a registered trademark of HarperCollins Publishers Limited

Mapping generated from CollinsBartholomew digital databases

Contains Ordnance Survey data © Crown copyright and database right (2019)

The grid on this map is the National Grid taken from the Ordnance Survey map with the permission of the Controller of Her Majesty's Stationery Office.

Printed in China by RR Donnelley APS Co Ltd

ISBN 9780008318703   10 9 8 7 6 5 4 3 2 1

e-mail: roadcheck@harpercollins.co.uk   facebook.com/collinsref   @collins_ref

© Natural England copyright. Contains Ordnance Survey data © Crown copyright and database right (2015)

Information for the alignment of the Wales Coast Path provided by © Natural Resources Wales. All rights reserved. Contains Ordnance Survey Data. Ordnance Survey Licence number 100019741. Crown Copyright and Database Right (2013).

Information for the alignment of several Long Distance Trails in Scotland provided by © walkhighlands

Information on fixed speed camera locations provided by PocketGPSWorld.com

With thanks to the Wine Guild of the United Kingdom for help with researching vineyards.

For the latest information on Blue Flag award beaches visit www.blueflag.global

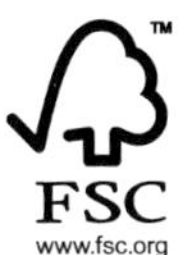

Contents

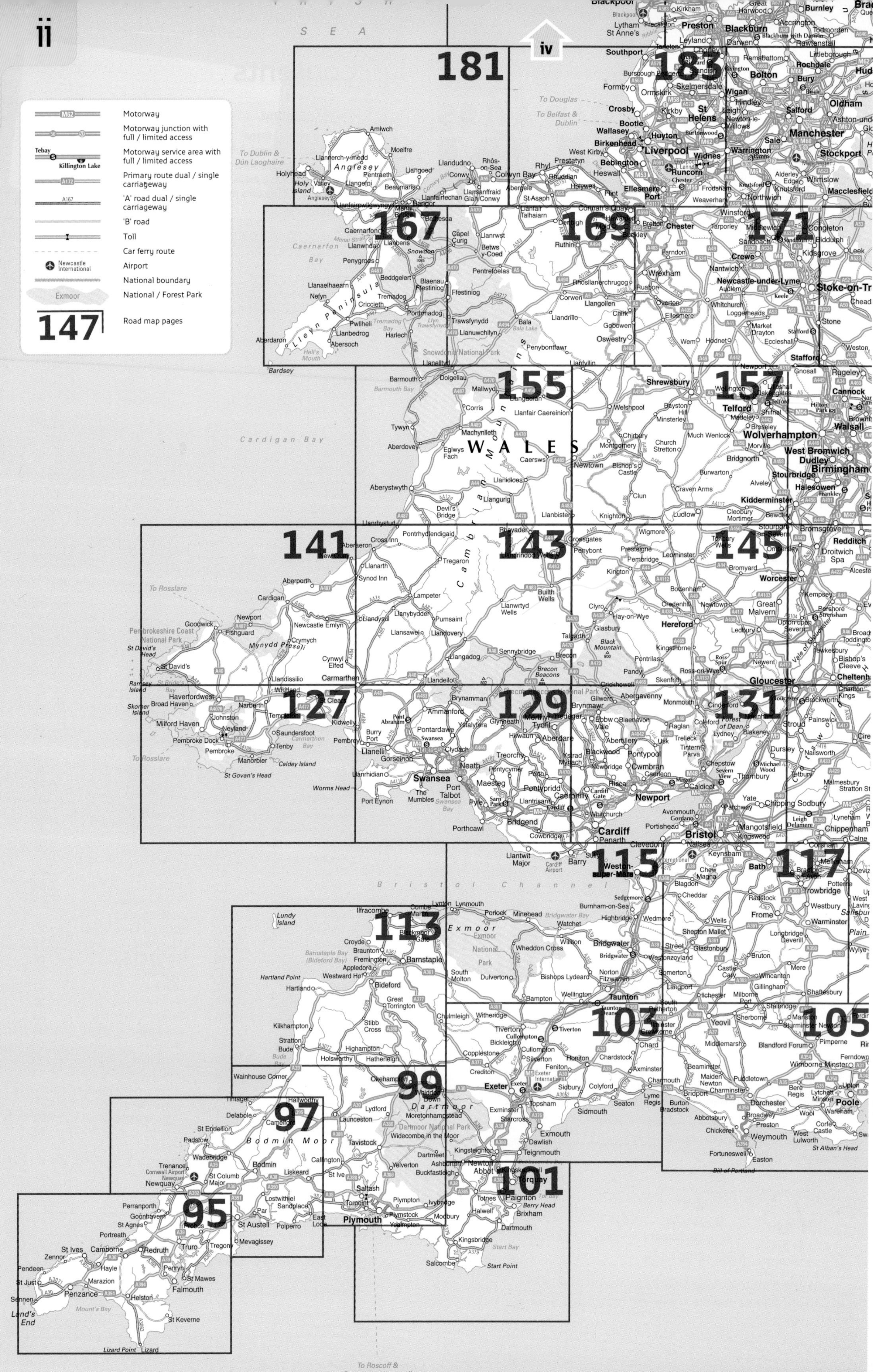
Motorway
Motorway junction with full / limited access
Tebay
Killington Lake
Motorway service area with full / limited access
Primary route dual / single carriageway
'A' road dual / single carriageway
'B' road
Toll
Car ferry route
Newcastle International
Airport
National boundary
Exmoor
National / Forest Park
147
Road map pages
iv
181
183
167
169
171
155
157
141
143
145
127
129
131
115
117
113
103
105
99
97
101
95
WALES
Cardigan Bay
Caernarfon Bay
Bristol Channel
Anglesey
Lleyn Peninsula
Snowdonia National Park
Cambrian Mountains
Pembrokeshire Coast National Park
Brecon Beacons National Park
Exmoor National Park
Dartmoor National Park
Bodmin Moor
To Dublin & Dún Laoghaire
To Douglas
To Belfast & Dublin
To Rosslare
To Roscoff & Santander (seasonal)
Liverpool
Manchester
Birmingham
Wolverhampton
Cardiff
Swansea
Newport
Bristol
Exeter
Plymouth
Taunton
Gloucester
Hereford
Worcester
Shrewsbury
Chester
Land's End
Lizard Point

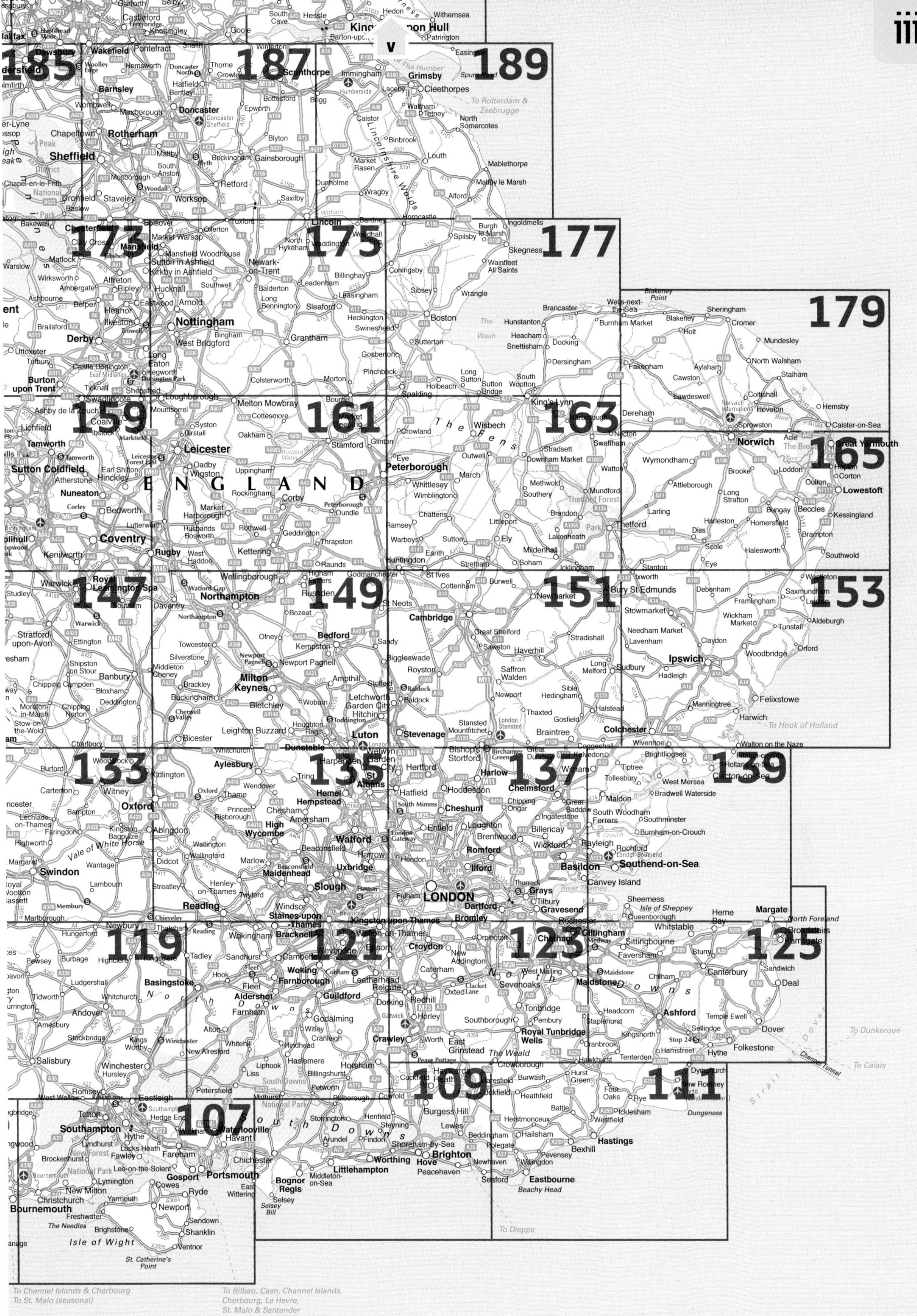

SCALE 1:1,478,872

| 0 | 10 | 20 | 30 | 40 miles |

| 0 | 10 | 20 | 30 | 40 | 50 | 60 kilometres |

23 miles to 1 inch / 15 km to 1 cm

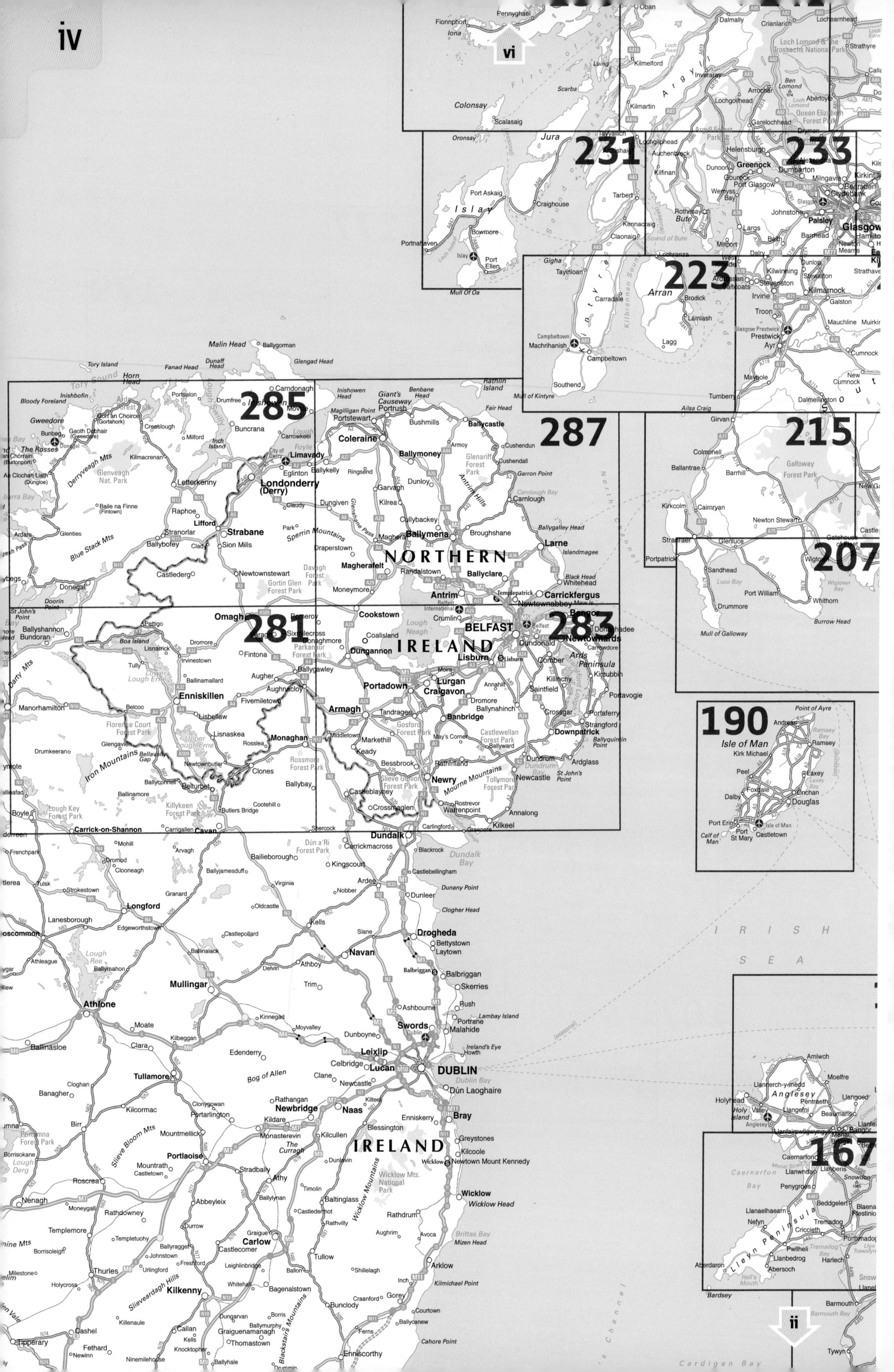

vi
231
233
223
285
287
215
281
283
207
190
167
ii
Colonsay
Jura
Islay
Arran
Isle of Man
NORTHERN
IRELAND
IRELAND
IRISH
SEA
Malin Head
Londonderry
(Derry)
Coleraine
Ballymoney
Ballymena
Larne
Carrickfergus
Antrim
BELFAST
Bangor
Newtownards
Lisburn
Lurgan
Craigavon
Portadown
Armagh
Dungannon
Cookstown
Magherafelt
Omagh
Enniskillen
Strabane
Lifford
Letterkenny
Monaghan
Banbridge
Newry
Downpatrick
Dundalk
Drogheda
Navan
Mullingar
Athlone
Longford
Tullamore
Portlaoise
Carlow
Kilkenny
Naas
Newbridge
Lucan
Leixlip
Swords
DUBLIN
Bray
Wicklow
Arklow
Greenock
Dumbarton
Paisley
Glasgow
Kilmarnock
Ayr
Irvine
Campbeltown
Stranraer
Douglas
Ramsey
Castletown
Peel
Anglesey
Holyhead
Llyn Peninsula
Mourne Mountains
Sperrin Mountains
Wicklow Mountains
Slieve Bloom Mts
North Channel
Dundalk Bay
Dublin Bay
Cardigan Bay

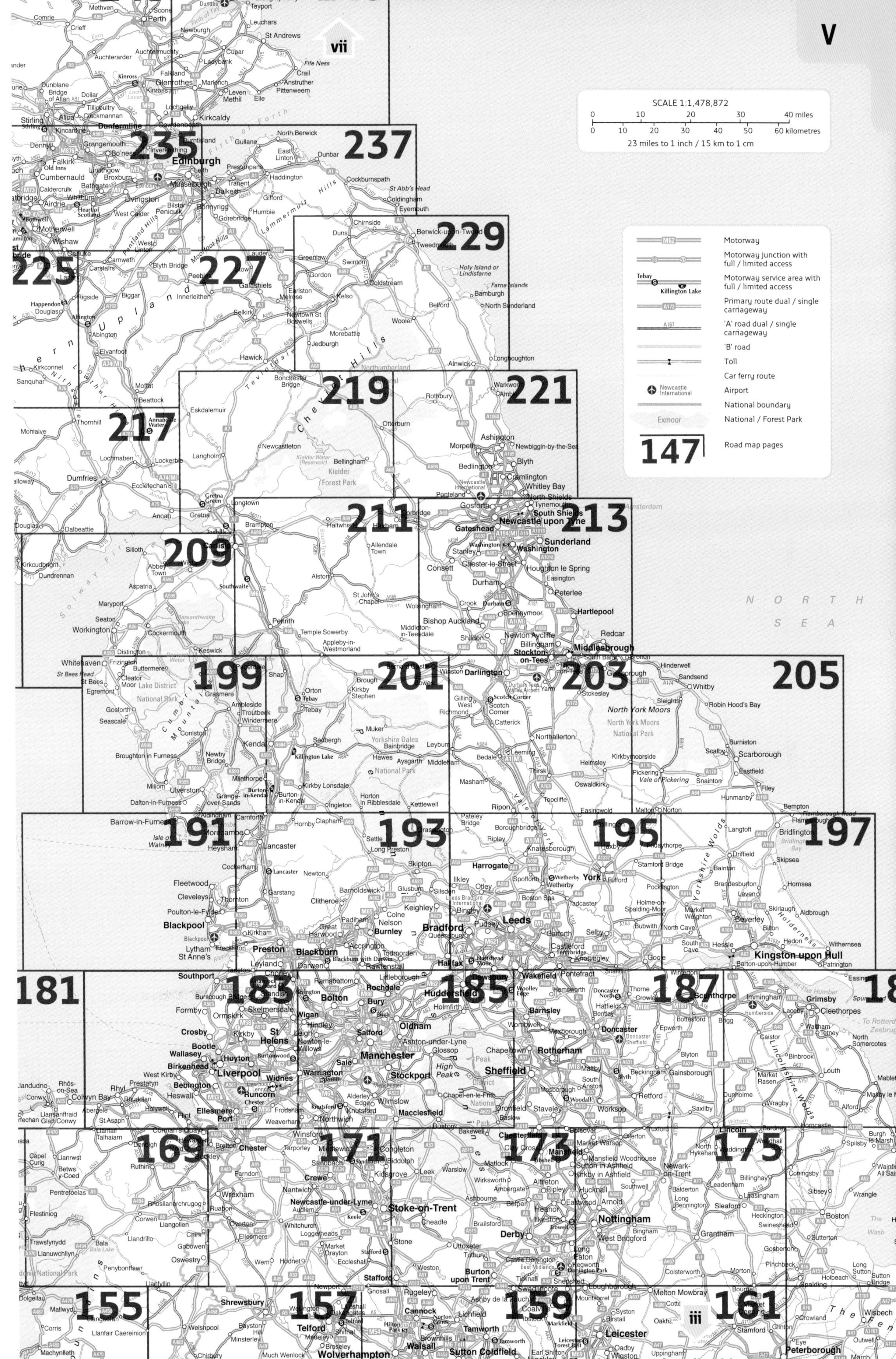

vii

SCALE 1:1,478,872

0   10   20   30   40 miles
0 10 20 30 40 50 60 kilometres
23 miles to 1 inch / 15 km to 1 cm

	Motorway
M62	Motorway junction with full / limited access
Tebay	Motorway service area with full / limited access
Killington Lake	
A172	Primary route dual / single carriageway
A167	'A' road dual / single carriageway
	'B' road
	Toll
	Car ferry route
Newcastle International	Airport
	National boundary
Exmoor	National / Forest Park
147	Road map pages

235 237
225 227 229
217 219 221
209 211 213
199 201 203 205
191 193 195 197
181 183 185 187 18
169 171 173 175
155 157 159 161

iii

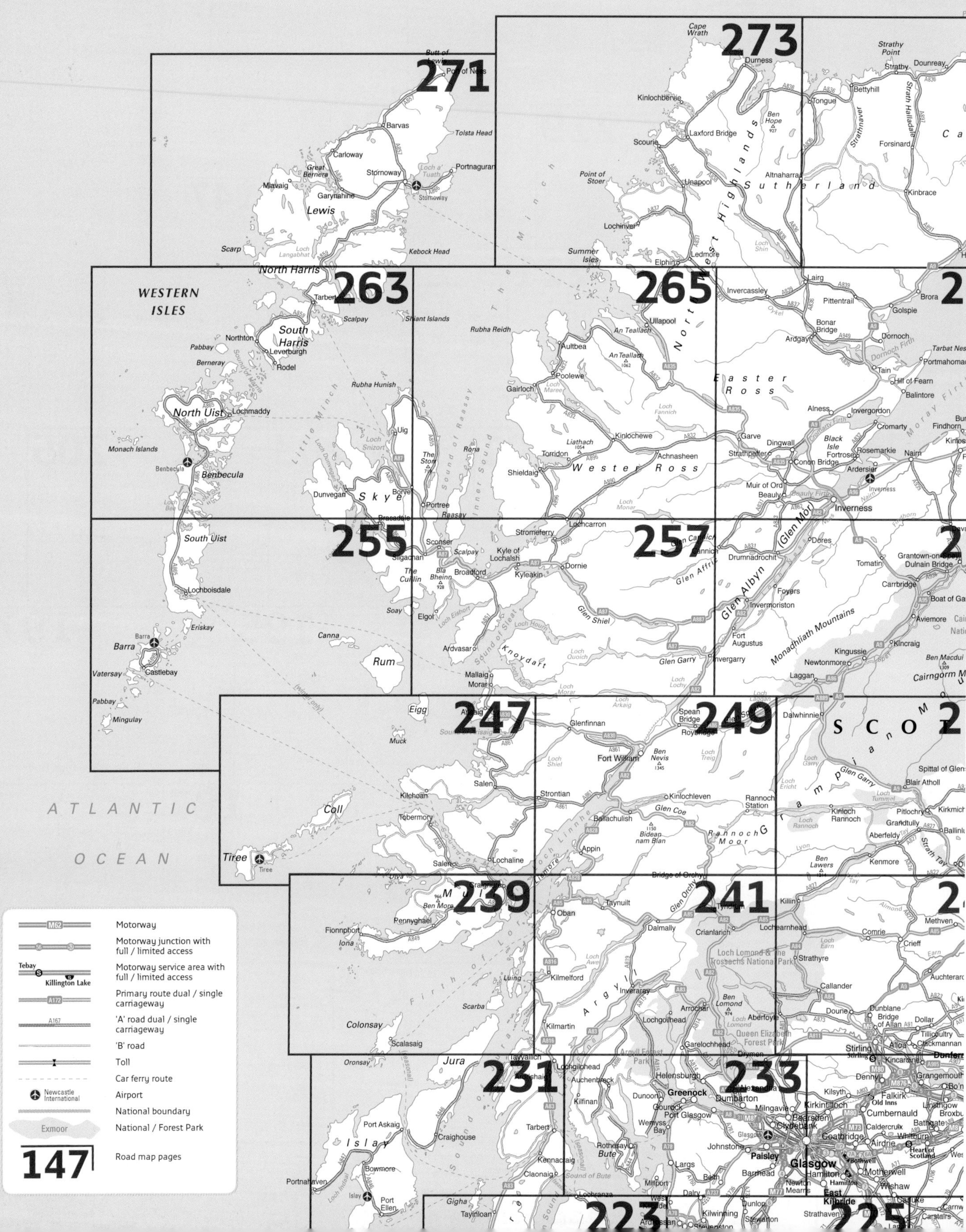

Legend

M62	Motorway
	Motorway junction with full / limited access
Tebay / Killington Lake	Motorway service area with full / limited access
A172	Primary route dual / single carriageway
A167	'A' road dual / single carriageway
	'B' road
	Toll
	Car ferry route
Newcastle International	Airport
	National boundary
Exmoor	National / Forest Park
147	Road map pages

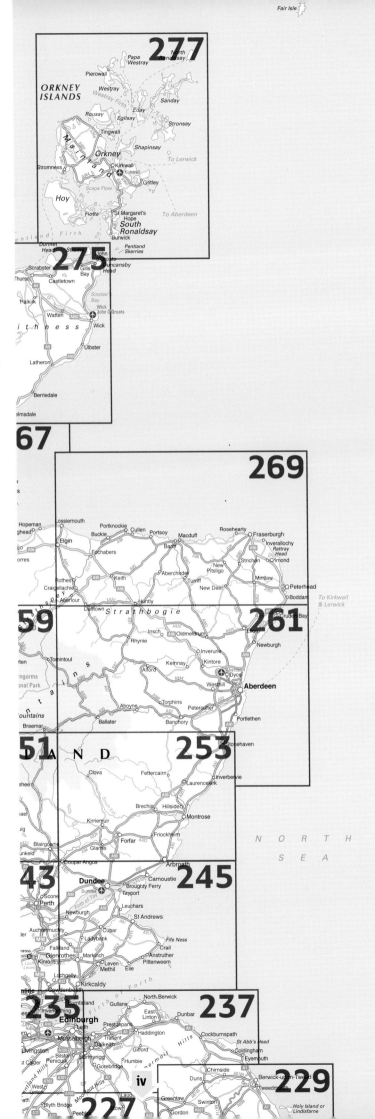

Fair Isle

277

ORKNEY ISLANDS

Papa Westray
Pierowall
Westray
Westray Firth
Sanday
Rousay
Eday
Egilsay
Stronsay
Tingwall
Shapinsay
Orkney
Mainland
Kirkwall
Kirkwall
To Lerwick
Stromness
Gritley
Hoy
Scapa Flow
To Aberdeen
Flotta
St Margaret's Hope
South Ronaldsay
Burwick
Pentland Skerries
Pentland Firth

275
Dunnet Head
Scrabster
Gills Bay
John O'Groats
Castletown
Duncansby Head
Thurso
Sinclair Bay
Halkirk
Wick
Watten
Wick
Caithness
Ulbster
Latheron
Berriedale
Helmsdale

67

269
Hopeman
Lossiemouth
Portknockie
Cullen
Portsoy
Macduff
Rosehearty
Fraserburgh
Elgin
Buckie
Banff
Inverallochy
Rattray Head
Fochabers
Forres
New Pitsligo
Strichen
Crimond
Rothes
Keith
Aberchirder
Turriff
Mintlaw
Peterhead
Craigellachie
New Deer
Aberlour
Huntly
Boddam
To Kirkwall & Lerwick
Dufftown
Strathbogie
261
Cruden Bay
59
Insch
Oldmeldrum
Ellon
Tomintoul
Rhynie
Inverurie
Newburgh
Kemnay
Alford
Kintore
Aberdeen
Cairngorms National Park
Westhill
Dyce
Aberdeen
Mountains
Aboyne
Torphins
Peterculter
Braemar
Ballater
Banchory
Portlethen
51
A N D
253
Stonehaven
Clova
Fettercairn
Inverbervie
shee
Laurencekirk
Brechin
Hillside
Kirriemuir
Montrose
Blairgowrie
Forfar
Friockheim
unkeld
Glamis
Coupar Angus
Arbroath
43
245
Dundee
Carnoustie
Scone
Dundee
Broughty Ferry
Perth
Tayport
Newburgh
Leuchars
Auchtermuchty
St Andrews
Cupar
Ladybank
Fife Ness
Falkland
Crail
Glenrothes
Markinch
Anstruther
Kinross
Leven
Pittenweem
Lochgelly
Methil
Elie
Kirkcaldy
Firth of Forth
235
Burntisland
Gullane
North Berwick
237
Inverkeithing
East Linton
Dunbar
Edinburgh
Prestonpans
Leith
Haddington
Cockburnspath
Livingston
Tranent
St Abb's Head
Musselburgh
Dalkeith
Gifford
Coldingham
Bilston
Humbie
Eyemouth
Penicuik
Bonnyrigg
Gorebridge
229
Chirnside
Berwick-upon-Tweed
West Calder
Duns
Tweedmouth
iv
Blyth Bridge
Lauder
Greenlaw
Swinton
Holy Island or Lindisfarne
227
Peebles
Gordon

N O R T H

S E A

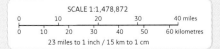
279
SHETLAND ISLANDS
Unst
Baltasound
Haroldswick
Belmont
Gutcher
Oddsta
Funzie
Yell
Ulsta
Hillswick
Toft
St. Magnus Bay
Brae
Vidlin
Whalsey
Out Skerries
Laxo
Symbister
Sandness
Aith
Shetland
Walls
Bressay
Lerwick
Scalloway
Sumburgh
Sumburgh
To Aberdeen & Kirkwall

Restricted motorway junctions

A1(M) LONDON TO NEWCASTLE

②
Northbound : No access
Southbound : No exit

③
Southbound : No access

⑤
Northbound : No exit
Southbound : No access
: No exit

④1
Northbound : No exit to M62 Eastbound

④3
Northbound : No exit to M1 Westbound

Dishforth
Southbound : No access from A168 Eastbound

⑤7
Northbound : No access
: Exit only to A66(M) Northbound
Southbound : Access only from A66(M) Southbound
: No exit

⑥5
Northbound : No access from A1
Southbound : No exit to A1

A3(M) PORTSMOUTH

①
Northbound : No exit
Southbound : No access

④
Northbound : No access
Southbound : No exit

A38(M) BIRMINGHAM

Victoria Road
Northbound : No exit
Southbound : No access

A48(M) CARDIFF

Junction with M4
Westbound : No access from M4 ㉙ Eastbound
Eastbound : No exit to M4 ㉙ Westbound

㉙A
Westbound : No exit to A48 Eastbound
Eastbound : No access from A48 Westbound

A57(M) MANCHESTER

Brook Street
Westbound : No exit
Eastbound : No access

A58(M) LEEDS

Westgate
Southbound : No access
Woodhouse Lane
Westbound : No exit

A64(M) LEEDS

Claypit Lane
Eastbound : No access

A66(M) DARLINGTON

Junction with A1(M)
Northbound : No access from A1(M) Southbound
: No exit
Southbound : No access
: No exit to A1(M) Northbound

A74(M) LOCKERBIE

⑱
Northbound : No access
Southbound : No exit

A167(M) NEWCASTLE

Campden Street
Northbound : No exit
Southbound : No access
: No exit

M1 LONDON TO LEEDS

②
Northbound : No exit
Southbound : No access

④
Northbound : No exit
Southbound : No access

⑥A
Northbound : Access only from M25 ㉑
: No exit
Southbound : No access
: Exit only to M25 ㉑

⑦
Northbound : Access only from A414
: No exit
Southbound : No access
: Exit only to A414

M1 LONDON TO LEEDS (continued)

⑰
Northbound : No access
: Exit only to M45
Southbound : Access only from M45
: No exit

⑲
Northbound : Exit only to M6
Southbound : Access only from M6

㉑A
Northbound : No access
Southbound : No exit

㉓A
Northbound : No access from A453
Southbound : No exit to A453

㉔A
Northbound : No exit
Southbound : No access

㉟A
Northbound : No access
Southbound : No exit

④3
Northbound : No access
: Exit only to M621
Southbound : No exit
: Access only from M621

④8
Northbound : No exit to A1(M) Southbound
: Access only from A1(M) Northbound
Southbound : Exit only to A1(M) Southbound
: No access

M2 ROCHESTER TO CANTERBURY

①
Westbound : No exit to A2 Eastbound
Eastbound : No access from A2 Westbound

M3 LONDON TO WINCHESTER

⑧
Westbound : No access
Eastbound : No exit

⑩
Northbound : No access
Southbound : No exit

⑬
Southbound : No exit to A335 Eastbound
: No access

⑭
Westbound : No access
Eastbound : No exit

M4 LONDON TO SWANSEA

①
Westbound : No access from A4 Eastbound
Eastbound : No exit to A4 Westbound

②
Westbound : No access from A4 Eastbound
: No exit to A4 Eastbound
Eastbound : No access from A4 Westbound
: No exit to A4 Westbound

㉑
Westbound : No access from M48 Eastbound
Eastbound : No exit to M48 Westbound

㉓
Westbound : No exit to M48 Eastbound
Eastbound : No access from M48 Westbound

㉕
Westbound : No access
Eastbound : No exit

㉕A
Westbound : No access
Eastbound : No exit

㉙
Westbound : No access
: Exit only to A48(M)
Eastbound : Access only from A48(M) Eastbound
: No exit

㊳
Westbound : No access

㊴
Westbound : No exit
Eastbound : No access
: No exit

④1
Westbound : No exit
Eastbound : No access

④2
Westbound : No exit to A48
Eastbound : No access from A48

M5 BIRMINGHAM TO EXETER

⑩
Northbound : No exit
Southbound : No access

⑪A
Northbound : No access from A417 Eastbound
Southbound : No exit to A417 Westbound

M6 COVENTRY TO CARLISLE

Junction with M1
Northbound : No access from M1 ⑲ Southbound
Southbound : No exit to M1 ⑲ Northbound

③A
Northbound : No access from M6 Toll
Southbound : No exit to M6 Toll

④
Northbound : No exit to M42 Northbound
: No access from M42 Southbound
Southbound : No exit to M42
: No access from M42 Southbound

④A
Northbound : No access from M42 ⑧
Northbound
: No exit
Southbound : No access
: Exit only to M42 ⑧

⑤
Northbound : No access
Southbound : No exit

⑩A
Northbound : No access
: Exit only to M54
Southbound : Access only from M54
: No exit

⑪A
Northbound : No exit to M6 Toll
Southbound : No access from M6 Toll

㉔
Northbound : No exit
Southbound : No access

㉕
Northbound : No access
Southbound : No exit

㉚
Northbound : Access only from M61 Northbound
: No exit
Southbound : No access
: Exit only to M61 Southbound

㉛A
Northbound : No access
Southbound : No exit

M6 Toll BIRMINGHAM

T1
Northbound : Exit only to M42
: Access only from A4097
Southbound : No exit
: Access only from M42 Southbound

T2
Northbound : No exit
: No access
Southbound : No access

T5
Northbound : No exit
Southbound : No access

T7
Northbound : No access
Southbound : No exit

T8
Northbound : No access
Southbound : No access

M8 EDINBURGH TO GLASGOW

⑥A
Westbound : No exit
Eastbound : No access

⑦
Westbound : No exit
Eastbound : No access

⑦A
Westbound : No access
Eastbound : No exit

⑧
Westbound : No access from M73 ② Southbound
: No access from A8 Eastbound
: No access from A89 Eastbound
Eastbound : No access from A89 Westbound
: No exit to M73 ② Northbound

⑨
Westbound : No exit
Eastbound : No access

⑬
Westbound : Access only from M80
Eastbound : Exit only to M80

⑭
Westbound : No exit
Eastbound : No access

⑯
Westbound : No access
Eastbound : No exit

M8 EDINBURGH TO GLASGOW (cont)

⑰
Eastbound : Access only from A82,
not central Glasgow
: Exit only to A82,
not central Glasgow

⑱
Westbound : No access
Eastbound : No access

⑲
Westbound : Access only from A814 Eastbound
Eastbound : Exit only to A814 Westbound,
not central Glasgow

⑳
Westbound : No access
Eastbound : No exit

㉑
Westbound : No exit
Eastbound : No access

㉒
Westbound : No access
: Exit only to M77 Southbound
Eastbound : Access only from M77 Northbound
: No exit

㉓
Westbound : No access
Eastbound : No exit

㉕A
Eastbound : No exit
Westbound : No access

㉘
Westbound : No access
Eastbound : No exit

㉘A
Westbound : No access
Eastbound : No exit

M9 EDINBURGH TO STIRLING

②
Westbound : No exit
Eastbound : No access

③
Westbound : No access
Eastbound : No exit

⑥
Westbound : No access
Eastbound : No access

⑧
Westbound : No access
Eastbound : No exit

M11 LONDON TO CAMBRIDGE

④
Northbound : No access from A1400 Westbound
: No exit
Southbound : No access
: No exit to A1400 Eastbound

⑤
Northbound : No access
Southbound : No exit

⑧A
Northbound : No access
Southbound : No exit

⑨
Northbound : No access
Southbound : No exit

⑬
Northbound : No access
Southbound : No exit

⑭
Northbound : No access from A428 Eastbound
: No exit to A428 Westbound
: No exit to A1307
Southbound : No access from A428 Eastbound
: No access from A1307
: No exit

M20 LONDON TO FOLKESTONE

②
Westbound : No exit
Eastbound : No access

③
Westbound : No access
: Exit only to M26 Westbound
Eastbound : Access only from M26 Eastbound
: No exit

⑪A
Westbound : No exit
Eastbound : No access

Restricted motorway junctions are shown on the maps as:

M23 LONDON TO CRAWLEY

⑦
Northbound : No exit to A23 Southbound
Southbound : No access from A23 Northbound
⑩A
Southbound : No access from B2036
Northbound : No exit to B2036

M25 LONDON ORBITAL MOTORWAY

①B
Clockwise : No access
Anticlockwise : No exit
⑤
Clockwise : No exit to M26 Eastbound
Anticlockwise : No access from M26 Westbound
Spur of M25 ⑤
Clockwise : No access from M26 Westbound
Anticlockwise : No exit to M26 Eastbound
⑲
Clockwise : No access
Anticlockwise : No exit
㉑
Clockwise : No access from M1 ⑥A Northbound
: No exit to M1 ⑥A Southbound
Anticlockwise : No access from M1 ⑥A Northbound
: No exit to M1 ⑥A Southbound
㉛
Clockwise : No exit
Anticlockwise : No access

M26 SEVENOAKS

Junction with M25 ⑤
Westbound : No exit to M25 Anticlockwise
: No exit to M25 spur
Eastbound : No access from M25 Clockwise
: No access from M25 spur
Junction with M20
Westbound : No access from M20 ③ Eastbound
Eastbound : No exit to M20 ③ Westbound

M27 SOUTHAMPTON TO PORTSMOUTH

④ West
Westbound : No exit
Eastbound : No access
④ East
Westbound : No access
Eastbound : No exit
⑩
Westbound : No access
Eastbound : No exit
⑫ West
Westbound : No exit
Eastbound : No access
⑫ East
Westbound : No access from A3
Eastbound : No exit

M40 LONDON TO BIRMINGHAM

③
Westbound : No access
Eastbound : No exit
⑦
Eastbound : No exit
⑧
Northbound : No access
Southbound : No exit
⑬
Northbound : No access
Southbound : No exit
⑭
Northbound : No exit
Southbound : No access
⑯
Northbound : No access
Southbound : No exit

M42 BIRMINGHAM

①
Northbound : No exit
Southbound : No access
⑦
Northbound : No access
: Exit only to M6 Northbound
Southbound : Access only from M6 Northbound
: No exit

M42 BIRMINGHAM

⑦A
Northbound : No access
: Exit only to M6 Eastbound
Southbound : No access
: No exit
⑧
Northbound : Access only from M6 Southbound
: No exit
Southbound : Access only from M6 Southbound
: Exit only to M6 Northbound

M45 COVENTRY

Junction with M1
Westbound : No access from M1 ⑰ Southbound
Eastbound : No exit to M1 ⑰ Northbound
Junction with A45
Westbound : No exit
Eastbound : No access

M48 CHEPSTOW

M4
Westbound : No exit to M4 Eastbound
Eastbound : No access from M4 Westbound

M49 BRISTOL

⑱A
Northbound : No access from M5 Southbound
Southbound : No access from M5 Northbound

M53 BIRKENHEAD TO CHESTER

⑪
Northbound : No access from M56 ⑮ Eastbound
: No exit to M56 ⑮ Westbound
Southbound : No access from M56 ⑮ Eastbound
: No exit to M56 ⑮ Westbound

M54 WOLVERHAMPTON TO TELFORD

Junction with M6
Westbound : No access from M6 ⑩A Southbound
Eastbound : No exit to M6 ⑩A Northbound

M56 STOCKPORT TO CHESTER

①
Westbound : No access from M60 Eastbound
: No access from A34 Northbound
Eastbound : No exit to M60 Westbound
: No exit to A34 Southbound
②
Westbound : No access
Eastbound : No exit
③
Westbound : No exit
Eastbound : No access
④
Westbound : No access
Eastbound : No exit
⑦
Westbound : No access
Eastbound : No exit
⑧
Westbound : No exit
Eastbound : No access
⑨
Westbound : No exit to M6 Southbound
Eastbound : No access from M6 Northbound
⑮
Westbound : No access
: No access from M53 ⑪
Eastbound : No exit
: No exit to M53 ⑪

M57 LIVERPOOL

③
Northbound : No exit
Southbound : No access
⑤
Northbound : Access only from A580 Westbound
: No exit
Southbound : No access
: Exit only to A580 Eastbound

M58 LIVERPOOL TO WIGAN

①
Westbound : No access
Eastbound : No exit

M60 MANCHESTER

②
Westbound : No exit
Eastbound : No access
③
Westbound : No access from M56 ①
: No access from A34 Southbound
: No exit to A34 Northbound

M60 MANCHESTER (continued)

③
Eastbound : No access from A34 Southbound
: No exit to M56 ①
: No exit to A34 Northbound
④
Westbound : No access
Eastbound : No exit to M56
⑤
Westbound : No access from A5103 Southbound
: No exit to A5103 Southbound
Eastbound : No access from A5103 Northbound
: No exit to A5103 Northbound
⑭
Westbound : No access from A580
: No exit to A580 Eastbound
Eastbound : No access from A580 Westbound
: No exit to A580
⑯
Westbound : No access
Eastbound : No exit
⑳
Westbound : No access
Eastbound : No exit
㉒
Westbound : No access
㉕
Westbound : No access
㉖
Eastbound : No access
: No exit
㉗
Westbound : No exit
Eastbound : No access

M61 MANCHESTER TO PRESTON

②
Northbound : No access from A580 Eastbound
: No access from A666
Southbound : No exit to A580 Westbound
③
Northbound : No access from A580 Eastbound
: No access from A666
Southbound : No exit to A580 Westbound
Junction with M6
Northbound : No exit to M6 ㉚ Southbound
Southbound : No access from M6 ㉚ Northbound

M62 LIVERPOOL TO HULL

㉓
Westbound : No exit
Eastbound : No access
㉜A
Westbound : No exit to A1(M) Southbound

M65 BURNLEY

⑨
Westbound : No exit
Eastbound : No access
⑪
Westbound : No access
Eastbound : No exit

M66 MANCHESTER TO EDENFIELD

①
Northbound : No access
Southbound : No exit
Junction with A56
Northbound : Exit only to A56 Northbound
Southbound : Access only from A56 Southbound

M67 MANCHESTER

①
Westbound : No exit
Eastbound : No access
②
Westbound : No access
Eastbound : No exit

M69 COVENTRY TO LEICESTER

②
Northbound : No exit
Southbound : No access

M73 GLASGOW

①
Northbound : No access from A721 Eastbound
Southbound : No exit to A721 Eastbound
②
Northbound : No access from M8 ⑧ Eastbound
Southbound : No exit to M8 ⑧ Westbound

M74 GLASGOW

①A
Westbound : No exit to M8 Kingston Bridge
Eastbound : No access from M8 Kingston Bridge

M74 GLASGOW (continued)

③
Westbound : No access
Eastbound : No exit
③A
Westbound : No exit
Eastbound : No access
⑦
Northbound : No exit
Southbound : No access
⑨
Northbound : No access
: No exit
Southbound : No access
⑩
Southbound : No access
⑪
Northbound : No exit
Southbound : No access
⑫
Northbound : Access only from A70 Northbound
Southbound : Exit only to A70 Southbound

M77 GLASGOW

Junction with M8
Northbound : No exit to M8 ㉒ Westbound
Southbound : No access from M8 ㉒ Eastbound
④
Northbound : No exit
Southbound : No access
⑥
Northbound : No exit to A77
Southbound : No access from A77
⑦
Northbound : No access
: No exit
⑧
Northbound : No access
Southbound : No access

M80 STIRLING

④A
Northbound : No access
Southbound : No exit
⑥A
Northbound : No exit
Southbound : No access
⑧
Northbound : No access from M876
Southbound : No exit to M876

M90 EDINBURGH TO PERTH

①
Northbound : No exit to A90
②A
Northbound : No access
Southbound : No exit
⑦
Northbound : No exit
Southbound : No access
⑧
Northbound : No access
Southbound : No exit
⑩
Northbound : No access from A912
: No exit to A912 Southbound
Southbound : No access from A912 Northbound
: No exit to A912

M180 SCUNTHORPE

①
Westbound : No exit
Eastbound : No access

M606 BRADFORD

Straithgate Lane
Northbound : No access

M621 LEEDS

②A
Northbound : No exit
Southbound : No access
⑤
Northbound : No access
Southbound : No exit
⑥
Northbound : No exit
Southbound : No access

M876 FALKIRK

Junction with M80
Westbound : No exit to M80 ⑧ Northbound
Eastbound : No access from M80 ⑧ Southbound
Junction with M9
Westbound : No access
Eastbound : No exit

Motorway services information

All motorway service areas have fuel, food, toilets, disabled facilities and free short-term parking

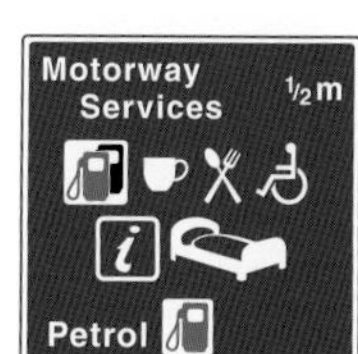

For further information on motorway services providers:
Moto www.moto-way.com
RoadChef www.roadchef.com
Welcome Break www.welcomebreak.co.uk
Euro Garages www.eurogarages.com
Extra www.extraservices.co.uk
Westmorland www.westmorland.com

Motorway	Junction	Service provider	Service name	Fuel supplier	Information	Accommodation	Conference facilities	Showers	M&S Simply Food	Waitrose	Costa Coffee	Starbucks	Burger King	KFC	McDonalds
A1(M)	1	Welcome Break	South Mimms	BP	●	●	●		●		●	●	●		
	10	Extra	Baldock	Shell	●	●		●				●		●	●
	17	Extra	Peterborough	Shell	●	●		●						●	●
	34	Moto	Blyth	Esso	●	●		●		●		●			
	46	Moto	Wetherby	BP	●	●		●		●		●			
	53	Moto	Scotch Corner	Esso		●		●		●		●			
	61	RoadChef	Durham	Shell	●	●	●			●					●
	64	Moto	Washington	BP	●	●									
A74(M)	16	RoadChef	Annandale Water	BP	●	●				●					●
	22	Welcome Break	Gretna Green	BP	●	●			●		●	●	●		●
M1	2-4	Welcome Break	London Gateway	Shell	●	●	●	●			●				
	11-12	Moto	Toddington	BP	●	●		●	●			●			
	14-15	Welcome Break	Newport Pagnell	Shell	●	●		●			●				
	15A	RoadChef	Northampton	BP							●				
	16-17	RoadChef	Watford Gap	BP	●	●	●	●			●				
	21-21A	Welcome Break	Leicester Forest East	Shell	●	●	●				●	●			
	22	Euro Garages	Markfield	BP	●	●					●				
	23A	Moto	Donington Park	BP	●	●	●	●	●			●			
	25-26	Moto	Trowell	BP	●	●		●		●		●			
	28-29	RoadChef	Tibshelf	Shell	●	●	●				●				
	30-31	Welcome Break	Woodall	Shell	●	●			●		●				
	38-39	Moto	Woolley Edge	BP	●	●			●			●			
M2	4-5	Moto	Medway	BP	●				●			●			
M3	4A-5	Welcome Break	Fleet	Shell	●	●	●	●			●	●	●		●
	8-9	Moto	Winchester	BP	●					●					
M4	3	Moto	Heston	BP	●	●	●	●	●			●			
	11-12	Moto	Reading	BP	●	●	●	●		●		●			
	13	Moto	Chieveley	BP	●	●		●		●		●			
	14-15	Welcome Break	Membury	BP	●	●			●		●	●	●		
	17-18	Moto	Leigh Delamere	BP	●	●	●	●		●		●			
	23A	RoadChef	Magor	Esso	●	●									●
	30	Welcome Break	Cardiff Gate	Shell	●		●					●	●		
	33	Moto	Cardiff West	Esso	●	●	●					●			
	36	Welcome Break	Sarn Park	Shell	●		●					●			
	47	Moto	Swansea	BP	●	●									
	49	RoadChef	Pont Abraham	Esso	●										
M5	3-4	Moto	Frankley	BP	●		●	●		●					
	8	RoadChef	Strensham (South)	BP	●		●					●			
	8	RoadChef	Strensham (North)	Texaco	●	●	●								
	11-12	Westmorland	Gloucester	Texaco				●							
	13-14	Welcome Break	Michaelwood	BP	●	●			●		●	●	●		
	19	Welcome Break	Gordano	Shell	●	●			●		●	●	●		
	21-22	RoadChef	Sedgemoor (South)	Shell	●					●					
	21-22	Welcome Break	Sedgemoor (North)	Shell	●	●			●						
	24	Moto	Bridgwater	BP	●	●			●			●			
	25-26	RoadChef	Taunton Deane	Shell	●	●					●				
	27	Moto	Tiverton	Shell	●	●						●			
	28	Extra	Cullompton	Shell	●				●						●
	29-30	Moto	Exeter	BP	●	●			●			●			
M6 Toll	T6-T7	RoadChef	Norton Canes	BP	●	●	●	●			●				●

Motorway	Junction	Service provider	Service name	Fuel supplier	Information	Accommodation	Conference facilities	Showers	M&S Simply Food	Waitrose	Costa Coffee	Starbucks	Burger King	KFC	McDonalds
M6	3-4	Welcome Break	Corley	Shell	●	●		●	●		●	●	●		
	10-11	Moto	Hilton Park	BP	●	●		●	●		●	●			
	14-15	RoadChef	Stafford (South)	Esso	●	●	●	●			●				●
	14-15	Moto	Stafford (North)	BP	●	●		●	●			●			
	15-16	Welcome Break	Keele	Shell	●	●		●			●	●	●		
	16-17	RoadChef	Sandbach	BP		●					●				
	18-19	Moto	Knutsford	BP	●	●		●	●			●			
	20	Moto	Lymm	BP	●	●		●		●		●			
	27-28	Welcome Break	Charnock Richard	Shell	●	●		●	●		●	●	●		
	32-33	Moto	Lancaster	BP	●	●		●	●			●			
	35A-36	Moto	Burton-in-Kendal (N)	BP	●	●		●		●		●			
	36-37	RoadChef	Killington Lake (S)	BP	●	●		●			●				
	38-39	Westmorland	Tebay	Total	●	●	●								
	41-42	Moto	Southwaite	BP	●	●		●	●			●			
	44-45	Moto	Todhills	BP/Shell	●										
M8	4-5	BP	Heart of Scotland	BP			●	●	●						
M9	9	Moto	Stirling	BP	●	●		●	●			●			
M11	8	Welcome Break	Birchanger Green	Shell	●	●	●	●	●		●	●	●		●
M18	5	Moto	Doncaster North	BP	●	●			●						
M20	8	RoadChef	Maidstone	Esso	●	●									●
	11	Stop 24	Stop 24	Shell	●						●				
M23	11	Moto	Pease Pottage	BP	●	●		●				●			●
M25	5-6	RoadChef	Clacket Lane	BP	●		●	●			●	●			●
	9-10	Extra	Cobham	Shell	●	●		●	●		●	●			●
	23	Welcome Break	South Mimms	BP	●	●	●	●	●		●	●	●		●
	30	Moto	Thurrock	Esso	●	●		●	●			●			
M27	3-4	RoadChef	Rownhams	BP	●	●									●
M40	2	Extra	Beaconsfield	Shell		●			●			●			●
	8	Welcome Break	Oxford	BP		●		●	●		●				●
	10	Moto	Cherwell Valley	Esso		●		●	●			●			●
	12-13	Welcome Break	Warwick	BP	●	●	●	●			●				●
M42	2	Welcome Break	Hopwood Park	Shell	●		●	●	●		●	●			
	10	Moto	Tamworth	Esso	●	●		●	●			●			
M48	1	Moto	Severn View	BP	●	●		●		●		●			
M54	4	Welcome Break	Telford	Shell	●	●			●		●				
M56	14	RoadChef	Chester	Shell	●	●	●				●				
M61	6-7	Euro Garages	Rivington	BP		●	●	●				●	●		
M62	7-9	Welcome Break	Burtonwood	Shell	●		●				●	●			●
	18-19	Moto	Birch	BP	●	●	●	●	●		●	●			
	25-26	Welcome Break	Hartshead Moor	Shell	●	●		●	●		●	●	●		
	33	Moto	Ferrybridge	BP	●	●		●	●			●			
M65	4	Extra	Blackburn with Darwen	Shell	●	●	●	●			●				●
M74	4-5	RoadChef	Bothwell (South)	Shell	●			●			●				●
	5-6	RoadChef	Hamilton (North)	Shell	●	●					●				●
	11-12	Cairn Lodge	Happendon	Shell	●	●					●				
	12-13	Welcome Break	Abington	Shell	●	●			●		●	●			
M80	6-7	Shell	Old Inns	Shell	●										●
M90	6	Moto	Kinross	BP	●	●		●	●			●			

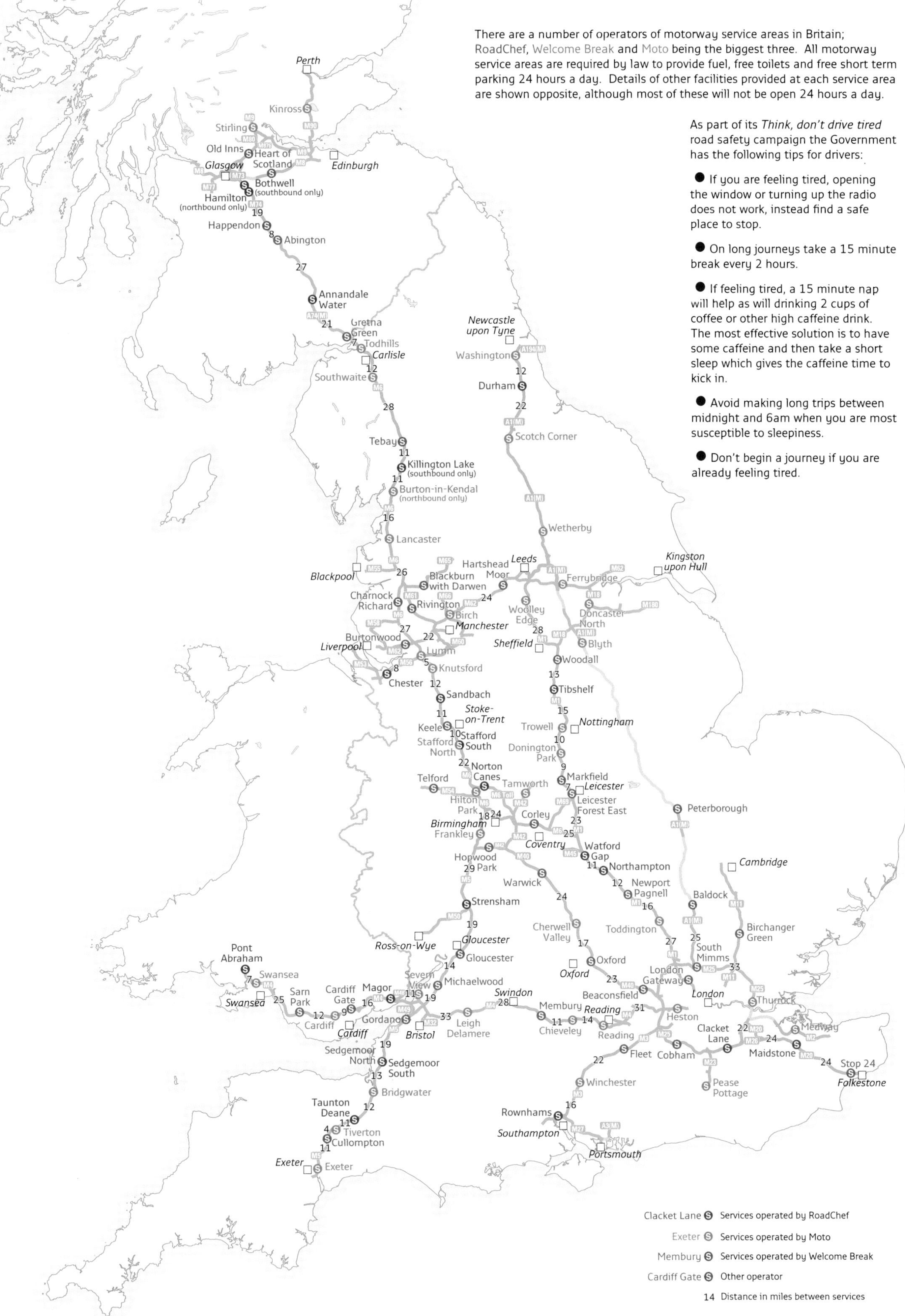

There are a number of operators of motorway service areas in Britain; RoadChef, Welcome Break and Moto being the biggest three. All motorway service areas are required by law to provide fuel, free toilets and free short term parking 24 hours a day. Details of other facilities provided at each service area are shown opposite, although most of these will not be open 24 hours a day.

As part of its *Think, don't drive tired* road safety campaign the Government has the following tips for drivers:

● If you are feeling tired, opening the window or turning up the radio does not work, instead find a safe place to stop.

● On long journeys take a 15 minute break every 2 hours.

● If feeling tired, a 15 minute nap will help as will drinking 2 cups of coffee or other high caffeine drink. The most effective solution is to have some caffeine and then take a short sleep which gives the caffeine time to kick in.

● Avoid making long trips between midnight and 6am when you are most susceptible to sleepiness.

● Don't begin a journey if you are already feeling tired.

Clacket Lane Ⓢ Services operated by RoadChef

Exeter Ⓢ Services operated by Moto

Membury Ⓢ Services operated by Welcome Break

Cardiff Gate Ⓢ Other operator

14 Distance in miles between services

M25 orbital map

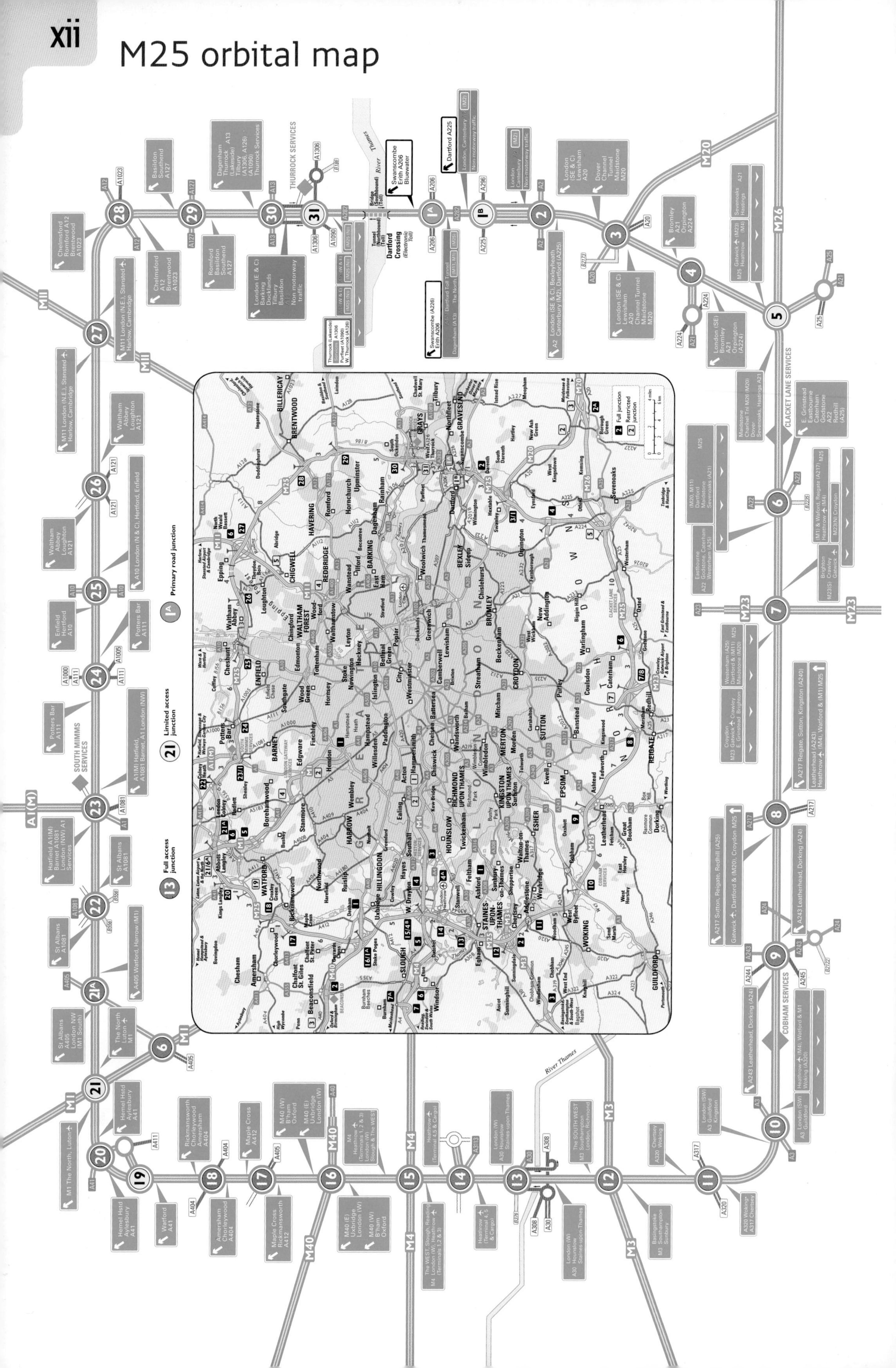

Full access junction
Limited access junction
Primary road junction
THURROCK SERVICES
SOUTH MIMMS SERVICES
CLACKET LANE SERVICES
COBHAM SERVICES
Dartford Crossing
River Thames

Motorway junction signs (M6 / M5 / M42 / M54 / M6 Toll)

M6

The SOUTH, B'ham
The S WEST (M5)

The SOUTH M6 Toll

A4601

A460

T8 — M6 Toll

A460 (M6 south) Wolverhampton

The NORTH WEST (M6, North) Stafford, telford — M6 Toll

A460 Wolverhampton Cannock

A460 Cannock

11 — M6

A460

HILTON PARK SERVICES

10ᴬ

M54 — NORTH (& MID) WALES Wolverhampton & Telford

The NORTH WEST & Stafford — M6

A454 Walsall

10 — A454

A454 Walsall, W'hampton (Cent. & East)

The North West, Telford (M54), W'hampton (N) — M6

A461 Wednesbury

The SOUTH & Birmingham — M6

9 — A4148

A461 Wednesbury

The NORTH WEST, Walsall & W'hampton — M6

London (M1 & M40) Birmingham (N.E. & Cen.) N.E.C. &

The SOUTH WEST M5 Birmingham (W & S) West Bromwich

M5 ◆ M6

8 — M6

A34 Birmingham (N)

London (M1 & M40) Birmingham (S & Cen.) N.E.C. & — M6

A34

8 — M6 — **7**

A34

The SOUTH WEST M5 Birmingham (W & S) West Bromwich

The NORTH WEST & Wolverhampton

A34 Birmingham (N) & Walsall

The NORTH WEST The SOUTH WEST B'ham (W & S) (M5) — M6

M6 London (M1 & M40) Walsall Birmingham (N & E) — M6

The NORTH WEST Walsall Wolverhampton

A41

1 — A41

A41 West Bromwich & B'ham (NW)

The NORTH (M1 & M6), Birmingham (N), N.E.C. & — M5

M5

West Bromwich, Sandwell & B'ham (N & W)

The SOUTH WEST & Birmingham (W & S) — M5

A4123 Birmingham (W) & Dudley

The SOUTH WEST & Birmingham (S) — M5

2 — A4123

A4123 Dudley, W'hampton & Sandwell

The NORTH (M1 & M6), Birmingham (N) — M5

A456 Kidderminster

The SOUTH WEST & Birmingham (S) — M5

3 — A456

A456 Birmingham (W & Cen)

FRANKLEY SERVICES

A38 B'ham (SW) Bromsgrove

4 — A38 — A491

A38 Birmingham (SW), A491 Stourbridge

M5

A42 London (M40) N.E.C. &

M42 & M5

M5 The SOUTH WEST Worcester

A38

4ᴬ — M42

M42 The NORTH EAST (M1) London (M40) N.E.C. &

M42 & M5

M5 The NORTH WEST (M6) B'ham (N, W & Cen)

M5 The NORTH WEST B'ham (W.N & Cen) Stourbridge (M6)

M5 The SOUTH WEST Worcester

1 — M42

A38 Bromsgrove

A441

A441 Birmingham (S)

2 — M42

A441 Birmingham (S)

HOPWOOD PARK SERVICES

B'ham (S), Redditch Evesham

A435

3 — M42

A435 B'ham (S), Redditch Evesham

(Right side — M6 Toll / M42)

A5148 Lichfield, (A38) Burton

The SOUTH, Tamworth — M6 Toll

A5148

A5 Tamworth (M42 North)

The SOUTH, Birmingham Sutton Coldfield — M6 Toll

A5

T5 — Toll

A5 — A38

A5195 Brownhills, Burntwood

The NORTH WEST (M6 North), Cannock — M6 Toll

A38 Burton, Lichfield A5 Tamworth

The NORTH WEST (M6 North), Cannock — M6 Toll

T4 — Toll

A5 — A38

A38 Birmingham Sutton Coldfield

M6 Toll London, Coventry, (M6, M42)

A38

T3 — Tolls

A38

A38 Sutton Coldfield

The NORTH WEST Cannock, Lichfield — M6 Toll

A446 (M42 North) Coleshill

M6 Toll London, Coventry, (M6, M42)(S)

A446

T2 — A4091

A446

M6 Toll

T1 — A446

M42

A446

A4097 A446 M42 — The N. EAST (M1), Tamworth

The NORTH WEST — M6 Toll

A4097

9 — M42

A446

M6(N) Birmingham (Cen, E, N, & T.) &

M42 The SOUTH WEST (M5) (M6, South M40) Birmingham (S), N.E.C. & — London, Coventry

M42 & M6 Toll Motorways merge in ¼ mile

A38(M) & A38 B'ham (E, Cen, & NE) & Lichfield

London (M1 & M40) N.E.C. & B'ham

A5127

A452

The NORTH (M1) The SOUTH (M40)

M42 & M6 — LONDON Coventry N.E.C.

8 — M42

A446

M42 The SOUTH WEST (M8) B'ham (S), N.E.C. & London, (S & W)

M6 London (N & E) (M1 Coventry (S & W))

Ring / central junctions

6 — A38(M) — A38

A5127

A452

5 — A452

B4147

M6

4ᴬ — M6

A452 B'ham (E) & Sutton Coldfield

The NORTH WEST & B'ham (Cen. N & W) — M6

A38(M)

A4540

A38 — A4540

Stay in lane through ◆ markings

M6 & A38(M), A38 B'ham (Cen & NE) — M6 M6

7ᴬ — M6

7 — **4** — M6 — **3ᴬ**

M6 London (M1), Coventry

The N. EAST (M6Toll) M42 & The N. EAST (M1), Tamworth — M42

M6 The NORTH WEST, B'ham

The NORTH WEST (M6Toll) The NORTH EAST (M1) — M42

A446

A45 B'ham (S.E.) N.E.C. Coventry

The SOUTH WEST, LONDON (M40) Birmingham (SE), Solihull — M42

6 — A45

A45 B'ham (S.E.) N.E.C., Coventry (S & W)

The NORTH, B'ham (E.N & Cen), Coventry (N & E) — M42

A41 Solihull

5 — A4141

A41 Solihull

A3400 Henley-in-Arden

A34 Shirley

4 — A3400 — M42

The NORTH M42 N.E.C. & B'ham

M42 & M40

London (M40) Warwick Stratford

M40 London, Warwick, Stratford

3ᴬ — M42

M40 London, Warwick, Stratford

M42 The SOUTH WEST (M5), Birmingham (S & W)

Legend

3 Full access junction

4ᴬ Limited access junction

T4 Full access junction M6 Toll

T1 Limited access junction M6 Toll

Inset maps (place names)

Norton Canes, Burntwood, LICHFIELD, Hammerwich, Cheslyn Hay, Great Wyrley, Brownhills, Shenstone, Essington, Aldridge, WALSALL, SUTTON COLDFIELD, DUDLEY, WEST BROMWICH, BIRMINGHAM, HALESOWEN, Coleshill, Water Orton, Curdworth

Full junction / Restricted junction

NORTON CANES SERVICES

DUDLEY, WEST BROMWICH, BIRMINGHAM, HALESOWEN, SUTTON COLDFIELD, Coleshill, Water Orton, Curdworth, Bickenhill, SOLIHULL, Knowle, Hampton in Arden, Wythall, Hopwood Park, Barnt Green, Alvechurch, Catshill, Cofton Hackett, Romsley, Frankley

FRANKLEY SERVICES

EuroRAP

This map shows the statistical risk of death or serious injury occurring on Britain's motorway and A road network for 2014-2016. More than half of Britain's road fatalities are on the British EuroRAP network, which covers 48,500km in total, representing around 10% of Britain's road network, and which carries almost 70% of the traffic.

The risk is calculated by comparing the frequency of road crashes resulting in death and serious injury on every stretch of road with how much traffic each road is carrying. For example, the risk on a road carrying 10,000 vehicles a day with 20 crashes is ten times the risk on a road that has the same number of crashes but which carries 100,000 vehicles.

Some of the roads shown have had improvements made to them recently but, during the survey period, the risk of a fatal or serious injury crash on the black road sections was almost 30 times that of the safest (green) roads.

For more information on the Road Safety Foundation go to **www.roadsafetyfoundation.org.**

For more information on the statistical background to this research, visit the EuroRAP website at **www.eurorap.org.**

Road Assessment Programme Risk Rating

- Low risk (safest) roads
- Low-medium risk roads
- Medium risk roads
- Medium-high risk roads
- High risk roads

- Motorway
- Single and dual carriageway
- Unrated roads

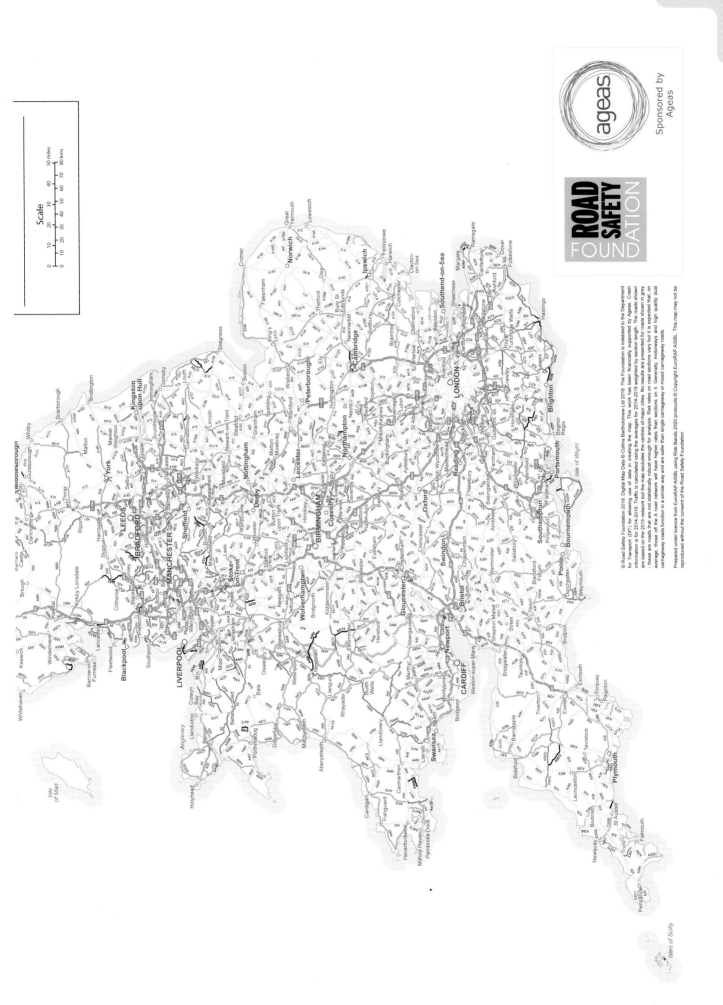
Scale
0 10 20 30 40 50 miles
0 10 20 30 40 50 60 70 80 kms
ROAD SAFETY FOUNDATION
ageas
Sponsored by Ageas
Isle of Man
Isles of Scilly
Isle of Wight
Anglesey
Whitehaven
Keswick
Brough
Barnard Castle
Middlesbrough
Darlington
Guisborough
Whitby
Windermere
Kendal
Thirsk
Scarborough
Kirkby Lonsdale
Ripon
Malton
Barrow-in-Furness
Lancaster
Bridlington
Harrogate
Skipton
York
Fleetwood
Clitheroe
Market Weighton
Blackpool
LEEDS
BRADFORD
Selby
Kingston upon Hull
Preston
Burnley
Goole
Southport
Huddersfield
Immingham
Scunthorpe
Bolton
Grimsby
MANCHESTER
Barnsley
Doncaster
LIVERPOOL
Sheffield
Louth
Holyhead
Llandudno
Colwyn Bay
Warrington
Gainsborough
Bangor
Worksop
Chester
Buxton
Macclesfield
Chesterfield
Lincoln
Mold
Skegness
Mansfield
Crewe
Leek
Newark-on-Trent
Betws-y-coed
Wrexham
Stoke-on-Trent
Sleaford
Ashbourne
Boston
Porthmadog
Nottingham
Bala
Uttoxeter
Derby
Grantham
Cromer
Oswestry
Stafford
Melton Mowbray
Spalding
Fakenham
Dolgellau
Burton upon Trent
King's Lynn
Shrewsbury
Newport
Lichfield
Stamford
Wisbech
Norwich
Great Yarmouth
Welshpool
Telford
Wolverhampton
Leicester
Machynlleth
Newtown
Bridgnorth
Hinckley
Peterborough
Lowestoft
Aberystwyth
BIRMINGHAM
Thetford
Diss
Kidderminster
Coventry
Kettering
Ely
Llanguria
Rugby
Huntingdon
Bury St Edmunds
Rhayader
Redditch
Warwick
Northampton
St Neots
Newmarket
Leominster
Daventry
Cambridge
Ipswich
Cardigan
Builth Wells
Worcester
Stratford-upon-Avon
Bedford
Sudbury
Llandovery
Evesham
Banbury
Royston
Fishguard
Hereford
Milton Keynes
Felixstowe
Harwich
Buckingham
Braintree
Carmarthen
Stevenage
Colchester
Gloucester
Cheltenham
Haverfordwest
Merthyr Tydfil
Abergavenny
Luton
Bicester
Aylesbury
Harlow
Clacton-on-Sea
St Albans
Chelmsford
Milford Haven
Pembroke Dock
Llanelli
Cirencester
Oxford
Watford
Swansea
Neath
Basildon
High Wycombe
Romford
Southend-on-Sea
Swindon
Pontypridd
Newport
Maidenhead
Reading
LONDON
Sheerness
Bridgend
CARDIFF
Bristol
Bracknell
Margate
Chippenham
Newbury
Bath
Dartford
Rochester
Ramsgate
Weston-super-Mare
Woking
Sevenoaks
Maidstone
Canterbury
Basingstoke
Shepton Mallet
Warminster
Andover
Farnham
Guildford
Ashford
Dover
Barnstaple
Bridgwater
Street
Folkestone
Bideford
Crawley
Salisbury
Winchester
Horsham
Royal Tunbridge Wells
Taunton
Yeovil
Petersfield
Tiverton
Blandford Forum
Southampton
Hastings
Ringwood
Fareham
Lewes
Brighton
Exeter
Bridport
Poole
Portsmouth
Bognor Regis
Dorchester
Bournemouth
Exmouth
Weymouth
Launceston
Tavistock
Newquay
Bodmin
Torquay
Paignton
St Austell
Plymouth
Truro
Penzance
Falmouth

Distance chart

Distances between two selected towns in this table are shown in miles and kilometres. In general, distances are based on the shortest routes by classified roads.

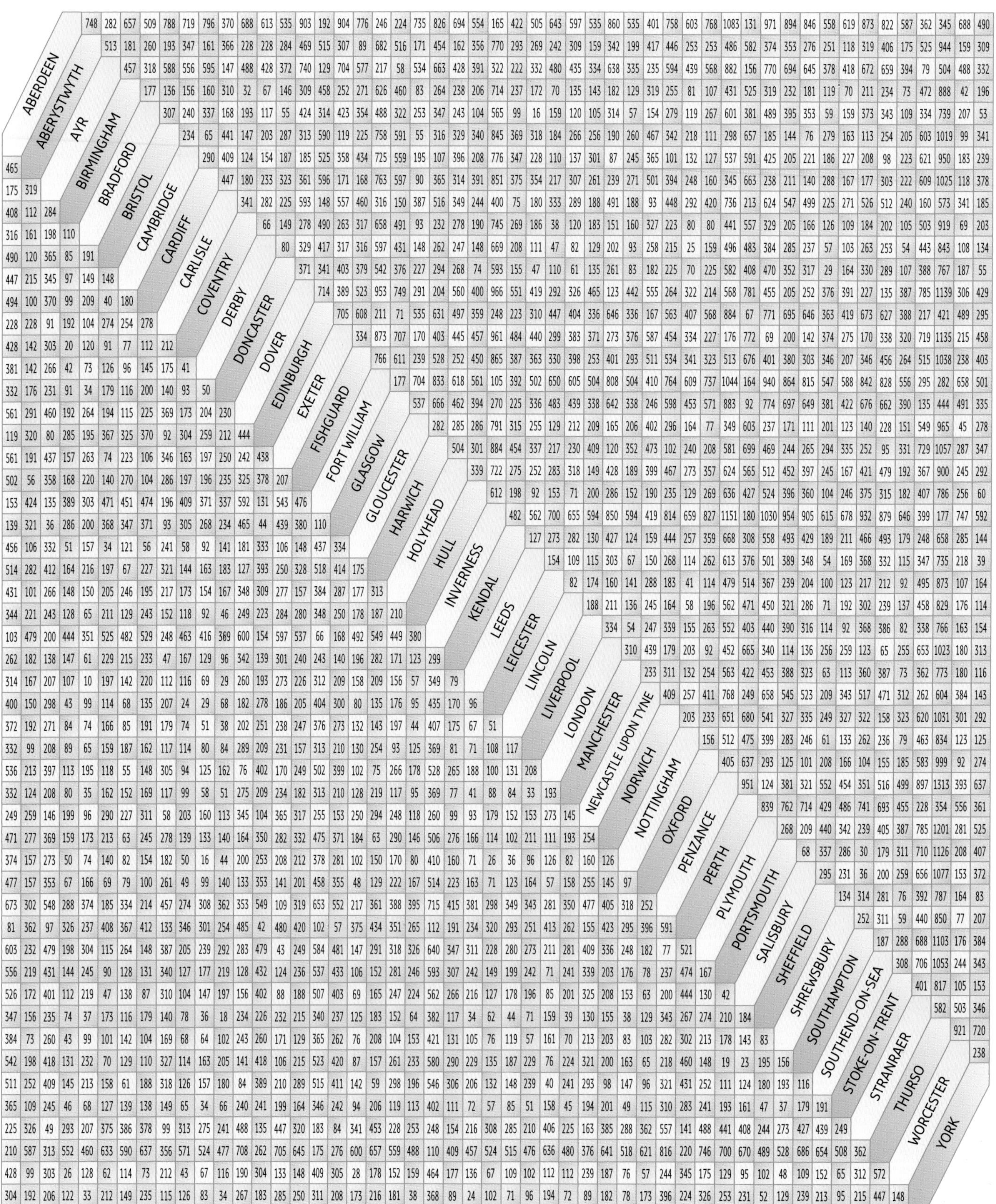

Distance in kilometres

	ABERDEEN	ABERYSTWYTH	AYR	BIRMINGHAM	BRADFORD	BRISTOL	CAMBRIDGE	CARDIFF	CARLISLE	COVENTRY	DERBY	DONCASTER	DOVER	EDINBURGH	EXETER	FISHGUARD	FORT WILLIAM	GLASGOW	GLOUCESTER	HARWICH	HOLYHEAD	HULL	INVERNESS	KENDAL	LEEDS	LEICESTER	LINCOLN	LIVERPOOL	LONDON	MANCHESTER	NEWCASTLE UPON TYNE	NORWICH	NOTTINGHAM	OXFORD	PENZANCE	PERTH	PLYMOUTH	PORTSMOUTH	SALISBURY	SHEFFIELD	SHREWSBURY	SOUTHAMPTON	SOUTHEND-ON-SEA	STOKE-ON-TRENT	STRANRAER	THURSO	WORCESTER	YORK
ABERDEEN		748	282	657	509	788	719	796	370	688	613	535	903	192	904	776	246	224	735	826	694	554	165	422	505	643	597	535	860	535	401	758	603	768	1083	131	971	894	846	558	619	873	822	587	362	345	688	490
ABERYSTWYTH	465		513	181	260	193	347	161	366	228	228	284	469	515	307	89	682	516	171	454	162	356	770	293	269	242	309	159	342	199	417	446	253	253	486	582	374	353	276	251	118	319	406	175	525	944	159	309
AYR	175	319		457	318	588	556	595	147	488	428	372	740	129	704	577	217	58	534	663	428	391	322	222	332	480	435	334	638	335	235	594	439	568	882	156	770	694	645	378	418	672	659	394	79	504	488	332
BIRMINGHAM	408	112	284		177	136	156	160	310	32	67	146	309	458	252	271	626	460	83	264	238	206	714	237	172	70	135	143	182	129	319	255	81	107	431	525	319	232	181	119	70	211	234	73	472	888	42	196
BRADFORD	316	161	198	110		307	240	337	168	193	117	55	424	314	423	354	488	322	253	347	243	104	565	99	16	159	120	105	314	57	154	279	119	267	601	381	489	395	353	59	159	373	343	109	334	739	207	53
BRISTOL	490	120	365	85	191		234	65	441	147	203	287	313	590	119	225	758	591	55	316	329	340	845	369	318	184	266	256	190	260	467	342	218	111	298	657	185	144	76	279	163	113	254	205	603	1019	99	341
CAMBRIDGE	447	215	345	97	149	148		290	409	124	154	187	185	525	358	434	725	559	195	107	396	208	776	347	228	110	137	301	87	245	365	101	132	127	537	591	425	205	221	186	227	208	98	223	621	950	183	239
CARDIFF	494	100	370	99	209	40	180		447	180	233	323	361	596	171	168	763	597	90	365	314	391	851	375	354	217	307	261	239	271	501	394	248	160	345	663	238	211	140	288	167	177	303	222	609	1025	118	378
CARLISLE	228	228	91	192	104	274	254	278		341	282	225	593	148	557	460	316	150	387	516	349	244	400	75	180	333	289	188	491	188	93	448	292	420	736	213	624	547	499	225	271	526	512	240	160	573	341	185
COVENTRY	428	142	303	20	120	91	77	112	212		66	149	278	490	263	317	658	491	93	232	278	190	745	269	186	38	120	183	151	160	327	223	80	80	441	557	329	205	166	126	109	184	202	105	503	919	69	203
DERBY	381	142	266	42	73	126	96	145	175	41		80	329	417	317	316	597	431	148	262	247	148	669	208	111	47	82	129	202	93	258	215	25	159	496	483	384	285	237	57	103	263	253	54	443	843	108	134
DONCASTER	332	176	231	91	34	179	116	200	140	93	50		371	341	403	379	542	376	227	294	268	74	593	155	47	110	61	135	261	83	182	225	70	225	582	408	470	352	317	29	164	330	289	107	388	767	187	55
DOVER	561	291	460	192	264	194	115	225	369	173	204	230		714	389	523	953	749	291	204	560	400	966	551	419	292	326	465	123	442	555	264	322	214	568	781	455	205	252	376	391	227	135	387	785	1139	306	429
EDINBURGH	119	320	80	285	195	367	325	370	92	304	259	212	444		705	608	211	71	535	631	497	359	248	223	310	447	404	336	646	336	167	563	407	568	884	67	771	695	646	363	419	673	627	388	217	421	489	295
EXETER	561	191	437	157	263	74	223	106	346	163	197	250	242	438		334	873	707	170	403	445	457	961	484	440	299	383	371	273	376	587	454	334	227	176	772	69	200	142	374	275	170	338	320	719	1135	215	458
FISHGUARD	502	56	358	168	220	140	270	104	286	197	196	235	325	378	207		766	611	239	528	252	450	865	387	363	330	398	253	401	293	511	534	341	323	513	676	401	380	303	346	207	346	456	264	515	1038	238	403
FORT WILLIAM	153	424	135	389	303	471	451	474	196	409	371	337	592	131	543	476		177	704	833	618	561	105	392	502	650	605	504	808	504	410	764	609	737	1044	164	940	864	815	547	588	842	828	556	295	282	658	501
GLASGOW	139	321	36	286	200	368	347	371	93	305	268	234	465	44	439	380	110		537	666	462	394	270	225	336	483	439	338	642	338	246	598	453	571	883	92	774	697	649	381	422	676	662	390	135	444	491	335
GLOUCESTER	456	106	332	51	157	34	121	56	241	58	92	141	181	333	106	148	437	334		282	285	286	791	315	255	129	212	209	165	206	402	296	164	77	349	603	237	171	111	201	123	140	228	151	549	965	45	278
HARWICH	514	282	412	164	216	197	67	227	321	144	163	183	127	393	250	328	518	414	175		504	301	884	454	337	217	230	409	120	352	473	102	240	208	581	699	469	244	265	294	335	252	95	331	729	1057	287	347
HOLYHEAD	431	101	266	148	150	205	246	195	217	173	154	167	348	309	277	157	384	287	177	313		339	722	275	252	283	318	149	428	189	399	467	273	357	624	565	512	452	397	245	167	421	479	192	367	900	245	292
HULL	344	221	243	128	65	211	129	243	152	118	92	46	249	223	284	280	348	250	178	187	210		612	198	92	153	71	200	286	152	190	235	129	269	636	427	524	396	360	104	246	375	315	182	407	786	256	60
INVERNESS	103	479	200	444	351	525	482	529	248	463	416	369	600	154	597	537	66	168	492	549	449	380		482	562	700	655	594	850	594	419	814	659	827	1151	180	1030	954	905	615	678	932	879	646	399	177	747	592
KENDAL	262	182	138	147	61	229	215	233	47	167	129	96	342	139	301	240	243	140	196	282	171	123	299		127	273	282	130	427	124	159	444	257	359	668	308	558	493	429	189	211	466	493	179	248	658	285	144
LEEDS	314	167	207	107	10	197	142	220	112	116	69	29	260	193	273	226	312	209	158	209	156	57	349	79		154	109	115	303	67	150	268	114	262	613	376	501	389	348	54	169	368	332	115	347	735	218	39
LEICESTER	400	150	298	43	99	114	68	135	207	24	29	68	182	278	186	205	404	300	80	135	176	95	435	170	96		82	174	160	141	288	183	41	114	479	514	367	239	204	100	123	217	212	92	495	873	107	164
LINCOLN	372	192	271	84	74	166	85	191	179	74	51	38	202	251	238	247	376	273	132	143	197	44	407	175	67	51		188	211	136	245	164	58	196	562	471	450	321	286	71	192	302	239	137	458	829	176	114
LIVERPOOL	332	99	208	89	65	159	187	162	117	114	80	84	289	209	231	157	313	210	130	254	93	125	369	81	71	108	117		334	54	247	339	155	263	552	403	440	390	316	114	92	368	386	82	338	766	163	154
LONDON	536	213	397	113	195	118	55	148	305	94	125	162	76	402	170	249	502	399	102	75	266	178	528	265	188	100	131	208		310	439	179	203	92	452	665	340	114	136	256	259	123	65	255	653	1023	180	313
MANCHESTER	332	124	208	80	35	162	152	169	117	99	58	51	275	209	234	182	313	210	128	219	117	95	369	77	41	88	84	33	193		233	311	132	254	563	422	453	388	323	63	113	360	387	73	362	773	180	116
NEWCASTLE UPON TYNE	249	259	146	199	96	290	227	311	58	203	160	113	345	104	365	317	255	153	250	294	248	118	260	99	93	179	152	153	273	145		409	257	411	768	249	658	545	523	209	343	517	471	312	262	604	384	143
NORWICH	471	277	369	159	173	213	63	245	278	139	133	140	164	350	282	332	475	371	184	63	290	146	506	276	166	114	102	211	111	193	254		203	233	651	680	541	327	335	249	327	322	158	323	620	1031	301	292
NOTTINGHAM	374	157	273	50	74	140	82	154	182	50	16	44	200	253	208	212	378	281	102	150	170	80	410	160	71	26	36	96	126	82	160	126		156	512	475	399	283	246	61	133	262	236	79	463	834	123	125
OXFORD	477	157	353	67	166	69	79	100	261	49	99	140	133	353	141	201	458	355	48	129	222	167	514	223	163	71	123	164	57	158	255	145	97		405	637	293	125	101	208	166	104	155	185	583	999	92	274
PENZANCE	673	302	548	288	374	185	334	214	457	274	308	362	353	549	109	319	653	552	217	361	388	395	715	415	381	298	349	343	281	350	477	405	318	252		951	124	381	321	552	454	351	516	499	897	1313	393	637
PERTH	81	362	97	326	237	408	367	412	133	346	301	254	485	42	480	420	102	57	375	434	351	265	112	191	234	320	293	251	413	262	155	423	295	396	591		839	762	714	429	486	741	693	455	228	354	556	361
PLYMOUTH	603	232	479	198	304	115	264	148	387	205	239	292	283	479	43	249	584	481	147	291	318	326	640	347	311	228	280	273	211	281	409	336	248	182	77	521		268	209	440	342	239	405	387	785	1201	281	525
PORTSMOUTH	556	219	431	144	245	90	128	131	340	127	177	219	128	432	124	236	537	433	106	152	281	246	593	307	242	149	199	242	71	241	339	203	176	78	237	474	167		68	337	286	30	179	311	710	1126	208	407
SALISBURY	526	172	401	112	219	47	138	87	310	104	147	197	156	402	88	188	507	403	69	165	247	224	562	266	216	127	178	196	85	201	325	208	153	63	200	444	130	42		295	231	36	200	259	656	1077	153	372
SHEFFIELD	347	156	235	74	37	173	116	179	140	78	36	18	234	226	232	215	340	237	125	183	152	64	382	117	34	62	44	71	159	39	130	155	38	129	343	267	274	210	184		134	314	281	76	392	787	164	83
SHREWSBURY	384	73	260	43	99	101	142	104	169	68	64	102	243	260	171	129	365	262	76	208	104	153	421	131	105	76	119	57	161	70	213	203	83	103	282	302	213	178	143	83		252	311	59	440	850	77	207
SOUTHAMPTON	542	198	418	131	232	70	129	110	327	114	163	205	141	418	106	215	523	420	87	157	261	233	580	290	229	135	187	229	76	224	321	200	163	65	218	460	148	19	23	195	156		187	288	688	1103	176	384
SOUTHEND-ON-SEA	511	252	409	145	213	158	61	188	318	126	157	180	84	389	210	289	515	411	142	59	298	196	546	306	206	132	148	239	40	241	293	98	147	96	321	431	252	111	124	180	193	116		308	706	1053	244	343
STOKE-ON-TRENT	365	109	245	46	68	127	139	138	149	65	34	66	240	241	199	164	346	242	94	206	119	113	402	111	72	57	85	51	158	45	194	201	49	115	310	283	241	193	161	47	37	179	191		401	817	105	153
STRANRAER	225	326	49	293	207	375	386	378	99	313	275	241	488	135	447	320	183	84	341	453	228	253	248	154	216	308	285	210	406	225	163	385	288	362	557	141	488	441	408	244	273	427	439	249		582	503	346
THURSO	210	587	313	552	460	633	590	637	356	571	524	477	708	262	705	645	175	276	600	657	559	488	110	409	457	524	515	476	636	480	376	641	518	621	816	220	746	700	670	489	528	686	654	508	362		921	720
WORCESTER	428	99	303	26	128	62	114	73	212	43	67	116	190	304	133	148	409	305	28	178	152	159	464	177	136	67	109	102	112	112	239	187	76	57	244	345	175	129	95	102	48	109	152	65	312	572		238
YORK	304	192	206	122	33	212	149	235	115	126	83	34	267	183	285	250	311	208	173	216	181	38	368	89	24	102	71	96	194	72	89	182	78	173	396	224	326	253	231	52	129	239	213	95	215	447	148	

Distance in miles

Symbols used on the map

Blue place of interest symbols e.g ★ are listed on page 93

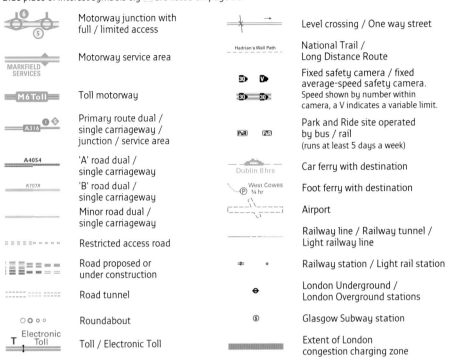

Motorway junction with full / limited access	
Motorway service area	
MARKFIELD SERVICES	
M6 Toll	Toll motorway
A316	Primary route dual / single carriageway / junction / service area
A4054	'A' road dual / single carriageway
B707B	'B' road dual / single carriageway
	Minor road dual / single carriageway
	Restricted access road
	Road proposed or under construction
	Road tunnel
○○○○	Roundabout
T Electronic Toll	Toll / Electronic Toll

	Level crossing / One way street
Hadrian's Wall Path	National Trail / Long Distance Route
30 V	Fixed safety camera / fixed average-speed safety camera. Speed shown by number within camera, a V indicates a variable limit.
P&R P&R	Park and Ride site operated by bus / rail (runs at least 5 days a week)
Dublin 8hrs	Car ferry with destination
West Cowes ¼ hr	Foot ferry with destination
	Airport
	Railway line / Railway tunnel / Light railway line
	Railway station / Light rail station
⊖	London Underground / London Overground stations
Ⓢ	Glasgow Subway station
	Extent of London congestion charging zone

	Notable building
H	Hospital
362 ▲	Spot height (in metres) / Lighthouse
	Built up area
	Woodland / Park
	National Park
	Heritage Coast
BRISTOL	County / Unitary Authority boundary and name
SEE PAGE 68	Area covered by street map

Locator map

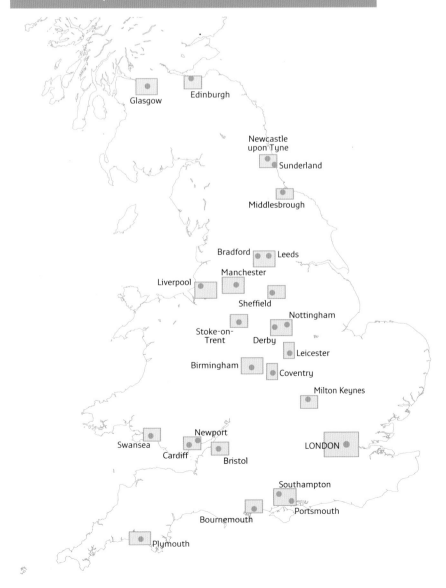

Urban approach maps	
Birmingham	14-15
Bournemouth	3
Bradford	26-27
Bristol	8
Cardiff	7
Coventry	16
Derby	18-19
Edinburgh	32
Glasgow	30-31
Greater Manchester	24-25
Leeds	26-27
Leicester	17
Liverpool	22-23
London	10-13
Manchester	24-25
Merseyside	22-23
Middlesbrough	29
Milton Keynes	9
Newcastle upon Tyne	28-29
Newport	7
Nottingham	18-19
Plymouth	2
Portsmouth	4-5
Sheffield	21
Southampton	4-5
Stoke-on-Trent	20
Sunderland	28-29
Swansea	6
West Midlands	14-15

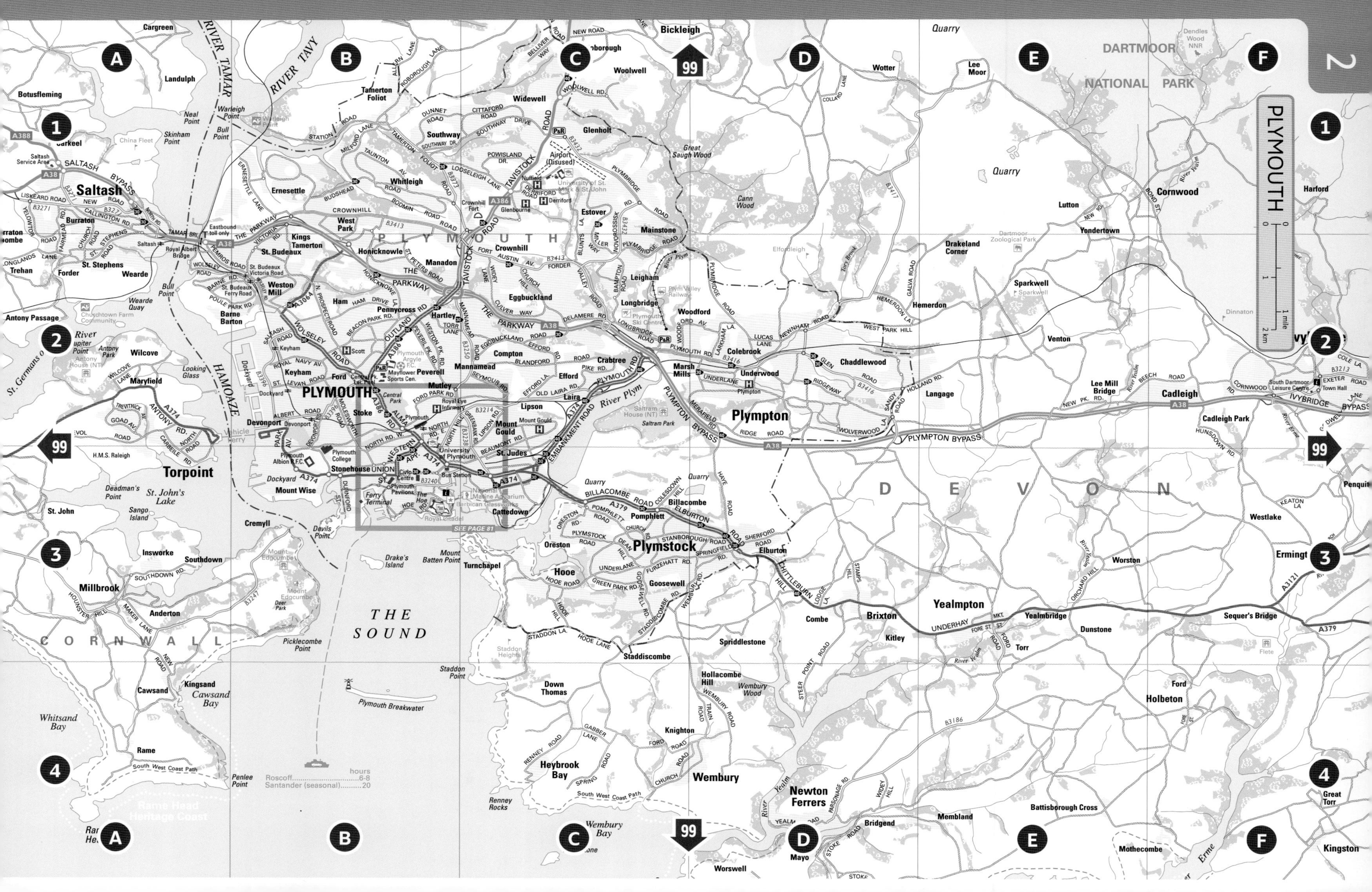
PLYMOUTH
0 1 mile
0 1 2 km
A
B
C
D
E
F
1
2
3
4
99
DARTMOOR
NATIONAL PARK
D E V O N
C O R N W A L L
THE SOUND
PLYMOUTH
Plympton
Plymstock
Saltash
Torpoint
Yealmpton
Cadleigh
Cornwood
Wembury
Newton Ferrers
Bickleigh
Plymouth Breakwater
Drake's Island
Mount Batten Point
HAMOAZE
RIVER TAMAR
RIVER TAVY
River Plym
Whitsand Bay
Cawsand Bay
Wembury Bay
SEE PAGE 81
hours
Roscoff.......6-8
Santander (seasonal).......20

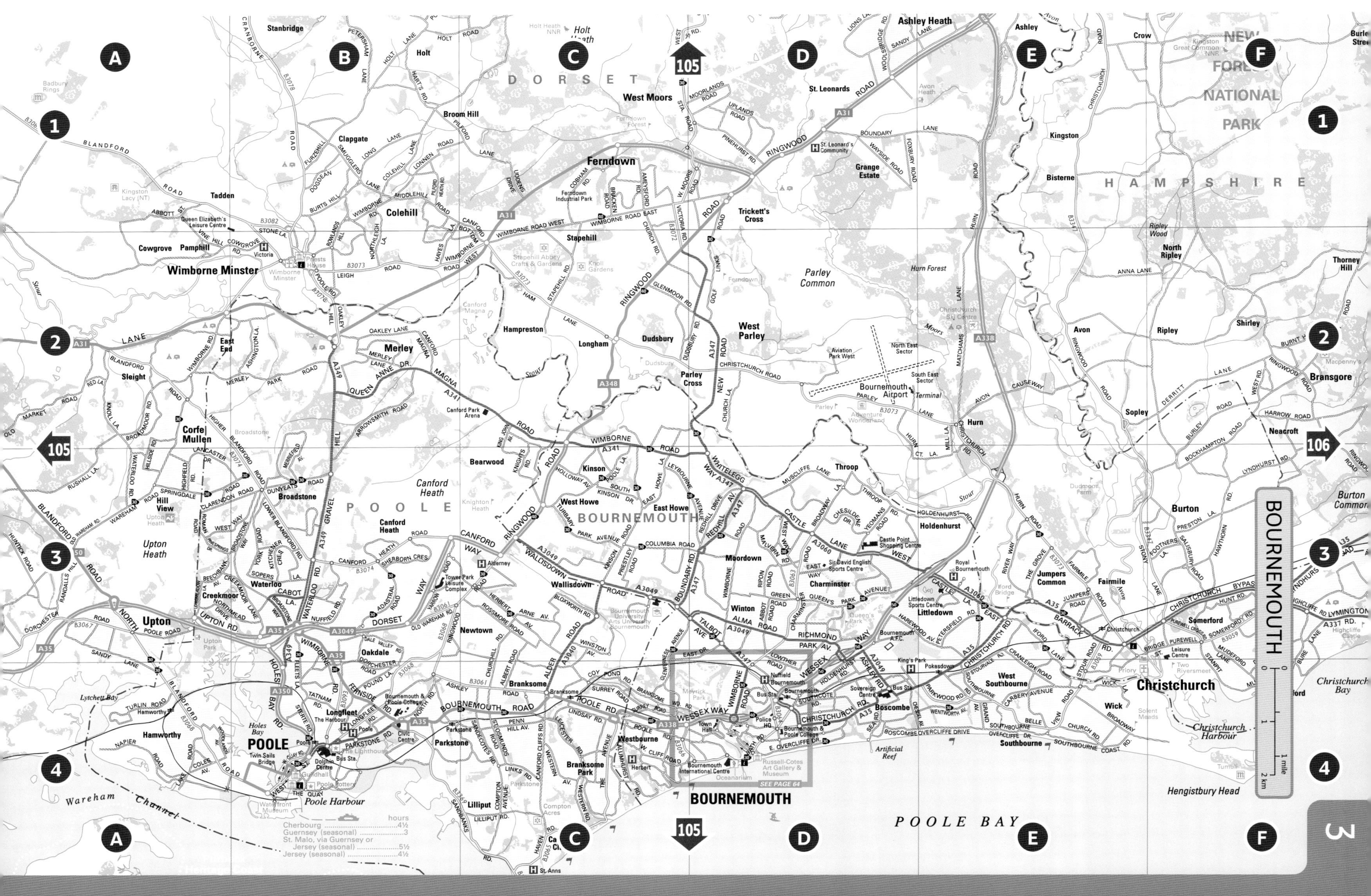
BOURNEMOUTH
1 mile
2 km
POOLE BAY
BOURNEMOUTH
SEE PAGE 64
POOLE
Christchurch
Christchurch Harbour
Christchurch Bay
Hengistbury Head
NEW FOREST NATIONAL PARK
HAMPSHIRE
DORSET
Wimborne Minster
Ferndown
West Moors
St. Leonards
Ashley Heath
West Parley
Bournemouth Airport
Boscombe
Southbourne
West Southbourne
Westbourne
Branksome
Parkstone
Poole Harbour
Holes Bay
Upton
Corfe Mullen
Broadstone
Colehill
Merley
Kinson
Moordown
Winton
Throop
Holdenhurst
Hurn
Sopley
Burton
Bransgore
Wick
Somerford
Hamworthy
Canford Heath
Parley Common
Longham
Hampreston
Stapehill
Holt
Wareham Channel
105
106
Cherbourg (seasonal) hours 4½
Guernsey (seasonal) 3
St. Malo, via Guernsey or Jersey (seasonal) 5½
Jersey (seasonal) 4½

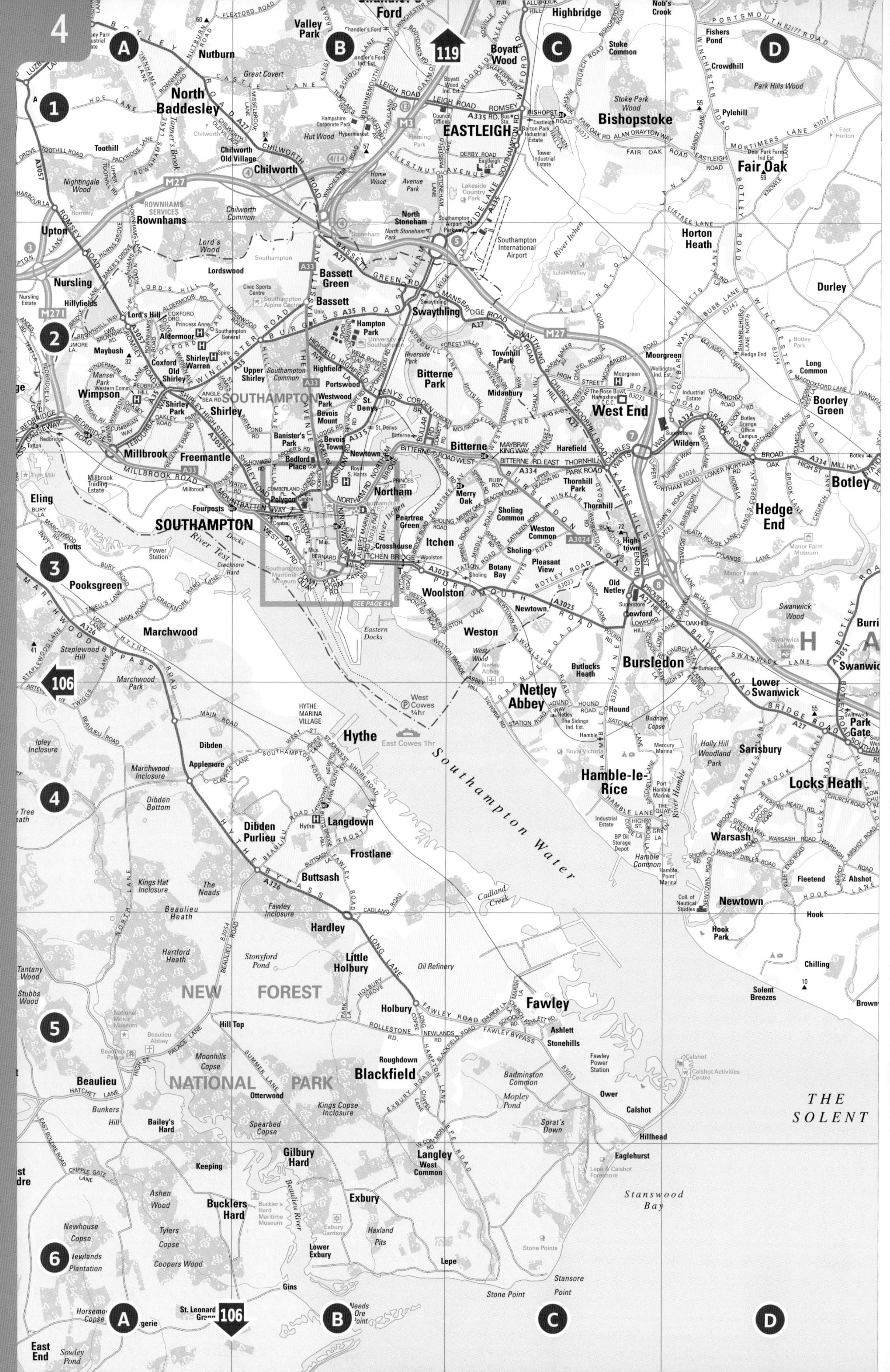

119
106
SEE PAGE 84
A
B
C
D
1
2
3
4
5
6
Valley Park
Nutburn
North Baddesley
Great Covert
Highbridge
Nob's Crook
Fishers Pond
Boyatt Wood
Stoke Common
Crowdhill
Park Hills Wood
Stoke Park Wood
Bishopstoke
Pylehill
EASTLEIGH
Fair Oak
Hut Wood
Toothill
Chilworth Old Village
Chilworth
Nightingale Wood
Home Wood
Avenue Park
Lakeside Country Park
North Stoneham
Rownhams
Chilworth Common
Upton
Lord's Wood
Southampton International Airport
Horton Heath
River Itchen
Itchen Valley
Durley
Nursling
Lordswood
Bassett Green
Bassett
Swaythling
Hillyfields
Lord's Hill
Aldermoor
Maybush
Coxford
Shirley Warren
Old Shirley
Upper Shirley
Southampton Common
Hampton Park
Highfield
Portswood
Townhill Park
Bitterne Park
Moorgreen
Long Common
Mansel Park
Wimpson
SOUTHAMPTON
Westwood Park
St. Denys
Bevois Mount
Midanbury
West End
Boorley Green
Shirley Park
Shirley
Banister's Park
Bevois Town
Millbrook
Freemantle
Newtown
Bitterne
Harefield
Wildern
Bedford Place
Polygon
Northam
Thornhill Park
Thornhill
Botley
Eling
Fourposts
Merry Oak
Sholing Common
Hedge End
SOUTHAMPTON
Peartree Green
Weston Common
River Test
Crosshouse
Itchen
Sholing
Hightown
Trotts
Power Station
Cracknore Hard
Botany Bay
Pleasant View
Pooksgreen
Woolston
Old Netley
Newtown
Eastern Docks
Swanwick Wood
Marchwood
Weston
Lowford
Staplewood Hill
West Wood
Butlocks Heath
Bursledon
Marchwood Park
Lower Swanwick
Netley Abbey
Hound
Hythe
Dibden
Applemore
Marchwood Inclosure
Ipley Inclosure
Holly Hill Woodland Park
Sarisbury
Park Gate
Southampton Water
Hamble-le-Rice
Locks Heath
Dibden Bottom
Dibden Purlieu
Langdown
Warsash
Frostlane
Buttsash
Fleetend
Abshot
Kings Hat Inclosure
The Noads
Cadland Creek
Newtown
Hook
Beaulieu Heath
Fawley Inclosure
Hardley
Hook Park
Hartford Heath
Stonyford Pond
Little Holbury
Oil Refinery
Chilling
NEW FOREST
Solent Breezes
Fawley
Holbury
Hill Top
Ashlett
Stonehills
Moonhills Copse
Roughdown
NATIONAL PARK
Blackfield
Badminston Common
Beaulieu
Otterwood
Mopley Pond
Ower
THE SOLENT
Bunkers Hill
Kings Copse Inclosure
Calshot
Bailey's Hard
Spearbed Copse
Sprat's Down
Hillhead
Gilbury Hard
Langley
West Common
Eaglehurst
Keeping
Ashen Wood
Bucklers Hard
Exbury
Stanswood Bay
Tylers Copse
Haxland Pits
Newhouse Copse
Newlands Plantation
Coopers Wood
Lower Exbury
Lepe
Stone Point
Stansore Point
Gins
Needs Ore Point
East End
Sowley Pond

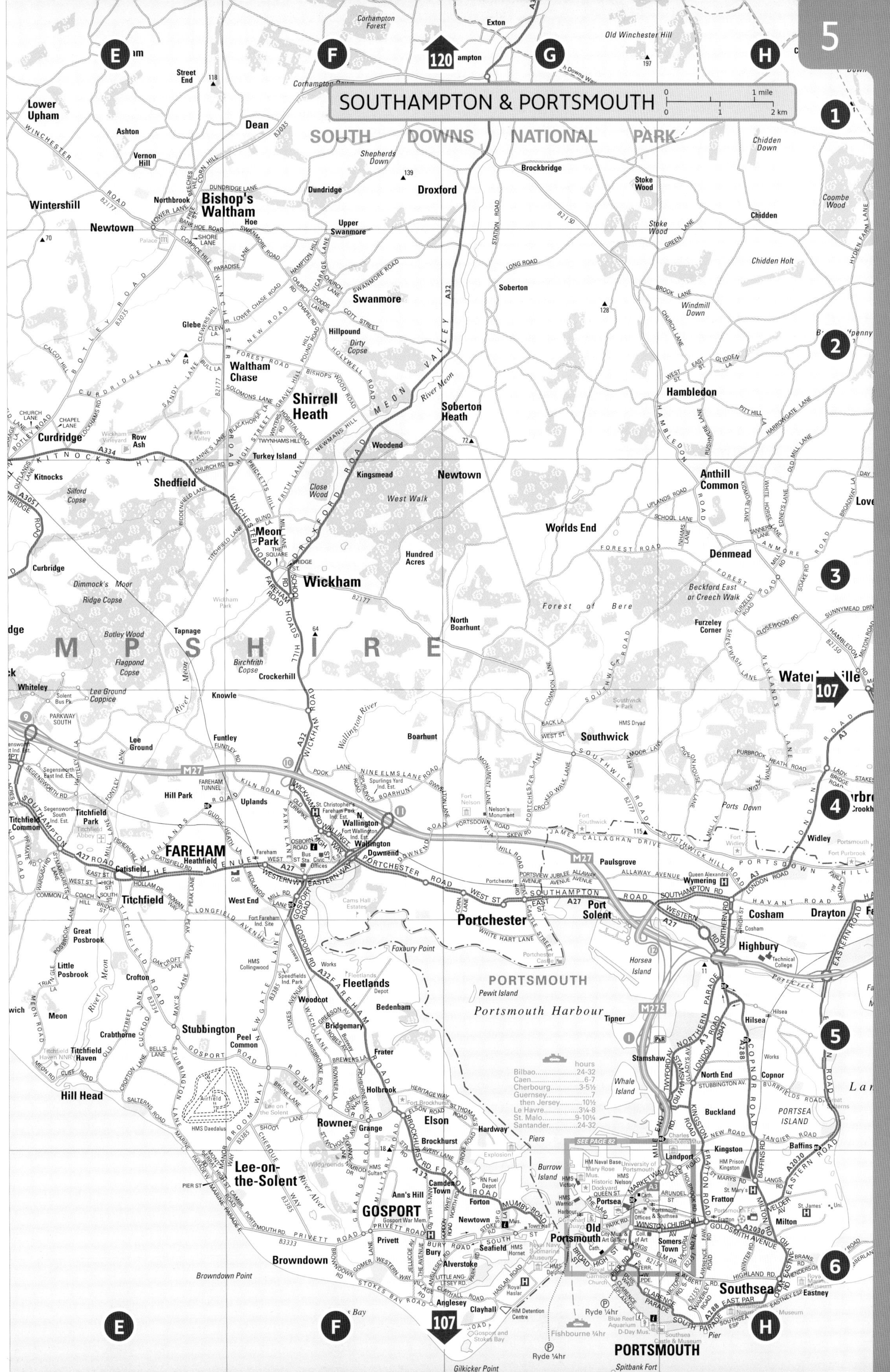
SOUTHAMPTON & PORTSMOUTH
0 1 mile
0 1 2 km
SOUTH DOWNS NATIONAL PARK
E
F
G
H
1
2
3
4
5
6
120
107
107
Corhampton Forest
Exton
Old Winchester Hill
Street End
Lower Upham
Ashton
Dean
Vernon Hill
Shepherds Down
Chidden Down
Brockbridge
Wintershill
Northbrook
Bishop's Waltham
Dundridge
Droxford
Stoke Wood
Coombe Wood
Hoe
Newtown
Upper Swanmore
Chidden
Chidden Holt
Soberton
Swanmore
Windmill Down
Glebe
Hillpound
Dirty Copse
Waltham Chase
Shirrell Heath
Hambledon
Soberton Heath
Curdridge
Row Ash
Woodend
Turkey Island
Kingsmead
Newtown
Anthill Common
Kitnocks
Silford Copse
Shedfield
Close Wood
West Walk
Worlds End
Meon Park
Hundred Acres
Denmead
Curbridge
Wickham
Dimmock's Moor
Ridge Copse
Beckford East or Creech Walk
Forest of Bere
North Boarhunt
Furzeley Corner
Tapnage
Botley Wood
HAMPSHIRE
Flagpond Copse
Birchfrith Copse
Crockerhill
Whiteley
Lee Ground Coppice
Knowle
Waterlooville
Southwick
Lee Ground
Funtley
Boarhunt
M27
Hill Park
Uplands
Titchfield Park
Titchfield Common
N. Wallington
Wallington
Downend
Ports Down
Widley
FAREHAM
Heathfield
Catisfield
Paulsgrove
Wymering
Titchfield
West End
Portchester
Port Solent
Cosham
Drayton
Great Posbrook
Foxbury Point
Highbury
Little Posbrook
Crofton
Fleetlands
PORTSMOUTH
Horsea Island
Pewit Island
Portsmouth Harbour
Tipner
Meon
Woodcot
Bedenham
Hilsea
Stubbington
Bridgemary
Peel Common
Crabthorne
Titchfield Haven
Frater
Stamshaw
Holbrook
Whale Island
North End
Copnor
Hill Head
Rowner
Grange
Elson
Hardway
Buckland
PORTSEA ISLAND
Brockhurst
Kingston
Baffins
Lee-on-the-Solent
Camden Town
Landport
Ann's Hill
Forton
Portsea
Fratton
GOSPORT
Newtown
Old Portsmouth
Milton
Privett
Bury
Seafield
Somers Town
Browndown
Alverstoke
Southsea
Eastney
Anglesey
Clayhall
Browndown Point
Gilkicker Point
Spitbank Fort
hours
Bilbao 24-32
Caen 6-7
Cherbourg 3-5½
Guernsey 7
then Jersey 10½
Le Havre 3¼-8
St. Malo 9-10¾
Santander 24-32
Ryde ¼hr
Fishbourne ¾hr
Ryde ¼hr
SEE PAGE 82

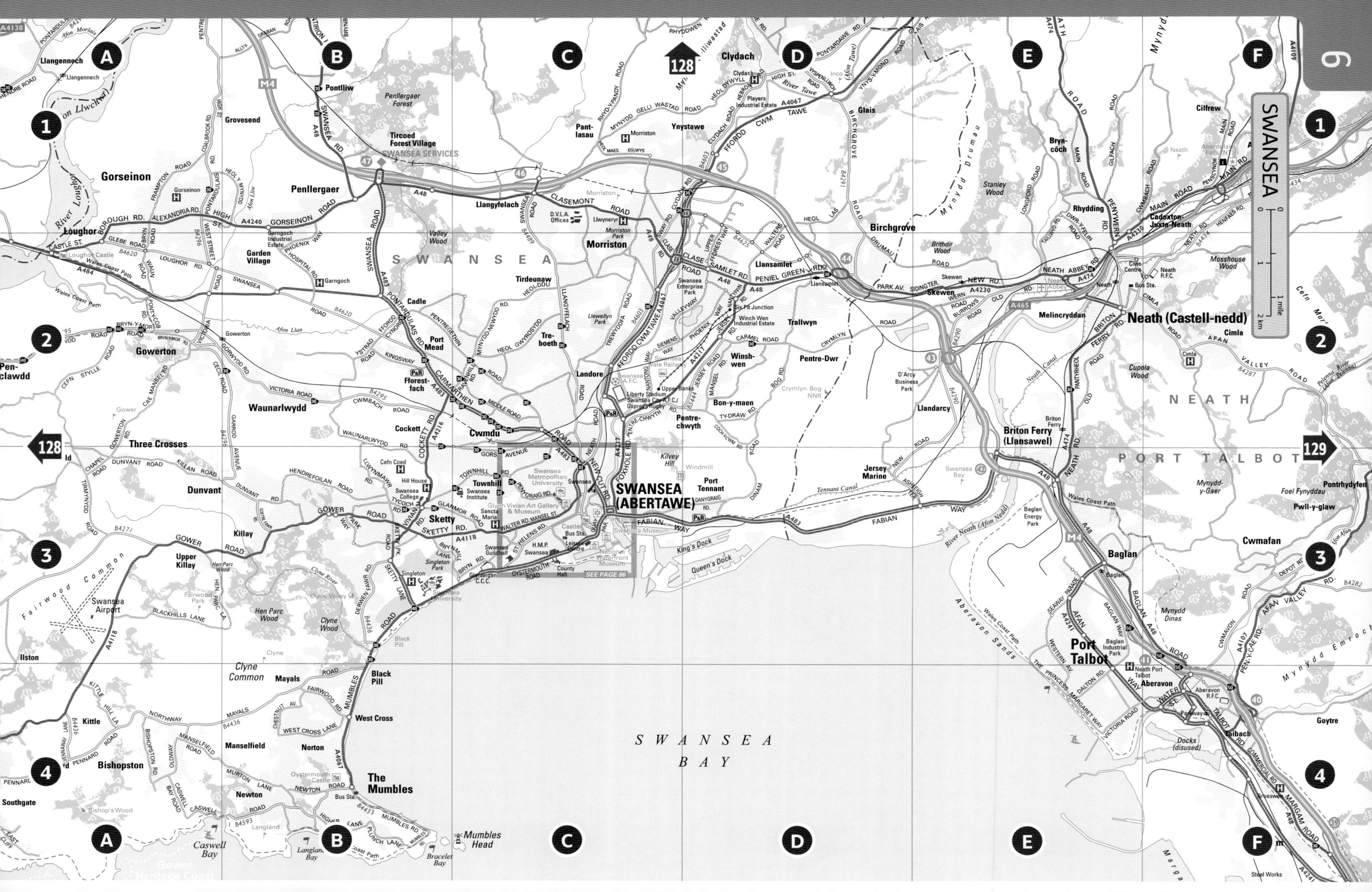
SWANSEA
0 1 mile
0 1 2 km
SWANSEA (ABERTAWE)
Neath (Castell-nedd)
Port Talbot
Aberavon
Briton Ferry (Llansawel)
Baglan
Skewen
Llandarcy
Jersey Marine
Port Tennant
Morriston
Llansamlet
Clydach
Ynystawe
Glais
Birchgrove
Trallwyn
Pentre-Dwr
Winsh-wen
Bon-y-maen
Pentre-chwyth
Landore
Tre-boeth
Tirdeunaw
Llangyfelach
Cwmdu
Townhill
Sketty
Cockett
Fforest-fach
Cadle
Port Mead
Penllergaer
Gorseinon
Loughor
Garden Village
Gowerton
Waunarlwydd
Dunvant
Killay
Upper Killay
Three Crosses
Black Pill
West Cross
The Mumbles
Mumbles Head
Mayals
Norton
Newton
Manselfield
Bishopston
Kittle
Ilston
Southgate
Caswell Bay
Swansea Airport
Fairwood Common
Clyne Common
SWANSEA BAY
Aberavon Sands
Mynydd Drumau
Cwmafan
Pontrhydyfen
Pwll-y-glaw
Goytre
Taibach
Melincryddan
Cimla
Cilfrew
Cadoxton-Juxta-Neath
Rhydding
Penywern
Bryn-coch
Llangennech
Pontlliw
Grovesend
Pant-lasau
Tircoed Forest Village
SWANSEA SERVICES
Pen-clawdd
NEATH
PORT TALBOT
SWANSEA
128
129
SEE PAGE 86
M4
A48
A483
A4067
A4118
A4217
A465
Fabian Way

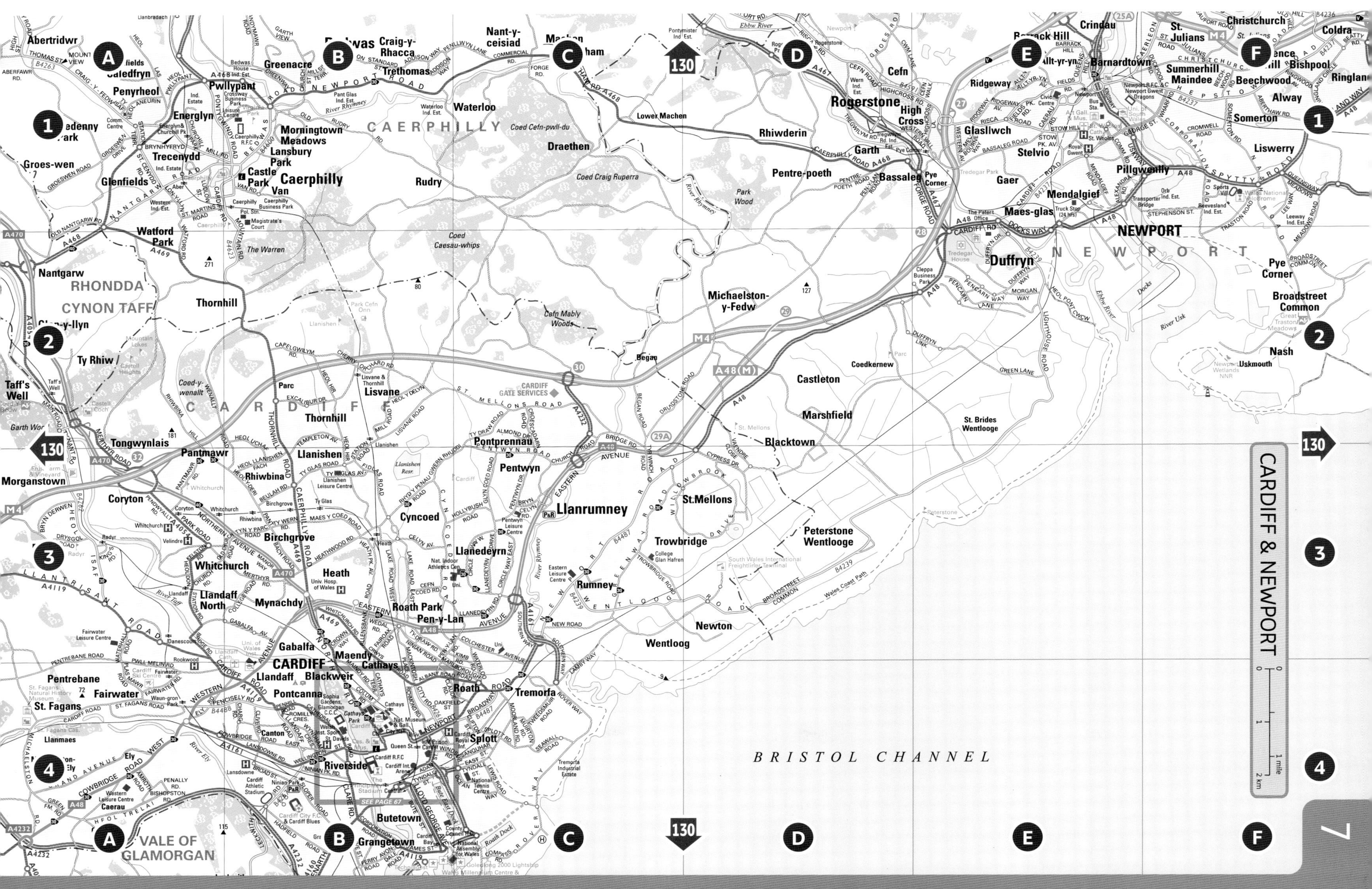
CARDIFF & NEWPORT
0 1 mile
0 1 2 km
130
BRISTOL CHANNEL
NEWPORT
CARDIFF
CAERPHILLY
RHONDDA CYNON TAFF
VALE OF GLAMORGAN
Abertridwr
Penyrheol
Groes-wen
Glenfields
Pwllypant
Energlyn
Trecenydd
Greenacre
Trethomas
Mornington Meadows
Lansbury Park
Castle Park
Van
Caerphilly
Waterloo
Nant-y-ceisiad
Draethen
Rudry
Lower Machen
Watford Park
Nantgarw
Thornhill
Ty Rhiw
Taff's Well
Tongwynlais
Morganstown
Coryton
Pantmawr
Rhiwbina
Llanishen
Lisvane
Parc
Whitchurch
Birchgrove
Heath
Llandaff North
Mynachdy
Gabalfa
Maendy
Cathays
Llandaff
Blackweir
Pontcanna
Canton
Riverside
Butetown
Grangetown
Roath
Splott
Tremorfa
Pentrebane
Fairwater
St. Fagans
Llanmaes
Ely
Caerau
Cyncoed
Llanedeyrn
Roath Park
Pen-y-Lan
Pentwyn
Pontprennau
Llanrumney
Rumney
Trowbridge
St.Mellons
Newton
Wentloog
Peterstone Wentlooge
Blacktown
Marshfield
Castleton
Coedkernew
St. Brides Wentlooge
Michaelston-y-Fedw
Began
Cefn Mably Woods
Coed Caesau-whips
Coed Craig Ruperra
Coed Cefn-pwll-du
Rhiwderin
Pentre-poeth
Garth
Bassaleg
Rogerstone
High Cross
Cefn
Ridgeway
Glasllwch
Stelvio
Gaer
Mendalgief
Maes-glas
Duffryn
Pillgwenlly
Allt-yr-yn
Barnardtown
Crindau
St. Julians
Summerhill
Maindee
Beechwood
Christchurch
Alway
Somerton
Lisvwerry
Ringland
Coldra
Bishpool
Pye Corner
Broadstreet Common
Nash
Uskmouth
River Usk
Ebbw River
River Rhymney
River Taff
River Ely
Cardiff Gate Services
SEE PAGE 67
A48(M)
M4
A48
A469
A470
A4232

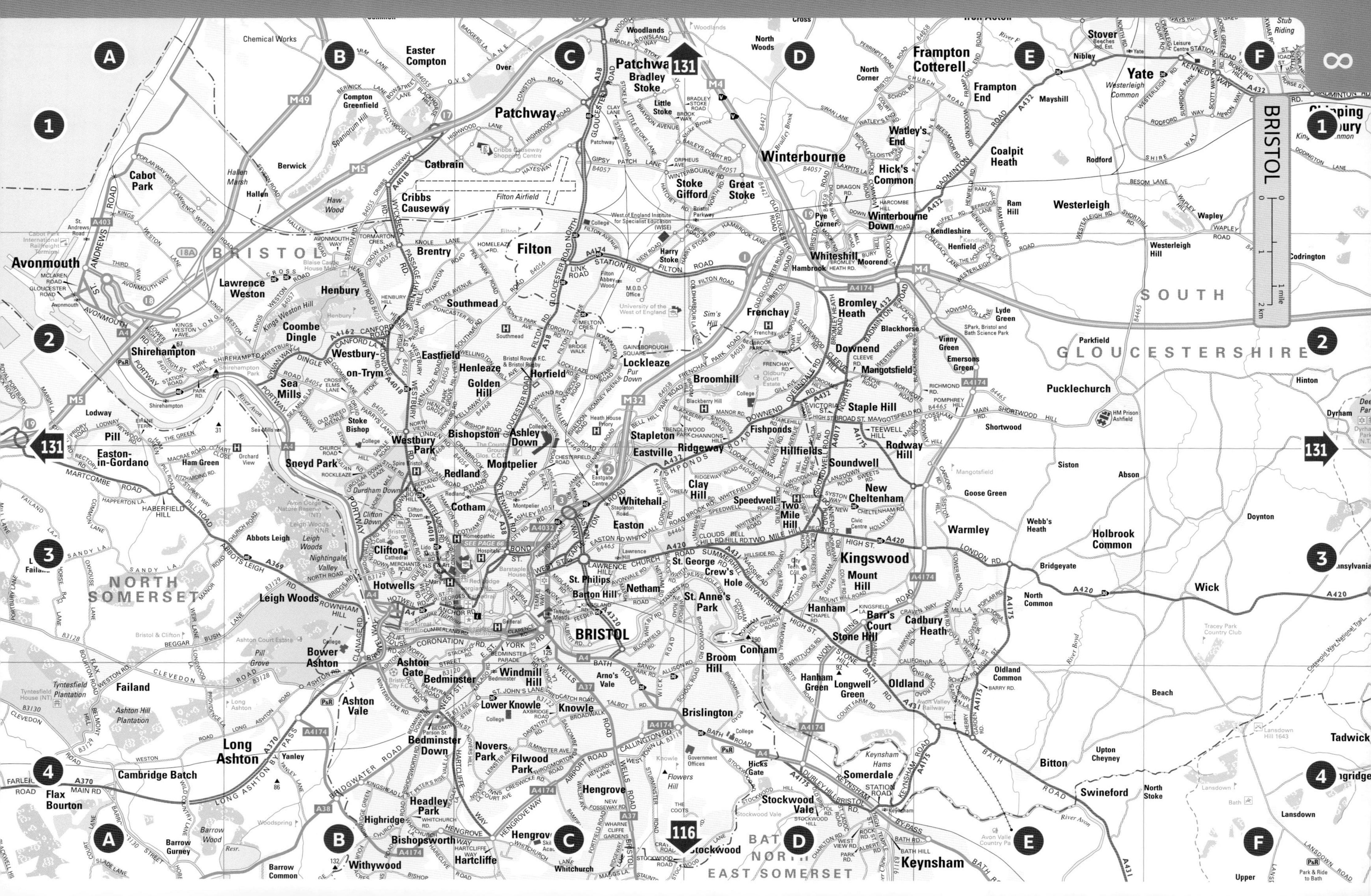
BRISTOL
0 1 mile
0 1 2 km
SOUTH GLOUCESTERSHIRE
NORTH SOMERSET
BATH & NORTH EAST SOMERSET
BRISTOL
Avonmouth
Cabot Park
Easter Compton
Compton Greenfield
Patchway
Bradley Stoke
Little Stoke
Stoke Gifford
Great Stoke
Winterbourne
Frampton Cotterell
Frampton End
Coalpit Heath
Yate
Stover
Nibley
Westerleigh
Pucklechurch
Lyde Green
Emersons Green
Filton
Filton Airfield
Cribbs Causeway
Catbrain
Brentry
Henbury
Lawrence Weston
Coombe Dingle
Shirehampton
Sea Mills
Westbury-on-Trym
Southmead
Henleaze
Horfield
Lockleaze
Frenchay
Bromley Heath
Downend
Mangotsfield
Staple Hill
Fishponds
Stapleton
Eastville
Ridgeway
Hillfields
Soundwell
Rodway Hill
New Cheltenham
Kingswood
Warmley
Siston
Abson
Wick
Holbrook Common
Bridgeyate
Doynton
Dyrham
Hinton
Stoke Bishop
Sneyd Park
Westbury Park
Bishopston
Ashley Down
Redland
Montpelier
Cotham
Clifton
Hotwells
Leigh Woods
Abbots Leigh
Pill
Easton-in-Gordano
Ham Green
Lodway
Failand
Long Ashton
Ashton Vale
Bower Ashton
Ashton Gate
Bedminster
Windmill Hill
Lower Knowle
Knowle
Bedminster Down
Novers Park
Filwood Park
Hengrove
Headley Park
Highridge
Bishopsworth
Withywood
Hartcliffe
Whitchurch
Brislington
Broom Hill
Conham
St. Anne's Park
St. George
Crew's Hole
Easton
Whitehall
Clay Hill
Speedwell
Two Mile Hill
St. Philips
Barton Hill
Netham
Hanham
Mount Hill
Barr's Court
Cadbury Heath
Stone Hill
Oldland
Oldland Common
Longwell Green
Hanham Green
Bitton
Swineford
Upton Cheyney
North Stoke
Lansdown
Tadwick
Keynsham
Somerdale
Stockwood
Stockwood Vale
Hicks Gate
Cambridge Batch
Flax Bourton
Barrow Gurney
Barrow Common
Yanley
M4
M5
M32
M49
A4
A38
A37
A420
A431
A432
A4174
131
116

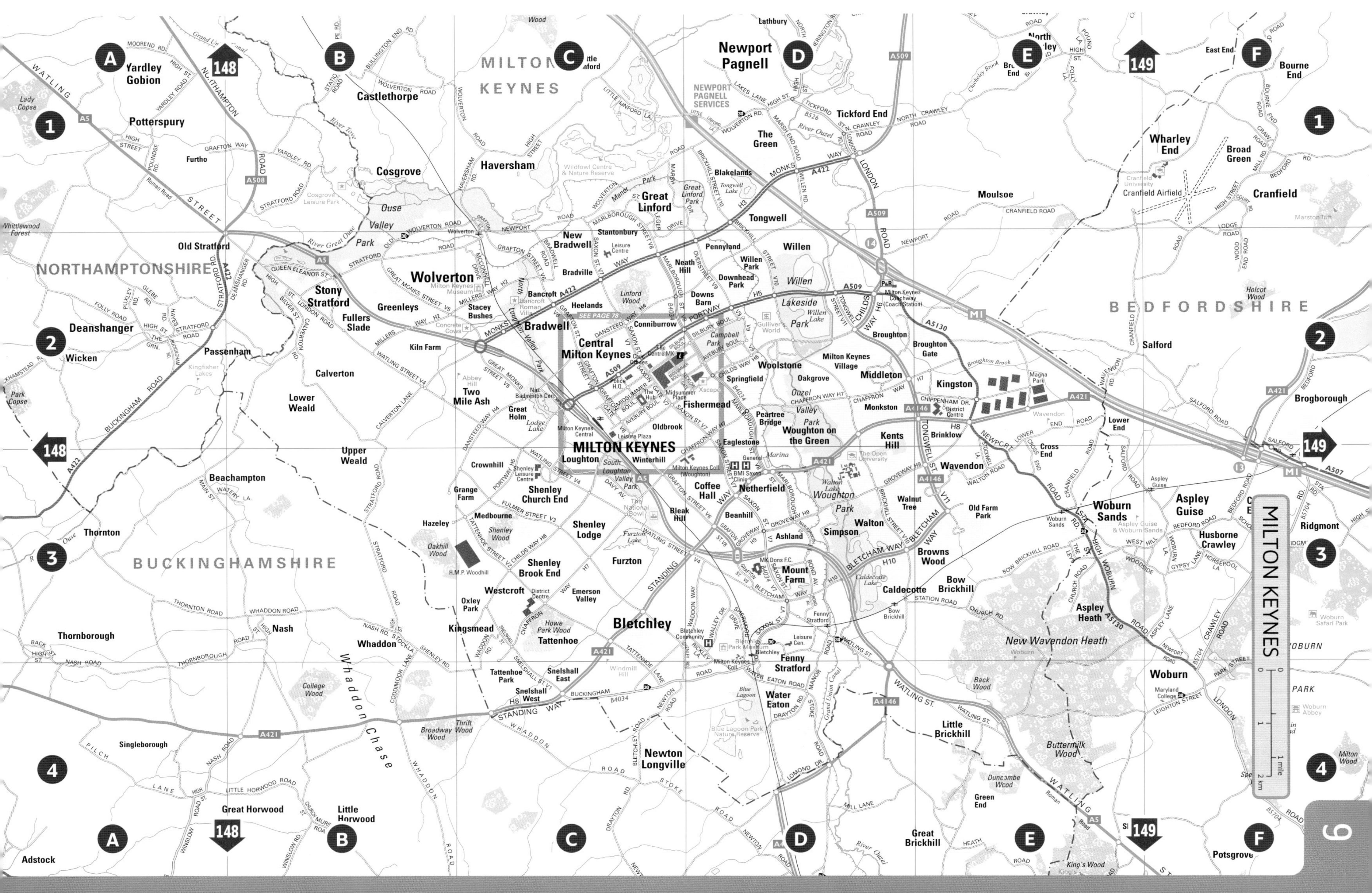
MILTON KEYNES
0 1 mile
0 1 2 km
BEDFORDSHIRE
BUCKINGHAMSHIRE
NORTHAMPTONSHIRE
MILTON KEYNES
Central Milton Keynes
SEE PAGE 78
Newport Pagnell
Wolverton
Stony Stratford
Bletchley
Woburn Sands
Woburn
Cranfield
New Wavendon Heath
Whaddon Chase
148
149

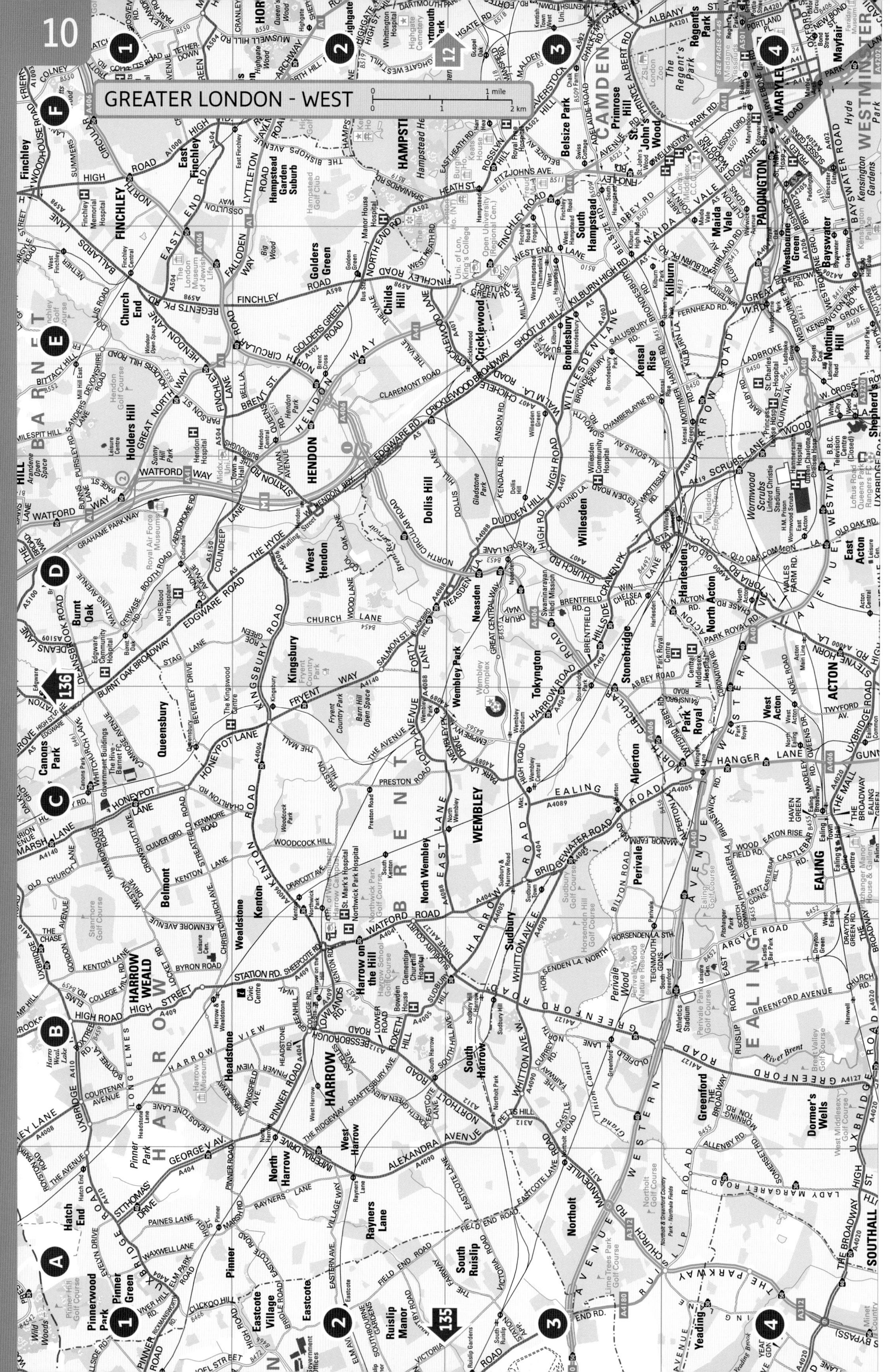
GREATER LONDON - WEST
0
1 mile
0
1
2 km
Finchley
FINCHLEY
East Finchley
Hampstead Garden Suburb
Golders Green
Childs Hill
Church End
Holders Hill
Hendon
HENDON
West Hendon
Burnt Oak
Canons Park
Queensbury
Kingsbury
Dollis Hill
Cricklewood
Neasden
Wembley Park
WEMBLEY
North Wembley
Tokyngton
Stonebridge
Alperton
Willesden
Harlesden
Brondesbury
Kensal Rise
Kilburn
Maida Vale
PADDINGTON
Westbourne Green
Bayswater
Notting Hill
Shepherd's Bush
East Acton
North Acton
ACTON
West Acton
Park Royal
EALING
Perivale
Greenford
Dormer's Wells
SOUTHALL
Yeading
Northolt
South Ruislip
Ruislip Manor
Eastcote
Eastcote Village
Rayners Lane
West Harrow
HARROW
Harrow on the Hill
South Harrow
Sudbury
Kenton
Wealdstone
Belmont
Headstone
North Harrow
Pinner
Pinner Green
Pinnerwood Park
Hatch End
HARROW WEALD
Belsize Park
Primrose Hill
St. John's Wood
South Hampstead
CAMDEN
Regent's Park
MARYLEBONE
Mayfair
WESTMINSTER
Kensington Gardens
Hyde Park
HAMPSTEAD
Wormwood Scrubs
BARNET
BRENT
HARROW
EALING
12
135
136
SEE PAGES 44-45

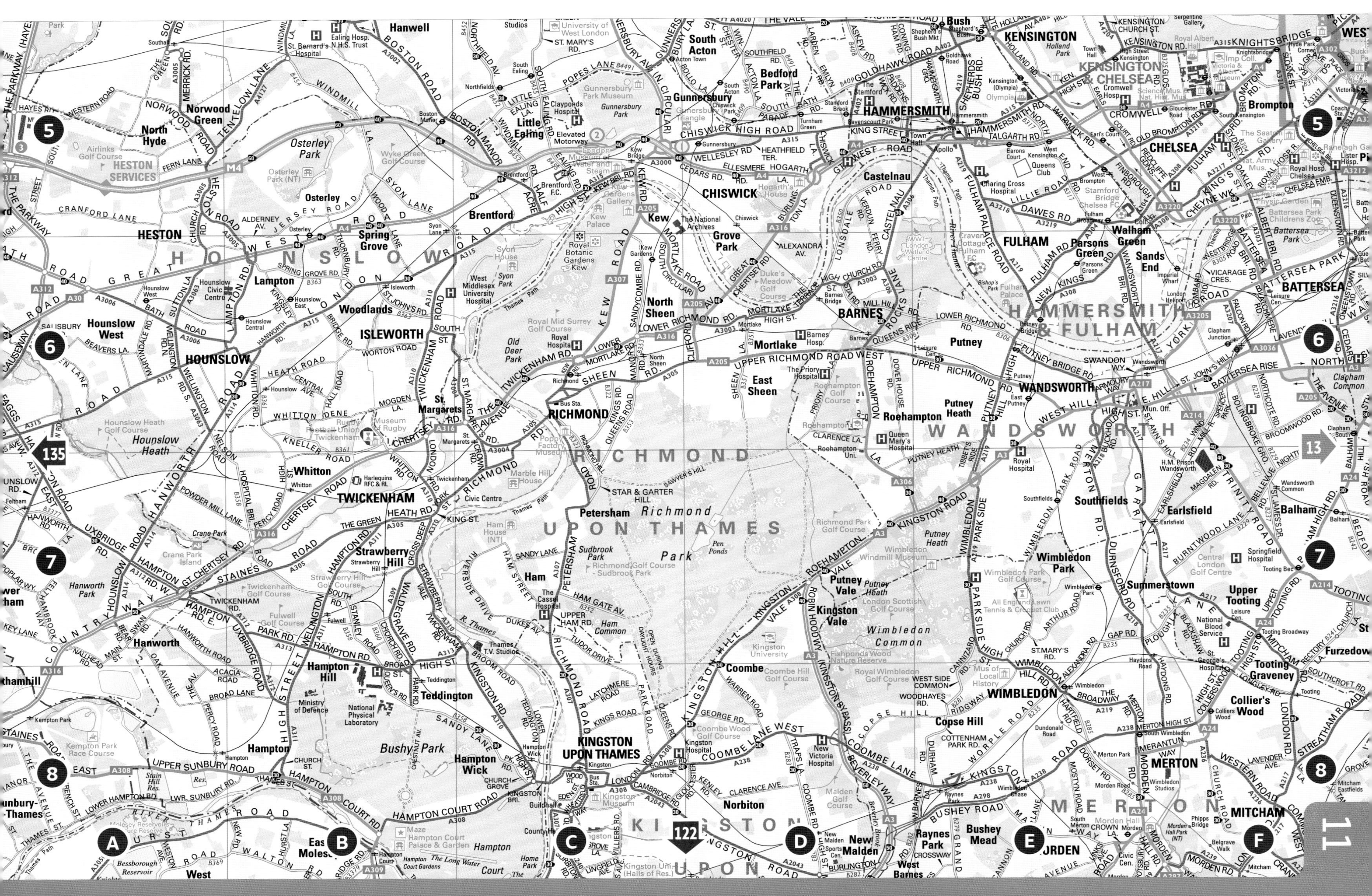

KENSINGTON
KENSINGTON & CHELSEA
CHELSEA
Brompton
FULHAM
HAMMERSMITH & FULHAM
HAMMERSMITH
BATTERSEA
WANDSWORTH
Putney
Roehampton
BARNES
Mortlake
East Sheen
CHISWICK
Grove Park
Kew
RICHMOND
Petersham
Ham
TWICKENHAM
Whitton
ISLEWORTH
Brentford
HOUNSLOW
Hounslow West
HESTON
Norwood Green
North Hyde
Hanwell
Osterley
Spring Grove
Lampton
Woodlands
St. Margarets
Teddington
Hampton Wick
KINGSTON UPON THAMES
Norbiton
Coombe
Kingston Vale
Putney Vale
WIMBLEDON
Wimbledon Park
Southfields
Earlsfield
Summerstown
Upper Tooting
Balham
Collier's Wood
MERTON
MITCHAM
New Malden
Raynes Park
Bushey Mead
Hampton
Hampton Hill
Strawberry Hill
Hanworth
Hounslow Heath
Richmond Park
Bushy Park
Wimbledon Common
HESTON SERVICES
RICHMOND UPON THAMES
HOUNSLOW
KINGSTON UPON THAMES
MERTON
13
122
135

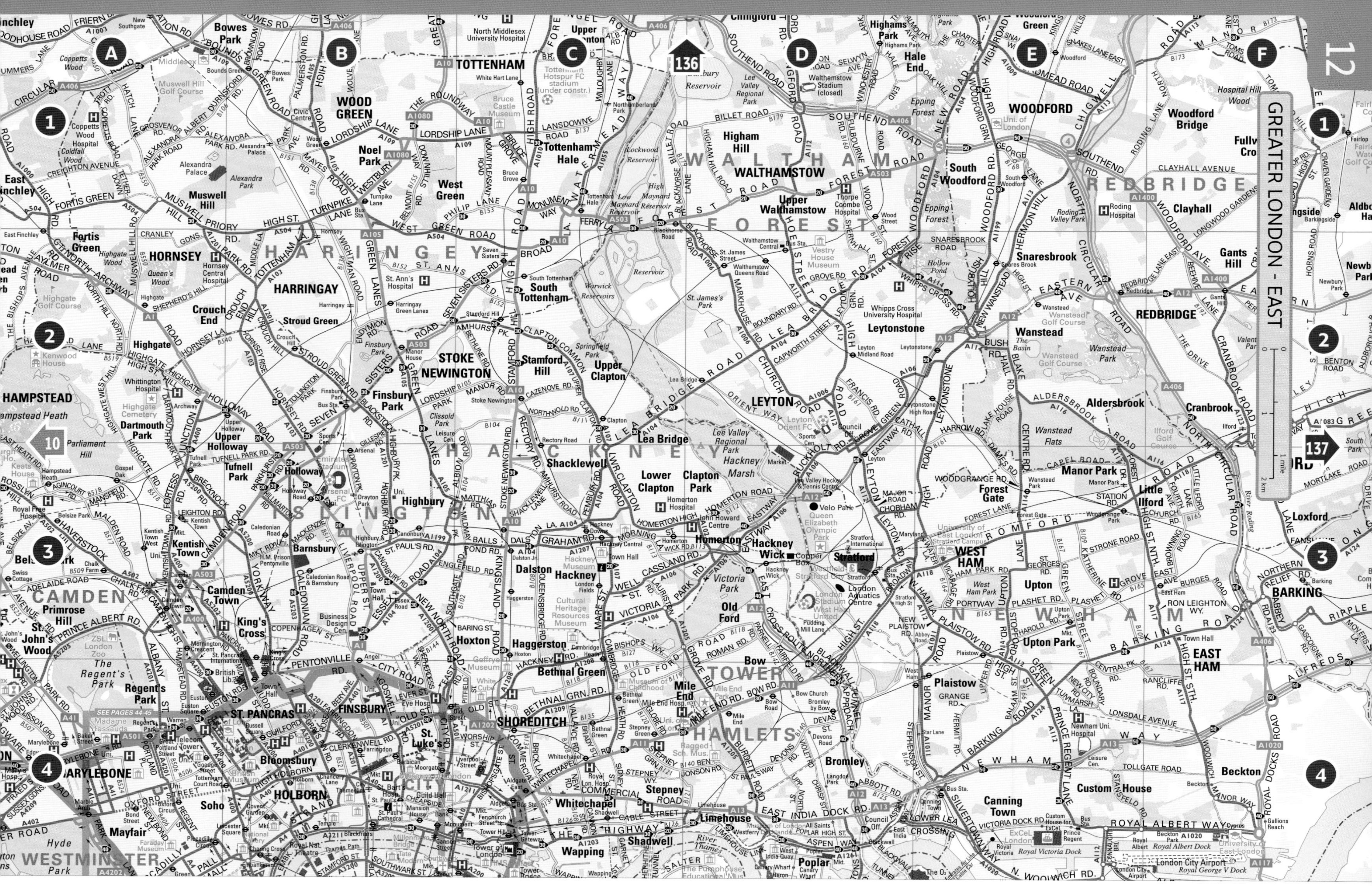
GREATER LONDON - EAST
0 1 mile
0 1 2 km
136
137
10
WOODFORD
Woodford Bridge
South Woodford
Snaresbrook
Wanstead
REDBRIDGE
Clayhall
Gants Hill
Cranbrook
Aldersbrook
Manor Park
Little Ilford
Forest Gate
WEST HAM
Upton
Upton Park
EAST HAM
BARKING
Loxford
Beckton
Custom House
Canning Town
Plaistow
Stratford
Leyton
Leytonstone
WALTHAMSTOW
Upper Walthamstow
Higham Hill
Hale End
Highams Park
TOTTENHAM
Tottenham Hale
South Tottenham
Upper Clapton
Lower Clapton
Clapton Park
Lea Bridge
Hackney Wick
Homerton
Old Ford
Bow
Bromley
Poplar
Limehouse
Stepney
Mile End
Bethnal Green
Shadwell
Wapping
Whitechapel
SHOREDITCH
Hoxton
Haggerston
Dalston
Hackney
Shacklewell
Stamford Hill
STOKE NEWINGTON
Highbury
Finsbury Park
Stroud Green
HARRINGAY
WOOD GREEN
Noel Park
West Green
Bowes Park
Muswell Hill
HORNSEY
Crouch End
Highgate
Upper Holloway
Tufnell Park
Holloway
Barnsbury
King's Cross
Camden Town
Kentish Town
Dartmouth Park
Fortis Green
FINSBURY
ST. PANCRAS
Bloomsbury
HOLBORN
Soho
Mayfair
MARYLEBONE
Regent's Park
Primrose Hill
HAMPSTEAD
CAMDEN
WESTMINSTER
HACKNEY
ISLINGTON
HARINGEY
WALTHAM FOREST
NEWHAM
TOWER HAMLETS
REDBRIDGE
NORTH CIRCULAR ROAD
London City Airport
SEE PAGES 44-45

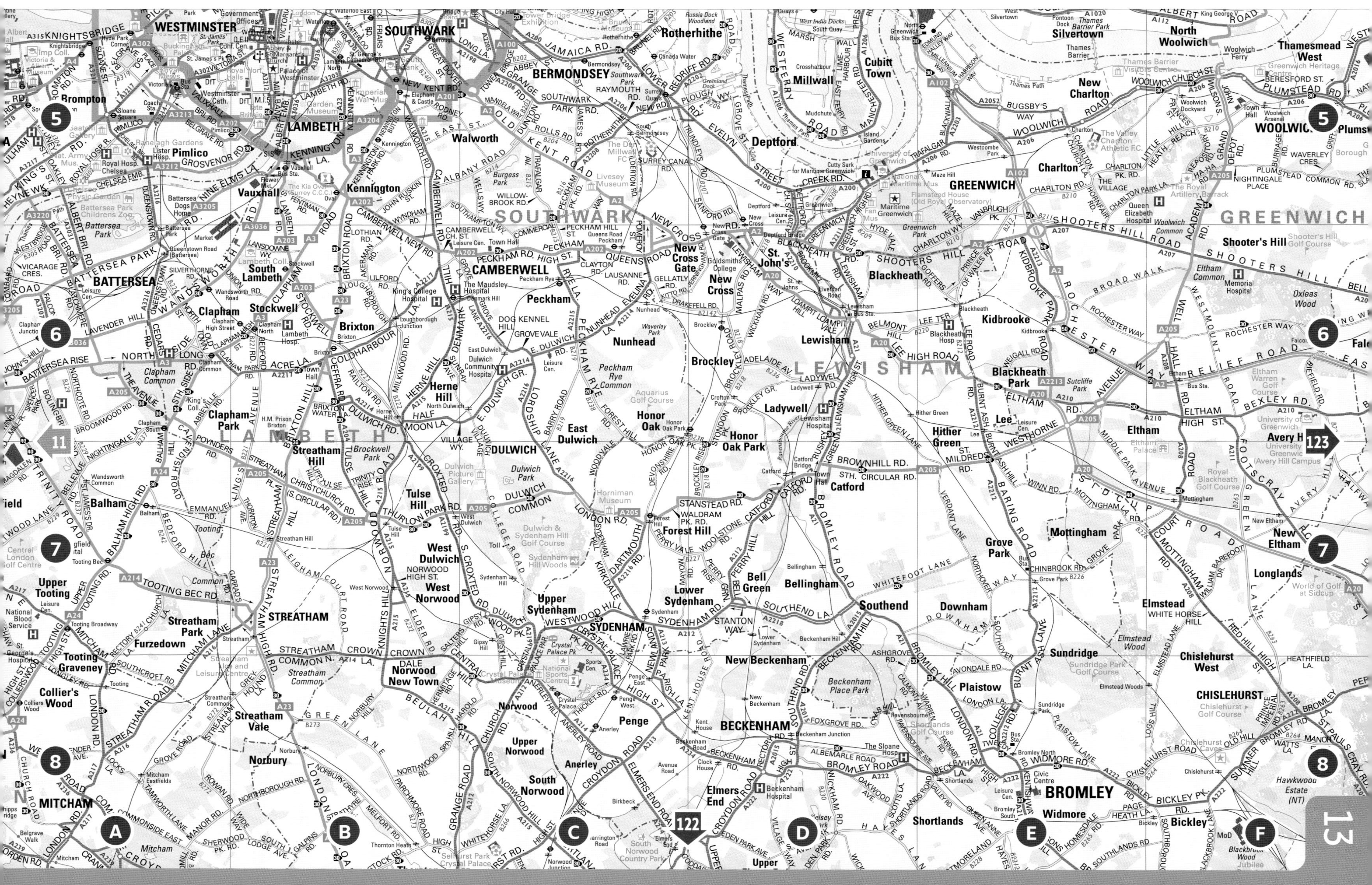
5
6
7
8
A
B
C
D
E
F
122
123
11
WESTMINSTER
SOUTHWARK
BERMONDSEY
Rotherhithe
Millwall
Cubitt Town
Silvertown
North Woolwich
Thamesmead West
Brompton
LAMBETH
Walworth
Deptford
New Charlton
Charlton
WOOLWICH
Plumstead
Pimlico
Vauxhall
Kennington
GREENWICH
SOUTHWARK
BATTERSEA
South Lambeth
CAMBERWELL
Peckham
New Cross Gate
New Cross
St. John's
Blackheath
Shooter's Hill
Clapham
Stockwell
Brixton
Nunhead
Brockley
Lewisham
Kidbrooke
LEWISHAM
Blackheath Park
Clapham Park
Herne Hill
Ladywell
Lee
Eltham
Avery Hill
LAMBETH
Streatham Hill
DULWICH
East Dulwich
Honor Oak
Honor Oak Park
Hither Green
Catford
Balham
Tulse Hill
Forest Hill
West Dulwich
West Norwood
Mottingham
Grove Park
New Eltham
Longlands
Upper Tooting
Upper Sydenham
Lower Sydenham
Bell Green
Bellingham
Southend
Downham
Elmstead
STREATHAM
SYDENHAM
Streatham Park
Furzedown
Tooting Graveney
Norwood New Town
New Beckenham
Sundridge
Chislehurst West
Plaistow
CHISLEHURST
Collier's Wood
Streatham Vale
Norwood
Penge
BECKENHAM
Norbury
Upper Norwood
Anerley
South Norwood
MITCHAM
Elmers End
BROMLEY
Widmore
Shortlands
Bickley

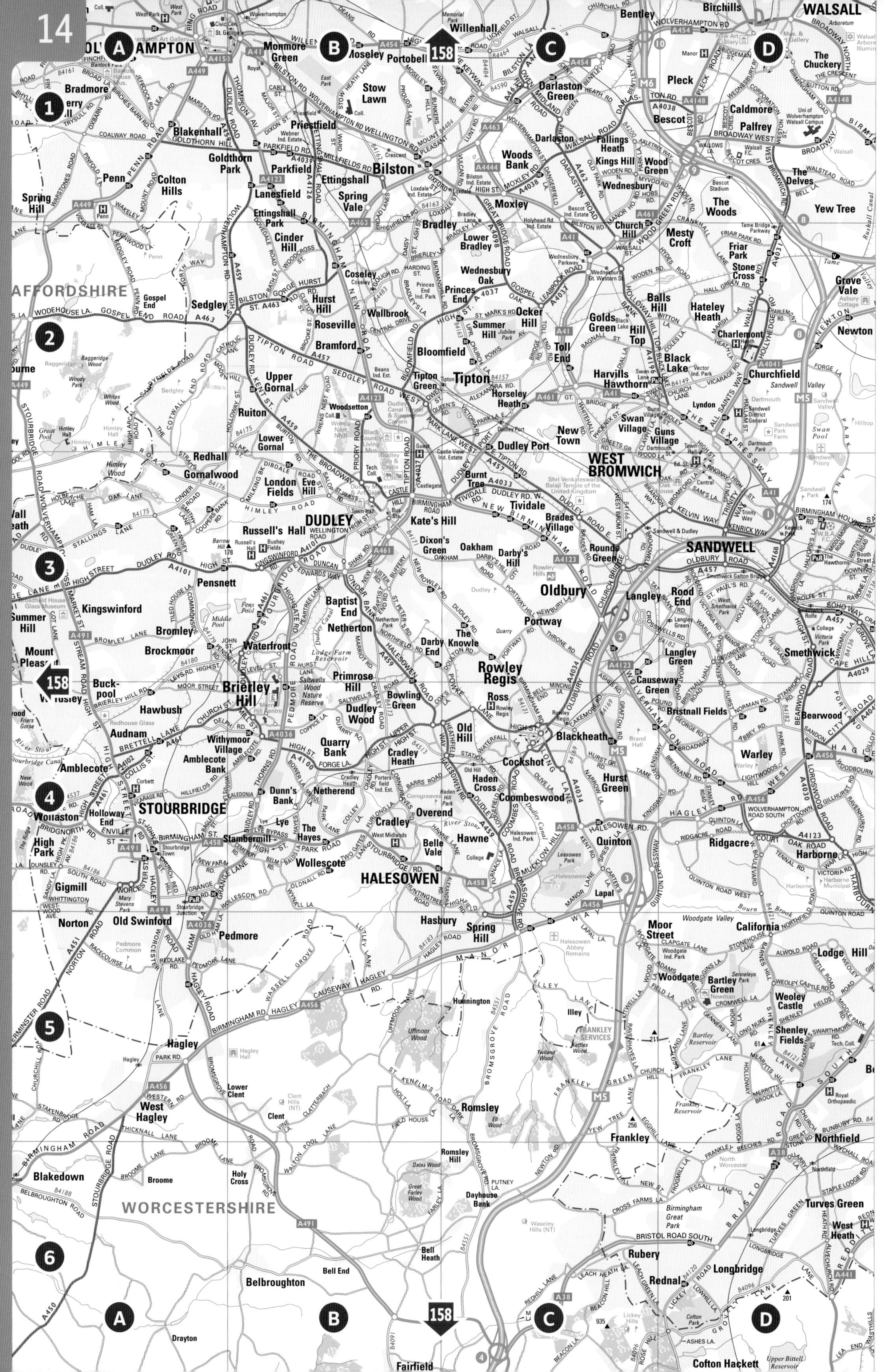
Wolverhampton
Bradmore
Blakenhall
Goldthorn Park
Penn
Colton Hills
Spring Hill
Monmore Green
Moseley
Portobello
Willenhall
Stow Lawn
Priestfield
Ettingshall
Parkfield
Lanesfield
Bilston
Spring Vale
Ettingshall Park
Cinder Hill
Darlaston Green
Darlaston
Woods Bank
Moxley
Bentley
Birchills
WALSALL
Pleck
Bescot
Caldmore
Palfrey
The Chuckery
Fallings Heath
Kings Hill
Wood Green
Wednesbury
The Delves
The Woods
Yew Tree
Bradley
Lower Bradley
Church Hill
Mesty Croft
Friar Park
Stone Cross
Wednesbury Oak
Princes End
Ocker Hill
Coseley
Hurst Hill
Wallbrook
Roseville
Bramford
Sedgley
Gospel End
STAFFORDSHIRE
Summer Hill
Bloomfield
Tipton Green
Tipton
Toll End
Golds Green
Hill Top
Balls Hill
Hateley Heath
Grove Vale
Newton
Charlemont
Black Lake
Harvills Hawthorn
Churchfield
Upper Gornal
Woodsetton
Horseley Heath
Swan Village
Guns Village
Lyndon
New Town
Ruiton
Lower Gornal
Redhall
Gornalwood
Dudley Port
WEST BROMWICH
London Fields
Eve Hill
Burnt Tree
Tividale
DUDLEY
Russell's Hall
Kate's Hill
Dixon's Green
Oakham
Darby's Hill
Brades Village
Rounds Green
SANDWELL
Pensnett
Kingswinford
Summer Hill
Mount Pleasant
Baptist End
Netherton
Oldbury
Langley
Rood End
Bromley
Brockmoor
Waterfront
Darby End
The Knowle
Portway
Langley Green
Smethwick
Buckpool
Wordsley
Hawbush
Brierley Hill
Primrose Hill
Bowling Green
Dudley Wood
Rowley Regis
Ross
Causeway Green
Bristnall Fields
Bearwood
Audnam
Withymoor Village
Amblecote
Amblecote Bank
Quarry Bank
Cradley Heath
Old Hill
Cockshot
Blackheath
Warley
Haden Cross
Hurst Green
Dunn's Bank
Netherend
Coombeswood
Wollaston
STOURBRIDGE
Holloway End
Lye
The Hayes
Cradley
Overend
Hawne
Belle Vale
Quinton
Ridgacre
Harborne
High Park
Stambermill
Wollescote
HALESOWEN
Gigmill
Norton
Old Swinford
Pedmore
Hasbury
Spring Hill
Lapal
Moor Street
California
Woodgate
Bartley Green
Lodge Hill
Weoley Castle
Shenley Fields
Hagley
Hunnington
Illey
West Hagley
Lower Clent
Clent
Romsley
Frankley
Northfield
Blakedown
Broome
Holy Cross
Romsley Hill
WORCESTERSHIRE
Dayhouse Bank
Turves Green
West Heath
Rubery
Rednal
Longbridge
Bell Heath
Bell End
Belbroughton
Drayton
Fairfield
Cofton Hackett
158

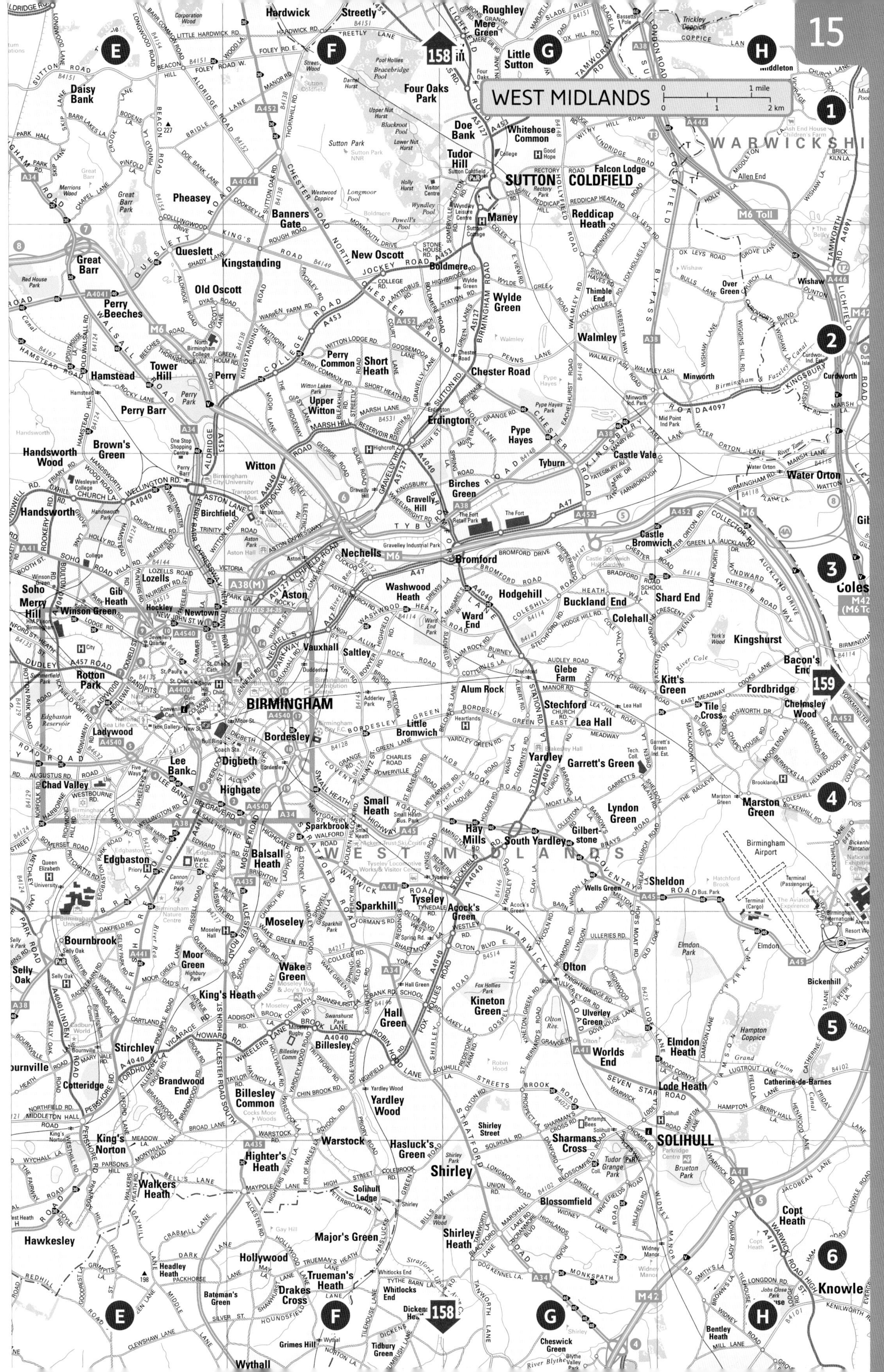
WEST MIDLANDS
0 1 mile
0 1 2 km
E
F
G
H
1
2
3
4
5
6
158
159
WARWICKSHIRE
Hardwick
Streetly
Roughley
Mere Green
Little Sutton
Middleton
Daisy Bank
Four Oaks Park
Doe Bank
Whitehouse Common
Tudor Hill
SUTTON COLDFIELD
Falcon Lodge
Reddicap Heath
Pheasey
Banners Gate
Maney
Great Barr
Queslett
Kingstanding
New Oscott
Boldmere
Old Oscott
Perry Beeches
Wylde Green
Thimble End
Over Green
Wishaw
Walmley
Minworth
Curdworth
Hamstead
Tower Hill
Perry
Perry Common
Short Heath
Chester Road
Perry Barr
Upper Witton
Erdington
Pype Hayes
Tyburn
Castle Vale
Water Orton
Handsworth Wood
Brown's Green
Witton
Birches Green
Gravelly Hill
Handsworth
Birchfield
Nechells
Bromford
Castle Bromwich
Soho
Lozells
Gib Heath
Aston
Washwood Heath
Hodgehill
Buckland End
Shard End
Merry Hill
Winson Green
Hockley
Newtown
Ward End
Colehall
Kingshurst
Vauxhall
Saltley
Glebe Farm
Bacon's End
Rotton Park
Alum Rock
Kitt's Green
Fordbridge
BIRMINGHAM
Stechford
Lea Hall
Tile Cross
Chelmsley Wood
Ladywood
Bordesley
Little Bromwich
Yardley
Garrett's Green
Lee Bank
Digbeth
Chad Valley
Highgate
Small Heath
Marston Green
Lyndon Green
Sparkbrook
Hay Mills
South Yardley
Gilbertstone
Balsall Heath
Edgbaston
Birmingham Airport
Sheldon
Tyseley
Sparkhill
Acock's Green
Wells Green
Moseley
Bournbrook
Selly Oak
Moor Green
Wake Green
Olton
Elmdon
Bickenhill
King's Heath
Kineton Green
Ulverley Green
Hall Green
Stirchley
Billesley
Worlds End
Elmdon Heath
Bournville
Cotteridge
Brandwood End
Catherine-de-Barnes
Lode Heath
Billesley Common
Yardley Wood
King's Norton
Warstock
Shirley Street
Sharmans Cross
SOLIHULL
Highter's Heath
Hasluck's Green
Shirley
Walkers Heath
Solihull Lodge
Blossomfield
Copt Heath
Hawkesley
Major's Green
Shirley Heath
Hollywood
Trueman's Heath
Headley Heath
Bateman's Green
Drakes Cross
Whitlocks End
Knowle
Bentley Heath
Cheswick Green
Grimes Hill
Tidbury Green
Wythall
M6
M42
M6 Toll
A38(M)
SEE PAGES 34-35

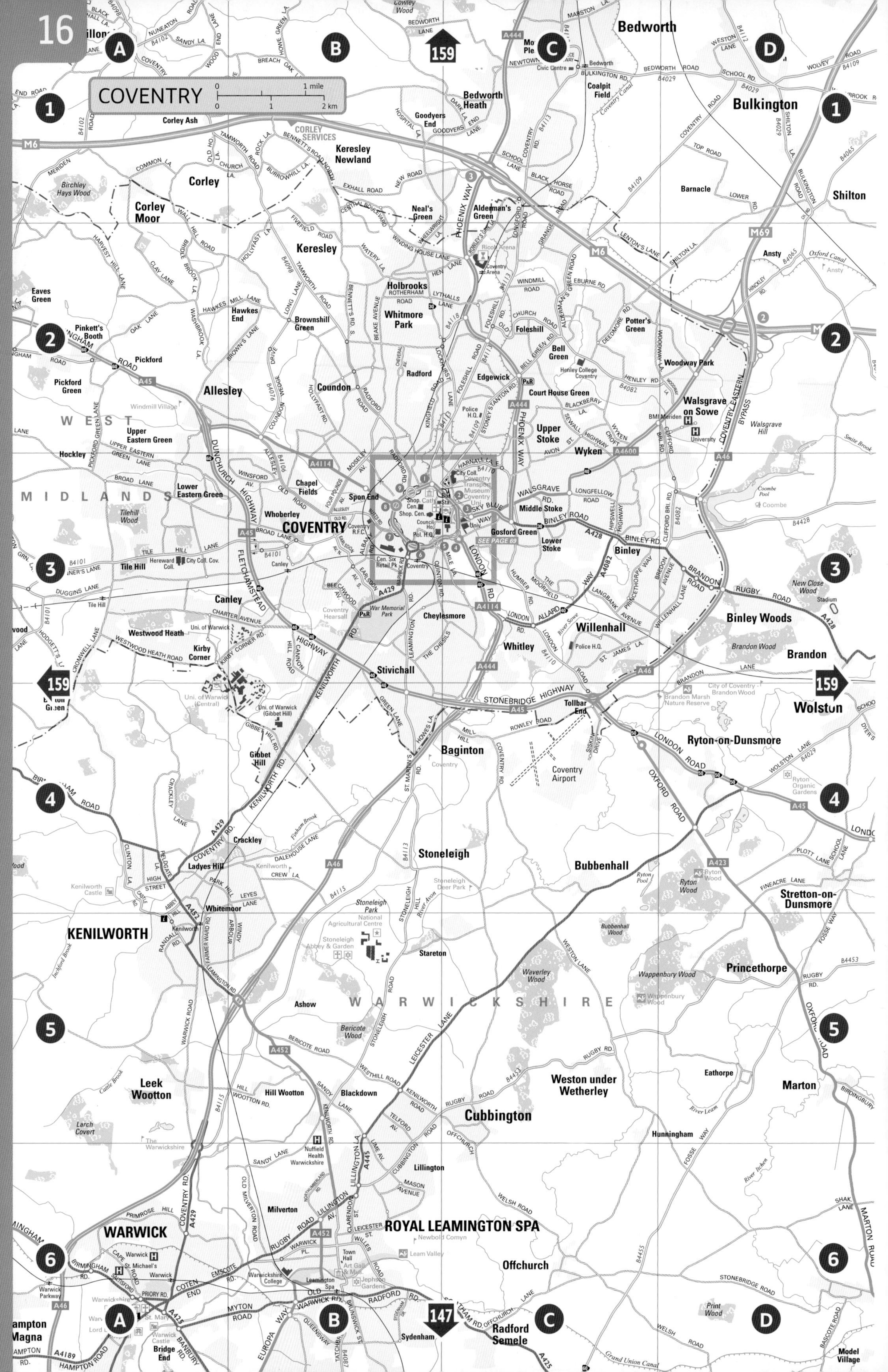
COVENTRY
0 1 mile
0 1 2 km
A
B
C
D
1
2
3
4
5
6
159
147
Bedworth
Bulkington
Bedworth Heath
Goodyers End
Corley Ash
CORLEY SERVICES
Keresley Newland
Corley
Birchley Hays Wood
Corley Moor
Neal's Green
Alderman's Green
Keresley
Coalpit Field
Coventry Canal
Barnacle
Shilton
Ansty
Oxford Canal
Eaves Green
Pinkett's Booth
Pickford
Pickford Green
Hawkes End
Brownshill Green
Holbrooks
Whitmore Park
Radford
Coundon
Foleshill
Potter's Green
Bell Green
Woodway Park
Edgewick
Henley College Coventry
Court House Green
Walsgrave on Sowe
Walsgrave Hill
University
Allesley
Windmill Village
WEST
MIDLANDS
Upper Eastern Green
Hockley
Upper Stoke
Wyken
Chapel Fields
Spon End
Lower Eastern Green
Whoberley
COVENTRY
Middle Stoke
Gosford Green
Lower Stoke
Binley
Coombe Pool
Coombe
Tilehill Wood
Tile Hill
Canley
SEE PAGE 69
Cen. Six Retail Pk
New Close Wood
Binley Woods
Brandon Wood
Brandon
Westwood Heath
Uni. of Warwick
Kirby Corner
War Memorial Park
Cheylesmore
Willenhall
Whitley
Police H.Q.
Stivichall
Wolston
Brandon Marsh Nature Reserve
City of Coventry Brandon Wood
Tollbar End
Uni. of Warwick (Central)
Uni. of Warwick (Gibbet Hill)
Gibbet Hill
Baginton
Ryton-on-Dunsmore
Coventry Airport
Ryton Organic Gardens
Crackley
Ladyes Hill
Kenilworth
Stoneleigh
Bubbenhall
Ryton Pool
Ryton Wood
Kenilworth Castle
Whitemoor
Stoneleigh Deer Park
Stretton-on-Dunsmore
KENILWORTH
Stoneleigh Park
National Agricultural Centre
Stoneleigh Abbey & Garden
Stareton
Bubbenhall Wood
Waverley Wood
Princethorpe
Wappenbury Wood
Ashow
WARWICKSHIRE
Bericote Wood
Eathorpe
Leek Wootton
Hill Wootton
Blackdown
Weston under Wetherley
Marton
Cubbington
River Leam
Larch Covert
Nuffield Health Warwickshire
Hunningham
Lillington
River Itchen
Milverton
WARWICK
ROYAL LEAMINGTON SPA
Newbold Comyn
Warwick
St. Michael's
Warwickshire College
Leamington Spa
Jephson Gardens
Offchurch
Town Hall
Art Gall. & Mus.
Warwick Parkway
Warwick Castle
Bridge End
Sydenham
Radford Semele
Print Wood
Hampton Magna
Model Village
Grand Union Canal
M6
M69
A45
A46
A444
A429
A428
A4114
A4082
A452
A423
A445
A425
A4600
A4189
B4101
B4109
B4029
B4113
B4115
B4082
B4453
B4455
B4087
COVENTRY EASTERN BYPASS
PHOENIX WAY
KENILWORTH RD.
FLETCHAMSTEAD HIGHWAY
STONEBRIDGE HIGHWAY
LONDON ROAD
OXFORD ROAD
RUGBY ROAD
BINLEY ROAD
LEICESTER LANE
FOSSE WAY
COVENTRY RD.
BANBURY
MYTON ROAD
EUROPA WAY

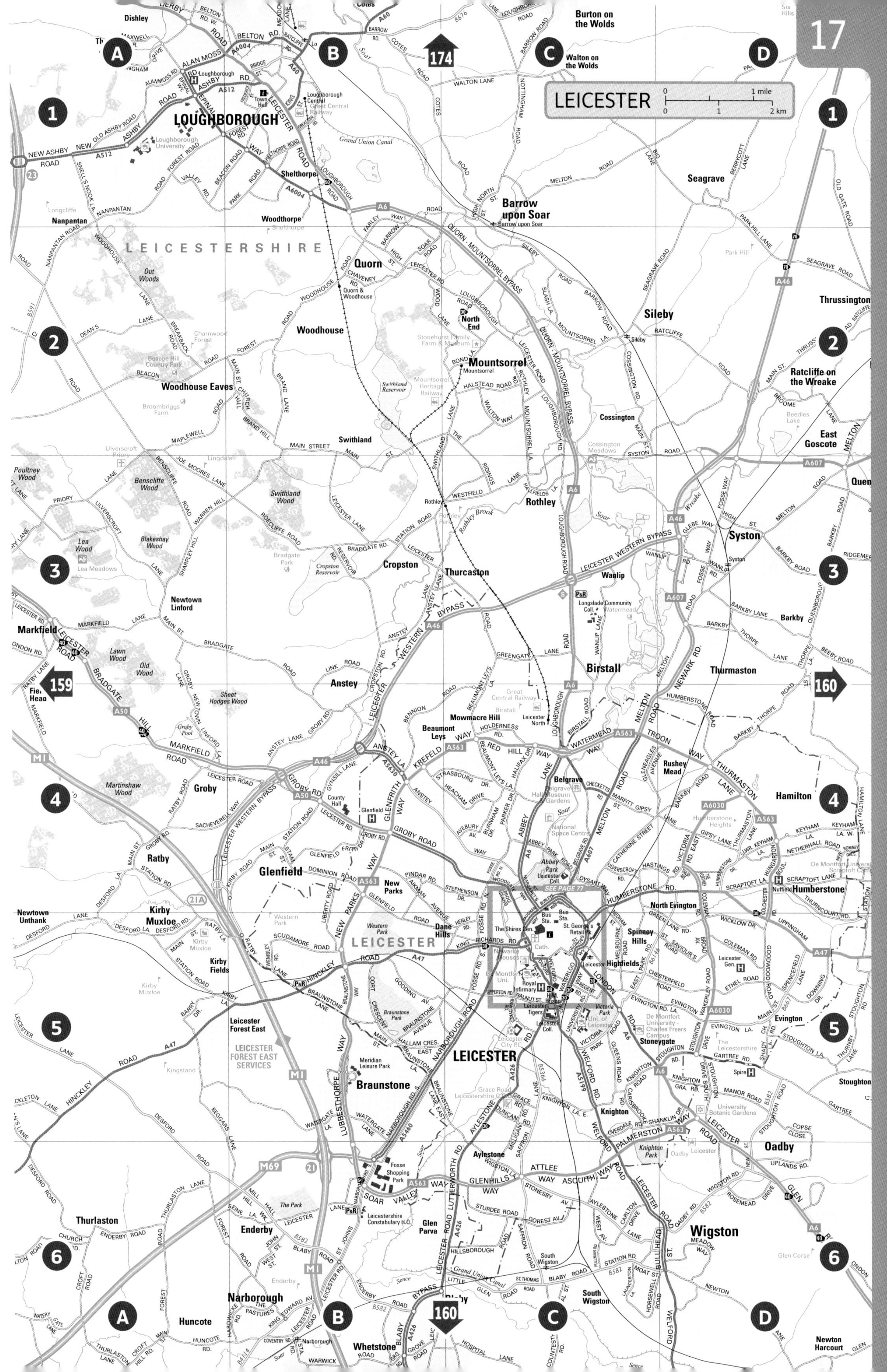
LEICESTER
0 1 mile
0 1 2 km
174
159
160
160
SEE PAGE 77
LOUGHBOROUGH
Loughborough University
Loughborough Central Great Central Railway
Grand Union Canal
Dishley
Burton on the Wolds
Walton on the Wolds
Shelthorpe
Nanpantan
Longcliffe
Woodthorpe
LEICESTERSHIRE
Barrow upon Soar
Seagrave
Quorn
Out Woods
Woodhouse
North End
Stonehurst Family Farm & Museum
Sileby
Thrussington
Charnwood Forest
Beacon Hill Country Park
Mountsorrel
Mountsorrel Heritage Railway
Swithland Reservoir
Woodhouse Eaves
Broombriggs Farm
Ratcliffe on the Wreake
Cossington
East Goscote
Swithland
Ulverscroft Priory
Poultney Wood
Benscliffe Wood
Swithland Wood
Cossington Meadows
Rothley
Rothley Brook
Lea Wood
Lea Meadows
Blakeshay Wood
Bradgate Park
Cropston Reservoir
Cropston
Thurcaston
Syston
Wanlip
Newtown Linford
Longslade Community Coll.
Watermead
Markfield
Lawn Wood
Old Wood
Sheet Hedges Wood
Anstey
Birstall
Thurmaston
Barkby
Great Central Railway
Leicester North
Mowmacre Hill
Beaumont Leys
Groby Pool
Groby
Martinshaw Wood
County Hall
Glenfield
Belgrave
Belgrave Hall Museum Gardens
National Space Centre
Rushey Mead
Hamilton
Humberstone Heights
Ratby
Abbey Park
Leicester Coll.
De Montfort University Scraptoft Campus
Humberstone
Glenfield
New Parks
North Evington
Newtown Unthank
Kirby Muxloe
Western Park
Dane Hills
The Shires Cen.
Bus Sta.
St. George's Retail Pk.
Cath.
Spinney Hills
Highfields
LEICESTER
Kirby Fields
Leicester Gen.
De Montfort Uni.
Royal Infirmary
Leicester Tigers
Leicester Coll.
Victoria Park
Uni. of Leicester
De Montfort University - Charles Frears Campus
Braunstone Park
Leicester City F.C.
Leicester Forest East
LEICESTER FOREST EAST SERVICES
Evington
Stoneygate
The Leicestershire Hospice
Meridian Leisure Park
LEICESTER
Braunstone
Kingstand
Spire
Stoughton
Grace Road Leicestershire C.C.C.
Knighton
University Botanic Gardens
Aylestone
Knighton Park
Oadby
Fosse Shopping Park
Thurlaston
Enderby
The Park
Leicestershire Constabulary H.Q.
Glen Parva
Wigston
Glen Corse
South Wigston
Enderby
Narborough
Huncote
Whetstone
Blaby
Newton Harcourt
M1
M69
A6
A46
A47
A50
A563
A607
A6030
A426
A5199
A5460
A512
A6004
A60
A47
A563
B582
B5366
B676
B591
B4114
B5327
B667
B6047
21A
21
23
QUORN - MOUNTSORREL BYPASS
LEICESTER WESTERN BYPASS
NEW ASHBY ROAD
HINCKLEY ROAD
NARBOROUGH ROAD
LONDON ROAD
WELFORD RD.
LOUGHBOROUGH ROAD
MELTON ROAD
GROBY ROAD
SOAR VALLEY WAY
GLENHILLS WAY
ATTLEE WAY
PALMERSTON WAY
LUBBESTHORPE WAY
NEW PARKS WAY
ABBEY LANE
HUMBERSTONE RD.
THURMASTON LANE
LEICESTER ROAD
MARKFIELD ROAD
BRADGATE HILL
FOSSE WAY
NEWARK RD.
TROON WAY
WATERMEAD WAY
KREFELD WAY
GLENFRITH WAY
STATION ROAD
MAIN STREET

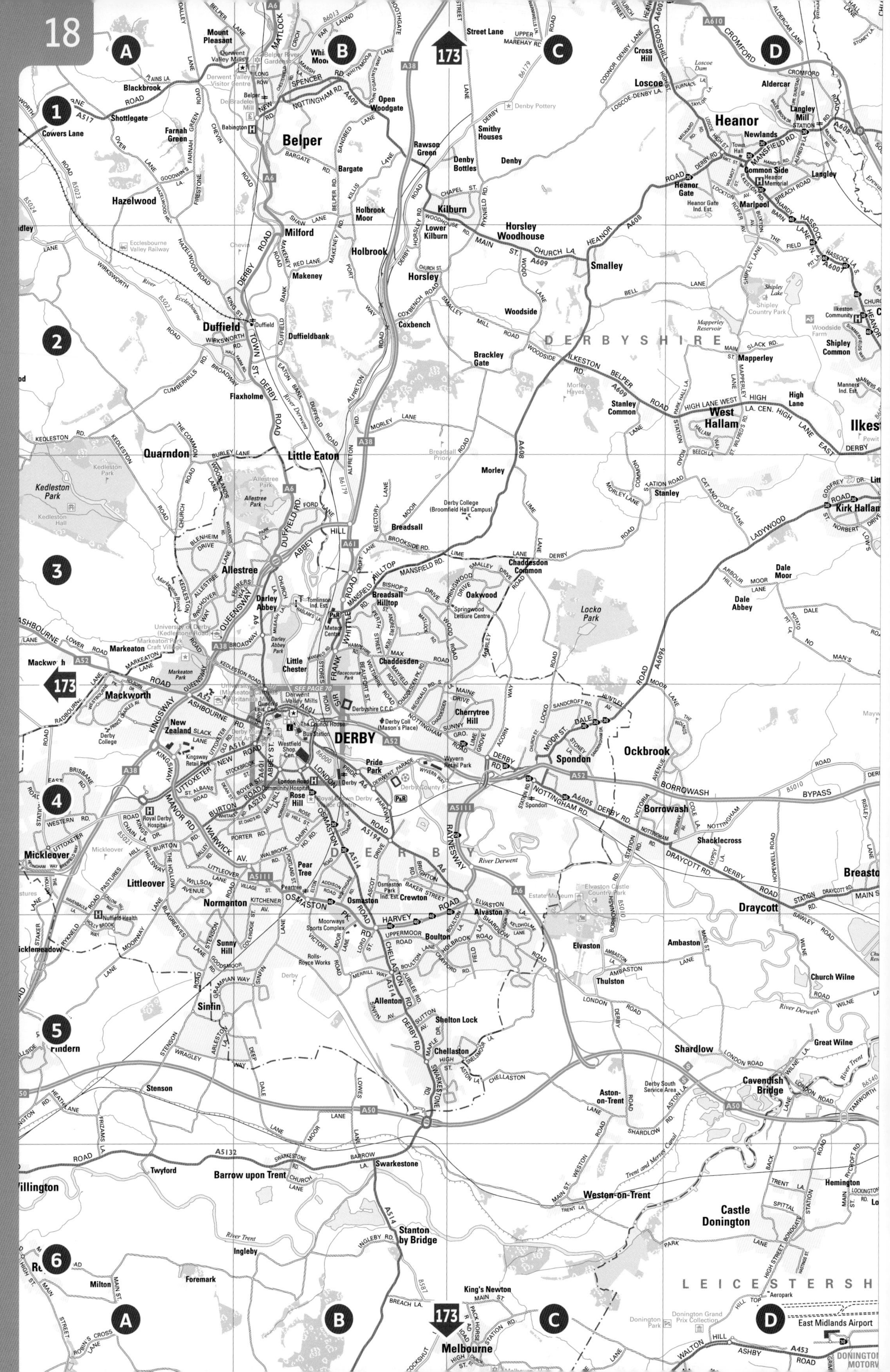
A
B
C
D
1
2
3
4
5
6
173
Mount Pleasant
Belper
Shottlegate
Cowers Lane
Farnah Green
Blackbrook
Hazelwood
Milford
Makeney
Holbrook
Holbrook Moor
Bargate
Open Woodgate
Rawson Green
Denby
Denby Bottles
Smithy Houses
Street Lane
Cross Hill
Loscoe
Heanor
Aldercar
Langley Mill
Newlands
Langley
Common Side
Heanor Gate
Marlpool
Kilburn
Lower Kilburn
Horsley
Horsley Woodhouse
Smalley
Coxbench
Woodside
Brackley Gate
Duffield
Duffieldbank
Flaxholme
Mapperley
Shipley Common
DERBYSHIRE
Stanley Common
West Hallam
High Lane
Quarndon
Little Eaton
Morley
Breadsall
Stanley
Kirk Hallam
Allestree
Darley Abbey
Breadsall Hilltop
Chaddesden Common
Oakwood
Dale Moor
Dale Abbey
Locko Park
Kedleston Park
Markeaton
Mackworth
Little Chester
Chaddesden
Cherrytree Hill
New Zealand
DERBY
Spondon
Ockbrook
Borrowash
Pride Park
Rose Hill
Mickleover
Littleover
Pear Tree
Normanton
Osmaston
Crewton
Alvaston
Boulton
Elvaston
Ambaston
Shacklecross
Draycott
Thulston
Sunny Hill
Sinfin
Allenton
Shelton Lock
Chellaston
Church Wilne
Great Wilne
Findern
Shardlow
Cavendish Bridge
Stenson
Aston-on-Trent
Twyford
Barrow upon Trent
Swarkestone
Weston-on-Trent
Hemington
Willington
Castle Donington
Stanton by Bridge
Ingleby
Milton
Foremark
King's Newton
Melbourne
LEICESTERSH
East Midlands Airport
River Derwent
River Trent
SEE PAGE 70

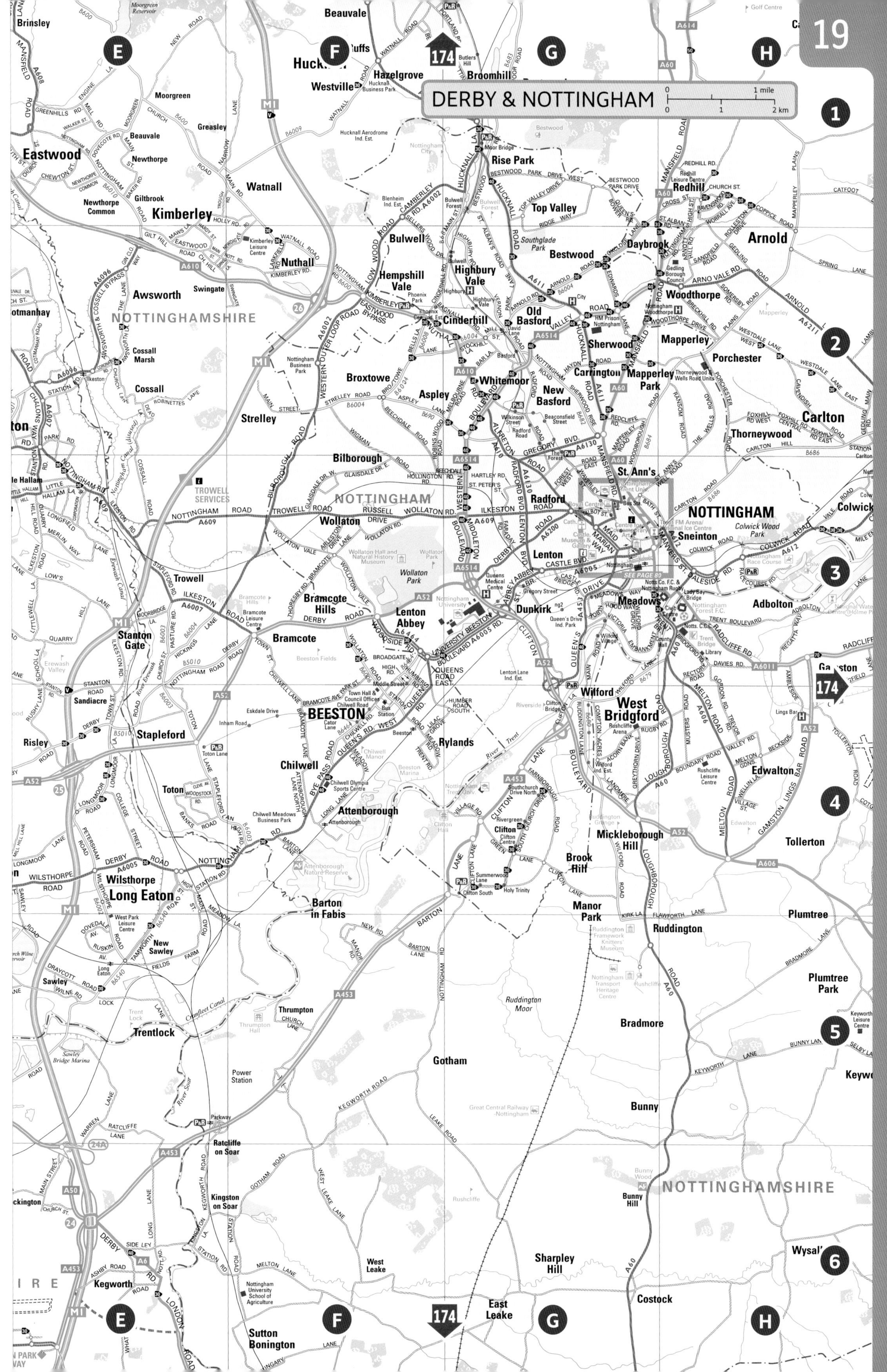
19
DERBY & NOTTINGHAM
0 1 mile
0 1 2 km
E
F
G
H
1
2
3
4
5
6
174
NOTTINGHAMSHIRE
NOTTINGHAM
Brinsley
Beauvale
Hazelgrove
Westville
Broomhill
Eastwood
Moorgreen
Greasley
Newthorpe
Newthorpe Common
Giltbrook
Kimberley
Watnall
Nuthall
Awsworth
Swingate
Cossall Marsh
Cossall
Strelley
Trowell
TROWELL SERVICES
Stanton Gate
Sandiacre
Risley
Stapleford
Toton
Wilsthorpe
Long Eaton
New Sawley
Sawley
Trentlock
Ratcliffe on Soar
Kingston on Soar
Kegworth
Sutton Bonington
Rise Park
Top Valley
Bestwood
Bulwell
Hempshill Vale
Highbury Vale
Cinderhill
Old Basford
Sherwood
Carrington
Mapperley
Mapperley Park
Redhill
Arnold
Daybrook
Woodthorpe
Porchester
Carlton
Thorneywood
Colwick
Broxtowe
Aspley
Whitemoor
New Basford
Bilborough
Wollaton
Radford
St. Ann's
Sneinton
Lenton
Lenton Abbey
Dunkirk
Meadows
Bramcote Hills
Bramcote
BEESTON
Chilwell
Attenborough
Rylands
Wilford
West Bridgford
Adbolton
Edwalton
Tollerton
Clifton
Brook Hill
Mickleborough Hill
Manor Park
Ruddington
Plumtree
Plumtree Park
Barton in Fabis
Thrumpton
Gotham
Bradmore
Bunny
Bunny Hill
West Leake
East Leake
Sharpley Hill
Costock
Wysall
SEE PAGE 80
Wollaton Park
Colwick Wood Park
Ruddington Moor
Power Station
Great Central Railway - Nottingham

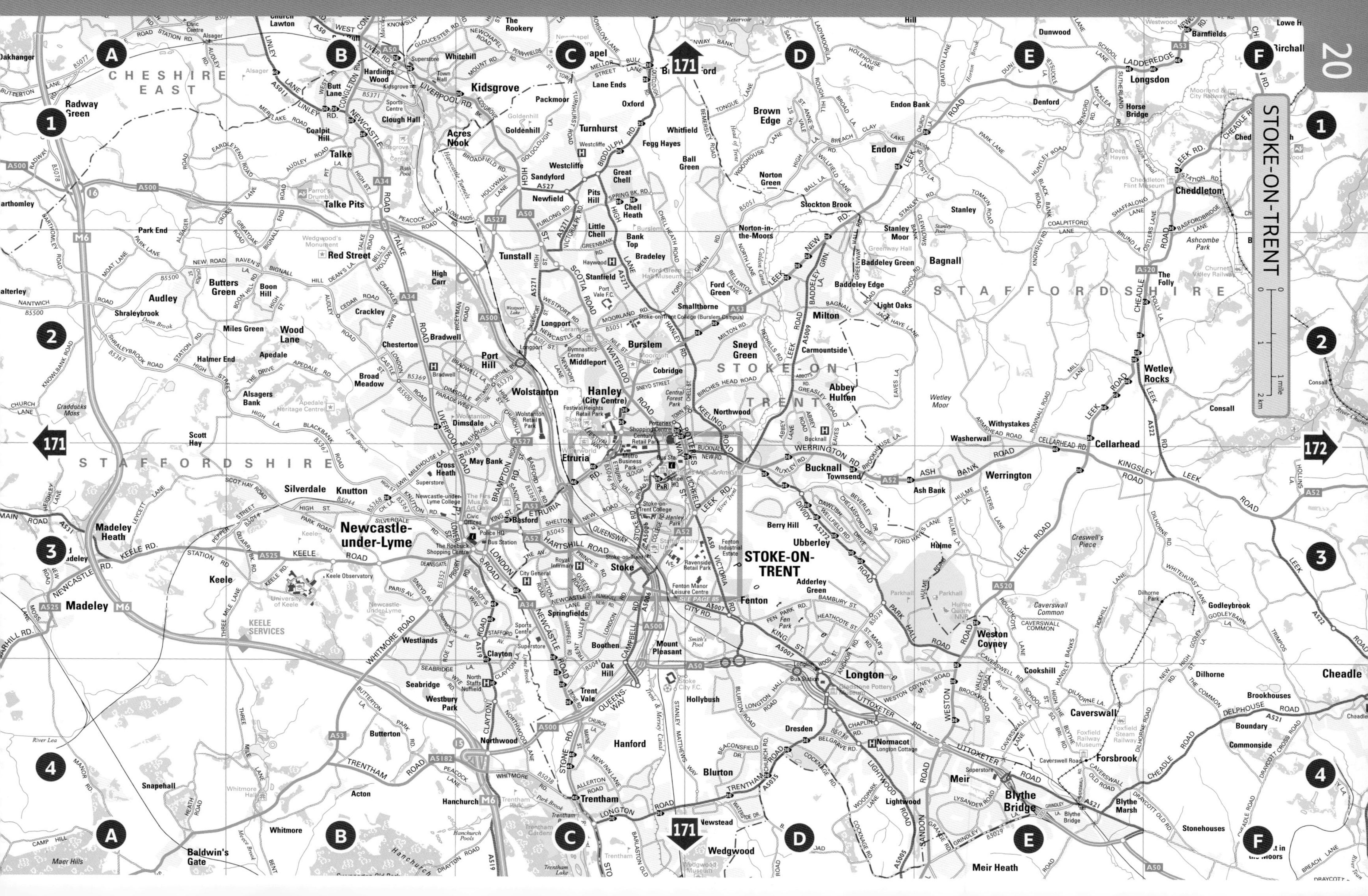
STOKE-ON-TRENT
0 1 mile
0 1 2 km
172
171
Cheadle
Cheddleton
Consall
Wetley Rocks
Cellarhead
Werrington
Longsdon
Endon
Stanley
Bagnall
Milton
Bucknall
Weston Coyney
Caverswall
Forsbrook
Blythe Bridge
Meir
Meir Heath
Longton
Normacot
Dresden
Fenton
Blurton
Hanley (City Centre)
Burslem
Tunstall
Kidsgrove
Wolstanton
Etruria
Stoke
Trentham
Hanford
Newcastle-under-Lyme
Clayton
Westlands
Keele
Silverdale
Knutton
Madeley
Madeley Heath
Audley
Talke
Talke Pits
Chesterton
Butterton
Whitmore
Baldwin's Gate
Wedgwood
STOKE-ON-TRENT
STAFFORDSHIRE
CHESHIRE EAST
KEELE SERVICES

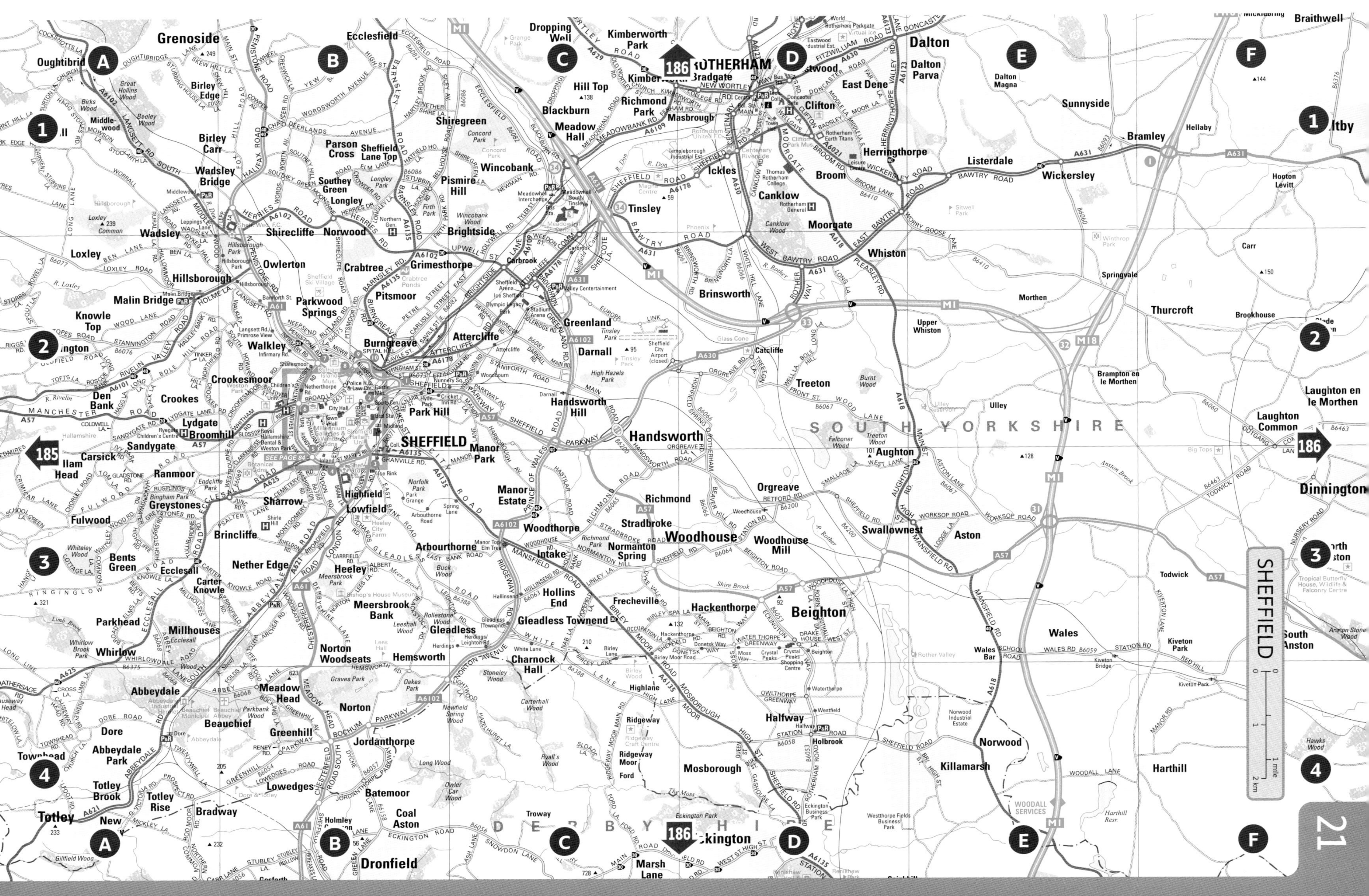
SHEFFIELD
0 1 mile
0 1 2 km
186
185
SOUTH YORKSHIRE
DERBYSHIRE
ROTHERHAM
SHEFFIELD
Dinnington
Laughton en le Morthen
Laughton Common
Thurcroft
Brampton en le Morthen
Bramley
Sunnyside
Wickersley
Listerdale
Dalton
Dalton Parva
Dalton Magna
Herringthorpe
East Dene
Clifton
Broom
Moorgate
Whiston
Upper Whiston
Canklow
Brinsworth
Treeton
Catcliffe
Orgreave
Handsworth
Aughton
Swallownest
Aston
Ulley
Morthen
Todwick
Kiveton Park
Harthill
Wales
Wales Bar
Norwood
Killamarsh
Beighton
Halfway
Holbrook
Woodhouse
Woodhouse Mill
Hackenthorpe
Mosborough
Marsh Lane
Ridgeway
Highlane
Frecheville
Richmond
Stradbroke
Normanton Spring
Gleadless Townend
Charnock Hall
Intake
Woodthorpe
Manor Estate
Manor Park
Darnall
Handsworth Hill
Greenland
Attercliffe
Tinsley
Kimberworth Park
Richmond Park
Masbrough
Ickles
Hill Top
Blackburn
Meadow Hall
Dropping Well
Ecclesfield
Shiregreen
Wincobank
Pismire Hill
Brightside
Grimesthorpe
Pitsmoor
Burngreave
Parkwood Springs
Crabtree
Norwood
Shirecliffe
Longley
Southey Green
Parson Cross
Sheffield Lane Top
Owlerton
Walkley
Crookesmoor
Crookes
Hillsborough
Wadsley
Wadsley Bridge
Birley Carr
Birley Edge
Grenoside
Loxley
Malin Bridge
Knowle Top
Den Bank
Lydgate
Broomhill
Sandygate
Carsick
Ranmoor
Greystones
Sharrow
Brincliffe
Nether Edge
Ecclesall
Carter Knowle
Bents Green
Fulwood
Millhouses
Whirlow
Parkhead
Abbeydale
Beauchief
Greenhill
Meadow Head
Norton
Norton Woodseats
Jordanthorpe
Batemoor
Coal Aston
Dronfield
Lowedges
Bradway
Totley Rise
Totley Brook
Totley
Abbeydale Park
Dore
New
Holmley
Heeley
Meersbrook Bank
Gleadless
Hemsworth
Arbourthorne
Highfield
Lowfield
Park Hill
Troway
Ford
Ridgeway Moor
Woodall Services
Hellaby
Hooton Levitt
Carr
Brookhouse
Springvale
Braithwell
M1
M18
A57
A61
A618
A630
A631
A6102
A6135

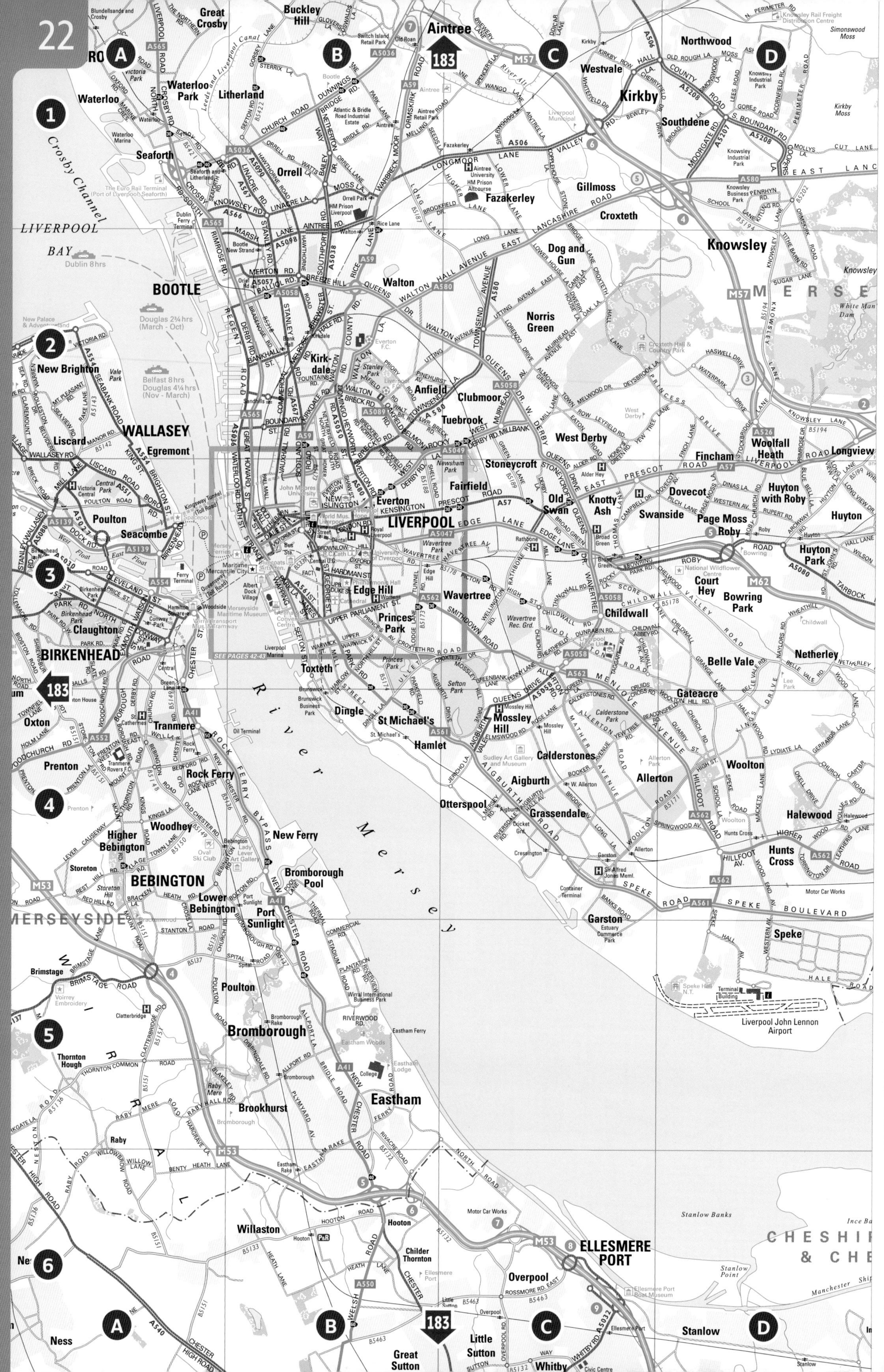

A
B
C
D
1
2
3
4
5
6
183
Great Crosby
Buckley Hill
Aintree
Northwood
Kirkby
Westvale
Southdene
Waterloo
Waterloo Park
Litherland
Seaforth
Orrell
Crosby Channel
LIVERPOOL BAY
Dublin 8hrs
BOOTLE
Douglas 2¾hrs (March - Oct)
Belfast 8hrs
Douglas 4¼hrs (Nov - March)
Fazakerley
Gillmoss
Croxteth
Knowsley
Walton
Dog and Gun
Norris Green
Kirkdale
Anfield
Clubmoor
Tuebrook
West Derby
Stoneycroft
Fairfield
Everton
LIVERPOOL
Old Swan
Knotty Ash
Dovecot
Swanside
Page Moss
Roby
Huyton with Roby
Huyton
Huyton Park
Woolfall Heath
Fincham
Longview
Court Hey
Bowring Park
New Brighton
WALLASEY
Liscard
Egremont
Poulton
Seacombe
Claughton
BIRKENHEAD
Oxton
Tranmere
Prenton
Rock Ferry
Woodhey
Higher Bebington
BEBINGTON
Lower Bebington
Port Sunlight
New Ferry
Bromborough Pool
Storeton
Edge Hill
Wavertree
Princes Park
Childwall
Toxteth
Dingle
St Michael's
Hamlet
Mossley Hill
Calderstones
Aigburth
Otterspool
Grassendale
Allerton
Belle Vale
Netherley
Gateacre
Woolton
Halewood
Hunts Cross
Garston
Speke
Liverpool John Lennon Airport
River Mersey
MERSEYSIDE
WIRRAL
Brimstage
Thornton Hough
Raby
Poulton
Bromborough
Brookhurst
Eastham
Willaston
Hooton
Childer Thornton
Overpool
ELLESMERE PORT
Stanlow Banks
Stanlow Point
Stanlow
Little Sutton
Great Sutton
Whitby
Ness
CHESHIRE & CHE
SEE PAGES 42-43

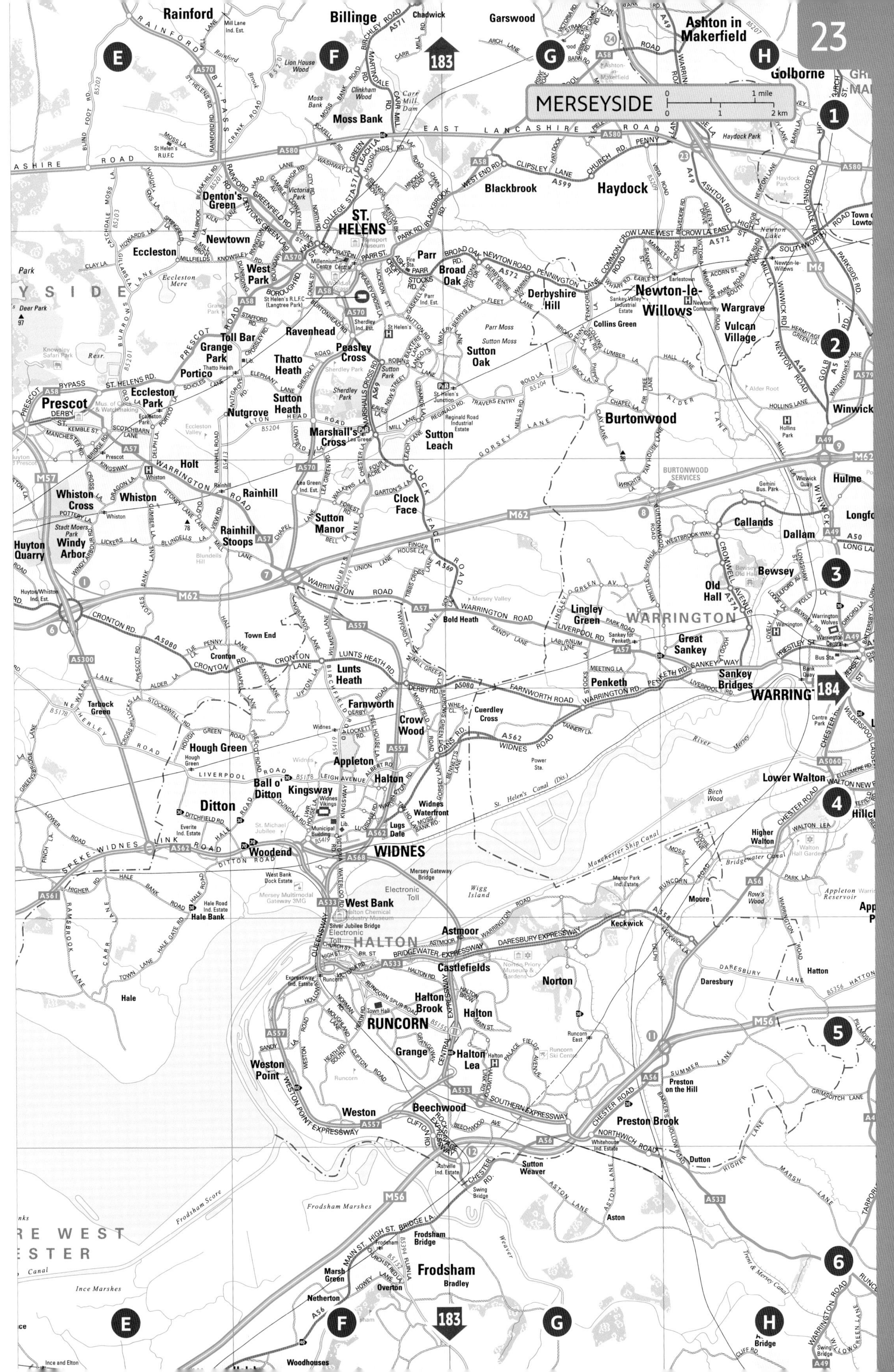
MERSEYSIDE
0
1 mile
0
1
2 km
183
184
183
E
F
G
H
E
F
G
H
1
2
3
4
5
6
Rainford
Billinge
Chadwick
Garswood
Ashton in Makerfield
Golborne
Moss Bank
Blackbrook
Haydock
Denton's Green
Newtown
Eccleston
ST. HELENS
Parr
Broad Oak
West Park
Derbyshire Hill
Newton-le-Willows
Wargrave
Vulcan Village
Collins Green
Ravenhead
Toll Bar
Grange Park
Thatto Heath
Peasley Cross
Sutton Oak
Portico
Eccleston Park
Prescot
Sutton Heath
Nutgrove
Marshall's Cross
Sutton Leach
Burtonwood
Winwick
Holt
Whiston Cross
Whiston
Rainhill
Clock Face
Hulme
Sutton Manor
Callands
Dallam
Rainhill Stoops
Huyton Quarry
Windy Arbor
Bewsey
Old Hall
Lingley Green
WARRINGTON
Bold Heath
Town End
Cronton
Lunts Heath
Great Sankey
Penketh
Sankey Bridges
WARRING
Tarbock Green
Farnworth
Crow Wood
Cuerdley Cross
Hough Green
Appleton
Halton
Ball o' Ditton
Kingsway
Ditton
Widnes Waterfront
Lugs Dale
Lower Walton
Higher Walton
Woodend
WIDNES
West Bank
Moore
Astmoor
Keckwick
HALTON
Castlefields
Norton
Daresbury
Hatton
Halton Brook
Halton
RUNCORN
Hale
Hale Bank
Grange
Halton Lea
Weston Point
Preston on the Hill
Weston
Beechwood
Preston Brook
Dutton
Sutton Weaver
Aston
Frodsham Bridge
Frodsham
Bradley
Marsh Green
Overton
Netherton
Woodhouses
Frodsham Marshes
Ince Marshes
M62
M57
M6
M56
A580
A58
A570
A572
A57
A49
A5080
A562
A557
A533
A568
A56
A561
A5300
A599
A571
A574
A5060
St. Helen's Canal
Manchester Ship Canal
Bridgewater Canal
River Mersey
BURTONWOOD SERVICES
EAST LANCASHIRE ROAD
WARRINGTON ROAD
SPEKE-WIDNES LINK ROAD
SOUTHERN EXPRESSWAY
DARESBURY EXPRESSWAY
BRIDGEWATER EXPRESSWAY
WESTON POINT EXPRESSWAY
CENTRAL EXPRESSWAY
Silver Jubilee Bridge
Mersey Gateway Bridge
Wigg Island
Power Sta.
Knowsley Safari Park
Clock Face
Frodsham Score

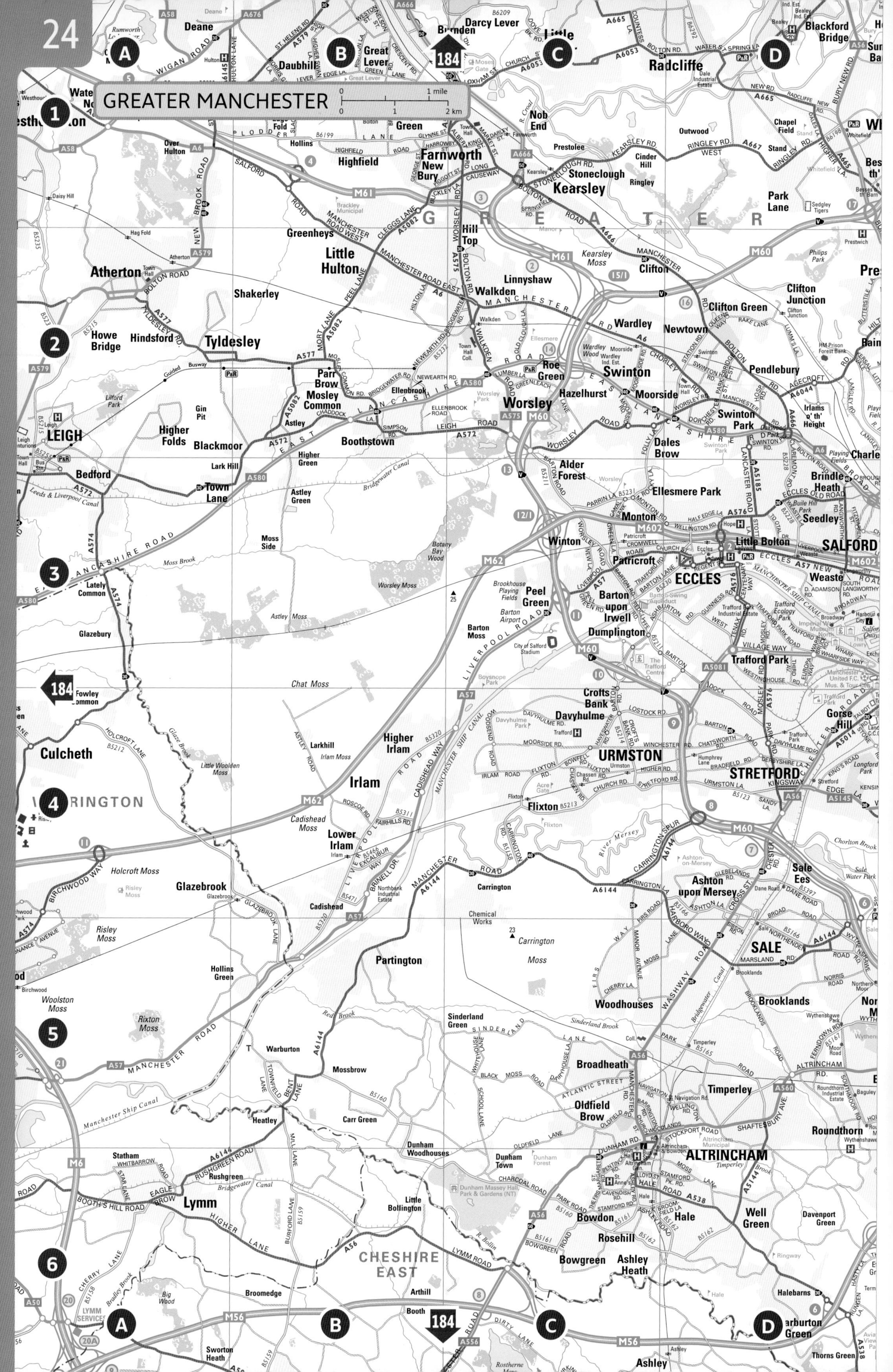

GREATER MANCHESTER
0 1 mile
0 1 2 km
A
B
C
D
1
2
3
4
5
6
184
Deane
Daubhill
Great Lever
Darcy Lever
Burnden
Little Lever
Radcliffe
Blackford Bridge
Westhoughton
Over Hulton
Hollins
Highfield
Green
Farnworth
New Bury
Nob End
Prestolee
Stoneclough
Kearsley
Outwood
Chapel Field
Cinder Hill
Ringley
Stand
Whitefield
Park Lane
Daisy Hill
Hag Fold
Greenheys
Little Hulton
Hill Top
Kearsley Moss
Clifton
Atherton
Shakerley
Linnyshaw
Walkden
Wardley
Newtown
Clifton Green
Clifton Junction
Pendlebury
Howe Bridge
Hindsford
Tyldesley
Parr Brow
Mosley Common
Ellenbrook
Roe Green
Swinton
Moorside
Worsley
Hazelhurst
Swinton Park
Irlams o' th' Height
Gin Pit
Higher Folds
Blackmoor
Astley
Boothstown
Dales Brow
LEIGH
Bedford
Lark Hill
Town Lane
Higher Green
Astley Green
Alder Forest
Ellesmere Park
Brindle Heath
Charlestown
Monton
Seedley
Moss Side
Botany Bay Wood
Winton
Patricroft
Little Bolton
SALFORD
ECCLES
Weaste
Lately Common
Worsley Moss
Peel Green
Barton upon Irwell
Glazebury
Astley Moss
Barton Moss
Dumplington
Trafford Park
Chat Moss
Fowley Common
Crofts Bank
Davyhulme
Gorse Hill
Culcheth
Larkhill
Higher Irlam
Irlam
URMSTON
STRETFORD
WARRINGTON
Flixton
Cadishead Moss
Lower Irlam
Holcroft Moss
Glazebrook
Carrington
Sale
Ashton upon Mersey
Cadishead
Chemical Works
Carrington Moss
Risley Moss
SALE
Partington
Hollins Green
Woolston Moss
Brooklands
Woodhouses
Rixton Moss
Sinderland Green
Warburton
Broadheath
Mossbrow
Timperley
Oldfield Brow
Heatley
Carr Green
Roundthorn
Statham
Dunham Woodhouses
Dunham Town
ALTRINCHAM
Rushgreen
Lymm
Little Bollington
Bowdon
Hale
Well Green
Davenport Green
Rosehill
CHESHIRE EAST
Bowgreen
Ashley Heath
Broomedge
Arthill
Big Wood
Halebarns
Booth
Warburton Green
Sworton Heath
Ashley
Thorns Green
Rostherne
GREATER
M61
M60
M62
M602
M6
M56
Manchester Ship Canal
Bridgewater Canal
Leeds & Liverpool Canal
River Mersey

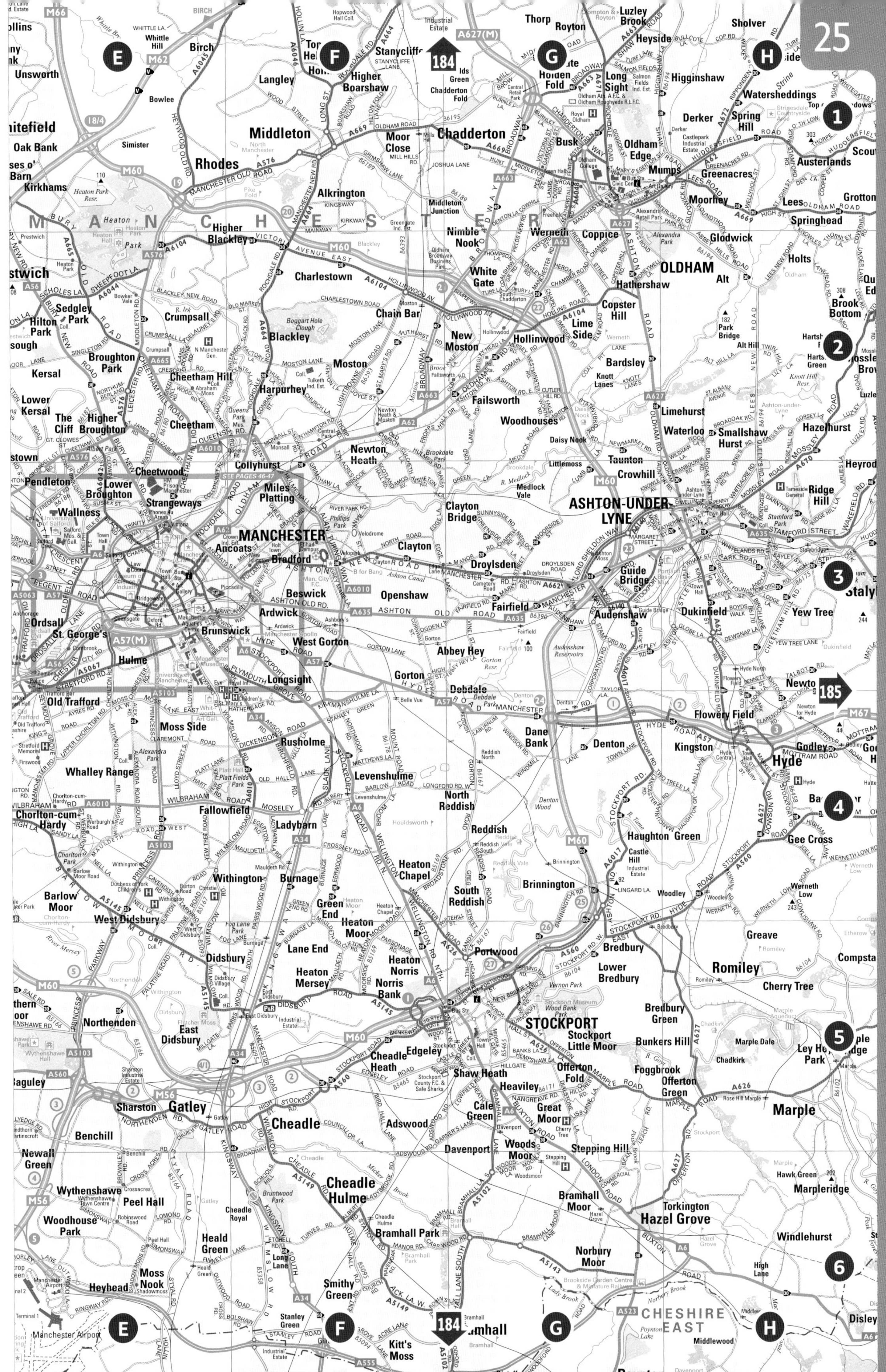
E
F
G
H
1
2
3
4
5
6
184
185
Unsworth
Whitefield
Oak Bank
Simister
Birch
Whitehill
Bowlee
Rhodes
Middleton
Langley
Higher Boarshaw
Stanycliffe
Chadderton
Moor Close
Alkrington
Royton
Thorp
Luzley Brook
Heyside
Sholver
Holden Fold
Long Sight
Higginshaw
Watersheddings
Derker
Spring Hill
Busk
Oldham Edge
Mumps
Greenacres
Austerlands
Moorhey
Lees
Springhead
Grotton
Kirkhams
MANCHESTER
Heaton Park
Higher Blackley
Prestwich
Middleton Junction
Nimble Nook
White Gate
Werneth
Coppice
Glodwick
OLDHAM
Alt
Hathershaw
Holts
Brook Bottom
Sedgley Park
Crumpsall
Charlestown
Chain Bar
Blackley
New Moston
Hollinwood
Lime Side
Copster Hill
Hilton Park
Broughton Park
Kersal
Moston
Bardsley
Cheetham Hill
Harpurhey
Failsworth
Woodhouses
Limehurst
Lower Kersal
The Cliff
Higher Broughton
Cheetham
Newton Heath
Waterloo
Smallshaw Hurst
Hazelhurst
Daisy Nook
Taunton
Crowhill
Littlemoss
Collyhurst
Pendleton
Lower Broughton
Cheetwood
Strangeways
Miles Platting
Medlock Vale
ASHTON-UNDER-LYNE
Ridge Hill
Heyrod
Wallness
Clayton Bridge
MANCHESTER
Ancoats
Bradford
Clayton
Droylsden
Guide Bridge
Stalybridge
Beswick
Openshaw
Fairfield
Audenshaw
Dukinfield
Yew Tree
Ordsall
Ardwick
St. George's
Brunswick
West Gorton
Abbey Hey
Hulme
Longsight
Gorton
Debdale
Newton
Old Trafford
Moss Side
Dane Bank
Denton
Flowery Field
Kingston
Godley
Hyde
Rusholme
Whalley Range
Levenshulme
Fallowfield
North Reddish
Chorlton-cum-Hardy
Ladybarn
Reddish
Haughton Green
Gee Cross
Heaton Chapel
Withington
Burnage
Barlow Moor
South Reddish
Brinnington
Woodley
Werneth Low
Green End
Heaton Moor
West Didsbury
Greave
Lane End
Portwood
Bredbury
Heaton Norris
Romiley
Didsbury
Heaton Mersey
Norris Bank
Lower Bredbury
Cherry Tree
Compstall
Northenden
East Didsbury
STOCKPORT
Stockport Little Moor
Bredbury Green
Bunkers Hill
Marple Dale
Chadkirk
Marple Bridge
Ley Hey Park
Cheadle Heath
Edgeley
Shaw Heath
Offerton Fold
Foggbrook
Offerton Green
Baguley
Sharston
Gatley
Heaviley
Great Moor
Marple
Cheadle
Adswood
Cale Green
Benchill
Davenport
Woods Moor
Stepping Hill
Newall Green
Cheadle Hulme
Mount Pleasant
Wythenshawe
Peel Hall
Bramhall Moor
Torkington
Hazel Grove
Marpleridge
Woodhouse Park
Heald Green
Bramhall Park
Windlehurst
Norbury Moor
Moss Nook
Heyhead
Smithy Green
High Lane
Manchester Airport
Stanley Green
Kitt's Moss
Bramhall
CHESHIRE EAST
Middlewood
Disley
M60
M62
M66
M56
M67
A627(M)
A57(M)
SEE PAGES 46-47

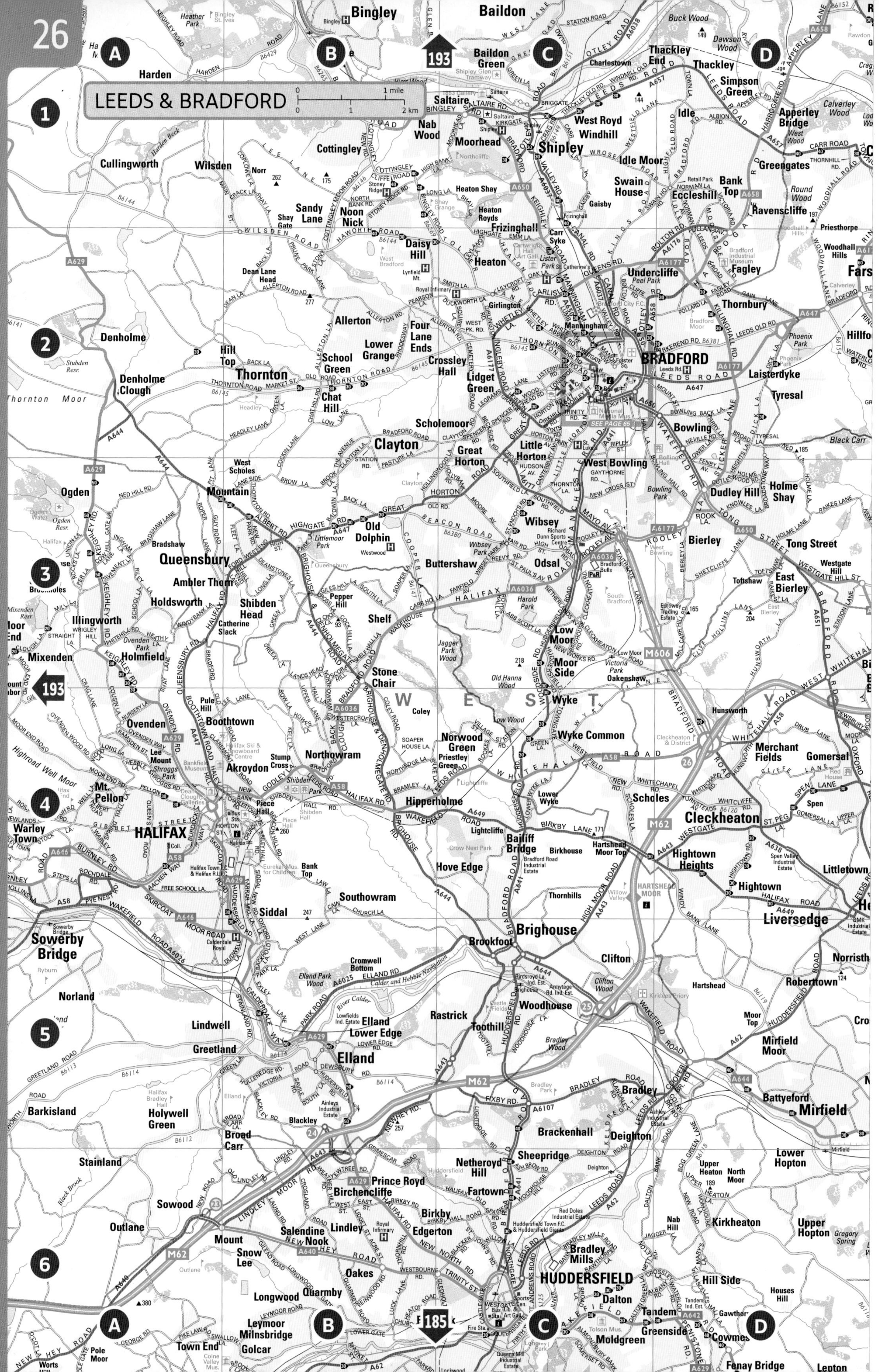
LEEDS & BRADFORD
0 1 mile
0 1 2 km
A
B
C
D
1
2
3
4
5
6
193
185
SEE PAGE 65
Bingley
Baildon
Baildon Green
Harden
Saltaire
Shipley
Thackley End
Thackley
Apperley Bridge
Idle
Cottingley
Cullingworth
Wilsden
Nab Wood
Moorhead
Windhill
West Royd
Idle Moor
Greengates
Simpson Green
Swain House
Eccleshill
Bank Top
Ravenscliffe
Heaton Shay
Sandy Lane
Shay Gate
Noon Nick
Heaton Royds
Frizinghall
Daisy Hill
Heaton
Undercliffe
Fagley
Thornbury
Girlington
Manningham
Allerton
Four Lane Ends
Lower Grange
Crossley Hall
Denholme
Hill Top
Thornton
School Green
Denholme Clough
Chat Hill
Lidget Green
BRADFORD
Laisterdyke
Tyresal
Scholemoor
Clayton
Great Horton
Little Horton
West Bowling
Bowling
Ogden
West Scholes
Mountain
Dudley Hill
Holme Shay
Old Dolphin
Queensbury
Ambler Thorn
Wibsey
Odsal
Bierley
Tong Street
Buttershaw
East Bierley
Holdsworth
Shibden Head
Illingworth
Shelf
Low Moor
Moor Side
Mixenden
Holmfield
Stone Chair
Ovenden
Boothtown
Wyke
Wyke Common
Hunsworth
Merchant Fields
Gomersal
Norwood Green
Northowram
Akroydon
Mt. Pellon
Hipperholme
Scholes
Cleckheaton
HALIFAX
Warley Town
Bailiff Bridge
Hightown Heights
Hove Edge
Hightown
Littletown
Siddal
Southowram
Liversedge
Sowerby Bridge
Brighouse
Brookfoot
Clifton
Norland
Rastrick
Woodhouse
Toothill
Lindwell
Greetland
Elland
Lower Edge
Mirfield Moor
Battyeford
Mirfield
Bradley
Barkisland
Holywell Green
Broad Carr
Brackenhall
Deighton
Stainland
Sheepridge
Netheroyd Hill
Prince Royd
Birchencliffe
Fartown
Sowood
Outlane
Lindley
Birkby
Edgerton
Salendine Nook
Kirkheaton
Upper Hopton
Mount
Snow Lee
Bradley Mills
Oakes
HUDDERSFIELD
Quarmby
Longwood
Dalton
Leymoor
Milnsbridge
Golcar
Tandem
Greenside
Moldgreen
Town End
Cowmes
Fenay Bridge
Hill Side
M62
M606

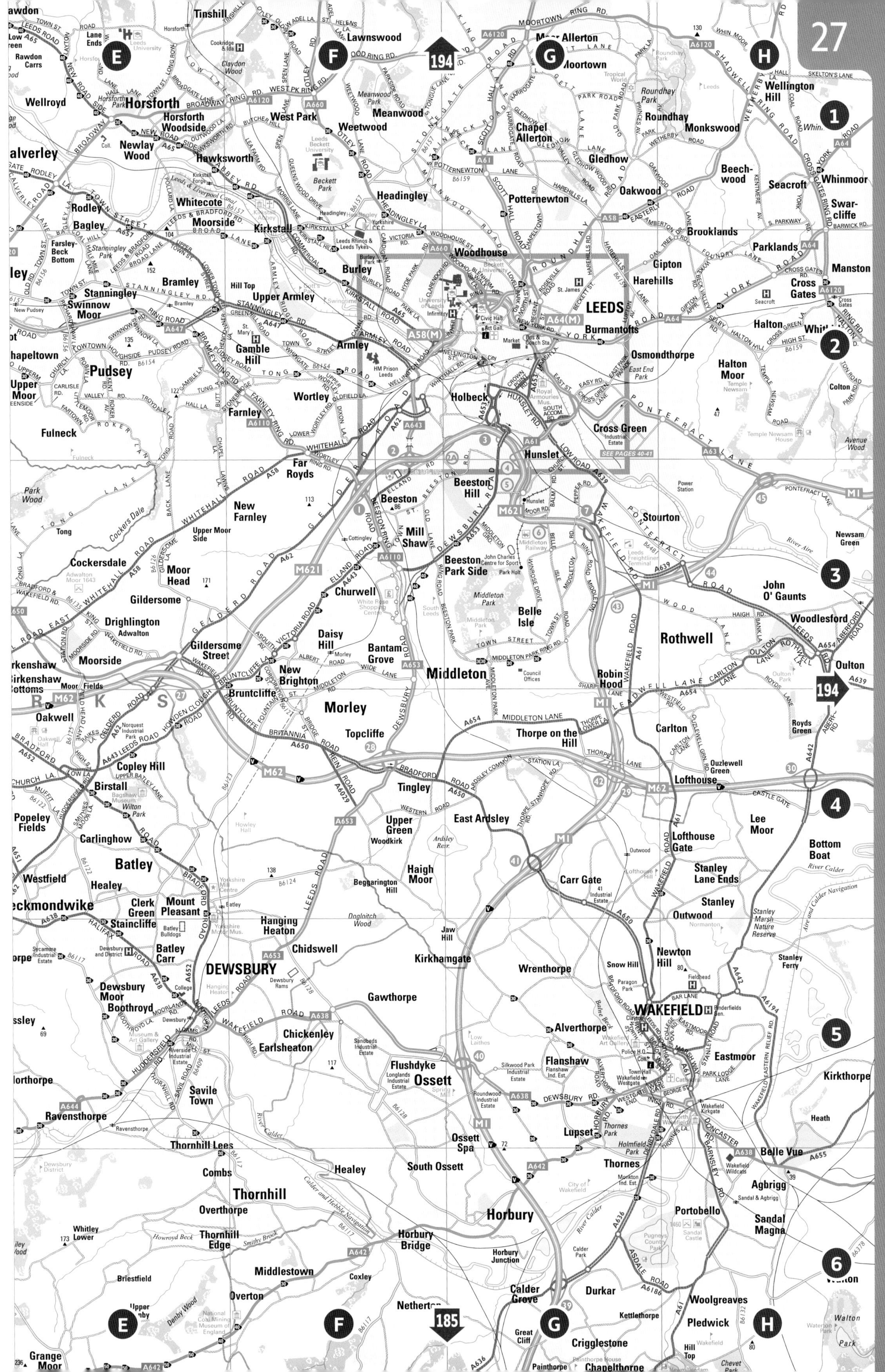
E
F
G
H
194
185
1
2
3
4
5
6
Horsforth
Tinshill
Lawnswood
Moor Allerton
Moortown
Wellington Hill
Rawdon Carrs
Lane Ends
Wellroyd
Horsforth Woodside
West Park
Weetwood
Meanwood
Chapel Allerton
Roundhay Park
Roundhay
Monkswood
Newlay Wood
Hawksworth
Gledhow
Beech-wood
Seacroft
Whinmoor
Calverley
Rodley
Whitecote
Moorside
Kirkstall
Headingley
Potternewton
Oakwood
Swarcliffe
Bagley
Farsley-Beck Bottom
Stanningley Park
Bramley
Hill Top
Upper Armley
Burley
Woodhouse
Gipton
Harehills
Brooklands
Parklands
Manston
Cross Gates
Stanningley
Swinnow Moor
Pudsey
Gamble Hill
Armley
LEEDS
Burmantofts
Halton
Whitkirk
Chapeltown
Upper Moor
Wortley
Farnley
Holbeck
Osmondthorpe
East End Park
Halton Moor
Colton
Fulneck
Far Royds
Hunslet
Cross Green
Beeston Hill
Beeston
Park Wood
New Farnley
Tong
Cockers Dale
Upper Moor Side
Mill Shaw
Stourton
Newsam Green
Cockersdale
Moor Head
Beeston Park Side
Churwell
Belle Isle
John O' Gaunts
Gildersome
Drighlington
Adwalton
Woodlesford
Rothwell
Daisy Hill
Bantam Grove
Moorside
Gildersome Street
New Brighton
Middleton
Robin Hood
Oulton
Birkenshaw
Birkenshaw Bottoms
Bruntcliffe
Morley
Oakwell
Topcliffe
Carlton
Thorpe on the Hill
Royds Green
Copley Hill
Birstall
Tingley
Lofthouse
Oulzlewell Green
Popeley Fields
Upper Green
East Ardsley
Lee Moor
Carlinghow
Lofthouse Gate
Bottom Boat
Batley
Haigh Moor
Stanley Lane Ends
Westfield
Healey
Beggarington Hill
Carr Gate
Stanley
Heckmondwike
Clerk Green
Mount Pleasant
Outwood
Staincliffe
Hanging Heaton
Dogloitch Wood
Jaw Hill
Batley Carr
Chidswell
Newton Hill
Stanley Ferry
DEWSBURY
Kirkhamgate
Wrenthorpe
Snow Hill
Dewsbury Moor
Gawthorpe
WAKEFIELD
Boothroyd
Alverthorpe
Chickenley
Earlsheaton
Flanshaw
Eastmoor
Flushdyke
Ossett
Kirkthorpe
Northorpe
Savile Town
Ravensthorpe
Lupset
Thornes Park
Thornhill Lees
Ossett Spa
Belle Vue
Heath
Combs
Healey
South Ossett
Thornes
Agbrigg
Thornhill
Overthorpe
Portobello
Sandal Magna
Horbury
Whitley Lower
Thornhill Edge
Horbury Bridge
Horbury Junction
Middlestown
Briestfield
Coxley
Calder Grove
Durkar
Woolgreaves
Overton
Netherton
Kettlethorpe
Pledwick
Great Cliff
Crigglestone
Grange Moor
Hill Top
Painthorpe
Chapelthorpe
Walton Park
M1
M62
M621
A58(M)
A64(M)
SEE PAGES 40-41

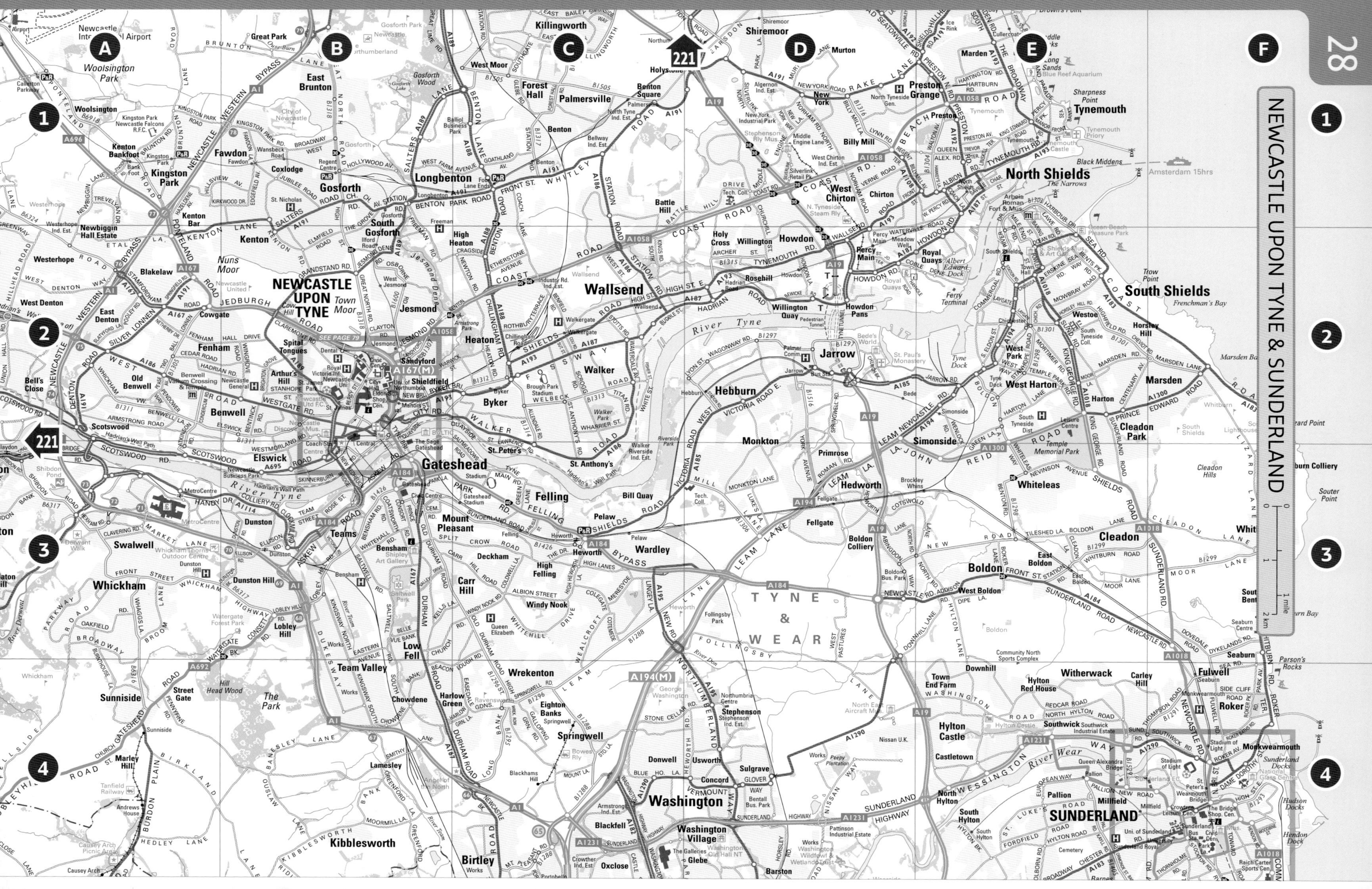
NEWCASTLE UPON TYNE & SUNDERLAND
0
1 mile
0
1
2 km
1
2
3
4
A
B
C
D
E
F
Tynemouth
North Shields
South Shields
Sunderland
Newcastle upon Tyne
Gateshead
Wallsend
Jarrow
Hebburn
Washington
Killingworth
Longbenton
Gosforth
Jesmond
Heaton
Byker
Walker
Felling
Whickham
Dunston
Kenton
Fenham
Benwell
Elswick
Scotswood
Cleadon
Whiteleas
Boldon
Birtley
Kibblesworth
Sunniside
Marley Hill
Lamesley
Team Valley
Low Fell
Chowdene
Springwell
Wrekenton
Usworth
Concord
Sulgrave
Fellgate
Hedworth
Monkton
Simonside
Westoe
Harton
Marsden
Cleadon Park
Horsley Hill
Seaburn
Fulwell
Roker
Monkwearmouth
Southwick
Pallion
Millfield
Hylton Castle
Castletown
Downhill
Witherwack
Carley Hill
Town End Farm
Hylton Red House
North Hylton
South Hylton
Preston
Preston Grange
Murton
New York
Shiremoor
West Moor
Forest Hall
Palmersville
Benton
Benton Square
Holystone
Battle Hill
Howdon
Willington Quay
Willington
Rosehill
Holy Cross
Percy Main
Chirton
West Chirton
Billy Mill
Marden
High Heaton
Sandyford
Shieldfield
Spital Tongues
Arthur's Hill
Cowgate
Blakelaw
Kenton Bar
Kingston Park
Fawdon
Coxlodge
East Brunton
Woolsington
Kenton Bankfoot
Newbiggin Hall Estate
Westerhope
West Denton
East Denton
Old Benwell
Swalwell
Teams
Bensham
Carr Hill
Deckham
High Felling
Windy Nook
Mount Pleasant
Pelaw
Wardley
Bill Quay
St. Anthony's
St. Peter's
Donwell
Blackfell
Oxclose
Harlow Green
Eighton Banks
Stephenson
Barmston
Washington Village
Glebe
Primrose
Boldon Colliery
West Boldon
East Boldon
Lobley Hill
Dunston Hill
Street Gate
River Tyne
River Wear
Tyne & Wear
221

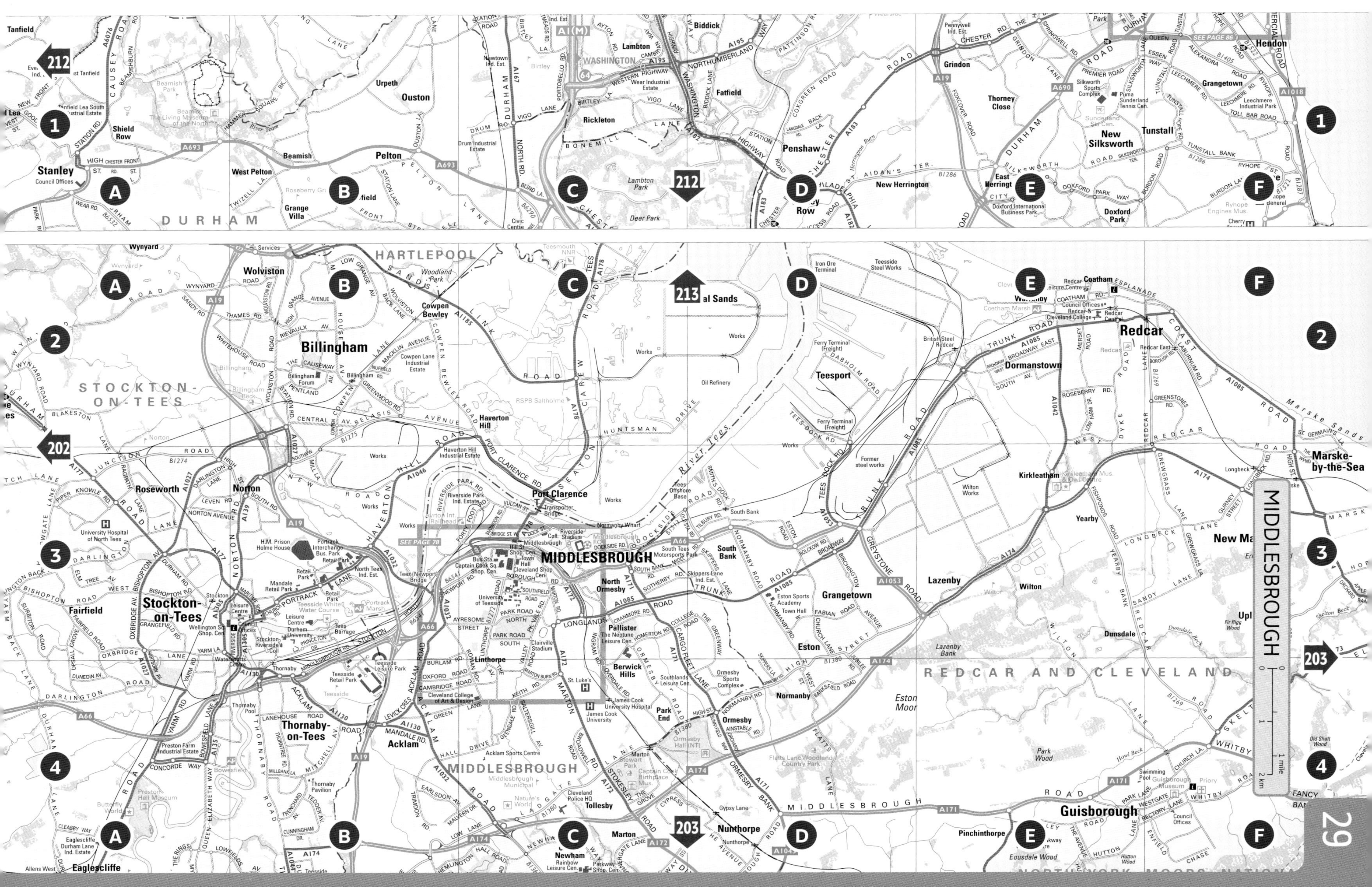
MIDDLESBROUGH
0 1 mile
0 1 2 km
Redcar
Marske-by-the-Sea
Guisborough
MIDDLESBROUGH
Stockton-on-Tees
Billingham
Thornaby-on-Tees
Eaglescliffe
HARTLEPOOL
Stanley
Washington
Teesport
Eston
Normanby
Ormesby
Nunthorpe
Marton
Acklam
Port Clarence
Norton
Roseworth
Fairfield
Wolviston
Dormanstown
Kirkleatham
Lazenby
Wilton
Grangetown
South Bank
Pelton
Ouston
Urpeth
Beamish
Penshaw
Tunstall
New Silksworth
Grindon
Hendon
REDCAR AND CLEVELAND
STOCKTON-ON-TEES
DURHAM
River Tees
212
213
202
203

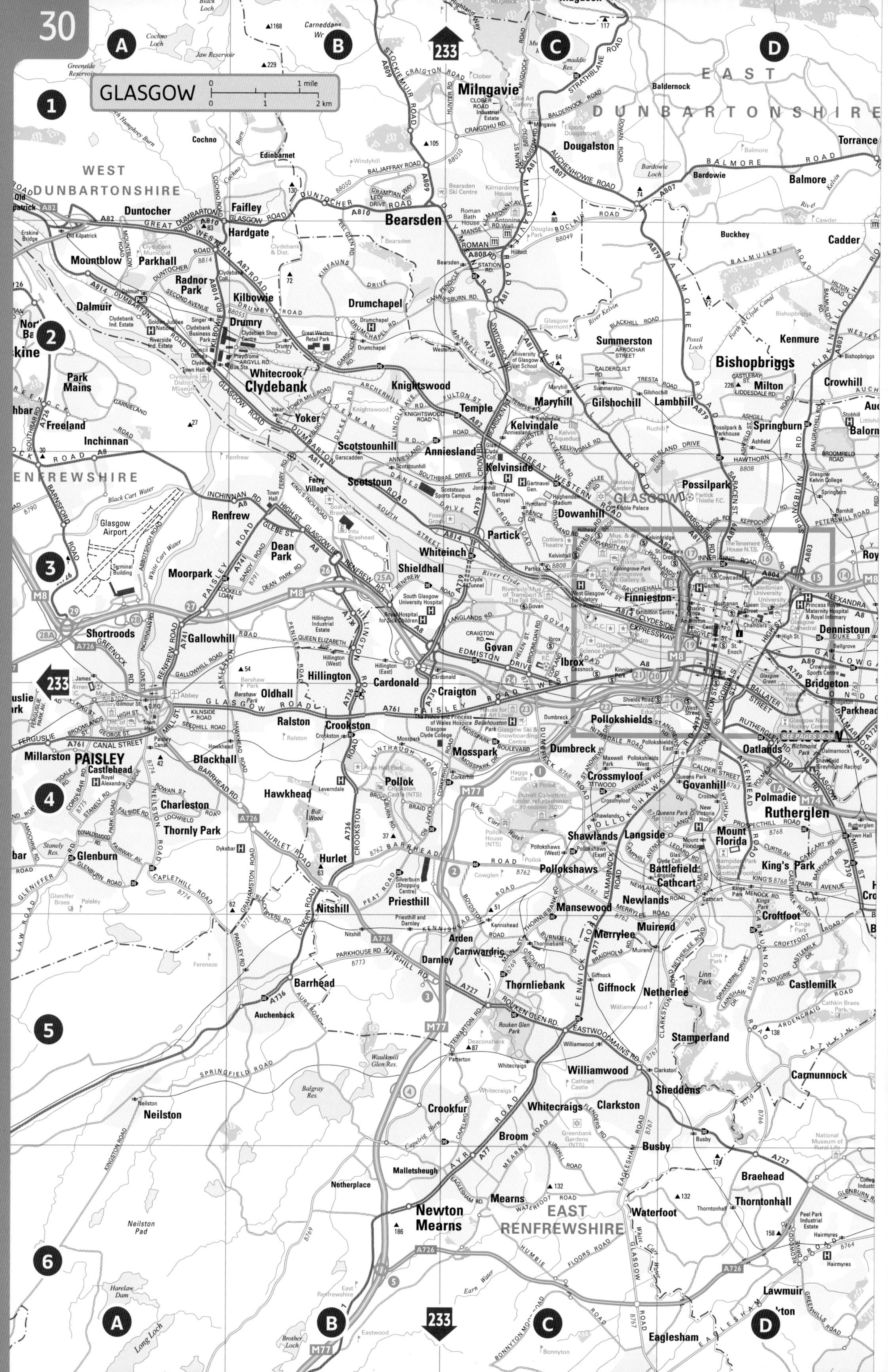
GLASGOW
0 1 mile
0 1 2 km
A
B
C
D
1
2
3
4
5
6
233
EAST DUNBARTONSHIRE
WEST DUNBARTONSHIRE
RENFREWSHIRE
EAST RENFREWSHIRE
Milngavie
Bearsden
Dougalston
Torrance
Balmore
Bardowie
Baldernock
Cadder
Buckhey
Duntocher
Faifley
Hardgate
Mountblow
Parkhall
Radnor Park
Kilbowie
Dalmuir
Drumry
Drumchapel
Whitecrook
Clydebank
Knightswood
Yoker
Scotstounhill
Anniesland
Scotstoun
Temple
Maryhill
Kelvindale
Kelvinside
Gilshochill
Lambhill
Summerston
Bishopbriggs
Kenmure
Milton
Crowhill
Springburn
Possilpark
Partick
Whiteinch
Shieldhall
Dowanhill
Finnieston
GLASGOW
Dennistoun
Bridgeton
Parkhead
Oatlands
Rutherglen
Polmadie
Govanhill
Mount Florida
King's Park
Croftfoot
Castlemilk
Carmunnock
Govan
Ibrox
Pollokshields
Dumbreck
Crossmyloof
Mosspark
Pollok
Craigton
Cardonald
Hillington
Oldhall
Ralston
Crookston
Renfrew
Dean Park
Moorpark
Glasgow Airport
Park Mains
Freeland
Inchinnan
Shortroods
Gallowhill
PAISLEY
Millarston
Castlehead
Charleston
Thornly Park
Blackhall
Hawkhead
Glenburn
Hurlet
Nitshill
Priesthill
Pollokshaws
Shawlands
Langside
Battlefield
Cathcart
Newlands
Muirend
Merrylee
Mansewood
Arden
Carnwadric
Darnley
Thornliebank
Giffnock
Netherlee
Stamperland
Barrhead
Auchenback
Williamwood
Sheddens
Clarkston
Whitecraigs
Crookfur
Broom
Busby
Neilston
Malletsheugh
Netherplace
Newton Mearns
Mearns
Waterfoot
Braehead
Thorntonhall
Eaglesham
Lawmuir
M8
M74
M77
A82
A81
A8
A726
A727
A736
A761
A739
A814
A803
A879
A807
A809
SEE PAGES 38-39

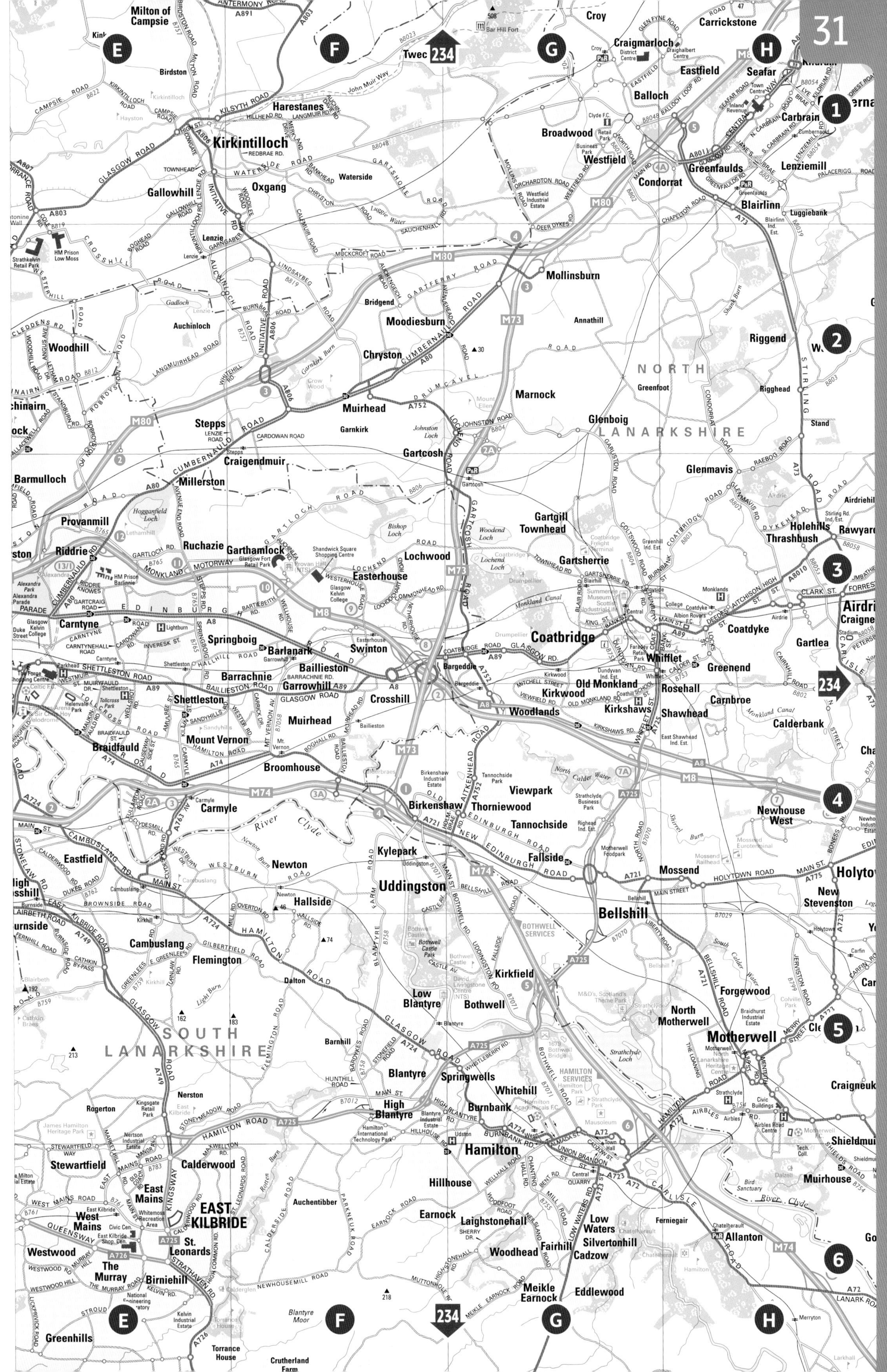
Milton of Campsie
Birdston
Harestanes
Kirkintilloch
Twec
234
Bar Hill Fort
Croy
Craigmarloch
Carrickstone
Eastfield
Seafar
Balloch
Carbrain
Broadwood
Westfield
Greenfaulds
Lenziemill
Condorrat
Blairlinn
Luggiebank
Waterside
Oxgang
Gallowhill
Lenzie
HM Prison Low Moss
Strathkelvin Retail Park
Mollinsburn
Annathill
Bridgend
Moodiesburn
Chryston
Auchinloch
Woodhill
Riggend
Rigghead
Stand
Marnock
Greenfoot
NORTH
LANARKSHIRE
Glenboig
Muirhead
Garnkirk
Stepps
Craigendmuir
Millerston
Gartcosh
Glenmavis
Barmulloch
Provanmill
Riddrie
Ruchazie
Garthamlock
Gartgill
Townhead
Holehills
Thrashbush
Lochwood
Easterhouse
Gartsherrie
Airdrie
Coatdyke
Carntyne
Springboig
Barlanark
Swinton
Coatbridge
Whifflet
Gartlea
Greenend
Barrachnie
Baillieston
Garrowhill
Crosshill
Bargeddie
Old Monkland
Kirkwood
Rosehall
Shettleston
Kirkshaws
Woodlands
Shawhead
Carnbroe
Calderbank
Mount Vernon
Muirhead
Braidfauld
Broomhouse
Viewpark
Thorniewood
Birkenshaw
Carmyle
Tannochside
Newhouse
West
Fallside
Kylepark
Eastfield
Newton
Uddingston
Mossend
Holytown
New Stevenston
Hallside
Bellshill
BOTHWELL SERVICES
Cambuslang
Flemington
Kirkfield
Dalton
Low Blantyre
Bothwell
Forgewood
North Motherwell
Motherwell
SOUTH
LANARKSHIRE
Barnhill
Blantyre
Springwells
Whitehill
HAMILTON SERVICES
Craigneuk
Nerston
Rogerton
High Blantyre
Burnbank
Hamilton
Shieldmuir
Stewartfield
Calderwood
Hillhouse
Muirhouse
East Mains
Auchentibber
Earnock
Laighstonehall
Low Waters
Silvertonhill
Ferniegair
Allanton
West Mains
EAST KILBRIDE
St. Leonards
Woodhead
Fairhill
Cadzow
Westwood
The Murray
Birniehill
Meikle Earnock
Eddlewood
Blantyre Moor
Greenhills
Torrance House
Crutherland Farm
River Clyde
M8
M73
M74
M80
A80
A8
A89
A721
A725
A724
A726
A749
A752
A73
E
F
G
H
1
2
3
4
5
6

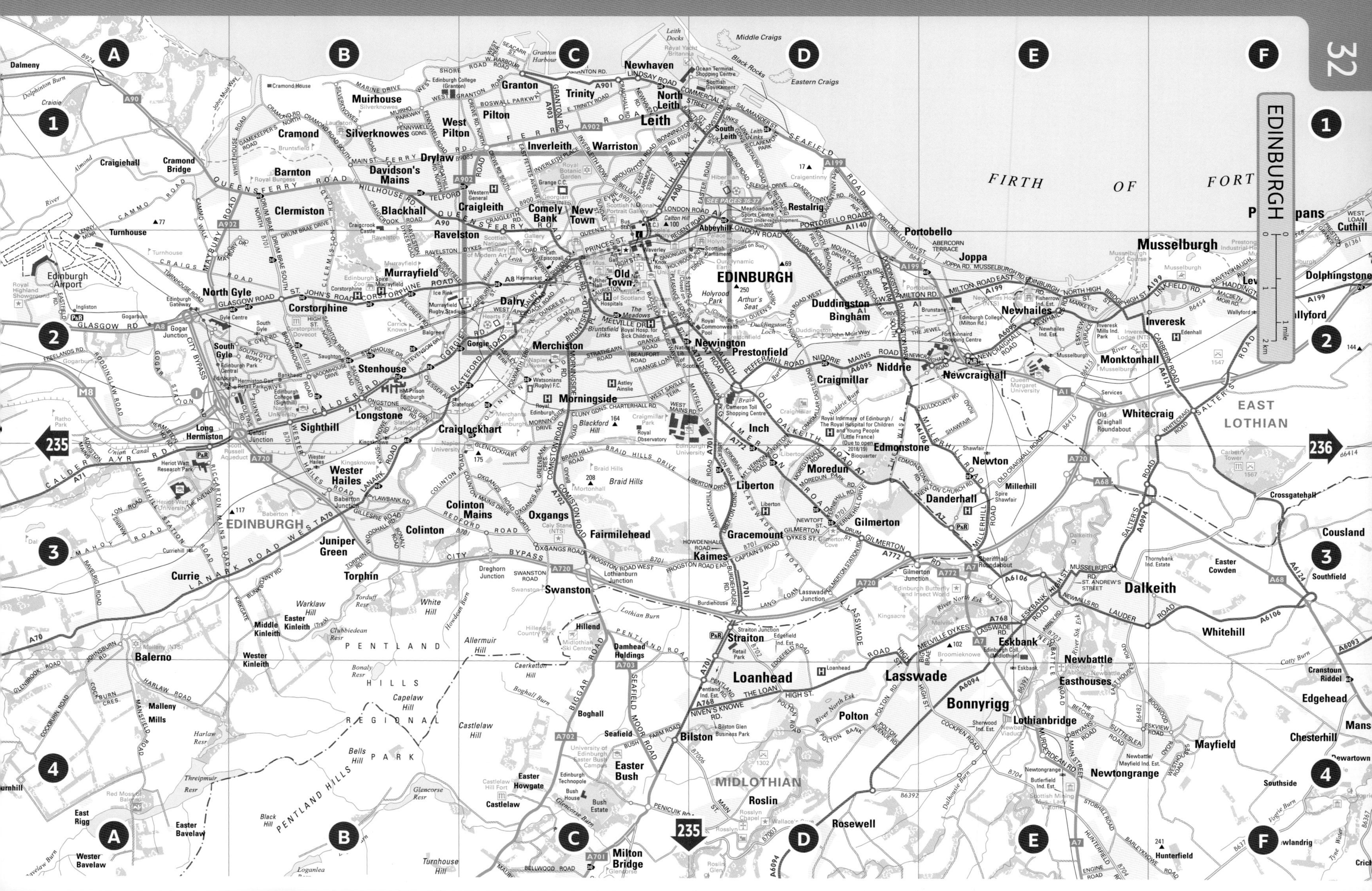
EDINBURGH
0 1 mile
0 1 2 km
FIRTH OF FORTH
EAST LOTHIAN
MIDLOTHIAN
PENTLAND HILLS REGIONAL PARK
SEE PAGES 36-37
236
235
Dalmeny
Cramond Bridge
Craigiehall
Turnhouse
Edinburgh Airport
Cramond
Muirhouse
Silverknowes
Barnton
Davidson's Mains
Clermiston
Blackhall
Drylaw
West Pilton
Pilton
Granton
Trinity
Newhaven
North Leith
Leith
South Leith
Inverleith
Warriston
Craigleith
Comely Bank
New Town
Ravelston
Murrayfield
Corstorphine
North Gyle
South Gyle
Gogar Junction
Long Hermiston
Calder Junction
Sighthill
Stenhouse
Longstone
Gorgie
Dalry
Merchiston
Old Town
EDINBURGH
Arthur's Seat
Holyrood Park
Restalrig
Portobello
Joppa
Duddingston
Bingham
Newington
Prestonfield
Niddrie
Craigmillar
Newcraighall
Newhailes
Musselburgh
Inveresk
Monktonhall
Whitecraig
Morningside
Craiglockhart
Wester Hailes
Colinton Mains
Colinton
Oxgangs
Juniper Green
Torphin
Currie
Fairmilehead
Swanston
Braid Hills
Inch
Liberton
Gracemount
Kaimes
Moredun
Gilmerton
Edmonstone
Newton
Danderhall
Millerhill
Sheriffhall Roundabout
Dalkeith
Whitehill
Cousland
Crossgatehall
Easter Cowden
Eskbank
Newbattle
Easthouses
Lasswade
Bonnyrigg
Lothianbridge
Newtongrange
Mayfield
Loanhead
Straiton
Bilston
Polton
Roslin
Rosewell
Hillend
Boghall
Seafield
Easter Bush
Easter Howgate
Castlelaw
Milton Bridge
Balerno
Malleny Mills
Middle Kinleith
Easter Kinleith
Wester Kinleith
East Rigg
Easter Bavelaw
Wester Bavelaw
Edgehead
Chesterhill
Southfield
Hunterfield
CITY BYPASS
A1
A7
A68
A70
A71
A90
A199
A720
A702
A701
A703
A772
A6106
A6094
M8

Symbols used on the map

M8	Motorway	Bus / Coach station	Embassy
A4	Primary route dual / single carriageway / Junction	Park and Ride site - rail operated (runs at least 5 days a week)	Cinema
A40	'A' road dual / single carriageway	Extent of London congestion charging zone	Cathedral / Church
B507	'B' road dual / single carriageway	Dublin 8hrs Vehicle / Pedestrian ferry	Mosque / Synagogue / Other place of worship
Toll	Other road dual / single carriageway / Toll	Car park	Leisure & tourism
	One way street / Orbital route	Theatre	Shopping
	Access restriction	Major hotel	Administration & law
	Pedestrian street	Public House	Health & welfare
	Street market	Police station	Education
	Minor road / Track	Library	Industry / Office
FB	Footpath / Footbridge	Post Office	Other notable building
	Road under construction	Visitor information centre (open all year / seasonally)	Park / Garden / Sports ground
	Main / other National Rail station	Toilet	Cemetery
	London Underground / Overground station		
	Light Rail / Station		

Locator map

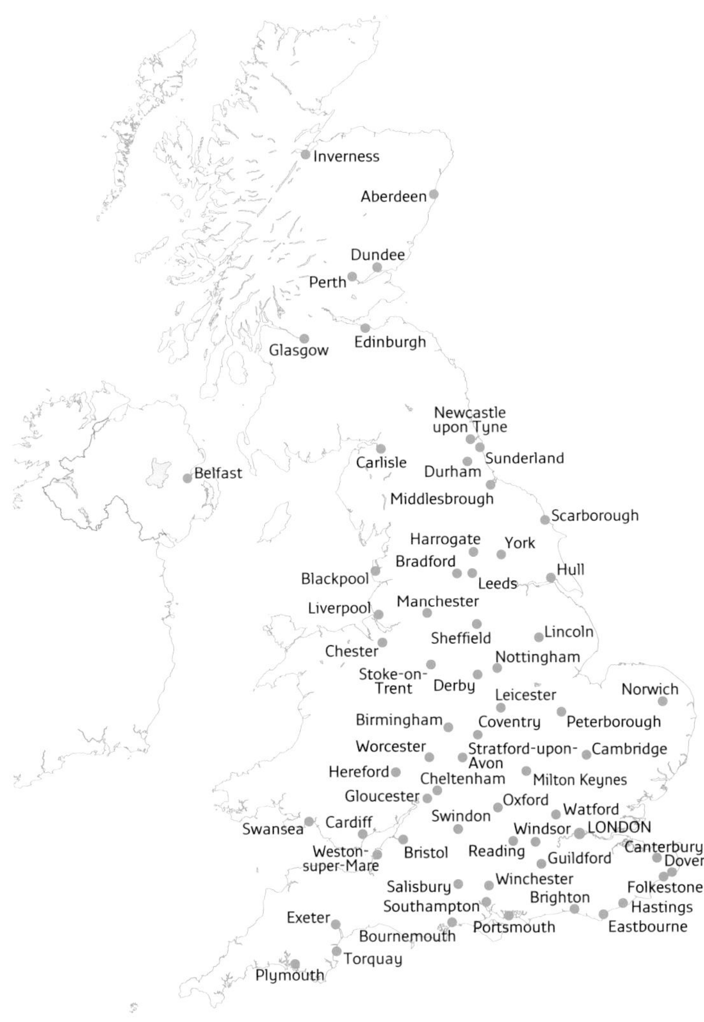

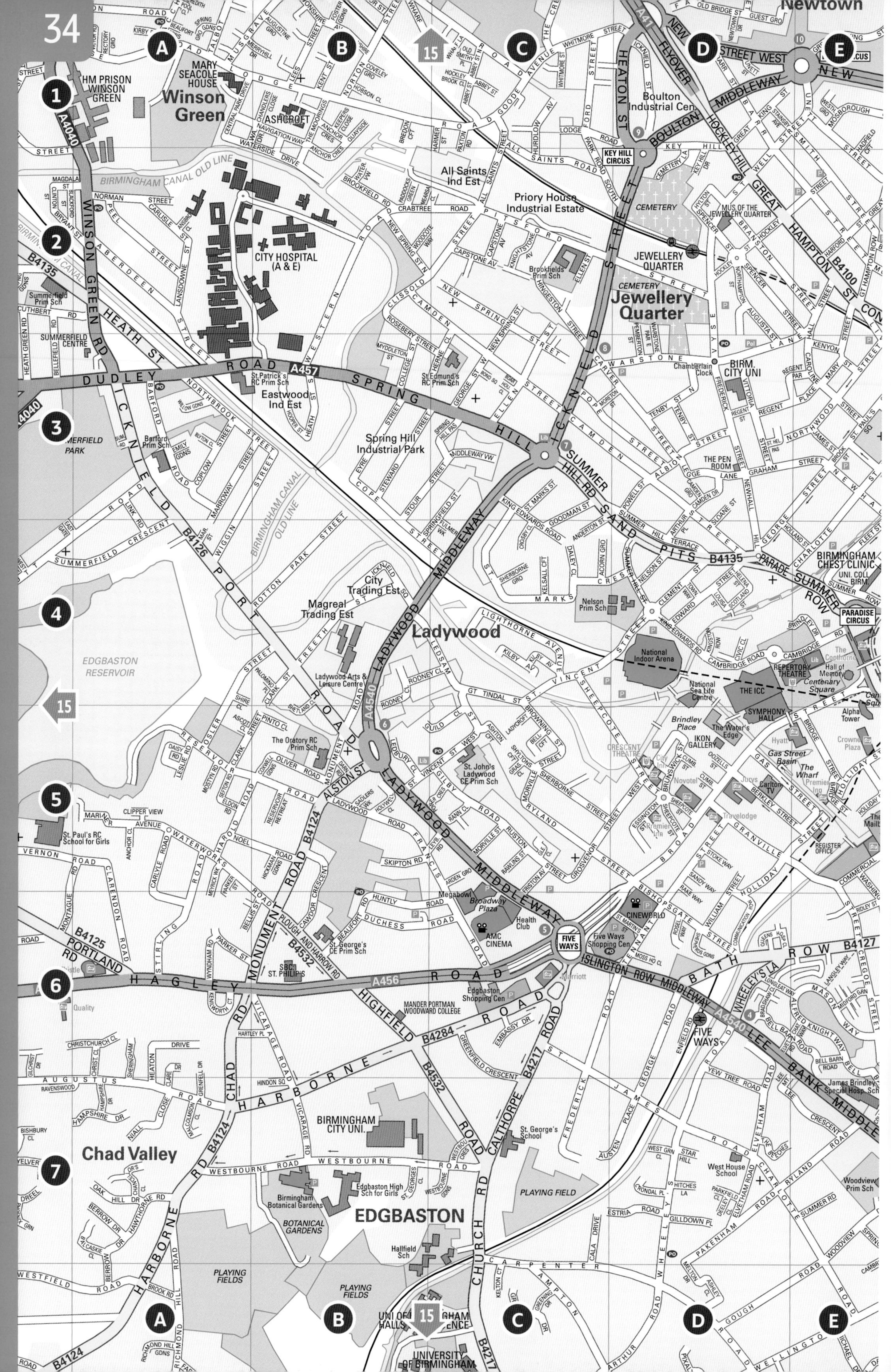
Newtown
Winson Green
HM PRISON WINSON GREEN
MARY SEACOLE HOUSE
ASHCROFT
BIRMINGHAM CANAL OLD LINE
CITY HOSPITAL (A & E)
All Saints Ind Est
Priory House Industrial Estate
Boulton Industrial Cen
KEY HILL CIRCUS
CEMETERY
MUS. OF THE JEWELLERY QUARTER
JEWELLERY QUARTER
Jewellery Quarter
Brookfields Prim Sch
Summerfield Prim Sch
SUMMERFIELD CENTRE
St.Patrick's RC Prim Sch
Eastwood Ind Est
St.Edmund's RC Prim Sch
Spring Hill Industrial Park
Chamberlain Clock
BIRM. CITY UNI
THE PEN ROOM
Barford Prim Sch
SUMMERFIELD PARK
BIRMINGHAM CHEST CLINIC
City Trading Est
Magreal Trading Est
Ladywood
Nelson Prim Sch
PARADISE CIRCUS
National Indoor Arena
EDGBASTON RESERVOIR
Ladywood Arts & Leisure Centre
National Sea Life Centre
THE ICC
REPERTORY THEATRE
SYMPHONY HALL
Centenary Square
Alpha Tower
Brindley Place
IKON GALLERY
The Water's Edge
CRESCENT THEATRE
The Oratory RC Prim Sch
St. John's Ladywood CE Prim Sch
Gas Street Basin
The Wharf
Crowne Plaza
Novotel
Travelodge
REGISTER OFFICE
St. Paul's RC School for Girls
Megabowl
Broadway Plaza
Health Club
AMC CINEMA
CINEWORLD
FIVE WAYS
Five Ways Shopping Cen
Marriott
St. George's CE Prim Sch
SBC ST. PHILIP'S
Edgbaston Shopping Cen
MANDER PORTMAN WOODWARD COLLEGE
James Brindley Special Hosp. Sch
BIRMINGHAM CITY UNI.
St. George's School
Chad Valley
West House School
Woodview Prim Sch
Edgbaston High Sch for Girls
Birmingham Botanical Gardens
BOTANICAL GARDENS
EDGBASTON
PLAYING FIELD
PLAYING FIELDS
Hallfield Sch
UNIVERSITY OF BIRMINGHAM
DUDLEY ROAD
SPRING HILL
HAGLEY ROAD
HARBORNE ROAD
LADYWOOD MIDDLEWAY
ICKNIELD STREET
WINSON GREEN RD
MONUMENT ROAD
CALTHORPE RD
CHURCH RD
A457
A456
A4540
A4040
A41
B4135
B4125
B4124
B4126
B4532
B4284
B4217
B4127
B4100
15

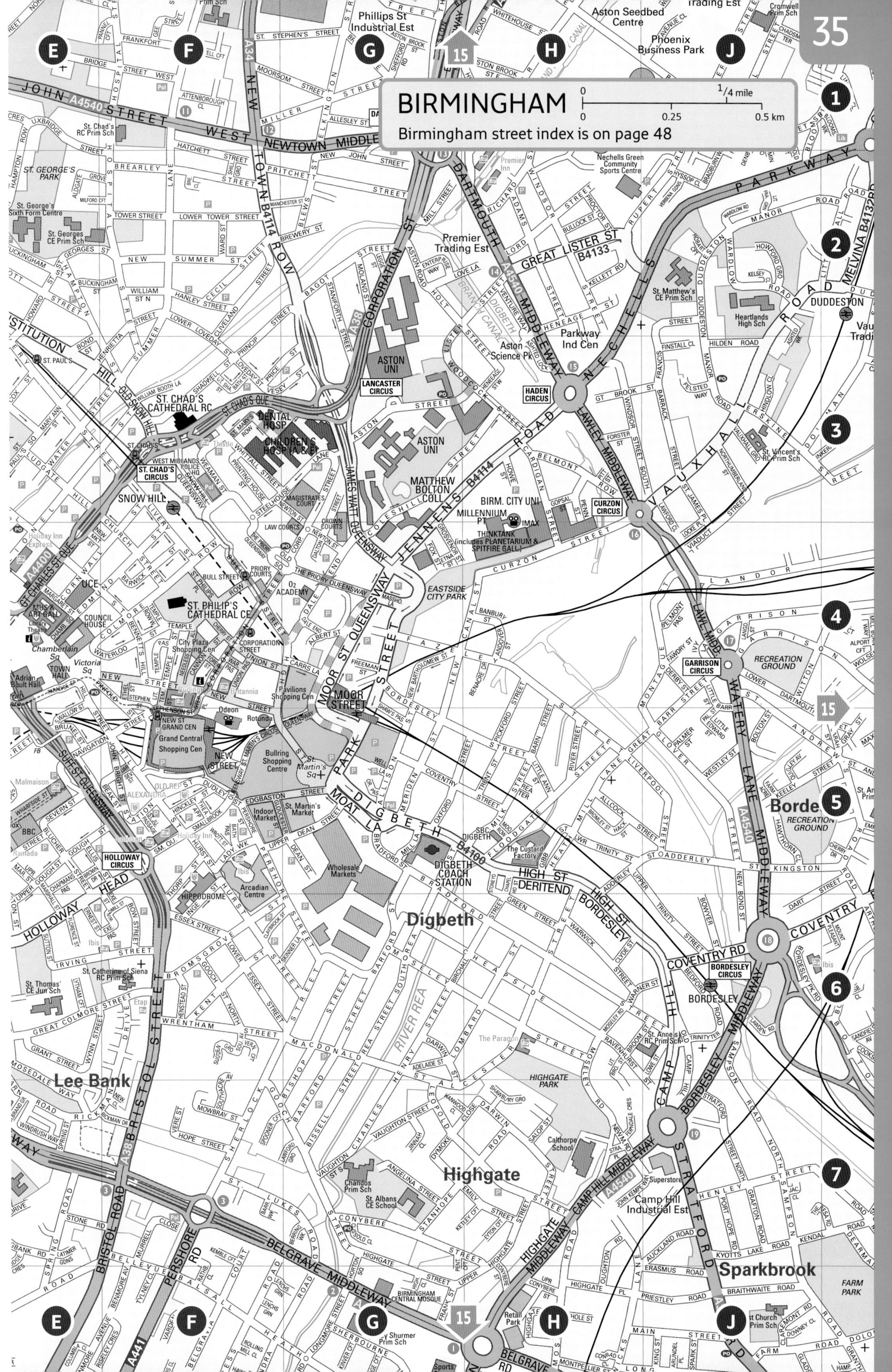
BIRMINGHAM
0 1/4 mile
0 0.25 0.5 km
Birmingham street index is on page 48
E
F
G
H
J
1
2
3
4
5
6
7
15
Aston Seedbed Centre
Phoenix Business Park
Phillips St Industrial Est
JOHN STREET WEST
NEWTOWN MIDDLEWAY
NEW TOWN ROW
ST. GEORGE'S PARK
St. George's Sixth Form Centre
St. Georges CE Prim Sch
St. Chad's RC Prim Sch
SUMMER LANE
TOWER STREET
LOWER TOWER STREET
HOSPITAL STREET
NEW SUMMER STREET
GREAT LISTER ST
DARTMOUTH MIDDLEWAY
Premier Trading Est
Nechells Green Community Sports Centre
NECHELLS PARKWAY
St. Matthew's CE Prim Sch
Heartlands High Sch
DUDDESTON
ASTON UNI
LANCASTER CIRCUS
CORPORATION ST
Aston Science Pk
Parkway Ind Cen
HADEN CIRCUS
LAWLEY MIDDLEWAY
ST. CHAD'S CATHEDRAL RC
ST. CHAD'S CIRCUS
SNOW HILL
DENTAL HOSP
CHILDREN'S HOSP (A & E)
JAMES WATT QUEENSWAY
MATTHEW BOLTON COLL
BIRM. CITY UNI MILLENNIUM PT
THINKTANK (includes PLANETARIUM & SPITFIRE GALL)
CURZON CIRCUS
VAUXHALL ROAD
St. Vincent's RC Prim Sch
EASTSIDE CITY PARK
ST. PHILIP'S CATHEDRAL CE
COUNCIL HOUSE
MUS & ART GALL
UCE
Victoria Sq
TOWN HALL
Chamberlain Sq
Adrian Boult Hall
O2 ACADEMY
MOOR ST QUEENSWAY
MOOR STREET
Pavilions Shopping Cen
City Plaza Shopping Cen
Grand Central Shopping Cen
NEW STREET
Odeon
Rotunda
Bullring Shopping Centre
St. Martin's Sq
St. Martin's Market
Indoor Market
DIGBETH
DIGBETH COACH STATION
HIGH ST DERITEND
HIGH ST BORDESLEY
The Custard Factory
GARRISON CIRCUS
RECREATION GROUND
WATERY LANE MIDDLEWAY
Wholesale Markets
Digbeth
Arcadian Centre
HIPPODROME
HOLLOWAY CIRCUS
HOLLOWAY HEAD
SUFFOLK ST QUEENSWAY
BRISTOL STREET
St. Catherine of Siena RC Prim Sch
St. Thomas' CE Jun Sch
Lee Bank
RIVER REA
HIGHGATE PARK
Calthorpe School
COVENTRY RD
BORDESLEY CIRCUS
BORDESLEY
St. Anne's RC Prim Sch
CAMP HILL MIDDLEWAY
Camp Hill Industrial Est
Highgate
Chandos Prim Sch
St. Albans CE School
BIRMINGHAM CENTRAL MOSQUE
BELGRAVE MIDDLEWAY
PERSHORE RD
BRISTOL ROAD
Sparkbrook
FARM PARK
Retail Park
STRATFORD ROAD
A4540
A38
A34
A441

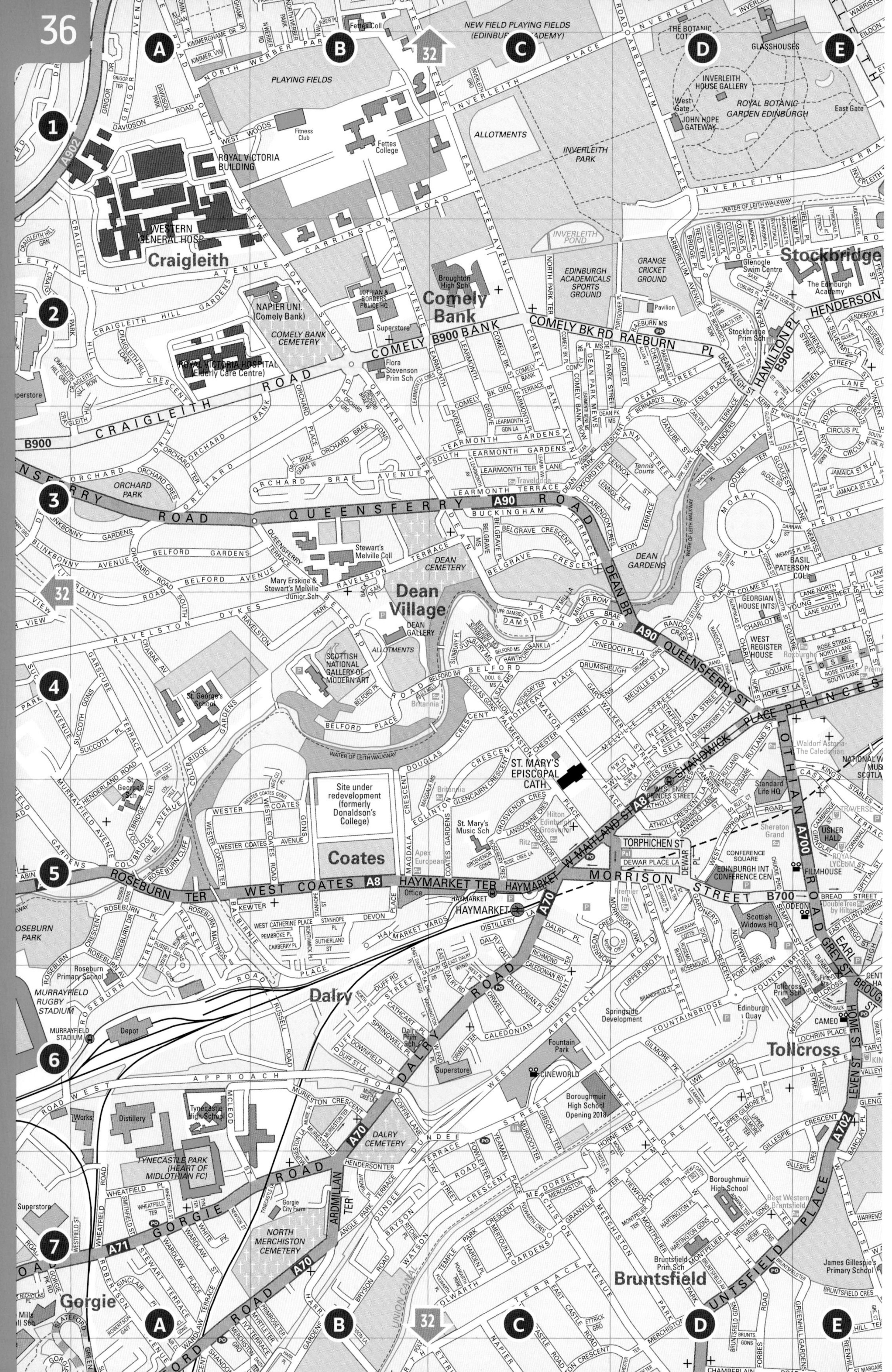
A
B
C
D
E
1
2
3
4
5
6
7
32
NEW FIELD PLAYING FIELDS
PLAYING FIELDS
THE BOTANIC COTTAGE
GLASSHOUSES
INVERLEITH HOUSE GALLERY
ROYAL BOTANIC GARDEN EDINBURGH
East Gate
West Gate
JOHN HOPE GATEWAY
ALLOTMENTS
INVERLEITH PARK
INVERLEITH POND
Fitness Club
Fettes College
Fettes Coll
ROYAL VICTORIA BUILDING
WESTERN GENERAL HOSP
Craigleith
NAPIER UNI. (Comely Bank)
COMELY BANK CEMETERY
ROYAL VICTORIA HOSPITAL (Elderly Care Centre)
LOTHIAN & BORDERS POLICE HQ
Superstore
Broughton High Sch
Comely Bank
Flora Stevenson Prim Sch
EDINBURGH ACADEMICALS SPORTS GROUND
GRANGE CRICKET GROUND
Pavilion
Glenogle Swim Centre
Stockbridge
The Edinburgh Academy
Stockbridge Prim Sch
ORCHARD PARK
Tennis Courts
Stewart's Melville Coll
DEAN CEMETERY
Mary Erskine & Stewart's Melville Junior Sch
Dean Village
DEAN GALLERY
DEAN GARDENS
BASIL PATERSON COLL
GEORGIAN HOUSE (NTS)
WEST REGISTER HOUSE
ALLOTMENTS
SCOTTISH NATIONAL GALLERY OF MODERN ART
St. George's School
St. George's Sch
WATER OF LEITH WALKWAY
Site under redevelopment (formerly Donaldson's College)
Coates
ST. MARY'S EPISCOPAL CATH
St. Mary's Music Sch
Standard Life HQ
Waldorf Astoria-The Caledonian
Sheraton Grand
USHER HALL
ROYAL LYCEUM
CONFERENCE SQUARE
EDINBURGH INT CONFERENCE CEN
FILMHOUSE
ODEON
Scottish Widows HQ
HAYMARKET
Office
ROSEBURN PARK
Roseburn Primary School
MURRAYFIELD RUGBY STADIUM
MURRAYFIELD STADIUM
Depot
Dalry
Dalry Prim Sch
Superstore
Springside Development
Edinburgh Quay
Tollcross Prim Sch
CAMEO
Tollcross
Fountain Park
CINEWORLD
Boroughmuir High School Opening 2018
Works
Distillery
Tynecastle High School
TYNECASTLE PARK (HEART OF MIDLOTHIAN FC)
DALRY CEMETERY
Gorgie City Farm
NORTH MERCHISTON CEMETERY
Superstore
Gorgie
Boroughmuir High School
Best Western Bruntsfield
Bruntsfield Prim Sch
Bruntsfield
James Gillespie's Primary School
UNION CANAL
QUEENSFERRY ROAD
A90
B900
A8
A70
A71
A700
A702
A902
B700
WEST COATES
HAYMARKET TER
MORRISON STREET
DALRY ROAD
GORGIE ROAD
CRAIGLEITH ROAD
COMELY BANK
INVERLEITH PLACE
PRINCES ST
LOTHIAN ROAD
BRUNTSFIELD PLACE
FOUNTAINBRIDGE
WEST APPROACH ROAD
DUNDEE STREET
MORAY PLACE
HERIOT ROW
RAVELSTON DYKES
ROSEBURN TER
BELFORD ROAD
DEAN BR
SHANDWICK PLACE
W MAITLAND ST
MELVILLE STREET
CHARLOTTE SQUARE
GEORGE STREET
CASTLE STREET
GILMORE PLACE
VIEWFORTH
MERCHISTON AVENUE
POLWARTH TERRACE
LEVEN ST
HOME ST
EARL GREY ST
SLATEFORD ROAD
ARDMILLAN TER
HAMILTON PL
RAEBURN PL
DEANHAUGH ST
HENDERSON ROW

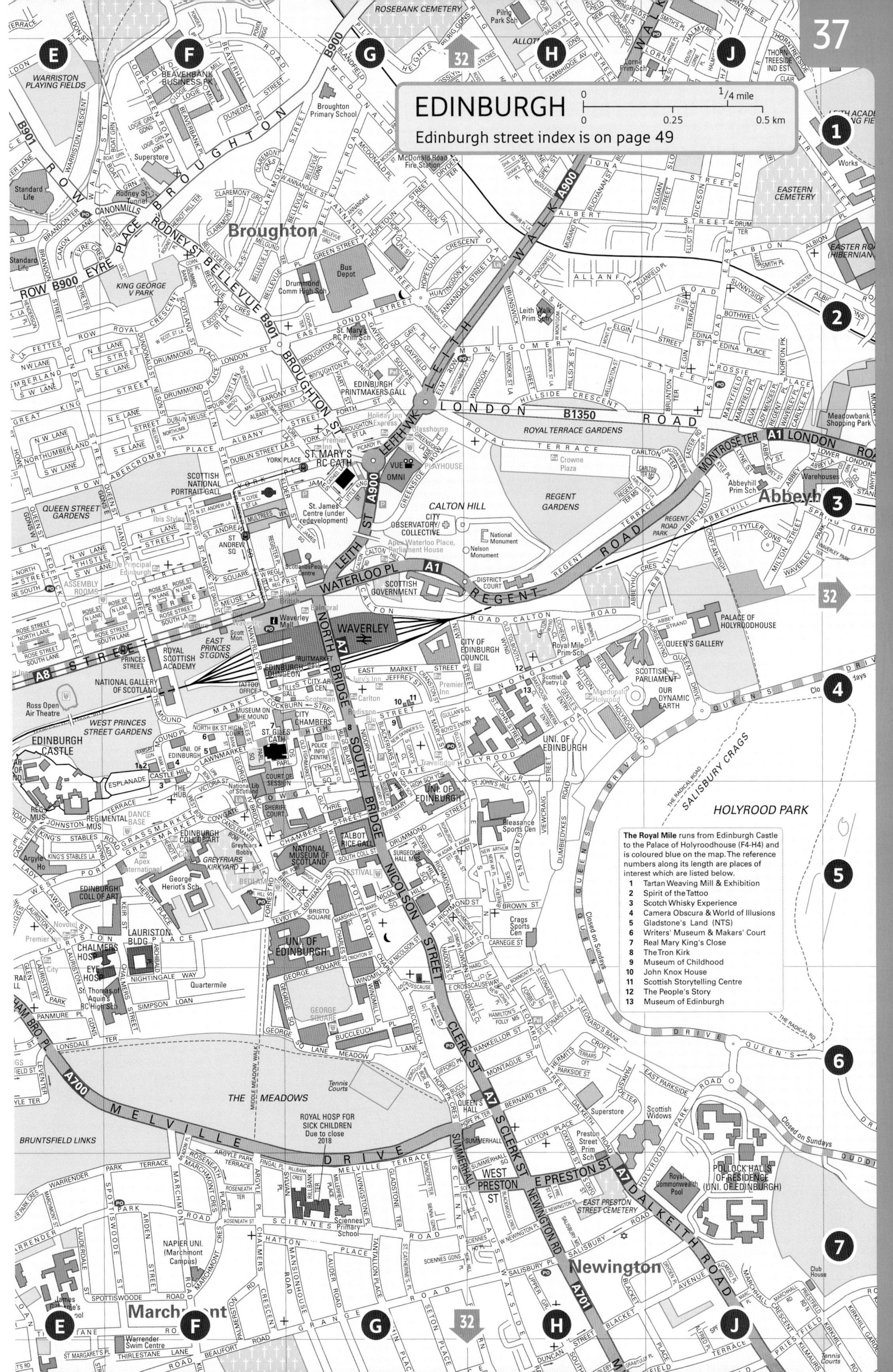

EDINBURGH

Edinburgh street index is on page 49

0 — 0.25 — 0.5 km / ¼ mile

The Royal Mile runs from Edinburgh Castle to the Palace of Holyroodhouse (F4-H4) and is coloured blue on the map. The reference numbers along its length are places of interest which are listed below.

1 Tartan Weaving Mill & Exhibition
2 Spirit of the Tattoo
3 Scotch Whisky Experience
4 Camera Obscura & World of Illusions
5 Gladstone's Land (NTS)
6 Writers' Museum & Makars' Court
7 Real Mary King's Close
8 The Tron Kirk
9 Museum of Childhood
10 John Knox House
11 Scottish Storytelling Centre
12 The People's Story
13 Museum of Edinburgh

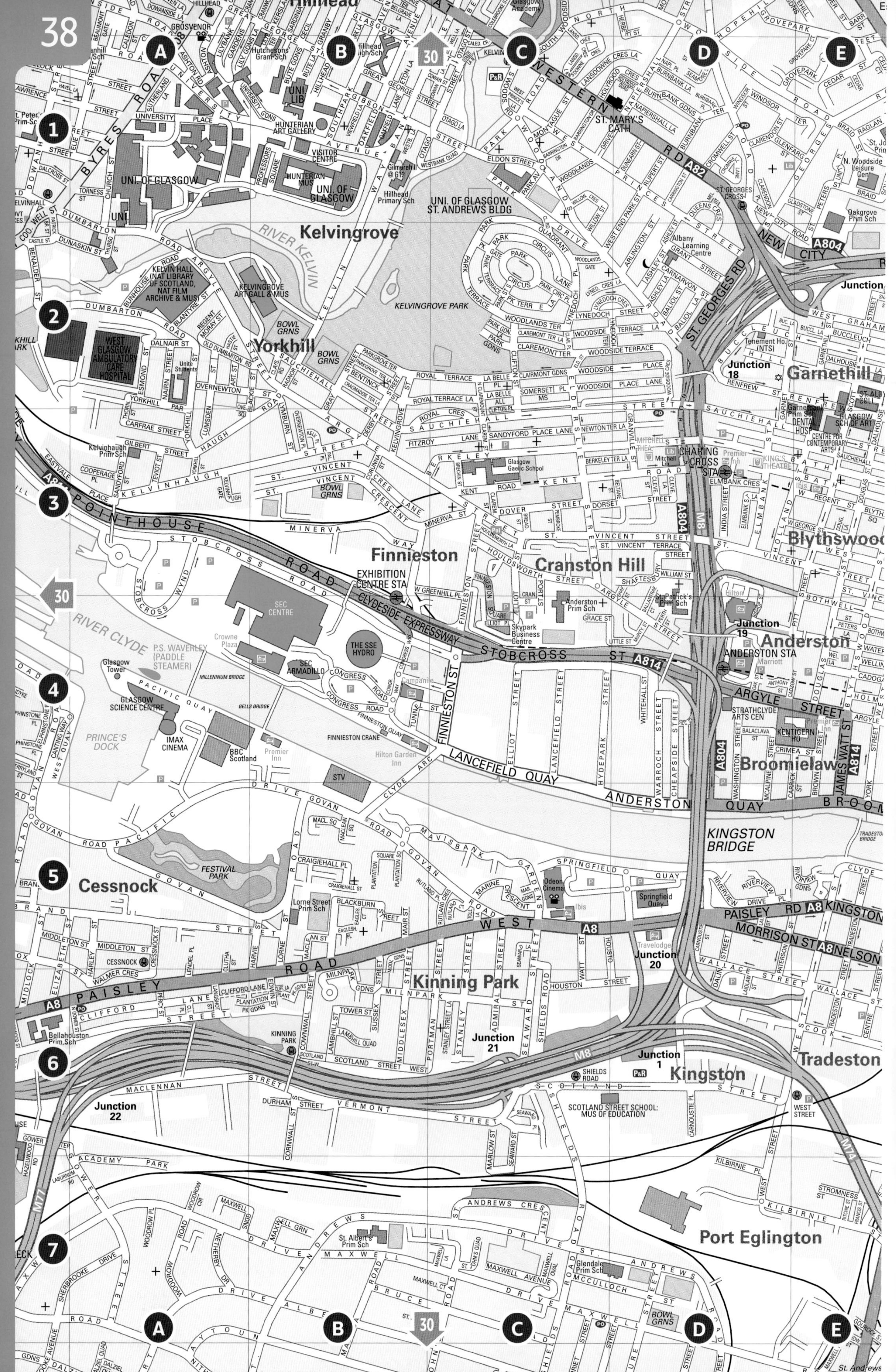
Hillhead
Kelvingrove
Yorkhill
Finnieston
Cranston Hill
Garnethill
Blythswood
Anderston
Broomielaw
Cessnock
Kinning Park
Kingston
Tradeston
Port Eglington
UNI. OF GLASGOW
HUNTERIAN ART GALLERY
HUNTERIAN MUS
UNI LIB
UNI. OF GLASGOW ST. ANDREWS BLDG
KELVINGROVE PARK
RIVER KELVIN
KELVINGROVE ARTGALL & MUS
KELVIN HALL (NAT LIBRARY OF SCOTLAND, NAT FILM ARCHIVE & MUS)
WEST GLASGOW AMBULATORY CARE HOSPITAL
ST. MARY'S CATH
SEC CENTRE
THE SSE HYDRO
SEC ARMADILLO
EXHIBITION CENTRE STA
CLYDESIDE EXPRESSWAY
STOBCROSS ROAD
POINTHOUSE
RIVER CLYDE
P.S. WAVERLEY (PADDLE STEAMER)
Glasgow Tower
GLASGOW SCIENCE CENTRE
IMAX CINEMA
BBC Scotland
PRINCE'S DOCK
STV
FINNIESTON CRANE
MILLENNIUM BRIDGE
BELLS BRIDGE
LANCEFIELD QUAY
ANDERSTON QUAY
KINGSTON BRIDGE
FESTIVAL PARK
CHARING CROSS STA
ANDERSTON STA
KING'S THEATRE
STRATHCLYDE ARTS CEN
KENTIGERN HO
GLASGOW SCH OF ART
CENTRE FOR CONTEMPORARY ARTS
Tenement Ho (NTS)
Mitchell Lib
Albany Learning Centre
Junction 18
Junction 19
Junction 20
Junction 21
Junction 22
Junction 1
PAISLEY ROAD WEST
A8
M8
M77
A804
A82
A814
M74
SCOTLAND STREET SCHOOL: MUS OF EDUCATION
SHIELDS ROAD
KINNING PARK
CESSNOCK
WEST STREET
Odeon Cinema
Springfield Quay
ST. GEORGES RD
GREAT WESTERN RD
SAUCHIEHALL STREET
ARGYLE STREET
KELVINHAUGH STREET
FINNIESTON ST
GOVAN ROAD
PACIFIC QUAY
30
A B C D E
1 2 3 4 5 6 7

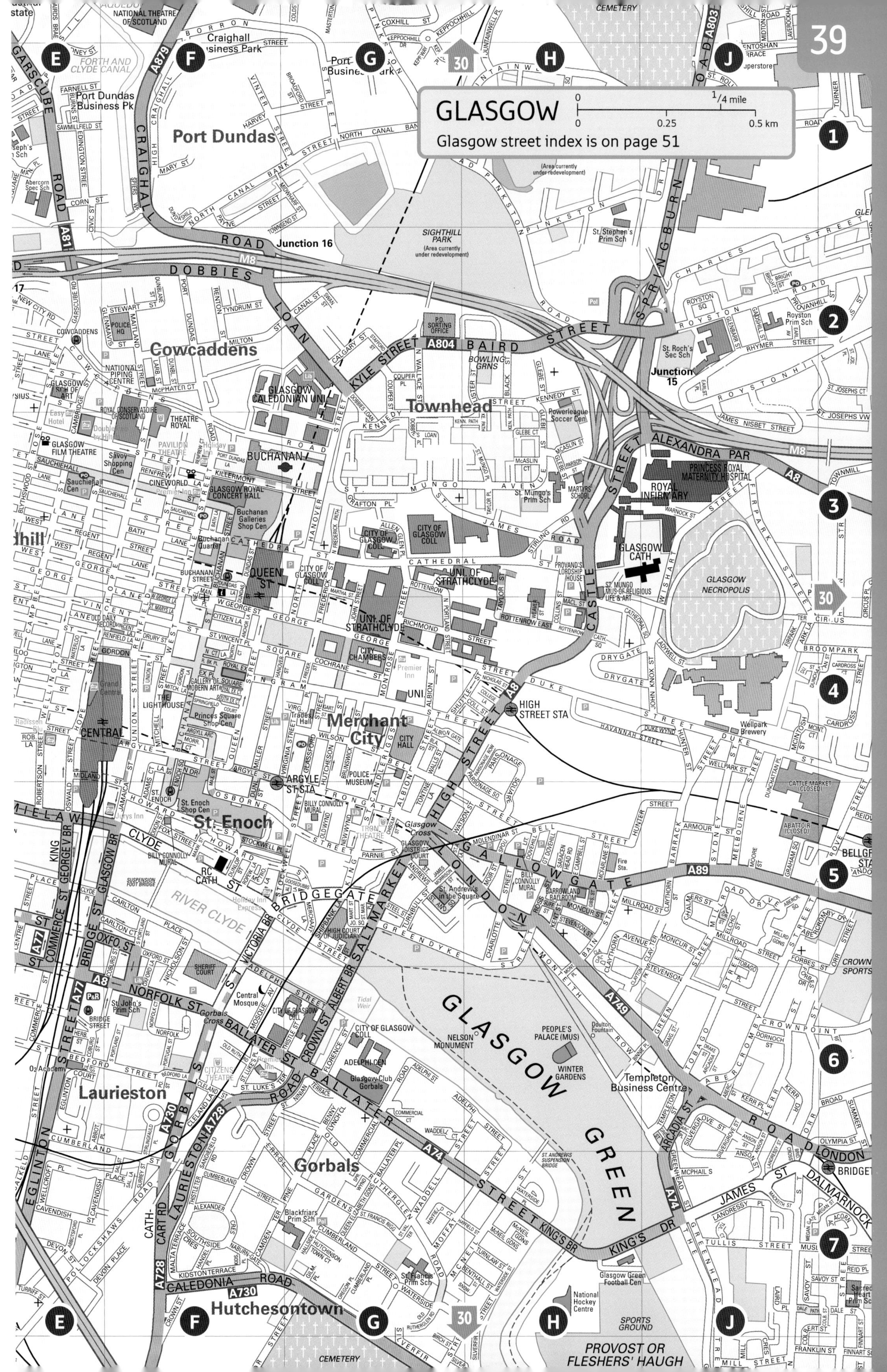
GLASGOW
0 1/4 mile
0 0.25 0.5 km
Glasgow street index is on page 51
E
F
G
H
J
1
2
3
4
5
6
7
30
Port Dundas
Cowcaddens
Townhead
Merchant City
St. Enoch
Laurieston
Gorbals
Hutchesontown
GLASGOW GREEN
RIVER CLYDE
Junction 16
Junction 15
M8
A8
A81
A879
A803
A804
A89
A749
A74
A77
A728
A730
SIGHTHILL PARK
(Area currently under redevelopment)
Craighall Business Park
Port Dundas Business Pk
Port Business Park
NATIONAL THEATRE OF SCOTLAND
FORTH AND CLYDE CANAL
CRAIGHALL ROAD
DOBBIES LOAN
NORTH CANAL BANK STREET
BAIRD STREET
KYLE STREET
SPRINGBURN ROAD
ROYSTON ROAD
ALEXANDRA PAR
CATHEDRAL ST
GEORGE SQUARE
ST VINCENT ST
SAUCHIEHALL STREET
BUCHANAN ST
ARGYLE ST
INGRAM ST
HIGH STREET
CASTLE STREET
DUKE STREET
GALLOWGATE
LONDON ROAD
SALTMARKET
BRIDGEGATE
CLYDE ST
NORFOLK ST
BALLATER ST
CALEDONIA ROAD
CROWN ST
KING'S DR
GLASGOW CALEDONIAN UNI
UNI. OF STRATHCLYDE
CITY OF GLASGOW COLL
ROYAL INFIRMARY
PRINCESS ROYAL MATERNITY HOSPITAL
GLASGOW CATH
GLASGOW NECROPOLIS
ST. MUNGO MUS. OF RELIGIOUS LIFE & ART
PROVAND'S LORDSHIP HOUSE
BUCHANAN
QUEEN ST
CENTRAL
HIGH STREET STA
ARGYLE ST STA
BELLGROVE STA
BRIDGETON
CITY HALL
POLICE MUSEUM
TRON THEATRE
Glasgow Cross
PEOPLE'S PALACE (MUS)
WINTER GARDENS
NELSON MONUMENT
Doulton Fountain
Templeton Business Centre
Wellpark Brewery
CATTLE MARKET (CLOSED)
ABATTOIR (CLOSED)
SHERIFF COURT
HIGH COURT OF JUDICIARY
Central Mosque
CITIZENS THEATRE
ADELPHI CEN
Glasgow Club Gorbals
Blackfriars Prim Sch
St. Francis Prim Sch
National Hockey Centre
Glasgow Green Football Cen
SPORTS GROUND
PROVOST OR FLESHERS' HAUGH
CEMETERY
GLASGOW ROYAL CONCERT HALL
Buchanan Galleries Shop Cen
ROYAL CONSERVATOIRE OF SCOTLAND
THEATRE ROYAL
GLASGOW SCH OF ART
GLASGOW FILM THEATRE
NATIONAL PIPING CENTRE
Savoy Shopping Cen
St. Enoch Shop Cen
Princes Square Shop Cen
GALLERY OF MODERN ART
Powerleague Soccer Cen
St. Mungo's Prim Sch
St. Roch's Sec Sch
Royston Prim Sch
P.O. SORTING OFFICE
BOWLING GRNS
CROWN SPORTS

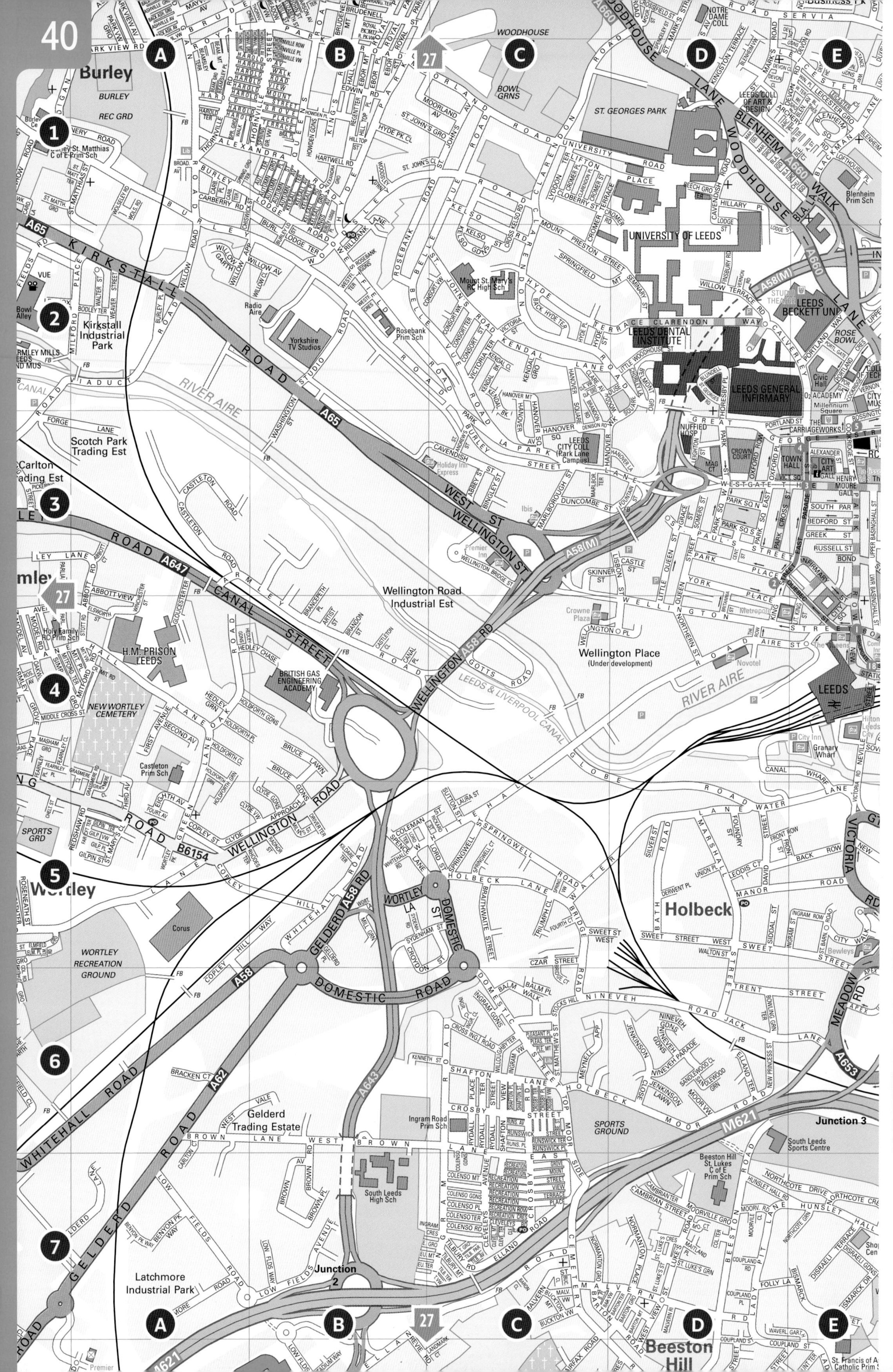

A
B
C
D
E
27
1
2
3
4
5
6
7
Burley
BURLEY REC GRD
WOODHOUSE
BOWL GRNS
NOTRE DAME COLL
ST. GEORGES PARK
UNIVERSITY OF LEEDS
LEEDS COLL OF ART & DESIGN
LEEDS BECKETT UNI
ROSE BOWL
Blenheim Prim Sch
LEEDS DENTAL INSTITUTE
LEEDS GENERAL INFIRMARY
NUFFIED HOSP
CROWN COURT
TOWN HALL
CITY ART GALL
HENRY MOORE GALL
Civic Hall
O2 ACADEMY
Millennium Square
THE CARRIAGEWORKS
Mount St. Mary's RC High Sch
Rosebank Prim Sch
Yorkshire TV Studios
Radio Aire
Kirkstall Industrial Park
VUE
Bowl Alley
Scotch Park Trading Est
RIVER AIRE
KIRKSTALL ROAD
A65
A660
A58(M)
WEST ST
WELLINGTON ST
Holiday Inn Express
Premier Inn
Ibis
Crowne Plaza
Metropole
Wellington Road Industrial Est
Wellington Place (Under development)
Novotel
LEEDS
City Inn
Granary Wharf
Hilton
LEEDS & LIVERPOOL CANAL
CANAL STREET
ARMLEY ROAD
A647
H.M. PRISON LEEDS
Holy Family RC Prim Sch
NEW WORTLEY CEMETERY
Castleton Prim Sch
BRITISH GAS ENGINEERING ACADEMY
WELLINGTON ROAD
B6154
SPORTS GRD
Wortley
Corus
WORTLEY RECREATION GROUND
GELDERD ROAD
A58
A62
A643
WHITEHALL ROAD
DOMESTIC ROAD
Holbeck
WATER LANE
SWEET ST WEST
NINEVEH ROAD
VICTORIA RD
MEADOW RD
A653
M621
Junction 3
Junction 2
SPORTS GROUND
South Leeds Sports Centre
Beeston Hill St. Lukes C of E Prim Sch
Ingram Road Prim Sch
South Leeds High Sch
Gelderd Trading Estate
Latchmore Industrial Park
ELLAND ROAD
Beeston Hill
St. Francis of A. Catholic Prim S

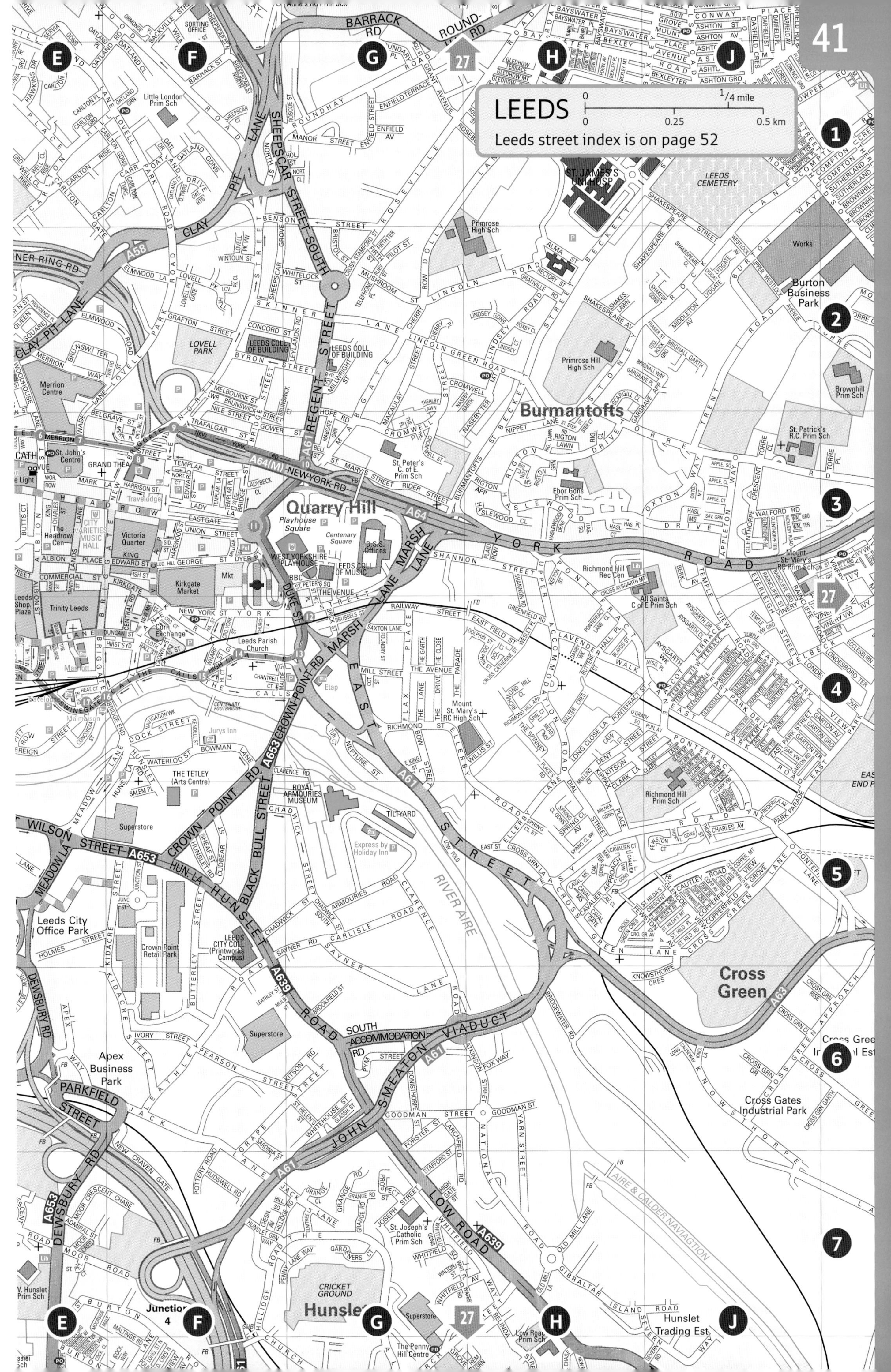
LEEDS
0 1/4 mile
0 0.25 0.5 km
Leeds street index is on page 52
E
F
G
H
J
1
2
3
4
5
6
7
27
Quarry Hill
Burmantofts
Cross Green
Hunslet
ST. JAMES'S UNI HOSP
LEEDS CEMETERY
Primrose High Sch
Primrose Hill High Sch
Burton Business Park
Works
Brownhill Prim Sch
St. Patrick's R.C. Prim Sch
Ebor Gdns Prim Sch
St. Peter's C. of E. Prim Sch
Little London Prim Sch
LOVELL PARK
LEEDS COLL OF BUILDING
Merrion Centre
St. John's Centre
GRAND THEA
Victoria Quarter
CITY VARIETIES MUSIC HALL
The Headrow Cen
Kirkgate Market
Mkt
Trinity Leeds
Leeds Shop. Plaza
Corn Exchange
Leeds Parish Church
Playhouse Square
Centenary Square
D.S.S. Offices
WEST YORKSHIRE PLAYHOUSE
LEEDS COLL OF MUSIC
THE VENUE
BBC
Richmond Hill Rec Cen
All Saints C of E Prim Sch
Mount St. Mary's RC High Sch
Mount St. Mary's RC Prim Sch
Richmond Hill Prim Sch
Etap
Jurys Inn
THE TETLEY (Arts Centre)
ROYAL ARMOURIES MUSEUM
TILTYARD
Express by Holiday Inn
RIVER AIRE
Superstore
Leeds City Office Park
Crown Point Retail Park
LEEDS CITY COLL (Printworks Campus)
Apex Business Park
Cross Gates Industrial Park
Hunslet Trading Est
CRICKET GROUND
St. Joseph's Catholic Prim Sch
Low Road Prim Sch
The Penny Hill Centre
AIRE & CALDER NAVIGATION
Junction 4
YORK ROAD
A64(M) NEW YORK RD
A61 REGENT STREET
SHEEPSCAR STREET SOUTH
CLAY PIT LANE
BARRACK RD
ROUNDHAY ROAD
A58
A64
A61
A653
A639
A63
CROWN POINT RD
BLACK BULL STREET
HUNSLET RD
WILSON STREET
DEWSBURY RD
PARKFIELD STREET
JOHN SMEATON VIADUCT
SOUTH ACCOMMODATION RD
LOW ROAD
EAST STREET
MARSH LANE
BECKETT STREET
LINCOLN GREEN ROAD
TEMPLE VIEW RD
PONTEFRACT LANE
CROSS GREEN LANE
KNOWSTHORPE LANE
MEADOW LANE
HOLMES STREET
CHURCH ST
DUKE ST
THE CALLS
KIRKGATE
VICAR LANE
EASTGATE
DOCK STREET
WATERLOO ST
BOWMAN LANE
ARMOURIES RD
CHADWICK ST
CLARENCE RD
SAYNER RD
CARLISLE RD
BRIDGEWATER RD
ATKINSON STREET
GOODMAN STREET
NATIONAL RD
YARN STREET
OLD MILL LANE
GIBRALTAR ISLAND ROAD
IVORY STREET
PEARSON STREET
KIDACRE STREET
BUTTERLEY STREET
JACK LANE
NEW CRAVEN GATE
MOOR CRESCENT CHASE
BURTON ROAD
YORK ST
SHANNON STREET
RICHMOND ROAD
EAST PARK PARADE
OSMONDTHORPE LANE

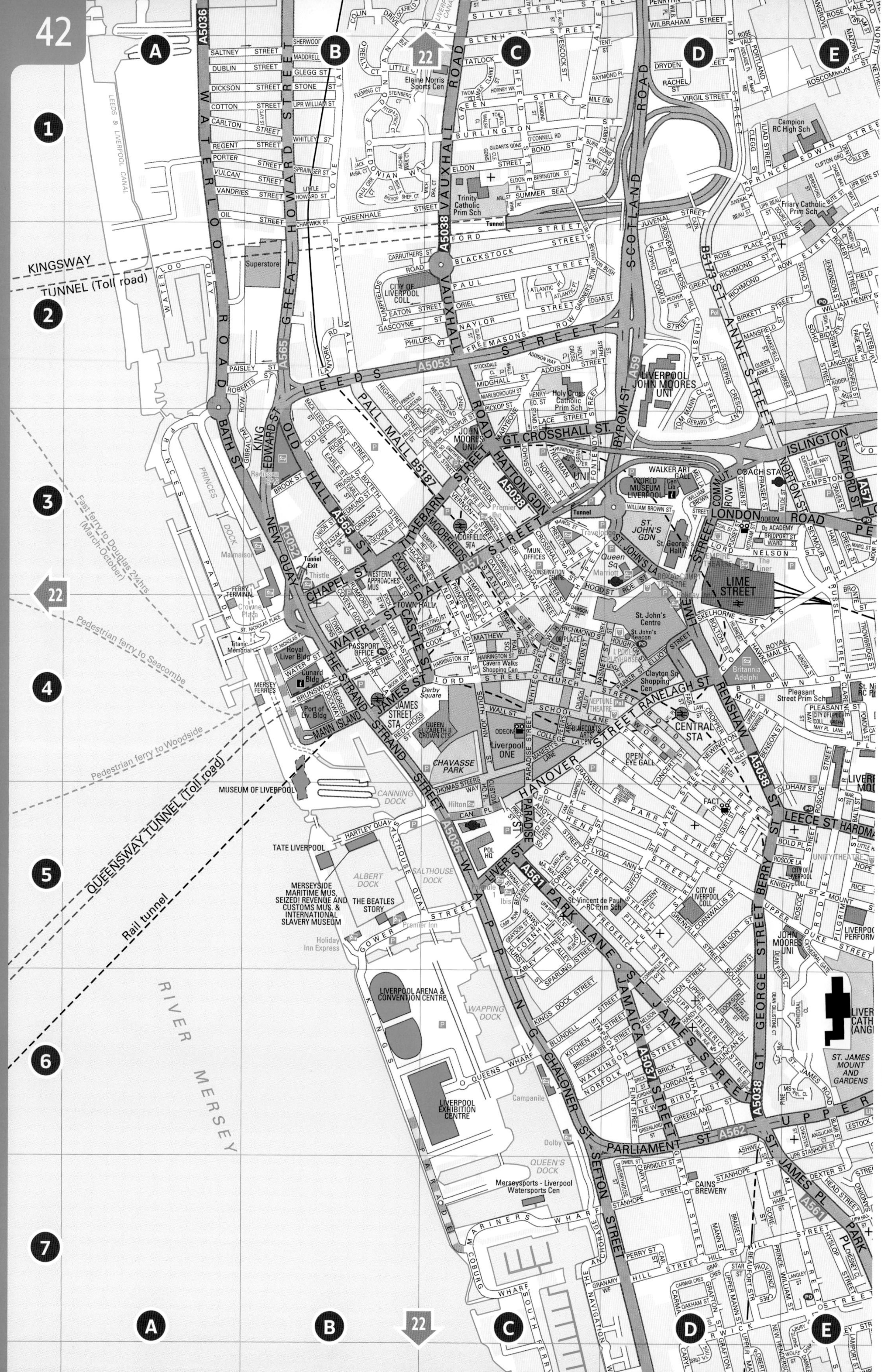
A
B
C
D
E
1
2
3
4
5
6
7
22
KINGSWAY
TUNNEL (Toll road)
QUEENSWAY TUNNEL (Toll road)
Rail tunnel
Fast ferry to Douglas 2¾hrs (March-October)
Pedestrian ferry to Seacombe
Pedestrian ferry to Woodside
RIVER MERSEY
LEEDS & LIVERPOOL CANAL
WATERLOO ROAD
GREAT HOWARD STREET
VAUXHALL ROAD
SCOTLAND ROAD
LEEDS STREET
PRINCES DOCK
PRINCES PARADE
NEW QUAY
THE STRAND
STRAND STREET
WAPPING
CHALONER ST
SEFTON STREET
PARLIAMENT ST
ST. JAMES STREET
GT. GEORGE STREET
ST. ANNE STREET
LONDON ROAD
LIME STREET
ISLINGTON
HANOVER STREET
RANELAGH ST
DALE STREET
TITHEBARN STREET
OLD HALL ST
WATER ST
CASTLE ST
JAMES ST
PARK LANE
JAMAICA STREET
BERRY ST
LEECE ST
RENSHAW ST
Elaine Norris Sports Cen
Trinity Catholic Prim Sch
Superstore
CITY OF LIVERPOOL COLL
LIVERPOOL JOHN MOORES UNI
Holy Cross Catholic Prim Sch
JOHN MOORES UNI
WALKER ART GALL
WORLD MUSEUM LIVERPOOL
ST. JOHN'S GDN
St. George's Hall
MOORFIELDS STA
Queen Sq
ROYAL COURT THEATRE
St. John's Centre
LIME STREET
Britannia Adelphi
Royal Liver Bldg
Cunard Bldg
Port of Liv. Bldg
MERSEY FERRIES
FERRY TERMINAL
Titanic Memorial
TOWN HALL
WESTERN APPROACHES MUS
PASSPORT OFFICE
JAMES STREET STA
Derby Square
QUEEN ELIZABETH II CROWN CTS
CHAVASSE PARK
Liverpool ONE
CENTRAL STA
OPEN EYE GALL
FACT
MUSEUM OF LIVERPOOL
CANNING DOCK
TATE LIVERPOOL
ALBERT DOCK
SALTHOUSE DOCK
MERSEYSIDE MARITIME MUS, SEIZED! REVENUE AND CUSTOMS MUS. & INTERNATIONAL SLAVERY MUSEUM
THE BEATLES STORY
LIVERPOOL ARENA & CONVENTION CENTRE
WAPPING DOCK
LIVERPOOL EXHIBITION CENTRE
Campanile
QUEEN'S DOCK
Merseysports - Liverpool Watersports Cen
CAINS BREWERY
ST. JAMES MOUNT AND GARDENS
Campion RC High Sch
Friary Catholic Prim Sch
St.Vincent de Paul RC Prim Sch
Pleasant Street Prim Sch
A5036
A565
A5038
A5053
A59
A57
A5052
A561
A562
A5037
B5173
B5187

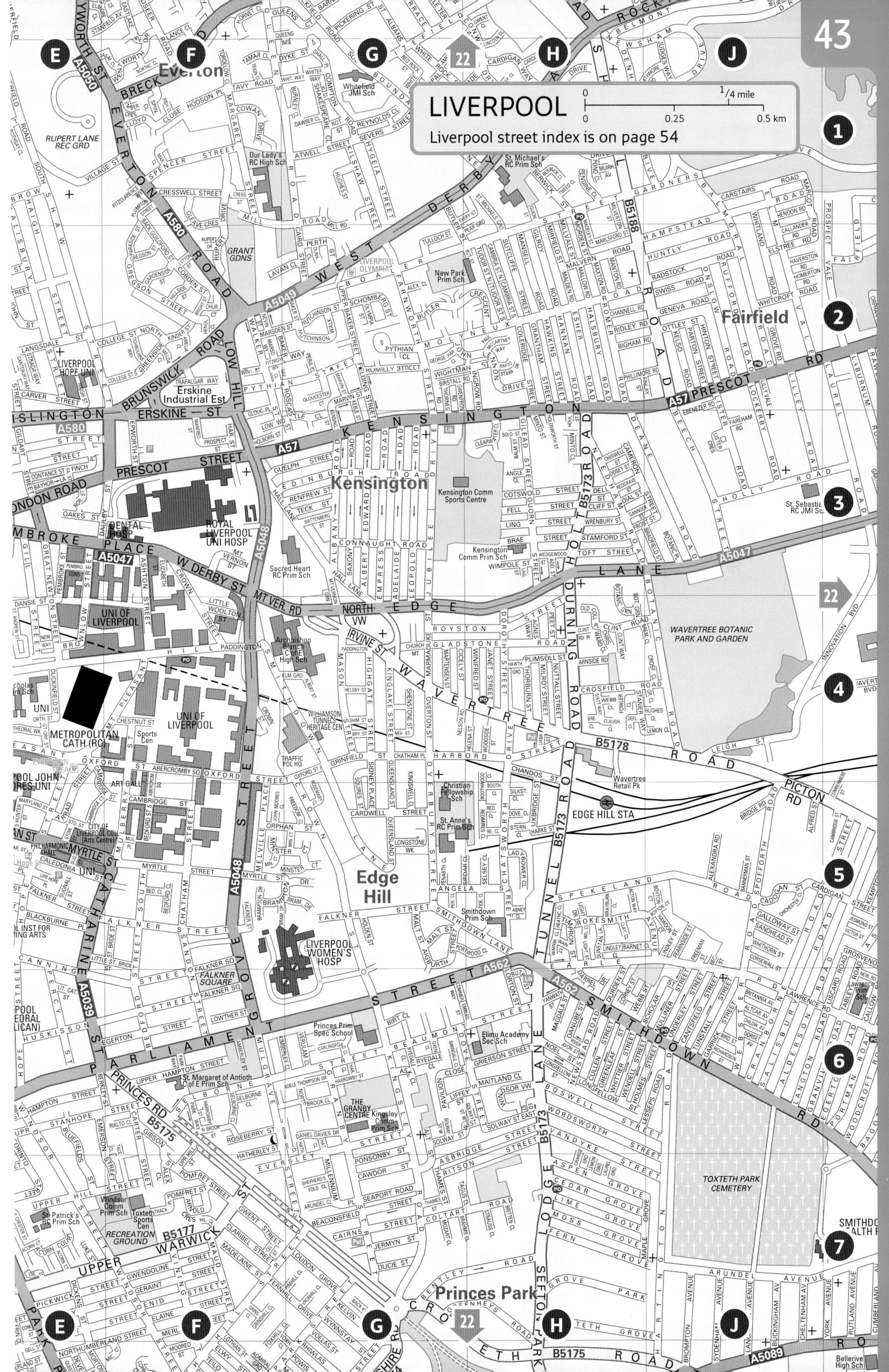
LIVERPOOL
0
1/4 mile
0
0.25
0.5 km
Liverpool street index is on page 54
22
E
F
G
H
J
1
2
3
4
5
6
7
Everton
Fairfield
Kensington
Edge Hill
Princes Park
RUPERT LANE REC GRD
GRANT GDNS
Whitefield JMI Sch
Our Lady's RC High Sch
St. Michael's RC Prim Sch
LIVERPOOL OLYMPIA
New Park Prim Sch
LIVERPOOL HOPE UNI
Erskine Industrial Est
DENTAL HOSP
ROYAL LIVERPOOL UNI HOSP
Sacred Heart RC Prim Sch
Kensington Comm Sports Centre
Kensington Comm Prim Sch
UNI OF LIVERPOOL
Archbishop Blanch C of E High Sch
WILLIAMSON TUNNELS HERITAGE CEN
TRAFFIC POL HQ
METROPOLITAN CATH (RC)
Sports Cen
ART GALL
WAVERTREE BOTANIC PARK AND GARDEN
Wavertree Retail Pk
EDGE HILL STA
Christian Fellowship Sch
St. Anne's RC Prim Sch
Smithdown Prim Sch
LIVERPOOL WOMEN'S HOSP
FALKNER SQUARE
Princes Prim Spec School
Elimu Academy Sec Sch
St. Margaret of Antioch C of E Prim Sch
THE GRANBY CENTRE
Kingsley Comm Prim Sch
Windsor Comm Prim Sch
St Patrick's RC Prim Sch
Toxteth Sports Cen
RECREATION GROUND
TOXTETH PARK CEMETERY
St. Sebastian's RC JMI Sch
Lawrence Prim Sch
Bellerive High Sch
A5050
A580
A5049
A57
A5048
A5047
B5173
B5188
B5178
A562
A5039
B5175
B5177
A5089
EVERTON ROAD
BRECK ROAD
WEST DERBY ROAD
BRUNSWICK ROAD
LOW HILL
ISLINGTON
ERSKINE ST
PRESCOT STREET
LONDON ROAD
PEMBROKE PLACE
W DERBY ST
MT VER. RD
KENSINGTON
PRESCOT RD
NORTH EDGE
EDGE LANE
DURNING ROAD
WAVERTREE ROAD
PICTON RD
GROVE STREET
SMITHDOWN ROAD
UPPER PARLIAMENT STREET
PRINCES RD
CATHARINE ST
UPPER WARWICK ST
LODGE LANE
TUNNEL ROAD
SMITHDOWN LANE
ARUNDEL AVENUE
TOXTETH GROVE
CROXTETH ROAD
SEFTON PARK RD
SHEIL ROAD
HALL LANE
MOSS GROVE
LIME GROVE
CEDAR GROVE
FERN GROVE

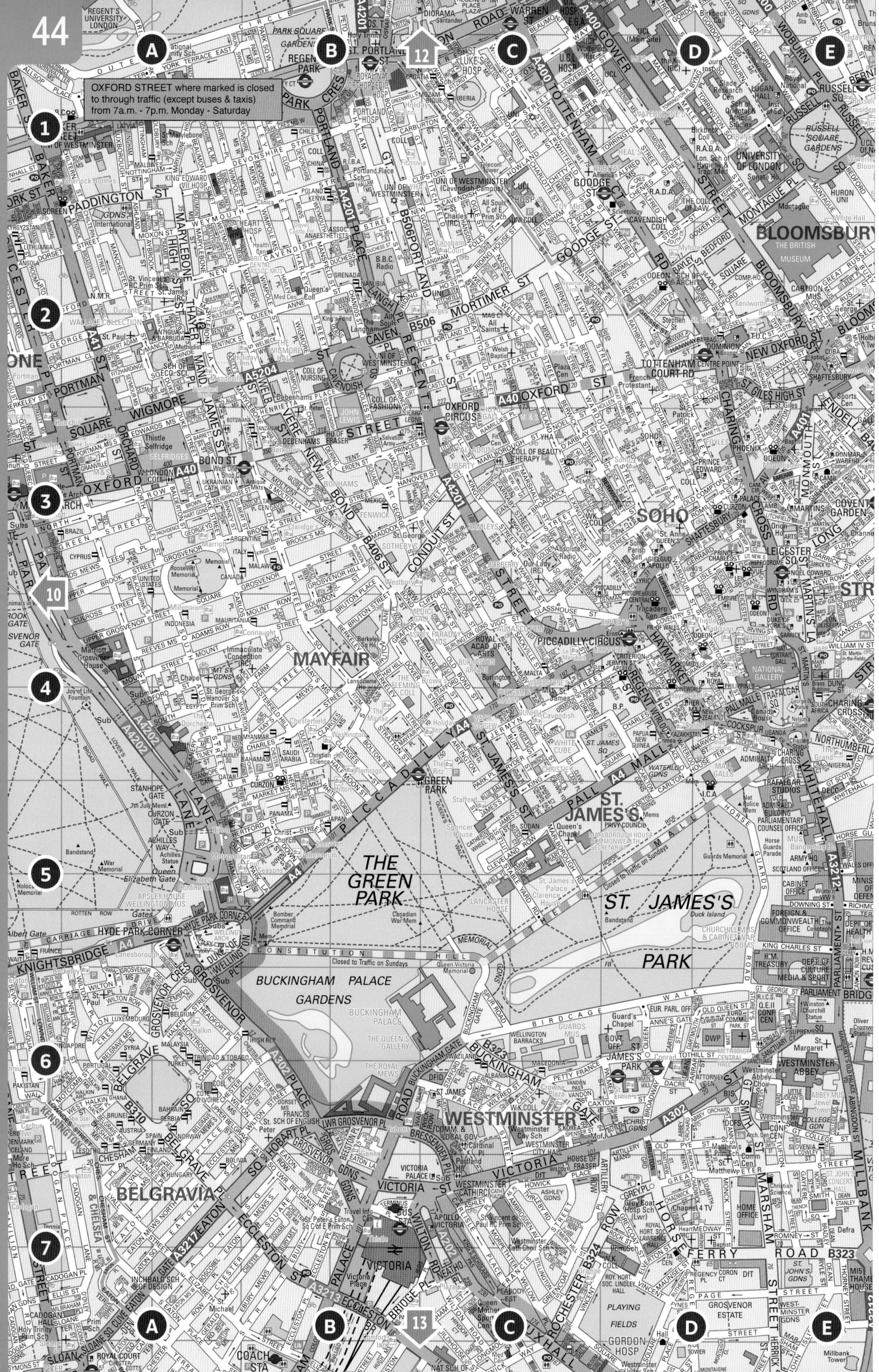

OXFORD STREET where marked is closed to through traffic (except buses & taxis) from 7 a.m. - 7 p.m. Monday - Saturday

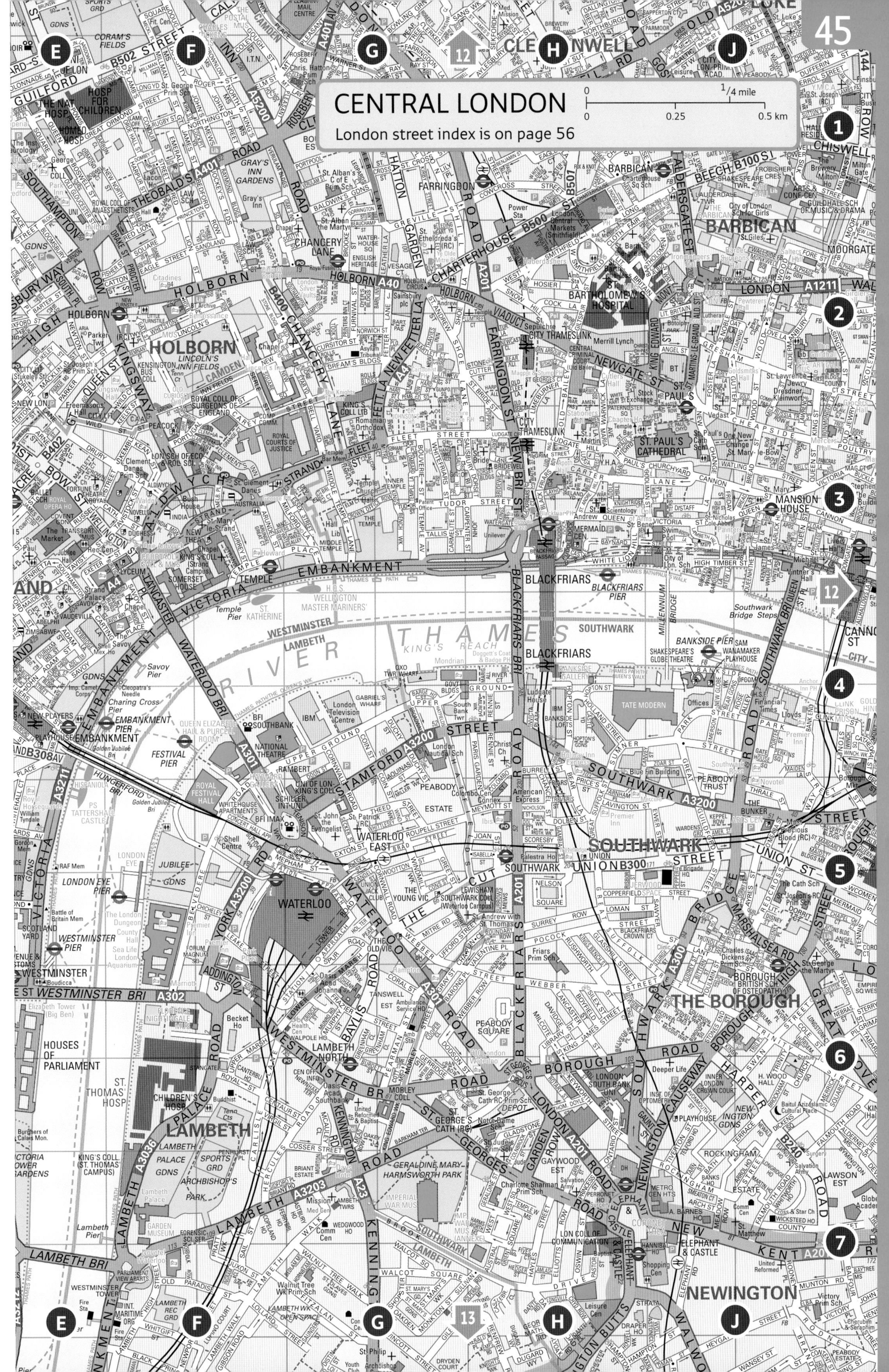
CENTRAL LONDON
London street index is on page 56
0
1/4 mile
0
0.25
0.5 km
E
F
G
H
J
12
13
1
2
3
4
5
6
7
CLERKENWELL
HOLBORN
BARBICAN
SOUTHWARK
THE BOROUGH
LAMBETH
NEWINGTON
RIVER THAMES
KING'S REACH
HOLBORN
CHANCERY LANE
FARRINGDON
BARBICAN
ST. PAUL'S
MANSION HOUSE
TEMPLE
BLACKFRIARS
EMBANKMENT
WATERLOO
WATERLOO EAST
SOUTHWARK
BOROUGH
LAMBETH NORTH
ELEPHANT & CASTLE
WESTMINSTER
CITY THAMESLINK
ST. PAUL'S CATHEDRAL
ROYAL COURTS OF JUSTICE
TATE MODERN
SHAKESPEARE'S GLOBE THEATRE
NATIONAL THEATRE
ROYAL FESTIVAL HALL
HOUSES OF PARLIAMENT
ST. THOMAS' HOSP
GERALDINE MARY HARMSWORTH PARK
IMPERIAL WAR MUS
ARCHBISHOP'S PARK
LAMBETH PALACE GDNS
JUBILEE GDNS
GRAY'S INN GARDENS
LINCOLN'S INN FIELDS
CORAM'S FIELDS
ST. BARTHOLOMEW'S HOSPITAL
CENTRAL CRIMINAL COURT (Old Bailey)
LONDON EYE
MILLENNIUM BRIDGE
BLACKFRIARS PIER
BANKSIDE PIER
FESTIVAL PIER
EMBANKMENT PIER
LONDON EYE PIER
WESTMINSTER PIER
VICTORIA EMBANKMENT
WATERLOO BRI
BLACKFRIARS BRI
SOUTHWARK BRI
WESTMINSTER BRI
LAMBETH BRI
HOLBORN
HOLBORN VIADUCT
FLEET STREET
STRAND
ALDWYCH
KINGSWAY
THEOBALD'S ROAD
CHARTERHOUSE ST
NEWGATE ST
LONDON WALL
QUEEN VICTORIA ST
CANNON ST
STAMFORD STREET
SOUTHWARK STREET
UNION ST
BOROUGH ROAD
BOROUGH HIGH ST
WESTMINSTER BR ROAD
ST GEORGE'S ROAD
LAMBETH ROAD
KENNINGTON ROAD
NEW KENT RD
NEWINGTON CAUSEWAY
LONDON ROAD
BLACKFRIARS ROAD
WATERLOO ROAD
THE CUT
YORK ROAD

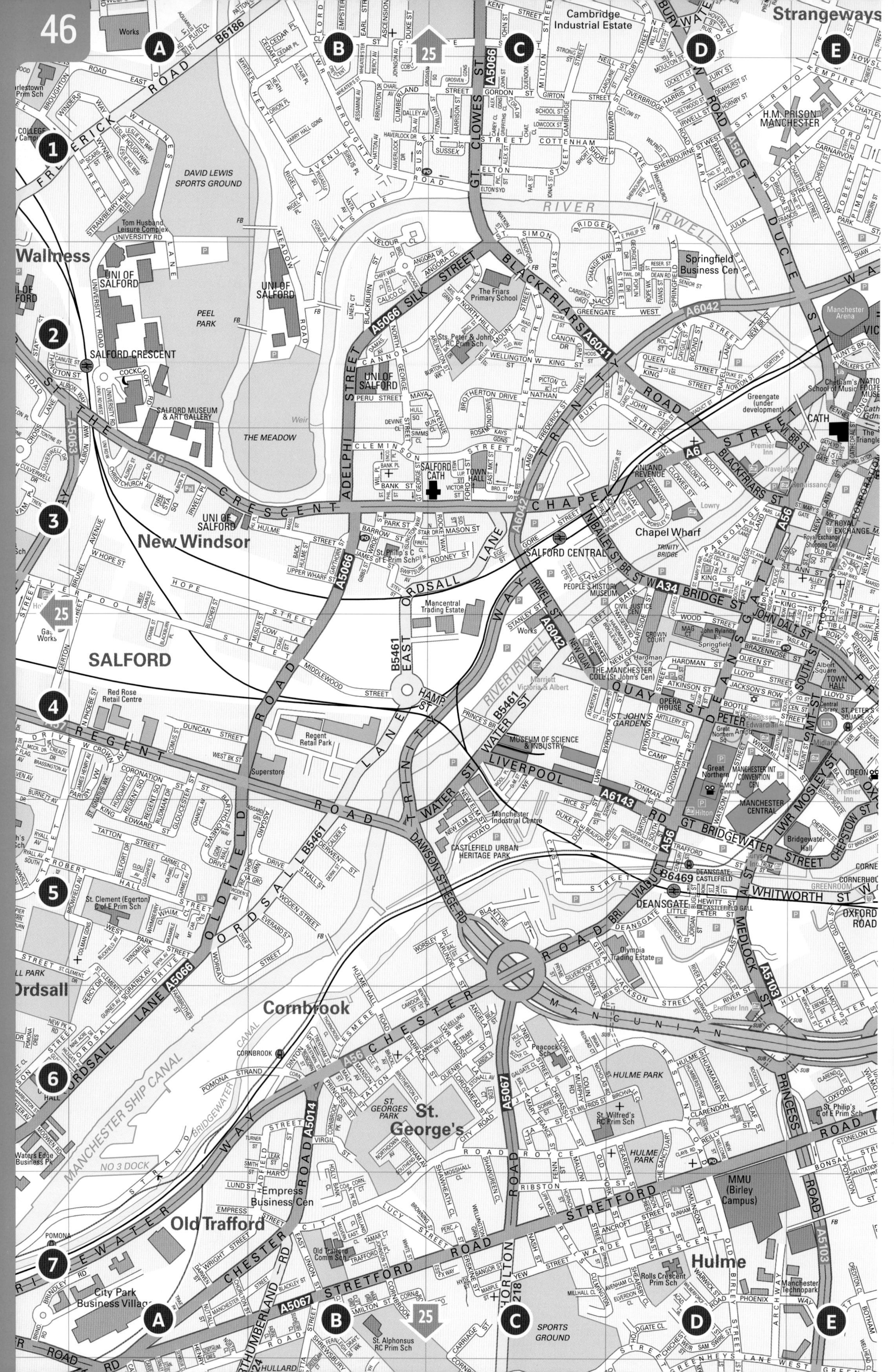
Strangeways
Cambridge Industrial Estate
H.M. PRISON MANCHESTER
Walness
DAVID LEWIS SPORTS GROUND
Tom Husband Leisure Complex
UNI OF SALFORD
PEEL PARK
SALFORD CRESCENT
SALFORD MUSEUM & ART GALLERY
THE MEADOW
RIVER IRWELL
Springfield Business Cen
The Friars Primary School
Sts. Peter & John RC Prim Sch
SALFORD CATH
TOWN HALL
Manchester Arena
Chetham's School of Music
CATH
Greengate (under development)
New Windsor
SALFORD CENTRAL
PEOPLE'S HISTORY MUSEUM
Chapel Wharf
Mancentral Trading Estate
SALFORD
Red Rose Retail Centre
Regent Retail Park
Superstore
MUSEUM OF SCIENCE & INDUSTRY
Manchester Industrial Centre
CASTLEFIELD URBAN HERITAGE PARK
Great Northern
MANCHESTER INT CONVENTION CEN
MANCHESTER CENTRAL
Bridgewater Hall
Albert Square
TOWN HALL
Central Library
ST. PETER'S SQUARE
DEANSGATE CASTLEFIELD
DEANSGATE
OXFORD ROAD
St. Clement (Egerton) C of E Prim Sch
Ordsall
Cornbrook
MANCHESTER SHIP CANAL
NO 3 DOCK
Olympia Trading Estate
Peacock Sch
HULME PARK
St. Wilfrid's RC Prim Sch
St. GEORGES PARK
St. George's
Empress Business Cen
Old Trafford
City Park Business Village
Old Trafford Comm Sch
St. Alphonsus RC Prim Sch
SPORTS GROUND
Rolls Crescent Prim Sch
Hulme
MMU (Birley Campus)
Manchester Technopark
St. Philip's C of E Prim Sch
REGENT ROAD
CHESTER ROAD
STRETFORD ROAD
TRINITY WAY
CHAPEL STREET
DEANSGATE
MANCUNIAN WAY
LIVERPOOL ROAD
OLDFIELD ROAD
ORDSALL LANE
BRIDGEWATER WAY
PRINCESS ROAD
A B C D E
1 2 3 4 5 6 7
25

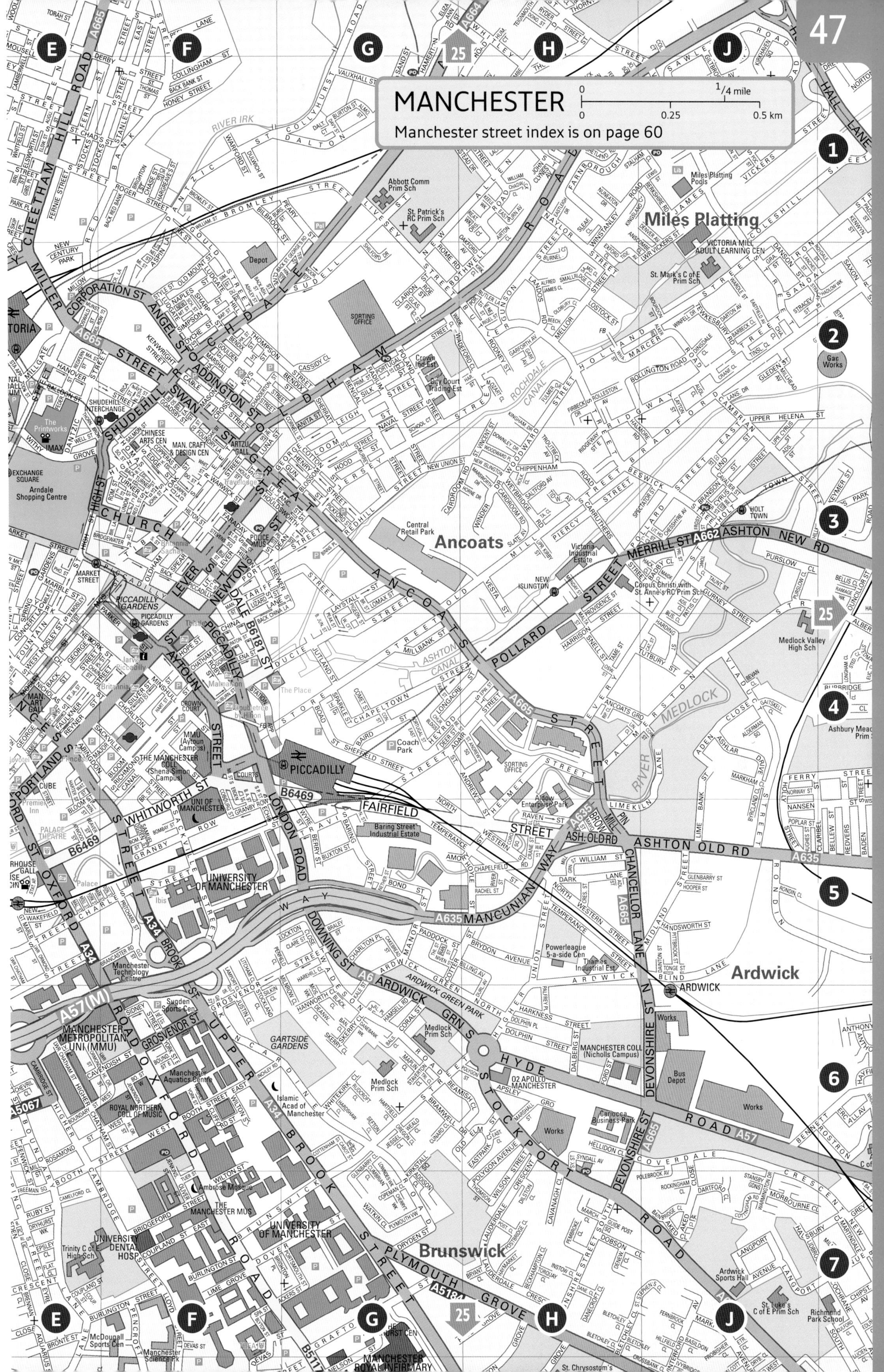
MANCHESTER
0
1/4 mile
0
0.25
0.5 km
Manchester street index is on page 60
E
F
G
H
J
1
2
3
4
5
6
7
25
Miles Platting
Ancoats
Ardwick
Brunswick
PICCADILLY
ARDWICK
NEW ISLANDTON
HOLT TOWN
VICTORIA MILL ADULT LEARNING CEN
St. Mark's C of E Prim Sch
Abbott Comm Prim Sch
St. Patrick's RC Prim Sch
Miles Platting Pools
SORTING OFFICE
Central Retail Park
Victoria Industrial Estate
Corpus Christi with St. Anne's RC Prim Sch
Medlock Valley High Sch
Ashbury Meadow Prim Sch
Crown Ind Est
City Court Trading Est
The Printworks
IMAX
EXCHANGE SQUARE
Arndale Shopping Centre
SHUDEHILL INTERCHANGE
CHINESE ARTS CEN
MAN. CRAFT & DESIGN CEN
PICCADILLY GARDENS
MARKET STREET
MMU (Aytoun Campus)
THE MANCHESTER COLL (Shena Simon Campus)
UNI OF MANCHESTER
UNIVERSITY OF MANCHESTER
Coach Park
Baring Street Industrial Estate
Aldow Enterprise Park
Powerleague 5-a-side Cen
Thames Industrial Est
Manchester Technology Centre
Sugden Sports Cen
MANCHESTER METROPOLITAN UNI (MMU)
Manchester Aquatics Centre
ROYAL NORTHERN COLL OF MUSIC
GARTSIDE GARDENS
Islamic Acad of Manchester
Medlock Prim Sch
O2 APOLLO MANCHESTER
MANCHESTER COLL (Nicholls Campus)
Bus Depot
Works
Carjacca Business Park
Ambrose Mosque
THE MANCHESTER MUS
UNIVERSITY DENTAL HOSP
Trinity C of E High Sch
McDougall Sports Cen
Manchester Science Pk
MANCHESTER ROYAL INFIRMARY
Ardwick Sports Hall
St. Luke's C of E Prim Sch
Richmond Park School
ROCHDALE CANAL
ASHTON CANAL
RIVER MEDLOCK
RIVER IRK
ASHTON NEW RD
ASHTON OLD RD
MANCUNIAN WAY
HYDE ROAD
STOCKPORT ROAD
DOWNING ST
LONDON ROAD
OXFORD ROAD
PORTLAND ST
WHITWORTH ST
GREAT ANCOATS ST
POLLARD STREET
CHANCELLOR LANE
DEVONSHIRE ST
UPPER BROOK STREET
PLYMOUTH GROVE
ROCHDALE ROAD
CHEETHAM HILL ROAD
MILLER ST
CORPORATION ST
SHUDEHILL
OLDHAM ROAD
A665
A664
A662
A635
A6
A34
A57
A57(M)
B6469
B6181
A5067
A5184

Indexes to street maps

General abbreviations

All	Alley	Chyd	Churchyard	Embk	Embankment	La	Lane	Pl	Place	W	West
App	Approach	Circ	Circus	Est	Estate	Lo	Lodge	Rd	Road	Wf	Wharf
Arc	Arcade	Clo	Close	Flds	Fields	Mans	Mansions	Ri	Rise	Wk	Walk
Av/Ave	Avenue	Cor	Corner	Gdn	Garden	Mkt/Mkts	Market/Markets	S	South	Yd	Yard
Bdy	Broadway	Cres	Crescent	Gdns	Gardens	Ms	Mews	Sq	Square		
Bldgs	Buildings	Ct	Court	Grd	Ground	N	North	St	Street		
Br/Bri	Bridge	Ctyd	Courtyard	Grn	Green	Par	Parade	St.	Saint		
Cen	Central, Centre	Dr	Drive	Gro	Grove	Pas	Passage	Ter	Terrace		
Ch	Church	E	East	Ho	House	Pk	Park	Twr	Tower		

Place names are shown in bold type

Birmingham street index

A

Abbey St 34 C1
Abbey St N 34 C1
Aberdeen St 34 A2
Acorn Gro 34 C4
Adams St 35 H2
Adderley St 35 H5
Adelaide St 35 G6
Albert St 35 G4
Albion St 34 D3
Alcester St 35 G7
Aldgate Gro 35 E2
Alfred Knight Way 34 E6
Allcock St 35 H5
Allesley St 35 G1
Allison St 35 G5
All Saints Rd 34 C1
All Saints St 34 C2
Alston St 34 B5
Anchor Cl 34 A5
Anchor Cres 34 B1
Anderton St 34 C4
Angelina St 35 G7
Ansbro Cl 34 A2
Arden Gro 34 C5
Arthur Pl 34 D4
Ascot Cl 34 A5
Ashted Lock 35 H3
Ashted Wk 35 J2
Ashton Cft 34 C5
Aston 35 H1
Aston Br 35 G1
Aston Brook St 35 G1
Aston Brook St E 35 H1
Aston Expressway 35 G2
Aston Rd 35 H1
Aston St 35 G3
Attenborough Cl 35 F1
Auckland Rd 35 J7
Augusta St 34 D2
Augustine Gro 34 B1
Austen Pl 34 C7
Autumn Gro 34 E1
Avenue Cl 35 J1
Avenue Rd 35 H1

B

Bacchus Rd 34 A1
Bagot St 35 G2
Balcaskie Cl 34 A7
Banbury St 35 G4
Barford Rd 34 A3
Barford St 35 G6
Barn St 35 H5
Barrack St 35 J3
Barrow Wk 35 F7
Barr St 34 D1
Bartholomew Row 35 G4
Bartholomew St 35 G4
Barwick St 35 F4
Bath Pas 35 F5
Bath Row 34 D6
Bath St 35 F3
Beak St 35 F5
Beaufort Gdns 34 A1
Beaufort Rd 34 B6
Bedford Rd 35 J6
Beeches, The 34 D7
Belgrave Middleway 35 F7
Bell Barn Rd 34 D6
Bellcroft 34 C5
Bellevue 35 F7
Bellis St 34 A6
Belmont Pas 35 J4
Belmont Row 35 H3
Benacre Dr 35 H4
Bennett's Hill 35 F4
Benson Rd 34 A1
Berkley St 34 D5
Berrington Wk 35 G7
Birchall St 35 G6
Bishopsgate St 34 D5
Bishop St 35 G7
Bissell St 35 G7
Blews St 35 G2
Bloomsbury St 35 J2
Blucher St 35 E5
Blyton Cl 34 A3
Boar Hound Cl 34 C3
Bodmin Gro 35 J1
Bolton St 35 J5
Bond Sq 34 C3
Bond St 35 E3
Bordesley 35 J5
Bordesley Circ 35 J6
Bordesley Middleway 35 J7
Bordesley Pk Rd 35 J6
Bordesley St 35 G4
Boulton Middleway 34 D1
Bow St 35 F6
Bowyer St 35 J6
Bracebridge St 35 G1
Bradburn Way 35 J2
Bradford St 35 G5
Branston St 34 D2
Brearley Cl 35 F2
Brearley St 35 F2
Bredon Cft 34 B1
Brewery St 35 G2
Bridge St 34 E5
Bridge St W 35 E1
Brindley Dr 34 D4
Brindley Pl 34 D5
Bristol St 35 F7
Broad St 34 D6
Broadway Plaza 34 C6
Bromley St 35 H5
Bromsgrove St 35 F6
Brookfield Rd 34 B2
Brook St 34 E3
Brook Vw Cl 34 E1
Broom St 35 H6
Brough Cl 35 J1
Browning St 34 C5
Brownsea Dr 35 E5
Brunel St 35 E5
Brunswick St 34 D5
Buckingham St 35 E2
Bullock St 35 H2
Bull St 35 F4

C

Cala Dr 34 C7
Calthorpe Rd 34 C7
Cambridge Rd 34 D4
Camden Dr 34 D3
Camden Gro 34 D3
Camden St 34 B2
Camp Hill 35 J7
Camp Hill Middleway 35 H7
Cannon St 35 F4
Capstone Av 34 C2
Cardigan St 35 H3
Carlisle St 34 A2
Carlyle Rd 34 A5
Caroline St 34 E3
Carpenter Rd 34 C7
Carrs La 35 G4
Carver St 34 C3
Cawdor Cres 34 B6
Cecil St 35 F2
Cemetery La 34 D2
Centenary Sq 34 E4
Central Pk Dr 34 A1
Central Sq 34 E5
Chad Rd 34 A7
Chadsmoor Ter 35 J1
Chad Valley 34 A7
Chamberlain Sq 35 E4
Chancellor's Cl 34 A7
Chandlers Cl 34 B1
Chapel Ho St 35 H5
Chapmans Pas 35 E5
Charles Henry St 35 G7
Charlotte Rd 34 D7
Charlotte St 34 E4
Chatsworth Way 34 E6
Cheapside 35 G6
Cherry St 35 F4
Chester St 35 H1
Chilwell Cft 35 F1
Christchurch Cl 34 A6
Church Rd 34 C7
Church St 35 F3
Civic Cl 34 D4
Clare Dr 34 A7
Clarendon Rd 34 A5
Clark St 34 A5
Claybrook St 35 F6
Clement St 34 D4
Clipper Vw 34 A5
Clissold Cl 35 G7
Clissold St 34 B2
Cliveland St 35 F3
Clyde St 35 H6
Colbrand Gro 35 E7
Coleshill St 35 G4
College St 34 B3
Colmore Circ 35 F3
Colmore Row 35 F4
Commercial St 34 E5
Communication Row 34 D6
Constitution Hill 34 E2
Conybere St 35 G7
Cope St 34 B3
Coplow St 34 A3
Cornwall St 35 E4
Corporation St 35 F4
Coveley Gro 34 B1
Coventry Rd 35 J6
Coventry St 35 G5
Cox St 35 E3
Coxwell Gdns 34 B5
Crabtree Rd 34 B2
Cregoe St 34 E6
Crescent, The 34 C1
Crescent Av 34 C1
Cromwell St 35 J1
Crondal Pl 34 D7
Crosby Cl 34 C4
Cumberland St 34 D5
Curzon Circ 35 H3
Curzon St 35 H4

D

Daisy Rd 34 A5
Dale End 35 G4
Daley Cl 34 C4
Dalton St 35 G4
Darnley Rd 34 B5
Dartmouth Circ 35 G1
Dartmouth Middleway 35 G2
Dart St 35 J6
Darwin St 35 G6
Dean St 35 G5
Deeley Cl 34 D7
Denby Cl 35 J2
Derby St 35 J4
Devonshire Av 34 B1
Devonshire St 34 B1
Digbeth 35 G6
Digbeth 35 G5
Dollman St 35 J3
Dover St 34 B1
Duchess Rd 34 B6
Duddeston Manor Rd 35 J2
Dudley St 35 F5
Dymoke Cl 35 G7

E

Edgbaston 34 B7
Edgbaston St 35 F5
Edmund St 35 E4
Edward St 34 D4
Eldon Rd 34 A5
Elkington St 35 G1
Ellen St 34 C3
Ellis St 35 E5
Elvetham Rd 34 D7
Embassy Dr 34 C6
Emily Gdns 34 A3
Emily St 35 G7
Enfield Rd 34 D6
Enterprise Way 35 G2
Ernest St 35 E6
Erskine St 35 J3
Essex St 35 F6
Essington St 34 D5
Estria Rd 34 C7
Ethel St 35 F4
Exeter Pas 35 F6
Exeter St 35 F6
Eyre St 34 B3
Eyton Cft 35 H7

F

Farmacre 35 J5
Farm Cft 34 D1
Farm St 34 D1
Fawdry St 35 J4
Fazeley St 35 G4
Felsted Way 35 J3
Ferndale Cres 35 H7
Finstall Cl 35 J3
Five Ways 34 C6
Fleet St 34 E4
Floodgate St 35 H5
Florence St 35 E6
Ford St 34 C1
Fore St 35 F4
Forster St 35 H3
Foster Gdns 34 B1
Fox St 35 G4
Francis Rd 34 B5
Francis St 35 J3
Frankfort St 35 F1
Frederick Rd 34 C7
Frederick St 34 D3
Freeman St 35 G4
Freeth St 34 B4
Friston Av 34 C6
Fulmer Wk 34 C4

G

Garrison Circ 35 J4
Garrison La 35 J4
Garrison St 35 J4
Gas St 34 D5
Gas St Basin 34 E5
Geach St 35 F1
Gee St 35 F1
George Rd 34 D7
George St 34 D4
George St W 34 C3
Gibb St 35 H5
Gilby Rd 34 C5
Gilldown Pl 34 D7
Glebeland Cl 34 C5
Gloucester St 35 F5
Glover St 35 J5
Gooch St 35 F7
Gooch St N 35 F6
Goode Av 34 C1
Goodman St 34 C4
Gopsal St 35 H3
Gough St 35 E5
Grafton Rd 35 J7
Graham St 34 D3
Grant St 35 E6
Granville St 34 D5
Graston Cl 34 C5
Great Barr St 35 H5
Great Brook St 35 H3
Great Charles St Queensway 35 E4
Great Colmore St 34 E6
Great Hampton Row 34 E2
Great Hampton St 34 D2
Great King St 34 D1
Great King St N 34 E1
Great Lister St 35 H2
Great Tindal St 34 C4
Greenfield Cres 34 C6
Green St 35 H6
Grenfell Dr 34 A7
Grosvenor St 35 G4
Grosvenor St W 34 C5
Guest Gro 34 D1
Guild Cl 34 B5
Guild Cft 35 F1
Guthrie Cl 35 E1

H

Hack St 35 H5
Hadfield Cft 34 E2
Hagley Rd 34 A6
Hall St 34 E3
Hampshire Dr 34 A7
Hampton St 35 E2
Hanley St 35 F2
Hanwood Cl 35 G7
Harborne Rd 34 A7
Harford St 34 E2
Harmer St 34 C2
Harold Rd 34 A5
Hartley Pl 34 A6
Hatchett St 35 F1
Hawthorn Cl 35 J5
Hawthorne Rd 34 A7
Heath Mill La 35 H5
Heath St S 34 B3
Heaton Dr 34 A7
Heaton St 34 D1
Helena St 34 D4
Heneage St 35 H2
Heneage St W 35 H3
Henley St 35 J7
Henrietta St 35 F3
Henstead St 35 F6
Herne Cl 34 C3
Hickman Gdns 34 B5
Highfield Rd 34 B6
Highgate 35 H7
Highgate St 35 G7
High St 35 G4
Hilden Rd 35 J3
Hill St 35 E4
Hinckley St 35 F5
Hindlow Cl 35 J3
Hindon Sq 34 B7
Hingeston St 34 C2
Hitches La 34 D7
Hobart Cft 35 J2
Hobson Cl 34 B1
Hockley Brook Cl 34 B1
Hockley Cl 35 F1
Hockley Hill 34 D1
Hockley St 34 D2
Holland St 34 D4
Holliday Pas 34 E5
Holliday St 34 E5
Holloway Circ 35 F5
Holloway Head 35 E6
Holt St 35 G2
Holywell Cl 34 B5
Hooper St 34 B3
Hope St 35 F7
Hospital St 35 F1
Howard St 35 E2
Howe St 35 H3
Howford Gro 35 J2
Hubert St 35 H1
Hunter's Vale 34 D1
Huntly Rd 34 B6
Hurdlow Av 34 C2
Hurst St 35 F5
Hylton St 34 D2
Hyssop Cl 35 J2

I

Icknield Port Rd 34 A3
Icknield Sq 34 B4
Icknield St 34 C3
Inge St 35 F6
Inkerman St 35 J3
Irving St 35 E6
Islington Row Middleway 34 C6
Ivy La 35 J4

J

Jackson Cl 35 J7
James St 34 E3
James Watt Queensway 35 G3
Jennens Rd 35 G4
Jewellery Quarter 34 D2
Jinnah Cl 35 G7
John Bright St 35 F5
John Kempe Way 35 H7

K

Keeley St 35 J5
Keepers Cl 34 B1
Kellett Rd 35 H2
Kelsall Cft 34 C4
Kelsey Cl 35 J2
Kemble Cft 35 F7
Kendal Rd 35 J7
Kenilworth Ct 34 A6
Kent St 35 F6
Kent St N 34 B1
Kenyon St 34 E3
Ketley Cft 35 G7
Key Hill 34 D2
Key Hill Dr 34 D2
Kilby Av 34 C4
King Edwards Rd 34 D4
Kingston Rd 35 J5
Kingston Row 34 D4
Kirby Rd 34 A1
Knightstone Av 34 C2
Kyotts Lake Rd 35 J7

L

Ladycroft 34 C5
Ladywell Wk 35 F5
Ladywood 34 C4
Ladywood Middleway 34 B5
Ladywood Rd 34 B5
Lancaster Circ 35 G3
Landor St 35 J4
Langdon St 35 J4
Lansdowne St 34 A2
Latimer Gdns 35 E7
Lawden Rd 35 J6
Lawford Cl 35 J3
Lawford Gro 35 G7
Lawley Middleway 35 H3
Ledbury Cl 34 B5
Ledsam St 34 C4
Lee Bk 35 E7
Lee Bk Middleway 34 D6
Lee Cres 34 D7
Lee Mt 34 D7
Lees St 34 B1
Legge La 34 D3
Legge St 35 G2
Lennox St 35 E1
Leopold St 35 G7
Leslie Rd 34 A5
Leyburn Rd 34 C5
Lighthorne Av 34 C4
Link Rd 34 A3
Lionel St 34 E4
Lister St 35 G3
Little Ann St 35 H5
Little Barr St 35 J4
Little Broom St 35 H6
Little Edward St 35 J5
Little Francis Grn 35 J2
Little Shadwell St 35 F3
Liverpool St 35 H5
Livery St 35 F3
Locke Pl 35 J4
Lodge Rd 34 A1
Lombard St 35 G6
Longleat Way 34 D6
Lord St 35 H2
Louisa St 34 D4
Loveday St 35 F3
Love La 35 G2
Lower Dartmouth St 35 J4
Lower Essex St 35 F6
Lower Loveday St 35 F2
Lower Severn St 35 F5
Lower Temple St 35 F4

Edinburgh street index

Glasgow street index

Houston St 38 C6
Howard St 39 F5
Hunter St 39 H5
Huntingdon Rd 39 H1
Huntingdon Sq 39 H1
Hutcheson St 39 G5
Hutchesontown 39 G7
Hutchinson Town Ct 39 G7
Hydepark St 38 C5

I

India St 38 D3
Ingram St 39 G4

J

Jamaica St 39 F5
James Morrison St 39 G5
James Nisbet St 39 J3
James St 39 J7
James Watt St 38 E5
Jocelyn Sq 39 G5
John Knox St 39 J4
John St 39 G4

K

Kelvingrove 38 B2
Kelvingrove St 38 B3
Kelvinhaugh 38 A3
Kelvinhaugh Gate 38 A3
Kelvinhaugh Pl 38 B3
Kelvinhaugh St 38 A3
Kelvin Way 38 B2
Kennedy Path 39 G3
Kennedy St 39 G3
Kent Rd 38 C3
Kent St 39 H5
Keppochhill Pl 39 G1
Keppochhill Way 39 G1
Kerr Dr 39 J6
Kerr Pl 39 J6
Kerr St 39 J6
Kidston Pl 39 F7
Kidston Ter 39 F7
Kilbarchan St 39 E6
Kilbirnie Pl 38 D7
Kilbirnie St 38 D7
Killermont St 39 F3
King George V Br 39 E5
King's Br 39 H7
King's Dr 39 H7
Kingston 38 D6
Kingston St 38 E5
King St 39 G5
Kinning Pk 38 B6
Kinning St 38 D6
Kyle St 39 G2

L

La Belle Allee 38 C2
La Belle Pl 38 C2
Ladywell St 39 J4
Laidlaw St 38 D6
Laird Pl 39 J7
Lambhill Quad 38 B6
Lambhill St 38 B6
Lanark St 39 H5
Lancefield Quay 38 C4
Lancefield St 38 C4
Landressy Pl 39 J7
Landressy St 39 J7
Langshot St 38 A6
Lansdowne Cres 38 C1
Lansdowne Cres La 38 C1
Larbert St 39 F2
Laurieston 39 F6
Laurieston Rd 39 F7
Lendel Pl 38 A6
Lilybank Gdns 38 A1
Lilybank Gdns La 38 A1
Lilybank Ter 38 B1
Lister St 39 H2
Little Dovehill 39 H5
Little St 38 C4
London Rd 39 G5
Lorne St 38 B5
Lumsden St 38 A3
Lymburn St 38 B2
Lynedoch Cres 38 C2
Lynedoch Cres La 38 C2
Lynedoch Pl 38 C2
Lynedoch St 38 C2
Lynedoch Ter 38 D2

M

Mcalpine St 38 D5
McAslin Ct 39 H3
Mcaslin St 39 H3
McCulloch St 38 C7
Mcfarlane St 39 H5
McIntosh Ct 39 J4
McIntosh St 39 J4
Mcintyre St 38 D4
MacKeith St 39 J7
MacKinlay St 39 E7
Maclean Sq 38 B5
Maclean St 38 B5
Maclennan St 38 A6
Macleod St 39 H4
McNeil Gdns 39 H7
McNeil St 39 G7
McPhail St 39 J7
McPhater St 39 F2
Mair St 38 B5
Maitland St 39 F2
Malta Ter 39 F7
Manresa Pl 39 E1
Marine Cres 38 C5
Marine Gdns 38 C5
Marlow St 38 C7
Martha St 39 G3
Mart St 39 G5
Mary St 39 F1
Mauchline St 38 E7
Mavisbank Gdns 38 B5
Maxwell Av 38 C7
Maxwell Ct 38 B7
Maxwell Dr 38 B7
Maxwell Gdns 38 A7
Maxwell Grn 38 B7
Maxwell La 38 C7
Maxwell Oval 38 C7
Maxwell Rd 38 C7
Maxwell St 39 F5
Megan Gate 39 J7
Megan St 39 J7
Melbourne St 39 J5
Melrose St 38 D1
Merchant City 39 G4
Merchant La 39 G5
Metropole La 39 F5
Middlesex Gdns 38 B6
Middlesex St 38 B6
Middleton St 38 A5
Midland St 39 E4
Midwharf St 39 F1
Miller St 39 F4
Millroad Dr 39 J5
Millroad Gdns 39 J5
Millroad St 39 H5
Milnpark Gdns 38 B6
Milnpark St 38 B6
Milton St 39 F2
Minerva St 38 B3
Minerva Way 38 B3
Mitchell La 39 F4
Mitchell St 39 F4
Moffat St 39 G7
Moir St 39 H5
Molendinar St 39 H5
Moncur St 39 H5
Montague St 38 C1
Monteith Pl 39 H6
Monteith Row 39 H5
Montrose St 39 G4
Moore St 39 J5
Morrison Ct 39 F4
Morrison St 38 D5
Mosque Av 39 F6
Muslin St 39 J7

N

Naburn Gate 39 F7
Nairn St 38 A2
Napiershall La 38 D1
Napiershall Pl 38 D1
Napiershall St 38 D1
Nelson Mandela Pl 39 F4
Nelson St 38 E5
Netherby Dr 38 A7
New City Rd 38 D2
Newton St 38 D2
Newton Ter La 38 C3
New Wynd 39 G5
Nicholas St 39 H4
Nicholson St 39 F6
Norfolk Ct 39 F6
Norfolk St 39 F6
North Canal Bk 39 G1
North Canal Bk St 39 F1
North Claremount St 38 C2
North Ct 39 F4
North Ct La 39 F4
North Dr 39 F4
North Frederick Path 39 G3
North Frederick St 39 G4
North Gower St 38 A6
North Hanover St 39 G4
North Portland St 39 G4
North St 38 D2
North Wallace St 39 G2

O

Oakfield Av 38 B1
Oakfield La 38 B1
Oak St 38 D4
Old Dumbarton Rd 38 A2
Old Rutherglen Rd 39 G6
Old Wynd 39 G5
Oregon Pl 39 G7
Orr St 39 J6
Osborne St 39 F5
Oswald St 39 E5
Otago La 38 C1
Otago La N 38 C1
Otago St 38 B1
Overnewton Pl 38 B3
Overnewton Sq 38 A3
Overnewton St 38 A2
Oxford La 39 F6
Oxford St 39 E5

P

Pacific Dr 38 A5
Pacific Quay 38 A4
Paisley Rd 38 D5
Paisley Rd W 38 C5
Palmerston Pl 38 B3
Parnie St 39 G5
Park Av 38 C1
Park Circ 38 C2
Park Circ La 38 C2
Park Circ Pl 38 C2
Park Dr 38 C1
Park Gdns 38 C2
Park Gdns La 38 C2
Park Gate 38 C2
Parkgrove Ter 38 B2
Parkgrove Ter La 38 B2
Park Quad 38 C2
Park Rd 38 C1
Park St S 38 C2
Park Ter 38 C2
Park Ter E La 38 C2
Park Terrrace La 38 C2
Parsonage Row 39 H4
Parsonage Sq 39 H4
Parson St 39 H3
Paterson St 38 D6
Payne St 39 F1
Pembroke St 38 C3
Percy St 38 A6
Perth St 38 D4
Piccadilly St 38 D4
Pine Pl 39 G7
Pinkston Dr 39 H2
Pinkston Rd 39 H1
Pitt St 38 E4
Plantation Pk Gdns 38 A6
Plantation Sq 38 B5
Port Dundas 39 F1
Port Dundas La 39 F3
Port Dundas Rd 39 F2
Port Eglington 38 D7
Portman St 38 C6
Port St 38 C3
Portugal St 39 F6
Possil Rd 39 E1
Professors Sq 38 B1
Provanhill St 39 J2

Q

Queen Elizabeth Gdns 39 G7
Queens Cres 38 D1
Queen St 39 F4

R

Radnor St 38 B2
Raglan St 38 E1
Regent Moray St 38 A2
Renfield La 39 E4
Renfield St 39 F4
Renfrew Ct 39 F3
Renfrew La 39 F3
Renfrew St 38 D2
Renton St 39 F2
Rhymer St 39 J2
Richmond St 39 G4
Ritchie St 38 E7
Riverview Dr 38 D5
Riverview Gdns 38 E5
Riverview Pl 38 D5
Robertson La 38 E4
Robertson St 39 E5
Rodney St 39 E1
Ropework La 39 F5
Rose St 39 E3
Ross St 39 H5
Rottenrow 39 G3
Rottenrow E 39 H4
Royal Bk Pl 39 F4
Royal Cres 38 B3
Royal Ex Ct 39 F4
Royal Ex Sq 39 F4
Royal Ter 38 B2
Royal Ter La 38 B2
Royston 39 J2
Roystonhill 39 J2
Royston Rd 39 J2
Royston Sq 39 J2
Rupert St 38 D1
Rutland Ct 38 C5
Rutland Cres 38 C5
Rutland Pl 38 B5

S

St. Andrews Cres 38 C7
St. Andrew's La 39 G5
St. Andrews Rd 38 C7
St. Andrews Sq 39 G5
St. Andrews St 39 G5
St. Clair St 38 D1
St. Enoch 39 F5
St. Enoch Sq 39 F4
St. Francis Rigg 39 G7
St. Georges Rd 38 D2
St. Georges Rd 38 D2
St. James Rd 39 G3
St. John's Ct 38 B7
St. John's Quad 38 C7
St. Josephs Vw 39 J2
St. Luke's Pl 39 F6
St. Luke's Ter 39 F6
St. Margaret's Pl 39 G5
St. Marys La 39 F4
St. Mungo Av 39 G3
St. Mungo Pl 39 H3
St. Ninian Ter 39 F6
St. Peters La 38 E4
St. Peters St 38 E2
St. Rollox Brae 39 J1
St. Valentine Ter 39 G7
St. Vincent Cres 38 B3
St. Vincent Cres La 38 B3
St. Vincent La 38 E3
St. Vincent Pl 39 F4
St. Vincent St 38 C3
St. Vincent Ter 38 C3
Salisbury La 39 F7
Salisbury St 39 F7
Salkeld St 38 E7
Saltmarket 39 G5
Sandiefield Rd 39 F7
Sandyford Pl La 38 C3
Sandyford St 38 A3
Saracen Head Rd 39 H5
Sauchiehall La 38 E3
Sauchiehall St 38 B2
Savoy St 39 J7
Sawmillfield St 39 E1
Scotland St 38 C6
Scotland St W 38 B6
Scott St 38 E3
Seamore St 38 D1
Seaward La 38 C5
Seaward Pl 38 C6
Seaward St 38 C6
Shaftesbury St 38 D3
Shamrock St 38 E2
Shields Rd 38 C6
Shipbank La 39 G5
Shuttle St 39 G4
Sighthill 39 H1
Silverfir St 39 G7
Silvergrove St 39 J6
Snowdon St 39 G7
Somerset Pl Ms 38 C2
South Ex Ct 39 F4
South Frederick St 39 G4
Southpark Av 38 B1
Southpark La 38 B1
South Portland St 39 F5
Southside Cres 39 F7
South Woodside Rd 38 C1
Spiers Wf 39 F1
Spoutmouth 39 H5
Springburn Rd 39 J2
Springfield Ct 39 F4
Springfield Quay 38 C5
Spring Wynd 39 G7
Stafford St 39 G2
Stanley St 38 C6
Stanley St La 38 C6
Steel St 39 G5
Stevenson St 39 J6
Stewart St 39 F2
Stirlingfauld Pl 39 F7
Stirling Rd 39 H3
Stobcross Rd 38 A3
Stobcross St 38 C4
Stobcross Wynd 38 A3
Stockwell Pl 39 F5
Stockwell St 39 F5
Stromness St 38 E7
Suffolk St 39 H5
Surrey St 39 F7
Sussex St 38 B6
Sutherland La 38 A1
Swan St 39 G2
Sydney St 39 J5

T

Taylor Pl 39 H3
Taylor St 39 H4
Templeton St 39 J6
Teviot St 38 A3
Thistle St 39 G6
Thistle Ter 39 F7
Thornbank St 38 A3
Thurso St 38 A2
Tobago Pl 39 J5
Tobago St 39 J6
Toll La 38 C5
Tontine La 39 G5
Torness St 38 A1
Tower St 38 B6
Townhead 39 G2
Townsend St 39 F2
Tradeston 38 E6
Tradeston St 38 E6
Trongate 39 G5
Tullis Ct 39 J7
Tullis St 39 J7
Tunnel St 38 B4
Tureen St 39 J5
Turnbull St 39 G5
Turnlaw St 39 H7
Turriff St 39 E7
Tyndrum St 39 F2

U

Union Pl 39 F4
Union St 39 F4
Unity Pl 38 E1
University Av 38 A1
University Gdns 38 A1
University Pl 38 A1

V

Vermont St 38 B6
Victoria Br 39 F5
Viewfield La 38 B1
Vinter St 39 F1
Virginia Pl 39 G4
Virginia St 39 G4

W

Waddell Ct 39 G6
Waddell St 39 G7
Wallace St 38 D5
Walls St 39 G4
Walmer Cres 38 A6
Warnock St 39 J3
Warroch St 38 D5
Washington St 38 D5
Waterloo La 39 E4
Waterloo St 39 E4
Waterside Pl 39 H7
Waterside St 39 G7
Watson St 39 G5
Watt St 38 C6
Weaver St 39 H4
Wellcroft Pl 39 E7
Wellington La 38 E4
Wellington St 39 E4
Wellpark St 39 J4
Westbank La 38 B1
Westbank Quad 38 B1
West Campbell St 38 E4
West End Pk St 38 C2
West George La 38 E3
West George St 39 E3
West Graham St 38 E2
West Greenhill Pl 38 B3
West Nile St 39 F4
West Prince's La 38 C1
West Princes St 38 C1
West Regent La 39 E3
West Regent St 39 E3
West St 38 D7
Whitehall St 38 D4
William St 38 D3
Willowbank Cres 38 C1
Willowbank St 38 C2
Wilson St 39 G4
Windsor St 38 D1
Windsor Ter 38 D1
Wishart St 39 J4
Woodlands Dr 38 C1
Woodlands Gate 38 C2
Woodlands Rd 38 C1
Woodlands Ter 38 C2
Woodrow Circ 38 A7
Woodrow Pl 38 A7
Woodrow Rd 38 A7
Woodside Cres 38 D2
Woodside Pl 38 C2
Woodside Pl La 38 C2
Woodside Ter 38 C2
Woodside Ter La 38 C2

Y

Yorkhill 38 B2
Yorkhill Par 38 A2
Yorkhill St 38 A3
York St 38 E5

Leeds street index

A

Abbey St 40 C3
Abbott Ct 40 A3
Abbott Rd 40 A4
Abbott Vw 40 A3
Admiral St 41 E7
Aire St 40 D4
Albion Pl 41 E3
Albion St 41 E3
Alexander St 40 C3
Alexandra Gro 40 B1
Alexandra Rd 40 A1
Alma St 41 H2
Anderson Av 41 H1
Anderson Mt 41 H1
Apex Vw 40 E6
Apex Way 41 E6
Appleton Cl 41 J3
Appleton Ct 41 J3
Appleton Sq 41 J3
Appleton Way 41 J3
Archery Pl 40 D1
Archery Rd 40 D1
Archery St 40 E1
Archery Ter 40 E1
Armley Rd 40 A3
Armouries Rd 41 G5
Artist St 40 B4
Ascot Ter 41 J4
Ashley Av 41 J1
Ashley Rd 41 J1
Ashley Ter 41 J1
Ashton Av 41 J1
Ashton Gro 41 J1
Ashton Mt 41 J1
Ashton Pl 41 J1
Ashton Ter 41 J1
Ashton Vw 41 J1
Ashville Vw 40 A1
Assembly St 41 F4
Atkinson St 41 G6
Autumn Av 40 B1
Autumn Gro 40 B1
Autumn Pl 40 B1
Autumn St 40 B1
Autumn Ter 40 B1
Avenue, The 41 G4
Aysgarth Cl 41 J4

Aysgarth Dr 41 J4
Aysgarth Pl 41 J4
Aysgarth Wk 41 J4

B

Back Ashville Av 40 A1
Back Hyde Ter 40 C2
Back Row 40 E5
Balm Pl 40 C6
Balm Wk 40 C6
Bank St 41 E4
Baron Cl 40 C7
Barrack St 41 F1
Barran Ct 41 H1
Barton Gro 40 D7
Barton Mt 40 D7
Barton Pl 40 C7
Barton Rd 40 C7
Barton Ter 40 D7
Barton Vw 40 C7
Bath Rd 40 D5
Bayswater Vw 41 H1
Beamsley Gro 40 A1
Beamsley Mt 40 A1
Beamsley Pl 40 A1
Beamsley Ter 40 A1
Beckett St 41 H3
Bedford St 40 E3
Beech Gro Ter 40 D1
Belgrave St 41 E3
Belinda St 41 H7
Belle Vue Rd 40 B2
Bell St 41 G3
Belmont Gro 40 D2
Benson St 41 F1
Benyon Pk Way 40 A7
Berking Av 41 J3
Bertrand St 40 C6
Bexley Av 41 H1
Bexley Gro 41 J1
Bexley Mt 41 H1
Bexley Pl 41 H1
Bexley Rd 41 J1
Bexley Ter 41 J1
Bingley St 40 C3
Bishopgate St 40 E4
Bismarck Dr 40 E7
Bismarck St 40 E7
Black Bull St 41 F5
Blackman La 40 E1
Blandford Gdns 40 D1
Blandford Gro 40 D1
Blayds St 41 H4
Blayd's Yd 41 E4
Blenheim Av 40 E1
Blenheim Ct 40 E1
Blenheim Cres 40 E1
Blenheim Gro 40 E1
Blenheim Sq 40 E1
Blenheim Vw 40 D1
Blenheim Wk 40 D1
Blundell St 40 D2
Boar La 40 E4
Bodley Ter 40 A2
Bond St 40 E3
Boundary Pl 41 G1
Boundary St 41 G1
Bourse, The 41 E4
Bowling Grn Ter 40 D6
Bowman La 41 F4
Bow St 41 G4
Bracken Ct 40 A6
Braithwaite St 40 C5
Brancepeth Pl 40 B4
Brandon Rd 40 C2
Brandon St 40 B4
Branksome Pl 40 B1
Brick St 41 G4
Bridge Ct 40 C5
Bridge End 41 E4
Bridge Rd 40 C5
Bridge St 41 F3
Bridgewater Rd 41 H6
Briggate 41 E4
Brignall Garth 41 J2
Brignall Way 41 H2
Bristol St 41 G2
Britannia St 40 D4
Broadway Av 40 A1
Brookfield St 41 G6
Brown Av 40 B7
Brown La E 40 B6
Brown La W 40 A6
Brown Pl 40 B7
Brown Rd 40 B7
Bruce Gdns 40 B4
Bruce Lawn 40 B4
Brunswick Ct 41 F3
Brunswick Ter 41 E2
Brussels St 41 G4
Buckton Cl 40 C7
Buckton Mt 40 C7
Buckton Vw 40 C7
Burley 40 A1
Burley Lo Pl 40 B2
Burley Lo Rd 40 A1
Burley Lo St 40 B2
Burley Lo Ter 40 B1
Burley Pl 40 A2
Burley Rd 40 A1
Burley St 40 C3
Burmantofts 41 H3
Burmantofts St 41 G3
Burton Row 41 E7
Burton St 41 E7
Burton Way 41 J2
Butterfield St 41 H4
Butterley St 41 F6
Butts Ct 41 E3
Byron St 41 F2

C

Cain Cl 41 H4
Call La 41 F4
Calls, The 41 F4
Calverley St 40 D2
Cambrian St 40 D7
Cambrian Ter 40 D7
Canal Pl 40 B4
Canal St 40 A3
Canal Wf 40 D4
Carberry Pl 40 A1
Carberry Rd 40 A1
Carberry Ter 40 A1
Carlisle Rd 41 G5
Carlton Carr 41 E1
Carlton Ct 40 A7
Carlton Gdns 41 E1
Carlton Gate 41 E1
Carlton Gro 41 E1
Carlton Hill 41 E1
Carlton Pl 41 E1
Carlton Ri 41 E1
Carlton Twrs 41 F1
Carlton Vw 41 E1
Castle St 40 D3
Castleton Cl 40 B4
Castleton Rd 40 A3
Cautley Rd 41 J5
Cavalier App 41 H5
Cavalier Cl 41 H5
Cavalier Ct 41 H5
Cavalier Gdns 41 H5
Cavalier Gate 41 H5
Cavalier Ms 41 H5
Cavalier Vw 41 H5
Cavendish Rd 40 D1
Cavendish St 40 C3
Cemetery Rd 40 C7
Central Rd 41 F4
Central St 40 D3
Chadwick St 41 F5
Chadwick St S 41 G5
Chantrell Ct 41 F4
Charles Av 41 J5
Charlton Gro 41 J4
Charlton Pl 41 J4
Charlton Rd 41 J4
Charlton St 41 J4
Cherry Pl 41 G2
Cherry Row 41 G2
Chesney Av 41 F7
Chiswick St 40 A2
Chorley La 40 D2
Churchill Gdns 40 E1
Church La 41 F4
City Sq 40 E4
City Wk 40 E5
Claremont Av 40 C2
Claremont Gro 40 C2
Claremont Vw 40 C2
Clarence Rd 41 G5
Clarendon Pl 40 C1
Clarendon Rd 40 C1
Clarendon Way 40 D2
Clark Av 41 J4
Clark Cres 41 J4
Clark Gro 41 J5
Clark La 41 H5
Clark Mt 41 J4
Clark Rd 41 J5
Clark Row 41 J5
Clark Ter 41 J4
Clark Vw 41 J5
Clay Pit La 41 E2
Cleveleys Av 40 C7
Cleveleys Mt 40 C7
Cleveleys Rd 40 C7
Cleveleys St 40 C7
Cleveleys Ter 40 C7
Cloberry St 40 C1
Close, The 41 G4
Cloth Hall St 41 F4
Clyde App 40 A5
Clyde Gdns 40 B5
Clyde Vw 40 A5
Coleman St 40 B5
Colenso Gdns 40 C7
Colenso Mt 40 C7
Colenso Pl 40 C7
Colenso Rd 40 C7
Colenso Ter 40 C7
Colville Ter 40 D7
Commercial St 41 E3
Compton Av 41 J1
Compton Cres 41 J1
Compton Gro 41 J1
Compton Mt 41 J1
Compton Pl 41 J1
Compton Rd 41 J1
Compton St 41 J1
Compton Ter 41 J1
Compton Vw 41 J1
Concordia St 41 E4
Concord St 41 F2
Consort St 40 C2
Consort Ter 40 C2
Consort Vw 40 B2
Consort Wk 40 C2
Constance Gdns 40 E1
Constance Way 40 E1
Cookridge St 40 E3
Copley Hill 40 A5
Copley Hill Way 40 A6
Copley St 40 A5
Copperfield Av 41 J5
Copperfield Cres 41 J5
Copperfield Gro 41 J5
Copperfield Mt 41 J5
Copperfield Pl 41 J5
Copperfield Row 41 J5
Copperfield Ter 41 J5
Copperfield Vw 41 J5
Copperfield Wk 41 J5
Copperfiield Dr 41 J5
Cotton St 41 G4
Coupland Pl 40 D7
Coupland Rd 40 D7
Cowper Av 41 J1
Cowper Cres 41 J1
Cowper Rd 41 J1
Cromer Pl 40 C1
Cromer Rd 40 C1
Cromer St 40 C1
Cromer Ter 40 C2
Cromwell Mt 41 G2
Cromwell St 41 G3
Crosby Pl 40 C6
Crosby Rd 40 C7
Crosby St 40 C6
Crosby Ter 40 C6
Crosby Vw 40 C6
Cross Aysgarth Mt 41 H4
Cross Belgrave St 41 F3
Cross Catherine St 41 H4
Cross Grn 41 J6
Cross Grn App 41 J6
Cross Grn Av 41 H5
Cross Grn Cl 41 J6
Cross Grn Cres 41 H5
Cross Grn Dr 41 J6
Cross Grn Garth 41 J6
Cross Grn La 41 H5
Cross Grn Ri 41 J6
Cross Grn Way 41 J6
Cross Ingram Rd 40 C6
Cross Kelso Rd 40 C2
Cross Mitford Rd 40 A4
Cross Stamford St 41 G2
Cross York St 41 F4
Crown Ct 41 F4
Crown Pt Rd 41 F5
Crown St 41 F4
Croydon St 40 B5
Cudbear St 41 F5
Czar St 40 C5

D

Danby Wk 41 H4
David St 40 D5
Dene Ho Ct 40 E1
Denison Rd 40 C3
Dent St 41 H4
Derwent Pl 40 D5
Devon Cl 40 D1
Devon Rd 40 D1
Dewsbury Rd 41 E6
Dial St 41 H5
Disraeli Gdns 40 E7
Disraeli Ter 40 E7
Dock St 41 F4
Dolly La 41 G2
Dolphin Ct 41 H4
Dolphin St 41 H4
Domestic Rd 40 B6
Domestic St 40 C5
Donisthorpe St 41 G6
Drive, The 41 G4
Driver Ter 40 B5
Dudley Way 41 E3
Duke St 41 F3
Duncan St 41 E4
Duncombe St 40 C3
Duxbury Ri 40 E1
Dyer St 41 F3

E

East Fld St 41 H4
Eastgate 41 F3
East King St 41 G4
East Par 40 E3
East Pk Dr 41 J4
East Pk Gro 41 J4
East Pk Mt 41 J4
East Pk Par 41 J4
East Pk Pl 41 J4
East Pk Rd 41 J4
East Pk St 41 J4
East Pk Ter 41 J4
East Pk Vw 41 J4
East St 41 G4
Easy Rd 41 H5
Ebor Mt 40 B1
Ebor Pl 40 B1
Ebor St 40 B1
Edgware Av 41 H1
Edgware Gro 41 H1
Edgware Mt 41 H1
Edgware Pl 41 H1
Edgware Row 41 H1
Edgware St 41 H1
Edgware Ter 41 H1
Edgware Vw 41 H1
Edward St 41 F3
Edwin Rd 40 B1
Eighth Av 40 A5
Elland Rd 40 C7
Elland Ter 40 D6
Ellerby La 41 H5
Ellerby Rd 41 G4
Elmtree La 41 G7
Elmwood La 41 F2
Elmwood Rd 41 E2
Elsworth St 40 A4
Enfield Av 41 G1
Enfield St 41 G1
Enfield Ter 41 G1
Euston Gro 40 B7
Euston Mt 40 B7
Euston Ter 40 B7
Everleigh St 41 J3

F

Far Cft Ter 40 A5
Fewston Av 41 H5
Fewston Ct 41 J5
Finsbury Rd 40 D2
First Av 40 A4
Firth St 41 G2
Firth Ter 41 G2
Fish St 41 F3
Flax Pl 41 G4
Florence Av 41 J1
Florence Gro 41 J1
Florence Mt 41 J1
Florence Pl 41 J1
Florence St 41 J1
Folly La 40 D7
Forster St 41 G6
Foundry St (Holbeck) 40 D5
Foundry St (Quarry Hill) 41 G4
Fountain St 40 D3
Fourteenth Av 40 A5
Fourth Ct 40 C5
Fox Way 41 H6
Fraser St 41 J2
Frederick Av 41 J5
Front Row 40 D5
Front St 40 D5

G

Gardeners Ct 41 G7
Gargrave App 41 H3
Gargrave Pl 41 H2
Garth, The 41 G4
Garton Av 41 J4
Garton Gro 41 J4
Garton Rd 41 J4
Garton Ter 41 J4
Garton Vw 41 J4
Gelderd Pl 40 B5
Gelderd Rd 40 A7
George St 41 F3
Gibraltar Island Rd 41 H7
Gilpin Pl 40 A5
Gilpin St 40 A5
Gilpin Ter 40 A5
Gilpin Vw 40 A5
Glasshouse St 41 G6
Gledhow Mt 41 H1
Gledhow Pl 41 H1
Gledhow Rd 41 H1
Gledhow Ter 41 H1
Glencoe Vw 41 J5
Glensdale Gro 41 J4
Glensdale Mt 41 J4
Glensdale Rd 41 J4
Glensdale St 41 J4
Glensdale Ter 41 J4
Glenthorpe Av 41 J3
Glenthorpe Cres 41 J3
Glenthorpe Ter 41 J3
Globe Rd 40 C4
Gloucester Ter 40 A4
Goodman St 41 G6
Gotts Rd 40 C4
Gower St 41 F3
Grace St 40 D3
Grafton St 41 F2
Grange Cl 41 G7
Grange Rd 41 G7
Grant Av 41 G1
Granville Rd 41 H2
Grape St 41 F7
Grasmere Cl 40 A5
Grassmere Rd 40 A5
Great George St 40 D3
Great Wilson St 40 E5
Greek St 40 E3
Greenfield Rd 41 H4
Green La 40 A5
Grosvenor Hill 41 E1

H

Hall Gro 40 B1
Hall La 40 A4
Hall Pl 41 H4
Hanover Av 40 C2
Hanover La 40 D3
Hanover Mt 40 C2
Hanover Sq 40 C2
Hanover Wk 40 C3
Harewood St 41 F3
Harold Av 40 A1
Harold Gro 40 A1
Harold Mt 40 A1
Harold Pl 40 A1
Harold Rd 40 A1
Harold St 40 A1
Harold Ter 40 A1
Harold Vw 40 A1
Harold Wk 40 A1
Harper St 41 F4
Harrison St 41 F3
Hartwell Rd 40 B1
Haslewood Cl 41 H3
Haslewood Ct 41 H3
Haslewood Dene 41 H3
Haslewood Dr 41 H3
Haslewood Ms 41 J3
Haslewood Pl 41 H3
Haslewood Sq 41 H3
Hawkins Dr 41 E1
Headrow, The 40 D3
Heaton's Ct 41 E4
Hedley Chase 40 A4
Hedley Gdns 40 A4
Hedley Grn 40 A4
High 41 G7
High Ct 41 F4
High Ct La 41 F4
Hillary Pl 40 D1
Hillidge Rd 41 F7
Hillidge Sq 41 F7
Hill Top Pl 40 B1
Hill Top St 40 B1
Hirst's Yd 41 F4
Holbeck 40 D5
Holbeck La 40 C5
Holbeck Moor Rd 40 C6
Holdforth Cl 40 A4
Holdforth Gdns 40 A4
Holdforth Grn 40 A4
Holdforth Pl 40 A4
Holmes St 41 E5
Holroyd St 41 G1
Hope Rd 41 G3
Howden Gdns 40 B1
Howden Pl 40 B1
Hudson Rd 41 J1
Hudswell Rd 41 F7
Hunslet 41 G7
Hunslet Grn Way 41 F7
Hunslet Hall Rd 40 E7
Hunslet La 41 F5
Hunslet Rd 41 F4
Hyde Pk Cl 40 B1
Hyde Pk Rd 40 B1
Hyde Pl 40 C2
Hyde St 40 C2
Hyde Ter 40 C2

I

Infirmary St 40 E3
Ingram Cl 40 C6
Ingram Cres 40 B7
Ingram Gdns 40 C6
Ingram Rd 40 C7
Ingram Row 40 E5
Ingram St 40 E5
Ingram Vw 40 C6
Inner Ring Rd 40 E2
Ivory St 41 F6

J

Jack La 40 D6
Jenkinson Cl 40 D6
Jenkinson Lawn 40 D6
John Smeaton Viaduct 41 G6
Joseph St 41 G7
Junction St 41 F5

K

Keeton St 41 H3
Kelsall Av 40 B1
Kelsall Gro 40 B2
Kelsall Pl 40 B1
Kelsall Rd 40 B1
Kelsall Ter 40 B1
Kelso Gdns 40 C1
Kelso Rd 40 C1
Kelso St 40 C2
Kendal Bk 40 C2
Kendal Cl 40 C2
Kendal Gro 40 C2
Kendal La 40 C2
Kendell St 41 F4
Kenneth St 40 B6
Kepler Gro 41 H1
Kepler Mt 41 H1
Kepler Ter 41 H1
Kidacre St 41 F5
Kildare Ter 40 B5
King Charles St 41 E3
King Edward St 41 F3
Kings Av 40 B2
King's Rd 40 B1
Kingston Ter 40 D1
King St 40 D4
Kippax Pl 41 H4
Kirkgate 41 F4
Kirkstall Rd 40 A2
Kitson Rd 41 G6
Kitson St 41 H4
Knowsthorpe Cres 41 H5
Knowsthorpe La 41 J6

L

Ladybeck Cl 41 F3
Lady La 41 F3
Lady Pit La 40 D7
Lands La 41 E3
Lane, The 41 G4
Larchfield Rd 41 G6
Latchmore Rd 40 A7
Laura St 40 C5
Lavender Wk 41 H4
Leathley Rd 41 F6
Leathley St 41 F6
Leicester Cl 40 E1
Leicester Gro 40 E1
Leicester Pl 40 D1
Leighton St 40 D3
Leodis Ct 40 D5
Leylands Rd 41 G2
Lifton Pl 40 C1
Lincoln Grn Rd 41 G2
Lincoln Rd 41 G2
Lindsey Ct 41 H2
Lindsey Gdns 41 H2
Lindsey Rd 41 H2
Lisbon St 40 D3
Little King St 40 E4
Little Queen St 40 D4
Little Woodhouse St 40 D2
Livinia Gro 40 E1
Lodge St 40 D1
Lofthouse Pl 40 E1
Londesboro Gro 41 J4
Long Causeway 41 H6
Long Cl La 41 H4
Lord St 40 C5
Lord Ter 40 B5
Lovell Pk Cl 41 F2
Lovell Pk Gate 41 F2
Lovell Pk Hill 41 F2
Lovell Pk Rd 41 F2
Lovell Pk Vw 41 F2
Lower Basinghall St 40 E3
Lower Brunswick St 41 F2
Low Flds Av 40 B7
Low Flds Rd 40 A7
Low Flds Way 40 B7
Low Fold 41 G5
Low Rd 41 G7
Low Whitehouse Row 41 G6
Ludgate Hill 41 F3
Lyddon Ter 40 C1
Lydgate 41 J2

Liverpool street index

Brahms Cl 43 G7
Brampton Dr 43 F5
Brassey St 42 D7
Breames Cl 43 H4
Breck Rd 43 F1
Bremner Cl 43 H4
Brick St 42 D6
Bridge Rd 43 J5
Bridgewater St 42 C6
Bridport St 42 D3
Bright St 43 F2
Brindley St 42 D7
Britannia Av 43 J6
Britten Cl 43 H7
Bronte St 42 E3
Brook St 42 B3
Brownlow Hill 42 D4
Brownlow St 43 E4
Brow Side 43 E1
Brunswick Rd 43 F3
Brunswick St 42 B4
Bryges St 43 G4
Brythen St 42 C4
Burlington St 42 C1
Burnley Cl 43 G1
Burroughs Gdns 42 C1
Burrows Ct 42 B1
Burton Cl 42 C5
Bute St 42 D2
Bute St (Edge Hill) 43 H6
Butler Cres 43 G2
Butler St 43 G1
Button St 42 C4
Byrom St 42 D3

C
Cadogan St 43 J5
Caird St 43 G2
Cairns St 43 G7
Caledonia St 43 E5
Callander Rd 43 J2
Cambria St N 43 H2
Cambria St S 43 H2
Cambridge Ct 43 E5
Cambridge St 43 E4
Camden St 42 D3
Cameo Cl 43 G1
Cameron St 43 H3
Campbell St 42 C5
Canada Boul 42 B4
Canning Pl 42 C4
Canning St 43 E5
Cantebury St 42 E2
Cantebury Way 43 E2
Cantsfield St 43 J6
Cardigan St 43 J5
Cardigan Way 43 H1
Cardwell St 43 G5
Carlingford Cl 43 G6
Carlton St 42 A1
Carmarthen Cres 42 D7
Carpenters Row 42 C5
Carruthers St 42 B2
Carstairs Rd 43 J1
Carter St 43 F6
Carver St 43 E2
Caryl St 42 D7
Castle St 42 B4
Catharine St 43 F5
Cathedral Cl 42 E6
Cathedral Gate 42 E5
Cathedral Wk 42 E4
Cawdor St 43 G7
Cazneau St 42 D1
Cedar Gro 43 H7
Celtic St 43 F7
Chadwick St 42 B2
Chaloner St 42 C6
Chandos St 43 H4
Channell Rd 43 H2
Chapel St 42 B4
Chase Way 42 E1
Chatham Pl 43 G4
Chatham St 43 F5
Chatsworth Dr 43 H5
Chaucer St 42 D2
Cheapside 42 C3
Chesney Cl 42 E7
Chesterfield St 42 E6
Chester St 42 E7
Chestnut St 43 F4
Chichester Cl 43 J5
Childwall Av 43 J6
Chisenhale St 42 B1
Chiswell St 43 H3
Christian St 42 D2
Chris Ward Cl 43 H4
Church All 42 C4
Church Mt 43 G4
Church St 42 C4
Churton Ct 43 F2
Cicely St 43 G4
Clarence St 42 E4
Claribel St 43 F7

Claughton Cl 43 H4
Claypole Cl 43 H5
Clay St 42 B1
Clearwater Cl 43 H3
Clegg St 42 D1
Clement Gdns 42 C1
Cleveland Sq 42 C5
Clifford St 42 E3
Cliff St 43 H3
Clifton Gro 42 E1
Clint Rd 43 H4
Clint Rd W 43 H4
Clint Way 43 H4
Coal St 42 D3
Cobden St 43 F2
Coburg Wf 42 C7
Cockspur St 42 C3
Coleridge St 43 H2
College La 42 C4
College St N 42 E2
College St S 43 F2
Colquitt St 42 D5
Coltart Rd 43 G7
Comberme St 43 E7
Commerce Way 43 G6
Commutation Row 42 D3
Compton Rd 43 G1
Comus St 42 D2
Concert St 42 D5
Connaught Rd 43 G3
Contance St 43 E3
Cookson St 42 D6
Cook St 42 C4
Copperas Hill 42 D4
Corinto St 42 E6
Corney St 43 H6
Cornhill 42 C5
Cornwallis St 42 D5
Corsewall St 43 J5
Cotswold St 43 H3
Cotton St 42 A1
Covent Gdn 42 B3
Cowan Dr 43 F1
Cranborne Rd 43 J6
Craven St 42 E3
Cresswell St 43 F1
Cropper St 42 D4
Crosfield Cl 43 J4
Crosfield Rd 43 H4
Crosshall St 42 C3
Crown St 43 F3
Croxteth Gro 43 H7
Croxteth Rd 43 G7
Crump St 42 D6
Cullen St 43 H6
Cumberland St 42 C3
Cunliffe St 42 C3
Custom Ho Pl 42 C5

D
Dale St 42 B4
Daniel Davies Dr 43 G6
Dansie St 43 E4
Danube St 43 H6
Darrel Dr 43 H6
Daulby St 43 F3
Davies St 42 C3
Dawber Cl 43 G1
Dawson St 42 C4
Dean Dillistone Ct 42 D6
Deane Rd 43 H3
Dean Patey Ct 42 D5
Deeley Cl 43 H4
Dell St 43 H3
Denham Dr 43 H1
Denham Way 43 H1
Dentdale Dr 42 E1
Devon St 42 E3
Dexter St 42 E7
Dial St 43 H3
Diamond St 42 C1
Dickens St 43 E7
Dickson St 42 A1
Dombey St 43 E7
Dorothy St 43 H4
Dorrit St 43 E7
Dorset Av 43 J6
Douro St 42 D1
Dovestone Cl 43 H5
Dove St 43 G6
Drury La 42 B4
Dryden St 42 D1
Dublin St 42 A1
Ducie St 43 G7
Duckinfield St 43 E4
Duke St 42 C5
Duncan St 42 D6
Dunkeld Cl 43 G2
Dunstan La 43 H5
Durden St 43 H6
Durning Rd 43 H3

Dwerryhouse St 43 H4
Dyke St 43 H5

E
Earle Rd 43 H6
Earle St 42 B3
East St 42 B3
Eaton St 42 B2
Ebenezer Rd 43 J3
Eden St 43 H6
Edgar St 42 C2
Edge Hill 43 G5
Edge La 43 G4
Edinburgh Rd 43 G3
Edmund St 42 B3
Egerton St 43 E6
Elaine St 43 F7
Eldonian Way 42 B1
Eldon Pl 42 C1
Eldon St 42 C1
Elizabeth St 43 F3
Elliot St 42 D4
Elm Gro 43 F4
Elm Vale 43 J1
Elstree Rd 43 J2
Ember Cres 43 F1
Embledon St 43 G6
Emerson St 43 E6
Empress Rd 43 G4
Enid St 43 F7
Epworth St 43 F3
Erin Cl 42 E7
Erskine St 43 F3
Esher Rd 43 H2
Eversley St 43 F7
Everton Brow 42 E2
Everton Rd 43 F1
Every St 43 G1
Exchange St E 42 B3
Exchange St W 42 B3

F
Fairclough St 42 D4
Fairfield 43 J2
Falkland St 43 E3
Falkner Sq 43 F6
Falkner St 43 E5
Fareham Rd 43 J3
Farnworth St 43 G2
Fazakerley St 42 B3
Fearnside St 43 J5
Fell St 43 H3
Fenwick St 42 B4
Fern Gro 43 H7
Fernhill Dr 43 F7
Fielding St 43 G2
Field St 42 E2
Finch Pl 43 E3
Finlay St 43 H2
Fishguard Cl 43 F1
Fitzclarence Way 43 F1
Fitzpatrick Ct 42 B1
Fitzroy Way 43 F2
Fleet St 42 D4
Fleming Ct 42 B1
Flint St 42 D6
Fontenoy St 42 C2
Ford St 42 C2
Forrest St 42 C5
Fowler Cl 43 H4
Foxhill Cl 43 F7
Fox St 42 D1
Fraser St 42 D3
Freedom Cl 43 G5
Freeman St 43 J5
Freemasons' Row 42 C2
Frost St 43 H3

G
Galloway St 43 J5
Gannock St 43 H3
Gardenside St 43 F2
Gardners Dr 43 H1
Gardner's Row 42 C2
Garrick St 43 J6
Gascoyne St 42 B2
Geneva Rd 43 J2
George Harrison Cl 43 G2
Georges Dockway 42 B4
George St 42 B3
Geraint St 43 F7
Gerard St 42 D3
Gibraltar Row 42 B3
Gibson St 43 F6
Gilbert St 42 C5
Gildarts Gdns 42 C1
Gildart St 43 E3
Gilead St 43 E4
Gill St 43 E3
Gilroy Rd 43 H2
Gladstone Rd 43 G4
Gladstone St 42 C2
Gleave Cres 43 F1
Glegg St 42 B1

Gloucester Ct 43 G2
Gloucester Pl 43 F3
Gore St 42 D7
Gower St 42 B5
Gradwell St 42 C4
Grafton Cres 42 D7
Grafton St 42 D6
Granary Wf 42 C7
Granby St 43 J3
Grantham St 43 H6
Granville Rd 42 C2
Grayson St 43 G5
Great Crosshall St 42 C3
Great George Pl 42 D6
Great George St 42 D6
Great Howard St 42 B2
Great Nelson St 42 D1
Great Newton St 43 E3
Great Orford St 42 D2
Great Richmond St 42 E3
Greek St 43 G7
Greenheys Rd 42 D6
Greenland St 42 E4
Green La 43 H6
Greenleaf St 43 H2
Greenside 42 C1
Green St 43 F2
Gregson St 42 D5
Grenville St S 43 J4
Gresley Cl 43 H6
Grierson St 43 G4
Grinfield St 43 F7
Grinshill Cl 43 H2
Grosvenor St 43 F7
Grove Pk 42 E2
Grove Rd 43 F1
Grove St 43 G1
Guelph St 42 B3
Guion St 42 B3
Gwendoline St 43 G2
Gwenfron Rd 43 G2
Gwent St 43 F7

H
Hackins Hey 42 B3
Haigh St 43 E1
Hale St 42 C3
Hall La 43 F3
Halsbury Rd 43 H2
Hampstead Rd 43 J2
Hampton St 42 B3
Hannan Rd 43 J5
Hanover St 43 H3
Harbord St 42 B4
Hardman St 43 H7
Hardy St 43 F7
Harewood St 43 G2
Harker St 42 E2
Harke St 43 E3
Harper St 43 H2
Harrington St 43 F1
Harrowby Cl 43 F1
Harrowby St 42 B1
Hartley Quay 43 F2
Hart St 42 D4
Hatherley Cl 42 B1
Hatherley St 42 D6
Hatton Gdn 42 C3
Haverston Rd 42 C2
Hawdon Ct 42 C5
Hawke St 43 H4
Hawkins St 43 F7
Hawthorn Gro 42 D1
Head St 42 D3
Heathcote Cl 43 G5
Heathfield St 43 J5
Helena St 42 C2
Helsby St 43 H3
Hendon Rd 43 G4
Henglers Cl 43 J1
Henry Edward St 43 F2
Henry St 42 C2
Hewitts Pl 42 C5
Highfield St 42 C2
Highgate St 42 B2
High St 43 G4
Hilbre St 42 B3
Hillaby Cl 43 J2
Hillside St 43 G2
Hill St 43 F7
Hinton St 42 D7
Hockenhall All 43 J2
Hodson Pl 42 C3
Holborn St 43 F1
Holden St 43 F3
Holdsworth St 43 G5
Holly Rd 43 J3
Holmes St 43 H6
Holt Rd 43 H3
Holy Cross Cl 42 C2
Homerton Rd 43 J2
Hood St 42 C2
Hope Pl 43 F1
Hope St 42 B1

Hornby Wk 43 G2
Hotham St 43 F3
Houghton St 42 D7
Houlton St 43 H3
Hughes Cl 42 C4
Hughes St 42 D7
Huntly Rd 42 D6
Hurst St 42 C7
Huskisson St 43 G6
Hutchinson St 43 H2
Hutchinson Wk 43 J6
Hygeia St 43 G1
Hyslop St 42 E7

I
Iliad St 42 D1
Ingrow Rd 43 H2
Innovation Bvd 43 E3
Irvine St 43 G4
Islington 42 D2
Ivatt Way 42 E3

J
Jack McBain Ct 42 B1
Jade Rd 43 H1
Jamaica St 42 D6
James Clarke St 42 C1
James St 42 B4
Janet St 43 H4
Jasmine Cl 43 E1
Jenkinson St 42 E2
Jermyn St 43 G7
Jet Cl 43 H1
John Lennon Dr 43 G2
John Moores Cl 43 F5
Johnson St 42 C3
John St 42 E2
Jordan St 42 D6
Jubilee Dr 43 G3
Judges Dr 43 J1
Judges Way 43 J1
Juvenal Pl 42 D1
Juvenal St 42 D2

K
Keble St 43 G2
Kelso Rd 43 J2
Kelvin Gro 43 G7
Kempston St 42 E3
Kenley Cl 43 H1
Kensington 43 E6
Kensington 43 G3
Kensington St 43 G2
Kent St 42 D5
Kilshaw St 43 G1
Kimberley Cl 43 F6
Kinder St 43 F2
King Edward St 42 B3
Kinglake St 43 G4
Kings Dock St 42 C6
Kingsley Rd 43 G6
Kings Par 42 B5
Kingsway Ct 42 C1
Kingswell Cl 43 G4
Kitchen St 42 C6
Knight St 42 D5

L
Lace St 42 C3
Ladybower Cl 43 H5
Laggan St 43 H3
Lairds Pl 42 C1
Lakeland Cl 42 C5
Lambert Way 42 E3
Lamport St 42 E7
Lance Cl 43 F1
Langley St 42 E7
Langsdale St 42 E2
Langton Rd 43 J1
Lanyork Rd 42 B2
Laurel Gro 43 H7
Lavan Cl 43 F2
Lawrence Rd 43 J6
Lawton St 42 D4
Laxey St 42 E7
Leece St 42 E5
Leeds St 42 B2
Leigh St 42 C4
Leigh St (Edge Hill) 43 H3
Lemon Cl 43 J4
Lemon Gro 43 H7
Leopold Rd 43 G4
Lesseps Rd 43 H6
Lestock St 42 E6
Liffey St 43 G6
Lightwood Dr 43 H5
Lightwood St 43 H5
Lilley Rd 43 J2
Lilly Vale 43 J2
Lime Gro 43 H7
Limekiln La 42 C1
Lime St 42 D4
Lincoln Cl 43 H1
Lindley Cl 43 H5

Lindley St 43 J5
Ling St 43 H3
Lister Cres 43 J3
Lister Rd 43 J2
Little Catherine St 43 E6
Little Ct 42 B1
Little Hardman St 42 E5
Little Howard St 42 B1
Little St. Bride St 43 E5
Little Woolton St 43 F4
Liver St 42 C5
Lloyd Cl 43 F1
Lockerby Rd 43 J2
Lodge La 43 H7
London Rd 42 D3
Longfellow St 43 H6
Longstone Wk 43 G5
Lord Nelson St 42 D3
Lord St 42 C4
Lorton St 43 H6
Lothian St 43 F7
Loudon Gro 43 G7
Love La 42 B1
Lower Castle St 42 B4
Low Hill 43 F2
Lowther St 43 F6
Low Wd St 43 F3
Luke St 43 E7
Lyceum Pl 42 D4
Lydia Ann St 42 C5
Lytton St 43 F2

M
Maddrell St 42 B1
Madelaine St 43 F7
Madeley St 43 H1
Magdala St 43 H6
Maitland Cl 43 H6
Malden Rd 43 H2
Mallow Rd 43 H2
Malt St 43 G5
Malvern Rd 43 H2
Manchester St 42 C3
Manesty's La 42 C4
Manfred St 43 F3
Mann Island 42 B4
Mann St 42 D7
Mansell Rd 43 H2
Mansfield St 42 D2
Manton Rd 43 H2
Maple Gro 43 H7
Marathon Cl 43 F1
Marcot Rd 43 J1
Margaret St 43 F1
Mariners Wf 42 C7
Maritime Pl 42 E2
Maritime Way 42 C5
Marlborough St 42 C2
Marlsford St 43 H2
Marmaduke St 43 G4
Marquis St 42 E3
Marsden St 43 F2
Marsden Way 43 F2
Marshall Pl 42 C1
Martensen St 43 G4
Marvin St 43 G2
Marybone 42 C3
Maryland St 43 E5
Mason St 43 G4
Mathew St 42 C4
Maud St 43 F7
Maxton Rd 43 H2
Mayfair Cl 43 H1
May Pl 42 E4
May St 42 E4
Melda Cl 43 F2
Melville Pl 43 F5
Merlin St 43 F7
Michael Dragonette Ct 42 C1
Midghall St 42 C2
Mile End 42 C1
Millennium Pl 43 G7
Mill La 42 D3
Mill Rd 43 F1
Mill St 42 E7
Millvale St 43 H1
Milroy St 43 H4
Milverton St 43 H1
Minshull St 43 F4
Minster Ct 43 F5
Minto Cl 43 H3
Minto St 43 H3
Mirfield St 43 H2
Molyneux Rd 43 G2
Montgomery Way 43 H1
Moorfields 42 C3
Moor Pl 42 E3
Moor St 42 B4
Morden St 43 H1
Moss Gro 43 H7
Mount Pleasant 42 D4
Mount St 42 E5

London street index

Bartlett Ct EC4 45 G2
Bartletts Pas EC4 45 G2
Barton St SW1 44 E6
Bastion Highwalk EC2 45 J2
Bateman's Bldgs W1 44 D3
Bateman St W1 44 D3
Bath Ct EC1 45 G1
Bath Ter SE1 45 J7
Bayley St WC1 44 D2
Baylis Rd SE1 45 G6
Beak St W1 44 C3
Bear All EC4 45 H2
Bear Gdns SE1 45 J4
Bear La SE1 45 H4
Bear St WC2 44 D3
Beauchamp St EC1 45 G2
Beaumont Ms W1 44 A1
Beaumont St W1 44 A1
Bedford Av WC1 44 D2
Bedfordbury WC2 44 E3
Bedford Ct WC2 44 E4
Bedford Pl WC1 44 E1
Bedford Row WC1 45 F1
Bedford Sq WC1 44 D2
Bedford St WC2 44 E3
Bedford Way WC1 44 D1
Bedlam Ms SE11 45 G7
Beech St EC2 45 J1
Beeston Pl SW1 44 B7
Belgrave Ms N SW1 44 A6
Belgrave Ms S SW1 44 A6
Belgrave Ms W SW1 44 A6
Belgrave Pl SW1 44 A6
Belgrave Sq SW1 44 A6
Belgrave Yd SW1 44 B7
Belgravia SW1 44 A7
Bell Wf La EC4 45 J4
Bell Yd WC2 45 G2
Belvedere Bldgs SE1 45 H6
Belvedere Pl SE1 45 H6
Belvedere Rd SE1 45 F5
Benjamin St EC1 45 H1
Bennet's Hill EC4 45 H3
Bennet St SW1 44 C4
Bennetts Yd SW1 44 D7
Bentinck Ms W1 44 A2
Bentinck St W1 44 A2
Berkeley Sq W1 44 B4
Berkeley St W1 44 B4
Bernard St WC1 44 E1
Berners Ms W1 44 C2
Berners Pl W1 44 C2
Berners St W1 44 C2
Berwick St W1 44 D3
Betterton St WC2 44 E3
Bingham Pl W1 44 A1
Binney St W1 44 A3
Birdcage Wk SW1 44 C6
Bird St W1 44 A3
Bishop's Ct EC4 45 H2
Bishop's Ct WC2 45 G2
Bishops Ter SE11 45 G7
Bittern St SE1 45 J6
Blackburne's Ms W1 44 A3
Blackfriars Br EC4 45 H3
Blackfriars Br SE1 45 H3
Blackfriars Ct EC4 45 H3
Black Friars La EC4 45 H3
Blackfriars Pas EC4 45 H3
Blackfriars Rd SE1 45 H6
Bleeding Heart Yd EC1 45 G2
Blenheim St W1 44 B3
Bloomfield Pl W1 44 B3
Bloomsbury WC1 44 D2
Bloomsbury Ct WC1 45 E2
Bloomsbury Pl WC1 45 E1
Bloomsbury Sq WC1 45 E2
Bloomsbury St WC1 44 D2
Bloomsbury Way WC1 44 E2
Blore Ct W1 44 D3
Blue Ball Yd SW1 44 C5
Bolsover St W1 44 B1
Bolt Ct EC4 45 G3
Bolton St W1 44 B4
Book Ms WC2 44 D3
Booth La EC4 45 J3
Booth's Pl W1 44 C2
Borough, The SE1 45 J6
Borough High St SE1 45 J6
Borough Rd SE1 45 H6
Borough Sq SE1 45 J6
Boscobel Pl SW1 44 A7
Boswell Ct WC1 45 E1
Boswell St WC1 45 E1
Boundary Row SE1 45 H5
Bourchier St W1 44 D3
Bourdon Pl W1 44 B3
Bourdon St W1 44 B3
Bourlet Cl W1 44 C2
Bourne Est EC1 45 G1
Bouverie St EC4 45 G3
Bow Chyd EC4 45 J3
Bow La EC4 45 J3
Bow St WC2 45 E3
Boyce St SE1 45 F5
Boyfield St SE1 45 H6
Boyle St W1 44 C3
Brackley St EC1 45 J1
Brad St SE1 45 G5
Bread St EC4 45 J3
Bream's Bldgs EC4 45 G2
Bressenden Pl SW1 44 B6
Brewer's Grn SW1 44 D6
Brewers Hall Gdns EC2 45 J2
Brewer St W1 44 C3
Briant Est SE1 45 G7
Briant Ho SE1 45 F7
Brick Ct EC4 45 G3
Brick St W1 44 B5
Bride Ct EC4 45 H3
Bride La EC4 45 H3
Bridewell Pl EC4 45 H3
Bridford Ms W1 44 B1
Bridge Pl SW1 44 B7
Bridge St SW1 44 E6
Bridgewater Sq EC2 45 J1
Bridgewater St EC2 45 J1
Bridle La W1 44 C3
Brinton Wk SE1 45 H5
Briset St EC1 45 H1
Britton St EC1 45 H1
Broadbent St W1 44 B3
Broad Ct WC2 45 E3
Broad Sanctuary SW1 44 D6
Broadstone Pl W1 44 A2
Broad Wk W1 44 A4
Broadwall SE1 45 G4
Broadway SW1 44 D6
Broadwick St W1 44 C3
Broad Yd EC1 45 H1
Brockham St SE1 45 J6
Broken Wf EC4 45 J3
Bromley Pl W1 44 C1
Brook Dr SE11 45 G7
Brooke's Ct EC1 45 G1
Brookes Mkt EC1 45 G1
Brooke St EC1 45 G2
Brook's Ms W1 44 B3
Brook St W1 44 A3
Brown Hart Gdns W1 44 A3
Browning Ms W1 44 B2
Brownlow Ms WC1 45 F1
Brownlow St WC1 45 F2
Brunswick Sq WC1 45 E1
Bruton La W1 44 B4
Bruton Pl W1 44 B4
Bruton St W1 44 B4
Brydges Pl WC2 44 E4
Buckingham Arc WC2 45 E4
Buckingham Gate SW1 44 C6
Buckingham Ms SW1 44 C6
Buckingham Pl SW1 44 C6
Buckingham St WC2 45 E4
Buckley St SE1 45 G5
Bucknall St WC2 44 D2
Bull Inn Ct WC2 45 E4
Bulstrode Pl W1 44 A2
Bulstrode St W1 44 A2
Burdett St SE1 45 G6
Burgon St EC4 45 H3
Burleigh St WC2 45 F3
Burlington Arc W1 44 C4
Burlington Gdns W1 44 C4
Burrell St SE1 45 H4
Burrows Ms SE1 45 H5
Bury Pl WC1 44 E2
Bury St SW1 44 C4
Butler Pl SW1 44 D6
Byng Pl WC1 44 D1
Bywell Pl W1 44 C2
C
Cadogan La SW1 44 A7
Cahill St EC1 45 J1
Caleb St SE1 45 J5
Cambridge Circ WC2 44 D3
Candover St W1 44 C2
Cannon St EC4 45 J3
Canon Row SW1 44 E6
Canterbury Ho SE1 45 F6
Canvey St SE1 45 H4
Capener's Cl SW1 44 A6
Capper St WC1 44 C1
Carburton St W1 44 B1
Carey La EC2 45 J2
Carey St WC2 45 F3
Carlisle La SE1 45 F7
Carlisle Pl SW1 44 C7
Carlisle St W1 44 D3
Carlos Pl W1 44 A4
Carlton Gdns SW1 44 D5
Carlton Ho Ter SW1 44 D5
Carlton St SW1 44 D4
Carmelite St EC4 45 G3
Carnaby St W1 44 C3
Carpenter St W1 44 B4
Carrington St W1 44 B5
Carteret St SW1 44 D6
Carter La EC4 45 H3
Carthusian St EC1 45 J1
Carting La WC2 45 E4
Castle Baynard St EC4 45 H3
Castlebrook Cl SE11 45 H7
Castle La SW1 44 C6
Castle Yd SE1 45 H4
Cathedral Piazza SW1 44 C7
Cathedral Wk SW1 44 C6
Catherine Pl SW1 44 C6
Catherine St WC2 45 F3
Catherine Wheel Yd SW1 44 C5
Catton St WC1 45 F2
Cavendish Ms N W1 44 B1
Cavendish Ms S W1 44 B2
Cavendish Pl W1 44 B2
Cavendish Sq W1 44 B2
Caxton St SW1 44 C6
Cecil Ct WC2 44 D4
Centaur St SE1 45 F6
Centrepoint WC1 44 D2
Chadwick St SW1 44 D7
Chancel St SE1 45 H4
Chancery La WC2 45 G2
Chandos Pl WC2 44 E4
Chandos St W1 44 B2
Chapel Pl W1 44 B3
Chapel St SW1 44 A6
Chaplin Cl SE1 45 G5
Chapone Pl W1 44 D3
Chapter Ho Ct EC4 45 J3
Charing Cross SW1 44 D4
Charing Cross Rd WC2 44 D2
Charles II St SW1 44 D4
Charles St W1 44 B4
Charlotte Ms W1 44 C1
Charlotte Pl W1 44 C2
Charlotte St W1 44 C1
Charterhouse, The EC1 45 H1
Charterhouse Bldgs EC1 45 H1
Charterhouse Ms EC1 45 H1
Charterhouse Sq EC1 45 H1
Charterhouse St EC1 45 G2
Cheapside EC2 45 J3
Chenies Ms WC1 44 D1
Chenies St WC1 44 D1
Chequer St EC1 45 J1
Cherry Tree Wk EC1 45 J1
Chesham Cl SW1 44 A7
Chesham Ms SW1 44 A6
Chesham Pl SW1 44 A7
Chesham St SW1 44 A7
Cheshire Ct EC4 45 G3
Chester Cl SW1 44 A6
Chesterfield Gdns W1 44 B4
Chesterfield Hill W1 44 B4
Chesterfield St W1 44 B4
Chester Ms SW1 44 B6
Chester Sq SW1 44 B7
Chester Sq Ms SW1 44 B7
Chester St SW1 44 A6
Chicheley St SE1 45 F5
Chichester Rents WC2 45 G2
Chiltern St W1 44 A1
Ching Ct WC2 44 E3
Chiswell St EC1 45 J1
Chitty St W1 44 C1
Christ Ch Pas EC1 45 H2
Church Entry EC4 45 H3
Church Pl SW1 44 C4
Churchyard Row SE11 45 H7
Clare Mkt WC2 45 F3
Clarges Ms W1 44 B4
Clarges St W1 44 B4
Clarke's Ms W1 44 A1
Clement's Inn WC2 45 F3
Clement's Inn Pas WC2 45 F3
Clennam St SE1 45 J5
Clerkenwell EC1 45 H1
Clerkenwell Grn EC1 45 G1
Clerkenwell Rd EC1 45 G1
Cleveland Ms W1 44 C1
Cleveland Pl SW1 44 C4
Cleveland Row SW1 44 C5
Cleveland St W1 44 C1
Clifford's Inn Pas EC4 45 G3
Clifford St W1 44 C4
Clink St SE1 45 J4
Clipstone Ms W1 44 C1
Clipstone St W1 44 B1
Cliveden Pl SW1 44 A7
Cloak La EC4 45 J3
Cloth Ct EC1 45 H2
Cloth Fair EC1 45 H2
Cloth St EC1 45 J1
Coach & Horses Yd W1 44 B3
Coburg Cl SW1 44 C7
Cock La EC1 45 H2
Cockpit Steps SW1 44 D6
Cockpit Yd WC1 45 F1
Cockspur Ct SW1 44 D4
Cockspur St SW1 44 D4
Coin St SE1 45 G4
Cole St SE1 45 J6
Coley St WC1 45 F1
College Hill EC4 45 J3
College Ms SW1 44 E6
College St EC4 45 J3
Collinson St SE1 45 J6
Collinson Wk SE1 45 J6
Colnbrook St SE1 45 H7
Colombo St SE1 45 H5
Colonnade WC1 44 E1
Colville Pl W1 44 C2
Computer Pass EC2 45 J2
Concert Hall App SE1 45 F5
Conduit Ct WC2 44 E3
Conduit St W1 44 B3
Cons St SE1 45 G5
Constitution Hill SW1 44 B5
Conway Ms W1 44 C1
Conway St W1 44 C1
Cooper Cl SE1 45 G6
Copeland Ho SE11 45 F7
Copperfield St SE1 45 H5
Coptic St WC1 44 E2
Coral St SE1 45 G6
Coram St WC1 44 E1
Cork St W1 44 C4
Cork St Ms W1 44 C4
Corner Ho St WC2 44 E4
Cornwall Rd SE1 45 G4
Cosmo Pl WC1 45 E1
Cosser St SE1 45 G6
Cottesloe Ms SE1 45 G6
County St SE1 45 J7
Covent Gdn WC2 45 E3
Covent Gdn Mkt WC2 45 E3
Coventry St W1 44 D4
Cowcross St EC1 45 H1
Cowley St SW1 44 E6
Craigs Ct SW1 44 E4
Cramer St W1 44 A2
Cranbourn St WC2 44 D3
Crane Ct EC4 45 G3
Cranfield Row SE1 45 G6
Craven Pas WC2 44 E4
Craven St WC2 44 E4
Crawford Pas EC1 45 G1
Creed La EC4 45 H3
Crescent Row EC1 45 J1
Cripplegate St EC2 45 J1
Cromwell Twr EC2 45 J1
Cross Keys Cl W1 44 A2
Cross Keys Sq EC1 45 J2
Crown Ct EC2 45 J3
Crown Ct WC2 45 E3
Crown Office Row EC4 45 G3
Crown Pas SW1 44 C5
Cubitts Yd WC2 45 E3
Culross St W1 44 A4
Cursitor St EC4 45 G2
Curzon Gate W1 44 A5
Curzon Sq W1 44 A5
Curzon St W1 44 A5
Cut, The SE1 45 G5
Cypress Pl W1 44 C1
D
Dacre St SW1 44 D6
Dane St WC1 45 F2
Dansey Pl W1 44 D3
Dante Pl SE11 45 H7
Dante Rd SE11 45 H7
D'Arblay St W1 44 C3
Dartmouth St SW1 44 D6
Davidge St SE1 45 H6
Davies Ms W1 44 B3
Davies St W1 44 B3
Dean Bradley St SW1 44 E7
Deanery Ms W1 44 A4
Deanery St W1 44 A4
Dean Farrar St SW1 44 D6
Dean Ryle St SW1 44 E7
Deans Ct EC4 45 H3
Deans Ms W1 44 B2
Dean Stanley St SW1 44 E7
Dean St W1 44 D2
Dean's Yd SW1 44 D6
Dean Trench St SW1 44 E7
Denman St W1 44 D4
Denmark Pl WC2 44 D2
Denmark St WC2 44 D3
Derby Gate SW1 44 E5
Derby St W1 44 A5
Dering St W1 44 B3
Devereux Ct WC2 45 G3
Devonshire Cl W1 44 B1
Devonshire Ms N W1 44 B1
Devonshire Ms S W1 44 B1
Devonshire Ms W W1 44 B1
Devonshire Pl W1 44 A1
Devonshire Pl Ms W1 44 A1
Devonshire Row Ms W1 44 B1
Devonshire St W1 44 A1
De Walden St W1 44 A2
Diadem Ct W1 44 D3
Dickens Ms EC1 45 H1
Dickens Sq SE1 45 J6
Disney Pl SE1 45 J5
Disney St SE1 45 J5
Distaff La EC4 45 J3
Doby Ct EC4 45 J3
Dodson St SE1 45 G6
Dolben St SE1 45 H5
Dombey St WC1 45 F1
Doon St SE1 45 G5
Dorrington St EC1 45 G1
Dorrit St SE1 45 J5
Dorset Bldgs EC4 45 H3
Dorset Ms SW1 44 B6
Dorset Ri EC4 45 H3
Doughty Ms WC1 45 F1
Dover St W1 44 B4
Dover Yd W1 44 B4
Downing St SW1 44 E5
Down St W1 44 B5
Down St Ms W1 44 B5
Doyce St SE1 45 J5
D'Oyley St SW1 44 A7
Drake St WC1 45 F2
Draper Ho SE1 45 H7
Drury La WC2 45 E3
Dryden St WC2 45 E3
Duchess Ms W1 44 B2
Duchess St W1 44 B2
Duchy Pl SE1 45 G4
Duchy St SE1 45 G4
Duck La W1 44 D3
Dufferin St EC1 45 J1
Dufour's Pl W1 44 C3
Dugard Way SE11 45 H7
Duke of Wellington Pl SW1 44 A5
Duke of York St SW1 44 C4
Duke's Ms W1 44 A2
Duke St SW1 44 C4
Duke St W1 44 A2
Duke's Yd W1 44 A3
Duncannon St WC2 44 E4
Dunns Pas WC1 45 E2
Dunstable Ms W1 44 A1
Durham Ho St WC2 45 E4
Dyer's Bldgs EC1 45 G2
Dyott St WC1 44 E2
E
Eagle Ct EC1 45 H1
Eagle Pl SW1 44 C4
Eagle St WC1 45 F2
Earlham St WC2 44 D3
Earnshaw St WC2 44 D2
Easley's Ms W1 44 A2
Eastcastle St W1 44 C2
East Harding St EC4 45 G2
East Pas EC1 45 H1
East Poultry Av EC1 45 H2
Eaton Gate SW1 44 A7
Eaton La SW1 44 B7
Eaton Ms N SW1 44 A7
Eaton Ms S SW1 44 A7
Eaton Ms W SW1 44 A7
Eaton Pl SW1 44 A7
Eaton Row SW1 44 B6
Eaton Sq SW1 44 B6
Eaton Ter SW1 44 A7
Eaton Ter Ms SW1 44 A7
Ebury Ms SW1 44 A7
Ebury Ms E SW1 44 B7
Ebury St SW1 44 B7
Eccleston Br SW1 44 B7
Eccleston Ms SW1 44 A7
Eccleston Pl SW1 44 B7
Eccleston St SW1 44 B7
Edwards Ms W1 44 A3
Elba Pl SE17 45 J7
Elephant & Castle SE1 45 H7
Elephant Rd SE17 45 J7
Elizabeth Ct SW1 44 D7
Elizabeth St SW1 44 A7
Ellington Ho SE1 45 J6
Elliotts Row SE11 45 H7
Elm Ct EC4 45 G3
Elm St WC1 45 F1
Elverton St SW1 44 D7
Ely Ct EC1 45 G2
Ely Pl EC1 45 G2
Embankment Pier WC2 45 F4
Embankment Pl WC2 45 E4
Emerald St WC1 45 F1
Emerson St SE1 45 J4
Emery Hill St SW1 44 C7
Emery St SE1 45 G6
Endell St WC2 44 E2
Errol St EC1 45 J1
Essex Ct EC4 45 G3
Essex St WC2 45 G3
Euston Rd NW1 44 B1
Evelyn Yd W1 44 D2
Ewer St SE1 45 J5
Excel Ct WC2 44 D4
Exchange Ct WC2 45 E4
Exeter St WC2 45 E3
Exton St SE1 45 G5
Eyre St Hill EC1 45 G1
F
Falconberg Ct W1 44 D2
Falconberg Ms W1 44 D2
Falcon Ct EC4 45 G3
Falmouth Rd SE1 45 J6
Fann St EC1 45 J1
Fann St EC2 45 J1
Fareham St W1 44 D2
Farm St W1 44 B4
Farnham Pl SE1 45 H5
Farringdon La EC1 45 G1
Farringdon St EC4 45 H2
Faulkner's All EC1 45 H1
Ferrybridge Ho SE11 45 F7
Fetter La EC4 45 G3
Field Ct WC1 45 F2
Fisher St WC1 45 E2
Fitzalan St SE11 45 G7
Fitzhardinge St W1 44 A2
Fitzmaurice Pl W1 44 B4
Fitzroy Ct W1 44 C1
Fitzroy Ms W1 44 C1
Fitzroy Sq W1 44 C1
Fitzroy St W1 44 C1
Fives Ct SE11 45 H7
Flaxman Ct W1 44 D3
Fleet St EC4 45 G3
Flitcroft St WC2 44 D2
Floral St WC2 44 E3
Florin Ct EC1 45 J1
Foley St W1 44 C2
Fore St EC2 45 J2
Fortune St EC1 45 J1
Forum Magnum Sq SE1 45 F5
Foster La EC2 45 J2
Foubert's Pl W1 44 C3
Fountain Ct EC4 45 G3
Fountain Sq SW1 44 B7
Fox & Knot St EC1 45 H1
Francis St SW1 44 C7
Frazier St SE1 45 G6
Friars Cl SE1 45 H5
Friar St EC4 45 H3
Friary Ct SW1 44 C5
Friday St EC4 45 J3
Frith St W1 44 D3
Fulwood Pl WC1 45 F2
Furnival St EC4 45 G2
Fynes St SW1 44 D7
G
Gabriel's Wf SE1 45 G4
Gage St WC1 45 E1
Galen Pl WC1 45 E2
Gambia St SE1 45 H5
Ganton St W1 44 C3
Garbutt Pl W1 44 A1
Garden Row SE1 45 H7
Gardners La EC4 45 J3
Garlick Hill EC4 45 J3
Garrick St WC2 44 E3
Garrick Yd WC2 44 E3
Gate Ho Sq SE1 45 J4
Gate St WC2 45 F2
Gaunt St SE1 45 H6
Gayfere St SW1 44 E7
Gaywood Est SE1 45 H7
Gaywood St SE1 45 H7
Gees Ct W1 44 A3
George Ct WC2 45 E4
George Mathers Rd SE11 45 H7
George Yd W1 44 A3
Geraldine St SE11 45 H7
Gerald Ms SW1 44 A7
Gerald Rd SW1 44 A7
Gerrard Pl W1 44 D3
Gerrard St W1 44 D3
Gerridge St SE1 45 G6
Gilbert Pl WC1 44 E2
Gilbert St W1 44 A3

Old Palace Yd SW1 **44** E6
Old Paradise St SE11 **45** F7
Old Pk La W1 **44** A5
Old Pye St SW1 **44** D6
Old Queen St SW1 **44** D6
Old Seacoal La EC4 **45** H2
Old Sq WC2 **45** F2
O'Meara St SE1 **45** J5
Onslow St EC1 **45** G1
Ontario St SE1 **45** H7
Orange St WC2 **44** D4
Orange Yd W1 **44** D3
Orchard St W1 **44** A3
Orde Hall St WC1 **45** F1
Orient St SE11 **45** H7
Ormond Cl WC1 **45** E1
Ormond Ms WC1 **45** E1
Ormond Yd SW1 **44** C4
Osnaburgh St NW1 **44** B1
Ossington Bldgs W1 **44** A1
Oswin St SE11 **45** H7
Outer Circle NW1 **44** A1
Oxendon St SW1 **44** D4
Oxford Circ Av W1 **44** C3
Oxford St W1 **44** C2
Oxo Twr Wf SE1 **45** G4

P

Paddington St W1 **44** A1
Pageantmaster Ct EC4 **45** H3
Page St SW1 **44** D7
Palace Pl SW1 **44** C6
Palace St SW1 **44** C6
Pall Mall SW1 **44** C5
Pall Mall E SW1 **44** D4
Palmer St SW1 **44** D6
Pancras La EC4 **45** J3
Panton St SW1 **44** D4
Panyer All EC4 **45** J3
Paris Gdn SE1 **45** H4
Park Cres W1 **44** B1
Park Cres Ms E W1 **44** B1
Park Cres Ms W W1 **44** B1
Parker Ms WC2 **45** E2
Parker St WC2 **45** E2
Park La W1 **44** A5
Park Pl SW1 **44** C5
Park Sq Ms NW1 **44** B1
Park St SE1 **45** J4
Park St W1 **44** A3
Parliament Sq SW1 **44** E6
Parliament St SW1 **44** E6
Parliament Vw Apts SE1 **45** F7
Passing All EC1 **45** H1
Pastor St SE11 **45** H7
Paternoster Row EC4 **45** J3
Paternoster Sq EC4 **45** H3
Paul's Wk EC4 **45** H3
Peabody Est EC1 **45** J1
Peabody Est SE1 **45** G5
Peabody Est SW1 **44** C7
Peabody Sq SE1 **45** H6
Peabody Trust SE1 **45** J5
Pearman St SE1 **45** G6
Pear Pl SE1 **45** G5
Pearson Sq W1 **44** C2
Pear Tree Ct EC1 **45** G1
Pemberton Row EC4 **45** G2
Pembroke Cl SW1 **44** A6
Penhurst Pl SE1 **45** F7
Pepper St SE1 **45** J5
Percy Ms W1 **44** D2
Percy Pas W1 **44** C2
Percy St W1 **44** D2
Perkin's Rents SW1 **44** D6
Perkins Sq SE1 **45** J4
Perrys Pl W1 **44** D2
Peters Hill EC4 **45** J3
Peter's La EC1 **45** H1
Peter St W1 **44** C3
Petty France SW1 **44** C6
Phipp's Ms SW1 **44** B7
Phoenix St WC2 **44** D3
Piccadilly W1 **44** B5
Piccadilly Arc SW1 **44** C4
Piccadilly Circ W1 **44** D4
Piccadilly Pl W1 **44** C4
Pickering Pl SW1 **44** C5
Pickwick St SE1 **45** J6
Picton Pl W1 **44** A3
Pilgrim St EC4 **45** H3
Pineapple Ct SW1 **44** C6
Pitt's Head Ms W1 **44** A5
Playhouse Yd EC4 **45** H3
Plaza Shop Cen, The W1 **44** C2
Pleydell Ct EC4 **45** G3
Pleydell St EC4 **45** G3
Plough Pl EC4 **45** G2
Plumtree Ct EC4 **45** G2
Pocock St SE1 **45** H5
Poland St W1 **44** C3
Pollen St W1 **44** B3
Polperro Ms SE11 **45** G7
Pontypool Pl SE1 **45** H5
Pooles Bldgs EC1 **45** G1
Poppins Ct EC4 **45** H3
Porter St SE1 **45** J4
Portland Ms W1 **44** C3
Portland Pl W1 **44** B1
Portman Ms S W1 **44** A3
Portman St W1 **44** A3
Portpool La EC1 **45** G1
Portsmouth St WC2 **45** F3
Portugal St WC2 **45** F3
Powis Pl WC1 **45** E1
Pratt Wk SE11 **45** F7
Price's St SE1 **45** H5
Priest Ct EC2 **45** J2
Primrose Hill EC4 **45** G3
Prince's Arc SW1 **44** C4
Princes Pl SW1 **44** C4
Princess St SE1 **45** H7
Princes St W1 **44** B3
Princeton St WC1 **45** F1
Printers Inn Ct EC4 **45** G2
Printer St EC4 **45** G2
Procter St WC1 **45** F2
Providence Ct W1 **44** A3
Prudent Pas EC2 **45** J2
Puddle Dock EC4 **45** H3

Q

Quadrant Arc W1 **44** C4
Quality Ct WC2 **45** G2
Queen Anne Ms W1 **44** B2
Queen Anne's Gate SW1 **44** D6
Queen Anne St W1 **44** B2
Queenhithe EC4 **45** J3
Queen's Head Pas EC4 **45** J2
Queen Sq WC1 **45** E1
Queen Sq Pl WC1 **45** E1
Queen St EC4 **45** J3
Queen St W1 **44** B4
Queen St Pl EC4 **45** J4
Queen's Wk SW1 **44** C5
Queen's Wk, The SE1 **45** F5
Queens Yd WC1 **44** C1
Queen Victoria St EC4 **45** H3
Quilp St SE1 **45** J5

R

Ramillies Pl W1 **44** C3
Ramillies St W1 **44** C3
Rathbone Pl W1 **44** D2
Rathbone St W1 **44** C2
Raymond Bldgs WC1 **45** F1
Ray St EC1 **45** G1
Ray St Br EC1 **45** G1
Redcross Way SE1 **45** J5
Red Lion Ct EC4 **45** G2
Red Lion Sq WC1 **45** F2
Red Lion St WC1 **45** F1
Red Lion Yd W1 **44** A4
Red Pl W1 **44** A3
Reeves Ms W1 **44** A4
Regency Pl SW1 **44** D7
Regency St SW1 **44** D7
Regent Pl W1 **44** C3
Regent Sq SW1 **44** D4
Regent St W1 **44** B2
Remnant St WC2 **45** F2
Renfrew Rd SE11 **45** H7
Rennie St SE1 **45** H4
Rex Pl W1 **44** A4
Richardson's Ms W1 **44** C1
Richbell Pl WC1 **45** F1
Richmond Bldgs W1 **44** D3
Richmond Ms W1 **44** D3
Richmond Ter SW1 **44** E5
Ridgmount Gdns WC1 **44** D1
Ridgmount Pl WC1 **44** D1
Ridgmount St WC1 **44** D1
Riding Ho St W1 **44** C2
Risborough St SE1 **45** H5
Rising Sun Ct EC1 **45** H2
River Ct SE1 **45** H4
Robert Adam St W1 **44** A2
Roberts Ms SW1 **44** A7
Robert St WC2 **45** E4
Rochester Row SW1 **44** C7
Rochester St SW1 **44** D7
Rockingham Est SE1 **45** J7
Rockingham St SE1 **45** J7
Rodney Pl SE17 **45** J7
Rodney Rd SE17 **45** J7
Roger St WC1 **45** F1
Rolls Bldgs EC4 **45** G2
Rolls Pas EC4 **45** G2
Romilly St W1 **44** D3
Romney Ms W1 **44** A1
Romney St SW1 **44** D7
Roscoe St EC1 **45** J1
Rose All SE1 **45** J4
Rose & Crown Ct EC2 **45** J2
Rose & Crown Yd SW1 **44** C4
Rosebery Av EC1 **45** G1
Rosebery Sq EC1 **45** G1
Rose St EC4 **45** H2
Rose St WC2 **44** E3
Rotary St SE1 **45** H6
Rotherham Wk SE1 **45** H5
Rotten Row SW1 **44** A5
Roupell St SE1 **45** G5
Royal Arc W1 **44** C4
Royal Ms, The SW1 **44** B6
Royal Opera Arc SW1 **44** D4
Royal St SE1 **45** F6
Royalty Ms W1 **44** D3
Rugby St WC1 **45** F1
Rupert Ct W1 **44** D3
Rupert St W1 **44** D3
Rushworth St SE1 **45** H5
Russell Ct SW1 **44** C5
Russell Sq WC1 **44** E1
Russell St WC2 **45** E3
Russia Row EC2 **45** J3
Rutherford St SW1 **44** D7
Rutland Pl EC1 **45** J1
Ryder Ct SW1 **44** C4
Ryder St SW1 **44** C4
Ryder Yd SW1 **44** C4

S

Sackville St W1 **44** C4
Saddle Yd W1 **44** B4
Saffron Hill EC1 **45** G1
Saffron St EC1 **45** G1
Sail St SE11 **45** F7
St. Albans Ct EC2 **45** J2
St. Albans St SW1 **44** D4
St. Alphage Gdn EC2 **45** J2
St. Andrew's Hill EC4 **45** H3
St. Andrew St EC4 **45** G2
St. Anne's Ct W1 **44** D3
St. Ann's La SW1 **44** D6
St. Ann's St SW1 **44** D6
St. Anselm's Pl W1 **44** B3
St. Brides Av EC4 **45** H3
St. Bride St EC4 **45** H2
St. Christopher's Pl W1 **44** A2
St. Clement's La WC2 **45** F3
St. Cross St EC1 **45** G1
St. Ermin's Hill SW1 **44** D6
St. Georges Circ SE1 **45** H6
St. Georges Ct EC4 **45** H2
St. Georges Ms SE1 **45** G6
St. Georges Rd SE1 **45** G6
St. George St W1 **44** B3
St. Giles High St WC2 **44** D2
St. Giles Pas WC2 **44** D3
St. James's SW1 **44** D5
St. James's Ct SW1 **44** C6
St. James's Mkt SW1 **44** D4
St. James's Palace SW1 **44** C5
St. James's Pk SW1 **44** D5
St. James's Pl SW1 **44** C5
St. James's Sq SW1 **44** C4
St. James's St SW1 **44** C4
St. John's La EC1 **45** H1
St. John's Path EC1 **45** H1
St. John's Pl EC1 **45** H1
St. John's Sq EC1 **45** H1
St. John St EC1 **45** H1
St. Margaret's Ct SE1 **45** J5
St. Margaret's St SW1 **44** E6
St. Martin's La WC2 **44** E3
St. Martin's-le-Grand EC1 **45** J2
St. Martin's Ms WC2 **44** E4
St. Martin's Pl WC2 **44** E4
St. Martin's St WC2 **44** D4
St. Mary's Gdns SE11 **45** G7
St. Mary's Wk SE11 **45** G7
St. Matthew St SW1 **44** D7
St. Olaves Gdns SE11 **45** G7
St. Paul's Chyd EC4 **45** H3
St. Vincent St W1 **44** A2
Salisbury Ct EC4 **45** H3
Salisbury Sq EC4 **45** G3
Sanctuary, The SW1 **44** D6
Sanctuary St SE1 **45** J6
Sandell St SE1 **45** G5
Sandland St WC1 **45** F2
Saperton Wk SE11 **45** F7
Sardinia St WC2 **45** F3
Savile Row W1 **44** C3
Savoy Bldgs WC2 **45** F4
Savoy Ct WC2 **45** E4
Savoy Hill WC2 **45** F4
Savoy Pl WC2 **45** E4
Savoy Row WC2 **45** F3
Savoy St WC2 **45** F3
Savoy Way WC2 **45** F4
Sawyer St SE1 **45** J5
Scala St W1 **44** C1
Scoresby St SE1 **45** H5
Scotland Pl SW1 **44** E4
Scovell Cres SE1 **45** J6
Scovell Rd SE1 **45** J6
Secker St SE1 **45** G5
Sedding St SW1 **44** A7
Sedley Pl W1 **44** B3
Sekforde St EC1 **45** H1
Serjeants Inn EC4 **45** G3
Serle St WC2 **45** F2
Sermon La EC4 **45** J3
Seymour Ms W1 **44** A2
Shaftesbury Av W1 **44** D3
Shaftesbury Av WC2 **44** D3
Shakespeare Twr EC2 **45** J1
Shavers Pl SW1 **44** D4
Sheffield St WC2 **45** F3
Shelton St WC2 **44** E3
Shepherd Mkt W1 **44** B4
Shepherd's Pl W1 **44** A3
Shepherd St W1 **44** B5
Sheraton St W1 **44** D3
Sherlock Ms W1 **44** A1
Sherwood St W1 **44** C3
Shoe La EC4 **45** G2
Shorts Gdns WC2 **44** E3
Short St SE1 **45** G5
Shropshire Pl WC1 **44** C1
Sicilian Av WC1 **45** E2
Sidford Pl SE1 **45** F7
Silex St SE1 **45** H6
Silk St EC2 **45** J1
Silver Pl W1 **44** C3
Silvester St SE1 **45** J6
Skinners La EC4 **45** J3
Slingsby Pl WC2 **44** E3
Smart's Pl WC2 **45** E2
Smeaton Ct SE1 **45** J7
Smithfield St EC1 **45** H2
Smith's Ct W1 **44** C3
Smith Sq SW1 **44** E7
Smokehouse Yd EC1 **45** H1
Snow Hill EC1 **45** H2
Snow Hill Ct EC1 **45** H2
Soho W1 **44** C3
Soho Sq W1 **44** D2
Soho St W1 **44** D2
Southampton Bldgs WC2 **45** G2
Southampton Pl WC1 **45** E2
Southampton Row WC1 **45** E1
Southampton St WC2 **45** E3
South Audley St W1 **44** A4
South Cres WC1 **44** D2
South Eaton Pl SW1 **44** A7
South Molton La W1 **44** B3
South Molton St W1 **44** B3
South Sq WC1 **45** G2
South St W1 **44** A4
Southwark SE1 **45** H5
Southwark Br EC4 **45** J4
Southwark Br SE1 **45** J4
Southwark Br Rd SE1 **45** H6
Southwark St SE1 **45** H4
Spanish Pl W1 **44** A2
Spenser St SW1 **44** C6
Spring Gdns SW1 **44** D4
Spur Rd SE1 **45** G5
Spur Rd SW1 **44** C6
Stable Yd SW1 **44** C5
Stable Yd Rd SW1 **44** C5
Stacey St WC2 **44** D3
Stafford Pl SW1 **44** C6
Stafford St W1 **44** C4
Staining La EC2 **45** J2
Stamford St SE1 **45** G5
Stangate SE1 **45** F6
Stanhope Gate W1 **44** A4
Stanhope Row W1 **44** B5
Staple Inn WC1 **45** G2
Staple Inn Bldgs WC1 **45** G2
Star Yd WC2 **45** G2
Station App SE1 **45** F5
Stedham Pl WC1 **44** E2
Stephen Ms W1 **44** D2
Stephen St W1 **44** D2
Stew La EC4 **45** J3
Stillington St SW1 **44** C7
Stone Bldgs WC2 **45** F2
Stonecutter St EC4 **45** H2
Stones End St SE1 **45** J6
Store St WC1 **44** D2
Storey's Gate SW1 **44** D6
Strand WC2 **44** E4
Strand WC2 **44** E4
Strand La WC2 **45** F3
Stratford Pl W1 **44** B3
Stratton St W1 **44** B4
Streatham St WC1 **44** D2
Strutton Grd SW1 **44** D6
Stukeley St WC1 **45** E2
Stukeley St WC2 **45** E2
Sturge St SE1 **45** J5
Sudrey St SE1 **45** J6
Suffolk Pl SW1 **44** D4
Suffolk St SW1 **44** D4
Sullivan Rd SE11 **45** G7
Summers St EC1 **45** G1
Sumner St SE1 **45** H4
Surrey Row SE1 **45** H5
Surrey St WC2 **45** F3
Sutton La EC1 **45** H1
Sutton Row W1 **44** D2
Sutton's Way EC1 **45** J1
Sutton Wk SE1 **45** F5
Swallow Pl W1 **44** B3
Swallow St W1 **44** C4
Swan St SE1 **45** J6
Swiss Ct W1 **44** D4
Sycamore St EC1 **45** J1

T

Tachbrook Ms SW1 **44** C7
Tallis St EC4 **45** G3
Tanswell Est SE1 **45** G6
Tanswell St SE1 **45** G6
Tarn St SE1 **45** J7
Tavistock St WC2 **45** E3
Telford Ho SE1 **45** J7
Temple Av EC4 **45** G3
Temple La EC4 **45** G3
Temple Pl WC2 **45** F3
Temple W Ms SE11 **45** H7
Tenison Ct W1 **44** C3
Tenison Way SE1 **45** G5
Tenterden St W1 **44** B3
Terminus Pl SW1 **44** B7
Thavies Inn EC1 **45** G2
Thayer St W1 **44** A2
Theed St SE1 **45** G5
Theobald's Rd WC1 **45** F1
Thirleby Rd SW1 **44** C7
Thomas Doyle St SE1 **45** H6
Thorney St SW1 **44** E7
Thornhaugh Ms WC1 **44** D1
Thornhaugh St WC1 **44** D1
Thrale St SE1 **45** J5
Three Barrels Wk EC4 **45** J4
Three Cups Yd WC1 **45** F2
Three Kings Yd W1 **44** B3
Tilney St W1 **44** A4
Tiverton St SE1 **45** J7
Took's Ct EC4 **45** G2
Torrington Pl WC1 **44** C1
Torrington Sq WC1 **44** D1
Tothill St SW1 **44** D6
Tottenham Ct Rd W1 **44** C1
Tottenham Ms W1 **44** C1
Tottenham St W1 **44** C2
Toulmin St SE1 **45** J6
Tower Ct WC2 **44** E3
Tower Royal EC4 **45** J3
Tower St WC2 **44** D3
Trafalgar Sq SW1 **44** D4
Trafalgar Sq WC2 **44** D4
Trebeck St W1 **44** B4
Treveris St SE1 **45** H5
Trig La EC4 **45** J3
Trinity Ch Sq SE1 **45** J6
Trinity St SE1 **45** J6
Trio Pl SE1 **45** J6
Trump St EC2 **45** J3
Trundle St SE1 **45** J5
Tudor St EC4 **45** G3
Tufton St SW1 **44** D6
Turk's Head Yd EC1 **45** H1
Turnagain La EC4 **45** H2
Turnmill St EC1 **45** G1
Tweezer's All WC2 **45** G3
Twyford Pl WC2 **45** F2
Tyler's Ct W1 **44** D3

U

Ufford St SE1 **45** G5
Ulster Pl NW1 **44** B1
Ulster Ter NW1 **44** B1
Union Jack Club SE1 **45** G5
Union St SE1 **45** H5
University St WC1 **44** C1
Upper Belgrave St SW1 **44** A6
Upper Brook St W1 **44** A4
Upper Grosvenor St W1 **44** A4
Upper Grd SE1 **45** G4
Upper James St W1 **44** C3
Upper John St W1 **44** C3
Upper Marsh SE1 **45** F6
Upper St. Martin's La WC2 **44** E3
Upper Tachbrook St SW1 **44** C7
Upper Thames St EC4 **45** H3
Upper Wimpole St W1 **44** B1

V

Valentine Pl SE1 **45** H5
Valentine Row SE1 **45** H6
Vandon Pas SW1 **44** C6
Vandon St SW1 **44** C6
Vane St SW1 **44** C7
Vauxhall Br Rd SW1 **44** C7
Vere St W1 **44** B3
Vernon Pl WC1 **45** E2
Verulam Bldgs WC1 **45** F1
Verulam St WC1 **45** G1
Vesage Ct EC1 **45** G2
Victoria Embk EC4 **45** F4
Victoria Embk SW1 **45** E5
Victoria Embk WC2 **45** F4
Victoria Pl SW1 **44** B7
Victoria Sq SW1 **44** B6
Victoria Sta SW1 **44** B7
Victoria St SW1 **44** C7
Vigo St W1 **44** C4
Villiers St WC2 **44** E4
Vincent Sq SW1 **44** C7
Vincent St SW1 **44** D7
Vine Hill EC1 **45** G1
Vine St W1 **44** C4
Vine St Br EC1 **45** G1
Vine Yd SE1 **45** J5
Vintners Ct EC4 **45** J3
Virgil St SE1 **45** F6
Viscount St EC1 **45** J1

W

Waithman St EC4 **45** H3
Walcot Sq SE11 **45** G7
Walcott St SW1 **44** C7
Walkers Ct W1 **44** D3
Wallis All SE1 **45** J5
Wallside EC2 **45** J2
Walnut Tree Wk SE11 **45** G7
Walworth Rd SE1 **45** J7
Walworth Rd SE17 **45** J7
Wardens Gro SE1 **45** J5
Wardour Ms W1 **44** C3
Wardour St W1 **44** D3
Wardrobe Ter EC4 **45** H3
Warner St EC1 **45** G1
Warner Yd EC1 **45** G1
Warren Ms W1 **44** C1
Warren St W1 **44** B1
Warwick Ct WC1 **45** F2
Warwick Ho St SW1 **44** D4
Warwick La EC4 **45** H3
Warwick Pas EC4 **45** H2
Warwick Row SW1 **44** B6
Warwick Sq EC4 **45** H2
Warwick St W1 **44** C3
Warwick Yd EC1 **45** J1
Watergate EC4 **45** H3
Watergate Wk WC2 **45** E4
Waterhouse Sq EC1 **45** G2
Waterloo Br SE1 **45** F4
Waterloo Br WC2 **45** F4
Waterloo Pl SW1 **44** D4
Waterloo Rd SE1 **45** G5
Waterloo Sta SE1 **45** G5
Water St WC2 **45** F3
Watling Ct EC4 **45** J3
Watling St EC4 **45** J3
Waverton St W1 **44** A4
Webber Row SE1 **45** G6
Webber St SE1 **45** G5
Wedgwood Ho SE11 **45** G7
Wedgwood Ms W1 **44** D3
Weighhouse St W1 **44** A3
Welbeck St W1 **44** B2
Welbeck Way W1 **44** B2
Well Ct EC4 **45** J3
Weller St SE1 **45** J5
Wellington St WC2 **45** E3
Wells Ms W1 **44** C2
Wells St W1 **44** C2
Wesley St W1 **44** A2
West Cen St WC1 **44** E2
West Eaton Pl SW1 **44** A7
West Eaton Pl Ms SW1 **44** A7
West Halkin St SW1 **44** A6
West Harding St EC4 **45** G2
Westminster SW1 **44** C6
Westminster Br SE1 **45** E6
Westminster Br SW1 **45** E6
Westminster Br Rd SE1 **45** F6
Westminster Gdns SW1 **44** E7
Westmoreland St W1 **44** A2
West One Shop Cen W1 **44** A3

Manchester street index

Elverdon Cl **46** D7
Empire St **46** E1
Empress St **46** A7
Encombe Pl **46** B3
Epping St **46** E6
Epsley Cl **47** E7
Epworth St **47** H4
Errington Dr **46** B1
Erskine St **46** C7
Essex St **46** E4
Essex Way **46** C7
Etruria Cl **47** J7
Evans St **46** D2
Everard St **46** B5
Every St **47** H4
Exford Cl **47** H2
Eyre St **47** E7

F

Fairbrother St **46** A6
Fairfield St **47** G5
Fair St **47** G4
Falkland Av **47** J1
Faraday St **47** F3
Farnborough Rd **47** H1
Farrell St **46** C1
Farwood Cl **46** B7
Faulkner St **47** E4
Federation St **47** E2
Fennel St **46** E2
Fenn St **46** C7
Fenwick St **47** E6
Ferdinan St **47** H1
Fernbrook Cl **47** J7
Fernie St **47** E1
Fernleigh Dr **46** B7
Fern St **47** E1
Ferry St **47** J4
Filby Wk **47** J1
Firbeck Dr **47** H2
Firefly Cl **46** B3
Fire Sta Sq **46** A3
Fir St **47** H1
Fitzwilliam St **46** C1
Flatley Cl **47** E7
Flora Dr **46** C1
Ford St **47** H6
Ford St (Salford) **46** C3
Foundry La **47** F3
Fountain St **47** E4
Four Yards **46** E4
Frances St **47** G6
Francis St **46** D1
Frederick St **46** C3
Freeman Sq **47** E7
Freya Gro **46** A5
Frobisher Cl **47** J7
Frost St **47** J3
Fulmer Dr **47** H2

G

Gaitskell Cl **47** J4
Galgate Cl **46** C6
Garden La **46** D3
Garden St **46** D2
Garden Wall Cl **46** A5
Garforth Av **47** H2
Gartside St **46** D4
Garwood St **46** D6
Gateaton St **46** E3
Gaythorn St **46** B3
George Leigh St **47** F3
George St **47** E4
Georgette Dr **46** D2
Gibbs St **46** B3
Gibson Pl **47** E1
Girton St **46** C1
Glasshouse St **47** G2
Gleden St **47** J2
Glenbarry Cl **47** G7
Glenbarry St **47** J5
Gloucester St **46** E5
Gloucester St (Salford) **46** A5
Goadsby St **47** F2
Gold St **47** F4
Gordon St **46** C1
Gore St **47** F4
Gore St (Salford) **46** C3
Gorton St **46** D2
Goulden St **47** F2
Gould St **47** F1
Grafton St **47** G7
Granby Row **47** F5
Granshaw St **47** J2
Gratrix Av **46** A6
Gravell La **46** D2
Grear Ducie St **46** E2
Great Ancoats St **47** F3
Great Bridgewater St **46** D5
Great Clowes St **46** C1
Great Ducie St **46** D1
Great George St **46** B3
Great Jackson St **46** C5
Great John St **46** C4
Great
Marlborough St **47** E5
Greek St **47** F6
Greengate W **46** C2
Grenham Av **46** B6
Griffiths Cl **46** C1
Groom St **47** F6
Grosvenor Gdns **46** C1
Grosvenor Sq **46** C1
Grosvenor St **47** F6
Guide Post Sq **47** H7
Gunson St **47** H2
Gun St **47** G3
Gurner Av **46** A6
Gurney St **47** J3

H

Hackleton Cl **47** J3
Hadfield St **46** B7
Half St **46** D2
Hall St **46** E4
Halmore Rd **47** H2
Halsbury Cl **47** J7
Halston St **46** D7
Hamerton Rd **47** G1
Hamilton Gro **46** B7
Hamilton St **46** B7
Hampson St **47** H1
Hamsell Rd **47** G6
Handsworth St **47** J5
Hanging Ditch **46** E3
Hanover St **47** E2
Hanworth Cl **47** G6
Harding St **47** J4
Hardman Sq **46** D4
Hardman St **46** D4
Hardshaw Cl **47** G6
Harehill Cl **47** G5
Hare St **47** F3
Hargreave's St **47** F1
Harkness St **47** H6
Harold St **46** B7
Harriett St **47** H2
Harrison St **47** H4
Harrison St (Salford) **46** C1
Harris St **46** D1
Harry Hall Gdns **46** B1
Harter St **47** E4
Hartfield Cl **47** G6
Hart St **47** F4
Hatter St **47** F2
Hatton Av **46** B1
Haverlock Dr **46** B1
Haymarket Cl **47** H7
Heath Av **46** B1
Helga St **47** H1
Hellidon Cl **47** H6
Helmet St **47** H5
Henry St **47** G3
Henry St
(Old Trafford) **46** A7
Hewitt St **46** D5
Heyrod St **47** G4
Higher Ardwick **47** H6
Higher Cambridge St **47** E6
Higher Chatham St **47** E6
Higher Ormond St **47** F6
Higher Oswald St **47** F2
Higher York St **47** F6
High St **47** E3
Hillcourt St **47** F6
Hillfield Cl **47** J7
Hillkirk St **47** J3
Hilton St **47** F3
Hinton St **47** G2
Hodson St **46** C2
Holdgate Cl **46** D7
Holkham Cl **47** H3
Holland St **47** H2
Holly Bk Cl **46** B6
Holly St **47** J4
Holt Town **47** J3
Honey St **47** F1
Hood St **47** G3
Hooper St **47** J5
Hope St **47** F4
Hope St (Salford) **46** A3
Hornby St **46** D1
Hornchurch St **46** C7
Horne Dr **47** H3
Houldsworth St **47** F3
Hoyle St **47** H5
Huddart Cl **46** A5
Hughes St **47** J5
Hull Sq **46** B2
Hulme **46** D7
Hulme Ct **46** C6
Hulme Hall Rd **46** B5
Hulme Pl **46** B3
Hulme St **46** D6
Hulme St (Salford) **46** B3
Humberstone Av **46** D6
Hunmanby Av **46** D6
Hunt's Bk **46** E2
Hyde Gro **47** G7
Hyde Pl **47** H7
Hyde Rd **47** H6
Hyde St **46** C7

I

Inchley Rd **47** F6
Instow Cl **47** H7
Ionas St **46** C1
Irk St **47** F1
Iron St **47** J2
Irwell Pl **46** A3
Irwell St **46** D1
Irwell St (Salford) **46** C3
Islington Way **46** B3

J

Jackson Cres **46** C6
Jackson's Row **46** D4
James Henry Av **46** A4
James St **47** J1
James St (Salford) **46** B3
Jenkinson St **47** F6
Jersey St **47** G3
Jerusalem Pl **46** D4
Jessamine Av **46** B1
Jessel Cl **47** G6
Joddrell St **46** D4
John Clynes Av **47** H1
John Dalton St **46** D3
Johnson Sq **47** H1
Johnson St **46** B7
Johnson St (Salford) **46** C3
John St **47** F3
John St
(Lower Broughton) **46** C1
John St (Salford) **46** D2
Joiner St **47** F3
Jordan St **46** D5
Joynson Av **46** B1
Julia St **46** D1
Jury St **46** D1
Justin Cl **47** F6
Jutland St **47** G4

K

Kale St **47** G6
Kays Gdns **46** C3
Keele Wk **47** H1
Kelling Wk **46** C6
Kelvin St **47** F3
Kennedy St **46** E4
Kenwright St **47** F2
Kincardine Rd **47** F6
King Edward St **46** A5
Kingham Dr **47** H2
Kingsfold Av **47** H1
Kingsland Cl **47** H1
King St **46** D3
King St (Salford) **46** D2
King St W **46** D3
Kirkgate Cl **47** H2
Kirkhaven Sq **47** J1
Kirkstall Sq **47** G7
Kirkwood Dr **47** H1

L

Lackford Dr **47** H1
Lamb La **46** C3
Lamport Cl **47** F5
Lanchester St **47** J2
Landos Rd **47** H2
Langholme Cl **46** C6
Langport Av **47** J7
Langston St **46** D1
Lanstead Dr **47** J2
Lauderdale Cres **47** H7
Laystall St **47** G3
Layton St **47** J2
Leaf St **46** D6
Leak St **46** B6
Ledburn Ct **46** C6
Left Bk **46** C4
Lena St **47** F4
Leslie Hough Way **46** A1
Lever St **47** F3
Lewis St **47** J1
Leycroft St **47** G4
Lidbrook Wk **47** J7
Lime Bk St **47** J5
Lime Gro **47** F7
Limekiln La **47** H5
Linby St **46** C6
Lind St **47** J3
Linen Ct **46** B2
Linsley St **46** D2
Linton Cl **47** H4
Litcham Cl **47** F5
Little Ancoats St **47** F3
Little Holme St **47** J3
Little John St **46** C4
Little Lever St **47** F3
Little Nelson St **47** F2
Little Peter St **46** D5
Little Pit St **47** G3
Little Quay St **46** D4
Liverpool Rd **46** C4
Livesey St **47** G1
Lizard St **47** F3
Lloyd St **46** D4
Lloyd St N **47** F7
Lockett St **46** D1
Lockton Cl **47** G5
Lomax St **47** G3
London Rd **47** F4
Longacre St **47** G4
Long Millgate **46** E2
Longworth St **46** D4
Loom St **47** G3
Lordsmead St **46** C6
Lord St **46** E1
Lostock St **47** H2
Lowcock St **46** C1
Lower Byrom St **46** C4
Lower Chatham St **47** E6
Lower Mosley St **46** D5
Lower Moss La **46** C6
Lower Ormond St **47** E5
Lower Vickers St **47** J2
Lowndes Wk **47** G6
Loxford St **46** E6
Lucy St **46** B7
Ludgate Hill **47** F2
Ludgate St **47** F2
Luna street **47** F3
Lund St **46** A7
Lupton St **46** C3
Lyceum Pl **47** E6

M

Maidford Cl **47** J3
Major St **47** E4
Makin St **47** E5
Mallard St **47** E5
Mallow St **46** C6
Malta St **47** H3
Malt St **46** B6
Malvern St **46** B7
Manchester St **46** A7
Mancunian Way **46** C6
Mangle St Street **47** F3
Manor St **47** G5
Manson Av **46** B6
Maplin Cl **47** G6
Marble St **47** E3
Marcer Rd **47** H2
Marchmont Cl **47** H7
Market St **46** E3
Markfield Av **47** J7
Markham Cl **47** J4
Marple St **46** C7
Marsden St **46** E3
Marshall St **47** F2
Marshall St (Ardwick) **47** H6
Marsworth Dr **47** H3
Mary France St **46** C6
Mary St **46** D1
Mason St **47** F2
Mason St (Salford) **46** C3
Massey St **46** B3
Mayan Av **46** B2
Mayes St **47** E2
Mayo St **47** H5
Mays St **47** F2
Meadow Rd **46** B1
Medlock St **46** D5
Melbourne St **46** C6
Mellor St **47** H2
Melville St **46** C3
Merrill St **47** H3
Middlewood St **46** B4
Midland St **47** J5
Miles Platting **47** J1
Milk St **47** E3
Millbank St **47** G4
Millbeck St **47** E6
Miller St **47** E2
Mill Grn St **47** H5
Millhall Cl **46** C7
Millhead Av **47** J2
Millow St **47** E2
Milnrow Cl **47** F5
Milton St **46** C1
Mincing St **47** F2
Minshull St **47** F4
Minshull St S **47** F4
Mistletoe Grn **46** C2
Moorhead St **47** G2
Morbourne Cl **47** J7
Mosley St **47** E4
Mosscott Wk **47** G5
Mosshall Cl **46** C7
Moulton St **46** D1
Mouncey St **47** E5
Mount Carmel Cres **46** A5
Mount St **46** E4
Mount St (Salford) **46** C2
Mozart Cl **47** H2
Mullberry St **46** D4
Munday St **47** H3
Munster St **47** E2
Murrey St **47** G3
Museum St **46** E4
Muslin St **46** B4
Myrtle Pl **46** A1

N

Nancy St **46** B6
Nansen St **47** J5
Naples St **47** F2
Nash St **46** C7
Nathan Dr **46** C2
Naval St **47** G3
Naylor St **47** H1
Neild St **47** G5
Neill St **46** C1
Nelson St **47** J1
Nether St **47** G5
New Allen St **47** G2
Newbeck St **47** F2
New Br St **46** D2
Newcastle St **46** E6
New Cath St **46** E3
New Century Park **47** E2
Newcombe St **46** E1
New Elm St **46** C4
New Gartside St **46** D4
New Islington **47** H3
New Mkt **46** E3
New Mkt St **46** E3
New Mt St **47** F2
New Quay St **46** C4
Newton St **47** F3
New Union St **47** G3
New Vine St **46** D6
New Wakefield St **47** E5
New Welcome St **46** D6
New Windsor **46** A3
New York St **47** E4
Nicholas St **47** E4
Nine Acre Dr **46** A6
Niven St **47** G5
North Bailey St **46** C3
Northdown Av **46** B6
North George St **46** B2
North Hill St **46** C2
North Phoebe St **46** A4
North Star Dr **46** B3
Northumberland Cl **46** A7
Northumberland
Cres **46** A7
North Western St **47** G5
North W Services Rd **46** D3
Norton St **46** D2
Norway St **47** J4
Nuneaton Dr **47** H1
Nuttall St **46** A7

O

Oakford Av **47** G1
Oak St **47** F3
Old Bk St **46** E3
Old Birley St **46** D7
Oldbury Cl **47** H2
Old Elm St **47** G6
Oldfield Rd **46** A5
Oldham Rd **47** F3
Oldham St **47** F3
Old Medlock St **46** C4
Old Mill St **47** G3
Old Mt St **47** F2
Old Trafford **46** A7
Old York St **46** C6
Oliver St **47** F7
Ordsall Dr **46** A6
Ordsall La **46** A5
Oregon Cl **47** G6
Orion Pl **46** B1
Ormsgill St **46** D7
Orsett Cl **47** H1
Osborne St **47** G1
Oswald St **47** E2
Oswald St (Ancoats) **47** H4
Overbridge Rd **46** D1
Oxford Rd **47** E5
Oxford St **46** E4

P

Paddock St **47** G5
Palfrey Pl **47** H6
Pall Mall **46** E4
Palmerston St **47** H4
Parish Vw **46** A4
Parker St **47** F3
Park Pl **47** E1
Park St **46** E1
Park St (Salford) **46** B3
Parsonage **46** D3
Parsonage La **46** D3
Parsonage Way **46** A5
Paton St **47** F4
Pattishall Cl **47** J4
Peak St **47** G3
Peary St **47** G1
Peel Mt **46** A1
Pegasus Sq **46** B1
Pembroke Cl **47** H7
Pencroft Way **47** F7
Penfield Cl **47** F5
Percy Dr **46** A6
Percy St **46** C7
Peru St **46** B2
Peter St **46** D4
Phoenix St **47** E3
Phoenix Way **46** D7
Piccadilly **47** F3
Pickford St **47** G3
Picton Cl **46** C2
Picton St **46** C1
Piercy Av **46** B1
Piercy St **47** H3
Pigeon St **47** G3
Pimblett St **46** E1
Pine St **47** E4
Pin Mill Brow **47** H5
Pittbrook St **47** J5
Plymouth Gro **47** G7
Plymouth Vw **47** G7
Pochin St **47** J1
Poland St **47** G2
Polebrook Av **47** H7
Police St **46** D3
Pollard St **47** H4
Pollard St E **47** H3
Polygon Av **47** H7
Polygon St **47** G6
Pomona Strand **46** A6
Poplar St **47** J5
Poplin Dr **46** D2
Portland St **47** E5
Portsmouth St **47** G7
Port St **47** F3
Portugal St **47** G2
Portugal St E **47** G4
Postal St **47** G3
Postbridge Cl **47** H7
Potato Wf **46** C5
Poynton St **46** E6
Price St **47** J3
Primrose St **47** G2
Prince's Br **46** C4
Princess Rd **46** D6
Princess St **46** E4
Princess St
(Cornbrook) **46** B6
Pritchard St **47** F5
Providence St **47** H4
Pryme St **46** C5
Purslow Cl **47** J3

Q

Quay St **46** C4
Quay St (Salford) **46** D3
Queen St **46** D4
Queen St (Salford) **46** D2
Quenby St **46** C6
Quendon Av **46** C1

R

Rachel St **47** H5
Radium St **47** G2
Ralli Cts **46** C3
Randerson St **47** G5
Rankin Cl **46** D7
Raven St **47** H5
Reather Wk **47** H1
Red Bk **47** E2
Redfern St **47** E2
Redhill St **47** G3
Red Lion St **47** F3
Regent Sq **46** A5
Reilly St **46** D6
Reservoir St **46** D2
Reyner St **47** E4
Rial Pl **47** E7
Ribston St **46** C7
Rice St **46** C5
Richmond St **47** F4
Richmond St
(Salford) **46** C2
Ridgefield **46** D3
Ridgeway St E **47** H3
Ridgway St **47** H3
Riga St **47** F2
Rigel Pl **46** B1
Rigel St **47** H2
Rimworth Dr **47** H1
Ringstead Dr **47** G1
Ripley Cl **47** H4
River Pl **46** D5
Riverside **46** B2
River St **46** D6
River St (Ardwick) **47** H5
Robert St **46** E1
Roby St **47** F4
Rochdale Rd **47** F2

Tourist Information Centre: 23 Union Street
Tel: 01224 269180

Albert Quay	C3	Hutcheon Street	B2
Albert Street	B2	Justice Mill Lane	B3
Albury Road	B3	King's Crescent	C1
Albyn Place	A3	King Street	C1
Argyll Place	A2	Langstane Place	B3
Ashgrove Road	A1	Leadside Road	B2
Ashgrove Road West	A1	Leslie Terrace	B1
Ash-hill Drive	A1	Links Road	C2
Ashley Road	A3	Linksfield Road	C1
Back Hilton Road	A1	Loch Street	B2
Baker Street	B2	Maberly Street	B2
Beach Boulevard	C2	Market Street	C3
Bedford Place	B1	Menzies Road	C3
Bedford Road	B1	Merkland Road East	C1
Beechgrove Terrace	A2	Mid Stocket Road	A2
Belgrave Terrace	A2	Mile-end Avenue	A2
Berryden Road	B1	Miller Street	C2
Blaikie's Quay	C3	Mount Street	B2
Bon-Accord Street	B3	Nelson Street	C2
Bonnymuir Place	A2	North Esplanade East	C3
Bridge Street	B2	North Esplanade West	C3
Brighton Place	A3	Orchard Street	C1
Cairncry Road	A1	Osborne Place	A3
Canal Road	B1	Palmerston Road	C3
Carden Place	A3	Park Road	C1
Carlton Place	A3	Park Street	C2
Cattofield Place	A1	Pittodrie Place	C1
Causewayend	B1	Pittodrie Street	C1
Chapel Street	B2	Powis Place	B1
Claremont Street	A3	Powis Terrace	B1
Clifton Road	A1	Queens Road	A3
College Bounds	B1	Queens Terrace	A3
College Street	C3	Regent Quay	C2
Commerce Street	C2	Rosehill Crescent	A1
Commercial Quay	C3	Rosehill Drive	A1
Constitution Street	C2	Rosemount Place	A2
Cornhill Drive	A1	Rose Street	B2
Cornhill Road	A1	Rubislaw Terrace	B3
Cornhill Terrace	A1	St. Swithin Street	A3
Cotton Street	C2	Schoolhill	B2
Cromwell Road	A3	Seaforth Road	C1
Desswood Place	A3	Sinclair Road	C3
Devonshire Road	A3	Skene Square	B2
Elmbank Terrace	B1	Skene Street	B2
Esslemont Avenue	B2	South Crown Street	B3
Ferryhill Road	B3	South Esplanade West	C3
Fonthill Road	B3	Spital	C1
Forest Road	A3	Springbank Terrace	B3
Forest Avenue	A3	Spring Gardens	B2
Fountainhall Road	A2	Stanley Street	A3
Froghall Terrace	B1	Sunnybank Road	B1
Gallowgate	C2	Sunnyside Road	B1
George Street	B1	Union Glen	B3
Gillespie Crescent	A1	Union Grove	A3
Gladstone Place	A3	Union Street	B2
Golf Road	C1	Urquhart Road	C2
Gordondale Road	A2	Victoria Bridge	C3
Great Southern Road	B3	Victoria Road	C3
Great Western Road	A3	Walker Road	C3
Guild Street	C3	Waterloo Quay	C2
Hamilton Place	A2	Waverley Place	B3
Hardgate	B3	Well Place	C3
Hilton Drive	A1	Westburn Drive	A1
Hilton Place	A1	Westburn Road	A2
Hilton Street	A1	West North Street	C2
Holburn Road	B3	Whitehall Place	A2
Holburn Street	B3	Whitehall Road	A2
Holland Street	B1	Willowbank Road	B3

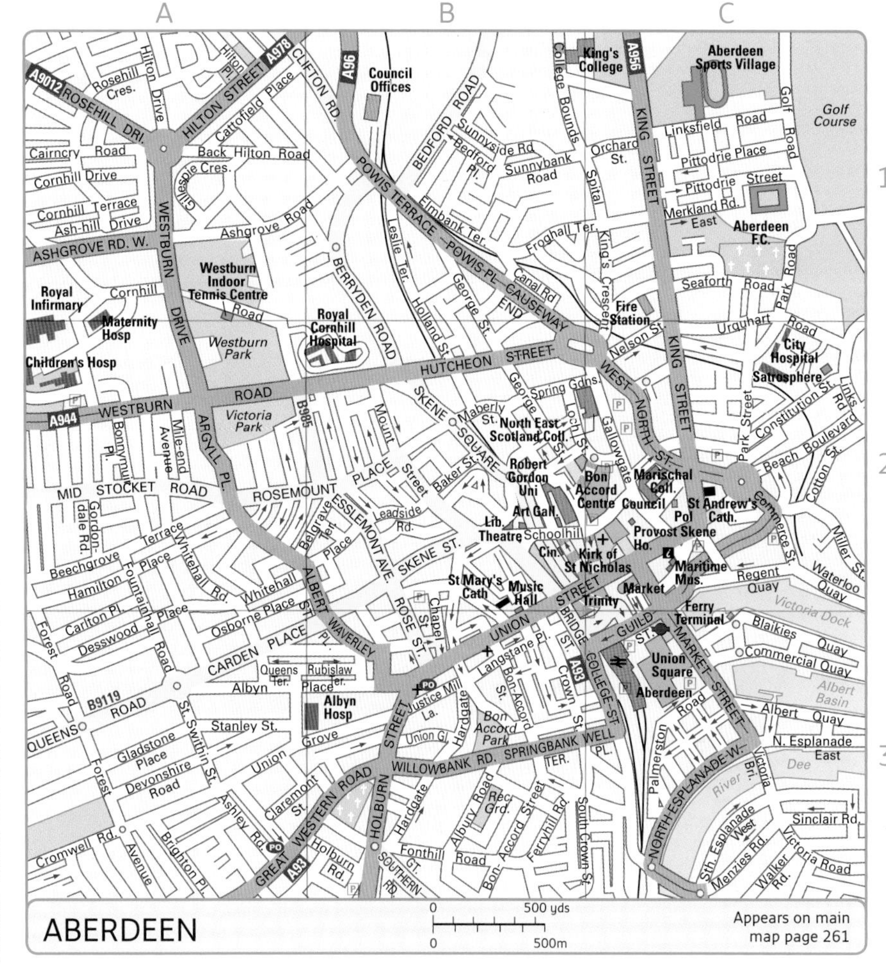

ABERDEEN

0   500 yds
0   500m

Appears on main
map page 261

Tourist Information Centre: 9 Donegall Square North
Tel: 028 9024 6609

Academy Street	A1	Millfield	A2
Adelaide Street	A3	Montgomery Street	B2
Albert Bridge	C3	Mount Pottinger Link	C2
Albert Bridge Road	C3	Nelson Street	B1
Albert Square	B2	North Queen Street	A1
Alfred Street	A3	North Street	A2
Amelia Street	A3	Old Channel Road	C1
Ann Street	B2	Ormeau Avenue	A3
Arran Street	C3	Oxford Street	B2
Arthur Street	A2	Queen Elizabeth Bridge	B2
Bedford Street	A3	Queen Street	B1
Berry Street	A2	Queen's Bridge	B2
Bridge End	C2	Queen's Quay	B2
Bridge Street	A2	Queen's Road	C1
Bruce Street	A3	Queen's Square	B2
Brunswick Street	A3	Raphael Street	B3
Callender Street	A2	Ravenhill Road	C3
Carrick Hill	A1	Regent Street	A1
Castle Place	A2	Rosemary Street	A2
Castle Street	A2	Royal Avenue	A2
Chapel Lane	A2	Short Strand	C2
Chichester Street	A3	Skipper Street	B2
Church Lane	B2	Station Street	C2
Clarence Street	A3	Stewart Street	B3
Clifton Street	A1	Sydenham Road	C1
College Square	A3	Talbot Street	A2
College Square North	A2	Tomb Street	B2
Cornmarket	A2	Union Street	A2
Corporation Square	B1	Upper Arthur Street	A3
Corporation Street	B2	Upper Queen Street	A3
Cromac Street	B3	Victoria Street	B2
Donegall Place	A2	Waring Street	A2
Donegall Quay	B2	Wellington Place	A3
Donegall Square East	A3	Westlink	A1
Donegall Square North	A3	York Street	A1
Donegall Square South	A3		
Donegall Square West	A3		
Donegall Street	A2		
Dunbar Link	B1		
Dunbar Street	B2		
East Bridge Street	B3		
Francis Street	A2		
Franklin Street	A3		
Frederick Street	A1		
Friendly Street	B3		
Gloucester Street	B3		
Great Georges Street	A1		
Great Patrick Street	A1		
Great Victoria Street	A3		
Gresham Street	A2		
Hamilton Street	B3		
High Street	A2		
Hill Street	A2		
Hope Street	A3		
Howard Street	A3		
Joy Street	B3		
Laganbank Road	C3		
Lanyon Place	B3		
Library Street	A1		
Linenhall Street	A3		
Little Donegall Street	A1		
Little Patrick Street	B1		
Lombard Street	A2		
Lower Stanfield Street	B3		
May Street	B3		
Middlepath Street	C2		

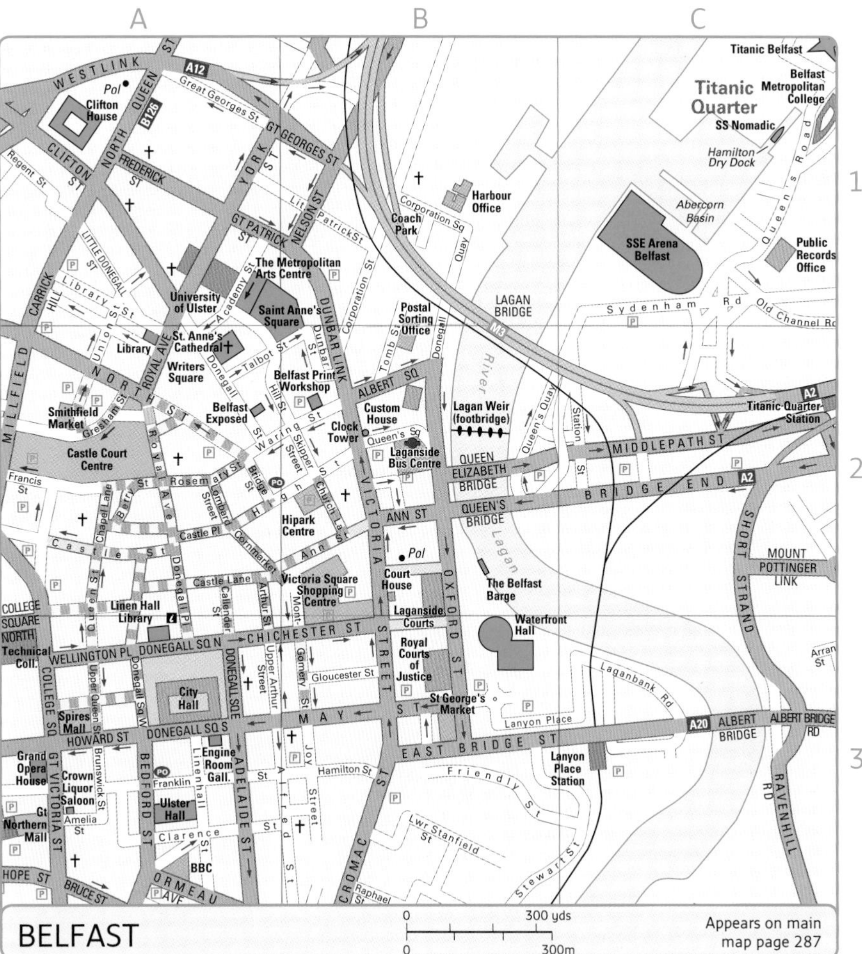

BELFAST

0   300 yds
0   300m

Appears on main
map page 287

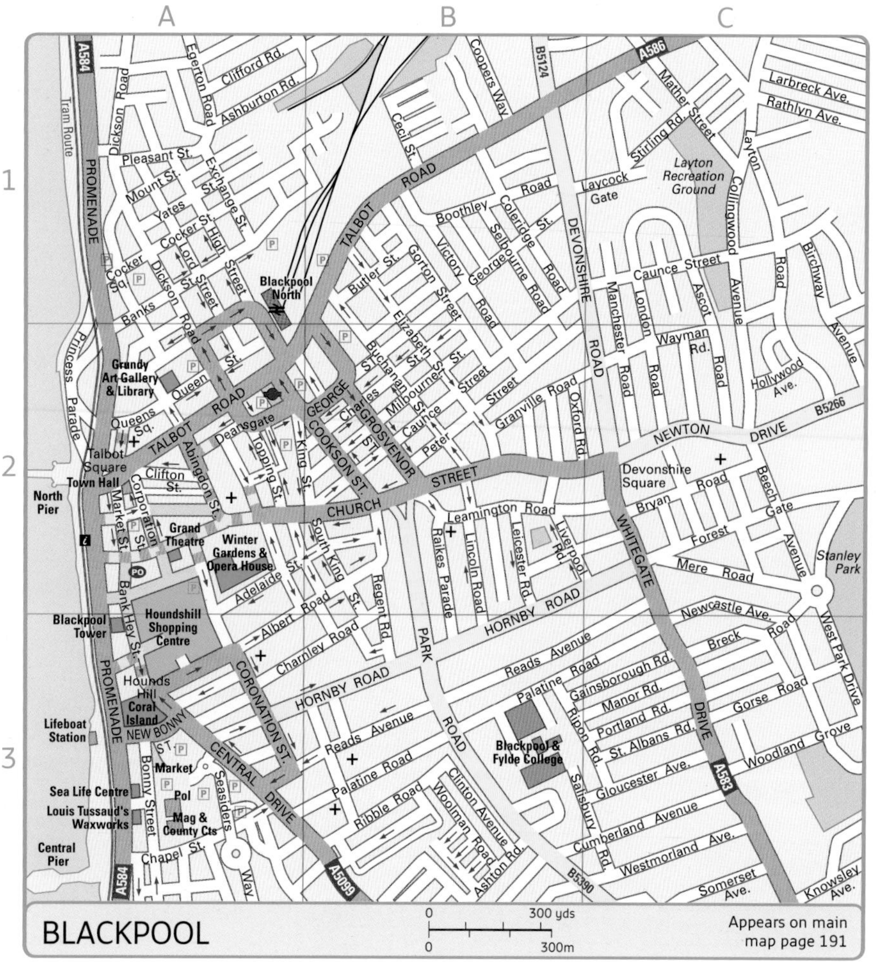

BLACKPOOL

0 ——— 300 yds
0 ——— 300m

Appears on main
map page 191

Tourist Information Centre: Festival House, Promenade
Tel: 01253 478222

Street	Grid	Street	Grid
Abingdon Street	A2	Manor Road	C3
Adelaide Street	A2	Market Street	A2
Albert Road	A3	Mather Street	C1
Ascot Road	C1	Mere Road	C2
Ashburton Road	A1	Milbourne Street	B2
Ashton Road	B3	Mount Street	A1
Bank Hey Street	A2	New Bonny Street	A3
Banks Street	A1	Newcastle Avenue	C2
Beech Avenue	C2	Newton Drive	C2
Birchway Avenue	C1	Oxford Road	B2
Bonny Street	A3	Palatine Road	B3
Boothley Road	B1	Park Road	B2
Breck Road	C3	Peter Street	B2
Bryan Road	C2	Pleasant Street	A1
Buchanan Street	B2	Portland Road	C3
Butler Street	B1	Princess Parade	A2
Caunce Street	B2/C1	Promenade	A1
Cecil Street	B1	Queens Square	A2
Central Street	A3	Queen Street	A2
Chapel Street	A3	Rathlyn Avenue	C1
Charles Street	B2	Reads Avenue	B3
Charnley Road	A3	Regent Road	B2
Church Street	B2	Ribble Road	B3
Clifford Road	A1	Ripon Road	B3
Clifton Street	A2	St. Albans Road	C3
Clinton Avenue	B3	Salisbury Road	C3
Cocker Square	A1	Seasiders Way	A3
Cocker Street	A1	Selbourne Road	B1
Coleridge Road	B1	Somerset Avenue	C3
Collingwood Avenue	C1	South King Street	B2
Cookson Street	B2	Stirling Road	C1
Coopers Way	B1	Talbot Road	A2/B1
Coronation Street	A3	Talbot Square	A2
Corporation Street	A2	Topping Street	A2
Cumberland Avenue	C3	Victory Road	B1
Deansgate	A2	Wayman Road	C2
Devonshire Road	B1	Westmorland Avenue	C3
Devonshire Square	C2	West Park Drive	C2
Dickson Road	A1	Whitegate Drive	C2/C3
Egerton Road	A1	Woodland Grove	C3
Elizabeth Street	B1	Woolman Road	B3
Exchange Street	A1	Yates Street	A1
Forest Gate	C2		
Gainsborough Road	B3		
George Street	B2/B1		
Gloucester Avenue	C3		
Gorse Road	C3		
Gorton Street	B1		
Granville Road	B2		
Grosvenor Street	B2		
High Street	A1		
Hollywood Avenue	C2		
Hornby Road	A3		
Hounds Hill	A3		
King Street	A2		
Knowsley Avenue	C3		
Larbreck Avenue	C1		
Laycock Gate	C1		
Layton Road	C1		
Leamington Road	B2		
Leicester Road	B2		
Lincoln Road	B2		
Liverpool Road	B2		
London Road	C1		
Lord Street	A1		
Manchester Road	C1		

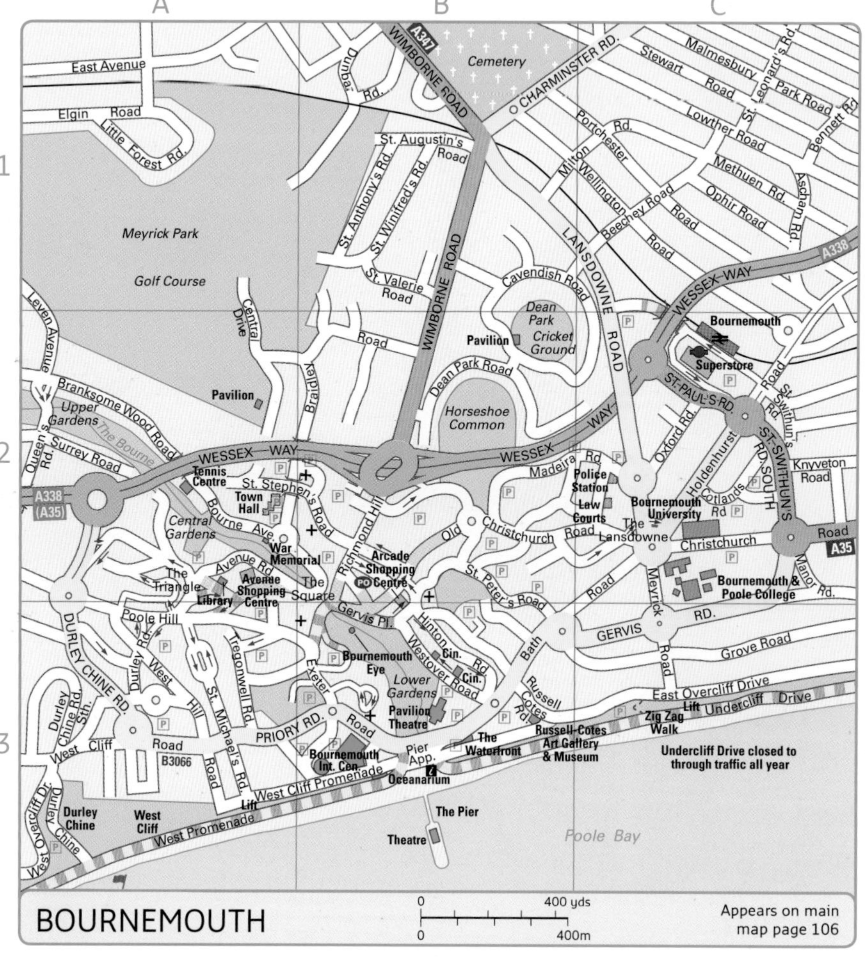

BOURNEMOUTH

0 ——— 400 yds
0 ——— 400m

Appears on main
map page 106

Tourist Information Centre: Pier Approach
Tel: 01202 451781

Street	Grid	Street	Grid
Ascham Road	C1	Undercliff Drive	C3
Avenue Road	A2	Wellington Road	C1
Bath Road	B3	Wessex Way	A2/C1
Beechey Road	C1	West Cliff Promenade	A3
Bennett Road	C1	West Cliff Road	A3
Bourne Avenue	A2	West Hill Road	A3
Braidley Road	B2	West Overcliff Drive	A3
Branksome Wood Road	A2	West Promenade	A3
Cavendish Road	B1	Westover Road	B3
Central Drive	A1	Wimborne Road	B2
Charminster Road	B1		
Christchurch Road	C2		
Cotlands	C2		
Dean Park Road	B2		
Dunbar Road	B1		
Durley Chine	A3		
Durley Chine Road	A3		
Durley Chine Road South	A3		
Durley Road	A3		
East Avenue	A1		
East Overcliff Drive	C3		
Elgin Road	A1		
Exeter Road	B3		
Gervis Place	B3		
Gervis Road	C3		
Grove Road	C3		
Hinton Road	B3		
Holdenhurst Road	C2		
Knyveton Road	C2		
Lansdowne Road	B1		
Leven Avenue	A1		
Little Forest Road	A1		
Lowther Road	C1		
Madeira Road	B2		
Malmesbury Park Road	C1		
Manor Road	C2		
Methuen Road	C1		
Meyrick Road	C2		
Milton Road	B1		
Old Christchurch Road	B2		
Ophir Road	C1		
Oxford Road	C2		
Pier Approach	B3		
Poole Hill	A3		
Portchester Road	C1		
Priory Road	A3		
Queen's Road	A2		
Richmond Hill	B2		
Russell Cotes Road	B3		
St. Augustin's Road	B1		
St. Anthony's Road	B1		
St. Leonard's Road	C1		
St. Michael's Road	A3		
St. Pauls' Road	C2		
St. Peter's Road	B2		
St. Stephen's Road	A2		
St. Swithun's Road	C2		
St. Swithun's Road South	C2		
St. Valerie Road	B1		
St. Winifred's Road	B1		
Stewart Road	C1		
Surrey Road	A2		
The Lansdowne	C2		
The Square	B2		
The Triangle	A2		
Tregonwell Road	A3		

Tourist Information Centre: Britannia House, Broadway
Tel: 01274 433678

Street	Grid	Street	Grid
Akam Road	A1	John Street	A2
Ann Place	A3	Kirkgate	B2
Ashgrove	A3	Leeds Road	C2
Balme Street	B1	Little Horton Lane	A3
Bank Street	B2	Lower Kirkgate	B2
Baptist Place	A1	Lumb Lane	A1
Barkerend Road	C1	Manchester Road	B3
Barry Street	A2	Manningham Lane	A1
Bolling Road	C3	Mannville Terrace	A3
Bolton Road	C1	Manor Row	B1
Brearton Street	A1	Melbourne Place	A3
Bridge Street	B2	Midland Road	B1
Britannia Street	B3	Moody Street	C3
Broadway	B2	Morley Street	A3
Burnett Street	C2	Neal Street	A3
Caledonia Street	B3	Nelson Street	B3
Canal Road	B1	North Parade	B1
Captain Street	C1	North Street	C1
Carlton Street	A2	North Wing	C1
Carter Street	C3	Nuttall Road	C1
Centenary Square	B2	Otley Road	C1
Chain Street	A1	Paradise Street	A1
Channing Way	B2	Park Road	B3
Chapel Street	C2	Peckover Street	C2
Charles Street	B2	Prince's Way	B2
Cheapside	B2	Prospect Street	C3
Chester Street	A3	Radwell Drive	B1
Churchbank	C2	Rawson Place	A1
Claremont	C1	Rawson Road	A1
Croft Street	B3	Rebecca Street	A1
Darfield Street	A1	Rouse Fold	C3
Darley Street	B1	Russell Street	A3
Drake Street	B2	Salem Street	B1
Drewton Road	A1	Sawrey Place	A3
Dryden Street	C3	Sedgwick Close	A1
Duke Street	B1	Sharpe Street	B3
Dyson Street	A1	Shipley Airedale Road	C1
East Parade	C2	Simes Street	A1
Edmund Street	A3	Snowden Street	A1
Edward Street	C3	Sunbridge Road	A1
Eldon Place	A1	Sylhet Close	A1
Fairfax Street	C3	Ternhill Grove	B3
Filey Street	C2	Tetley Street	A2
Fitzwilliam Street	C3	The Tyrls	B2
Fountain Street	A1	Thornton Road	A2
George Street	C2	Trafalgar Street	A1
Godwin Street	B2	Trinity Road	A3
Gracechurch Street	A1	Tumbling Hill Street	A2
Grafton Street	A3	Valley Road	B1
Grattan Road	A2	Vaughan Street	A1
Great Horton Road	A3	Vicar Lane	C2
Grove Terrace	A3	Vincent Street	A2
Guy Street	C3	Wakefield Road	C3
Hall Ings	B2	Wapping Road	C1
Hall Lane	C3	Water Lane	A2
Hallfield Road	A1	Westgate	A1
Hamm Strasse	B1	Wigan Street	A2
Hammerton Street	C2		
Hanover Square	A1		
Harris Street	C2		
Heap Lane	C1		
Houghton Place	A1		
Howard Street	A3		
Hustlergate	B2		
Ivegate	B2		
James Street	B2		

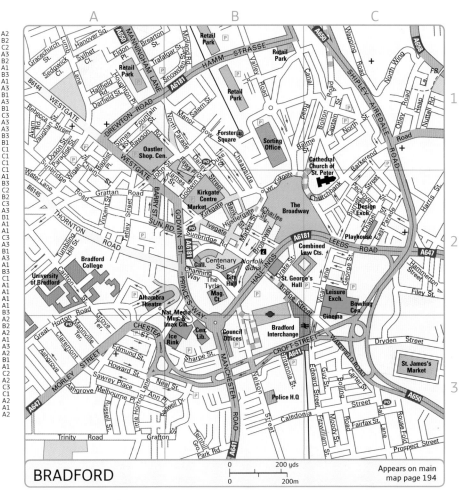

BRADFORD

0   200 yds
0   200m

Appears on main
map page 194

Tourist Information Centre: The Brighton Centre
Tel: 01273 290337

Street	Grid	Street	Grid
Addison Road	A1	Southover Street	C2
Albion Hill	C2	Springfield Road	B1
Beaconsfield Road	B1	Stafford Road	A1
Brunswick Square	A2	Stanford Road	B1
Buckingham Place	B1	Sussex Street	C2
Buckingham Road	B2	Terminus Road	B2
Carlton Hill	C2	The Lanes	B3
Cheapside	B2	The Upper Drive	A1
Church Street	B2	Trafalgar Street	B2
Churchill Square	B3	Union Road	C1
Clifton Hill	A2	Upper Lewes Road	C1
Clyde Road	B1	Upper North Street	A2
Davigdor Road	A1	Upper Rock Gardens	C3
Ditchling Rise	B1	Viaduct Road	B1
Ditchling Road	C1	Victoria Road	A2
Dyke Road	B2	Waterloo Street	A2
Dyke Road Drive	B1	Wellington Road	C1
Eastern Road	C3	West Drive	C2
Edward Street	C3	West Street	B3
Elm Grove	C1	Western Road	A2
Fleet Street	B2	Wilbury Crescent	A1
Florence Road	B1	York Avenue	A2
Freshfield Road	C3	York Place	C2
Furze Hill	A2		
Gloucester Road	B2		
Grand Junction Road	B3		
Hamilton Road	B1		
Hanover Street	C2		
Highdown Road	A1		
Holland Road	A2		
Hollingdean Road	C1		
Howard Place	B1		
Islingword Road	C1		
John Street	C2		
King's Road	A3		
Lansdowne Road	A2		
Lewes Road	C1		
London Road	B1		
Lyndhurst Road	A1		
Madeira Drive	C3		
Marine Parade	C3		
Montefiore Road	A1		
Montpelier Road	A2		
New England Road	B1		
New England Street	B1		
Nizells Avenue	A1		
Norfolk Terrace	A2		
North Road	B2		
North Street	B2		
Old Shoreham Road	A1		
Old Steine	C3		
Park Crescent Terrace	C1		
Park Street	C2		
Port Hall Road	A1		
Preston Circus	B1		
Preston Road	B1		
Preston Street	A3		
Prince's Crescent	C1		
Queen's Park Road	C2		
Queen's Road	B2		
Richmond Place	C2		
Richmond Road	C1		
Richmond Street	C2		
Richmond Terrace	C2		
St. James's Street	C3		
Somerhill Road	A2		

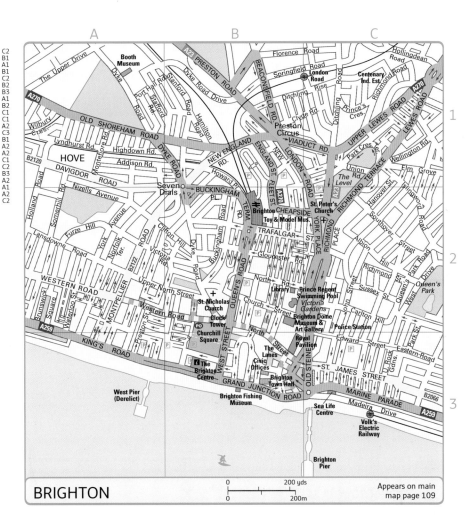

BRIGHTON

0   200 yds
0   200m

Appears on main
map page 109

BRISTOL

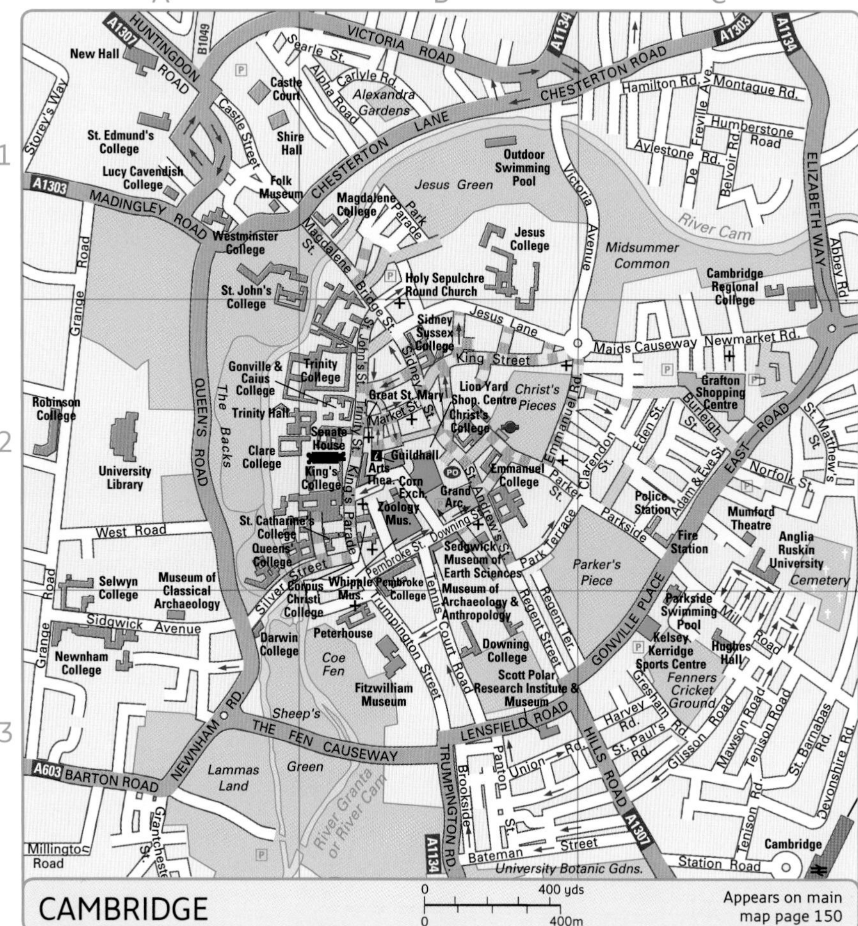

Appears on main map page 131

0   200 yds
0   200m

Tourist Information Centre: E Shed 1, Canons Road
Tel: 0906 711 2191

Alfred Hill	A1
Anchor Road	A3
Avon Street	C2
Baldwin Street	A2
Bath Road	C3
Bond Street	B1
Bridge Street	B2
Brigstowe Street	C1
Bristol Bridge	B2
Broadmead	B1
Broad Quay	A2
Broad Street	B2
Broad Weir	C1
Brunswick Square	B1
Cannon Street	B1
Canon's Road	A3
Canon's Way	A3
Castle Street	C2
Charles Street	B1
Cheese Lane	C2
Christmas Steps	A1
Church Lane	C2
College Green	A2
Colston Avenue	A2
Colston Street	A2
Concorde Street	C1
Corn Street	B2
Countership	B2
Eugene Street	A1
Fairfax Street	B1
Frogmore Street	A2
George White Street	C1
High Street	B2
Horfield Road	A1
Houlton Street	C1
John Street	B2
King Street	A2
Lewins Mead	A1
Lower Castle Street	C1
Lower Maudlin Street	B1
Marlborough Street	B1
Marsh Street	A2
Merchant Street	B1
Nelson Street	B1
Newfoundland Street	C1
Newgate	B2
New Street	C1
North Street	B1
Old Bread Street	C2
Old Market Street	C2
Park Row	A2
Park Street	A2
Passage Street	C2
Penn Street	C1
Pero's Bridge	A3
Perry Road	A2
Pipe Lane	A2
Portwall Lane	B3
Prewett Street	B3
Prince Street	A3
Prince Street Bridge	C1
Quakers' Friars	B1
Queen Charlotte Street	B2
Queen Square	A3
Queen Street	C2
Redcliff Backs	B3

Redcliffe Bridge	B3
Redcliffe Parade	B3
Redcliff Hill	B3
Redcliff Mead Lane	C3
Redcliff Street	B2
Redcross Street	C1
River Street	C1
Rupert Street	A1
St. James Barton	B1
St. Matthias Park	C1
St. Michael's Hill	A1
St. Nicholas Street	B2
St. Thomas Street	B2
Small Street	A2
Somerset Street	C3
Southwell Street	A1
Station Approach Road	C3
Straight Street	C2
Surrey Street	C1
Temple Back	C2
Temple Gate	C3
Temple Street	B2
Temple Way	C3
Terrell Street	A1
The Grove	A3
The Haymarket	B1
The Horsefair	B1
Thomas Lane	B2
Trenchard Street	A2
Tyndall Avenue	A1
Union Street	B1
Unity Street	A2
Unity Street	C2
Upper Maudlin Street	A1
Victoria Street	B2
Wapping Road	A3
Water Lane	C2
Welsh Back	B2
Wilder Street	B1
Wine Street	B2

CAMBRIDGE

0   400 yds
0   400m

Appears on main map page 150

Tourist Information Centre: The Guildhall, Peas Hill
Tel: 01223 791500

Adam and Eve Street	C2
Alpha Road	B1
Aylestone Road	C1
Barton Road	A3
Bateman Street	B3
Belvior Road	C1
Brookside	B3
Burleigh Street	C2
Carlyle Road	B1
Castle Street	A1
Chesterton Lane	B1
Chesterton Road	B1
Clarendon Street	C2
De Freville Avenue	C1
Devonshire Road	C3
Downing Street	B2
East Road	C2
Eden Street	C2
Elizabeth Way	C1
Emmanuel Road	B2
Fen Causeway, The	A3
Glisson Road	C3
Gonville Place	C3
Granchester Street	A3
Grange Road	A3
Gresham Road	C3
Hamilton Road	C1
Harvey Road	C3
Hills Road	C3
Humberstone Road	C1
Huntingdon Road	A1
Jesus Lane	B2
King's Parade	B2
King Street	B2
Lensfield Road	B3
Madingley Road	A1
Magdalene Bridge Street	B1
Maids Causeway	C2
Market Street	B2
Mawson Road	C3
Millington Road	A3
Mill Road	C3
Montague Road	C1
Newmarket Road	C2
Newnham Road	A3
Norfolk Street	C2
Panton Street	B3
Parker Street	B2
Park Parade	B1
Parkside	C2
Park Terrace	B2
Pembroke Street	B2
Queen's Road	A2
Regent Street	B2
Regent Terrace	B2
St. Andrew's Street	B2
St. Barnabas Road	C3
St. John's Street	B2
St. Matthew's Street	C2
St. Paul's Road	C3
Searce Street	A1
Sidgwick Avenue	A3
Sidney Street	B2
Silver Street	A3
Station Road	C3
Storey's Way	A1

Tenison Road	C3
Tennis Court Road	B2
Trinity Street	B2
Trumpington Road	B3
Trumpington Street	B3
Union Road	B3
Victoria Avenue	B1
Victoria Road	B1
West Road	A2

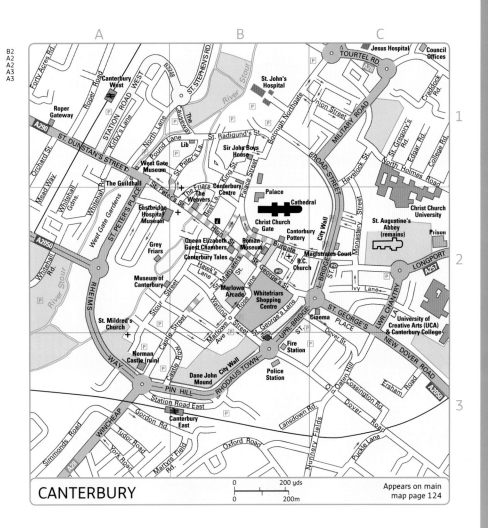

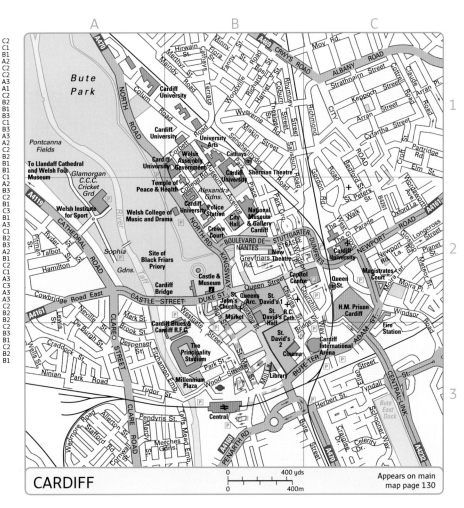

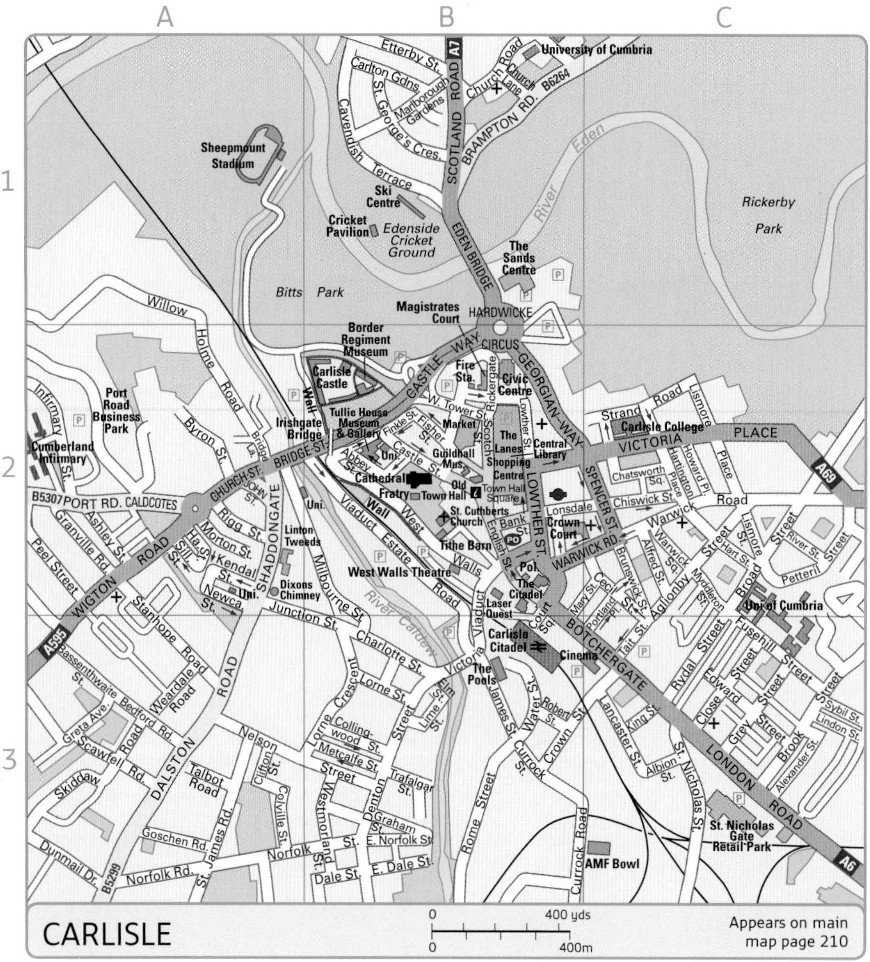

CARLISLE

0   400 yds
0   400m

Appears on main map page 210

Tourist Information Centre: Old Town Hall, Green Market
Tel: 01228 598596

Abbey Street	B2	Lancaster Street	C3
Aglionby Street	C2	Lime Street	B3
Albion Street	C3	Lindon Street	C3
Alexander Street	C3	Lismore Place	C2
Alfred Street	C2	Lismore Street	C2
Ashley Street	A2	London Road	C3
Bank Street	B2	Lonsdale	B2
Bassenthwaite Street	A3	Lorne Crescent	B3
Bedford Road	A3	Lorne Street	B3
Botchergate	B3	Lowther Street	B2
Brampton Road	B1	Marlborough Gardens	B1
Bridge Lane	A2	Mary Street	B3
Bridge Street	A2	Metcalfe Street	B3
Broad Street	C2	Milbourne Street	A2
Brook Street	C3	Morton Street	A2
Brunswick Street	C2	Myddleton Street	C2
Byron Street	A2	Nelson Street	A3
Caldcotes	A2	Newcastle Street	A2
Carlton Gardens	B1	Norfolk Road	A3
Castle Street	B2	Norfolk Street	A3
Castle Way	B2	Peel Street	A2
Cavendish Terrace	B1	Petteril Street	C2
Cecil Street	C2	Port Road	A2
Charlotte Street	B3	Portland Place	C3
Chatsworth Square	C2	Rickergate	B2
Chiswick Street	C2	Rigg Street	A2
Church Lane	B1	River Street	C2
Church Road	B1	Robert Street	B3
Church Street	A2	Rome Street	B3
Clifton Street	A3	Rydal Street	C3
Close Street	C3	St. George's Crescent	B1
Collingwood Street	B3	St. James Road	A3
Colville Street	A3	St. Nicholas Street	C3
Crown Street	B3	Scawfell Road	A3
Currock Road	B3	Scotch Street	B2
Currock Street	B3	Scotland Road	B1
Dale Street	B3	Shaddongate	A2
Denton Street	B3	Silloth Street	A2
Dunmail Drive	A3	Skiddaw Road	A3
East Dale Street	B3	Spencer Street	C2
East Norfolk Street	B3	Stanhope Road	A2
Eden Bridge	B1	Strand Road	C2
Edward Street	C3	Sybil Street	C3
Elm Street	B3	Tait Street	C3
English Street	B2	Talbot Road	A3
Etterby Street	B1	Trafalgar Street	B3
Finkle Street	B2	Viaduct Estate Road	B2
Fisher Street	B2	Victoria Place	C2
Fusehill Street	C3	Victoria Viaduct	B3
Georgian Way	B2	Warwick Road	B2
Goschen Road	A3	Warwick Square	C2
Graham Street	B3	Water Street	B3
Granville Road	A2	Weardale Road	A3
Greta Avenue	A3	West Tower Street	B2
Grey Street	C3	West Walls	B2
Hardwicke Circus	B1	Westmorland Street	B3
Hart Street	C2	Wigton Road	A2
Hartington Place	C2	Willow Holme Road	A1
Hawick Street	A2		
Howard Place	C2		
Infirmary Street	A2		
James Street	B3		
John Street	A2		
Junction Street	A2		
Kendal Street	A2		
King Street	C3		

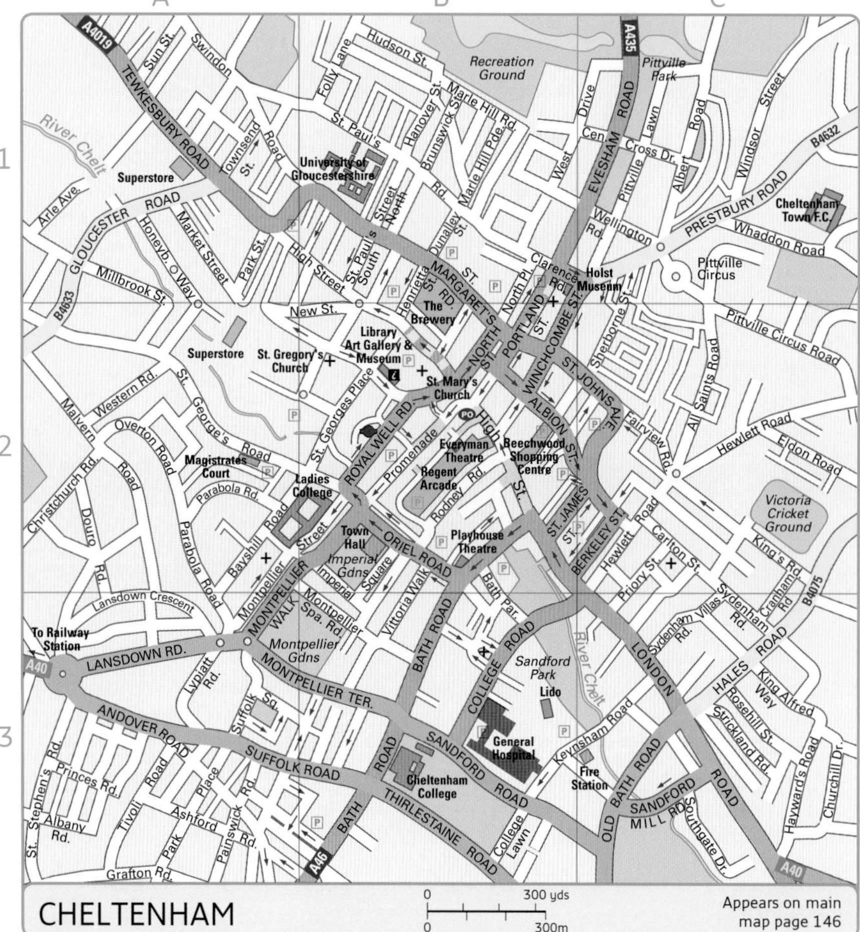

CHELTENHAM

0   300 yds
0   300m

Appears on main map page 146

Tourist Information Centre: The Wilson, Cheltenham Art Gallery and Museum, Clarence Street   Tel: 01242 387492

Albany Road	A3	Portland Street	B2
Albert Road	C1	Prestbury Road	C1
Albion Street	B2	Princes Road	A3
All Saints Road	C2	Priory Street	C3
Andover Road	A3	Promenade	B2
Arle Avenue	A1	Rodney Road	B2
Ashford Road	A3	Rosehill Street	C3
Bath Parade	B2	Royal Well Road	B2
Bath Road	B3	St. George's Place	B2
Bayshill Road	A2	St. George's Road	A2
Berkeley Street	B2	St. James Street	B2
Brunswick Street	B1	St. Johns Avenue	B2
Carlton Street	C2	St. Margaret's Road	B1
Central Cross Drive	C1	St. Paul's Road	B1
Christchurch Road	A2	St. Paul's Street North	B1
Churchill Drive	C3	St. Paul's Street South	B1
Clarence Road	B1	St. Stephen's Road	A3
College Lawn	B3	Sandford Mill Road	C3
College Road	B3	Sandford Road	B3
Cranham Road	C3	Sherborne Street	C2
Douro Road	A2	Southgate Drive	C3
Dunalley Street	B1	Strickland Road	C3
Eldon Road	C2	Suffolk Road	A3
Evesham Road	C1	Suffolk Square	A3
Fairview Road	B2	Sun Street	A1
Folly Lane	B1	Swindon Road	A1
Gloucester Road	A2	Sydenham Road	C2
Grafton Road	A3	Sydenham Villas Road	C3
Hales Road	C3	Tewkesbury Road	A1
Hanover Street	B1	Thirlestaine Road	A3
Hayward's Road	C3	Tivoli Road	A3
Henrietta Street	B2	Townsend Street	A1
Hewlett Road	C2	Vittoria Walk	B3
High Street	B1	Wellington Road	C1
Honeybourne Way	A1	West Drive	B1
Hudson Street	B1	Western Road	A2
Imperial Square	B2	Whaddon Road	C1
Keynsham Road	B3	Winchcombe Street	B2
King Alfred Way	C3	Windsor Street	C1
King's Road	C2		
Lansdown Crescent	A3		
Lansdown Road	A3		
London Road	C3		
Lypiatt Road	A3		
Malvern Road	A2		
Market Street	A1		
Marle Hill Parade	B1		
Marle Hill Road	B1		
Millbrook Street	A1		
Montpellier Spa Road	B3		
Montpellier Street	A3		
Montpellier Terrace	A3		
Montpellier Walk	A3		
New Street	A2		
North Place	B2		
North Street	B2		
Old Bath Road	C3		
Oriel Road	B2		
Overton Road	A2		
Painswick Road	A3		
Parabola Road	A2		
Park Place	A3		
Park Street	A1		
Pittville Circus	C1		
Pittville Circus Road	C2		
Pittville Lawn	C1		

Tourist Information Centre: Town Hall, Northgate Street
Tel: 0845 647 7868

Bath Street	C2	Queen's Park Road	B3
Bedward Row	A2	Queen's Road	C1
Black Diamond Street	B1	Queen Street	B2
Black Friars	A3	Raymond Street	A1
Bold Square	B2	Russel Street	C2
Boughton	C2	St. Anne Street	B1
Bouverie Street	A1	St. George's Crescent	C3
Bridge Street	B2	St. John's Road	C3
Brook Street	B1	St. John Street	B2
Canal Street	A1	St. Martins Way	A1
Castle Drive	A3	St. Oswalds Way	B1
Charles Street	B1	St. Werburgh Street	B2
Cheyney Road	A1	Seller Street	C2
Chichester Street	A1	Sibell Street	C1
City Road	C2	Souter's Lane	B3
City Walls Road	A2	Stanley Street	A2
Commonhall Street	A2	Station Road	C1
Cornwall Street	B1	Steam Mill Street	C2
Crewe Street	C1	Talbot Street	B1
Cuppin Street	A3	The Bars	C2
Dee Hills Park	C2	The Groves	B3
Dee Lane	C2	Trafford Street	B1
Deva Terrace	C2	Union Street	B2
Duke Street	B3	Upper Northgate Street	A1
Eastgate Street	B2	Vicar's Lane	B2
Edinburgh Way	C3	Victoria Crescent	C3
Egerton Street	B1	Victoria Place	B2
Elizabeth Crescent	C3	Victoria Road	C1
Foregate Street	B2	Walker Street	B1
Forest Street	B2	Walpole Street	A1
Francis Street	C1	Walter Street	B1
Frodsham Street	B2	Watergate Street	A2
Garden Lane	A1	Water Tower Street	A2
George Street	B1	Weaver Street	A2
Gloucester Street	B1	White Friars	A3
Grey Friars	A3	York Street	B2
Grosvenor Park Terrace	C2		
Grosvenor Road	A3		
Grosvenor Street	A3		
Handbridge	B3		
Hoole Road	B1		
Hoole Way	B1		
Hunter Street	A2		
King Street	A2		
Leadworks Lane	C2		
Lightfoot Street	C1		
Louise Street	A1		
Love Street	B2		
Lower Bridge Street	B3		
Lower Park Road	C3		
Mill Street	C2		
Milton Street	B1		
Newgate Street	B2		
Nicholas Street	A2		
Nicholas Street Mews	A2		
Northern Pathway	C3		
Northgate Avenue	B1		
Northgate Street	A2		
Nun's Road	A3		
Old Dee Bridge	B3		
Pepper Street	B3		
Phillip Street	C1		
Prince's Avenue	C1		
Princess Street	A2		
Queen's Avenue	C1		
Queen's Drive	C3		

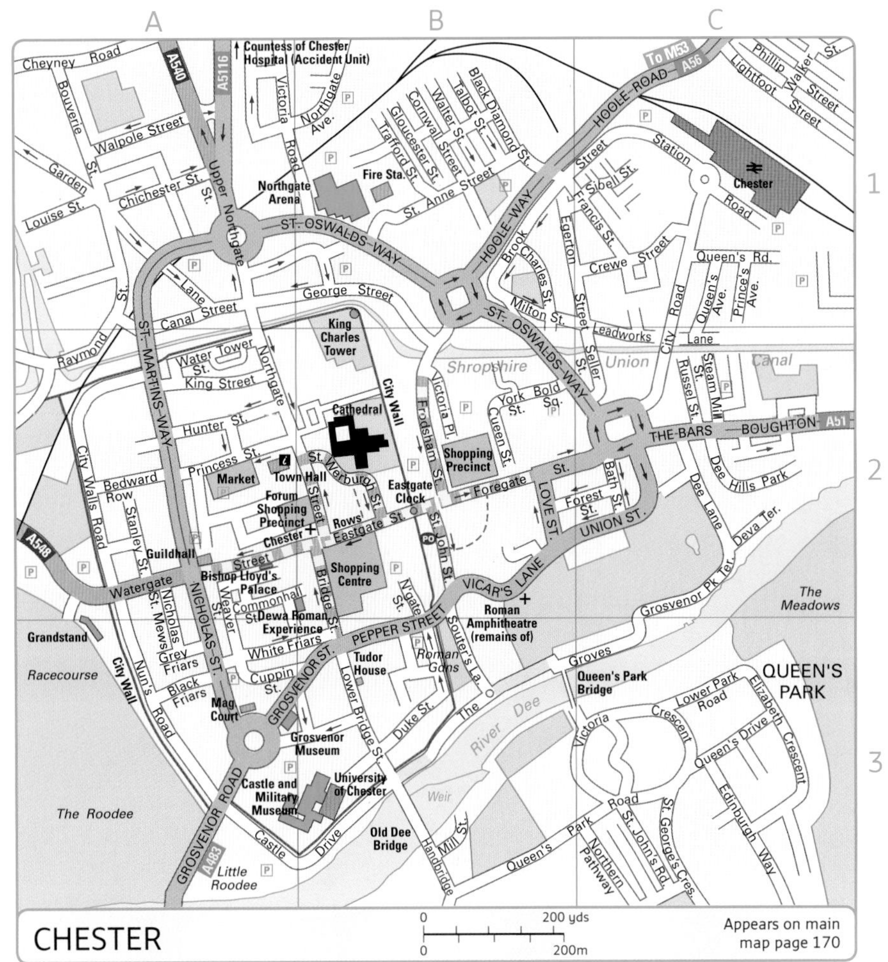

CHESTER

0   200 yds
0   200m

Appears on main
map page 170

Tourist Information Centres: St. Michael's Tower, Coventry
Cathedral   Tel: 024 7622 5616
Herbert Art Gallery & Museum, Jordan Well
Tel: 024 7623 7521

Abbott's Lane	A1	Minster Road	A2
Acacia Avenue	C3	Much Park Street	B2
Albany Road	A3	New Union Street	B2
Alma Street	C2	Norfolk Street	A2
Asthill Grove	B3	Oxford Street	C2
Barker's Butts Lane	A1	Park Road	B3
Barras Lane	A2	Parkside	B3
Berry Street	C1	Primrose Hill Street	C1
Bishop Street	B1	Priory Street	B2
Blythe Road	C1	Puma Way	B3
Bond Street	A2	Quarryfield Lane	C3
Bramble Street	C2	Queen's Road	A3
Bretts Close	C1	Queen Street	C1
Broadway	A3	Queen Victoria Road	A2
Burges	B2	Quinton Road	B3
Butts Road	A2	Radford Road	A1
Cambridge Street	C1	Raglan Street	C2
Canterbury Street	C1	Regent Street	A3
Clifton Street	C1	Ringway Hill Cross	A2
Colchester Street	C1	Ringway Queens	A2
Cornwall Road	C3	Ringway Rudge	A2
Corporation Street	B2	Ringway St. Johns	B3
Coundon Road	A1	Ringway St. Nicholas	B1
Coundon Street	A1	Ringway St. Patricks	B3
Cox Street	C2	Ringway Swanswell	B2
Croft Road	A2	Ringway Whitefriars	C2
Drapers Fields	B1	St. Nicholas Street	B1
Earl Street	B2	Sandy Lane	B1
East Street	C2	Seagrave Road	C3
Eaton Road	B3	Silver Street	B1
Fairfax Street	B2	Sky Blue Way	C2
Far Gosford Street	C2	South Street	C2
Foleshill Road	B1	Spencer Avenue	A3
Fowler Road	A1	Spon Street	A2
Gordon Street	A3	Strathmore Avenue	C3
Gosford Street	C2	Stoney Road	B3
Greyfriars Road	A2	Stoney Stanton Road	B1
Gulson Road	C2	Swanswell Street	B1
Hales Street	B2	The Precinct	B2
Harnall Lane East	C1	Tomson Avenue	A1
Harnall Lane West	B1	Trinity Street	B2
Harper Road	C2	Upper Hill Street	A2
Harper Street	B2	Upper Well Street	B2
Hertford Street	B2	Vauxhall Street	C2
Hewitt Avenue	A1	Vecqueray Street	C2
High Street	B2	Victoria Street	C1
Hill Street	A2	Vine Street	C1
Holyhead Road	A2	Warwick Road	A3
Hood Street	C2	Waveley Road	A2
Howard Street	B1	Westminster Road	A3
Jordan Well	B2	White Street	B1
King William Street	C1	Windsor Street	A2
Lamb Street	B2	Wright Street	C1
Leicester Row	B1		
Leigh Street	C1		
Little Park Street	B3		
London Road	C3		
Lower Ford Street	C2		
Market Way	B2		
Meadow Street	A2		
Michaelmas Road	A3		
Middleborough Road	A1		
Mile Lane	B3		
Mill Street	A1		

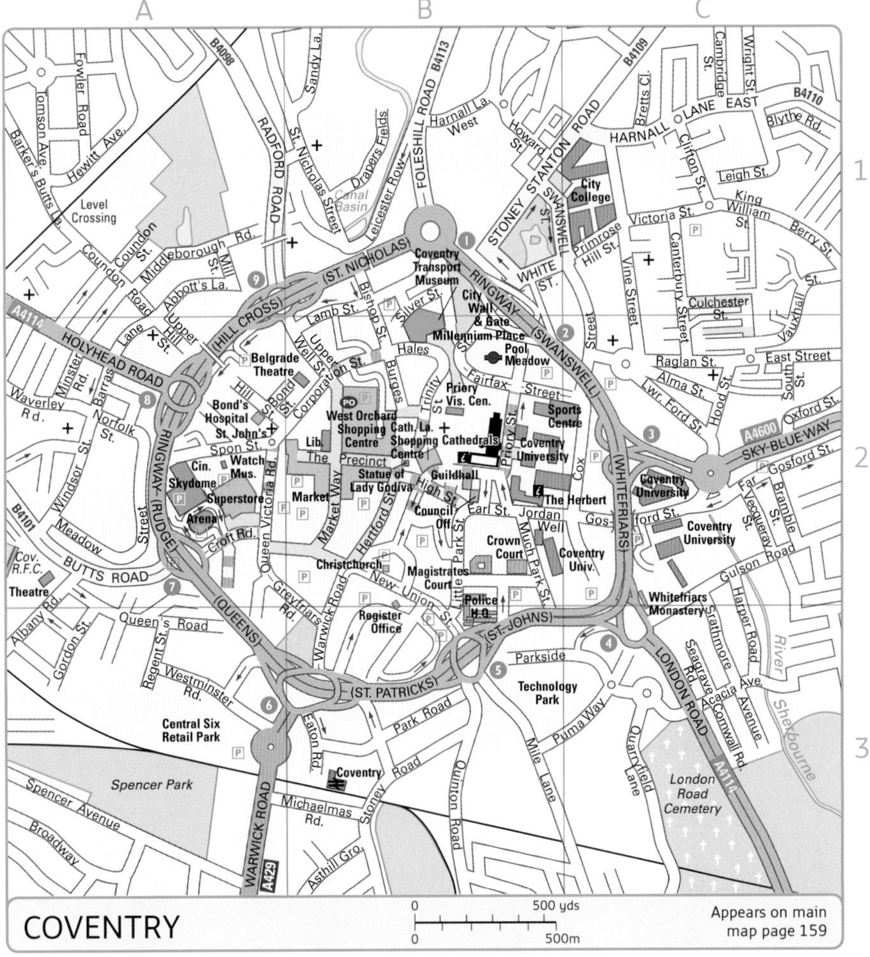

COVENTRY

0   500 yds
0   500m

Appears on main
map page 159

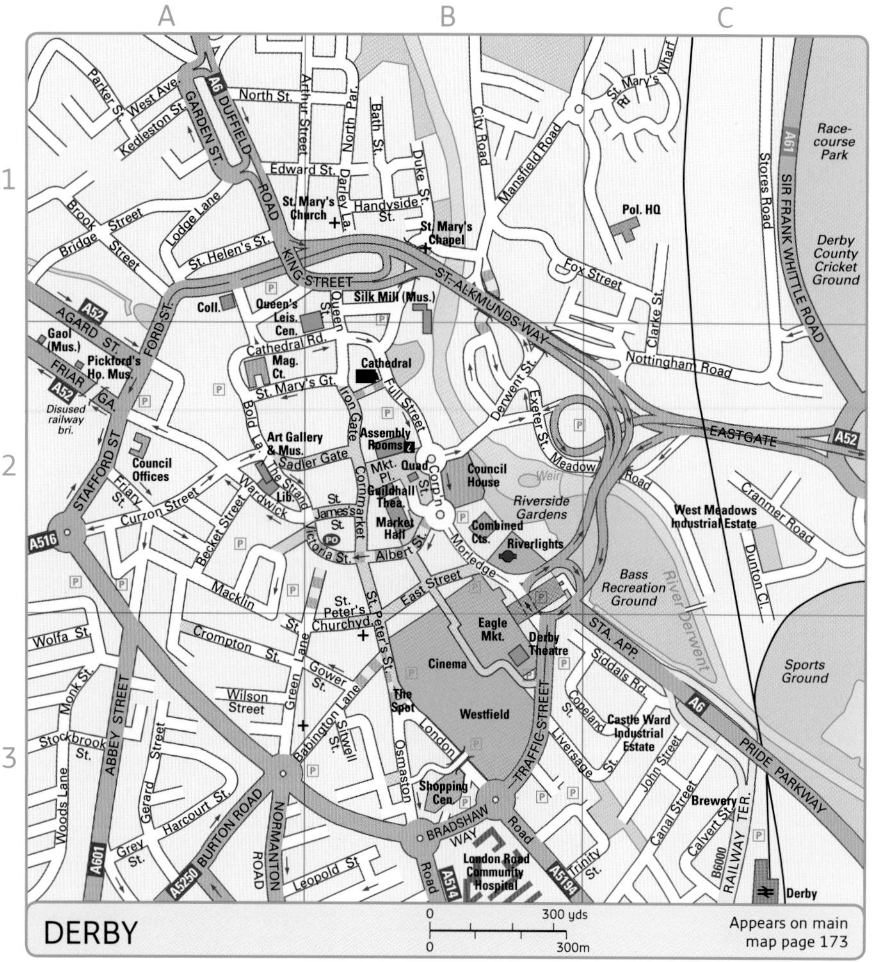

DERBY

Appears on main map page 173

Tourist Information Centre: Assembly Rooms, Market Place
Tel: 01332 643411

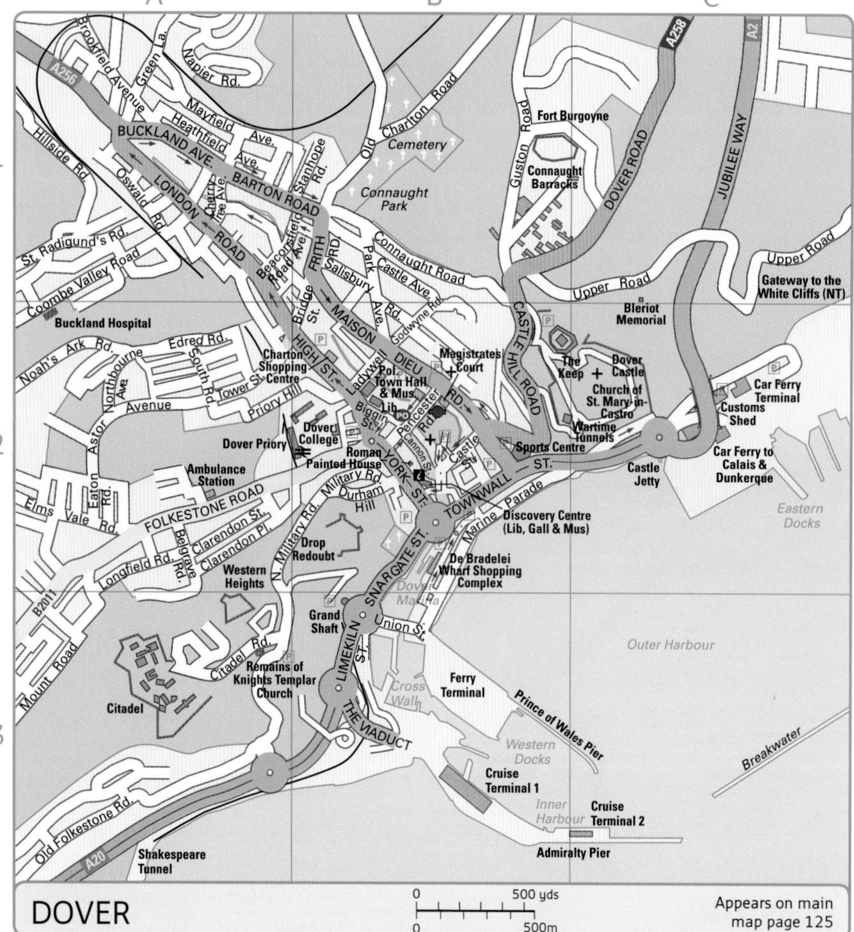

DOVER

Appears on main map page 125

Tourist Information Centre: Dover Museum, Market Square
Tel: 01304 201066

Tourist Information Centre: 16 City Square
Tel: 01382 527527

Adelaide Place	A1
Albany Terrace	A1
Albert Street	C2
Alexander Street	B1
Ann Street	B2
Arbroath Road	C2
Arklay Street	C1
Arklay Terrace	C1
Arthurstone Terrace	C2
Barrack Road	A2
Blackness Road	A2
Blinshall Street	A2
Brewery Lane	A2
Brook Street	A2
Broughty Ferry Road	C2
Brown Street	A2
Bruce Street	A1
Byron Street	A1
Canning Street	B1
City Square	B3
Clepington Road	C1
Constitution Road	B2
Constitution Street	B1
Court Street	C1
Cowgate Street	B2
Dens Road	B1
Douglas Street	A2
Dudhope Street	A1
Dudhope Terrace	C1
Dundonald Street	C1
Dura Street	C2
East Dock Street	C2
East Marketgait	B2
Fairbairn Street	B1
Greenmarket	B3
Guthrie Street	A2
Hawkhill	A2
High Street	B3
Hill Street	B1
Hilltown	B1
Kenmore Terrace	A1
Killin Avenue	A1
Kinghorne Road	A1
King Street	B2
Larch Street	A2
Law Crescent	A1
Lawside Avenue	A1
Law Street	A1
Leng Street	A1
Lochee Road	A2
Lower Princes Street	C2
Mains Road	B1
Main Street	B1
Meadowside	B2
Morgan Street	C2
Murraygate	B2
Nelson Street	B2
Nethergate	A3
North Marketgait	A2
Perth Road	A3
Polepark Road	A2
Princes Street	C2
Riverside Drive	A3
Roseangle	A3
Rosebank Road	B2
Seagate	B2

South Marketgait	B3
South Tay Street	A3
Strathmartine Road	B1
Tannadice Street	B1
Tay Road Bridge	B3
Trades Lane	B2
Upper Constitution Street	A1
Victoria Road	B2
Victoria Street	C2
Ward Road	A2
West Marketgait	A2
West Port	A2
William Street	C2

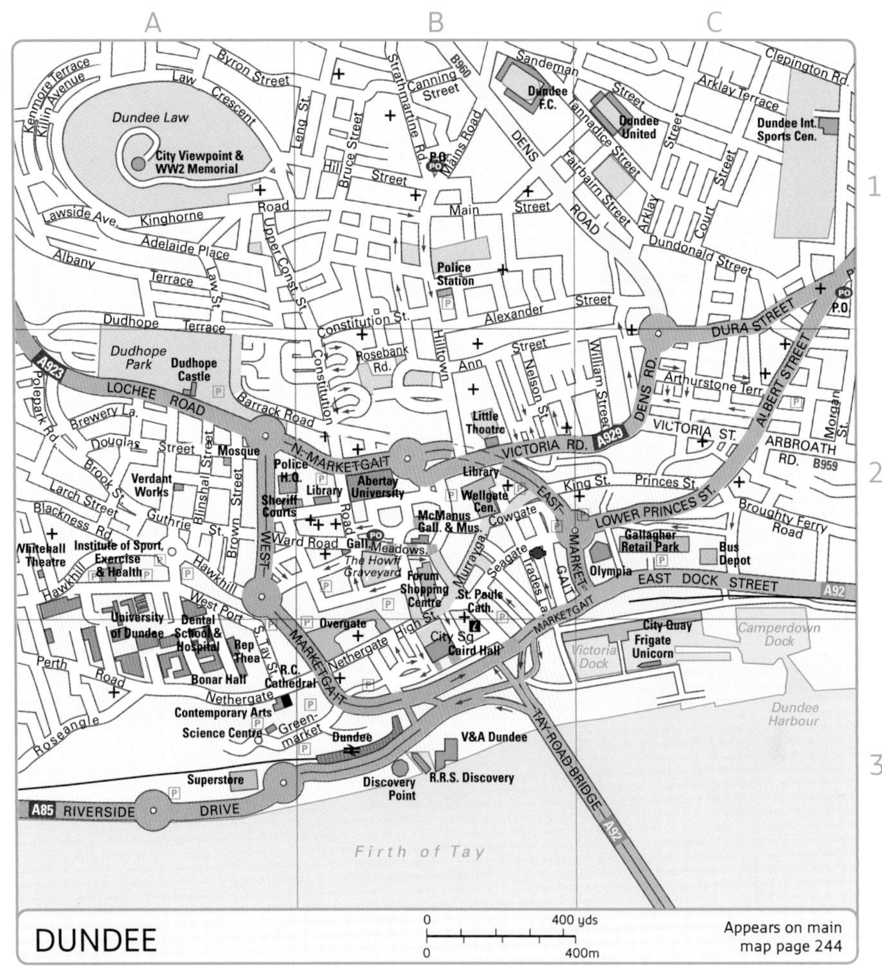

Tourist Information: Telephone Service
Tel: 03000 262626

Aykley Heads	A1
Church Street	B3
Clay Lane	A3
Claypath	B2
Crossgate	B2
Crossgate Peth	A3
Darlington Road	A3
Dryburn Road	A1
Durham Road	A1
Fieldhouse Lane	A1
Framwelgate	B2
Framwelgate Peth	B1
Framwelgate Waterside	B2
Gilesgate	C2
Great North Road	A1
Green Lane	C2
Grove Street	B3
Hallgarth Street	C3
Hawthorn Terrace	A2
Leazes Road	B2
Margery Lane	B3
Market Place	B2
Millburngate Bridge	B2
Newcastle Road	A1
New Elvet	B2
North Bailey	B2
North End	A1
North Road	B2
Old Elvet	C2
Pity Me Bypass	A1
Potters Bank	A3
Quarryheads Lane	B3
Providence Row	B2
Redhills Lane	A2
St. Monica Grove	A2
Sidegate	B2
Silver Street	B2
South Bailey	B3
South Road	B3
South Street	B3
Southfield Way	A1
Stockton Road	B3
Sutton Street	B2
The Avenue	A2
Toll House Road	A2
Western Hill	A2
Whinney Hill	C3
Whitesmocks	A1

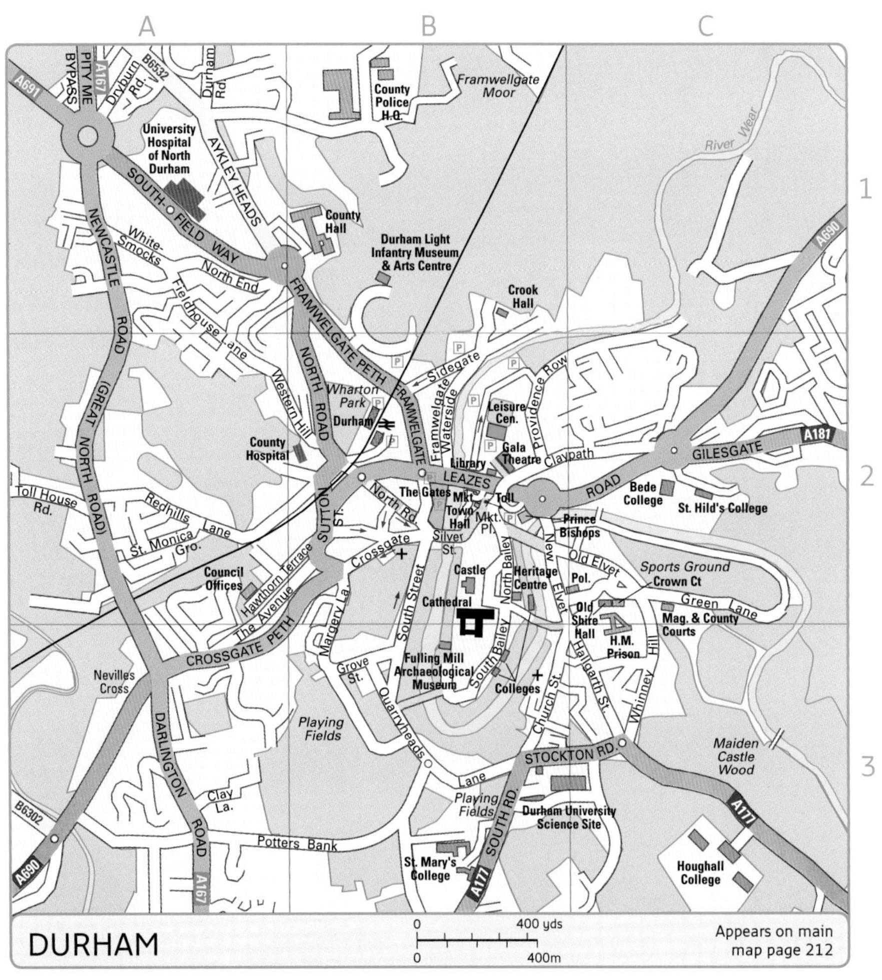

Edinburgh street map on pages 36-37

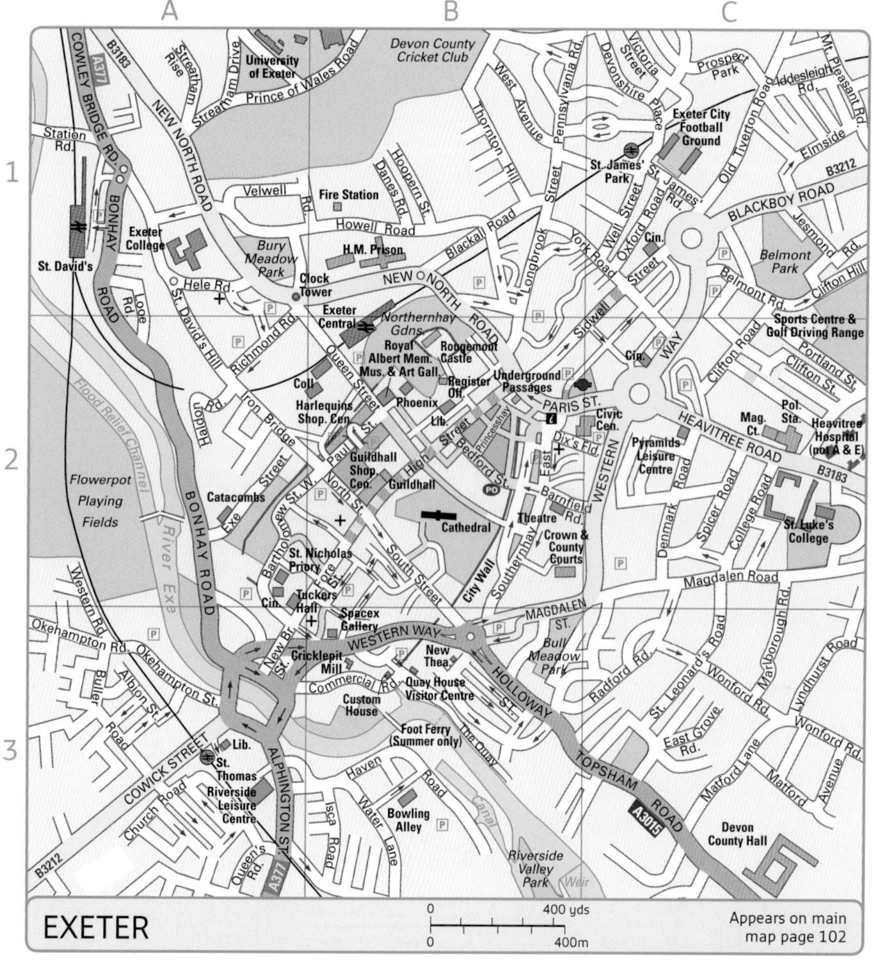

EASTBOURNE

0	200 yds
0	200m

Appears on main map page 110

Tourist Information Centre: 3 Cornfield Road
Tel: 01323 415415

Arlington Road	A2	The Avenue	B2
Arundel Road	B1	The Goffs	A1
Ashford Road	B2/C2	Trinity Trees	C2
Avondale Road	C1	Upper Avenue	B1
Bedfordwell Road	B1	Upperton Lane	B2
Belmore Road	C1	Upperton Road	A1
Blackwater Road	B3	Watts Lane	A1
Borough Lane	A1	Whitley Road	A1
Bourne Street	C2	Willingdon Road	A1
Carew Road	A1/B1	Winchcombe Road	C1
Carlisle Road	A3		
Cavendish Avenue	C1		
Cavendish Place	C2		
College Road	B3		
Commercial Road	B2		
Compton Place Road	A2		
Compton Street	B3		
Cornfield Terrace	B2		
Denton Road	A3		
Devonshire Place	B2		
Dittons Road	A2		
Dursley Road	C2		
Enys Road	B1		
Eversfield Road	B1		
Fairfield Road	A3		
Firle Road	C1		
Furness Road	B3		
Gaudick Road	A3		
Gilbert Road	C1		
Gildredge Road	B2		
Gorringe Road	B1		
Grand Parade	C3		
Grange Road	B3		
Grassington Road	B3		
Grove Road	B2		
Hartfield Road	B1		
Hartington Place	C2		
High Street	A1		
Hyde Gardens	B2		
King Edward's Parade	B3		
Langney Road	C2		
Lewes Road	B1		
Marine Parade	C2		
Mark Lane	B2		
Meads Road	A3		
Melbourne Road	C1		
Mill Gap Road	A1		
Mill Road	A1		
Moat Croft Road	A1		
Moy Avenue	C1		
Ratton Road	A1		
Royal Parade	C2		
Saffrons Park	A3		
Saffrons Road	A2		
St. Anne's Road	A1		
St. Leonard's Road	B2		
Seaside	C2		
Seaside Road	C2		
Selwyn Road	A1		
Silverdale Road	B3		
South Street	B2		
Southfields Road	A2		
Station Parade	B2		
Susan's Road	C2		
Sydney Road	C2		
Terminus Road	B2		

EXETER

0	400 yds
0	400m

Appears on main map page 102

Tourist Information Centre: Dix's Field
Tel: 01392 665700

Albion Street	A3	St. James' Road	C1
Alphington Street	A3	St. Leonard's Road	C3
Barnfield Road	B2	Sidwell Street	B2
Bartholomew Street West	A2	Southernhay East	B2
Bedford Street	B2	South Street	B2
Belmont Road	C1	Spicer Road	C2
Blackboy Road	C1	Station Road	A1
Blackall Road	B1	Streatham Drive	A1
Bonhay Road	A2	Streatham Rise	A1
Buller Road	A3	The Quay	B3
Church Road	A3	Thornton Hill	B1
Clifton Hill	C1	Topsham Road	B3
Clifton Road	C2	Velwell Road	A1
Clifton Street	C2	Victoria Street	C1
College Road	C2	Water Lane	B3
Commercial Road	B3	Well Street	C1
Cowick Street	A3	West Avenue	B1
Cowley Bridge Road	A1	Western Road	A2
Danes Road	B1	Western Way	C2
Denmark Road	C2	Wonford Road	C3
Devonshire Place	C1	York Road	B1
Dix's Field	B2		
East Grove Road	C3		
Elmside	C1		
Exe Street	A2		
Fore Street	B2		
Haldon Road	A2		
Haven Road	B3		
Heavitree Road	C2		
Hele Road	A1		
High Street	B2		
Holloway Street	B3		
Hoopern Street	B1		
Howell Road	B1		
Iddesleigh Road	C1		
Iron Bridge	A2		
Isca Road	B3		
Jesmond Road	C1		
Longbrook Street	B1		
Looe Road	A1		
Lyndhurst Road	C3		
Magdalen Road	C2		
Magdalen Street	B3		
Marlborough Road	C3		
Matford Avenue	C3		
Matford Lane	C3		
Mount Pleasant Road	C1		
New Bridge Street	A3		
New North Road	A1/B1		
North Street	B2		
Okehampton Road	A3		
Okehampton Street	A3		
Old Tiverton Road	C1		
Oxford Road	C1		
Paris Street	B2		
Paul Street	B2		
Pennsylvania Road	B1		
Portland Street	C2		
Prince of Wales Road	A1		
Princesshay	B2		
Prospect Park	C1		
Queen's Road	A3		
Queen Street	B2		
Radford Road	C3		
Richmond Road	A2		
St. David's Hill	A1		

Folkestone

Tourist Information Centre: Town Hall, 1-2 Guildhall Street
Tel: 01303 257946

Alder Road	B2
Archer Road	C2
Bathurst Road	A2
Beatty Road	C1
Black Bull Road	B2
Bournemouth Road	B2
Bouverie Road West	A3
Bradstone Road	B2
Broadfield Road	A2
Broadmead Road	B2
Brockman Road	B2
Canterbury Road	C1
Castle Hill Avenue	B3
Cheriton Gardens	B3
Cheriton Road	A2/B2
Cherry Garden Avenue	A1
Christ Church Road	B3
Churchill Avenue	B1
Clifton Crescent	A3
Coniston Road	A1
Coolinge Road	B2
Cornwallis Avenue	A2
Dawson Road	B2
Dixwell Road	A3
Dolphins Road	B1
Dover Hill	C1
Dover Road	C1
Downs Road	B1
Earles Avenue	A3
Foord Road	B2
Godwyn Road	A3
Grimston Avenue	A3
Grimston Gardens	A3
Guildhall Street	B2
Guildhall Street North	B2
Harbour Way	C2
Hill Road	C1
Ivy Way	C1
Joyes Road	C1
Linden Crescent	B2
Links Way	A1
Lower Sandgate Road	A3
Lucy Avenue	A1
Manor Road	B3
Marine Parade	B3
Marshall Street	C1
Mead Road	B2
Old High Street	C3
Park Farm Road	B1
Pavilion Road	B2
Radnor Bridge Road	C2
Radnor Park Avenue	A2
Radnor Park Road	B2
Radnor Park West	A2
Sandgate Hill	A3
Sandgate Road	B3
Shorncliffe Road	A2
Sidney Street	C2
The Leas	B3
The Stade	C3
The Tram Road	C2
Tontine Street	C2
Turketel Road	A3
Tyson Road	C1
Wear Bay Crescent	C2
Wear Bay Road	C1
Westbourne Gardens	A3
Wingate Road	B1
Wood Avenue	C1
Wilton Road	A2

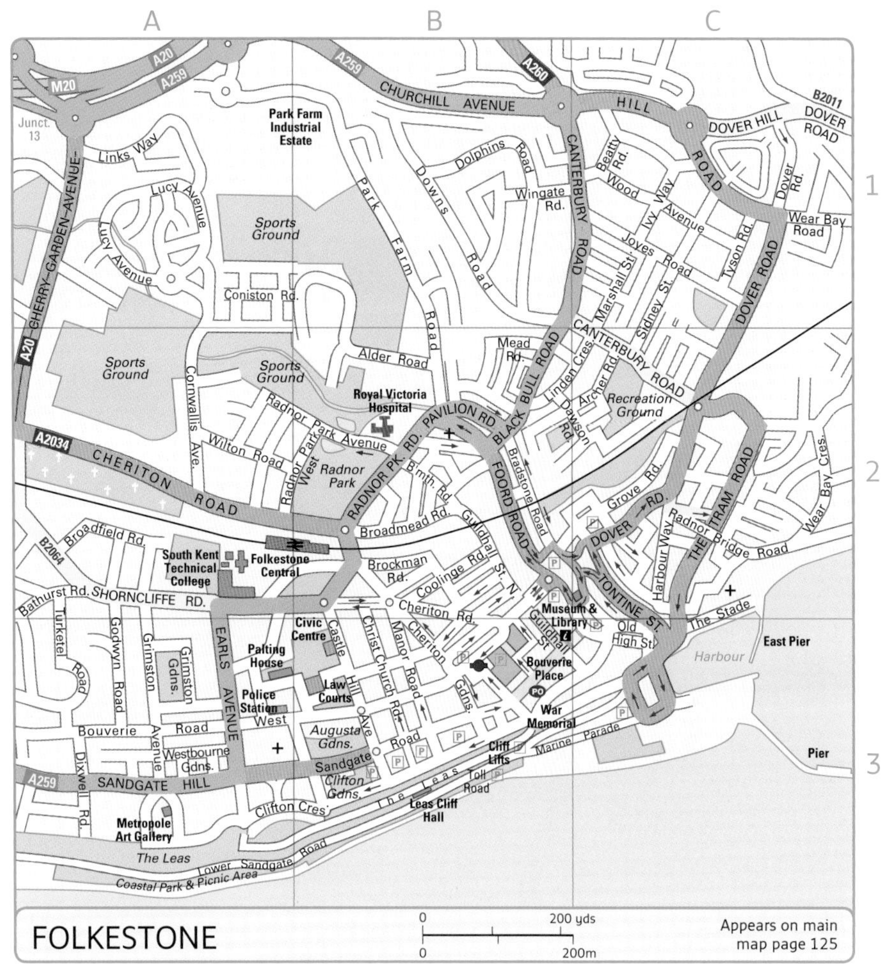

FOLKESTONE

0 200 yds
0 200m

Appears on main
map page 125

Gloucester

Tourist Information Centre: 28 Southgate Street
Tel: 01452 396572

Adelaide Street	B3
Alexandra Road	B1
Alfred Street	C2
Alma Place	A3
Alvin Street	B1
Archdeacon Street	A1
Argyll Road	C1
Askwith Road	C3
Barnwood Road	C1
Barton Street	B2
Black Dog Way	B1
Bristol Road	A3
Brunswick Road	B2
Bruton Way	B2
Calton Road	B3
Castle Meads Way	A1
Cecil Road	A3
Cheltenham Road	C1
Churchill Road	A3
Clifton Road	A3
Conduit Street	B3
Coney Hill Road	C3
Dean's Way	B1
Denmark Road	B1
Derby Road	B2
Estcourt Road	B1
Eastern Avenue	C3
Eastgate Street	B2
Frampton Road	A3
Gouda Way	A1
Great Western Road	B2
Greyfriars	B2
Hatherley Road	B3
Heathville Road	B1
Hempsted Lane	A2
Henry Road	B1
High Street	B3
Hopewell Street	B3
Horton Road	C2
Howard Street	B3
India Road	C2
King Edward's Avenue	B3
Kingsholm Road	B1
Lansdown Road	B1
Linden Road	A3
Llanthony Road	A2
London Road	B1
Lower Westgate Street	A1
Marlborough Road	C3
Merevale Road	C1
Metz Way	B2
Midland Road	B3
Millbrook Street	B2
Myers Road	C2
Northgate Street	B1
Oxford Road	B1
Oxstalls Lane	C1
Painswick Road	C3
Park Road	B2
Parkend Road	B3
Pitt Street	B1
Quay Street	A2
Regent Street	B3
Robinson Road	A3
Ryecroft Street	B3
St. Ann Way	A3
St. Oswald's Road	A1
Secunda Way	A3
Severn Road	A2
Seymour Road	A3
Southgate Street	A2
Spa Road	A2
Stanley Road	B3
Station Road	B2
Stroud Road	A3
The Quay	A2
Tredworth Road	B3
Trier Way	A3
Upton Street	B3
Vicarage Road	C3
Victoria Street	B2
Wellington Street	B2
Westgate Street	A1
Weston Road	A3
Wheatstone Road	B3
Willow Avenue	C3
Worcester Street	B1

GLOUCESTER

0 500 yds
0 500m

Appears on main
map page 132

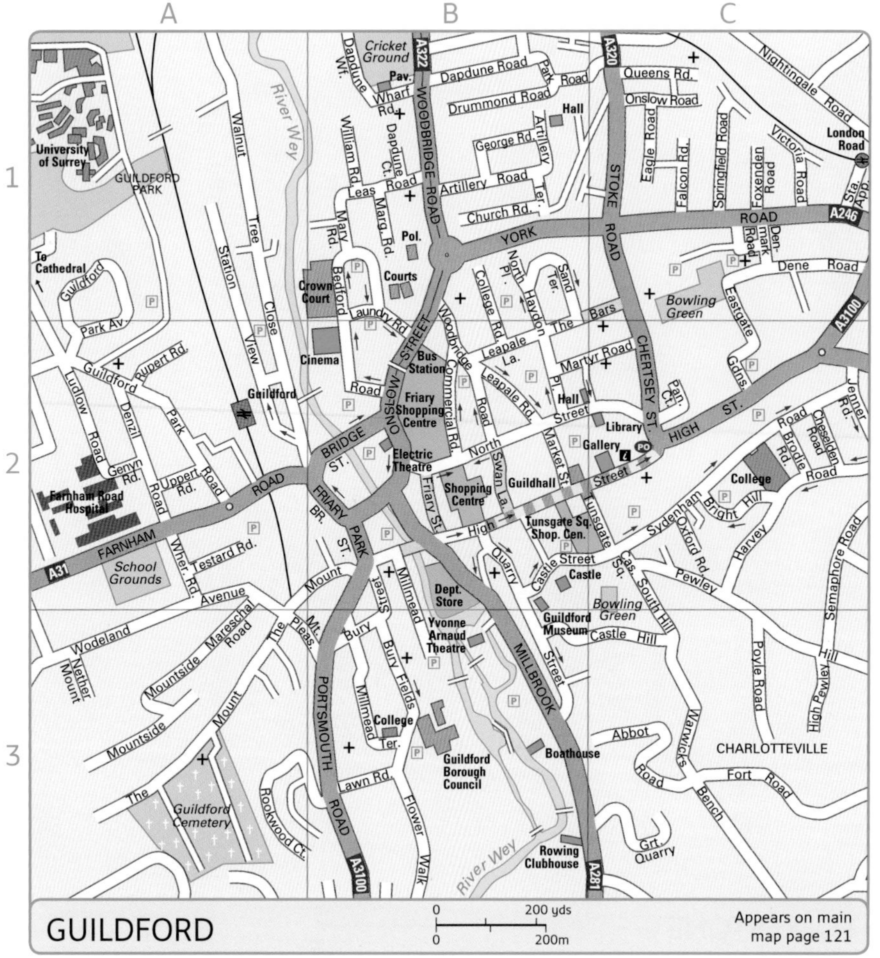

GUILDFORD

Map grid labels: A B C (columns), 1 2 3 (rows)

Map features: Cricket Ground, University of Surrey, Guildford Park, To Cathedral, Farnham Road Hospital, FARNHAM, School Grounds, Guildford Cemetery, The, Crown Court, Courts, Cinema, Guildford, Bus Station, Friary Shopping Centre, Electric Theatre, Shopping Centre, Guildhall, Library, Gallery, P.O., College, Dept. Store, Yvonne Arnaud Theatre, Tunsgate Sq. Shop. Cen., Castle, Guildford Museum, Bowling Green, Boathouse, Guildford Borough Council, Abbot, CHARLOTTEVILLE, Rowing Clubhouse, Grt. Quarry, Bowling Green, Hall, London Road, River Wey

Scale: 0 — 200 yds / 0 — 200m

Appears on main map page 121

Tourist Information Centre: 155 High Street
Tel: 01483 444333

Street	Grid	Street	Grid
Abbot Road	C3	Portsmouth Road	B3
Artillery Road	B1	Poyle Road	C3
Artillery Terrace	B1	Quarry Street	B2
Bedford Road	B1	Queens Road	C1
Bridge Street	B2	Rookwood Court	A3
Bright Hill	C2	Rupert Road	A2
Brodie Road	C2	Sand Terrace	B1
Bury Fields	B3	Semaphore Road	C3
Bury Street	B3	South Hill	C2
Castle Hill	C3	Springfield Road	C1
Castle Square	C2	Station Approach	C1
Castle Street	B2	Station View	A1
Chertsey Street	C1	Stoke Road	C1
Cheselden Road	C2	Swan Lane	B2
Commercial Road	B2	Sydenham Road	C2
Dapdune Court	B1	Testard Road	A2
Dapdune Road	B1	The Bars	B2
Dapdune Wharf	B1	The Mount	A3
Dene Road	C1	Tunsgate	C2
Denmark Road	C1	Upperton Road	A2
Denzil Road	A2	Victoria Road	C1
Drummond Road	B1	Walnut Tree Close	A1
Eagle Road	C1	Warwicks	C3
Eastgate Gardens	C2	Wharf Road	B1
Falcon Road	C1	Wherwell Road	A2
Farnham Road	A2	William Road	B1
Flower Walk	B3	Wodeland Avenue	A3
Fort Road	C3	Woodbridge Road	B1
Foxenden Road	C1	York Road	B1
Friary Bridge	B2		
Friary Street	B2		
Genyn Road	A2		
George Road	B1		
Great Quarry	C3		
Guildford Park Avenue	A1		
Guildford Park Road	A2		
Harvey Road	C2		
Haydon Place	B1		
High Pewley	C3		
High Street	B2/C2		
Laundry Road	B1		
Lawn Road	B3		
Leap Lane	B2		
Leas Road	B1		
Ludlow Road	A2		
Mareschal Road	A3		
Margaret Road	B1		
Market Street	B2		
Martyr Road	B2		
Mary Road	B1		
Millbrook	B3		
Millmead	B2		
Millmead Terrace	B3		
Mount Pleasant	A3		
Mountside	A3		
Nether Mount	A3		
Nightingale Road	C1		
North Place	B1		
North Street	B2		
Onslow Road	C1		
Onslow Street	B2		
Oxford Road	C2		
Pannells Court	C2		
Park Road	B1		
Park Street	B2		
Pewley Hill	C2		

HARROGATE

Map grid labels: A B C (columns), 1 2 3 (rows)

Map features: KNAPPING MOUNT, Coach Park, Rugby Football Ground, Ladies College, International Centre, Royal Hall, Council Offices, Royal Baths, Mercer Art Gallery, Royal Pump Room Museum, Sun Pavilion, Valley Gardens, Harrogate Theatre, Harrogate Cinema, Harrogate Shopping Centre, Police Station, Christ Church, Library, Magistrates's Court, West Park, The Stray, Tewit Well, Stray Walk, Stray Rein

Scale: 0 — 150 yds / 0 — 150m

Appears on main map page 194

Tourist Information Centre: Royal Baths, Crescent Road
Tel: 01423 537300

Street	Grid	Street	Grid
Ainsty Road	C1	Regent Grove	C1
Albert Street	B2	Regent Parade	C1
Alexandra Road	B1	Regent Street	C1
Arthington Avenue	B2	Regent Terrace	C1
Beech Grove	A3	Ripon Road	A1
Belford Road	B2	Robert Street	B3
Bower Road	B1	St. James Drive	C3
Bower Street	B2	St. Mary's Walk	A3
Cambridge Street	B2	Skipton Road	C1
Cavendish Avenue	C3	South Park Road	B3
Chelmsford Road	B2	Springfield Avenue	A1
Cheltenham Mount	B1	Spring Grove	A1
Chudleigh Road	C1	Spring Mount	A1
Clarence Drive	A2	Station Avenue	B2
Claro Road	C1	Station Parade	B2
Cold Bath Road	A3	Stray Rein	B3
Commercial Street	B1	Stray Walk	C3
Coppice Drive	A1	Studley Road	B1
Cornwall Road	A2	Swan Road	A2
Crescent Gardens	A2	The Grove	C1
Dragon Avenue	B1	Tower Street	B3
Dragon Parade	B1	Trinity Road	B3
Dragon Road	B1	Valley Drive	A2
Duchy Road	A1	Victoria Avenue	B2
East Parade	B2	Victoria Road	A3
East Park Road	B2	West End Avenue	A3
Franklin Mount	B1	West Park	B2
Franklin Road	B1	Woodside	B2
Gascoigne Crescent	C1	York Place	B3
Glebe Avenue	A2	York Road	A2
Glebe Road	A3		
Grove Park Terrace	C1		
Grove Road	B1		
Harcourt Drive	C2		
Harcourt Road	C1		
Heywood Road	A3		
Hollins Road	A1		
Homestead Road	B2		
James Street	B2		
Kent Road	A1		
King's Road	A2		
Knaresborough Road	C2		
Lancaster Road	A3		
Leeds Road	B3		
Lime Grove	C1		
Lime Street	C1		
Mayfield Grove	B1		
Montpellier Hill	A2		
Montpellier Street	A2		
Mowbray Square	C1		
North Park Road	C2		
Oatlands Drive	C3		
Otley Road	A3		
Oxford Street	B2		
Park Chase	C1		
Park Drive	B3		
Park Parade	C2		
Park Road	A3		
Park View	B2		
Parliament Street	A2		
Princes Villa Road	B2		
Providence Terrace	B1		
Queen Parade	C2		
Queen's Road	A3		
Raglan Street	B2		
Regent Avenue	C1		

Tourist Information Centre: Muriel Matters House, 2 Breeds Pl
Tel: 01424 451111

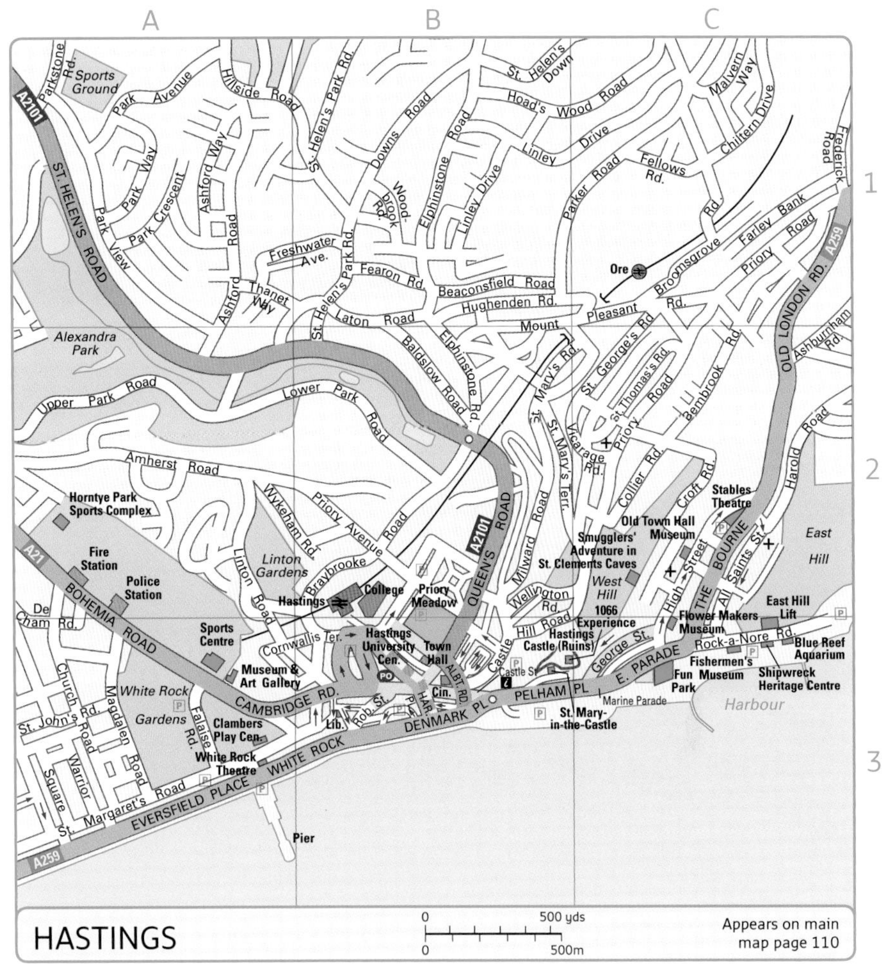

HASTINGS

0   500 yds
0   500m

Appears on main
map page 110

Tourist Information Centre: The Butter Market, High Town,
Maylord St   Tel: 01432 370514

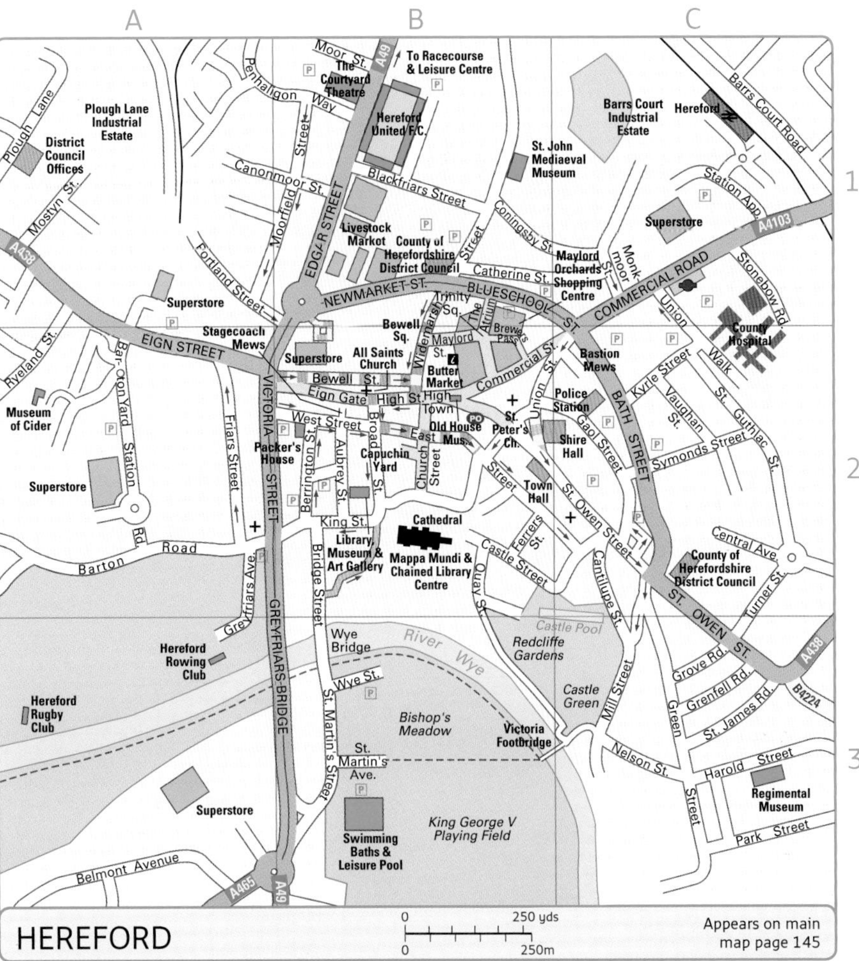

HEREFORD

0   250 yds
0   250m

Appears on main
map page 145

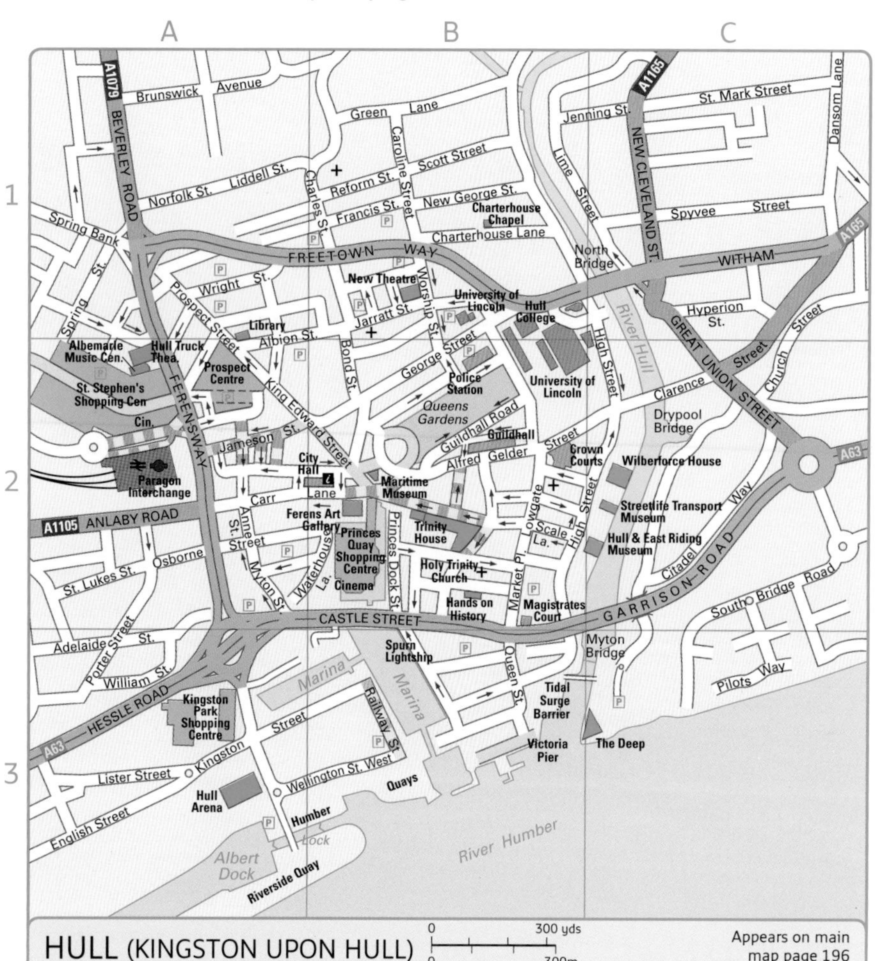

HULL (KINGSTON UPON HULL)

0   300 yds
0   300m

Appears on main map page 196

Tourist Information Centre: Hull City Hall, 1 Paragon Street
Tel: 01482 223559

Adelaide Street	A3
Albion Street	A2
Alfred Gelder Street	B2
Anlaby Road	A2
Anne Street	A2
Beverley Road	A1
Bond Street	B2
Brunswick Avenue	A1
Caroline Street	B1
Carr Lane	A2
Castle Street	B2
Charles Street	B1
Charterhouse Lane	B1
Church Street	C2
Citadel Way	C2
Clarence Street	C2
Cleveland Street	C1
Dansom Lane	C1
English Street	A3
Ferensway	A2
Francis Street	B1
Freetown Way	A1
Garrison Road	C2
George Street	B2
Great Union Street	C1
Green Lane	B1
Guildhall Road	B2
Hessle Road	A3
High Street	C1
Hyperion Street	C1
Jameson Street	A2
Jarratt Street	B1
Jenning Street	B1
King Edward Street	A2
Kingston Street	A3
Liddell Street	A1
Lime Street	B1
Lister Street	A3
Lowgate	B2
Market Place	B2
Myton Street	A2
New Cleveland Street	C1
New George Street	B1
Norfolk Street	A1
North Bridge	B1
Osborne Street	A2
Pilots Way	C3
Porter Street	A3
Princes Dock Street	B2
Prospect Street	A1
Queen Street	B3
Reform Street	B1
St. Lukes Street	A2
St. Mark Street	C1
Scale Lane	B2
Scott Street	B1
Scott Street Bridge	B1
South Bridge Road	C2
Spring Bank	A1
Spring Street	A2
Spyvee Street	C1
Waterhouse Lane	A2
Wellington Street West	A3
William Street	A3
Witham	C1
Worship Street	B1
Wright Street	A1

INVERNESS

0   300 yds
0   300m

Appears on main map page 266

Tourist Information Centre: 36 High Street
Tel: 01463 252401

Abban Street	A1	Lochalsh Road	A1
Academy Street	B2	Longman Road	C1
Alexander Place	B2	Maxwell Drive	A3
Anderson Street	B1	Mayfield Road	B3
Ardconnel Street	B3	Midmills Road	C2
Ardconnel Terrace	C2	Millburn Road	C2
Ardross Place	B3	Montague Row	A2
Ardross Street	B3	Muirfield Road	C3
Argyle Street	C3	Nelson Street	A1
Argyle Terrace	C3	Ness Bank	B3
Attadale Road	A2	Ness Bridge	B2
Auldcastle Road	C2	Ness Walk	B3
Bank Street	B2	Old Edinburgh Road	B3
Baron Taylor's Street	B2	Park Road	A3
Benula Road	A1	Perceval Road	A2
Bishop's Road	A3	Planefield Road	A2
Bridge Street	B2	Queensgate	B2
Broadstone Park	C3	Rangemore Road	A2
Bruce Gardens	A3	Riverside Street	B1
Burnett Road	C1	Ross Avenue	A2
Carse Road	A1	Shore Street	B1
Castle Road	B2	Smith Avenue	A3
Castle Street	B2	Southside Place	C3
Castle Wynd	B2	Southside Road	C3
Cawdor Road	C2	Stephen's Brae	C2
Celt Street	A2	Strother's Lane	B2
Chapel Street	B1	Telford Road	A1
Charles Street	C2	Telford Street	A1
Church Street	B2	Tomnahurich Street	A3
Columba Road	A3	Union Road	C3
Crown Avenue	C2	Union Street	B2
Crown Circus	C2	View Place	B3
Crown Drive	C2	Walker Road	B1
Crown Road	C2	Waterloo Bridge	B1
Crown Street	C3	Wells Street	A2
Culduthel Road	B3	Young Street	B2
Denny Street	C3		
Dochfour Drive	A3		
Douglas Row	B1		
Duffy Drive	B3		
Duncraig Street	A2		
Eastgate	C2		
Fairfield Road	A2		
Falcon Square	B2		
Friars Bridge	A1		
Friars Lane	B2		
Friars Street	B2		
Gilbert Street	A1		
Glebe Street	B1		
Glen Urquhart Road	A3		
Gordon Terrace	B3		
Grant Street	A1		
Greig Street	A2		
Harbour Road	B1		
Harrowden Road	A2		
Haugh Road	B3		
High Street	B2		
Hill Street	C2		
Hontly Place	A1		
Huntly Street	A2		
Innes Street	B1		
Kenneth Street	A2		
Kingsmills Road	C2		
King Street	A2		
Leys Drive	C3		
Lindsay Avenue	A3		

Tourist Information Centre: 51 Gallowtree Gate
Tel: 0116 299 4444

Abbey Street	B1	Market Place South	B2
Albion Street	B2	Market Street	B2
All Saints Road	A2	Mill Lane	A3
Aylestone Road	B3	Millstone Lane	B2
Bassett Street	A1	Montreal Road	C1
Bath Lane	A2	Morledge Street	C2
Bedford Street North	C1	Narborough Road	A3
Belgrave Gate	B1	Narborough Road North	A2
Bell Lane	C1	Nelson Street	C3
Belvoir Street	B2	Newarke Close	A3
Braunstone Gate	A2	Newarke Street	B2
Burgess Street	B1	Northgate Street	A1
Burleys Way	B1	Ottawa Road	C1
Byron Street	B1	Oxford Street	B2
Cank Street	B2	Pasture Lane	A1
Castle Street	A2	Peacock Lane	B2
Charles Street	C2	Pocklingtons Walk	B2
Christow Street	C1	Prebend Street	C3
Church Gate	B1	Princess Road East	C3
Clarence Street	B1	Pringle Street	A1
Clyde Street	C1	Queen Street	C2
College Street	C2	Regent Road	B3
Colton Street	C2	Regent Street	C3
Conduit Street	C2	Repton Street	A1
Crafton Street East	C1	Rutland Street	C2
Cravan Street	A1	Samuel Street	C2
De Montfort Street	C3	Sanvey Gate	A1
Deacon Street	B3	Saxby Street	C3
Dryden Street	B1	Slater Street	A1
Duns Lane	A2	Soar Lane	A1
Dunton Street	A1	South Albion Street	C2
Eastern Boulevard	A3	Southampton Street	C2
Friar Lane	B2	Sparkenhoe Street	C2
Friday Street	B1	St. George Street	C2
Frog Island	A1	St. George's Way	C2
Gallowtree Gate	B2	St. John's Street	B1
Gaul Street	A3	St. Margaret's Way	A1
Glebe Street	C2	St. Matthew's Way	C1
Gotham Street	C3	St. Nicholas Circle	A2
Granby Street	B2	Swain Street	C2
Grange Lane	B3	Swan Street	A1
Grasmere Street	A3	Taylor Road	C1
Great Central Street	A1	Thames Street	B1
Halford Street	B2	The Gateway	A3
Havelock Street	B3	The Newarke	A2
Haymarket	B1	Tigers Way	B3
High Street	B2	Tower Street	B3
Highcross Street	A1	Tudor Road	A1
Hobart Street	C2	Ullswater Street	A3
Horsfair Street	B2	University Road	C3
Humberstone Gate	B2	Upperton Road	A3
Humberstone Road	C1	Vaughan Way	A1
Infirmary Road	B3	Vestry Street	C2
Jarrom Street	A3	Walnut Street	A3
Jarvis Street	A2	Waterloo Way	C3
Kamloops Crescent	C1	Welford Road	B2
Kent Street	C1	Wellington Street	B2
King Richard's Road	A2	West Street	B3
King Street	B2	Western Boulevard	A3
Lancaster Road	B3	Western Road	A3
Lee Street	B1	Wharf Street North	C1
Lincoln Street	C2	Wharf Street South	C1
London Road	C3	Wilberforce Road	A3
Loseby Lane	B2	Windermere Street	A3
Lower Brown Street	B2	Woodboy Street	C1
Manitoba Road	C1	Yeoman Street	B2
Mansfield Street	B1	York Road	B2

Tourist Information Centre: 9 Castle Hill
Tel: 01522 545458

Alexandra Terrace	A2	Spa Road	C3
Baggholme Road	C2	St. Anne's Road	C2
Bailgate	B1	St. Giles Avenue	C1
Beaumont Fee	B2	St. Mark Street	B3
Beevor Street	A3	St. Mary's Street	B3
Brayford Way	A3	St. Rumbold Street	B2
Brayford Wharf North	A2	Steep Hill	B2
Broadgate	B2	The Avenue	A2
Broadway	B1	The Avenue	A2
Bruce Road	C1	Tritton Road	A3
Burton Road	A1	Union Row	B2
Canwick Road	B3	Upper Lindum Street	C2
Carholme Road	A2	Upper Long Leys Road	A1
Carline Road	A1	Vere Street	B1
Carr Street	A2	Vine Street	C2
Cheviot Street	C2	Waterside North	B3
Church Lane	B1	Waterside South	B3
Clasketgate	B2	West Parade	A2
Croft Street	B2	Westgate	B1
Cross Street	B3	Wigford Way	B2
Curle Avenue	C1	Wilson Street	A1
Drury Lane	B2	Winn Street	C2
East Gate	B2	Wragby Road	C2
Firth Road	A3	Yarborough Road	A1
George Street	C3		
Great Northern Terrace	B3		
Greetwell Close	C1		
Greetwell Road	C2		
Gresham Street	A2		
Hampton Street	A2		
Harvey Street	A2		
High Street	B3		
John Street	C2		
Langworthgate	B1		
Lee Road	C1		
Lindum Road	B2		
Lindum Terrace	C2		
Long Leys Road	A1		
Mainwaring Road	C1		
Mill Road	A1		
Milman Road	C2		
Monks Road	C2		
Monson Street	B3		
Moor Street	C2		
Mount Street	A1		
Nettleham Road	B1		
Newland	A2		
Newland Street West	A2		
Newport	B1		
Northgate	B1		
Orchard Street	A2		
Pelham Bridge	B3		
Portland Street	B3		
Portland Street	B3		
Pottergate	B2		
Queensway	C1		
Rasen Lane	B1		
Richmond Road	A2		
Ripon Street	B3		
Rope Walk	A3		
Rosemary Lane	B2		
Ruskin Avenue	C1		
Saltergate	B2		
Sewell Road	C2		
Silver Street	B2		
Sincil Bank	B3		

LEICESTER

0   200 yds
0   200m

Appears on main map page 160

LINCOLN

0   200 yds
0   200m

Appears on main map page 187

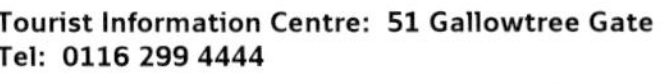

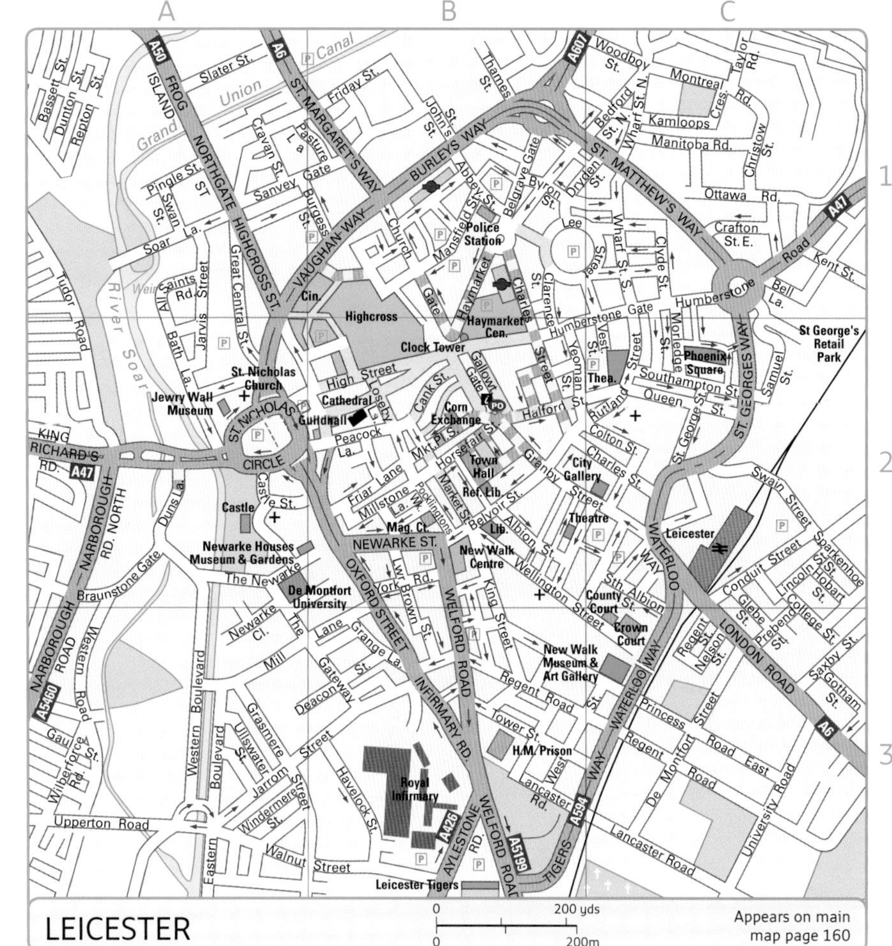

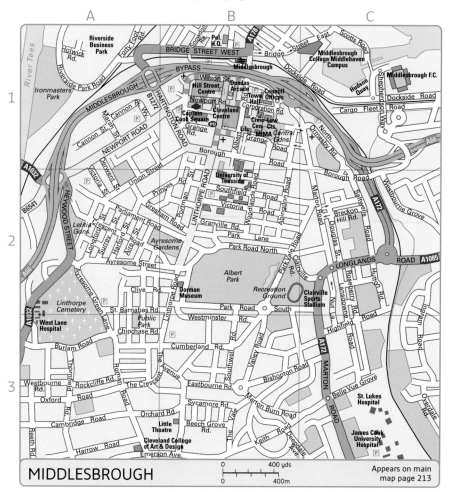

MIDDLESBROUGH

400 yds
400m

Appears on main
map page 213

Abingdon Road	B2
Aire Street	A2
Albert Road	B1
Ayresome Green Lane	A2
Ayresome Street	A2
Beech Grove Road	B3
Belle Vue Grove	C3
Bishopton Road	B3
Borough Road	B1/C3
Breckon Hill Road	C2
Bridge Street East	B1
Bridge Street West	B1
Burlam Road	A3
Cambridge Road	A3
Cannon Park Way	A1
Cannon Street	A1
Cargo Fleet Road	C1
Chipchase Road	A3
Clairville Road	B2
Clive Road	A2
Corporation Road	B1
Crescent Road	A2
Cumberland Road	B3
Deepdale Avenue	B3
Derwent Street	A1
Dockside Road	B1/C1
Douglas Street	C2
Eastbourne Road	B3
Emerson Avenue	B3
Forty Foot Road	A1
Grange Road	B1
Granville Road	B2
Gresham Road	A2
Harford Street	A2
Harrow Road	A3
Hartington Road	A1
Heywood Street	A2
Highfield Road	C3
Holwick Road	A1
Hudson Quay	C1
Hutton Road	C2
Ingram Road	C2
Keith Road	B3
Lansdowne Road	C2
Linthorpe Road	B3
Longford Street	A2
Longlands Road	C2
Marsh Street	A1
Marton Burn Road	B3
Marton Road	C2/C3
Newport Road	A1/B1
North Ormesby Road	C1
Nut Lane	C2
Orchard Road	A3
Overdale Road	C3
Oxford Road	A3
Park Lane	B2
Park Road North	B2
Park Road South	B2
Park Vale Road	B2
Parliament Road	A2
Portman Street	B2
Princes Road	A2
Reeth Road	A3
Riverside Park Road	A1
Rockcliffe Road	A3
Roman Road	A3
Roseberry Road	C2
Saltwells Road	C2
Scotts Road	C1
Sheperdson Way	C1
Snowdon Road	B1
Southfield Road	B2
Southwell Road	B3
St. Barnabas Road	A2
Surrey Street	A2
Sycamore Road	B3
The Avenue	B3
The Crescent	A3
The Vale	B3
Thornfield Road	A3
Union Street	A2
Valley Road	B3
Victoria Road	B2
Victoria Street	A1
Westbourne Grove	C2
Westbourne Road	A3
Westminster Road	B3
Wilson Street	B1
Woodlands Road	B2

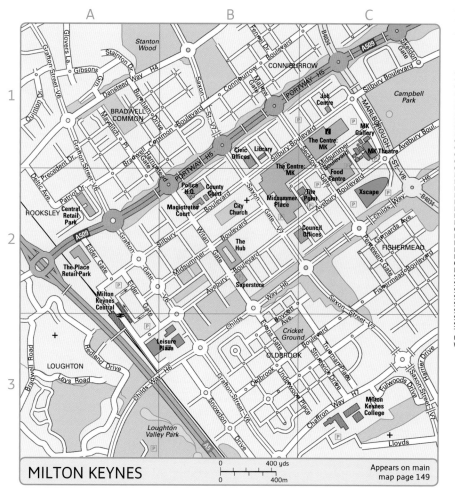

MILTON KEYNES

400 yds
400m

Appears on main
map page 149

Tourist Information Centre: Silbury Arcade
Tel: 01908 688293

Avebury Boulevard	B2/C1
Boycott Avenue	B3
Bradwell Common Boulevard	A1
Bradwell Road	A3
Burnham Drive	A1
Chaffron Way	C3
Childs Way	A3/C2
Conniburrow Boulevard	B1
Dansteed Way	A1
Deltic Avenue	A2
Elder Gate	A2
Evans Gate	B3
Fennel Drive	B1
Fishermead Boulevard	C2
Fulwoods Drive	C3
Gibsons Green	A1
Glovers Lane	A1
Grafton Gate	A2
Grafton Street	A1/B3
Gurnards Avenue	C2
Hampstead Gate	A1
Harrier Drive	C3
Leys Road	A3
Lloyds	C3
Mallow Gate	B1
Marlborough Street	C1
Mayditch Place	A1
Midsummer Boulevard	B2/C1
Oldbrook Boulevard	B3
Patriot Drive	A2
Pentewan Gate	C2
Portway	B2/C1
Precedent Drive	A2
Quinton Drive	A1
Redland Drive	A3
Saxon Gate	B2
Saxon Street	B1/C3
Secklow Gate	C1
Silbury Boulevard	B2/C1
Skeldon Gate	C1
Snowdon Drive	B3
Stainton Drive	A1
Strudwick Drive	C3
Trueman Place	C3
Underwood Place	B3
Witan Gate	B2

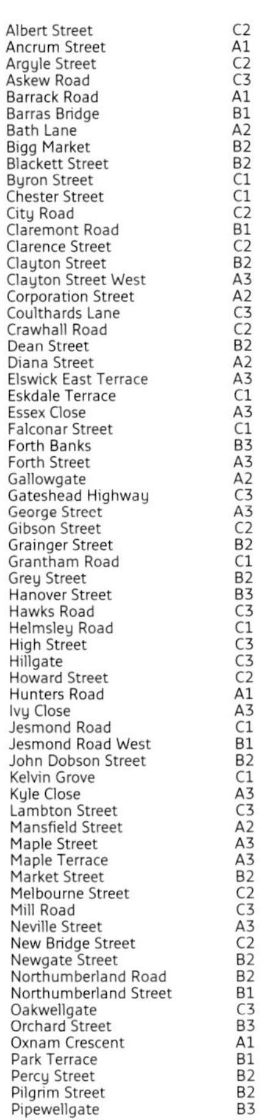

Newcastle upon Tyne

Street	Grid		Street	Grid
Albert Street	C2		Pitt Street	A2
Ancrum Street	A1		Portland Road	C1
Argyle Street	C2		Portland Terrace	C1
Askew Road	C3		Pottery Lane	A3
Barrack Road	A1		Quarryfield Road	C3
Barras Bridge	B1		Quayside	C3
Bath Lane	A2		Queen Victoria Road	B1
Bigg Market	B2		Railway Street	A3
Blackett Street	B2		Redheugh Bridge	A3
Byron Street	C1		Richardson Road	A1
Chester Street	C1		Rye Hill	A3
City Road	C2		St. James Boulevard	A3
Claremont Road	B1		St. Mary's Place	B1
Clarence Street	C2		St. Thomas Street	B1
Clayton Street	B2		Sandyford Road	B1/C1
Clayton Street West	A3		Scotswood Road	A3
Corporation Street	A2		Skinnerburn Road	B3
Coulthards Lane	C3		South Shore Road	C3
Crawhall Road	C2		Stanhope Street	A2
Dean Street	B2		Starbeck Avenue	C1
Diana Street	A2		Stodart Street	C1
Elswick East Terrace	A3		Stowell Street	A2
Eskdale Terrace	C1		Strawberry Place	A2
Essex Close	A3		Summerhill Grove	A2
Falconar Street	C1		Swing Bridge	B3
Forth Banks	B3		The Close	B3
Forth Street	A3		Tyne Bridge	C3
Gallowgate	A2		Union Street	C2
Gateshead Highway	C3		Warwick Street	C1
George Street	A3		Wellington Street	A2
Gibson Street	C2		West Street	C3
Grainger Street	B2		Westgate Road	A2
Grantham Road	C1		Westmorland Road	A3
Grey Street	B2		Windsor Terrace	B1
Hanover Street	B3		York Street	A2
Hawks Road	C3			
Helmsley Road	C1			
High Street	C3			
Hillgate	C3			
Howard Street	C2			
Hunters Road	A1			
Ivy Close	A3			
Jesmond Road	C1			
Jesmond Road West	B1			
John Dobson Street	B2			
Kelvin Grove	C1			
Kyle Close	A3			
Lambton Street	C3			
Mansfield Street	A2			
Maple Street	A3			
Maple Terrace	A3			
Market Street	B2			
Melbourne Street	C2			
Mill Road	C3			
Neville Street	A3			
New Bridge Street	C2			
Newgate Street	B2			
Northumberland Road	B2			
Northumberland Street	B1			
Oakwellgate	C3			
Orchard Street	B3			
Oxnam Crescent	A1			
Park Terrace	B1			
Percy Street	B2			
Pilgrim Street	B2			
Pipewellgate	B3			

NEWCASTLE UPON TYNE

0   400 yds
0   400m

Appears on main map page 212

Norwich

Tourist Information Centre: The Forum, Millennium Plain
Tel: 01603 213999

Street	Grid		Street	Grid
Albion Way	C3		Queens Road	B3
All Saints Green	B3		Rampant Horse Street	B2
Ashby Street	B3		Recorder Road	C2
Bakers Road	A1		Red Lion Street	B2
Bank Plain	B2		Riverside	C3
Barker Street	A1		Riverside Road	C2
Barn Road	A2		Rosary Road	C2
Barrack Street	B1		Rose Lane	B2
Bedford Street	B2		Rouen Road	B3
Ber Street	B3		Rupert Street	A3
Bethel Street	A2		Russell Street	A1
Bishopbridge Road	C2		St. Andrew's Street	B2
Bishopgate	C2		St. Augustine's Street	A1
Botolph Street	B1		St. Benedict's Street	A2
Brazen Gate	B3		St. Crispin's Road	A1
Britannia Road	C1		St. Faiths Lane	B2
Brunswick Road	A3		St. George's Street	B1
Bullclose Road	B1		St. Giles Street	A2
Canary Way	C3		St. James Close	C1
Carrow Hill	C3		St. Leonards Road	C2
Carrow Road	C3		St. Martin's Road	A1
Castle Meadow	B2		St. Stephen's Road	A3
Chapel Field Road	A2		St. Stephen's Street	B3
Chapelfield North	A2		Silver Road	B1
City Road	B3		Silver Street	B1
Clarence Road	C3		Southwell Road	B3
Colegate	B1		Surrey Street	B3
Coslany Street	A2		Sussex Street	A1
Cowgate	B1		Theatre Street	A2
Dereham Road	A2		Thorn Lane	B3
Duke Street	B1		Thorpe Road	C2
Earlham Road	A2		Tombland	B2
Edward Street	B1		Trinity Street	A3
Elm Hill	B2		Trory Street	A2
Fishergate	B1		Union Street	A3
Gas Hill	C1		Unthank Road	A3
Grapes Hill	A2		Vauxhall Street	A3
Grove Avenue	A3		Victoria Street	A3
Grove Road	A3		Wensum Street	B1
Grove Walk	A3		Wessex Street	A3
Gurney Road	C1		Westwick Street	A1
Hall Road	B3		Wherry Road	C3
Hardy Road	C3		Whitefriars	B1
Heathgate	C1		Wodehouse Street	B1
Heigham Street	A1		York Street	A3
Horns Lane	B3			
Ipswich Road	A3			
Ketts Hill	C1			
King Street	B3			
Koblenz Avenue	C3			
Lothian Street	A1			
Lower Clarence Road	C2			
Magdalen Street	B1			
Magpie Road	B1			
Market Avenue	B2			
Marlborough Road	B1			
Mountergate	C1			
Mousehold Street	C1			
Newmarket Road	A3			
Newmarket Street	A3			
Oak Street	A1			
Orchard Street	A1			
Palace Street	B2			
Pitt Street	B1			
Pottergate	A2			
Prince of Wales Road	B2			

NORWICH

0   400 yds
0   400m

Appears on main map page 178

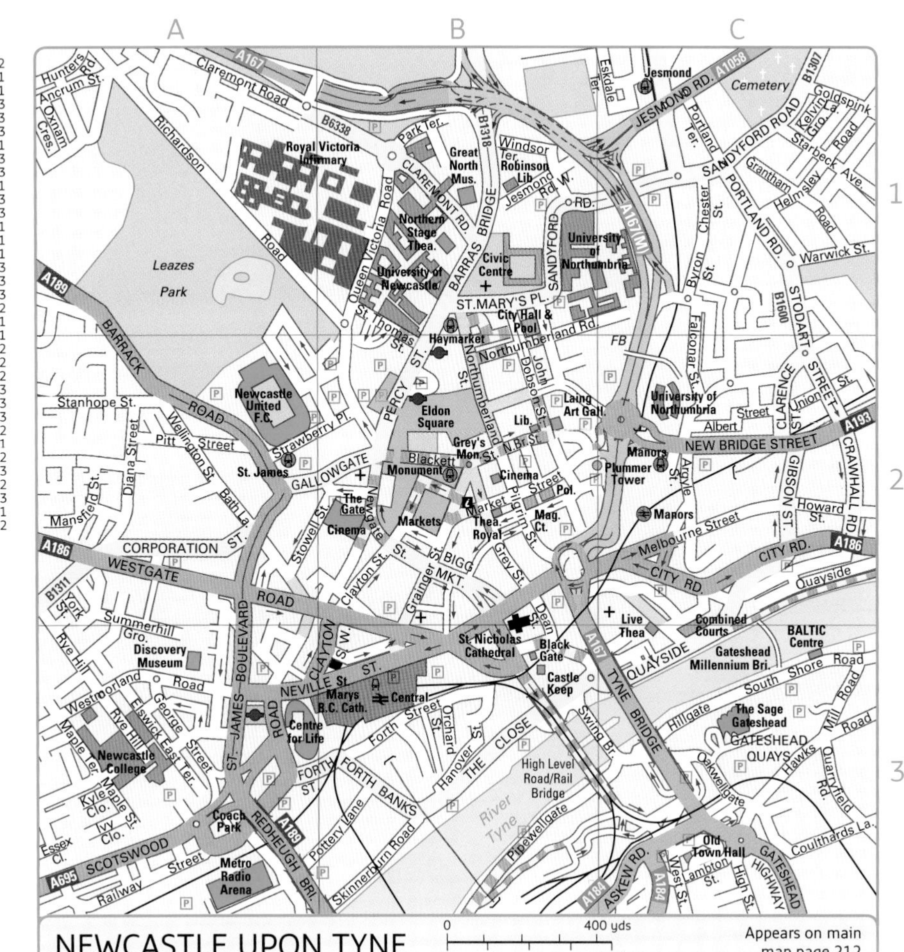

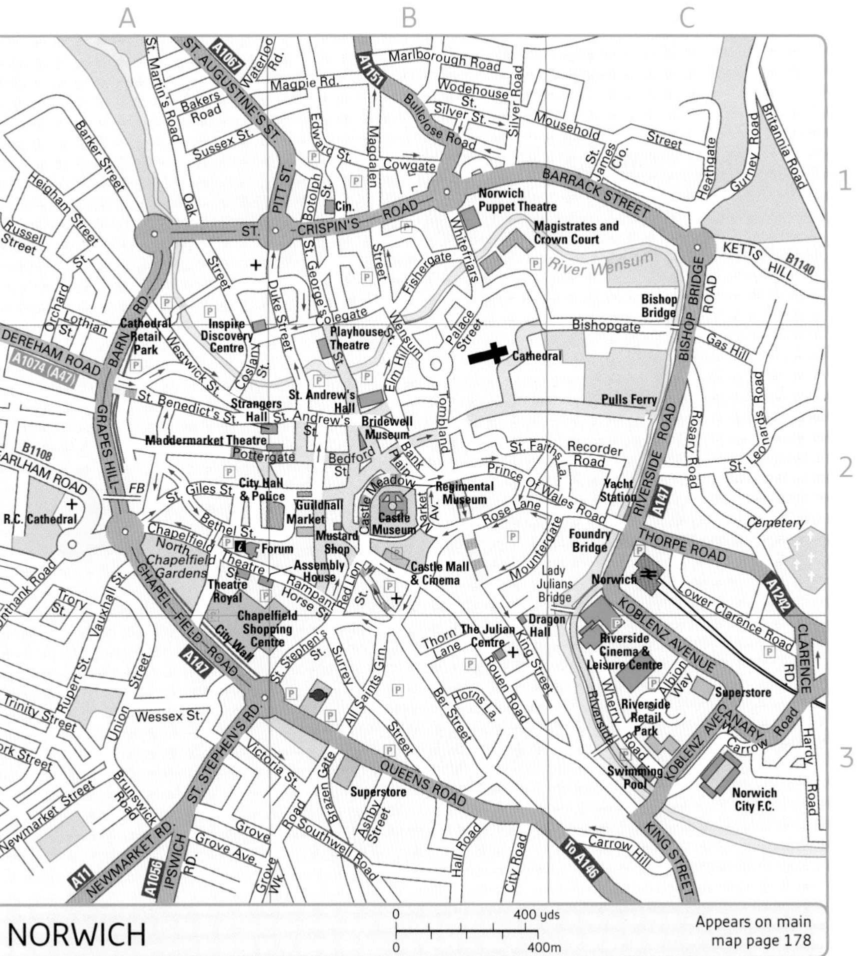

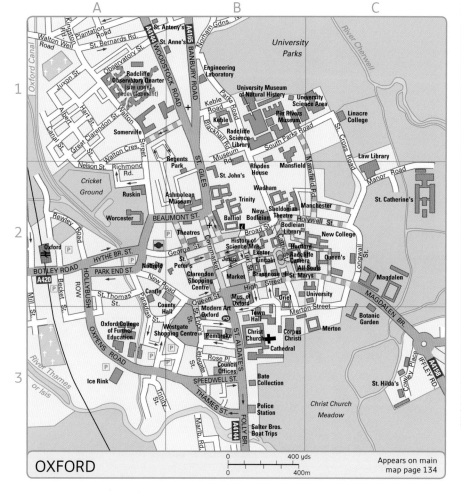

Tourist Information Centre: 1-4 Smithy Row
Tel: 0844 477 5678

Abbotsford Drive	B1	Maid Marian Way	A2
Albert Street	B2	Mansfield Road	B1
Angel Row	A2	Manvers Street	C2
Barker Gate	C2	Market Street	B2
Bath Street	C1	Middle Pavement	B2
Beacon Hill Rise	C1	Milton Street	B1
Bellar Gate	C2	Mount Street	A2
Belward Street	C2	North Church Street	B1
Bridlesmith Gate	B2	North Sherwood Street	B1
Broad Street	B2	Park Row	A2
Brook Street	C1	Park Terrace	A2
Burton Street	A1	Park Valley	A2
Canal Street	B3	Peel Street	A1
Carlton Street	B2	Pelham Street	B2
Carrington Street	B3	Pennyfoot Street	C2
Castle Boulevard	A3	Peveril Drive	A3
Castle Gate	B2	Pilcher Gate	B2
Castle Meadow Road	A3	Plantagenet Street	C1
Castle Road	A3	Popham Street	B3
Chapel Bar	A2	Poplar Street	C2
Chaucer Street	A1	Queens Road	B3
Cheapside	B2	Queen Street	B2
City Link	C3	Regent Street	A2
Clarendon Street	A1	Robin Hood Street	C1
Cliff Road	B3	Roden Street	C1
Clumber Street	B2	St. Ann's Well Road	C1
College Street	A2	St. James Street	A2
Collin Street	B3	St. Mary's Gate	B2
Cranbrook Street	C2	St. Peter's Gate	B2
Cromwell Street	A1	Shakespeare Street	A1
Curzon Street	B1	Shelton Street	B1
Derby Road	A2	Sneinton Road	C2
Dryden Street	A1	South Parade	B2
Fisher Gate	C2	South Sherwood Street	B1
Fishpond Drive	A3	Southwell Road	C2
Fletcher Gate	B2	Station Street	B3
Forman Street	B2	Stoney Street	C2
Friar Lane	A2	Talbot Street	A1
Gedling Street	C2	The Great Northern Close	C3
George Street	B2	The Rope Walk	A2
Gill Street	A1	Union Road	B1
Glasshouse Street	B1	Upper Parliament Street	B2
Goldsmith Street	A1	Victoria Street	B2
Goose Gate	C2	Warser Gate	B2
Hamilton Drive	A3	Waverley Street	A1
Hampden Street	A1	Wheeler Gate	B2
Handel Street	C2	Wilford Street	A3
Heathcote Street	B2	Wollaton Street	A2
High Pavement	B2	Woolpack Lane	C2
Hockley	C2		
Hollowstone	C2		
Hope Drive	A3		
Huntingdon Drive	A2		
Huntingdon Street	B1		
Instow Rise	C1		
Kent Street	B1		
King Edward Street	B2		
King Street	B2		
Lamartine Street	C1		
Lenton Road	A3		
Lincoln Street	B2		
Lister Gate	B3		
London Road	C3		
Long Row	B2		
Low Pavement	B2		
Lower Parliament Street	B2		

NOTTINGHAM

0 — 400 yds
0 — 400m

Appears on main
map page 173

Tourist Information Centre: 15-16 Broad Street
Tel: 01865 686430

Albert Street	A1
Banbury Road	B1
Beaumont Street	A2
Becket Street	A2
Blackhall Road	B1
Botley Road	A2
Broad Street	B2
Canal Street	A1
Cattle Street	B2
Cornmarket	B2
Cowley Place	C3
Folly Bridge	B3
George Street	A2
Great Clarendon Street	A1
Hart Street	A1
High Street	B2
Hollybush Row	A2
Holywell Street	B2
Hythe Bridge Street	A2
Iffley Road	C3
Juxon Street	A1
Keble Road	B1
Kingston Road	A1
Littlegate Street	B3
Longwall Street	C2
Magdalen Bridge	C2
Manor Road	C2
Mansfield Road	C1
Marlborough Road	B3
Merton Street	B3
Mill Street	A2
Museum Road	B1
Nelson Street	A2
New Road	A2
Norham Gardens	B1
Observatory Street	A1
Oxpens Road	A3
Paradise Street	A2
Park End Street	A2
Parks Road	B1
Plantation Road	A1
Queen Street	B2
Rewley Road	A2
Richmond Road	A2
Rose Place	B3
St. Aldate's	B3
St. Bernards Road	A1
St. Cross Road	C1
St. Ebbe's Street	B3
St. Giles	B1
St. Thomas' Street	A2
South Parks Road	B1
Speedwell Street	B3
Thames Street	B3
Trinity Street	A3
Turl Street	B2
Walton Crescent	A1
Walton Street	A1
Walton Well Road	A1
Woodstock Road	A1

OXFORD

0 — 400 yds
0 — 400m

Appears on main
map page 134

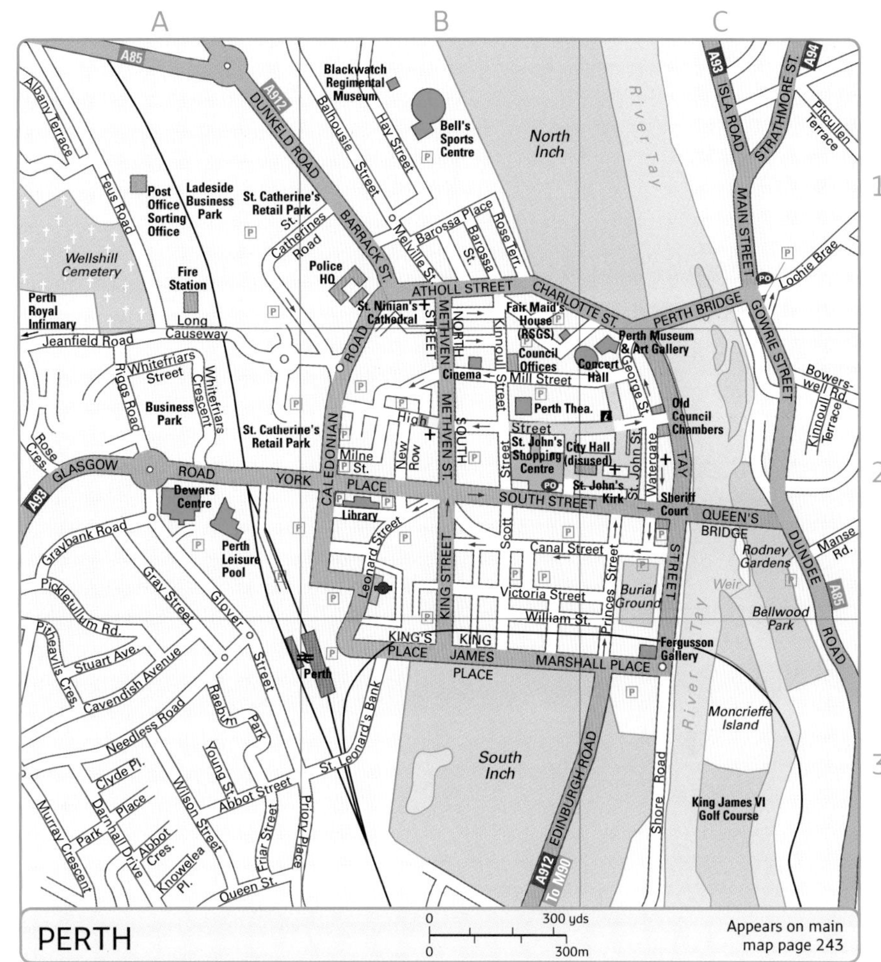

PERTH

Tourist Information Centre: 45 High Street
Tel: 01738 450600

Abbot Crescent	A3
Abbot Street	A3
Albany Terrace	A1
Atholl Street	B1
Balhousie Street	B1
Barossa Place	B1
Barossa Street	B1
Barrack Street	B1
Bowerswell Road	C2
Caledonian Road	B2
Canal Street	B2
Cavendish Avenue	A3
Charlotte Street	B1
Clyde Place	A3
Darnhall Drive	A3
Dundee Road	C2
Dunkeld Road	A1
Edinburgh Road	B3
Feus Road	A1
Friar Street	A3
George Street	C2
Glasgow Road	A2
Glover Street	A2
Gowrie Street	C1
Gray Street	A2
Graybank Road	A2
Hay Street	B1
High Street	B2
Isla Road	C1
Jeanfield Road	A2
King's Place	B3
King James Place	B3
King Street	B2
Kinnoull Street	B1
Kinnoull Terrace	C2
Knowelea Place	A3
Leonard Street	B2
Lochie Brae	C1
Long Causeway	A1
Main Street	C1
Manse Road	C2
Marshall Place	B3
Melville Street	B1
Mill Street	B2
Milne Street	B2
Murray Crescent	A3
Needless Road	A3
New Row	B2
North Methven Street	B1
Park Place	A3
Perth Bridge	C1
Pickletullum Road	A2
Pitcullen Terrace	C1
Pitheavlis Crescent	A3
Princes Street	C3
Priory Place	B3
Queen Street	A3
Queens Bridge	C2
Raeburn Park	A3
Riggs Road	A2
Rose Crescent	A2
Rose Terrace	B1
St. Catherines Road	A1
St. John Street	C2
St. Leonard's Bank	B3
Scott Street	B2
Shore Road	C3
South Methven Street	B2
South Street	B2
Strathmore Street	C1
Stuart Avenue	A3
Tay Street	C2
Victoria Street	B2
Watergate	C2
Whitefriars Crescent	A2
Whitefriars Street	A2
William Street	B2
Wilson Street	A3
Young Street	A3
York Place	A2

Appears on main map page 243

PLYMOUTH

Tourist Information Centre: Plymouth Mayflower Centre,
3-5 The Barbican Tel: 01752 306330

Alexandra Road	C1
Alma Road	A1
Armada Street	B2
Armada Way	B2
Ashford Road	C1
Barbican Approach	C3
Beaumont Road	C2
Beechwood Avenue	B1
Belgrave Road	C1
Bretonside	B2
Buckwell Street	B3
Camden Street	B2
Cattledown Road	C3
Cecil Street	A2
Central Park Avenue	A1
Charles Street	B2
Citadel Road	A3
Clarence Place	A2
Cliff Road	A3
Clifton Place	B1
Clovelly Road	C3
Cobourg Street	B2
Coleridge Road	C1
Connaught Avenue	C1
Cornwall Street	B2
Dale Road	B1
De-La-Hay Avenue	A1
Desborough Road	C2
Drake Circus	B2
East Street	A3
Ebrington Street	B2
Elliot Street	A3
Embankment Road	C2
Exeter Street	B2
Ford Park Road	B1
Furzehill Road	C1
Gdynia Way	C3
Glen Park Avenue	B1
Grand Parade	A3
Greenbank Avenue	C2
Greenbank Road	C1
Grenville Road	C2
Harwell Street	A2
Hill Park Crescent	B1
Hoe Road	B3
Houndiscombe Road	B1
James Street	B2
King Street	A2
Knighton Road	C2
Lipson Hill	C1
Lipson Road	C2
Lisson Grove	C1
Lockyer Street	B3
Looe Street	B2
Madeira Road	B3
Manor Road	A2
Martin Street	A3
Mayflower Street	B2
Millbay Road	A3
Mount Gould Road	C1
Mutley Plain	B1
New George Street	A2
North Cross	B2
North Hill	B2
North Road East	B2
North Road West	A2
North Street	B2
Notte Street	B3
Oxford Street	A2
Pentillie Road	B1
Ponsonby Road	A1
Princess Street	B3
Queen's Road	C1
Royal Parade	B2
Salisbury Road	C2
Saltash Road	A1
Seaton Avenue	B1
Seymour Avenue	C2
Southside Street	B3
Stoke Road	A2
Stuart Road	A1
Sutton Road	C2
Sydney Street	A2
Teats Hill Road	C3
The Crescent	A3
Tothill Avenue	C2
Tothill Road	C2
Union Street	A2
Vauxhall Street	B3
West Hoe Road	A3
Western Approach	A2
Whittington Street	A1
Wilton Street	A2
Wyndham Street	A2

Appears on main map page 100

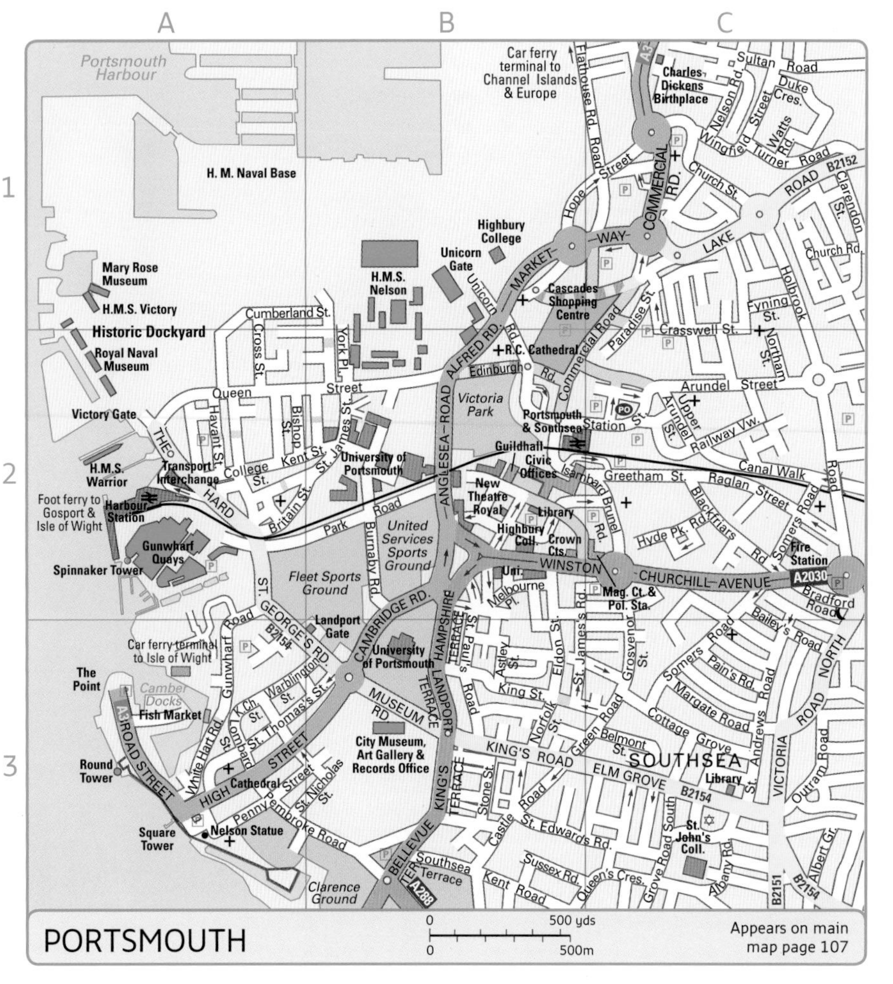

PORTSMOUTH

Albany Road	C3	Penny Street	A3
Albert Grove	C3	Queen's Crescent	C3
Alfred Road	B2	Queen Street	A2
Anglesea Road	B2	Raglan Street	C2
Arundel Street	C2	Railway View	C2
Astley Street	B3	St. Andrews Road	C3
Bailey's Road	C2	St. Edward's Road	B3
Bellevue Terrace	B3	St. George's Road	A2
Belmont Street	C3	St. James Road	B3
Bishop Street	A1	St. James Street	B2
Blackfriars Road	C2	St. Paul's Road	B2
Bradford Road	C3	St. Thomas's Street	A3
Britain Street	A2	Somers Road	C2
Broad Street	A3	Southsea Terrace	B3
Burnaby Road	B2	Station Street	C2
Cambridge Road	B3	Stone Street	B3
Canal Walk	C2	Sultan Road	C1
Castle Road	B3	Sussex Street	B3
Church Street	C1	The Hard	A2
Church Street	C1	Turner Road	C1
Clarendon Street	C1	Unicorn Road	B1
College Street	A2	Upper Arundel Street	C2
Commercial Road	B2	Victoria Road North	C3
Cottage Grove	C3	Warblington Street	A3
Crasswell Street	C1	Watts Road	C1
Cross Street	A1	White Hart Road	A3
Cumberland Street	A1	Wingfield Street	C1
Duke Crescent	C1	Winston Churchill Avenue	B2
Edinburgh Road	B2	York Place	B2
Eldon Street	B3		
Elm Grove	C3		
Flathouse Road	C1		
Fyning Street	C1		
Green Road	B3		
Greetham Street	C2		
Grosvenor Street	C3		
Grove Road South	C3		
Gunwharf Road	A3		
Hampshire Terrace	B3		
Havant Street	A2		
High Street	A3		
Holbrook Road	C1		
Hope Street	B1		
Hyde Park Road	C2		
Isambard Brunel Road	B2		
Kent Road	B3		
Kent Street	A1		
King Charles Street	A3		
King's Road	B3		
King's Terrace	B3		
King Street	B3		
Lake Road	C1		
Landport Terrace	B3		
Lombard Street	A3		
Margate Road	C3		
Market Way	B1		
Melbourne Place	B2		
Museum Road	B3		
Nelson Road	C1		
Norfolk Street	B3		
Northam Street	C2		
Outram Road	C3		
Pain's Road	C3		
Paradise Street	C2		
Park Road	B2		
Pembroke Road	A3		

Appears on main map page 107

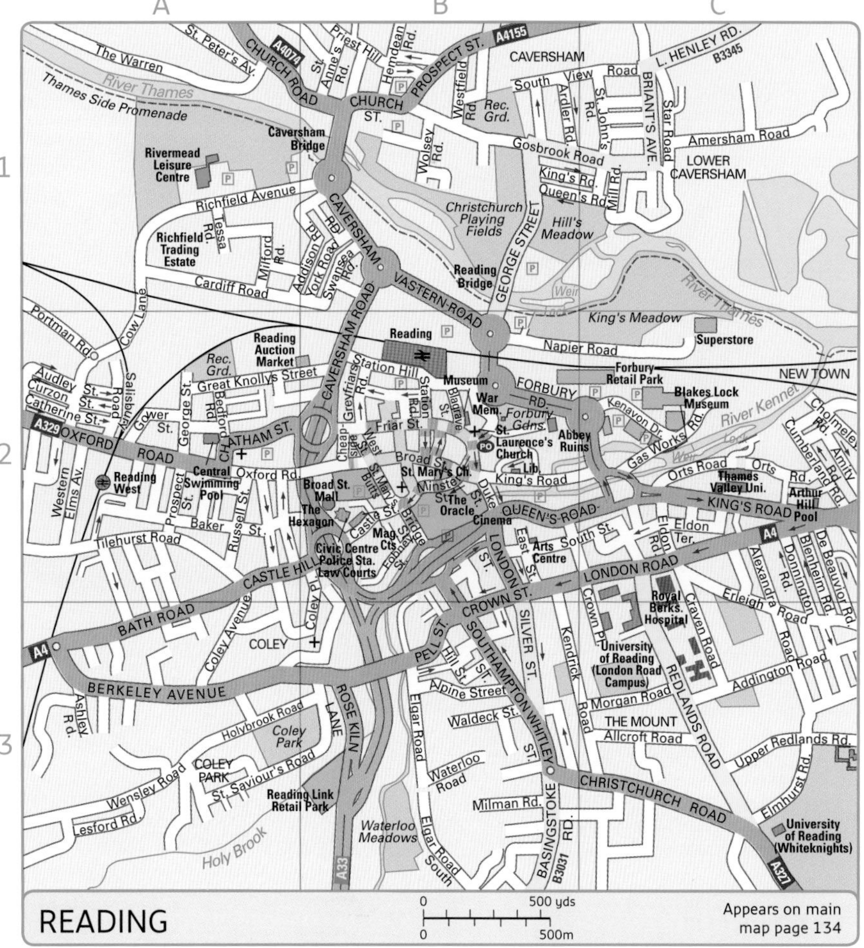

READING

Addington Road	C3	Lesford Road	A3
Addison Road	A1	London Road	C2
Alexandra Road	C2	London Street	B2
Allcroft Road	C3	Lower Henley Road	C1
Alpine Street	B3	Mill Road	C1
Amersham Road	C1	Milford Road	A1
Amity Road	A2	Milman Road	B3
Ardler Road	B1	Minster Street	B2
Ashley Road	A3	Morgan Road	C3
Audley Street	A2	Napier Road	B2
Baker Street	A2	Orts Road	C2
Basingstoke Road	B3	Oxford Road	A2
Bath Road	A3	Pell Street	B3
Bedford Road	A2	Portman Road	A1
Berkeley Avenue	A3	Priest Hill	B1
Blagrave Street	B2	Prospect Street Caversham	B1
Blenheim Road	C2	Prospect Street Reading	A2
Briant's Avenue	C1	Queen's Road Caversham	B1
Bridge Street	B2	Queen's Road Reading	B2
Broad Street	B2	Richfield Avenue	A1
Cardiff Road	A1	Rose Kiln Lane	B3
Castle Hill	A2	Russell Street	A2
Castle Street	B2	St. Anne's Road	B1
Catherine Street	A2	St. John's Road	C1
Caversham Road	B2	St. Mary's Butts	B2
Chatham Street	A2	St. Peters Avenue	A1
Cheapside	B2	St. Saviours Road	A3
Cholmeley Road	C2	Silver Street	B3
Christchurch Road	C3	South Street	B2
Church Road	A1	Southampton Street	B3
Church Street	B1	South View Road	B1
Coley Avenue	A3	Star Road	C1
Coley Place	B2	Station Hill	B2
Cow Lane	A2	Station Road	B2
Craven Road	C3	Swansea Road	B1
Crown Place	C2	Tessa Road	A1
Crown Street	B3	The Warren	A1
Cumberland Road	C2	Tilehurst Road	A2
Curzon Street	A2	Upper Redlands Road	C3
De Beauvoir Road	C2	Vastern Road	B1
Donnington Road	C2	Waldelk Street	B3
Duke Street	B2	Waterloo Road	B3
East Street	B2	Wensley Road	A3
Eldon Road	C2	Western Elms Avenue	A2
Eldon Terrace	C2	Westfield Road	B1
Elgar Road	B3	West Street	B2
Elgar Road South	B3	Whitley Street	B3
Elmhurst Road	C3	Wolsey Road	B1
Erleigh Road	C2	York Road	B1
Fobney Street	B2		
Forbury Road	B2		
Friar Street	B2		
Gas Work Road	C2		
George Street Caversham	B1		
George Street Reading	A2		
Gosbrook Road	B1		
Gower Street	A2		
Great Knollys Street	A2		
Greyfriars Road	B2		
Hemdean Road	B1		
Hill Street	B3		
Holybrook Road	A3		
Kenavon Drive	C2		
Kendrick Road	B3		
King's Road Caversham	B1		
King's Road Reading	B2		

Appears on main map page 134

Tourist Information Centre: Fish Row
Tel: 01722 342860

Albany Road	B1	Salt Lane	B2
Ashley Road	A1	Scots Lane	B2
Avon Terrace	A1	Silver Street	B2
Barnard Street	C2	Southampton Road	C3
Bedwin Street	B1	Swaynes Close	B1
Belle Vue Road	B1	Tollgate Road	C2
Bishops Walk	B3	Trinity Street	C2
Blackfriars Way	C3	Wain-a-long Road	C1
Blue Boar Row	B2	West Walk	B3
Bourne Avenue	C1	Wilton Road	A1
Bourne Hill	C1	Winchester Street	B2
Bridge Street	B2	Windsor Road	A2
Brown Street	B2	Wyndham Road	B1
Butcher Row	B2	York Road	A1
Carmelite Way	B3		
Castle Street	B1		
Catherine Street	B2		
Chipper Lane	B2		
Churchfields Road	A2		
Churchill Way East	C2		
Churchill Way North	B1		
Churchill Way South	C3		
Churchill Way West	A1		
Clifton Road	A1		
College Street	C1		
Crane Bridge Road	A2		
Crane Street	B2		
De Vaux Place	B3		
Devizes Road	A1		
Elm Grove Road	C2		
Endless Street	B1		
Estcourt Road	C1		
Exeter Street	B3		
Fairview Road	C1		
Fisherton Street	A2		
Fowlers Hill	C2		
Fowlers Road	C2		
Friary Lane	C3		
Gas Lane	A1		
Gigant Street	C2		
Greencroft Street	C1		
Hamilton Road	B1		
High Street	B2		
Ivy Street	B2		
Kelsey Road	C1		
Laverstock Road	C2		
Manor Road	C1		
Marsh Lane	A1		
Meadow Road	A1		
Milford Hill	C2		
Milford Street	B2		
Mill Road	A2		
Millstream Approach	B1		
Minster Street	B2		
New Canal	B2		
New Street	B2		
North Walk	B3		
Park Street	C1		
Pennyfarthing Street	B2		
Queens Road	B1		
Rampart Road	C2		
Rollestone Street	B1		
St. Ann Street	C3		
St. John's Street	B2		
St. Marks Road	C1		
St. Paul's Road	A1		

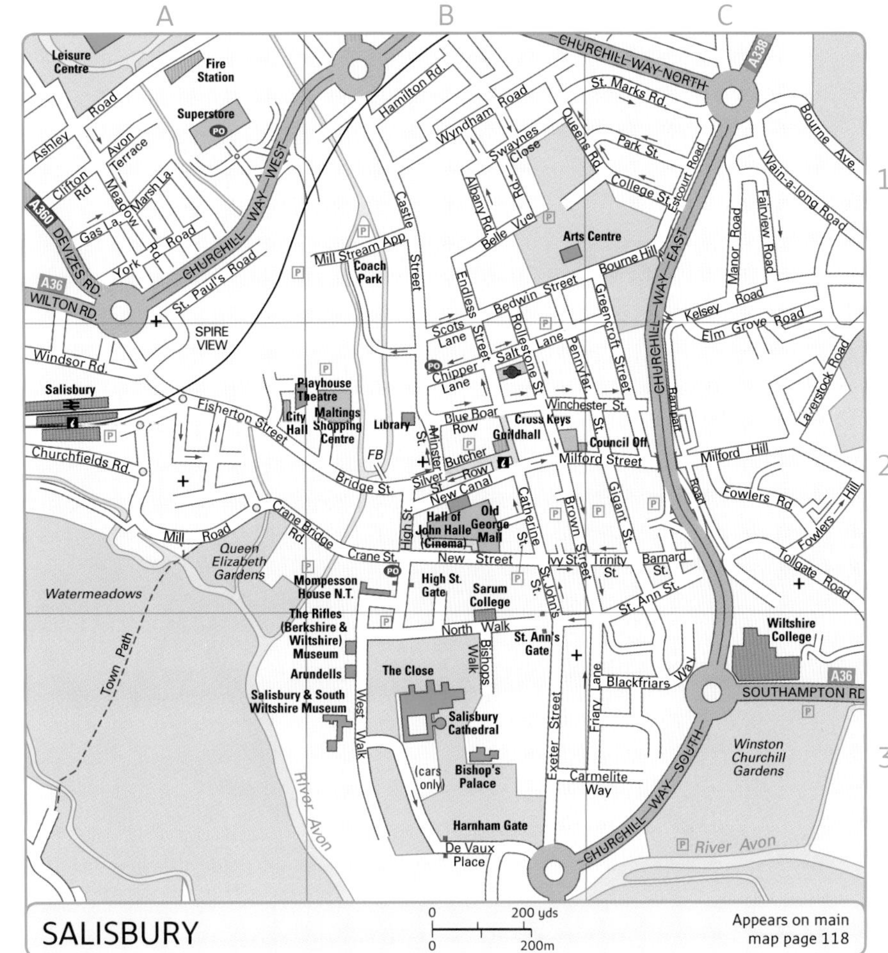

SALISBURY

0   200 yds
0   200m

Appears on main
map page 118

Tourist Information Centre: Brunswick Shopping Centre,
Unit 15a, Westborough   Tel: 01723 383636

Aberdeen Walk	B2	Valley Bridge Road	B2
Albion Road	B3	Valley Road	A3
Ashville Avenue	A2	Vernon Road	B2
Avenue Road	A3	Victoria Park Mount	A1
Belmont Road	B3	Victoria Road	A3
Candler Street	A2	Victoria Street	B2
Castle Road	B2	West Street	B3
Chatsworth Gardens	A1	Westborough	A3
Columbus Ravine	A2	Westbourne Grove	B3
Commercial Street	A3	Westover Road	A3
Cross Street	B2	Westwood	B3
Dean Road	A2	Westwood Road	A3
Eastborough	B2	Weydale Avenue	A1
Esplanade	B3	Wykeham Street	A3
Falconers Rd	B2		
Falsgrave Road	A3		
Foreshore Road	B2		
Franklin Street	A2		
Fnargate	B2		
Friarsway	B2		
Garfield Road	A2		
Gladstone Road	A2		
Gladstone Street	A2		
Gordon Street	A2		
Grosvenor Road	B3		
Highfield	A3		
Hoxton Road	A2		
Longwestgate	C2		
Manor Road	A2		
Marine Drive	C1		
Mayville Avenue	A2		
Moorland Road	A1		
New Queen Street	B1		
Newborough	B2		
North Marine Road	B1		
North Street	B2		
Northstead Manor Drive	A1		
Northway	A2		
Norwood Street	A2		
Oak Road	A3		
Peasholm Crescent	A1		
Peasholm Drive	A1		
Peasholm Road	A1		
Prince Of Wales Terrace	B3		
Princess Street	C2		
Prospect Road	A2		
Queen Street	B2		
Queen's Parade	B1		
Raleigh Street	A2		
Ramshill Road	B3		
Roscoe Street	A3		
Rothbury Street	A2		
Royal Albert Drive	B1		
Royal Avenue	B3		
Sandside	C2		
Seamer Road	A3		
St. James Road	A3		
St. John's Avenue	A3		
St. John's Road	A3		
St. Thomas Street	B2		
Tollergate	B1		
Trafalgar Road	A1		
Trafalgar Square	B1		
Trafalgar Street West	A2		
Trinity Road	A3		
Valley Bridge Parade	B3		

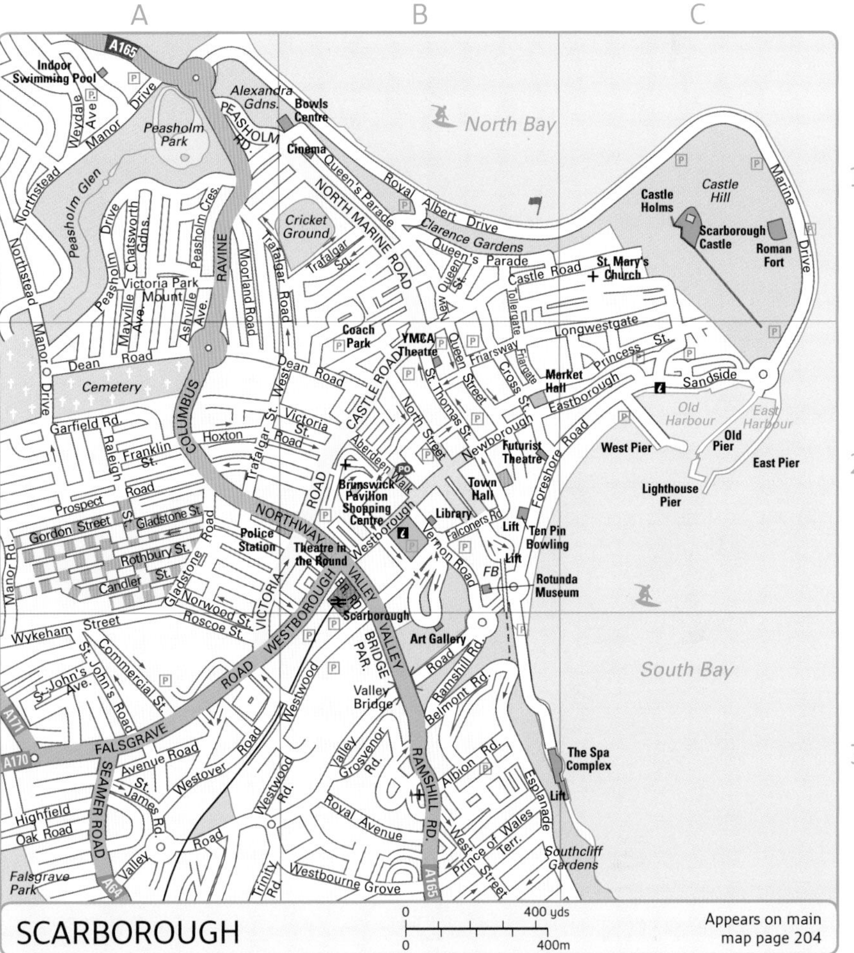

SCARBOROUGH

0   400 yds
0   400m

Appears on main
map page 204

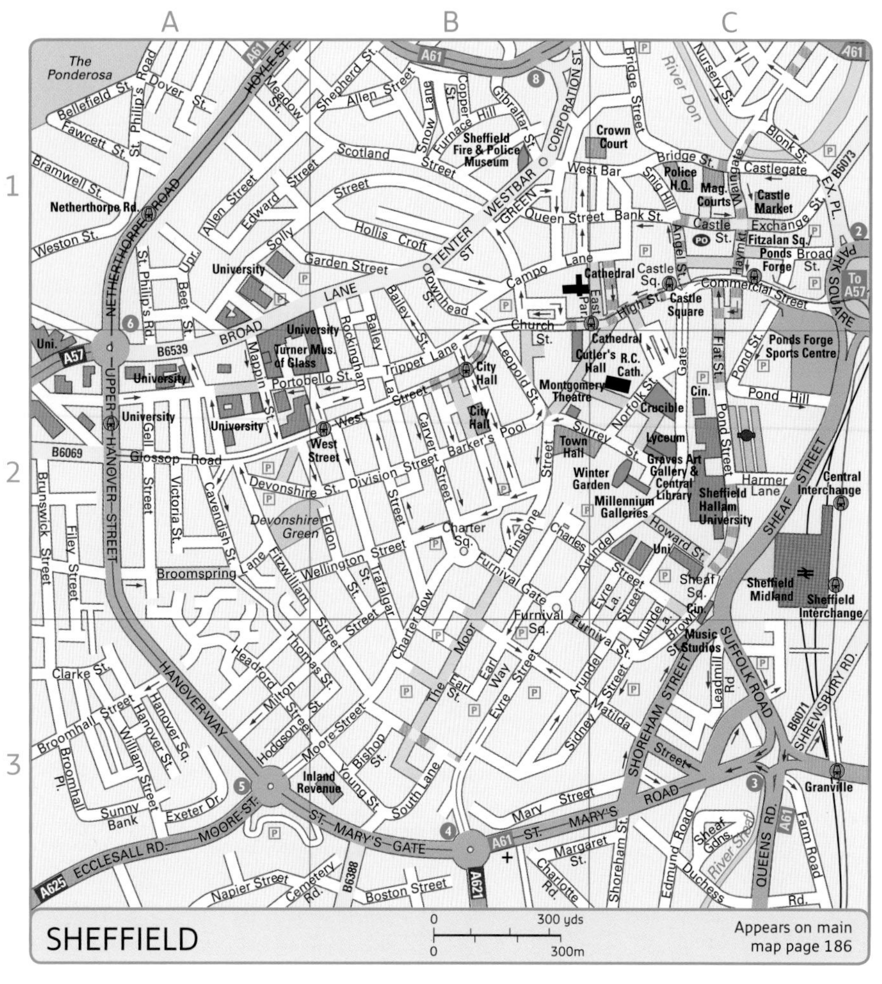

SHEFFIELD

Allen Street	B1	Hanover Square	A3
Angel Street	C1	Hanover Street	A3
Arundel Gate	B2	Hanover Way	A3
Arundel Lane	C3	Harmer Lane	C2
Arundel Street	B3	Haymarket	C1
Bailey Lane	B1	Headford Street	A3
Bailey Street	B1	High Street	C1
Bank Street	C1	Hodgson Street	A3
Barker's Pool	B2	Hollis Croft	B1
Beet Street	A1	Howard Street	C2
Bellefield Street	A1	Hoyle Street	A1
Bishop Street	B3	Leadmill Road	C3
Blonk Street	C1	Leopold Street	B2
Boston Street	B3	Mappin Street	A2
Bower Street	B1	Margaret Street	B3
Bramwell Street	A1	Mary Street	B3
Bridge Street	C1	Matilda Street	B3
Broad Lane	A2	Meadow Street	A1
Broad Street	C1	Milton Street	A3
Broomhall Street	A3	Moore Street	A3
Broomhall Place	A3	Napier Street	A3
Broomspring Lane	A2	Netherthorpe Road	A1
Brown Street	C3	Norfolk Street	C2
Brunswick Street	A2	Nursery Street	C1
Campo Lane	B1	Pinstone Street	B2
Carver Street	B2	Pond Hill	C2
Castle Square	C1	Pond Hill	C2
Castle Street	C1	Pond Street	C2
Castlegate	C1	Portobello Street	A2
Cavendish Street	A2	Queen Street	B1
Cemetery Road	A3	Queens Road	C3
Charles Street	B2/C2	Rockingham Street	B2
Charlotte Road	B3	St. Mary's Gate	B3
Charter Row	B3	St. Mary's Road	B3
Charter Square	B2	St. Philip's Road	A1
Church Street	B1	Scotland Street	B1
Clarke Street	A3	Sheaf Gardens	C3
Commercial Street	C1	Sheaf Square	C2
Copper Street	B1	Sheaf Street	C2
Corporation Street	B1	Shepherd Street	B1
Devonshire Street	A2	Shoreham Street	C3
Division Street	B2	Shrewsbury Road	C3
Dover Street	A1	Sidney Street	B3
Duchess Road	C3	Snig Hill	C1
Earl Street	B3	Snow Lane	B1
Earl Way	B3	Solly Street	A1
East Parade	C1	South Lane	B3
Ecclesall Road	A3	Spring Street	B1
Edmund Road	C3	Suffolk Road	C3
Edward Street	A1	Sunny Bank	A3
Eldon Street	B2	Surrey Street	B2
Exchange Street	C1	Tenter Street	B1
Exeter Drive	A3	The Moor	B3
Eyre Lane	C2	Thomas Street	A3
Eyre Street	B3	Townhead Street	B1
Farm Road	C3	Trafalgar Street	B2
Fawcett Street	A1	Trippet Lane	B2
Filey Street	A2	Upper Allen Street	A1
Fitzwilliam Street	A2	Upper Hanover Street	A2
Flat Street	C1	Victoria Street	A2
Furnace Hill	B1	Waingate	C1
Furnival Gate	B2	Wellington Street	B2
Furnival Square	B2	West Bar	B1
Furnival Street	B2	West Street	B2
Garden Street	A1	Westbar Green	B1
Gell Street	A2	Weston Street	A1
Gibraltar Street	B1	William Street	A3
Glossop Road	A2	Young Street	B3

Appears on main
map page 186

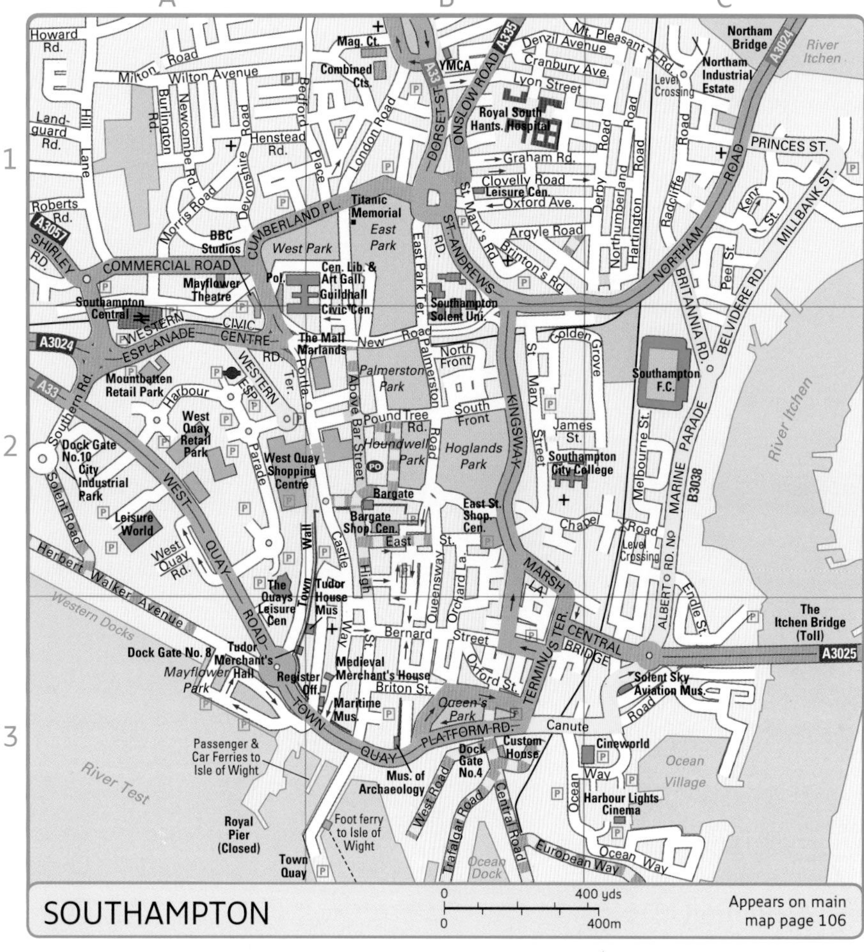

SOUTHAMPTON

Above Bar Street	B2	Queensway	B3
Albert Road North	C3	Radcliffe Road	C1
Argyle Road	B1	Roberts Road	A1
Bedford Place	A1	St. Andrews Road	B1
Belvidere Road	C2	St. Mary's Road	B1
Bernard Street	B3	St. Mary Street	B2
Brintons Road	B1	Shirley Road	A1
Britannia Road	C1	Solent Road	A2
Briton Street	B3	Southern Road	A2
Burlington Road	A1	South Front	B2
Canute Road	B3	Terminus Terrace	B3
Castle Way	B2	Town Quay	A3
Central Bridge	B3	Trafalgar Road	B3
Central Road	B3	West Quay Road	A2
Chapel Road	B2	West Road	B3
Civic Centre Road	A2	Western Esplanade	A2
Clovelly Road	B1	Wilton Avenue	A1
Commercial Road	A1		
Cranbury Avenue	B1		
Cumberland Place	A1		
Denzil Avenue	B1		
Derby Road	C1		
Devonshire Road	A1		
Dorset Street	B1		
East Park Terrace	B1		
East Street	B2		
Endle Street	C2		
European Way	B3		
Golden Grove	B2		
Graham Road	B1		
Harbour Parade	A2		
Hartington Road	C1		
Henstead Road	A1		
Herbert Walker Avenue	A2		
High Street	B2		
Hill Lane	A1		
Howard Road	A1		
James Street	B2		
Kent Street	C1		
Kingsway	B2		
Landguard Road	A1		
London Road	B1		
Lyon Street	B1		
Marine Parade	C2		
Marsh Lane	B2		
Melbourne Street	C2		
Millbank Street	C1		
Milton Road	A1		
Morris Road	A1		
Mount Pleasant Road	B1		
Newcombe Road	A1		
New Road	B2		
Northam Road	C1		
North Front	B2		
Northumberland Road	C1		
Ocean Way	B3		
Onslow Road	B1		
Orchard Lane	B3		
Oxford Avenue	B1		
Oxford Street	B3		
Palmerston Road	B2		
Peel Street	C1		
Platform Road	B3		
Portland Terrace	A2		
Pound Tree Road	B2		
Princes Street	C1		

Appears on main
map page 106

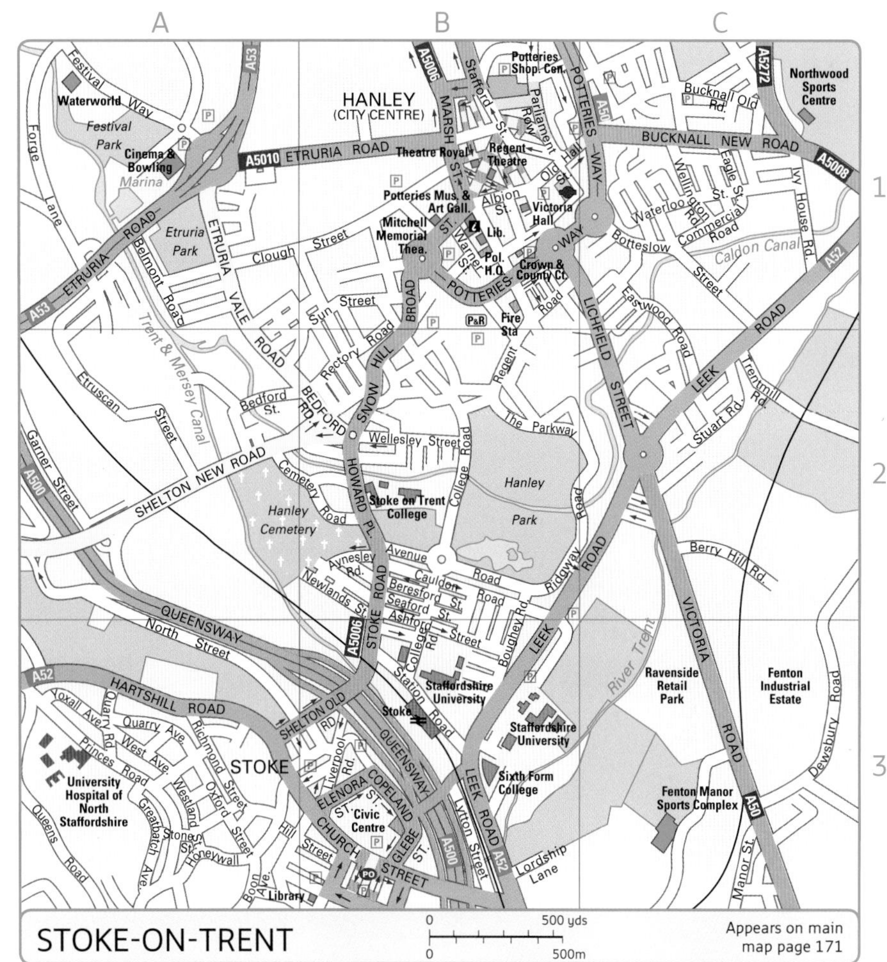

STOKE-ON-TRENT

0	500 yds
0	500m

Appears on main map page 171

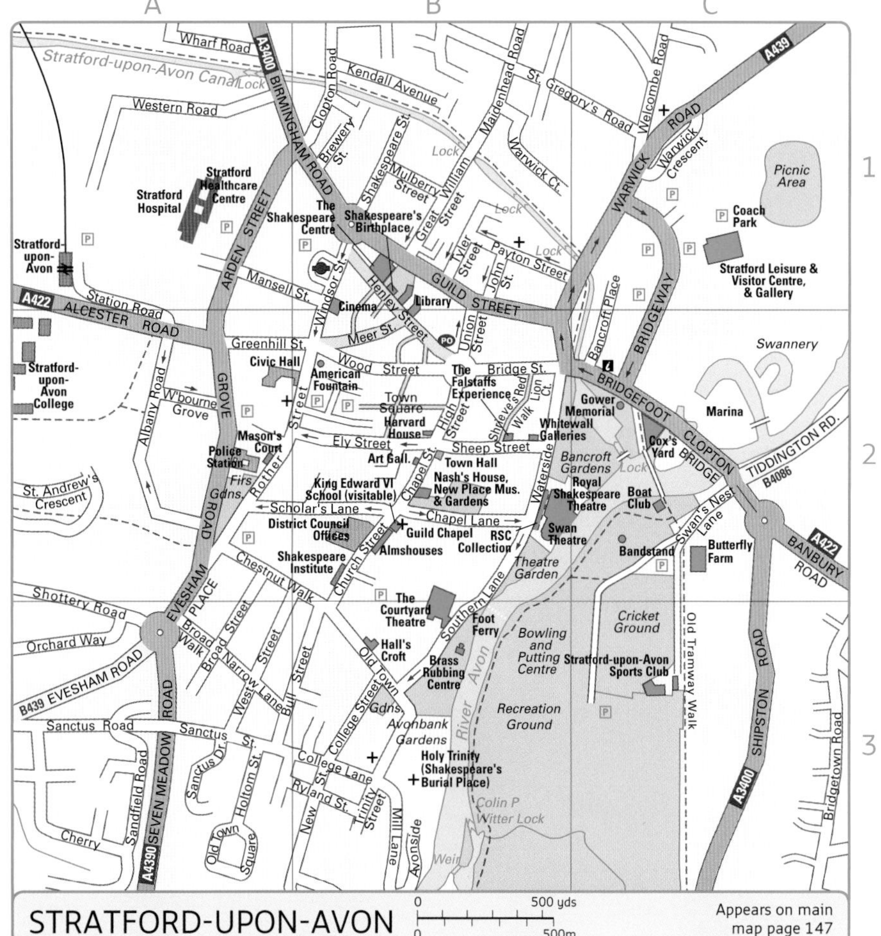

STRATFORD-UPON-AVON

0	500 yds
0	500m

Appears on main map page 147

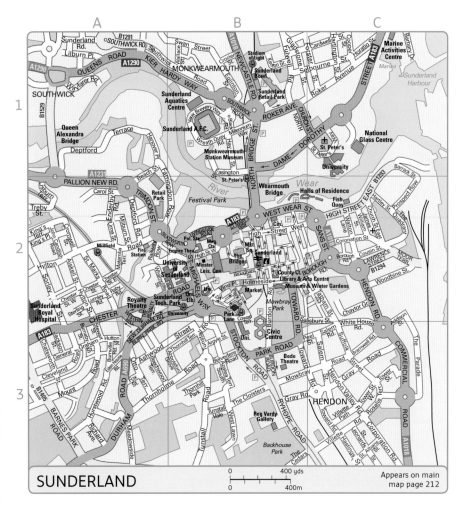

Tourist Information Centre: 50 Fawcett Street
Tel: 0191 553 2000

Street	Grid	Street	Grid
Abbotsford Grove	B3	Lime Street	A2
Addison Street	C3	Livingstone Road	B2
Aiskell Street	A2	Lumley Road	A2
Argyle Street	B3	Matamba Terrace	A2
Ashwood Street	A3	Milburn Street	A2
Azalea Terace South	B3	Millennium Way	B1
Barnes Park Road	A3	Moor Terrace	C2
Barrack Street	C1	Mount Road	A3
Beach Street	A2	Mowbray Road	B3
Beechwood Terrace	A3	New Durham Road	A3
Belvedere Road	B3	Newcastle Road	B1
Black Road	B1	North Bridge Street	B2
Borough Road	B2/C2	Otto Terrace	A3
Bramwell Road	C3	Pallion New Road	A2
Brougham Street	B2	Park Lane	B2
Burdon Road	B3	Park Road	B3
Burn Park Road	A3	Peel Street	B3
Burnaby Street	A3	Prospect Row	C2
Burnville Road	A3	Queens Road	A1
Carol Street	A2	Raby Road	A2
Chatsworth Street	A3	Railway Row	A2
Chaytor Grove	C2	Roker Avenue	B1/C1
Chester Road	A2	Rosalie Terrace	C3
Chester Street	A2	Ryhope Road	B3
Church Street East	C2	St. Albans Street	C3
Church Street North	B1	St. Leonards Street	C3
Cleveland Road	A3	St. Marks Road	A2
Commercial Road	C3	St. Mary's Way	B2
Cooper Street	C1	St. Michaels Way	B2
Coronation Street	C2	St. Peter's Way	C1
Corporation Road	C3	Salem Road	C3
Cousin Street	C2	Salem Street	C3
Cromwell Street	A2	Salisbury Street	B2
Crozier Street	B1	Sans Street	C2
Dame Dorothy Street	B1	Selbourne Street	B1
Deptford Road	A2	Silksworth Row	A2
Deptford Terrace	A1	Sorley Street	A2
Durham Road	A3	Southwick Road	A1
Easington Street	B1	Southwick Road	B1
Eden House Road	A3	Stewart Street	A3
Eglinton Street	B1	Stockton Road	B3
Enderby Road	A2	Suffolk Street	C3
Farringdon Row	A1	Sunderland Road	A1
Forster Street	C1	Swan Street	B1
Fox Street	A3	Tatham Street	C2
Fulwell Road	B1	The Cedars	B3
General Graham Street	A3	The Cloisters	B3
Gladstone Street	B1	The Parade	C3
Gray Road	B3/C3	The Quadrant	C2
Hanover Place	A1	The Royalty	A2
Hartington Street	C1	Thornhill Park	B3
Hartley Street	C2	Thornhill Terrace	B3
Hastings Street	C3	Thornholme Road	A3
Hay Street	B1	Toward Road	B2/C3
Hendon Road	C2	Tower Street	C3
Hendon Valley Road	C3	Tower Street West	C3
High Street East	C2	Trimdon Street	A2
High Street West	B2	Tunstall Road	B3
Holmeside	B2	Tunstall Vale	B3
Horatio Street	C1	Vaux Brewery Way	B1
Hurstwood Road	A3	Villette Road	C3
Hutton Street	A3	Vine Place	B2
Hylton Road	A2	Wallace Street	B1
Hylton Street	A2	West Lawn	B3
Jackson Street	A3	West Wear Street	B2
James William Street	C2	Western Hill	A2
Kenton Grove	B1	Wharncliffe Street	A2
Kier Hardy Way	A1	White House Road	C3
King's Place	A2	Woodbine Street	C2
Lawrence Street	C2	Wreath Quay Road	B1

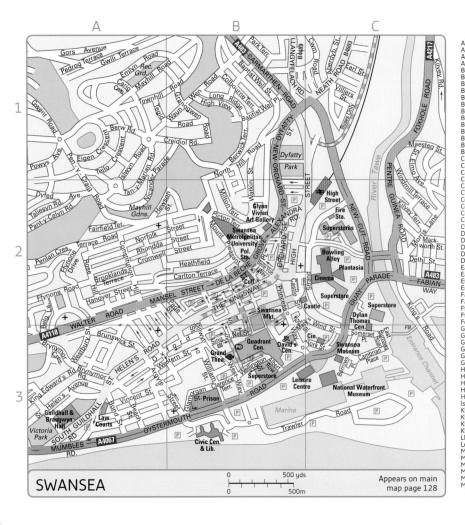

Street	Grid	Street	Grid
Aberdyberthi Street	C1	Mount Pleasant	B2
Albert Row	B3	Mumbles Road	A3
Alexandra Road	B2	Neath Road	C1
Argyle Street	A3	Nelson Street	B3
Baptist Well Place	B1	New Cut Road	C2
Baptist Well Street	B1	New Orchard Street	B1
Beach Street	A3	Nicander Parade	A2
Belgrave Lane	A3	Norfolk Street	A2
Belle Vue Way	B2	North Hill Road	B1
Berw Road	A1	Orchard Street	B2
Berwick Terrace	B1	Oxford Street	A3
Bond Street	A3	Oystermouth Road	A3
Brooklands Terrace	A2	Page Street	B2
Brunswick Street	A3	Pant-y-Celyn Road	A2
Brynymor Crescent	A3	Park Terrace	B1
Brynymor Road	A3	Pedrog Terrace	A1
Burrows Place	C3	Penlan Crescent	A2
Cambrian Place	C3	Pentre Guinea Road	C1
Carig Crescent	A1	Pen-y-Craig Road	A1
Carlton Terrace	B2	Picton Terrace	B2
Carmarthen Road	B1	Powys Avenue	A1
Castle Street	B2	Princess Way	B2
Clarence Terrace	B3	Quay Parade	C2
Colbourne Terrace	B1	Rhondda Street	A2
Constitution Hill	A2	Rose Hill	A2
Creidiol Road	A1	St. Elmo Avenue	C1
Cromwell Street	A2	St. Helen's Avenue	A3
Cwm Road	C1	St. Helen's Road	A3
De La Beche Street	B2	St. Mary Street	B2
Delhi Street	C2	Singleton Street	B3
Dillwyn Street	B3	Somerset Place	C3
Dyfatty Street	B1	South Guildhall Road	A3
Dyfed Avenue	A2	Strand	C2
Earl Street	C1	Taliesyn Road	A2
East Burrows Road	C3	Tan-y-Marian Road	A2
Eigen Crescent	A1	Tegid Road	A1
Emlyn Road	A1	Teilo Crescent	A1
Fabian Way	C2	Terrace Road	A2
Fairfield Terrace	A2	The Kingsway	B2
Ffynone Drive	A2	Townhill Road	A1
Ffynone Road	A2	Trawler Road	B3
Foxhole Road	C1	Villiers Street	C1
Glamorgan Street	B3	Vincent Street	A3
Gors Avenue	A1	Walter Road	A3
Granagwen Road	B1	Watkin Street	B2
Grove Place	B2	Waun-Wen Road	B1
Gwent Road	A1	Wellington Street	B3
Gwili Terrace	A1	West Way	B3
Hanover Street	A2	Westbury Street	A3
Heathfield	B2	Western Street	A3
Hewson Street	A2	William Street	B3
High Street	B2	Windmill Terrace	C1
High View	B1	York Street	C3
Islwyn Road	A1		
Kilvey Road	C1		
Kilvey Terrace	C2		
King Edward's Road	A3		
King's Road	C2		
Llangyfelach Road	B1		
Long Ridge	B1		
Mackworth Street	C2		
Maesteg Street	C1		
Mansel Street	A2		
Mayhill Road	A1		
Milton Terrace	B2		
Morris Lane	C2		

Tourist Information Centre: Central Library, Regent Circus
Tel: 01793 466454

Street	Grid	Street	Grid
Albion Street	A3	Upham Road	C3
Bath Road	B3	Victoria Road	C2
Beatrice Street	B1	Westcott Place	A3
Beckhampton Street	C2	Western Street	C3
Birch Street	A2	William Street	A3
Bridge Street	B2	York Road	C2
Broad Street	C1		
Canal Walk	B2		
Caulfield Road	C1		
Church Place	A2		
Cirencester Way	C1		
Clifton Street	B3		
Commercial Road	B2		
County Road	C1		
Cricklade Street	C3		
Curtis Street	B2		
Dean Street	A2		
Drove Road	C3		
Eastcott Hill	B3		
Edmund Street	B2		
Elmina Road	C1		
Euclid Street	C2		
Faringdon Road	A2		
Farnsby Street	B2		
Fleet Street	B2		
Fleming Way	B2		
Gladstone Street	C1		
Goddard Avenue	B3		
Great Western Way	A1		
Grosvenor Road	A3		
Groundwell Road	C2		
Hawksworth Way	A1		
High Street	C3		
Holbrook Way	B2		
Hythe Road	B3		
Islington Street	B2		
Jennings Street	A2		
Kemble Drive	A1		
Kent Road	B3		
Kingshill Street	A3		
Lansdown Road	B3		
Manchester Road	B1		
Market Street	B2		
Milford Street	B2		
Milton Road	B2		
Morris Street	A1		
Newburn Crescent	A2		
Newcombe Drive	A1		
North Star Avenue	B1		
Ocotal Way	C1		
Okus Road	A3		
Park Lane	A2		
Penzance Drive	A2		
Plymouth Street	C2		
Princes Street	C2		
Queen Street	B2		
Radnor Street	A3		
Redcliffe Street	A2		
Regent Street	B2		
Rodbourne Road	A1		
Rosebery Street	C1		
Spring Gardens	C2		
Stafford Street	B3		
Station Road	B1		
Swindon Road	B3		
The Parade	B2		

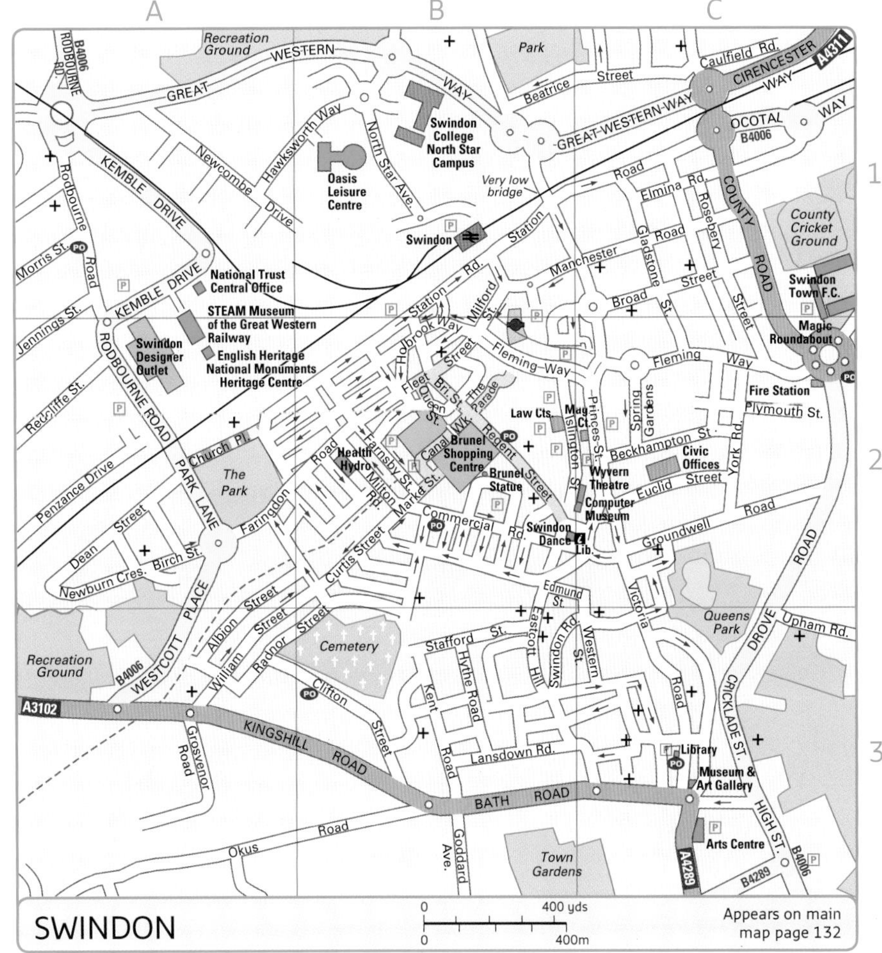

SWINDON

Appears on main map page 132

Tourist Information Centre: 5 Vaughan Parade
Tel: 01803 211211

Street	Grid	Street	Grid
Abbey Road	B2	Thurlow Road	B1
Ash Hill Road	B1	Tor Hill Road	B2
Avenue Road	A2	Torbay Road	A3
Bampfylde Road	A2	Torwood Gardens Road	C3
Barton Road	A1	Torwood Street	C3
Belgrave Road	A2	Union Street	B2
Belmont Road	C1	Upton Hill	B1
Braddons Hill Road East	C2	Upton Road	A1
Bridge Road	A2	Vanehill Road	C3
Bronshill Road	B1	Victoria Parade	C3
Brunswick Square	B1	Walnut Road	A3
Carlton Road	C1	Warbro Road	C1
Cary Parade	C3	Warren Road	B2
Cedars Road	C2	Windsor Road	C1
Chestnut Avenue	A2		
Cockington Lane	A3		
Croft Road	B2		
Crownhill Park	A1		
Dunmere Road	C1		
East Street	A1		
Ellacombe Church Road	C1		
Ellacombe Road	B1		
Falkland Road	A2		
Falkland Road	A2		
Fleet Street	B2		
Forest Road	B1		
Goshen Road	A2		
Hatfield Road	B1		
Hennapyn Road	A3		
Higher Warberry Road	C2		
Hillesdon Road	C2		
Kenwyn Road	C1		
Lower Warberry Road	C2		
Lucius Street	A2		
Lymington Road	B1		
Mallock Road	A2		
Market Street	B2		
Marnham Road	C1		
Meadfoot Lane	C3		
Meadfoot Road	C3		
Middle Warberry Road	C2		
Mill Lane	A2		
Newton Road	A1		
Old Mill Road	A2		
Old Mill Road	A3		
Parkfield Road	B1		
Parkhill Road	C3		
Prince's Road	C2		
Princes Road East	C2		
Quinta Road	C1		
Rathmore Road	A3		
Reddenhill Road	C1		
Rosehill Road	C2		
Sanford Road	A2		
Seaway Lane	A3		
Shedden Hill	A2		
Sherwell Lane	A2		
Solsbro Road	A3		
South Street	A2		
St. Lukes Road	B2		
St. Marychurch Road	B2		
St. Michael's Road	A1		
Stitchill Road	C2		
Strand	C3		
Teignmouth Road	A1		
The King's Drive	A2		

TORQUAY

Appears on main map page 101

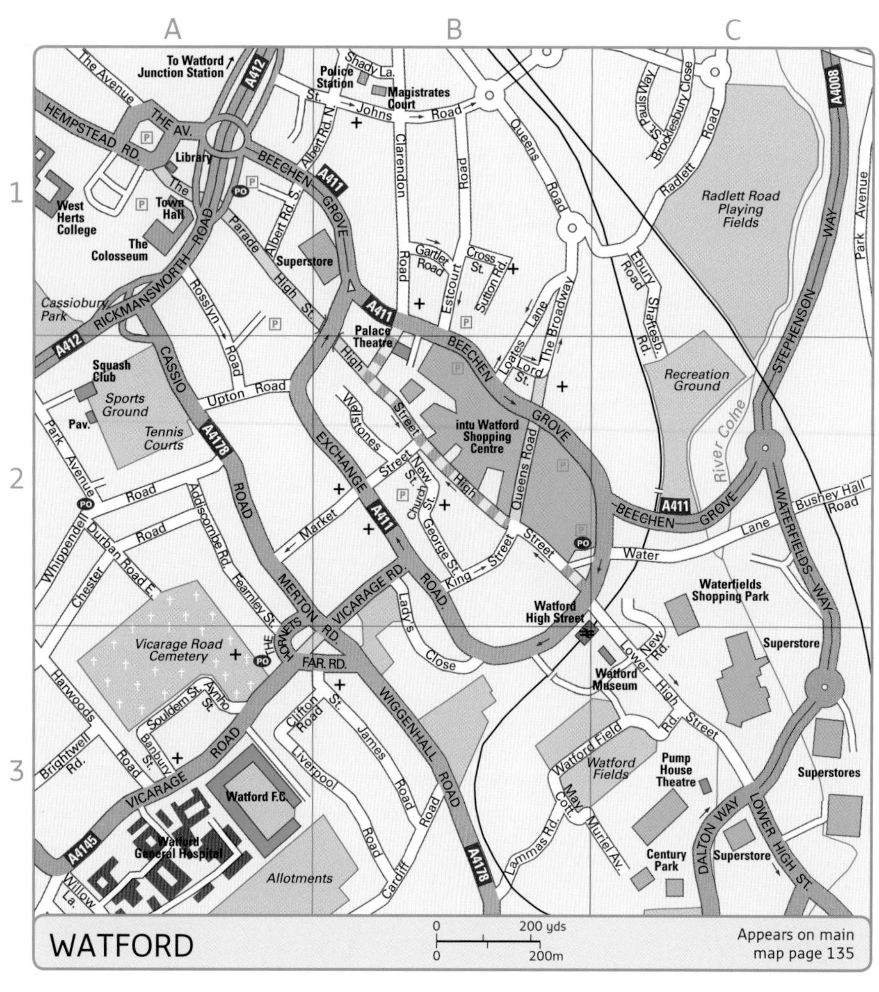

WATFORD

0   200 yds
0   200m

Appears on main
map page 135

Addiscombe Road	A2
Albert Road North	A1
Albert Road South	A1
Aynho Street	A3
Banbury Street	A3
Beechen Grove	A1/C2
Brightwell Road	A3
Brocklesbury Close	C1
Bushey Hall Road	C2
Cardiff Road	B3
Cassio Road	A2
Chester Road	A2
Church Street	B2
Clarendon Road	B1
Clifton Road	A3
Cross Street	B1
Dalton Way	C3
Durban Road East	A2
Ebury Road	C1
Estcourt Road	B1
Exchange Road	A2
Farraline Road	A3
Fearnley Street	A2
Garlet Road	B1
George Street	B2
Harwoods Road	A3
Hempstead Road	A1
High Street	A1/B2
King Street	B2
Lady's Close	B2
Lammas Road	B3
Liverpool Road	A3
Loates Lane	B2
Lord Street	B2
Lower High Street	C3
Market Street	A2
May Cottages	B3
Merton Road	A2
Muriel Avenue	B3
New Road	C3
New Street	B2
Park Avenue	C1
Park Avenue	A2
Queens Road	B1/B2
Radlett Road	C1
Rickmansworth Road	A2
Rosslyn Road	A1
Shaftesbury Road	C1
Souldern Street	A3
St. James Road	B3
St. Johns Road	A1
St. Pauls Way	C1
Stephenson Way	C2
Sutton Road	B1
The Avenue	A1
The Broadway	B2
The Hornets	A3
The Parade	A1
Upton Road	A2
Vicarage Road	A3/B2
Water Lane	C2
Waterfields Way	C2
Watford Field Road	B3
Wellstones	B2
Whippendell Road	A2
Wiggenhall Road	B3
Willow Lane	A3

Tourist Information Centre: Tropicana, Marine Parade
Tel: 01934 888877

Addicott Road	B3	Stafford Road	C2
Albert Avenue	B3	Station Road	B2
Alexandra Parade	B2	Sunnyside Road	B3
Alfred Street	B2	Swiss Road	C2
All Saints Road	B1	The Centre	B2
Amberey Road	C3	Trewartha Park	C1
Arundell Road	B1	Upper Church Road	A1
Ashcombe Gardens	C1	Walliscote Road	B3
Ashcombe Road	C2	Waterloo Street	B2
Atlantic Road	A1	Whitecross Road	B3
Baker Street	B2	Winterstoke Road	C3
Beach Road	B3		
Beaconsfield Road	B2		
Birnbeck Road	A1		
Boulevard	B2		
Brendon Avenue	C1		
Bridge Road	C2		
Brighton Road	B3		
Bristol Road	B1		
Carlton Street	B2		
Cecil Road	B1		
Clarence Road North	B3		
Clarendon Road	C2		
Clevedon Road	B3		
Clifton Road	B3		
Drove Road	C3		
Earlham Grove	C2		
Ellenborough Park North	B3		
Ellenborough Park South	B3		
Exeter Road	B3		
George Street	B2		
Gerard Road	B2		
Grove Park Road	B1		
High Street	B2		
Highbury Road	A1		
Hildesheim Bridge	B2		
Hill Road	C1		
Jubilee Road	B2		
Kenn Close	C3		
Kensington Road	C3		
Knightstone Road	A1		
Langford Road	C3		
Lewisham Grove	C2		
Locking Road	C2		
Lower Bristol Road	C1		
Lower Church Road	A1		
Manor Road	C1		
Marchfields Way	C3		
Marine Parade	B3		
Meadow Street	B2		
Milton Road	C2		
Montpelier	B1		
Neva Road	B2		
Norfolk Road	C3		
Oxford Street	B2		
Queen's Road	B1		
Rectors Way	C3		
Regent Street	B2		
Ridgeway Avenue	B3		
Royal Crescent	A1		
St. Paul's Road	B3		
Sandford Road	C2		
Severn Road	B3		
Shrubbery Road	A1		
South Road	A1		
Southside	B1		

WESTON-SUPER-MARE

0   400 yds
0   400m

Appears on main
map page 115

WINCHESTER

Tourist Information Centre: Guildhall, High Street
Tel: 01962 840500

Street	Grid
Alison Way	A1
Andover Road	A1
Archery Lane	A2
Bar End Road	C3
Barfield Close	C3
Beaufort Road	A3
Beggar's Lane	C2
Blue Ball Hill	C2
Bridge Stret	C2
Broadway	B2
Canon Street	B3
Chesil Street	C3
Christchurch Road	A3
City Road	A1
Clifton Hill	A2
Clifton Road	A1
Clifton Terrace	A2
Colebrook Street	B2
College Street	B3
College Walk	B3
Compton Road	A3
Cranworth Road	A1
Culver Road	B3
Domum Road	C3
Durngate	C2
East Hill	C3
Eastgate Street	C2
Easton Lane	C1
Ebden Road	C1
Edgar Road	A3
Elm Road	A1
Fairfield Road	A1
Friarsgate	B2
Gordon Road	B1
Great Minster Street	B2
Hatherley Road	A1
High Street	B2
Hyde Abbey Road	B1
Hyde Close	B1
Hyde Street	B1
Jewry Street	B2
King Alfred Place	B1
Kingsgate Street	B3
Little Minster Street	B2
Lower Brook Street	B2
Magdalen Hill	C2
Market Lane	B2
Middle Brook Street	B2
Middle Road	A2
Milland Road	C3
North Walls	A1
Parchment Street	B2
Park Avenue	B1
Peninsula Square	A2
Portal Road	C3
Quarry Road	C3
Romans' Road	A3
Romsey Road	A2
St. Catherine's Road	C3
St. Cross Road	A3
St. George's Street	B2
St. James Lane	A2
St. James Villas	A3
St. John's Street	C2
St. Michael's Road	A3
St. Paul's Hill	A1
St. Peter Street	B2
St. Swithun Street	B3
St. Thomas Street	B3
Saxon Road	B1
Silver Hill	B2
Southgate Street	A3
Staple Gardens	B2
Station Road	A1
Step Terrace	A2
Stockbridge Road	A1
Sussex Street	A2
Swan Lane	B1
Symond's Street	B3
Tanner Street	B2
The Square	B2
Tower Street	A2
Union Street	C2
Upper Brook Street	B2
Upper High Street	A2
Wales Street	C2
Water Lane	C2
Wharf Hill	C3
Worthy Lane	A1

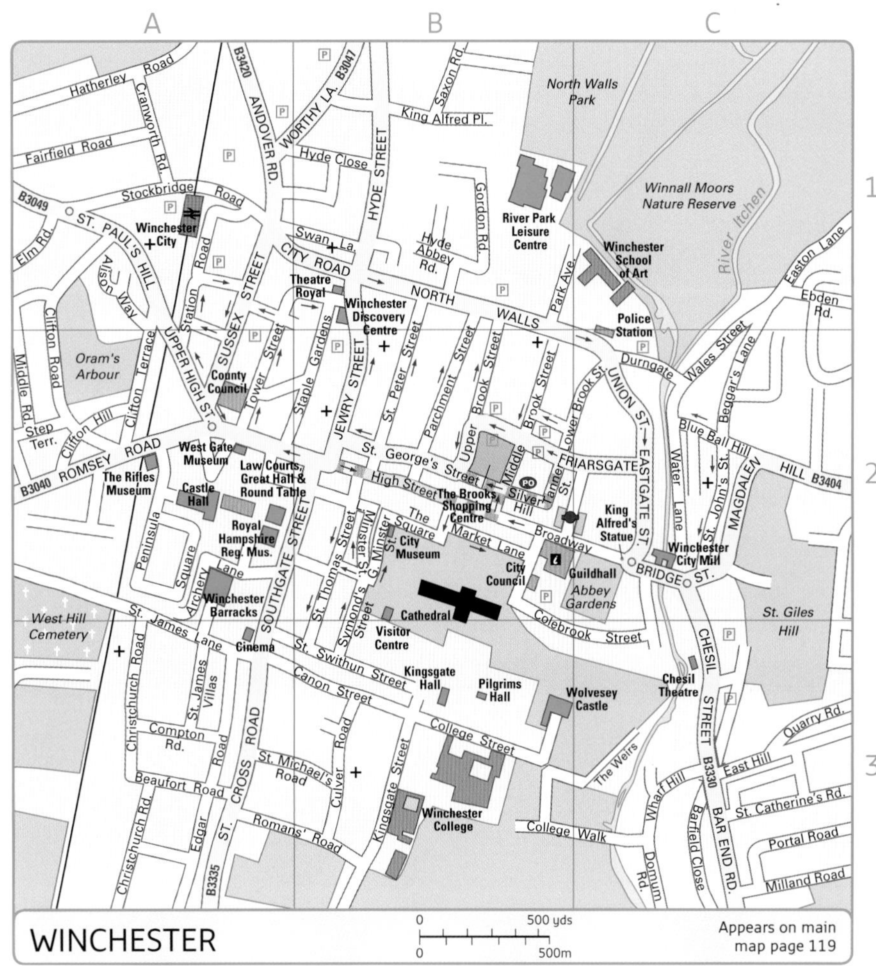

WINCHESTER

0   500 yds
0   500m

Appears on main
map page 119

WINDSOR

Tourist Information Centre: Old Booking Hall, Central Station
Tel: 01753 743900

Street	Grid
Adelaide Square	C3
Albert Street	A2
Alexandra Road	B3
Alma Road	B2/B3
Arthur Road	B2
Barry Avenue	B1
Bexley Street	B2
Bolton Avenue	B3
Bolton Crescent	B3
Bolton Road	B3
Bulkeley Avenue	A3
Castle Hill	C2
Charles Street	B2
Clarence Crescent	B2
Clarence Road	A2
College Crescent	A3
Dagmar Road	B2
Datchet Road	C1
Frances Road	B3
Goslar Way	A2
Goswell Road	B2
Green Lane	A2
Grove Road	B2
Helston Lane	A2
High Street (Eton)	B1
High Street (Windsor)	C2
Imperial Road	A3
King Edward VII Avenue	C1
Kings Road	C3
Meadow Lane	B1
Mill Lane	A1
Osborne Road	B3
Oxford Road	B2
Park Street	C2
Parsonage Lane	A2
Peascod Street	B2
Peel Close	A3
Princess Avenue	A3
Romney Lock Road	C1
St. Leonards Road	B3
St. Marks Road	B2
Sheet Street	C2
South Meadow Lane	B1
Springfield Road	A3
Stovell Road	A1
Thames Street	C1
The Long Walk	C3
Upcroft	A3
Vansittart Road	B2
Victoria Street	B2
Victor Road	B3
Westmead	A3
Windsor & Eton Relief Road	A2
York Avenue	A3
York Road	A3

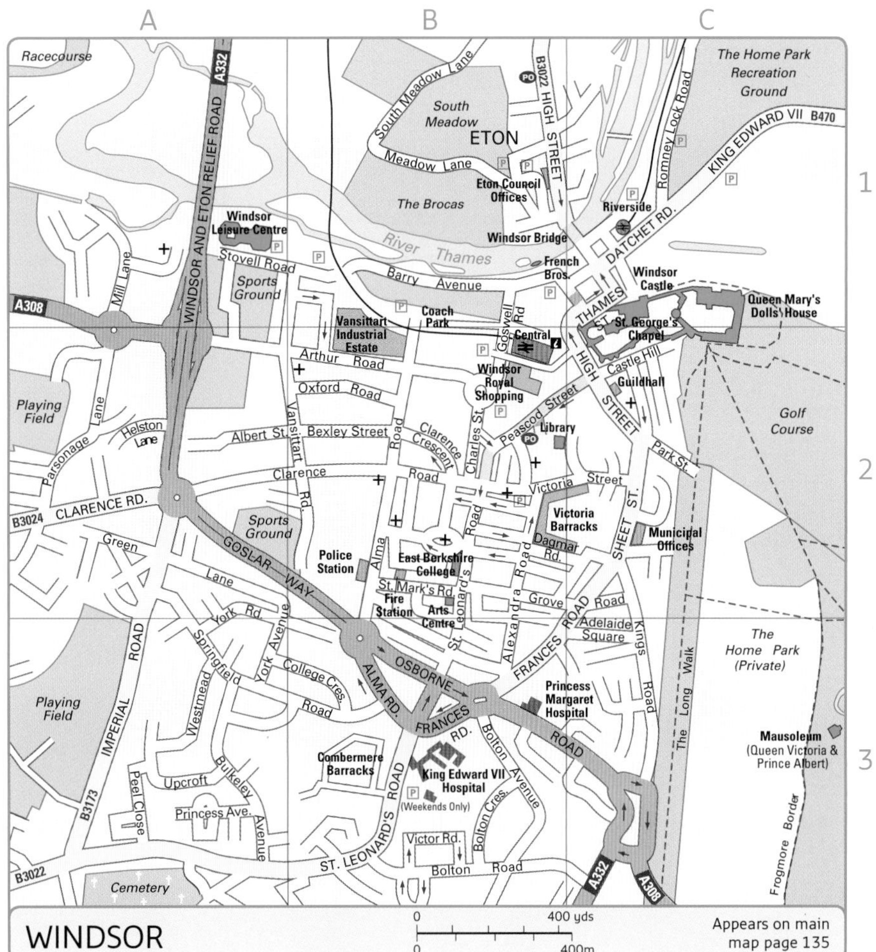

WINDSOR

0   400 yds
0   400m

Appears on main
map page 135

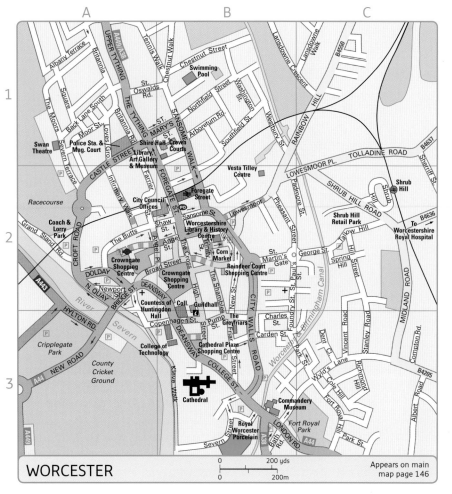

WORCESTER

0   200 yds
0   200m

Appears on main
map page 146

Tourist Information Centre: The Guildhall, High Street
Tel: 01905 726311

Albany Terrace	A1	Sherriff Street	C1
Albert Road	C3	Shrub Hill	C2
Angel Place	A2	Shrub Hill Road	C2
Angel Street	B2	Sidbury	B3
Arboretum Road	B1	Southfield Street	B1
Back Lane South	A1	Spring Hill	C2
Bath Road	B3	Stanley Road	C3
Bridge Street	A2	Tallow Hill	C2
Britannia Road	A1	Tennis Walk	A1
Britannia Square	A1	The Butts	A2
Broad Street	A2	The Cross	B2
Carden Street	B3	The Moors	A1
Castle Street	A2	The Shambles	B2
Charles Street	B3	The Tything	A1
Chestnut Street	B1	Tolladine Road	C1
Chestnut Walk	B1	Trinity Street	B2
City Walls Road	B2	Upper Tything	A1
Cole Hill	C3	Vincent Road	C3
College Street	B3	Washington Street	B1
Compton Road	C3	Westbury Street	B1
Copenhagen Street	A3	Wyld's Lane	C3
Croft Road	A2		
Deansway	A2		
Dent Close	C3		
Dolday	A2		
Farrier Street	A2		
Foregate Street	B2		
Fort Royal Hill	C3		
Foundry Street	B3		
Friar Street	B3		
George Street	C2		
Grand Stand Road	A2		
High Street	B2		
Hill Street	C2		
Hylton Road	A2		
Infirmary Walk	A2		
Kleve Walk	B3		
Lansdowne Crescent	B1		
Lansdowne Walk	C1		
London Road	B3		
Loves Grove	A1		
Lowesmoor	B2		
Lowesmoor Place	B2		
Midland Road	C3		
Moor Street	A1		
Newport Street	A2		
New Road	A3		
New Street	B2		
Northfield Street	B1		
North Quay	A2		
Padmore Street	B2		
Park Street	B3		
Park Street	C3		
Pheasant Street	B2		
Pump Street	B3		
Rainbow Hill	B1		
Richmond Hill	C3		
St. Martin's Gate	B2		
St. Mary's Street	A1		
St. Oswalds Road	A1		
St. Paul's Street	B2		
Sansome Street	B2		
Sansome Walk	B1		
Severn Street	B3		
Severn Terrace	A1		
Shaw Street	A2		

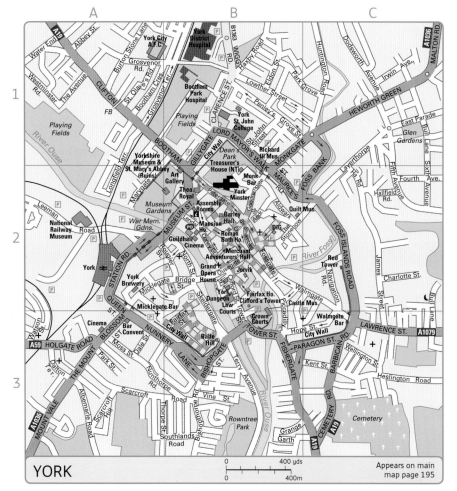

YORK

0   400 yds
0   400m

Appears on main
map page 195

Tourist Information Centre: 1 Museum Street
Tel: 01904 550099

Abbey Street	A1	Paragon Street	B3
Albermarle Road	A3	Park Grove	B1
Aldwark	B2	Park Street	A3
Barbican Road	C3	Penley's Grove Street	B1
Bishopthorpe Road	B3	Petergate	B2
Bishopgate Street	B3	Piccadilly	B2
Blossom Street	A3	Queen Street	A2
Bootham	A1	Rougier Street	A2
Bootham Crescent	A1	St. Andrewgate	B2
Bridge Street	B2	St. John Street	B1
Bull Lane	C1/C2	St. Maurice's Road	B2
Burton Stone Lane	A1	St. Olave's Road	A1
Cemetery Road	C3	Scarcroft Hill	A3
Charlotte Street	C2	Scarcroft Road	A3
Church Street	B2	Shambles	B2
Clarence Street	B1	Sixth Avenue	C1
Clifford Street	B2	Skeldergate	B2
Clifton	A1	Southlands Road	A3
Coney Street	B2	Station Road	A2
Dale Street	A3	Terry Avenue	B3
Dalton Terrace	A3	The Avenue	A1
Dodsworth Avenue	C1	The Mount	A3
East Parade	C1	The Stonebow	B2
Eldon Street	B1	Thorpe Street	A3
Fairfax Street	B3	Tower Street	B2
Fifth Avenue	C1	Vine Street	B3
Fishergate	B3	Walmgate	B2
Foss Bank	C2	Water End	A1
Fossgate	B2	Watson Street	A3
Foss Islands Road	C2	Wellington Street	C3
Fourth Avenue	C2	Westminster Road	A1
Gillygate	B1	Wigginton Road	B1
Goodramgate	B2		
Grange Garth	B3		
Grosvenor Road	A1		
Grosvenor Terrace	A1		
Hallfield Road	C2		
Haxby Road	B1		
Heslington Road	C3		
Heworth Green	C1		
Holgate Road	A3		
Hope Street	B3		
Huntington Road	C1		
Irwin Avenue	C1		
James Street	B2		
Kent Street	C3		
Lawrence Street	C3		
Layerthorpe	C2		
Leeman Road	A2		
Lendal	B2		
Longfield Terrace	A2		
Lord Mayor's Walk	B1		
Lowther Street	B1		
Malton Road	C1		
Marygate	A2		
Maurices Road	A2		
Micklegate	A2		
Monkgate	B1		
Moss Street	A3		
Mount Vale	A3		
Museum Street	B2		
Navigation Road	C2		
North Street	B2		
Nunnery Lane	A3		
Nunthorpe Road	A3		
Ousegate	B2		

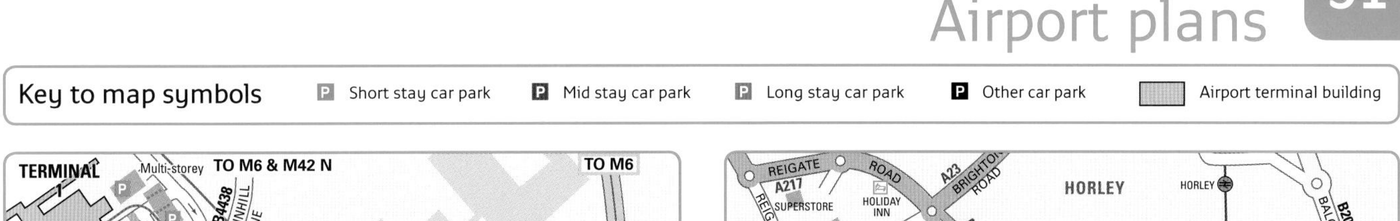

Key to map symbols
- **P** Short stay car park
- **P** Mid stay car park
- **P** Long stay car park
- **P** Other car park
- Airport terminal building

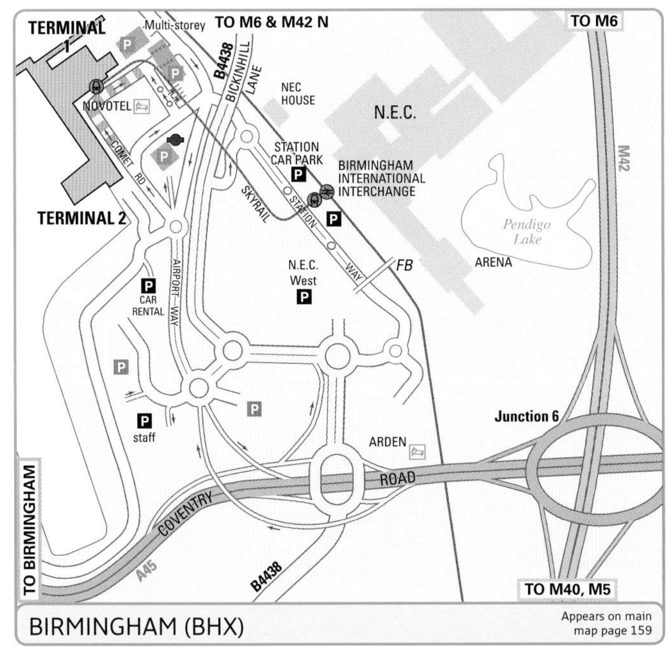

BIRMINGHAM (BHX)

Appears on main map page 159

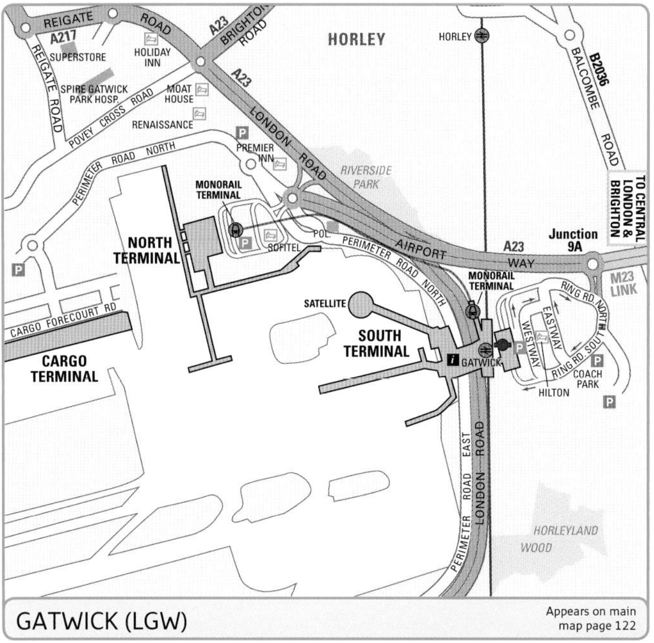

GATWICK (LGW)

Appears on main map page 122

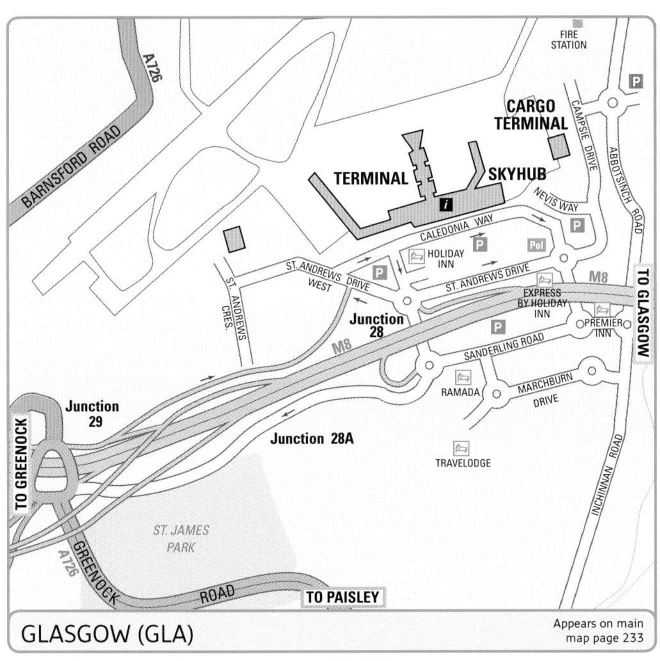

GLASGOW (GLA)

Appears on main map page 233

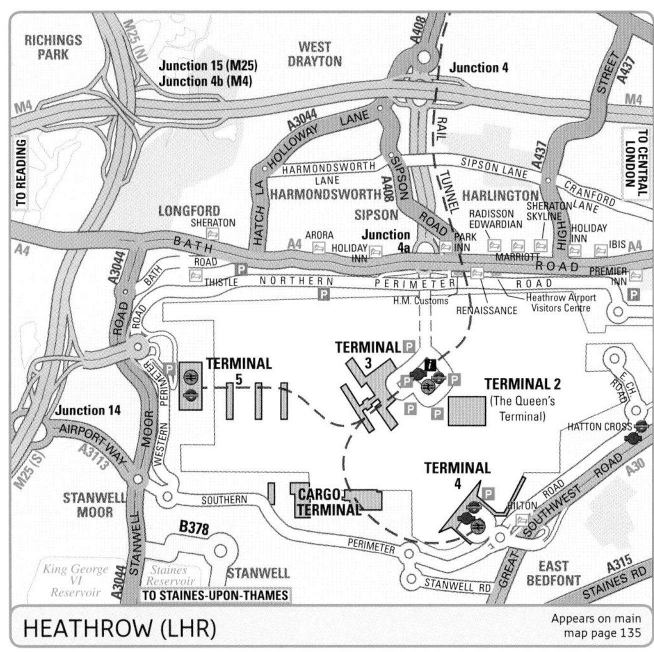

HEATHROW (LHR)

Appears on main map page 135

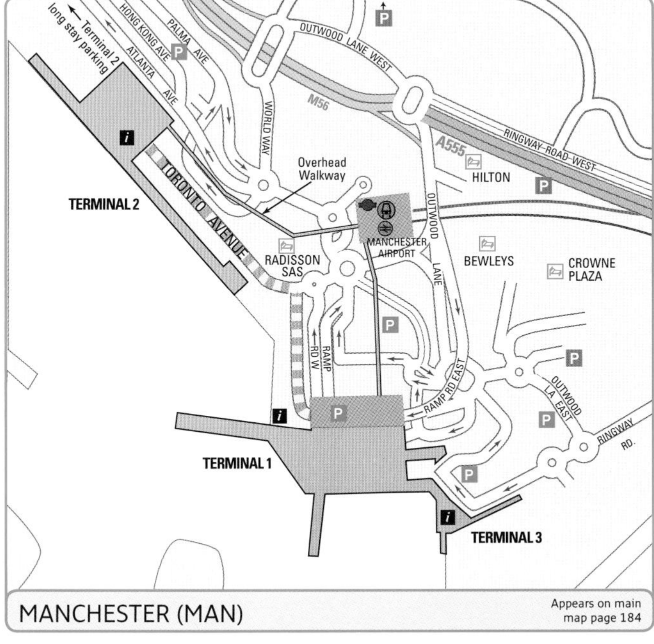

MANCHESTER (MAN)

Appears on main map page 184

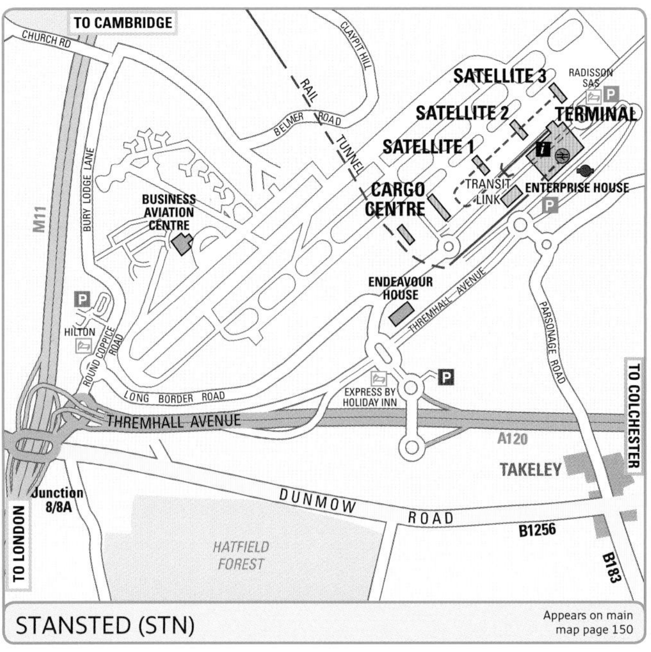

STANSTED (STN)

Appears on main map page 150

Symbols used on the map

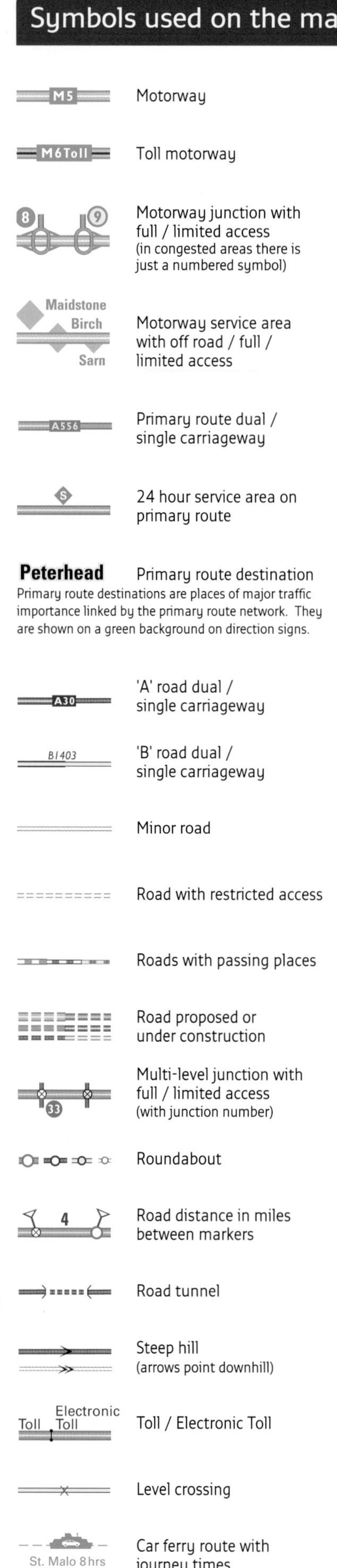

M5	Motorway
M6Toll	Toll motorway
8 9	Motorway junction with full / limited access (in congested areas there is just a numbered symbol)
Maidstone / Birch / Sarn	Motorway service area with off road / full / limited access
A556	Primary route dual / single carriageway
S	24 hour service area on primary route
Peterhead	Primary route destination

Primary route destinations are places of major traffic importance linked by the primary route network. They are shown on a green background on direction signs.

A30	'A' road dual / single carriageway
B1403	'B' road dual / single carriageway
	Minor road
	Road with restricted access
	Roads with passing places
	Road proposed or under construction
33	Multi-level junction with full / limited access (with junction number)
	Roundabout
4	Road distance in miles between markers
	Road tunnel
	Steep hill (arrows point downhill)
Toll / Electronic Toll	Toll / Electronic Toll
	Level crossing
St. Malo 8hrs	Car ferry route with journey times
	Railway line / station / tunnel
Wales Coast Path	National Trail / Long Distance Route

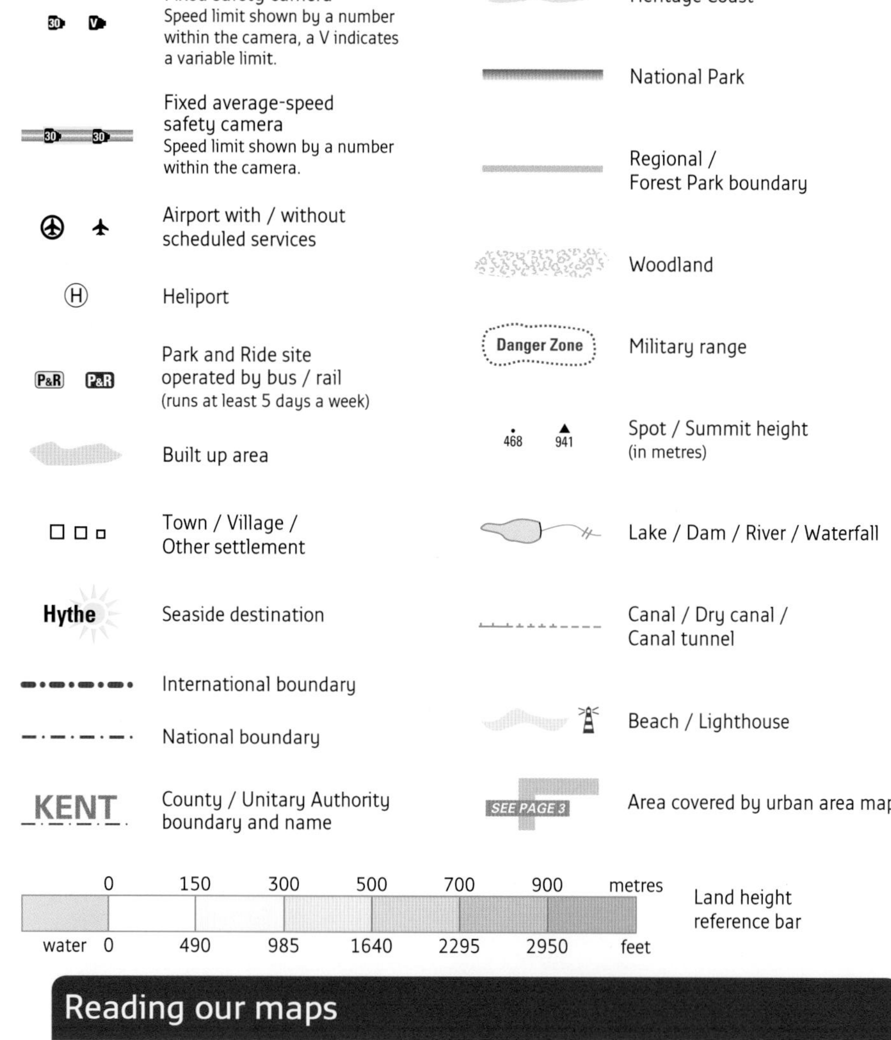

30 V	Fixed safety camera Speed limit shown by a number within the camera, a V indicates a variable limit.
30 30	Fixed average-speed safety camera Speed limit shown by a number within the camera.
⊕ ✈	Airport with / without scheduled services
Ⓗ	Heliport
P&R P&R	Park and Ride site operated by bus / rail (runs at least 5 days a week)
	Built up area
□ ▫ ▫	Town / Village / Other settlement
Hythe	Seaside destination
	International boundary
	National boundary
KENT	County / Unitary Authority boundary and name

	Heritage Coast
	National Park
	Regional / Forest Park boundary
	Woodland
Danger Zone	Military range
468 ▲941	Spot / Summit height (in metres)
	Lake / Dam / River / Waterfall
	Canal / Dry canal / Canal tunnel
	Beach / Lighthouse
SEE PAGE 3	Area covered by urban area map

water	0	150	300	500	700	900	metres	Land height reference bar
	0	490	985	1640	2295	2950	feet	

Reading our maps

Safety Camera The number inside the camera shows the speed limit at the camera location.

Multi-level junctions Non-motorway junctions where slip roads are used to access the main roads.

Distances Blue numbers give distances in miles between junctions shown with a blue marker.

Park & Ride Sites are shown that operate at least 5 days a week. Bus operated sites have a yellow symbol and rail operated sites a pink symbol.

Motorway service area

World Heritage site Places of interest defined by UNESCO as special on a world scale.

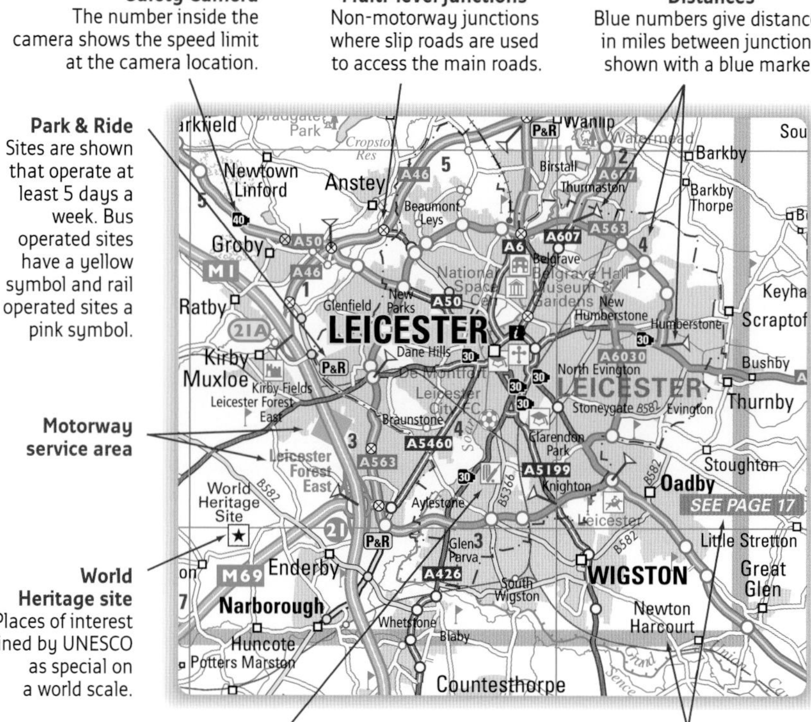

Places of interest Blue symbols indicate places of interest. See the section at the bottom of the page for the different types of feature represented on the map.

More detailed maps Green boxes indicate busy built-up-areas. More detailed mapping is available.

Places of interest

A selection of tourist detail is shown on the mapping. It is advisable to check with the local tourist information centre regarding opening times and facilities available.

Any of the following symbols may appear on the map in maroon ★ which indicates that the site has World Heritage status.

i	Tourist information centre (open all year)
i	Tourist information centre (open seasonally)
m	Ancient monument
⌐	Aquarium
🏛	Aqueduct / Viaduct
♣	Arboretum
⚔ 1643	Battlefield
⚑	Blue flag beach
▲ ⌂	Camp site / Caravan site
🏰	Castle
⌂	Cave
🏞	Country park
🏏	County cricket ground
🍶	Distillery
✝	Ecclesiastical feature
🎪	Event venue
🐑	Farm park
❀	Garden
⚐	Golf course
🏠	Historic house
⛵	Historic ship
⚽	Major football club
£	Major shopping centre / Outlet village
🏟	Major sports venue
🏎	Motor racing circuit
🚴	Mountain bike trail
🏛	Museum / Art gallery
🐾	Nature reserve (NNR indicates a National Nature Reserve)
🏇	Racecourse
🚂	Rail Freight Terminal
⛷ ⛷	Ski slope (artificial / natural)
🐾	Spotlight nature reserve (Best sites for access to nature)
🚂⊷⊷⊷	Steam railway centre / preserved railway
🏄	Surfing beach
🎢	Theme park
🎓	University
🍇	Vineyard
🐘	Wildlife park / Zoo
🦋	Wildlife Trust nature reserve
★	Other interesting feature
(NT) (NTS)	National Trust / National Trust for Scotland property

Map scale

A scale bar appears at the bottom of every page to help with distances.

0		2		4		6 miles
0	2	4	6	8	10 km

England, Wales & Southern Scotland are at a scale of 1:200,000 or 3.2 miles to 1 inch
Northern Scotland & Northern Ireland are at a scale of 1:263,158 or 4.2 miles to 1 inch.

Map pages

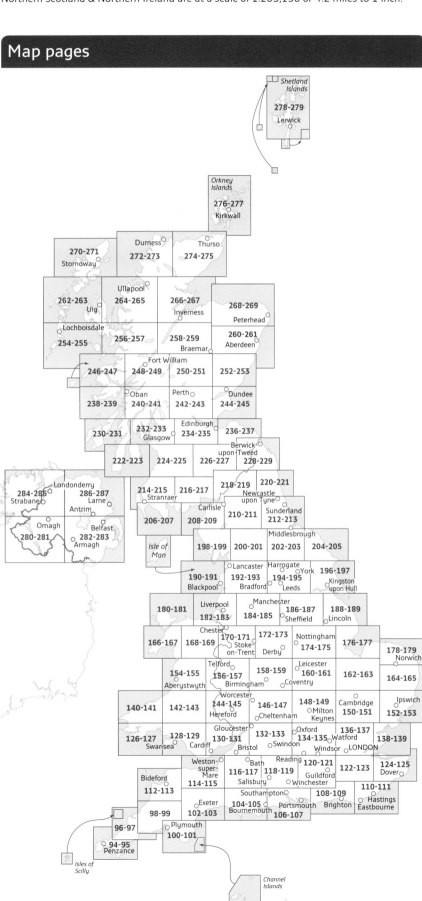

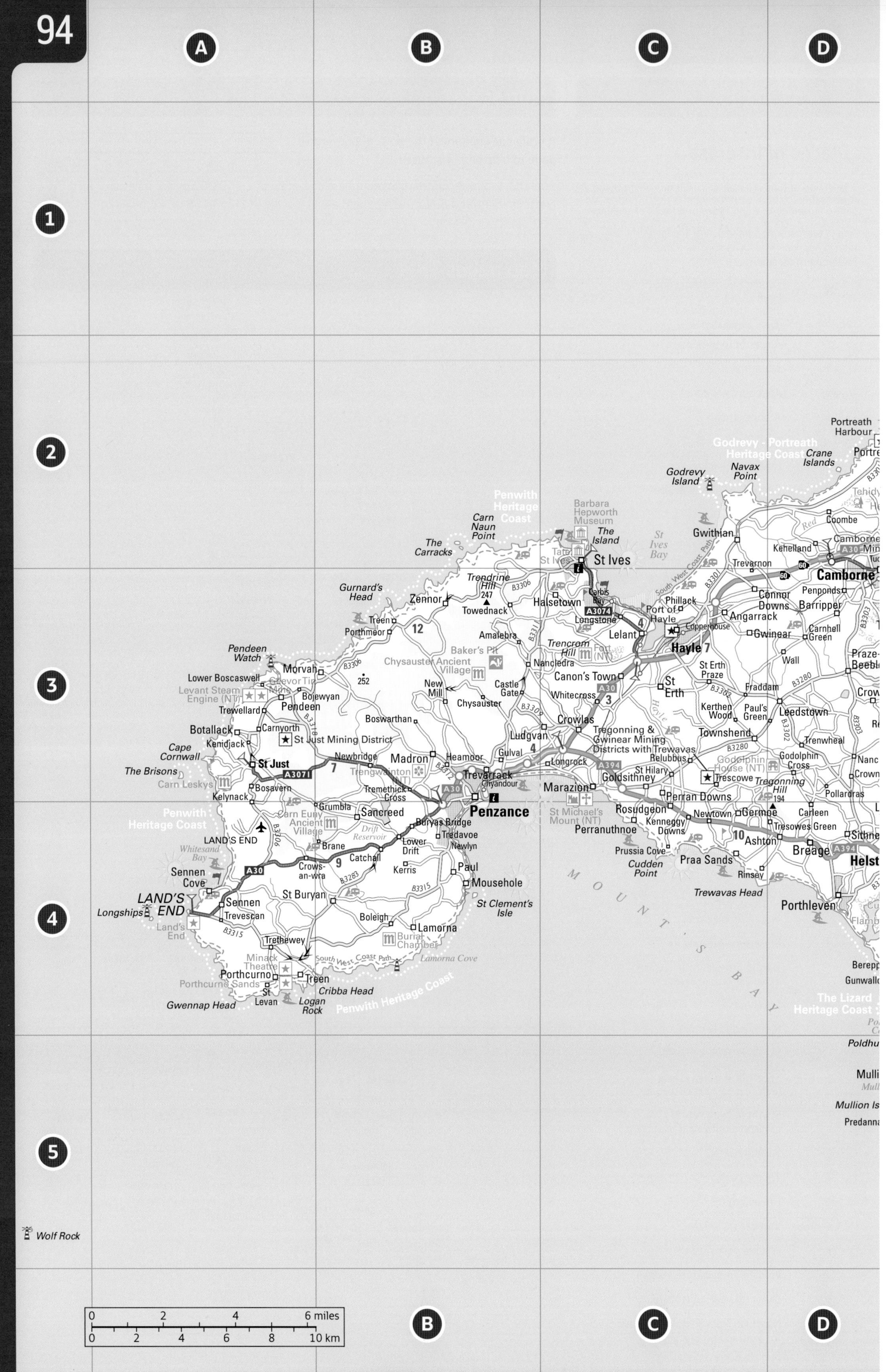

A B C D

1

2

Portreath Harbour
Godrevy - Portreath Heritage Coast
Crane Islands
Portr
Godrevy Island
Navax Point
Tehidy
Coombe
Penwith Heritage Coast
Barbara Hepworth Museum
The Island
St Ives Bay
Gwithian
Kehelland
Camborne
Carn Naun Point
The Carracks
Trendrine Hill 247
St Ives
Carbis Bay
South West Coast Path
Phillack
Connor Downs
Camborne
Penponds
A30
Gurnard's Head
Zennor
Towednack
Halsetown
Longstone
Port of Hayle
Copperhouse
Trevarnon
Angarrack
Gwinear
Barripper
Carnhell Green
Praze-Beebl
Crow

3

Treen
Porthmeor
12
Amalebra
A3074
Lelant
Hayle 7
St Erth Praze
Wall
Pendeen Watch
Morvah
Baker's Pit
Chysauster Ancient Village
Nancledra
Trencrom Hill Fort (NT)
St Erth
Fraddam
B3280
Leedstown
Lower Boscaswell
Trevor Tin Mine
252
New Mill
Castle Gate
Canon's Town
A30
Kerthen Wood
Paul's Green
Trenwheal
Levant Steam Engine (NT)
Bojewyan
Pendeen
Boswarthan
Chysauster
Whitecross
3
St Dolphin Cross
Crown
Trewellard
Carnyorth
Crowlas
Tregonning & Gwinear Mining Districts with Trewavas
Townshend
B3302
B3303
Botallack
Kenidjack
St Just Mining District
Ludgvan
Gulval
4
Longrock
Relubbus
St Hilary
Godolphin House (NT)
Dolphin Cross
Crown
Cape Cornwall
Newbridge
Madron
Heamoor
A394
Trescowe
Tregonning Hill 194
Pollardras
The Brisons
St Just
A3071
Trengwainton
Chyandour
Trevarrack
Marazion
Goldsithney
Perran Downs
Carleen
Carn Leskys
7
Tremethick Cross
A30
Penzance
St Michael's Mount (NT)
Rosudgeon
Newtown
Germoe
Tresowes Green
Sithne
Kelynack
Bosavern
Sancreed
Grumbla
Buryas Bridge
Kenneggy Downs
10
Ashton
Breage
A394
Helst
Carn Euny Ancient Village
Brane
Tredavoe
Newlyn
Perranuthnoe
Prussia Cove
Praa Sands
Rinsey
Porthleven
LAND'S END
Crows-an-wra
9
Lower Drift
Cudden Point
Whitesand Bay
Catchall
Kerris
Paul
B3283
Trewavas Head
Sennen Cove
A30
St Buryan
B3315
Mousehole
MOUNT'S
7
Sennen
Trevescan
Boleigh
St Clement's Isle
BAY
Berepp
LAND'S END
B3315
Lamorna
Gunwallo

4

Longships
Land's End
Trethewey
Burial Chamber
Lamorna Cove
The Lizard Heritage Coast
Minack Theatre
South West Coast Path
Porthcurno
Treen
Porthcurno Sands
St Levan
Cribba Head
Gwennap Head
Logan Rock
Penwith Heritage Coast
Poldhu

Mulli
Mull

Mullion Is
Predanna

5

Wolf Rock

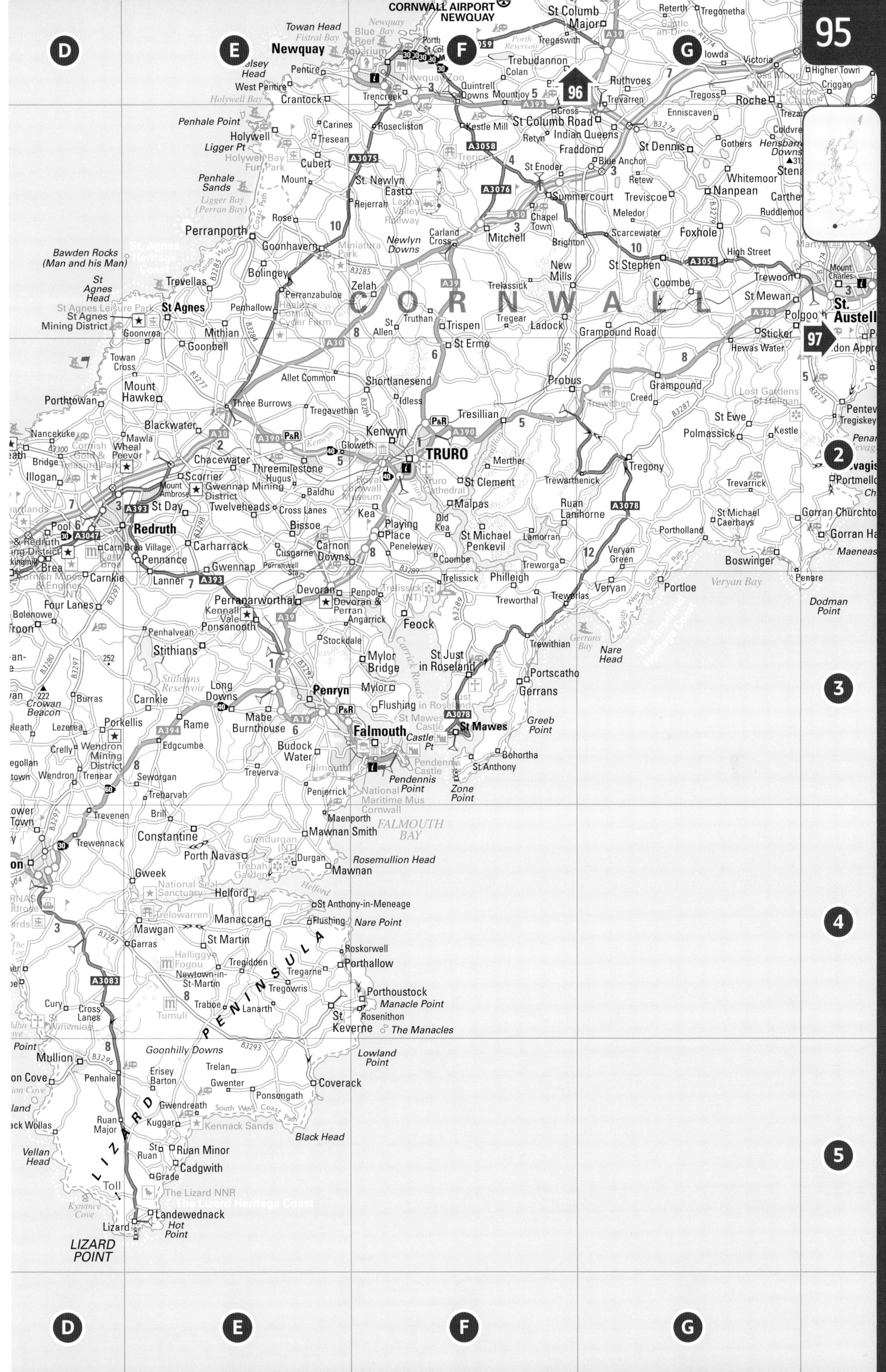
D
E
F
G
CORNWALL AIRPORT NEWQUAY
Newquay
Towan Head
Fistral Bay
Blue Reef Aquarium
Newquay Zoo
Pentire
West Pentire
Holywell Bay
Crantock
Penhale Point
Holywell
Ligger Pt
Holywell Bay Fun Park
Cubert
Penhale Sands
Ligger Bay (Perran Bay)
Perranporth
Bawden Rocks (Man and his Man)
St Agnes Head
St Agnes Leisure Park
St Agnes Mining District
St Agnes
Trevellas
Goonhavern
Bolingey
Perranzabuloe
Healey's Cornish Cyder Farm
Zelah
Goonvrea
Mithian
Goonbell
Towan Cross
Mount Hawke
Porthtowan
Three Burrows
Blackwater
Nancekuke
Mawla
Wheal Peevor
Cornish Gold & Treasure Park
Bridge
Illogan
Chacewater
Scorrier
Mount Ambrose
Gwennap Mining District
St Day
Twelveheads
Pool
Redruth
Carn Brea Village
Brea
Carharrack
Pennance
Gwennap
Lanner
Carnkie
Cornish Mines & Engines (NT)
Four Lanes
Bolenowe
Troon
Penhalvean
Stithians
Stithians Reservoir
Crowan Beacon
Burras
Carnkie
Porkellis
Rame
Lezerea
Crelly
Wendron Mining District
Wendron
Trenear
Edgcumbe
Seworgan
Trebarvah
Trevenen
Brill
Trewennack
Constantine
Porth Navas
Gweek
National Seal Sanctuary
Trelowarren
Mawgan
Garras
Halligye Fogou
Newtown-in-St-Martin
Cury
Cross Lanes
St Winwaloe
Mullion
Penhale
Goonhilly Downs
Erisey Barton
Trelan
Gwenter
Ponsongath
Gwendreath
Kuggar
Kennack Sands
Ruan Major
St Ruan
Ruan Minor
Cadgwith
Grade
Toll
The Lizard NNR
The Lizard Heritage Coast
Kynance Cove
Landewednack
Lizard
Hot Point
LIZARD POINT
Vellan Head
LIZARD PENINSULA
Black Head
Coverack
Lowland Point
St Keverne
The Manacles
Rosenithon
Manacle Point
Porthoustock
Porthallow
Roskorwell
Tregarne
Tregowris
Tregidden
Traboe
Lanarth
Tumuli
St Martin
Manaccan
Flushing
Nare Point
St Anthony-in-Meneage
Helford
Trebah Garden
Glendurgan (NT)
Durgan
Mawnan
Rosemullion Head
Mawnan Smith
Maenporth
FALMOUTH BAY
National Maritime Mus Cornwall
Penjerrick
Treverva
Budock Water
Mabe Burnthouse
Long Downs
Penryn
Mylor
Mylor Bridge
Flushing
Falmouth
Pendennis Castle
Pendennis Point
St Mawes Castle
Castle Pt
St Mawes
St Just in Roseland
Zone Point
St Anthony
Bohortha
Greeb Point
Gerrans
Portscatho
Trewithian
Gerrans Bay
Nare Head
The Roseland Heritage Coast
Veryan Bay
Portloe
Veryan
Veryan Green
Treworlas
Treworthal
Philleigh
Treworga
Trelissick
Trelissick (NT)
Feock
Devoran
Devoran & Perran
Penpol
Angarrick
Stockdale
Carrick Roads
Perranarworthal
Kennall Vale
Ponsanooth
Perranwell Sta
Cusgarne
Carnon Downs
Penelewey
Playing Place
Kea
Old Kea
Coombe
St Michael Penkevil
Lamorran
Ruan Lanihorne
Malpas
St Clement
Merther
Trewarthenick
Tregony
Truro Cathedral
TRURO
Royal Cornwall Museum
Baldhu
Cross Lanes
Bissoe
Hugus
Threemilestone
Gloweth
Kenwyn
Tregavethan
Allet Common
Shortlanesend
Idless
Tresillian
St Allen
Truthan
Trispen
St Erme
Tregear
Ladock
Grampound Road
Probus
Trewithen
Creed
Grampound
CORNWALL
Newlyn Downs
Miniatura Park
Carland Cross
Mitchell
Chapel Town
Summercourt
Brighton
Trelassick
New Mills
St Enoder
Fraddon
Blue Anchor
Indian Queens
St Columb Road
Retyn
Trerice (NT)
Kestle Mill
Quintrell Downs
Mountjoy
Colan
Trebudannon
Porth Reservoir
Tregaswith
St Columb Major
Trencreek
Rosecliston
Carines
Tresean
Mount
St. Newlyn East
Lappa Valley Railway
Rejerrah
Rose
Ruthvoes
Trevarren
Reterth
Tregonetha
Castle-an-Dinas
Iowda
Victoria
Goss Moor NNR
Higher Town
Criggan
Tregoss
Roche
Enniscaven
St Dennis
Gothers
Hensbarrow Downs
Whitemoor
Nanpean
Retew
Treviscoe
Meledor
Scarcewater
Foxhole
St Stephen
High Street
Coombe
Trewoon
St Mewan
Mount Charles
St. Austell
Polgooth
Sticker
Hewas Water
Lost Gardens of Heligan
St Ewe
Polmassick
Kestle
Trevarrick
Portmellon
St Michael Caerhays
Gorran Churchtown
Portholland
Boswinger
Penare
Dodman Point
Tregiskey
96
97
A30
A39
A390
A392
A393
A394
A3058
A3075
A3076
A3078
A3083
A3047
B3285
B3284
B3277
B3298
B3297
B3289
B3293
B3296
B3287
B3275
B3279
B3274
2
3
4
5

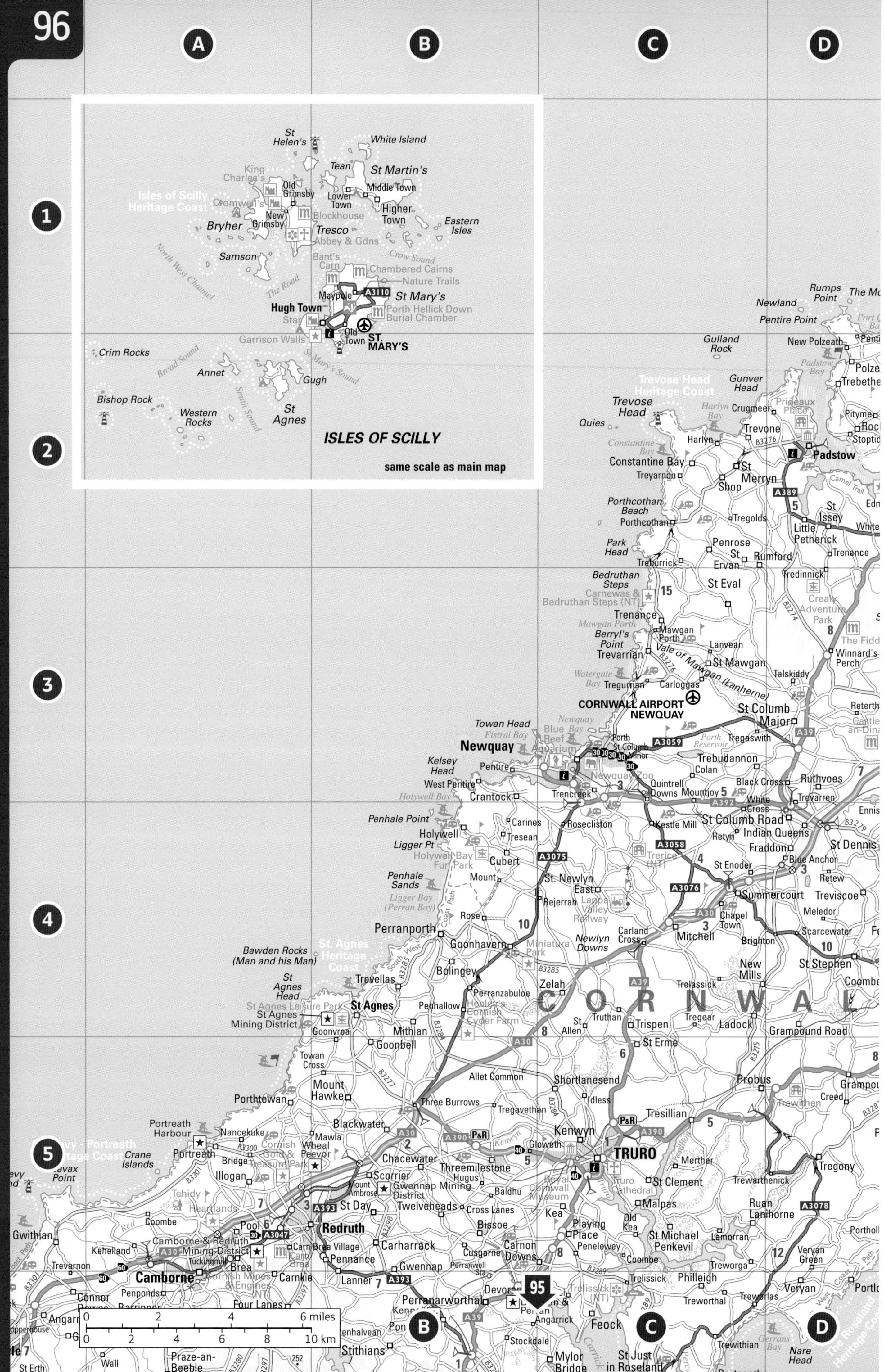
A
B
C
D
1
2
3
4
5
ISLES OF SCILLY
same scale as main map
St Helen's
White Island
Tean
St Martin's
King Charles's
Old Grimsby
Middle Town
Lower Town
Higher Town
Isles of Scilly Heritage Coast
Cromwell's
New Grimsby
Blockhouse
Eastern Isles
Bryher
Tresco
Abbey & Gdns
Samson
Crow Sound
North West Channel
Bant's Carn
Chambered Cairns
Nature Trails
The Road
Maypole
A3110
St Mary's
Hugh Town
Porth Hellick Down Burial Chamber
Star
Old Town
ST. MARY'S
Garrison Walls
Crim Rocks
Broad Sound
St Mary's Sound
Annet
Gugh
Bishop Rock
Smith Sound
Western Rocks
St Agnes
Rumps Point
Newland
Pentire Point
Gulland Rock
New Polzeath
Trevose Head Heritage Coast
Gunver Head
Padstow Bay
Trevose Head
Harlyn Bay
Crugmeer
Prideaux Place
Quies
Trevone
Constantine Bay
Harlyn
B3276
Padstow
St Merryn
Treyarnon
Shop
A389
Camel Trail
Porthcothan Beach
Porthcothan
Tregolds
St Issey
Little Petherick
Park Head
Penrose
St Ervan
Rumford
Trenance
Treburrick
Tredinnick
Bedruthan Steps
Carnewas & Bedruthan Steps (NT)
St Eval
Crealy Adventure Park
B3274
Trenance
Mawgan Porth
Mawgan Porth
Berryl's Point
Lanvean
Trevarrian
Vale of Mawgan (Lanherne)
St Mawgan
Winnard's Perch
Watergate Bay
Tregurrian
Carloggas
Talskiddy
CORNWALL AIRPORT NEWQUAY
St Columb Major
Towan Head
Newquay Bay
Fistral Bay
Blue Reef Aquarium
Newquay
Porth
St Columb Minor
A3059
Porth Reservoir
Tregaswith
Kelsey Head
Pentire
Newquay Zoo
Trebudannon
Colan
A39
West Pentire
Quintrell Downs
Mountjoy
Black Cross
Ruthvoes
Holywell Bay
Crantock
Trencreek
A392
White Cross
Trevarren
Penhale Point
Carines
Rosecliston
Kestle Mill
St Columb Road
Holywell
Tresean
Retyn
Indian Queens
St Dennis
Ligger Pt
A3075
Trerice (NT)
A3058
Fraddon
Holywell Bay Fun Park
Cubert
Blue Anchor
Penhale Sands
Mount
St. Newlyn East
St Enoder
Retew
A3076
Summercourt
Treviscoe
Ligger Bay (Perran Bay)
Rejerrah
Lappa Valley Railway
Rose
Chapel Town
Meledor
A30
Perranporth
Carland Cross
Mitchell
Brighton
Scarcewater
Bawden Rocks (Man and his Man)
St. Agnes Heritage Coast
Goonhavern
Miniatura Park
Newlyn Downs
St Stephen
St Agnes Head
Trevellas
Bolingey
B3285
New Mills
Coombe
A39
Zelah
Trelassick
St Agnes Leisure Park
St Agnes
Perranzabuloe
CORNWALL
St Agnes Mining District
Penhallow
Healey's Cornish Cyder Farm
Truthan
St Allen
Trispen
Tregear
Ladock
Grampound Road
Goonvrea
Mithian
A30
St Erme
Goonbell
Towan Cross
B3277
B3275
Mount Hawke
Allet Common
Shortlanesend
Probus
Porthtowan
Three Burrows
Idless
Trewithen
Creed
Portreath Harbour
Blackwater
Tregavethan
Tresillian
Nancekuke
Mawla
A390
Kenwyn
Crane Islands
Cornish Gold & Treasure Park
Wheal Peevor
Gloweth
TRURO
Portreath
Chacewater
Threemilestone
Merther
Tregony
Bridge
Illogan
Scorrier
Gwennap Mining District
Hugus
Royal Cornwall Museum
Truro Cathedral
St Clement
Trewarthenick
Tehidy
Mount Ambrose
Baldhu
Heartlands
St Day
Twelveheads
Cross Lanes
Kea
Malpas
Ruan Lanihorne
A3078
Gwithian
Coombe
Pool
A393
A3047
Redruth
Bissoe
Playing Place
Old Kea
St Michael Penkevil
Camborne & Redruth Mining District
Carn Brea Village
Carharrack
Carnon Downs
Lamorran
Veryan Green
Kehelland
Tuckingmill
Brea
Pennance
Cusgarne
Penelewey
Coombe
Trevarnon
Camborne
Cornish Mines & Engines (NT)
Carnkie
Lanner
Gwennap
Perranwell Sta
Trelissick
Phillleigh
Treworga
Veryan
Connor Downs
Penponds
Perranarworthal
Devoran
95
Trelissick (NT)
Treworthal
Trewarlas
Four Lanes
Kennall
Pon
Angarrick
Feock
Trewithian
Gerrans Bay
Nare Head
The Roseland Heritage Coast
Angarr
Penhalvean
Stithians
Stockdale
Mylor Bridge
St Just in Roseland
Portscatho
Wall
Praze-an-Beeble
St Erth
0 2 4 6 miles
0 2 4 6 8 10 km

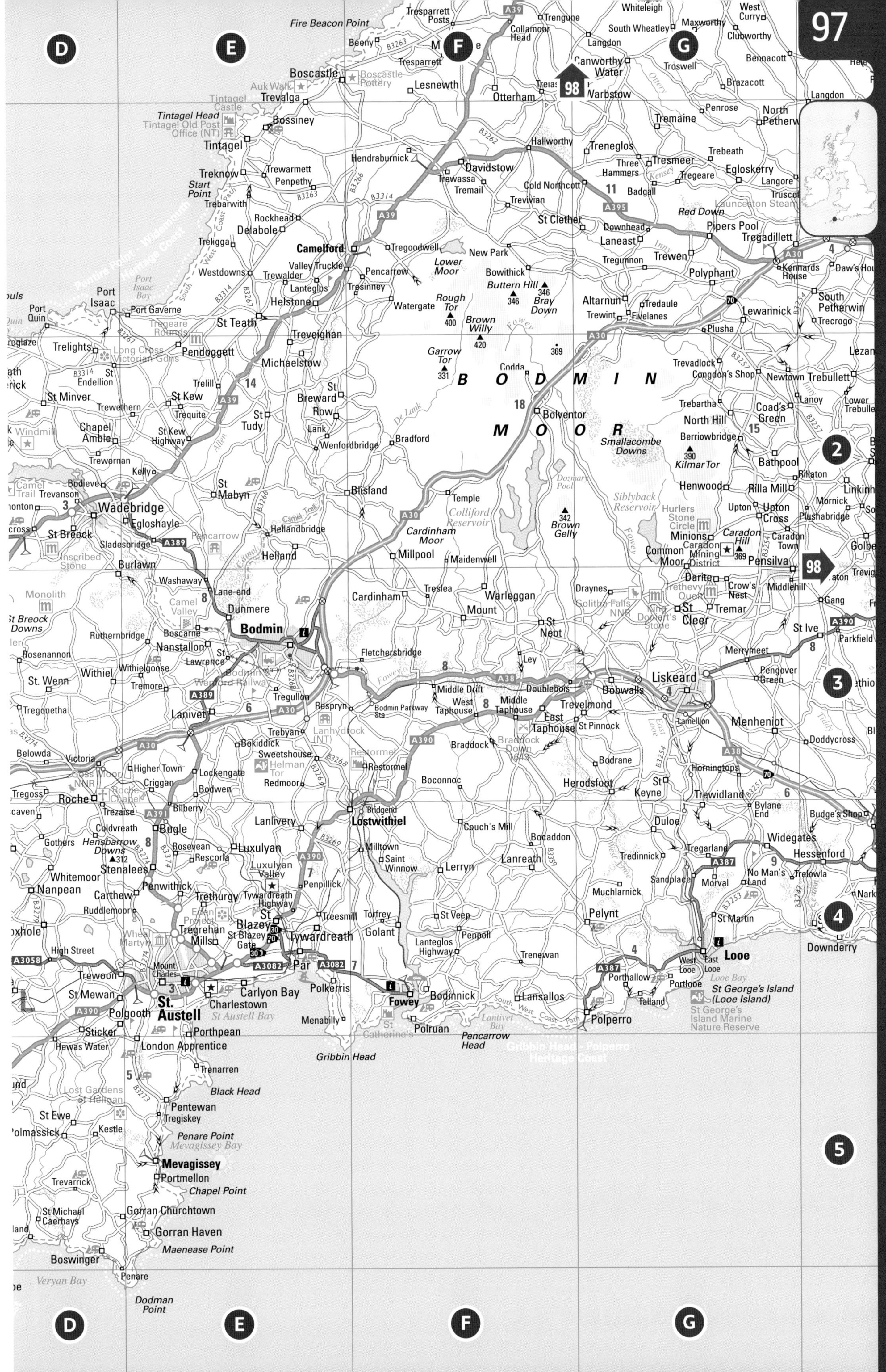
D
E
F
G
98
Fire Beacon Point
Trespassett Posts
Beeny
Trespassett
Boscastle
Boscastle Pottery
Auk Walk
Tintagel Castle
Trevalga
Tintagel Head
Tintagel Old Post Office (NT)
Bossiney
Tintagel
Lesnewth
Collamoor Head
Trengune
Otterham
Whiteleigh
West Curry
South Wheatley
Maxworthy
Clubworthy
Langdon
Canworthy Water
Bennacott
Troswell
Warbstow
Brazacott
Langdon
Penrose
North Petherwin
Tremaine
Hallworthy
Treneglos
Trebeath
Three Hammers
Tresmeer
Egloskerry
Tregeare
Badgall
Langore
Hendraburnick
Davidstow
Trewassa
Tremail
Cold Northcott
Trevivian
Red Down
Launceston Steam
St Clether
Downhead
Pipers Pool
Laneast
Tregadillett
Trewen
Tregunnon
Polyphant
Kennards House
Daw's House
South Petherwin
Trecrogo
Treknow
Start Point
Trebarwith
Trewarmett
Penpethy
Rockhead
Delabole
Treligga
Westdowns
Port Isaac Bay
Pentire Point - Widemouth Heritage Coast
Port Isaac
Port Quin
Port Gaverne
Tregeare Rounds
Camelford
Tregoodwell
New Park
Lower Moor
Bowithick
Buttern Hill
Bray Down
Valley Truckle
Pencarrow
Trewalder
Lanteglos
Tresinney
Helstone
Watergate
Rough Tor
Brown Willy
Altarnun
Tredaule
Trewint
Fivelanes
Lewannick
Plusha
St Teath
Treveighan
Trelights
Long Cross Victorian Gdns
Pendoggett
Michaelstow
Garrow Tor
Codda
St Endellion
BODMIN MOOR
Trevadlock
Congdon's Shop
Newtown
Trebullett
Lezant
Trelill
St Minver
Trewethern
St Kew
Trequite
St Breward
Row
St Tudy
Lank
Bolventor
Trebartha
North Hill
Coad's Green
Lanoy
Lower Trebullett
Chapel Amble
Windmill
St Kew Highway
De Lank
Wenfordbridge
Bradford
Smallacombe Downs
Berriowbridge
Kilmar Tor
Bathpool
Trewornan
Kelly
Camel Trail
Bodieve
Trevanson
St Mabyn
Blisland
Temple
Dozmary Pool
Henwood
Rilla Mill
Rillaton
Linkinhorne
Wadebridge
Egloshayle
Colliford Reservoir
Siblyback Reservoir
Hurlers Stone Circle
Upton Cross
Mornick
Plushabridge
St Breock
Sladesbridge
Pencarrow
Hellandbridge
Cardinham Moor
Brown Gelly
Minions
Caradon Hill
Caradon Town
Inscribed Stone
Helland
Millpool
Maidenwell
Common Moor
Caradon Mining District
Pensilva
Burlawn
Washaway
Monolith
Lane-end
Camel Valley
Cardinham
Treslea
Warleggan
Draynes
Golitha Falls NNR
Trethevy Quoit
Darite
Crow's Nest
Middlehill
St Breock Downs
Dunmere
Bodmin
Mount
St Cleer
King Doniert's Stone
Tremar
Gang
Rutherbridge
Boscarne
Nanstallon
St Neot
St Ive
Parkfield
Rosenannon
St Lawrence
Fletchersbridge
Ley
Merrymeet
Withiel
Withielgoose
Bodmin & Wenford Railway
Liskeard
Pengover Green
St. Wenn
Tremore
Tregullon
Middle Drift
Doublebois
Dobwalls
West Taphouse
Middle Taphouse
Trevelmond
East Taphouse
St Pinnock
Tregonetha
Lanivet
Respryn
Bodmin Parkway Sta
Lamellion
Menheniot
Trebyan
Lanhydrock (NT)
Braddock
Braddock Down 1643
Doddycross
Belowda
Victoria
Bokiddick
Sweetshouse
Helman Tor
Restormel
Bodrane
Goss Moor NNR
Higher Town
Lockengate
Redmoor
Boconnoc
Hormingtops
Tregoss
Criggan
Bodwen
Herodsfoot
St Keyne
Trewidland
Roche
Roche Chapel
Trezaise
Bilberry
Bridgend
Bylane End
Lanlivery
Lostwithiel
Couch's Mill
Duloe
Budge's Shop
Coldvreath
Bugle
Bocaddon
Widegates
Gothers
Hensbarrow Downs
Rosevean
Luxulyan
Milltown
Tredinnick
Tregarland
Hessenford
Rescorla
Saint Winnow
Lanreath
Stenalees
Luxulyan Valley
Lerryn
Sandplace
No Man's Land
Trelowla
Whitemoor
Nanpean
Penwithick
Penpillick
Morval
Narkurs
Carthew
Trethurgy
Tywardreath Highway
Muchlarnick
Ruddlemoor
Eden Project
Treesmill
Torfrey
St Veep
Pelynt
St Martin
Downderry
Wheal Martyn
Tregrehan Mills
St Blazey
St Blazey Gate
Tywardreath
Golant
Penpoll
Lanteglos Highway
Trenewan
Looe
East Looe
West Looe
High Street
Trewoon
Mount Charles
Par
Polkerris
Carlyon Bay
Porthallow
Portlooe
Talland
Looe Bay
St George's Island (Looe Island)
St George's Island Marine Nature Reserve
St Mewan
St. Austell
Charlestown
St Austell Bay
Fowey
Bodinnick
Lansallos
Polperro
Lantivet Bay
Polgooth
Menabilly
St Catherine's
Polruan
Sticker
Porthpean
Pencarrow Head
Gribbin Head - Polperro Heritage Coast
Hewas Water
London Apprentice
Gribbin Head
Trenarren
Black Head
Lost Gardens of Heligan
Pentewan
Tregiskey
St Ewe
Kestle
Polmassick
Penare Point
Mevagissey Bay
Mevagissey
Portmellon
Trevarrick
Chapel Point
St Michael Caerhays
Gorran Churchtown
Gorran Haven
Maenease Point
Boswinger
Penare
Veryan Bay
Dodman Point
A39
A30
A38
A389
A390
A391
A395
A387
A3082
A3058
B3263
B3266
B3314
B3267
B3262
B3254
B3257
B3268
B3269
B3274
B3279
B3359
B3253
B3273
B3251
B3247

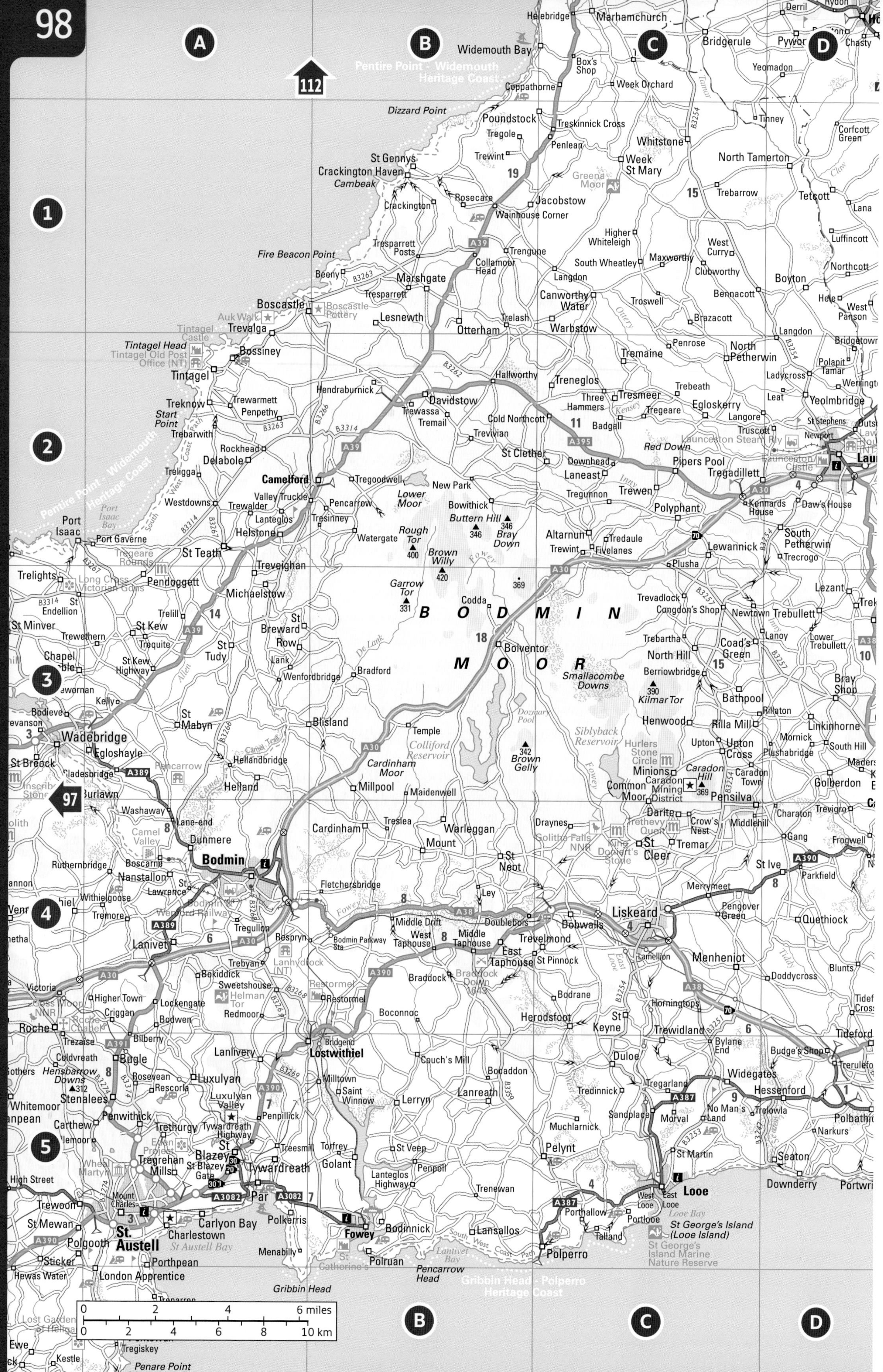
A
B
C
D
1
2
3
4
5
112
97
Widemouth Bay
Pentire Point - Widemouth Heritage Coast
Helebridge
Marhamchurch
Bridgerule
Pyworthy
Chasty
Derril
Rydon
Box's Shop
Yeomadon
Coppathorne
Week Orchard
Tamar
Dizzard Point
Poundstock
Treskinnick Cross
Tinney
Corfcott Green
Tregole
Whitstone
Penlean
Trewint
St Gennys
Crackington Haven
Cambeak
19
Week St Mary
Greena Moor
North Tamerton
15
Trebarrow
Tetcott
Lana
Rosecare
Jacobstow
Wainhouse Corner
Crackington
Higher Whiteleigh
Luffincott
Trengune
A39
Tresparrett Posts
Fire Beacon Point
Collamoor Head
South Wheatley
Maxworthy
West Curry
Clubworthy
Northcott
Beeny
B3263
Marshgate
Langdon
Tresparrett
Canworthy Water
Troswell
Bennacott
Boyton
Hele
West Panson
Boscastle
Boscastle Pottery
Auk Walk
Lesnewth
Trelash
Brazacott
Otterham
Warbstow
Tintagel Castle
Trevalga
Langdon
Tintagel Head
Tintagel Old Post Office (NT)
Bossiney
Penrose
North Petherwin
Bridgetown
Tremaine
Polapit Tamar
Tintagel
B3262
Hallworthy
Treneglos
Ladycross
Werrington
Hendraburnick
Trebeath
Three Hammers
Tresmeer
Egloskerry
Leat
Yeolmbridge
Treknow
Trewarmett
Davidstow
Trewassa
Tremail
Start Point
Penpethy
B3266
B3314
Cold Northcott
Tregeare
Langore
Kensey
St Stephens
Trebarwith
11
Badgall
Truscott
Newport
A395
Trevivian
Rockhead
Launceston Steam Rly
Red Down
Delabole
St Clether
Downhead
Pipers Pool
Tregadillett
Launceston Castle
Treligga
Camelford
Tregoodwell
New Park
Laneast
Westdowns
Valley Truckle
Lower Moor
Pencarrow
Tregunnon
Trewen
A30
Kennards House
Daw's House
Trewalder
Bowithick
Polyphant
Port Isaac Bay
Lanteglos
Buttern Hill
346
Port Isaac
Helstone
Tresinney
Rough Tor
Bray Down
South Petherwin
Port Gaverne
Watergate
400
Altarnun
Tredaule
Lewannick
Tregeare Rounds
St Teath
Brown Willy
420
Trewint
Fivelanes
Trecrogo
Trelights
Treveighan
Plusha
Long Cross Victorian Gdns
Pendoggett
369
Garrow Tor
331
Codda
Lezant
St Endellion
Michaelstow
Trevadlock
Congdon's Shop
Newtown
Trebullett
Trelill
B O D M I N
St Minver
14
St Kew
St Breward
Trewethern
Trequite
Row
18
Bolventor
Trebartha
Coad's Green
Lanoy
Lower Trebullett
Chapel
St Kew Highway
St Tudy
Lank
M O O R
North Hill
10
Wenfordbridge
Bradford
De Lank
Smallacombe Downs
Berriowbridge
15
Bray Shop
Kelly
Allen
390
Kilmar Tor
Bathpool
Bodieve
St Mabyn
Blisland
Dozmary Pool
Rillaton
Wadebridge
Temple
Henwood
Rilla Mill
Linkinhorne
Egloshayle
Colliford Reservoir
Siblyback Reservoir
Hurlers Stone Circle
Upton
Upton Cross
Mornick
South Hill
St Breock
Pencarrow
Hellandbridge
342
Brown Gelly
Plushabridge
Cardinham Moor
Minions
Caradon Hill
Caradon Town
Sladesbridge
A389
Helland
Millpool
Maidenwell
Common Moor
Caradon Mining District
Golberdon
Burlawn
Pensilva
Washaway
Lane-end
Cardinham
Treslea
Warleggan
Draynes
Darite
Trethevy Quoit
Crow's Nest
Middlehill
Charaton
Trevigro
Camel Valley
Dunmere
Mount
Golitha Falls NNR
King Doniert's Stone
St Cleer
Tremar
Gang
Frogwell
Ruthernbridge
Boscarne
Bodmin
St Neot
St Ive
Parkfield
A390
Nanstallon
Lawrence
Fletchersbridge
Merrymeet
Withielgoose
Bodmin & Wenford Railway
Ley
Liskeard
Tremore
Middle Drift
Doublebois
Dobwalls
Pengover Green
Quethiock
A38
Tregullon
West Taphouse
Middle Taphouse
Trevelmond
Lanivet
Respryn
Bodmin Parkway Sta
East Taphouse
St Pinnock
Lamellion
Menheniot
Trebyan
Lanhydrock (NT)
Bokiddick
Sweetshouse
Braddock
Braddock Down 1643
East Looe
Blunts
Doddycross
Victoria
Higher Town
Helman Tor
Restormel
Lockengate
Criggan
Redmoor
Bodrane
Tideford Cross
Goss Moor NNR
Bodwen
Boconnoc
Herodsfoot
St Keyne
Horningtops
Roche
Roche Chapel
Trewidland
Tideford
Trezaise
Bilberry
Lanlivery
Bridgend
Lostwithiel
Bylane End
Budge's Shop
Coldvreath
Bugle
Couch's Mill
Duloe
Trerulefoot
Hensbarrow Downs
312
Rosevean
Luxulyan
Bocaddon
Widegates
Stenalees
Rescorla
Milltown
Saint Winnow
Lanreath
Tredinnick
Tregarland
Hessenford
Luxulyan Valley
Lerryn
Polbathic
Whitemoor
Penwithick
Penpillick
A387
No Man's Land
Trelowla
Carthew
Trethurgy
Tywardreath Highway
Sandplace
Morval
Muchlarnick
Narkurs
Eden Project
St Blazey
Treesmill
Torfrey
St Veep
Seaton
Tregrehan Mills
Blazey Gate
Tywardreath
Golant
Pelynt
St Martin
Wheal Martyn
Penpoll
High Street
Lanteglos Highway
Trenewan
Looe
Downderry
Portwrinkle
Mount Charles
Par
A3082
Trewoon
Carlyon Bay
Polkerris
Porthallow
West Looe
Looe Bay
St Mewan
St. Austell
Charlestown
Bodinnick
St Austell Bay
Fowey
Lansallos
Talland
Portlooe
St George's Island (Looe Island)
St George's Island Marine Nature Reserve
Polgooth
Menabilly
Sticker
Porthpean
St Catherine's
Polruan
Lantivet Bay
South West Coast Path
Polperro
Hewas Water
London Apprentice
Pencarrow Head
Gribbin Head
Gribbin Head - Polperro Heritage Coast
Trenarren
Lost Gardens of Heligan
Ewe
Tregiskey
Kestle
Penare Point
0
2
4
6 miles
0
2
4
6
8
10 km

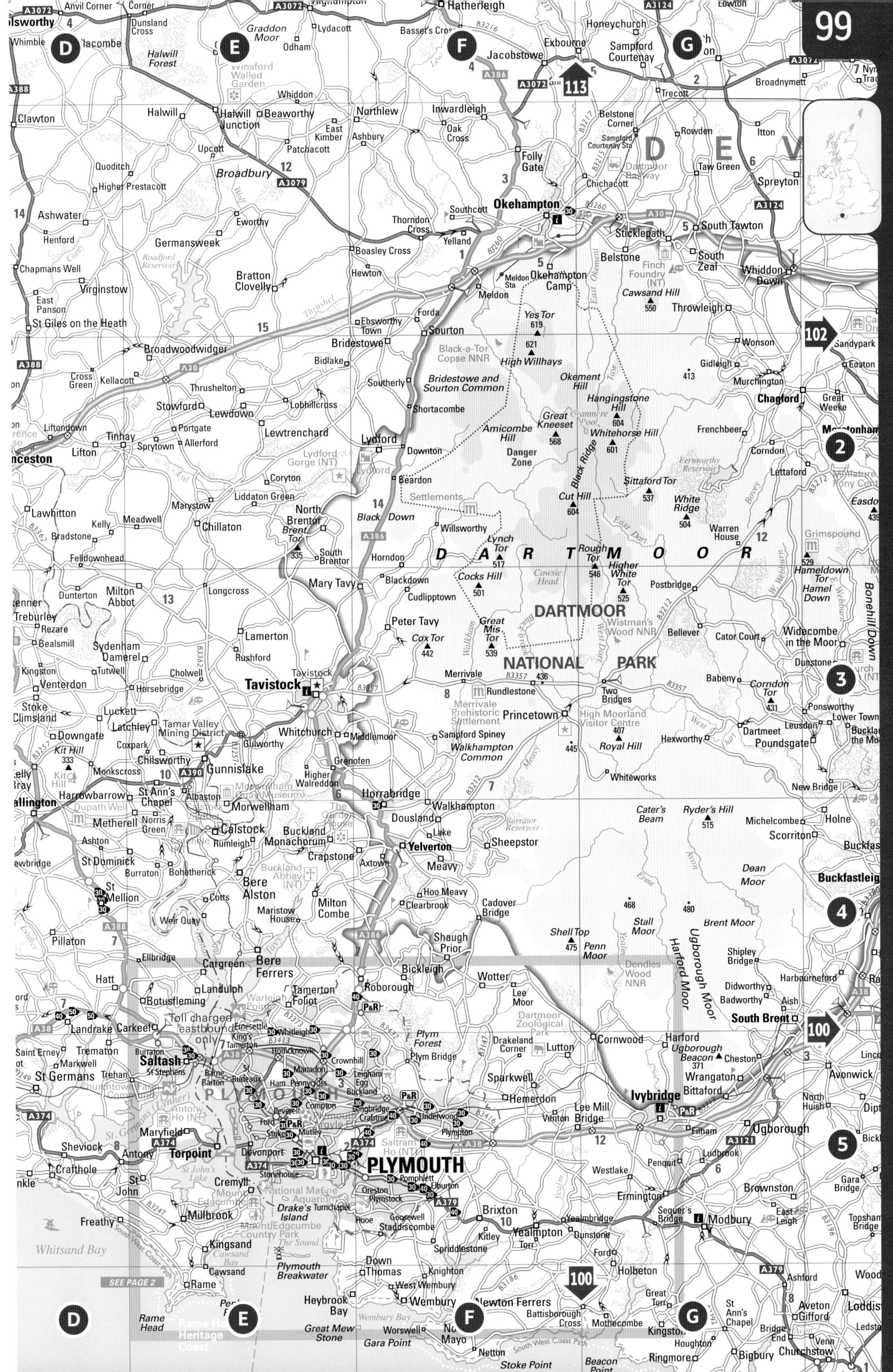

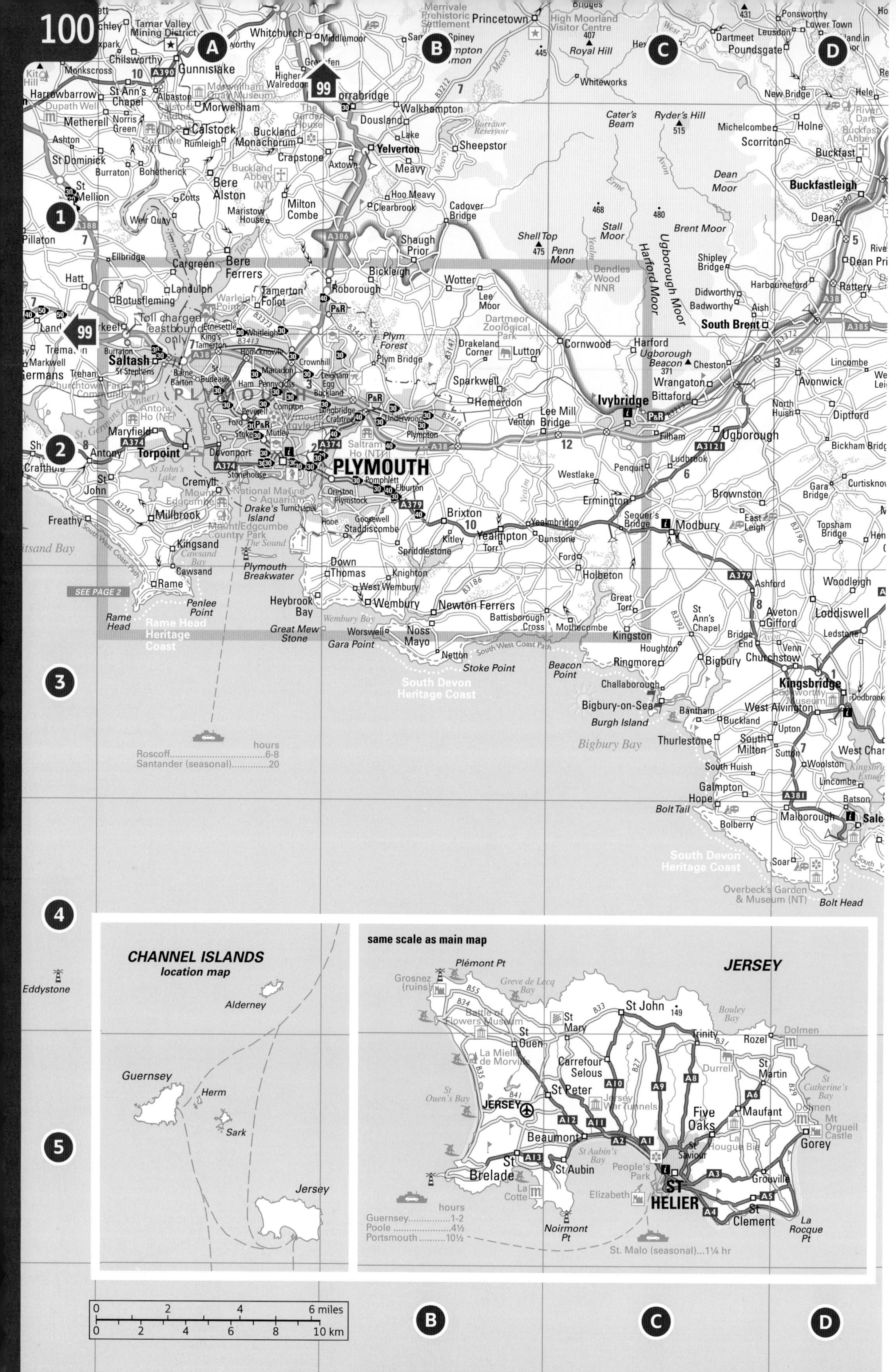

Tamar Valley Mining District
Gunnislake
Whitchurch
Middlemoor
Merrivale Prehistoric Settlement
Princetown
High Moorland Visitor Centre
Royal Hill
Whiteworks
Dartmeet
Poundsgate
Ponsworthy
Leusdon
Lower Town
Chilsworthy
Monkscross
Harrowbarrow
St Ann's Chapel
Albaston
Morwellham Quay Museum
Morwellham
Dupath Well
Metherell
Norris Green
Calstock
Calstock Viaduct
Cotehele (NT)
Rumleigh
Buckland Monachorum
The Garden House
Horrabridge
Walkhampton
Dousland
Lake
Yelverton
Burrator Reservoir
Sheepstor
Cater's Beam
Ryder's Hill
Michelcombe
Holne
Scorriton
Buckfast
Buckfast Abbey
Buckfastleigh
New Bridge
River Dart
Ashton
St Dominick
Burraton
Bohetherick
Bere Alston
Buckland Abbey (NT)
Crapstone
Axtown
Meavy
Hoo Meavy
Clearbrook
Dean Moor
St Mellion
Cotts
Maristow House
Milton Combe
Cadover Bridge
Weir Quay
Shaugh Prior
Shell Top
Penn Moor
Stall Moor
Brent Moor
Dean
Pillaton
Ellbridge
Cargreen
Bere Ferrers
Bickleigh
Roborough
Wotter
Lee Moor
Dendles Wood NNR
Harford Moor
Ugborough Moor
Shipley Bridge
Dean Prior
Didworthy
Badworthy
Harbourneford
Rattery
Aish
South Brent
Hatt
Landulph
Botusfleming
Warleigh Point
Tamerton Foliot
Toll charged eastbound only
Ernesettle
Whitleigh
King's Tamerton
Honicknowle
Crownhill
Plym Forest
Plym Bridge
Dartmoor Zoological Park
Drakeland Corner
Lutton
Cornwood
Harford
Ugborough Beacon
Cheston
Lincombe
Wrangaton
Bittaford
Avonwick
Saltash
St Stephens
Burraton
Trematon
Markwell
St Germans
Trehan
Churchtown Farm Community
Barne Barton
St Budeaux
Manadon
Leigham
Egg Buckland
Ham
Pennycross
PLYMOUTH
Sparkwell
Hemerdon
Ivybridge
North Huish
Diptford
Antony Ho (NT)
Maryfield
Antony
Torpoint
Peverell
Compton
Longbridge
Crabtree
Underwood
Plympton
Plymouth Argyle FC
Ford
Stoke
Mutley
Venton
Lee Mill Bridge
Filham
Ugborough
Devonport
Saltram Ho (NT)
Crafthole
St John's Lake
Stonehouse
Pomphlett
Elburton
Oreston
Plymstock
Westlake
Penquit
Ludbrook
Bickham Bridge
St John
Cremyll
Mount Edgcumbe
National Marine Aquarium
Turnchapel
Drake's Island
Ermington
Brownston
Gara Bridge
Curtisknowle
Freathy
Millbrook
Mount Edgcumbe Country Park
Hooe
Goosewell
Staddiscombe
Brixton
Yealmpton
Kitley
Yealmbridge
Torr
Dunstone
Sequer's Bridge
Modbury
East Leigh
Topsham Bridge
Whitsand Bay
Kingsand
Cawsand Bay
Cawsand
The Sound
Plymouth Breakwater
Spriddlestone
Ford
Holbeton
Ashford
Woodleigh
SEE PAGE 2
Rame
Down Thomas
Knighton
West Wembury
Wembury
Heybrook Bay
Newton Ferrers
Battisborough Cross
Mothecombe
Great Torr
St Ann's Chapel
Aveton Gifford
Loddiswell
Ledstone
Penlee Point
Rame Head
Rame Head Heritage Coast
Great Mew Stone
Wembury Bay
Worswell
Gara Point
Noss Mayo
Netton
Kingston
Houghton
Bridge End
Venn
Churchstow
Stoke Point
Beacon Point
Ringmore
Bigbury
South Devon Heritage Coast
Challaborough
Kingsbridge
Cookworthy Museum
Dodbrooke
Bigbury-on-Sea
Burgh Island
Bantham
Buckland
West Alvington
Upton
Bigbury Bay
Thurlestone
South Milton
Sutton
West Charleton
hours
Roscoff...........6-8
Santander (seasonal)...........20
South Huish
Woolston
Lincombe
Galmpton
Hope
Bolt Tail
Bolberry
Batson
Malborough
Salcombe
South Devon Heritage Coast
Soar
Overbeck's Garden & Museum (NT)
Bolt Head
Eddystone
CHANNEL ISLANDS location map
Alderney
Guernsey
Herm
Sark
Jersey
same scale as main map
JERSEY
Plémont Pt
Grosnez (ruins)
Greve de Lecq Bay
Battle of Flowers Museum
St John
St Mary
Bouley Bay
Trinity
Rozel
Dolmen
St Ouen
La Mielle de Morville
Carrefour Selous
Durrell
St Martin
St Ouen's Bay
St Peter
Jersey War Tunnels
St Catherine's Bay
JERSEY
Five Oaks
Maufant
Mt Orgueil Castle
Beaumont
St Aubin's Bay
St Saviour
La Hougue Bie
Gorey
St Brelade
St Aubin
People's Park
ST HELIER
Grouville
La Cotte
Elizabeth Castle
hours
Guernsey...........1-2
Poole...........4½
Portsmouth...........10½
Noirmont Pt
St Clement
La Rocque Pt
St. Malo (seasonal)...1¼ hr
0 2 4 6 miles
0 2 4 6 8 10 km

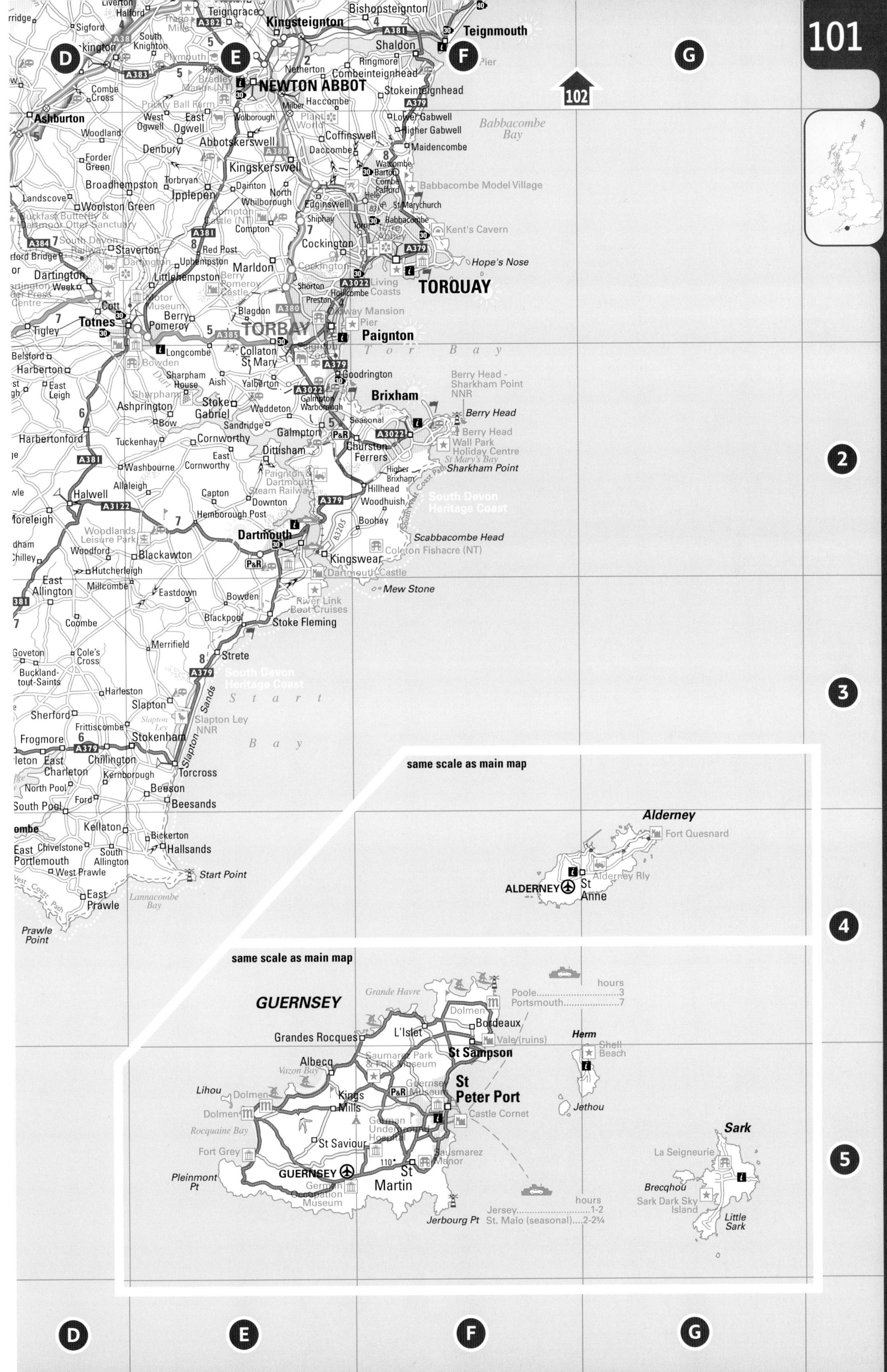

A map of South Devon (including Torquay, Newton Abbot, Dartmouth, Brixham, Paignton, Totnes and Torbay) with inset maps of Alderney and Guernsey/Sark (Channel Islands).

Main map labels (selected):

Bishopsteignton, Teignmouth, Shaldon, Kingsteignton, Teigngrace, Combeinteignhead, Ringmore, Stokeinteignhead, NEWTON ABBOT, Haccombe, Coffinswell, Lower Gabwell, Higher Gabwell, Maidencombe, Babbacombe Bay, Wolborough, Milber, Plant World, South Knighton, Netherton, Abbotskerswell, Denbury, Kingskerswell, Edginswell, Daccombe, Watcombe, Babbacombe, Babbacombe Model Village, Kent's Cavern, Ashburton, Woodland, Forder Green, Broadhempston, Woolston Green, Torbryan, Dainton, North Whilborough, Compton, Shiphay, Torre, St Marychurch, Landscove, Buckfast Butterfly & Dartmoor Otter Sanctuary, Red Post, Uphempston, Cockington, Hope's Nose, Staverton, Marldon, Blagdon, Hele, TORQUAY, Dartington, Littlehempston, Berry Pomeroy Castle, Shorton, Preston, Living Coasts, Week, Dartington Hall, Cott, Berry Pomeroy, Collaton St Mary, Paignton, Tigley, Totnes, Longcombe, Sharpham House, Goodrington, Tor Bay, Belsford, Harberton, Bowden, Sharpham, Aish, Yalberton, Stoke Gabriel, Berry Head - Sharkham Point NNR, East Leigh, Ashprington, Waddeton, Sandridge, Warborough, Galmpton, Brixham, Berry Head, Harbertonford, Tuckenhay, Bow, Cornworthy, Dittisham, Churston Ferrers, Berry Head Wall Park Holiday Centre, St Mary's Bay, Washbourne, East Cornworthy, Higher Brixham, Sharkham Point, Halwell, Allaleigh, Capton, Hillhead, Woodhuish, South Devon Heritage Coast, Moreleigh, Downton, Boohay, Woodlands Leisure Park, Hemborough Post, Woodford, Blackawton, Dartmouth, Scabbacombe Head, Coleton Fishacre (NT), Hutcherleigh, Kingswear, East Allington, Millcombe, Eastdown, Bowden, Dartmouth Castle, Coombe, Blackpool, Mew Stone, Goveton, Cole's Cross, Merrifield, Strete, River Link Boat Cruises, Buckland-tout-Saints, Harleston, Stoke Fleming, South Devon Heritage Coast, Slapton, Frogmore, Frittiscombe, Stokenham, Slapton Ley NNR, Start Bay, Slapton Sands, Sherford, Chillington, Kernborough, Torcross, North Pool, East Charleton, Beeson, Beesands, South Pool, Ford, Kellaton, Bickerton, Hallsands, Chivelstone, South Allington, East Portlemouth, West Prawle, Start Point, East Prawle, Prawle Point, Lannacombe Bay, West Coast Path

Road numbers: A38, A382, A383, A381, A380, A3022, A379, A385, A384, A3122, B205, A3121

↑ 102

Inset map 1 (same scale as main map):

Alderney
Fort Quesnard, ALDERNEY, St Anne, Alderney Rly

Inset map 2 (same scale as main map):

GUERNSEY

Grande Havre, Grandes Rocques, L'Islet, Bordeaux, Vale (ruins), *Herm*, Shell Beach, Albecq, St Sampson, Saumarez Park & Folk Museum, Lihou, Dolmen, Kings Mills, Guernsey Museum, St Peter Port, Vazon Bay, Dolmen, German Underground Hospital, Castle Cornet, Jethou, Rocquaine Bay, St Saviour, Saumarez Manor, Fort Grey, German Occupation Museum, Pleinmont Pt, GUERNSEY, St Martin, Jerbourg Pt

Sark, La Seigneurie, Brecqhou, Sark Dark Sky Island, Little Sark

	hours
Poole	3
Portsmouth	7

	hours
Jersey	1-2
St. Malo (seasonal)	2-2¾

D E F G

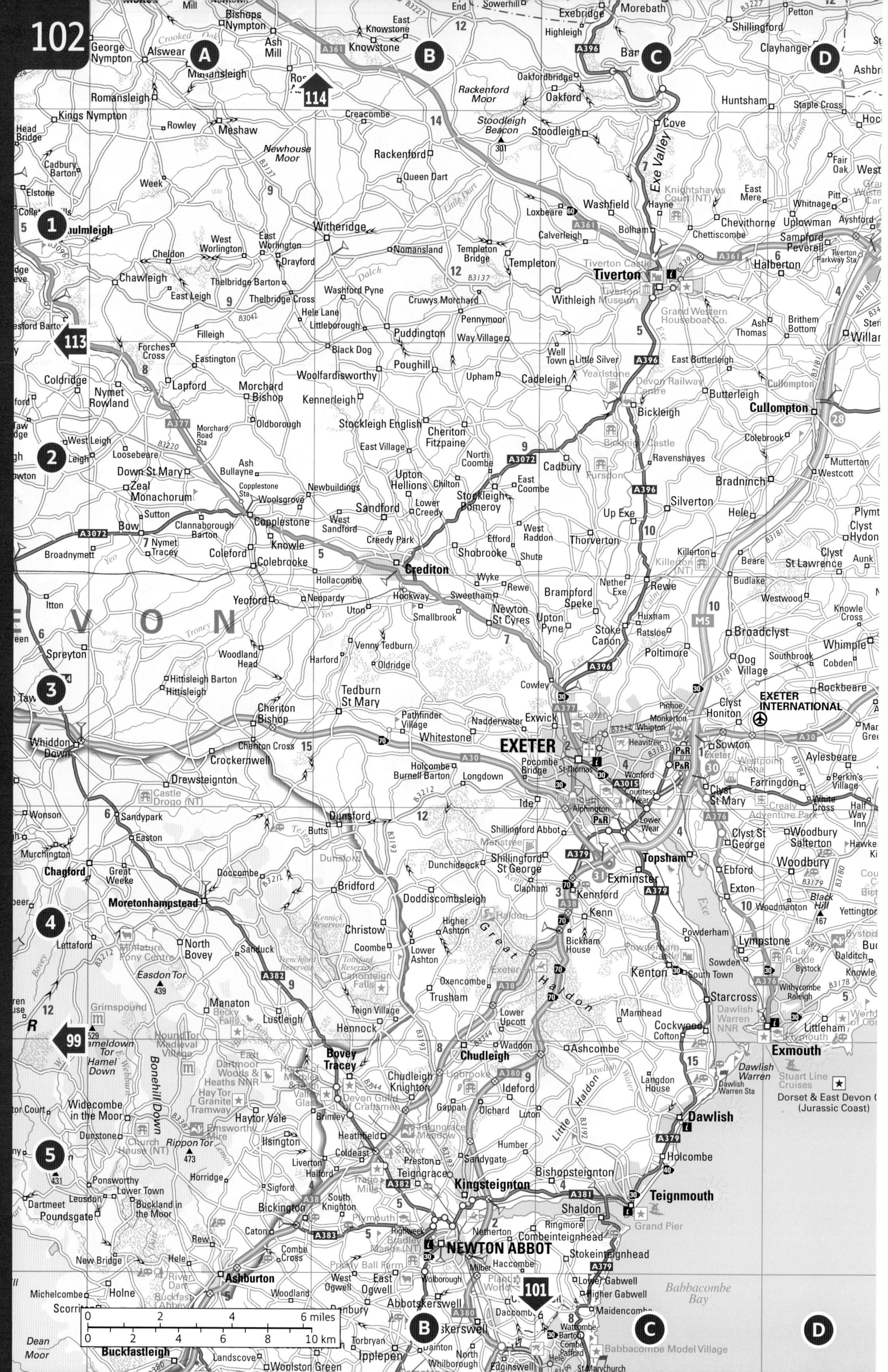

A
B
C
D
1
2
3
4
5
George Nympton
Alswear
Mariansleigh
Romansleigh
Bishops Nympton
Ash Mill
Knowstone
East Knowstone
114
Rackenford Moor
Oakfordbridge
Oakford
Exebridge
Morebath
Highleigh
Bampton
Shillingford
Petton
Clayhanger
Huntsham
Staple Cross
Kings Nympton
Rowley
Meshaw
Creacombe
Stoodleigh Beacon
301
Stoodleigh
Cove
Exe Valley
Head Bridge
Cadbury Barton
Newhouse Moor
Rackenford
Queen Dart
Fair Oak
Elstone
Week
Washfield
Hayne
Knightshayes Court (NT)
East Mere
Pitt
Whitnage
Chulmleigh
Witheridge
Loxbeare
Bolham
Chevithorne
Uplowman
Ayshford
West Worlington
East Worlington
Calverleigh
Chettiscombe
Sampford Peverell
Tiverton Parkway Sta
Cheldon
Drayford
Nomansland
Templeton Bridge
Templeton
Tiverton Castle
Tiverton
Tiverton Museum
Halberton
Chawleigh
Thelbridge Barton
Dalch
East Leigh
Thelbridge Cross
Washford Pyne
Cruwys Morchard
Withleigh
Grand Western Houseboat Co.
Hele Lane
Pennymoor
Ash Thomas
Brithem Bottom
Littleborough
Puddington
Way Village
Filleigh
113
Forches Cross
Eastington
Black Dog
Poughill
Well Town
Little Silver
East Butterleigh
Yearlstone
Upham
Cadeleigh
Devon Railway Centre
Butterleigh
Cullompton
Coldridge
Nymet Rowland
Lapford
Morchard Bishop
Woolfardisworthy
Kennerleigh
Bickleigh
Morchard Road Sta
Oldborough
Stockleigh English
Cheriton Fitzpaine
Bickleigh Castle
Colebrook
West Leigh
Leigh
Loosebeare
East Village
North Coombe
Cadbury
Ravenshayes
Mutterton
Westcott
Ash
Bullayne
Down St Mary
Zeal Monachorum
Copplestone Sta
Woolsgrove
Newbuildings
Upton Hellions
Chilton
Lower Creedy
Stockleigh Pomeroy
East Coombe
Fursdon
Bradninch
Silverton
Sutton
Bow
Clannaborough Barton
Copplestone
Sandford
West Sandford
Up Exe
Hele
Plymtree
Clyst Hydon
Nymet Tracey
Knowle
Creedy Park
Efford
West Raddon
Thorverton
Broadnymett
Coleford
Colebrooke
Crediton
Shobrooke
Shute
Killerton
Killerton (NT)
Beare
Clyst St Lawrence
Aunk
Hollacombe
Wyke
Rewe
Budlake
Nether Exe
Itton
DEVON
Yeoford
Neopardy
Hookway
Uton
Sweetham
Brampford Speke
Westwood
Knowle Cross
Smallbrook
Newton St Cyres
Upton Pyne
Huxham
Stoke Canon
Ratsloe
Broadclyst
Spreyton
Venny Tedburn
Woodland Head
Harford
Oldridge
Poltimore
Dog Village
Southbrook
Whimple
Cobden
Hittisleigh Barton
Hittisleigh
Tedburn St Mary
Cowley
Rockbeare
Pinhoe
Clyst Honiton
EXETER INTERNATIONAL
Cheriton Bishop
Pathfinder Village
Nadderwater
Exwick
Whipton
Monkerton
Whiddon Down
Cheriton Cross
Whitestone
Heavitree
Sowton
EXETER
Crockernwell
Holcombe Burnell Barton
Longdown
Pocombe Bridge
St Thomas
Wonford
Westpoint Arena
Aylesbeare
Drewsteignton
Castle Drogo (NT)
Countess Wear
Farringdon
Perkin's Village
Ide
Alphington
Clyst St Mary
White Cross
Crealy Adventure Park
Half Way Inn
Wonson
Sandypark
Dunsford
Butts
Shillingford Abbot
Lower Wear
Clyst St George
Woodbury Salterton
Easton
Murchington
Chagford
Great Weeke
Doccombe
Bridford
Dunchideock
Shillingford St George
Topsham
Woodbury
Exminster
Ebford
Clapham
Exton
Kennford
Moretonhampstead
Doddiscombsleigh
Haldon
Woodmanton
Black Hill
167
Yettington
Kennick Reservoir
Christow
Higher Ashton
Kenn
Bickham House
Powderham
Lympstone
Bystock
Lettaford
Miniature Pony Centre
North Bovey
Sanduck
Trenchford Reservoir
Tottiford Reservoir
Coombe
Lower Ashton
Powderham Castle
Great Haldon
Sowden
A La Ronde
Dalditch
Easdon Tor
439
Canonteign Falls
Exeter Racecourse
Oxencombe
Kenton
South Town
Knowle
Withycombe Raleigh
Manaton
Becky Falls
Trusham
Starcross
Grimspound
Lustleigh
Teign Village
Lower Upcott
Mamhead
Dawlish Warren NNR
Cockwood
Cofton
Exmouth
Littleham
World of Country Life
99
Hameldown Tor
Hamel Down
529
Hound Tor Medieval Village
Hennock
Bovey Tracey
Chudleigh
Waddon
Ashcombe
Bonehill Down
East Dartmoor Woods & Heaths NNR
House of Marbles & Teign Valley Glass
Chudleigh Knighton
Ugbrooke
Ideford
Langdon House
Dawlish Warren
Dawlish Warren Sta
Stuart Line Cruises
Dorset & East Devon Coast (Jurassic Coast)
Widecombe in the Moor
Hay Tor Granite Tramway
Haytor Vale
Devon Guild of Craftsmen
Brimley
Gappah
Olchard
Luton
Little Haldon
Dawlish
Dunstone
Church House (NT)
Rippon Tor
473
Emsworthy Mire
Ilsington
Heathfield
Teigngrace Meadow
Humber
Sandygate
Holcombe
Liverton
Halford
Coldeast
Stover
Preston
Teigngrace
Trago Mills
Kingsteignton
Bishopsteignton
Teignmouth
431
Ponsworthy
Leusdon
Lower Town
Buckland in the Moor
Sigford
South Knighton
Horridge
Dartmeet
Poundsgate
Bickington
Highweek
Netherton
Shaldon
Grand Pier
Ringmore
Combeinteignhead
Caton
Rew
Bradley Manor (NT)
NEWTON ABBOT
Combe Cross
Prickly Ball Farm
Haccombe
Stokeinteignhead
New Bridge
Hele
Milber
Plant World
Lower Gabwell
Higher Gabwell
Babbacombe Bay
Ashburton
River Dart
West Ogwell
East Ogwell
Wolborough
101
Maidencombe
Michelcombe
Holne
Buckfast Abbey
Woodland
Abbotskerswell
Daccombe
Scorriton
Denbury
Kingskerswell
Watcombe
Barton
Combe Pafford
Babbacombe Model Village
Dean Moor
Buckfastleigh
Landscove
Torbryan
Ipplepen
Dainton
North Whilborough
Edginswell
St Marychurch
Woolston Green
0 2 4 6 miles
0 2 4 6 8 10 km
A361
A396
A3072
A377
A30
A38
A382
A380
A383
A379
A381
A376
A3015
M5
B3227
B3137
B3042
B3220
B3212
B3193
B3344
B3387
B3181
B3179
B3180
B3178
B3192
B3391
B3183
B3184

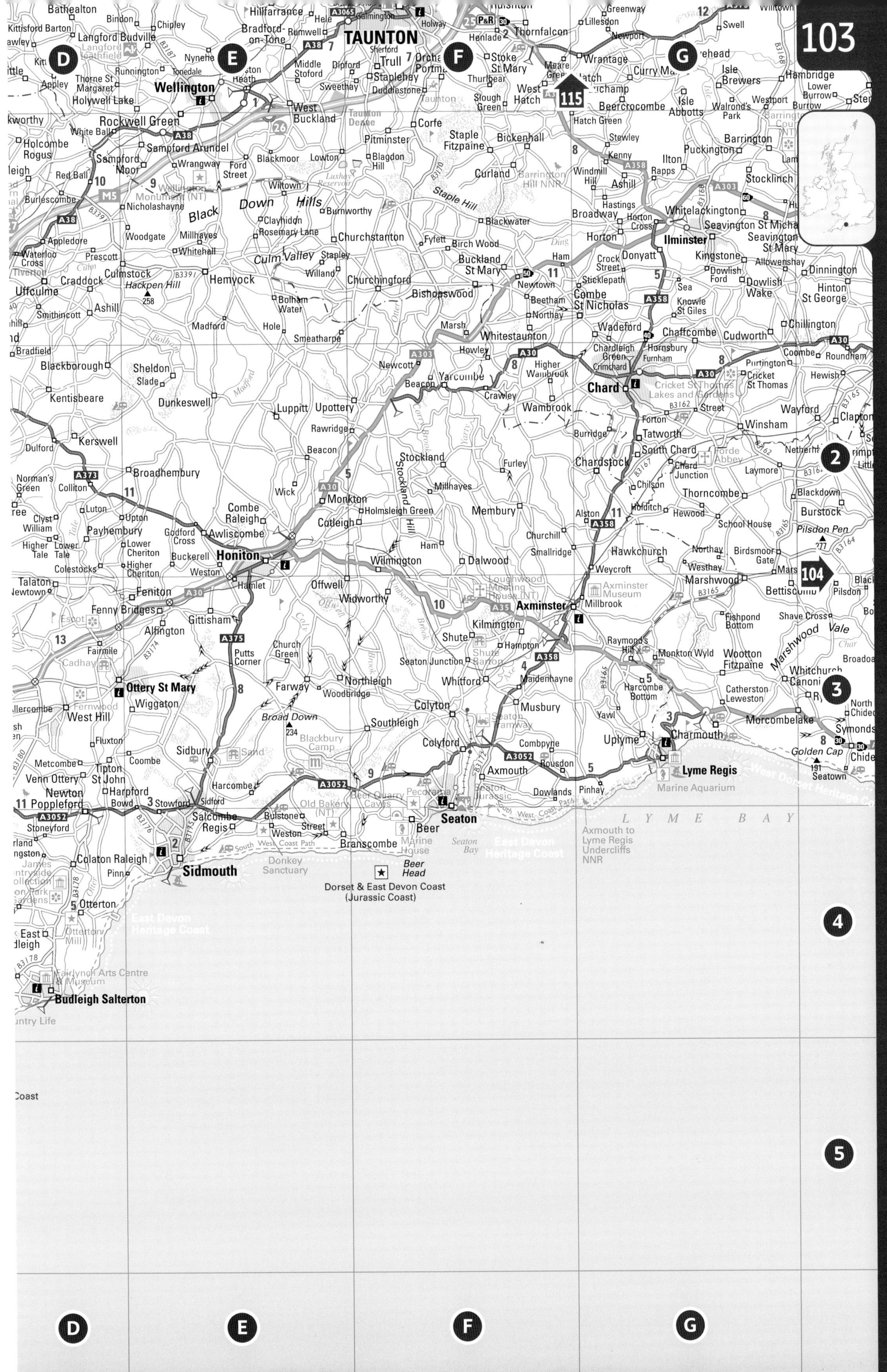

103
D
E
F
G
Bathealton
Bindon
Chipley
Kittisford Barton
Langford Budville
Langford Heathfield
Nynehead
Hillfarrance
Bradford-on-Tone
Rumwell
Hele
A3065
TAUNTON
Holway
P&R
Henlade
Thornfalcon
Greenway
Lillesdon
Newport
Swell
Wrantage
Curry Mallet
Isle Brewers
Hambridge
Lower Burrow
Burrow
Westport
Walrond's Park
Isle Abbotts
Beercrocombe
Hatch Green
Stewley
Kenny
Ilton
Rapps
Puckington
Barrington
Stocklinch
Ashill
Windmill Hill
Hastings
Broadway
Horton Cross
Whitelackington
Seavington St Michael
Seavington St Mary
Ilminster
Kingstone
Allowenshay
Dowlish Ford
Dowlish Wake
Dinnington
Hinton St George
Chillington
Cudworth
Chaffcombe
Knowle St Giles
Sea
Donyatt
Crock Street
Horton
Ham
Stoke St Mary
Thurlbear
West Hatch
Slough Green
Meare Green
115
Sherford
Trull
Orchard Portman
Middle Stoford
Dipford
Staplehay
Sweethay
Duddlestone
Taunton Deane
West Buckland
Corfe
Pitminster
Staple Fitzpaine
Bickenhall
Curland
Barrington Hill NNR
Blagdon Hill
Lowton
Blackmoor
Luxhay Reservoir
Staple Hill
Blackwater
Wellington
Runnington
Tonedale
Thorne St Margaret
Appley
Holywell Lake
Rockwell Green
White Ball
Holcombe Rogus
Sampford Arundel
Sampford Moor
Wrangway
Ford Street
Wiltown
Wellington Monument (NT)
Nicholashayne
Black Down Hills
Burnworthy
Clayhidon
Rosemary Lane
Churchstanton
Fyfett
Birch Wood
Buckland St Mary
Red Ball
Burlescombe
M5
A38
Appledore
Waterloo Cross
Prescott
Tiverton
Woodgate
Millhayes
Whitehall
Culm Valley
Stapley
Willand
Churchingford
Bishopswood
Newtown
Beetham
Northay
Combe St Nicholas
Sticklepath
Uffculme
Craddock
Culmstock
Hackpen Hill
258
Hemyock
Bolham Water
Smithincott
Ashill
Madford
Hole
Smeatharpe
Marsh
Whitestaunton
Wadeford
Bradfield
Blackborough
Sheldon
Slade
Newcott
Howley
A303
A30
Chardleigh Green
Crimchard
Hornsbury
Furnham
Purtington
Coombe
Roundham
Cricket St Thomas
Hewish
Cricket St Thomas Lakes and Gardens
Kentisbeare
Dunkeswell
Beacon
Yarcombe
Higher Wambrook
Crawley
Wambrook
Chard
Forton
Street
Wayford
Clapton
Winsham
Luppitt
Upottery
Rawridge
Burridge
Tatworth
Dulford
Kerswell
South Chard
Forde Abbey
Chard Junction
Laymore
Netherhay
Stockland
Furley
Chardstock
Chilson
Thorncombe
Blackdown
Broadhembury
Norman's Green
Colliton
A373
Wick
Monkton
Millhayes
Stockland Hill
Membury
Holditch
Hewood
School House
Burstock
Pilsdon Pen
277
Luton
Upton
Clyst William
Payhembury
Combe Raleigh
Awliscombe
Cotleigh
Holmsleigh Green
Alston
A358
Churchill
Smallridge
Hawkcombe
Northay
Birdsmoor Gate
Westhay
Higher Tale
Lower Tale
Lower Cheriton
Higher Cheriton
Godford Cross
Honiton
Buckerell
Weston
Colestocks
Ham
Wilmington
Dalwood
Weycroft
Marshwood
104
Bettiscombe
Pilsdon
Talaton
Newtown
Feniton
Hamlet
Offwell
Widworthy
Loughwood Meeting House (NT)
Axminster
Axminster Museum
Millbrook
Fenny Bridges
Gittisham
Escot
Alfington
A35
Kilmington
Shute
Hampton
Shute Barton
Raymond's Hill
Fishpond Bottom
Shave Cross
Marshwood Vale
Fairmile
Cadhay
A375
Putts Corner
Church Green
Seaton Junction
Monkton Wyld
Wootton Fitzpaine
Broadoak
Ottery St Mary
Fernwood
Wiggaton
West Hill
Farway
Woodbridge
Northleigh
Whitford
Maidenhayne
Harcombe Bottom
Catherston Leweston
Whitchurch Canonicorum
North Chideock
Symondsbury
Broad Down
234
Southleigh
Colyton
Musbury
Yawl
Uplyme
Charmouth
Morcombelake
Golden Cap
191
Seatown
Chideock
Fluxton
Blackbury Camp
Colyford
Seaton Tramway
Combpyne
Rousdon
A3052
Metcombe
Coombe
Sidbury
Sand
Venn Ottery
Tipton St John
Newton Poppleford
Harpford
Bowd
Stowford
Sidford
Harcombe
Axmouth
Dowlands
Pinhay
Lyme Regis
Marine Aquarium
West Dorset Heritage Coast
Seaton Jurassic
Pecorama
Beer Quarry Caves
Old Bakery (NT)
Seaton
Beer
Stoneyford
Salcombe Regis
Bulstone
Weston
Street
Branscombe
Marine House
Seaton Bay
East Devon Heritage Coast
South West Coast Path
LYME BAY
Axmouth to Lyme Regis Undercliffs NNR
Colaton Raleigh
Pinn
Sidmouth
Donkey Sanctuary
Beer Head
Dorset & East Devon Coast (Jurassic Coast)
Otterton
Otterton Mill
East Budleigh
Fairlynch Arts Centre & Museum
Budleigh Salterton
Coast

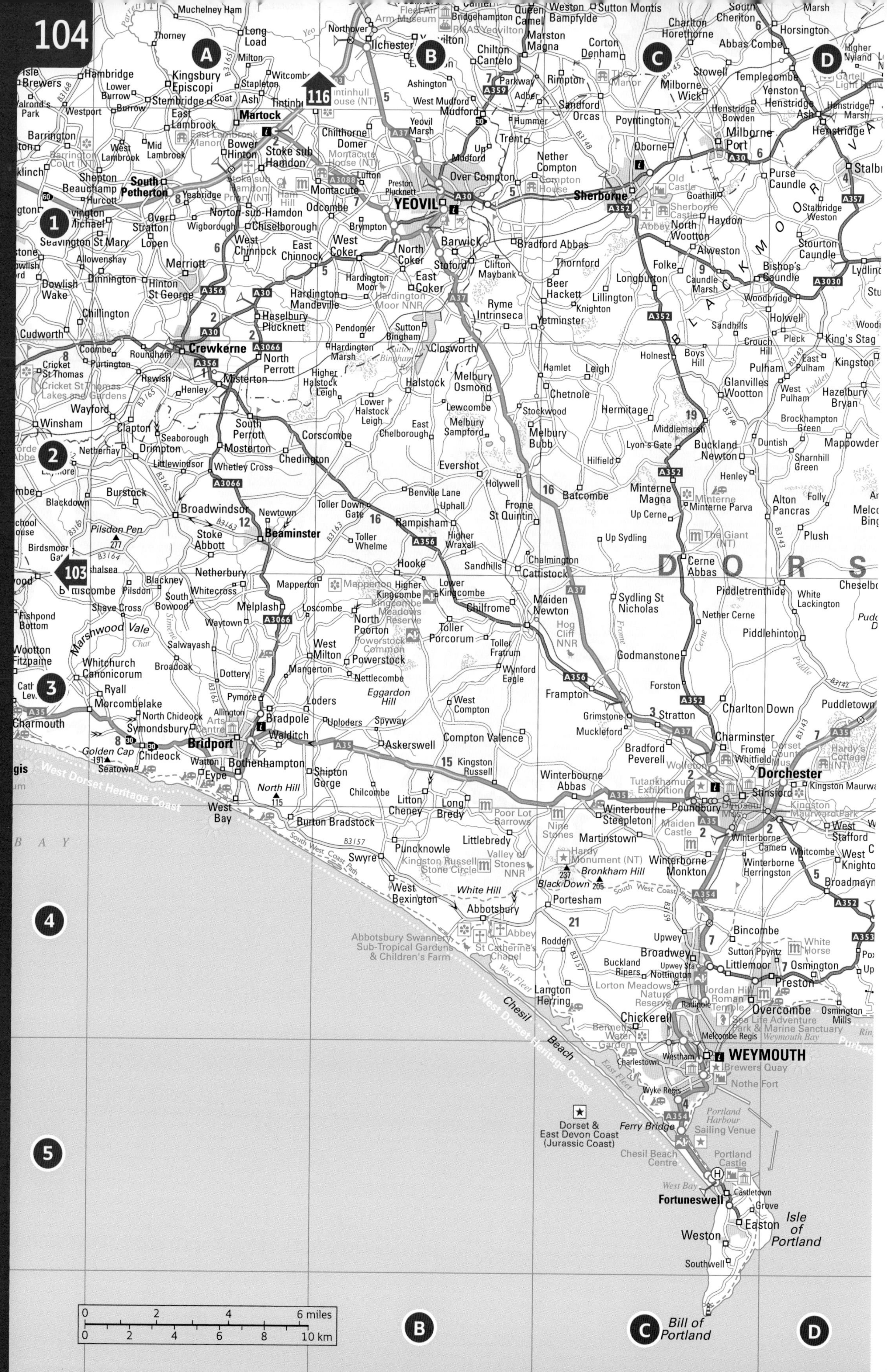

YEOVIL
Sherborne
Crewkerne
Beaminster
Bridport
Dorchester
WEYMOUTH
Fortuneswell
Isle of Portland
Bill of Portland
Chesil Beach
West Dorset Heritage Coast
Martock
South Petherton
Maiden Newton
Abbotsbury
Chickerell
Charmouth
Marshwood Vale
BLACKMOOR VALE
DORSET
116
103
0 2 4 6 miles
0 2 4 6 8 10 km

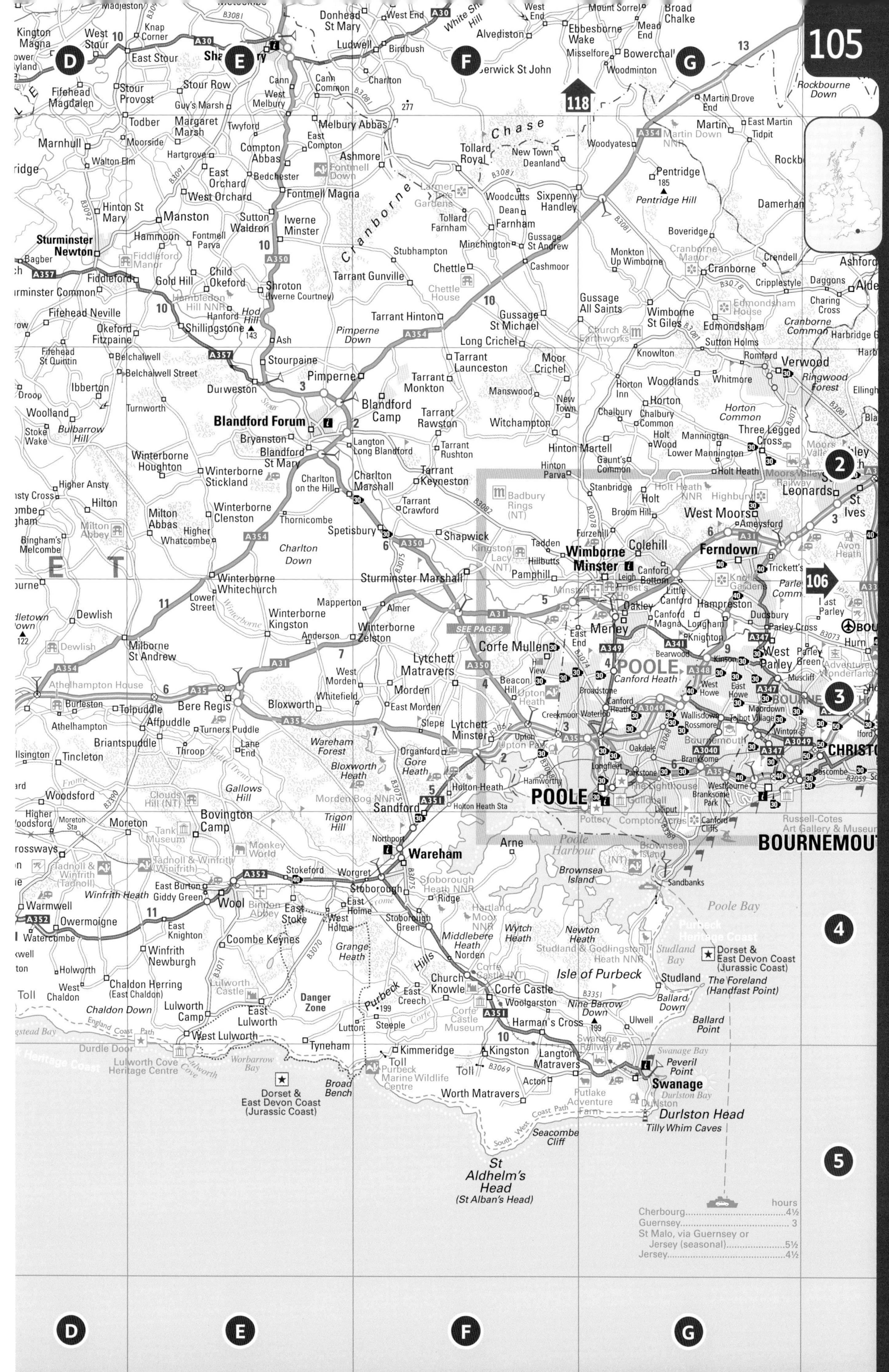
D
E
F
G
2
3
4
5
118
106
13
Kington Magna
West Stour
Knap Corner
Donhead St Mary
West End
White Sheet Hill
West End
Alvediston
Mount Sorrel
Ebbesborne Wake
Broad Chalke
Mead End
Misselfore
Bowerchalke
Woodminton
Berwick St John
East Stour
Ludwell
Birdbush
Cann
Cann Common
Charlton
Fifehead Magdalen
Stour Provost
Stour Row
West Melbury
Guy's Marsh
277
Rockbourne Down
Martin Drove End
Todber
Margaret Marsh
Twyford
Melbury Abbas
Martin
East Martin
Tidpit
Martin Down NNR
Marnhull
Moorside
Compton Abbas
East Compton
Chase
Tollard Royal
New Town
Deanland
Woodyates
Walton Elm
Hartgrove
Ashmore
Fontmell Down
Rockbourne
East Orchard
Bedchester
Pentridge
185
Pentridge Hill
Fontmell Magna
Larmer Tree Gardens
Woodcutts
Sixpenny Handley
West Orchard
Hinton St Mary
Manston
Sutton Waldron
Iwerne Minster
Tollard Farnham
Dean
Farnham
Damerham
Cranborne
Sturminster Newton
Hammoon
Fontmell Parva
Minchington
Gussage St Andrew
Boveridge
Bagber
Fiddleford Manor
Stubhampton
Monkton Up Wimborne
Cranborne Manor
Crendell
Ashford
A357
Fiddleford
Child Okeford
Gold Hill
Shroton (Iwerne Courtney)
Tarrant Gunville
Chettle
Cashmoor
Cranborne
Cripplestyle
Daggons
Alderholt
Sturminster Common
Hambledon Hill NNR
Hod Hill
Chettle House
10
Gussage All Saints
Wimborne St Giles
Edmondsham House
Charing Cross
Fifehead Neville
Hanford
Shillingstone
143
Tarrant Hinton
Gussage St Michael
Edmondsham
Cranborne Common
Harbridge Green
Okeford Fitzpaine
Ash
Pimperne Down
A354
Long Crichel
Church & Earthworks
Sutton Holms
Fifehead St Quintin
Belchalwell
Stourpaine
Tarrant Launceston
Moor Crichel
Knowlton
Romford
Verwood
Belchalwell Street
Pimperne
Tarrant Monkton
Horton Inn
Woodlands
Whitmore
Ringwood Forest
Ellingham
Ibberton
Durweston
Manswood
New Town
Horton
Droop
Turnworth
Blandford Camp
Tarrant Rawston
Chalbury
Chalbury Common
Horton Common
Woolland
Blandford Forum
Witchampton
Three Legged Cross
Stoke Wake
Bulbarrow Hill
Bryanston
Langton Long Blandford
Tarrant Rushton
Holt Wood
Mannington
Lower Mannington
Moors Valley
Winterborne Houghton
Blandford St Mary
Hinton Martell
Gaunt's Common
Hinton Parva
Holt Heath
Moors Valley Railway
Higher Ansty
Winterborne Stickland
Charlton on the Hill
Charlton Marshall
Tarrant Keyneston
Badbury Rings (NT)
Stanbridge
Holt Heath NNR
Highbury
St Leonards
Ansty Cross
Hilton
Tarrant Crawford
Holt
St Ives
Milton Abbas
Winterborne Clenston
Thornicombe
Broom Hill
West Moors
Milton Abbey
Higher Whatcombe
Spetisbury
Shapwick
Furzehill
Ameysford
Bingham's Melcombe
A354
Charlton Down
Kingston Lacy (NT)
Tadden
Wimborne Minster
Colehill
Ferndown
Avon Heath
Hillbutts
Trickett's Cross
Sturminster Marshall
Pamphill
Canford Bottom
Knoll Gardens
Parley Common
Winterborne Whitechurch
Leigh
Priest's House
Little Canford
Hampreston
Dewlish
Lower Street
Mapperton
Almer
Minster
Oakley
Dudsbury
East Parley
Winterborne Kingston
A31
Canford Magna
Longham
Parley Cross
SEE PAGE 3
Merley
Knighton
A341
Milborne St Andrew
Anderson
Winterborne Zelston
Corfe Mullen
East End
A349
Bearwood
West Parley
Dewlish
A354
West Morden
Lytchett Matravers
Hill View
POOLE
Kinson
Parley Green
Adventure Wonderland
Athelhampton House
A35
Whitefield
Morden
Canford Heath
A348
Muscliff
Burleston
Tolpuddle
Bere Regis
Bloxworth
East Morden
Beacon Hill
Upton Heath
Broadstone
West Howe
East Howe
A347
Athelhampton
Affpuddle
Turners Puddle
Slepe
Lytchett Minster
Creekmoor
Waterloo
Canford Heath
A3049
Wallisdown
Talbot Village
Moordown
Rossmore
Winton
Briantspuddle
Lane End
Wareham Forest
Upton
Upton Park
Oakdale
Bournemouth
A3049
Iford
Tincleton
Throop
Organford
Gore Heath
A3040
Branksome
CHRISTCHURCH
Bloxworth Heath
Longfleet
Parkstone
Boscombe
Woodsford
Gallows Hill
Clouds Hill (NT)
Holton Heath
Hamworthy
Lighthouse
Westbourne
Branksome Park
Morden Bog NNR
Sandford
Holton Heath Sta
POOLE
Guildhall
Lilliput
Higher Woodsford
Moreton Sta
Moreton
Bovington Camp
Trigon Hill
Pottery
Compton Acres
Canford Cliffs
Russell-Cotes Art Gallery & Museum
Tank Museum
Northport
Arne
Poole Harbour
Brownsea Island
BOURNEMOUTH
Crossways
Monkey World
Wareham
Tadnoll & Winfrith
Winfrith (Tadnoll)
A352
Stokeford
Worgret
Brownsea Island
Sandbanks
East Burton
Stoborough
Stoborough Heath NNR
Winfrith Heath
Giddy Green
Wool
Bindon Abbey
East Holme
Ridge
Hartland Moor NNR
Poole Bay
Warmwell
East Stoke
West Holme
Stoborough Green
Purbeck Heritage Coast
A352
Owermoigne
East Knighton
Middlebere Heath
Wytch Heath
Newton Heath
Watercombe
Coombe Keynes
Grange Heath
Norden
Studland & Godlingston Heath NNR
Studland Bay
Dorset & East Devon Coast (Jurassic Coast)
Winfrith Newburgh
Hills
Corfe Castle (NT)
Isle of Purbeck
Holworth
Lulworth Castle
Church Knowle
Corfe Castle
Studland
The Foreland (Handfast Point)
West Chaldon
Chaldon Herring (East Chaldon)
Danger Zone
Purbeck
East Creech
B3351
Ballard Down
Toll
Chaldon Down
Lulworth Camp
East Lulworth
199
Woolgarston
Nine Barrow Down
Corfe Castle Museum
A351
Ulwell
Ballard Point
Steeple
Harman's Cross
199
Lutton
West Lulworth
England Coast Path
Swanage Railway
Swanage Bay
Durdle Door
Tyneham
Kimmeridge
Kingston
Langton Matravers
Peveril Point
Heritage Coast
Lulworth Cove
Lulworth Cove Heritage Centre
Worbarrow Bay
Toll
Purbeck Marine Wildlife Centre
B3069
Toll
Swanage
Dorset & East Devon Coast (Jurassic Coast)
Broad Bench
Acton
Durlston Bay
Worth Matravers
Putlake Adventure Farm
Durlston
Durlston Head
South West Coast Path
Tilly Whim Caves
Seacombe Cliff
St Aldhelm's Head (St Alban's Head)
hours
Cherbourg....................4½
Guernsey.......................3
St Malo, via Guernsey or Jersey (seasonal)..........5½
Jersey............................4½

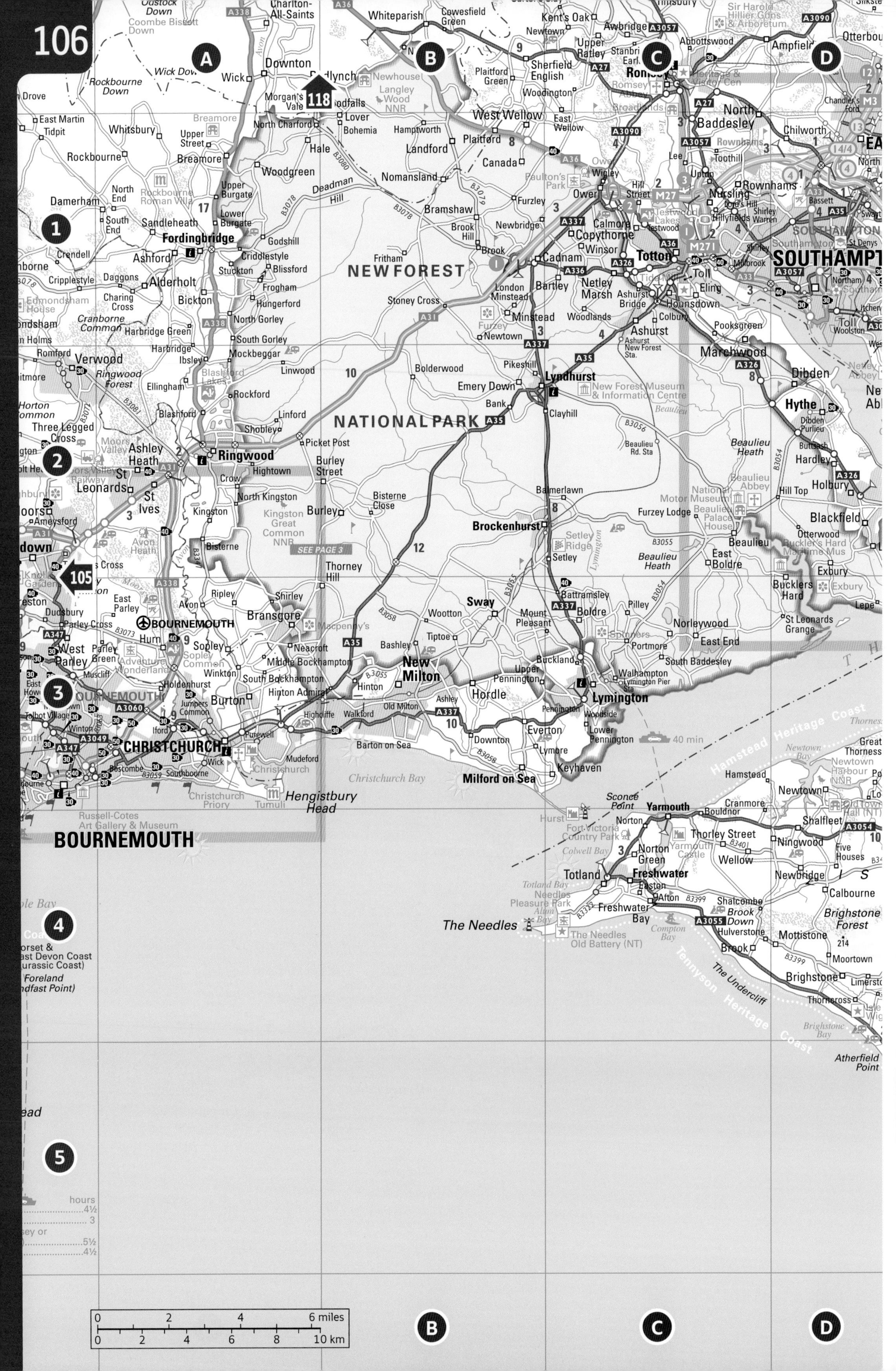
A
B
C
D
1
2
3
4
5
118
105
NEW FOREST
NATIONAL PARK
Whiteparish
Cowesfield Green
Kent's Oak
Awbridge
Sir Harold Hillier Gdns & Arboretum
Ampfield
Otterbourne
Coombe Bissett Down
Charlton-All-Saints
Downton
Wick
Wick Down
Rockbourne Down
Drove
East Martin
Tidpit
Whitsbury
Breamore
Upper Street
Rockbourne
Damerham
North End
South End
Rockbourne Roman Villa
Sandleheath
Fordingbridge
Crendell
Cripplestyle
Daggons
Alderholt
Ashford
Edmondsham House
Charing Cross
Cranborne Common
Harbridge Green
Harbridge
Verwood
Ringwood Forest
Ibsley
Ellingham
Three Legged Cross
Ashley Heath
St Leonards
St Ives
Ameysford
Ringwood
Moors Valley
Hightown
Crow
North Kingston
Kingston
Bisterne
Avon Heath
Ripley
Avon
Bransgore
East Parley
BOURNEMOUTH
Hurn
Sopley
Sopley Common
Winkton
Holdenhurst
Burton
Jumpers Common
Iford
CHRISTCHURCH
Purewell
Mudeford
Christchurch
Christchurch Priory
Tumuli
Hengistbury Head
Russell-Cotes Art Gallery & Museum
BOURNEMOUTH
West Parley
Parley Green
Muscliff
Dudsbury
Parley Cross
Adventure Wonderland
Talbot Village
Winton
Bascombe
Southbourne
Morgan's Vale
Redlynch
Woodfalls
Lover
Bohemia
North Charford
Hale
Woodgreen
Upper Burgate
Lower Burgate
Godshill
Criddlestyle
Stuckton
Blissford
Frogham
Hungerford
Bickton
North Gorley
South Gorley
Mockbeggar
Blashford Lakes
Rockford
Blashford
Linwood
Linford
Shobley
Picket Post
Burley Street
Burley
Bisterne Close
Kingston Great Common NNR
SEE PAGE 3
Thorney Hill
Shirley
Neacroft
Macpenny's
Middle Bockhampton
South Bockhampton
Hinton Admiral
Highcliffe
Walkford
Barton on Sea
Christchurch Bay
Newhouse
Langley Wood NNR
Hamptworth
Landford
Nomansland
Deadman Hill
Bramshaw
Brook Hill
Brook
Fritham
Stoney Cross
Linwood
Bolderwood
Emery Down
Bank
Lyndhurst
New Forest Museum & Information Centre
Clayhill
Pikeshill
Plaitford Green
West Wellow
East Wellow
Plaitford
Canada
Sherfield English
Woodington
Newtown
Upper Ratley
Romsey
Romsey Abbey
Broadlands
Heritage & Visitor Cen
Abbottswood
North Baddesley
Chilworth
Rownhams
Toothill
Lee
Upton
Nursling
Wigley
Ower
Hill Street
Paulton's Park
Testwood Lakes
Testwood
Calmore
Copythorne
Winsor
Cadnam
Furzley
Newbridge
London Minstead
Minstead
Furzey
Newtown
Bartley
Netley Marsh
Woodlands
Ashurst Bridge
Totton
Tide Mill
Eling
Hounsdown
Colbury
Ashurst
Ashurst New Forest Sta.
Pooksgreen
Marchwood
Dibden
Dibden Purlieu
Hythe
Butts Ash
Hardley
Holbury
Hill Top
Blackfield
Otterwood
Buckler's Hard Maritime Mus
Exbury
Bucklers Hard
Lepe
St Leonards Grange
SOUTHAMPTON
Southampton
Shirley
Millbrook
Bassett
Shirley Warren
Hillyfields
Toll
Woolston
Northam
Itchen
St Denys
Chandler's Ford
Netley Abbey
Beaulieu
Beaulieu Heath
Beaulieu Rd. Sta
Balmerlawn
Brockenhurst
Setley Ridge
Setley
National Motor Museum
Beaulieu Abbey
Beaulieu Palace House
Furzey Lodge
East Boldre
Battramsley
Boldre
Pilley
Norleywood
East End
Sway
Mount Pleasant
Wootton
Tiptoe
Bashley
New Milton
Hinton
Old Milton
Ashley
Hordle
Upper Pennington
Pennington
Buckland
Spinners
Portmore
South Baddesley
Walhampton
Lymington Pier Sta
Lymington
Woodside
Lower Pennington
Everton
Downton
Lymore
Keyhaven
Milford on Sea
40 min
Hurst
Sconce Point
Yarmouth
Norton
Fort Victoria Country Park
Colwell Bay
Norton Green
Yarmouth Castle
Thorley Street
Wellow
Totland
Freshwater
Totland Bay
Needles Pleasure Park
Alum Bay
Freshwater Bay
Afton
The Needles
The Needles Old Battery (NT)
Compton Bay
Shalcombe
Brook Down
Hulverstone
Brook
Mottistone
Bouldnor
Cranmore
Hamstead
Newtown
Newtown Bay
Newtown Harbour NNR
Shalfleet
Ningwood
Five Houses
Newbridge
Calbourne
Brighstone Forest
Moortown
Brighstone
Thorncross
Brighstone Bay
Atherfield Point
The Undercliff
Tennyson Heritage Coast
Hamstead Heritage Coast
Thorness
Great Thorness
Old Town Hall (NT)
Dorset & East Devon Coast (Jurassic Coast)
Foreland (Handfast Point)
hours
4½
3
5½
4½
0
2
4
6 miles
0
2
4
6
8
10 km

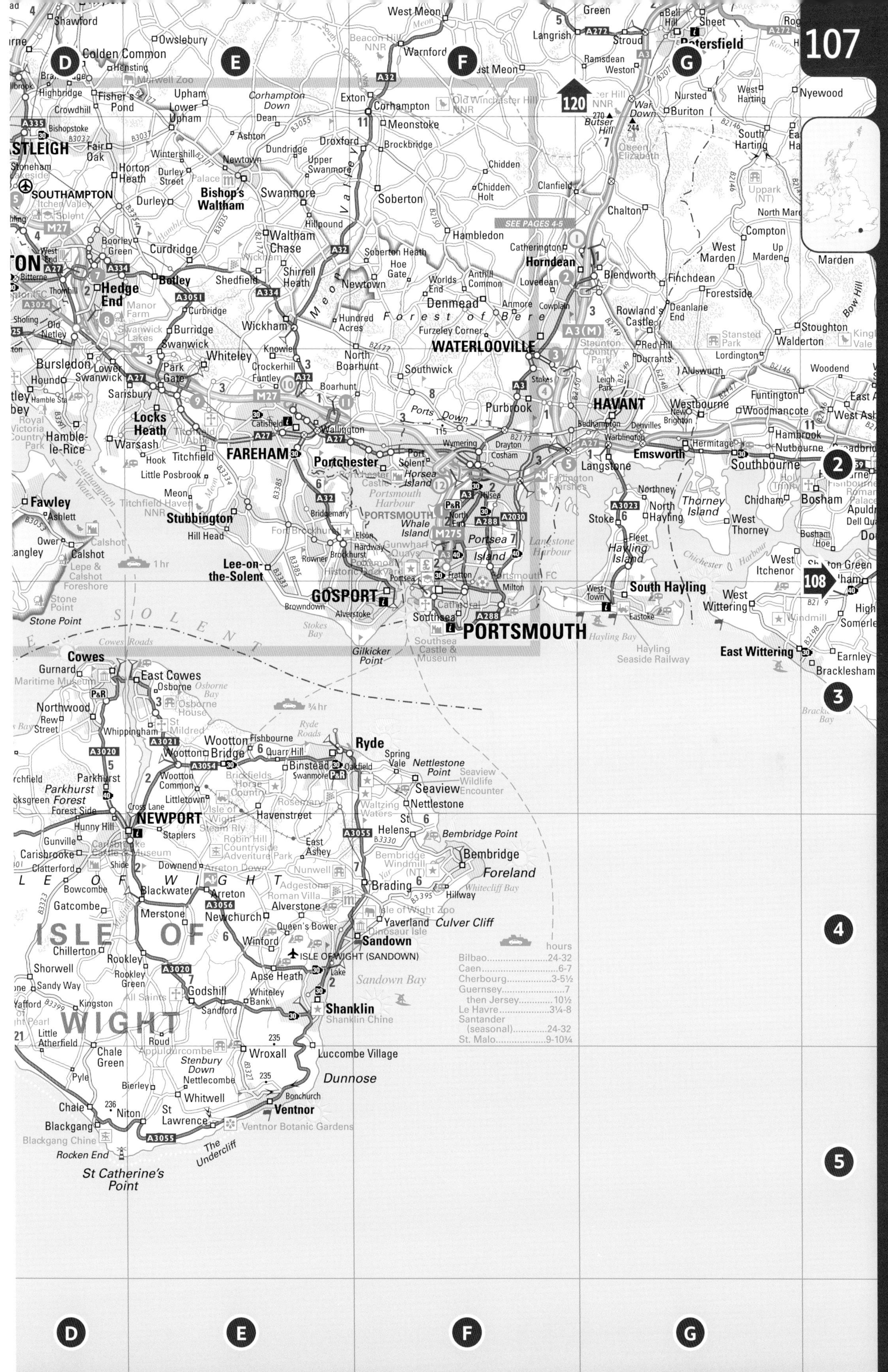

Shawford
Colden Common
Owslebury
West Meon
Beacon Hill NNR
Warnford
Langrish
Stroud
Sheet
Petersfield
Ramsdean
Weston
Henstring
Marwell Zoo
Highbridge
Fisher's Pond
Upham
Lower Upham
Corhampton Down
Exton
Corhampton
Old Winchester Hill NNR
Nurstead
Buriton
West Harting
Nyewood
Crowdhill
Bishopstoke
Dean
Meonstoke
Butser Hill
War Down
Queen Elizabeth
South Harting
Fair Oak
Ashton
Droxford
Brockbridge
Wintershill
Newtown
Dundridge
Upper Swanmore
Chidden
Chidden Holt
Clanfield
Uppark (NT)
Stoneham
Horton Heath
Durley Street
Palace
Bishop's Waltham
Swanmore
Soberton
SOUTHAMPTON
Durley
Itchen Valley
Hillpound
Chalton
North Marden
M27
Boorley Green
Curdridge
Waltham Chase
Hambledon
SEE PAGES 4-5
Compton
Up Marden
West Marden
Marden
Catherington
Horndean
Soberton Heath
Hoe Gate
West End
Bitterne
Hedge End
Botley
Shedfield
Shirrell Heath
Newtown
Worlds End
Anthill Common
Lovedean
Blendworth
Finchdean
Forestside
Manor Farm
Curbridge
Hundred Acres
Forest of Bere
Denmead
Anmore
Cowplain
Rowland's Castle
Deanlane End
Bow Hill
Sholing
Old Netley
Burridge
Swanwick
Wickham
Furzeley Corner
A3(M)
Stansted Park
Stoughton
Walderton
WATERLOOVILLE
Staunton Country Park
Red Hill
Durrants
Lordington
Knowle
Whiteley
North Boarhunt
Bursledon
Lower Swanwick
Park Gate
Crockerhill
Funtley
Southwick
Leigh Park
Aldsworth
Woodend
Hound
Sarisbury
Boarhunt
Stokes
HAVANT
Westbourne
Funtington
East Ashling
Locks Heath
Catisfield
Wallington
Ports Down
Purbrook
Woodmancote
New Brighton
West Ashling
Hamble-le-Rice
Royal Victoria Country Park
Titchfield Abbey
Warsash
FAREHAM
Wymering
Drayton
Bedhampton
Denvilles
Warblington
Hermitage
Hambrook
Nutbourne
Hook
Titchfield
Portchester
Port Solent
Cosham
Emsworth
Langstone
Southbourne
Little Posbrook
Portchester Castle
Horsea Island
Farlington Marshes
Holy Trinity
Fishbourne
Fawley
Meon
Portsmouth Harbour
Hilsea
Northney
North Hayling
Thorney Island
Chidham
Bosham
Ashlett
Titchfield Haven NNR
Stubbington
PORTSMOUTH
Bridgemary
North End
Stoke
West Thorney
Apuldram
Dell Quay
Ower
Calshot
Hill Head
Fort Brockhurst
Elson
Whale Island
M275
Portsea Island
Langstone Harbour
Fleet
Hayling Island
Bosham Hoe
Langley
Lepe & Calshot Foreshore
1 hr
Lee-on-the-Solent
Rowner
Brockhurst
Hardway
Gunwharf Quays
Portsmouth Historic Dockyard
Fratton
Portsmouth FC
Chichester Harbour
West Itchenor
Stone Point
GOSPORT
Portsea
Milton
West Town
South Hayling
West Wittering
Browndown
Alverstoke
Cathedral
Southsea
SOLENT
Stokes Bay
Cowes Roads
Gilkicker Point
Southsea Castle & Museum
Hayling Bay
Hayling Seaside Railway
Eastoke
East Wittering
Earnley
Bracklesham
Bracklesham Bay
Cowes
Gurnard
Maritime Museum
East Cowes
Osborne
Osborne Bay
Osborne House
Northwood
Rew Street
St Mildred
¾ hr
Whippingham
Ryde Roads
Wootton
Wootton Bridge
Fishbourne
Quarr Hill
Ryde
Spring Vale
Nettlestone Point
Binstead
Swanmore
Oakfield
Seaview
Seaview Wildlife Encounter
Parkhurst
Parkhurst Forest
Wootton Common
Brickfields Horse Country
Forest Side
Cross Lane
Littletown
Rosemary
Nettlestone
Hunny Hill
NEWPORT
Isle of Wight Steam Rly
Havenstreet
Waltzing Waters
St Helens
Gunville
Staplers
Robin Hill Countryside Adventure Park
East Ashey
Bembridge Point
Carisbrooke
Carisbrooke Castle & Museum
Bembridge
Bembridge Windmill (NT)
Shide
Clatterford
Downend
Arreton Down
Nunwell
Foreland
ISLE OF WIGHT
Bowcombe
Blackwater
Arreton
Adgestone
Roman Villa
Brading
Whitecliff Bay
Hillway
Gatcombe
Alverstone
Merstone
Newchurch
Isle of Wight Zoo
Yaverland
Culver Cliff
Queen's Bower
Dinosaur Isle
Sandown
Winford
Chillerton
ISLE OF WIGHT (SANDOWN)
Rookley
Shorwell
Rookley Green
Apse Heath
Lake
Sandown Bay
Sandy Way
Godshill
Whiteley Bank
All Saints
Kingston
Sandford
Shanklin
Shanklin Chine
Little Atherfield
Roud
Wroxall
Luccombe Village
Chale Green
Appuldurcombe
Stenbury Down
Nettlecombe
Dunnose
Pyle
Bierley
Whitwell
Bonchurch
Ventnor
Chale
Niton
St Lawrence
Ventnor Botanic Gardens
Blackgang
Blackgang Chine
The Undercliff
Rocken End
St Catherine's Point
hours
Bilbao 24-32
Caen 6-7
Cherbourg 3-5½
Guernsey 7
then Jersey 10½
Le Havre 3¼-8
Santander (seasonal) 24-32
St. Malo 9-10¾

120
108

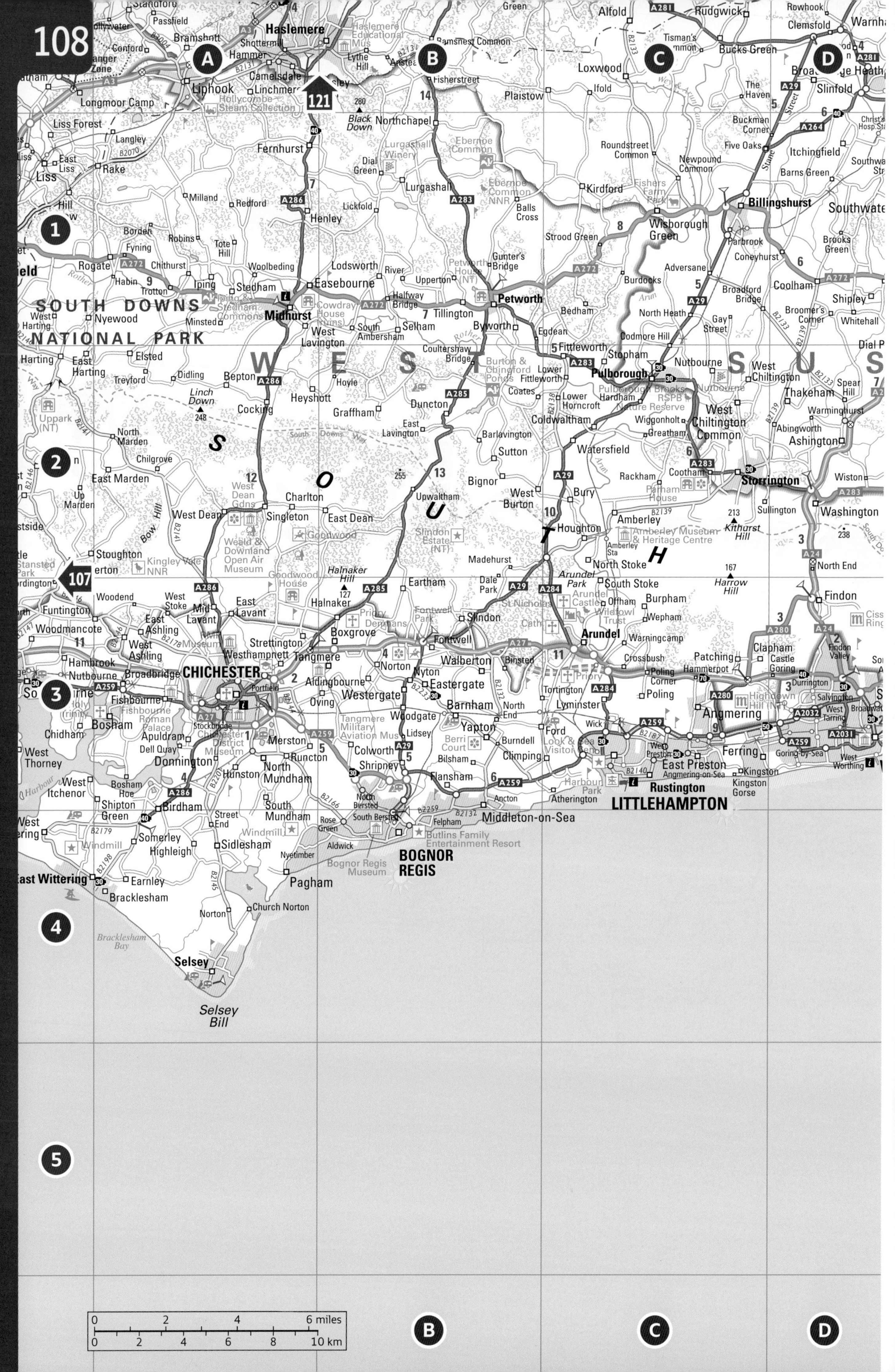
A
B
C
D
1
2
3
4
5
121
107
Haslemere
Haslemere Educational Mus
Bramshott
Passfield
Conford
Shottermill
Hammer
Camelsdale
Liphook
Linchmere
Longmoor Camp
Hollycombe Steam Collection
Liss Forest
Langley
East Liss
Liss
Rake
Lythe Hill
Ramsnest Common
Fisherstreet
Black Down
280
Northchapel
Fernhurst
Lurgashall Winery
Ebernoe Common
Dial Green
Lurgashall
Ebernoe Common NNR
Balls Cross
Milland
Redford
Lickfold
Henley
Borden
Robins
Tote Hill
Fyning
Rogate
Chithurst
Woolbeding
Lodsworth
River
Gunter's Bridge
Petworth House (NT)
Habin
Trotton
Iping
Stedham
Iping & Stedham Commons
Easebourne
Upperton
Petworth
Midhurst
Cowdray House (ruins)
Halfway Bridge
Tillington
SOUTH DOWNS
NATIONAL PARK
West Harting
Nyewood
Minsted
West Lavington
South Ambersham
Selham
Byworth
Harting
East Harting
Elsted
Treyford
Didling
Bepton
Cocking
Heyshott
Hoyle
Graffham
Coultershaw Bridge
Burton & Chingford Ponds
Duncton
East Lavington
Linch Down
248
Uppark (NT)
North Marden
Chilgrove
East Marden
Up Marden
West Dean Gdns
West Dean
Charlton
Singleton
East Dean
Goodwood
Weald & Downland Open Air Museum
Kingley Vale NNR
Stoughton
Stansted Park
Goodwood House
Halnaker Hill
127
Halnaker
Eartham
Slindon Estate (NT)
Upwaltham
255
Barlavington
Sutton
Bignor
West Burton
Bury
Houghton
Madehurst
Dale Park
Slindon
Fontwell Park
Fontwell
Boxgrove
Priory
Denmans
Woodend
Funtington
West Stoke
Mid Lavant
East Lavant
East Ashling
West Ashling
Woodmancote
Hambrook
Nutbourne
Broadbridge
CHICHESTER
Strettington
Westhampnett
Tangmere
Aldingbourne
Westergate
Oving
Tangmere Military Aviation Mus
Norton
Nyton
Eastergate
Barnham
Woodgate
Walberton
Binsted
Yapton
Lidsey
Berri Court
Colworth
Merston
Runcton
North Mundham
Shripney
North Bersted
South Bersted
Flansham
Bilsham
Burndell
Climping
Ford
Fishbourne
Fishbourne Roman Palace
Bosham
Chidham
West Thorney
Apuldram
Dell Quay
Stockbridge
Chichester District Museum
Donnington
Hunston
Portfield
Bosham Hoe
West Itchenor
Shipton Green
Birdham
Street End
Sidlesham
Somerley
Highleigh
Windmill
South Mundham
Rose Green
Aldwick
Nyetimber
Pagham
Church Norton
Norton
East Wittering
West Wittering
Earnley
Bracklesham
Bracklesham Bay
Selsey
Selsey Bill
Bognor Regis Museum
BOGNOR REGIS
Felpham
Butlins Family Entertainment Resort
Middleton-on-Sea
Ancton
Atherington
Harbour Park
Look & Sea Visitor Centre
Wick
LITTLEHAMPTON
Rustington
East Preston
Angmering-on-Sea
West Preston
Ferring
Kingston
Kingston Gorse
Goring-by-Sea
West Worthing
Angmering
Highdown Hill (NT)
Lyminster
Tortington
Arundel
Arundel Castle
Arundel Park
Wildfowl Trust
Offham
South Stoke
North Stoke
Amberley Sta
Amberley
Amberley Museum & Heritage Centre
Burpham
Wepham
Warningcamp
Crossbush
Poling Corner
Poling
Patching
Hammerpot
Clapham
Castle Goring
Durrington
Salvington
West Tarring
Findon
Findon Valley
Cissbury Ring
Harrow Hill
167
Kithurst Hill
213
238
North End
Washington
Sullington
Wiston
Storrington
Parham House
Rackham
Cootham
Watersfield
Coldwaltham
Lower Horncroft
Lower Fittleworth
Coates
Fittleworth
Egdean
Bedham
Stopham
Pulborough
Pulborough Brooks RSPB Nature Reserve
Hardham
Wiggonholt
Greatham
West Chiltington Common
Nutbourne
West Chiltington
Thakeham
Spear Hill
Warminghurst
Abingworth
Ashington
Codmore Hill
North Heath
Gay Street
Burdocks
Adversane
Broadford Bridge
Coolham
Shipley
Broomer's Corner
Whitehall
Dial Post
Strood Green
Wisborough Green
Parbrook
Coneyhurst
Brooks Green
Southwater
Billingshurst
Kirdford
Fishers Farm Park
Roundstreet Common
Newpound Common
Five Oaks
Itchingfield
Barns Green
Buckman Corner
The Haven
Slinfold
Broadbridge Heath
Clemsford
Rowhook
Warnham
Bucks Green
Rudgwick
Tisman's Common
Alfold
Loxwood
Ifold
Plaistow
Green
Christ's Hosp. Sta
Southwater Str
Stane Street
WEST SUSSEX
SOUTH
A3
A272
A286
A283
A285
A29
A27
A259
A284
A280
A24
A2032
A2031
A264
A281
B2070
B2131
B2133
B2138
B2139
B2141
B2146
B2178
B2179
B2198
B2145
B2166
B2201
B2259
B2132
B2233
B2187
B2140
B2144
B2004
0 2 4 6 miles
0 2 4 6 8 10 km

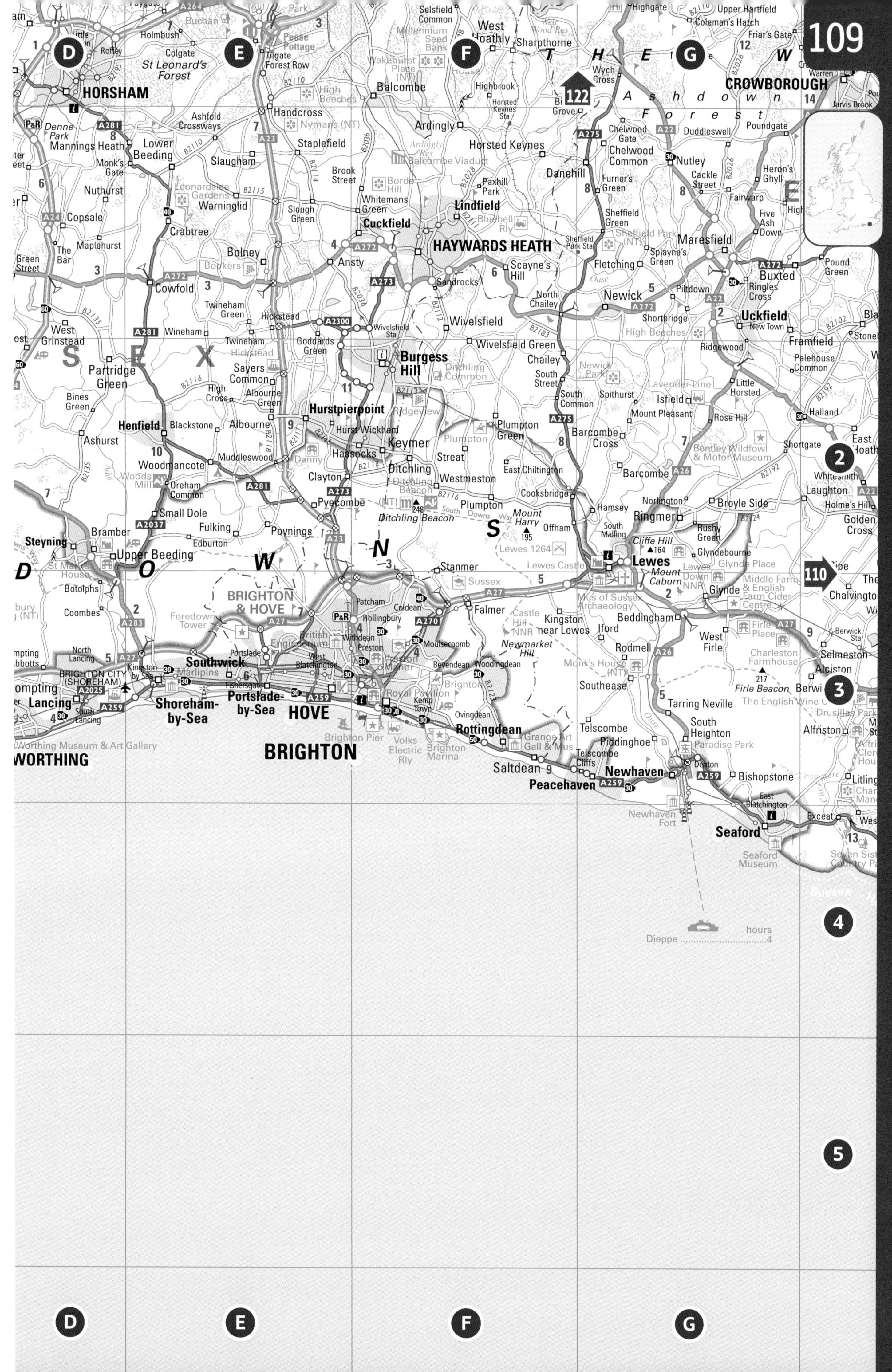
D
E
F
G
1
2
3
4
5
HORSHAM
Roffey
Holmbush
Buchan
Colgate
St Leonard's Forest
Pease Pottage
Tilgate Forest Row
Selsfield Common
Millennium Seed Bank
Wakehurst Place (NT)
West Hoathly
Sharpthorne
Highgate
Upper Hartfield
Coleman's Hatch
Friar's Gate
CROWBOROUGH
Warren
Jarvis Brook
Wych Cross
T H E W E A L D
A s h d o w n F o r e s t
Handcross
Nymans (NT)
High Beeches
Balcombe
Highbrook
Horsted Keynes Sta
Ardingly
Ardingly Res
Balcombe Viaduct
Horsted Keynes
Danehill
Chelwood Gate
Chelwood Common
Furner's Green
Nutley
Duddleswell
Poundgate
Cackle Street
Heron's Ghyll
Fairwarp
Five Ash Down
Denne Park
Mannings Heath
Lower Beeding
Ashfold Crossways
Staplefield
Slaugham
Monk's Gate
Nuthurst
Leonardslee Gardens
Warninglid
Brook Street
Borde Hill
Paxhill Park
Whitemans Green
Cuckfield
Lindfield
Bluebell Rly
Sheffield Green
Sheffield Park (NT)
Sheffield Park Sta
Maresfield
Splayne's Green
Copsale
Maplehurst
Crabtree
Bolney
Bookers
Ansty
Slough Green
HAYWARDS HEATH
Scayne's Hill
Fletching
Newick
North Chailey
Piltdown
Buxted
Ringles Cross
Pound Green
Uckfield
New Town
Shortbridge
High Beeches
Framfield
Stonehill
Green Street
The Bar
Cowfold
Twineham Green
Hickstead
Sandrocks
Wivelsfield
Wivelsfield Sta
Wivelsfield Green
West Grinstead
Wineham
Twineham
Goddards Green
Burgess Hill
Ditchling Common
Chailey
South Street
Newick Park
Ridgewood
Palehouse Common
S U S S E X
Partridge Green
Sayers Common
High Cross
Albourne Green
Bines Green
Hurstpierpoint
Ridgeview
South Common
Spithurst
Lavender Line
Isfield
Little Horsted
Mount Pleasant
Rose Hill
Halland
Henfield
Blackstone
Albourne
Hurst Wickham
Plumpton Green
Ashurst
Hassocks
Keymer
Plumpton
Barcombe Cross
Bentley Wildfowl & Motor Museum
Shortgate
East Hoathly
Woodmancote
Muddleswood
Danny
Clayton
Ditchling
Streat
Westmeston
East Chiltington
Barcombe
Whitesmith
Laughton
Woods Mill
Oreham Common
Pyecombe
Ditchling Beacon
Cooksbridge
Norlington
Broyle Side
Holme's Hill
Small Dole
South Downs Way
Mount Harry
Offham
Hamsey
Ringmer
Rushy Green
Golden Cross
Steyning
Bramber
Fulking
Poynings
Edburton
S O U T H   D O W N S
Lewes 1264
South Malling
Cliffe Hill
Glyndebourne
Upper Beeding
St Mary's House
Botolphs
Stanmer
Sussex
Lewes Castle
Lewes
Mount Caburn
Lewes Down NNR
Glynde Place
Glynde
Middle Farm & English Farm Cider Centre
Chalvington
BRIGHTON & HOVE
Patcham
Coldean
Falmer
Castle Hill NNR
Kingston near Lewes
Mus of Sussex Archaeology
Beddingham
Coombes
Foredown Tower
Hollingbury
Withdean
Preston
Moulsecoomb
Newmarket Hill
Iford
Rodmell
West Firle
Firle Place
Berwick Sta
Selmeston
Alciston
North Lancing
Portslade
Southwick
British Engineerium
Preston Manor
West Blatchington
Bevendean
Woodingdean
Monk's House (NT)
Charleston Farmhouse
Firle Beacon
Berwick
Drusillas Park
Alfriston
BRIGHTON CITY (SHOREHAM)
Kingston by Sea
Marlipins
Fishersgate
Portslade-by-Sea
Shoreham-by-Sea
Lancing
South Lancing
HOVE
Royal Pavilion
Kemp Town
Ovingdean
Southease
Tarring Neville
South Heighton
The English Wine Centre
Worthing Museum & Art Gallery
WORTHING
Compting
BRIGHTON
Brighton Pier
Volks Electric Rly
Brighton Marina
Rottingdean
Grange Art Gall & Mus
Saltdean
Telscombe
Piddinghoe
Telscombe Cliffs
Peacehaven
Newhaven
Denton
Paradise Park
Bishopstone
Littlington
East Blatchington
Newhaven Fort
Seaford
Seaford Museum
Exceat
Seven Sisters Country Park
Dieppe 4
hours
122
110

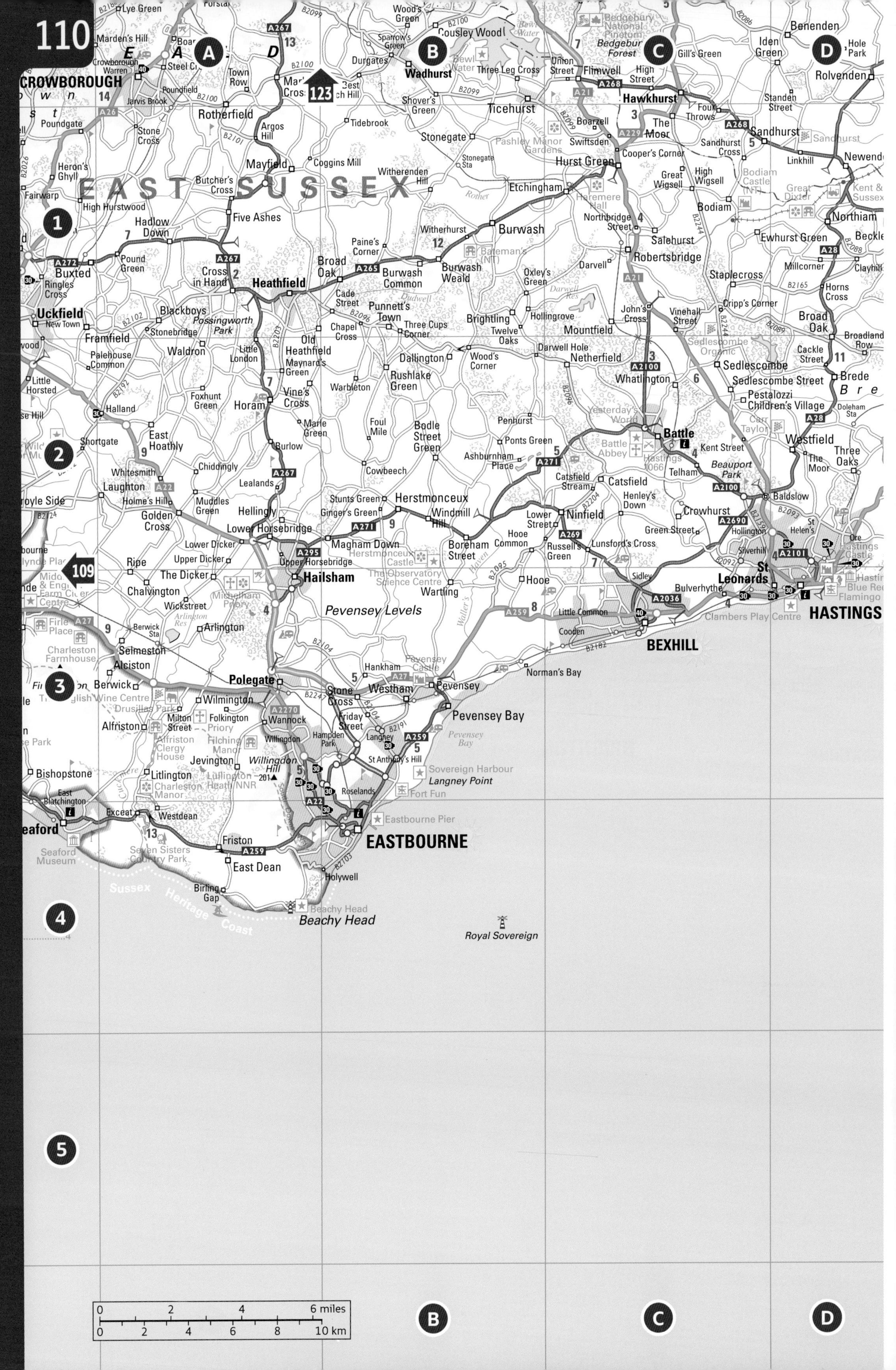
EAST SUSSEX
CROWBOROUGH
Lye Green
Marden's Hill
Crowborough Warren
Steel Cross
Jarvis Brook
Poundfield
Poundgate
Town Row
Mark Cross
Rotherfield
Stone Cross
Argos Hill
Heron's Ghyll
Fairwarp
Mayfield
Coggins Mill
Butcher's Cross
High Hurstwood
Five Ashes
Hadlow Down
Pound Green
Buxted
Ringles Cross
Uckfield
New Town
Framfield
Stonebridge
Blackboys
Possingworth Park
Cross in Hand
Heathfield
Waldron
Palehouse Common
Little Horsted
Little London
Old Heathfield
Halland
Foxhunt Green
Horam
Shortgate
East Hoathly
Whitesmith
Laughton
Chiddingly
Holme's Hill
Muddles Green
Golden Cross
Lealands
Hellingly
Lower Horsebridge
Lower Dicker
Upper Dicker
Upper Horsebridge
Ripe
The Dicker
Hailsham
Chalvington
Wickstreet
Michelham Priory
Arlington
Arlington Res
Berwick Sta
Selmeston
Charleston Farmhouse
Alciston
Berwick
Polegate
Wilmington
Drusillas Park
Milton Street
Folkington
Wannock
Alfriston
Priory
Willingdon
Filching Manor
Alfriston Clergy House
Jevington
Willingdon Hill
Litlington
Lullington Heath NNR
Charleston Manor
Bishopstone
East Blatchington
Seaford
Exceat
Westdean
Seaford Museum
Seven Sisters Country Park
Friston
East Dean
Birling Gap
Sussex Heritage Coast
Beachy Head
Royal Sovereign
EASTBOURNE
Eastbourne Pier
Holywell
Roselands
Fort Fun
Hampden Park
Langney
St Anthony's Hill
Sovereign Harbour
Langney Point
Pevensey Bay
Friday Street
Stone Cross
Westham
Pevensey
Pevensey Castle
Hankham
Pevensey Levels
Wartling
The Observatory Science Centre
Herstmonceux Castle
Magham Down
Herstmonceux
Stunts Green
Ginger's Green
Windmill Hill
Boreham Street
Hooe Common
Hooe
Norman's Bay
Cooden
Little Common
BEXHILL
Sidley
Bulverhythe
St Leonards
HASTINGS
Clambers Play Centre
Blue Reef
Flamingo
Hastings Castle
Ore
St Helen's
Silverhill
Hollington
Baldslow
Crowhurst
Green Street
Lunsford's Cross
Russell's Green
Lower Street
Ninfield
Henley's Down
Catsfield
Catsfield Stream
Ashburnham Place
Ponts Green
Penhurst
Cowbeech
Bodle Street Green
Foul Mile
Marle Green
Burlow
Vine's Cross
Warbleton
Rushlake Green
Maynard's Green
Chapel Cross
Punnett's Town
Three Cups Corner
Dallington
Wood's Corner
Twelve Oaks
Brightling
Hollingrove
Mountfield
Darwell Hole
Netherfield
Whatlington
Battle
Battle Abbey
Hastings 1066
Yesterday's World
Telham
Beauport Park
Kent Street
Westfield
The Moor
Three Oaks
Carr Taylor
Pestalozzi Children's Village
Sedlescombe Street
Sedlescombe
Sedlescombe Organic
Cackle Street
Brede
Broad Oak
Broadland Row
Horns Cross
Cripp's Corner
Staplecross
Vinehall Street
John's Cross
Darwell
Darwell Res
Oxley's Green
Burwash Weald
Burwash Common
Burwash
Bateman's (NT)
Witherhurst
Paine's Corner
Broad Oak
Cade Street
Dudwell
Etchingham
Haremere Hall
Northbridge Street
Salehurst
Robertsbridge
Bodiam
Bodiam Castle (NT)
Great Dixter
Northiam
Ewhurst Green
Beckley
Millcorner
Clayhill
Great Wigsell
High Wigsell
Hurst Green
Cooper's Corner
Swiftsden
Boarzell
The Moor
Hawkhurst
Four Throws
Sandhurst Cross
Sandhurst
Linkhill
Newenden
Kent & East Sussex
Standen Street
Rolvenden
Benenden
Iden Green
Hole Park
Gill's Green
High Street
Flimwell
Union Street
Bedgebury National Pinetum
Bedgebury Forest
Three Leg Cross
Bewl Water
Cousley Wood
Wood's Green
Sparrow's Green
Durgates
Wadhurst
Best Beech Hill
Shover's Green
Ticehurst
Tidebrook
Stonegate
Stonegate Sta
Pashley Manor Gardens
Witherenden Hill
Rother
109
123
0 2 4 6 miles
0 2 4 6 8 10 km

Channel Tunnel terminal maps

Eurotunnel: Access from the UK

FOLKESTONE TERMINAL

Departures

1 Leave M20/A20 at junction 11a

2 Check-In

3 Passenger Terminal Building

4 UK and French frontier controls and security

5 Vehicle allocation zone

6 Vehicles drive onto platform via overbridges

7 Vehicles board the shuttle train

8 Eurotunnel's shuttle train enters tunnel

Arrivals

1 The shuttle train exits tunnel and loops round terminal to stop at platform

2 Vehicles disembark from the shuttle train and join exit road via overbridges

3 Vehicles follow exit road to M20/A20

Arrivals
Passenger vehicles
Freight

Departures
Passenger vehicles
Freight

Eurotunnel: Access from France

CALAIS/COQUELLES TERMINAL

Arrivals

1 The shuttle train exits tunnel and loops round terminal to stop at platform

2 Vehicles disembark from the shuttle train and join exit road via overbridges

3 Vehicles follow exit road to A16

Departures

1 Leave A16 at junction 42

2 Check-In

3 Passenger Terminal Building

4 French and UK frontier controls and security

5 Vehicle allocation zone

6 Vehicles drive onto platforms via overbridges

7 Vehicles board the shuttle train

8 Eurotunnel's shuttle train enters tunnel

Arrivals
Passenger vehicles
Freight

Departures
Passenger vehicles
Freight

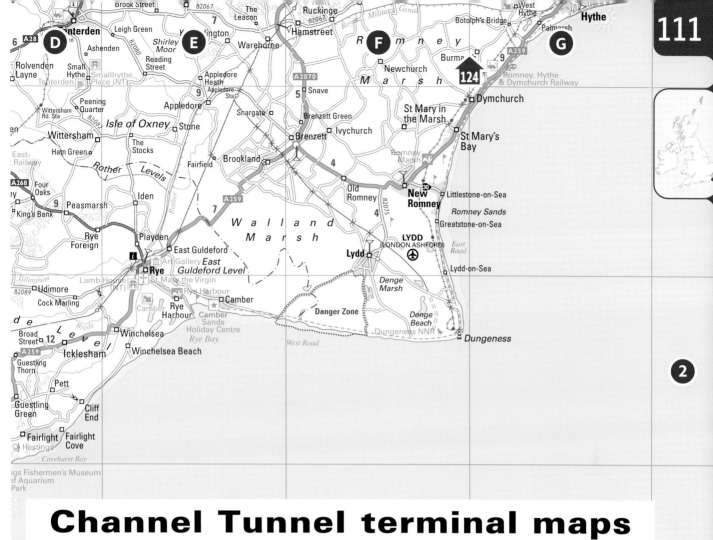

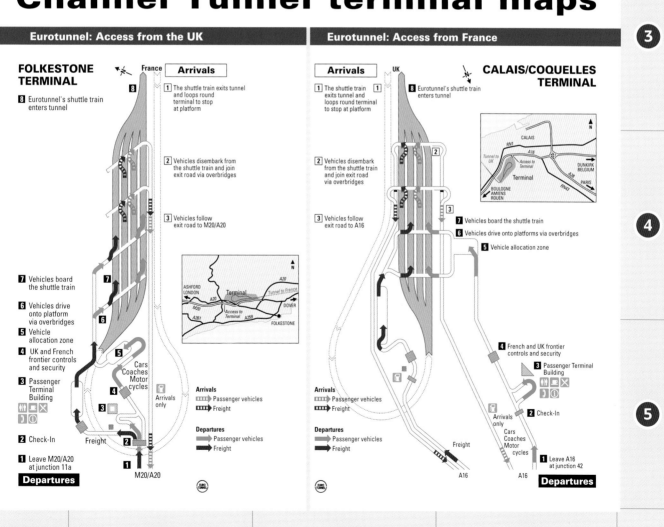

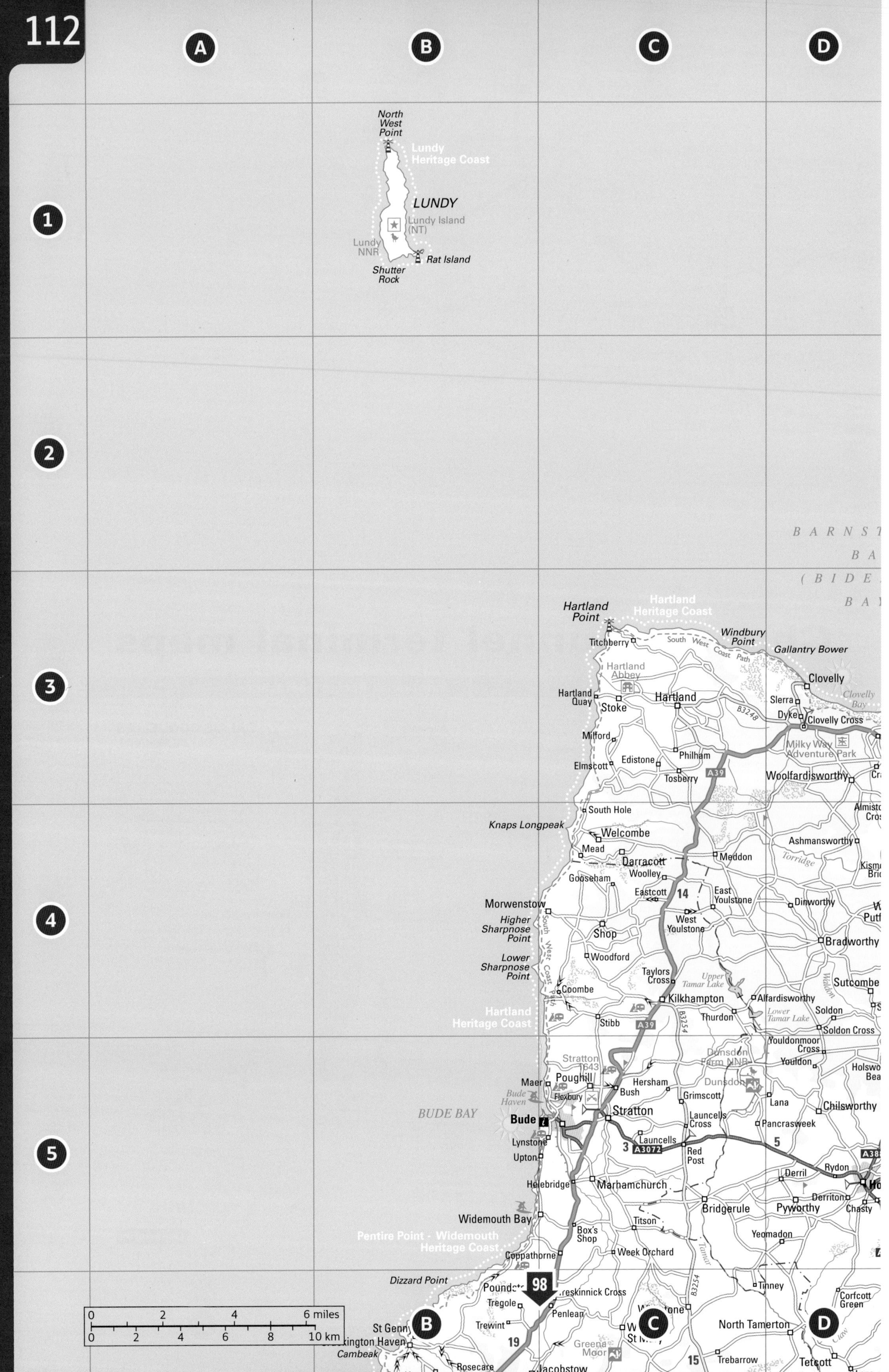

A   B   C   D

1
2
3
4
5

North West Point

Lundy Heritage Coast

LUNDY

Lundy NNR

Lundy Island (NT)

Rat Island

Shutter Rock

Hartland Point

Hartland Heritage Coast

Titchberry

South West Coast Path

Windbury Point

Gallantry Bower

Clovelly

Hartland Abbey

Slerra

Clovelly Bay

Hartland Quay   Stoke   Hartland   Dyke   Clovelly Cross

Milford   B3248

Philham   Milky Way Adventure Park

Elmscott   Edistone   A39   Woolfardisworthy

Tosberry

South Hole

Knaps Longpeak

Ashmansworthy

Welcombe   *Torridge*

Mead   Meddon   Kisme...

Darracott   Bri...

Gooseham   Woolley   East Youlstone   Dinworthy

Eastcott   14

Morwenstow   West Youlstone   Bradworthy

Higher Sharpnose Point   Shop   Putf...

Woodford

Lower Sharpnose Point   *South West Coast*   Taylors Cross   *Upper Tamar Lake*   Sutcombe

Coombe   Kilkhampton   Alfardisworthy

Thurdon   Soldon   *Lower Tamar Lake*   Soldon Cross

Stibb   A39   B3254

Youldonmoor Cross

Dunsdon Farm NNR   Youldon

Stratton 1643   Dunsdon   Holsw... Bea...

Maer   Poughill   Hersham   Bush   Grimscott   Lana   Chilsworthy

Bude Haven   Flexbury   Stratton   Launcells Cross   Pancrasweek

BUDE BAY   **Bude**   3   Launcells   5   A38...

Lynstone   A3072   Red Post   Derril

Upton   Rydon   Ho...

Helebridge   Marhamchurch   Bridgerule   Pyworthy   Chasty   Derriton

Titson   Yeomadon

Widemouth Bay   Box's Shop   Week Orchard

Pentire Point - Widemouth Heritage Coast   Coppathorne   *Tamar*   Tinney   Corfcott Green

Dizzard Point   98

Poundst...   reskinnick Cross   North Tamerton   Tetcott

Tregole   Penlean   C   D

St Genn   B

Trewint   19   W St I...   15   Trebarrow

kington Haven   Greena Moor

Cambeak   Rosecare   Jacobstow

BARNST...

BA...

(BIDE...

BA...

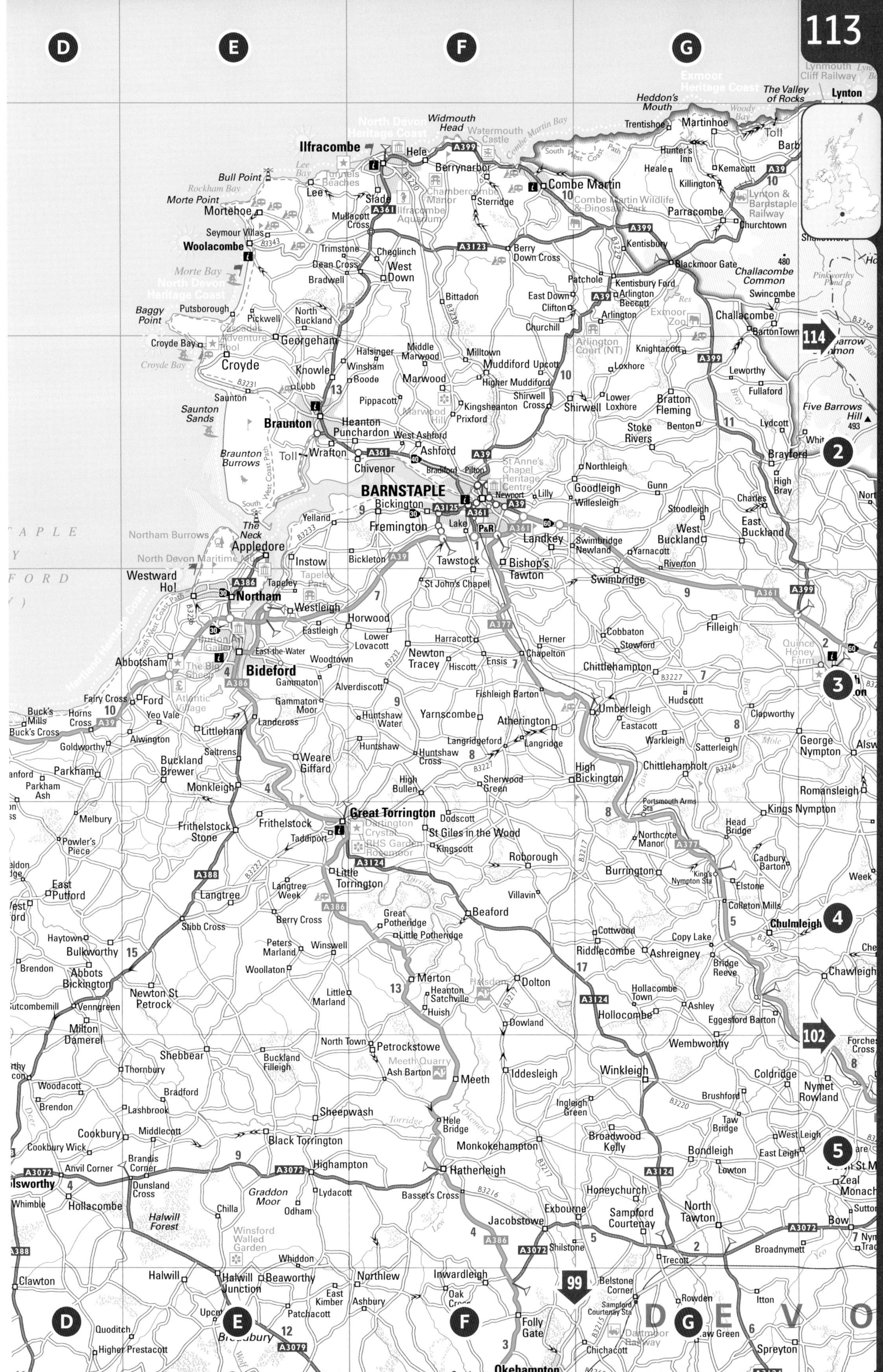
D
E
F
G
Lynmouth Cliff Railway
Lynton
The Valley of Rocks
Heddon's Mouth
Exmoor Heritage Coast
Widmouth Head
North Devon Heritage Coast
Watermouth Castle
Combe Martin Bay
Trentishoe
Martinhoe
Toll
Ilfracombe
Hele
Berrynarbor
South West Coast Path
Hunter's Inn
Heale
Kemacott
Bull Point
Lee Bay
Tunnels Beaches
Chambercombe Manor
Sterridge
Combe Martin
Killington
Rockham Bay
Lee
Slade
Ilfracombe Aquarium
Combe Martin Wildlife & Dinosaur Park
Lynton & Barnstaple Railway
Morte Point
Mortehoe
Mullacott Cross
Parracombe
Churchtown
Seymour Villas
Woolacombe
Trimstone
Cheglinch
Berry Down Cross
Kentisbury
Blackmoor Gate
Morte Bay
Dean Cross
West Down
Challacombe Common
Bradwell
Patchole
Kentisbury Ford
Arlington Beccott
Baggy Point
Putsborough
Pickwell
North Buckland
Bittadon
East Down
Clifton
Arlington
Exmoor Zoo
Swincombe
Challacombe
Barton Town
114
Churchill
Croyde Bay
Cascades Adventure Pool
Georgeham
Halsinger
Middle Marwood
Milltown
Arlington Court (NT)
Knightacott
Croyde
Knowle
Winsham
Muddiford
Upcott
Loxhore
Lewortny
Croyde Bay
Boode
Marwood
Higher Muddiford
Fullaford
Saunton
Lobb
Pippacott
Shirwell Cross
Shirwell
Lower Loxhore
Bratton Fleming
Five Barrows Hill
Saunton Sands
Marwood Hill
Kingsheanton
Prixford
Benton
Lydcott
Braunton
Heanton Punchardon
Stoke Rivers
West Ashford
Ashford
Braunton Burrows
Toll
Wrafton
Chivenor
Bradiford
Pilton
St Anne's Chapel Heritage Centre
Northleigh
Brayford
High Bray
BARNSTAPLE
Newport
Lilly
Goodleigh
Gunn
Willesleigh
Charles
Bickington
Stoodleigh
The Neck
Yelland
Fremington
Lake
West Buckland
East Buckland
Northam Burrows
Appledore
Landkey
Swimbridge Newland
Yarnacott
North Devon Maritime Museum
Instow
Bickleton
Tawstock
Bishop's Tawton
Riverton
Westward Ho!
Tapeley
Tapeley Park
Swimbridge
Northam
St John's Chapel
Westleigh
Horwood
Eastleigh
Lower Lovacott
Cobbaton
Filleigh
Burton Gallery
Harracott
Herner
Stowford
Quince Honey Farm
East-the-Water
Woodtown
Newton Tracey
Ensis
Chapelton
Abbotsham
The Big Sheep
Bideford
Hiscott
Chittlehampton
Gammaton
Alverdiscott
Fishleigh Barton
Hudscott
Fairy Cross
Ford
Atlantic Village
Gammaton Moor
Umberleigh
Buck's Mills
Horns Cross
Yeo Vale
Huntshaw Water
Yarnscombe
Atherington
Eastacott
Clapworthy
Buck's Cross
Littleham
Landcross
Langridgeford
Langridge
Warkleigh
Satterleigh
George Nympton
Goldworthy
Alwington
Huntshaw
Huntshaw Cross
Parkham
Saltrens
Weare Giffard
Chittlehamholt
Buckland Brewer
High Bickington
Parkham Ash
Monkleigh
High Bullen
Sherwood Green
Romansleigh
Portsmouth Arms Sta
Kings Nympton
Melbury
Great Torrington
Frithelstock
Dodscott
Head Bridge
Frithelstock Stone
Dartington Crystal
St Giles in the Wood
Northcote Manor
Powler's Piece
Taddiport
RHS Garden Rosemoor
Kingscott
Cadbury Barton
Roborough
Little Torrington
Burrington
King's Nympton Sta
Week
East Putford
Langtree
Langtree Week
Elstone
Villavin
Colleton Mills
Beaford
Great Potheridge
Chulmleigh
Berry Cross
Stibb Cross
Little Potheridge
Cottwood
Copy Lake
Haytown
Peters Marland
Winswell
Riddlecombe
Ashreigney
Bulkworthy
Bridge Reeve
Brendon
Abbots Bickington
Woollaton
Chawleigh
Merton
Halsdon
Dolton
Hollacombe Town
Newton St Petrock
Little Marland
Heanton Satchville
Huish
Ashley
Venngreen
Hollocombe
Milton Damerel
Dowland
Eggesford Barton
102
North Town
Petrockstowe
Wembworthy
Shebbear
Thornbury
Buckland Filleigh
Meeth Quarry
Ash Barton
Meeth
Iddesleigh
Winkleigh
Coldridge
Woodacott
Brendon
Bradford
Nymet Rowland
Brushford
Lashbrook
Sheepwash
Ingleigh Green
Hele Bridge
Middlecott
Broadwood Kelly
Taw Bridge
West Leigh
Cookbury
Cookbury Wick
Black Torrington
Monkokehampton
Bondleigh
East Leigh
Anvil Corner
Brandis Corner
Highampton
Hatherleigh
Lowton
Zeal Monachorum
Holsworthy
Dunsland Cross
Graddon Moor
Lydacott
Basset's Cross
Honeychurch
North Tawton
Whimble
Hollacombe
Chilla
Odham
Exbourne
Sampford Courtenay
Bow
Halwill Forest
Jacobstowe
Winsford Walled Garden
Shilstone
Broadnymett
Whiddon
Trecott
Clawton
Halwill
Halwill Junction
Beaworthy
Northlew
Inwardleigh
Belstone Corner
East Kimber
Oak Cross
Ashbury
Rowden
Itton
Patchacott
Sampford Courtenay Sta
D
E
F
G
DEVON
Quoditch
Folly Gate
Dartmoor Railway
Higher Prestacott
Chichacott
Spreyton
Okehampton
99
2
3
4
5

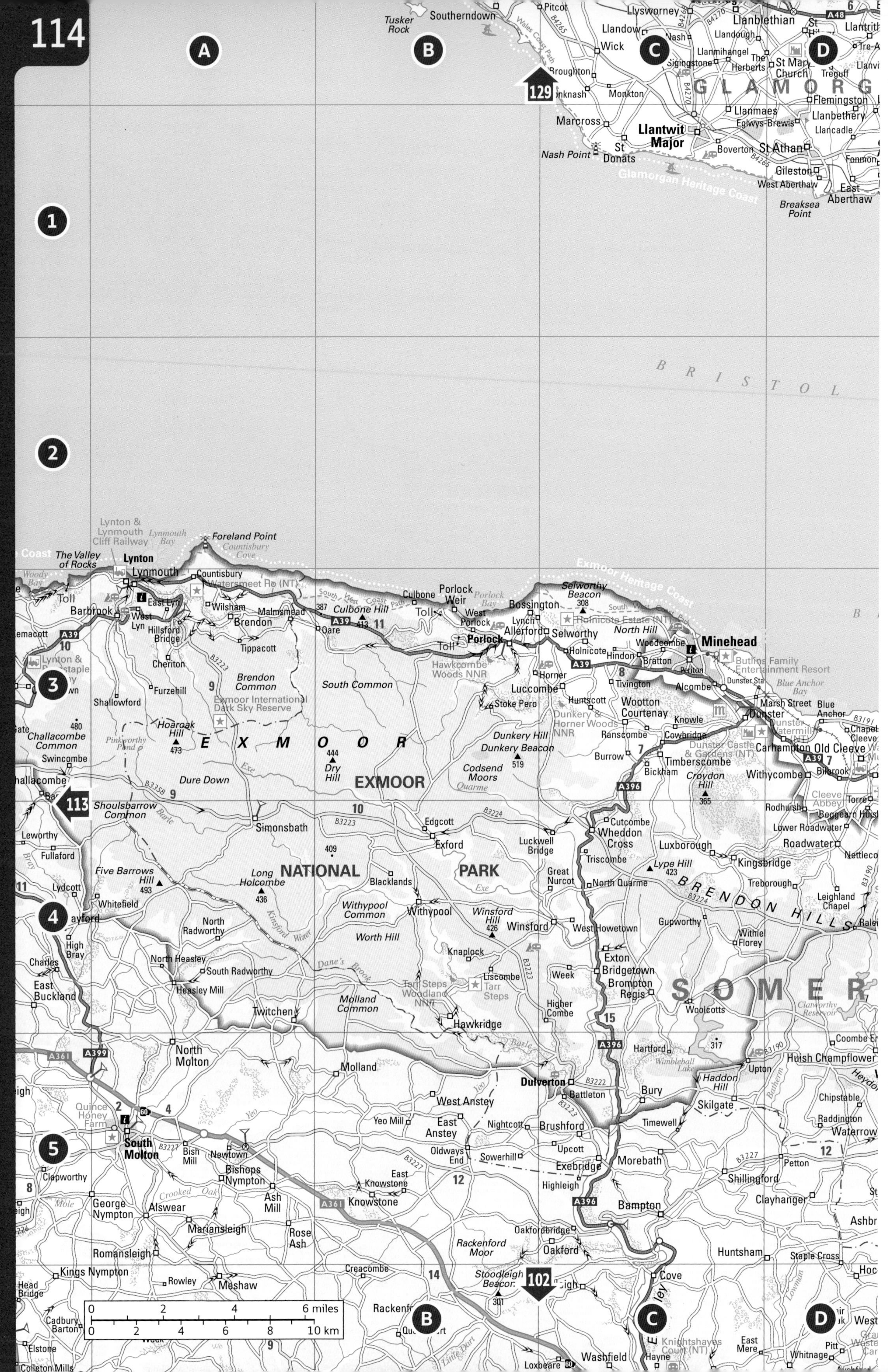
A
B
C
D
1
2
3
4
5
Tusker Rock
Southerndown
Pitcot
Llysworney
Llandow
Wick
Nash
Llanblethian
Llandough
Llanmihangel
Sigingstone
The Herberts
St Mary Church
Treguff
Broughton
Monkton
129
GLAMORG
Flemingston
Llanmaes
Eglwys-Brewis
Llanbethery
Llancadle
Marcross
Llantwit Major
St Donats
Nash Point
Boverton
St Athan
Fonmon
Gileston
West Aberthaw
East Aberthaw
Breaksea Point
Glamorgan Heritage Coast
Wales Coast Path
A48
BRISTOL
Lynton & Lynmouth Cliff Railway
Lynmouth Bay
Foreland Point
Countisbury Cove
The Valley of Rocks
Lynton
Lynmouth
Countisbury
Watersmeet Ho (NT)
Woody Bay
Toll
Barbrook
East Lyn
West Lyn
Wilsham
Brendon
Malmsmead
Hillsford Bridge
Cheriton
Tippacott
Oare
Culbone Hill
Culbone
Porlock Weir
Porlock Bay
West Porlock
Porlock
Bossington
Lynch
Allerford
Selworthy
Selworthy Beacon
Holnicote Estate (NT)
North Hill
Exmoor Heritage Coast
Woodcombe
Minehead
Bratton
Periton
Butlins Family Entertainment Resort
Hindon
Holnicote
Hawkcombe Woods NNR
Horner
Luccombe
Stoke Pero
Tivington
Alcombe
Dunster Sta
Blue Anchor Bay
Huntscott
Wootton Courtenay
Marsh Street
Blue Anchor
Dunkery & Horner Woods NNR
Knowle
Dunster
Dunster Watermill (NT)
Chapel Cleeve
Ranscombe
Cowbridge
Dunster Castle & Gardens (NT)
Carhampton
Old Cleeve
Burrow
Timberscombe
Bickham
Croydon Hill
Withycombe
Bilbrook
Cleeve Abbey
Rodhuish
Torre
Beggearn Huish
Lower Roadwater
Roadwater
Nettlecombe
Brendon Common
South Common
Exmoor International Dark Sky Reserve
Shallowford
Furzehill
Hoaroak Hill
Pinkworthy Pond
Challacombe Common
Swincombe
Challacombe
EXMOOR
Dry Hill
Dunkery Hill
Dunkery Beacon
Codsend Moors
Quarme
Dure Down
113
Shoulsbarrow Common
Barle
Simonsbath
Edgcott
Exford
Luckwell Bridge
Cutcombe
Wheddon Cross
Triscombe
Luxborough
Kingsbridge
Lype Hill
Treborough
Leworthy
Fullaford
Bray
Five Barrows Hill
Long Holcombe
NATIONAL
PARK
Blacklands
Great Nurcot
North Quarme
BRENDON HILLS
Leighland Chapel
Lydcott
Whitefield
Withypool Common
Withypool
Winsford Hill
Winsford
West Howetown
Gupworthy
Withiel Florey
Brayford
High Bray
North Radworthy
Kinsford Water
Worth Hill
Knaplock
Exton
Bridgetown
Charles
North Heasley
South Radworthy
Heasley Mill
Dane's Brook
Tarr Steps Woodland NNR
Liscombe
Tarr Steps
Week
Brompton Regis
SOMER
Clatworthy Reservoir
East Buckland
Twitchen
Molland Common
Hawkridge
Higher Combe
Woolcotts
North Molton
Molland
Dulverton
Hartford
Wimbleball Lake
Haddon Hill
Upton
Coombe
Huish Champflower
Battleton
Bury
Quince Honey Farm
South Molton
West Anstey
Skilgate
Chipstable
Yeo Mill
East Anstey
Nightcott
Brushford
Timewell
Raddington
Waterrow
Bish Mill
Newtown
Oldways End
Sowerhill
Upcott
Morebath
Petton
Clapworthy
Bishops Nympton
East Knowstone
Exebridge
Shillingford
Highleigh
Crooked Oak
George Nympton
Alswear
Ash Mill
Knowstone
Bampton
Clayhanger
Mole
Mariansleigh
Rose Ash
Oakfordbridge
Rackenford Moor
Oakford
Huntsham
Staple Cross
Romansleigh
Kings Nympton
Creacombe
Rowley
Meshaw
Stoodleigh Beacon
102
Cove
Head Bridge
Cadbury Barton
Rackenford
Elstone
Colleton Mills
Little Dart
Washfield
Knightshayes Court (NT)
Hayne
East Mere
Whitnage
Pitt
Loxbeare
A39
B3223
B3358
B3224
A396
B3222
B3227
A361
A399
B3190
B3191
0 2 4 6 miles
0 2 4 6 8 10 km

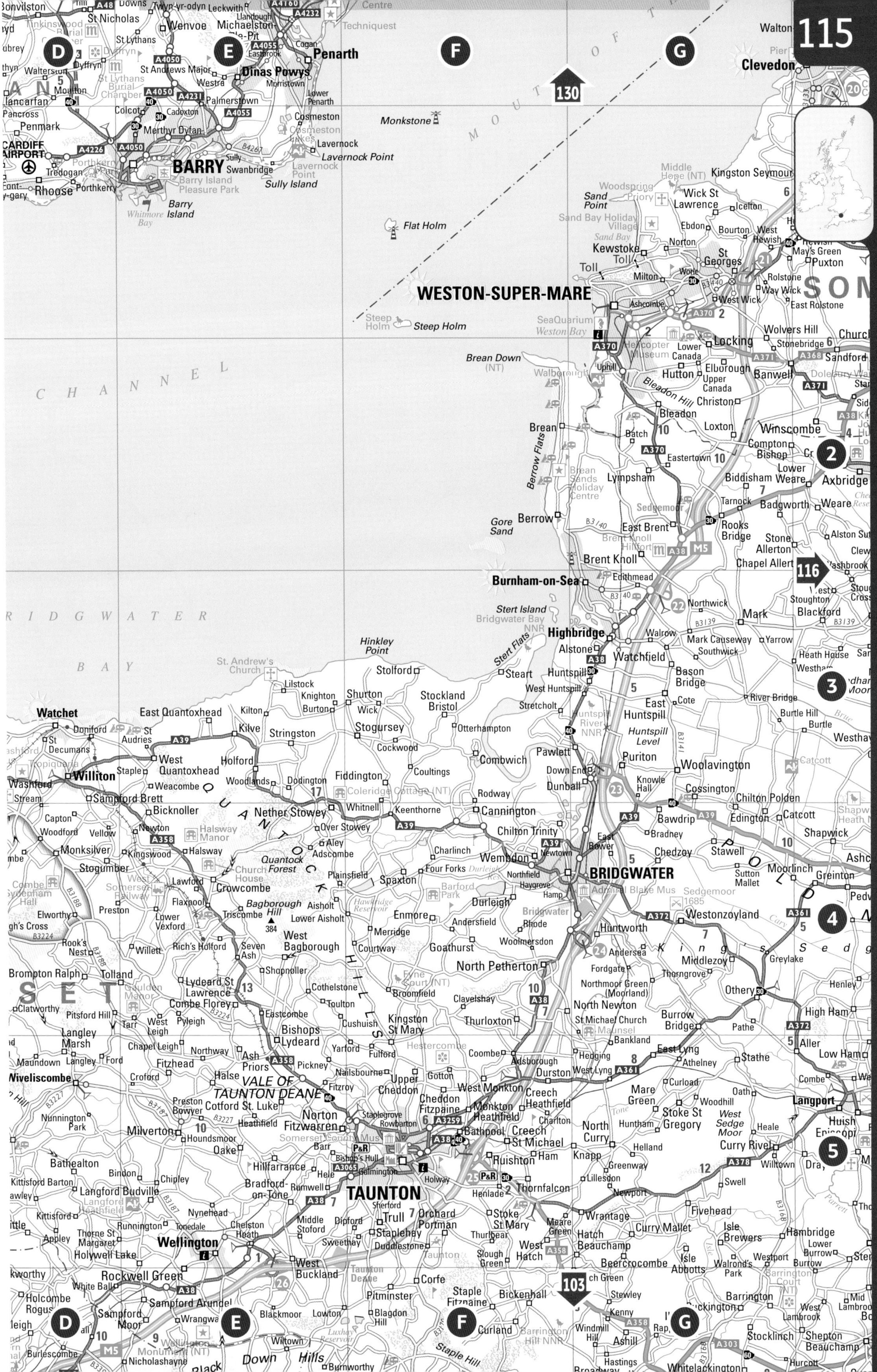
130
116
103
D
E
F
G
2
3
4
5
Bonvilston
St Nicholas
Wenvoe
Michaelston-le-Pit
Leckwith
St Lythans
Dyffryn
Penarth
Cogan
Dinas Powys
St Andrews Major
Walterston
Moulton
Llancarfan
Pancross
Penmark
Colcot
Palmerstown
Cadoxton
Merthyr Dyfan
Cosmeston
Lower Penarth
Lavernock
Lavernock Point
Monkstone
Sully
Swanbridge
Sully Island
CARDIFF AIRPORT
Tredogan
Rhoose
Porthkerry
BARRY
Barry Island Pleasure Park
Barry Island
Whitmore Bay
Flat Holm
Steep Holm
Techniquest
Walton
Clevedon
Middle Hope (NT)
Kingston Seymour
Woodspring Priory
Sand Point
Sand Bay Holiday Village
Sand Bay
Wick St Lawrence
Icelton
Ebdon
Bourton
West Hewish
May's Green
Puxton
Kewstoke
Norton
Toll
St Georges
Worle
Milton
Rolstone
Way Wick
West Wick
East Rolstone
WESTON-SUPER-MARE
Ashcombe
SeaQuarium
Weston Bay
Helicopter Museum
Lower Canada
Locking
Wolvers Hill
Stonebridge
Sandford
Churchill
Uphill
Hutton
Elborough
Upper Canada
Banwell
Brean Down (NT)
Walborough
Bleadon Hill
Bleadon
Christon
Brean
Batch
Loxton
Winscombe
Compton Bishop
Eastertown
Berrow Flats
Brean Sands Holiday Centre
Lympsham
Biddisham
Lower Weare
Axbridge
Sedgemoor
Tarnock
Badgworth
Weare
Berrow
Gore Sand
East Brent
Rooks Bridge
Brent Knoll Hillfort
Brent Knoll
Stone Allerton
Chapel Allerton
Burnham-on-Sea
Edithmead
Northwick
Stert Island
Bridgwater Bay NNR
Highbridge
Mark
Stoughton
Blackford
Walrow
Mark Causeway
Yarrow
Southwick
Alstone
Watchfield
Heath House
Westham
Hinkley Point
Stert Flats
Stolford
Steart
Huntspill
West Huntspill
Bason Bridge
Cote
River Bridge
Burtle Hill
Burtle
Westhay
Lilstock
Knighton
Shurton
Burton
Wick
Kilton
Stockland Bristol
Stretcholt
East Huntspill
Huntspill River NNR
Huntspill Level
Watchet
East Quantoxhead
Doniford
St Audries
Kilve
Stringston
Stogursey
Cockwood
Otterhampton
Pawlett
Puriton
Woolavington
Catcott
St Decumans
West Quantoxhead
Holford
Combwich
Williton
Staple
Woodlands
Dodington
Fiddington
Coultings
Down End
Knowle Hall
Dunball
Cossington
Chilton Polden
Washford
Stream
Sampford Brett
Weacombe
Coleridge Cottage (NT)
Rodway
Bicknoller
Nether Stowey
Whitnell
Keenthorne
Cannington
Bawdrip
Edington
Catcott
Capton
Newton
Halsway Manor
Over Stowey
Chilton Trinity
Bradney
Woodford
Vellow
Aley
Adscombe
Shapwick
Monksilver
Kingswood
Halsway
Charlinch
East Bower
Newtown
Chedzoy
Stawell
Quantock Forest
Wembdon
Stogumber
Four Forks
Northfield
Sutton Mallet
Moorlinch
Greinton
Church House
Plainsfield
Spaxton
Hawkridge Reservoir
Barford Park
Hamp
BRIDGWATER
Admiral Blake Mus
Sedgemoor 1685
West Somerset Railway
Lawford
Crowcombe
Flaxpool
Preston
Bagborough Hill
Aisholt
Lower Aisholt
Durleigh
Triscombe
Enmore
Andersfield
Rhode
Huntworth
Westonzoyland
Elworthy
Lower Vexford
Merridge
Woolmersdon
West Bagborough
Courtway
Goathurst
Andersea
Middlezoy
Rook's Nest
Willett
Rich's Holford
Seven Ash
Fordgate
Thorngrove
Greylake
Brompton Ralph
Tolland
Shopnoller
North Petherton
Northmoor Green (Moorland)
Gaulden Manor
Lydeard St Lawrence
Cothelstone
Fyne Court (NT)
Broomfield
Othery
Henley
Combe Florey
Toulton
Clavelshay
North Newton
Clatworthy
Pitsford Hill
West Leigh
Pyleigh
Eastcombe
Cushuish
Kingston St Mary
Thurloxton
St Michael Church
Burrow Bridge
Maunsel
Pathe
High Ham
Langley Marsh
Tarr
Bishops Lydeard
Bankland
Aller
Chapel Leigh
Northway
Yarford
Fulford
Hestercombe
Coombe
Adsborough
Hedging
East Lyng
Athelney
Stathe
Low Ham
Maundown
Langley
Ford
Fitzhead
Ash Priors
Pickney
Nailsbourne
Durston
West Lyng
Wiveliscombe
Croford
Halse
Upper Cheddon
Gotton
West Monkton
Creech Heathfield
Curload
Oath
Combe
Langport
VALE OF TAUNTON DEANE
Fitzroy
Cheddon Fitzpaine
Monkton Heathfield
Mare Green
Woodhill
Preston Bowyer
Cotford St. Luke
Staplegrove
Rowbarton
Charlton
Stoke St Gregory
West Sedge Moor
Huish Episcopi
Nunnington Park
Heathfield
Norton Fitzwarren
Bathpool
Creech St Michael
North Curry
Huntham
Heale
Milverton
Houndsmoor
Somerset County Mus
Curry Rivel
Oake
Barr
Helland
Bathealton
Bishop's Hull
Ham
Knapp
Willtown
Drayton
Bindon
Hillfarrance
Hele
Galmington
Holway
Ruishton
Greenway
Kittisford Barton
Chipley
Lillesdon
Swell
Langford Budville
Bradford-on-Tone
Rumwell
TAUNTON
Henlade
Thornfalcon
Newport
Langford Heathfield
Sherford
Trull
Orchard Portman
Stoke St Mary
Wrantage
Fivehead
Kittisford
Nynehead
Runnington
Tonedale
Chelston Heath
Middle Stoford
Dipford
Staplehay
Meare Green
Hatch Beauchamp
Curry Mallet
Isle Brewers
Hambridge
Thorne St Margaret
Sweethay
Duddlestone
Thurlbear
Slough Green
West Hatch
Lower Burrow
Appley
Wellington
Holywell Lake
West Buckland
Taunton Deane
Beercrocombe
Isle Abbotts
Walrond's Park
Westport
Barrington Court (NT)
Rockwell Green
White Ball
Corfe
Ash Green
Stewley
Holcombe Rogus
Sampford Arundel
Pitminster
Staple Fitzpaine
Bickenhall
Barrington
Puckington
West Lambrook
Mid Lambrook
Sampford Moor
Wrangway
Blackmoor
Lowton
Blagdon Hill
Curland
Barrington Hill NNR
Kenny
Windmill Hill
Ashill
Stocklinch
Shepton Beauchamp
Burlescombe
Wellington Monument (NT)
Nicholashayne
Luxhay Reservoir
Widcombe
Black Down Hills
Staple Hill
Burnworthy
Hastings
Whitelackington
Hurcott
Broadway
BRISTOL CHANNEL
BRIDGWATER BAY
MOUTH OF THE SEVERN
QUANTOCK HILLS
King's Sedgemoor
POLDEN HILLS
SOMERSET
A48
A4160
A4232
A4055
A4050
A4231
A4226
B4267
A370
A371
A368
A38
M5
B3140
B3139
B3141
A39
A372
A361
A358
A3259
A3065
A378
A303
B3224
B3188
B3227
B3187
B3168
B3170

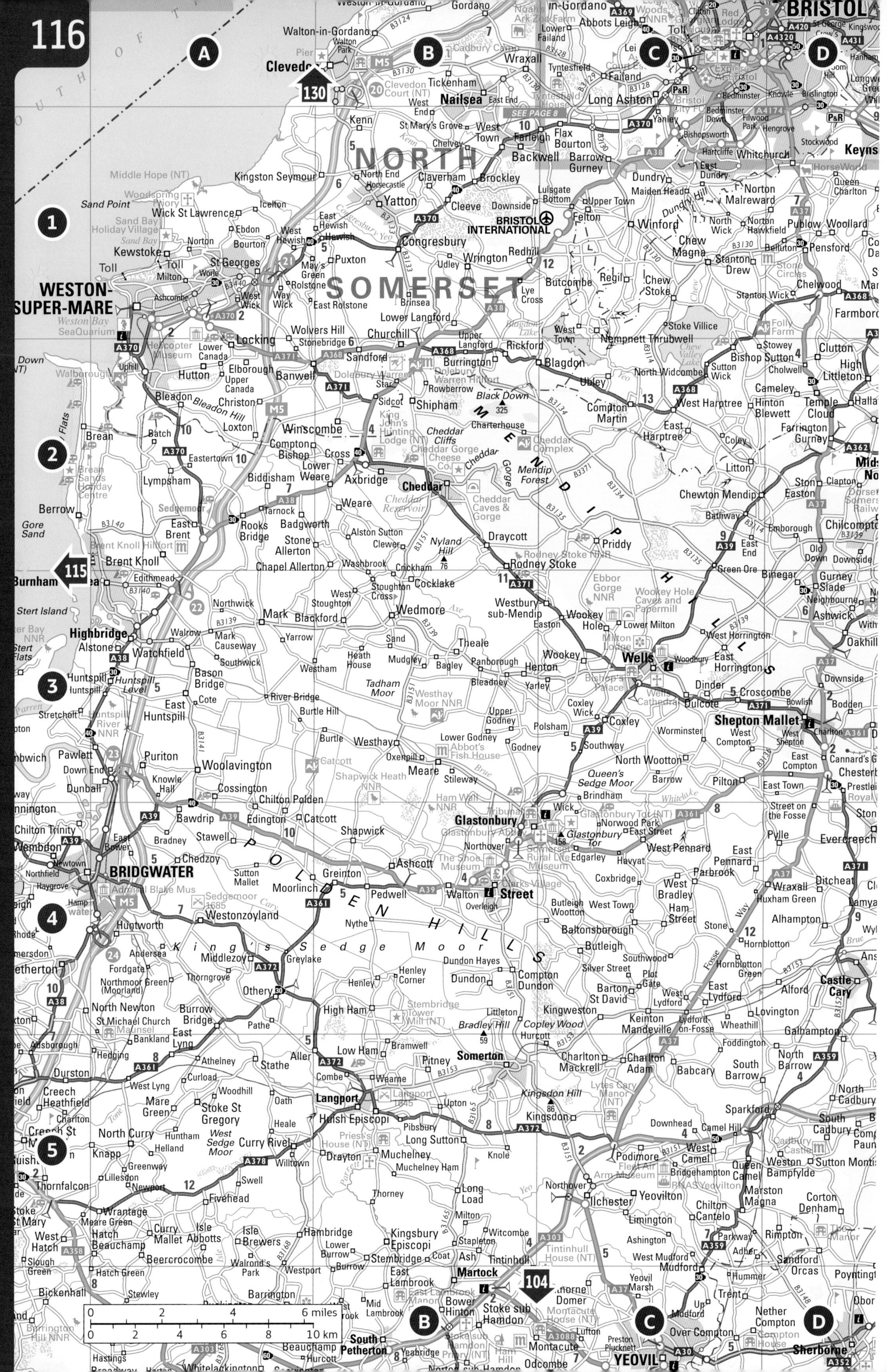

A
B
C
D
1
2
3
4
5
BRISTOL
Clevedon
130
Walton-in-Gordano
Gordano
Abbots Leigh
Wraxall
Tickenham
Nailsea
Long Ashton
Failand
Flax Bourton
Backwell
Barrow Gurney
Farleigh
West Town
Kenn
Bishopsworth
Whitchurch
Hartcliffe
Keynsham
Bedminster
Yanley
Hengrove
Stockwood
Brislington
Knowle
NORTH
SOMERSET
Kingston Seymour
Middle Hope (NT)
Woodspring Priory
Sand Point
Sand Bay Holiday Village
Sand Bay
Wick St Lawrence
Kewstoke
Toll
Milton
Worle
St Georges
Ashcombe
WESTON-SUPER-MARE
Weston Bay
SeaQuarium
Uphill
Walborough
Helicopter Museum
Locking
Hutton
Lower Canada
Upper Canada
Elborough
Banwell
Bleadon
Bleadon Hill
Christon
Loxton
Brean
Brean Sands Holiday Centre
Berrow
Gore Sand
Lympsham
Eastertown
Batch
Sedgemoor
East Brent
Brent Knoll
Brent Knoll Hillfort
Burnham
115
Stert Island
Edithmead
Highbridge
Alstone
Watchfield
Huntspill
Huntspill Level
East Huntspill
Huntspill River NNR
Stretcholt
Pawlett
Down End
Dunball
Puriton
Woolavington
Knowle Hall
Cossington
Chilton Polden
Bawdrip
Edington
Catcott
Chilton Trinity
Wembdon
BRIDGWATER
Admiral Blake Mus
Northfield
Haygrove
Hamp
Huntworth
Andersea
Fordgate
North Petherton
Northmoor Green (Moorland)
North Newton
St Michael Church
Maunsel
Bankland
Burrow Bridge
East Lyng
Hedging
Athelney
Durston
West Lyng
Creech Heathfield
Charlton
Creech St Michael
Mare Green
Stoke St Gregory
North Curry
Huntham
Helland
West Sedge Moor
Curry Rivel
Knapp
Greenway
Lillesdon
Newport
Thornfalcon
Wrantage
Meare Green
Hatch Beauchamp
West Hatch
Curry Mallet
Isle Abbotts
Isle Brewers
Beercrocombe
Walrond's Park
Hatch Green
Stewley
Slough Green
Bickenhall
Barrington
Westport
Fivehead
Swell
Hastings
Whitelackington
Barrington Hill NNR
Yatton
Claverham
Brockley
Cleeve
Congresbury
Puxton
Hewish
West Hewish
East Hewish
Icelton
Ebdon
Bourton
Norton
West Wick
Way Wick
May's Green
Rolstone
East Rolstone
Wrington
Udley
Redhill
Brinsea
Lower Langford
Churchill
Wolvers Hill
Stonebridge
Sandford
Upper Langford
Burrington
Dolebury Warren
Star
Rowberrow
Sidcot
Shipham
Winscombe
Compton Bishop
Cross
Axbridge
Lower Weare
Biddisham
Weare
Cheddar
Cheddar Cliffs
Cheddar Gorge
Cheddar Reservoir
Cheddar Caves & Gorge
Tarnock
Badgworth
Rooks Bridge
Stone Allerton
Alston Sutton
Clewer
Chapel Allerton
Washbrook
Nyland Hill
Draycott
Rodney Stoke
Rodney Stoke NNR
Crickham
Cocklake
Stoughton Cross
West Stoughton
Northwick
Mark
Blackford
Wedmore
Mark Causeway
Southwick
Yarrow
Sand
Theale
Westham
Heath House
Mudgley
Bagley
Panborough
Bason Bridge
Cote
River Bridge
Burtle Hill
Burtle
Tadham Moor
Westhay Moor NNR
Westhay
Catcott
Shapwick Heath NNR
Meare
Oxenpill
Abbot's Fish House
Stileway
Ham Wall NNR
Shapwick
Glastonbury
Glastonbury Abbey
Glastonbury Tor
Northover
Somerset Rural Life Museum
The Shoe Museum
Ashcott
Walton
Street
Overleigh
Clarks Village
Greinton
Moorlinch
Sutton Mallet
Pedwell
Stawell
Chedzoy
Bradney
East Bower
Sedgemoor 1685
Westonzoyland
Nythe
King's Sedge Moor
Middlezoy
Greylake
Thorngrove
Othery
Henley
Henley Corner
Dundon Hayes
Dundon
Compton Dundon
High Ham
Stembridge Tower Mill (NT)
Littleton
Bradley Hill
Pathe
Stathe
Aller
Low Ham
Bramwell
Pitney
Somerton
Combe
Wearne
Langport
Oath
Upton
Huish Episcopi
Heale
Pibsbury
Long Sutton
Priest's House (NT)
Drayton
Muchelney
Muchelney Ham
Wiltown
Thorney
Long Load
Knole
Kingsbury Episcopi
Hambridge
Lower Burrow
Burrow
Stembridge
Coat
Ash
Stapleton
Milton
Witcombe
Tintinhull
Tintinhull House (NT)
Martock
East Lambrook
East Lambrook Manor
Mid Lambrook
Bower Hinton
Stoke sub Hamdon
South Petherton
Yeabridge
Beauchamp
Hurcott
Montacute
Montacute House (NT)
Odcombe
104
Lufton
Preston Plucknett
YEOVIL
Over Compton
Nether Compton
Compton House
Sherborne
Trent
Mudford
Yeovil Marsh
West Mudford
Ashington
Limington
Yeovilton
Ilchester
Northover
Fleet Air Arm Museum
RNAS Yeovilton
Podimore
West Camel
Queen Camel
Bridgehampton
Downhead
Camel Hill
Sparkford
Kingsdon
Kingsdon Hill
Lytes Cary Manor (NT)
Charlton Mackrell
Charlton Adam
Babcary
Keinton Mandeville
Lydford-on-Fosse
Wheathill
Kingweston
Copley Wood
Hurcott
Barton St David
West Lydford
East Lydford
Butleigh
Butleigh Wootton
Silver Street
Southwood
Plot Gate
Baltonsborough
West Town
Coxbridge
Havyat
Edgarley
Chilton Cantelo
Marston Magna
Rimpton
Sandford Orcas
Corton Denham
Weston Bampfylde
Sutton Montis
South Cadbury
North Cadbury
Cadbury Castle
South Barrow
North Barrow
Lovington
Galhampton
Foddington
Alford
Castle Cary
Hornblotton
Hornblotton Green
Alhampton
Ditcheat
Wraxall
Huxham Green
Stone
West Bradley
Ham Street
East Pennard
Parbrook
West Pennard
East Street
Norwood Park
Glastonbury Tor (NT)
Brindham
Wick
Queen's Sedge Moor
Barrow
North Wootton
Worminster
Southway
Polsham
Godney
Upper Godney
Lower Godney
Bleadney
Yarley
Henton
Wookey
Coxley
Coxley Wick
Wells
Wells Cathedral
Bishop's Palace
Dulcote
Dinder
Croscombe
Shepton Mallet
West Compton
East Compton
Pilton
East Town
Street on the Fosse
Pylle
Evercreech
Chesterblade
Prestleigh
Cannard's Grave
Charlton
Bowlish
Bodden
Downside
Oakhill
Ashwick
Neighbourne
Gurney Slade
Binegar
Green Ore
East End
Old Down
Emborough
Chilcompton
Bathway
Chewton Mendip
Stone Easton
Clapton
Litton
Coley
East Harptree
West Harptree
Hinton Blewett
Temple Cloud
Farrington Gurney
Cameley
High Littleton
Clutton
Bishop Sutton
Sutton Wick
Cholwell
Stowey
North Widcombe
Chew Valley Lake
Nempnett Thrubwell
Stoke Villice
West Town
Blagdon
Blagdon Lake
Rickford
Ubley
Compton Martin
Black Down
MENDIP HILLS
Charterhouse
Mendip Forest
Cheddar Complex
Priddy
Ebbor Gorge NNR
Wookey Hole Caves and Papermill
Wookey Hole
Lower Milton
Milton Lodge
Easton
Westbury-sub-Mendip
West Horrington
East Horrington
Woodbury
BRISTOL INTERNATIONAL
Lulsgate Bottom
Felton
Upper Town
Downside
Butcombe
Lye Cross
Regil
Chew Stoke
Winford
Chew Magna
North Wick
Norton Hawkfield
Stanton Drew
Stanton Wick
Stone Circles
Belluton
Pensford
Publow
Woolard
Norton Malreward
Queen Charlton
Dundry
Maiden Head
East Dundry
Chelwood
Farmborough
Folly Farm
POLDEN HILLS
6 miles
10 km

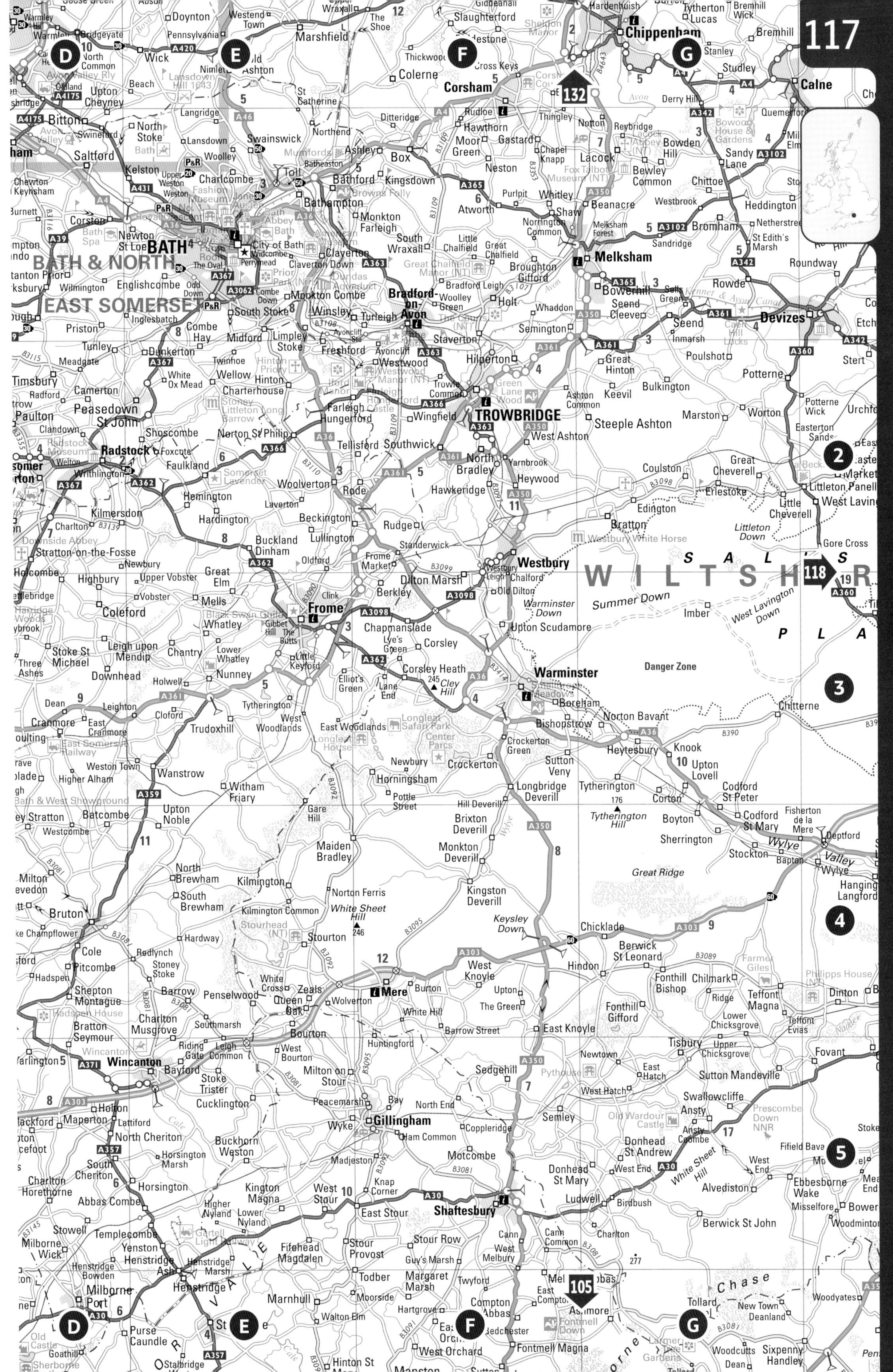

Chippenham
Calne
Corsham
Marshfield
Colerne
Box
Wick
Bitton
Saltford
Kelston
Charlcombe
Swainswick
Batheaston
Bathford
Bathampton
Bath
BATH
BATH & NORTH EAST SOMERSET
Englishcombe
Combe Hay
South Stoke
Monkton Combe
Winsley
Bradford-on-Avon
Limpley Stoke
Freshford
Westwood
Holt
Atworth
Melksham
Lacock
Bowerhill
Seend
Devizes
Semington
Hilperton
TROWBRIDGE
North Bradley
Steeple Ashton
Keevil
Edington
Westbury
Dilton Marsh
Frome
Rode
Beckington
Radstock
Paulton
Peasedown St John
Timsbury
Midford
Dunkerton
Norton St Philip
Farleigh Hungerford
Southwick
Mells
Coleford
Nunney
Chapmanslade
Corsley Heath
Warminster
Upton Scudamore
Imber
W I L T S H I R E
SALISBURY PLAIN
Danger Zone
Bishopstrow
Heytesbury
Codford St Mary
Longbridge Deverill
Horningsham
Wanstrow
Witham Friary
Bruton
Maiden Bradley
Kilmington
Stourton
Mere
Zeals
Wincanton
Hindon
Chicklade
Tisbury
Fovant
Semley
Gillingham
Motcombe
Shaftesbury
Milborne Port
Henstridge
Stalbridge
Marnhull
Fontmell Magna
Ashmore
Tollard Royal
Cranborne Chase
132
105
118
D
E
F
G
2
3
4
5

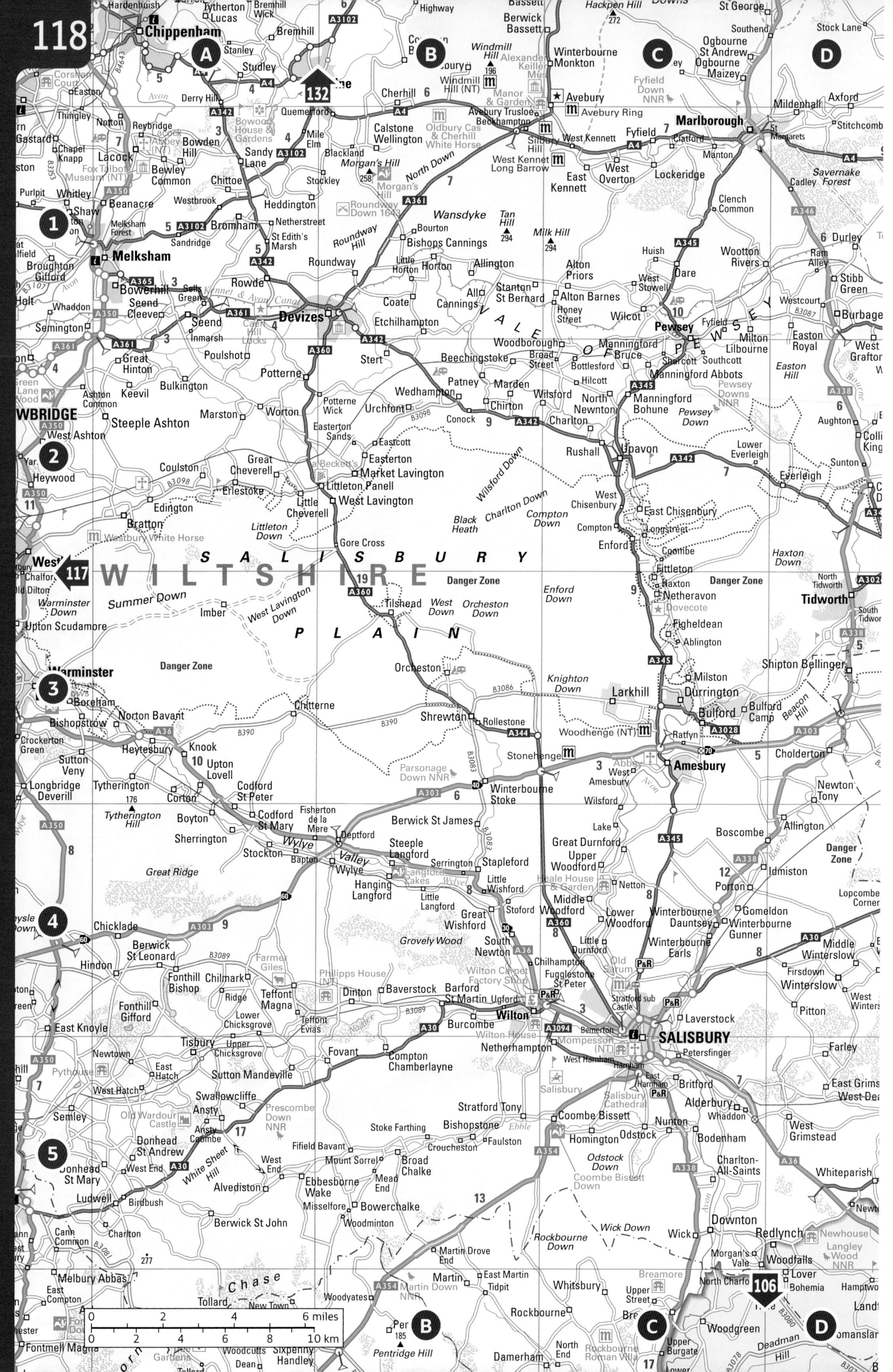
Chippenham
Hardenhuish
Tytherton Lucas
Bremhill Wick
Bremhill
Highway
Berwick Bassett
Hackpen Hill
272
St George
Southend
Stock Lane
Stanley
Studley
Derry Hill
Windmill Hill
196
Alexander Keiller Mus
Winterbourne Monkton
Ogbourne St Andrew
Ogbourne Maizey
Fyfield Down NNR
Corsham Court
Easton
Thingley
Notton
Reybridge
Lacock Abbey (NT)
Bowden Hill
Bowood House & Gardens
Quemerford
Cherhill
Calstone Wellington
Oldbury Cas & Cherhill White Horse
Manor & Garden
Avebury
Avebury Ring
Avebury Trusloe
Beckhampton
Silbury Hill
West Kennett
Fyfield
Marlborough
Clatford
Mildenhall
Axford
Stitchcombe
St Margarets
Manton
Gastard
Chapel Knapp
Lacock
Fox Talbot Museum (NT)
Bewley Common
Sandy Lane
Mile Elm
Blackland
Morgan's Hill
258
North Down
West Kennet Long Barrow
East Kennett
West Overton
Lockeridge
Savernake Forest
Cadley
Purlpit
Whitley
Shaw
Beanacre
Chittoe
Westbrook
Stockley
Heddington
Roundway Down 1643
Clench Common
Melksham Forest
Bromham
Netherstreet
St Edith's Marsh
Wansdyke
Tan Hill
294
Milk Hill
294
Durley
Melksham
Sandridge
Roundway Hill
Bourton
Bishops Cannings
Huish
Wootton Rivers
Ram Alley
Broughton Gifford
Holt
Whaddon
Bowerhill
Sells Green
Seend Cleeve
Kennet & Avon Canal
Rowde
Roundway
Little Horton
Horton
Allington
Alton Priors
Alton Barnes
Stanton St Bernard
All Cannings
West Stowell
Oare
Stibb Green
Semington
Seend
Inmarsh
Caen Hill Locks
Devizes
Coate
Etchilhampton
Honey Street
Wilcot
Pewsey
Fyfield
Westcourt
Burbage
Milton Lilbourne
Easton Royal
West Grafton
Great Hinton
Poulshot
Stert
Beechingstoke
Broad Street
Woodborough
Manningford Bruce
Bottlesford
Sharcott
Southcott
Manningford Abbots
Easton Hill
Vale of Pewsey
Green Lane Wood
Ashton Common
Keevil
Bulkington
Potterne
Patney
Marden
Hilcott
Pewsey Downs NNR
Wedhampton
Chirton
Wilsford
North Newnton
Manningford Bohune
Pewsey Down
Aughton
Collingbourne Kingston
Trowbridge
West Ashton
Steeple Ashton
Marston
Worton
Potterne Wick
Urchfont
Conock
Charlton
Easterton Sands
Eastcott
Rushall
Upavon
Lower Everleigh
Sunton
Yarnbrook
Heywood
Coulston
Great Cheverell
Erlestoke
a Beckett's
Easterton
Market Lavington
Littleton Panell
Little Cheverell
West Lavington
Wilsford Down
Charlton Down
West Chisenbury
East Chisenbury
Everleigh
Edington
Bratton
Westbury White Horse
Littleton Down
Gore Cross
Black Heath
Compton Down
Compton
Longstreet
Enford
Coombe
Haxton Down
Westbury
Chalford
Old Dilton
117
Salisbury Plain
Wiltshire
Danger Zone
Fittleton
Haxton
Netheravon
North Tidworth
Tidworth
South Tidworth
Warminster Down
Summer Down
Imber
West Lavington Down
Tilshead
West Down
Orcheston Down
Enford Down
Dovecote
Upton Scudamore
Figheldean
Ablington
Warminster
Boreham
Orcheston
Knighton Down
Milston
Shipton Bellinger
Larkhill
Durrington
Bulford
Bulford Camp
Beacon Hill
Norton Bavant
Bishopstrow
Chitterne
Shrewton
Rollestone
Woodhenge (NT)
Crockerton Green
Heytesbury
Knook
Upton Lovell
Ratfyn
Stonehenge
Abbey
West Amesbury
Amesbury
Cholderton
Sutton Veny
Longbridge Deverill
Tytherington
Corton
Codford St Peter
Parsonage Down NNR
Winterbourne Stoke
Wilsford
Newton Tony
Tytherington Hill
176
Boyton
Codford St Mary
Fisherton de la Mere
Berwick St James
Lake
Allington
Boscombe
Sherrington
Deptford
Wylye Valley
Stockton
Bapton
Wylye
Steeple Langford
Serrington
Stapleford
Great Durnford
Upper Woodford
Danger Zone
Idmiston
Great Ridge
Hanging Langford
Langford Lakes
Little Wishford
Heale House & Garden
Netton
Porton
Lopcombe Corner
Little Langford
Stoford
Middle Woodford
Lower Woodford
Winterbourne Dauntsey
Gomeldon
Winterbourne Gunner
Deverill Down
Chicklade
Great Wishford
Grovely Wood
South Newton
Little Durnford
Winterbourne Earls
Middle Winterslow
Berwick St Leonard
Hindon
Farmer Giles
Philipps House (NT)
Wilton Carpet Factory Shop
Chilhampton
Fugglestone St Peter
Old Sarum
Firsdown
Winterslow
Fonthill Bishop
Chilmark
Ridge
Teffont Magna
Dinton
Baverstock
Barford St Martin
Ugford
Wilton
Stratford sub Castle
Laverstock
West Winterslow
Pitton
Fonthill Gifford
East Knoyle
Lower Chicksgrove
Teffont Evias
Burcombe
Wilton House
Bemerton
Salisbury
Netherhampton
Mompesson (NT)
Petersfinger
Farley
Newtown
Tisbury
Upper Chicksgrove
Fovant
Compton Chamberlayne
West Harnham
Harnham
East Harnham
Britford
East Grimstead
West Dean
Pythouse
East Hatch
Sutton Mandeville
West Hatch
Swallowcliffe
Salisbury Cathedral
Alderbury
Whaddon
Semley
Old Wardour Castle
Ansty
Prescombe Down NNR
Stratford Tony
Coombe Bissett
Nunton
West Grimstead
Ansty Coombe
Stoke Farthing
Bishopstone
Ebble
Faulston
Croucheston
Homington
Odstock
Bodenham
Donhead St Andrew
White Sheet Hill
West End
Fifield Bavant
Mount Sorrel
Broad Chalke
Odstock Down
Coombe Bissett Down
Charlton-All-Saints
Whiteparish
Donhead St Mary
West End
Alvediston
Ebbesborne Wake
Mead End
Ludwell
Birdbush
Misselfore
Bowerchalke
Woodminton
Wick Down
Downton
Newhouse
Cann Common
Charlton
Berwick St John
Rockbourne Down
Wick
Redlynch
Langley Wood NNR
277
Martin Drove End
Morgan's Vale
Woodfalls
Melbury Abbas
Cranborne Chase
Martin
Martin Down NNR
East Martin
Tidpit
Whitsbury
Breamore
North Charford
106
Lover
Bohemia
Hamptworth
Landford
East Compton
Tollard Royal
New Town
Woodyates
Upper Street
Rockbourne
Woodgreen
Fontmell Magna
Pentridge Hill
185
Woodcutts
Sixpenny Handley
Dean
Gardens
Damerham
North End
Rockbourne Roman Villa
Upper Burgate
Deadman Hill
Nomansland
0 2 4 6 miles
0 2 4 6 8 10 km

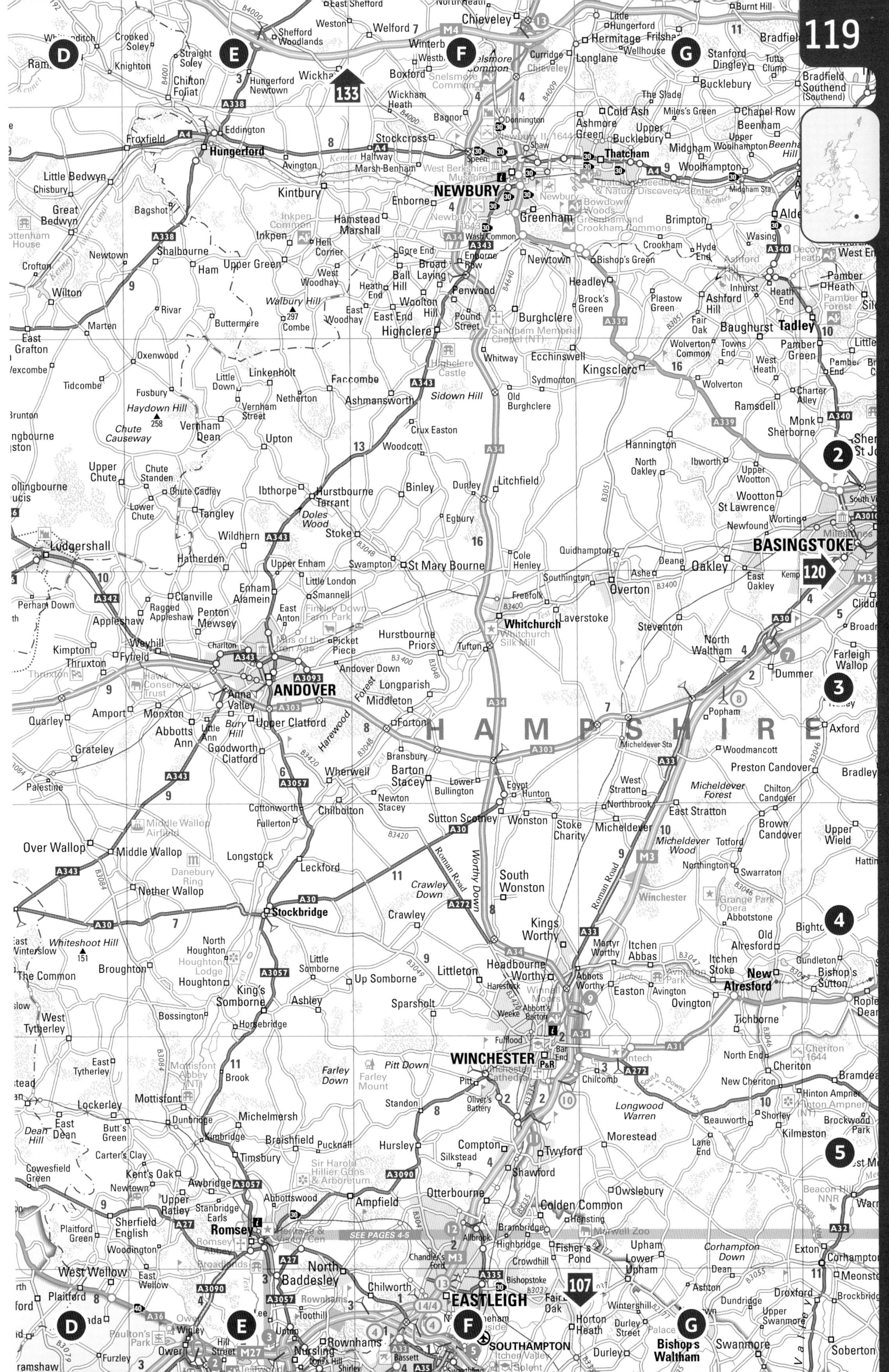
NEWBURY
ANDOVER
BASINGSTOKE
WINCHESTER
EASTLEIGH
SOUTHAMPTON
Hungerford
Thatcham
Tadley
Whitchurch
Stockbridge
Romsey
New Alresford
Bishop's Waltham
HAMPSHIRE
133
120
107
SEE PAGES 4-5

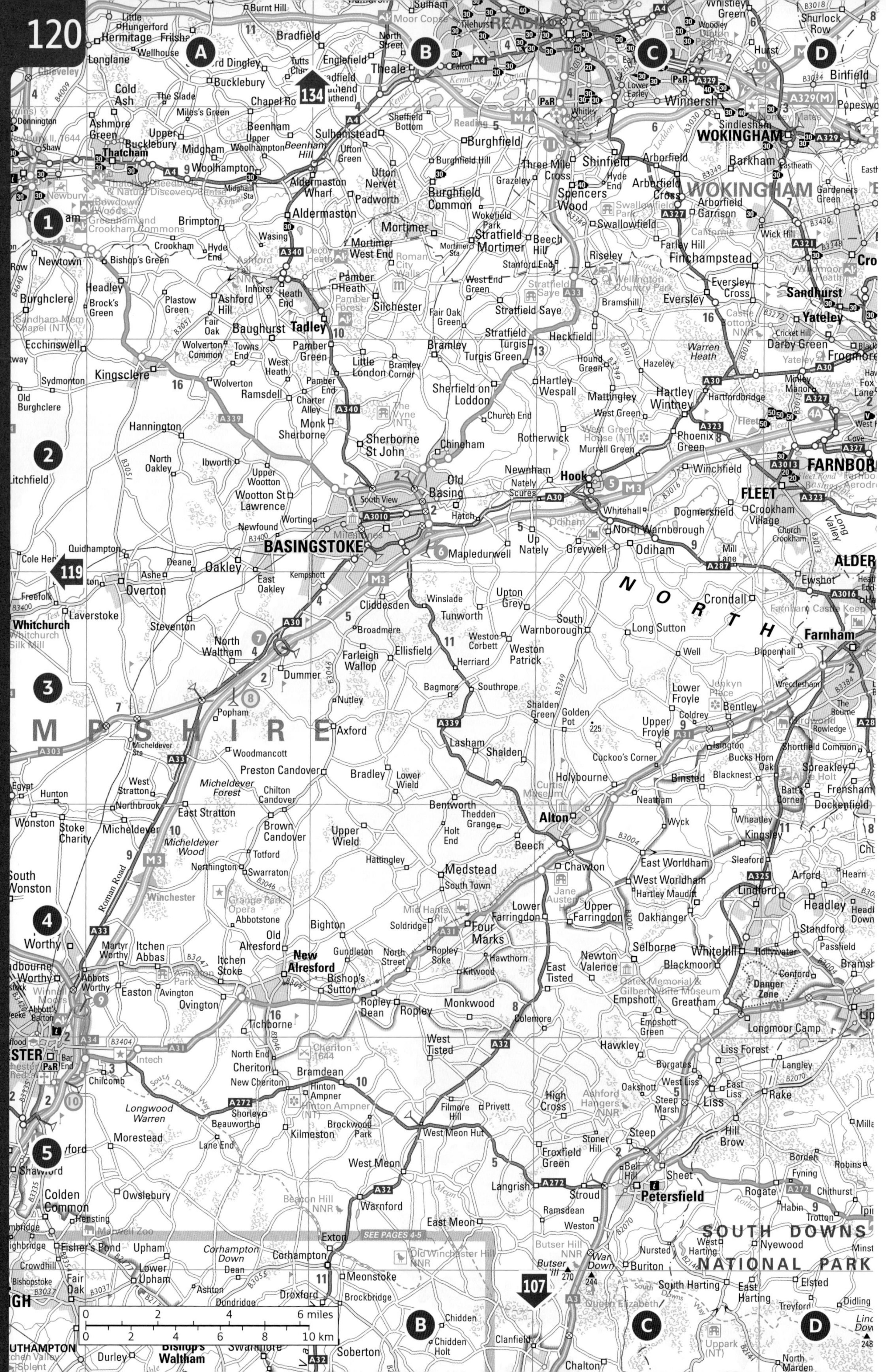
A
B
C
D
1
2
3
4
5
134
119
107
Hermitage
Little Hungerford
Frilsham
Longlane
Wellhouse
Burnt Hill
Bradfield
Bucklebury
Cold Ash
The Slade
Miles's Green
Chapel Row
Tutts Clump
Englefield
North Street
Theale
Sulham
Moor Copse
Tilehurst
Calcot
READING
Woodley
Whistley Green
Shurlock Row
Hurst
Binfield
Lower Earley
Winnersh
Sindlesham
WOKINGHAM
Whitley
Shinfield
Three Mile Cross
Spencers Wood
Arborfield
Arborfield Cross
Arborfield Garrison
Barkham
Eastheath
Gardeners Green
Swallowfield
Burghfield
Burghfield Hill
Burghfield Common
Grazeley
Sheffield Bottom
Sulhamstead
Ufton Green
Ufton Nervet
Padworth
Beenham
Upper Woolhampton
Beenham Hill
Woolhampton
Midgham
Upper Bucklebury
Bucklebury
Thatcham
Ashmore Green
Donnington
Newbury
Aldermaston Wharf
Aldermaston
Brimpton
Wasing
Crookham
Hyde End
Bishop's Green
Newtown
Greenham and Crookham Commons
Bowdown Woods
Mortimer
Mortimer West End
Stratfield Mortimer
Wokefield Park
Beech Hill
Riseley
Stanford End
Farley Hill
Finchampstead
California
Wick Hill
Nine Mile Ride
Sandhurst
Crowthorne
Eversley Cross
Eversley
Castle Bottom NNR
Yateley
Cricket Hill
Darby Green
Frogmore
Wellington Country Park
Bramshill
Stratfield Saye
Heckfield
Hound Green
Hazeley
Mattingley
Hartley Wintney
Hartfordbridge
Minley Manor
West Green
West Green House (NT)
Murrell Green
Phoenix Green
Winchfield
FLEET
Crookham Village
Church Crookham
FARNBOROUGH
Hook
Newnham
Nately Scures
Rotherwick
Hartley Wespall
Stratfield Turgis
Turgis Green
Bramley
Bramley Corner
Little London
Sherfield on Loddon
Church End
Chineham
Old Basing
Silchester
Pamber Heath
Pamber End
Pamber Green
Pamber Forest
Tadley
Baughurst
Heath End
Inhurst
Ashford Hill
Plastow Green
Headley
Brock's Green
Burghclere
Sandham Mem Chapel (NT)
Ecchinswell
Kingsclere
Sydmonton
Old Burghclere
Wolverton Common
Towns End
Wolverton
West Heath
Ramsdell
Charter Alley
Monk Sherborne
Sherborne St John
The Vyne (NT)
Hannington
North Oakley
Ibworth
Upper Wootton
Wootton St Lawrence
South View
BASINGSTOKE
Worting
Newfound
Quidhampton
Deane
Oakley
East Oakley
Kempshott
Cole Henley
Ashe
Overton
Freefolk
Laverstoke
Whitchurch
Whitchurch Silk Mill
Litchfield
Steventon
North Waltham
Dummer
Cliddesden
Broadmere
Farleigh Wallop
Ellisfield
Winslade
Tunworth
Upton Grey
Weston Corbett
Weston Patrick
Herriard
South Warnborough
Mapledurwell
Hatch
Up Nately
Greywell
Odiham
North Warnborough
Whitehall
Dogmersfield
Mill Lane
ALDERSHOT
Ewshot
Crondall
Farnham Castle Keep
Long Sutton
Well
Dippenhall
Farnham
Wrecclesham
Lower Froyle
Upper Froyle
Coldrey
Bentley
Jenkyn Place
The Bourne
Rowledge
Shortfield Common
Spreakley
Alice Holt
Frensham
Batt's Corner
Dockenfield
Isington
Bucks Horn Oak
Blacknest
Binsted
Neatham
Wyck
Wheatley
Kingsley
NORTH
HAMPSHIRE
Popham
Micheldever Sta
Woodmancott
Axford
Preston Candover
Chilton Candover
Bradley
Lower Wield
Upper Wield
Nutley
Bagmore
Southrope
Lasham
Shalden
Shalden Green
Golden Pot
Cuckoo's Corner
Holybourne
Curtis Museum
Alton
Bentworth
Thedden Grange
Holt End
Beech
Chawton
Jane Austen's House
East Worldham
West Worldham
Hartley Mauditt
Sleaford
Lindford
Arford
Headley
Headley Down
Standford
Passfield
Bramshott
Whitehill
Hollywater
Conford
Danger Zone
Blackmoor
Greatham
Longmoor Camp
Liphook
Oakhanger
Selborne
Newton Valence
Gilbert White Museum
Oates Memorial
Empshott
Empshott Green
Upper Farringdon
Lower Farringdon
East Tisted
Medstead
South Town
Mid Hants Rly
Four Marks
Soldridge
Hawthorn
Kitwood
Ropley Soke
Ropley
Ropley Dean
Monkwood
Colemore
Hattingley
Brown Candover
Totford
Northington
Swarraton
Grange Park Opera
Abbotstone
Bighton
Old Alresford
Gundleton
North Street
New Alresford
Bishop's Sutton
Itchen Stoke
Itchen Abbas
Martyr Worthy
Avington Park
Avington
Easton
Ovington
Tichborne
Micheldever
Micheldever Forest
Micheldever Wood
East Stratton
Northbrook
West Stratton
Hunton
Egypt
Stoke Charity
Wonston
South Wonston
Worthy
Headbourne Worthy
Kings Worthy
Abbots Worthy
Winnall Moors
Abbott's Barton
Winchester
WINCHESTER
Intech
Chilcomb
Roman Road
South Downs Way
Longwood Warren
Morestead
Cheriton 1644
North End
Cheriton
New Cheriton
Bramdean
Hinton Ampner
Hinton Ampner (NT)
Shorley
Beauworth
Kilmeston
Brockwood Park
Lane End
Owslebury
Shawford
Colden Common
Hensting
Marwell Zoo
Fisher's Pond
Upham
Lower Upham
Crowdhill
Bishopstoke
Fair Oak
Corhampton Down
Dean
Corhampton
Ashton
Droxford
Exton
Meonstoke
Brockbridge
Old Winchester Hill NNR
Beacon Hill NNR
Warnford
West Meon
West Meon Hut
Filmore Hill
Privett
West Tisted
East Meon
Langrish
High Cross
Ashford Hangers NNR
Stoner Hill
Froxfield Green
Steep
Bell Hill
Stroud
Petersfield
Sheet
Ramsdean
Weston
Butser Hill NNR
Butser Hill
War Down
Buriton
Nursted
Queen Elizabeth
South Harting
West Harting
East Harting
Nyewood
Elsted
Didling
Treyford
Uppark (NT)
North Marden
Chalton
Clanfield
Chidden
Chidden Holt
Soberton
Swanmore
Bishop's Waltham
Durley
SOUTHAMPTON
Itchen Valley
Hawkley
Liss Forest
Burgates
Liss
West Liss
East Liss
Steep Marsh
Oakshott
Langley
Rake
Hill Brow
Milland
Borden
Robins
Fyning
Rogate
Chithurst
Habin
Trotton
SOUTH DOWNS NATIONAL PARK
SEE PAGES 4-5
0 2 4 6 miles
0 2 4 6 8 10 km

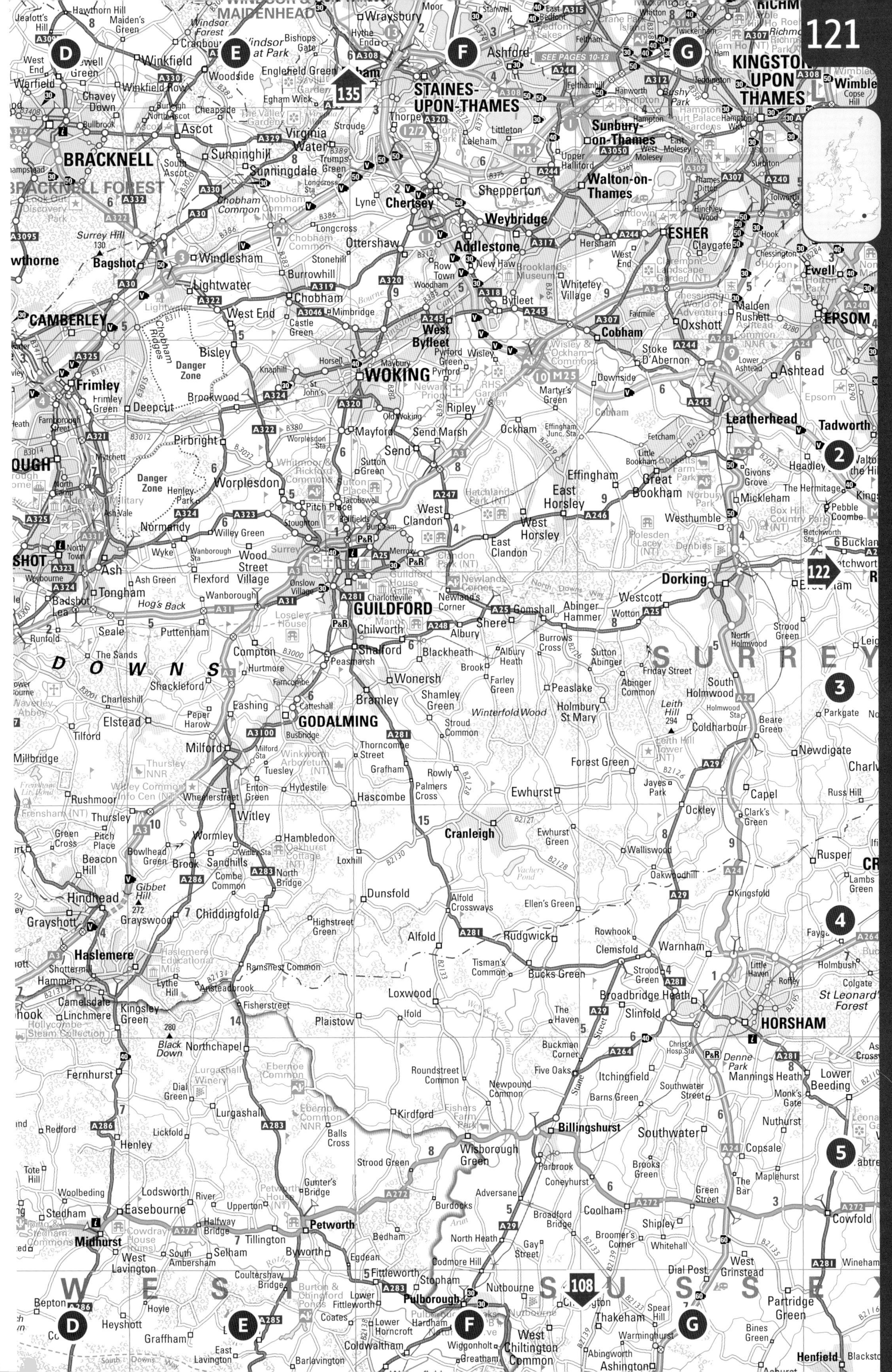
SEE PAGES 10-13
135
122
108
KINGSTON UPON THAMES
STAINES-UPON-THAMES
BRACKNELL
BRACKNELL FOREST
Winkfield
Ascot
Sunninghill
Sunningdale
Virginia Water
Egham Wick
Englefield Green
Windsor Great Park
Wraysbury
Ashford
Feltham
Twickenham
Sunbury-on-Thames
Walton-on-Thames
Shepperton
Chertsey
Weybridge
Addlestone
ESHER
Claygate
Ewell
EPSOM
Bagshot
Windlesham
Lightwater
CAMBERLEY
Frimley
Deepcut
Chobham
West End
Bisley
WOKING
West Byfleet
Byfleet
Cobham
Oxshott
Ashtead
Leatherhead
Tadworth
Pirbright
Worplesdon
Ripley
Send
Ockham
Effingham
Great Bookham
East Horsley
West Horsley
West Clandon
East Clandon
GUILDFORD
Chilworth
Shalford
Shere
Gomshall
Abinger Hammer
Westcott
Dorking
Ash
Tongham
Hog's Back
Seale
Puttenham
Compton
DOWNS
SURREY
GODALMING
Milford
Elstead
Bramley
Wonersh
Cranleigh
Ewhurst
Holmbury St Mary
Leith Hill
Capel
Ockley
Newdigate
Hindhead
Grayshott
Haslemere
Witley
Chiddingfold
Dunsfold
Alfold
Rudgwick
Warnham
Loxwood
Slinfold
HORSHAM
Billingshurst
Southwater
Kirdford
Wisborough Green
Petworth
Midhurst
Easebourne
Pulborough
Storrington
West Chiltington Common
Thakeham
Cowfold
Henfield
WEST SUSSEX

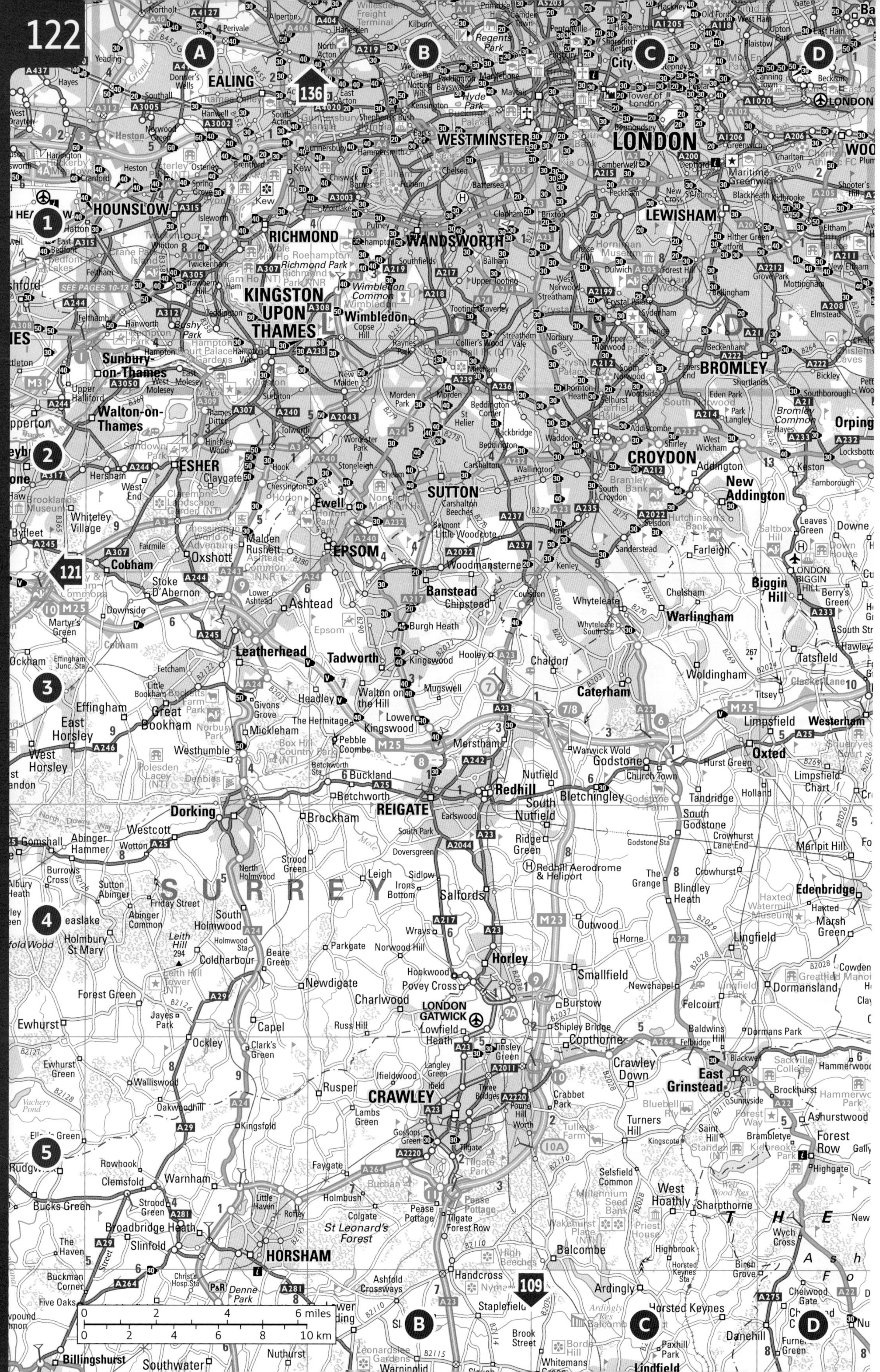
A
B
C
D
136
EALING
LONDON
City
WESTMINSTER
Regents Park
Hyde Park
HOUNSLOW
RICHMOND
WANDSWORTH
LEWISHAM
KINGSTON UPON THAMES
Wimbledon
BROMLEY
CROYDON
SUTTON
EPSOM
ESHER
Sunbury-on-Thames
Walton-on-Thames
Cobham
121
Oxshott
Leatherhead
Ashtead
Banstead
Tadworth
Caterham
Warlingham
Biggin Hill
New Addington
Oxted
Westerham
Godstone
Redhill
REIGATE
Dorking
Bletchingley
Great Bookham
East Horsley
West Horsley
SURREY
Salfords
Horley
LONDON GATWICK
CRAWLEY
Crawley Down
East Grinstead
Edenbridge
Lingfield
Dormansland
HORSHAM
Broadbridge Heath
Slinfold
Billingshurst
Southwater
Nuthurst
Handcross
Staplefield
Balcombe
Ardingly
West Hoathly
Forest Row
Horsted Keynes
Danehill
Lindfield
109
Ockley
Capel
Warnham
Rusper
Faygate
Pease Pottage
St Leonard's Forest
Lowfield Heath
Charlwood
Newdigate
Coldharbour
Ewhurst
Forest Green
SEE PAGES 10-13
0 2 4 6 miles
0 2 4 6 8 10 km

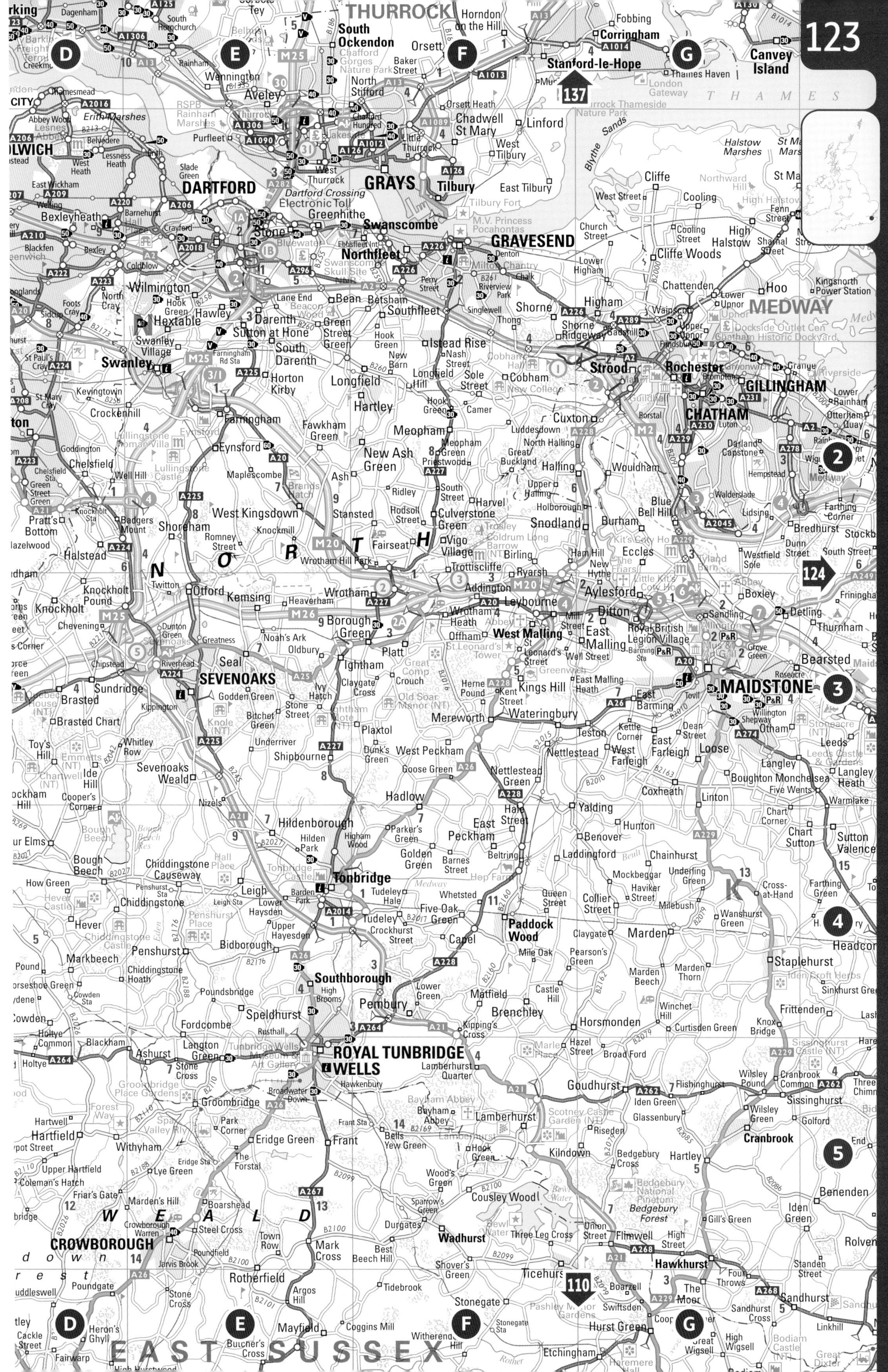
THURROCK
South Ockendon
Orsett
Horndon on the Hill
Fobbing
Corringham
Stanford-le-Hope
Canvey Island
Thames Haven
London Gateway
THAMES
137
Dagenham
Rainham
Wennington
Aveley
Purfleet
North Stifford
Chadwell St Mary
Linford
West Tilbury
East Tilbury
Tilbury
GRAYS
West Thurrock
Erith Marshes
Belvedere
Lessness Heath
Slade Green
DARTFORD
Dartford Crossing
Bexleyheath
Crayford
Stone
Greenhithe
Swanscombe
Northfleet
GRAVESEND
Denton
Cliffe
Cooling
High Halstow
Cliffe Woods
Chattenden
Hoo
MEDWAY
Higham
Shorne
Strood
Rochester
GILLINGHAM
CHATHAM
Wilmington
Hextable
Hawley
Darenth
Sutton at Hone
South Darenth
Swanley
Southfleet
Betsham
Longfield
Hartley
Istead Rise
Cobham
Sole Street
Farningham
Eynsford
Crockenhill
Horton Kirby
Fawkham Green
Meopham
New Ash Green
Cuxton
Luddesdown
Halling
Wouldham
Borstal
Chelsfield
Shoreham
West Kingsdown
Stansted
Culverstone Green
Vigo Village
Trottiscliffe
Snodland
Burham
Eccles
Blue Bell Hill
Halstead
Knockholt
Otford
Kemsing
Wrotham
Borough Green
Addington
Leybourne
West Malling
Ditton
Aylesford
Larkfield
Boxley
Detling
Bearsted
MAIDSTONE
124
SEVENOAKS
Seal
Riverhead
Sundridge
Brasted
Ightham
Platt
Kings Hill
East Malling
Wateringbury
Mereworth
Teston
Barming
Loose
Coxheath
Linton
Otham
Leeds
Langley
Sevenoaks Weald
Shipbourne
Plaxtol
West Peckham
Hadlow
East Peckham
Yalding
Hunton
Hildenborough
Tonbridge
Leigh
Chiddingstone
Penshurst
Tudeley
Five Oak Green
Capel
Paddock Wood
Marden
Staplehurst
Southborough
Pembury
Matfield
Brenchley
Horsmonden
Goudhurst
Lamberhurst
ROYAL TUNBRIDGE WELLS
Groombridge
Speldhurst
Langton Green
Frant
Eridge Green
Hartfield
Withyham
Rotherfield
Mark Cross
Wadhurst
Ticehurst
Stonegate
Mayfield
Flimwell
Hawkhurst
Cranbrook
Sissinghurst
Benenden
Sandhurst
Hurst Green
Etchingham
CROWBOROUGH
WEALD
EAST SUSSEX
110

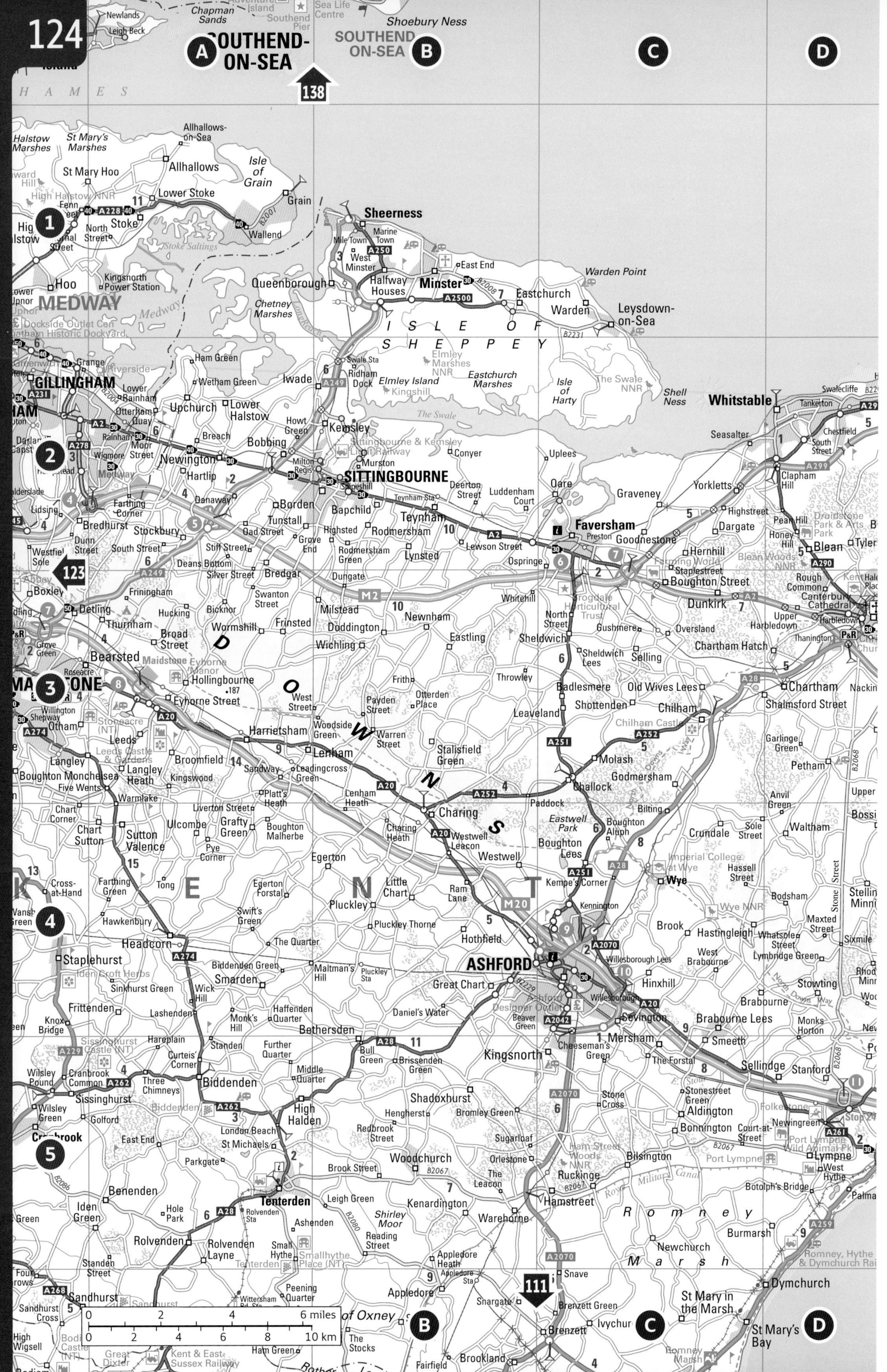

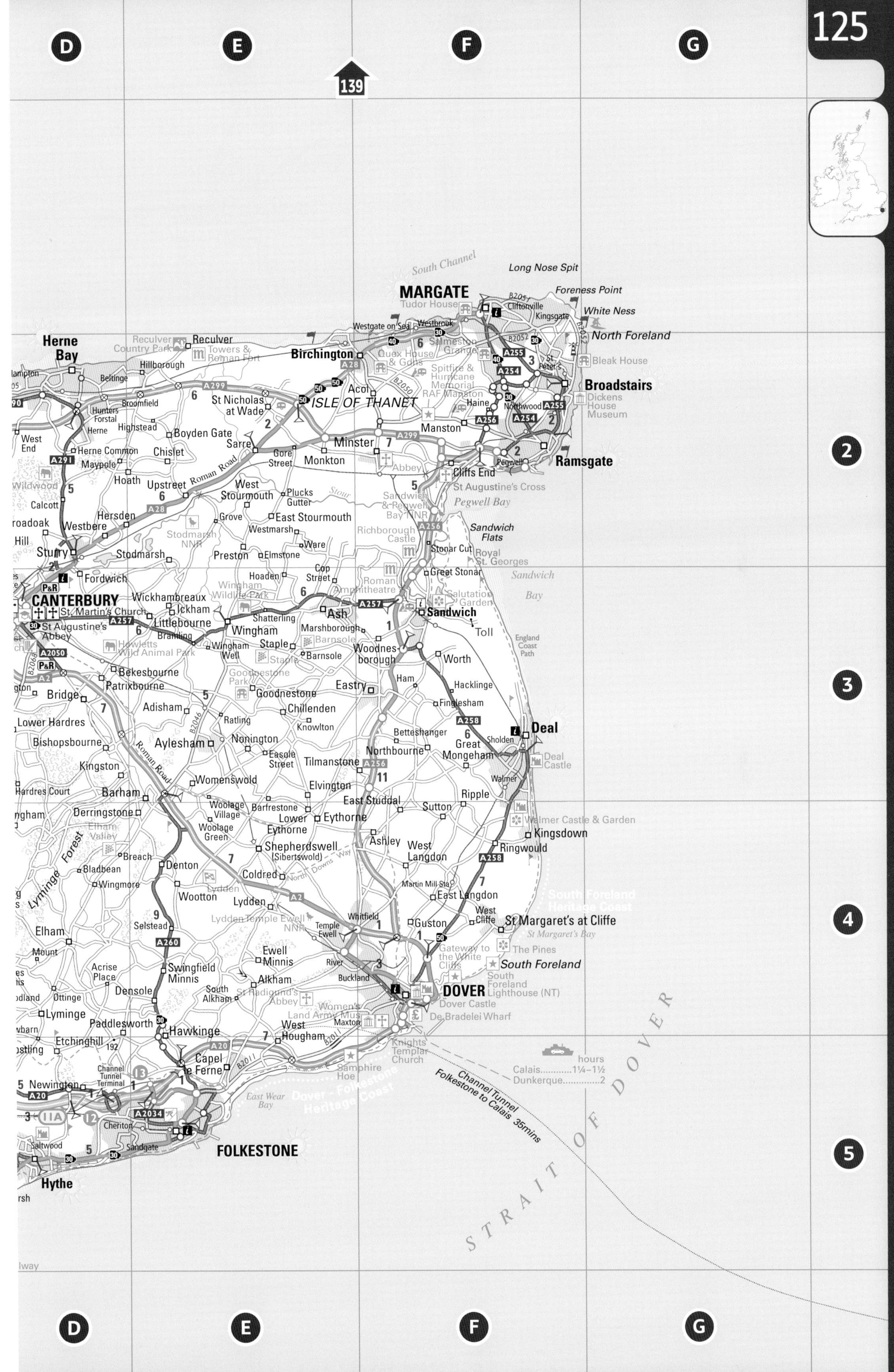

D E F G

139

MARGATE

South Channel
Long Nose Spit
Foreness Point
White Ness
North Foreland

Tudor House
Westgate on Sea Westbrook
B2052 Cliftonville
Kingsgate
Salmestone Grange
Birchington
Quex House & Gdns
Spitfire & Hurricane Memorial
RAF Manston
Haine
Northwood
Broadstairs
Dickens House Museum
Bleak House
St Peter's

Herne Bay
Reculver Country Park
Reculver Towers & Roman Fort
Hillborough
Beltinge
Broomfield
Hunters Forstal
Herne
Highstead
Herne Common
Maypole
Hoath
Upstreet
Chislet
Boyden Gate
Sarre
Gore Street
Monkton
Minster
Manston
Abbey
Cliffs End
Pegwell
Ramsgate
St Augustine's Cross

ISLE OF THANET
Acol
St Nicholas at Wade

West End
Hampton
Calcott
Westbere
Hersden
Broadoak
Hill
Sturry
Stodmarsh
Fordwich
West Stourmouth
East Stourmouth
Plucks Gutter
Grove
Westmarsh
Ware
Preston
Elmstone
Cop Street
Hoaden
Stodmarsh NNR
Wingham Wildlife Park
Roman Amphitheatre
Sandwich & Pegwell Bay NNR
Pegwell Bay
Sandwich Flats
Richborough Castle
Stonar Cut
Great Stonar
Sandwich Bay
Royal St Georges

CANTERBURY
St Martin's Church
St Augustine's Abbey
Howletts Wild Animal Park
Wickhambreaux
Ickham
Littlebourne
Bramling
Wingham
Wingham Well
Staple
Staple
Goodnestone Park
Ash
Shatterling
Marshborough
Barnsole
Barnsole
Woodnesborough
Sandwich
Salutation Garden
Toll
England Coast Path

Bridge
Bekesbourne
Patrixbourne
Lower Hardres
Bishopsbourne
Adisham
Ratling
Nonington
Knowlton
Goodnestone
Chillenden
Eastry
Ham
Worth
Hacklinge
Findlesham
Bettesbanger
Northbourne
Great Mongeham
Sholden
Deal
Deal Castle

Kingston
Barham
Derringstone
Aylesham
Easole Street
Tilmanstone
Northbourne
Elvington
Walmer

Hardres Court
Elham Valley
Lyminge Forest
Womenswold
Woolage Village
Woolage Green
Barfrestone
Lower Eythorne
Eythorne
East Studdal
Sutton
Ripple
Kingsdown
Ringwould
Walmer Castle & Garden

Breach
Bladbean
Wingmore
Denton
Shepherdswell (Sibertswold)
Ashley
West Langdon
Martin Mill Sta
East Langdon
St Margaret's at Cliffe
South Foreland Heritage Coast

Elham
Mount
Acrise Place
Densole
Wootton
Lydden
Coldred
North Downs Way
West Cliffe
Guston
Whitfield
St Margaret's Bay
Gateway to the White Cliffs
The Pines
South Foreland
South Foreland Lighthouse (NT)

Lyminge
Paddlesworth
Swingfield Minnis
Selstead
Lydden Temple Ewell NNR
Temple Ewell
Ewell Minnis
River
Alkham
South Alkham
St Radigund's Abbey
Buckland
Maxton
Dover
Dover Castle
De Bradelei Wharf
Women's Land Army Mus

Etchinghill
Hawkinge
Capel le Ferne
Channel Tunnel Terminal
Cheriton
Sandgate
Saltwood
Folkestone
West Hougham
Knights Templar Church
Samphire Hoe
Dover - Folkestone Heritage Coast
East Wear Bay

Hythe
Newington
Marsh
ilway

STRAIT OF DOVER

Calais.............1¼–1½ hours
Dunkerque..............2

Channel Tunnel
Folkestone to Calais 35mins

A299 A28 A291 A2050 A257 A256 A255 A254 A258 A260 A2034 A20 A2 A291 B2050 B2052 B2205 B2046 B2011 B206

2

3

4

5

D E F G

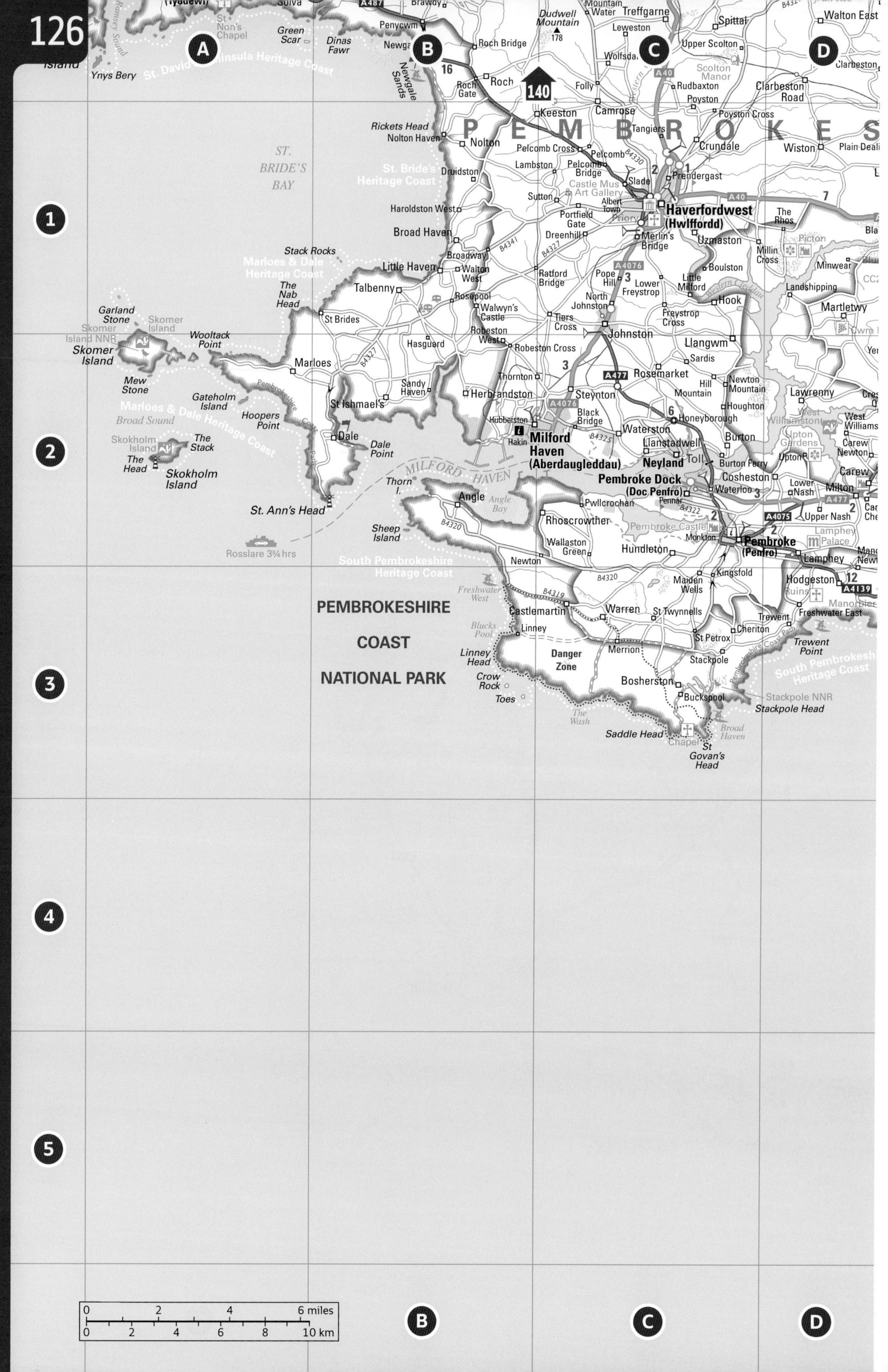

PEMBROKESHIRE
COAST
NATIONAL PARK

St. David's Peninsula Heritage Coast

ST.
BRIDE'S
BAY

St. Bride's
Heritage Coast

Marloes & Dale
Heritage Coast

Marloes & Dale Heritage Coast

Broad Sound

South Pembrokeshire
Heritage Coast

South Pembrokeshire
Heritage Coast

MILFORD HAVEN

Ynys Bery
Island
St Non's Chapel
Green Scar
Dinas Fawr
Solva
Brawdy
A487
Penycwm
Newga
Newgale Sands
Roch Gate
Roch
Roch Bridge
16
140
Dudwell Mountain 178
Mountain Water
Treffgarne
Lewesdon
Spittal
Walton East
Wolfsdale
Upper Scolton
Clarbeston
Scolton Manor
Rudbaxton
Clarbeston Road
A40
Keeston
Camrose
Tangiers
Folly
Poyston
Crundale
Poyston Cross
Wiston
Plain Deali-

Rickets Head
Nolton Haven
Nolton
Pelcomb Cross
Pelcomb
Lambston
Pelcomb Bridge
B4330
2
1
Prendergast
The Rhos
Picton
CC2
Druidston
Sutton
Castle Mus
Art Gallery
Albert Town
Slade
Priory
Haverfordwest
(Hwlffordd)
A40
Uzmaston
Millin Cross
Minwear

Haroldston West
Portfield Gate
Dreenhill
Merlin's Bridge
Boulston
Landshipping

Broad Haven
Broadway
Little Haven
Walton West
Rosepool
Ratford Bridge
B4341
B4327
Pope Hill
North Johnston
A4076
Lower Freystrop
Little Milford
Freystrop Cross
Hook
Martletwy

Stack Rocks
The Nab Head
Talbenny
St Brides
Walwyn's Castle
Roberston West
Tiers Cross
Johnston
Llangwm
Sardis
Yel-

Garland Stone
Skomer Island
Skomer Island NNR
Skomer Island
Wooltack Point
Marloes
Hasguard
Roberston Cross
3
A477
Rosemarket
Hill Mountain
Newton Mountain
Houghton
Lawrenny

Mew Stone
Gateholm Island
Hoopers Point
Sandy Haven
Thornton
Herbrandston
Steynton
A4076
Black Bridge
B4325
6
Honeyborough
Burton
West Williamston
West Williams
Carew Newton

Skokholm Island
The Stack
The Head
Skokholm Island
Dale
Dale Point
St Ishmael's
Hubberston
Hakin
Milford Haven
(Aberdaugleddau)
Waterston
Llanstadwell
Neyland
Burton Ferry
Coshseton
Upton Gardens
Upton
Lower Nash
Carew
Milton

St. Ann's Head
Thorn I.
Angle
Angle Bay
Pwllcrochan
Pembroke Dock
(Doc Penfro)
Pennar
B4322
Waterloo
3
2
Upper Nash

Sheep Island
Rosslare 3¾ hrs
Rhoscrowther
Wallaston Green
Hundleton
Pembroke Castle
Monkton
Pembroke
(Penfro)
2
A4075
Lamphey Palace
Lamphey
Lampher New

Freshwater West
Newton
B4320
Maiden Wells
Kingsfold
Hodgeston
12
A4139

Blucks Pool
Castlemartin
Linney
B4319
Warren
St Twynnells
Trewent
Freshwater East

Linney Head
Danger Zone
Merrion
St Petrox
Cheriton
Trewent Point

Crow Rock
Toes
Bosherston
Stackpole
South Pembrokesh-
Heritage Coast

The Wash
Saddle Head
Chapel
St Govan's Head
Buckspool
Broad Haven
Stackpole NNR
Stackpole Head

0   2   4   6 miles
0 2 4 6 8 10 km

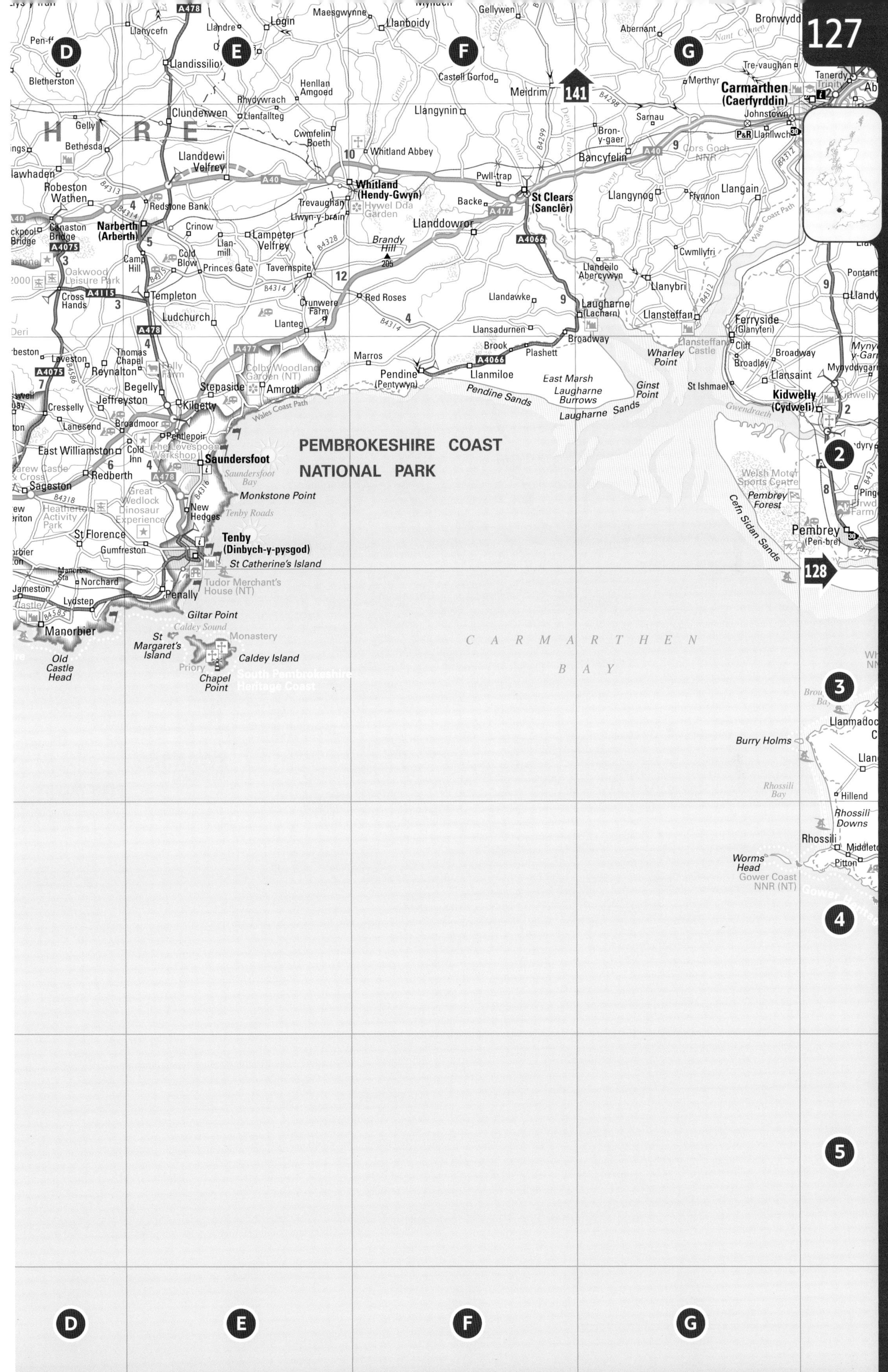
D
E
F
G
PEMBROKESHIRE COAST
NATIONAL PARK
C A R M A R T H E N
B A Y
Carmarthen
(Caerfyrddin)
Whitland
(Hendy-Gwyn)
St Clears
(Sanclêr)
Narberth
(Arberth)
Saundersfoot
Tenby
(Dinbych-y-pysgod)
Kidwelly
(Cydweli)
Pembrey
(Pen-bre)
Laugharne
(Lacharn)
Llanboidy
Login
Llandissilio
Clunderwen
Llanddewi Velfrey
Robeston Wathen
Redstone Bank
Lampeter Velfrey
Templeton
Ludchurch
Kilgetty
Stepaside
Amroth
Pendine
(Pentywyn)
Llanmiloe
Llanddowror
Bancyfelin
Llangynog
Llanstephan
Ferryside
(Glanyferi)
Meidrim
Llangynin
Castell Gorfod
Whitland Abbey
Hywel Dda Garden
Red Roses
Marros
Pendine Sands
Laugharne Sands
East Marsh
Laugharne Burrows
Ginst Point
Wharley Point
St Ishmael
Cefn Sidan Sands
Pembrey Forest
Welsh Motor Sports Centre
Monkstone Point
St Catherine's Island
Tudor Merchant's House (NT)
Penally
Giltar Point
Caldey Island
St Margaret's Island
Chapel Point
Manorbier
Old Castle Head
Lydstep
St Florence
Redberth
Sageston
Jeffreyston
Begelly
Reynalton
Oakwood Leisure Park
Colby Woodland Garden (NT)
Brandy Hill
205
Burry Holms
Rhossili
Rhossili Bay
Rhossili Downs
Hillend
Worms Head
Gower Coast NNR (NT)
A40
A477
A478
A4066
A4075
A4115
141
128
1
2
3
4
5

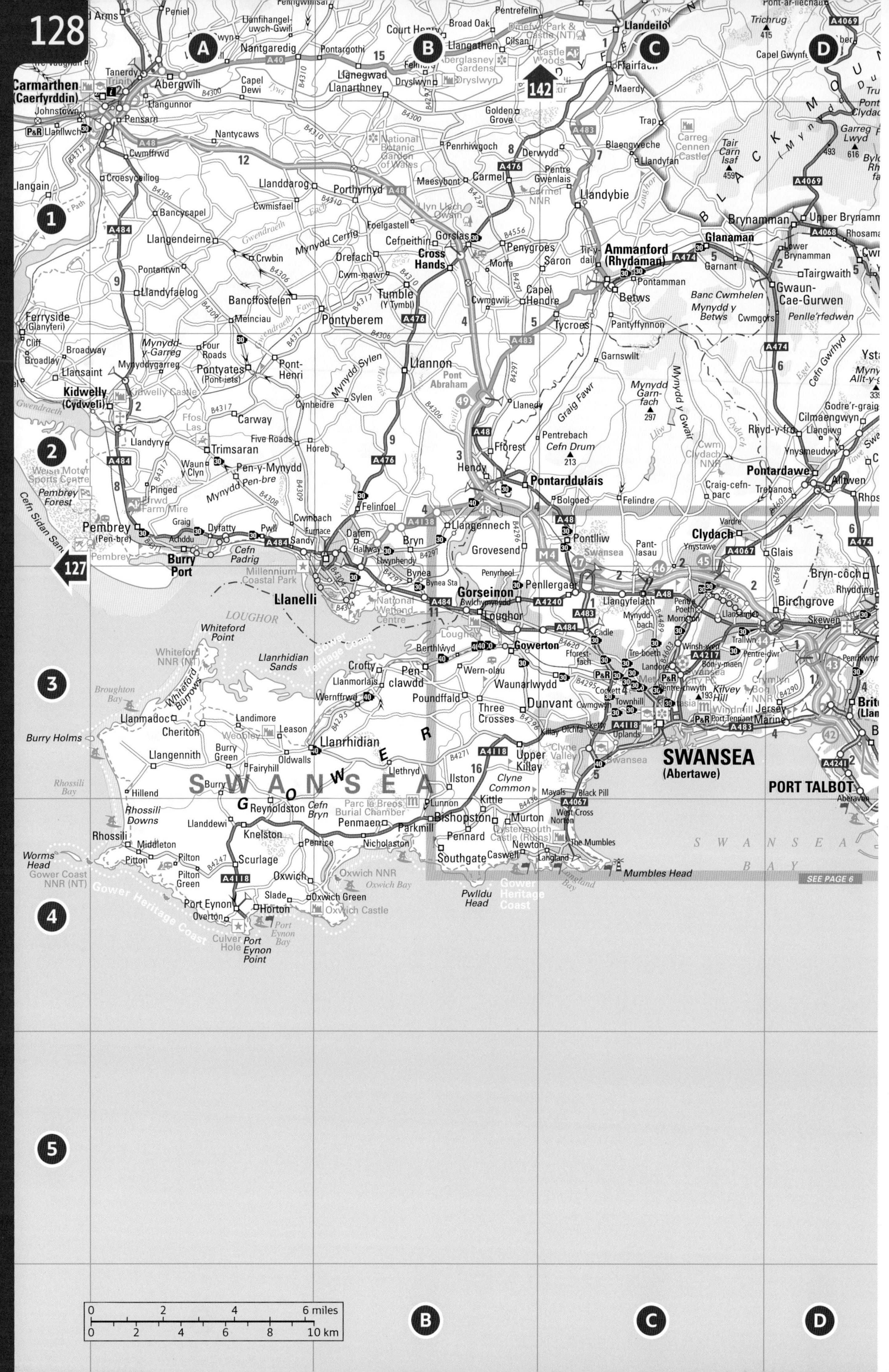
A
B
C
D
1
2
3
4
5
Carmarthen
(Caerfyrddin)
Abergwili
Nantgaredig
Llandeilo
Ffairfach
Llangathen
Court Henry
Broad Oak
Pentrefelin
Dinefwr Park & Castle (NT)
Aberglasney Gardens
Dryslwyn
Llanegwad
Llanarthney
Capel Dewi
Johnstown
Llangunnor
Pensarn
Llanllwch
Cwmffrwd
Nantycaws
National Botanic Garden of Wales
Golden Grove
Trap
Carreg Cennen Castle
Llandyfan
Blaengweche
Derwydd
Penrhiwgoch
Carmel
Maesybont
Llandybie
Llanddarog
Porthyrhyd
Cwmisfael
Croesyceiliog
Llangain
Bancycapel
Llangendeirne
Crwbin
Foelgastell
Cefneithin
Gorslas
Cross Hands
Drefach
Cwm-mawr
Tumble
(Y Tymbl)
Penygroes
Morfa
Saron
Ammanford
(Rhydaman)
Pontamman
Betws
Capel Hendre
Cwmgwili
Tycroes
Pantyffynnon
Garnant
Glanaman
Brynamman
Upper Brynamman
Gwaun-Cae-Gurwen
Tairgwaith
Cwmgors
Banc Cwmhelen
Mynydd y Betws
Penlle'rfedwen
Pontantwn
Llandyfaelog
Bancffosfelen
Pontyberem
Meinciau
Ferryside
(Glanyferi)
Cliff
Broadway
Broadlay
Llansaint
Mynyddygarreg
Four Roads
Pontyates
(Pont-iets)
Pont-Henri
Llannon
Pont Abraham
Garnswllt
Mynydd Garn-fach
Mynydd y Gwair
Kidwelly
(Cydweli)
Kidwelly Castle
Carway
Cynheidre
Sylen
Llanedy
Graig Fawr
Pentrebach
Cefn Drum
Landyry
Trimsaran
Five Roads
Horeb
Ffos Las
Fforest
Hendy
Pontarddulais
Bolgoed
Felindre
Craig-cefn-parc
Trebanos
Pontardawe
Alltwen
Rhyd-y-fro
Cilmaengwyn
Ynysmeudwy
Welsh Motor Sports Centre
Pembrey Forest
Waun y Clyn
Pen-y-Mynydd
Mynydd Pen-bre
Pinged
Ffrwd Farm Mire
Cefn Sidan Sands
Pembrey
(Pen-bre)
Graig
Dyfatty
Pwll
Cwmbach
Furnace
Felinfoel
Dafen
Halfway
Llwynhendy
Bryn
Llangennech
Grovesend
Pontlliw
Pant-lasau
Clydach
Ynystawe
Vardre
Glais
Bryn-côch
Rhydding
Burry Port
Achddu
Sandy
Cefn Padrig
Millennium Coastal Park
Llanelli
Bynea
National Wetland Centre
Gorseinon
Penllergaer
Llangyfelach
Mynydd-bach
Birchgrove
Skewen
Loughor
LOUGHOR
Whiteford Point
Whiteford NNR (NT)
Whiteford Burrows
Llanrhidian Sands
Gower Heritage Coast
Crofty
Llanmorlais
Pen-clawdd
Wern-olau
Gowerton
Waunarlwydd
Cadle
Fforest-fach
Tre-boeth
Landore
Morriston
Winsh-wen
Bon-y-maen
Trallwn
Crymlyn Bog NNR
Jersey Marine
Kilvey Hill
Broughton Bay
Burry Holms
Llanmadoc
Cheriton
Landimore
Weobley
Leason
Wernffrwd
Llanrhidian
Oldwalls
Poundffald
Three Crosses
Dunvant
Cwmgwrach
Cockett
Townhill
Uplands
Sketty
Killay
Olchfa
Clyne Valley
Upper Killay
Swansea
SWANSEA
(Abertawe)
PORT TALBOT
Aberavon
Llangennith
Burry Green
Fairyhill
Llethryd
Ilston
Clyne Common
Mayals
Black Pill
Rhossili Bay
Hillend
Burry
GOWER
SWANSEA
Reynoldston
Cefn Bryn
Parc le Breos Burial Chamber
Lunnon
Kittle
Bishopston
Murton
West Cross
Norton
Rhossili Downs
Llanddewi
Knelston
Penmaen
Parkmill
Pennard
Oystermouth Castle (Ruins)
The Mumbles
Rhossili
Middleton
Penrice
Nicholaston
Southgate
Caswell
Newton
Langland
Worms Head
Gower Coast NNR (NT)
Pitton
Pilton
Pilton Green
Scurlage
Oxwich
Oxwich NNR
Oxwich Bay
Mumbles Head
Langland Bay
SWANSEA BAY
SEE PAGE 6
Pwlldu Head
Gower Heritage Coast
Port Eynon
Slade
Oxwich Green
Oxwich Castle
Horton
Overton
Culver Hole
Port Eynon Point
Port Eynon Bay
Trichrug
Capel Gwynfe
BLACK MOUNTAIN
Tair Carn Isaf
Garreg Lwyd
Brynamman
Rhosaman
Cefn Gwrhyd
A40
A48
A476
A483
A484
A474
A4069
A4068
A4138
A4240
A4217
A4067
A4118
A483
A4241
M4
B4300
B4310
B4306
B4317
B4309
B4308
B4297
B4295
B4247
B4271
B4436
B4620
B4489
B4603
B4290
142
127
0 2 4 6 miles
0 2 4 6 8 10 km

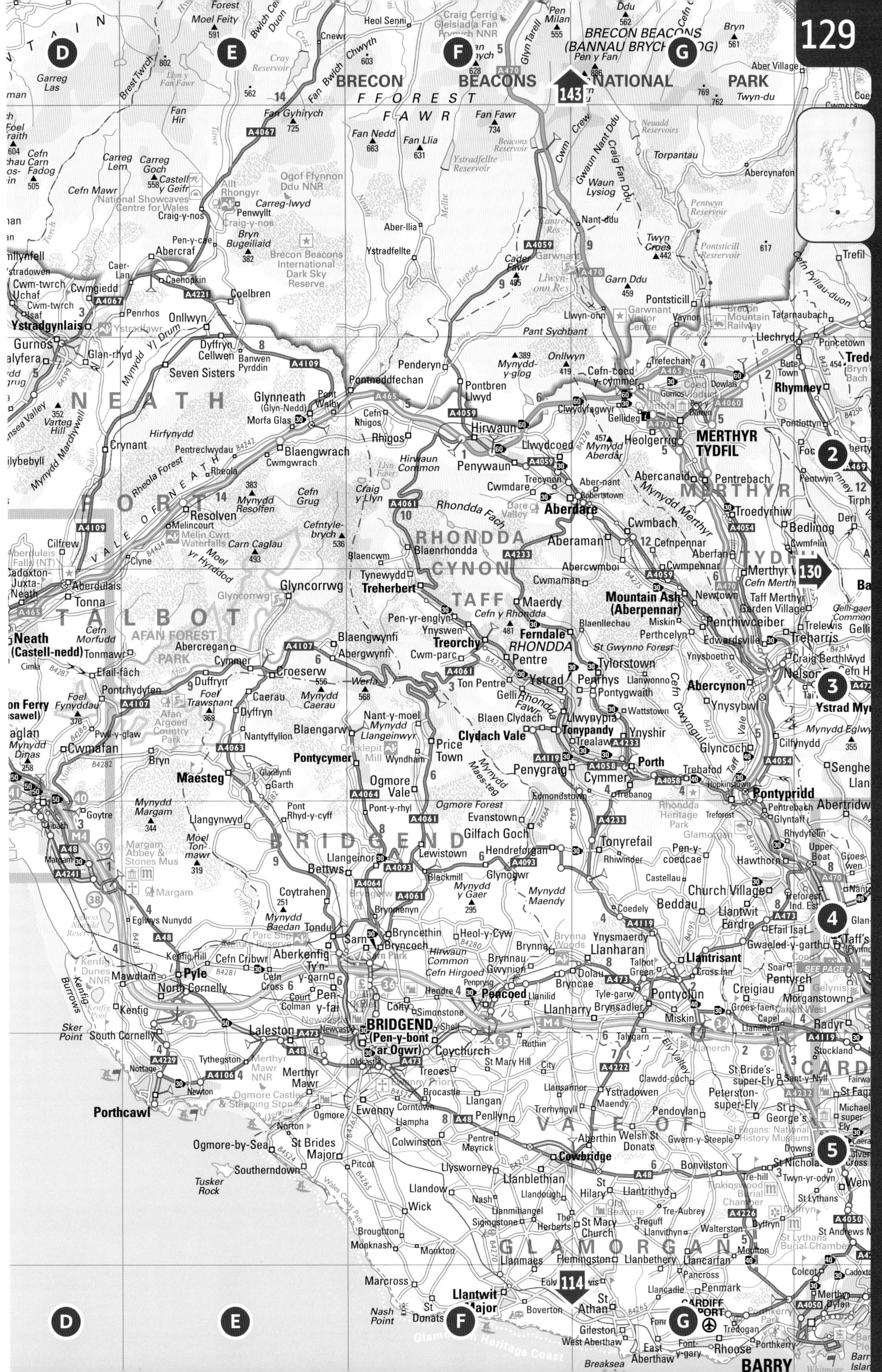
D
E
F
G
BRECON BEACONS (BANNAU BRYCHEINIOG) NATIONAL PARK
BRECON
BEACONS
FFOREST FAWR
143
Moel Feity
591
Cray Reservoir
Heol Senni
Cnewr
Fan Bwlch Chwyth
603
Craig Cerrig Gleisiad a Fan Frynych NNR
628
Pen y Fan
886
Pen Milan
555
Glyn Tarell
A470
Bryn
561
Aber Village
Twyn-du
769
762
Garreg Las
802
Llyn y Fan Fawr
562
14
Fan Gyhirych
725
A4067
Fan Hir
Fan Nedd
663
Fan Llia
631
Fan Fawr
734
Beacons Reservoir
Ystradfellte Reservoir
Neuadd Reservoirs
Torpantau
Abercynafon
Cwm Crew
Gwaun Nant Ddu
Craig Fan Ddu
Waun Lysiog
Carreg Lem
Carreg Goch
558
Castell y Geifr
Cefn Carn Fadog
505
Cefn Mawr
National Showcaves Centre for Wales
Allt Rhongyr
Ogof Ffynnon Ddu NNR
Penwyllt
Craig-y-nos
Carreg-lwyd
Bryn Bugeiliaid
382
Pen-y-cae
Abercraf
Brecon Beacons International Dark Sky Reserve
Aber-llia
Ystradfellte
Cantref Res
Nant-ddu
Pentwyn Reservoir
Pontsticill Reservoir
Twyn Croes
442
617
Trefil
Cefn Pyllau-duon
A4059
Cader Fawr
495
Garwnant
Llwyn-onn Res
Garn Ddu
459
Pontsticill
Caer-Lan
Cwm-twrch Uchaf
Cwmgiedd
Caehopkin
A4221
Coelbren
A4067
Cwm-twrch Isaf
Penrhos
Onllwyn
Ystradgynlais
Ystradfawr
Gurnos
Glan-rhyd
Mynydd y Drum
Dyffryn Cellwen
Banwen Pyrddin
8
A4109
Seven Sisters
Llwyn-onn
Garwnant Visitor Centre
Vaynor
Brecon Mountain Railway
Tafarnaubach
Pant Sychbant
Llechryd
Princetown
Penderyn
389
Mynydd-y-glog
Onllwyn
419
Cefn-coed-y-cymmer
Trefechan
Pontneddfechan
Pontbren Llwyd
Dowlais
Rhymney
Bute Town
NEATH
Glynneath (Glyn-Nedd)
Pont Walby
A465
Cefn Rhigos
Morfa Glas
Rhigos
Hirwaun
A4059
Clwydyfagwyr
Gellideg
Cyfarthfa
Gurnos
Pen-y-Darren
A4060
MERTHYR TYDFIL
Pontlottyn
352
Varteg Hill
Swansea Valley
Crynant
Hirfynydd
Pentreclwydau
B4242
Blaengwrach
Cwmgwrach
Mynydd Marchywel
Rheola Forest
Rheola
Hirwaun Common
Penywaun
Llwydcoed
457
Mynydd Aberdar
Heolgerrig
Abercanaid
Pentrebach
MERTHYR
Pentwyn
Troedyrhiw
Bedlinog
Deri
Cwmfelin
Dare Valley
Aberdare
Aber-nant
Robertstown
Trecynon
Cwmdare
Mynydd Merthyr
383
Mynydd Resolfen
Cefn Grug
Craig y Llyn
A4061
Rhondda Fach
Resolven
PORT
VALE OF NEATH
Melincourt
Melin Cwrt Waterfalls
Carn Caglau
493
Cefntyle-brych
536
A4109
Cilfrew
Aberdulais Falls (NT)
Cadoxton-Juxta-Neath
Aberdulais
Clyne
Moel yr Hyrddod
Blaencwm
Blaenrhondda
RHONDDA CYNON TAFF
Cwmbach
Cefnpennar
Aberaman
A4233
Abercwmboi
Cwmaman
Aberfan
Cwmpennar
Merthyr Vale
Cefn Merthyr
130
Taff Merthyr Garden Village
Gelli-gaer Common
Tonna
A465
TALBOT
Neath (Castell-nedd)
Cefn Morfudd
Tonmawr
AFAN FOREST PARK
Abercregan
Glyncorrwg
Tynewydd
Treherbert
Maerdy
Cefn y Rhondda
481
Ferndale
Blaenllechau
Mountain Ash (Aberpennar)
Miskin
Penrhiwceiber
Perthcelyn
Trelewis
Treharris
Edwardsville
Cymmer
Cimla
Efail-fâch
Pontrhydyfen
Croeserw
Blaengwynfi
Abergwynfi
A4107
556
Werfa
568
Pen-yr-englyn
Ynyswen
Treorchy
Cwm-parc
RHONDDA
Pentre
St Gwynno Forest
Tylorstown
Ynysboeth
Craig Berthlwyd
Nelson
Ystrad
Ton Pentre
Gelli
Penrhys
Pontygwaith
Llanwonno
Abercynon
Ynysybwl
Ystrad Mynach
Foel Fynyddau
370
Duffryn
Foel Trawsnant
369
Caerau
Mynydd Caerau
Dyffryn
Afan Argoed Country Park
Pwll-y-glaw
Nantyffyllon
Nant-y-moel
Mynydd Llangeinwyr
Blaengarw
Clydach Vale
Blaen Clydach
Llwynypia
Tonypandy
Trealaw
Wattstown
Ynyshir
Glyncoch
Cilfynydd
Mynydd Eglwysilan
355
Aglan
Mynydd Dinas
258
Cwmafan
Bryn
A4063
Cricklepit Mill
Pontycymer
Wyndham
Price Town
Mynydd Maes-teg
Penygraig
Cymmer
Porth
Trehafod
Hopkinstown
A4054
Pontypridd
Senghenydd
Maesteg
Garth
Ogmore Vale
A4064
Pont-y-rhyl
Ogmore Forest
Edmondstown
Trebanog
Rhondda Heritage Park
Treforest
Pentrebach
Glyntaff
Abertridwr
Goytre
Taibach
M4
Mynydd Margam
344
Llangynwyd
Pont Rhyd-y-cyff
BRIDGEND
A4061
Evanstown
Gilfach Goch
A4233
Tonyrefail
Glamorgan
Rhydyfelin
Upper Boat
Margam
A48
Moel Ton-mawr
319
Margam Abbey & Stones Mus
Llangeinor
Bettws
A4093
Lewistown
Hendreforgan
Glynogwr
Rhiwinder
Pen-y-coedcae
Hawthorn
Castellau
Church Village
Treforest Ind. Est
A4241
Margam
Coytrahen
251
Blackmill
Mynydd y Gaer
295
Mynydd Maendy
Bryngarw
Brynmenyn
Beddau
Llantwit Fardre
Coedely
A4119
Efail Isaf
Gwaelod-y-garth
Eglwys Nunydd
Mynydd Baedan
Tondu
Parc Slip Nature Reserve
Bryncethin
Bryncoch
Heol-y-Cyw
Brynna Woods
Brynna
Ynysmaerdy
Llanharan
Llantrisant
Kenfig Dunes NNR
Kenfig Burrows
Kenfig Hill
Pyle
Cefn Cribwr
Aberkenfig
Sarn
Sarn Park
Hirwaun Common
Cefn Hirgoed
Brynnau Gwynion
Dolau
Talbot Green
Cross Inn
Creigiau
Pentyrch
Mawdlam
North Cornelly
Cefn Cross
Ty'n-y-garn
Court Colman
Pen-y-fai
Penprysg
Pencoed
Llanilid
Brynsadler
Pontyclun
Tyle-garw
Llanharry
Miskin
Groes-faen
Morganstown
Capel Llanilltern
Kenfig
Sker Point
South Cornelly
Laleston
A473
Newcastle
BRIDGEND (Pen-y-bont ar Ogwr)
Coity
Simonstone
Shelf
Hendre
M4
Ruthin
Talygarn
Ely Valley
Llanerch
Radyr
Stockland
CARDIFF
A4229
Tythegston
Merthyr Mawr NNR
Merthyr Mawr
Oldcastle
A473
Coychurch
Treoes
St Mary Hill
City
A4222
Clawdd-coch
St Bride's-super-Ely
Sant-y-Nyll
Nottage
Newton
A4106
Ogmore Castle & Stepping Stones
Brocastle
Llangan
Llansannor
Ystradowen
Maendy
Peterston-super-Ely
St Fagans
Porthcawl
Ogmore
Ewenny
Corntown
A48
Penllyn
Trerhyngyll
Pendoylan
St George's
Norton
Llampha
Colwinston
Pentre Meyrick
VALE OF GLAMORGAN
Aberthin
Welsh St Donats
Gwern-y-Steeple
St Fagans: National History Museum
Ogmore-by-Sea
St Brides Major
Pitcot
Cowbridge
Bonvilston
St Nicholas
Southerndown
Llysworney
Llanblethian
St Hilary
Llantrithyd
Tre-hill
Twyn-yr-odyn
Tinkinswood Burial Chamber
Tusker Rock
Wales Coast Path
Llandow
Llandough
Wick
Nash
Llanmihangel
The Herberts
St Mary Church
Old Beaupre
Tre-Aubrey
Treguff
Llanvithyn
Walterston
Dyffryn
St Lythans
St Lythans Burial Chamber
St Andrews Major
Broughton
Monknash
Monkton
Llanmaes
Flemingston
Llanbethery
Llancarfan
Moulton
Pancross
Colcot
Cadoxton
Marcross
114
Eglwys Brewis
Llancadle
Penmark
Merthyr Dyfan
Nash Point
St Donats
Llantwit Major
Boverton
St Athan
CARDIFF AIRPORT
Porthkerry Park
Gileston
West Aberthaw
Font-y-gary
Tredogan
Porthkerry
Rhoose
East Aberthaw
Breaksea
BARRY
Glamorgan Heritage Coast
2
3
4
5

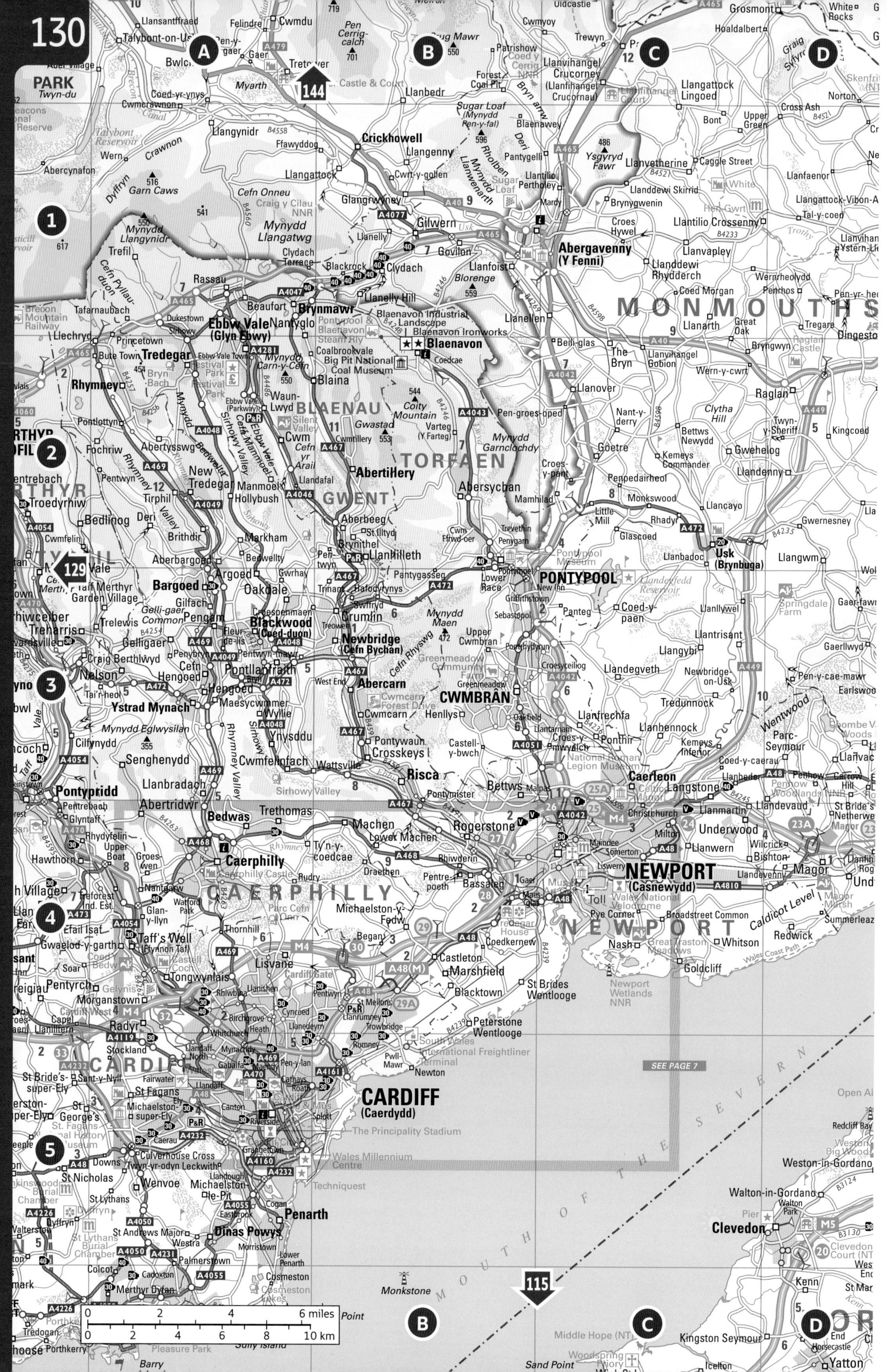

PARK
Twyn-du
Talybont-on-Usk
Llansantffraed
Felindre
Cwmdu
Pen Cerrig-calch
Crug Mawr
Patrishow
Cwmyoy
Trewyn
Grosmont
Hoaldalbert
Graig Syfyrddin
Bwlch
Tretower
Castle & Court
144
Myarth
Forest Coal Pit
Llanbedr
Llanvihangel Crucorney (Llanfihangel Crucornau)
Llanfihangel Court
Llangattock Lingoed
Coed-yr-ynys
Cwmcrawnon
Talybont Reservoir
Llangynidr
Crickhowell
Sugar Loaf (Mynydd Pen-y-fal)
Blaenawey
Bont
Upper Green
Cross Ash
Norton
Ffawyddog
Llangenny
Pantygelli
Ysgyryd Fawr
Llanvetherine
Caggle Street
Wern
Crawnon
Abercynafon
Llangattock
Cwrt-y-gollen
Rholben
Mynydd Llanwenarth
Llantilio Pertholey
Llanddewi Skirrid
White Castle
Llanfaenor
Garn Caws
Dyffryn Crawnon
Cefn Onneu
Craig y Cilau NNR
Glangrwyney
Mardy
Brynygwenin
Hen Gwrt
Llangattock-Vibon-Avel
Tal-y-coed
Mynydd Llangatwg
Mynydd Llangynidr
Gilwern
Llanelly
Govilon
Croes Hywel
Llantilio Crossenny
Trefil
Clydach Terrace
Blackrock
Clydach
Llanfoist
Abergavenny (Y Fenni)
Llanvapley
Llanddewi Rhydderch
Cefn Pyllau-duon
Rassau
Llanelly Hill
Blorenge
Coed Morgan
Wernrheolydd
Penrhos
Pen-yr-heol
Beaufort
Brynmawr
Blaenavon Industrial Landscape
Llanellen
MONMOUTHSHIRE
Brecon Mountain Railway
Tafarnaubach
Dukestown
Ebbw Vale (Glyn Ebbwy)
Nantyglo
Pontypool & Blaenavon Steam Rly
Blaenavon Ironworks
Blaenavon
Great Oak
Llanarth
Tregare
Dingestow
Llechryd
Princetown
Tredegar
Sirhowy
Coalbrookvale
Big Pit National Coal Museum
Coedcae
Bettws
The Bryn
Llanvihangel Gobion
Bryngwyn
Raglan Castle
Bute Town
Ebbw Vale Town
Festival Park
Mynydd Carn-y-Cefn
Blaina
Wern-y-cwrt
Rhymney
Bryn Bach
Llanover
Raglan
Waun-Lwyd
Coity Mountain
Pen-groes-oped
Nant-y-derry
Clytha Hill
Twyn-y-Sheriff
Kingcoed
Pontlottyn
Mynydd Bedwellte
Ebbw Vale (Parkway)
BLAENAU
Silent Valley
Gwastad
Varteg (Y Farteg)
Mynydd Garnclochdy
Bettws Newydd
Gwehelog
Fochriw
Abertysswg
Sirhowy Valley
Cwm
Cwmtillery
Goetre
Kemeys Commander
Rhymney
Cefn Manmoel
Cefn yr Arail
TORFAEN
Croes-y-pant
Llandenny
New Tredegar
Pentwyn
Manmoel
Llandafal
Abertillery
Penpedairheol
Troedyrhiw
Tirphil
Hollybush
GWENT
Abersychan
Mamhilad
Monkswood
Llancayo
Bedlinog
Deri
Valley
Aberbeeg
Little Mill
Rhadyr
Cwmfelin
Brithdir
Markham
St Illtyd
Cwm Ffrwd-oer
Trevethin
Penygarn
Glascoed
Usk (Brynbuga)
Gwernesney
129
Aberbargoed
Bedwellty
Brynithel
Llanhilleth
Pen-twyn
Pontypool Museum
Llanbadoc
Llangwm
Merthyr Vale
Argoed
Gwrhay
Pantygasseg
Lower Race
Pontnewynydd
PONTYPOOL
Llandegfedd Reservoir
Taff Merthyr Garden Village
Bargoed
Oakdale
Trinant
Hafodyrynys
New Inn
Gilfach
Croespenmaen
Swffryd
Griffithstown
Coed-y-paen
Springdale Farm
Gaer-fawr
Gelli-gaer Common
Pengam
Crumlin
Mynydd Maen
Sebastopol
Panteg
Llanllywel
Treharris
Trelewis
Fleur-de-lis
Blackwood (Coed-duon)
Treowen
Upper Cwmbran
Llantrisant
Gelligaer
Newbridge (Cefn Bychan)
Cefn Rhyswg
Pontrhydyrun
Llangybi
Gaerllwyd
Craig Berthlwyd
Penybryn
Pentwyn-mawr
Greenmeadow Community Farm
Croesyceiliog
Llandegveth
Newbridge-on-Usk
Pen-y-cae-mawr
Nelson
Cefn
Hengoed
Pontllanfraith
Earlswood
Tai'r-heol
Ystrad Mynach
Maesycwmmer
West End
Abercarn
Cwmcarn Forest Drive
CWMBRÂN
Tredunnock
Wentwood
Mynydd Eglwysilan
Wyllie
Cwmcarn
Henllys
Oakfield
Llanfrechfa
Llanhennock
Parc-Seymour
Cilfynydd
Ynysddu
Pontywaun
Crosskeys
Llantarnam
Croes-y-mwyalch
Ponthir
Kemeys Inferior
Coed-y-caerau
Llanvaches
Senghenydd
Castell-y-bwch
National Roman Legion Museum
Cwmfelinfach
Wattsville
Risca
Caerleon
Llanbeder
Penhow
Carrow Hill
Pontypridd
Llanbradach
Sirhowy Valley
Bettws
Malpas
Celtic Manor
Langstone
Pentrebach
Abertridwr
Trethomas
Pontymister
Penhow Woodlands
Llandevaud
St Bride's Netherwent
Glyntaff
Bedwas
Machen
Rogerstone
Christchurch
Llanmartin
Rhydyfelin
Lower Machen
Maindee
Milton
Underwood
Magor
Upper Boat
Groes-wen
Caerphilly
Ty'n-y-coedcae
Rhiwderin
Somerton
Llanwern
Wilcrick
Hawthorn
Caerphilly Castle
Rudry
Draethen
Liswerry
Bishton
Treforest Ind. Est.
Nantgarw
CAERPHILLY
Pentre-poeth
Bassaleg
Gaer
NEWPORT (Casnewydd)
Llandevenny
Church Village
Watford Park
Parc Cefn Onn
Michaelston-y-Fedw
Maesglas
Wales National Velodrome
Tolll
Caldicot Level
Magor Marsh
Glan-y-llyn
Tredegar House
Pye Corner
Broadstreet Common
Summerleaze
Efail Isaf
Taff's Well (Ffynnon Taf)
Thornhill
Began
Coedkernew
NEWPORT
Redwick
Gwaelod-y-garth
Castell Coch
Castleton
Nash
Great Traston Meadows
Whitson
Wales Coast Path
Soar
Lisvane
Cardiff Gate
Marshfield
Goldcliff
Pentyrch
Tongwynlais
Llanishen
Blacktown
St Brides Wentlooge
Newport Wetlands NNR
Morganstown
Rhiwbina
Pentwyn
St Mellons
Cardiff West
Birchgrove
Cyncoed
Llanrumney
Capel Llanilltern
Radyr
Whitchurch
Heath
Llanedeyrn
Trowbridge
Peterstone Wentlooge
Llandaff North
Mynachdy
Rumney
South Wales International Freightliner Terminal
Stockland
Gabalfa
Maendy
Pen-y-lan
Pwll-Mawr
SEE PAGE 7
CARDIFF
Fairwater
Llandaff
Cathays
Roath
Newton
St Bride's-super-Ely
Sant-y-Nyll
St Fagans
Michaelston-super-Ely
Canton
Riverside
Splott
CARDIFF (Caerdydd)
Open Air
St George's
St. Fagans National History Museum
The Principality Stadium
Redcliff Bay
Caerau
Grangetown
Culverhouse Cross
Wales Millennium Centre
Weston Big Wood
Downs
Twyn-yr-odyn
Leckwith
St Nicholas
Llandough
Weston-in-Gordano
Techniquest
Walton-in-Gordano
St Lythans
Wenvoe
Michaelston-le-Pit
Cogan
Dyffryn
Eastbrook
Penarth
Walton Park
Pier
Clevedon
Dinas Powys
St Andrews Major
Westra
St Lythans Burial Chamber
Clevedon Court (NT)
Morristown
Palmerstown
Lower Penarth
Colcot
Cadoxton
Cosmeston
Cosmeston Lakes
Merthyr Dyfan
115
Kenn
St Mary
Monkstone
Tredogan
Porthkerry
Point
Middle Hope (NT)
Kingston Seymour
Pleasure Park
Sully Island
Horsecastle
Barry
Sand Point
Woodspring Priory
Icelton
End
Yatton
MOUTH OF THE SEVERN
0 2 4 6 miles
0 2 4 6 8 10 km

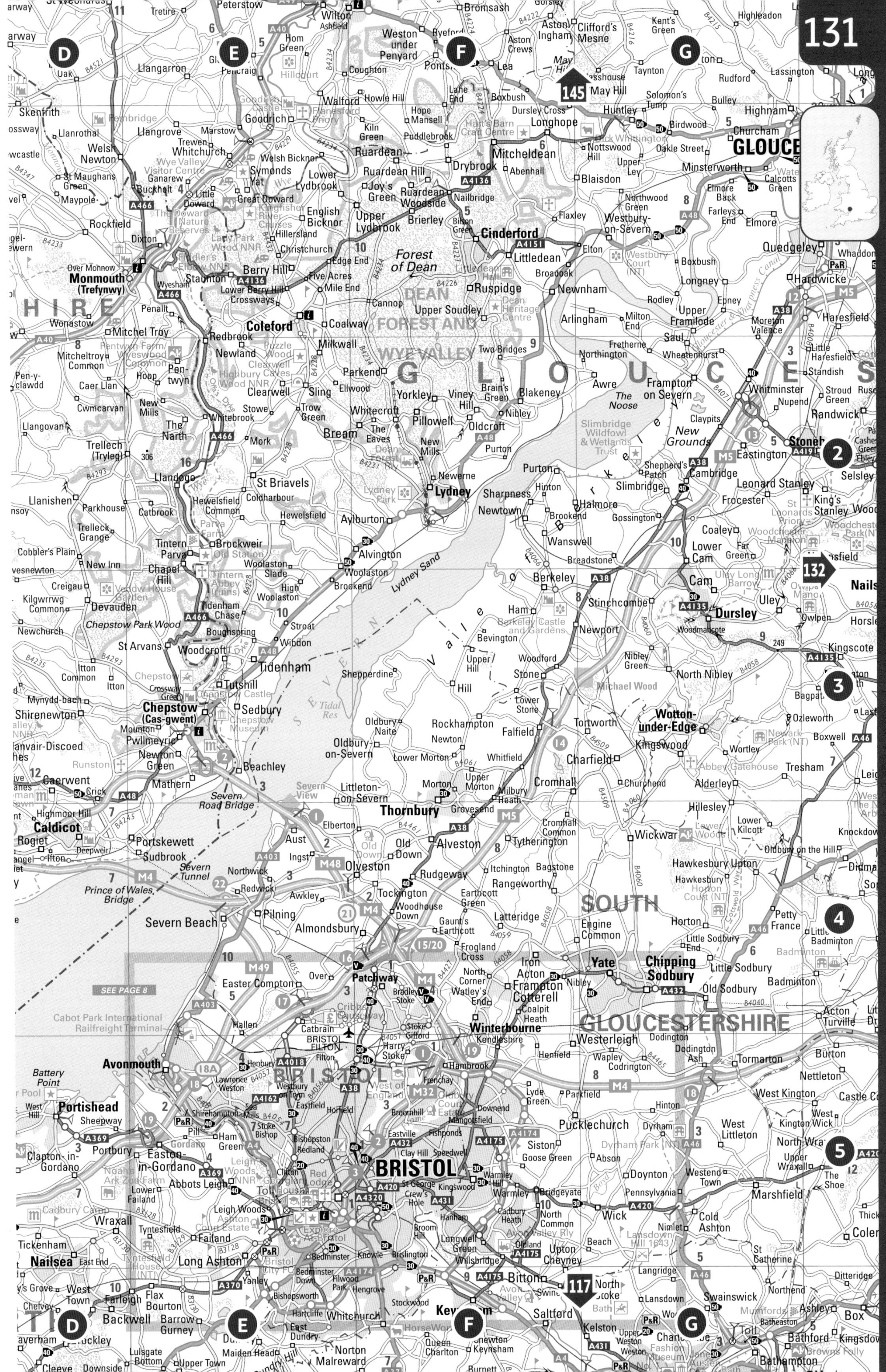
D
E
F
G
145
132
117
SEE PAGE 8
Peterstow
Wilton
Bromsash
Aston Ingham
Clifford's Mesne
Kent's Green
Highleadon
Weston under Penyard
Ryeford
Aston Crews
Tayton
Rudford
Lassington
Llangarron
Hom Green
Coughton
Pontshill
Lea
May Hill
Solomon's Tump
Bulley
Highnam
Skenfrith
Goodrich Castle
Walford
Howle Hill
Lane End
Boxbush
Dursley Cross
Huntley
Churcham
GLOUCESTER
Llanrothal
Pembridge
Llangrove
Marstow
Goodrich
Flanesford Priory
Hope Mansell
Hart's Barn Craft Centre
Longhope
Birdwood
Welsh Newton
Trewen
Whitchurch
Kiln Green
Puddlebrook
Mitcheldean
Nottswood Hill
Oakle Street
Welsh Bicknor
Ruardean
Drybrook
Abenhall
Upper Ley
Minsterworth
Wye Valley Visitor Centre
Symonds Yat
Lower Lydbrook
Ruardean Hill
St Maughans Green
Ganarew
Joy's Green
Ruardean Woodside
Blaisdon
Calcotts Green
Buckholt
Little Doward
Great Doward
Nailbridge
Elmore Back
Maypole
English Bicknor
Upper Lydbrook
Brierley
Northwood Green
Rockfield
The Doward Nature Reserves
Kingfisher River Cruises
Hillersland
Bilson Green
Cinderford
Flaxley
Westbury-on-Severn
Farleys End
Elmore
Dixton
Lady Park Wood NNR
Christchurch
Forest of Dean
Littledean
Elton
Quedgeley
Over Monnow
Monmouth (Trefynwy)
Staunton
Berry Hill
Edge End
Five Acres
Mile End
Ruspidge
Newnham
Westbury Court (NT)
Boxbush
Longney
Hardwicke
Wyesham
Lower Berry Hill
Crossways
Cannop
DEAN
Dean Heritage Centre
Upper Soudley
Rodley
Epney
Haresfield
Penallt
Coleford
Coalway
FOREST AND
Arlingham
Milton End
Upper Framilode
Moreton Valence
Wonastow
Mitchel Troy
Redbrook
Milkwall
WYE VALLEY
Two Bridges
Saul
Fretherne
Wheatenhurst
Little Haresfield
Mitcheltroy Common
Pentwyn Farm/Wyeswood Common
Newland
Puzzle Wood
Northington
Standish
Clearwell Highbury Caves
Parkend
G L O U C E S
Pen-y-clawdd
Caer Llan
Pen-twyn
Hoop
Clearwell
Sling
Ellwood
Yorkley
Viney Hill
Brain's Green
Blakeney
Awre
The Noose
Frampton on Severn
Whitminster
Stroud Green
Cwmcarvan
New Mills
Stowe
Trow Green
Whitecroft
Pillowell
Oldcroft
Nibley
Nupend
Randwick
Llangovan
The North
Whitebrook
Bream
The Eaves
Slimbridge Wildfowl & Wetlands Trust
Claypits
New Grounds
Stonehouse
Trellech (Tryleg)
Mork
New Mills
Purton
Eastington
Dean Forest Rly
Shepherd's Patch
Cambridge
Leonard Stanley
Selsley
Llandogo
St Briavels
Coldharbour
Lydney Park
Newerne
Lydney
Purton
Hinton
Slimbridge
Llanishen
Parkhouse
Catbrook
Hewelsfield Common
Hewelsfield
Aylburton
Sharpness
Halmore
Frocester
King's Stanley
Newtown
Brookend
Gossington
Trelleck Grange
Parva Farm
Coaley
Woodchester Mansion
Tintern Parva
Brockweir
Old Station
Wanswell
Lower Cam
Far Green
Cobbler's Plain
New Inn
Chapel Hill
Tintern Abbey (ruins)
Woolaston Slade
Alvington
Lydney Sand
Breadstone
Cam
Uley Long Barrow
Creigau
Kilgwrrwg Common
Veddw House Garden
Devauden
Woolaston
Brookend
Berkeley
Uley
Owlpen
High Woolaston
Tidenham Chase
Stinchcombe
Dursley
Woodmancote
Newchurch
Chepstow Park Wood
Boughspring
Stroat
Ham
Berkeley Castle and Gardens
Newport
Kingscote
St Arvans
Woodcroft
Wibdon
Bevington
Itton Common
Itton
Tidenham
Upper Hill
Woodford
Nibley Green
North Nibley
Chepstow Racecourse
Crossway Green
Tutshill
Shepperdine
Hill
Stone
Michael Wood
Mynydd-bach
Chepstow Castle
Lower Stone
Shirenewton
Chepstow (Cas-gwent)
Sedbury
Chepstow Museum
Tidal Res
Oldbury Naite
Rockhampton
Falfield
Tortworth
Wotton-under-Edge
Ozleworth
Mounton
Pwllmeyric
Oldbury-on-Severn
Newton
Kingswood
Newark Park (NT)
Boxwell
Llanvair-Discoed
Runston
Newton Green
Beachley
Lower Morton
Whitfield
Charfield
Wortley
Abbey Gatehouse
Tresham
Caerwent
Crick
Mathern
Severn View
Littleton-upon-Severn
Morton
Upper Morton
Cromhall
Churchend
Alderley
Severn Road Bridge
Thornbury
Milbury Heath
Grovesend
Hillesley
Highmoor Hill
Caldicot
Elberton
Cromhall Common
Lower Kilcott
Rogiet
Portskewett
Aust
Old Down
Alveston
Tytherington
Wickwar
Knockdown
Sudbrook
Deepweir
Ingst
Olveston
Oldbury on the Hill
Severn Tunnel
Northwick
Rudgeway
Itchington
Bagstone
Hawkesbury Upton
Didmarton
Prince of Wales Bridge
Redwick
Tockington
Rangeworthy
Hawkesbury
Horton Court (NT)
Awkley
Woodhouse Down
Earthcott Green
SOUTH
Petty France
Severn Beach
Pilning
Almondsbury
Gaunt's Earthcott
Latteridge
Engine Common
Horton
Little Badminton
Little Sodbury End
Frogland Cross
Iron Acton
Yate
Chipping Sodbury
Little Sodbury
Badminton
Easter Compton
Over
Patchway
North Corner
Watley's End
Frampton Cotterell
Nibley
Old Sodbury
Cribbs Causeway
Bradley Stoke
Coalpit Heath
Cabot Park International Railfreight Terminal
Hallen
Acton Turville
GLOUCESTERSHIRE
Catbrain
Stoke Gifford
Winterbourne
Westerleigh
Dodington
Bristol Filton
Filton
Harry Stoke
Kendleshire
Henfield
Dodington Ash
Burton
Battery Point
Avonmouth
Henbury
Hambrook
Wapley
Codrington
Tormarton
Lawrence Weston
Westbury on Trym
BRISTOL
West of England
Frenchay
Lyde Green
Parkfield
Nettleton
Portishead
Sheepway
Shirehampton
Sea Mills
Eastfield
Horfield
Clubs Court Estate
Downend
Hinton
West Kington
Castle Combe
Pill
Stoke Bishop
Broomhill
Mangotsfield
Pucklechurch
Dyrham
West Littleton
Kington Wick
Ham Green
Bishopston
Eastville
Fishponds
Redland
Clay Hill
Speedwell
Siston
Dyrham Park (NT)
North Wraxall
Portbury
Easton-in-Gordano
Leigh Woods NNR
Georgian House
Goose Green
Abson
Upper Wraxall
Clapton-in-Gordano
Noah's Ark Zoo Farm
Abbots Leigh
Clifton
Red Lodge
BRISTOL
St George
Kingswood
Warmley Hill
Warmley
Doynton
Westend Town
The Shoe
Lower Failand
Crew's Hole
Bridgeyate
Pennsylvania
Marshfield
Cadbury Camp
Leigh Woods
Ashton Court Estate
Hanham
Cadbury Heath
North Common
Wick
Avon Valley Rly
Cold Ashton
Wraxall
Tyntesfield
Explore-At-Bristol
Broom Hill
Oldland
Nimlet
Tickenham
Failand
Bedminster
Knowle
Brislington
Longwell Green
Upton Cheyney
Lansdown Hill 1643
St Catherine
Nailsea
East End
Tyntesfield House (NT)
Long Ashton
Bristol City FC
Willsbridge
Beach
Yanley
Bedminster Down
Filwood Park
Hengrove
Bitton
Avon Valley
Swineford
North Stoke
Langridge
Ditteridge
Northend
West Town
Farleigh
Flax Bourton
Bishopsworth
Stockwood
Keynsham
Saltford
Lansdown
Swainswick
Mumfords
Ashley
Box
Backwell
Barrow Gurney
Hartcliffe
Whitchurch
Bath
Batheaston
Charlcombe
Bathford
Kingsdown
East Dundry
Horseworld
Queen Charlton
Chewton Keynsham
Kelston
Upper Weston
Fashion Museum
Brockley
Lulsgate Bottom
Maiden Head
Norton Malreward
Weston
Bathampton
Cleeve
Downside
Upper Town
Burnett
Browns Folly

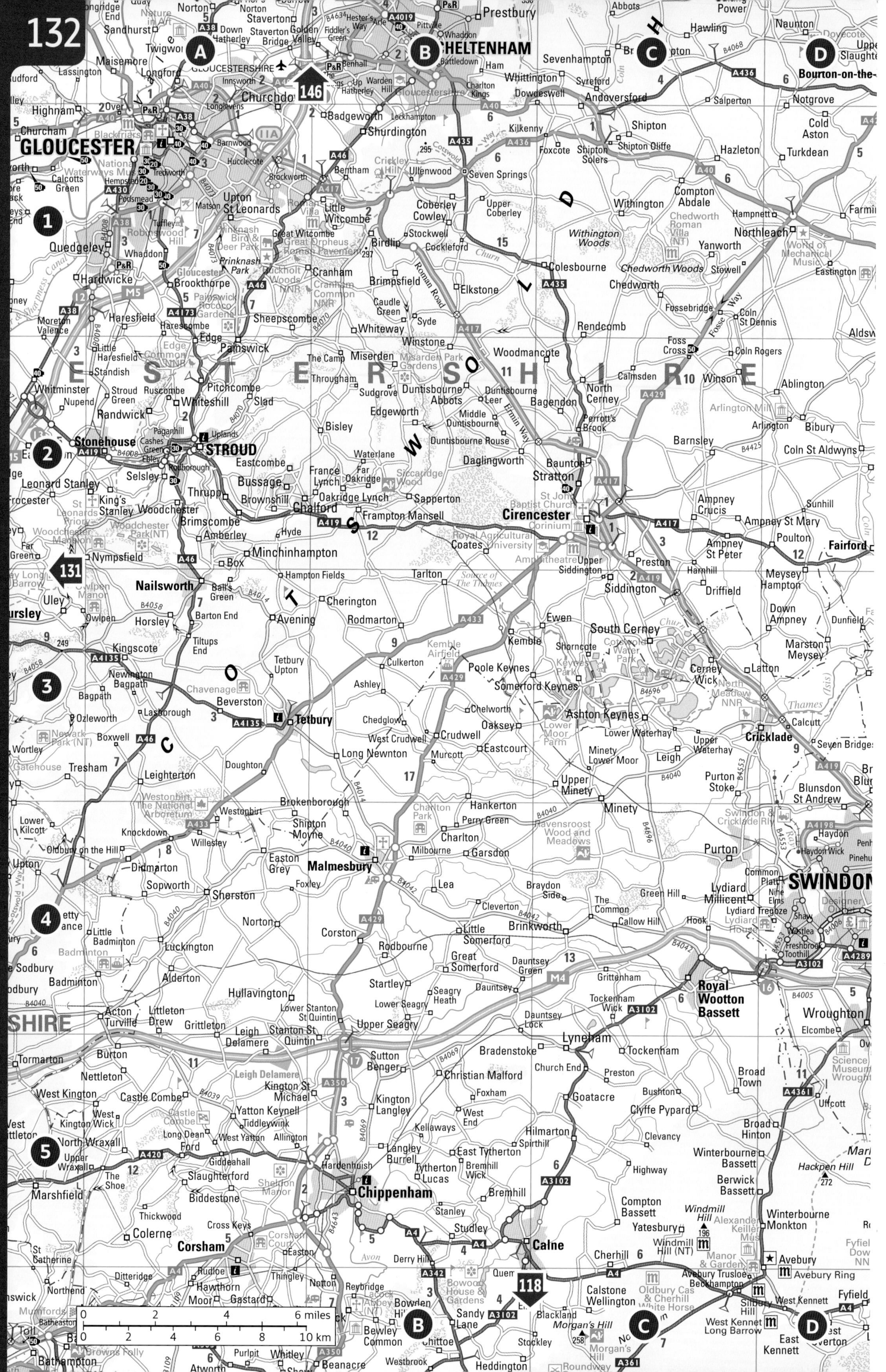
A
B
C
D
1
2
3
4
5
146
131
118
GLOUCESTER
CHELTENHAM
Prestbury
Sandhurst
Norton
Staverton
Down Hatherley
Twigworth
Longford
Maisemore
Lassington
Highnam
Churcham
Churchdown
Innsworth
Longlevens
Barnwood
Hucclecote
Brockworth
Tredworth
Hempsted
Podsmead
Matson
Tuffley
Upton St Leonards
Quedgeley
Whaddon
Robinswood Hill
Hardwicke
Brookthorpe
Haresfield
Moreton Valence
Standish
Whitminster
Stonehouse
STROUD
Leonard Stanley
Frocester
King's Stanley
Selsley
Woodchester
Nympsfield
Nailsworth
Uley
Owlpen
Horsley
Kingscote
Newington Bagpath
Beverston
Tetbury
Ozleworth
Boxwell
Tresham
Leighterton
Westonbirt
Knockdown
Didmarton
Sopworth
Sherston
Luckington
Badminton
Alderton
Acton Turville
Littleton Drew
Grittleton
Burton
Nettleton
West Kington
Castle Combe
Yatton Keynell
North Wraxall
Ford
Marshfield
Biddestone
Slaughterford
Colerne
Corsham
Chippenham
Hardenhuish
Kington Langley
Langley Burrell
Calne
Lyneham
Royal Wootton Bassett
SWINDON
Wroughton
Avebury
Malmesbury
Corston
Rodbourne
Great Somerford
Little Somerford
Brinkworth
Hullavington
Stanton St Quintin
Sutton Benger
Christian Malford
Cricklade
Purton
Minety
Ashton Keynes
South Cerney
Siddington
Kemble
Crudwell
Oaksey
Cirencester
Preston
Ampney Crucis
Fairford
Poulton
Barnsley
Bibury
Coln St Aldwyns
North Cerney
Bagendon
Rendcomb
Chedworth
Northleach
Withington
Compton Abdale
Shipton
Andoversford
Dowdeswell
Whittington
Sevenhampton
Naunton
Bourton-on-the-Water
Notgrove
Turkdean
Hazleton
Cold Aston
Birdlip
Cowley
Coberley
Seven Springs
Elkstone
Brimpsfield
Cranham
Painswick
Sheepscombe
Miserden
Bisley
Duntisbourne Abbots
Daglingworth
Chalford
Sapperton
Bussage
Brimscombe
Thrupp
Minchinhampton
Avening
Cherington
Rodmarton
Tarlton
Coates
Ewen
Somerford Keynes
Poole Keynes
Leigh
Lydiard Millicent
Charlton
Garsdon
Lea
Foxley
Norton
Easton Grey
Shipton Moyne
Long Newnton
Tockenham
Hilmarton
Goatacre
Bremhill
Studley
Stanley
Lacock
Bowden Hill
Sandy Lane
Heddington
Cherhill
Calstone Wellington
Yatesbury
Winterbourne Monkton
Winterbourne Bassett
Broad Hinton
Broad Town
West Kennett
East Kennett
Fyfield
G L O U C E S T E R S H I R E
C O T S W O L D S
SHIRE
0 2 4 6 miles
0 2 4 6 8 10 km

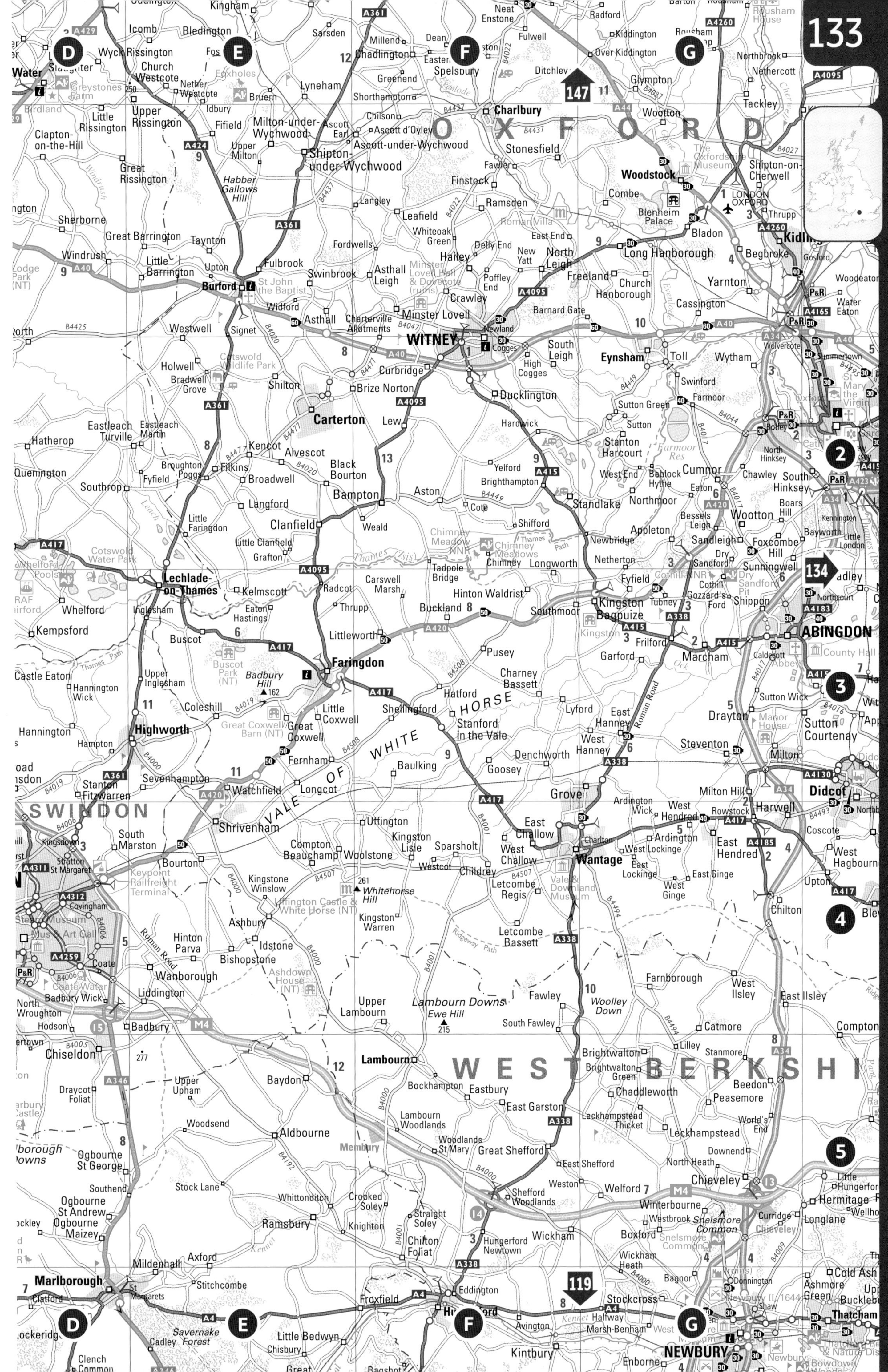
Kingham
Icomb
Bledington
Sarsden
A361
Neat Enstone
Radford
Rousham House
A4260
Millend
Dean
Kiddington
Rousham
D
E
F
G
A429
Wyck Rissington
Fos
12
Chadlington
Eastend
Spelsbury
Fulwell
Over Kiddington
Northbrook
Church Westcote
Foxholes
Nether Westcote
Greystones Farm
Lyneham
Greenend
Ditchley
147
11
Glympton
Nethercott
A4095
Bruern
Shorthampton
Charlbury
Tackley
Birdland
Idbury
Little Rissington
Upper Rissington
Fifield
Milton-under-Wychwood
Ascott Earl
Chilson
Ascott d'Oyley
Ascott-under-Wychwood
O X F O R D
Wootton
Clapton-on-the-Hill
A424
Upper Milton
Shipton-under-Wychwood
Stonesfield
The Oxfordshire Museum
Shipton-on-Cherwell
B4027
Great Rissington
Habber Gallows Hill
Fawler
Woodstock
Finstock
Combe
Blenheim Palace
LONDON OXFORD
Thrupp
Langley
Ramsden
Sherborne
A361
Leafield
Roman Villa
Kidlington
Great Barrington
Taynton
Whiteoak Green
East End
Bladon
A4260
Windrush
Fordwells
Delly End
New Yatt
North Leigh
Long Hanborough
Begbroke
Gosford
Little Barrington
Fulbrook
Hailey
9
A40
Upton
Swinbrook
Asthall Leigh
Minster Lovell Hall & Dovecote (ruins)
Poffley End
Freeland
Church Hanborough
Yarnton
Woodeaton
Burford
St John the Baptist
Crawley
A4095
Water Eaton
Widford
Asthall
Charterville Allotments
Minster Lovell
Barnard Gate
Cassington
P&R
A4165
Westwell
Signet
B4425
WITNEY
Newland
Cogges
10
A40
Wolvercote
Summertown
Holwell
Cotswold Wildlife Park
8
Curbridge
South Leigh
High Cogges
Eynsham
Toll
Wytham
St Mary the Virgin
Bradwell Grove
Shilton
Brize Norton
Ducklington
Swinford
Oxford
A361
A4095
Farmoor
Carterton
Sutton Green
Eastleach Turville
Eastleach Martin
Lew
Hardwick
Sutton
B4044
Botley
Hatherop
Kencot
Alvescot
13
Stanton Harcourt
Farmoor Res
North Hinksey
8
Broughton Poggs
Filkins
Black Bourton
Yelford
West End
Bablock Hythe
Cumnor
Chawley
South Hinksey
Quenington
Fyfield
Broadwell
Brighthampton
A415
Eaton
Southrop
Aston
Bampton
Standlake
Northmoor
A420
Boars Hill
Kennington
Langford
Cote
B4449
Bessels Leigh
Wootton
Little Faringdon
Clanfield
Weald
Shifford
Appleton
Bayworth
Chimney Meadow NNR
Chimney Meadows
Newbridge
Sandleigh
Foxcombe Hill
Little London
A417
Cotswold Water Park
Little Clanfield
Grafton
Thames Path
Chimney
Longworth
Netherton
Dry Sandford
Sunningwell
Whelford Pools
A4095
Tadpole Bridge
Carswell Marsh
Fyfield
Cothill NNR
Cothill
Dry Sandford Pit
134
Radley
Lechlade-on-Thames
Kelmscott
Radcot
Hinton Waldrist
Kingston Bagpuize
Gozzard's Ford
Shippon
Northcourt
RAF Fairford
Whelford
Inglesham
Eaton Hastings
Thrupp
Buckland
Southmoor
Tubney
A4183
Kempsford
6
Littleworth
A420
Kingston
A415
A338
ABINGDON
Buscot
A417
Pusey
Frilford
Marcham
Caldecott
County Hall
Castle Eaton
Buscot Park (NT)
Badbury Hill
Faringdon
Garford
Abbey
Hannington Wick
Upper Inglesham
162
Charney Bassett
Ock
Sutton Wick
Coleshill
Little Coxwell
Shellingford
Hatford
Lyford
East Hanney
Drayton
Manor House
Sutton Courtenay
Hannington
Highworth
Great Coxwell Barn (NT)
Great Coxwell
HORSE
Stanford in the Vale
West Hanney
Roman Road
Steventon
Hampton
Fernham
WHITE
Denchworth
Milton
Stanton Fitzwarren
Sevenhampton
Baulking
Goosey
A338
A4130
Watchfield
OF
Longcot
Grove
Milton Hill
Didcot
SWINDON
A420
VALE
Ardington Wick
West Hendred
Rowstock
Harwell
Kingsdown
Shrivenham
Uffington
East Challow
Ardington
Coscote
South Marston
Compton Beauchamp
Woolstone
Kingston Lisle
Sparsholt
West Challow
Charlton
West Locking
East Hendred
A4185
West Hagbourne
Stratton St Margaret
Bourton
Westcot
Childrey
Wantage
East Lockington
Keypoint Railfreight Terminal
Kingstone Winslow
261
Whitehorse Hill
Letcombe Regis
Vale & Downland Museum
West Ginge
East Ginge
Upton
A4312
Covingham
Uffington Castle & White Horse (NT)
Chilton
Steam Museum
Mus & Art Gall
Ashbury
Kingston Warren
Ridgeway Path
Letcombe Bassett
Hinton Parva
Idstone
Bishopstone
A4259
Coate
Coate Water
Wanborough
Ashdown House (NT)
Farnborough
West Ilsley
East Ilsley
Badbury Wick
Liddington
Upper Lambourn
Lambourn Downs
Ewe Hill
Fawley
Woolley Down
North Wroughton
Hodson
Badbury
215
South Fawley
Catmore
Compton
Chiseldon
277
Lambourn
Brightwalton
Lilley
Stanmore
W E S T B E R K S H I
Brightwalton Green
A346
Upper Upham
Baydon
Bockhampton
Eastbury
Chaddleworth
Beedon
Draycot Foliat
Peasemore
Lambourn Woodlands
East Garston
Leckhampstead Thicket
World's End
Woodsend
Aldbourne
Leckhampstead
Membury
Woodlands St Mary
Great Shefford
Downend
Marlborough Downs
Ogbourne St George
East Shefford
North Heath
Chieveley
Little Hungerford
Stock Lane
Weston
Welford
Hermitage
Southend
Whittonditch
Crooked Soley
Shefford Woodlands
Winterbourne
Wellhouse
Ogbourne St Andrew
Straight Soley
Westbrook
Snelsmore Common
Curridge
Longlane
Ogbourne Maizey
Ramsbury
Knighton
Chilton Foliat
Hungerford Newtown
Wickham
Boxford
Snelsmore Common
Mildenhall
Axford
Wickham Heath
Cold Ash
Marlborough
St Margarets
Stitchcombe
Eddington
119
Bagnor
Donnington
Ashmore Green
Clatford
Froxfield
Hungerford
Stockcross
Newbury II, 1644
Bucklebury
Thatcham
Savernake Forest
A4
Avington
Halfway
Marsh Benham
West
Lockeridge
Cadley
Little Bedwyn
Chisbury
Kintbury
Enborne
NEWBURY
Clench Common

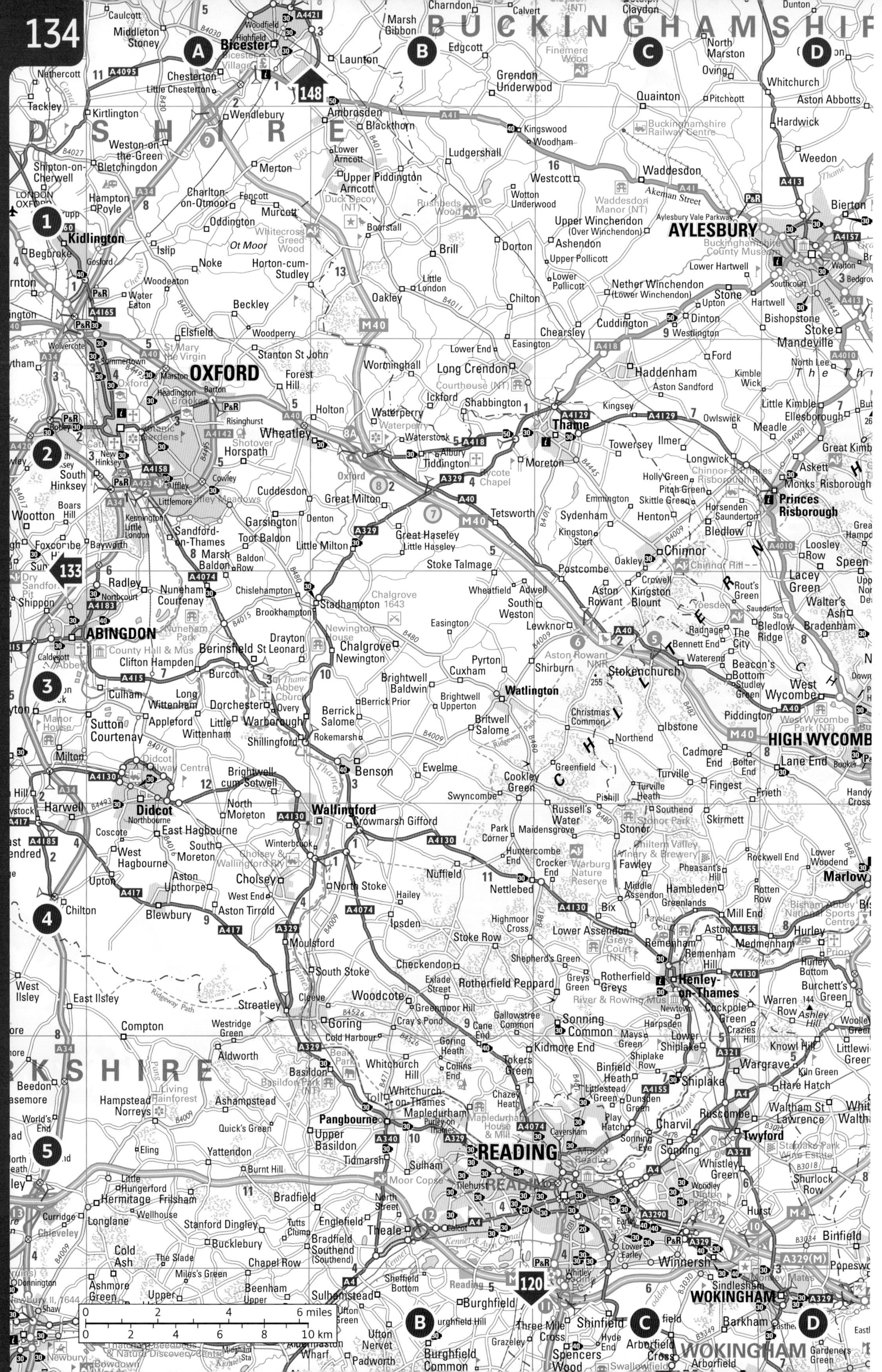
BUCKINGHAMSHIRE
OXFORDSHIRE
BERKSHIRE
CHILTERN HILLS
A
B
C
D
1
2
3
4
5
148
133
120
Caulcott
Middleton Stoney
Bicester
Bicester Village
Woodfield
Highfield
Charndon
Calvert
Claydon
Dunton
Marsh Gibbon
Edgcott
North Marston
Launton
Finemere Wood
Oving
Nethercott
Chesterton
Little Chesterton
Grendon Underwood
Quainton
Pitchcott
Whitchurch
Aston Abbotts
Tackley
Kirtlington
Wendlebury
Ambrosden
Blackthorn
Kingswood
Woodham
Buckinghamshire Railway Centre
Hardwick
Weston-on-the-Green
Lower Arncott
Ludgershall
Weedon
Shipton-on-Cherwell
Bletchingdon
Merton
Upper Arncott
Piddington
Westcott
Waddesdon
Akeman Street
London Oxford Airport
Hampton Poyle
Charlton-on-Otmoor
Fencott
Murcott
Duck Decoy (NT)
Rushbeds Wood
Wotton Underwood
Waddesdon Manor (NT)
Upper Winchendon (Over Winchendon)
Aylesbury Vale Parkway
AYLESBURY
Bierton
Kidlington
Begbroke
Oddington
Boarstall
Whitecross Green Wood
Ot Moor
Islip
Noke
Horton-cum-Studley
Brill
Dorton
Ashendon
Upper Pollicott
Lower Pollicott
Buckinghamshire County Museum
Lower Hartwell
Walton
Southcourt
Bedgrove
Gosford
Woodeaton
Water Eaton
Oakley
Little London
Chilton
Nether Winchendon (Lower Winchendon)
Stone
Upton
Hartwell
Dinton
Bishopstone
Stoke Mandeville
Beckley
Woodperry
Elsfield
Cuddington
Westlington
Chearsley
Easington
Wolvercote
Summertown
St Mary the Virgin
OXFORD
Stanton St John
Forest Hill
Worminghall
Lower End
Long Crendon
Courthouse (NT)
Haddenham
Aston Sandford
Ford
Kimble Wick
North Lee
Marston
Headington
Barton
Brookes
Risinghurst
Holton
Ickford
Shabbington
Thame
Kingsey
Towersey
Owlswick
Little Kimble
Ellesborough
Meadle
Great Kimble
Botley
Wheatley
Waterperry
Waterstock
Albury
Tiddington
Rycote Chapel
Moreton
Ilmer
Longwick
Askett
Monks Risborough
Princes Risborough
Chinnor & Princes Risborough Rly
Holly Green
Pitch Green
Skittle Green
Horsenden
Saunderton
New Hinksey
South Hinksey
Shotover
Horspath
Cowley
Iffley
Iffley Meadows
Littlemore
Cuddesdon
Great Milton
Emmington
Sydenham
Henton
Bledlow
Boars Hill
Wootton
Kennington
Little London
Sandford-on-Thames
Garsington
Denton
Tetsworth
Kingston Stert
Great Haseley
Little Haseley
Chinnor
Chinnor Hill
Foxcombe
Bayworth
Marsh Baldon
Toot Baldon
Baldon Row
Little Milton
Stoke Talmage
Postcombe
Oakley
Crowell
Loosley Row
Speen
Lacey Green
Radley
Nuneham Courtenay
Northcourt
Chislehampton
Stadhampton
Chalgrove 1643
Wheatfield
Adwell
South Weston
Aston Rowant
Kingston Blount
Rout's Green
Walter's Ash
Saunderton Sta
Bledlow Ridge
Bradenham
Shippon
Dry Sandford Pit
ABINGDON
Brookhampton
Newington House
Easington
Lewknor
Yoesden
Radnage
The City
Bennett End
Caldecott
Abbey
County Hall & Mus
Clifton Hampden
Berinsfield
Drayton St Leonard
Chalgrove
Newington
Pyrton
Aston Rowant NNR
Waterend
Beacon's Bottom
Studley Green
West Wycombe
Culham
Burcot
Dorchester
Abbey Church
Overy
Cuxham
Brightwell Baldwin
Brightwell Upperton
Watlington
Shirburn
Stokenchurch
Long Wittenham
Little Wittenham
Warborough
Berrick Prior
Berrick Salome
Britwell Salome
Christmas Common
Northend
Ibstone
Piddington
West Wycombe Park (NT)
HIGH WYCOMBE
Sutton Courtenay
Appleford
Manor House
Rokemarsh
Shillingford
Milton
Didcot Railway Centre
Brightwell-cum-Sotwell
Benson
Ewelme
Cookley Green
Greenfield
Cadmore End
Bolter End
Lane End
Booker
Turville
Turville Heath
Fingest
Frieth
Handy Cross
Harwell
Didcot
Northbourne
North Moreton
Wallingford
Crowmarsh Gifford
Swyncombe
Pishill
Russell's Water
Southend
Stonor Park
Stonor
Skirmett
Maidensgrove
Park Corner
Coscote
East Hagbourne
Winterbrook
Cholsey & Wallingford Rly
Chiltern Valley Winery & Brewery
Rockwell End
Lower Woodend
West Hagbourne
South Moreton
Huntercombe End
Crocker End
Warburg Nature Reserve
Fawley
Pheasant's Hill
Marlow
Upton
Aston Upthorpe
Cholsey
North Stoke
Nuffield
Nettlebed
Middle Assendon
Hambleden
Greenlands
Rotten Row
Chilton
Blewbury
West End
Aston Tirrold
Hailey
Ipsden
Highmoor Cross
Bix
Mill End
Bisham Abbey National Sports Centre
Moulsford
Stoke Row
Lower Assendon
Aston
Remenham
Medmenham
Hurley
Priory
Checkendon
Shepherd's Green
Greys Court (NT)
Remenham Hill
Hurley Bottom
Burchett's Green
South Stoke
Exlade Street
Rotherfield Peppard
Greys Green
Rotherfield Greys
Henley-on-Thames
River & Rowing Mus
West Ilsley
East Ilsley
Cleeve
Woodcote
Streatley
Greenmoor Hill
Gallowstree Common
Sonning Common
Newtown
Cockpole Green
Warren Row
Ashley Hill
Crazies Hill
Woolley Green
Compton
Westridge Green
Goring
Cray's Pond
Cane End
Harpsden
Mays Green
Lower Shiplake
Cold Harbour
Goring Heath
Kidmore End
Shiplake Row
Knowl Hill
Littlewick Green
Aldworth
Basildon
Beale Park
Whitchurch Hill
Collins End
Tokers Green
Binfield Heath
Wargrave
Kiln Green
Basildon Park (NT)
Shiplake
Hare Hatch
Beedon
Hampstead Norreys
Living Rainforest
Ashampstead
Whitchurch-on-Thames
Chazey Heath
Littlestead Green
Dunsden Green
Ruscombe
Waltham St Lawrence
World's End
Quick's Green
Pangbourne
Mapledurham
Purley on Thames
Mapledurham House & Mill
Caversham
Play Hatch
Charvil
Twyford
Upper Basildon
Tidmarsh
READING
Sonning Eye
Sonning
Mus of Reading
Stanlake Park Wine Estate
Eling
Yattendon
Sulham
Whistley Green
Shurlock Row
Burnt Hill
Moor Copse
Tilehurst
Woodley
Dinton Pastures
Little Hungerford
Hermitage
Frilsham
Bradfield
North Street
Hurst
Curridge
Longlane
Wellhouse
Stanford Dingley
Tutts Clump
Englefield
Theale
Calcot
Earley
Lower Earley
Winnersh
Binfield
Chieveley
Bucklebury
Bradfield Southend (Southend)
Kennet & Avon Canal
Cold Ash
The Slade
Chapel Row
Sheffield Bottom
Whitley
Popeswood
Ashmore Green
Miles's Green
Beenham
Sulhamstead
Reading
Burghfield
Sindlesham
Newbury II 1644
Shaw
Upper Green
Burghfield Hill
Three Mile Cross
Shinfield
Arborfield
Arborfield Cross
Barkham
WOKINGHAM
Ufton Nervet
Grazeley
Spencers Wood
Hyde End
Swallowfield
Gardeners Green
Newbury
Bowdown
Thatcham Reedbeds & Nature Discovery Centre
Midgham Sta
Padworth
Burghfield Common
Aldermaston Wharf
0 2 4 6 miles
0 2 4 6 8 10 km
A4095
A4421
A41
A413
A4157
A34
A4165
A40
A418
A4129
A4010
A420
A4142
A4158
A423
A329
A4074
A4183
A415
A4130
A417
A4185
A4155
A321
A4
A340
A3290
A329(M)
M40
M4
B4030
B430
B4027
B4011
B4017
B4495
B4015
B480
B4009
B4016
B4493
B4443
B4445
B482
B481
B4526
B471
B3018
B3034
B3030
B3349

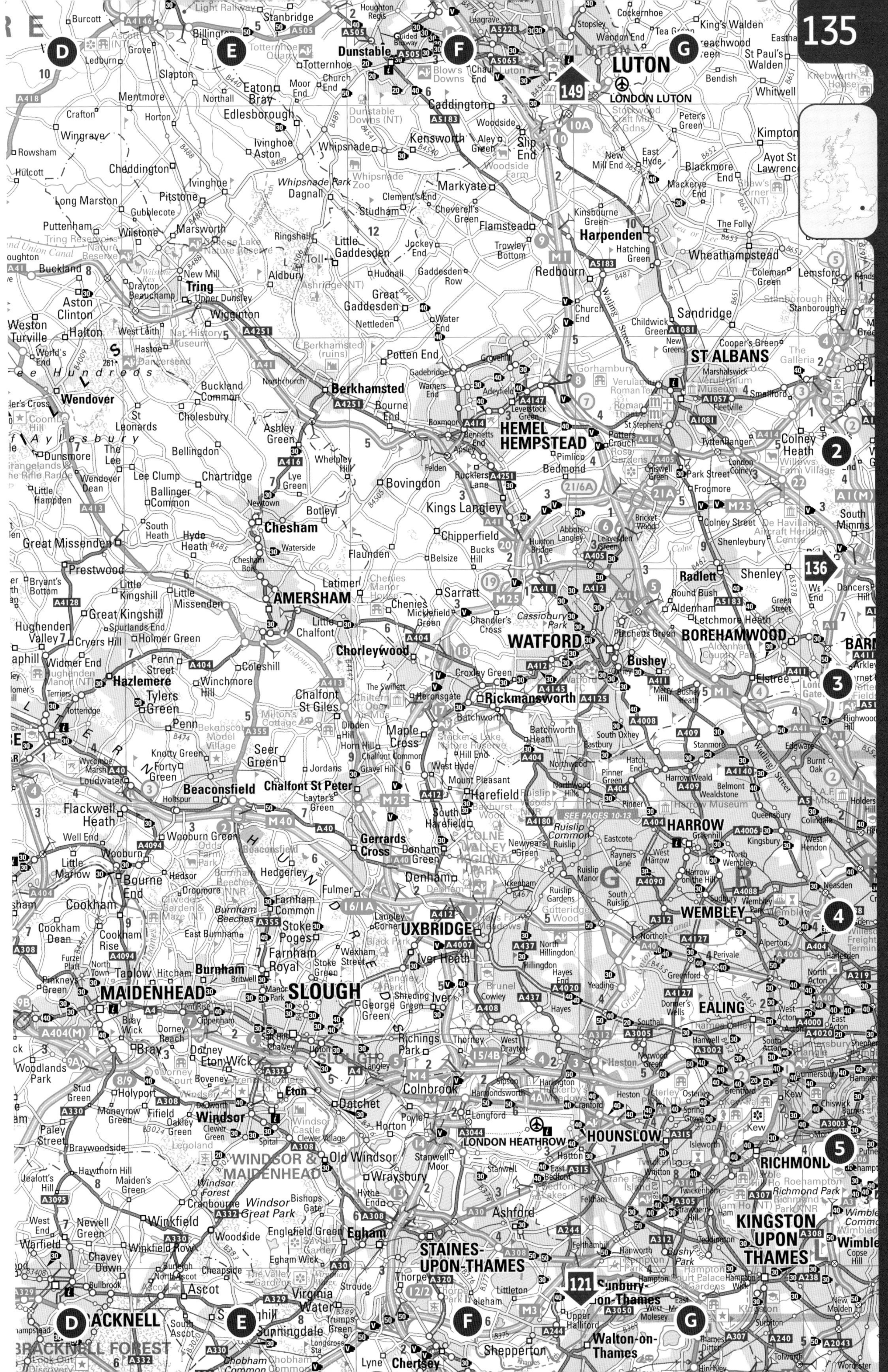
LUTON
LONDON LUTON
Dunstable
Houghton Regis
Caddington
Kensworth
Slip End
Markyate
Flamstead
Harpenden
Redbourn
Wheathampstead
Sandridge
ST ALBANS
Kimpton
Whitwell
Lemsford
Leighton Buzzard
Billington
Stanbridge
Totternhoe
Eaton Bray
Edlesborough
Ivinghoe
Ivinghoe Aston
Whipsnade
Dagnall
Studham
Cheddington
Pitstone
Marsworth
Long Marston
Wingrave
Tring
Wigginton
Aldbury
Little Gaddesden
Great Gaddesden
Nettleden
Potten End
Berkhamsted
Bourne End
Northchurch
Wendover
Aston Clinton
Halton
Weston Turville
Buckland
HEMEL HEMPSTEAD
Kings Langley
Bovingdon
Chipperfield
Abbots Langley
Bedmond
Chesham
AMERSHAM
Chenies
Latimer
Flaunden
Sarratt
Chorleywood
WATFORD
Bushey
Radlett
Shenley
BOREHAMWOOD
Elstree
London Colney
Colney Heath
South Mimms
Great Missenden
Prestwood
Little Kingshill
Great Kingshill
Little Missenden
Hazlemere
Tylers Green
Penn
Chalfont St Giles
Chalfont St Peter
Rickmansworth
Harefield
Beaconsfield
Seer Green
Gerrards Cross
Denham
UXBRIDGE
HARROW
WEMBLEY
EALING
Flackwell Heath
Wooburn Green
Bourne End
Cookham
Marlow
MAIDENHEAD
Burnham
Farnham Royal
Stoke Poges
SLOUGH
Iver Heath
Iver
Eton
Windsor
Datchet
Colnbrook
LONDON HEATHROW
HOUNSLOW
RICHMOND
KINGSTON UPON THAMES
Old Windsor
Wraysbury
Egham
STAINES-UPON-THAMES
Ashford
Sunbury-on-Thames
Walton-on-Thames
Shepperton
Chertsey
Virginia Water
Sunningdale
Ascot
Winkfield
BRACKNELL
BRACKNELL FOREST
WINDSOR & MAIDENHEAD
Windsor Great Park
Legoland
M1
M25
M40
M4
M3
A1(M)
SEE PAGES 10-13
149
136
121

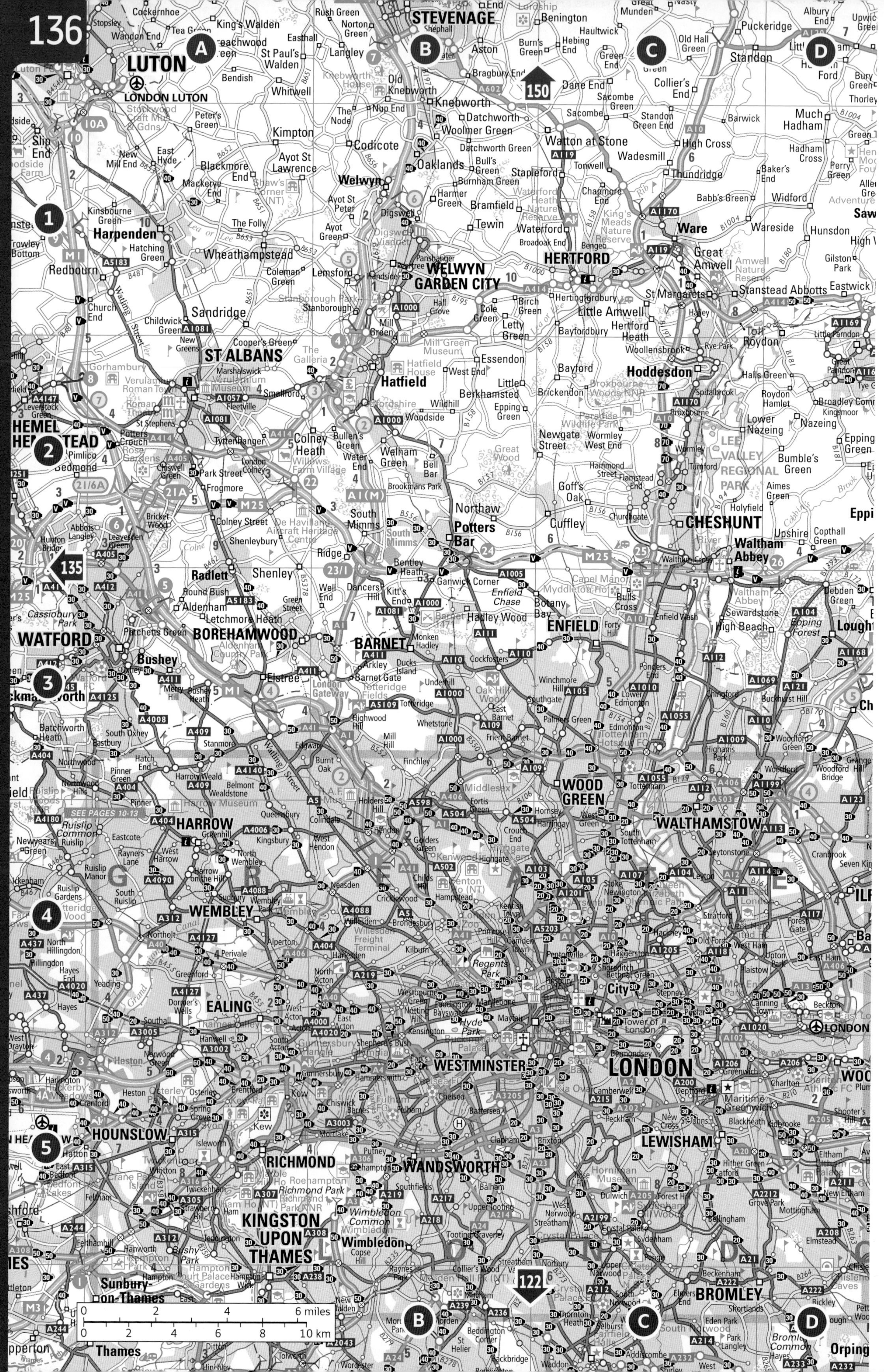
LUTON
LONDON LUTON
STEVENAGE
150
Harpenden
Redbourn
Wheathampstead
Welwyn
WELWYN GARDEN CITY
HERTFORD
Ware
Hoddesdon
ST ALBANS
Hatfield
HEMEL HEMPSTEAD
Sandridge
Colney Heath
South Mimms
Potters Bar
CHESHUNT
Waltham Abbey
135
WATFORD
Radlett
Shenley
BOREHAMWOOD
BARNET
ENFIELD
Bushey
Elstree
WOOD GREEN
WALTHAMSTOW
HARROW
WEMBLEY
EALING
WESTMINSTER
LONDON
LEWISHAM
HOUNSLOW
RICHMOND
WANDSWORTH
KINGSTON UPON THAMES
Wimbledon
BROMLEY
122
Sunbury-on-Thames
Thames
SEE PAGES 10-13
0 2 4 6 miles
0 2 4 6 8 10 km

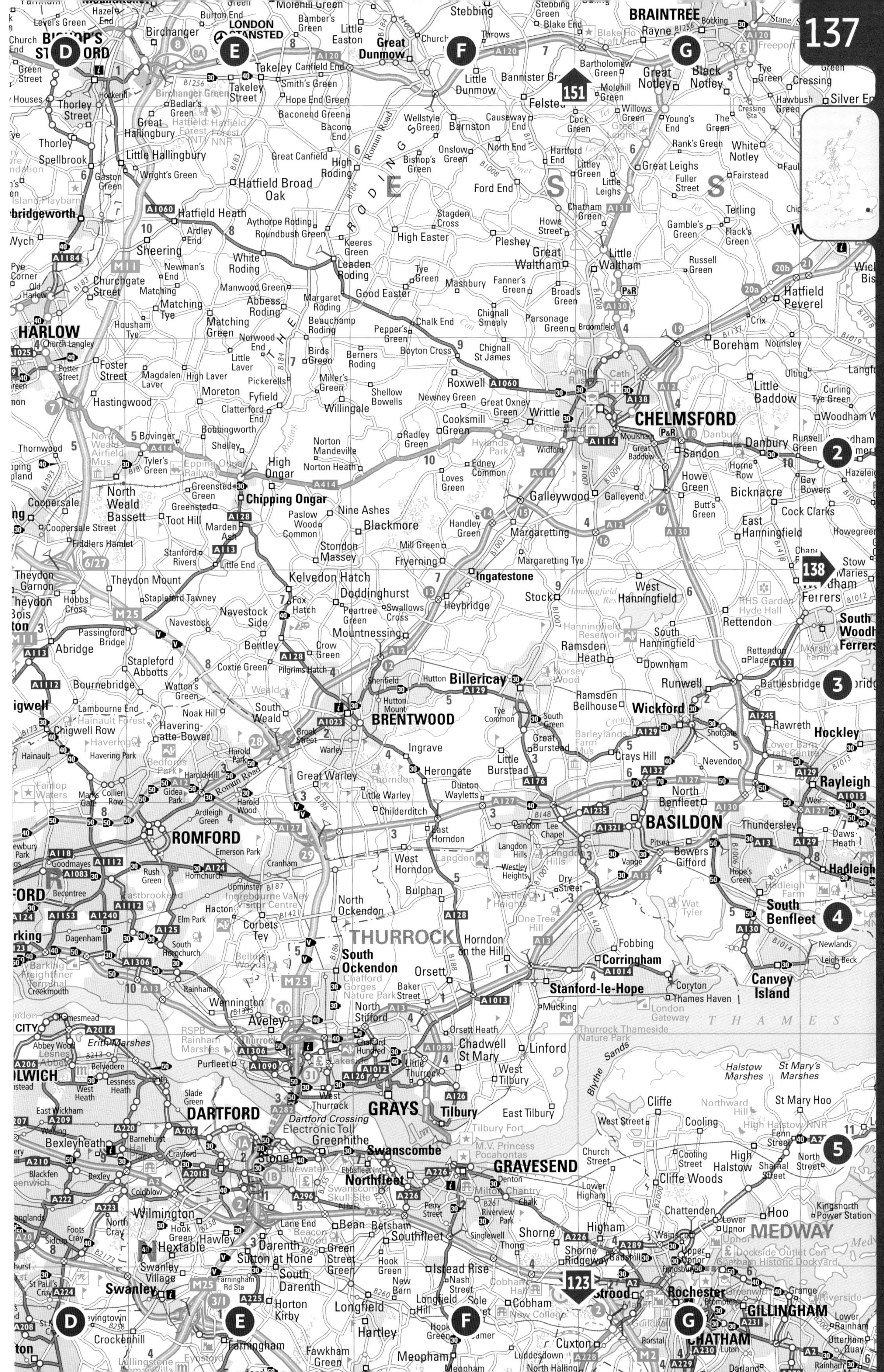
BISHOP'S STORTFORD
LONDON STANSTED
Great Dunmow
BRAINTREE
Rayne
Great Notley
Black Notley
Felsted
Takeley
Birchanger
Hatfield Broad Oak
Hatfield Heath
Sheering
HARLOW
THE RODINGS
High Roding
Leaden Roding
Good Easter
Pleshey
Great Waltham
Little Waltham
Broomfield
Hatfield Peverel
Boreham
CHELMSFORD
Writtle
Danbury
Sandon
Galleywood
Margaretting
Ingatestone
Stock
West Hanningfield
Hanningfield Reservoir
South Woodham Ferrers
Chipping Ongar
High Ongar
Fyfield
Blackmore
Kelvedon Hatch
Doddinghurst
Mountnessing
Billericay
BRENTWOOD
Wickford
Rayleigh
Hockley
BASILDON
North Benfleet
Thundersley
Hadleigh
South Benfleet
Canvey Island
Stanford-le-Hope
Corringham
Fobbing
Horndon on the Hill
Orsett
THURROCK
South Ockendon
North Stifford
Aveley
Chadwell St Mary
GRAYS
Tilbury
West Tilbury
East Tilbury
Linford
ROMFORD
Abridge
Theydon Bois
Chigwell Row
Havering-atte-Bower
Hornchurch
Upminster
Rainham
Dagenham
DARTFORD
Swanscombe
Northfleet
GRAVESEND
Higham
Cliffe
Cliffe Woods
Strood
Rochester
GILLINGHAM
CHATHAM
MEDWAY
Hoo
High Halstow
Shorne
Cobham
Meopham
Longfield
Hartley
Swanley
Sutton at Hone
Hextable
Wilmington
Bexleyheath
Crockenhill
Farningham
Horton Kirby
South Darenth
Darenth
THAMES
Dartford Crossing Electronic Toll
M25
M11
A12
A13
A127
A130
A120
151
138
123

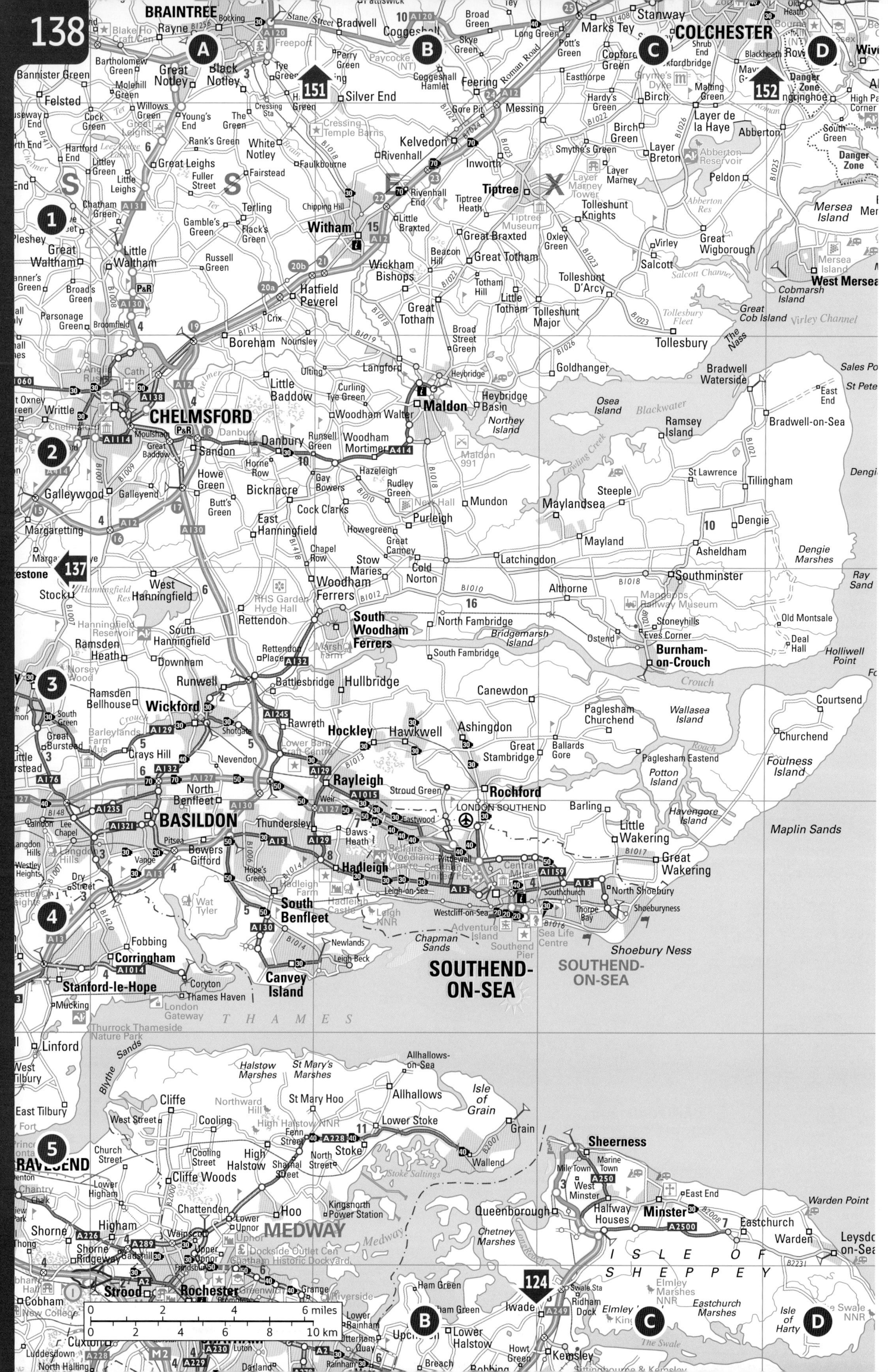
BRAINTREE
Rayne
Bocking
Bradwell
Coggeshall
Broad Green
Skye Green
Long Green
Marks Tey
Stanway
COLCHESTER
Pott's Green
Copford Green
Shrub End
Blackheath
Rowhedge
Bartholomew Green
Bannister Green
Great Notley
Black Notley
Perry Green
Paycocke (NT)
Tye Green
151
Silver End
Coggeshall Hamlet
Feering
Roman Road
Easthorpe
Gryme's Dyke
Malting Green
Danger Zone
Fingringhoe
High Park Corner
152
Felsted
Molehill Green
Willows Green
Cressing Sta
Cock Green
Young's End
The Green
Cressing Temple Barns
Gore Pit
Messing
Hardy's Green
Birch
Layer de la Haye
Abberton
South Green
Hartford End
Great Leighs
Rank's Green
White Notley
Kelvedon
Rivenhall
Faulkbourne
Birch Green
Smythe's Green
Layer Breton
Abberton Reservoir
Danger Zone
Littley Green
Little Leighs
Fuller Street
Fairstead
Inworth
Layer Marney
Layer Marney Tower
Peldon
Chatham Green
Terling
Chipping Hill
Rivenhall End
Tiptree
Tiptree Heath
Tollesbunt Knights
Abberton Res
Mersea Island
Pleshey
Great Waltham
Gamble's Green
Flack's Green
Witham
Little Braxted
Great Braxted
Tiptree Museum
Oxley Green
Virley
Great Wigborough
Little Waltham
Russell Green
Wickham Bishops
Beacon Hill
Great Totham
Salcott
Salcott Channel
Mersea Island
West Mersea
Broad's Green
P&R
Hatfield Peverel
Totham Hill
Tolleshunt D'Arcy
Cobmarsh Island
Parsonage Green
Broomfield
Crix
Great Totham
Little Totham
Tolleshunt Major
Tollesbury Fleet
Great Cob Island
Virley Channel
Boreham
Nounsley
Broad Street Green
Tollesbury
The Nass
Ulting
Langford
Goldhanger
Bradwell Waterside
Sales Point
St Peter's
Heybridge
East End
Writtle
Little Baddow
Curling Tye Green
Heybridge Basin
Osea Island
Blackwater
Chelmsford
CHELMSFORD
Woodham Walter
Maldon
Northey Island
Ramsey Island
Bradwell-on-Sea
Moulsham
Danbury Park
Runsell Green
Woodham Mortimer
Maldon 991
Great Baddow
Sandon
Danbury
Lawling Creek
Horne Row
Hazeleigh
Gay Bowers
St Lawrence
Tillingham
Dengie
Howe Green
Rudley Green
New Hall
Steeple
Galleywood
Galleyend
Bicknacre
Mundon
Maylandsea
Butt's Green
Cock Clarks
Purleigh
Margaretting
East Hanningfield
Howegreen
Dengie
Great Canney
Mayland
Asheldham
Dengie Marshes
Chapel Row
Stow Maries
Cold Norton
Latchingdon
137
West Hanningfield
Hanningfield Res
Stock
Woodham Ferrers
Southminster
Ray Sand
RHS Garden Hyde Hall
Althorne
Mangapps Railway Museum
Rettendon
South Woodham Ferrers
North Fambridge
Stoneyhills
Old Montsale
Hanningfield Reservoir
South Hanningfield
Ramsden Heath
Bridgemarsh Island
Ostend
Eves Corner
Deal Hall
Holliwell Point
Downham
Rettendon Place
Marsh Farm
South Fambridge
Burnham-on-Crouch
Norsey Wood
Runwell
Battlesbridge
Hullbridge
Crouch
Ramsden Bellhouse
Wickford
Canewdon
Courtsend
South Green
Rawreth
Paglesham Churchend
Wallasea Island
Great Burstead
Barleylands Farm Mus
Shotgate
Hockley
Hawkwell
Ashingdon
Churchend
Crays Hill
Nevendon
Lower Barn Farm Craft Centre
Great Stambridge
Ballards Gore
Paglesham Eastend
Foulness Island
Roach
Potton Island
North Benfleet
Rayleigh
Stroud Green
Rochford
Weir
LONDON SOUTHEND
Barling
Havengore Island
BASILDON
Eastwood
Little Wakering
Maplin Sands
Lee Chapel
Pitsea
Thundersley
Daws Heath
Langdon Hills
Bowers Gifford
Vange
Belfairs Woodland Centre
Prittlewell
Southend United FC
Great Wakering
Hadleigh
Hope's Green
Central Mus
Southchurch
North Shoebury
Dry Street
Wat Tyler
Hadleigh Farm
Leigh-on-Sea
South Benfleet
Hadleigh Castle
Leigh NNR
Westcliff-on-Sea
Thorpe Bay
Shoeburyness
Fobbing
Adventure Island
Southend Pier
Sea Life Centre
Newlands
Chapman Sands
Shoebury Ness
Corringham
Leigh Beck
Stanford-le-Hope
Canvey Island
SOUTHEND-ON-SEA
Coryton
Thames Haven
Mucking
London Gateway
THAMES
Thurrock Thameside Nature Park
Linford
Blythe Sands
Allhallows-on-Sea
West Tilbury
Halstow Marshes
St Mary's Marshes
Isle of Grain
Cliffe
Northward Hill
St Mary Hoo
Allhallows
East Tilbury
West Street
Cooling
High Halstow NNR
Lower Stoke
Grain
Fenn Street
Stoke
Sheerness
Church Street
Cooling Street
High Halstow
Shamal Street
North Street
Wallend
Marine Town
GRAVESEND
Cliffe Woods
Stoke Saltings
Mile Town
West Minster
Chantry
Lower Higham
East End
Chalk
Chattenden
Hoo
Kingsnorth Power Station
Queenborough
Halfway Houses
Minster
Warden Point
Higham
Lower Upnor
Upnor
MEDWAY
Medway
Chetney Marshes
Eastchurch
Shorne
Shorne Ridgeway
Wainscott
Dockside Outlet Cen
Chatham Historic Dockyard
Warden
Leysdown-on-Sea
Gadshill
ISLE OF SHEPPEY
Frindsbury
Strood
Rochester
Grange
Riverside
Ham Green
124
Swale Sta
Elmley Marshes NNR
Cobham
Ridham Dock
Eastchurch Marshes
Isle of Harty
Swale NNR
Iwade
0 2 4 6 miles
0 2 4 6 8 10 km
Lower Rainham
Upchurch
Lower Halstow
The Swale
Cuxton
Otterham Quay
Luddesdown
Luton
Breach
Howt Green
Kemsley
North Halling
Darland
Rainham
A
B
C
D
1
2
3
4
5
ESSEX

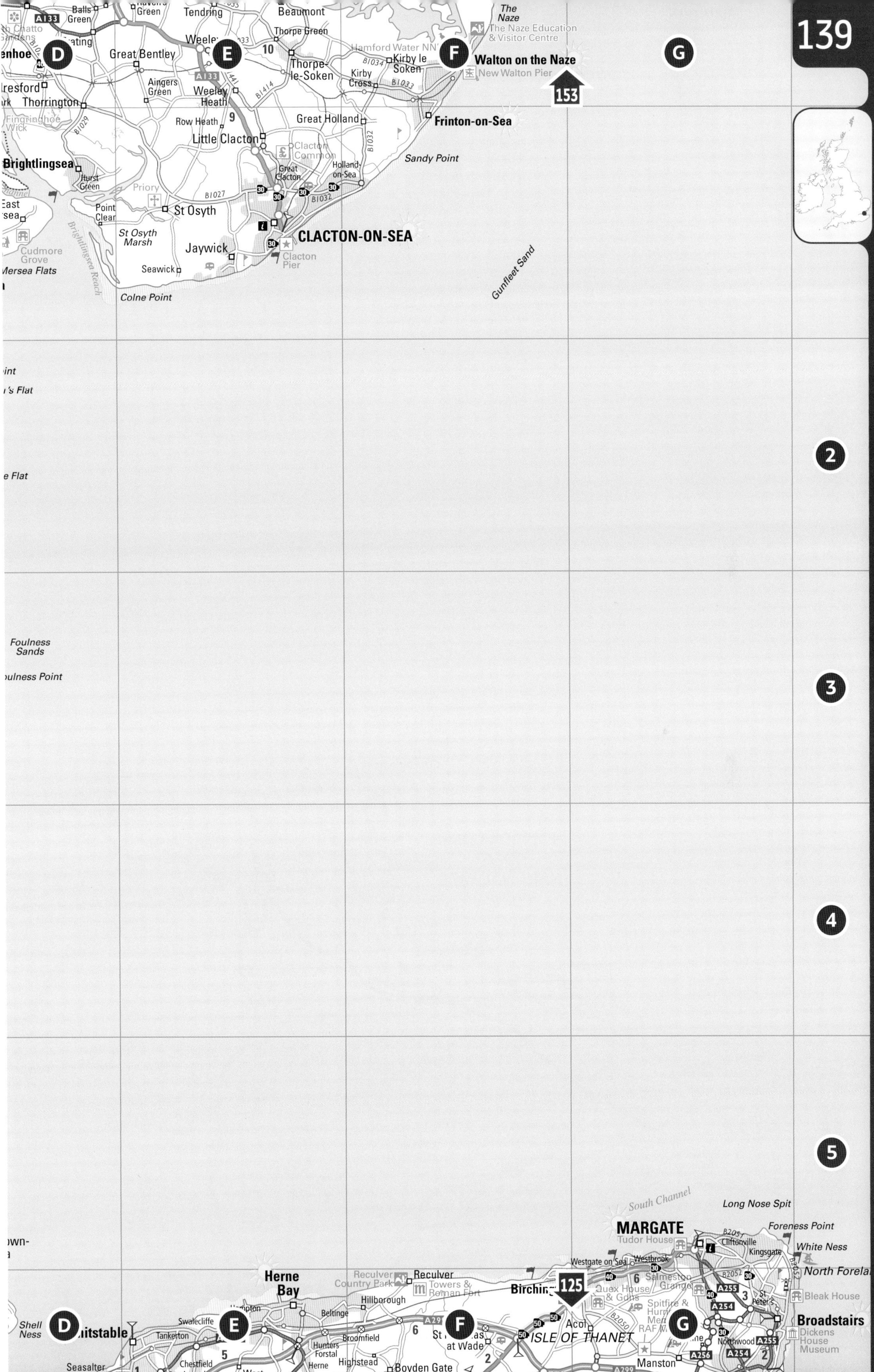

A133

Balls Green
Tendring
Beaumont
The Naze
The Naze Education
& Visitor Centre

Weeley
E
10
Thorpe Green

Great Bentley
Thorpe-le-Soken
Hamford Water NN
F
Walton on the Naze

enhoe
D
B1034
Kirby le Soken
New Walton Pier

Aingers Green
A133
Weeley Heath
Kirby Cross
B1033
153
G

resford
Thorrington
Row Heath
9
Great Holland
Frinton-on-Sea

Fingringhoe
Wick
B1029
Little Clacton
B1032
Sandy Point

Brightlingsea
Hurst Green
£
Clacton Common
Holland-on-Sea

East
sea
Priory
90
Great Clacton
30

Point Clear
St Osyth
B1027
30
B1032

Cudmore Grove
St Osyth Marsh
i
90
CLACTON-ON-SEA
Gunfleet Sand

Mersea Flats
Jaywick
Clacton Pier

Colne Point
Seawick

int

's Flat

e Flat

2

Foulness Sands

oulness Point

3

4

5

South Channel
Long Nose Spit

MARGATE
Tudor House
Foreness Point

Westgate on Sea
Westbrook
Cliftonville
White Ness
Kingsgate

North Forela

own-

Herne Bay
Reculver
Reculver Country Park
Reculver Towers & Roman Fort

Birchin
125
Quex House & Gdns
Salmeston Grange
A255
St Peter's
Bleak House

Shell Ness
D
hitstable
E
Hampton
Swalecliffe
Tankerton
Beltinge
Hillborough
6
A29
St as at Wade
F
50
50
Acol
ISLE OF THANET
Spitfire & Hurri
RAF M
G
Northwood
A255
Broadstairs
Dickens House Museum

Seasalter
Chestfield
Broomfield
Hunters Forstal
Highstead
Boyden Gate
Manston
A256
A254

5
West
2
A299

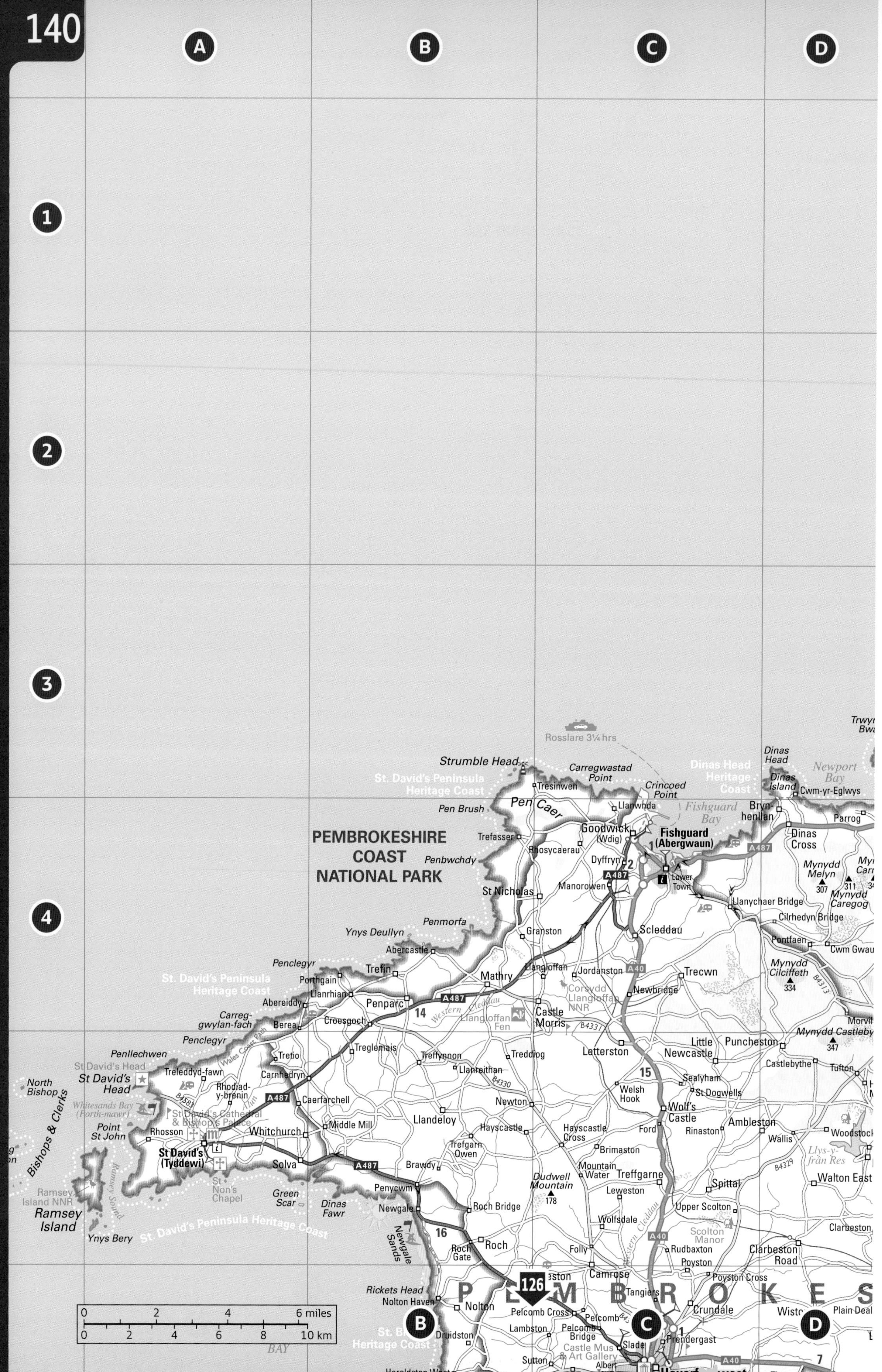

A   B   C   D

1

2

3

Rosslare 3¼ hrs

Strumble Head

Carregwastad Point

Trwyn Bwa

Dinas Head

Newport Bay

St. David's Peninsula Heritage Coast

Dinas Head Heritage Coast

Dinas Island

Crincoed Point

Cwm-yr-Eglwys

Tresinwen

Pen Brush

Pen Caer

Llanwnda

Fishguard Bay

Bryn-henllan

Parrog

PEMBROKESHIRE COAST NATIONAL PARK

Penbwchdy

Trefasser

Goodwick (Wdig)

Rhosycaerau

Fishguard (Abergwaun)

Dinas Cross

Dyffryn

A487

Lower Town

Mynydd Melyn
307

Myr Carr

Mynydd Caregog

St Nicholas

Manorowen

Llanychaer Bridge

4

Granston

Scleddau

Cilrhedyn Bridge

Pontfaen

Cwm Gwau

Penmorfa

Ynys Deullyn

Abercastle

Llangloffan

Jordanston

A40

Trecwn

Mynydd Cilciffeth
334

B4313

Penclegyr

Trefin

Mathry

Castle Morris

Corsydd Llangloffan NNR

Newbridge

Mynydd Castleby
347

Porthgain

Penparc

14

Western Cleddau

B433

Little Newcastle

Puncheston

Tufton

St. David's Peninsula Heritage Coast

Llanrhian

Abereiddy

Croesgoch

Llangloffan Fen

Letterston

15

Castlebythe

Carreg-gwylan-fach

Berea

Treglemais

Treffynnon

Treddiog

Welsh Hook

Sealyham

St Dogwells

Ambleston

Woodstock

Penclegyr

Tretio

Wolf's Castle

Rinaston

Wallis

Llys-y-frân Res

Penllechwen

St David's Head

Treleddyd-fawr

Carnhedryn

Llanreithan

B4330

Newton

Ford

B4329

North Bishop

St David's Head

Rhodiad-y-brenin

A487

Caerfarchell

Llandeloy

Hayscastle

Hayscastle Cross

Brimaston

Walton East

Whitesands Bay (Porth-mawr)

St David's Cathedral & Bishop's Palace

Middle Mill

Trefgarn Owen

Mountain Water

Treffgarne

Spittal

Point St John

Rhosson

Whitchurch

Brawdy

Dudwell Mountain
178

Leweston

Upper Scolton

Clarbeston

St Non's Chapel

St David's (Tyddewi)

Solva

A487

Penycwm

Roch Bridge

Wolfsdale

Scolton Manor

Clarbeston Road

Ramsey Island NNR

Green Scar

Dinas Fawr

Newgale

Folly

Rudbaxton

Poyston Cross

Ramsey Island

Ynys Bery

St. David's Peninsula Heritage Coast

16

Roch Gate

Roch

Camrose

Tangiers

Crundale

Wisto

Plain Deal

Newgale Sands

126

PEMBROKES

Rickets Head

Nolton Haven

Nolton

Pelcomb Cross

Pelcomb

Lambston

Pelcomb Bridge

Castle Mus Art Gallery

A40

St. B Heritage Coast

Druidston

Sutton

Slade

Prendergast

Haverfordwest

7

Bishops & Clerks

BAY

B   C   D

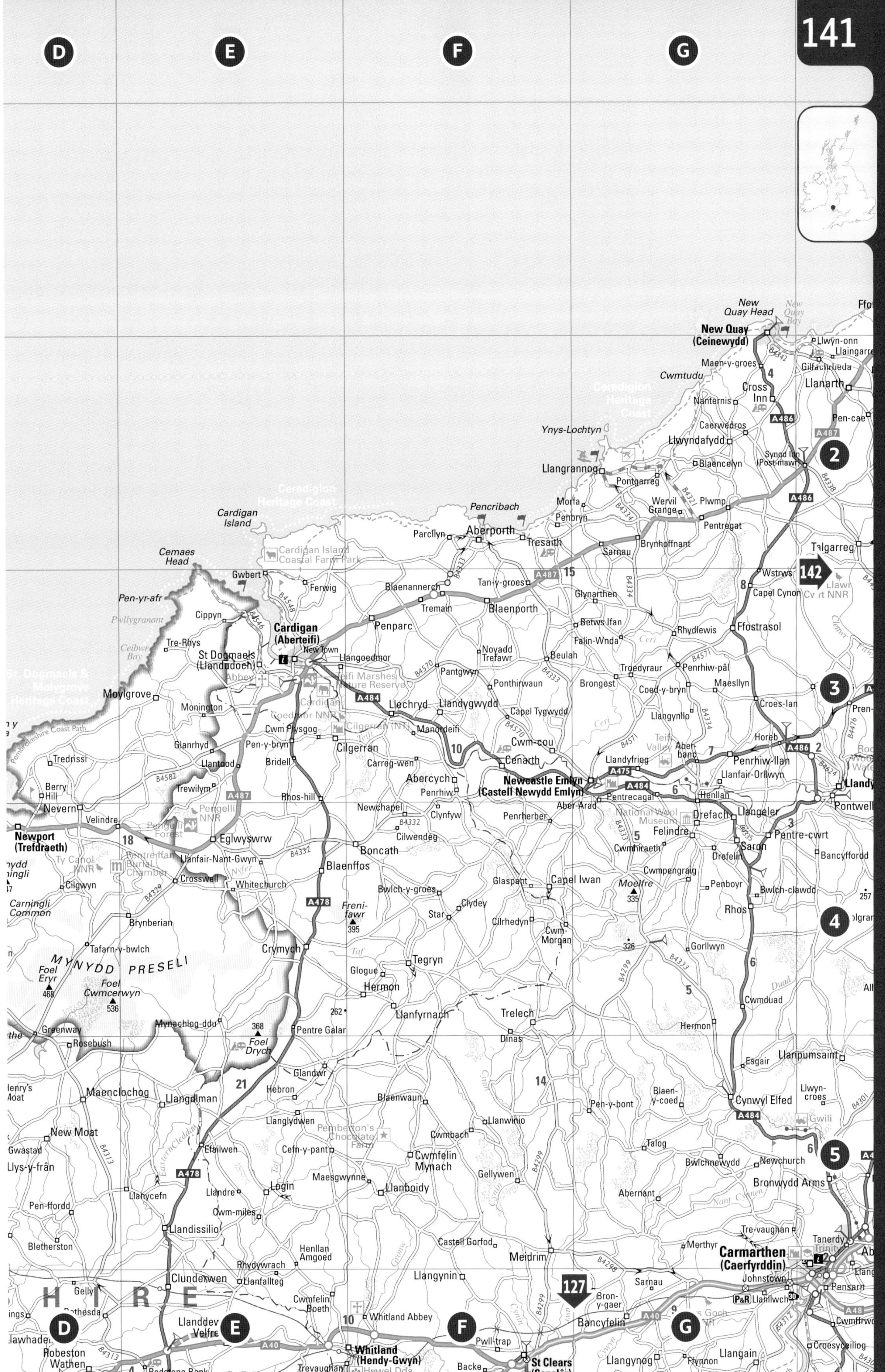

New Quay Head
New Quay (Ceinewydd)
Cwmtudu
Ceredigion Heritage Coast
Ynys-Lochtyn
Llangrannog
Cross Inn
Llanarth
Synod Inn (Post-mawr)
Pencribach
Aberporth
Tresaith
Cardigan Island
Cemaes Head
Gwbert
Cardigan (Aberteifi)
St Dogmaels (Llandudoch)
Moylgrove
Newport (Trefdraeth)
Eglwyswrw
Cilgerran
Llechryd
Cenarth
Newcastle Emlyn (Castell Newydd Emlyn)
Drefach
Felindre
Crymych
Boncath
Blaenffos
Tegryn
Hermon
Llanfyrnach
Trelech
MYNYDD PRESELI
Foel Cwmcerwyn 536
Foel Eryr 468
Maenclochog
Llangolman
New Moat
Llys-y-frân
Efailwen
Login
Llanboidy
Cwmfelin Mynach
Llandissilio
Clunderwen
Whitland (Hendy-Gwyn)
St Clears (Sanclêr)
Meidrim
Carmarthen (Caerfyrddin)
Cynwyl Elfed
Llanpumsaint
Bronwydd Arms
Newchurch
Bancyfelin
Llangynog
Llangain
Robeston Wathen
Llanddewi Velfrey
142
127

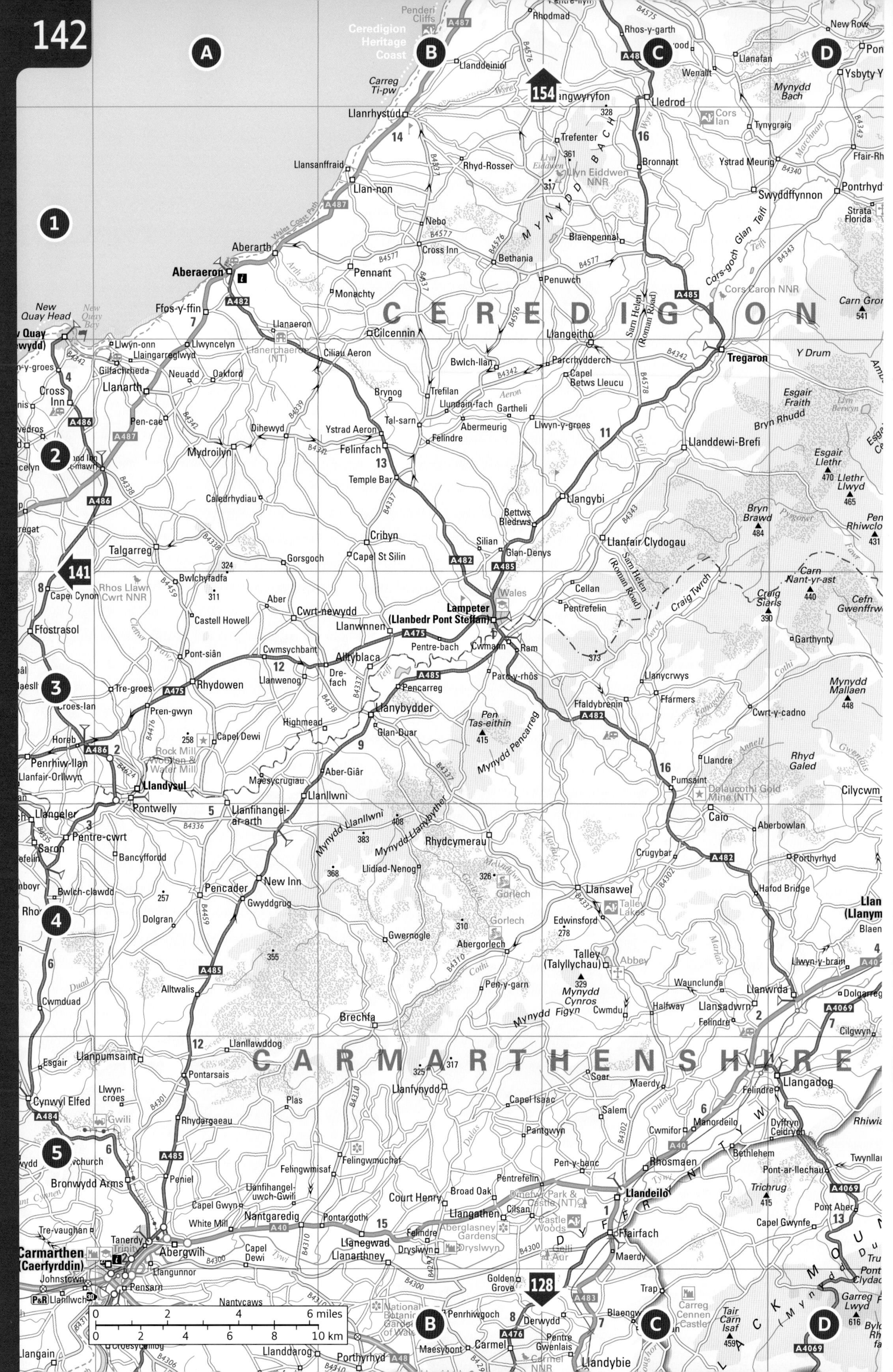

A
B
C
D
1
2
3
4
5
154
141
128
Penderi Cliffs
Ceredigion Heritage Coast
Carreg Ti-pw
Rhodmad
Rhos-y-garth
Llanddeiniol
New Row
Llanafan
Wenallt
Ysbyty Ystwyth
Mynydd Bach
Lledrod
Cors Ian
Tynygraig
Llanrhystud
Trefenter
Rhyd-Rosser
Llyn Eiddwen
Llyn Eiddwen NNR
Bronnant
Ystrad Meurig
Ffair-Rhos
Llansanffraid
Llan-non
Swyddffynnon
Pontrhydfendigaid
Strata Florida
Nebo
Cross Inn
Mynydd Bach
Blaenpennal
Wales Coast Path
Aberarth
Aberaeron
Pennant
Bethania
Penuwch
Cors-goch Glan Teifi
Cors Caron NNR
Monachty
Ffos-y-ffin
New Quay Head
New Quay Bay
CEREDIGION
Sarn Helen (Roman Road)
Carn Gron
541
Llanaeron
Llanerchaeron (NT)
Cilcennin
Llangeitho
Tregaron
Y Drum
Llwyn-onn
Llwyncelyn
Llaingarreglwyd
Gilfachreda
Ciliau Aeron
Bwlch-llan
Parcrhydderch
Capel Betws Lleucu
Cross Inn
Llanarth
Neuadd
Oakford
Brynog
Trefilan
Llundain-fach
Gartheli
Aeron
Esgair Fraith
Llyn Berwyn
Bryn Rhudd
Pen-cae
Dihewyd
Ystrad Aeron
Tal-sarn
Abermeurig
Llwyn-y-groes
Mydroilyn
Felinfach
Felindre
Llanddewi-Brefi
Esgair Llethr
470
Llethr Llwyd
465
Temple Bar
Caledrhydiau
Llangybi
Bryn Brawd
484
Pen Rhiwclochdy
431
Cribyn
Bettws Bledrws
Llanfair Clydogau
Talgarreg
Capel St Silin
Silian
Glan-Denys
324
Gorsgoch
Bwlchyfadfa
Carn Nant-yr-ast
440
Rhos Llawr Cwrt NNR
Capel Cynon
311
Cellan
Craig Twrch
Craig Siarls
390
Cefn Gwenffrwd
Aber
Lampeter (Llanbedr Pont Steffan)
Pentrefelin
Castell Howell
Cwrt-newydd
Ffostrasol
Llanwnnen
Pentre-bach
Cwmann
Ram
Garthynty
Pont-siân
Cwmsychbant
Alltyblaca
373
Dre-fach
Rhydowen
Llanwenog
Llanycrwys
Cothi
Tre-groes
Pencarreg
Parc-y-rhôs
Mynydd Mallaen
448
Croes-lan
Ffaldybrenin
Ffarmers
Pren-gwyn
Llanybydder
Cwrt-y-cadno
Pen Tas-eithin
415
Horeb
Highmead
Glan-Duar
258
Capel Dewi
Mynydd Pencarreg
Penrhiw-llan
Rock Mill Woollen & Water Mill
Llandre
Rhyd Galed
Llanfair-Orllwyn
Aber-Giâr
Pumsaint
Dolaucothi Gold Mine (NT)
Cilycwm
Maesycrugiau
Llandysul
Llanllwni
Pontwelly
Llanfihangel-ar-arth
Llangeler
Caio
Aberbowlan
Mynydd Llanllwni
408
Pentre-cwrt
Rhydcymerau
Saron
383
Mynydd Llanybydder
Bancyffordd
Crugybar
Porthyrhyd
368
Llidiad-Nenog
Bwlch-clawdd
326
New Inn
Hafod Bridge
257
Pencader
Gorlech
Llansawel
Talley Lakes
Gwyddgrug
Llanymddyfri (Llandovery)
Dolgran
310
Edwinsford
278
Blaen
Gwernogle
Abergorlech
355
Talley (Talyllychau)
Abbey
Llwyn-y-brain
Alltwalis
329
Mynydd Cynros
Wauncunda
Llanwrda
Cwmduad
Pen-y-garn
Dolgarreg
Cwmdu
Halfway
Llansadwrn
Brechfa
Mynydd Figyn
Felindre
Cilgwyn
Llanllawddog
CARMARTHENSHIRE
Esgair
Llanpumsaint
325
317
Pontarsais
Soar
Maerdy
Llangadog
Llwyn-croes
Llanfynydd
Cynwyl Elfed
Plas
Capel Isaac
Felindre
Salem
Gwili
Rhydargaeau
Manordeilo
Cwmifor
Dyffryn Ceidrych
Rhiwiau
Pantgwyn
Bethlehem
Felingwmuchaf
Bronwydd Arms
Felingwmisaf
Pen-y-banc
Rhosmaen
Twynllanan
Peniel
Pentrefelin
Pont-ar-llechau
Llanfihangel-uwch-Gwili
Court Henry
Broad Oak
Dinefwr Park & Castle (NT)
Llandeilo
Trichrug
415
Capel Gwyn
Nantgaredig
Pontargothi
Llangathen
Cilsan
Pont Aber
Tre-vaughan
White Mill
Castle Woods
Capel Gwynfe
Tanerdy
Felindre
Aberglasney Gardens
Ffairfach
Carmarthen (Caerfyrddin)
Trinity
Abergwili
Capel Dewi
Llanegwad
Llanarthney
Dryslwyn
Dryslwyn
Gelli Aur
Maerdy
Johnstown
Llangunnor
Golden Grove
Trap
Carreg Cennen Castle
Garreg Lwyd
616
Pensarn
Llanllwch
Nantycaws
National Botanic Garden of Wales
Penrhiwgoch
Derwydd
Blaengwyn
Tair Carn Isaf
459
Pentre Gwenlais
Carmel
Carmel NNR
Maesybont
Llangain
Croesyceiliog
Llanddarog
Porthyrhyd
Llandybie
Black Mountain
Mynydd Du
DYFFRYN TYWI
0 2 4 6 miles
0 2 4 6 8 10 km

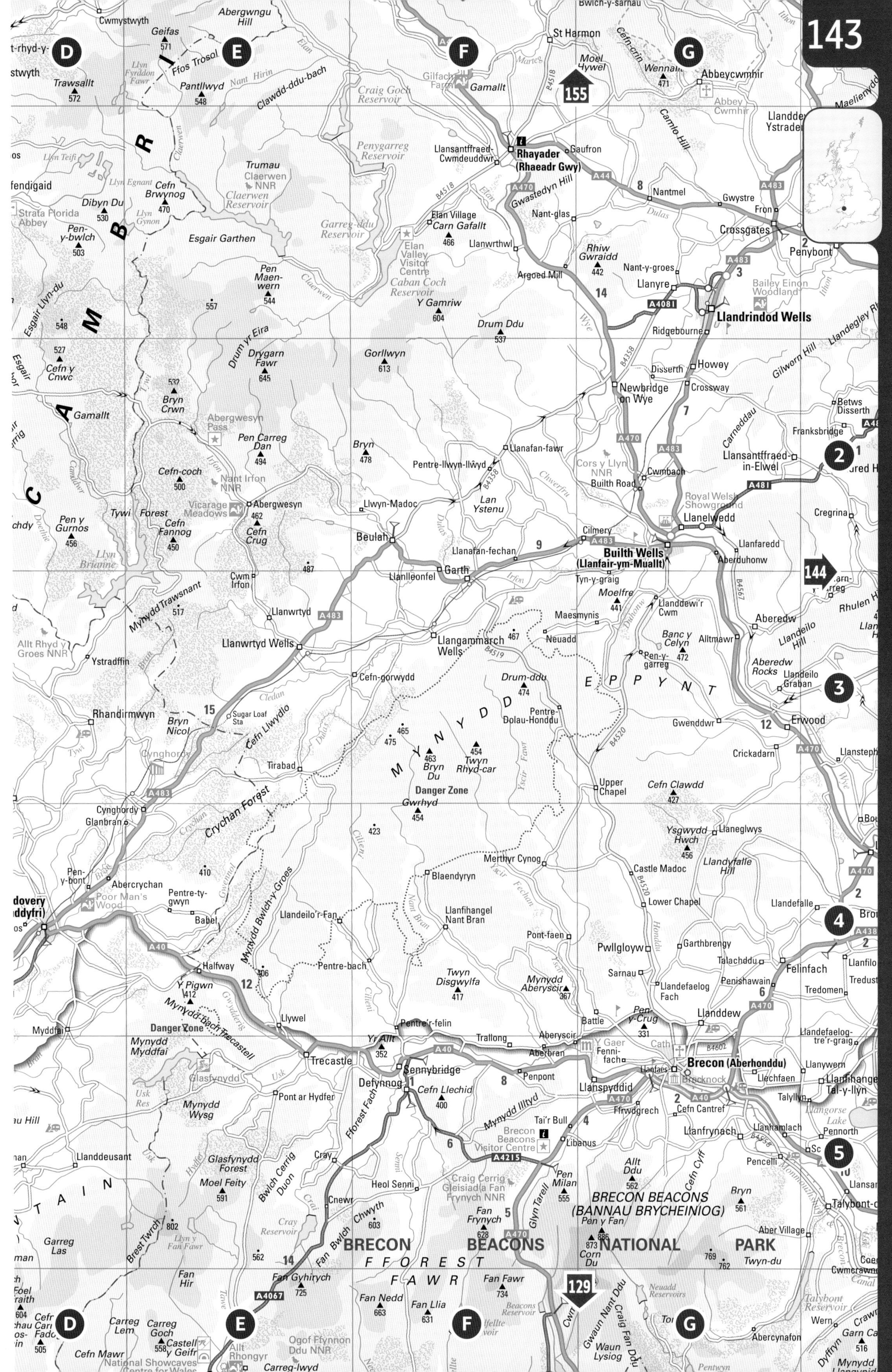
Rhayader (Rhaeadr Gwy)
St Harmon
Abbeycwmhir
Llandrindod Wells
Crossgates
Penybont
Newbridge on Wye
Builth Wells (Llanfair-ym-Muallt)
Llanelwedd
Beulah
Garth
Llanwrtyd Wells
Llangammarch Wells
Abergwesyn
Erwood
Rhandirmwyn
Cynghordy
Llandovery (Llanymddyfri)
Trecastle
Sennybridge
Defynnog
Brecon (Aberhonddu)
Llanspyddid
Libanus
Llanfrynach
Talybont-on-Usk
Felinfach
Llandefalle
Upper Chapel
Merthyr Cynog
Elan Village
Elan Valley Visitor Centre
Craig Goch Reservoir
Penygarreg Reservoir
Garreg-ddu Reservoir
Caban Coch Reservoir
Claerwen Reservoir
Claerwen NNR
Llyn Brianne
Tywi Forest
Crychan Forest
Mynydd Eppynt
Danger Zone
Brecon Beacons Visitor Centre
BRECON BEACONS (BANNAU BRYCHEINIOG)
BRECON BEACONS NATIONAL PARK
FFOREST FAWR
Pen y Fan
Corn Du
Fan Gyhirych
Fan Nedd
Fan Llia
Fan Fawr
Cray Reservoir
Usk Res
Glasfynydd Forest
Mynydd Myddfai
Strata Florida Abbey
Royal Welsh Showground
Cors y Llyn NNR
Nant Irfon NNR
Allt Rhyd y Groes NNR
Craig Cerrig Gleisiad a Fan Frynych NNR
Ogof Ffynnon Ddu NNR
155
144
129

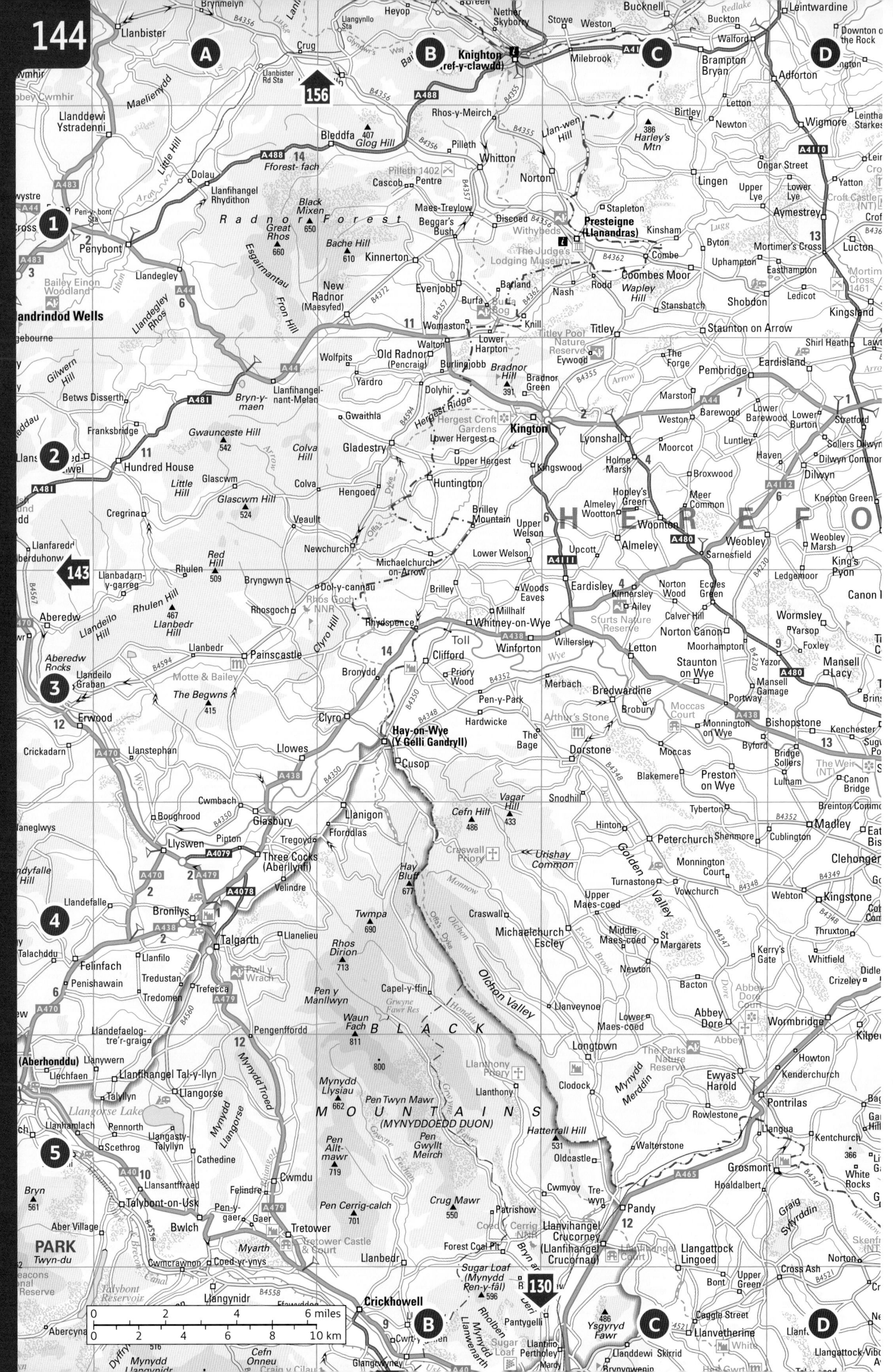
156
143
130
A
B
C
D
1
2
3
4
5
Llanbister
Knighton
(Tref-y-clawdd)
Bucknell
Leintwardine
Brampton Bryan
Adforton
Wigmore
Llanddewi Ystradenni
Bleddfa
Glog Hill
Radnor Forest
Whitton
Norton
Presteigne
(Llanandras)
Pilleth 1402
Penybont
Llandegley
Llandrindod Wells
New Radnor
(Maesyfed)
Kinnerton
Evenjobb
Lingen
Aymestrey
Mortimer's Cross
Kinsham
Combe
Coombes Moor
Shobdon
Kingsland
Titley
Staunton on Arrow
Old Radnor
(Pencraig)
Burlingjobb
Kington
Pembridge
Eardisland
Hergest Ridge
Hergest Croft Gardens
Gladestry
Huntington
Lyonshall
Almeley
Weobley
Eardisley
Dilwyn
Hundred House
Glascwm
Colva
Newchurch
Painscastle
Clyro
Whitney-on-Wye
Winforton
Clifford
Hay-on-Wye
(Y Gelli Gandryll)
Cusop
Bredwardine
Dorstone
Arthur's Stone
Moccas
Preston on Wye
Madley
Erwood
Llanstephan
Llowes
Glasbury
Llyswen
Three Cocks
(Aberllynfi)
Bronllys
Talgarth
Llanigon
Hay Bluff
Twmpa
Rhos Dirion
Craswall
Michaelchurch Escley
Peterchurch
Golden Valley
Vowchurch
Kingstone
Abbey Dore
Longtown
Llanthony
Llanthony Priory
Olchon Valley
Ewyas Harold
Pontrilas
Kentchurch
Grosmont
Pandy
Black Mountains
(Mynyddoedd Duon)
Waun Fach
811
Pen y Manllwyn
Pen Twyn Mawr
Pen Allt-mawr
Pen Cerrig-calch
Crug Mawr
Sugar Loaf
(Mynydd Pen-y-fâl)
Hatterall Hill
Llanvihangel Crucorney
(Llanfihangel Crucornau)
Llangattock Lingoed
Ysgyryd Fawr
Llanfihangel Tal-y-llyn
Llangorse
Llangorse Lake
Bwlch
Tretower
Cwmdu
Talybont-on-Usk
Crickhowell
Llangynidr
(Aberhonddu)
Felinfach
Pengenffordd
Mynydd Troed
0
2
4
6 miles
0
2
4
6
8
10 km

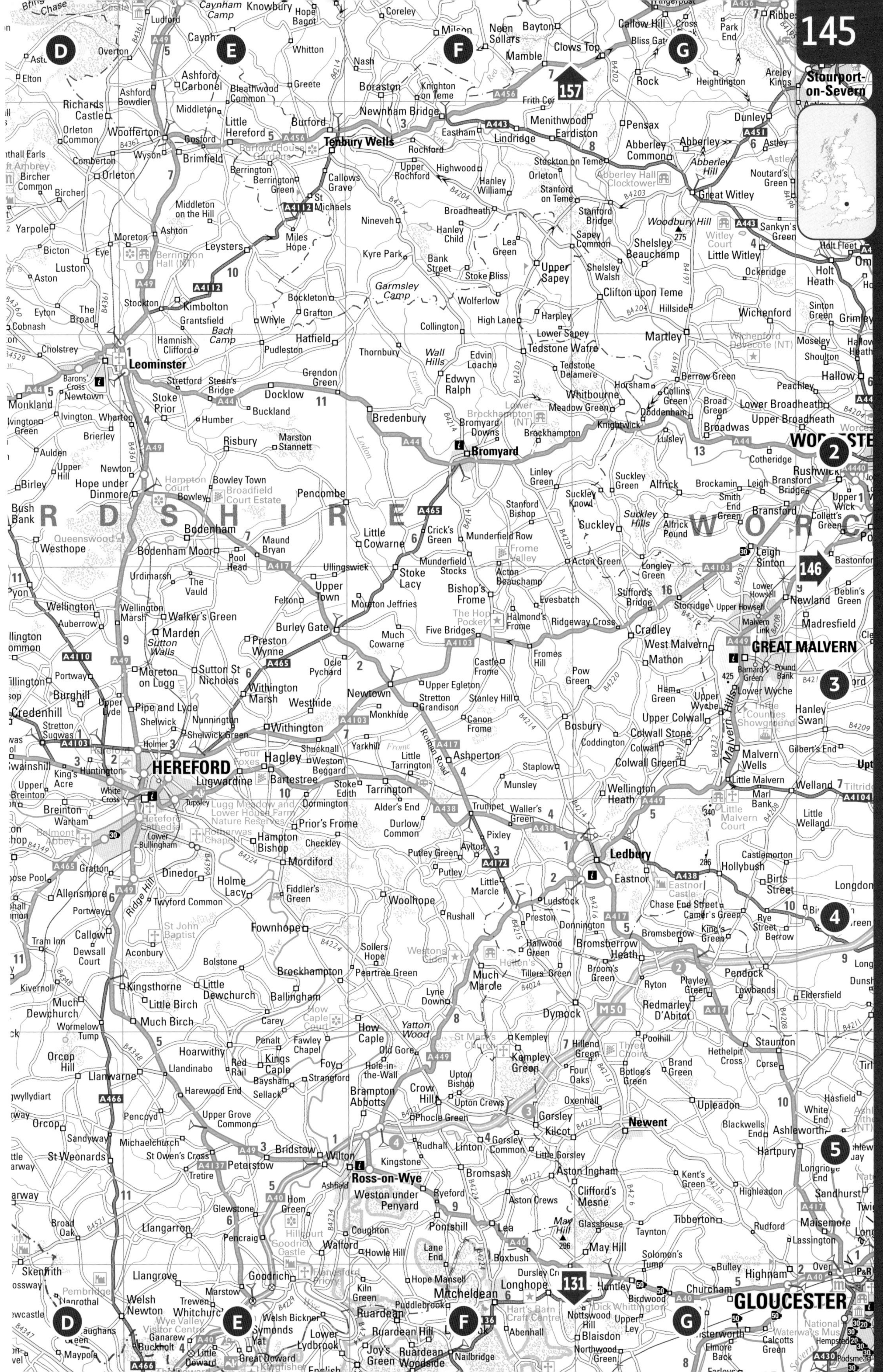
D
E
F
G
157
Caynham Camp
Knowbury
Hope Bagot
Coreley
Milson
Neen Sollars
Bayton
Callow Hill
Bliss Gate
Cross
Park End
Clows Top
Mamble
Ludford
Overton
Whitton
Nash
Ashford Carbonel
Ashford Bowdler
Bleathwood Common
Greete
Boraston
Knighton on Teme
Richards Castle
Elton
Orleton Common
Woofferton
Middleton
Little Hereford
Burford
Tenbury Wells
Newnham Bridge
Eastham
Frith Cor
Menithwood
Lindridge
Eardiston
Pensax
Rock
Heightington
Areley Kings
Stourport-on-Severn
Dunley
Abberley
Abberley Common
Abberley Hill
Astley
Noutard's Green
Gosford
Wyson
Brimfield
Burford House Gardens
Rochford
Upper Rochford
Highwood
Stockton on Teme
Orleton
Abberley Hall Clocktower
Great Witley
Comberton
Orleton
Birchet Common
Bircher
Berrington
Berrington Green
Callows Grave
St Michaels
Hanley William
Stanford on Teme
Middleton on the Hill
Nineveh
Broadheath
Stanford Bridge
Woodbury Hill
275
Sankyn's Green
Yarpole
Moreton
Ashton
Miles Hope
Hanley Child
Sapey Common
Witley Court
Little Witley
Holt Fleet
Bicton
Eye
Berrington Hall (NT)
Leysters
Kyre Park
Bank Street
Lea Green
Shelsley Beauchamp
Holt Heath
Luston
Aston
Stoke Bliss
Upper Sapey
Shelsley Walsh
Ockeridge
Garmsley Camp
Clifton upon Teme
Eyton
The Broad
Stockton
Kimbolton
Bockleton
Wolferlow
Hillside
Sinton Green
Grimley
Cobnash
Grantsfield
Whyle
Grafton
Collington
High Lane
Harpley
Wichenford
Hamnish Clifford
Bach Camp
Hatfield
Lower Sapey
Martley
Wichenford Dovecote (NT)
Moseley
Cholstrey
Leominster
Pudleston
Thornbury
Wall Hills
Edvin Loach
Tedstone Wafre
Shoulton
Hallow
Barons' Cross
Newtown
Stretford
Steen's Bridge
Grendon Green
Edwyn Ralph
Tedstone Delamere
Berrow Green
Horsham
Collins Green
Peachley
Monkland
Stoke Prior
Docklow
Whitbourne
Broad Green
Lower Broadheath
Ivington
Wharton
Humber
Buckland
Bredenbury
Lower Brockhampton (NT)
Bromyard Downs
Meadow Green
Doddenham
Upper Broadheath
Ivington Green
Brierley
Risbury
Marston Stannett
Brockhampton
Knightwick
Broadwas
Lulsley
Aulden
Bromyard
WORCESTER
Upper Hill
Newton
Linley Green
Cotheridge
Rushwick
Birley
Hope under Dinmore
Hampton Court
Bowley Town
Bowley
Broadfield Court Estate
Pencombe
Suckley Green
Alfrick
Brockamin
Leigh
Bransford Bridge
Smith End Green
Upper Wick
Bush Bank
Stanford Bishop
Suckley Knowl
Bransford
Collett's Green
Queenswood
Bodenham
Little Cowarne
Crick's Green
Suckley Hills
Suckley
Alfrick Pound
Westhope
Bodenham Moor
Maund Bryan
Munderfield Row
Frome Valley
Leigh Sinton
Pool Head
Ullingswick
Munderfield Stocks
Acton Green
Longley Green
Bastonford
146
Urdimarsh
The Vault
Upper Town
Stoke Lacy
Acton Beauchamp
Lower Howsell
Newland
Deblin's Green
Pyon
Felton
Bishop's Frome
Evesbatch
Stifford's Bridge
Storridge
Upper Howsell
Wellington
Wellington Marsh
Walker's Green
Moreton Jeffries
The Hop Pocket
Halmond's Frome
Ridgeway Cross
Malvern Link
Madresfield
Auberrow
Marden
Burley Gate
Much Cowarne
Five Bridges
Cradley
West Malvern
GREAT MALVERN
Sutton Walls
Preston Wynne
Fromes Hill
Mathon
Moreton on Lugg
Sutton St Nicholas
Ocle Pychard
Castle Frome
Pow Green
Barnard's Green
Pound Bank
Portway
Withington Marsh
Newtown
Upper Egleton
Ham Green
Upper Wyche
Lower Wyche
Burghill
Upper Lyde
Pipe and Lyde
Westhide
Stretton Grandison
Stanley Hill
Three Counties Showground
Hanley Swan
Credenhill
Shelwick
Nunnington
Withington
Monkhide
Canon Frome
Bosbury
Upper Colwall
Stretton Sugwas
Holmer
Shelwick Green
Shucknall
Yarkhill
Coddington
Colwall Stone
Colwall
Gilbert's End
Swainshill
Huntington
Hereford
HEREFORD
Four Foxes
Hagley
Weston Beggard
Little Tarrington
Roman Road
Ashperton
Staplow
Colwall Green
Malvern Hills
Malvern Wells
King's Acre
Lugwardine
Bartestree
Stoke Edith
Tarrington
Munsley
Little Malvern
Welland
Upper Breinton
White Cross
Tupsley
Dormington
Alder's End
Trumpet
Waller's Green
Wellington Heath
Marl Bank
Breinton
Warham
Lugg Meadow and Lower House Farm Nature Reserves
Prior's Frome
Durlow Common
Pixley
Little Malvern Court
Little Welland
Belmont Abbey
Hereford Cathedral
Lower Bullingham
Rotherwas Chapel
Hampton Bishop
Checkley
Aylton
Ledbury
340
Castlemorton
Grafton
Mordiford
Putley Green
Putley
Eastnor
Hollybush
Birts Street
Dinedor
Holme Lacy
Fiddler's Green
Little Marcle
Eastnor Castle
Longdon
Allensmore
Twyford Common
Woolhope
Ludstock
Chase End Street
Camer's Green
Portway
Rushall
Preston
Donnington
Rye Street
Berrow
Ridge Hill
St John Baptist
Fownhope
Bromsberrow
King's Green
Tram Inn
Callow
Dewsall Court
Aconbury
Sollers Hope
Westons Cider
Hallwood Green
Bromsberrow Heath
Bolstone
Hellens
Much Marcle
Tillers Green
Broom's Green
Pendock
Kivernoll
Kingsthorne
Little Dewchurch
Brockhampton
Peartree Green
Ryton
Playley Green
Lowbands
Eldersfield
Much Dewchurch
Little Birch
Ballingham
How Caple Court
Lyne Down
Dymock
Redmarley D'Abitot
M50
Wormelow Tump
Much Birch
Carey
How Caple
Yatton Wood
St Mary's Church
Kempley
Three Choirs
Poolhill
Orcop Hill
Hoarwithy
Penalt
Fawley Chapel
Kings Caple
Foy
Old Gore
Kempley Green
Hillend Green
Hethelpit Cross
Staunton
Corse
Llandinabo
Red Rail
Hole-in-the-Wall
Upton Bishop
Four Oaks
Brand Green
Llanwarne
Baysham
Strangford
Botloe's Green
Harewood End
Sellack
Brampton Abbotts
Crow Hill
Upton Crews
Oxenhall
Upleadon
Hasfield
Llangunnock
Pencoyd
Upper Grove Common
Phocle Green
Gorsley
Newent
White End
Orcop
Michaelchurch
Bridstow
Wilton
Rudhall
Linton
Kilcot
Gorsley Common
Blackwells End
Ashleworth
Sandyway
St Owen's Cross
Little Gorsley
Hartpury
St Weonards
Tretire
Peterstow
Kingstone
Ross-on-Wye
Aston Ingham
Bromsash
Kent's Green
Longridge End
Ashfield
Weston under Penyard
Ryeford
Clifford's Mesne
Highleadon
Sandhurst
Hom Green
Glewstone
Aston Crews
Pontshill
Tibberton
Maisemore
Broad Oak
Llangarron
Pencraig
Hill Court
Goodrich Castle
Coughton
Walford
Howle Hill
Lea
May Hill
296
Glasshouse
Taynton
Rudford
Lassington
Lane End
Boxbush
May Hill
Solomon's Tump
Skenfrith
Llangrove
Goodrich
Flanesford Priory
Hope Mansell
Kiln Green
Dursley Cross
Bulley
Highnam
Over
Pembridge
Marstow
Longhope
131
Huntley
Churcham
GLOUCESTER
Welsh Newton
Trewen
Whitchurch
Mitcheldean
Puddlebrook
Ruardean
Hart's Barn Craft Centre
Nottswood Hill
Dick Whittington
Birdwood
Upper Ley
Wye Valley Visitor Centre
Ganarew
Welsh Bicknor
Symonds Yat
Lower Lydbrook
Ruardean Hill
Abenhall
Blaisdon
Minsterworth
National Waterways Museum
Hempsted
Maypole
Buckholt
Little Doward
Great Doward
Joy's Green
Ruardean Woodside
Nailbridge
Northwood Green
Elmore Back
Calcotts Green
Llangrove
Garway
Upper Breinton
Marstow
HEREFORDSHIRE
WORCESTERSHIRE

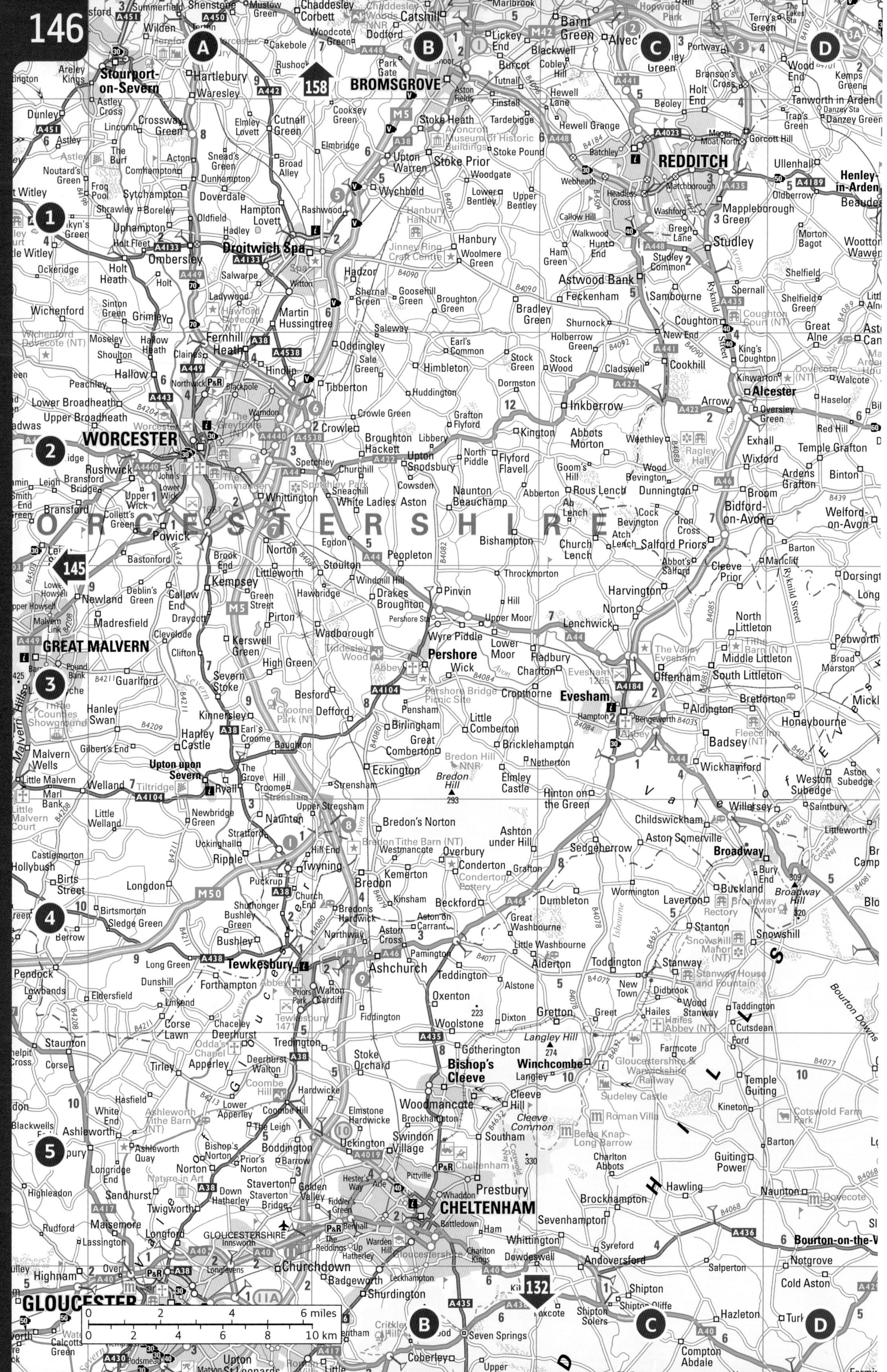
A
B
C
D
1
2
3
4
5
158
145
132
WORCESTERSHIRE
Stourport-on-Severn
BROMSGROVE
REDDITCH
Henley-in-Arden
Droitwich Spa
WORCESTER
Alcester
GREAT MALVERN
Pershore
Evesham
Upton upon Severn
Tewkesbury
Broadway
Ashchurch
Bishop's Cleeve
Winchcombe
CHELTENHAM
GLOUCESTER
Bourton-on-the-W
Vale of Evesham
Malvern Hills
Bredon Hill
Cleeve Common
Langley Hill
Broadway Hill
Studley
Inkberrow
Bidford-on-Avon
Kempsey
Bredon
Prestbury
Churchdown
Shurdington
0 2 4 6 miles
0 2 4 6 8 10 km

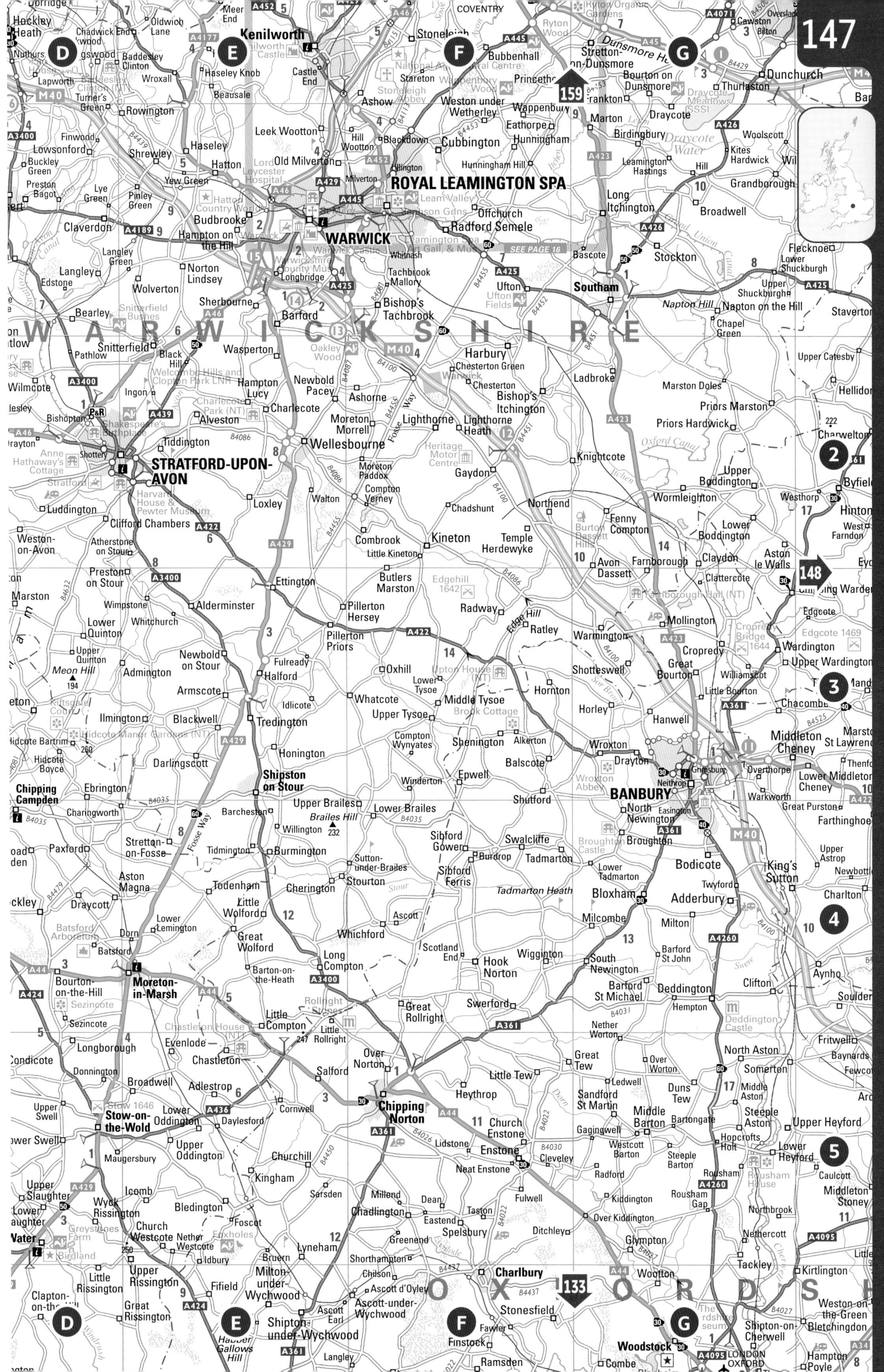
Hockley Heath
Chadwick End
Oldwich Lane
Meer End
Kenilworth
Kenilworth Castle
COVENTRY
Stoneleigh
Ryton Wood
Ryton Organic Gardens
Cawston
Bilton
Overslade
Dunsmore Heath
Nuthurst
Baddesley Clinton
Haseley Knob
Wroxall
Castle End
National Agricultural Centre
Bubbenhall
Stretton-on-Dunsmore
Bourton on Dunsmore
Dunchurch
Thurlaston
Lapworth
Turner's Green
Rowington
Beausale
Stareton
Stoneleigh Abbey
Ashow
Weston under Wetherley
Princethorpe
Wappenbury
Eathorpe
Frankton
Marton
Draycote
Draycote Meadows SSSI
Birdingbury
Draycote Water
Woolscott
Kites Hardwick
Finwood
Lowsonford
Buckley Green
Preston Bagot
Shrewley
Haseley
Hatton
Leek Wootton
Hill Wootton
Blackdown
Cubbington
Hunningham
Hunningham Hill
Leamington Hastings
Hill
Grandborough
Broadwell
Lye Green
Pinley Green
Yew Green
Old Milverton
Lord Leycester Hospital
Milverton
Lillington
ROYAL LEAMINGTON SPA
Long Itchington
Hatton Country World
Leam Valley
Jephson Gdns
Offchurch
Radford Semele
Claverdon
Budbrooke
Hampton on the Hill
WARWICK
Warwick Castle
Leamington Spa Art Gall. & Mus.
SEE PAGE 16
Bascote
Stockton
Flecknoe
Lower Shuckburgh
Langley Green
Langley
Edstone
Norton Lindsey
Wolverton
Warwickshire County Mus.
Longbridge
Whitnash
Tachbrook Mallory
Ufton
Ufton Fields
Southam
Upper Shuckburgh
Napton Hill
Napton on the Hill
Staverton
Snitterfield Bushes
Bearley
Sherbourne
Barford
Bishop's Tachbrook
Chapel Green
WARWICKSHIRE
Snitterfield
Pathlow
Black Hill
Wasperton
Oakley Wood
Harbury
Chesterton Green
Chesterton
Upper Catesby
Wilmcote
Welcombe Hills and Clopton Park LNR
Hampton Lucy
Newbold Pacey
Ashorne
Bishop's Itchington
Ladbroke
Marston Doles
Priors Marston
Hellidon
Ingon
Charlecote Park (NT)
Charlecote
Moreton Morrell
Fosse Way
Lighthorne
Lighthorne Heath
Priors Hardwick
Charwelton
Bishopton
Alveston
Shakespeare's Birthplace
Tiddington
Wellesbourne
Heritage Motor Centre
Oxford Canal
Anne Hathaway's Cottage
Shottery
STRATFORD-UPON-AVON
Moreton Paddox
Gaydon
Knightcote
Upper Boddington
Byfield
Stratford
Harvard House & Pewter Museum
Walton
Compton Verney
Chadshunt
Northend
Wormleighton
Westhorp
Hinton
Luddington
Loxley
Clifford Chambers
Burton Dassett Hills
Fenny Compton
Lower Boddington
West Farndon
Weston-on-Avon
Atherstone on Stour
Combrook
Kineton
Little Kineton
Temple Herdewyke
Avon Dassett
Farnborough
Claydon
Aston le Walls
Preston on Stour
Ettington
Butlers Marston
Edgehill 1642
Clattercote
Chipping Warden
Marston
Wimpstone
Alderminster
Pillerton Hersey
Radway
Farnborough Hall (NT)
Edgcote
Lower Quinton
Whitchurch
Edge Hill
Ratley
Mollington
Cropredy Bridge 1644
Edgcote 1469
Upper Quinton
Pillerton Priors
Warmington
Cropredy
Wardington
Upper Wardington
Meon Hill
Newbold on Stour
Fulready
Oxhill
Lower Tysoe
Upton House (NT)
Shotteswell
Great Bourton
Williamscot
Admington
Halford
Middle Tysoe
Hornton
Little Bourton
Armscote
Idlicote
Whatcote
Upper Tysoe
Brook Cottage
Horley
Chacombe
Kiftsgate Court
Ilmington
Blackwell
Tredington
Hanwell
Middleton Cheney
Marston St Lawrence
Hidcote Bartrim
Hidcote Manor Gardens (NT)
Compton Wynyates
Shenington
Alkerton
Wroxton
Hidcote Boyce
Darlingscott
Honington
Epwell
Balscote
Drayton
Grimsbury
Overthorpe
Thenford
Chipping Campden
Ebrington
Shipston on Stour
Winderton
Wroxton Abbey
Neithrop
BANBURY
Lower Middleton Cheney
Warkworth
Charingworth
Upper Brailes
Lower Brailes
Shutford
North Newington
Easington
Great Purston
Barcheston
Brailes Hill
Willington
Sibford Gower
Swalcliffe
Broughton Castle
Broughton
Farthinghoe
Paxford
Stretton-on-Fosse
Tidmington
Burmington
Sutton-under-Brailes
Burdrop
Tadmarton
Lower Tadmarton
Bodicote
King's Sutton
Upper Astrop
Aston Magna
Todenham
Stourton
Cherington
Sibford Ferris
Tadmarton Heath
Bloxham
Twyford
Adderbury
Newbottle
Charlton
Draycott
Little Wolford
Batsford Arboretum
Lower Lemington
Great Wolford
Ascott
Whichford
Milcombe
Milton
Dorn
Batsford
Scotland End
Hook Norton
Wigginton
South Newington
Barford St John
Bourton-on-the-Hill
Moreton-in-Marsh
Long Compton
Barton-on-the-Heath
Barford St Michael
Deddington
Clifton
Aynho
Souldern
Sezincote
Rollright Stones
Great Rollright
Swerford
Hempton
Deddington Castle
Little Compton
Little Rollright
Chastleton House (NT)
Nether Worton
Longborough
Evenlode
Chastleton
Over Norton
Great Tew
Over Worton
North Aston
Fritwell
Baynards
Condicote
Donnington
Broadwell
Adlestrop
Salford
Little Tew
Ledwell
Somerton
Fewcott
Upper Swell
Stow 1646
Stow-on-the-Wold
Lower Oddington
Daylesford
Cornwell
Chipping Norton
Heythrop
Sandford St Martin
Duns Tew
Middle Aston
Lower Swell
Upper Oddington
Church Enstone
Middle Barton
Bartongate
Steeple Aston
Upper Heyford
Lidstone
Enstone
Cleveley
Gagingwell
Westcott Barton
Hopcrofts Holt
Maugersbury
Churchill
Neat Enstone
Steeple Barton
Lower Heyford
Caulcott
Kingham
Radford
Rousham
Rousham House
Upper Slaughter
Lower Slaughter
Icomb
Sarsden
Milland
Dean
Fulwell
Kiddington
Rousham Gap
Middleton Stoney
Wyck Rissington
Bledington
Chadlington
Eastend
Taston
Over Kiddington
Northbrook
Greystones Farm
Church Westcote
Nether Westcote
Foxholes
Foscot
Spelsbury
Ditchley
Glympton
Nethercott
Bourton-on-the-Water
Birdland
Idbury
Lyneham
Greenend
Tackley
Little Rissington
Upper Rissington
Bruern
Shorthampton
Chilson
Charlbury
Wootton
Kirtlington
Clapton-on-the-Hill
Great Rissington
Fifield
Milton-under-Wychwood
Ascott d'Oyley
Ascott-under-Wychwood
Ascott Earl
OXFORDSHIRE
Stonesfield
Fawler
Finstock
Weston-on-the-Green
Bletchingdon
Shipton-on-Cherwell
Idbury
Shipton-under-Wychwood
Habber Gallows Hill
Langley
Ramsden
Woodstock
Combe
LONDON OXFORD
Hampton Poyle
M40
A46
A429
A3400
A422
A361
A44
A423
A425
A426
A445
A452
A424
A436
A4260
A4095
B4035
B4086
B4100
B4455
159
148
133
D
E
F
G
2
3
4
5

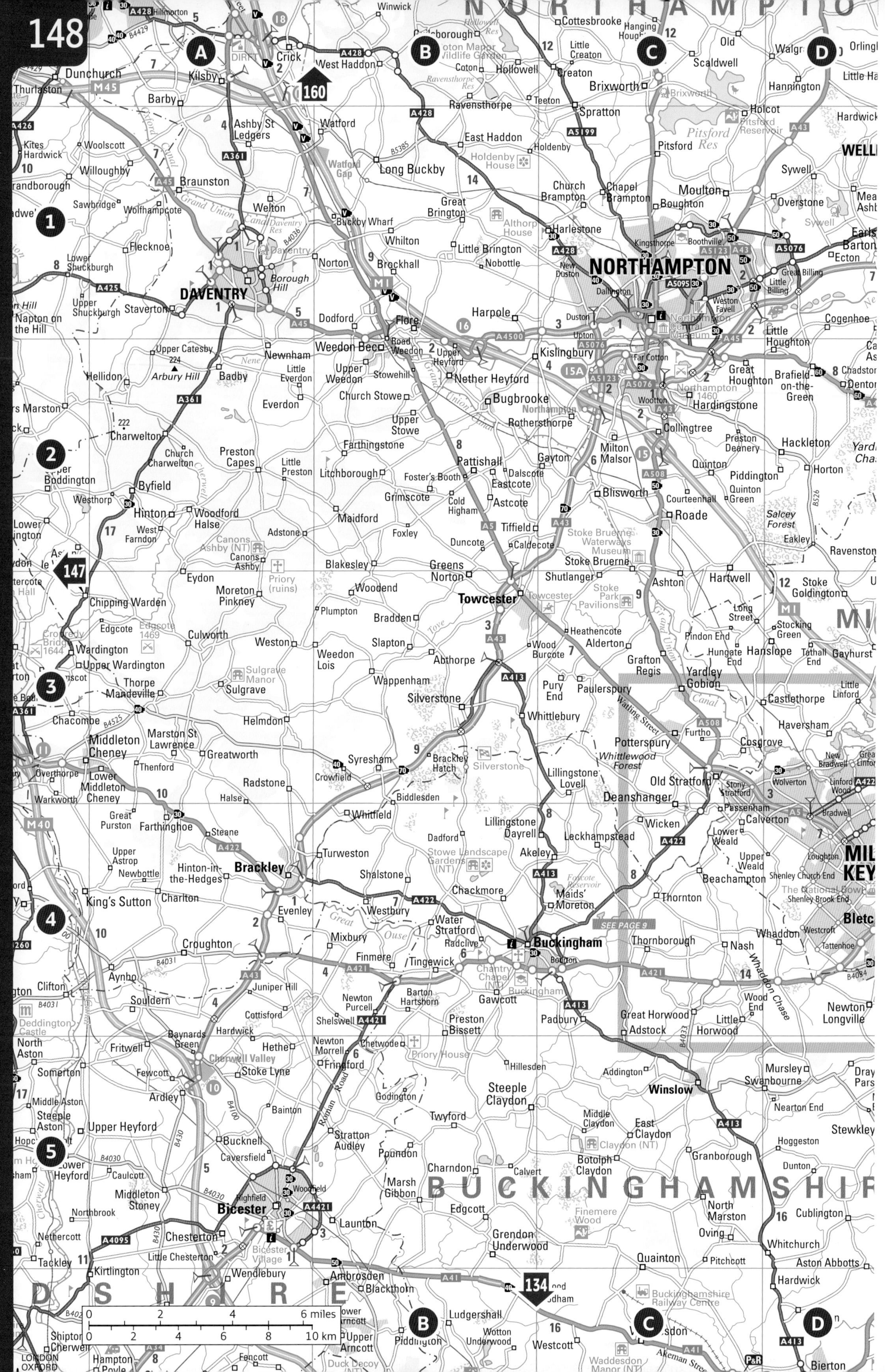
NORTHAMPTON
BUCKINGHAMSHIRE
NORTHAMPTON
DAVENTRY
Towcester
Brackley
Buckingham
Bicester
Winslow
Dunchurch
Crick
West Haddon
Kilsby
Barby
Braunston
Long Buckby
Watford
Ashby St Ledgers
Welton
Norton
Brockhall
Flore
Dodford
Weedon Bec
Badby
Newnham
Staverton
Harpole
Kislingbury
Upper Heyford
Nether Heyford
Bugbrooke
Rothersthorpe
Gayton
Milton Malsor
Blisworth
Roade
Collingtree
Hardingstone
Great Houghton
Pattishall
Tiffield
Greens Norton
Stoke Bruerne
Shutlanger
Hartwell
Ashton
Yardley Gobion
Potterspury
Deanshanger
Old Stratford
Stony Stratford
Whittlebury
Silverstone
Syresham
Byfield
Hinton
Woodford Halse
Chipping Warden
Wardington
Middleton Cheney
Farthinghoe
King's Sutton
Aynho
Croughton
Evenley
Westbury
Finmere
Tingewick
Gawcott
Padbury
Steeple Claydon
Twyford
Marsh Gibbon
Launton
Ambrosden
Blackthorn
Chesterton
Kirtlington
Upper Heyford
Souldern
Fritwell
Ardley
Stoke Lyne
Fringford
Brixworth
Pitsford
Moulton
Boughton
Spratton
Creaton
Cottesbroke
Harlestone
Chapel Brampton
Church Brampton
Great Brington
Little Brington
Holdenby
Althorp House
Duston
Upton
Cogenhoe
Hackleton
Piddington
Quinton
Hanslope
Castlethorpe
Cosgrove
Calverton
Beachampton
Thornborough
Nash
Great Horwood
Little Horwood
Swanbourne
Granborough
North Marston
Oving
Quainton
Whitchurch
Hardwick
Waddesdon
Westcott
Grendon Underwood
Edgcott
Charndon
Poundon
Stratton Audley
Bucknell
Caversfield
Middleton Stoney
Wendlebury
Piddington
Ludgershall
0 2 4 6 miles
0 2 4 6 8 10 km
160
147
134

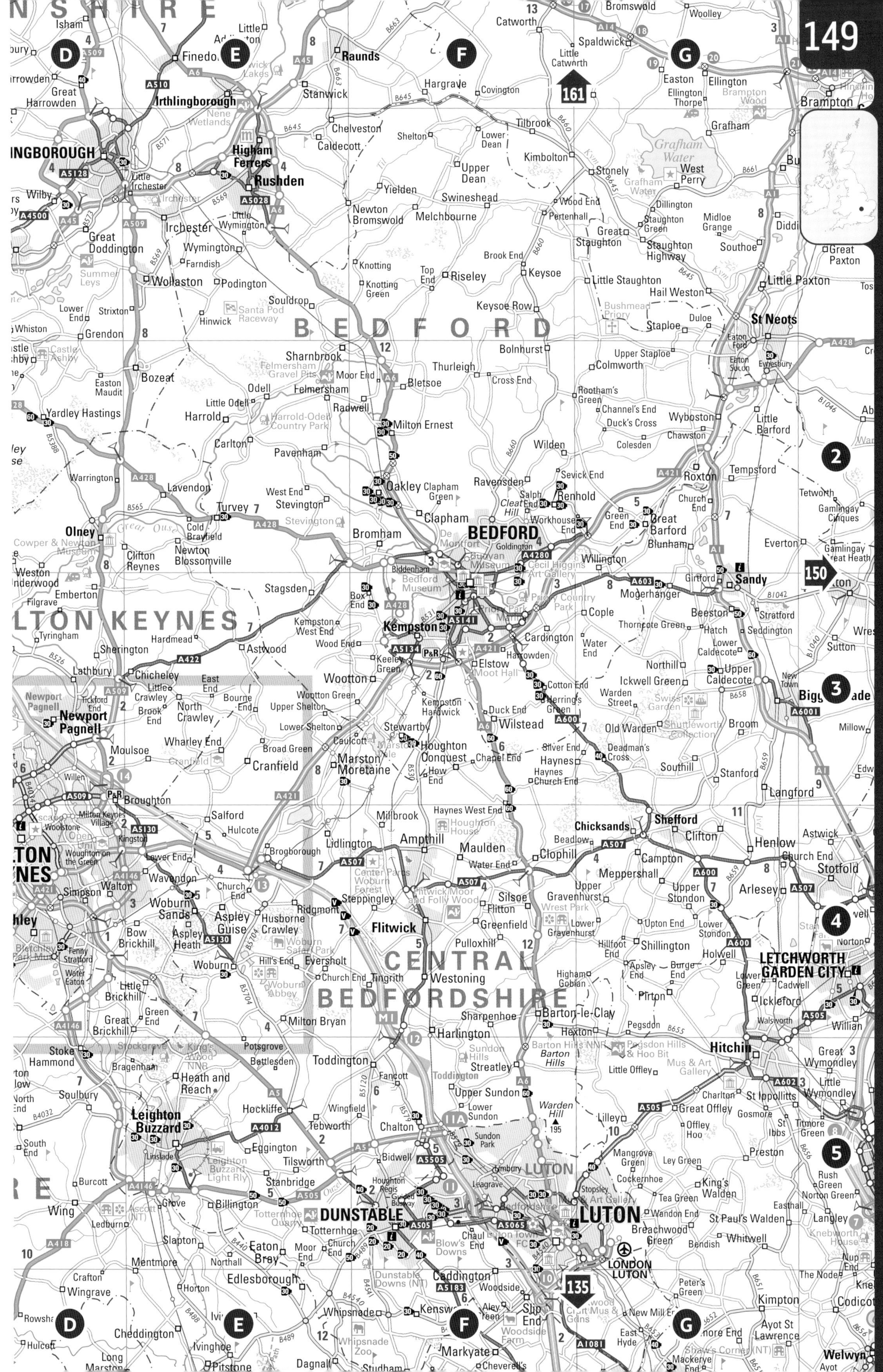
149
D
E
F
G
161
150
135
2
3
4
5
BEDFORD
CENTRAL
BEDFORDSHIRE
MILTON KEYNES
BEDFORD
LUTON
DUNSTABLE
LETCHWORTH
GARDEN CITY
Kempston
Sandy
St Neots
Rushden
Higham
Ferrers
Irthlingborough
Raunds
Finedon
Olney
Newport
Pagnell
Leighton
Buzzard
Flitwick
Ampthill
Shefford
Hitchin
Biggleswade
Stotfold
Arlesey
Toddington
Houghton Regis
Harlington
Barton-le-Clay
Woburn
Woburn
Sands
Aspley
Guise
Marston
Moretaine
Cranfield
Sharnbrook
Oakley
Clapham
Bromham
Riseley
Kimbolton
Tempsford
Little Paxton
Potton
Wilstead
Cardington
Willington
Great
Barford
Renhold
Wootton
Stewartby
Lidlington
Maulden
Clophill
Silsoe
Westoning
Eaton
Bray
Edlesborough
Caddington
Slip
End
Kensworth
Whipsnade
Markyate
Cheddington
Ivinghoe
Pitstone
Wing
Grafham
Water
Brampton
Easton
Tilbrook
Swineshead
Yielden
Melchbourne
Keysoe
Wilden
Roxton
Blunham
Moggerhanger
Northill
Old Warden
Southill
Stanford
Langford
Henlow
Clifton
Campton
Meppershall
Shillington
Pirton
Ickleford
Great Offley
Lilley
Streatley
Sundon
Wollaston
Bozeat
Harrold
Carlton
Turvey
Lavendon
Emberton
Sherington
Chicheley
North
Crawley
Salford
Hulcote
Brogborough
Ridgmont
Eversholt
Tingrith
Milton Bryan
Hockliffe
Tebworth
Chalton
Tilsworth
Stanbridge
Totternhoe
London
Luton
A1
A6
A5
M1
A421
A428
A509
A507
A600
A603
A505
A5120

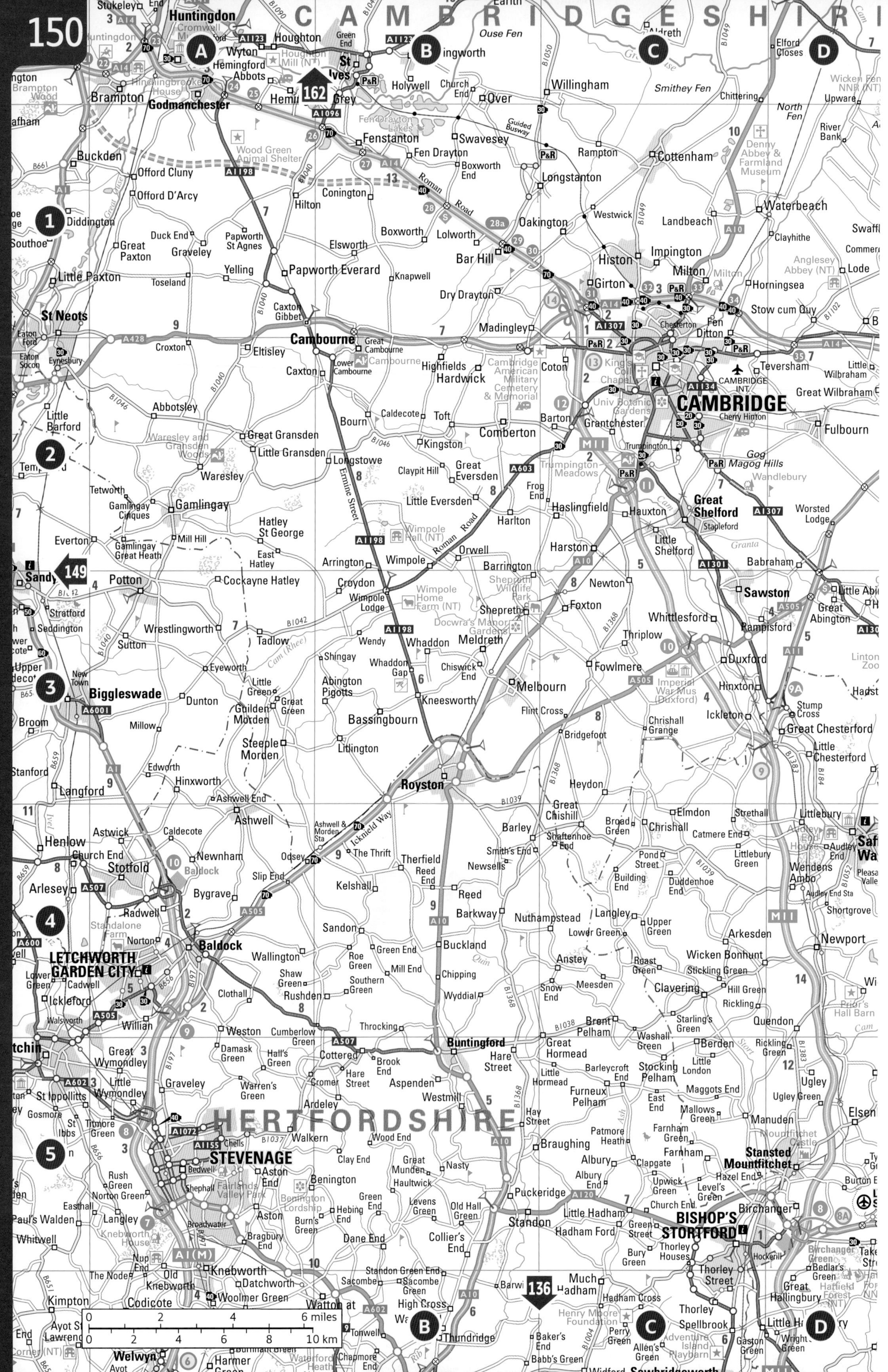
CAMBRIDGESHIRE
HERTFORDSHIRE
CAMBRIDGE
Huntingdon
St Ives
Godmanchester
Brampton
Buckden
Offord Cluny
Offord D'Arcy
Diddington
Southoe
Great Paxton
Little Paxton
St Neots
Eaton Socon
Eynesbury
Hemingford Abbots
Houghton
Wyton
Holywell
Fenstanton
Fen Drayton
Swavesey
Over
Willingham
Rampton
Cottenham
Longstanton
Oakington
Westwick
Landbeach
Waterbeach
Histon
Impington
Milton
Girton
Horningsea
Stow cum Quy
Fen Ditton
Chesterton
Teversham
Fulbourn
Cherry Hinton
Great Wilbraham
Little Wilbraham
Bar Hill
Dry Drayton
Lolworth
Boxworth
Elsworth
Knapwell
Conington
Hilton
Papworth Everard
Papworth St Agnes
Graveley
Yelling
Toseland
Duck End
Caxton Gibbet
Cambourne
Great Cambourne
Lower Cambourne
Caxton
Eltisley
Croxton
Madingley
Coton
Highfields
Hardwick
Cambridge American Military Cemetery & Memorial
Toft
Comberton
Barton
Grantchester
Trumpington
Trumpington Meadows
Univ Botanic Gardens
King's Coll Chapel
Cambridge Int.
Bourn
Caldecote
Kingston
Great Gransden
Little Gransden
Waresley
Waresley and Gransden Woods
Abbotsley
Little Barford
Tempsford
Tetworth
Gamlingay
Gamlingay Cinques
Gamlingay Great Heath
Everton
Mill Hill
Hatley St George
East Hatley
Longstowe
Claypit Hill
Great Eversden
Little Eversden
Harlton
Haslingfield
Frog End
Hauxton
Great Shelford
Little Shelford
Stapleford
Worsted Lodge
Babraham
Sawston
Little Abington
Great Abington
Pampisford
Harston
Newton
Barrington
Shepreth
Shepreth Wildlife Park
Foxton
Orwell
Wimpole
Wimpole Hall (NT)
Wimpole Home Farm (NT)
Arrington
Croydon
Wimpole Lodge
Sandy
Potton
Cockayne Hatley
Stratford
Seddington
Wrestlingworth
Tadlow
Sutton
Eyeworth
Biggleswade
Dunton
Millow
Broom
Little Green
Guilden Morden
Great Green
Steeple Morden
Abington Pigotts
Shingay
Wendy
Whaddon
Whaddon Gap
Meldreth
Melbourn
Chiswick End
Kneesworth
Bassingbourn
Litlington
Docwra's Manor Gardens
Whittlesford
Thriplow
Fowlmere
Duxford
Imperial War Mus (Duxford)
Hinxton
Ickleton
Stump Cross
Great Chesterford
Little Chesterford
Chrishall Grange
Flint Cross
Bridgefoot
Heydon
Great Chishill
Royston
Ashwell
Ashwell End
Hinxworth
Edworth
Langford
Stanford
Henlow
Astwick
Caldecote
Church End
Stotfold
Arlesey
Newnham
Baldock
Bygrave
Radwell
Norton
Letchworth Garden City
Ickleford
Walsworth
Willian
Hitchin
Great Wymondley
Little Wymondley
St Ippolitts
Gosmore
St Ibbs
Titmore Green
Graveley
Weston
Clothall
Wallington
Rushden
Shaw Green
Sandon
Roe Green
Green End
Mill End
Southern Green
Kelshall
Therfield
Reed End
Reed
The Thrift
Odsey
Ashwell & Morden Sta
Slip End
Barkway
Buckland
Chipping
Wyddial
Throcking
Buntingford
Cumberlow Green
Cottered
Brook End
Hare Street
Cromer
Aspenden
Westmill
Ardeley
Walkern
Wood End
Clay End
Great Munden
Haultwick
Nasty
Levens Green
Old Hall Green
Collier's End
Puckeridge
Standon
Braughing
Hay Street
Barley
Smith's End
Newsells
Nuthampstead
Shaftenhoe End
Great Hormead
Little Hormead
Brent Pelham
Furneux Pelham
Barleycroft End
Stocking Pelham
Anstey
Snow End
Meesden
Langley
Upper Green
Lower Green
Roast Green
Clavering
Starling's Green
Berden
Little London
Washall Green
Maggots End
East End
Mallows Green
Patmore Heath
Farnham Green
Farnham
Albury
Albury End
Clapgate
Upwick Green
Hazel End
Level's Green
Church End
Little Hadham
Hadham Ford
Green Street
Bishop's Stortford
Thorley Houses
Bury Green
Thorley Street
Thorley
Much Hadham
Hadham Cross
Henry Moore Foundation
Perry Green
Allen's Green
Spellbrook
Gaston Green
Birchanger
Stansted Mountfitchet
Manuden
Ugley
Ugley Green
Quendon
Rickling
Rickling Green
Hill Green
Stickling Green
Wicken Bonhunt
Arkesden
Newport
Shortgrove
Wendens Ambo
Littlebury
Littlebury Green
Strethall
Elmdon
Catmere End
Chrishall
Broad Green
Pond Street
Building End
Duddenhoe End
Stevenage
Bedwell
Shephall
Chells
Aston
Aston End
Benington
Bragbury End
Broadwater
Knebworth
Old Knebworth
Datchworth
Woolmer Green
Codicote
Nup End
The Node
Kimpton
Langley
Rush Green
Norton Green
Easthall
St Paul's Walden
Whitwell
Hebing End
Burn's Green
Dane End
Green End
Standon Green End
Sacombe
Sacombe Green
High Cross
Thundridge
Barwick
Baker's End
Babb's Green
Watton at Stone
Tonwell
Chapmore End
Welwyn
Harmer Green
Ayot St Lawrence
Cambridge American Military Cemetery
Denny Abbey & Farmland Museum
Anglesey Abbey (NT)
Lode
Swaffham
Wicken Fen NNR (NT)
Upware
North Fen
River Bank
Chittering
Smithey Fen
Elford Closes
Aldreth
Earith
Ouse Fen
Houghton Mill (NT)
Hinchingbrooke House
Wood Green Animal Shelter
Fen Drayton Lakes
Roman Road
Guided Busway
Ermine Street
Icknield Way
Wandlebury
Gog Magog Hills
Linton Zoo
Hadstock
Fairlands Valley Park
Benington Lordship
Knebworth House
Standalone Farm
Mountfitchet Castle
Prior's Hall Barn
Hatfield Forest (NT)
Great Hallingbury
Little Hallingbury
Wrights Green
Adventure Island Playbarn
Burton End
162
149
136
0 2 4 6 miles
0 2 4 6 8 10 km

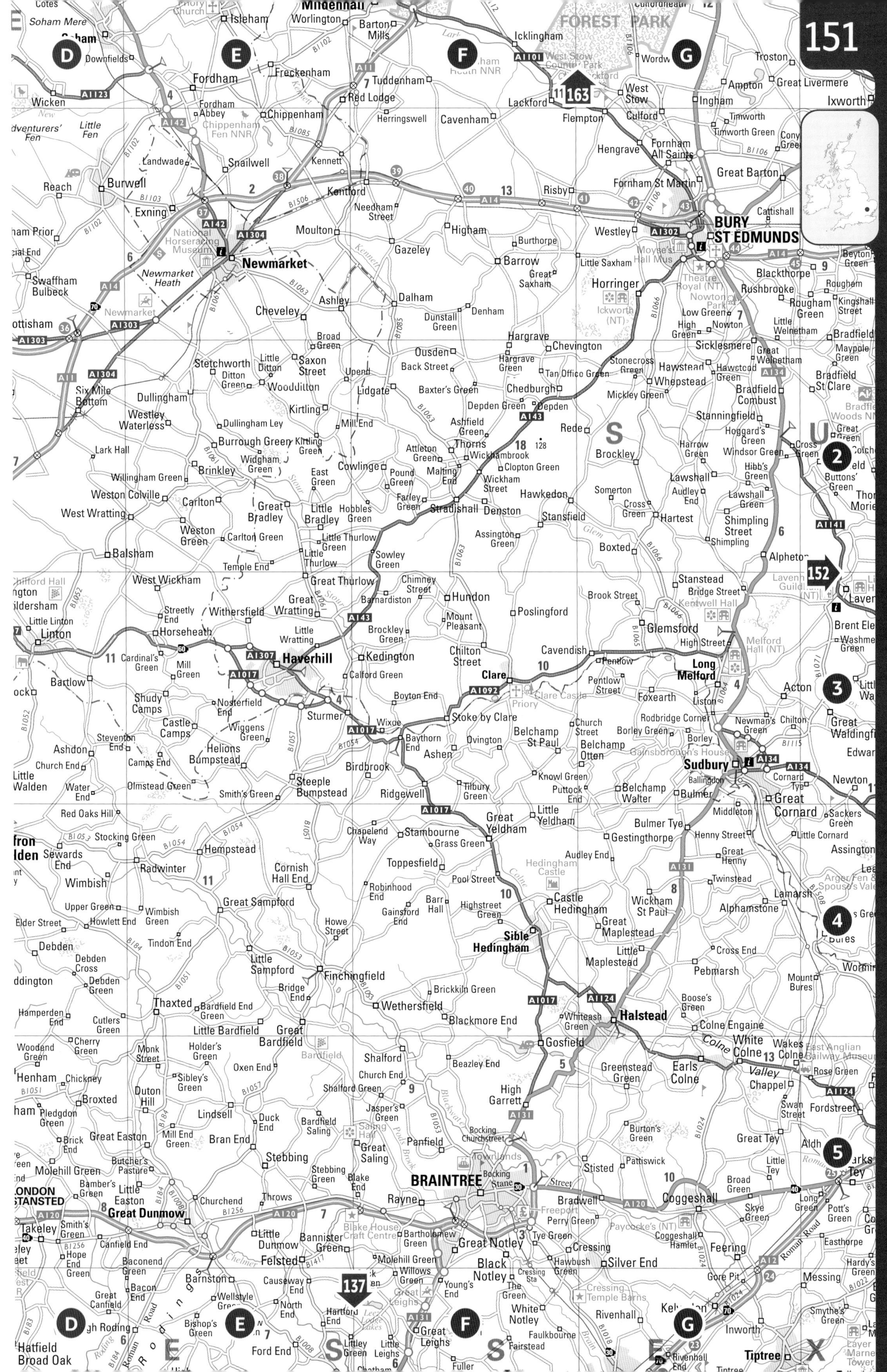
FOREST PARK
Soham Mere
Isleham
Worlington
Barton Mills
Icklingham
West Stow Country Park
Wordwell
Troston
Downfields
Fordham
Freckenham
Tuddenham
Lackford
West Stow
Ampton
Great Livermere
Ixworth
Wicken
Chippenham
Chippenham Fen NNR
Red Lodge
Herringswell
Cavenham
Flempton
Culford
Ingham
Timworth
Timworth Green
Little Fen
Landwade
Snailwell
Kennett
Hengrave
Fornham All Saints
Great Barton
Burwell
Reach
Kentford
Risby
Fornham St Martin
Exning
Needham Street
Moulton
Higham
Westley
BURY ST EDMUNDS
Cattishall
National Horseracing Museum
Newmarket
Newmarket Heath
Gazeley
Burthorpe
Barrow
Little Saxham
Great Saxham
Moyse's Hall Mus
Theatre Royal (NT)
Blackthorpe
Rushbrooke
Rougham
Kingshall Street
Rougham Green
Swaffham Bulbeck
Ashley
Dalham
Denham
Dunstall Green
Horringer
Ickworth (NT)
Nowton Park
Low Green
Nowton
High Green
Little Welnetham
Bradfield
Cheveley
Broad Green
Hargrave
Chevington
Sicklesmere
Great Welnetham
Maypole Green
Stetchworth
Little Ditton
Saxon Street
Ousden
Back Street
Hargrave Green
Tan Office Green
Stonecross Green
Hawstead
Hawstead Green
Whepstead
Bradfield St Clare
Ditton Green
Woodditton
Upend
Lidgate
Baxter's Green
Chedburgh
Depden Green
Depden
Mickley Green
Bradfield Combust
Six Mile Bottom
Dullingham
Kirtling
Westley Waterless
Dullingham Ley
Mill End
Ashfield Green
Rede
Stanningfield
Hoggard's Green
Burrough Green
Kirtling Green
Thorns
Attleton Green
Wickhambrook
Clopton Green
Brockley
Harrow Green
Windsor Green
Cross Green
Lark Hall
Widgham Green
Brinkley
Cowlinge
Pound Green
Malting End
Wickham Street
Lawshall
Hibb's Green
Buttons' Green
Willingham Green
Weston Colville
East Green
Somerton
Audley End
Lawshall Green
Carlton
Farley Green
Stradishall
Denston
Hawkedon
Cross Green
Great Bradley
Little Bradley
Hobbles Green
Hartest
Shimpling Street
Shimpling
West Wratting
Weston Green
Carlton Green
Little Thurlow Green
Assington Green
Stansfield
Boxted
Balsham
Little Thurlow
Temple End
Sowley Green
Alpheton
West Wickham
Great Thurlow
Chimney Street
Stanstead
Bridge Street
Kentwell Hall
Lavenham Guild. (NT)
Streetly End
Withersfield
Great Wratting
Barnardiston
Hundon
Brook Street
Poslingford
Mount Pleasant
Glemsford
Little Linton
Linton
Horseheath
Little Wratting
Brockley Green
High Street
Melford Hall (NT)
Cardinal's Green
Mill Green
Haverhill
Kedington
Chilton Street
Cavendish
Pentlow
Long Melford
Clare
Calford Green
Pentlow Street
Bartlow
Boyton End
Clare Castle
Foxearth
Acton
Shudy Camps
Nosterfield End
Sturmer
Priory
Liston
Castle Camps
Wiggens Green
Wixoe
Stoke by Clare
Church Street
Rodbridge Corner
Newman's Green
Chilton
Great Waldingfield
Steventon End
Ashdon
Helions Bumpstead
Baythorn End
Ovington
Belchamp St Paul
Borley Green
Borley
Belchamp Otten
Gainsborough's House
Church End
Camps End
Ashen
Birdbrook
Knowl Green
Sudbury
Ballingdon
Cornard Tye
Newton
Little Walden
Water End
Olmstead Green
Smith's Green
Steeple Bumpstead
Ridgewell
Tilbury Green
Puttock End
Belchamp Walter
Bulmer
Great Cornard
Little Yeldham
Red Oaks Hill
Great Yeldham
Bulmer Tye
Middleton
Sackers Green
Stocking Green
Chapelend Way
Stambourne
Grass Green
Gestingthorpe
Henny Street
Little Cornard
Sewards End
Hempstead
Audley End
Great Henny
Assington
Radwinter
Toppesfield
Hedingham Castle
Wimbish
Cornish Hall End
Pool Street
Twinstead
Robinhood End
Barr Hall
Highstreet Green
Castle Hedingham
Wickham St Paul
Lamarsh
Upper Green
Great Sampford
Gainsford End
Alphamstone
Elder Street
Howlett End
Wimbish Green
Howe Street
Sible Hedingham
Great Maplestead
Debden
Tindon End
Little Maplestead
Cross End
Debden Cross
Little Sampford
Finchingfield
Pebmarsh
Debden Green
Bridge End
Brickkiln Green
Mount Bures
Thaxted
Bardfield End Green
Wethersfield
Hamperden End
Cutlers Green
Blackmore End
Whiteash Green
Halstead
Boose's Green
Little Bardfield
Colne Engaine
Great Bardfield
Woodend Green
Cherry Green
Monk Street
Holder's Green
Gosfield
White Colne
Wakes Colne
East Anglian Railway Museum
Oxen End
Shalford
Beazley End
Greenstead Green
Earls Colne
Colne Valley
Henham
Chickney
Sibley's Green
Church End
Rose Green
Shalford Green
Chappel
Duton Hill
Broxted
High Garrett
Pledgdon Green
Jasper's Green
Swan Street
Fordstreet
Lindsell
Duck End
Bardfield Saling
Saling Hall
Bocking Churchstreet
Burton's Green
Great Easton
Mill End Green
Bran End
Brick End
Great Saling
Panfield
Great Tey
Aldham
Butcher's Pasture
Stebbing
Townlands
Stisted
Pattiswick
Little Tey
Molehill Green
Stebbing Green
Blake End
BRAINTREE
Bocking
Stane Street
Bradwell
Coggeshall
Broad Green
LONDON STANSTED
Bamber's Green
Little Easton
Churchend
Throws
Rayne
Skye Green
Long Green
Pott's Green
Great Dunmow
Freeport
Perry Green
Paycocke's (NT)
Coggeshall Hamlet
Takeley
Smith's Green
Little Dunmow
Bannister Green
Blake House Craft Centre
Bartholomew Green
Great Notley
Tye Green
Cressing
Feering
Easthorpe
Canfield End
Hope End Green
Baconend Green
Felsted
Molehill Green
Black Notley
Hawbush Green
Silver End
Hardy's Green
Barnston
Causeway End
Willows Green
Young's End
Cressing Sta
Cressing Temple Barns
Gore Pit
Messing
Great Canfield
Bacon End
Wellstyle Green
North End
Great Leighs
The Green
Kelvedon
Smythe's Green
Bishop's Green
Hartford End
White Notley
Rivenhall
Inworth
Hatfield Broad Oak
Ford End
Littley Green
Little Leighs
Faulkbourne
Fairstead
Tiptree
Rivenhall End
Roman Road
Fuller
Chatham
Roding
S
E
X
D
E
F
G
U
2
3
4
5
152
163
137
Fen NNR
Cotes
Adventurers' Fen
Tottisham

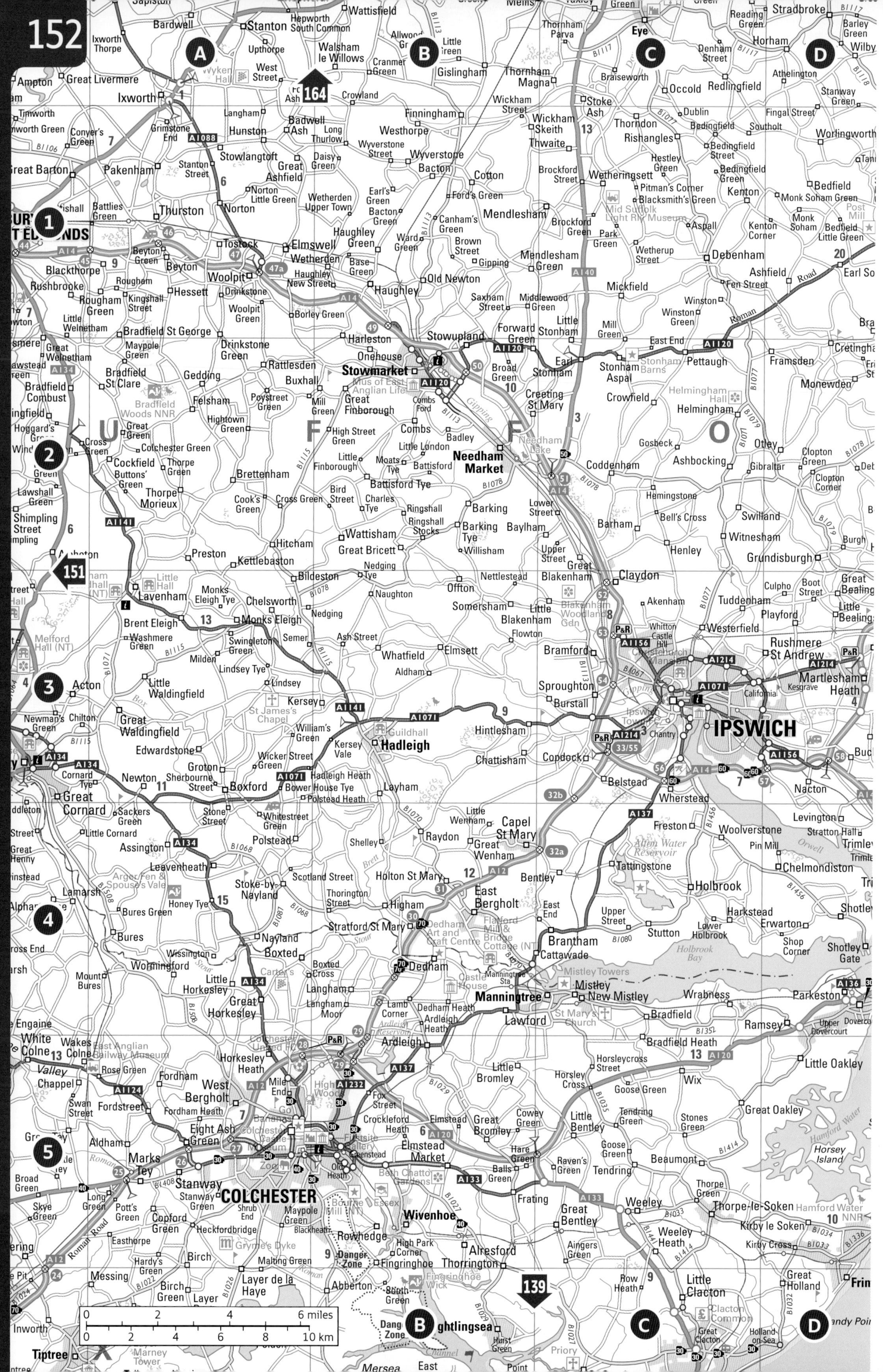

A
B
C
D
1
2
3
4
5
164
151
139
Bardwell
Stanton
Hepworth South Common
Wattisfield
Ixworth Thorpe
Upthorpe
Walsham le Willows
Allwood Green
Little Green
Cranmer Green
Gislingham
Thornham Magna
Thornham Parva
Eye
Braiseworth
Occold
Redlingfield
Denham Street
Horham
Stradbroke
Reading Green
Barley Green
Wilby
Athelington
Stanway Green
Ampton
Great Livermere
Ixworth
West Street
Crowland
Langham
Hunston
Badwell Ash
Long Thurlow
Finningham
Westhorpe
Wyverstone Street
Wyverstone
Wickham Street
Wickham Skeith
Stoke Ash
Thwaite
Thorndon
Rishangles
Dublin
Bedingfield
Southolt
Bedingfield Street
Bedingfield Green
Hestley Green
Fingal Street
Worlingworth
Timworth Green
Conyer's Green
Grimstone End
Stowlangtoft
Daisy Green
Great Ashfield
Stanton Street
Pakenham
Great Barton
Norton Little Green
Norton
Thurston
Battlies Green
Bacton
Cotton
Earl's Green
Bacton Green
Ford's Green
Wetherden Upper Town
Brockford Street
Wetheringsett
Pitman's Corner
Blacksmith's Green
Mid Suffolk Light Rly Museum
Kenton
Bedfield
Monk Soham Green
Monk Soham
Bedfield Little Green
Kenton Corner
Aspall
Canham's Green
Mendlesham
Brockford Green
Park Green
Bury St Edmunds
Tostock
Elmswell
Haughley Green
Wetherden
Ward Green
Brown Street
Gipping
Mendlesham Green
Wetherup Street
Debenham
Ashfield
Earl Soham
Beyton Green
Beyton
Blackthorpe
Rushbrooke
Rougham
Kingshall Street
Rougham Green
Hessett
Woolpit
Drinkstone
Woolpit Green
Haughley New Street
Base Green
Haughley
Old Newton
Saxham Street
Middlewood Green
Mickfield
Fen Street
Winston
Winston Green
Little Welnetham
Great Welnetham
Bradfield St George
Borley Green
Harleston
Onehouse
Stowupland
Forward Green
Little Stonham
Mill Green
East End
Pettaugh
Cretingham
Framsden
Stowmarket
Drinkstone Green
Rattlesden
Maypole Green
Bradfield St Clare
Bradfield Combust
Gedding
Buxhall
Mus of East Anglian Life
Broad Green
Earl Stonham
Stonham Aspal
Stonham Barns
Bradfield Woods NNR
Felsham
Poystreet Green
Mill Green
Great Finborough
Combs Ford
Creeting St Mary
Crowfield
Helmingham Hall
Helmingham
Monewden
Hoggard's Green
Great Green
Cross Green
Hightown Green
Colchester Green
High Street Green
Combs
Badley
Needham Lake
Gosbeck
Otley
Clopton Green
Cockfield
Thorpe Green
Buttons' Green
Little London
Little Finborough
Moats Tye
Battisford
Needham Market
Coddenham
Ashbocking
Gibraltar
Clopton Corner
Lawshall Green
Brettenham
Thorpe Morieux
Battisford Tye
Bird Street
Cook's Green
Cross Green
Charles Tye
Ringshall
Ringshall Stocks
Barking
Barking Tye
Lower Street
Baylham
Hemingstone
Bell's Cross
Swilland
Shimpling Street
Wattisham
Great Bricett
Willisham
Barham
Witnesham
Henley
Burgh
Grundisburgh
Hitcham
Preston
Kettlebaston
Upper Street
Great Blakenham
Nedging Tye
Nettlestead
Claydon
Little Hall
Lavenham
Bildeston
Offton
Akenham
Tuddenham
Culpho
Boot Street
Great Bealings
Little Bealings
Monks Eleigh Tye
Chelsworth
Naughton
Somersham
Little Blakenham
Blakenham Woodland Gdn
Playford
Brent Eleigh
Monks Eleigh
Nedging
Whitton
Castle Hill
Westerfield
Melford Hall (NT)
Washmere Green
Swingleton Green
Semer
Ash Street
Flowton
Rushmere St Andrew
Milden
Lindsey Tye
Whatfield
Elmsett
Bramford
Christchurch Mansion
Aldham
Martlesham Heath
Kesgrave
California
Acton
Little Waldingfield
Lindsey
Kersey
Sproughton
Burstall
Newman's Green
Chilton
Great Waldingfield
St James's Chapel
William's Green
Hadleigh
Guildhall
Hintlesham
Ipswich Town FC
Chantry
IPSWICH
Edwardstone
Kersey Vale
Wicker Street Green
Groton
Chattisham
Copdock
Cornard Tye
Newton
Sherbourne Street
Boxford
Hadleigh Heath
Bower House Tye
Polstead Heath
Layham
Belstead
Wherstead
Nacton
Great Cornard
Sackers Green
Stone Street
Whitestreet Green
Little Wenham
Capel St Mary
Freston
Levington
Little Cornard
Assington
Polstead
Shelley
Raydon
Great Wenham
Woolverstone
Stratton Hall
Pin Mill
Trimley
Alton Water Reservoir
Tattingstone
Chelmondiston
Leavenheath
Arger Fen & Spouse's Vale
Stoke-by-Nayland
Scotland Street
Holton St Mary
East Bergholt
Bentley
Holbrook
Lamarsh
Honey Tye
Thorington Street
Higham
East End
Upper Street
Harkstead
Erwarton
Bures Green
Bures
Nayland
Stratford St Mary
Dedham Art and Craft Centre
Flatford Mill & Bridge Cottage (NT)
Brantham
Stutton
Lower Holbrook
Holbrook Bay
Shop Corner
Shotley Gate
Wissington
Boxted
Boxted Cross
Dedham
Cattawade
Mistley Towers
Mistley
Wormingford
Carter's
Mount Bures
Little Horkesley
Langham
Langham Moor
Castle House
Manningtree Sta
Manningtree
New Mistley
Wrabness
Parkeston
Great Horkesley
Lamb Corner
Dedham Heath
Ardleigh Heath
Lawford
St Mary's Church
Bradfield
Ramsey
Upper Dovercourt
Dovercourt
Ardleigh Reservoir
Ardleigh
Bradfield Heath
White Colne
Wakes Colne
East Anglian Railway Museum
Colchester United FC
Horkesley Heath
Horsleycross Street
Little Oakley
Chappel
Rose Green
Fordham
West Bergholt
Mile End
High Woods
Little Bromley
Horsley Cross
Wix
Goose Green
Swan Street
Fordstreet
Fordham Heath
Fox Street
Crockleford Heath
Elmstead
Great Bromley
Cowey Green
Little Bentley
Tendring Green
Stones Green
Great Oakley
Eight Ash Green
Colchester Castle
Firstsite Gallery
Greenstead
Elmstead Market
Hare Green
Goose Green
Horsey Island
Aldham
Marks Tey
Museum
Zoo
Old Heath
Beth Chatto Gardens
Balls Green
Raven's Green
Tendring
Beaumont
Broad Green
Stanway
Stanway Green
COLCHESTER
Frating
Weeley
Thorpe Green
Thorpe-le-Soken
Hamford Water NNR
Long Green
Skye Green
Pott's Green
Copford Green
Shrub End
Maypole Green
Blackheath
Bourne Mill (NT)
Essex
Wivenhoe
Great Bentley
Kirby le Soken
Heckfordbridge
Easthorpe
Rowhedge
High Park Corner
Alresford
Weeley Heath
Kirby Cross
Grymes Dyke
Hardy's Green
Birch
Malting Green
Danger Zone
Fingringhoe
Thorrington
Aingers Green
Great Holland
Frinton
Messing
Layer de la Haye
Abberton
Fingringhoe Wick
Row Heath
Little Clacton
Birch Green
Layer
South Green
Brightlingsea
Clacton Common
Holland-on-Sea
Great Clacton
Inworth
Tiptree
Marney Tower
Hurst Green
Priory
Mersea
East
Point
Danger Zone
Roman Road
Valley
Gipping
Deben
Orwell
Stour
Brett
Box
Hamford Water
Colne
0 2 4 6 miles
0 2 4 6 8 10 km

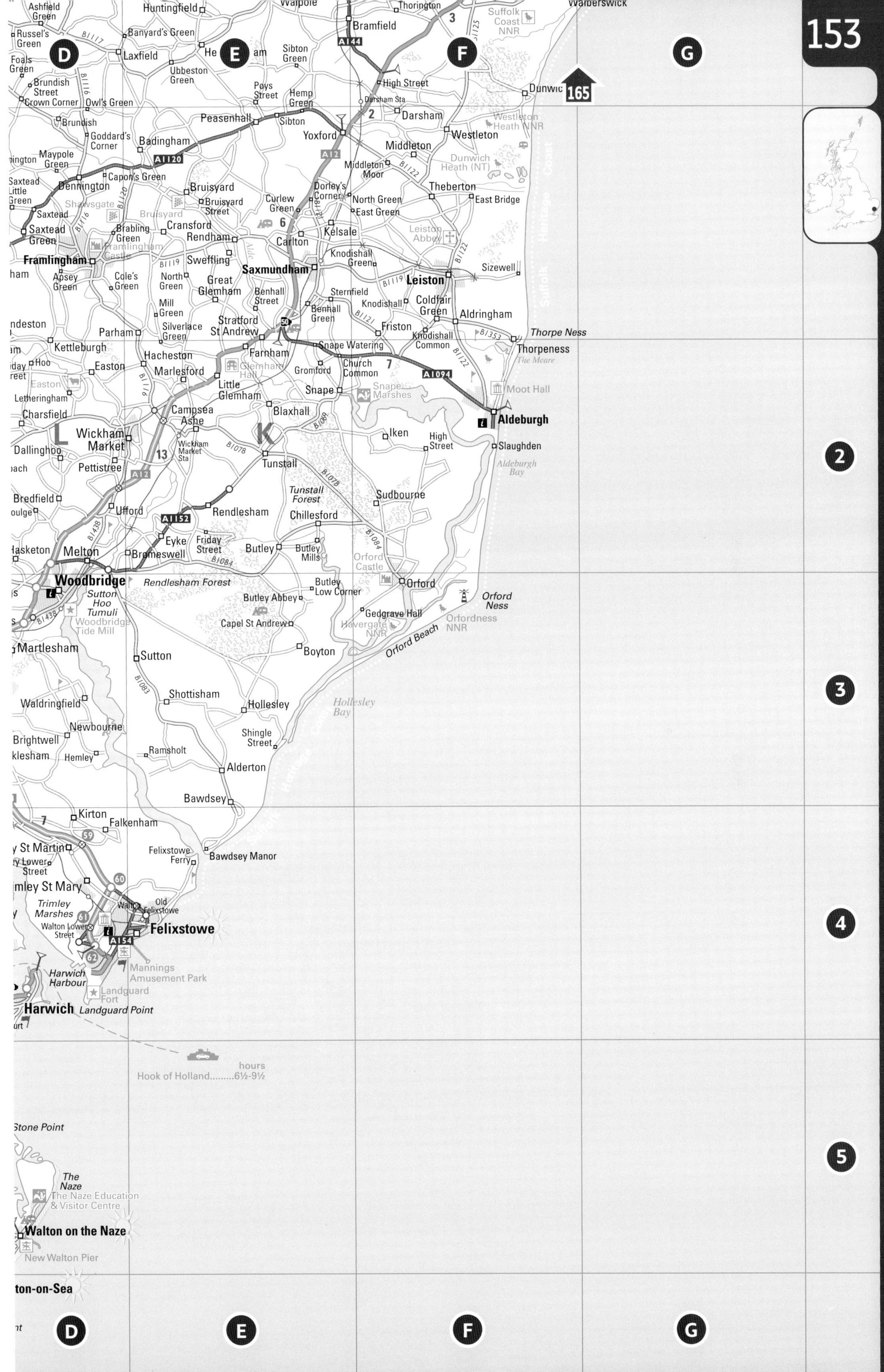

Huntingfield
Walpole
Thorington
Walberswick
Bramfield
Suffolk Coast NNR
Laxfield
Banyard's Green
Ubbeston Green
Sibton Green
High Street
Darsham Sta
Darsham
Dunwich
165
Westleton Heath NNR
Westleton
Peasenhall
Sibton
Yoxford
Middleton
Badingham
Dunwich Heath (NT)
Middleton Moor
Theberton
East Bridge
Bruisyard
Bruisyard Street
Curlew Green
Dorley's Corner
North Green
East Green
Cransford
Rendham
Kelsale
Carlton
Leiston Abbey
Knodishall Green
Framlingham
Framlingham Castle
Sweffling
Saxmundham
Sizewell
Leiston
Great Glemham
Benhall Street
Sternfield
Knodishall
Coldfair Green
Aldringham
Friston
Thorpe Ness
Thorpeness
The Meare
Parham
Stratford St Andrew
Farnham
Snape Watering
Church Common
Gromford
Snape
Snape Marshes
Moot Hall
Aldeburgh
Slaughden
Aldeburgh Bay
Iken
High Street
Blaxhall
Little Glemham
Glemham Hall
Hacheston
Marlesford
Easton
Kettleburgh
Campsea Ashe
Wickham Market
Wickham Market Sta
Pettistree
Tunstall
Tunstall Forest
Sudbourne
Rendlesham
Chillesford
Ufford
Eyke
Friday Street
Butley
Butley Mills
Orford Castle
Orford
Melton
Bromeswell
Woodbridge
Rendlesham Forest
Sutton Hoo Tumuli
Woodbridge Tide Mill
Butley Low Corner
Butley Abbey
Orford Ness
Gedgrave Hall
Havergate NNR
Orfordness NNR
Capel St Andrew
Orford Beach
Martlesham
Sutton
Boyton
Shottisham
Hollesley
Hollesley Bay
Waldringfield
Newbourne
Brightwell
Hemley
Ramsholt
Shingle Street
Alderton
Bawdsey
Suffolk Heritage Coast
Kirton
Falkenham
Felixstowe Ferry
Bawdsey Manor
Trimley Marshes
Walton Lower Street
Old Felixstowe
Felixstowe
Mannings Amusement Park
Harwich Harbour
Landguard Fort
Harwich
Landguard Point
Hook of Holland.........6½-9½ hours
Stone Point
The Naze
The Naze Education & Visitor Centre
Walton on the Naze
New Walton Pier
D
E
F
G
2
3
4
5

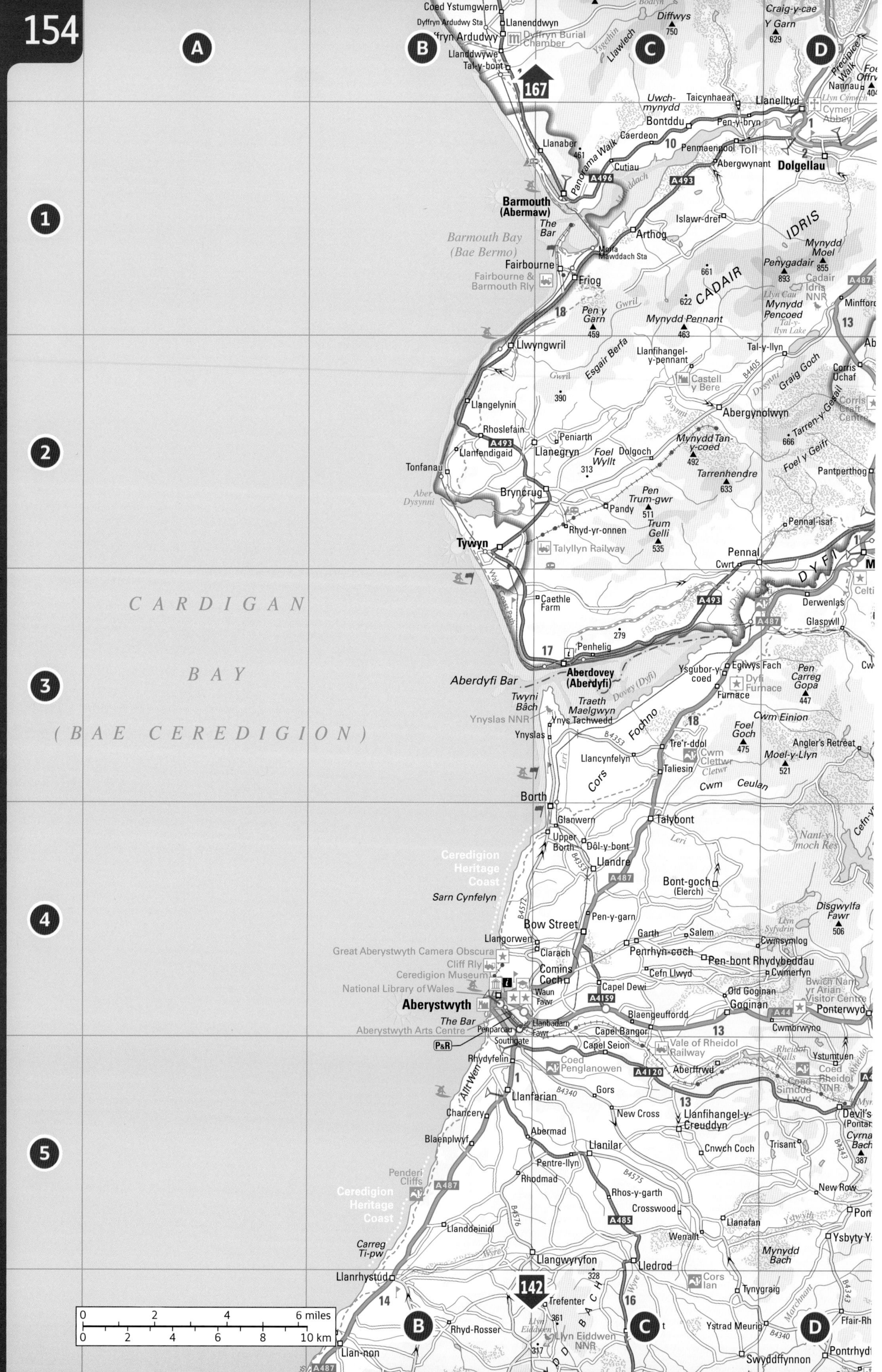

A   B   C   D

Coed Ystumgwern
Dyffryn Ardudwy Sta
'fryn Ardudwy
Llanenddwyn
Dyffryn Burial Chamber
Craig-y-cae
Y Garn
629
Bodlyn
Diffwys
750
Llawlech

Llanddwywe
Tal-y-bont
167

Uwch-mynydd
Taicynhaeaf
Llanelltyd
Cymer Abbey
Precipice Walk
Nannau
404
Llyn Cynwch

Bontddu
Pen-y-bryn
Caerdeon
Penmaenpool Toll
Abergwynant
10
Dolgellau

Llanaber
461
Cutiau
A496
A493

Barmouth (Abermaw)
The Bar
Islaw'r-dref
Arthog
IDRIS
Mynydd Moel
855

Barmouth Bay (Bae Bermo)
Morfa Mawddach Sta
Penygadair
893
Cadair Idris NNR
A487

Fairbourne
Friog
CADAIR
661
Mynydd Pencoed
Minffor
13

Fairbourne & Barmouth Rly
18
Pen y Garn
459
622
Mynydd Pennant
463
Tal-y-llyn Lake

Llwyngwril
Llanfihangel-y-pennant
Tal-y-llyn
Corris Uchaf

Esgair Berfa
Castell y Bere
Graig Goch
Corris Craft Centre

Llangelynin
390
Peniarth
Abergynolwyn
Tarren-y-
666
Foel y Geifr

Rhoslefain
Llanegryn
Foel Wyllt
Dolgoch
Mynydd Tan-y-coed
492

Llanfendigaid
313
Tarrenhendre
633
Pantperthog

Tonfanau
Bryncrug
Pen Trum-gwr
Pennal-isaf

Aber Dysynni
Pandy
511
Trum Gelli
535

Rhyd-yr-onnen
DYFI
M

Tywyn
Talyllyn Railway
Pennal
Cwrt

C A R D I G A N
Caethle Farm
279
A493
Derwenlas
Glaspwll

17
Penhelig
A487

B A Y
Aberdovey (Aberdyfi)
Ysgubor-y-coed
Eglwys Fach
Pen Carreg Gopa
447

Aberdyfi Bar
Twyni Bâch
Traeth Maelgwyn
Dyfi Furnace
Furnace

Ynyslas NNR
Ynys Tachwedd
Cwm Einion

(B A E   C E R E D I G I O N)
Ynyslas
18
Foel Goch
475
Moel-y-Llyn
521

Leri
Llancynfelyn
Fochno
Tre'r-ddol
Cwm Ceulan

Cors
Llandre
Taliesin
Cwm Clettwr
Cletwr

Borth
Talybont

Glanwern
Leri
Nant-y-moch Res

Upper Borth
Dôl-y-bont

Ceredigion Heritage Coast
Llandre
A487
Bont-goch (Elerch)

Sarn Cynfelyn
Pen-y-garn
Garth
Salem
Cwmsymlog
Disgwylfa Fawr
506

Bow Street
Penrhyn-coch
Pen-bont Rhydybeddau
Bwlch Nant yr Arian Visitor Centre

Great Aberystwyth Camera Obscura
Llangorwen
Clarach
Cefn Llwyd
Cwmerfyn

Cliff Rly
Comins Coch
Capel Dewi
Old Goginan
Goginan
A44
Ponterwyd

Ceredigion Museum
National Library of Wales
Waun Fawr
A4159
Blaengeuffordd
13
Cwmbrwyno

Aberystwyth
Llanbadarn Fawr
Capel Bangor
Vale of Rheidol Railway
Rheidol Falls
Ystumtuen

The Bar
Aberystwyth Arts Centre
Penparcau
Southgate
Capel Seion
Aberffrwd
Coed Rheidol NNR
Devil's
P&R
Rhydyfelin
Coed Penglanowen
A4120

Allt Wen
Llanfarian
Gors
13
Cyrna Bach

Chancery
New Cross
Llanfihangel-y-Creuddyn
Devil's (Pontar

Blaenplwyf
Abermad
Cnwch Coch
Trisant
387

Llanilar
New Row

Penderi Cliffs
A487
Pentre-llyn
Rhos-y-garth
Llanafan

Ceredigion Heritage Coast
Rhodmad
Crosswood
A485
Ysbyty Y

Carreg Ti-pw
Llanddeiniol
Wenallt
Mynydd Bach

Llanrhystud
Llangwyryfon
Lledrod
328
Cors Ian
Tynygraig
Marchnant

142
Trefenter
16

14
Rhyd-Rosser
361
Llyn Eiddwen NNR
t
Ystrad Meurig
Ffair-Rh

Llan-non
317
Swyddffynnon
B

A487
Pontrhyd

0   2   4   6 miles
0   2   4   6   8   10 km

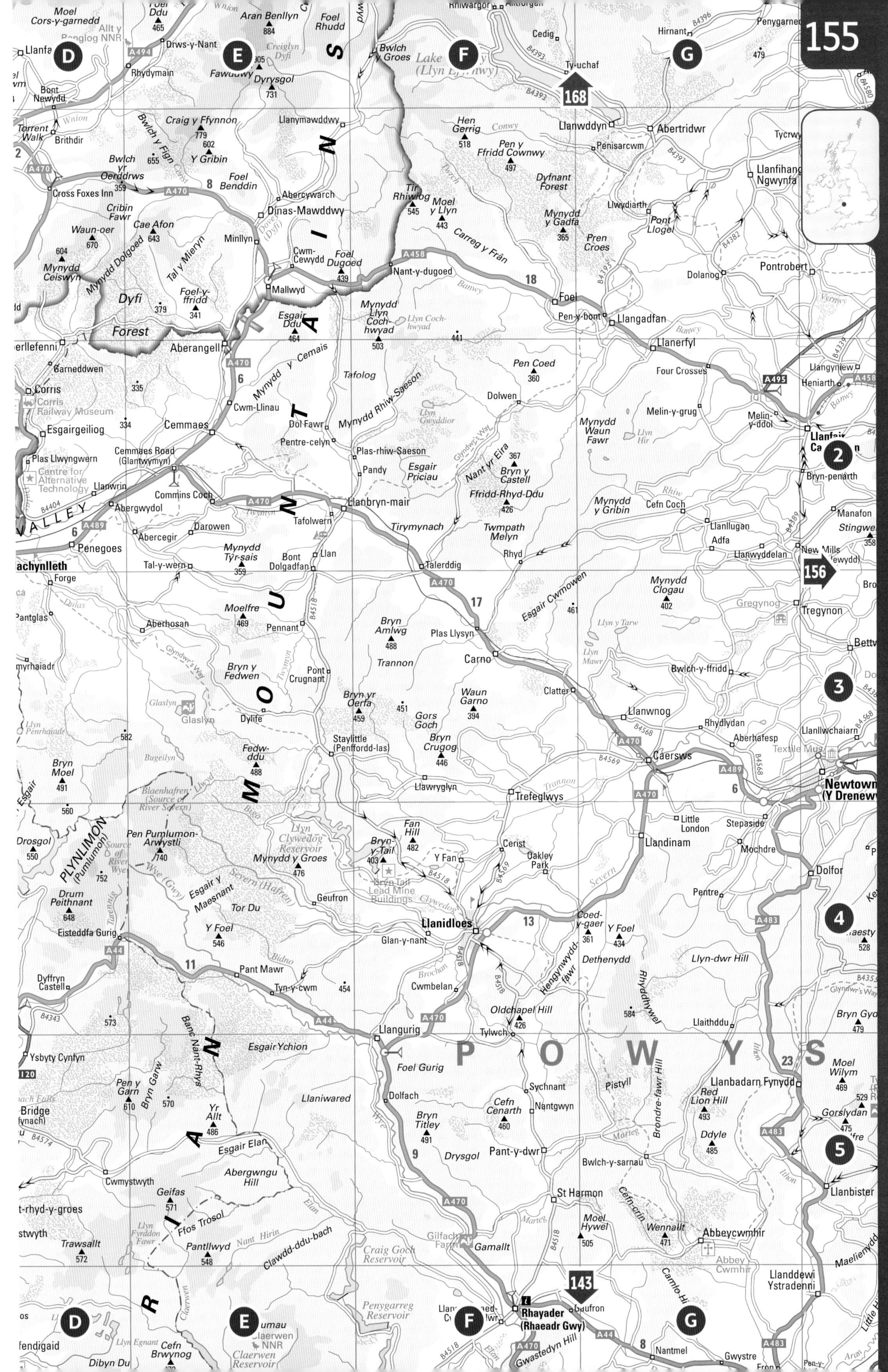

Moel Cors-y-garnedd
Allt y Genlog NNR
Llanfa
Foel Ddu
465
Drws-y-Nant
Rhydymain
Aran Benllyn
884
Creiglyn Dyfi
905
Fawddwy
Dyrysgol
731
Foel Rhudd
Bwlch y Groes
Lake Vyrnwy (Llyn Efyrnwy)
Cedig
Ty-uchaf
168
Hirnant
Penygarnedd
479
Bont Newydd
Torrent Walk
Brithdir
Wnion
Craig y Ffynnon
779
602
Y Gribin
655
Bwlch y Fign
Llanymawddwy
Hen Gerrig
518
Conwy
Llanwddyn
Abertridwr
Penisarcwm
Pen y Ffridd Cownwy
497
Dyfnant Forest
Tycrwyn
Llanfihangel-yng-Ngwynfa
Bwlch yr Oerddrws
359
Cross Foxes Inn
A470
Foel Benddin
Abercywarch
Dinas-Mawddwy
Tir Rhiwiog
545
Moel y Llyn
443
Carreg y Frân
Mynydd y Gadfa
365
Llwydiarth
Pont Llogel
Pren Croes
Cribin Fawr
Cae Afon
643
Waun-oer
670
604
Mynydd Ceiswyn
Mynydd Dolgoed
Tal y Mieryn
Minllyn
Dovey (Dyfi)
Cwm-Cewydd
Foel Dugoed
439
A458
Nant-y-dugoed
Dolanog
Pontrobert
Mallwyd
Dyfi Forest
379
Foel-y-ffridd
341
18
Banwy
Foel
Pen-y-bont
Llangadfan
Vyrnwy
Esgair Ddu
464
Mynydd Llyn Coch-hwyad
503
Llyn Coch-hwyad
441
Llanerfyl
Aberllefenni
Aberangell
Barneddwen
Mynydd y Cemais
Tafolog
Pen Coed
360
Four Crosses
Llangyniew
Heniarth
A495
Corris
Corris Railway Museum
335
Cwm-Llinau
Mynydd Rhiw-Saeson
Dolwen
Melin-y-grug
Melin-y-ddol
334
Esgairgeiliog
Cemmaes
Llyn Gwyddior
Dol Fawr
Mynydd Waun Fawr
Llyn Hir
Llanfair Caereinion
Pentre-celyn
Glyndŵr's Way
Plas Llwyngwern
Cemmaes Road (Glantwymyn)
Plas-rhiw-Saeson
Nant yr Eira
367
Bryn y Castell
Centre for Alternative Technology
Llanwrin
Pandy
Esgair Priciau
Bryn-penarth
Commins Coch
Ffridd-Rhyd-Ddu
426
Rhiw
B4404
VALLEY
Abergwydol
Llanbrynmair
Twymyn
Mynydd y Gribin
Cefn Coch
Manafon
A489
Tafolwern
Tirymynach
Twmpath Melyn
Llanllugan
Stingwern
Penegoes
Abercegir
Darowen
Adfa
358
Machynlleth
Mynydd Tŷr-sais
359
Bont Dolgadfan
Llan
Rhyd
Llanwyddelan
New Mills (Felindre)
Tal-y-wern
Talerddig
156
Forge
Mynydd Clogau
402
Dulas
A470
17
Esgair Cwmowen
461
Gregynog
Tregynon
Pantglas
Moelfre
469
Pennant
B4518
Bryn Amlwg
488
Plas Llysyn
Llyn y Tarw
Aberhosan
Carno
Bettws
Trannon
Llyn Mawr
Glyndŵr's Way
Bryn y Fedwen
Pont Crugnant
Bwlch-y-ffridd
3
Bryn yr Oerfa
Waun Garno
394
459
451
Clatter
Glaslyn
Dylife
Gors Goch
Llanwnog
Rhydlydan
Llyn Penrhaiadr
582
Staylittle (Penffordd-las)
Bryn Crugog
446
B4568
Aberhafesp
Llanllwchaiarn
Textile Museum
Fedw-ddu
488
Caersws
A489
Bryn Moel
491
Bugeilyn
Llawryglyn
B4569
Trefeglwys
Trannon
Newtown (Y Drenewydd)
560
Blaenhafren (Source of River Severn)
Llyn Clywedog Reservoir
Fan Hill
482
Little London
Stepaside
Llandinam
Drosgol
550
Pen Pumlumon-Arwystli
740
PLYNLIMON (Pumlumon)
Source of River Wye
752
Mynydd y Groes
476
Bryn-y-Tail
403
Y Fan
Bryn Tail Lead Mine Buildings
Cerist
Oakley Park
Mochdre
Dolfor
Esgair y Maesnant
Severn (Hafren)
Wye (Gwy)
Drum Peithnant
648
Tor Du
Geufron
Clywedog
Pentre
Kerry
4
Eisteddfa Gurig
Y Foel
546
Llanidloes
13
Coed-y-gaer
361
Y Foel
434
Glan-y-nant
A483
A44
11
Pant Mawr
Bidno
Dethenydd
Lyn-dwr Hill
Dyffryn Castell
Tyn-y-cwm
454
Brochan
Cwmbelan
Hengynwydd-fawr
Rhyddhywel
B4343
573
Oldchapel Hill
426
584
Llaithddu
Bryn Gydfa
479
Banc Nant-Rhys
Esgair Ychion
Llangurig
Tylwch
Ysbyty Cynfyn
P O W Y S
23
Moel Wilym
469
Foel Gurig
Pistyll
Llanbadarn Fynydd
Red Lion Hill
493
Pen y Garn
610
Bryn Garw
570
Dolfach
Sychnant
Llaniwared
Cefn Cenarth
460
Nantgwyn
Brondre-fawr Hill
529
Gorslydan
475
Devil's Bridge
Yr Allt
486
Bryn Titley
491
Marteg
Ddyle
485
B4574
Esgair Elan
9
Drysgol
Pant-y-dwr
Bwlch-y-sarnau
5
Cwmystwyth
Abergwngu Hill
Llanbister
Geifas
571
St Harmon
Cefn-crin
Pont-rhyd-y-groes
Ffos Trosol
Llyn Fyrddon Fawr
Nant Hirin
Elan
Moel Hywel
505
Wennallt
471
Abbeycwmhir
Trawsallt
572
Pantllwyd
548
Clawdd-ddu-bach
Craig Goch Reservoir
Gilfach Farm
Gamallt
Abbey Cwmhir
Maelienydd
Llanddewi Ystradenni
143
Camlo Hill
Penygarreg Reservoir
Rhayader (Rhaeadr Gwy)
Gaufron
Dibyn Du
Llyn Egnant
Cefn Brwynog
Claerwen NNR
Claerwen Reservoir
Elan
A470
Gwastedyn Hill
8
Nantmel
Gwystre
B4518
A483
R
A
D
N
O
R
I
A
N
S
M
O
U
N
T
A
I
N
S

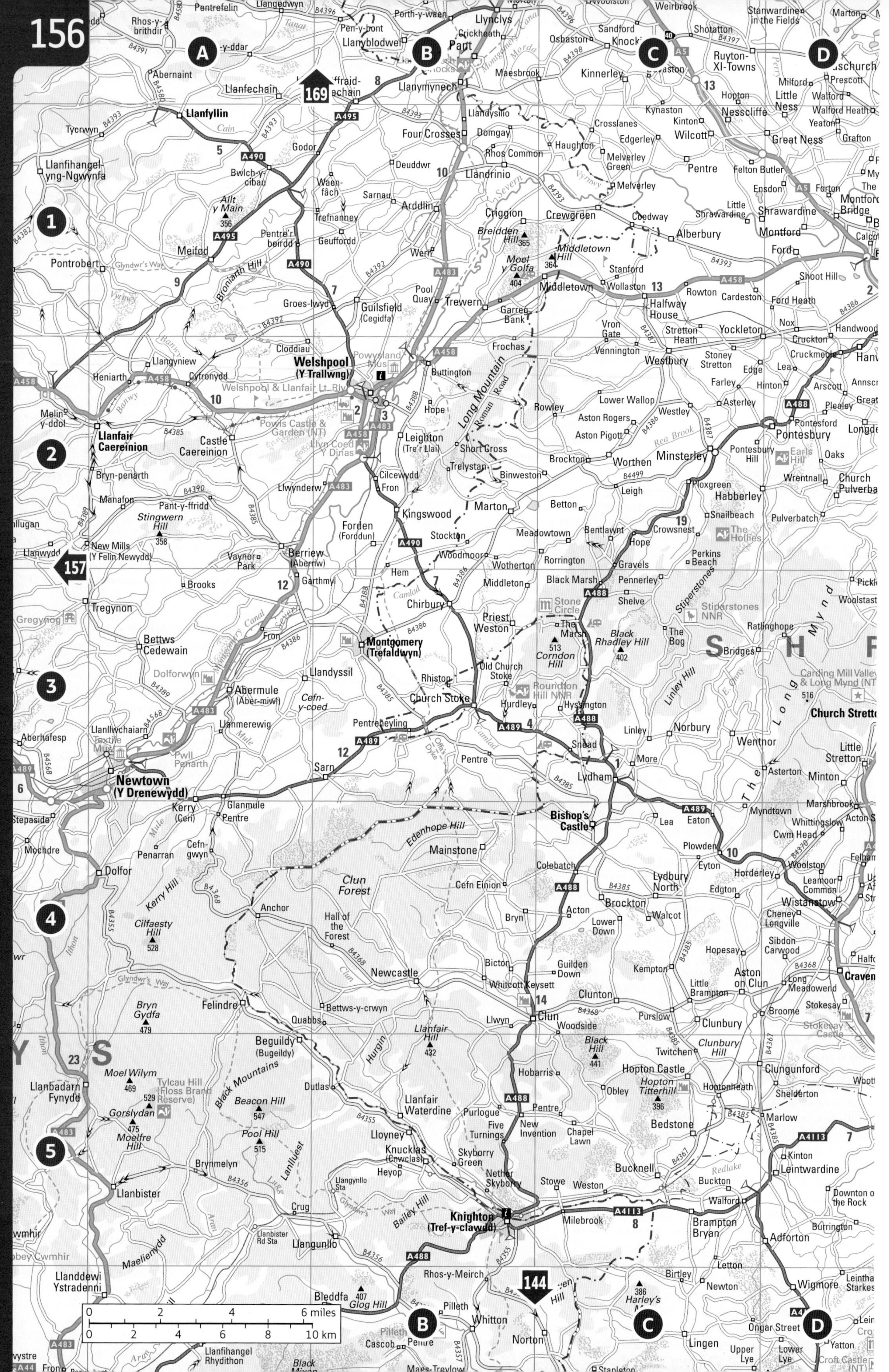

Pentrefelin
Llangedwyn
Porth-y-waen
Llynclys
Weirbrook
Stanwardine in the Fields
Marton
Rhos-y-brithdir
Pen-y-bont
Llanyblodwel
Crickheath
Pant
Sandford
Knockin
Shotatton
Ruyton-XI-Towns
Osbaston
Abernaint
Llanfechain
169
Llanymynech
Maesbrook
Kinnerley
Milford
Prescott
Little Ness
Walford
Hopton
Nesscliffe
Llanfyllin
Tycrwyn
Llandysilio
Four Crosses
Domgay
Crosslanes
Kynaston
Kinton
Walford Heath
Yeaton
Godor
Rhos Common
Haughton
Edgerley
Wilcott
Great Ness
Grafton
Llanfihangel-yng-Ngwynfa
Bwlch-y-cibau
Deuddwr
Llandrinio
Melverley Green
Pentre
Felton Butler
Waen-fâch
Sarnau
Melverley
Ensdon
Forton
Arddlin
Criggion
Crewgreen
Coedway
Little Shrawardine
Shrawardine
Montford Bridge
Trefnanney
Alberbury
Montford
Allt y Main
356
Meifod
Pentre'r beirdd
Geuffordd
Breidden Hill
365
Middletown Hill
364
Ford
Pontrobert
Glyndŵr's Way
Broniarth Hill
Welli
Moel y Golfa
404
Stanford
Shoot Hill
Wollaston
Middletown
Rowton
Cardeston
Ford Heath
Pool Quay
Trewern
Halfway House
Groes-lwyd
Guilsfield (Cegidfa)
Garreg Bank
Vron Gate
Nox
Stretton Heath
Yockleton
Cruckton
Handwood
Cloddiau
Frochas
Vennington
Westbury
Stoney Stretton
Cruckmeole
Powysland Mus
Llangyniew
Welshpool (Y Trallwng)
Buttington
Long Mountain
Roman Road
Edge
Lea
Farley
Hinton
Arscott
Heniarth
Cyfronydd
Welshpool & Llanfair Lt. Rly
Hope
Rowley
Lower Wallop
Westley
Asterley
Pontesford
Pontesbury
Melin-y-ddôl
Llanfair Caereinion
Powis Castle & Garden (NT)
Leighton (Tre'r Llai)
Aston Rogers
Aston Pigott
Rea Brook
Castle Caereinion
Llyn Coed Y Dinas
Short Cross
Minsterley
Pontesbury Hill
Earls Hill
Oaks
Trelystan
Brockton
Worthen
Bryn-penarth
Cilcewydd
Binweston
Leigh
Wrentnall
Church Pulverbatch
Llwynderw
Fron
Ploxgreen
Habberley
Manafon
Pant-y-ffridd
Marton
Betton
Snailbeach
Pulverbatch
Stingwern Hill
358
Kingswood
Forden (Forddun)
Bentlawnt
Crowsnest
The Hollies
Stockton
Meadowtown
Hope
New Mills (Y Felin Newydd)
Llanwyddelan
157
Vaynor Park
Berriew (Aberriw)
Woodmoor
Wotherton
Rorrington
Perkins Beach
Hem
Gravels
Brooks
Garthmyl
Middleton
Black Marsh
Pennerley
Camlad
Chirbury
Stone Circle
Shelve
Stiperstones
Stiperstones NNR
Tregynon
Gregynog
Priest Weston
The Marsh
Black Rhadley Hill
402
The Bog
Ratlinghope
Bettws Cedewain
Montgomery (Trefaldwyn)
Corndon Hill
513
Bridges
Llandyssil
Old Church Stoke
Rhiston
Linley Hill
Carding Mill Valley & Long Mynd (NT)
516
Dolforwyn
Cefn-y-coed
Roundton Hill NNR
Abermule (Aber-miwl)
Church Stoke
Hurdley
Hyssington
Church Stretton
Llanllwchaiarn
Llanmerewig
Pentrebeyling
Linley
Norbury
Wentnor
Little Stretton
Aberhafesp
Textile Mus
Pwll Penarth
Offa's Dyke
Snead
More
Asterton
Minton
Newtown (Y Drenewydd)
Sarn
Pentre
Lydham
Kerry (Ceri)
Glanmule
Bishop's Castle
Lea
Eaton
Myndtown
Marshbrook
Acton Scott
Stepaside
Whittingslow
Cwm Head
Mochdre
Edenhope Hill
Mainstone
Plowden
Cefn-gwyn
Penarran
Eyton
Horderley
Woolston
Dolfor
Colebatch
Lydbury North
Leamoor Common
Clun Forest
Cefn Einion
Edgton
Kerry Hill
Brockton
Wistanstow
Anchor
Acton
Walcot
Cheney Longville
Cilfaesty Hill
528
Hall of the Forest
Bryn
Lower Down
Sibdon Carwood
Hopesay
Kempton
Aston on Clun
Newcastle
Bicton
Guilden Down
Craven Arms
Whitcott Keysett
Little Brampton
Long Meadowend
Stokesay
Felindre
Bettws-y-crwyn
Clunton
Bryn Gydfa
479
Quabbs
Llwyn
Clun
Purslow
Clunbury
Broome
Stokesay Castle
Llanfair Hill
432
Woodside
Black Hill
441
Clunbury Hill
Beguildy (Bugeildy)
Hurgin
Twitchen
Moel Wilym
469
Hobarris
Hopton Castle
Clungunford
Llanbadarn Fynydd
Tylcau Hill (Floss Brand Reserve)
Black Mountains
Dutlas
Obley
Hopton Titterhill
396
Hoptonheath
Shelderton
Beacon Hill
547
Llanfair Waterdine
Purlogue
Pentre
Gorslydan
475
Bedstone
Marlow
Moelfre Hill
Pool Hill
515
Lloyney
Five Turnings
New Invention
Chapel Lawn
Knucklas (Cnwclas)
Skyborry Green
Kinton
Leintwardine
Brynmelyn
Lanlluest
Heyop
Nether Skyborry
Stowe
Weston
Bucknell
Redlake
Llanbister
Llangynllo Sta
Buckton
Downton on the Rock
Crug
Bailey Hill
Knighton (Tref-y-clawdd)
Milebrook
Walford
Brampton Bryan
Burrington
Llanbister Rd Sta
Llangunllo
Adforton
Maelienydd
Rhos-y-Meirch
Birtley
Letton
Llanddewi Ystradenni
Bleddfa
407
Glog Hill
144
Harley's Mountain
386
Newton
Wigmore
Leinthall Starkes
Pilleth
Whitton
Onger Street
Lingen
Norton
Cascob
Pentre
Upper Lye
Lower Lye
Yatton
Croft Castle
Llanfihangel Rhydithon
Black Mixen
Maes-Treylow
Stapleton
0 2 4 6 miles
0 2 4 6 8 10 km
A B C D
1 2 3 4 5

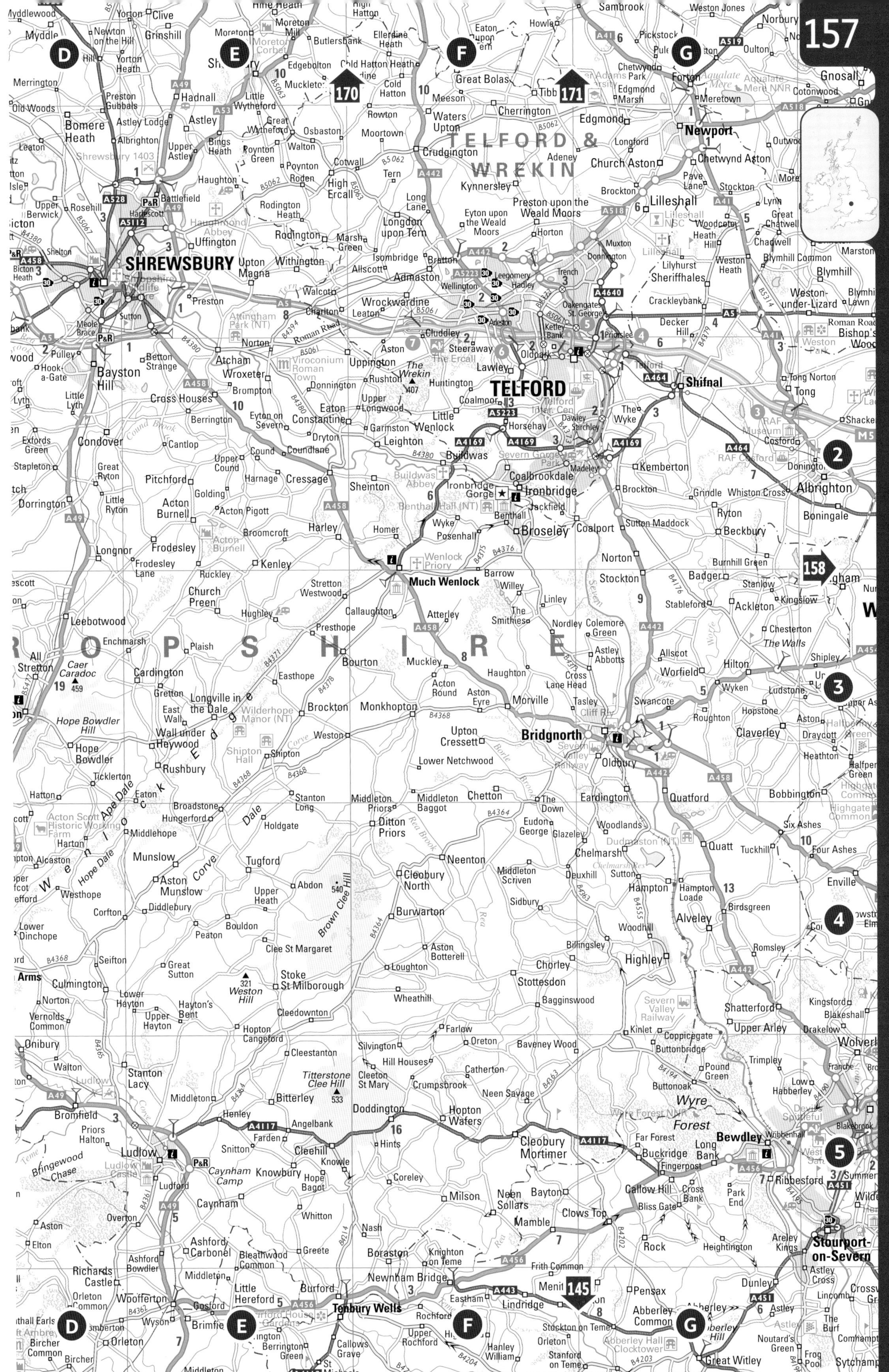

D
E
F
G
170
171
158
145
2
3
4
5
TELFORD & WREKIN
SHROPSHIRE
SHREWSBURY
TELFORD
Much Wenlock
Bridgnorth
Ludlow
Bewdley
Stourport-on-Severn
Tenbury Wells
Newport
Shifnal
Albrighton
Lilleshall
Wellington
Oakengates
Ironbridge
Broseley
Madeley
Dawley
Cleobury Mortimer
Wyre Forest
Highley
Alveley
Worfield
Claverley
Church Stretton
Wenlock Edge
Ape Dale
Corve Dale
Hope Dale
Brown Clee Hill
Titterstone Clee Hill
The Wrekin
Myddle
Grinshill
Clive
Hadnall
Astley
Bomere Heath
Atcham
Wroxeter
Cross Houses
Bayston Hill
Condover
Dorrington
Acton Burnell
Cressage
Harley
Kenley
Longnor
Cardington
Rushbury
Munslow
Culmington
Onibury
Bromfield
Caynham
Burford
Brimfield
Orleton
Woofferton
Abberley
Great Witley
Pensax
Lindridge
Menith
Newnham Bridge
Boraston
Neen Sollars
Mamble
Clows Top
Bliss Gate
Rock
Callow Hill
Far Forest
Buckridge
Kinlet
Stottesdon
Chorley
Billingsley
Burwarton
Cleobury North
Ditton Priors
Middleton Priors
Neenton
Chetton
Morville
Monkhopton
Brockton
Bourton
Shipton
Stanton Long
Holdgate
Tugford
Abdon
Clee St Margaret
Stoke St Milborough
Doddington
Bitterley
Cleehill
Hopton Wafers
Quatford
Eardington
Oldbury
Chelmarsh
Hampton Loade
Kemberton
Beckbury
Badger
Ackleton
Stockton
Norton
Coalport
Sutton Maddock
Ryton
Boningale
Donington
Cosford
Tong
Weston-under-Lizard
Blymhill
Sheriffhales
Crackleybank
Priorslee
Donnington
Muxton
Church Aston
Chetwynd Aston
Edgmond
Forton
Gnosall
Norbury
High Ercall
Rodington
Withington
Upton Magna
Uffington
Wrockwardine
Admaston
Uppington
Eaton Constantine
Leighton
Buildwas
Coalbrookdale
Little Wenlock
Lawley
Horsehay
Kynnersley
Crudgington
Waters Upton
Cherrington
Great Bolas
Preston upon the Weald Moors
Eyton upon the Weald Moors
Longdon upon Tern
Shatterford
Upper Arley
Kingsford
Enville
Bobbington
Six Ashes
Romsley
Trimpley
Ribbesford
Astley
Dunley
Areley Kings
Heightington
Far Forest
Nash
Knowle
Hints
Farden
Henley
Stanton Lacy
Hopton Cangeford
Cleestanton
Silvington
Catherton
Neen Savage
Baveney Wood
Farlow
Oreton
Wheathill
Loughton
Aston Botterell
Middleton Scriven
Deuxhill
Sidbury
Glazeley
Eudon George
Severn Valley Railway
Wyre Forest NNR
Dudmaston (NT)
Attingham Park (NT)
Benthall Hall (NT)
Wilderhope Manor (NT)
Shipton Hall
Acton Scott Historic Working Farm
Viroconium Roman Town
Buildwas Abbey
Wenlock Priory
Ludlow Castle
Burford House Gardens
Abberley Hill Clocktower
RAF Museum
RAF Cosford
Weston Park
Lilleshall NSC
Aqualate Mere NNR
Ironbridge Gorge
Caer Caradoc 459
Weston Hill 321
Hope Bowdler Hill
Bringewood Chase
Caynham Camp
A5
A41
A49
A442
A458
A464
A4169
A456
A4117
A443
A451
A518
A519
M54

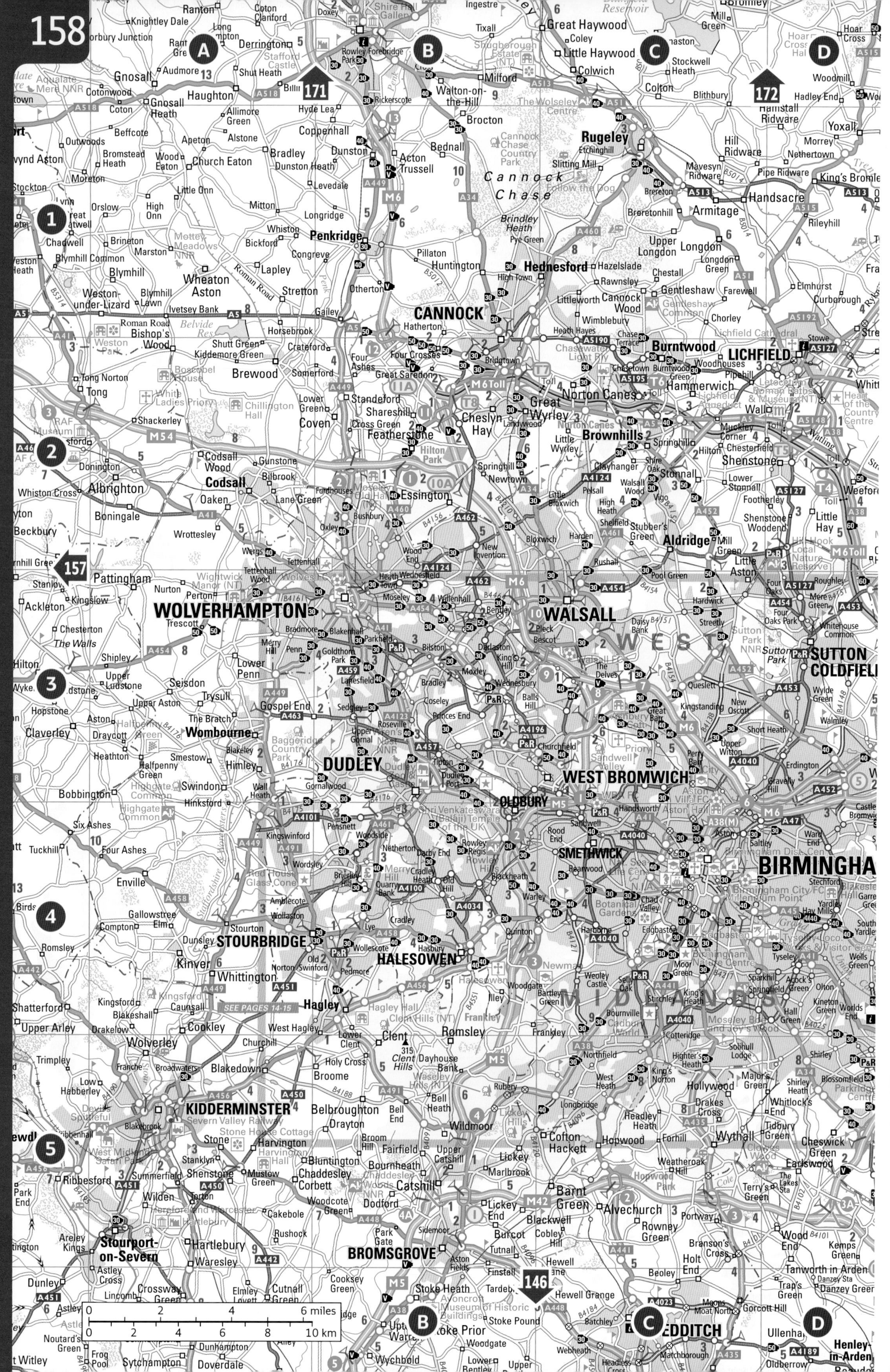
A
B
C
D
171
172
157
146
1
2
3
4
5
Ranton
Knightley Dale
Coton Clanford
Derrington
Doxey
Shire Hall Gallery
Ingestre
Tixall
Great Haywood
Coley
Little Haywood
Colwich
Shugborough Estate
Bromley
Mill Green
Hoar Cross
Stockwell Heath
Colton
Blithbury
Woodmill
Hadley End
Hamstall Ridware
Yoxall
Gnosall
Audmore
Shut Heath
Stafford Castle
Rowley Park
Forebridge
Milford
Walton-on-the-Hill
The Wolseley Centre
Cotonwood
Coton
Gnosall Heath
Haughton
Allimore Green
Hyde Lea
Rickerscote
Brocton
Rugeley
Etchinghill
Beffcote
Outwoods
Apeton
Alstone
Coppenhall
Cannock Chase Country Park
Hill Ridware
Morrey
Nethertown
Bromstead Heath
Wood Eaton
Church Eaton
Bradley
Dunston
Dunston Heath
Acton Trussell
Bednall
Slitting Mill
Mavesyn Ridware
Pipe Ridware
King's Bromley
Moreton
Levedale
Cannock Chase
Follow the Dog
Brereton
Handsacre
Stockton
Little Onn
Brereton hill
Armitage
Orslow
High Onn
Mitton
Longridge
Brindley Heath
Pye Green
Rileyhill
Chadwell
Brineton
Marston
Mottey Meadows NNR
Whiston
Bickford
Penkridge
Pillaton
Upper Longdon
Longdon
Longdon Green
Blymhill Common
Blymhill
Wheaton Aston
Lapley
Congreve
Huntington
Hednesford
Hazelslade
Chestall
Rawnsley
Gentleshaw
Farewell
Elmhurst
Curborough
Weston-under-Lizard
Blymhill Lawn
Ivetsey Bank
Roman Road
Stretton
Otherton
High Town
Littleworth
Cannock Wood
Gentleshaw Common
Chorley
CANNOCK
Wimblebury
Bishop's Wood
Belvide Res
Horsebrook
Gailey
Hatherton
Heath Hayes
Chase Terrace
Burntwood
LICHFIELD
Lichfield Cathedral
Stowe
Weston Park
Shutt Green
Kiddemore Green
Crateford
Four Ashes
Four Crosses
Great Saredon
Bridgtown
Chasewater Light Rly
Chasetown
Burntwood Green
Woodhouses
Pipehill
Tong Norton
Boscobel House
Brewood
Somerford
Norton Canes
Hammerwich
Letocetum Roman Baths & Museum (NT)
Tong
White Ladies Priory
Chillington Hall
Standeford
Shareshill
Cheslyn Hay
Great Wyrley
Landywood
Lichfield Aqueduct
Wall
Heart of the Country Centre
RAF Museum
Shackerley
Lower Green
Coven
Cross Green
Featherstone
Brownhills
Muckley Corner
Hilton Park
Little Wyrley
Springhill
Hilton
Chesterfield
Shenstone
Donington
Codsall Wood
Gunstone
Springhill
Newtown
Clayhanger
Shire Oak
Stonnall
Lower Stonnall
Weeford
Albrighton
Whiston Cross
Codsall
Bilbrook
Lane Green
Fordhouses
Moseley Old Hall
Essington
Pelsall
Walsall Wood
Vigo
Footherley
Boningale
Oaken
Bushbury
Little Bloxwich
High Heath
Shenstone Woodend
Little Hay
Beckbury
Wrottesley
Oxley
Bloxwich
Shelfield
Stubber's Green
Aldridge
Mill Green
Hill Hook Local Nature Reserve
Wergs
Tettenhall
Wood End
New Invention
Harden
Rushall
Little Aston
Tettenhall Wood
Wightwick Manor (NT)
Wolves FC
Heath Town
Wednesfield
Pool Green
Four Oaks
Roughley
Pattingham
Nurton
Perton
Moseley
Willenhall
Bentley
Hardwick
Mere Green
Stanlow
Kingslow
Ackleton
WOLVERHAMPTON
WALSALL
Four Oaks Park
Trescott
Bradmore
Blakenhall
Parkfield
Darlaston
Pleck
Bescot
Daisy Bank
Streetly
Whitehouse Common
Chesterton
The Walls
Merry Hill
Penn
Goldthorn Park
Bilston
King's Hill
Walsall FC
WEST
Sutton Park NNR
Sutton Park
SUTTON COLDFIELD
Hilton
Shipley
Lower Penn
Moxley
Wednesbury
The Delves
Upper Ludstone
Ludstone
Seisdon
Lanesfield
Bradley
Balls Hill
Great Barr
Queslett
Wylde Green
Hopstone
Trysull
Upper Aston
Gospel End
Sedgley
Coseley
Kingstanding
New Oscott
Aston
Halfpenny Green
The Birch
Wombourne
Roseville
Princes End
Churchfield
Priory
Short Heath
Walmley
Claverley
Draycott
Baggeridge Country Park
Upper Gornal
Wren's Nest NNR
Sandwell Valley
Perry Barr
Upper Witton
Heathton
Smestow
Blakeley
Himley
DUDLEY
Tipton
Dudley Port
WEST BROMWICH
Erdington
Gravelly Hill
Halfpenny Green
Highgate Common
Swindon
Gornalwood
Bobbington
Wall Heath
Hinksford
OLDBURY
WBA FC
Handsworth
Aston Villa FC
Aston Hall
Castle Bromwich
Shri Venkateswara (Balaji) Temple of the UK
Pensnett
Sandwell
Six Ashes
Kingswinford
Woodside
Rowley Regis
Rood End
Ward End
Saltley
Tuckhill
Four Ashes
Netherton
Darby End
Rowley Hill
SMETHWICK
Birmingham Dis. Cen
BIRMINGHAM
Wordsley
Red House Glass Cone
Brierley Hill
Merry Hill
Cradley Heath
Old Hill
Blackheath
Bearwood
Nat. Sea Life Cen
Enville
Quarry Bank
Stechford
Birmingham City FC
Millennium Point
Amblecote
Wollaston
Cradley
Warley
Botanical Gardens
Chad Valley
Yardley
Hay Mills
Gallowstree Elm
Compton
Lye
Quinton
Harborne
Edgbaston
South Yardley
Stourton
Dunsley
STOURBRIDGE
Wollescote
Hasbury
HALESOWEN
Tyseley
Tyseley Loco. Works & Visitor Cen
Romsley
Kinver
Whittington
Norton
Old Swinford
Pedmore
Newman
Weoley Castle
Selly Oak
Moor Green
Birmingham Nature Centre
Sparkhill
Acock's Green
Wells Green
Olton
Shatterford
Kingsford
Kingsford
Caunsall
SEE PAGES 14-15
Hagley
Hagley Hall
Halesowen
Woodgate
Bartley Green
MIDLANDS
Bournville
Cadbury World
Stirchley
King's Heath
Springfield
Kineton Green
Hall Green
Worlds End
Upper Arley
Blakeshall
Drakelow
Cookley
West Hagley
Clent Hills (NT)
Frankley
Moseley Bog and Joy's Wood
Wolverley
Churchill
Lower Clent
Clent
Romsley
Northfield
Cotteridge
Solihull Lodge
Trimpley
Franche
Broadwaters
Blakedown
315 Clent Hills
Holy Cross
Dayhouse Bank
Higher's Heath
Major's Green
Shirley
Shirley Heath
Blossomfield
Parkridge Centre
Low Habberley
Broome
Waseley Hills (NT)
Rubery
West Heath
King's Norton
Hollywood
Whitlock's End
Devil's Spittleful
KIDDERMINSTER
Severn Valley Railway
Bell End
Bell Heath
Drakes Cross
Belbroughton
Longbridge
Headley Heath
Tidbury Green
Trimpley
Blakebrook
Stone House Cottage
Stone
Drayton
Wildmoor
Lickey Hills
Cofton Hackett
Hopwood
Forhill
Wythall
Cheswick Green
Ribbesford
West Midland Safari Park
Stanklyn
Harvington
Harvington Hall
Broom Hill
Fairfield
Upper Catshill
Lickey
Weatheroak Hill
Earlswood
Summerfield
Shenstone
Mustow Green
Bluntington
Chaddesley Corbett
Bournheath
Chaddesley Woods NNR
Catshill
Marlbrook
Barnt Green
Alvechurch
Hopwood Park
Terry's Green
The Lakes Sta
Park End
Wilden
Torton
Hereford and Worcester
Hartlebury
Cakebole
Woodcote Green
Dodford
Lickey End
Blackwell
Rowney Green
Portway
Wood End
Kemps Green
Areley Kings
Stourport-on-Severn
Hartlebury
Rushock
Park Gate
Sidemoor
Burcot
Tutnall
Cobley Hill
Branson's Cross
Waresley
BROMSGROVE
Aston Fields
Hewell Lane
Holt End
Tanworth in Arden
Danzey Sta
Danzey Green
Astley Cross
Dunley
Crossway Green
Lincomb
Elmley Lovett
Cutnall Green
Cooksey Green
Finstall
Tardebigge
Stoke Heath
Avoncroft Museum of Historic Buildings
Beoley
Trap's Green
Hewell Grange
Batchley
Moons Moat North
Gorcott Hill
Astley
Upton Warren
Stoke Prior
Stoke Pound
REDDITCH
Ullenhall
Henley-in-Arden
Noutard's Green
Dunhampton
Woodgate
Webheath
Matchborough
Oldberrow
Witley
Frog Pool
Sytchampton
Doverdale
Wychbold
Lower Bentley
Upper Bentley
Headless Cross
0 2 4 6 miles
0 2 4 6 8 10 km

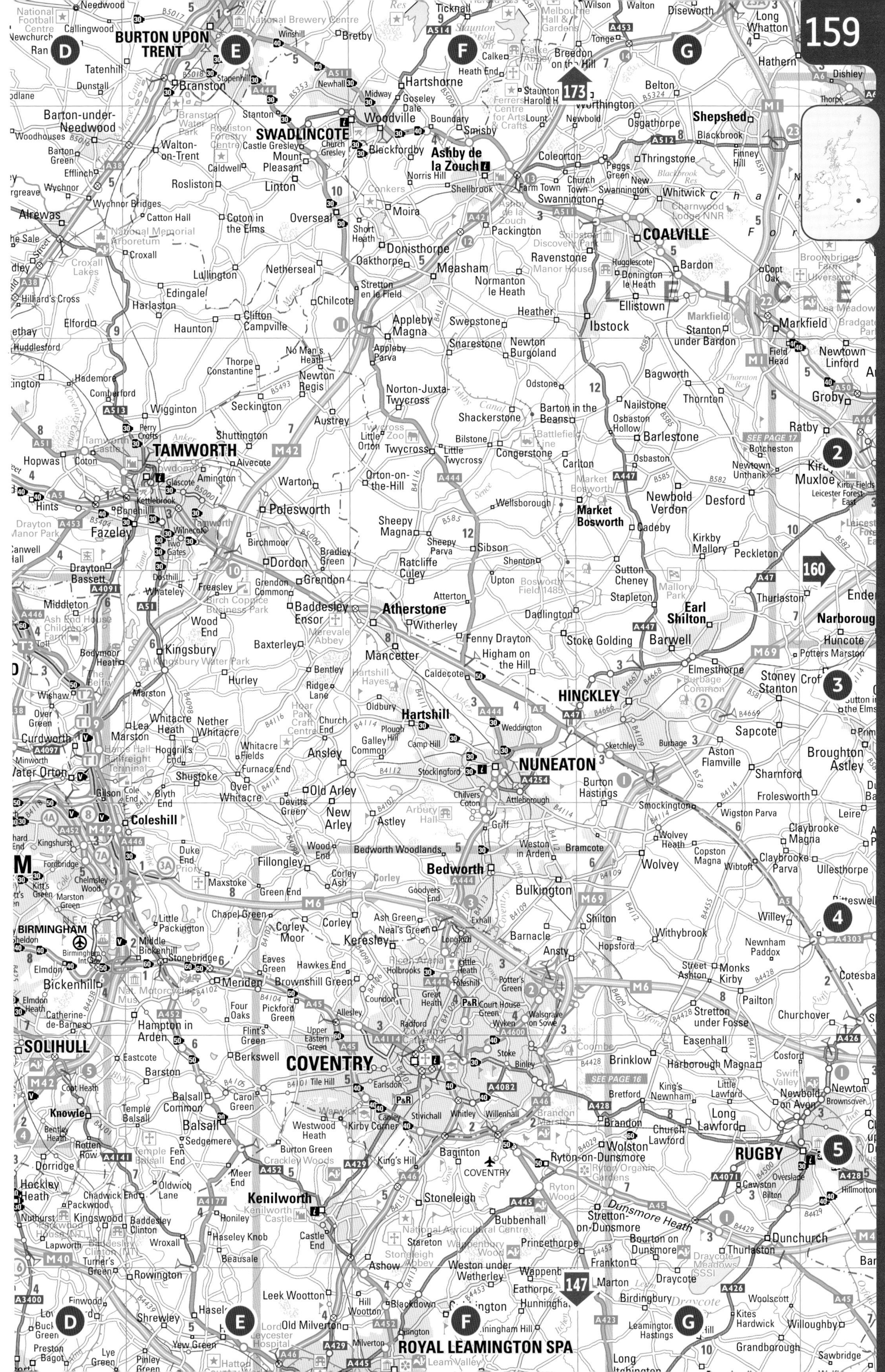
BURTON UPON TRENT
SWADLINCOTE
Ashby de la Zouch
COALVILLE
Shepshed
Markfield
Ibstock
Hathern
Long Whatton
Diseworth
Breedon on the Hill
Melbourne Hall & Gardens
Ticknall
National Brewery Centre
Branston
Barton-under-Needwood
Walton-on-Trent
Rosliston Forestry Centre
Woodville
Hartshorne
Linton
Overseal
Moira
Measham
Donisthorpe
Oakthorpe
Packington
Ravenstone
Ellistown
Bardon
Whitwick
Thringstone
Alrewas
National Memorial Arboretum
Croxall
Elford
Edingale
Harlaston
Clifton Campville
No Man's Heath
Appleby Magna
Snarestone
Newton Burgoland
Heather
Stanton under Bardon
Groby
Ratby
Newtown Linford
Thornton
Bagworth
Nailstone
Barlestone
Shackerstone
Twycross Zoo
Twycross
Congerstone
Carlton
Market Bosworth
Newbold Verdon
Desford
Kirby Muxloe
Leicester Forest East
TAMWORTH
Wigginton
Seckington
Shuttington
Austrey
Polesworth
Warton
Dordon
Grendon
Sheepy Magna
Sibson
Ratcliffe Culey
Atherstone
Mancetter
Witherley
Fenny Drayton
Higham on the Hill
Bosworth Field 1485
Sutton Cheney
Stapleton
Dadlington
Stoke Golding
Earl Shilton
Barwell
HINCKLEY
Burbage
Sapcote
Stoney Stanton
Thurlaston
Narborough
Huncote
Fazeley
Kingsbury
Kingsbury Water Park
Hurley
Baxterley
Hartshill
Ansley
Galley Common
NUNEATON
Weddington
Burton Hastings
Sharnford
Broughton Astley
Frolesworth
Claybrooke Magna
Ullesthorpe
Wolvey
Bulkington
Bedworth
Old Arley
New Arley
Astley
Fillongley
Coleshill
Water Orton
Curdworth
Shustoke
Over Whitacre
Maxstoke
Corley
Keresley
Ash Green
Shilton
Ansty
Barnacle
Withybrook
Monks Kirby
Pailton
Churchover
Stretton under Fosse
Brinklow
Harborough Magna
Newbold on Avon
RUGBY
Dunchurch
Thurlaston
BIRMINGHAM
Bickenhill
Meriden
Hampton in Arden
SOLIHULL
Knowle
Balsall Common
Berkswell
COVENTRY
Kenilworth
Kenilworth Castle
Stoneleigh
Baginton
Coventry
Wolston
Ryton-on-Dunsmore
Stretton-on-Dunsmore
Long Lawford
Bubbenhall
Princethorpe
Ashow
Leek Wootton
Hill Wootton
Blackdown
ROYAL LEAMINGTON SPA
Draycote
Birdingbury
Marton
Kingswood
Hockley Heath
Lapworth
Rowington
Shrewley
Hatton
Dorridge
Baddesley Clinton
Packwood House (NT)
173
160
147
D
E
F
G

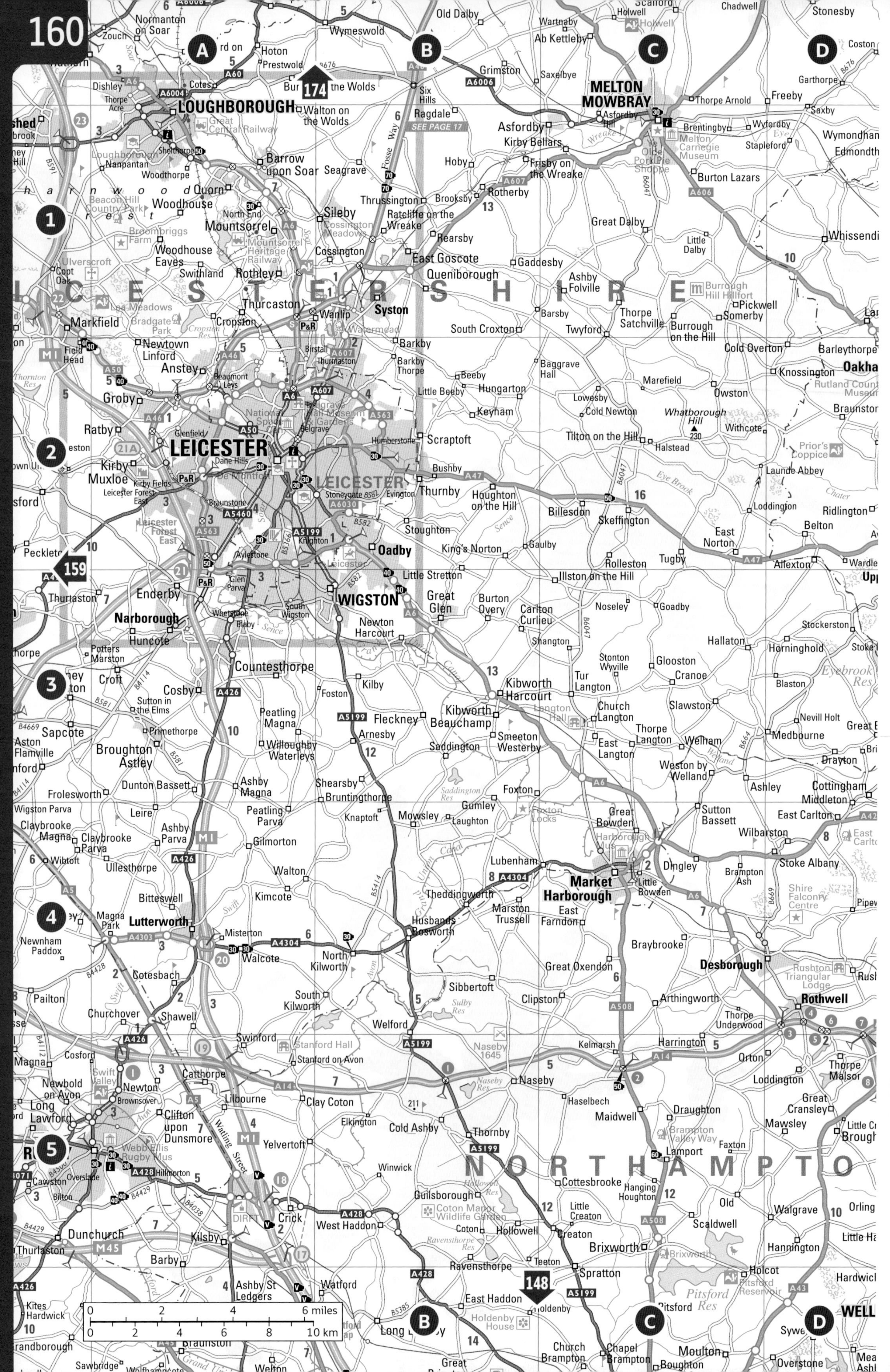

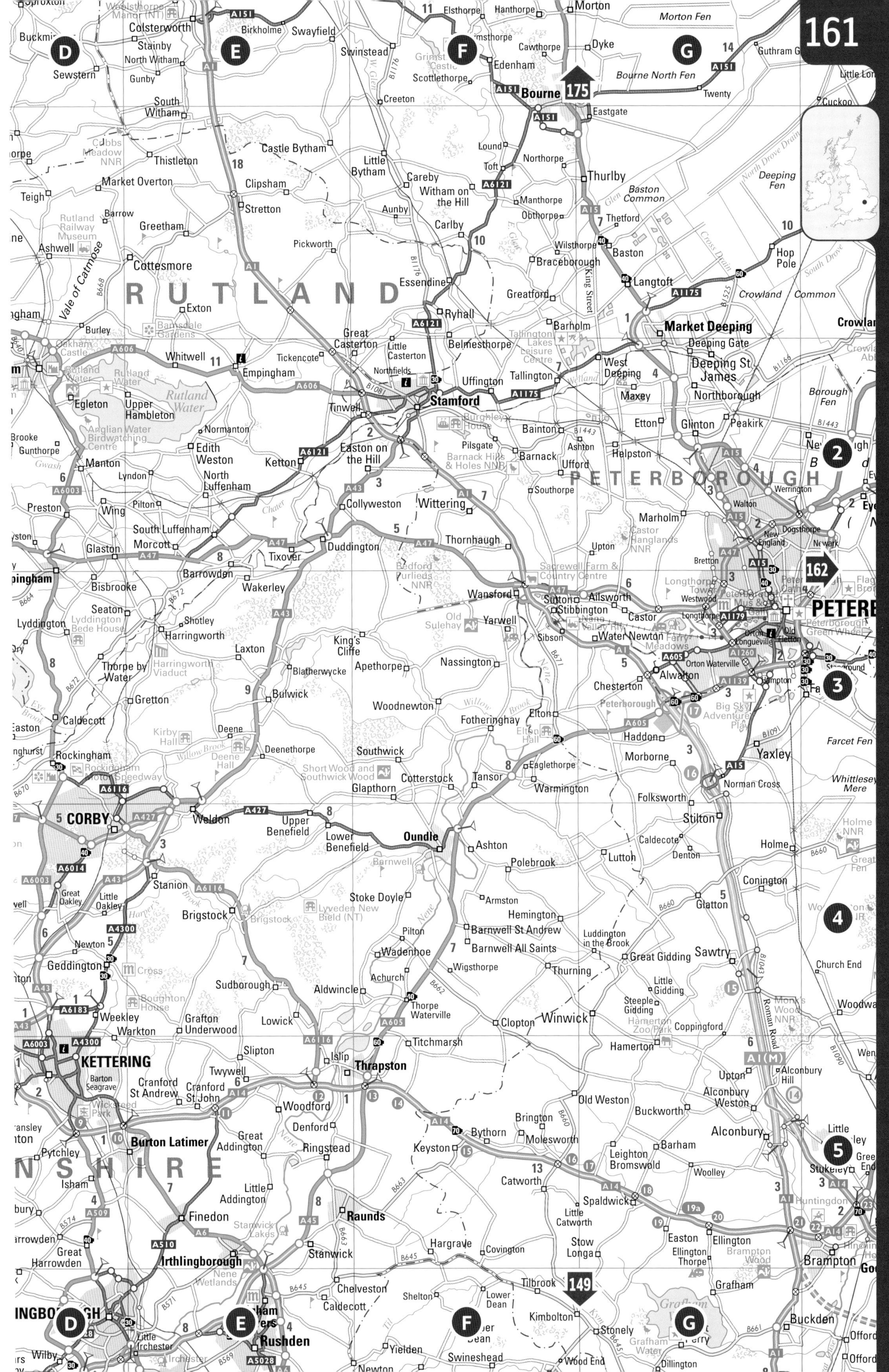

Sproxton
Woolsthorpe Manor (NT)
Colsterworth
Birkholme
Swayfield
Elsthorpe
Hanthorpe
Morton
Morton Fen
Buckminster
Stainby
North Witham
Gunby
Swinstead
Grimsthorpe Castle
Scottlethorpe
Edenham
Cawthorpe
Dyke
Bourne North Fen
Guthram Gowt
Twenty
Little London
Cuckoo
Sewstern
South Witham
Creeton
Bourne
175
Eastgate
D
E
F
G
Cribbs Meadow NNR
Thistleton
Castle Bytham
Little Bytham
Lound
Toft
Northorpe
Thurlby
North Drove Drain
Deeping Fen
Market Overton
Teigh
Clipsham
Careby
Witham on the Hill
Manthorpe
Obthorpe
Baston Common
Thetford
Barrow
Stretton
Aunby
Carlby
Rutland Railway Museum
Greetham
Pickworth
Wilsthorpe
Baston
Hop Pole
Ashwell
Cottesmore
Vale of Catmose
Braceborough
King Street
Cross Drain
South Drove
RUTLAND
Essendine
Greatford
Langtoft
Crowland
Common
Exton
Ryhall
Barholm
Market Deeping
Crowland
Burley
Barnsdale Gardens
Great Casterton
Little Casterton
Belmesthorpe
Tallington Lakes Leisure Centre
Deeping Gate
Oakham Castle
Whitwell
Tickencote
Northfields
Uffington
West Deeping
Deeping St James
Rutland Water
Empingham
Tallington
Maxey
Northborough
Borough Fen
Egleton
Upper Hambleton
Tinwell
Stamford
Burghley House
Bainton
Etton
Glinton
Peakirk
Anglian Water Birdwatching Centre
Normanton
Easton on the Hill
Pilsgate
Barnack Hills & Holes NNR
Ashton
Barnack
Helpston
Brooke
Gunthorpe
Edith Weston
Ketton
Ufford
PETERBOROUGH
Newborough
Manton
Lyndon
North Luffenham
Collyweston
Wittering
Southorpe
Werrington
Preston
Wing
Pilton
Walton
Marholm
Dogsthorpe
Castor Hanglands NNR
New England
Newark
South Luffenham
Morcott
Duddington
Thornhaugh
Upton
Glaston
Tixover
Bretton
162
Uppingham
Barrowden
Bedford Purlieus NNR
Sacrewell Farm & Country Centre
Longthorpe Tower
Bisbrooke
Wakerley
Wansford
Sutton
Ailsworth
Westwood
Seaton
Lyddington Bede House
Shotley
Stibbington
Castor
PETERBOROUGH
Lyddington
Harringworth
Old Sulehay
Yarwell
Nene Valley Rly
Longthorpe
Peterborough Green Wheel
Laxton
King's Cliffe
Sibson
Water Newton
Ferry Meadows
Orton Longueville
Old Fletton
Thorpe by Water
Harringworth Viaduct
Apethorpe
Nassington
Orton Waterville
Stanground
Blatherwycke
Alwalton
Gretton
Bulwick
Chesterton
Hampton
Woodnewton
Willow Brook
Peterborough
Big Sky Adventure Play
Caldecott
Eye Brook
Fotheringhay
Elton
Elton Hall
Kirby Hall
Deene
Haddon
Farcet Fen
Easton
Deenethorpe
Deene Hall
Southwick
Morborne
Yaxley
Rockingham
Rockingham Motor Speedway
Short Wood and Southwick Wood
Eaglethorpe
Whittlesey Mere
Cotterstock
Tansor
Warmington
Norman Cross
Glapthorn
Folksworth
CORBY
Weldon
Upper Benefield
Lower Benefield
Oundle
Stilton
Holme Fen NNR
Ashton
Caldecote
Denton
Holme
Barnwell
Lutton
Polebrook
Great Fen
Great Oakley
Little Oakley
Stanion
Brigstock
Lyveden New Bield (NT)
Stoke Doyle
Armston
Conington
Hemington
Glatton
Barnwell St Andrew
Luddington in the Brook
Barnwell All Saints
Pilton
Newton
Wadenhoe
Great Gidding
Sawtry
Geddington
Cross
Wigsthorpe
Thurning
Church End
Achurch
Little Gidding
Sudborough
Aldwincle
Steeple Gidding
Monks Wood NNR
Woodwalton
Boughton House
Thorpe Waterville
Weekley
Grafton Underwood
Lowick
Clopton
Winwick
Hamerton Zoo Park
Coppingford
Warkton
Titchmarsh
Hamerton
KETTERING
Slipton
Roman Road
Barton Seagrave
Twywell
Islip
Thrapston
Upton
Alconbury Hill
Cranford St Andrew
Cranford St John
Alconbury Weston
Wicksteed Park
Woodford
Old Weston
Buckworth
Brington
Molesworth
Alconbury
Little Stukeley
Broughton
Pytchley
Burton Latimer
Great Addington
Denford
Bythorn
Keyston
Barham
Ringstead
Leighton Bromswold
Woolley
Great Stukeley
NORTHAMPTONSHIRE
Isham
Little Addington
Catworth
Spaldwick
Huntingdon
Finedon
Raunds
Little Catworth
Easton
Ellington
Stanwick Lakes
Ellington Thorpe
Brampton Wood
Great Harrowden
Irthlingborough
Stanwick
Hargrave
Covington
Stow Longa
Brampton
Nene Wetlands
Chelveston
Tilbrook
149
Grafham
Grafham Water
Caldecott
Shelton
Lower Dean
WELLINGBOROUGH
Higham Ferrers
Kimbolton
Stonely
Perry
Buckden
Little Irchester
Irchester
Rushden
Upper Dean
Yielden
Swineshead
Wood End
Dillington
Offord
Newton
Wilby

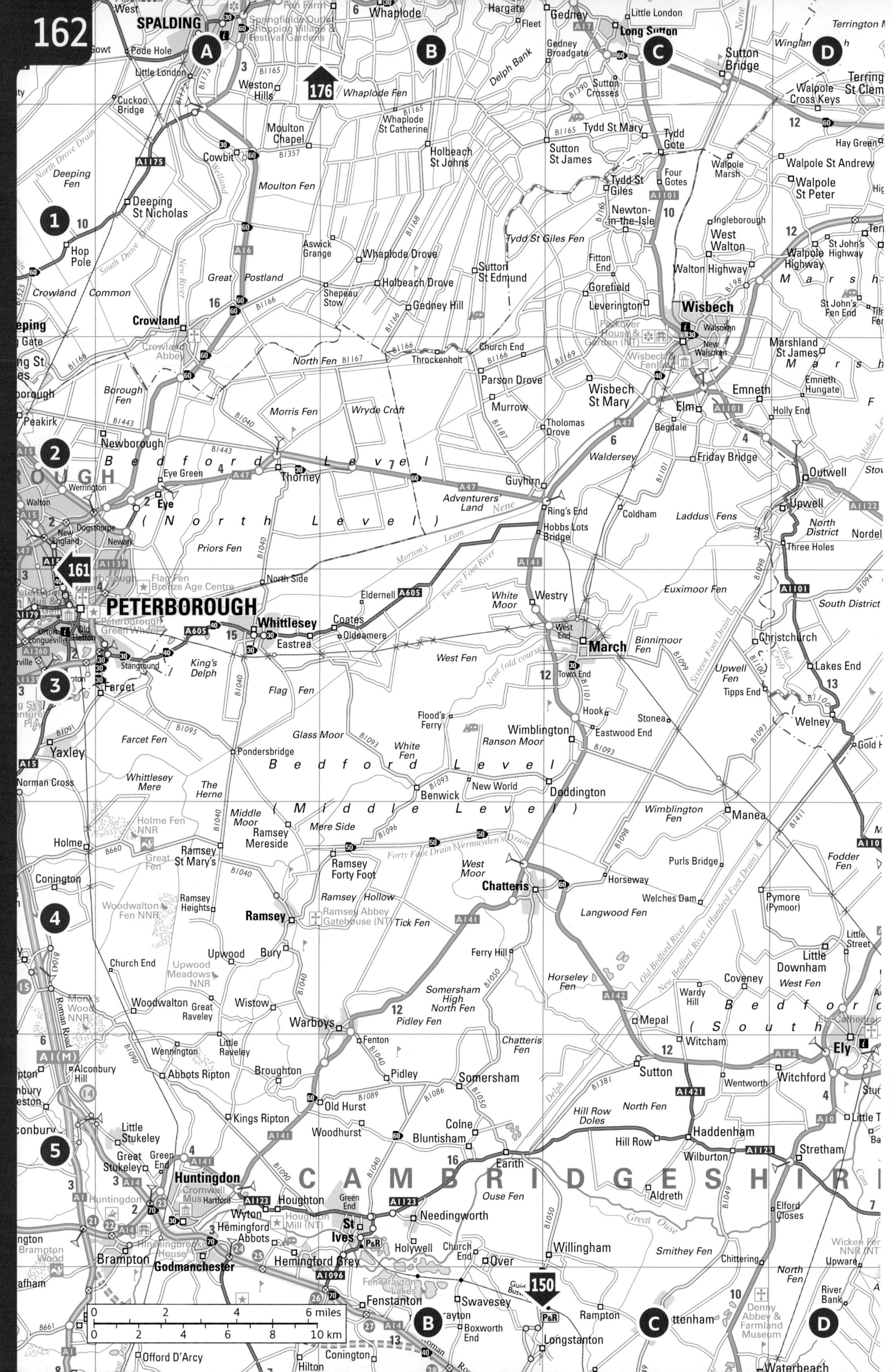

SPALDING
Whaplode
Gedney
Long Sutton
Sutton Bridge
Terrington
176
Holbeach St Johns
Moulton Chapel
Cowbit
Deeping St Nicholas
Hop Pole
Crowland
Whaplode Drove
Holbeach Drove
Gedney Hill
Sutton St Edmund
Tydd St Giles
Tydd St Mary
Sutton St James
Wisbech
Walpole St Andrew
Walpole St Peter
West Walton
Walton Highway
Leverington
Parson Drove
Murrow
Wisbech St Mary
Emneth
Elm
Outwell
Upwell
Thorney
Eye
Newborough
Guyhirn
Bedford Level
(North Level)
161
PETERBOROUGH
Whittlesey
Eastrea
Coates
March
Westry
Yaxley
Farcet
Wimblington
Doddington
Benwick
Bedford Level
(Middle Level)
Ramsey
Ramsey St Mary's
Chatteris
Manea
Welney
Warboys
Somersham
Sutton
Mepal
Witcham
Ely
Witchford
Haddenham
Stretham
Huntingdon
Godmanchester
Brampton
Houghton
St Ives
Hemingford Grey
Fenstanton
Swavesey
Over
Willingham
Longstanton
Rampton
Earith
Bluntisham
Colne
CAMBRIDGESHIRE
150
0 2 4 6 miles
0 2 4 6 8 10 km

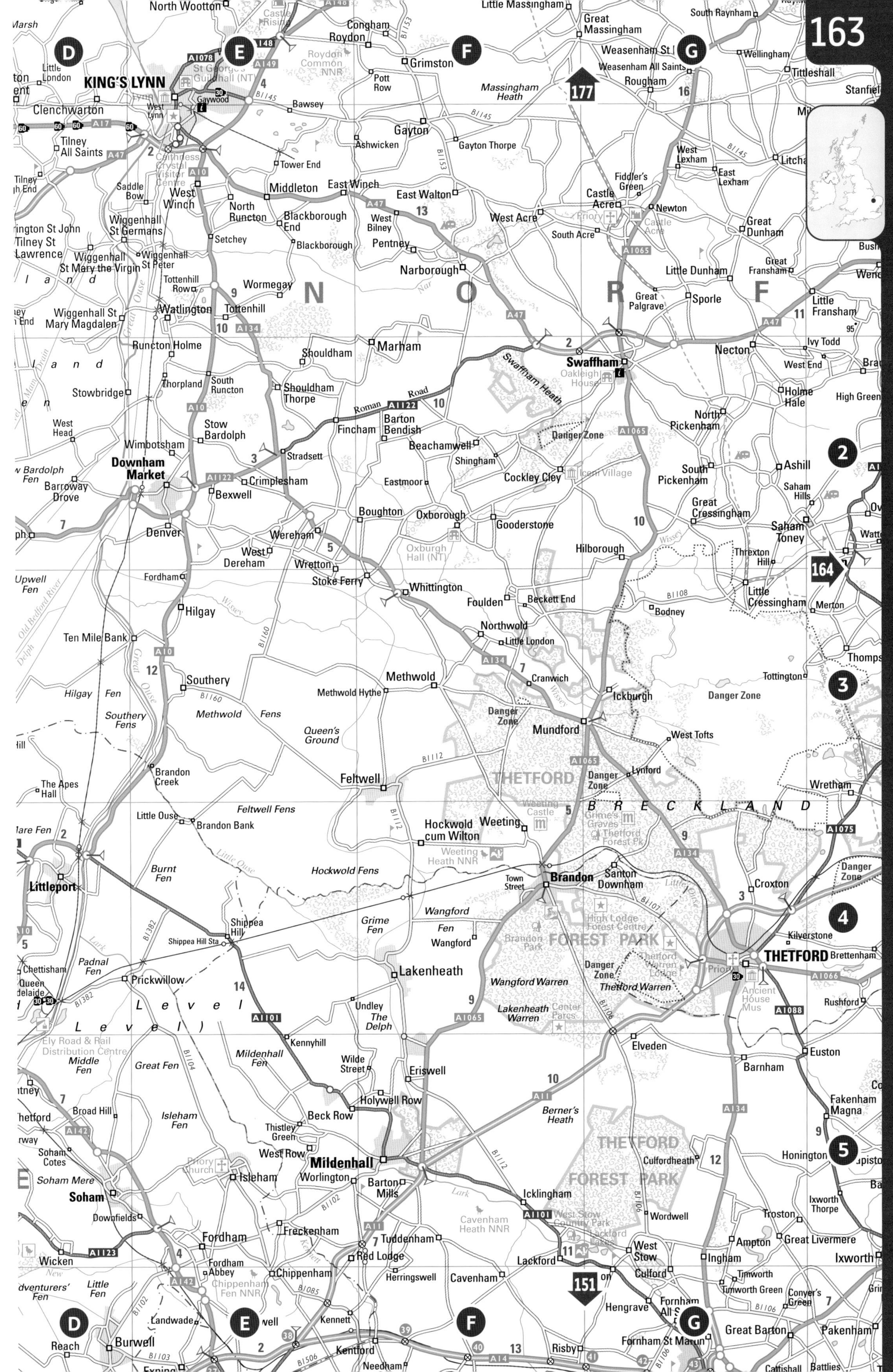
North Wootton
Castle Rising
Congham
Roydon
Little Massingham
Great Massingham
South Raynham
Weasenham St Peter
Weasenham All Saints
Wellingham
Tittleshall
Stanfield
D
E
F
G
Little London
KING'S LYNN
St George's Guildhall (NT)
Lynn
West Lynn
Gaywood
Roydon Common NNR
Grimston
Pott Row
Massingham Heath
177
Rougham
Clenchwarton
Bawsey
Gayton
Gayton Thorpe
Ashwicken
Tilney All Saints
Tilney High End
Caithness Crystal Visitor Centre
Tower End
West Lexham
East Lexham
Litcham
Saddle Bow
West Winch
Middleton
East Winch
East Walton
Fiddler's Green
Castle Acre
Newton
North Runcton
Blackborough End
West Bilney
West Acre
Priory
Castle Acre
Great Dunham
Wiggenhall St Germans
Tilney St Lawrence
Setchey
Blackborough
Pentney
South Acre
Wiggenhall St Mary the Virgin
Wiggenhall St Peter
Narborough
Little Dunham
Great Fransham
Tottenhill Row
Wormegay
N
O
R
F
Great Palgrave
Sporle
Little Fransham
Wiggenhall St Mary Magdalen
Watlington
Tottenhill
Runcton Holme
Shouldham
Marham
Swaffham Heath
Swaffham
Oakleigh House
Necton
Ivy Todd
West End
Stowbridge
Thorpland
South Runcton
Shouldham Thorpe
Roman Road
Holme Hale
High Green
West Head
Stow Bardolph
Fincham
Barton Bendish
Danger Zone
North Pickenham
Wimbotsham
Beachamwell
Stradsett
Shingham
Downham Market
Crimplesham
Eastmoor
Cockley Cley
Iceni Village
South Pickenham
Ashill
Saham Hills
Barroway Drove
Bexwell
West Bardolph Fen
Denver
Boughton
Oxborough
Gooderstone
Great Cressingham
Saham Toney
Wereham
Hilborough
Threxton Hill
West Dereham
Oxburgh Hall (NT)
Wretton
Stoke Ferry
Fordham
164
Upwell Fen
Whittington
Foulden
Beckett End
Little Cressingham
Merton
Hilgay
Bodney
Northwold
Little London
Ten Mile Bank
Thompson
Methwold
Cranwich
Tottington
Ickburgh
Danger Zone
Southery
Methwold Hythe
Hilgay Fen
Southery Fens
Methwold Fens
Queen's Ground
Danger Zone
Mundford
West Tofts
Brandon Creek
The Apes Hall
Feltwell
THETFORD
Lynford
Danger Zone
Wretham
Feltwell Fens
Little Ouse
Brandon Bank
Hockwold cum Wilton
Weeting
Weeting Castle
Grime's Graves
Thetford Forest Pk
BRECKLAND
Littleport
Burnt Fen
Hockwold Fens
Weeting Heath NNR
Town Street
Brandon
Santon Downham
Croxton
Danger Zone
Wangford
Grime Fen
Shippea Hill
Shippea Hill Sta
Fen
Wangford
High Lodge Forest Centre
Brandon Park
FOREST PARK
Kilverstone
Thetford Warren Lodge
THETFORD
Brettenham
Chettisham
Padnal Fen
Prickwillow
Lakenheath
Danger Zone
Thetford Warren
Wangford Warren
Priory
Ancient House Mus
Rushford
Queen Adelaide
Level
Undley
The Delph
Lakenheath Warren
Center Parcs
Ely Road & Rail Distribution Centre
Kennyhill
Elveden
Euston
Middle Fen
Great Fen
Mildenhall Fen
Wilde Street
Eriswell
Barnham
Littleport
Broad Hill
Isleham Fen
Holywell Row
Berner's Heath
Fakenham Magna
Beck Row
Thistley Green
Soham Cotes
West Row
THETFORD
Culfordheath
Honington
Soham Mere
Priory Church
Isleham
Mildenhall
Worlington
Barton Mills
FOREST PARK
Soham
Icklingham
Ixworth Thorpe
Downfields
Freckenham
Cavenham Heath NNR
Wordwell
Troston
West Stow Country Park
Lackford Lakes
Fordham
Tuddenham
Ampton
Great Livermere
Wicken
Fordham Abbey
Red Lodge
West Stow
Ingham
Ixworth
Chippenham
Chippenham Fen NNR
Herringswell
Cavenham
Lackford
Culford
Timworth
Timworth Green
Conyer's Green
Adventurers' Fen
Little Fen
151
Hengrave
Fornham All Saints
Landwade
Kennett
Great Barton
Pakenham
Reach
Burwell
Kentford
Risby
Fornham St Martin
Needham
Exning
Battlies
Catishall

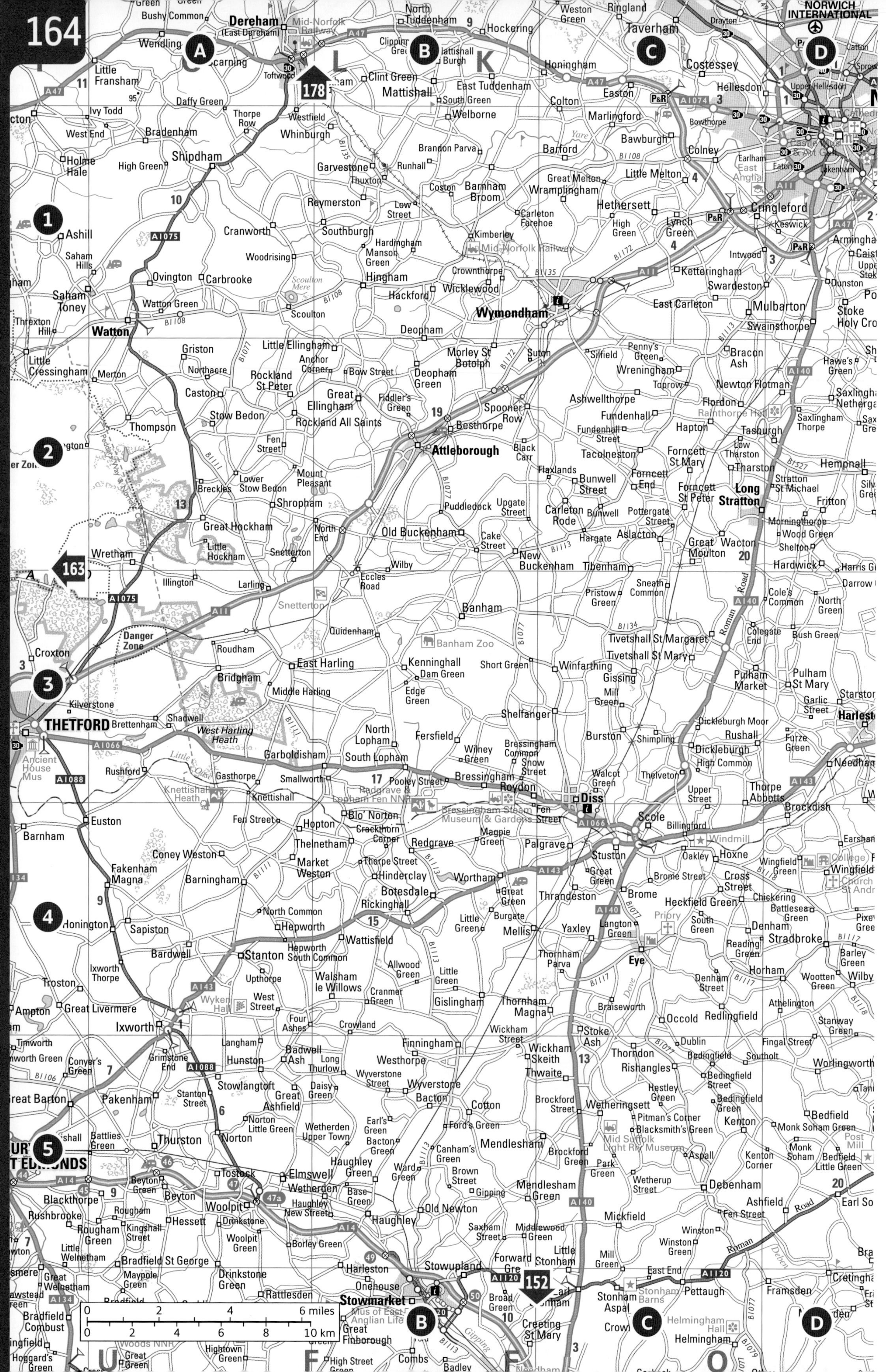

A
B
C
D
1
2
3
4
5
178
163
152
Dereham (East Dereham)
Mid-Norfolk Railway
North Tuddenham
Hockering
Weston Green
Ringland
Taverham
NORWICH INTERNATIONAL
Drayton
Catton
Bushy Common
Wendling
Scarning
Toftwood
Little Fransham
Clippings Green
Mattishall Burgh
Clint Green
Mattishall
East Tuddenham
Honingham
Costessey
Hellesdon
Upper Hellesdon
Daffy Green
Ivy Todd
Thorpe Row
Westfield
South Green
Welborne
Colton
Easton
Marlingford
Bawburgh
Bowthorpe
West End
Bradenham
Whinburgh
Brandon Parva
Barford
Yare
Colney
Earlham
East Anglia
Eaton
Lakenham
Holme Hale
High Green
Shipdham
Garvestone
Runhall
Thuxton
Coston
Barnham Broom
Great Melton
Wramplingham
Little Melton
Reymerston
Low Street
Carleton Forehoe
Hethersett
High Green
Lynch Green
Cringleford
Keswick
Ashill
Cranworth
Southburgh
Hardingham
Kimberley
Intwood
Arminghall
Saham Hills
Woodrising
Manson Green
Mid-Norfolk Railway
Ketteringham
Ovington
Carbrooke
Scoulton Mere
Hingham
Crownthorpe
Swardeston
Saham Toney
Watton Green
Scoulton
Hackford
Wicklewood
Wymondham
East Carleton
Mulbarton
Threxton Hill
Watton
Deopham
Swainsthorpe
Stoke Holy Cross
Griston
Little Ellingham
Morley St Botolph
Suton
Silfield
Penny's Green
Bracon Ash
Little Cressingham
Merton
Northacre
Rockland St Peter
Anchor Corner
Bow Street
Deopham Green
Wreningham
Toprow
Newton Flotman
Hawe's Green
Caston
Great Ellingham
Fiddler's Green
Spooner Row
Ashwellthorpe
Flordon
Saxlingham Nethergate
Thompson
Stow Bedon
Rockland All Saints
Besthorpe
Fundenhall
Rainthorpe Hall
Saxlingham Thorpe
Fen Street
Attleborough
Black Carr
Fundenhall Street
Hapton
Tasburgh
Low Tharston
Tacolneston
Forncett St Mary
Tharston
Hempnall
Lower Stow Bedon
Mount Pleasant
Flaxlands
Bunwell Street
Forncett End
Stratton St Michael
Breckles
Long Stratton
Shropham
Puddledock
Upgate Street
Carleton Rode
Bunwell
Pottergate Street
Forncett St Peter
Fritton
Great Hockham
North End
Old Buckenham
Cake Street
Hargate
Aslacton
Morningthorpe
Wood Green
Wacton
Great Moulton
Shelton
Little Hockham
Snetterton
New Buckenham
Tibenham
Hardwick
Wretham
Wilby
Eccles Road
Sneath Common
Pristow Green
Cole's Common
North Green
Illington
Larling
Snetterton
Banham
Roman Road
Danger Zone
Quidenham
Banham Zoo
Tivetshall St Margaret
Colegate End
Bush Green
Croxton
Roudham
Tivetshall St Mary
East Harling
Kenninghall
Dam Green
Short Green
Winfarthing
Gissing
Pulham Market
Pulham St Mary
Starston
Bridgham
Middle Harling
Edge Green
Mill Green
Garlic Street
Kilverstone
Shelfanger
Harleston
THETFORD
Brettenham
Shadwell
West Harling Heath
North Lopham
Fersfield
Burston
Dickleburgh Moor
Rushall
Ancient House Mus
Garboldisham
South Lopham
Wilney Green
Bressingham Common
Snow Street
Shimpling
Dickleburgh
High Common
Furze Green
Needham
Rushford
Gasthorpe
Smallworth
Pooley Street
Bressingham
Roydon
Walcot Green
Thelveton
Diss
Upper Street
Thorpe Abbotts
Brockdish
Knettishall Heath
Knettishall
Redgrave & Lopham Fen NNR
Bressingham Steam Museum & Gardens
Fen Street
Euston
Fen Street
Hopton
Blo' Norton
Crackthorn Corner
Scole
Billingford
Windmill
Barnham
Thelnetham
Redgrave
Maggie Green
Palgrave
Stuston
Oakley
Hoxne
Earsham
Coney Weston
Market Weston
Thorpe Street
Hinderclay
Wortham
Great Green
Brome Street
Wingfield Green
College
Wingfield
Fakenham Magna
Barningham
Botesdale
Great Green
Thrandeston
Brome
Cross Street
Church
Rickinghall
Heckfield Green
Chickering
North Common
Little Green
Burgate
Priory
Battlesea Green
Honington
Hepworth
Mellis
Yaxley
Langton Green
South Green
Denham
Sapiston
Wattisfield
Stradbroke
Bardwell
Stanton
Hepworth South Common
Thornham Parva
Eye
Reading Green
Barley Green
Ixworth Thorpe
Allwood Green
Little Green
Horham
Troston
Upthorpe
Walsham le Willows
Denham Street
Wootten Green
Wilby
Great Livermere
Ampton
Wyken Hall
West Street
Cranmer Green
Gislingham
Thornham Magna
Braiseworth
Athelington
Occold
Redlingfield
Stanway Green
Ixworth
Four Ashes
Crowland
Wickham Street
Stoke Ash
Dublin
Fingal Street
Ixworth
Langham
Finningham
Wickham Skeith
Bedingfield
Southolt
Grimstone End
Hunston
Badwell Ash
Long Thurlow
Westhorpe
Thorndon
Rishangles
Bedingfield Street
Worlingworth
Conyer's Green
Wyverstone Street
Thwaite
Stowlangtoft
Daisy Green
Wyverstone
Hestley Green
Great Barton
Pakenham
Stanton Street
Great Ashfield
Bacton
Cotton
Brockford Street
Wetheringsett
Bedingfield Green
Norton Little Green
Earl's Green
Pitman's Corner
Bedfield
Battlies Green
Wetherden Upper Town
Ford's Green
Blacksmith's Green
Kenton
Monk Soham Green
Thurston
Norton
Bacton Green
Canham's Green
Mendlesham
Mid Suffolk Light Rly Museum
Monk Soham
Post Mill
Bury St Edmunds
Tostock
Haughley Green
Brockford Green
Aspall
Kenton Corner
Bedfield Little Green
Beyton Green
Elmswell
Ward Green
Brown Street
Park Green
Blackthorpe
Beyton
Wetherden
Base Green
Gipping
Wetherup Street
Debenham
Rushbrooke
Rougham
Woolpit
Haughley New Street
Mendlesham Green
Ashfield
Earl Soham
Rougham Green
Kingshall Street
Hessett
Drinkstone
Haughley
Old Newton
Mickfield
Fen Street
Little Welnetham
Woolpit Green
Borley Green
Saxham Street
Middlewood Green
Winston
Winston Green
Roman Road
Bradfield St George
Harleston
Stowupland
Forward Green
Little Stonham
Mill Green
East End
Great Welnetham
Maypole Green
Drinkstone Green
Onehouse
Broad Green
Earl Stonham
Stonham Barns
Pettaugh
Framsden
Cretingham
Bradfield Combust
Rattlesden
Stowmarket
Mus of East Anglian Life
Stonham Aspal
Crowfield
Helmingham Hall
Great Finborough
Creeting St Mary
Helmingham
Hoggard's Green
Woods NNR
Hightown Green
High Street Green
Combs
Badley
Gipping
0 2 4 6 miles
0 2 4 6 8 10 km

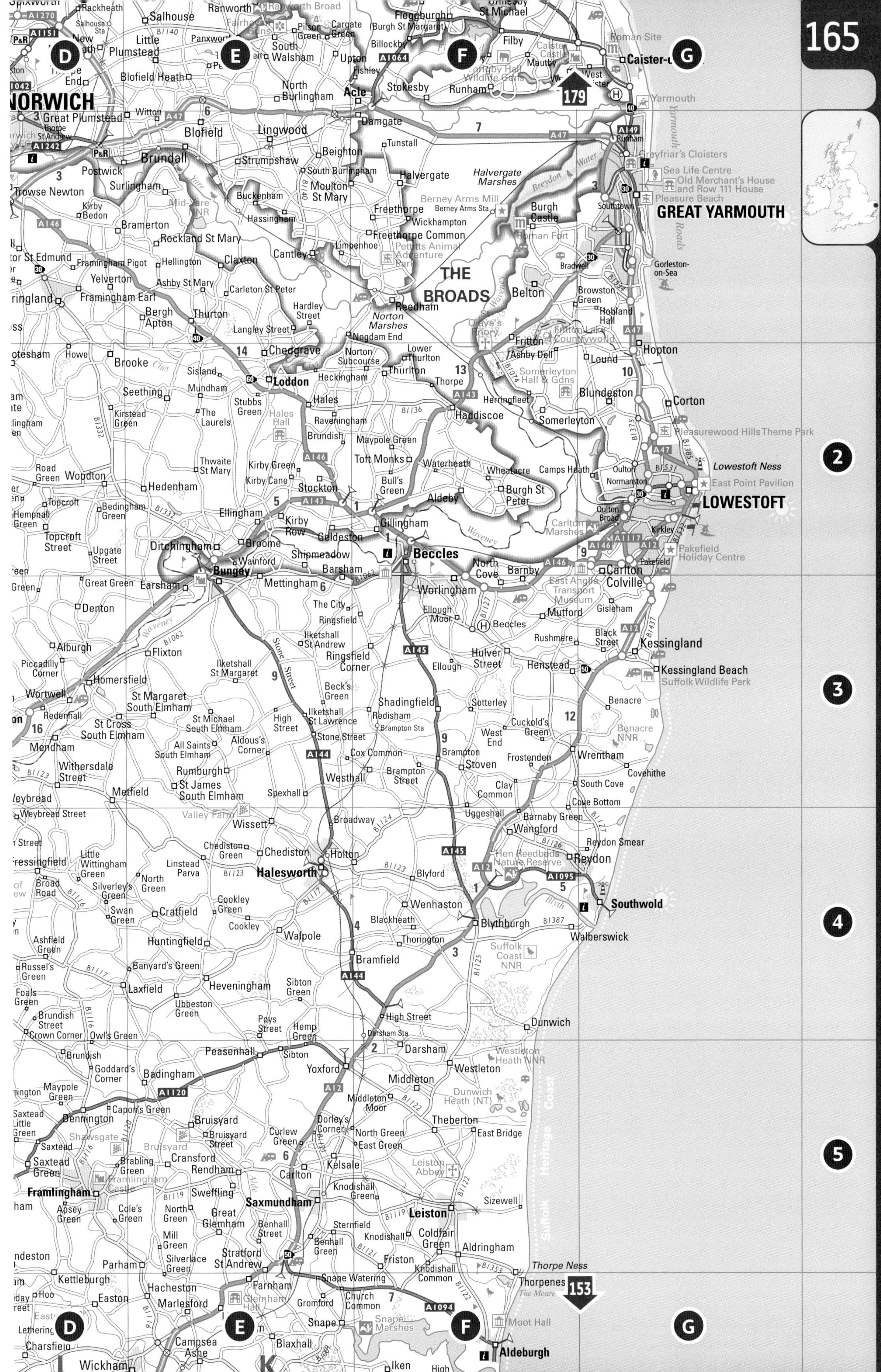
NORWICH
GREAT YARMOUTH
LOWESTOFT
THE BROADS
Caister-on-Sea
Roman Site
Yarmouth
Greyfriar's Cloisters
Sea Life Centre
Old Merchant's House and Row 111 House
Pleasure Beach
Gorleston-on-Sea
Burgh Castle
Roman Fort
Breydon Water
Halvergate Marshes
Berney Arms Mill
Berney Arms Sta
Pettitts Animal Adventure Park
Rackheath
Salhouse
Ranworth
Ranworth Broad
Fleggburgh
Burgh St Margaret
Ormesby St Michael
Filby
Caister Castle
Mautby
Thrigby Hall Wildlife Gdns
West Caister
Little Plumstead
Blofield Heath
Pilson Green
Cargate Green
South Walsham
Upton
Billockby
Fishley
Acle
Stokesby
Runham
North Burlingham
Great Plumstead
Thorpe St Andrew
Witton
Blofield
Lingwood
Damgate
Tunstall
Brundall
Strumpshaw
Beighton
South Burlingham
Halvergate
Postwick
Surlingham
Moulton St Mary
Trowse Newton
Kirby Bedon
Mid-Yare NNR
Buckenham
Hassingham
Freethorpe
Wickhampton
Freethorpe Common
Bramerton
Rockland St Mary
Limpenhoe
Cantley
Claxton
Hellington
Framingham Pigot
Yelverton
Ashby St Mary
Carleton St Peter
Framingham Earl
Bergh Apton
Thurton
Hardley Street
Reedham
Norton Marshes
Nogdam End
Langley Street
Chedgrave
Norton Subcourse
Lower Thurlton
Thurlton
Howe
Brooke
Sisland
Loddon
Heckingham
Thorpe
Seething
Mundham
Stubbs Green
Hales
Hales Hall
Kirstead Green
The Laurels
Raveningham
Haddiscoe
Herringfleet
Brundish
Maypole Green
Toft Monks
Thwaite St Mary
Kirby Green
Kirby Cane
Stockton
Bull's Green
Waterheath
Aldeby
Wheatacre
Burgh St Peter
Road Green
Woodton
Hedenham
Topcroft
Bedingham Green
Hempnall Green
Topcroft Street
Upgate Street
Ellingham
Kirby Row
Gillingham
Geldeston
Ditchingham
Broome
Wainford
Shipmeadow
Beccles
Bungay
Barsham
Earsham
Great Green
Mettingham
North Cove
Barnby
Worlingham
Denton
The City
Ringsfield
Ellough Moor
Beccles
Mutford
East Anglia Transport Museum
Alburgh
Flixton
Ilketshall St Andrew
Ilketshall St Margaret
Ringsfield Corner
Ellough
Hulver Street
Henstead
Rushmere
Gisleham
Black Street
Kessingland
Kessingland Beach
Suffolk Wildlife Park
Piccadilly Corner
Homersfield
Wortwell
Redenhall
St Margaret South Elmham
St Michael South Elmham
St Cross South Elmham
Beck's Green
Shadingfield
Redisham
Brampton Sta
Sotterley
Cuckold's Green
Benacre
Benacre NNR
Mendham
All Saints South Elmham
Aldous's Corner
High Street
Ilketshall St Lawrence
Stone Street
West End
Brampton
Frostenden
Wrentham
Covehithe
Withersdale Street
Rumburgh
St James South Elmham
Cox Common
Brampton Street
Stoven
Clay Common
South Cove
Cove Bottom
Metfield
Weybread
Weybread Street
Valley Farm
Spexhall
Westhall
Wissett
Broadway
Uggeshall
Barnaby Green
Wangford
Reydon Smear
Reydon
Hen Reedbeds Nature Reserve
Fressingfield
Little Wittingham Green
Linstead Parva
Chediston Green
Chediston
Holton
Halesworth
Blyford
Southwold
Broad Road
Silverley's Green
North Green
Cookley Green
Cookley
Wenhaston
Swan Green
Cratfield
Blackheath
Blythburgh
Walberswick
Ashfield Green
Huntingfield
Walpole
Thorington
Suffolk Coast NNR
Russel's Green
Banyard's Green
Laxfield
Bramfield
Heveningham
Sibton Green
Ubbeston Green
Foals Green
Brundish Street
Crown Corner
Owl's Green
Poys Street
Hemp Green
High Street
Darsham Sta
Darsham
Dunwich
Westleton Heath NNR
Westleton
Brundish
Goddard's Corner
Peasenhall
Sibton
Yoxford
Badingham
Middleton
Maypole Green
Middleton Moor
Dunwich Heath (NT)
Saxtead Little Green
Dennington
Capon's Green
Bruisyard
Dorley's Corner
North Green
East Green
Theberton
East Bridge
Saxtead
Shawsgate
Bruisyard Street
Curlew Green
Saxtead Green
Brabling Green
Cransford
Kelsale
Leiston Abbey
Framlingham Castle
Rendham
Carlton
Framlingham
Sweffling
Knodishall Green
Sizewell
Apsey Green
Cole's Green
North Green
Saxmundham
Great Glemham
Leiston
Benhall Street
Sternfield
Mill Green
Knodishall
Coldfair Green
Aldringham
Benhall Green
Silverlace Green
Stratford St Andrew
Parham
Friston
Knodishall Common
Thorpe Ness
Kettleburgh
Snape Watering
Thorpeness
The Meare
Hoo
Easton
Hacheston
Farnham
Church Common
Glemham Hall
Marlesford
Gromford
Snape
Snape Marshes
Moot Hall
Letheringham
Charsfield
Campsea Ashe
Blaxhall
Aldeburgh
Wickham
Iken
Ashby Dell
Fritton
Fritton Lake Countryworld
Olave's Priory
Somerleyton Hall & Gdns
Somerleyton
Lound
Blundeston
Bradwell
Belton
Browston Green
Hobland Hall
Hopton
Corton
Pleasurewood Hills Theme Park
Lowestoft Ness
East Point Pavilion
Oulton
Normanston
Oulton Broad
Carlton Marshes
Kirkley
Pakefield
Pakefield Holiday Centre
Carlton Colville
Camps Heath
Suffolk Heritage Coast
Yare
Chet
Waveney
Blyth
Alde
179
153
D
E
F
G
2
3
4
5

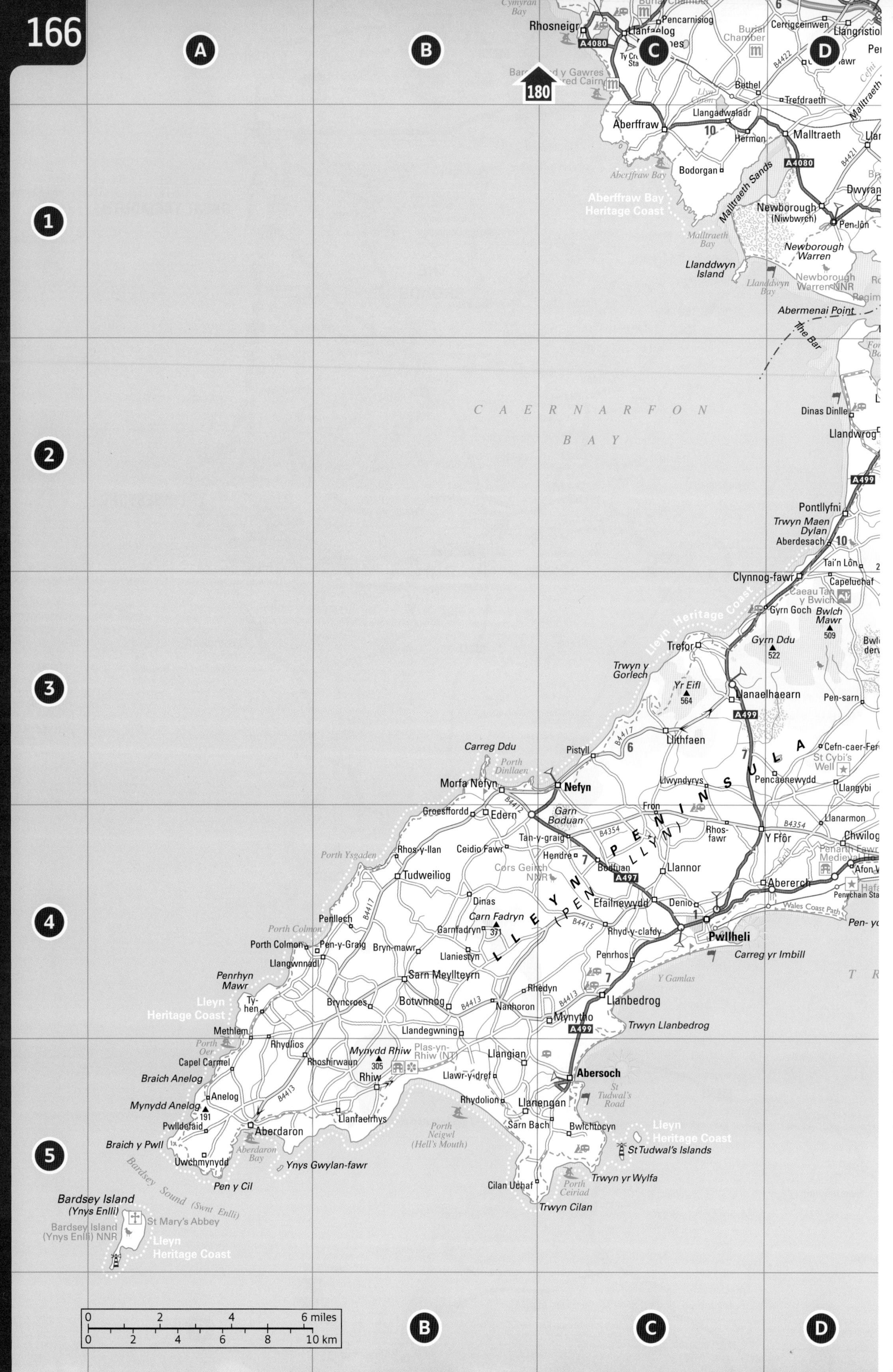

A · B · C · D

1

2

3

4

5

CAERNARFON BAY

Cymyran Bay
Rhosneigr
Llanfaelog
Pencarnisiog
Cerrigceinwen
Llangristiolus
A4080
Ty Croes Sta
180
Burial Chamber
Aberffraw
Bethel
Trefdraeth
Llangadwaladr
10
Hermon
Malltraeth
Bodorgan
A4080
Aberffraw Bay
Aberffraw Bay Heritage Coast
Malltraeth Sands
Newborough (Niwbwrch)
Pen-lôn
Dwyran
Malltraeth Bay
Newborough Warren
Llanddwyn Island
Llanddwyn Bay
Newborough Warren NNR
Abermenai Point
The Bar
Dinas Dinlle
Llandwrog
A499
Pontllyfni
Trwyn Maen Dylan
Aberdesach
10
Tai'n Lôn
Clynnog-fawr
Capeluchaf
Caeau Tan y Bwlch
Gyrn Goch
Bwlch Mawr
509
Lleyn Heritage Coast
Trefor
Gyrn Ddu
522
Trwyn y Gorlech
Yr Eifl
564
Llanaelhaearn
Pen-sarn
Cefn-caer-Fer
A499
Carreg Ddu
Pistyll
6
Llithfaen
Llwyndyrys
Pencaenewydd
Llangybi
St Cybi's Well
Porth Dinllaen
7
Nefyn
Garn Boduan
Fron
Rhos-fawr
Y Ffôr
Llanarmon
Chwilog
B4354
Morfa Nefyn
B4412
Tan-y-graig
Hendre
7
Bodfuan
Llannor
Penarth Fawr Medieval H
Groesffordd
Edern
B4354
Afon V
Rhos-y-llan
Ceidio Fawr
Cors Geirch NNR
A497
Abererch
Tudweiliog
Dinas
Efailnewydd
Denio
Penychain
Wales Coast Path
Carn Fadryn
371
Rhyd-y-clafdy
1
Pen-
Penllech
B4417
Garnfadryn
B4415
Pwllheli
Porth Colmon
Pen-y-Graig
Bryn-mawr
Llaniestyn
Carreg yr Imbill
Porth Colmon
Llangwnnadl
Sarn Meyllteyrn
Penrhos
7
Y Gamlas
Penrhyn Mawr
Bryncroes
Botwnnog
B4413
Rhedyn
B4413
Llanbedrog
Lleyn Heritage Coast
Ty-hen
Llandegwning
Nanhoron
Mynytho
Trwyn Llanbedrog
Methlem
Rhydlios
Mynydd Rhiw
305
Plas-yn-Rhiw (NT)
Llangian
A499
Porth Oer
Capel Carmel
Rhoshirwaun
Rhiw
Llawr-y-dref
Abersoch
Braich Anelog
B4413
Rhydolion
Llanengan
St Tudwal's Road
Mynydd Anelog
Anelog
Llanfaelrhys
Sarn Bach
Bwlchtocyn
191
Lleyn Heritage Coast
Pwlldefaid
Aberdaron
Porth Neigwl (Hell's Mouth)
St Tudwal's Islands
Braich y Pwll
Aberdaron Bay
Ynys Gwylan-fawr
Cilan Uchaf
Porth Ceiriad
Trwyn yr Wylfa
Uwchmynydd
Pen y Cil
Trwyn Cilan
Bardsey Island (Ynys Enlli)
St Mary's Abbey
Bardsey Island (Ynys Enlli) NNR
Lleyn Heritage Coast

LLEYN (PEN LLYN) PENINSULA

0   2   4   6 miles
0 2 4 6 8 10 km

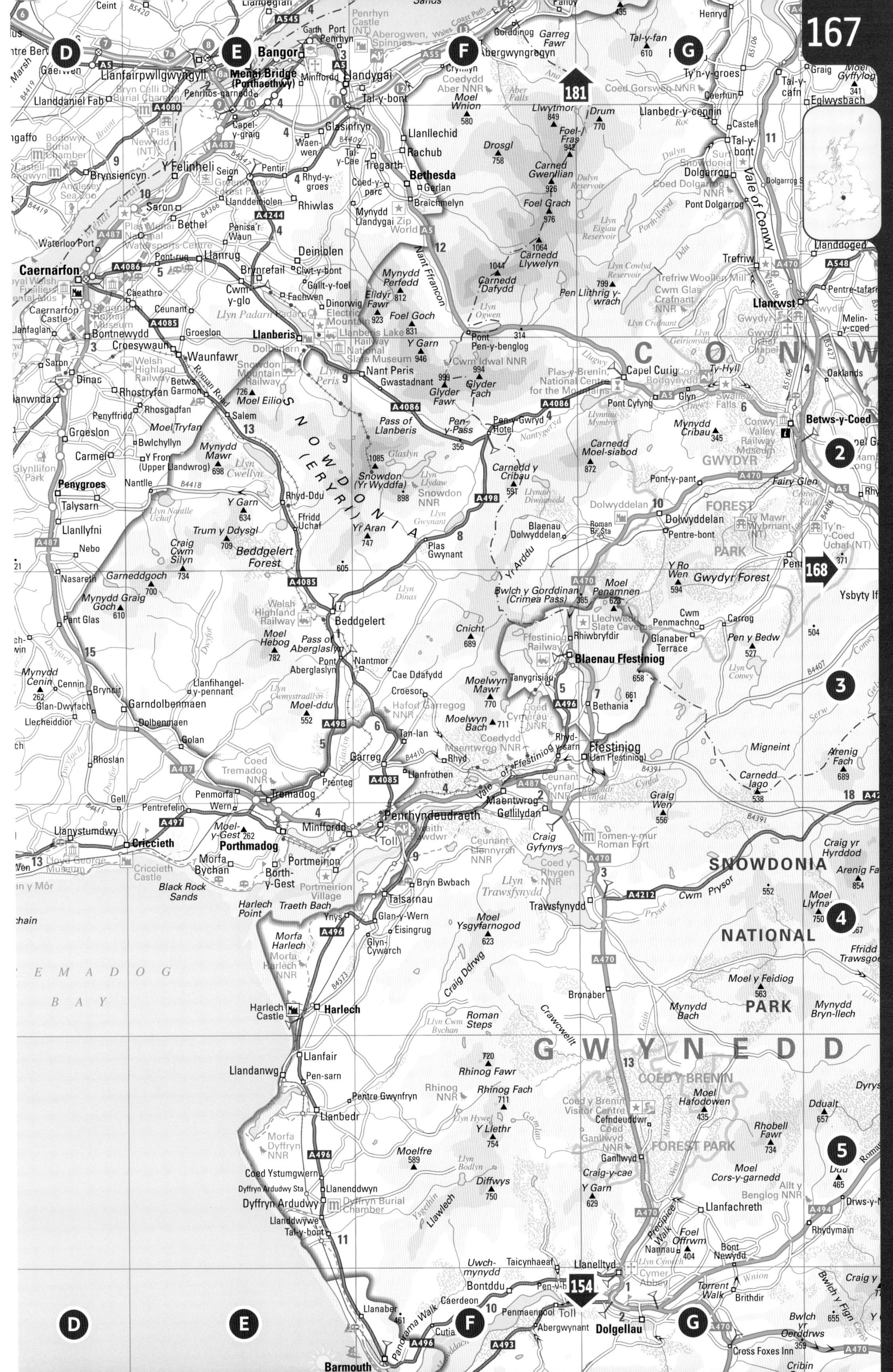

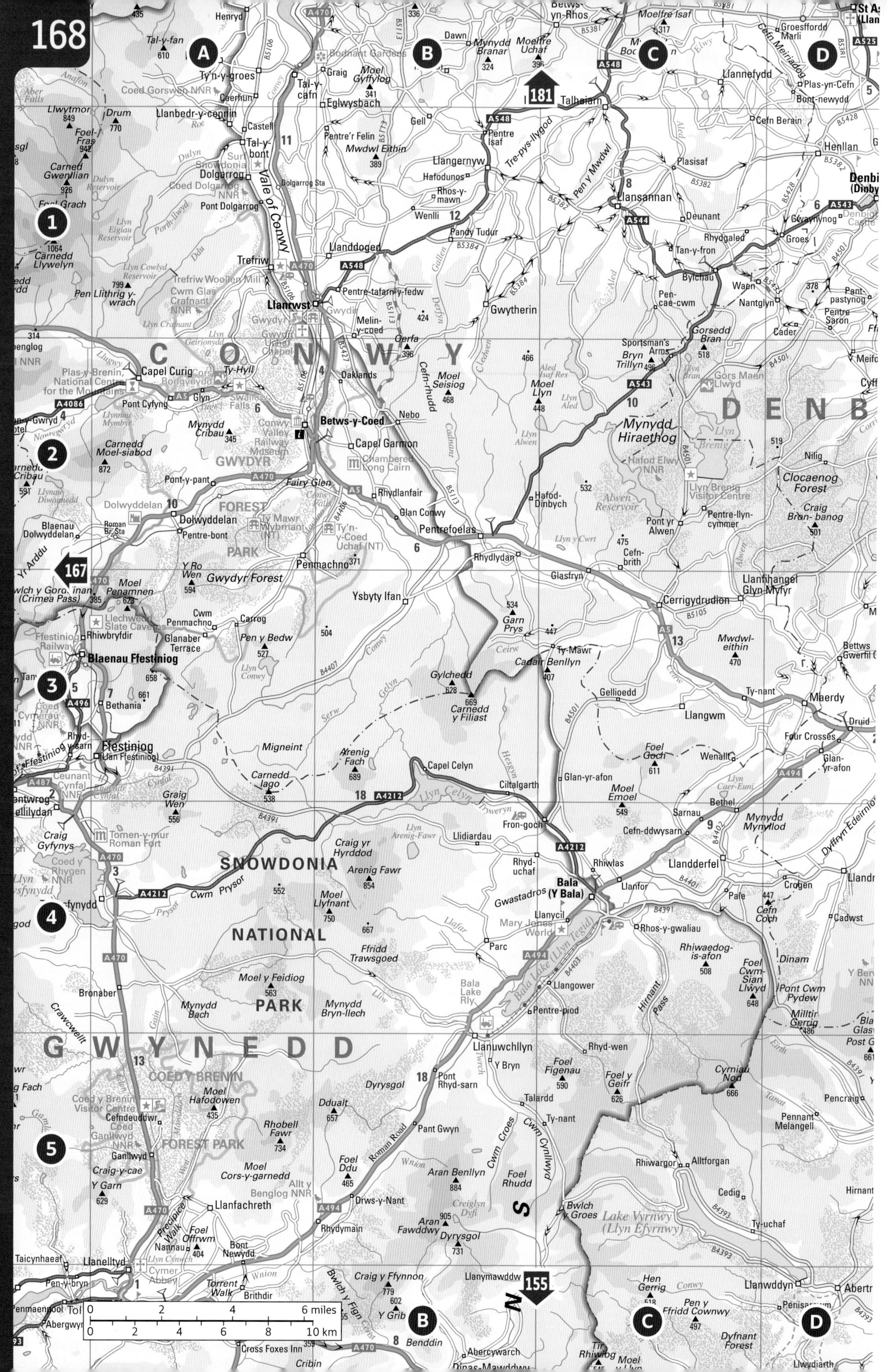
A
B
C
D
Henryd
Tal-y-fan
610
Dawn
Mynydd Branar
324
Moelfre Uchaf
396
Moelfre Isaf
317
Groesffordd Marli
St Asaph (Llanelwy)
A525
181
Bodnant Gardens
Ty'n-y-groes
Coed Gorswen NNR
Caerhun
Tal-y-cafn
Graig
Moel Gyffylog
341
Eglwysbach
Llannefydd
Cefn Meiriadog
Plas-yn-Cefn
Bont-newydd
Talhaiarn
A548
Llwytmor
849
Drum
770
Foel-Fras
942
Carnedd Gwenllian
926
Llanbedr-y-cennin
Castell
Tal-y-bont
Snowdonia
Vale of Conwy
Gell
Pentre Isaf
Tre-pys-llygod
Cefn Berain
Henllan
Pentre'r Felin
Mwdwl Eithin
389
Llangernyw
Hafodunos
Rhos-y-mawn
Wenlli
Pen y Mwdwl
Plasisaf
Denbigh (Dinbych)
Dolgarrog
Coed Dolgarrog NNR
Pont Dolgarrog
Dolgarrog Sta
Llansannan
Deunant
Foel Grach
Carnedd Llywelyn
1064
Llyn Eigiau Reservoir
Dulyn Reservoir
Porth-llwyd
Pandy Tudur
B5384
Rhydgaled
Gwaynynog
Groes
Tan-y-fron
Llanddoged
A548
Trefriw
Trefriw Woollen Mill
Llyn Cowlyd Reservoir
799
Pen Llithrig y-wrach
Cwm Glas Crafnant NNR
Llyn Crafnant
Llanrwst
Gwydyr
Gwydir Uchaf Chapel
Pentre-tafarn-y-fedw
Melin-y-coed
424
Gwytherin
Bylchau
Waen
Nantglyn
378
Pant-pastynog
Pentre Saron
Cader
Pen-cae-cwm
CONWY
DENB
Capel Curig
Plas-y-Brenin, National Centre for the Mountains
Ty-Hyll
Swallow Falls
Oakslands
Oerfa
396
Cefn-rhudd
Moel Seisiog
468
466
Aled Isaf Res
Moel Llyn
448
Llyn Aled
Gorsedd Bran
518
Sportsman's Arms
Bryn Trillyn
496
Gors Maen Llwyd
A543
A4086
Pont Cyfyng
Glyn
Betws-y-Coed
Nebo
Conwy Valley Railway Museum
Mynydd Cribau
345
Carnedd Moel-siabod
872
Capel Garmon
Chambered Long Cairn
GWYDYR
Mynydd Hiraethog
Llyn Brenig
Llyn Alwen
Hafod Elwy NNR
Llyn Brenig Visitor Centre
Nilig
519
Clocaenog Forest
Pont-y-pant
A470
Fairy Glen
Conwy Falls
Rhydlanfair
Glan Conwy
Pentrefoelas
Hafod-Dinbych
532
Alwen Reservoir
Pentre-llyn-cymmer
Craig Bron-banog
501
Pont yr Alwen
Dolwyddelan
FOREST
PARK
Dolwyddelan
Pentre-bont
Blaenau Dolwyddelan
Roman Br. Sta
Ty Mawr Wybrnant (NT)
Ty'n-y-Coed Uchaf (NT)
Penmachno
371
Rhydlydan
Llyn y Cwrt
475
Cefn-brith
Glasfryn
167
Moel Penamnen
623
Y Ro Wen
594
Gwydyr Forest
Ysbyty Ifan
Llanfihangel Glyn Myfyr
Cerrigydrudion
B5105
Bwlch y Gorddinan (Crimea Pass)
385
Llechwedd Slate Caverns
Cwm Penmachno
Carrog
504
534
Garn Prys
447
Ffestiniog Railway
Rhiwbryfdir
Blaenau Ffestiniog
Glanaber Terrace
Pen y Bedw
527
Llyn Conwy
Ty-Mawr
Cadair Benllyn
407
Mwdwl-eithin
470
Bettws Gwerfil Goch
658
661
Bethania
Gylchedd
628
669
Carnedd y Filiast
Gellioedd
Ty-nant
Maerdy
Llangwm
Druid
Coed Cymerau NNR
Rhyd-y-sarn
Ffestiniog (Llan Ffestiniog)
Migneint
Arenig Fach
689
Capel Celyn
Foel Goch
611
Wenallt
Four Crosses
Glan-yr-afon
Ceunant Cynfal NNR
Carnedd Iago
538
Ciltalgarth
Glan-yr-afon
Moel Emoel
549
Llyn Caer-Euni
Graig Wen
556
A4212
Llyn Celyn
Tryweryn
Fron-goch
Sarnau
Bethel
Mynydd Mynyllod
Dyffryn Edeirnion
Craig Gyfynys
Tomen-y-mur Roman Fort
Coed y Rhygen NNR
Llyn Trawsfynydd
Trawsfynydd
Craig yr Hyrddod
Llyn Arenig-Fawr
Llidiardau
Rhyd-uchaf
Cefn-ddwysarn
SNOWDONIA
Arenig Fawr
854
Rhiwlas
Llandderfel
Cwm Prysor
552
Moel Llyfnant
750
667
Gwastadros
Bala (Y Bala)
Llanfor
Crogen
Cefn Coch
447
Cadwst
Pale
NATIONAL
Llanycil
Mary Jones World
Rhos-y-gwaliau
Ffridd Trawsgoed
Parc
Rhiwaedog-is-afon
508
Foel Cwm-Sian Llwyd
648
Dinam
Bala Lake (Llyn Tegid)
Llangower
Bronaber
Moel y Feidiog
563
Bala Lake Rly
Hirnant Pass
Pont Cwm Pydew
Mynydd Bach
PARK
Mynydd Bryn-llech
Pentre-piod
Milltir Gerrig
486
Crawcwellt
GWYNEDD
Llanuwchllyn
Rhyd-wen
COED Y BRENIN
Moel Hafodowen
435
Dyrysgol
Pont Rhyd-sarn
Y Bryn
Foel Figenau
590
Foel y Geifr
626
Cyrniau Nod
666
Pencraig
Pennant Melangell
Coed y Brenin Visitor Centre
Cefndeuddwr
Coed Ganllwyd NNR
FOREST PARK
Dduallt
657
Rhobell Fawr
734
Pant Gwyn
Roman Road
Talardd
Ty-nant
Cwm Cynllwyd
Cwm Croes
Ganllwyd
Craig-y-cae
Y Garn
629
Moel Cors-y-garnedd
Allt y Benglog NNR
Foel Ddu
465
Aran Benllyn
884
Foel Rhudd
Rhiwargor
Alltforgan
Cedig
Hirnant
Llanfachreth
Drws-y-Nant
905
Aran Fawddwy
Creiglyn Dyfi
Dyrysgol
731
Bwlch y Groes
Lake Vyrnwy (Llyn Efyrnwy)
Tŷ-uchaf
Precipice Walk
Foel Offrwm
404
Nannau
Bont Newydd
Rhydymain
Taicynhaeaf
Llanelltyd
Cymer Abbey
Llyn Cynwch
Torrent Walk
Brithdir
Wnion
Bwlch y Fign
Craig y Ffynnon
779
602
Y Grib
Llanymawddwy
155
Hen Gerrig
518
Pen y Ffridd Cownwy
497
Dyfnant Forest
Llanwddyn
Abertridwr
Penisarcwm
Pen-y-bryn
Penmaenpool
Abergwynant
Cross Foxes Inn
359
Cribin
Benddin
Abercywarch
Dinas-Mawddwy
Moel y Llyn
Llwydiarth
0 2 4 6 miles
0 2 4 6 8 10 km

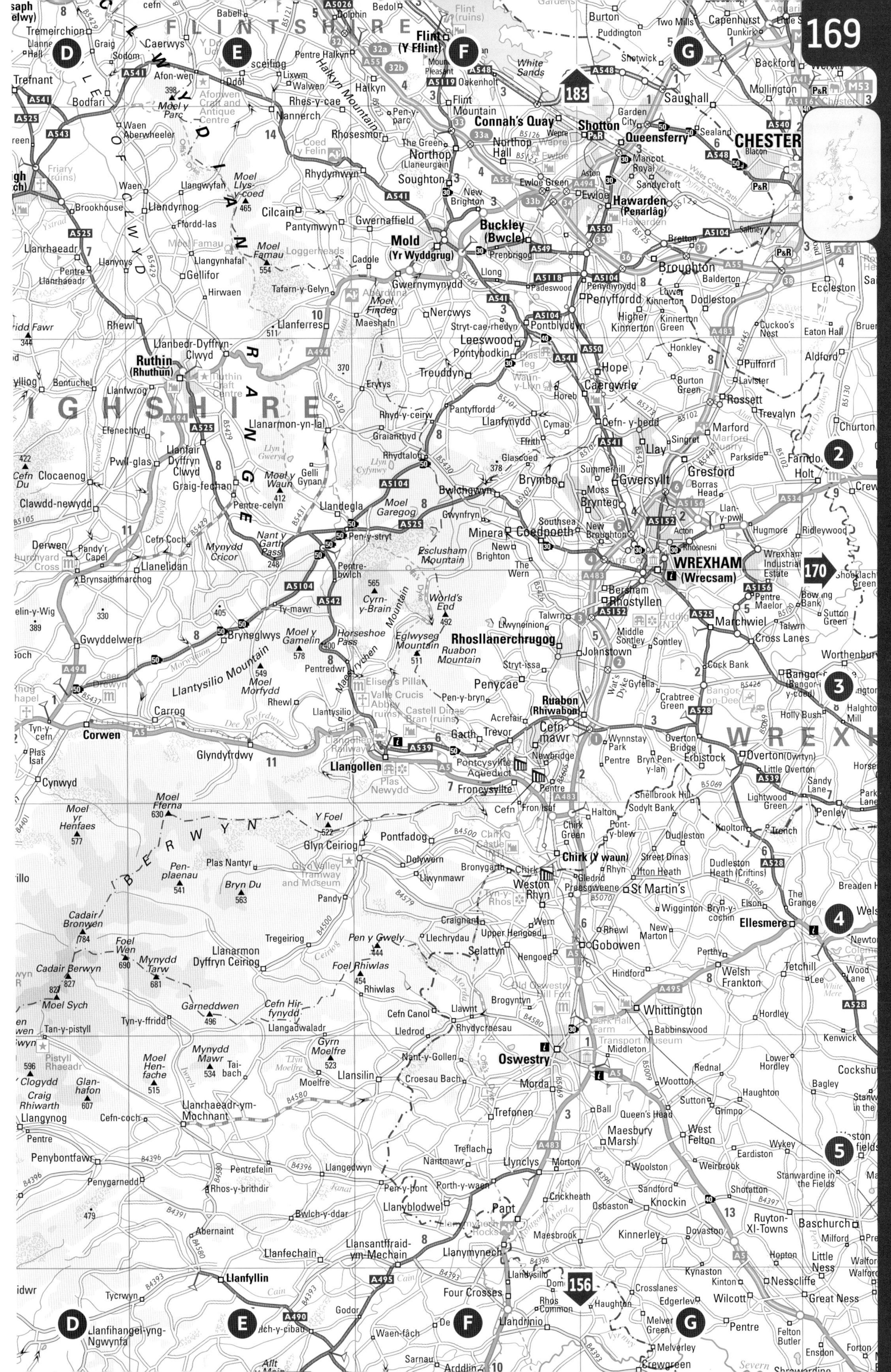
FLINTSHIRE
DENBIGHSHIRE
CLWYDIAN RANGE
VALE OF CLWYD
BERWYN
WREXHAM
D
E
F
G
2
3
4
5
183
170
156
Tremeirchion
Caerwys
Babell
Flint (ruins)
Flint (Y Fflint)
Bedol
Burton
Two Mills
Capenhurst
Puddington
Dunkirk
Backford
Shotwick
Mollington
Saughall
Chester
CHESTER
Blacon
Sealand
Queensferry
Shotton
Garden City
Connah's Quay
White Sands
Oakenholt
Flint Mountain
Mount Pleasant
Pentre Halkyn
Halkyn
Halkyn Mountain
Lixwm
Walwen
Rhes-y-cae
Ysceifiog
Afon-wen
Dôl
Afonwen Craft and Antique Centre
Moel y Parc
Trefnant
Bodfari
Waen
Aberwheeler
Friary (ruins)
Nannerch
Rhosesmor
Coed y Felin
Pen-y-parc
The Green
Northop
Northop (Llaneurgain)
Northop Hall
Soughton
Mancot
Aston
Sandycroft
Wales Coast Path
Ewloe
Ewloe Green
Hawarden (Penarlâg)
New Brighton
Buckley (Bwcle)
Prenbrigog
Mold (Yr Wyddgrug)
Rhydymwyn
Cilcain
Pantymwyn
Gwernaffield
Moel Llys-y-coed
Llangwyfan
Llandyrnog
Brookhouse
Ffordd-las
Moel Famau
Loggerheads
Cadole
Llangynhafal
Llanrhaeadr
Pentre
Llanynys
Gellifor
Hirwaen
Tafarn-y-Gelyn
Gwernymynydd
Llong
Padeswood
Penymynydd
Penyffordd
Higher Kinnerton
Kinnerton Green
Lower Kinnerton
Broughton
Bretton
Saltney
Balderton
Dodleston
Eccleston
Eaton Hall
Cuckoo's Nest
Pulford
Aldford
Lavister
Rossett
Trevalyn
Burton Green
Honkley
Churton
Farndon
Holt
Marford
Marford Quarry
Gresford
Borras Head
Parkside
Llan-y-pwll
Hugmore
Ridleywood
Wrexham Industrial Estate
Llay
Singret
Gwersyllt
Summerhill
Moss
Brynteg
Southsea
New Broughton
Acton
Rhosnesni
WREXHAM (Wrecsam)
Bersham
Rhostyllen
Erddig (NT)
Marchwiel
Cross Lanes
Sutton Green
Bowling Bank
Pentre Maelor
Talwrn
Middle Sontley
Sontley
Johnstown
Rhosllanerchrugog
Ruabon Mountain
Stryt-issa
Penycae
Ruabon (Rhiwabon)
Wat's Dyke
Gyfelia
Crabtree Green
Bangor-on-Dee
Bangor-is-y-coed
Holly Bush
Worthenbury
Overton Bridge
Erbistock
Overton (Owrtyn)
Little Overton
Wynnstay Park
Pentre
Bryn Pen-y-lan
Cefn-mawr
Newbridge
Acrefair
Trevor
Garth
Pontcysyllte Aqueduct
Froncysyllte
Fron Isaf
Cefn
Llangollen
Plas Newydd
Llangollen Railway
Castell Dinas Bran (ruins)
Valle Crucis Abbey (ruins)
Eliseg's Pillar
Pen-y-bryn
Llantysilio
Horseshoe Pass
Eglwyseg Mountain
World's End
Esclusham Mountain
Minera
Coedpoeth
New Brighton
The Wern
Brymbo
Glascoed
Bwlchgwyn
Gwynfryn
Ffrith
Cymau
Llanfynydd
Pantyffordd
Rhydtalog
Graianrhyd
Rhyd-y-ceirw
Treuddyn
Leeswood
Pontybodkin
Pontblyddyn
Stryt-cae-rhedyn
Plas Teg
Waun-y-Llyn
Hope
Caergwrle
Horeb
Cefn-y-bedd
Nercwys
Maeshafn
Moel Findeg
Llanferres
Eryrys
Llanarmon-yn-Iâl
Llyn Gweryd
Moel y Waun
Gelli Gynan
Llandegla
Moel Garegog
Pen-y-stryt
Nant y Garth Pass
Pentre-bwlch
Cyrn-y-Brain
Ty-mawr
Bryneglwys
Moel y Gamelin
Llantysilio Mountain
Moel Morfydd
Rhewl
Pentredwr
Ruthin (Rhuthun)
Ruthin Craft Centre
Llanbedr-Dyffryn-Clwyd
Rhewl
Bontuchel
Llanfwrog
Efenechtyd
Llanfair Dyffryn Clwyd
Pwll-glas
Graig-fechan
Pentre-celyn
Clocaenog
Clawdd-newydd
Derwen
Pandy'r Capel
Cefn Coch
Llanelidan
Mynydd Cricor
Brynsaithmarchog
Gwyddelwern
Caer Drewyn
Carrog
Corwen
Glyndyfrdwy
Tyn-y-cefn
Plas Isaf
Cynwyd
Moel yr Henfaes
Moel Fferna
Y Foel
Pontfadog
Glyn Ceiriog
Plas Nantyr
Pen-plaenau
Bryn Du
Glyn Valley Tramway and Museum
Dolywern
Llwynmawr
Pandy
Chirk Castle (NT)
Chirk (Y waun)
Chirk Green
Halton
Pont-y-blew
Shellbrook Hill
Sodylt Bank
Dudleston
Street Dinas
Ifton Heath
St Martin's
Preesgweene
Gledrid
Rhyn
Weston Rhyn
Tyn-y-Rhos
Bronygarth
Dudleston Heath (Criftins)
Elson
The Grange
Ellesmere
Wigginton
Bryn-y-cochin
New Marton
Lightwood Green
Knolton
Trench
Penley
Sandy Lane
Cadair Bronwen
Cadair Berwyn
Moel Sych
Foel Wen
Mynydd Tarw
Tregeiriog
Llanarmon Dyffryn Ceiriog
Pen y Gwely
Foel Rhiwlas
Rhiwlas
Llechrydau
Craignant
Upper Hengoed
Hengoed
Selattyn
Wern
Gobowen
Rhewl
Perthy
Welsh Frankton
Tetchill
Lee
Hindford
Whittington
Babbinswood
Hordley
Old Oswestry Hill Fort
Park Hall Farm
Transport Museum
Middleton
Brogyntyn
Llawnt
Cefn Canol
Rhydycroesau
Lledrod
Garneddwen
Cefn Hir-fynydd
Llangadwaladr
Tyn-y-ffridd
Tan-y-pistyll
Pistyll Rhaeadr
Mynydd Mawr
Moel Hen-fache
Tai-bach
Gyrn Moelfre
Llyn Moelfre
Moelfre
Llansilin
Nant-y-Gollen
Croesau Bach
Oswestry
Morda
Trefonen
Lower Hordley
Rednal
Wootton
Haughton
Sutton
Grimpo
Ball
Queen's Head
Maesbury Marsh
West Felton
Wykey
Eardiston
Weirbrook
Stanwardine in the Fields
Bagley
Cockshutt
Kenwick
Glan-hafon
Craig Rhiwarth
Clogydd
Llangynog
Llanrhaeadr-ym-Mochnant
Cefn-coch
Pentre
Penybontfawr
Penygarnedd
Pentrefelin
Rhos-y-brithdir
Llangedwyn
Treflach
Nantmawr
Llynclys
Morton
Woolston
Sandford
Porth-y-waen
Pen-y-bont
Llanyblodwel
Crickheath
Osbaston
Knockin
Shotatton
Ruyton-XI-Towns
Baschurch
Milford
Pant
Llanymynech Rocks
Maesbrook
Kinnerley
Dovaston
Llanymynech
Llansantffraid-ym-Mechain
Llanfechain
Bwlch-y-ddar
Abernaint
Llanfyllin
Tycrwyn
Llanfihangel-yng-Ngwynfa
Four Crosses
Llandysilio
Domgay
Rhos Common
Haughton
Crosslanes
Edgerley
Kynaston
Kinton
Nesscliffe
Little Ness
Great Ness
Wilcott
Pentre
Melverley Green
Melverley
Crewgreen
Felton Butler
Llandrinio
Deuddwr
Waen-fâch
Godor
Sarnau
Arddlin
Forton
Ensdon
Severn

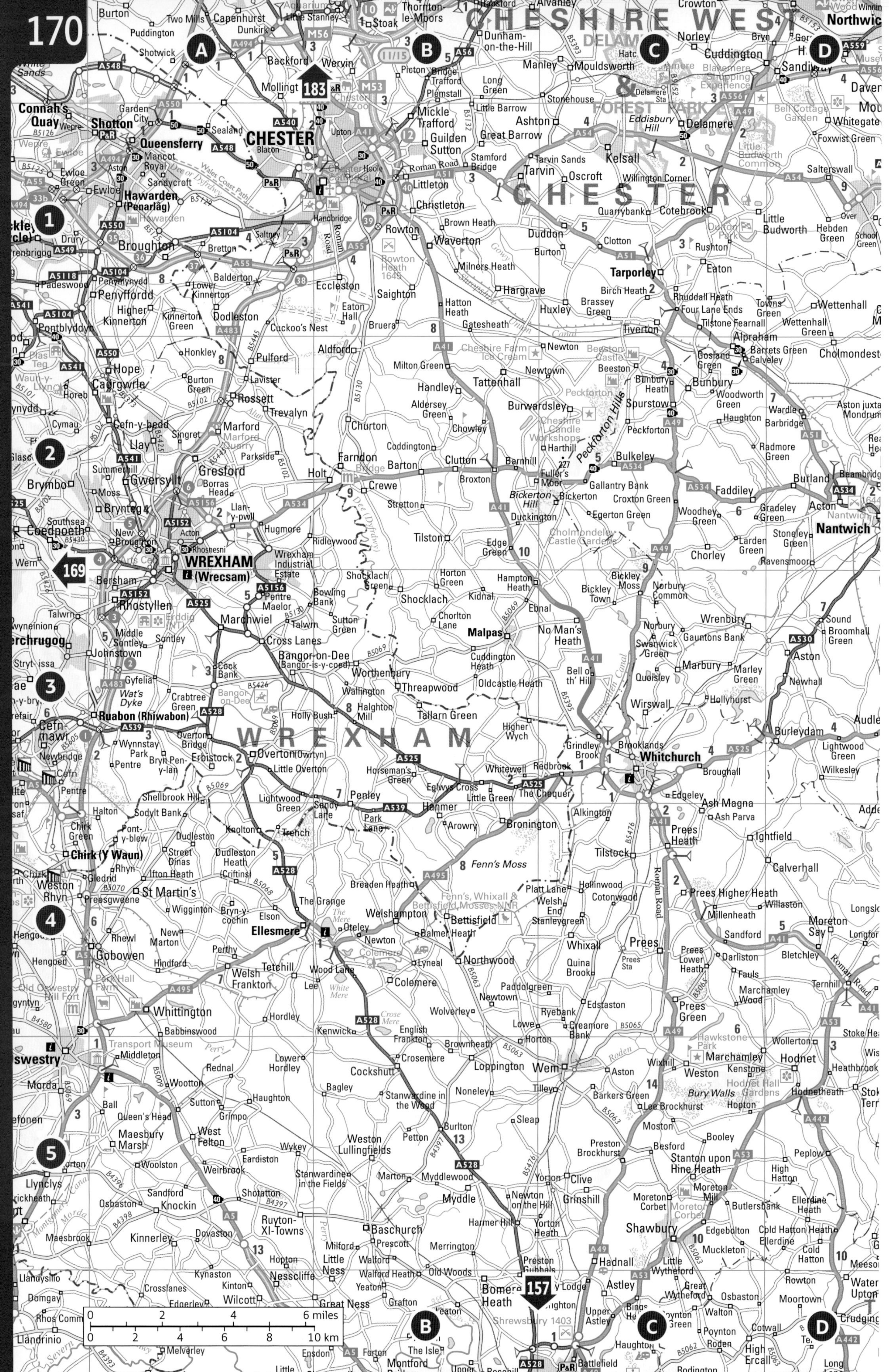
CHESHIRE WEST & CHESTER
DELAMERE FOREST PARK
WREXHAM
CHESTER
WREXHAM (Wrecsam)
Whitchurch
Nantwich
Northwich
Ellesmere
Wem
Oswestry
Shrewsbury 1403
Burton
Two Mills
Capenhurst
Puddington
Shotwick
Dunkirk
Aquarium
Little Stanney
Stoak
Thornton-le-Moors
Hapsford
Alvanley
Crowton
Backford
Wervin
Picton
Bridge Trafford
Dunham-on-the-Hill
Manley
Mouldsworth
Norley
Cuddington
Sandiway
Mollington
Plemstall
Long Green
Little Barrow
Stonehouse
Blakemere Shopping Experience
Davenham
Connah's Quay
Wepre
Garden City
Shotton
Queensferry
Sealand
Blacon
Upton
Mickle Trafford
Guilden Sutton
Great Barrow
Ashton
Eddisbury Hill
Delamere
Whitegate
Ewloe
Ewloe Green
Mancot Royal
Aston
Sandycroft
Hawarden (Penarlâg)
Wales Coast Path
Hoole
Chester Cathedral
Roman Road
Stamford Bridge
Tarvin Sands
Tarvin
Oscroft
Kelsall
Willington Corner
Little Budworth Common
Foxwist Green
Salterswall
Littleton
Christleton
Quarrybank
Cotebrook
Little Budworth
Over
Hebden Green
Broughton
Bretton
Saltney
Handbridge
Rowton
Brown Heath
Waverton
Duddon
Clotton
Rushton
Burton
Tarporley
Eaton
Drury
Penymynydd
Padeswood
Lower Kinnerton
Balderton
Eccleston
Rowton Heath 1645
Milners Heath
Hargrave
Birch Heath
Rhuddall Heath
Penyffordd
Higher Kinnerton
Kinnerton Green
Dodleston
Saighton
Eaton Hall
Huxley
Brassey Green
Four Lane Ends
Towns Green
Wettenhall
Tilstone Fearnall
Wettenhall Green
Pontblyddyn
Cuckoo's Nest
Bruera
Hatton Heath
Gatesheath
Tiverton
Alpraham
Plas Teg
Hope
Honkley
Pulford
Aldford
Milton Green
Cheshire Farm Ice Cream
Newton
Beeston Castle
Beeston
Bunbury
Bunbury Heath
Gosland Green
Barrets Green
Calveley
Cholmondeston
Caergwrle
Horeb
Burton Green
Lavister
Rossett
Trevalyn
Handley
Tattenhall
Newtown
Aldersey Green
Burwardsley
Peckforton
Peckforton Hills
Spurstow
Woodworth Green
Haughton
Wardle
Barbridge
Aston juxta Mondrum
Cefn-y-bedd
Cymau
Llay
Singret
Marford
Marford Quarry
Churton
Chowley
Cheshire Candle Workshops
Harthill
Radmore Green
Summerhill
Gwersyllt
Gresford
Parkside
Farndon
Holt
Barton
Coddington
Clutton
Barnhill
Fuller's Moor
Bulkeley
Gallantry Bank
Croxton Green
Faddiley
Burland
Brymbo
Moss
Borras Head
Crewe
Broxton
Bickerton Hill
Bickerton
Egerton Green
Woodhey Green
Gradeley Green
Acton
Brynteg
Southsea
Coedpoeth
New Broughton
Acton
Rhosnesni
Llan-y-pwll
Hugmore
Stretton
Ridleywood
Tilston
Duckington
Cholmondeley Castle Gardens
Larden Green
Stoneley Green
Chorley
Ravensmoor
Bersham
Wrexham Industrial Estate
Shocklach Green
Horton Green
Edge Green
Hampton Heath
Bickley Moss
Bickley Town
Norbury Common
Rhostyllen
Erddig (NT)
Pentre Maelor
Bowling Bank
Shocklach
Kidnal
Ebnal
Chorlton Lane
Talwrn
Middle Sontley
Sontley
Marchwiel
Sutton Green
Malpas
No Man's Heath
Norbury
Wrenbury
Gauntons Bank
Sound
Broomhall Green
Erchrugog
Johnstown
Cross Lanes
Bangor-on-Dee (Bangor-is-y-coed)
Cuddington Heath
Swanwick Green
Marbury
Marley Green
Aston
Stryt-issa
Cock Bank
Gyfelia
Worthenbury
Wallington
Threapwood
Oldcastle Heath
Bell o' th' Hill
Quoisley
Newhall
Wat's Dyke
Crabtree Green
Halghton Mill
Wirswall
Hollyhurst
Ruabon (Rhiwabon)
Holly Bush
Tallarn Green
Higher Wych
Cefn-mawr
Wynnstay Park
Overton Bridge
Grindley Brook
Brooklands
Burleydam
Audlem
Newbridge
Pentre
Bryn Pen-y-lan
Erbistock
Overton (Owrtyn)
Little Overton
Horseman's Green
Whitewell
Redbrook
Broughall
Lightwood Green
Wilkesley
Eglwys Cross
The Chequer
Little Green
Edgeley
Ash Magna
Ash Parva
Shellbrook Hill
Lightwood Green
Sodylt Bank
Penley
Sandy Lane
Hanmer
Alkington
Halton
Chirk Green
Pont-y-blew
Dudleston
Knolton
Trench
Park Lane
Arowry
Bronington
Prees Heath
Ightfield
Chirk (Y Waun)
Street Dinas
Dudleston Heath (Criftins)
Fenn's Moss
Tilstock
Calverhall
Rhyn
Ifton Heath
Weston Rhyn
Gledrid
St Martin's
Breaden Heath
Platt Lane
Hollinwood
Cotonwood
Prees Higher Heath
Preesgweene
Wigginton
Bryn-y-cochin
Elson
The Grange
The Mere
Fenn's, Whixall & Bettisfield Mosses NNR
Welsh End
Stanleygreen
Willaston
Millenheath
Moreton Say
Welshampton
Bettisfield
Balmer Heath
Roman Road
Longslow
Rhewl
New Marton
Otele
Newton
Sandford
Longford
Gobowen
Perthy
Hindford
Welsh Frankton
Tetchill
Wood Lane
Colemere
Lyneal
Northwood
Whixall
Quina Brook
Prees
Prees Sta
Prees Lower Heath
Darliston
Fauls
Bletchley
Hengoed
Park Hall Farm
Old Oswestry Hill Fort
Lee
White Mere
Colemere
Paddolgreen
Newtown
Edstaston
Marchamley Wood
Prees Green
Ternhill
Whittington
Babbinswood
Hordley
Crose Mere
Kenwick
Wolverley
Ryebank
Lowe
Creamore Bank
Hawkstone Park
Stoke Heath
Transport Museum
Middleton
English Frankton
Brownheath
Horton
Wollerton
Hodnet
Lower Hordley
Crosemere
Loppington
Aston
Wixhill
Marchamley
Kenstone
Heathbrook
Rednal
Cockshutt
Weston
Hodnet Hall Gardens
Hodnetheath
Morda
Wootton
Haughton
Bagley
Noneley
Tilley
Barkers Green
Bury Walls
Hopton
Ball
Sutton
Grimpo
Stanwardine in the Wood
Lee Brockhurst
Queen's Head
Sleap
West Felton
Burlton
Moston
Booley
Maesbury Marsh
Weston Lullingfields
Petton
Preston Brockhurst
Besford
Peplow
Morton
Llynclys
Woolston
Weirbrook
Wykey
Eardiston
Stanwardine in the Fields
Marton
Myddlewood
Yorton
Clive
Stanton upon Hine Heath
High Hatton
Sandford
Osbaston
Knockin
Shotatton
Myddle
Newton on the Hill
Grinshill
Moreton Corbet
Moreton Mill
Butlersbank
Ellerdine Heath
Maesbrook
Kinnerley
Dovaston
Ruyton-XI-Towns
Baschurch
Harmer Hill
Yorton Heath
Shawbury
Edgebolton
Cold Hatton Heath
Ellerdine
Prescott
Merrington
Muckleton
Cold Hatton
Milford
Little Ness
Walford
Hopton
Preston Gubbals
Hadnall
Little Wytheford
Rowton
Meeson
Llandysilio
Kynaston
Nesscliffe
Walford Heath
Old Woods
Astley
Great Wytheford
Moortown
Waters Upton
Crosslanes
Kinton
Yeaton
Bomere Heath
Osbaston
Domgay
Edgerley
Wilcott
Great Ness
Grafton
Upper Astley
Walton
Crudgington
Rhos Common
Poynton Green
Poynton
Cotwall
High Ercall
Llandrinio
Haughton
Roden
Melverley
Ensdon
Forton
The Isle
Montford Bridge
Battlefield
Rodington
Little
Upper
Rosehill
Long
Severn
0 2 4 6 miles
0 2 4 6 8 10 km
183
169
157

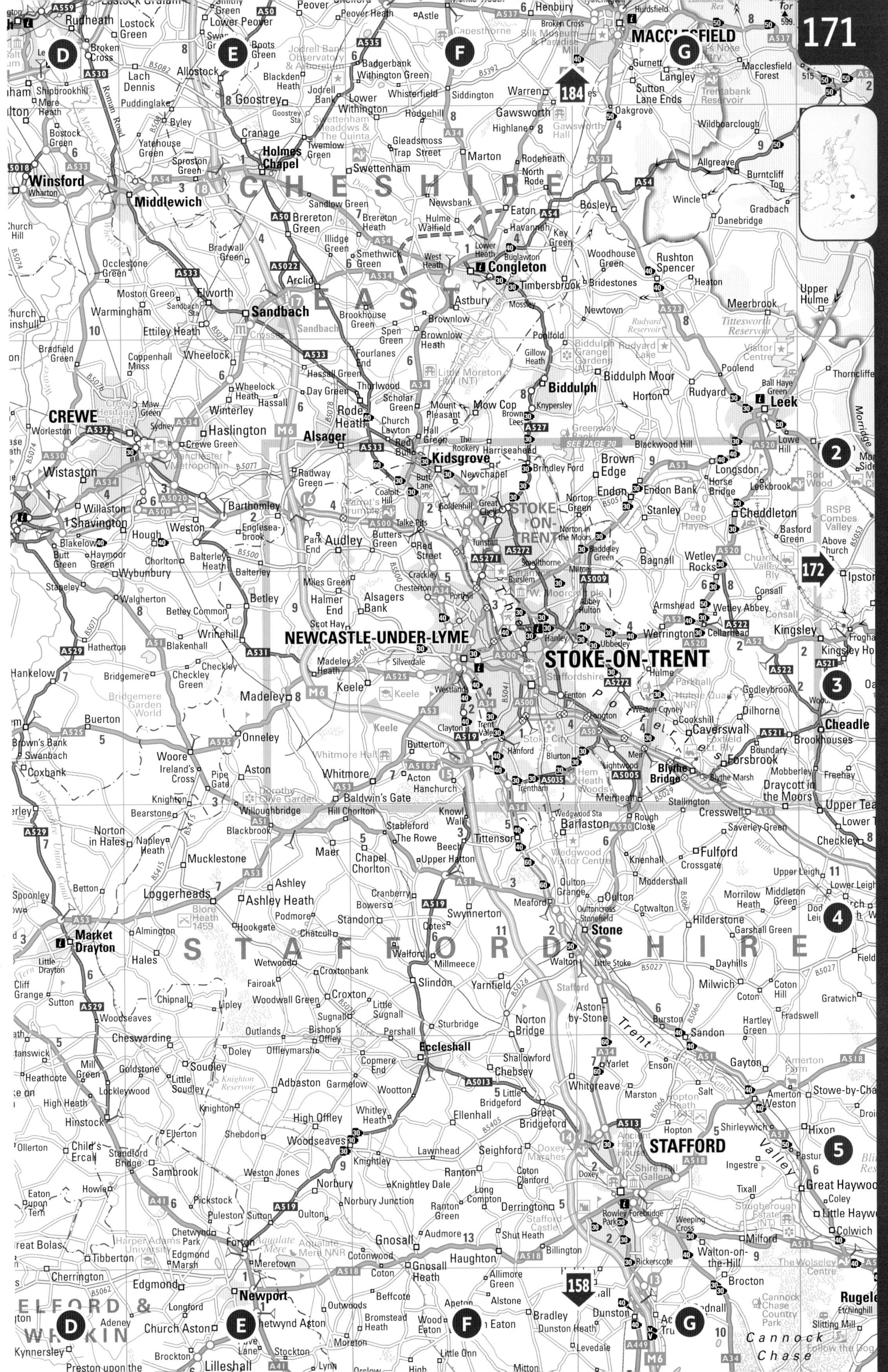
CHESHIRE EAST
STAFFORDSHIRE
TELFORD & WREKIN
MACCLESFIELD
Congleton
Sandbach
Middlewich
Winsford
CREWE
Alsager
Kidsgrove
Biddulph
Leek
NEWCASTLE-UNDER-LYME
STOKE-ON-TRENT
Cheadle
Market Drayton
Stone
Eccleshall
STAFFORD
Newport
Holmes Chapel
Haslington
Audley
Madeley
Loggerheads
Gnosall
Rugeley
Cannock Chase
The Potteries
Trent
M6
A34
A50
A500
A51
A53
A54
A519
A520
A523
A529
A533
A5013
184
172
158
SEE PAGE 20
D
E
F
G
2
3
4
5

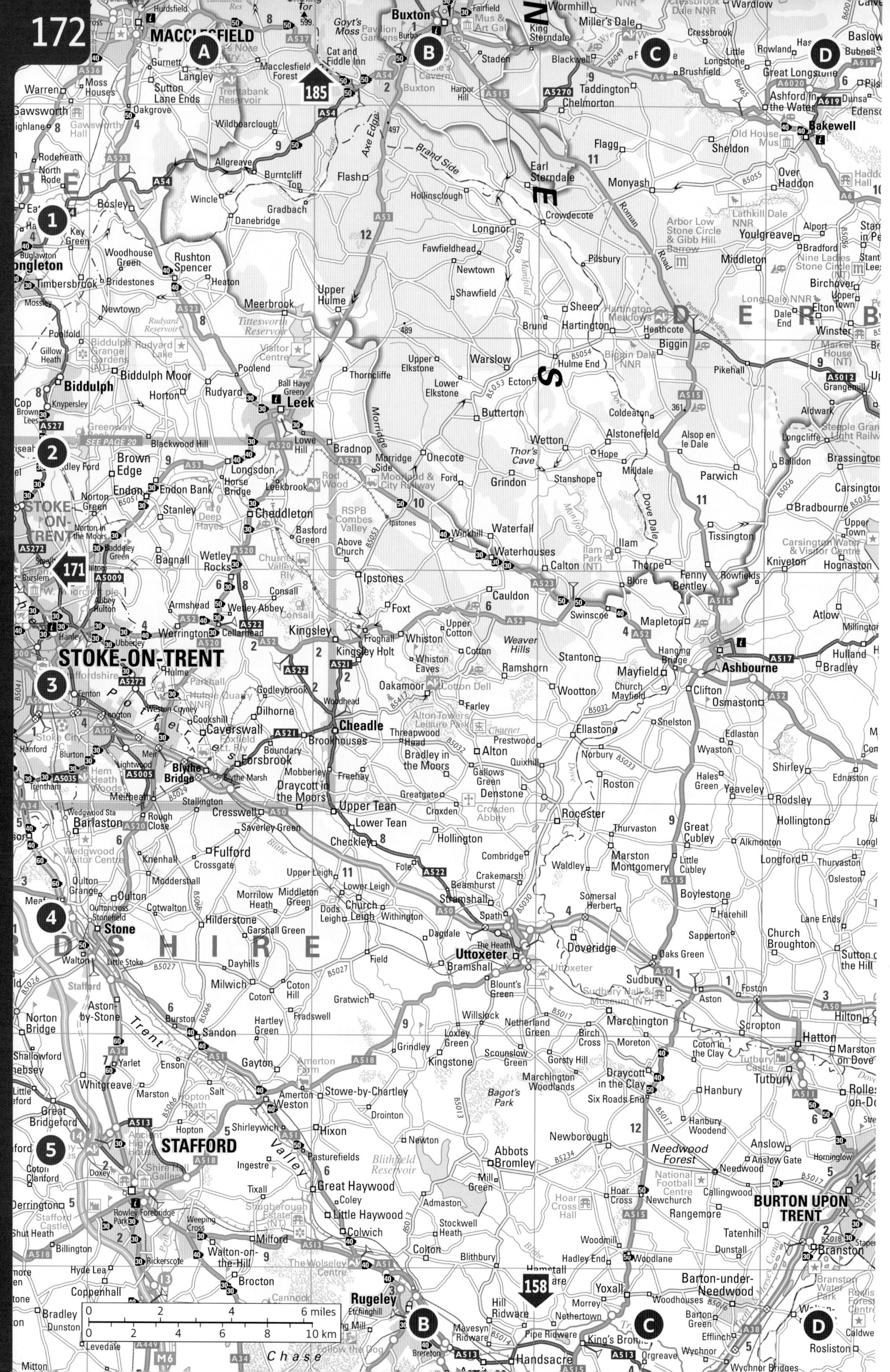
MACCLESFIELD
A
B
C
D
185
Buxton
Wormhill
Miller's Dale
Wardlow
Baslow
Cressbrook
Fairfield
King Sterndale
Goyt's Moss
Pavilion Gardens
Cat and Fiddle Inn
Macclesfield Forest
Langley
Gurnett
Sutton Lane Ends
Trentabank Reservoir
Warren
Moss Houses
Gawsworth
Oakgrove
Wildboarclough
Staden
Blackwell
Taddington
Chelmorton
Harpur Hill
Rowland
Little Longstone
Great Longstone
Brushfield
Hassop
Bubnell
Ashford in the Water
Bakewell
Old House Mus
Sheldon
Flagg
Earl Sterndale
Monyash
Over Haddon
Axe Edge
Brand Side
Flash
Hollinsclough
Allgreave
Burntcliff Top
Gradbach
Wincle
Danebridge
Rodeheath
North Rode
Bosley
Key Green
Congleton
Buglawton
Timbersbrook
Woodhouse Green
Rushton Spencer
Bridestones
Heaton
Longnor
Crowdecote
Fawfieldhead
Newtown
Shawfield
Pilsbury
Roman Road
Arbor Low Stone Circle & Gibb Hill Barrow
Lathkill Dale NNR
Youlgreave
Middleton
Alport
Bradford
Nine Ladies Stone Circle
Birchover
Long Dale NNR
Elton
Upper Hulme
Meerbrook
Tittesworth Reservoir
Rudyard Reservoir
Rudyard Lake
Mossley
Poolfold
Gillow Heath
Biddulph Grange Gardens
Biddulph
Biddulph Moor
Knypersley
Sheen
Hartington
Hartington Meadows
Brund
Heathcote
Biggin
Dale End
Winster
Market House (NT)
Warslow
Hulme End
Biggin Dale NNR
Pikehall
Grangemill
Upper Elkstone
Lower Elkstone
Thorncliffe
Poolend
Horton
Rudyard
Ball Haye Green
Leek
Visitor Centre
Ecton
Butterton
Coldeaton
Aldwark
Longcliffe
Brown Lees
Greenway Bank
SEE PAGE 20
Blackwood Hill
Lowe Hill
Bradnop
Morridge
Morridge Side
Onecote
Wetton
Thor's Cave
Alstonefield
Hope
Alsop en le Dale
Milldale
Ballidon
Brassington
Brown Edge
Endon
Endon Bank
Longsdon
Horse Bridge
Leekbrook
Rod Wood
Moorland & City Railway
Ford
Grindon
Stanshope
Dove Dale
Parwich
Carsington
Bradbourne
Norton Green
Stanley
Deep Hayes
Cheddleton
RSPB Coombes Valley
Ipstones
Winkhill
Waterfall
Waterhouses
Ilam
Ilam Park
Tissington
Upper Town
Carsington Water & Visitor Centre
STOKE-ON-TRENT
Norton in the Moors
Baddeley Green
Bagnall
Wetley Rocks
Basford Green
Above Church
Calton
Thorpe
Blore
Fenny Bentley
Rowfields
Kniveton
Hognaston
171
Burslem
Abbey Hulton
Armshead
Wetley Abbey
Consall
Churnet Valley Rly
Ipstones
Foxt
Cauldon
Swinscoe
Mapleton
Atlow
Hanley
Ubberley
Werrington
Cellarhead
Kingsley
Froghall
Whiston
Upper Cotton
Cotton
Weaver Hills
Stanton
Hanging Bridge
Ashbourne
Hulland
Bradley
Kingsley Holt
Whiston Eaves
Ramshorn
Mayfield
Church Mayfield
Clifton
Osmaston
Hulme
Parkhall
Hulme Quarry NNR
Godleybrook
Oakamoor
Cotton Dell
Wootton
Fenton
Longton
Weston Coyney
Cookshill
Dilhorne
Woodhead
Farley
Alton Towers Leisure Park
Snelston
Edlaston
Stoke City FC
Caverswall
Foxfield Lt Rly
Cheadle
Brookhouses
Threapwood
Head
Prestwood
Ellastone
Wyaston
Hanford
Blurton
Meir
Lightwood
Boundary
Forsbrook
Bradley in the Moors
Alton
Quixhill
Norbury
Shirley
Ednaston
Trentham
Hem Heath Woods
Blythe Bridge
Blythe Marsh
Mobberley
Freehay
Gallows Green
Denstone
Roston
Hales Green
Yeaveley
Rodsley
Meirheath
Stallington
Draycott in the Moors
Greatgate
Croxden
Croxden Abbey
Upper Tean
Lower Tean
Wedgwood Sta
Barlaston
Rough Close
Cresswell
Saverley Green
Rocester
Thurvaston
Great Cubley
Hollington
Wedgwood Visitor Centre
Fulford
Knenhall
Crossgate
Checkley
Hollington
Combridge
Marston Montgomery
Alkmonton
Longford
Waldley
Little Cubley
Osleston
Oulton Grange
Moddershall
Upper Leigh
Lower Leigh
Fole
Crakemarsh
Beamhurst
Boylestone
Oulton
Oultoncross
Stonefield
Cotwalton
Morrilow Heath
Middleton Green
Church Leigh
Dods Leigh
Withington
Stramshall
Somersal Herbert
Harehill
Lane Ends
Stone
Hilderstone
Garshall Green
Dagdale
Spath
Sapperton
Church Broughton
Uttoxeter
The Heath
Bramshall
Doveridge
Oaks Green
Sutton on the Hill
Walton
Little Stoke
Dayhills
Field
Milwich
Coton
Coton Hill
Gratwich
Blount's Green
Sudbury
Sudbury Hall & Museum (NT)
Foston
Aston
Stafford
Aston-by-Stone
Norton Bridge
Burston
Sandon
Hartley Green
Fradswell
Willslock
Netherland Green
Marchington
Loxley Green
Birch Cross
Hilton
Scropton
Hatton
Marston on Dove
Trent
Shallowford
Yarlet
Enson
Gayton
Amerton Farm
Grindley
Kingstone
Scounslow Green
Gorsty Hill
Moreton
Coton in the Clay
Tutbury Castle
Tutbury
Rolleston-on-Dove
Whitgreave
Marston
Salt
Hopton Heath 1643
Amerton
Weston
Stowe-by-Chartley
Drointon
Bagot's Park
Marchington Woodlands
Draycott in the Clay
Six Roads End
Hanbury
Hanbury Woodend
Great Bridgeford
Ancient High House
STAFFORD
Hopton
Shirleywich
Hixon
Trent Valley
Newton
Abbots Bromley
Newborough
Needwood Forest
Anslow
Anslow Gate
Horninglow
Coton Clanford
Doxey
Shire Hall Gallery
Ingestre
Pasturefields
Blithfield Reservoir
Mill Green
National Football Centre
Needwood
Derrington
Tixall
Great Haywood
Coley
Admaston
Hoar Cross Hall
Hoar Cross
Newchurch
Callingwood
BURTON UPON TRENT
Stafford Castle
Rowley Park
Forebridge
Shugborough Estate (NT)
Little Haywood
Rangemore
Shut Heath
Weeping Cross
Colwich
Stockwell Heath
Tatenhill
Billington
Milford
Colton
Woodmill
Dunstall
Branston
Walton-on-the-Hill
Blithbury
Hadley End
Woodlane
Rickerscote
The Wolseley Centre
Hamstall Ridware
Hyde Lea
Brocton
158
Yoxall
Barton-under-Needwood
Branston Water Park
Coppenhall
Cannock Chase
Rugeley
Etchinghill
Hill Ridware
Morrey
Nethertown
Woodhouses
Barton Green
Rosliston Forestry Centre
Bradley
Dunston
Mavesyn Ridware
Pipe Ridware
King's Bromley
Efflinch
Walton-on-Trent
Caldwell
Levedale
Brereton
Follow the Dog
Handsacre
Orgreave
Wychnor
Wychnor Bridges
Rosliston
Mitton
M6
0 2 4 6 miles
0 2 4 6 8 10 km
R E
S
N E
D E R B Y
S H I R E

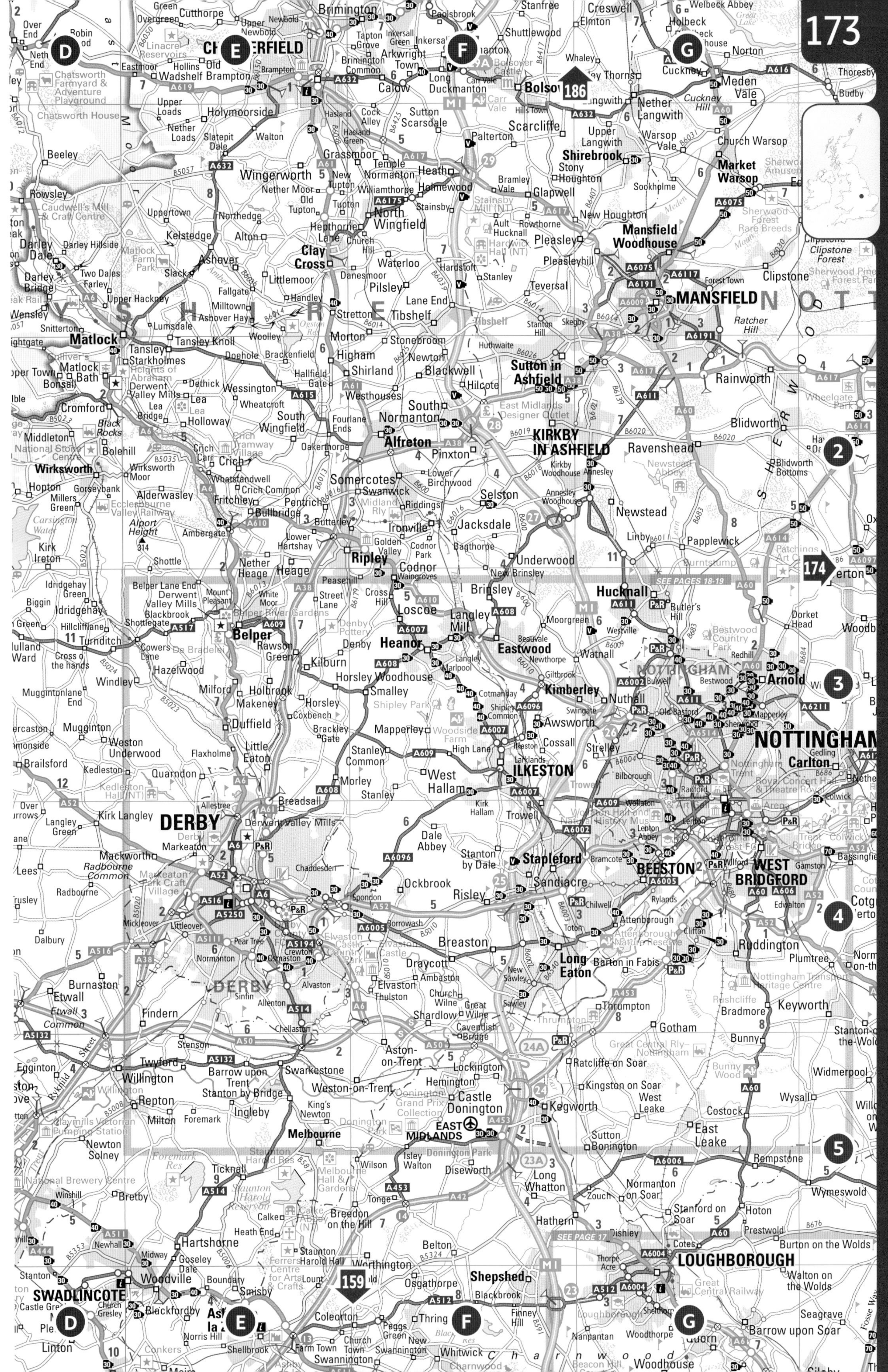
Over End
Cutthorpe
Brimington
Poolsbrook
Stanfree
Creswell
Welbeck Abbey
Holbeck
Newbold
Overgreen
Linacre Reservoirs
Tapton Grove
Inkersall Green
Shuttlewood
Elmton
Whaley
Norton
Cuckney
Meden Vale
Thoresby
Budby
Eastmoor
Hollins
Wadshelf
Brampton
Brimington Common
Arkwright Town
Bolsover Castle
Calow
Long Duckmanton
Carr Vale
Bolsover
186
Nether Langwith
Cuckney Hill
Chatsworth Farmyard & Adventure Playground
Chatsworth House
Upper Loads
Holymoorside
Nether Loads
Slatepit Dale
Walton
Hasland
Cock Alley
Sutton Scarsdale
Hills Town
Scarcliffe
Upper Langwith
Warsop Vale
Church Warsop
Beeley
Grassmoor
Temple Normanton
Heath
Palterton
Shirebrook
Market Warsop
Wingerworth
Nether Moor
New Tupton
Williamthorpe
Holmewood
Bramley Vale
Stony Houghton
Glapwell
Sookholme
Rowsley
Caudwell's Mill & Craft Centre
Old Tupton
Tupton
North Wingfield
Stainsby
Stainsby Mill (NT)
Uppertown
Northedge
Hepthorne Lane
Ault Hucknall
Rowthorne
New Houghton
Sherwood Forest Rare Breeds
Kelstedge
Alton
Mansfield Woodhouse
Darley Dale
Darley Hillside
Matlock Farm Park
Ashover
Clay Cross
Church Hill
Hardwick Hall (NT)
Pleasley
Pleasleyhill
Clipstone Forest
Two Dales
Farley
Darley Bridge
Slack
Littlemoor
Waterloo
Danesmoor
Hardstoft
Stanley
Teversal
Clipstone
Sherwood Pines Forest Park
Upper Hackney
Fallgate
Handley
Pilsley
Lane End
Forest Town
Mansfield
Milltown
Ashover Hay
Stretton
Tibshelf
Ratcher Hill
Wensley
Snitterton
Lumsdale
Woolley
Ogston Res
Morton
Stanton Hill
Skegby
Matlock
Tansley
Tansley Knoll
Stonebroom
Huthwaite
Starkholmes
Heights of Abraham
Doehole
Brackenfield
Higham
Newton
Sutton in Ashfield
Rainworth
Matlock Bath
Shirland
Blackwell
Gulliver's Kingdom
Derwent Valley Mills
Dethick
Hallfield Gate
Hilcote
Bonsall
Lea
Wessington
Westhouses
Cromford
Lea Bridge
Wheatcroft
South Normanton
East Midlands Designer Outlet
Wheelgate Park
Blidworth
Black Rocks
Holloway
South Wingfield
Fourlane Ends
Middleton
National Stone Centre
Crich Tramway Village
Alfreton
Kirkby in Ashfield
Ravenshead
Bolehill
Oakerthorpe
Pinxton
Kirkby Woodhouse
Annesley
Newstead Abbey
Blidworth Bottoms
Wirksworth
Crich Carr
Crich
Wirksworth Moor
Whatstandwell
Lower Birchwood
Hopton
Gorseybank
Crich Common
Somercotes
Swanwick
Selston
Annesley Woodhouse
Newstead
Millers Green
Alderwasley
Fritchley
Pentrich
Midland Rly
Riddings
Ecclesbourne Valley Railway
Bullbridge
Carsington Water
Alport Height
Ambergate
Butterley
Ironville
Jacksdale
Linby
Papplewick
Lower Hartshay
Golden Valley
Codnor Park
Bagthorpe
Kirk Ireton
Shottle
Nether Heage
Heage
Ripley
Codnor
Underwood
New Brinsley
Burntstump
174
Idridgehay Green
Belper Lane End
Mount Pleasant
Waingroves
Brinsley
Hucknall
Biggin
Idridgehay
Derwent Valley Mills
White Moor
Street Lane
Cross Hill
Loscoe
Langley Mill
Butler's Hill
Dorket Head
Blackbrook
Shottlegate
Belper River Gardens
Denby Pottery
Moorgreen
Westville
Bestwood Country Park
Hillcliff Lane
Turnditch
Belper
Rawson Green
Denby
Heanor
Eastwood
Watnall
Redhill
Cowers Lane
Cross o' the hands
Kilburn
Langley
Marlpool
Beauvale
Newthorpe
Nottingham
Bestwood
Arnold
Hazelwood
Windley
Giltbrook
Kimberley
Bulwell
Muggintonlane End
Milford
Holbrook
Horsley Woodhouse
Smalley
Cotmanhay
Nuthall
Makeney
Horsley
Shipley Park
Shipley Common
Swingate
Old Basford
Mapperley
Coxbench
Duffield
Mugginton
Brackley Gate
Mapperley
Woodside Farm
Awsworth
Sherwood
Weston Underwood
Cossall
Strelley
Brailsford
Flaxholme
Little Eaton
Stanley Common
High Lane
Ilkeston
Larklands
Gedling
Carlton
Kedleston
Quarndon
West Hallam
Bilborough
Nottingham Trent
Kedleston Hall (NT)
Morley
Stanley
Trowell
Radford
Royal Concert Hall & Theatre Royal
Breadsall
Allestree
Kirk Hallam
Wollaton
Colwick
Over Burrows
Langley Green
Kirk Langley
Derby
Derwent Valley Mills
Wollaton Hall and Natural History Mus
Lenton
Arena
Derby Markeaton
Dale Abbey
Lenton Abbey
Trent Bridge
Colwick
Mackworth
Radbourne Common
Markeaton Park Craft Village
Chaddesden
Stanton by Dale
Stapleford
Bramcote
Beeston
Wilford
West Bridgford
Gamston
Bassingfield
Lees
Ockbrook
Sandiacre
Trent FC
Radbourne
Spondon
Risley
Chilwell
Rylands
Edwalton
Cotgrave
Trusley
Mickleover
Littleover
Borrowash
Attenborough
Toton
Attenborough Nature Reserve
Clifton
Dalbury
Pear Tree
Elvaston Castle Country Park
Breaston
Ruddington
Plumtree
Normanton
Crewton
Osmaston
Draycott
Long Eaton
Barton in Fabis
Burnaston
Etwall
Alvaston
Ambaston
Elvaston
Thulston
New Sawley
Nottingham Transport Heritage Centre
Sinfin
Church Wilne
Great Wilne
Rushcliffe
Keyworth
Etwall Common
Findern
Allenton
Shardlow
Sawley
Thrumpton
Bradmore
Chellaston
Cavendish Bridge
Gotham
Bunny
Stanton-on-the-Wolds
Stenson
Aston-on-Trent
Great Central Rly Nottingham
Egginton
Twyford
Barrow upon Trent
Swarkestone
Lockington
Ratcliffe on Soar
Bunny Wood
Willington
Stanton by Bridge
Hemington
Weston-on-Trent
Kingston on Soar
Widmerpool
Repton
Castle Donington
Donington Grand Prix Collection
West Leake
Wysall
Claymills Victorian Pumping Station
Milton
Foremark
Ingleby
King's Newton
Kegworth
Costock
East Midlands
Melbourne
Donington Park
Newton Solney
Sutton Bonington
East Leake
Foremark Res
Staunton Harold Res
Isley Walton
Rempstone
Ticknall
Wilson
Diseworth
National Brewery Centre
Bretby
Melbourne Hall & Gardens
Long Whatton
Normanton on Soar
Wymeswold
Winshill
Staunton Harold Reservoir
Tonge
Zouch
Calke Abbey (NT)
Breedon on the Hill
Stanford on Soar
Hoton
Calke
Heath End
Hathern
Dishley
Prestwold
Hartshorne
Newhall
Staunton Harold Hall
Belton
Cotes
Burton on the Wolds
Midway
Goseley Dale
Ferrers Centre for Arts & Crafts
Worthington
Shepshed
Thorpe Acre
Loughborough
Woodville
Boundary
Lount
159
Osgathorpe
Blackbrook
Walton on the Wolds
Stanton
Swadlincote
Smisby
Great Central Railway
Castle Gresley
Church Gresley
Blackfordby
Ashby-de-la-Zouch
Coleorton
Thringstone
Finney Hill
Seagrave
Norris Hill
Peggs Green
Nanpantan
Woodthorpe
Quorn
Barrow upon Soar
Linton
Conkers
Shellbrook
Farm Town
Church Town
Swannington
New Swannington
Whitwick
Charnwood
Beacon Hill
Woodhouse
SEE PAGES 18-19
SEE PAGE 17

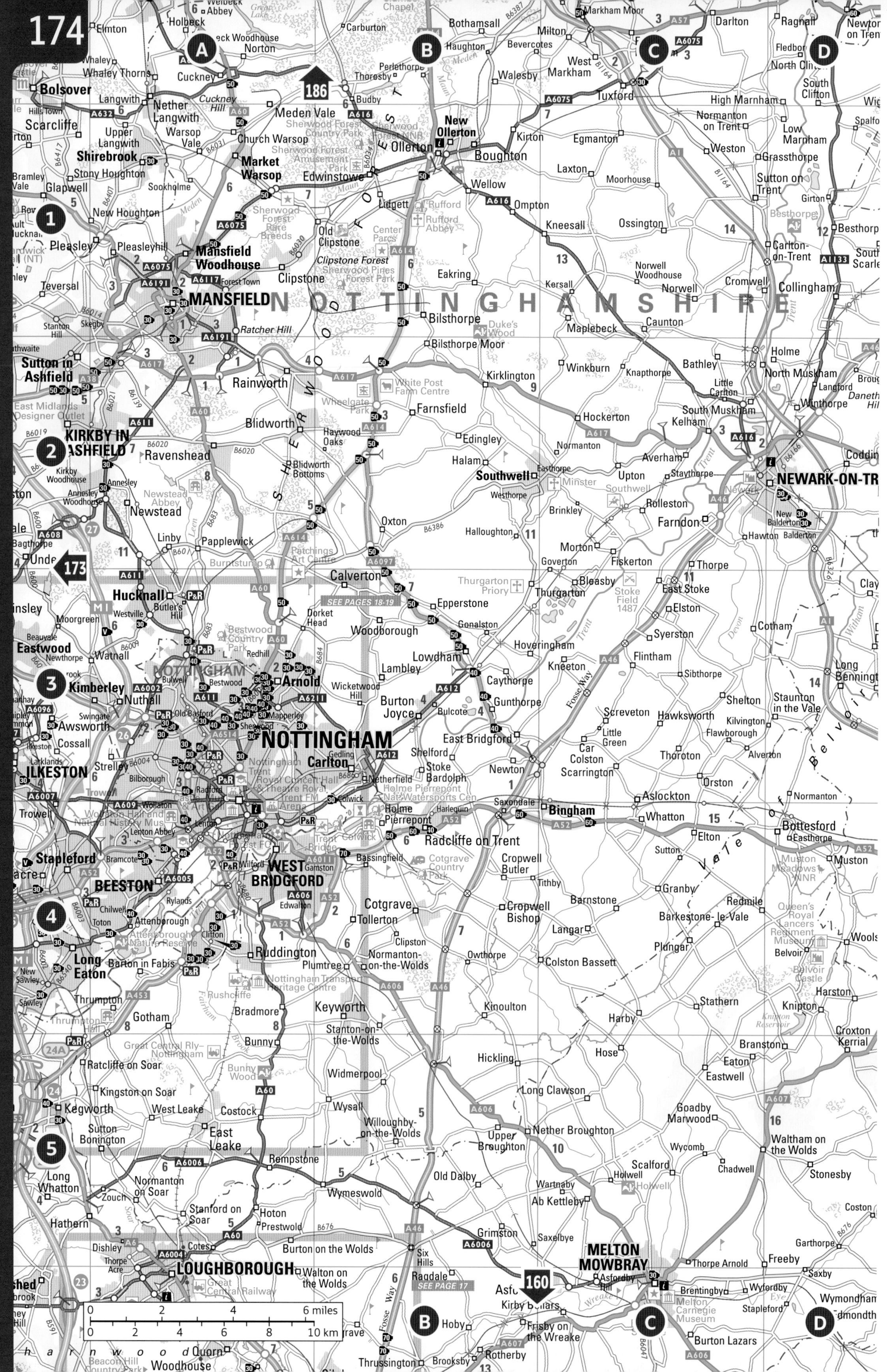
NOTTINGHAMSHIRE
NOTTINGHAM
MANSFIELD
NEWARK-ON-TRENT
MELTON MOWBRAY
LOUGHBOROUGH
WEST BRIDGFORD
BEESTON
ILKESTON
Long Eaton
Stapleford
Kimberley
Eastwood
Hucknall
Arnold
Carlton
KIRKBY IN ASHFIELD
Sutton in Ashfield
Mansfield Woodhouse
Market Warsop
Bolsover
Shirebrook
New Ollerton
Ollerton
Southwell
Bingham
Radcliffe on Trent
Cotgrave
Keyworth
Ruddington
Gotham
Kegworth
East Leake
Tuxford
Collingham
Bottesford
Rainworth
Blidworth
Ravenshead
Calverton
Lowdham
Burton Joyce
Farnsfield
Bilsthorpe
Clipstone
Edwinstowe
Boughton
Kirklington
Hockerton
Upton
Rolleston
Farndon
East Stoke
Elston
Syerston
Aslockton
Whatton
Orston
Long Bennington
Cropwell Bishop
Langar
Long Clawson
Nether Broughton
Old Dalby
Waltham on the Wolds
Asfordby
Kirby Bellars
Frisby on the Wreake
Rempstone
Wymeswold
Burton on the Wolds
Sutton Bonington
Hathern
Quorn
Woodhouse
Vale of Belvoir
Sherwood Forest
Charnwood
186
173
160
SEE PAGES 18-19
SEE PAGE 17
0 2 4 6 miles
0 2 4 6 8 10 km

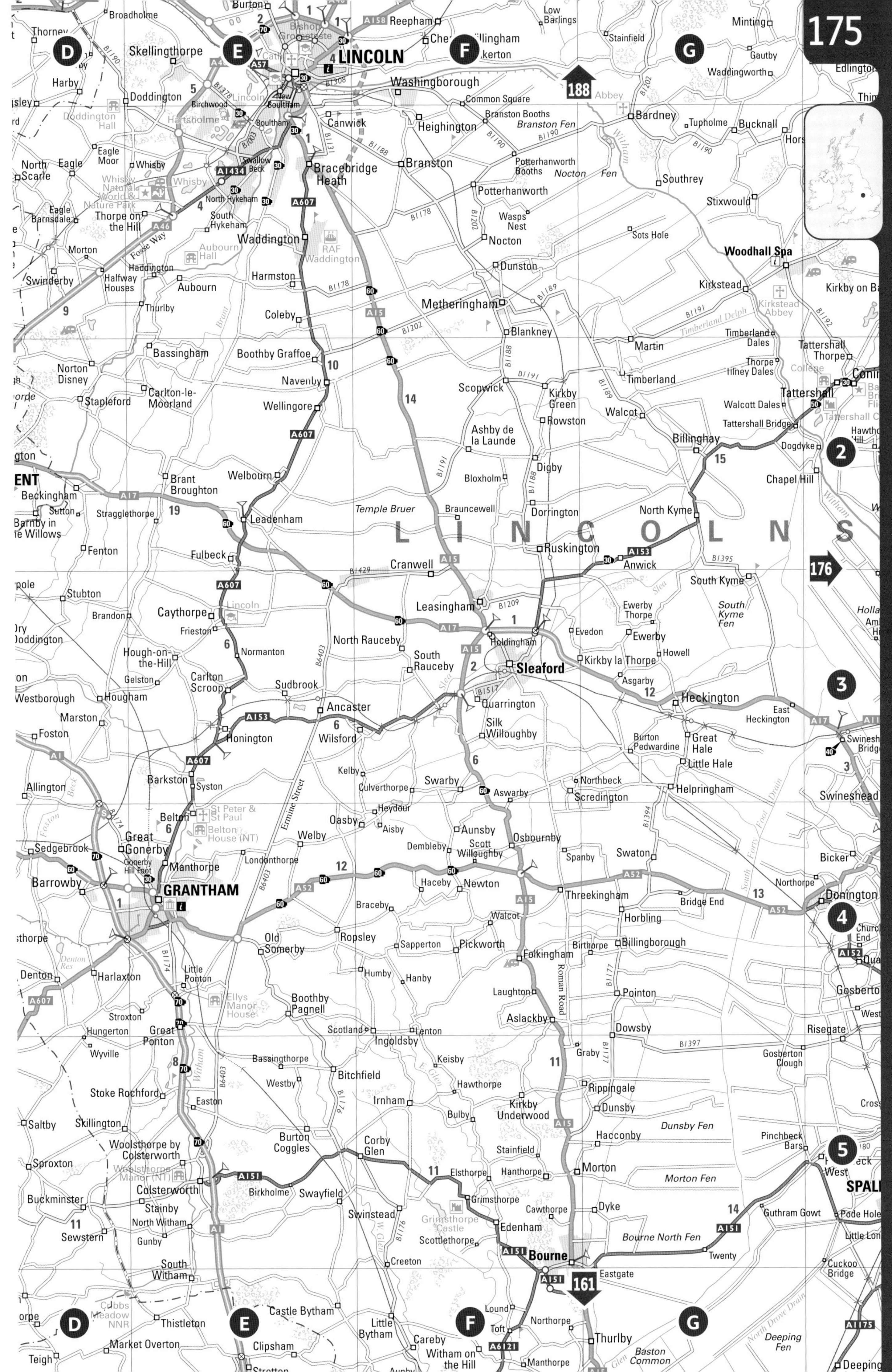
Burton
Broadholme
Thorney
Skellingthorpe
Bishop Grosseteste
LINCOLN
Reepham
Low Barlings
Minting
Stainfield
Gautby
Waddingworth
Edlington
Harby
Doddington
Birchwood
Lincoln
New Boultham
Washingborough
Common Square
188
Abbey
Bardney
Tupholme
Bucknall
Doddington Hall
Hartsholme
Boultham
Canwick
Heighington
Branston Booths
Branston Fen
Eagle Moor
Whisby
Swallow Beck
Bracebridge Heath
Branston
Potterhanworth Booths
Nocton
Fen
Southrey
North Scarle
Eagle
Whisby Nature World & Nature Park
North Hykeham
Potterhanworth
Stixwould
Eagle Barnsdale
Thorpe on the Hill
South Hykeham
Fosse Way
Wasps Nest
Nocton
Sots Hole
Waddington
RAF Waddington
Morton
Aubourn Hall
Woodhall Spa
Haddington
Dunston
Swinderby
Halfway Houses
Aubourn
Harmston
Kirkstead
Kirkby on Bain
Thurlby
Kirkstead Abbey
Coleby
Metheringham
Timberland Delph
Blankney
Martin
Timberland Dales
Tattershall Thorpe
Bassingham
Boothby Graffoe
Norton Disney
Navenby
Thorpe Tilney Dales
Timberland
Scopwick
Kirkby Green
Carlton-le-Moorland
Stapleford
Wellingore
Walcot
Walcott Dales
Tattershall
Tattershall Bridge
Rowston
Ashby de la Launde
Billinghay
Dogdyke
Digby
Welbourn
Bloxholm
Chapel Hill
Brant Broughton
Beckingham
Sutton
Stragglethorpe
Barnby in the Willows
Leadenham
Temple Bruer
Brauncewell
Dorrington
North Kyme
LINCOLNS
Fenton
Fulbeck
Ruskington
Anwick
176
Cranwell
South Kyme
Stubton
South Kyme Fen
Brandon
Caythorpe
Lincoln
Leasingham
Ewerby Thorpe
Frieston
Evedon
Ewerby
North Rauceby
Holdingham
Normanton
Howell
Hough-on-the-Hill
South Rauceby
Sleaford
Kirkby la Thorpe
Gelston
Carlton Scroop
Asgarby
Westborough
Hougham
Sudbrook
Quarrington
Heckington
Ancaster
East Heckington
Marston
Silk Willoughby
Foston
Honington
Wilsford
Burton Pedwardine
Great Hale
Swineshead Bridge
Little Hale
Kelby
Barkston
Allington
Syston
Culverthorpe
Swarby
Aswarby
Northbeck
Scredington
Helpringham
Swineshead
Heydour
St Peter & St Paul
Belton
Belton House (NT)
Oasby
Aisby
Aunsby
Ermine Street
Great Gonerby
Welby
Sedgebrook
Dembleby
Scott Willoughby
Osbournby
Spanby
Swaton
Bicker
Gonerby Hill Foot
Manthorpe
Londonthorpe
Barrowby
Haceby
Newton
Threekingham
Northorpe
Donington
GRANTHAM
Bridge End
Braceby
Horbling
Walcot
Church End
Ropsley
Old Somerby
Birthorpe
Billingborough
Sapperton
Pickworth
Folkingham
Denton Res
Denton
Harlaxton
Little Ponton
Humby
Hanby
Roman Road
Pointon
Gosberton
Laughton
Boothby Pagnell
Ellys Manor House
Stroxton
Aslackby
Dowsby
West
Hungerton
Great Ponton
Scotland
Lenton
Risegate
Ingoldsby
Wyville
Graby
Gosberton Clough
Bassingthorpe
Keisby
Bitchfield
Westby
Rippingale
Hawthorpe
Stoke Rochford
Easton
Irnham
Dunsby
Kirkby Underwood
Bulby
Cross
Saltby
Skillington
Dunsby Fen
Burton Coggles
Corby Glen
Hacconby
Pinchbeck Bars
Woolsthorpe by Colsterworth
Woolsthorpe Manor (NT)
Stainfield
Sproxton
Elsthorpe
Hanthorpe
Morton
Morton Fen
West
SPALDING
Colsterworth
Birkholme
Swayfield
Buckminster
Stainby
Grimsthorpe
Guthram Gowt
Pode Hole
North Witham
Swinstead
Cawthorpe
Dyke
Grimsthorpe Castle
Edenham
Sewstern
Gunby
Bourne North Fen
Little London
Scottlethorpe
Twenty
South Witham
Creeton
Bourne
Cuckoo Bridge
Eastgate
161
Cribbs Meadow NNR
Castle Bytham
Lound
Thistleton
Little Bytham
Northorpe
Toft
Market Overton
Clipsham
Careby
Witham on the Hill
Thurlby
Deeping Fen
Baston Common
North Drove Drain
Teigh
Stretton
Manthorpe
Deeping

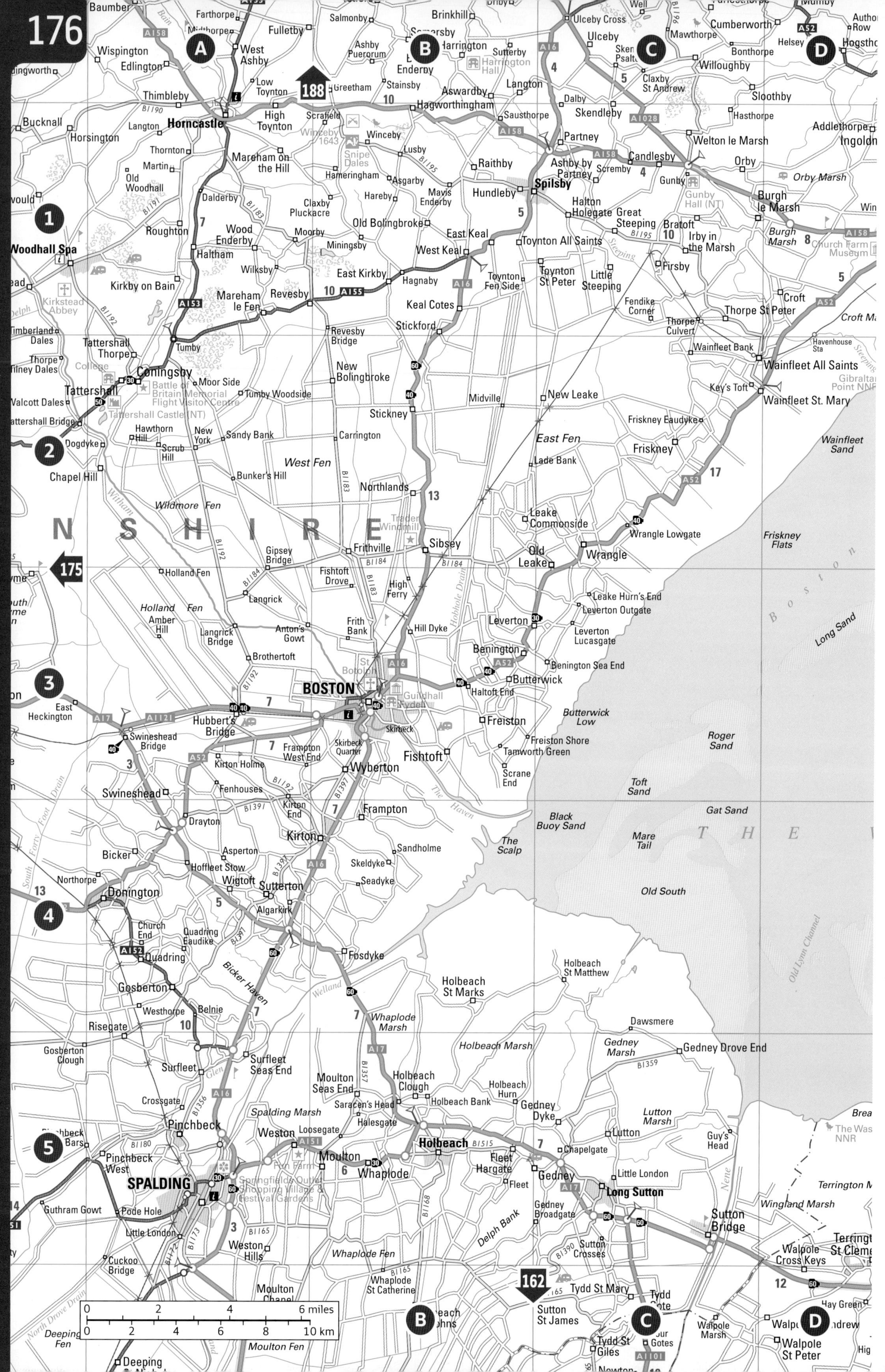
A
B
C
D
188
175
162
1
2
3
4
5
Baumber
Farthorpe
Midthorpe
Fulletby
Salmonby
Brinkhill
Somersby
Harrington
Ulceby Cross
Ulceby
Cumberworth
Mawthorpe
Bonthorpe
Willoughby
Helsey
Hogsthorpe
Wispington
Edlington
West Ashby
Ashby Puerorum
Bag Enderby
Harrington Hall
Skendleby Psalter
Claxby St Andrew
Sloothby
Hasthorpe
Low Toynton
Greetham
Stainsby
Aswardby
Langton
Dalby
Thimbleby
High Toynton
Scrafield
Hagworthingham
Sausthorpe
Skendleby
Bucknall
Horsington
Langton
Horncastle
Winceby 1643
Winceby
Partney
Welton le Marsh
Addlethorpe
Ingoldmells
Thornton
Martin
Old Woodhall
Mareham on the Hill
Snipe Dales
Lusby
Raithby
Ashby by Partney
Candlesby
Scremby
Gunby
Orby
Orby Marsh
Hameringham
Asgarby
Hundleby
Spilsby
Gunby Hall (NT)
Burgh le Marsh
Dalderby
Claxby Pluckacre
Hareby
Mavis Enderby
Halton Holegate
Great Steeping
Bratoft
Irby in the Marsh
Burgh Marsh
Church Farm Museum
Woodhall Spa
Roughton
Wood Enderby
Moorby
Old Bolingbroke
West Keal
East Keal
Toynton All Saints
Haltham
Miningsby
Toynton St Peter
Little Steeping
Firsby
Wilksby
East Kirkby
Hagnaby
Toynton Fen Side
Kirkby on Bain
Kirkstead Abbey
Mareham le Fen
Revesby
Keal Cotes
Fendike Corner
Croft
Thorpe St Peter
Thorpe Culvert
Croft Marsh
Stickford
Timberland Dales
Tattershall Thorpe
Tumby
Revesby Bridge
Wainfleet Bank
Havenhouse Sta
Thorpe Tilney Dales
College
Coningsby
Moor Side
New Bolingbroke
Wainfleet All Saints
Tattershall
Battle of Britain Memorial Flight Visitor Centre
Tumby Woodside
Key's Toft
Gibraltar Point NNR
Walcott Dales
Midville
New Leake
Wainfleet St. Mary
Tattershall Bridge
Tattershall Castle (NT)
Stickney
Friskney Eaudyke
Hawthorn Hill
New York
Sandy Bank
Carrington
East Fen
Dogdyke
Scrub Hill
Wainfleet Sand
Friskney
Lade Bank
Chapel Hill
West Fen
Bunker's Hill
Northlands
Wildmore Fen
Leake Commonside
Trader Windmill
Wrangle Lowgate
Friskney Flats
Sibsey
Frithville
Gipsey Bridge
Old Leake
Wrangle
Holland Fen
Fishtoft Drove
High Ferry
Langrick
Leake Hurn's End
Leverton Outgate
Holland Fen
Amber Hill
Langrick Bridge
Anton's Gowt
Frith Bank
Hill Dyke
Leverton
Leverton Lucasgate
Long Sand
Brothertoft
St Botolph
Benington
Benington Sea End
Butterwick
BOSTON
Guildhall
Haltoft End
East Heckington
Hubbert's Bridge
Freiston
Butterwick Low
Swineshead Bridge
Skirbeck
Frampton West End
Skirbeck Quarter
Freiston Shore
Tamworth Green
Roger Sand
Fishtoft
Kirton Holme
Wyberton
Scrane End
Swineshead
Fenhouses
Toft Sand
Kirton End
Frampton
Gat Sand
Drayton
Black Buoy Sand
Kirton
Mare Tail
The Scalp
Bicker
Asperton
Sandholme
Hoffleet Stow
Skeldyke
Northorpe
Donington
Wigtoft
Sutterton
Seadyke
Old South
Algarkirk
Church End
Quadring Eaudike
Quadring
Fosdyke
Holbeach St Matthew
Gosberton
Bicker Haven
Holbeach St Marks
Westhorpe
Belnie
Whaplode Marsh
Dawsmere
Risegate
Gosberton Clough
Surfleet Seas End
Holbeach Marsh
Gedney Marsh
Gedney Drove End
Surfleet
Moulton Seas End
Holbeach Clough
Crossgate
Holbeach Hurn
Saracen's Head
Holbeach Bank
Gedney Dyke
Lutton Marsh
Spalding Marsh
Pinchbeck
Loosegate
Weston
Halesgate
Lutton
Guy's Head
The Wash NNR
Pinchbeck Bars
Holbeach
Chapelgate
Moulton
Fleet Hargate
Pinchbeck West
Fen Farm
Whaplode
Gedney
Little London
SPALDING
Springfields Outlet Shopping Village & Festival Gardens
Fleet
Long Sutton
Terrington Marsh
Wingland Marsh
Guthram Gowt
Pode Hole
Gedney Broadgate
Sutton Bridge
Little London
Delph Bank
Weston Hills
Sutton Crosses
Walpole Cross Keys
Terrington St Clement
Cuckoo Bridge
Whaplode Fen
Whaplode St Catherine
Tydd St Mary
Tydd Gote
Moulton Chapel
Sutton St James
Hay Green
Deeping Fen
Moulton Fen
Tydd St Giles
Four Gotes
Walpole Marsh
Walpole St Peter
Deeping
Newton
Witham
The Haven
Welland
Nene
Old Lynn Channel
North Drove Drain
South Forty Foot Drain
Hobhole Drain
Steeping
Glen
Delph
N S H I R E
T H E W
B o s t o n
A158
A16
A153
A155
A52
A1028
A17
A1121
A152
A151
A1101
B1190
B1191
B1183
B1195
B1192
B1184
B1397
B1391
B1357
B1356
B1180
B1165
B1172
B1173
B1168
B1515
B1359
B1390
0 2 4 6 miles
0 2 4 6 8 10 km

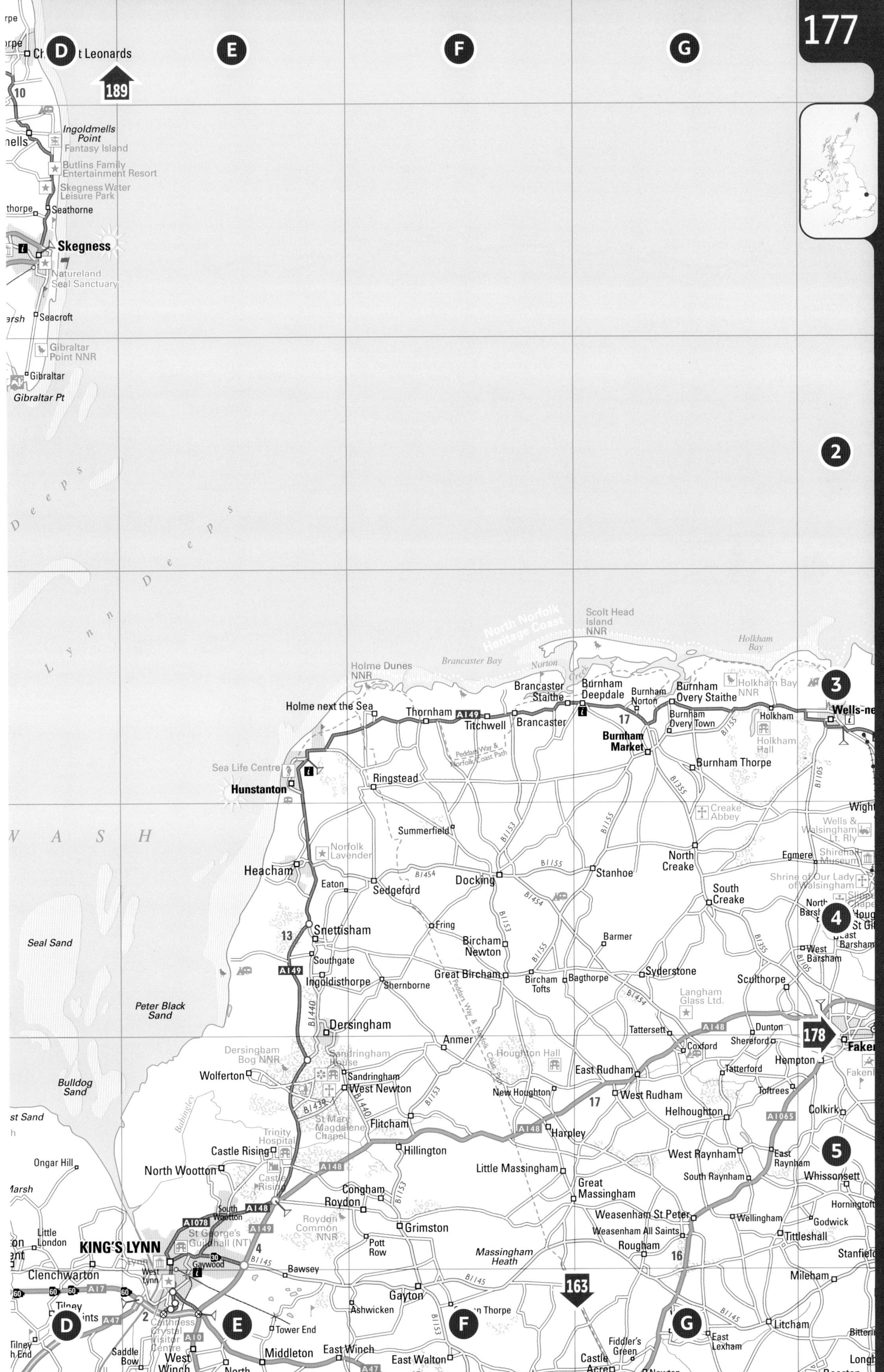

D t Leonards
E
F
G

189

10

Ingoldmells Point
Fantasy Island
Butlins Family Entertainment Resort
Skegness Water Leisure Park
thorpe   Seathorne
nells

Skegness
Natureland Seal Sanctuary

rsh   Seacroft

Gibraltar Point NNR

Gibraltar
Gibraltar Pt

2

D   e   e   p   s

L   y   n   n   D   e   e   p   s

North Norfolk Heritage Coast

Scolt Head Island NNR

Holkham Bay

3

Holme Dunes NNR
Brancaster Bay   *Norton*   Wells-ne

Holme next the Sea
Thornham   A149
Titchwell   Brancaster
Brancaster Staithe
Burnham Deepdale
Burnham Norton
Burnham Overy Staithe
Burnham Overy Town
Holkham
Holkham Bay NNR
Holkham Hall

Sea Life Centre

Hunstanton
Ringstead

17

Burnham Market
Burnham Thorpe

B1355

W A S H
N

Creake Abbey

Wight

Summerfield

B1153

Wells & Walsingham Lt. Rly
Egmere   Shireha Museum

Norfolk Lavender

Heacham
Eaton
Sedgeford
B1454
Docking
B1153
Stanhoe
B1155
North Creake
South Creake
Shrine of Our Lady of Walsingham

North Barsh   Houg St Gi

4

East Barsham

13

Snettisham
Southgate
A149
Ingoldisthorpe
Shernborne

Fring
B1153
Bircham Newton
Great Bircham
Bircham Tofts
Bagthorpe
B1454
Barmer
Syderstone
B1355
Sculthorpe
West Barsham
B1105

Langham Glass Ltd.

Peter Black Sand

B1440
Dersingham
Anmer
Houghton Hall
Tattersett
A148
Coxford
Shereford
Dunton
Hempton
178   Fake

Seal Sand

Dersingham Bog NNR
Sandringham House
Sandringham
West Newton
B1153
New Houghton
East Rudham
17   West Rudham
Helhoughton
Tatterford
Toftrees
Fakenh

Bulldog Sand

Wolferton
St Mary Magdalene Chapel
Flitcham
B1440
Harpley
A148
A1065
Colkirk

t Sand

Trinity Hospital
Castle Rising
Hillington
Little Massingham
West Raynham
East Raynham
5
Whissonsett

Marsh

North Wootton
Castle Rising
A148
Congham
Roydon
Grimston
Little Massingham
Great Massingham
South Raynham

Horningtoft
Godwick
Tittleshall
Stanfiel

Ongar Hill

Little London

KING'S LYNN
St George's Guildhall (NT)
A1078   A148
South Wootton
A149
4
B1145
Gaywood
Bawsey
Pott Row
Roydon Common NNR
n Thorpe
Massingham Heath
Weasenham St Peter
Weasenham All Saints
Rougham
16

Clenchwarton
West lynn
Caithness Crystal Visitor Centre
A47   2
A10
Tower End
Gayton
B1145
Ashwicken
163
Mileham

Tilney
ints
60   60   A17   60
Saddle Bow
West Winch
Middleton
East Winch
East Walton
Fiddler's Green
Castle Acre
Litcham
Bitterin
Longh

h End
ton
t

Clenchwarton
North
A47
Newton
Beeston

D
E
F
G

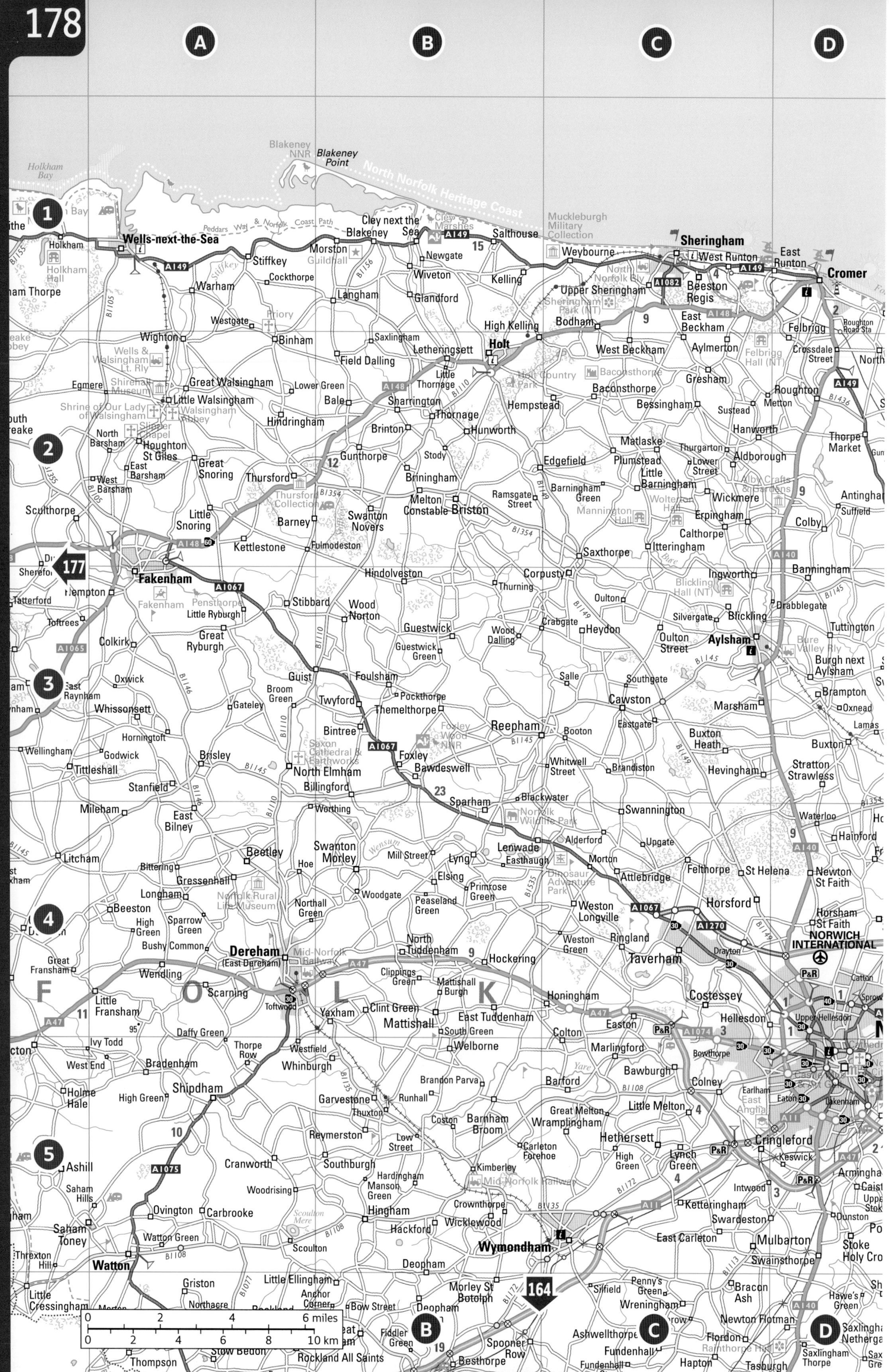
A
B
C
D
1
2
3
4
5
Holkham Bay
Blakeney NNR
Blakeney Point
North Norfolk Heritage Coast
Peddars Way & Norfolk Coast Path
Wells-next-the-Sea
Holkham
Holkham Hall
Stiffkey
Morston
Blakeney
Cley next the Sea
Cley Marshes
Salthouse
Muckleburgh Military Collection
Weybourne
Sheringham
West Runton
East Runton
Cromer
Warham
Cockthorpe
Langham
Wiveton
Glandford
Newgate
Kelling
Upper Sheringham
Sheringham Park (NT)
Beeston Regis
North Norfolk Rly
Binham
Priory
Westgate
Wighton
Wells & Walsingham Lt. Rly
Saxlingham
Field Dalling
Letheringsett
Holt
High Kelling
Bodham
West Beckham
East Beckham
Aylmerton
Felbrigg
Felbrigg Hall (NT)
Crossdale Street
Roughton Road Sta
Egmere
Shirehall Museum
Great Walsingham
Little Walsingham
Shrine of Our Lady of Walsingham
Walsingham Abbey
Slipper Chapel
Lower Green
Bale
Little Thornage
Sharrington
Thornage
Holt Country Park
Hempstead
Baconsthorpe
Bessingham
Gresham
Sustead
Metton
Roughton
Hindringham
Brinton
Hunworth
Stody
North Barsham
Houghton St Giles
East Barsham
West Barsham
Great Snoring
Thursford
Thursford Collection
Gunthorpe
Briningham
Edgefield
Matlaske
Plumstead
Little Barningham
Barningham Green
Thurgarton
Lower Street
Aldborough
Hanworth
Thorpe Market
Alby Crafts & Gardens
Wickmere
Antingham
Suffield
Melton Constable
Briston
Ramsgate Street
Swanton Novers
Barney
Mannington Hall
Wolterton Hall
Erpingham
Calthorpe
Colby
Sculthorpe
Little Snoring
Kettlestone
Fulmodeston
Saxthorpe
Itteringham
Banningham
Fakenham
Hempton
Tatterford
Toftrees
Hindolveston
Corpusty
Thurning
Ingworth
Blickling Hall (NT)
Oulton
Drabblegate
Stibbard
Pensthorpe
Little Ryburgh
Great Ryburgh
Wood Norton
Guestwick
Guestwick Green
Wood Dalling
Crabgate
Heydon
Oulton Street
Silvergate
Blickling
Aylsham
Bure Valley Rly
Tuttington
Burgh next Aylsham
Colkirk
Oxwick
East Raynham
Whissonsett
Guist
Foulsham
Broom Green
Gateley
Twyford
Pockthorpe
Themelthorpe
Salle
Southgate
Cawston
Eastgate
Brampton
Oxnead
Marsham
Lamas
Horningtoft
Godwick
Wellingham
Tittleshall
Brisley
Bintree
Saxon Cathedral & Earthworks
Foxley Wood NNR
Foxley
Bawdeswell
Reepham
Booton
Whitwell Street
Brandiston
Buxton Heath
Hevingham
Buxton
Stratton Strawless
Stanfield
North Elmham
Billingford
Worthing
Sparham
Blackwater
Norfolk Wildlife Park
Swannington
Waterloo
Hainford
Mileham
East Bilney
Beetley
Swanton Morley
Hoe
Mill Street
Lyng
Lenwade
Easthaugh
Alderford
Upgate
Litcham
Bittering
Gressenhall
Norfolk Rural Life Museum
Elsing
Primrose Green
Dinosaur Adventure Park
Morton
Attlebridge
Felthorpe
St Helena
Newton St Faith
Longham
Beeston
High Green
Sparrow Green
Bushy Common
Northall Green
Woodgate
Peaseland Green
Weston Longville
Horsford
Horsham St Faith
NORWICH INTERNATIONAL
Great Fransham
Dereham (East Dereham)
Mid-Norfolk Railway
North Tuddenham
Hockering
Weston Green
Ringland
Taverham
Drayton
Catton
Wendling
Scarning
Clippings Green
Mattishall Burgh
Little Fransham
Toftwood
Yaxham
Clint Green
Mattishall
East Tuddenham
Honingham
Costessey
Easton
Hellesdon
Upper Hellesdon
Sprowston
Ivy Todd
Daffy Green
South Green
Welborne
Colton
Marlingford
Bowthorpe
West End
Bradenham
Thorpe Row
Westfield
Whinburgh
Bawburgh
Holme Hale
High Green
Shipdham
Brandon Parva
Runhall
Barford
Colney
Earlham
East Anglia
Eaton
Lakenham
Garvestone
Thuxton
Coston
Barnham Broom
Great Melton
Wramplingham
Little Melton
Reymerston
Low Street
Carleton Forehoe
Hethersett
Cringleford
Ashill
Cranworth
Southburgh
Hardingham
Manson Green
Kimberley
High Green
Lynch Green
Keswick
Arminghall
Caistor
Saham Hills
Woodrising
Scoulton Mere
Crownthorpe
Intwood
Ketteringham
Ovington
Carbrooke
Hingham
Wicklewood
Swardeston
Dunston
Saham Toney
Watton Green
Hackford
Scoulton
Wymondham
East Carleton
Mulbarton
Stoke Holy Cross
Threxton Hill
Watton
Deopham
Swainsthorpe
Griston
Little Ellingham
Morley St Botolph
Silfield
Penny's Green
Bracon Ash
Hawe's Green
Little Cressingham
Northacre
Anchor Corner
Bow Street
Deopham Green
Wreningham
Newton Flotman
Saxlingham Nethergate
Fiddler Green
Ashwellthorpe
Flordon
Fundenhall
Rainthorpe Hall
Saxlingham Thorpe
Stow Bedon
Thompson
Rockland All Saints
Spooner Row
Besthorpe
Fundenhall Street
Hapton
Tasburgh
Fen
177
164
F
O
L
K
A149
A148
A1067
A1065
A1082
A140
A47
A1074
A1270
A11
A1075
B1105
B1156
B1110
B1354
B1149
B1145
B1146
B1135
B1108
B1172
B1113
B1436
B1535
0 2 4 6 miles
0 2 4 6 8 10 km

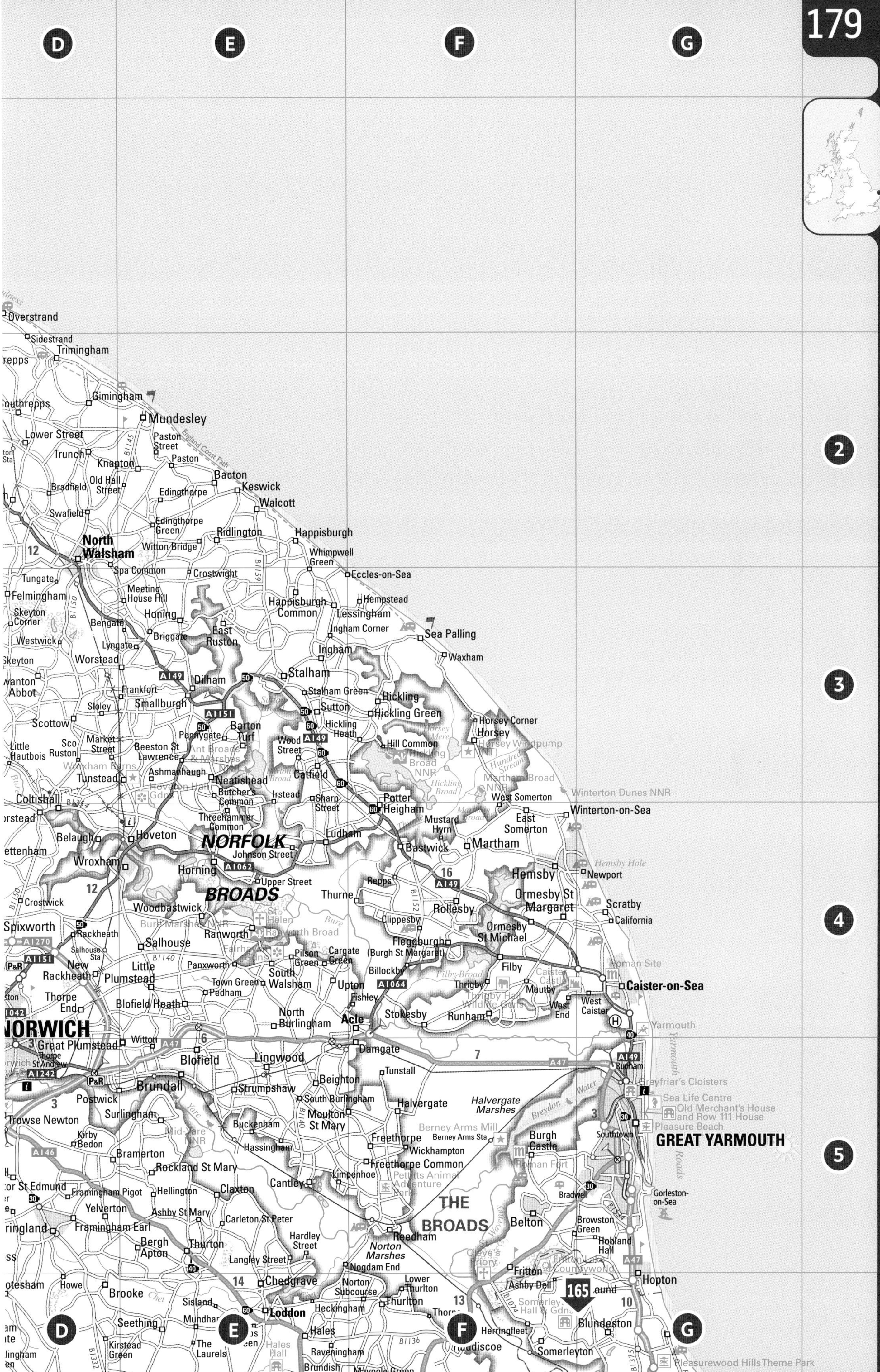

D
E
F
G
2
3
4
5
Overstrand
Sidestrand
Trimingham
Southrepps
Gimingham
Mundesley
Lower Street
Paston Street
Trunch
Knapton
Paston
England Coast Path
Bacton
Old Hall Street
Bradfield
Edingthorpe
Keswick
Walcott
Swafield
Edingthorpe Green
Ridlington
Happisburgh
North Walsham
Witton Bridge
Whimpwell Green
Tungate
Spa Common
Crostwight
Eccles-on-Sea
Felmingham
Meeting House Hill
Happisburgh Common
Hempstead
Skeyton Corner
Honing
Lessingham
Bengate
East Ruston
Ingham Corner
Westwick
Briggate
Sea Palling
Lyngate
Ingham
Waxham
Worstead
Stalham
Dilham
Frankfort
Stalham Green
Hickling
Sloley
Smallburgh
Sutton
Hickling Green
Scottow
Barton Turf
Hickling Heath
Horsey Corner
Pennygate
Horsey
Market Street
Wood Street
Hill Common
Horsey Windpump
Little Hautbois
Sco Ruston
Beeston St Lawrence
Ant Broads & Marshes NNR
Hickling Broad NNR
Wroxham Barns
Tunstead
Ashmanhaugh
Catfield
Martham Broad NNR
Winterton Dunes NNR
Hoveton Hall Gdns
Neatishead
Butcher's Common
Irstead
Sharp Street
Potter Heigham
West Somerton
Winterton-on-Sea
Coltishall
Threehammer Common
East Somerton
Mustard Hyrn
Belaugh
Hoveton
NORFOLK
Ludham
Martham
Wroxham
Johnson Street
Bastwick
Hemsby Hole
Horning
Hemsby
Newport
Upper Street
Repps
BROADS
Thurne
Ormesby St Margaret
Scratby
Crostwick
Rollesby
California
Woodbastwick
Spixworth
Bure Marshes NNR
Clippesby
Ormesby St Michael
Rackheath
Ranworth
Ranworth Broad
Salhouse
Fleggburgh (Burgh St Margaret)
Salhouse Sta
Pilson Green
Cargate Green
Filby
Roman Site
New Rackheath
Little Plumstead
Panxworth
South Walsham
Billockby
Thrigby
Caister Castle
Caister-on-Sea
Town Green
Upton
Mautby
Thorpe End
Pedham
Fishley
Thrigby Hall Wildlife Gdns
West Caister
Blofield Heath
North Burlingham
Stokesby
Runham
West End
NORWICH
Acle
Yarmouth
Great Plumstead
Witton
Damgate
Blofield
Lingwood
Runham
Thorpe St Andrew
Tunstall
Greyfriar's Cloisters
Brundall
Beighton
Strumpshaw
Postwick
South Burlingham
Halvergate
Halvergate Marshes
Sea Life Centre
Surlingham
Moulton St Mary
Breydon Water
Old Merchant's House and Row 111 House
Trowse Newton
Buckenham
Berney Arms Mill
Pleasure Beach
Kirby Bedon
Mid-Yare NNR
Berney Arms Sta
Southtown
GREAT YARMOUTH
Hassingham
Freethorpe
Burgh Castle
Wickhampton
Bramerton
Rockland St Mary
Freethorpe Common
Roman Fort
Cantley
Limpenhoe
Pettitts Animal Adventure Park
Framingham Pigot
Hellington
Claxton
Bradwell
Gorleston-on-Sea
Yelverton
THE BROADS
Ashby St Mary
Carleton St Peter
Belton
Browston Green
Framingham Earl
Hardley Street
Reedham
Hobland Hall
Bergh Apton
Thurton
Norton Marshes
Langley Street
Nogdam End
Fritton
Fritton Lake Countryworld
Howe
Chedgrave
Norton Subcourse
Lower Thurlton
Ashby Dell
Hopton
Brooke
Sisland
Thurlton
Somerleyton Hall & Gdns
Mundham
Loddon
Heckingham
Thorpe
Seething
Hales
Herringfleet
Blundeston
Kirstead Green
The Laurels
Hales Hall
Haddiscoe
Ravingham
Somerleyton
Brundish
Maypole Green
Pleasurewood Hills Theme Park
165
A149
A1151
A1062
A1064
A1270
A1242
A1042
A47
A146
B1150
B1145
B1159
B1152
B1140
B1332
B1136
B1074
B1375

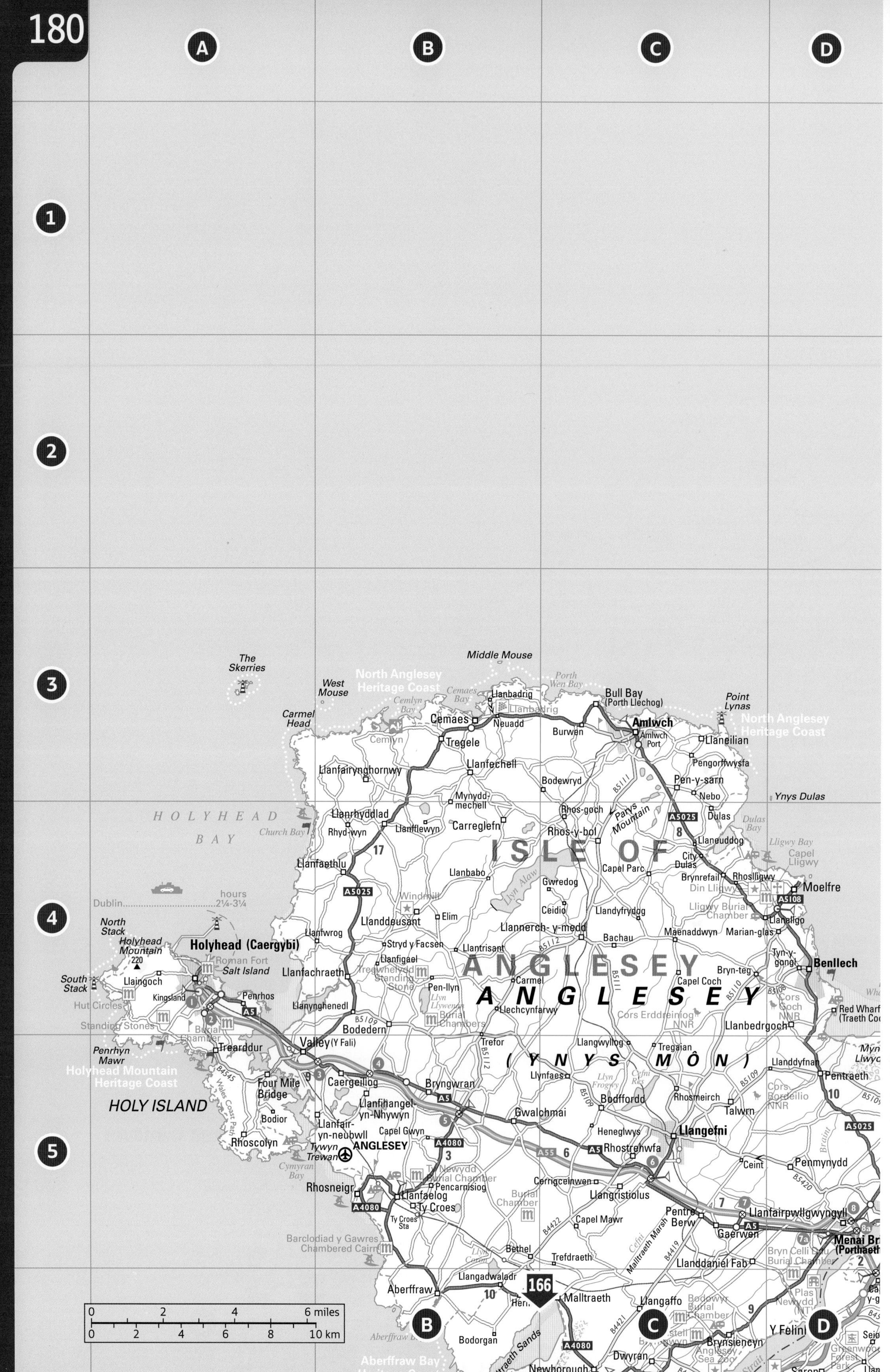

A **B** **C** **D**

1

2

The Skerries

Middle Mouse

3

West
Mouse

North Anglesey
Heritage Coast

Cemaes
Bay

Porth
Wen Bay

Bull Bay
(Porth Llechog)

Point
Lynas

Carmel
Head

Cemlyn
Bay

Llanbadrig

Amlwch

North Anglesey
Heritage Coast

Cemlyn

Cemaes

Neuadd

Amlwch
Port

Llaneilian

Tregele

Burwen

Llanfairynghornwy

Llanfechell

Bodewryd

Pengorffwysfa

Pen-y-sarn

HOLYHEAD

BAY

Church Bay

Llanrhyddlad

Mynydd
mechell

Rhos-goch

Nebo

Ynys Dulas

Rhyd-wyn

Llanfflewyn

Carreglefn

Rhos-y-bol

Parys
Mountain

A5025

Dulas

Dulas
Bay

17

Llanfaethlu

Llanbabo

ISLE OF

City
Dulas

8

Llaneuddog

Lligwy Bay

Capel
Lligwy

A5025

Windmill

Gwredog

Capel Parc

Brynrefail

Rhoslligwy

Din Lligwy

Moelfre

Dublin........ hours
2¼-3¼

Llanddeusant

Elim

Ceidio

Llandyfrydog

Lligwy Burial
Chamber

Llanallgo

A5108

North
Stack

Holyhead
Mountain
220

Llanfwrog

Stryd y Facsen

Llannerch- y- medd

Bachau

Maenaddwyn

Marian-glas

Tyn-y-
gongl

Benllech

Holyhead (Caergybi)

Roman Fort
Salt Island

Llanfigael

Llanfachraeth

Treawhelyd
Standing
Stone

Pen-llyn

Llantrisant

ANGLESEY

Carmel

Bryn-teg

South
Stack

Llaingoch

Kingsland

Penrhos

A5

Llanynghenedl

Llyn
Llywenan
Burial
Chambers

Llechcynfarwy

ANGLESEY

Capel Coch

Cors
NNR

Red Wharf
(Traeth Coch)

Hut Circles

Standing Stones

Burial
Chamber

Bodedern

Trefor

Llangwyllog

Cors Erddreiniog
NNR

Llanbedrgoch

Penrhyn
Mawr

Holyhead Mountain
Heritage Coast

Trearddur

Valley (Y Fali)

(YNYS MÔN)

Llynfaes

Llyn
Frogwy

Cefni
Res

Cors
Bodeilio
NNR

Llanddyfnan

Pentraeth

Myn
Llwyd

HOLY ISLAND

Four Mile
Bridge

Caergeiliog

Bryngwran

Gwalchmai

Bodffordd

Rhosmeirch

Tregaian

10

B4545

Bodior

Llanfihangel-
yn-Nhywyn

A5

Heneglwys

A55

Talwrn

B5109

Rhoscolyn

Wales Coast Path

Capel Gwyn

Llangefni

A5025

Cymyran
Bay

Tywyn
Trewan

ANGLESEY

A4080

3

Rhostrehwfa

A5

6

Ceint

Penmynydd

Rhosneigr

Llanfaelog

Pencarnisiog

Cerrigceinwen

Llangristiolus

7

Llanfairpwllgwyngyll

8

A4080

Ty Croes

Burial
Chamber

Pentre
Berw

Gaerwen

Menai Br
(Porthaeth)

Ty Croes
Sta

Capel Mawr

Bryn Celli Ddu
Burial Chamber

Barclodiad y Gawres
Chambered Cairn

Bethel

Trefdraeth

Llanddaniel Fab

Plas
Newydd

Y Felin

Llangadwaladr

Aberffraw

10

166

Malltraeth

Llangaffo

Bodowyr
Burial
Chamber

9

Brynsiencyn

Anglesey
Sea Zoo

Sejo

Greenwood
Forest

Aberffraw
Bay

A4080

Bodorgan

Altraeth Sands

Newborough

Dwyran

Saron

0   2   4   6 miles

0 2 4 6 8 10 km

B **C** **D**

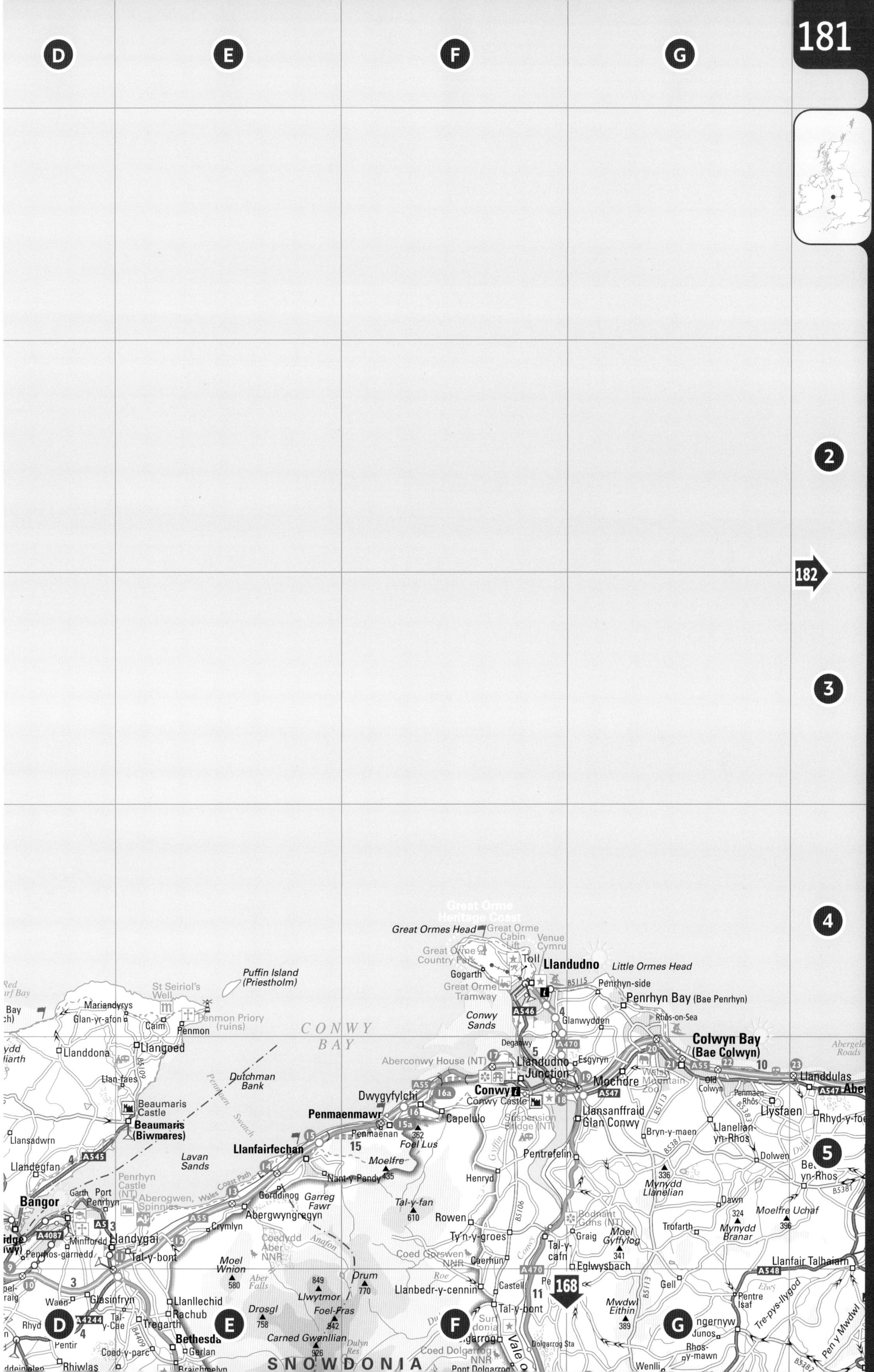
D
E
F
G
2
182
3
4
5
Great Orme Heritage Coast
Great Ormes Head
Great Orme Cabin Lift
Venue Cymru
Great Orme Country Park
Toll
Llandudno
Little Ormes Head
Gogarth
Great Orme Tramway
Penrhyn-side
Penrhyn Bay (Bae Penrhyn)
Rhos-on-Sea
Colwyn Bay (Bae Colwyn)
Glanwydden
Conwy Sands
Deganwy
Puffin Island (Priestholm)
St Seiriol's Well
Mariandyrys
Glan-yr-afon
Caim
Penmon
Penmon Priory (ruins)
CONWY BAY
Llanddona
Llangoed
Llan-faes
Dutchman Bank
Beaumaris Castle
Beaumaris (Biwmares)
Llansadwrn
Llandegfan
Lavan Sands
Aberconwy House (NT)
Llandudno Junction
Esgyryn
Mochdre
Welsh Mountain Zoo
Old Colwyn
Llanddulas
Abergele Roads
Dwygyfylchi
Conwy
Conwy Castle
Suspension Bridge (NT)
Capelulo
Penmaenmawr
Penmaenan
Foel Lus
Llanfairfechan
Moelfre
Nant-y-Pandy
Llansanffraid Glan Conwy
Bryn-y-maen
Llanelian-yn-Rhos
Penmaen-Rhôs
Llysfaen
Rhyd-y-foel
Pentrefelin
Henryd
Mynydd Llanelian
Dolwen
Bangor
Garth
Port Penrhyn
Penrhyn Castle (NT)
Aberogwen, Wales Coast Path
Spinnies
Gorddinog
Garreg Fawr
Abergwyngregyn
Tal-y-fan
Rowen
Crymlyn
Minffordd
Llandygai
Penrhos-garnedd
Tal-y-bont
Coedydd Aber NNR
Ty'n-y-groes
Bodnant Gdns (NT)
Graig
Moel Gyffylog
Tal-y-cafn
Eglwysbach
Trofarth
Dawn
Mynydd Branar
Moelfre Uchaf
Moel Wnion
Aber Falls
Llwytmor
Drum
Coed Gorswen NNR
Caerhun
Llanbedr-y-cennin
Castell
Gell
Llanfair Talhaiarn
Pentre Isaf
Tre-pys-llygod
Waen
Glasinfryn
Llanllechid
Rachub
Drosgl
Foel-Fras
Mwdwl Eithin
Tal-y-Cae
Tregarth
Bethesda
Carned Gwenllian
Dulyn Res
Rhyd
Pentir
Coed-y-parc
Gerlan
SNOWDONIA
Coed Dolgarrog NNR
Dolgarrog Sta
Pont Dolgarrog
Junos
Rhos-y-mawn
Wenlli
Pen y Mwdwl
168
A55
A545
A546
A547
A470
A548
A5
A4087
A4244
B5109
B5115
B5113
B5106
B5383
B5381
B4409
B5382

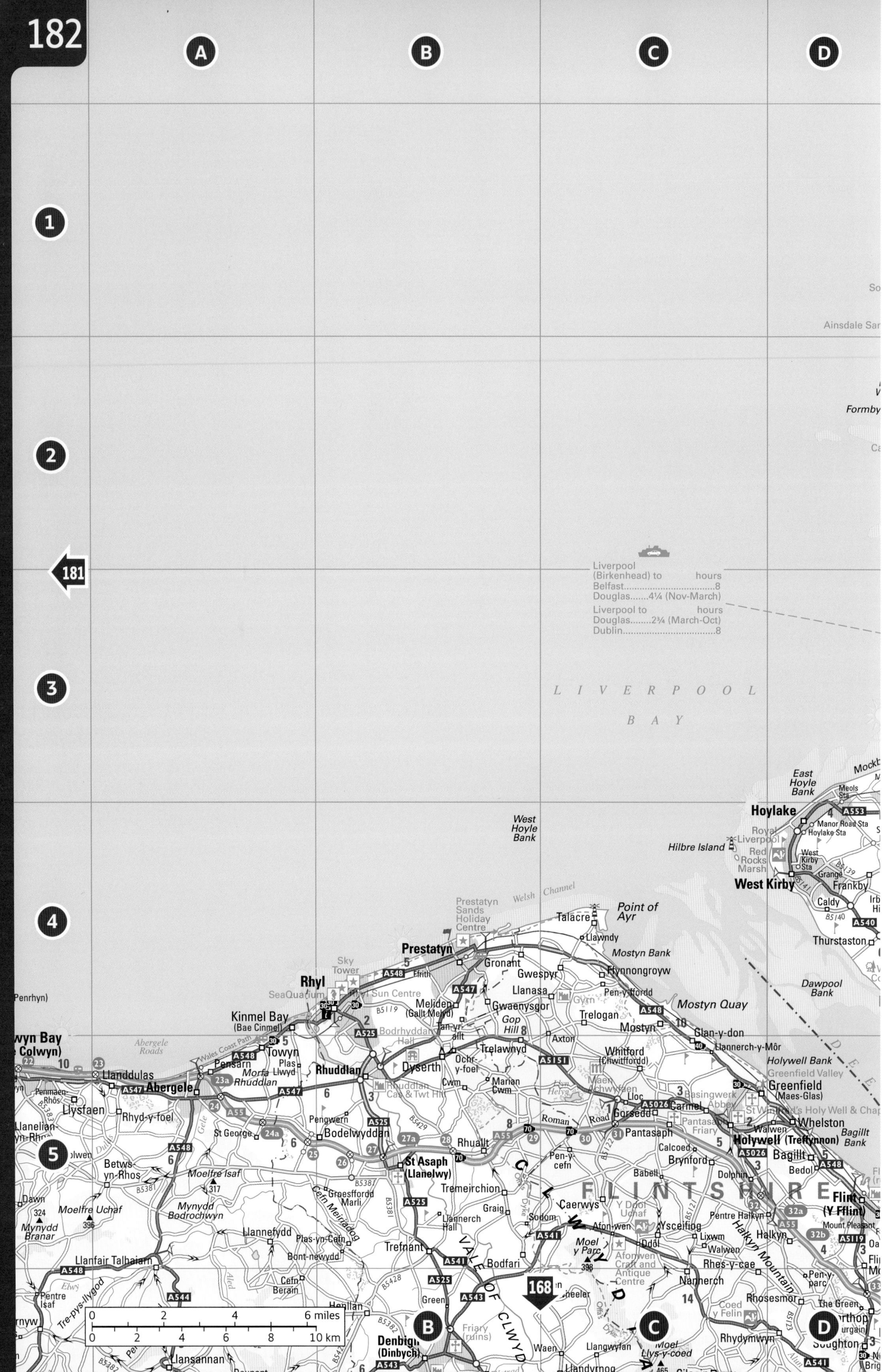

A   B   C   D

1

2

181

3

L I V E R P O O L

B A Y

Liverpool
(Birkenhead) to   hours
Belfast..8
Douglas.......4¼ (Nov-March)
Liverpool to   hours
Douglas........2¾ (March-Oct)
Dublin....................................8

East
Hoyle
Bank

Meols
Sta

West
Hoyle
Bank

A553

Hoylake

Manor Road Sta
Hoylake Sta

Royal
Liverpool

Hilbre Island

Red
Rocks
Marsh

West
Kirby
Sta

Grange
Frankby

West Kirby

Caldy

Irb
Hi

B5140

A540

Thurstaston

4

Welsh Channel

Dawpool
Bank

Prestatyn
Sands
Holiday
Centre

Talacre

Point of
Ayr

Llawndy

Mostyn Bank

Prestatyn

Sky
Tower

A548

Efrith

Gronant

Gwespyr

Flynnongroyw

Pen-y-ffordd

Mostyn Quay

Rhyl

SeaQuarium

Rhyl Sun Centre

B5119

A547

Meliden
(Gallt Melyd)

Llanasa

Gwaenysgor

Gyrn

Trelogan

Mostyn

A548

Glan-y-don

10

Kinmel Bay
(Bae Cinmel)

B5119

2

A525

Bodrhyddan
Hall

Gop
Hill 8

Axton

Whitford
(Chwitffordd)

40

Llannerch-y-Môr

wyn Bay
e Colwyn)

Abergele
Roads

Wales Coast Path

30

Towyn

Plas
Llwyd

5

Dyserth

Fan-y-
allt

Ochr-
y-foel

Trelawnyd

A5151

Maen
chwyfan

Lloc

Holywell Bank

Greenfield
(Maes-Glas)

22

10

23

Llanddulas

A548

Pensarn

Rhuddlan

6

Cwm

Marian
Cwm

Roman
Road

A5026

Basingwerk
Abbey

St Winifred's Holy Well & Chap

Penrhyn)

Abergele

A547

A55

Gele

Rhuddlan
Cas & Twt Hi

3

8

Gorsedd

Carmel

Pantasaph
Friary

2

Walwen

Whelston

Llysfaen

Rhyd-y-foel

St George

24

Pengwern

A525

B5429

Roman

70

Pantasaph

A5026

Holywell (Treffynnon)

Bagillt
Bank

Llanelian
n-Rhos

24a

Bodelwyddan

27

28

Rhuallt

A55

70

Pen-y-
cefn

30

31

Calcoed

Brynford

Dolphin

Bagillt

Bedol

A548

Betws
yn-Rhos

A548

6

St Asaph
(Llanelwy)

27a

70

Babell

Dawn

Moelfre Isaf

317

Tremeirchion

Graig

Sodom

Caerwys

Y Ddol
Uchaf

Ysceifiog

Pentre Halkyn

Flint
(Y Fflint)

32a

Moelfre Uchaf

396

Cefn Meiriadog

B5381

Llannerch
Hall

A525

Afon-wen

Moel
y Parc

Afonwen
Craft and
Antique
Centre

Lixwm

Walwen

Mount Pleasant

A55

32b

Mynydd
Branar

324

Llannefydd

Plas-yn-Cefn

Trefnant

Bodfari

A541

398

Rhes-y-cae

A5119

Oa

Halkyn
Mountain

Pen-y-
parc

Llanfair Talhaiarn

Bont-newydd

A541

Nannerch

14

Coed
y Felin

rthop
urgain

Pentre
Isaf

Elwy

Aled

Cefn
Berain

B5382

Henllan

A525

A543

Green

heeler

168

Coed
y Felin

Rhosesmor

The Green

Suughton

D

rnyw

A544

Tre-pys-llygod

0   2   4   6 miles
0   2   4   6   8   10 km

B5382

B

Denbigh
(Dinbych)

Friary
(ruins)

VALE OF CLWYD

Waen

Llangwyfan

C

Moel
Llys-y-coed

Rhydymwyn

A541

llansannan

A543

Llandyrnog

FLINTSHIRE

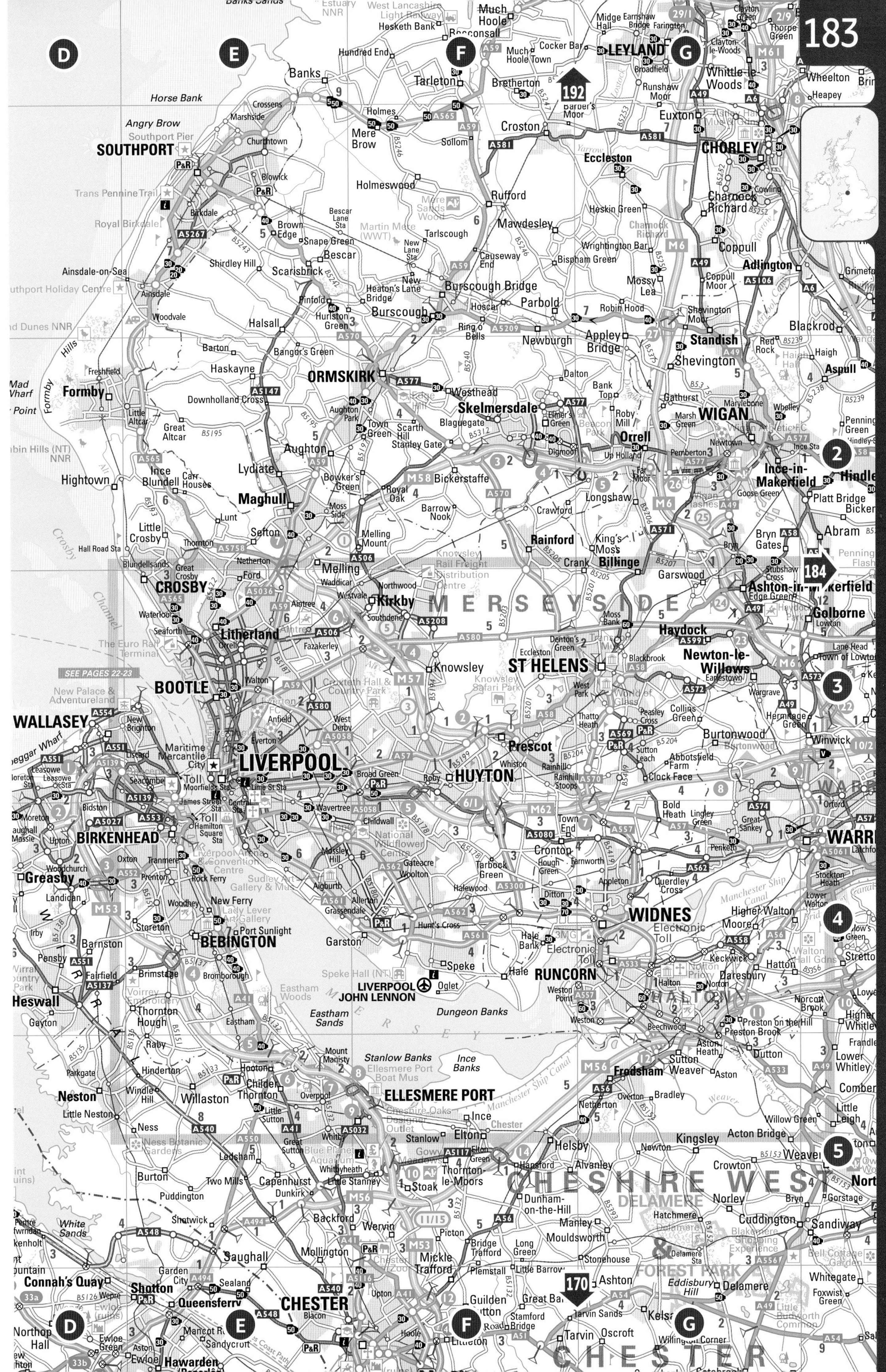
SOUTHPORT
Formby
CROSBY
BOOTLE
Litherland
Maghull
ORMSKIRK
Skelmersdale
WIGAN
CHORLEY
LEYLAND
Standish
Orrell
ST HELENS
Haydock
Newton-le-Willows
Ashton-in-Makerfield
Golborne
Kirkby
Prescot
HUYTON
LIVERPOOL
WALLASEY
BIRKENHEAD
BEBINGTON
Heswall
Neston
ELLESMERE PORT
WIDNES
RUNCORN
Fredsham
CHESTER
Connah's Quay
Shotton
Queensferry
Hawarden
MERSEYSIDE
CHESHIRE WEST
DELAMERE
FOREST PARK
HALTON
LIVERPOOL JOHN LENNON
Tarleton
Croston
Eccleston
Burscough Bridge
Scarisbrick
Rainford
Billinge
Knowsley
Rufford
Mawdesley
Adlington
Abram
Ince-in-Makerfield
Coppull
Euxton
Speke
Garston
Hale
Helsby
Frodsham
Kingsley
Norley
Cuddington
Sandiway
Tarvin
Kelsall
Delamere
192
184
170
SEE PAGES 22-23

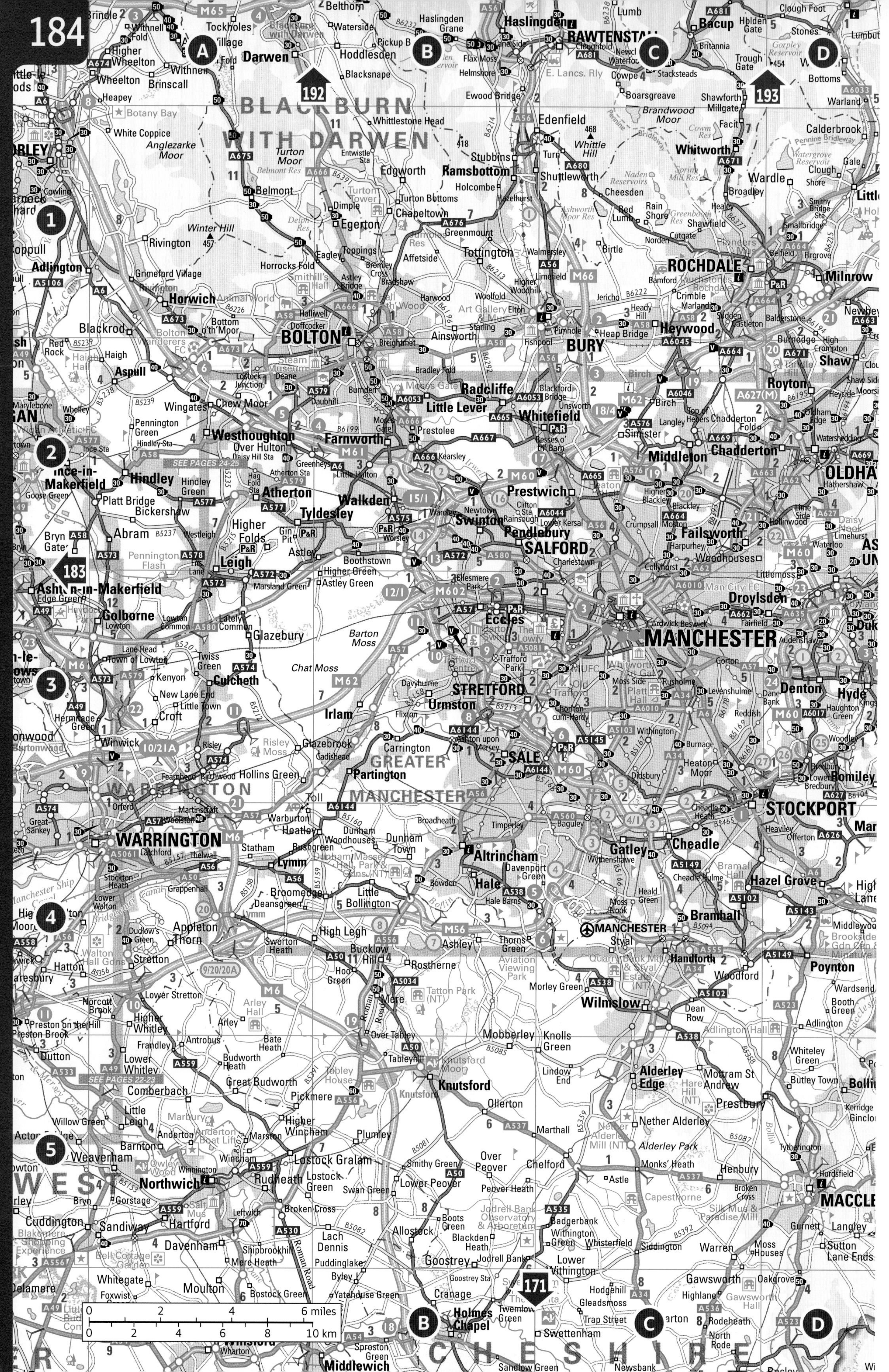

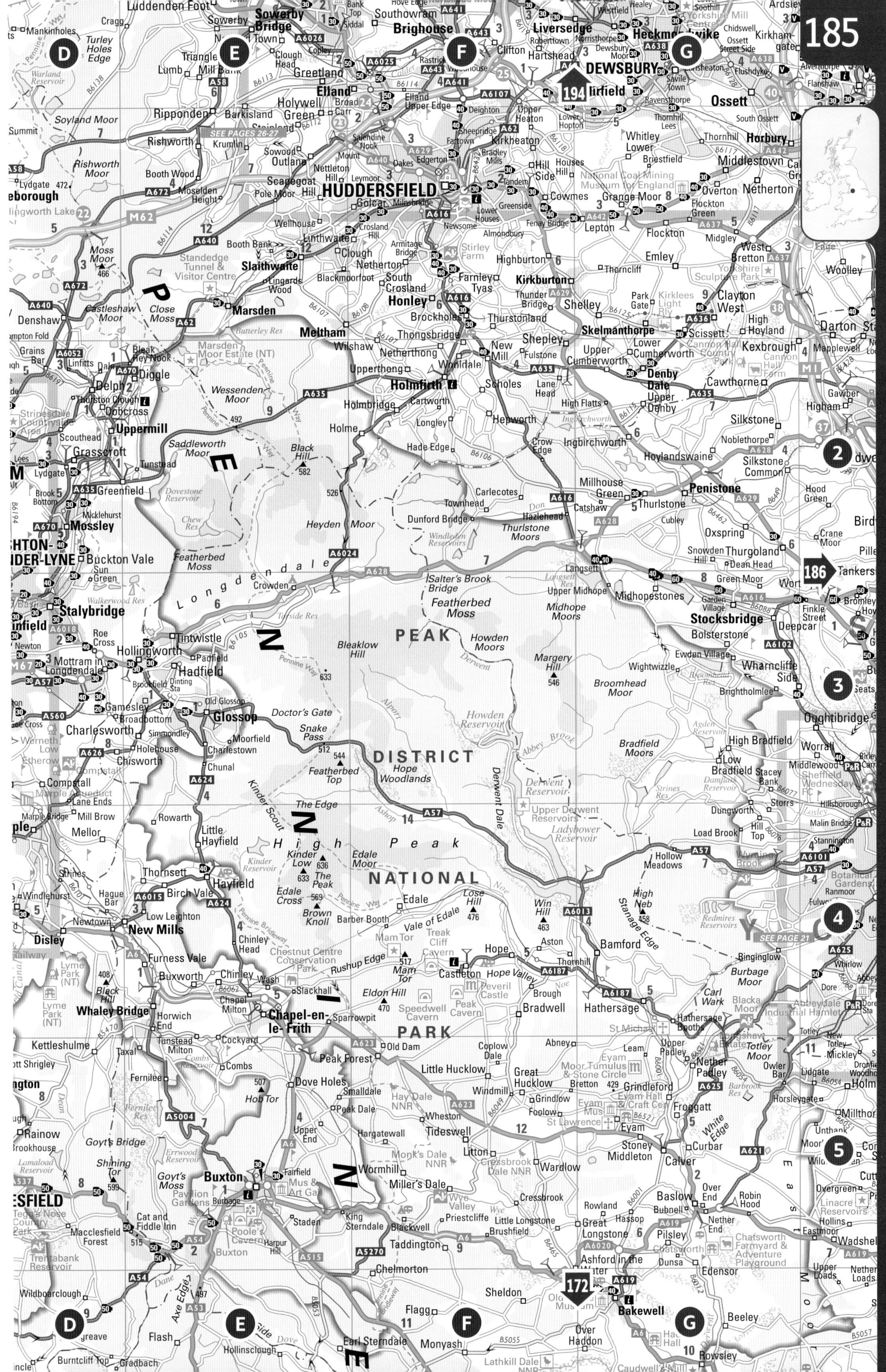

Luddenden Foot
Sowerby Bridge
Southowram
Brighouse
Liversedge
Heckmondwike
Mankinholes
Turley Holes Edge
Triangle
Mill Bank
Lumb
Greetland
Elland
Clifton
Hartshead
DEWSBURY
Ossett
Soyland Moor
Ripponden
Barkisland
Holywell Green
SEE PAGES 26-27
Rishworth
Krumlin
Rishworth Moor
Booth Wood
Sowood
Outlane
Kirkheaton
Whitley Lower
Thornhill
Horbury
Middlestown
Lydgate
Moselden Height
Scapegoat Hill
HUDDERSFIELD
Golcar
Milnsbridge
National Coal Mining Museum for England
Grange Moor
Overton
Netherton
Lepton
Flockton
Flockton Green
Almondbury
Fenay Bridge
Midgley
M62
Moss Moor
Standedge Tunnel & Visitor Centre
Booth Bank
Slaithwaite
Linthwaite
Netherton
Stirley Farm
Highburton
Emley
West Bretton
Woolley
Yorkshire Sculpture Park
Denshaw
Castleshaw Moor
Close Moss
Marsden
Farnley Tyas
Kirkburton
Thurstonland
Shelley
Clayton West
Skelmanthorpe
Scissett
High Hoyland
Darton
Meltham
Marsden Moor Estate (NT)
Wilshaw
Netherthong
Honley
Brockholes
Thongsbridge
Shepley
Upper Cumberworth
Kexbrough
Mapplewell
Delph
Diggle
Wessenden Moor
Holmfirth
New Mill
Scholes
Denby Dale
Cawthorne
Dobcross
Uppermill
Holmbridge
Cartworth
Hepworth
Upper Denby
Silkstone
Higham
Holme
Saddleworth Moor
Black Hill
Hade Edge
Ingbirchworth
Hoylandswaine
Silkstone Common
Greenfield
Mossley
Dovestone Reservoir
Chew Res
Carlecotes
Millhouse Green
Penistone
Thurlstone
Townhead
Dunford Bridge
Hazlehead
Catshaw
Heyden Moor
Thurlstone Moors
Cubley
Oxspring
Thurgoland
Crane Moor
Buckton Vale
Featherbed Moss
Longdendale
Crowden
Salter's Brook Bridge
Langsett
Upper Midhope
Midhopestones
Green Moor
Stocksbridge
Deepcar
Stalybridge
Featherbed Moss
Midhope Moors
Bolsterstone
Tintwistle
Hollingworth
PEAK
Bleaklow Hill
Howden Moors
Margery Hill
Ewden Village
Wharncliffe Side
Mottram in Longdendale
Hadfield
Wightwizzle
Broomhead Moor
Brightholmlee
Gamesley
Glossop
Doctor's Gate
Snake Pass
Howden Reservoir
Oughtibridge
Charlesworth
Moorfield
Charlestown
DISTRICT
Bradfield Moors
High Bradfield
Worrall
Chisworth
Featherbed Top
Hope Woodlands
Low Bradfield
Compstall
Chunal
Derwent Reservoir
Dungworth
Mellor
Rowarth
The Edge
Kinder Scout
Upper Derwent Reservoirs
Ladybower Reservoir
Little Hayfield
High Peak
Load Brook
Hill Top
Kinder Low
Edale Moor
Hollow Meadows
Thornsett
Hayfield
Edale Cross
The Peak
NATIONAL
Birch Vale
Brown Knoll
Edale
Lose Hill
Win Hill
High Neb
Stanage Edge
Disley
New Mills
Low Leighton
Barber Booth
Vale of Edale
Mam Tor
Treak Cliff Cavern
Hope
Aston
Bamford
Redmires Reservoirs
SEE PAGE 21
Chinley Head
Furness Vale
Chestnut Centre Conservation Park
Rushup Edge
Castleton
Hope Valley
Thornhill
Ringinglow
Burbage Moor
Lyme Park (NT)
Black Hill
Buxworth
Chinley
Peveril Castle
Brough
Carl Wark
Whaley Bridge
Chapel Milton
Chapel-en-le-Frith
Sparrowpit
Speedwell Cavern
Peak Cavern
Eldon Hill
Bradwell
Hathersage
Hathersage Booths
PARK
Kettleshulme
Taxal
Tunstead Milton
Cockyard
Combs
Old Dam
Peak Forest
Coplow Dale
Abney
Little Hucklow
Great Hucklow
Bretton
Upper Padley
Nether Padley
Totley Moor
Fernilee
Hob Tor
Dove Holes
Hay Dale NNR
Windmill
Grindlow
Foolow
Eyam
Grindleford
Eyam Hall & Craft Centre
Froggatt
White Edge
Rainow
Goyt's Bridge
Upper End
Peak Dale
Wheston
Tideswell
Hargatewall
Litton
Stoney Middleton
Curbar
Calver
Shining Tor
Buxton
Goyt's Moss
Monk's Dale NNR
Cressbrook Dale NNR
Wardlow
Wormhill
Miller's Dale
Fairfield
Pavilion Gardens
Cressbrook
Wye Valley
Priestcliffe
Little Longstone
Rowland
Hassop
Great Longstone
Baslow
Bubnell
Over End
Robin Hood
Nether End
Chatsworth Farmyard & Adventure Playground
Tegg's Nose Country Park
Macclesfield Forest
Cat and Fiddle Inn
Poole's Cavern
Harpur Hill
Staden
King Sterndale
Blackwell
Taddington
Brushfield
Pilsley
Chatsworth
Dunsa
Edensor
Trentabank Reservoir
Chelmorton
Ashford in the Water
Wildboarclough
Axe Edge
Sheldon
Flagg
Bakewell
Beeley
Flash
Earl Sterndale
Monyash
Over Haddon
Hollinsclough
Lathkill Dale
Burntcliff Top
Gradbach
Rowsley
Caudwell's Mill
194
186
172

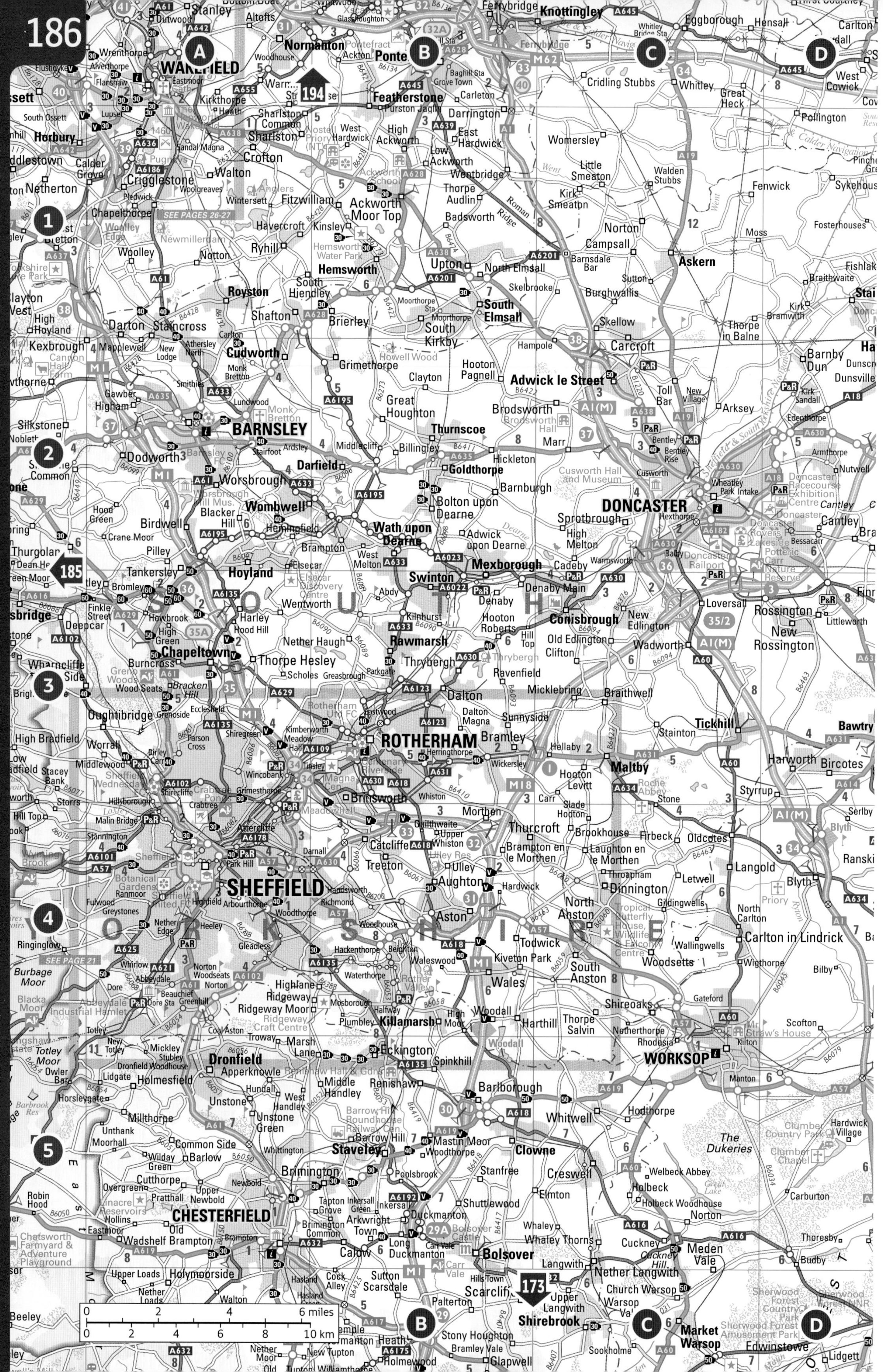

WAKEFIELD
Stanley
Altofts
Normanton
Pontefract
Ferrybridge
Knottingley
Eggborough
Hensall
Carlton
Whitley Bridge Sta
Whitley
Great Heck
West Cowick
Pollington
Cridling Stubbs
Womersley
Little Smeaton
Walden Stubbs
Kirk Smeaton
Fenwick
Sykehouse
Fosterhouses
Norton
Campsall
Askern
Moss
Fishlake
Braithwaite
Kirk Bramwith
Thorpe in Balne
Barnby Dun
Dunsville
Kirk Sandall
Arksey
Edenthorpe
Armthorpe
Nutwell
Cantley
Bessacarr
Rossington
New Rossington
Finningley
Littleworth
DONCASTER
Hexthorpe
Wheatley Park Intake
Doncaster Racecourse Exhibition Centre
Potteric Carr Nature Reserve
Loversall
Wadworth
Old Edlington
New Edlington
Conisbrough
Denaby Main
Cadeby
Warmsworth
High Melton
Sprotbrough
Cusworth Hall and Museum
Cusworth
Bentley
Bentley Rise
Toll Bar
New Village
Carcroft
Skellow
Adwick le Street
Brodsworth
Brodsworth Hall
Marr
Hooton Pagnell
Hampole
Burghwallis
Sutton
Skelbrooke
Barnsdale Bar
North Elmsall
South Elmsall
Upton
Badsworth
Thorpe Audlin
Wentbridge
Low Ackworth
High Ackworth
East Hardwick
Darrington
Carleton
Featherstone
Purston Jaglin
Sharlston
Sharlston Common
Crofton
Walton
Crigglestone
Horbury
Netherton
Calder Grove
South Ossett
Ossett
Middlestown
Sandal Magna
Kirkthorpe
Heath
Woodhouse
Warmfield
West Hardwick
Nostell Priory (NT)
Ackworth Moor Top
Fitzwilliam
Wintersett
Havercroft
Kinsley
Hemsworth
Hemsworth Water Park
Ryhill
Notton
Woolley
Woolley Edge
Newmillerdam
Chapelthorpe
West Bretton
Royston
South Hiendley
Shafton
Brierley
Grimethorpe
South Kirkby
Moorthorpe
Howell Wood
Clayton
Great Houghton
Thurnscoe
Billingley
Goldthorpe
Hickleton
Barnburgh
Bolton upon Dearne
Adwick upon Dearne
Mexborough
Swinton
Denaby
Hooton Roberts
Wath upon Dearne
West Melton
Brampton
Wombwell
Darfield
Middlecliffe
BARNSLEY
Stairfoot
Ardsley
Cudworth
Carlton
Athersley North
Monk Bretton
Lundwood
Staincross
Darton
Mapplewell
New Lodge
Smithies
Gawber
Higham
Kexbrough
Cannon Hall Farm
High Hoyland
Clayton West
Silkstone
Dodworth
Silkstone Common
Worsbrough
Worsbrough Mill Mus.
Birdwell
Blacker Hill
Hemingfield
Elsecar
Elsecar Discovery Centre
Hoyland
Tankersley
Pilley
Hood Green
Crane Moor
Thurgoland
Bromley
Finkle Street
Harley
Hood Hill
Wentworth
Nether Haugh
Thorpe Hesley
Scholes
Greasbrough
Parkgate
Rawmarsh
Kilnhurst
Thrybergh
Ravenfield
Micklebring
Braithwell
Dalton
Dalton Magna
Sunnyside
Bramley
Hellaby
Wickersley
Maltby
Hooton Levitt
Roche Abbey
Stainton
Tickhill
Harworth
Bircotes
Bawtry
Styrrup
Serlby
Blyth
Oldcotes
Langold
Letwell
Firbeck
Stone
Carr
Slade Hooton
Brookhouse
Laughton en le Morthen
Throapham
Dinnington
Gildingwells
North Carlton
Carlton in Lindrick
Wallingwells
Woodsetts
Wigthorpe
Bilby
North Anston
South Anston
Tropical Butterfly House, Wildlife & Falconry Centre
Todwick
Kiveton Park
Wales
Thurcroft
Brampton en le Morthen
Morthen
Whiston
Herringthorpe
ROTHERHAM
Rotherham Utd FC
Eastwood
Kimberworth
Meadow Hall
Tinsley
Magna
Centenary Riverside
Brinsworth
Meadowhall
Catcliffe
Treeton
Upper Whiston
Ulley
Ulley Res
Aughton
Guilthwaite
Hardwick
Aston
Swallownest
Woodhouse
Handsworth
Richmond
Darnall
Attercliffe
SHEFFIELD
Park Hill
Arbourthorne
Heeley
Highfield
Nether Edge
Botanical Gardens
Ranmoor
Fulwood
Greystones
Ringinglow
Burbage Moor
Dore
Abbeydale
Whirlow
Norton Woodseats
Norton
Beauchief
Greenhill
Gleadless
Hackenthorpe
Beighton
Waleswood
Waterthorpe
Rother Valley
Halfway
Highlane
Ridgeway
Ridgeway Moor
Ridgeway Craft Centre
Mosborough
Plumbley
Killamarsh
High Moor
Woodall
Harthill
Thorpe Salvin
Shireoaks
Netherthorpe
Rhodesia
Gateford
WORKSOP
Kilton
Mr Straw's House
Scofton
Manton
Hodthorpe
Whitwell
Barlborough
Spinkhill
Renishaw
Renishaw Hall & Gdns
Eckington
Marsh Lane
Troway
Coal Aston
Dronfield
Dronfield Woodhouse
Apperknowle
Hundall
Unstone
Unstone Green
West Handley
Middle Handley
Barrow Hill Roundhouse Railway Cen.
Barrow Hill
Staveley
Mastin Moor
Woodthorpe
Clowne
Creswell
Elmton
Stanfree
Shuttlewood
Poolsbrook
Whittington
Brimington
Newbold
Upper Newbold
CHESTERFIELD
Brampton
Old Brampton
Wadshelf
Holymoorside
Walton
Hasland
Cock Alley
Calow
Duckmanton
Long Duckmanton
Inkersall
Inkersall Green
Arkwright Town
Tapton Grove
Brimington Common
Bolsover
Bolsover Castle
Carr Vale
Hills Town
Scarcliffe
Palterton
Sutton Scarsdale
Stony Houghton
Bramley Vale
Glapwell
Heath
Holmewood
Temple Normanton
Nether Moor
New Tupton
Shirebrook
Upper Langwith
Langwith
Nether Langwith
Whaley
Whaley Thorns
Cuckney
Church Warsop
Warsop Vale
Market Warsop
Meden Vale
Sookholme
Edwinstowe
Budby
Thoresby
Carburton
Norton
Holbeck
Holbeck Woodhouse
Welbeck Abbey
Great Lake
The Dukeries
Clumber Country Park
Clumber Chapel
Hardwick Village
Sherwood Forest Country Park
Sherwood Forest NNR
Sherwood Forest Amusement Park
Lidgett
Ollerton
Stannington
Malin Bridge
Hillsborough
Crabtree
Grimesthorpe
Wincobank
Shiregreen
Parson Cross
Ecclesfield
Grenoside
Burncross
Chapeltown
High Green
Howbrook
Wharncliffe Side
Oughtibridge
Worrall
Middlewood
High Bradfield
Stacey Bank
Storrs
Loxley
Deepcar
Stocksbridge
Wood Seats
Bracken Hill
Birley Carr
Shirecliffe
Totley
Totley Moor
New Totley
Mickley
Stubley
Holmesfield
Lidgate
Owler Bar
Horsleygate
Millthorpe
Unthank
Moorhall
Common Side
Barlow
Wilday Green
Cutthorpe
Overgreen
Pratthall
Linacre Reservoirs
Hollins
Eastmoor
Robin Hood
Chatsworth Farmyard & Adventure Playground
Upper Loads
Nether Loads
Beeley
SOUTH YORKSHIRE
SEE PAGES 26-27
SEE PAGE 27
194
185
173
0 2 4 6 miles
0 2 4 6 8 10 km

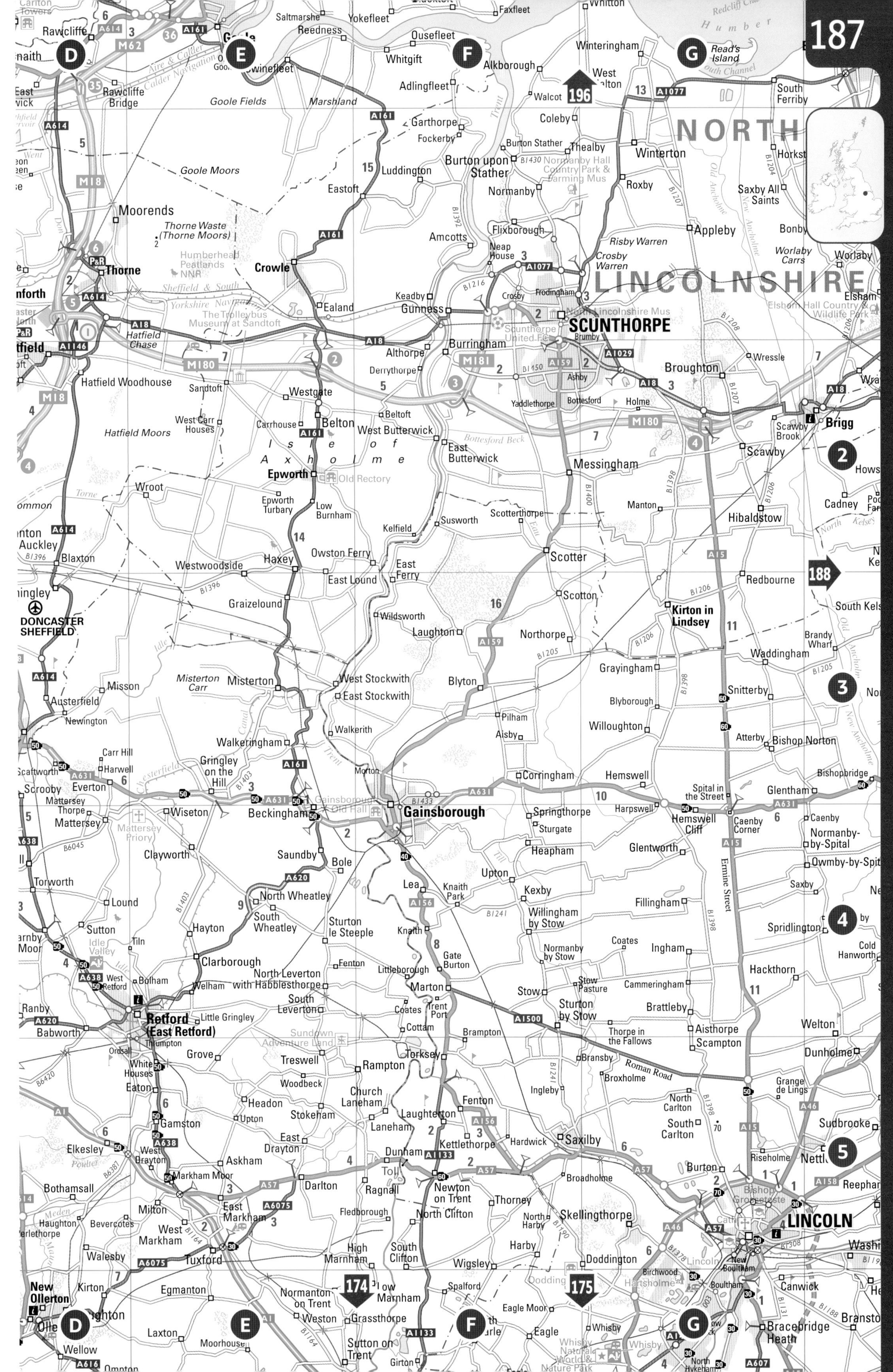

NORTH
LINCOLNSHIRE
Humber
Read's Island
Rawcliffe
Goole
Saltmarshe
Reedness
Yokefleet
Faxfleet
Whitton
Ousefleet
Whitgift
Winteringham
Alkborough
West Halton
Swinefleet
Adlingfleet
Walcot
196
South Ferriby
Rawcliffe Bridge
Goole Fields
Marshland
Garthorpe
Fockerby
Coleby
Burton Stather
Thealby
Winterton
Horkstow
Burton upon Stather
Normanby Hall Country Park & Farming Mus
Goole Moors
Luddington
Eastoft
Normanby
Roxby
Saxby All Saints
Moorends
Thorne Waste (Thorne Moors)
Humberhead Peatlands NNR
Amcotts
Flixborough
Appleby
Bonby
Risby Warren
Neap House
Crosby Warren
Worlaby Carrs
Worlaby
Thorne
Crowle
Sheffield & South Yorkshire Navigation
Keadby
Crosby
Frodingham
Elsham
Elsham Hall Country & Wildlife Park
Ealand
Gunness
The Trolleybus Museum at Sandtoft
North Lincolnshire Mus
SCUNTHORPE
Scunthorpe United FC
Brumby
Hatfield Chase
Burringham
Althorpe
Derrythorpe
Wressle
Broughton
Ashby
Bottesford
Holme
Yaddlethorpe
Hatfield Woodhouse
Sandtoft
Westgate
Beltoft
Brigg
Scawby Brook
West Carr Houses
Carrhouse
Belton
West Butterwick
Hatfield Moors
Isle of Axholme
East Butterwick
Bottesford Beck
Messingham
Scawby
Epworth
Old Rectory
Wroot
Epworth Turbary
Low Burnham
Manton
Cadney
Hibaldstow
Scotterthorpe
Susworth
Kelfield
Auckley
Blaxton
Westwoodside
Haxey
Owston Ferry
East Ferry
East Lound
Scotter
Redbourne
188
Graizelound
Wildsworth
Scotton
Kirton in Lindsey
South Kelsey
DONCASTER SHEFFIELD
Laughton
Northorpe
Brandy Wharf
Waddingham
Grayingham
Misterton Carr
Misterton
West Stockwith
East Stockwith
Blyton
Missonn
Austerfield
Newington
Blyborough
Snitterby
Pilham
Willoughton
Walkerith
Aisby
Atterby
Bishop Norton
Walkeringham
Carr Hill
Harwell
Gringley on the Hill
Scaftworth
Everton
Scrooby
Mattersey Thorpe
Mattersey
Mattersey Priory
Wiseton
Beckingham
Gainsborough
Gainsborough Old Hall
Corringham
Hemswell
Bishopbridge
Glentham
Spital in the Street
Springthorpe
Sturgate
Harpswell
Hemswell Cliff
Caenby Corner
Caenby
Normanby-by-Spital
Owmby-by-Spital
Clayworth
Saundby
Bole
Heapham
Glentworth
Torworth
Lea
Knaith Park
Upton
Kexby
Saxby
Lound
North Wheatley
South Wheatley
Fillingham
Ermine Street
Sutton
Hayton
Sturton le Steeple
Knaith
Willingham by Stow
Spridlington
Idle Valley
Tiln
Gate Burton
Normanby by Stow
Coates
Ingham
Cold Hanworth
Clarborough
Fenton
Littleborough
North Leverton with Habblesthorpe
Marton
Stow
Stow Pasture
Cammeringham
Hackthorn
West Retford
Bolham
Welham
South Leverton
Coates
Trent Port
Sturton by Stow
Brattleby
Ranby
Retford (East Retford)
Little Gringley
Cottam
Thorpe in the Fallows
Aisthorpe
Scampton
Welton
Babworth
Brampton
Thrumpton
Sundown Adventure Land
Ordsall
Grove
Torksey
Dunholme
Treswell
Rampton
Bransby
Roman Road
White Houses
Broxholme
Woodbeck
Grange de Lings
Eaton
Church Laneham
Ingleby
North Carlton
Headon
Fenton
Gamston
Upton
Stokeham
Laughterton
South Carlton
Sudbrooke
Laneham
Kettlethorpe
Hardwick
Saxilby
Elkesley
East Drayton
West Drayton
Askham
Dunham
Burton
Riseholme
Nettleham
Markham Moor
Darlton
Toll
Broadholme
Newton on Trent
Thorney
Reepham
Bothamsall
Milton
East Markham
Ragnall
North Clifton
Bishop Grosseteste
Haughton
Bevercotes
Fledborough
North Harby
Skellingthorpe
LINCOLN
West Markham
Harby
Walesby
Tuxford
High Marnham
South Clifton
Wigsley
Doddington
Birchwood
Hartsholme
New Boultham
Kirton
Egmanton
174
Low Marnham
175
Spalford
Boultham
Canwick
New Ollerton
Normanton on Trent
Eagle Moor
Weston
Grassthorpe
Eagle
Whisby
Bracebridge Heath
Wellow
Laxton
Moorhouse
Sutton on Trent
Whisby Nature Park
Girton
North Hykeham
M62
M18
M180
M181
A614
A161
A18
A1077
A1029
A159
A1146
A631
A620
A638
A156
A1500
A57
A6075
A1133
A1
A15
A46
A158
A616
A607
B1396
B1403
B1205
B1206
B1207
B1208
B1398
B1400
B1216
B1430
B1450
B1392
B1241
B1190
B1378
B1164
B6045
B6420
B6387
B1433

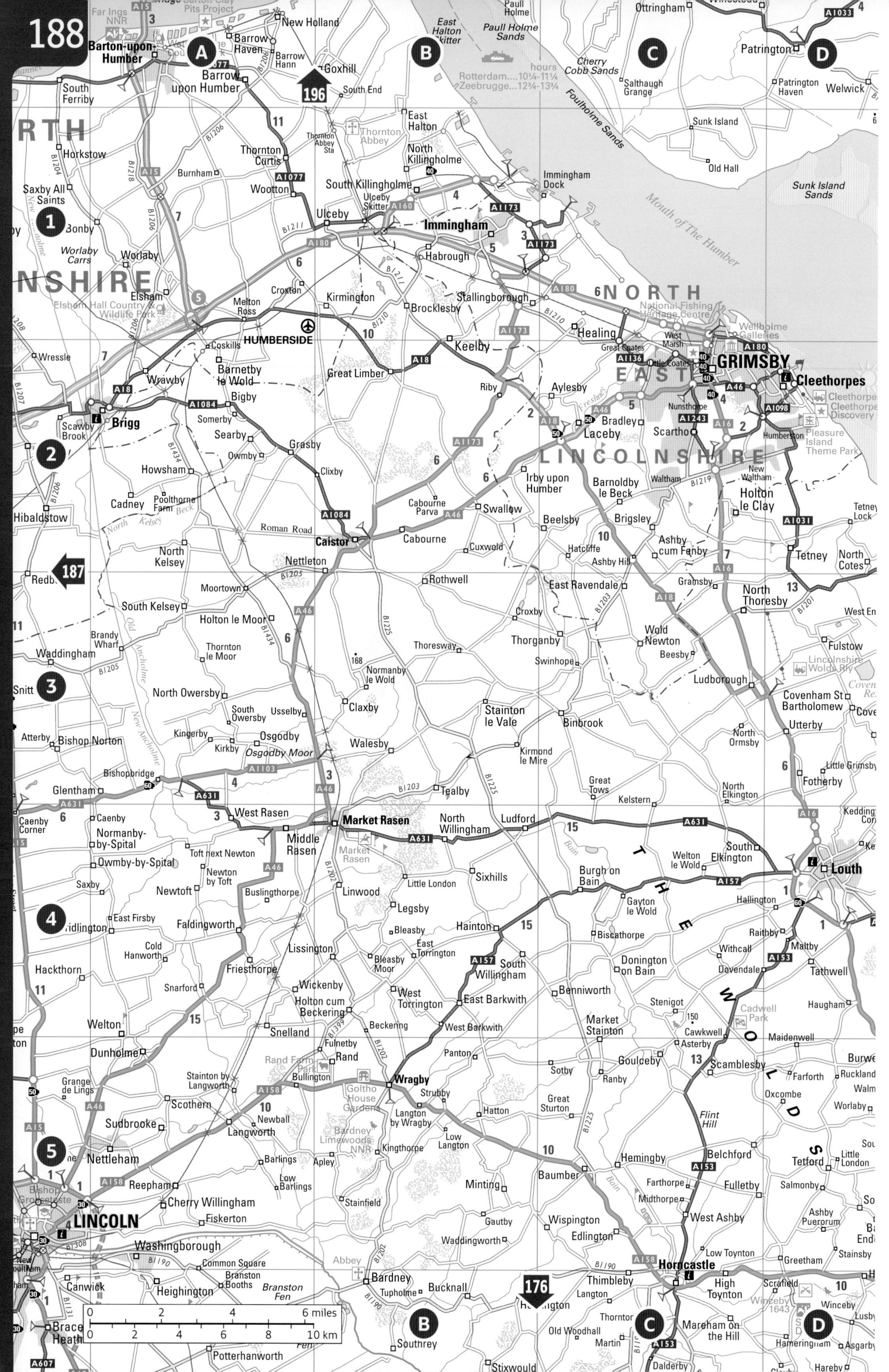

A
B
C
D
1
2
3
4
5
196
187
176
Barton-upon-Humber
Barrow upon Humber
Barrow Haven
Barrow Hann
New Holland
Goxhill
South End
East Halton Skitter
East Halton
Thornton Abbey
Thornton Curtis
North Killingholme
South Killingholme
Ulceby
Ulceby Skitter
Immingham
Immingham Dock
Habrough
Stallingborough
Brocklesby
Kirmington
Croxton
Melton Ross
HUMBERSIDE
Elsham
Elsham Hall Country & Wildlife Park
Worlaby
Worlaby Carrs
Bonby
Saxby All Saints
Horkstow
South Ferriby
Burnham
Wootton
Paull Holme
Paull Holme Sands
Rotterdam...10¼-11¼
Zeebrugge...12¾-13¾
hours
Cherry Cobb Sands
Ottringham
Salthaugh Grange
Foulholme Sands
Patrington
Patrington Haven
Welwick
Sunk Island
Old Hall
Sunk Island Sands
Mouth of The Humber
NORTH EAST LINCOLNSHIRE
National Fishing Heritage Centre
Welholme Galleries
GRIMSBY
Cleethorpes
Cleethorpes Discovery
Pleasure Island Theme Park
Humberston
Great Coates
West Marsh
Little Coates
Healing
Keelby
Riby
Aylesby
Laceby
Bradley
Scartho
Nunsthorpe
Waltham
New Waltham
Holton le Clay
Tetney
Tetney Lock
North Cotes
Barnoldby le Beck
Irby upon Humber
Brigsley
Ashby cum Fenby
Beelsby
Hatcliffe
Ashby Hill
East Ravendale
Grainsby
North Thoresby
Swallow
Cuxwold
Cabourne
Cabourne Parva
Caistor
Great Limber
Grasby
Clixby
Bigby
Barnetby le Wold
Coskills
Wrawby
Brigg
Scawby Brook
Somerby
Searby
Owmby
Howsham
Cadney
Poolthorne Farm
Hibaldstow
Redbourne
Wressle
North Kelsey
South Kelsey
Moortown
Holton le Moor
Nettleton
Rothwell
Roman Road
North Kelsey Beck
Brandy Wharf
Waddingham
Snitterby
Thornton le Moor
North Owersby
South Owersby
Usselby
Kingerby
Kirkby
Osgodby
Osgodby Moor
Atterby
Bishop Norton
Bishopbridge
Glentham
Caenby Corner
Caenby
Normanby-by-Spital
Owmby-by-Spital
Toft next Newton
Newton by Toft
Newtoft
Saxby
Buslingthorpe
West Rasen
Middle Rasen
Market Rasen
Walesby
Claxby
Normanby le Wold
Thoresway
Croxby
Thorganby
Swinhope
Wold Newton
Beesby
Binbrook
Stainton le Vale
Kirmond le Mire
Tealby
North Willingham
Ludford
Sixhills
Little London
Linwood
Legsby
Bleasby
East Torrington
Bleasby Moor
Lissington
Faldingworth
Friesthorpe
East Firsby
Ingham
Cold Hanworth
Hackthorn
Snarford
Wickenby
West Torrington
Holton cum Beckering
Snelland
Beckering
Fulnetby
Rand
Rand Farm Park
Welton
Dunholme
Grange de Lings
Stainton by Langworth
Bullington
Wragby
Goltho House Gardens
Strubby
Langton by Wragby
Low Langton
Bardney Limewoods NNR
Kingthorpe
Apley
Barlings
Low Barlings
Langworth
Newball
Scothern
Sudbrooke
Nettleham
Reepham
Cherry Willingham
Fiskerton
LINCOLN
Bishop Grosseteste
Washingborough
Common Square
Branston Booths
Branston Fen
Heighington
Canwick
Bracebridge Heath
Potterhanworth
Bardney
Abbey
Tupholme
Bucknall
Southrey
Stainfield
Gautby
Waddingworth
Minting
Hatton
Panton
West Barkwith
East Barkwith
South Willingham
Hainton
Benniworth
Biscathorpe
Gayton le Wold
Burgh on Bain
Donington on Bain
Stenigot
Market Stainton
Goulceby
Ranby
Sotby
Great Sturton
Baumber
Wispington
Edlington
Hemingby
Horncastle
Thimbleby
Langton
Thornton
Martin
Old Woodhall
Horsington
Stixwould
Dalderby
Mareham on the Hill
High Toynton
Low Toynton
Winceby 1643
Scrafield
Hameringham
Asgarby
Hareby
Greetham
West Ashby
Midthorpe
Farthorpe
Fulletby
Belchford
Flint Hill
Tetford
Little London
Salmonby
Ashby Puerorum
Stainsby
Scamblesby
Asterby
Cawkwell
Cadwell Park
Farforth
Oxcombe
Ruckland
Worlaby
Maidenwell
Haugham
Tathwell
Maltby
Raithby
Withcall
Dovendale
Hallington
Louth
South Elkington
Welton le Wold
North Elkington
Kelstern
Great Tows
Fotherby
Little Grimsby
Utterby
North Ormsby
Covenham St Bartholomew
Ludborough
Fulstow
Lincolnshire Wolds Rly
THE WOLDS
LINCOLNSHIRE
Freshney
Bain
Old Ancholme
New Ancholme
0 2 4 6 miles
0 2 4 6 8 10 km

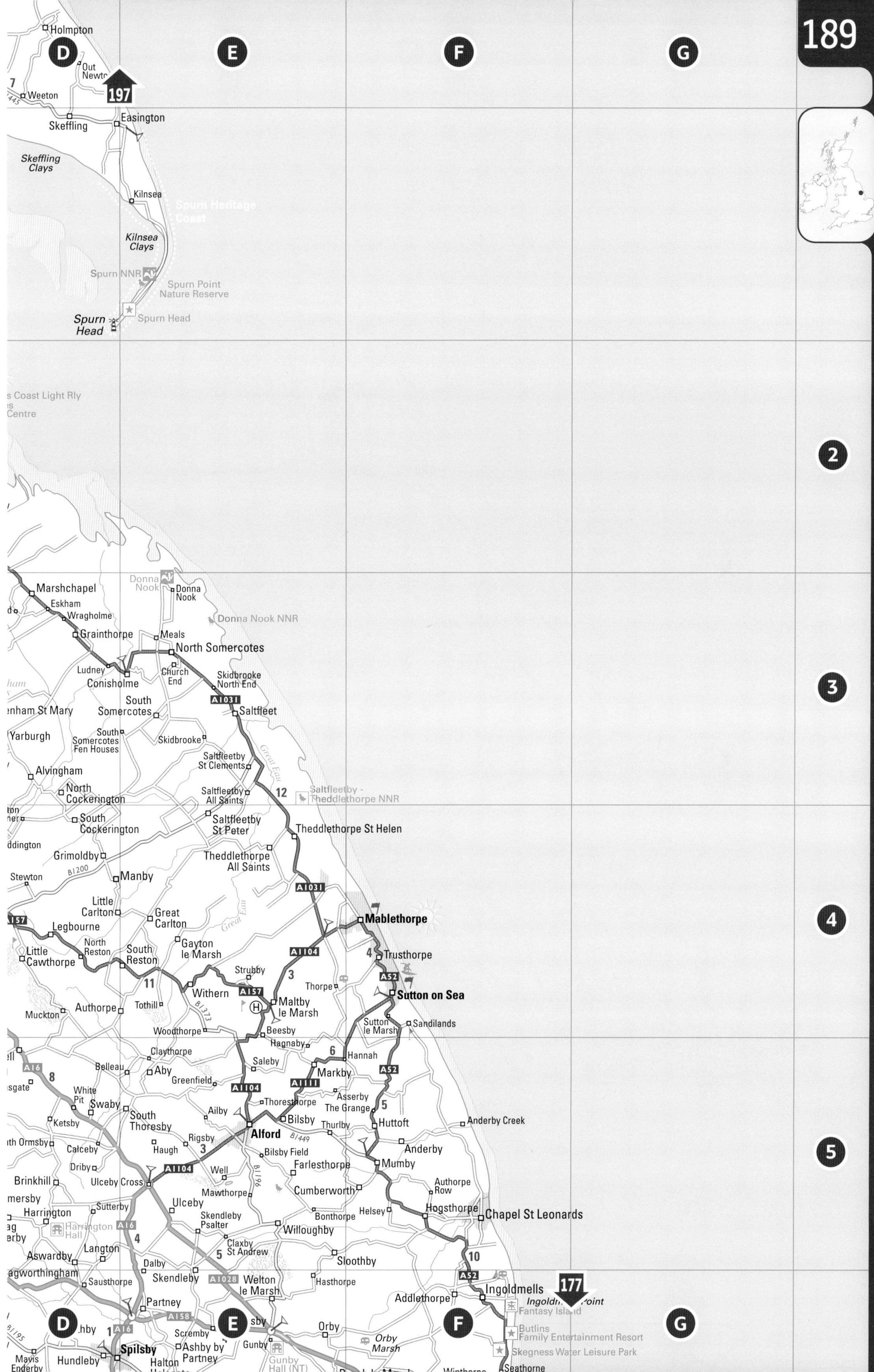

Holmpton
Out Newto
Weeton
D
197
Skeffling
Easington
E
F
G

Skeffling Clays

Kilnsea

Spurn Heritage Coast

Kilnsea Clays

Spurn NNR

Spurn Point
Nature Reserve

Spurn Head
Spurn Head

2

s Coast Light Rly
s
Centre

Marshchapel
Eskham
Wragholme
Donna Nook
Donna Nook
Donna Nook NNR

Grainthorpe
Meals
North Somercotes

3

Ludney
Conisholme
Church End
Skidbrooke North End
A1031
Saltfleet

enham St Mary
South Somercotes
Skidbrooke

Yarburgh
South Somercotes Fen Houses
Saltfleetby St Clements

Alvingham
North Cockerington
Saltfleetby All Saints
12
Saltfleetby - Theddlethorpe NNR

ddington
South Cockerington
Saltfleetby St Peter
Theddlethorpe St Helen

Grimoldby
B1200
Theddlethorpe All Saints

Stewton
Manby

4

Little Carlton
Great Carlton
A1031

A157
Legbourne
North Reston
South Reston
Gayton le Marsh
A1104
Mablethorpe

Little Cawthorpe
Strubby
4 Trusthorpe

Muckton
Authorpe
11
Withern
A157
3
Thorpe
A52

Tothill
Maltby le Marsh
Sutton on Sea

B1373
Woodthorpe
Beesby
Sutton le Marsh
Sandilands

ll
A16
8
Belleau
Claythorpe
Saleby
Hagnaby
6
Hannah

White Pit
Aby
Greenfield
Markby
A52

sgate
Swaby
Ailby
A1104
A1111
Asserby
5

Ketsby
South Thoresby
Thoresthorpe
The Grange
Huttoft
Anderby Creek

th Ormsby
Calceby
Rigsby
Bilsby
Thurlby
Anderby

Driby
Haugh
Alford
B1449
Bilsby Field
Mumby
Authorpe Row

Brinkhill
Ulceby Cross
Well
A1104
Farlesthorpe
Hogsthorpe

mersby
Sutterby
Ulceby
Mawthorpe
Cumberworth
Helsey
Chapel St Leonards

Harrington
Harrington Hall
Skendleby Psalter
Bonthorpe

ag
erby
Langton
A16
4
Claxby St Andrew
Willoughby
10

Aswardby
Dalby
5
Skendleby
Welton le Marsh
Sloothby

agworthingham
Sausthorpe
A1028
Hasthorpe
A52
Ingoldmells
177

Partney
Addlethorpe
Ingoldm   Point
Fantasy Isla d

D
hby
1
A16
Scremby
A158
sby
E
Orby
F
Butlins
Family Entertainment Resort
G

Mavis
Enderby
Hundleby
Spilsby
Ashby by Partney
Gunby
Orby Marsh
Skegness Water Leisure Park

Halton
Gunby Hall (NT)
Wintharna
Seathorne

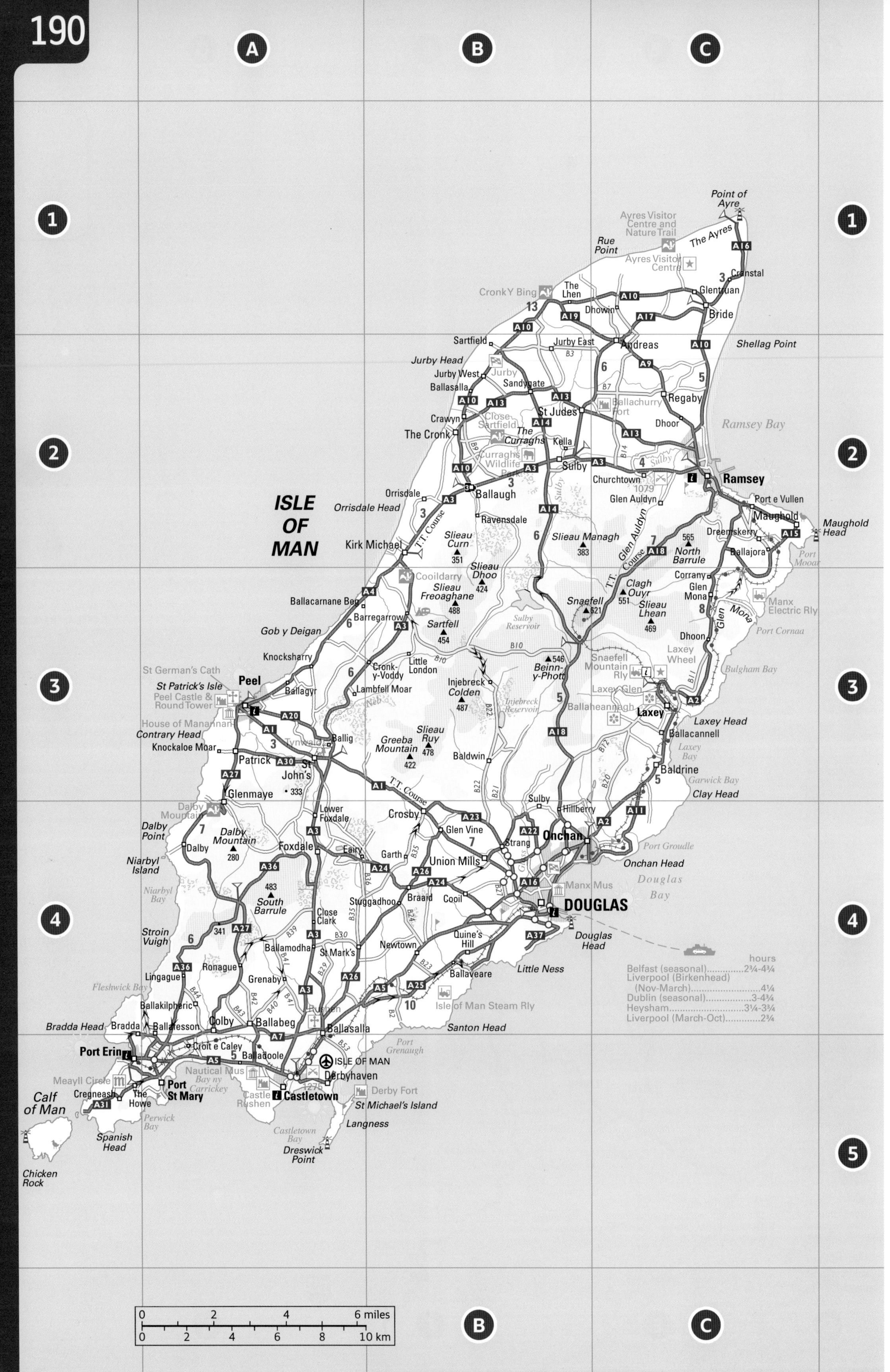

ISLE
OF
MAN

Point of Ayre
The Ayres
Ayres Visitor Centre and Nature Trail
Rue Point
Ayres Visitor Centre
A16
Cranstal
Glentruan
Bride
Shellag Point
Cronk Y Bing
The Lhen
Dhowin
A10
A19
A17
A16
Sartfield
Jurby East
Andreas
B3
Jurby Head
Jurby West
Sandygate
Jurby
A9
Regaby
Ballasalla
Ballachurry Fort
B7
Crawyn
St Judes
A13
A14
Dhoor
A13
The Cronk
The Curraghs
Kella
Ramsey Bay
Curraghs Wildlife Park
A10
Churchtown
Sulby
A3
A13
Ramsey
Orrisdale
A3
Ballaugh
1079
Glen Auldyn
Port e Vullen
Orrisdale Head
Ravensdale
Sulby
A14
Maughold
Slieau Curn 351
Slieau Managh 383
North Barrule 565
Dreemskerry
Maughold Head
Kirk Michael
Slieau Dhoo 424
A18
Ballajora
A15
Port Mooar
Cooildarry
Slieau Freoaghane 488
Snaefell 621
Clagh Ouyr 551
Corrany
Glen Mona
Manx Electric Rly
Ballacarnane Beg
Sartfell 454
Slieau Lhean 469
Dhoon
Glen Mona
Port Cornaa
Barregarrow
A3
B10
Gob y Deigan
Snaefell Mountain Rly
Laxey Wheel
Bulgham Bay
Knocksharry
Little London
Beinn-y-Phott 546
Laxey Glen
Cronk-y-Voddy
Injebreck Colden 487
Lambfell Moar
Injebreck Reservoir
Ballaheannagh
St German's Cath
Peel
A18
Laxey
St Patrick's Isle
Ballagyr
Slieau Ruy 478
Laxey Head
Peel Castle & Round Tower
Ballacannell
House of Manannan
Greeba Mountain 422
Baldwin
Laxey Bay
A2
Contrary Head
A20
Baldrine
Knockaloe Moar
A1
Ballig
Sulby
Garwick Bay
Patrick
Tynwald
St John's 333
Clay Head
A30
A1
Hillberry
Crosby
A23
A2
Glenmaye
A27
Dalby Mountain
Lower Foxdale
Glen Vine
Strang
A11
Dalby Point
Dalby
Dalby Mountain 280
Fairy
Union Mills
A22
Onchan
Port Groudle
Niarbyl Island
Foxdale
Garth
A26
A16
Onchan Head
Niarbyl Bay
A36
South Barrule 483
Stuggadhoo
Braaid
Cooil
Manx Mus
Douglas Bay
Stroin Vuigh
341
A27
Close Clark
Newtown
Quine's Hill
DOUGLAS
Lingague
A36
Ronague
Ballamodha
Little Ness
A37
Douglas Head
Fleshwick Bay
Grenaby
A3
Ballaveare
Belfast (seasonal)............2¾-4¾ hours
Ballakilpheric
Colby
A26
A5
A25
Liverpool (Birkenhead)
Bradda Head
Bradda
Ballabeg
10
Isle of Man Steam Rly
(Nov-March).....................4¼
Ballaresson
A7
Ballasalla
Santon Head
Dublin (seasonal).............3-4¾
Port Erin
Croit e Caley
A5
Port Grenaugh
Heysham.........................3¼-3¾
Meayll Circle
5
Balladoole
Liverpool (March-Oct)............2¾
Cregneash
The Howe
Port St Mary
Nautical Mus
Bay ny Carrickey
ISLE OF MAN
Derbyhaven
Calf of Man
A31
Castle Rushen
Castletown
Derby Fort
Spanish Head
Perwick Bay
St Michael's Island
Castletown Bay
Langness
Chicken Rock
Dreswick Point

0   2   4   6 miles
0 2 4 6 8 10 km

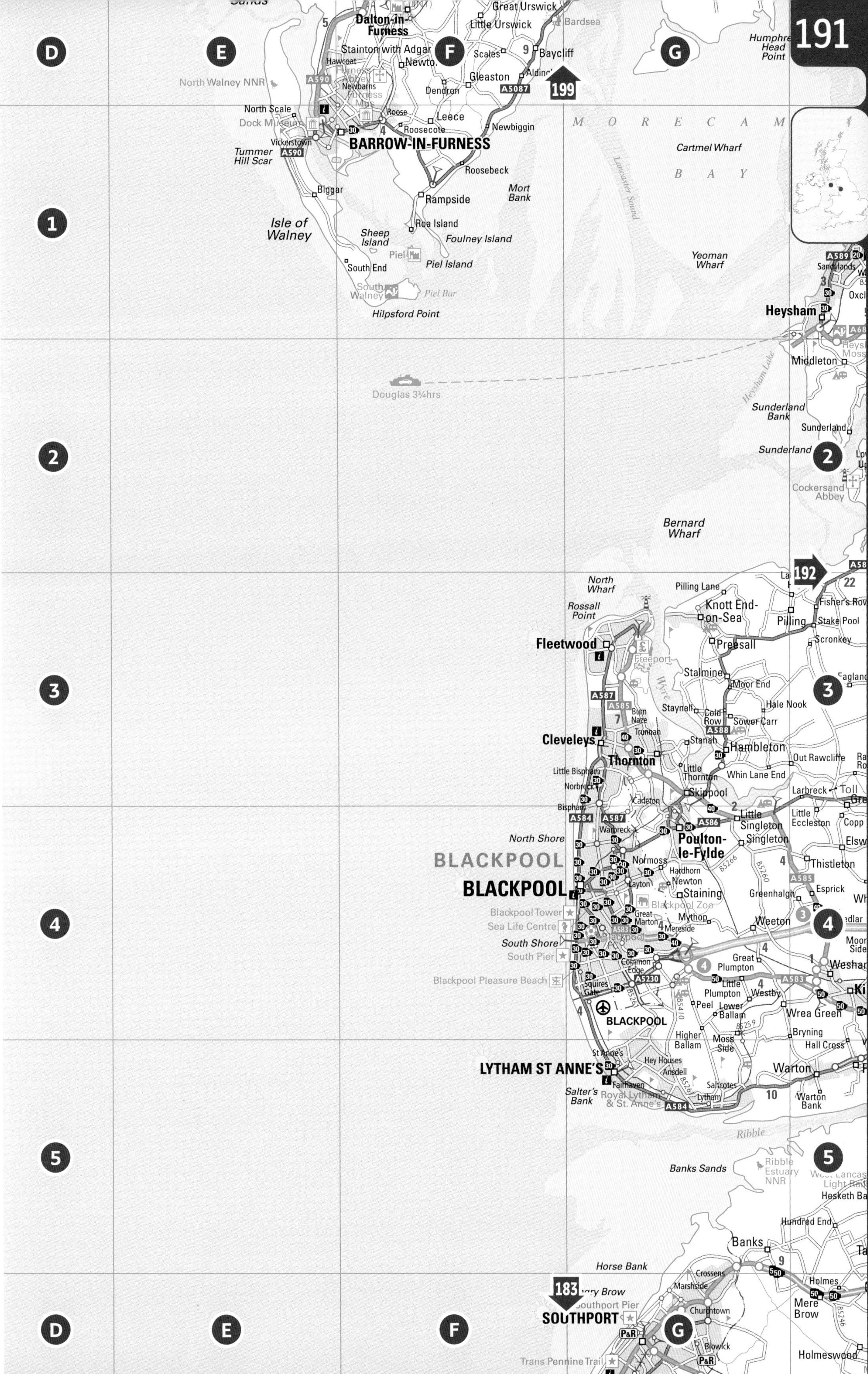

Sands

D **E** **F** **G**

Great Urswick
Dalton-in-Furness
Little Urswick
Bardsea
Stainton with Adgar
Scales 9 Bayliff
Newto.
Hawcoat
North Walney NNR
Gleaston
Aldingh
A5087
Dendron
199
North Scale
Furness Abbey
Dock Museum
Roose
Leece
Newbiggin
Vickerstown
A590
4
Roosecote
BARROW-IN-FURNESS
Tummer
Hill Scar
A590
Roosebeck
M O R E C A M
Biggar
Rampside
Mort
Bank
Cartmel Wharf
*Isle of
Walney*
Roa Island
B A Y
Sheep
Island
Foulney Island
Piel
Piel Island
Yeoman
Wharf
Sandylands
Oxcl
South End
South
Walney
Piel Bar
Heysham
Hilpsford Point
Heysham
Moss
Middleton

1

2

Douglas 3¾hrs

Sunderland
Bank
Sunderland

Sunderland
2
Cockersand
Abbey

*Bernard
Wharf*

192
A58
22
Fisher's Rov
North
Wharf
Pilling Lane
La
Rossall
Point
Knott End-
on-Sea
Pilling
Stake Pool
Scronkey
Fleetwood
Freeport
Preesall
A587
Stalmine
Eagland
A585
Moor End
3
Staynall
Cold
Row
Hale Nook
Burn
Naze
Sower Carr
3
Trunnah
Stanah
Cleveleys
40
Hambleton
Out Rawcliffe
Ra
Ro
Thornton
Stanah
Little Bispham
Little
Thornton
Whin Lane End
Larbreck Toll
Norbreck
Skippool
Gre
Bispham
Carleton
A587
40
2 Little
Singleton
Little
Eccleston
Copp
A584
Watbreck
A586
Singleton
Elsw
North Shore
Normoss
**Poulton-
le-Fylde**
BLACKPOOL
Hardhorn
Newton
4
Thistleton
Layton
Staining
Greenhalgh
Esprick
Wh
BLACKPOOL
Blackpool Zoo
Mythop
Weeton
3
dlar
Blackpool Tower
Great
Marton
Mereside
Moor
Side
Sea Life Centre
A583
4
4
South Shore
South Pier
Common
Edge
Great
Plumpton
1
Wesha
Blackpool Pleasure Beach
A5230
Squires
Gate
Little
Plumpton
50
Westby
4
A583
Ki
50
BLACKPOOL
4
Peel
Lower
Ballam
Wrea Green
50
Higher
Ballam
Moss
Side
Bryning
Hall Cross
Warton
LYTHAM ST ANNE'S
Hey Houses
Ansdell
Saltcotes
Warton
Bank
Salter's
Bank
Fairhaven
Lytham
10
Royal Lytham
& St. Anne's
A584
Ribble

5
Banks Sands
Ribble
Estuary
NNR
West Lancas
Light Ra
5
Hesketh Ba

Hundred End

Banks
9
Horse Bank
Crossens
50
Holmes
183
ry Brow
Marshside
Mere
Brow
SOUTHPORT
Churchtown
P&R
G
Blowick
Holmeswood
Trans Pennine Trail
P&R

D **E** **F**

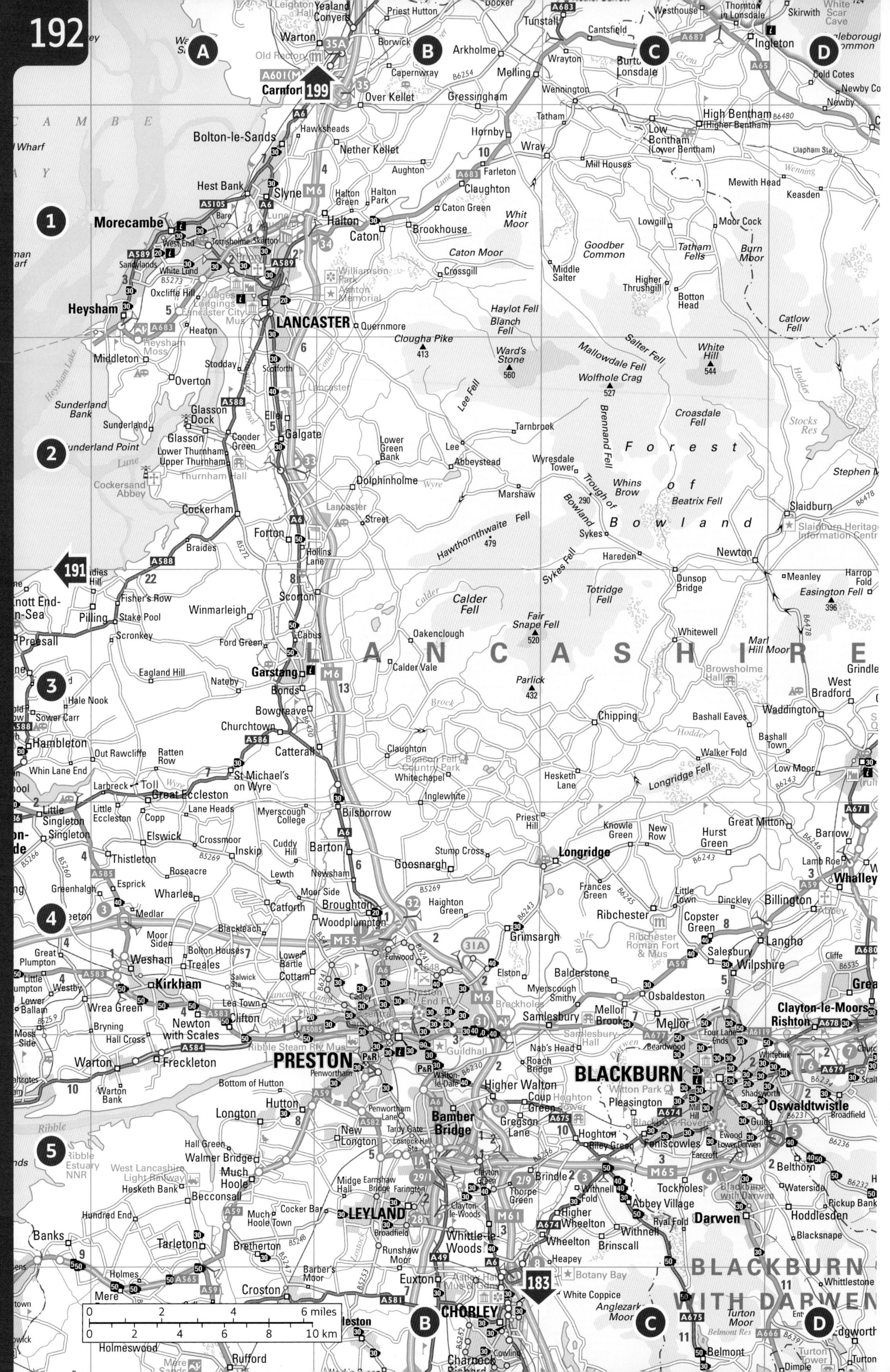
A
B
C
D
1
2
3
4
5
Priest Hutton
Yealand Conyers
Warton
Borwick
Arkholme
Tunstall
Cantsfield
Westhouse
Thornton in Lonsdale
Skirwith
White Scar Cave
Ingleton
Old Rectory
Capernwray
Melling
Wrayton
Burton in Lonsdale
Carnforth
199
Over Kellet
Gressingham
Wennington
Cold Cotes
Newby Cote
Newby
Hawksheads
Bolton-le-Sands
Nether Kellet
Hornby
Tatham
Wray
Low Bentham (Lower Bentham)
High Bentham (Higher Bentham)
Clapham Sta
Aughton
Farleton
Mill Houses
Wenning
Hest Bank
Slyne
Halton Green
Halton Park
Claughton
Mewith Head
Keasden
Morecambe
Bare
Torrisholme
West End
Sandylands
White Lund
Halton
Caton
Caton Green
Brookhouse
Whit Moor
Lowgill
Moor Cock
Caton Moor
Crossgill
Goodber Common
Tatham Fells
Burn Moor
Middle Salter
Higher Thrushgill
Botton Head
Williamson Park
Ashton Memorial
Oxcliffe Hill
Judges Lodgings
Lancaster City Mus
Heysham
Heaton
Heysham Moss
LANCASTER
Quernmore
Haylot Fell
Blanch Fell
Clougha Pike
413
Catlow Fell
Salter Fell
White Hill
544
Ward's Stone
560
Mallowdale Fell
Wolfhole Crag
527
Middleton
Stodday
Scotforth
Overton
Heysham Lake
Lancaster University
Lee Fell
Sunderland Bank
Sunderland
Glasson Dock
Glasson
Conder Green
Ellel
Galgate
Brennand Fell
Croasdale Fell
Stocks Res
Tarnbrook
Sunderland Point
Lower Thurnham
Upper Thurnham
Lower Green Bank
Lee
Abbeystead
Wyresdale Tower
Forest of Bowland
Whins Brow
Thurnham Hall
Cockersand Abbey
Dolphinholme
Marshaw
Trough of Bowland
290
Beatrix Fell
Stephen Moor
Slaidburn
Cockerham
Street
Lancaster
Slaidburn Heritage Information Centre
Forton
Hawthornthwaite Fell
479
Sykes
Braides
Hollins Lane
Hareden
Newton
191
Pilling
Fisher's Row
Stake Pool
Winmarleigh
Scorton
Sykes Fell
Calder Fell
Totridge Fell
Dunsop Bridge
Meanley
Harrop Fold
Easington Fell
396
Preesall
Scronkey
Ford Green
Cabus
Oakenclough
Fair Snape Fell
520
Whitewell
Marl Hill Moor
LANCASHIRE
Grindleton
West Bradford
Eagland Hill
Nateby
Garstang
Calder Vale
Parlick
432
Browsholme Hall
Hale Nook
Bonds
Sower Carr
Bowgreave
Hambleton
Churchtown
Chipping
Bashall Eaves
Waddington
Out Rawcliffe
Ratten Row
Catterall
Claughton
Beacon Fell Country Park
Whitechapel
Walker Fold
Bashall Town
Whin Lane End
Larbreck
Toll
St Michael's on Wyre
Hesketh Lane
Longridge Fell
Low Moor
Great Eccleston
Inglewhite
Little Singleton
Singleton
Little Eccleston
Copp
Lane Heads
Myerscough College
Bilsborrow
Priest Hill
Knowle Green
New Row
Hurst Green
Great Mitton
Barrow
Elswick
Crossmoor
Inskip
Cuddy Hill
Barton
Stump Cross
Longridge
Thistleton
Roseacre
Lewth
Newsham
Goosnargh
Lamb Roe
Whalley
Greenhalgh
Esprick
Wharles
Moor Side
Frances Green
Little Town
Dinckley
Billington
Medlar
Catforth
Broughton
Haighton Green
Ribchester
Copster Green
Woodplumpton
Blackleach
Moor Side
Bolton Houses
Treales
Grimsargh
Ribchester Roman Fort & Mus
Langho
Great Plumpton
Wesham
Lower Bartle
Fulwood
Salesbury
Wilpshire
Cliffe
Westby
Kirkham
Salwick Sta
Cottam
Elston
Balderstone
Little Plumpton
Lower Ballam
Wrea Green
Cadley
Preston North End FC
Myerscough Smithy
Osbaldeston
Lea Town
Brockholes
Clayton-le-Moors
Rishton
Bryning
Newton with Scales
Clifton
Mellor Brook
Samlesbury
Mellor
Four Lane Ends
Moss Side
Hall Cross
Ribble Steam Rly Mus
Samlesbury Hall
Nab's Head
Beardwood
Whitebirk
Warton
Freckleton
PRESTON
Guildhall
Walton-le-Dale
Roach Bridge
BLACKBURN
Shadsworth
Penwortham
Witton Park
Bottom of Hutton
Higher Walton
Pleasington
Warton Bank
Hutton
Coup Green
Hoghton Tower
Oswaldtwistle
Broadfield
Longton
Penwortham Lane
Bamber Bridge
Gregson Lane
Mill Hill
Guide
New Longton
Tardy Gate
Lostock Hall Sta
Hoghton
Riley Green
Blackburn Rovers FC
Ewood
Lower Darwen
Ribble
Feniscowles
Earcroft
Belthorn
Ribble Estuary NNR
Hall Green
Walmer Bridge
Brindle
Much Hoole
Clayton Green
Thorpe Green
Withnell Fold
Tockholes
Blackburn with Darwen
Waterside
West Lancashire Light Railway
Midge Hall
Earnshaw Bridge
Farington
Abbey Village
Pickup Bank
Hesketh Bank
Becconsall
Clayton-le-Woods
Higher Wheelton
Withnell
Ryal Fold
Darwen
Hoddlesden
Hundred End
Much Hoole Town
Cocker Bar
LEYLAND
Broadfield
Whittle-le-Woods
Wheelton
Brinscall
Blacksnape
Banks
Tarleton
Bretherton
Runshaw Moor
Heapey
Holmes
Barber's Moor
Euxton
Astley Hall Mus & Gallery
Botany Bay
183
BLACKBURN WITH DARWEN
Whittlestone Head
Mere Brow
Croston
White Coppice
Anglezarke Moor
Turton Moor
Belmont Res
Edgworth
CHORLEY
Belmont
Turton Tower
Holmeswood
Rufford
Charnock Richard
Cowling
Dimple
0 2 4 6 miles
0 2 4 6 8 10 km

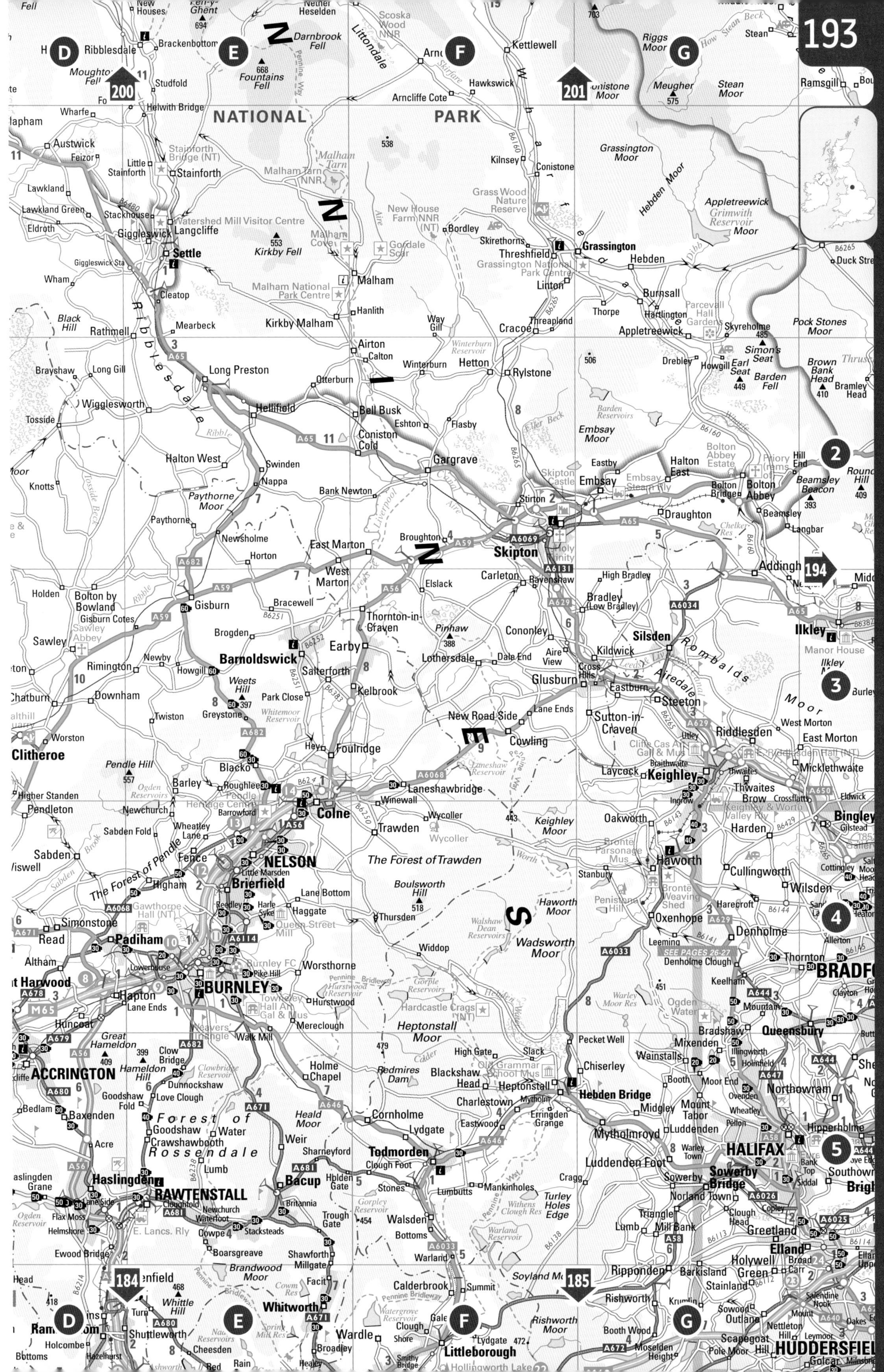

Ribblesdale
Brackenbottom
Darnbrook Fell
Littondale
Kettlewell
Riggs Moor
Stean
Ramsgill
Moughton Fell
Studfold
668
Fountains Fell
Hawkswick
Arncliffe Cote
Meugher
575
Stean Moor
200
201
Conistone Moor
Helwith Bridge
Wharfe
NATIONAL
PARK
Austwick
Feizor
Little Stainforth
Stainforth Bridge (NT)
Stainforth
Malham Tarn
538
Kilnsey
Conistone
Grassington Moor
Hebden Moor
Appletreewick
Grimwith Reservoir
Moor
Lawkland
Lawkland Green
Stackhouse
Watershed Mill Visitor Centre
Eldroth
Giggleswick
Langcliffe
Malham Tarn NNR
New House Farm NNR (NT)
Grass Wood Nature Reserve
553
Kirkby Fell
Malham Cove
Gordale Scar
Bordley
Skirethorns
Threshfield
Grassington
Hebden
B6265
Duck Street
Settle
Giggleswick Sta
Grassington National Park Centre
Wham
Cleatop
Malham
Malham National Park Centre
Linton
Burnsall
Hartlington
Parcevall Hall Gardens
Thorpe
Black Hill
Rathmell
Mearbeck
Kirkby Malham
Hanlith
Way Gill
Cracoe
Threapland
Appletreewick
Skyreholme
485
Simon's Seat
Pock Stones Moor
Airton
Calton
Winterburn Reservoir
Winterburn
Hetton
Rylstone
506
Drebley
Howgill
Earl Seat
449
Barden Fell
Brown Bank Head
410
Bramley Head
Brayshaw
Long Gill
Long Preston
Otterburn
Wigglesworth
Tosside
Hellifield
Bell Busk
Eshton
Flasby
Barden Reservoirs
Embsay Moor
Bolton Abbey Estate
Halton West
Coniston Cold
Gargrave
Eastby
Halton East
Priory (rems of)
Hill End
Round Hill
409
Beamsley Beacon
393
Swinden
Nappa
Knotts
Paythorne Moor
Bank Newton
Skipton Castle
Embsay
Embsay Steam Rly
Bolton Bridge
Bolton Abbey
Stirton
Draughton
Beamsley
Paythorne
Newsholme
Horton
East Marton
Broughton
Skipton
Holy Trinity
Chelker Res
Langbar
Addingham
194
West Marton
Elslack
Carleton
Ravenshaw
High Bradley
Holden
Bolton by Bowland
Gisburn Cotes
Gisburn
Bracewell
Bradley (Low Bradley)
Sawley Abbey
Sawley
Brogden
Thornton-in-Craven
Pinhaw
388
Cononley
Silsden
Ilkley
Manor House
Earby
Barnoldswick
Rimington
Newby
Howgill
Lothersdale
Dale End
Aire View
Kildwick
Salterforth
Cross Hills
Glusburn
Eastburn
Ilkley Moor
Chatburn
Downham
Weets Hill
397
Kelbrook
Park Close
Whitemoor Reservoir
Steeton
Rombalds Moor
Airedale
Twiston
Greystone
Worston
New Road Side
Lane Ends
Sutton-in-Craven
Riddlesden
West Morton
East Morton
Clitheroe
Hey
Foulridge
Cowling
Utley
Cliffe Cas Art Gall & Mus
East Riddlesden Hall (NT)
Pendle Hill
557
Blacko
Lumb
Laneshaw Reservoir
Laycock
Keighley
Braithwaite
Micklethwaite
Barley
Roughlee
Thwaites
Thwaites Brow
Crossflatts
Higher Standen
Pendleton
Ogden Reservoirs
Heritage Centre
Barrowford
Colne
Laneshawbridge
Winewall
Ingrow
Keighley & Worth Valley Rly
Eldwick
Bingley
Newchurch
Wycoller
Trawden
443
Keighley Moor
Oakworth
Harden
Gilstead
Sabden Fold
Wheatley Lane
Sabden
Fence
Nelson
Little Marsden
The Forest of Pendle
The Forest of Trawden
Brontë Parsonage Mus
Haworth
Stanbury
Cullingworth
Cottingley
Wilsden
Higham
Brierfield
Lane Bottom
Boulsworth Hill
518
Haworth Moor
Penistone Hill
Brontë Weaving Shed
Harecroft
Gawthorpe Hall (NT)
Reedley
Harle Syke
Haggate
Queen Street Mill
Thursden
Walshaw Dean Reservoirs
Wadsworth Moor
Oxenhope
Denholme
Simonstone
Read
Padiham
Leeming
SEE PAGES 26-27
Denholme Clough
Allerton
Thornton
Altham
Lowerhouse
Burnley FC
Pike Hill
Worsthorne
Widdop
Bradford
Great Harwood
Hapton
Burnley
Towneley Hall Art Gal & Mus
Pennine Bridleway
Gorple Reservoirs
Hurstwood Reservoir
Hurstwood
Hardcastle Crags (NT)
Warley Moor Res
451
Ogden Water
Keelham
Clayton
Lane Ends
Huncoat
Weavers' Triangle
Walk Mill
Mereclough
Heptonstall Moor
Mountain
Queensbury
Bradshaw
Great Harwood
Hameldon
399
409
Clow Bridge
479
High Gate
Slack
Pecket Well
Mixenden
Illingworth
Holmfield
Accrington
Hameldon Hill
Clowbridge Reservoir
Dunnockshaw
Holme Chapel
Redmires Dam
Blackshaw Head
Old Grammar School Mus
Heptonstall
Chiserley
Wainstalls
Booth
Moor End
Northowram
Goodshaw Fold
Love Clough
Hebden Bridge
Mytholm
Ovenden
Bedlam
Baxenden
Forest of Rossendale
Heald Moor
Cornholme
Charlestown
Eastwood
Erringden Grange
Midgley
Mount Tabor
Wheatley
Goodshaw
Water
Lydgate
Mytholmroyd
Luddenden
Pellon
Hipperholme
Acre
Crawshawbooth
Weir
Todmorden
Warley Town
Halifax
Shelf
Sharneyford
Clough Foot
Luddenden Foot
Sowerby
Sowerby Bridge
Bank Top
Southowram
Brighouse
Haslingden Grane
Haslingden
Rawtenstall
Lumb
Bacup
Hbden Gate
Stones
Lumbutts
Mankinholes
Cragg
Norland Town
Turley Holes Edge
Withens Clough Res
Ogden Reservoir
Flax Moss
Helmshore
Lane Side
Cloughfold
Newchurch
Waterfoot
E. Lancs. Rly
Cowpe
Stacksteads
Britannia
Gorpley Reservoir
454
Trough Gate
Walsden
Bottoms
Warland Reservoir
Triangle
Clough Head
Greetland
Copley
Lumb
Mill Bank
Elland
Ewood Bridge
Boarsgreave
Shawforth
Millgate
Brandwood Moor
Warland
Soyland Moor
Ripponden
Barkisland
Holywell Green
Broad Carr
Stainland
184
185
Whittle Hill
468
Cowm Res
Facit
Calderbrook
Summit
Rishworth
Krumlin
Sowood
Outlane
Nettleton Hill
Turn
Whitworth
Watergrove Reservoir
Gale
Clough
Shore
Rishworth Moor
Booth Wood
Scapegoat Hill
Huddersfield
Holcombe
Shuttleworth
Naden Reservoirs
Spring Mill Res
Wardle
Lydgate
472
Littleborough
Moselden Height
Pole Moor
Golcar
Milnsbridge
Bottoms
Hazlehurst
Cheesden
Rain
Broadley
Healey
Smithy Bridge
Hollingworth Lake

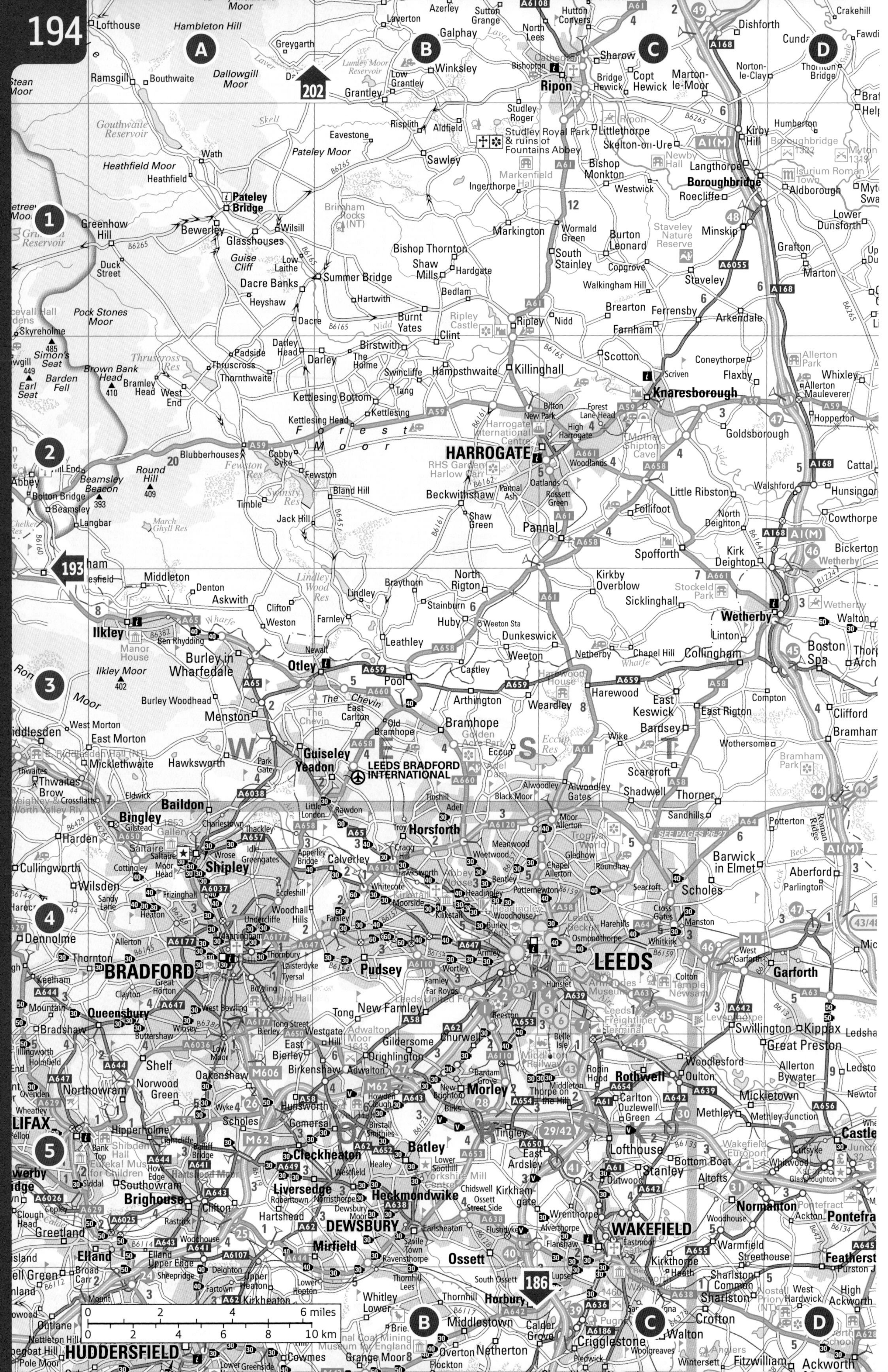
A
B
C
D
1
2
3
4
5
Lofthouse
Hambleton Hill
Azerley
Sutton Grange
Hutton Conyers
Laverton
Galphay
North Lees
Dishforth
Crakehill
Greygarth
Ramsgill
Bouthwaite
Dallowgill Moor
202
Low Grantley
Winksley
Grantley
Sharow
Copt Hewick
Bridge Hewick
Marton-le-Moor
Norton-le-Clay
Thornton Bridge
Bishopton
Ripon
Cathedral
Studley Roger
Studley Royal Park & ruins of Fountains Abbey
Littlethorpe
Skelton-on-Ure
Kirby Hill
Humberton
Boroughbridge
Langthorpe
Aldborough
Isurium Roman Town
Roecliffe
Gouthwaite Reservoir
Risplith
Aldfield
Eavestone
Pateley Moor
Sawley
Wath
Heathfield Moor
Heathfield
Markenfield Hall
Ingerthorpe
Bishop Monkton
Westwick
Newby Hall
Pateley Bridge
Brimham Rocks (NT)
Greenhow Hill
Bewerley
Wilsill
Glasshouses
Markington
Wormald Green
Burton Leonard
Staveley Nature Reserve
Minskip
Lower Dunsforth
Grafton
Marton
Guise Cliff
Low Laithe
Bishop Thornton
Shaw Mills
Hardgate
South Stainley
Copgrove
Staveley
Duck Street
Summer Bridge
Dacre Banks
Hartwith
Heyshaw
Bedlam
Walkingham Hill
Pock Stones Moor
Skyreholme
Dacre
Burnt Yates
Ripley Castle
Ripley
Nidd
Brearton
Ferrensby
Arkendale
Farnham
Clint
Simon's Seat
Barden Fell
Thruscross Res
Padside
Darley Head
Darley
Birstwith
The Holme
Scotton
Coneythorpe
Allerton Park
Thruscross
Thornthwaite
Swincliffe
Hampsthwaite
Killinghall
Scriven
Flaxby
Whixley
Brown Bank Head
Bramley Head
West End
Earl Seat
Kettlesing Bottom
Tang
Knaresborough
Allerton Mauleverer
Kettlesing Head
Kettlesing
Forest Moor
Bilton
New Park
Forest Lane Head
Goldsborough
Hopperton
Harrogate International Centre
High Harrogate
Mother Shipton's Cave
Blubberhouses
Fewston Res
Cobby Syke
HARROGATE
Woodlands
Cattal
Round Hill
Beamsley Beacon
Fewston
RHS Garden Harlow Carr
Abbey
Bolton Bridge
Beamsley
Bland Hill
Beckwithshaw
Pannal Ash
Oatlands
Rossett Green
Little Ribston
Walshford
Hunsingore
Langbar
Swinsty Res
Timble
March Ghyll Res
Jack Hill
Shaw Green
Pannal
Follifoot
North Deighton
Cowthorpe
Spofforth
Kirk Deighton
Bickerton
Wetherby
193
Middleton
Denton
Askwith
Lindley Wood Res
Lindley
Braythorn
North Rigton
Stainburn
Kirkby Overblow
Stockeld Park
Sicklinghall
Clifton
Weston
Huby
Weeton Sta
Ilkley
Ben Rhydding
Manor House
Farnley
Leathley
Dunkeswick
Linton
Walton
Burley in Wharfedale
Ilkley Moor
Newall
Otley
Weeton
Netherby
Chapel Hill
Collingham
Boston Spa
Thorp Arch
Pool
Castley
Harewood House
Harewood
The Chevin
East Carlton
Arthington
Weardley
East Keswick
Compton
Burley Woodhead
Menston
Bramhope
Old Bramhope
Golden Acre Park
Bardsey
East Rigton
Clifford
West Morton
East Morton
Eccup
Eccup Res
Wike
Wothersome
Bramham
Micklethwaite
Hawksworth
Guiseley
Yeadon
LEEDS BRADFORD INTERNATIONAL
Adel Dam
Scarcroft
Bramham Park
Thwaites Brow
Park Gate
Alwoodley
Alwoodley Gates
Shadwell
Thorner
Eldwick
Baildon
Tinshill
Black Moor
Adel
Sandhills
Bingley
Gilstead
Charlestown
Little London
Rawdon
Moor Allerton
Potterton
Harden
Saltaire
1853 Gallery
Horsforth
Tropical World
SEE PAGES 26-27
Barwick in Elmet
Roman Ridge
Cullingworth
Cottingley
Wrose
Idle
Thackley
Greengates
Apperley Bridge
Calverley
Cragg Hill
Meanwood
Weetwood
Gledhow
Chapel Allerton
Roundhay
Aberford
Parlington
Shipley
Moor Head
Hawksworth
Abbey House
Bentley
Potternewton
Seacroft
Scholes
Wilsden
Frizinghall
Eccleshill
Whitecote
Kirkstall
Moorside
Headingley
Woodhouse
Harehills
Cross Gates
Manston
Sandy Lane
Heaton
Undercliffe
Woodhall Hills
Farsley
Burley
Osmondthorpe
Whitkirk
Dennolme
Allerton
Manningham
Thornbury
Armley
Leeds Beckett
LEEDS
West Garforth
Garforth
Thornton
BRADFORD
Laisterdyke
Tyersal
Pudsey
Wortley
Hunslet
Colton
Temple Newsam
Keelham
Great Horton
Clayton
Bowling
Bolling Hall
Farnley
Far Royds
Leeds United FC
Royal Armouries Museum
Leeds Freightliner Terminal
Mountain
Queensbury
West Bowling
Tong
New Farnley
Beeston
Swillington
Kippax
Ledsham
Bradshaw
Buttershaw
Wibsey
Tong Street
Bierley
Westgate Hill
Adwalton Moor 1643
Churwell
Belle Isle
Great Preston
Illingworth
Holmfield
Low Moor
East Bierley
Gildersome
Middleton Railway
Robin Hood
Rothwell
Woodlesford
Oulton
Allerton Bywater
Ledston
Shelf
Norwood Green
Oakenshaw
Birkenshaw
Adwalton
Drighlington
Bantam Grove
Morley
Middleton
Thorpe on the Hill
Carlton
Oulton
Mickletown
Newton
Ovenden
Northowram
Hunsworth
Howden Clough
New Brighton
Birks
Oulzewell Green
Methley
Methley Junction
Wheatley
HALIFAX
Hipperholme
Lightcliffe
Scholes
Gomersal
Birstall Smithies
Tingley
Lofthouse
Castleford
Shibden Hall
Bank Top
Eureka! Museum for Children
Hove Edge
Bailiff Bridge
Hartshead Moor
Cleckheaton
Batley
Lower Soothill
East Ardsley
Bottom Boat
Wakefield Europort
Cutsyke
Whitwood
Glasshoughton
Sowerby Bridge
Siddal
Southowram
Westfield
Healey
Yorkshire Mill
Stanley
Altofts
Outwood
Brighouse
Clifton
Liversedge
Roberttown
Norristhorpe
Heckmondwike
Chidswell
Ossett Street Side
Kirkhamgate
Wrenthorpe
Normanton
Pontefract
Ackton
Clough Head
Copley
Rastrick
Hartshead
Dewsbury Moor
Alverthorpe
Woodhouse
Greetland
DEWSBURY
Earlsheaton
Flushdyke
WAKEFIELD
Eastmoor
Warmfield
Elland
Upper Edge
Woodhouse
Mirfield
Savile Town
Ravensthorpe
Ossett
Flanshaw
Kirkthorpe
Streethouse
Featherstone
Purston Jaglin
Holywell Green
Broad Carr
Sheepridge
Deighton
Upper Heaton
Lower Hopton
Thornhill Lees
South Ossett
186
Lupset
Sharlston Common
Sharlston
Nostell Priory (NT)
West Hardwick
High Ackworth
Outlane
Fartown
Kirkheaton
Whitley Lower
Thornhill
Horbury
Calder Grove
Sandal
Crofton
Middlestown
Pugneys
Nettleton Hill
HUDDERSFIELD
Cowmes
Lower Greenside
Grange Moor
Overton
Flockton
Netherton
Crigglestone
Walton
Woolgreaves
Wintersett
Fitzwilliam
Ackworth
Pole Moor
National Coal Mining Museum for England
0 2 4 6 miles
0 2 4 6 8 10 km

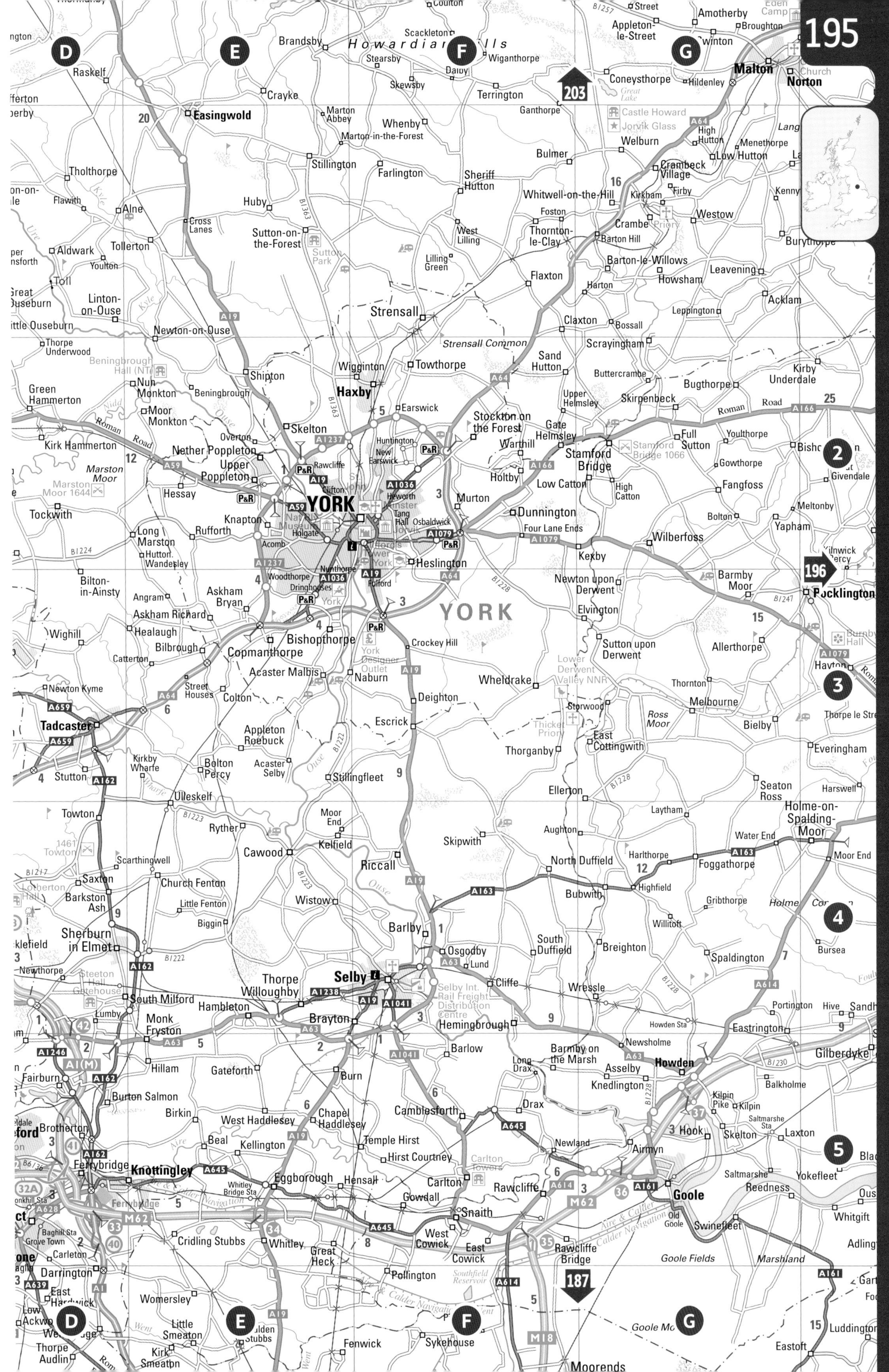
Howardian Hills
Brandsby
Scackleton
Stearsby
Dalby
Wiganthorpe
Appleton-le-Street
Amotherby
Broughton
Swinton
Malton
Norton
Hildenley
Coneysthorpe
Great Lake
Castle Howard
Jorvik Glass
Raskelf
Easingwold
Crayke
Marton Abbey
Skewsby
Terrington
Ganthorpe
Whenby
Marton-in-the-Forest
Welburn
High Hutton
Menethorpe
Low Hutton
Stillington
Farlington
Bulmer
Crambeck Village
Firby
Kirkham
Kirkham Priory
Tholthorpe
Sheriff Hutton
Whitwell-on-the-Hill
Flawith
Alne
Huby
Cross Lanes
Foston
Crambe
Westow
Sutton-on-the-Forest
Sutton Park
West Lilling
Thornton-le-Clay
Barton Hill
Barton-le-Willows
Aldwark
Tollerton
Youlton
Lilling Green
Leavening
Howsham
Toll
Flaxton
Harton
Acklam
Great Ouseburn
Linton-on-Ouse
Leppington
Strensall
Claxton
Bossall
Little Ouseburn
Newton-on-Ouse
Strensall Common
Scrayingham
Thorpe Underwood
Beningbrough Hall (NT)
Wigginton
Towthorpe
Sand Hutton
Buttercrambe
Kirby Underdale
Green Hammerton
Nun Monkton
Shipton
Beningbrough
Haxby
Upper Helmsley
Skirpenbeck
Bugthorpe
Moor Monkton
Earswick
Stockton on the Forest
Gate Helmsley
Roman Road
Kirk Hammerton
Skelton
Huntington
New Earswick
Warthill
Full Sutton
Youlthorpe
Overton
Nether Poppleton
Rawcliffe
Stamford Bridge
Stamford Bridge 1066
Bishop Wilton
Marston Moor
Upper Poppleton
Clifton
Holtby
Gowthorpe
Givendale
Marston Moor 1644
Hessay
Heworth
Low Catton
High Catton
Fangfoss
YORK
Murton
Tockwith
Knapton
Minster
Tang Hall
Osbaldwick
Dunnington
Meltonby
Long Marston
Rufforth
Holgate
Four Lane Ends
Bolton
Yapham
Acomb
Wilberfoss
Hutton Wandesley
Heslington
Kexby
Pocklington
Bilton-in-Ainsty
Nunthorpe
Woodthorpe
Dringhouses
Fulford
Newton upon Derwent
Barmby Moor
Angram
Askham Bryan
Askham Richard
Elvington
Wighill
Healaugh
Bishopthorpe
Crockey Hill
Sutton upon Derwent
Allerthorpe
Burnby Hall
Bilbrough
Catterton
Copmanthorpe
York Designer Outlet
Lower Derwent Valley NNR
Hayton
Acaster Malbis
Naburn
Wheldrake
Thornton
Newton Kyme
Street Houses
Colton
Deighton
Storwood
Melbourne
Tadcaster
Escrick
Ross Moor
Bielby
Thorpe le Street
Appleton Roebuck
Thicket Priory
East Cottingwith
Kirkby Wharfe
Bolton Percy
Acaster Selby
Thorganby
Everingham
Stutton
Stillingfleet
Ellerton
Seaton Ross
Harswell
Ulleskelf
Towton
Ryther
Moor End
Laytham
Holme-on-Spalding-Moor
1461 Towton
Kelfield
Skipwith
Aughton
Water End
Cawood
Moor End
Scarthingwell
Riccall
North Duffield
Harlthorpe
Foggathorpe
Saxton
Church Fenton
Highfield
Barkston Ash
Little Fenton
Wistow
Bubwith
Gribthorpe
Holme
Biggin
Willitoft
Sherburn in Elmet
Barlby
South Duffield
Breighton
Bursea
Osgodby
Lund
Spaldington
Newthorpe
Steeton Hall
Selby
Thorpe Willoughby
Cliffe
Wressle
South Milford
Selby Int. Rail Freight Distribution Centre
Hambleton
Portington
Hive
Lumby
Monk Fryston
Brayton
Hemingbrough
Howden Sta
Eastrington
Newsholme
Barlow
Barmby on the Marsh
Gilberdyke
Hillam
Gateforth
Long Drax
Asselby
Howden
Fairburn
Knedlington
Balkholme
Burn
Burton Salmon
Birkin
Camblesforth
Drax
Kilpin Pike
Kilpin
Brotherton
West Haddlesey
Chapel Haddlesey
Hook
Saltmarshe Sta
Skelton
Laxton
Beal
Kellington
Temple Hirst
Newland
Airmyn
Ferrybridge
Knottingley
Hirst Courtney
Carlton Towers
Saltmarshe
Yokefleet
Eggborough
Hensall
Carlton
Rawcliffe
Goole
Reedness
Whitley Bridge Sta
Gowdall
Snaith
Aire & Calder Navigation
Old Goole
Whitgift
Baghill Sta
Cridling Stubbs
Whitley
West Cowick
Swinefleet
Grove Town
Carleton
Great Heck
East Cowick
Rawcliffe Bridge
Adlingfleet
Darrington
Pollington
Goole Fields
Marshland
East Hardwick
Southfield Reservoir
Calder Navigation
Womersley
Little Smeaton
Went
Goole Moor
Thorpe Audlin
Kirk Smeaton
Fenwick
Sykehouse
Moorends
Eastoft
Luddington
203
196
187
D
E
F
G
2
3
4
5
A19
A64
A59
A1237
A1036
A1079
A166
A659
A162
A163
A63
A1238
A1041
A645
A614
A161
A1246
A1(M)
A628
A639
M62
M18
B1363
B1224
B1222
B1223
B1217
B1228
B1247
B1230
B1257

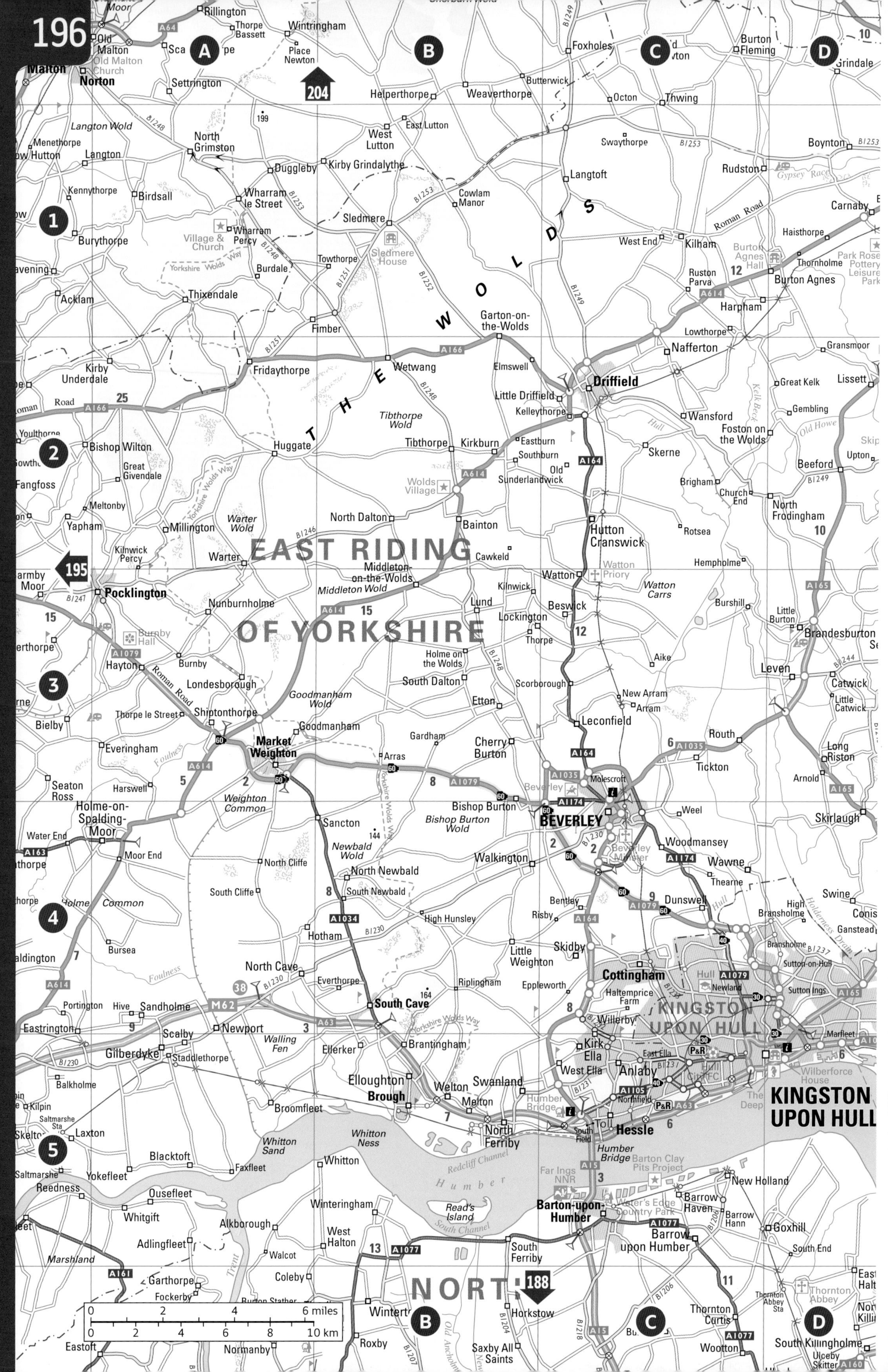

Malton
Old Malton
Old Malton Church
Norton
Rillington
Thorpe Bassett
Wintringham
Place Newton
204
A
B
C
D
Settrington
Helperthorpe
Weaverthorpe
Butterwick
Foxholes
Burton Fleming
Grindale
Octon
Thwing
Langton Wold
199
East Lutton
West Lutton
North Grimston
Menethorpe
Langton
Swaythorpe
Boynton
Duggleby
Kirby Grindalythe
Langtoft
Rudston
Gypsey Race
Kennythorpe
Birdsall
Wharram le Street
Cowlam Manor
Carnaby
1
Sledmere
Roman Road
Village & Church
Wharram Percy
Burythorpe
Sledmere House
West End
Kilham
Haisthorpe
Burton Agnes Hall
Park Rose Pottery Leisure Park
Yorkshire Wolds Way
Towthorpe
Burdale
Thornholme
Ruston Parva
12
Burton Agnes
Acklam
Thixendale
Harpham
THE WOLDS
Fimber
Garton-on-the-Wolds
Lowthorpe
Nafferton
Gransmoor
Kirby Underdale
Fridaythorpe
Wetwang
Elmswell
Driffield
Great Kelk
Lissett
Road
25
Little Driffield
Kelleythorpe
Gembling
Wansford
Foston on the Wolds
Old Howe
Youlthorpe
Bishop Wilton
Tibthorpe Wold
Huggate
Tibthorpe
Kirkburn
Eastburn
Southburn
Skerne
Upton
2
Great Givendale
Old
Sunderlandwick
Beeford
Fangfoss
Wolds Village
Brigham
Church End
Meltonby
North Dalton
North Frodingham
Yapham
Millington
Warter Wold
Bainton
Hutton Cranswick
Rotsea
10
EAST RIDING OF YORKSHIRE
Kilnwick Percy
Warter
Cawkeld
Hempholme
195
Middleton-on-the-Wolds
Watton
Watton Priory
Watton Carrs
Pocklington
Middleton Wold
Kilnwick
Nunburnholme
Lund
Beswick
Burshill
15
Lockington
Little Burton
Burnby Hall
Thorpe
Brandesburton
Holme on the Wolds
Aike
Hayton
Burnby
South Dalton
Scorborough
Leven
Catwick
3
Londesborough
New Arram
Arram
Little Catwick
Goodmanham Wold
Etton
Bielby
Thorpe le Street
Shiptonthorpe
Goodmanham
Leconfield
Routh
Everingham
Gardham
Cherry Burton
Long Riston
Market Weighton
Arras
Tickton
Seaton Ross
Harswell
Molescroft
Arnold
Beverley
Holme-on-Spalding-Moor
Weighton Common
Bishop Burton
Water End
Sancton
Bishop Burton Wold
BEVERLEY
Weel
Skirlaugh
Moor End
Newbald Wold
144
Beverley Minster
Woodmansey
Walkington
North Cliffe
Wawne
North Newbald
Thearne
Swine
Holme Common
South Cliffe
South Newbald
Bentley
Dunswell
4
High Hunsley
Risby
Hull
Bransholme
High Bransholme
Ganstead
Holderness Drain
Hotham
Skidby
Bursea
Little Weighton
North Cave
Cottingham
Sutton-on-Hull
Foulness
Everthorpe
Riplingham
Eppleworth
Haltemprice Farm
Newland
Sutton Ings
Portington
Hive
Sandholme
South Cave
164
KINGSTON UPON HULL
Eastrington
Newport
Scalby
Walling Fen
Willerby
Marfleet
Gilberdyke
Staddlethorpe
Brantingham
Ellerker
Kirk Ella
East Ella
Anlaby
Hull City FC
Wilberforce House
Balkholme
Elloughton
Welton
Swanland
West Ella
Kilpin
Brough
Melton
Humber Bridge
Northfield
The Deep
KINGSTON UPON HULL
Broomfleet
Saltmarshe Sta
Laxton
North Ferriby
South Field
Toll
Hessle
5
Whitton Sand
Whitton Ness
Redcliff Channel
Humber Bridge
Barton Clay Pits Project
Blacktoft
Faxfleet
Whitton
Far Ings NNR
Saltmarshe
Yokefleet
Humber
New Holland
Reedness
Ousefleet
Winteringham
Water's Edge Country Park
Barrow Haven
Read's Island
Barton-upon-Humber
Whitgift
Alkborough
South Channel
Barrow Hann
Goxhill
West Halton
Barrow upon Humber
Adlingfleet
South Ferriby
South End
Walcot
Marshland
Trent
Coleby
Garthorpe
NORTH
188
Thornton Abbey Sta
Thornton Abbey
Fockerby
Burton Stather
Thornton Curtis
Winterton
Horkstow
Roxby
Saxby All Saints
Wootton
South Killingholme
Ulceby Skitter
Eastoft
Normanby
Old Ancholme
0 2 4 6 miles
0 2 4 6 8 10 km
A64
A166
A614
A1079
A163
A614
A164
A1035
A1174
A1034
A1079
M62
A63
A1105
A15
A1077
A161
A165
A1033
B1248
B1253
B1249
B1251
B1252
B1246
B1247
B1230
B1237
B1244
B1206
B1204
B1207
B1218
B1231

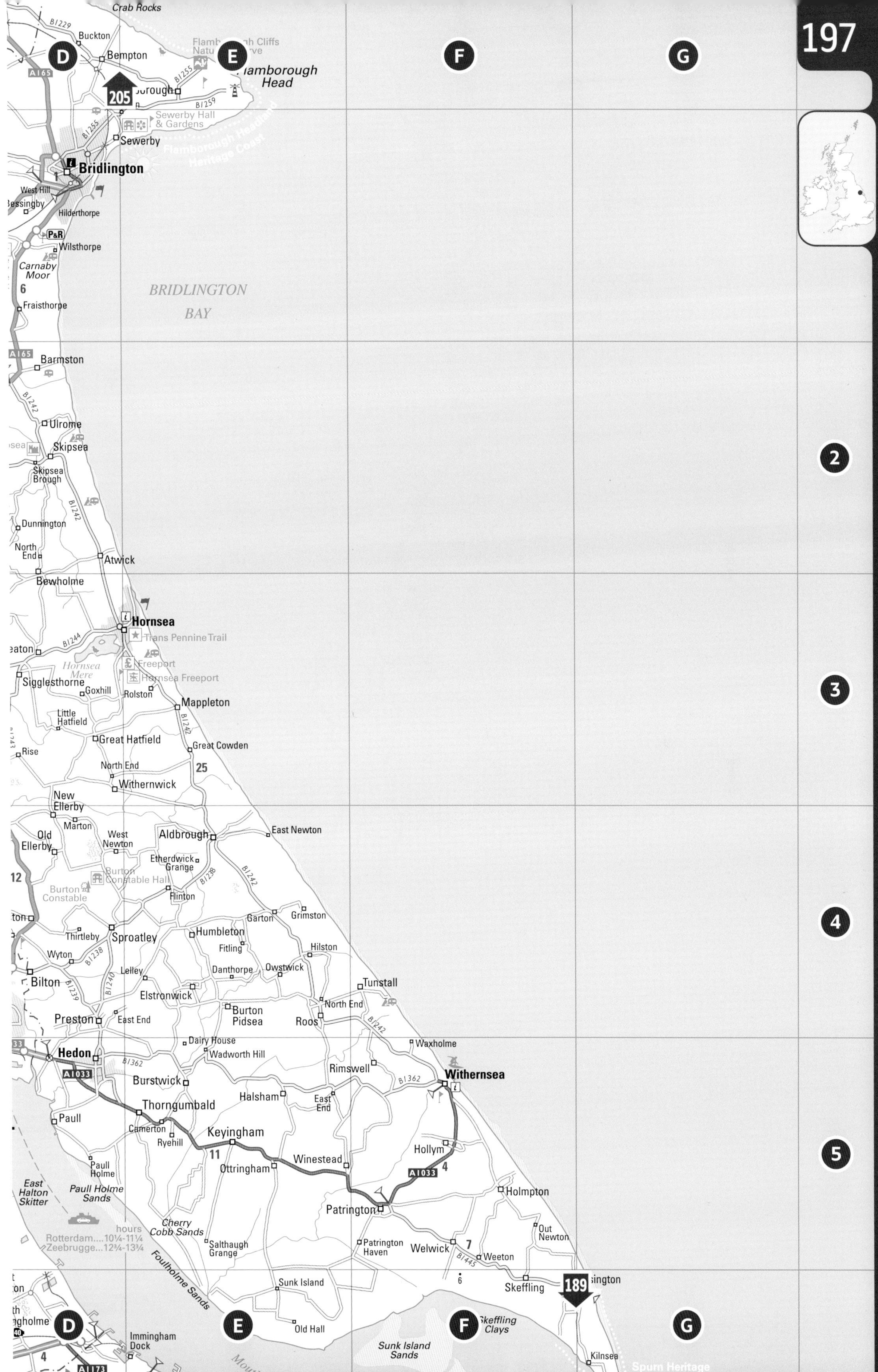
Crab Rocks
Buckton
Bempton
Flamborough Head
205
Sewerby Hall & Gardens
Sewerby
Flamborough Headland Heritage Coast
Bridlington
West Hill
Bessingby
Hilderthorpe
P&R
Wilsthorpe
Carnaby Moor
Fraisthorpe
BRIDLINGTON BAY
Barmston
Ulrome
Skipsea
Skipsea Brough
Dunnington
North End
Atwick
Bewholme
Hornsea
Trans Pennine Trail
Hornsea Mere
Freeport
Hornsea Freeport
Sigglesthorne
Goxhill
Rolston
Mappleton
Little Hatfield
Great Hatfield
Great Cowden
Rise
North End
Withernwick
New Ellerby
Marton
Old Ellerby
West Newton
Aldbrough
East Newton
Etherdwick Grange
Burton Constable Hall
Burton Constable
Flinton
Garton
Grimston
Thirtleby
Sproatley
Humbleton
Fitling
Hilston
Wyton
Lelley
Danthorpe
Owstwick
Bilton
Elstronwick
Tunstall
North End
Burton Pidsea
Roos
Preston
East End
Dairy House
Wadworth Hill
Waxholme
Hedon
Rimswell
Burstwick
Withernsea
Halsham
East End
Thorngumbald
Paull
Camerton
Ryehill
Keyingham
Hollym
Ottringham
Winestead
Paull Holme
East Halton Skitter
Paull Holme Sands
Holmpton
Patrington
hours
Rotterdam....10¼-11¼
Zeebrugge...12¾-13¾
Cherry Cobb Sands
Salthaugh Grange
Patrington Haven
Welwick
Out Newton
Weeton
Foulholme Sands
Sunk Island
Skeffling
189
Old Hall
Skeffling Clays
Sunk Island Sands
Immingham Dock
Kilnsea
Spurn Heritage
D
E
F
G
2
3
4
5

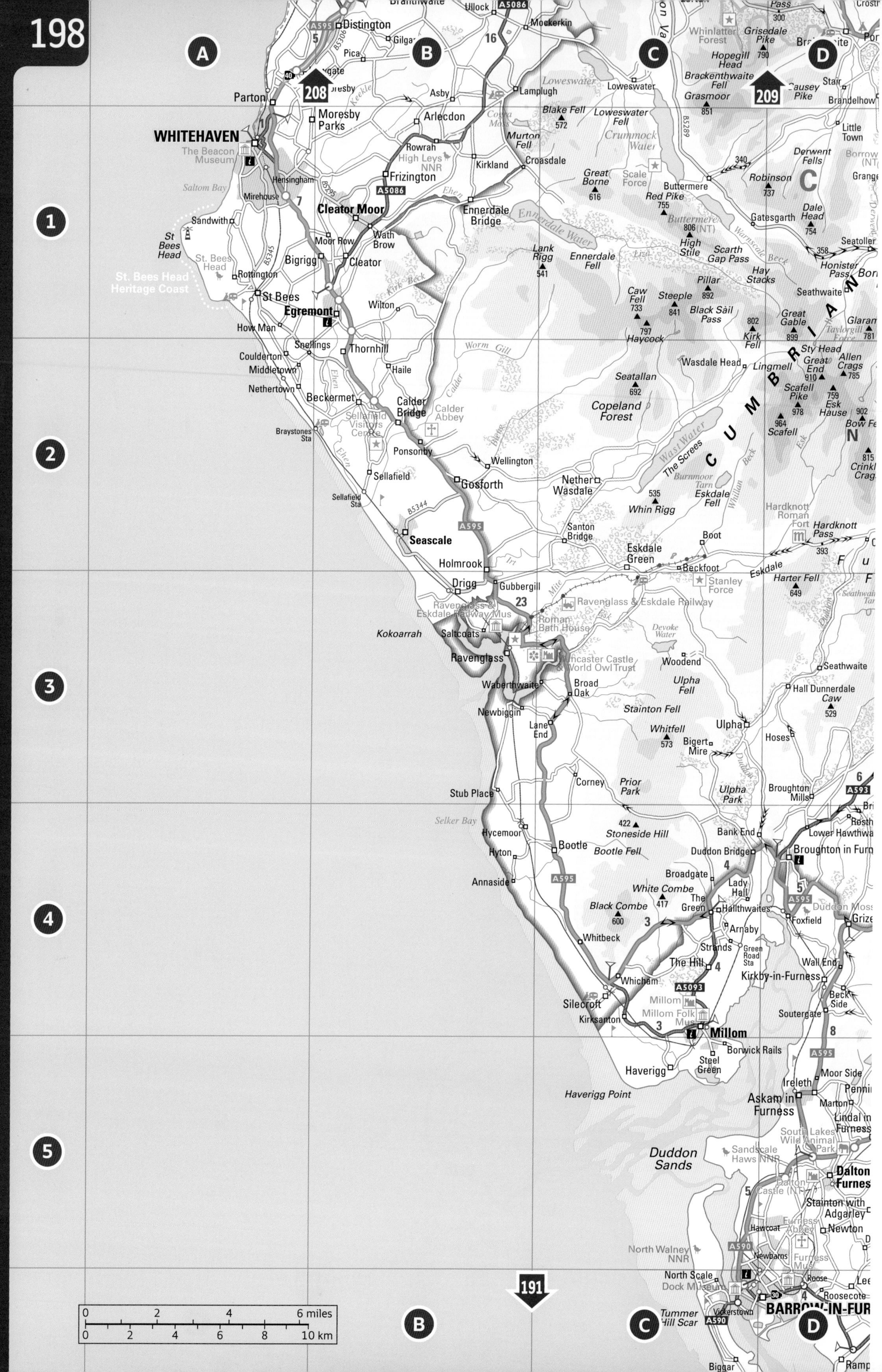
A
B
C
D
1
2
3
4
5
208
209
191
Distington
Gilgarran
Pica
Parton
Moresby Parks
WHITEHAVEN
The Beacon Museum
Hensingham
Mirehouse
Saltom Bay
Sandwith
St Bees Head
St. Bees Head
St. Bees Head Heritage Coast
Rottington
St Bees
How Man
Egremont
Bigrigg
Moor Row
Cleator Moor
Cleator
Wath Brow
Frizington
Rowrah
High Leys NNR
Arlecdon
Asby
Lamplugh
Ullock
Mockerkin
Kirkland
Croasdale
Ennerdale Bridge
Ennerdale Water
Loweswater
Loweswater Fell
Blake Fell
572
Murton Fell
Crummock Water
Great Borne
616
Scale Force
Buttermere
Red Pike
755
Buttermere (NT)
806
High Stile
Scarth Gap Pass
Lank Rigg
541
Ennerdale Fell
Whinlatter Forest
Grisedale Pike
790
Hopegill Head
Brackenthwaite Fell
Grasmoor
851
Causey Pike
Stair
Braithwaite
Brandelhow
Little Town
Derwent Fells
Robinson
737
Dale Head
754
Gatesgarth
Seatoller
Honister Pass
Seathwaite
Hay Stacks
Pillar
892
Caw Fell
733
Steeple
841
Black Sàil Pass
Haycock
797
802
Kirk Fell
Great Gable
899
Glaramara
781
Sty Head
Great End
910
Allen Crags
785
Wasdale Head
Lingmell
Scafell Pike
978
759
Esk Hause
964
Scafell
902
Bow Fell
815
Crinkle Crags
CUMBRIAN
Wilton
Snellings
Thornhill
Coulderton
Middletown
Nethertown
Haile
Beckermet
Calder Bridge
Calder Abbey
Worm Gill
Sellafield Visitors Centre
Braystones Sta
Ponsonby
Wellington
Sellafield
Sellafield Sta
Gosforth
Seatallan
692
Copeland Forest
Wast Water
The Screes
Burnmoor Tarn
Eskdale Fell
535
Whin Rigg
Nether Wasdale
Hardknott Roman Fort
Hardknott Pass
393
Seascale
Santon Bridge
Boot
Eskdale Green
Beckfoot
Stanley Force
Eskdale
Harter Fell
649
Holmrook
Drigg
Gubbergill
Ravenglass & Eskdale Railway Mus
Ravenglass & Eskdale Railway
Roman Bath House
Kokoarrah
Saltcoats
Ravenglass
Muncaster Castle & World Owl Trust
Devoke Water
Woodend
Seathwaite
Hall Dunnerdale
Caw
529
Waberthwaite
Broad Oak
Ulpha Fell
Newbiggin
Stainton Fell
Lane End
Whitfell
573
Bigert Mire
Ulpha
Hoses
Corney
Prior Park
Ulpha Park
Broughton Mills
Stub Place
Selker Bay
Hycemoor
422
Stoneside Hill
Bank End
Lower Hawthwaite
Broughton in Furness
Hyton
Bootle
Bootle Fell
Duddon Bridge
Annaside
Broadgate
Lady Hall
White Combe
417
The Green
Hallthwaites
Duddon Moss
Foxfield
Black Combe
600
Arnaby
Whitbeck
Strands
Green Road Sta
The Hill
Wall End
Whicham
Kirkby-in-Furness
Silecroft
Millom
Millom Folk Mus
Beck Side
Kirksanton
Soutergate
Borwick Rails
Steel Green
Haverigg
Haverigg Point
Moor Side
Ireleth
Askam in Furness
Marton
Lindal in Furness
South Lakes Wild Animal Park
Duddon Sands
Sandscale Haws NNR
Dalton Castle (NT)
Dalton in Furness
Stainton with Adgarley
Hawcoat
Furness Abbey
Newton
North Walney NNR
Newbarns
Furness Mus
North Scale
Dock Museum
Roose
Roosecote
Vickerstown
BARROW-IN-FURNESS
Tummer Hill Scar
Biggar
A595
A5086
A5093
A593
A590
B5306
B5295
B5345
B5344
B5289
0 2 4 6 miles
0 2 4 6 8 10 km

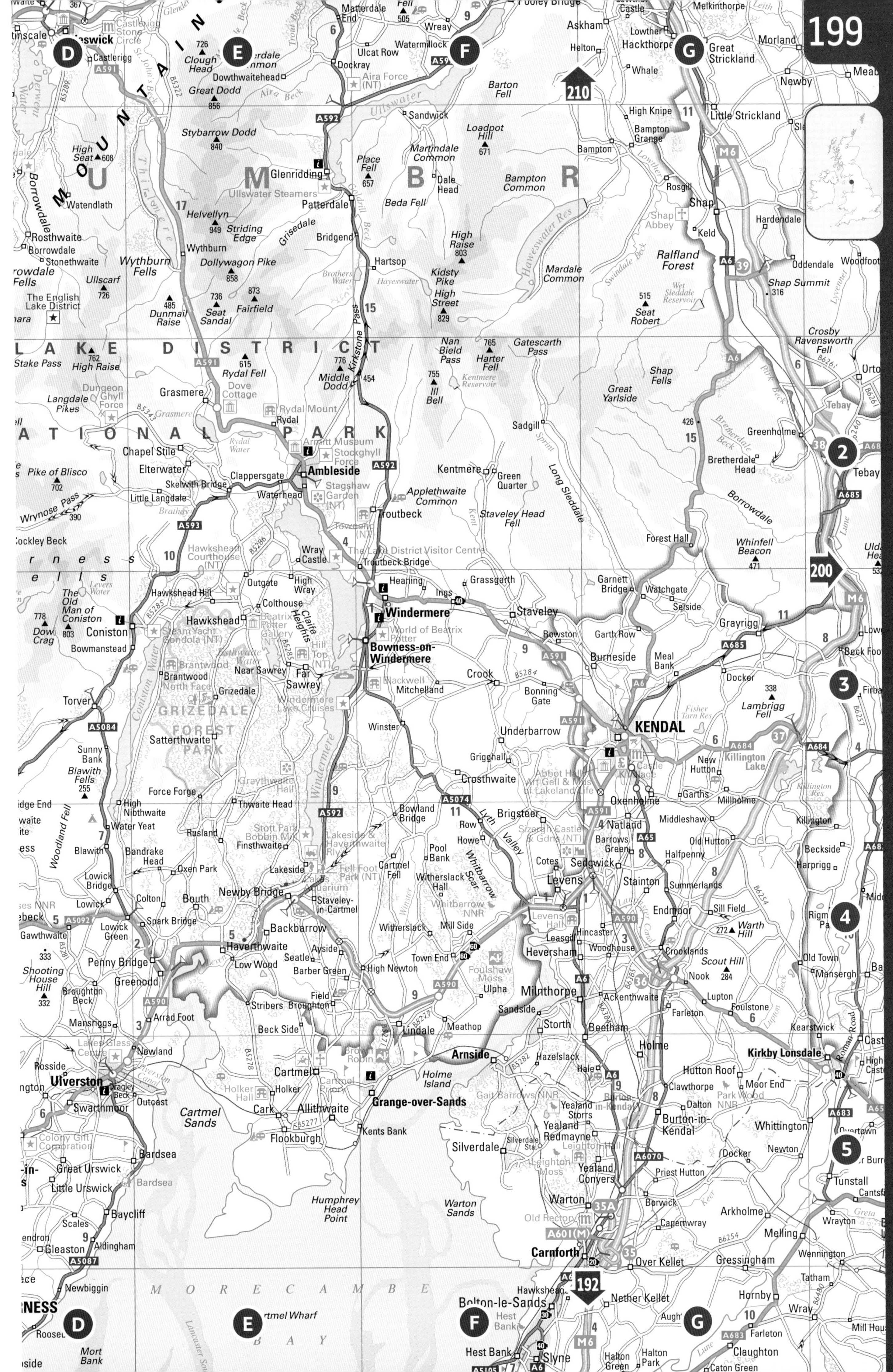
Matterdale End
Wreay
Pooley Bridge
Askham
Helton
Lowther
Hackthorpe
Great Strickland
Morland
Melkinthorpe
Castlerigg Stone Circle
Castlerigg
Clough Head
Great Dodd
Dowthwaitehead
Ulcat Row
Dockray
Watermillock
Aira Force (NT)
Ullswater
Sandwick
Barton Fell
Loadpot Hill
Whale
Newby
High Knipe
Little Strickland
Bampton Grange
Bampton
Stybarrow Dodd
High Seat
Glenridding
Ullswater Steamers
Patterdale
Place Fell
Martindale Common
Dale Head
Bampton Common
Beda Fell
Rosgill
Shap
Shap Abbey
Keld
Hardendale
Watendlath
Helvellyn
Striding Edge
Grisedale
Bridgend
Rosthwaite
Borrowdale
Stonethwaite
Wythburn
Wythburn Fells
Dollywagon Pike
Hartsop
Brothers Water
Hayeswater
High Raise
Kidsty Pike
High Street
Haweswater Res
Mardale Common
Ralfland Forest
Oddendale
Woodfoot
Shap Summit
Wet Sleddale Reservoir
Ullscarf
The English Lake District
Dunmail Raise
Seat Sandal
Fairfield
Kirkstone Pass
Nan Bield Pass
Harter Fell
Gatescarth Pass
Seat Robert
Crosby Ravensworth Fell
LAKE DISTRICT
NATIONAL PARK
Stake Pass
High Raise
Rydal Fell
Middle Dodd
Ill Bell
Kentmere Reservoir
Shap Fells
Great Yarlside
Tebay
Dungeon Ghyll Force
Langdale Pikes
Grasmere
Dove Cottage
Rydal Mount
Rydal
Rydal Water
Sadgill
Greenholme
Bretherdale Head
Armitt Museum
Stockghyll Force
Chapel Stile
Elterwater
Pike of Blisco
Skelwith Bridge
Clappersgate
Ambleside
Kentmere
Green Quarter
Long Sleddale
Borrowdale
Little Langdale
Waterhead
Stagshaw Garden (NT)
Applethwaite Common
Wrynose Pass
Troutbeck
Staveley Head Fell
Cockley Beck
Hawkshead Courthouse (NT)
Wray Castle
The Lake District Visitor Centre
Troutbeck Bridge
Forest Hall
Whinfell Beacon
Outgate
High Wray
Hawkshead Hill
Colthouse
Hawkshead
Beatrix Potter Gallery (NT)
Claife Heights
Hening
Ings
Grassgarth
Staveley
Garnett Bridge
Watchgate
Selside
The Old Man of Coniston
Dow Crag
Coniston
Steam Yacht Gondola (NT)
Bowmanstead
Windermere
World of Beatrix Potter
Bowness-on-Windermere
Bowston
Garth Row
Grayrigg
Brantwood
Near Sawrey
Hill Top (NT)
Far Sawrey
Blackwell
Crook
Burneside
Meal Bank
Beck Foot
Docker
Torver
Grizedale
GRIZEDALE FOREST PARK
Windermere Lake Cruises
Mitchelland
Bonning Gate
KENDAL
Lambrigg Fell
Fisher Tarn Res
Killington Lake
Sunny Bank
Blawith Fells
Satterthwaite
Winster
Underbarrow
New Hutton
Grigghall
Crosthwaite
Abbot Hall Art Gall & Mus of Lakeland Life
Castle
Kendal
Garths
Millholme
Oxenholme
Graythwaite Hall
Force Forge
High Nibthwaite
Thwaite Head
Bowland Bridge
Lyth Valley
Brigsteer
Row
Howe
Sizergh Castle & Gdns (NT)
Natland
Middleshaw
Killington
Water Yeat
Rusland
Stott Park Bobbin Mill
Finsthwaite
Lakeside & Haverthwaite Rly
Pool Bank
Barrows Green
Old Hutton
Halfpenny
Beckside
Blawith
Bandrake Head
Oxen Park
Lakeside
Fell Foot Park (NT)
Cartmel Fell
Witherslack Hall
Whitbarrow Scar
Cotes
Sedgwick
Stainton
Harprigg
Lowick Bridge
Colton
Bouth
Newby Bridge
Aquarium
Staveley-in-Cartmel
Whitbarrow NNR
Levens
Levens Hall
Summerlands
Endmoor
Sill Field
Warth Hill
Lowick
Lowick Green
Spark Bridge
Backbarrow
Witherslack
Mill Side
Hincaster
Leasgill
Crooklands
Rigmaden Park
Gawthwaite
Penny Bridge
Greenodd
Haverthwaite
Low Wood
Ayside
Seatle
Barber Green
High Newton
Town End
Foulshaw Moss
Ulpha
Heversham
Woodhouse
Scout Hill
Old Town
Mansergh
Shooting House Hill
Broughton Beck
Arrad Foot
Stribers
Broughton
Field
Milnthorpe
Sandside
Ackenthwaite
Nook
Lupton
Farleton
Foulstone
Mansriggs
Lakes Glass Centre
Newland
Beck Side
Lindale
Meathop
Storth
Beetham
Kearstwick
Rosside
Cartmel
Cartmel Priory
Holker
Holker Hall
Arnside
Hazelslack
Holme Island
Hale
Holme
Kirkby Lonsdale
Hutton Roof
Ulverston
Dragley Beck
Outcast
Swarthmoor
Ulverston Canal
Cartmel Sands
Cark
Allithwaite
Grange-over-Sands
Kents Bank
Flookburgh
Gait Barrows NNR
Yealand Storrs
Clawthorpe
Moor End
Park Wood NNR
Dalton
Burton-in-Kendal
Whittington
Colony Gift Corporation
Bardsea
Silverdale
Yealand Redmayne
Leighton Hall
Leighton Moss
Docker
Newton
Great Urswick
Little Urswick
Yealand Conyers
Priest Hutton
Tunstall
Humphrey Head Point
Warton Sands
Warton
Borwick
Arkholme
Baycliff
Scales
Old Rectory
Capernwray
Wrayton
Gleaston
Aldingham
Carnforth
Over Kellet
Melling
Gressingham
Wennington
Newbiggin
MORECAMBE BAY
Hawkshead
Tatham
Hornby
Wray
Bolton-le-Sands
Nether Kellet
Hest Bank
Cartmel Wharf
Mort Bank
Farleton
Claughton
Slyne
Halton Green
Halton Park
Caton Green
Mill House
A591
A592
A593
A5084
A5092
A590
A5074
A6
A65
A685
A684
A683
A6070
A601(M)
A5087
M6
B5289
B5322
B5343
B5285
B5286
B5284
B5278
B5277
B5282
B6254
B6257
B6260
B6261
B6480
210
200
192
D
E
F
G
2
3
4
5

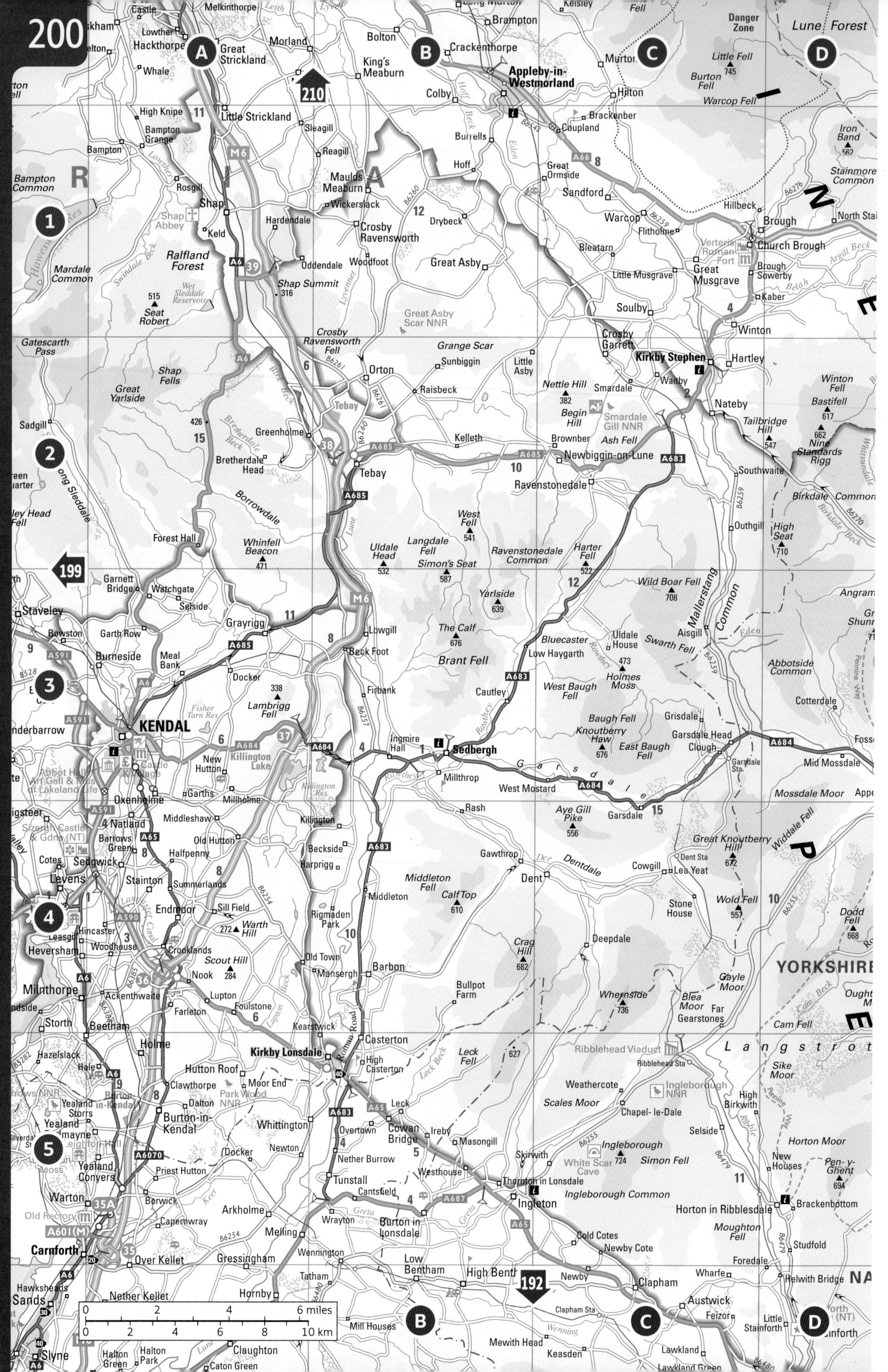
Castle
Melkinthorpe
Brampton
Lowther
Hackthorpe
Great Strickland
Morland
Bolton
Crackenthorpe
Murton
Danger Zone
Lune Forest
Little Fell
745
Burton Fell
Whale
King's Meaburn
Appleby-in-Westmorland
Colby
Hilton
Warcop Fell
210
High Knipe
Little Strickland
Bampton Grange
Sleagill
Brackenber
Coupland
Burrells
Iron Band
562
Bampton
Reagill
Hoff
Great Ormside
Stainmore Common
Bampton Common
Rosgill
Maulds Meaburn
Sandford
Shap
Wickerslack
Drybeck
Hillbeck
Brough
North Stainmore
Shap Abbey
Keld
Hardendale
Crosby Ravensworth
Warcop
Flitholme
Church Brough
Ralfland Forest
Oddendale
Woodfoot
Great Asby
Bleatarn
Verteris Roman Fort
Brough Sowerby
Mardale Common
Shap Summit
316
Little Musgrave
Great Musgrave
Kaber
515
Seat Robert
Wet Sleddale Reservoir
Great Asby Scar NNR
Soulby
Winton
Gatescarth Pass
Crosby Ravensworth Fell
Grange Scar
Crosby Garrett
Kirkby Stephen
Hartley
Shap Fells
Orton
Sunbiggin
Little Asby
Great Yarlside
Raisbeck
Nettle Hill
382
Smardale
Waitby
Winton Fell
Bastifell
617
Tebay
Begin Hill
Smardale Gill NNR
Nateby
Tailbridge Hill
662
547
Nine Standards Rigg
Sadgill
426
Greenholme
Kelleth
Brownber
Ash Fell
Newbiggin-on-Lune
Bretherdale Head
Tebay
Ravenstonedale
Southwaite
Long Sleddale
Borrowdale
Birkdale Common
West Fell
541
Outhgill
High Seat
710
Forest Hall
Whinfell Beacon
471
Uldale Head
532
Langdale Fell
Simon's Seat
587
Ravenstonedale Common
Harter Fell
522
199
Garnett Bridge
Watchgate
Selside
Yarlside
639
Wild Boar Fell
708
Angram
Mallerstang Common
Staveley
Grayrigg
Lowgill
The Calf
676
Bluecaster
Uldale House
Swarth Fell
Aisgill
Bowston
Garth Row
Low Haygarth
Burneside
Meal Bank
Beck Foot
Brant Fell
473
Holmes Moss
Abbotside Common
Docker
338
Lambrigg Fell
Firbank
Cautley
West Baugh Fell
Fisher Tarn Res
Cotterdale
Underbarrow
KENDAL
Baugh Fell
Grisdale
Knoutberry Haw
676
East Baugh Fell
Garsdale Head
Ingmire Hall
Sedbergh
Clough
New Hutton
Killington Lake
Garsdale Sta
Mid Mossdale
Abbot Hall Art Gall & Mus of Lakeland Life
Castle
Millthrop
West Mostard
Garsdale
Garths
Millholme
Killington Res
Oxenholme
Mossdale Moor
Rash
Aye Gill Pike
556
Sizergh Castle & Gdns (NT)
Natland
Middleshaw
Killington
Great Knoutberry Hill
672
Widdale Fell
Barrows Green
Old Hutton
Beckside
Dent Sta
Cowgill
Lea Yeat
Gawthrop
Dentdale
Cotes
Sedgwick
Halfpenny
Harprigg
Dent
Levens
Stainton
Summerlands
Middleton Fell
Middleton
Calf Top
610
Stone House
Wold Fell
557
Dodd Fell
668
Endmoor
Sill Field
Rigmaden Park
272
Warth Hill
Leasgill
Hincaster
Heversham
Woodhouse
Crooklands
Crag Hill
682
Deepdale
Scout Hill
284
Old Town
Barbon
Mansergh
YORKSHIRE
Gayle Moor
Milnthorpe
Nook
Ackenthwaite
Lupton
Bullpot Farm
Whernside
736
Blea Moor
Far Gearstones
Foulstone
Farleton
Storth
Beetham
Kearstwick
Cam Fell
Holme
Casterton
Ribblehead Viaduct
Langstrothdale
Hazelslack
Kirkby Lonsdale
High Casterton
Leck Fell
627
Ribblehead Sta
Sike Moor
Hutton Roof
Moor End
Weathercote
Ingleborough NNR
Clawthorpe
Park Wood NNR
High Birkwith
Yealand Storrs
Dalton
Leck
Scales Moor
Chapel-le-Dale
Burton-in-Kendal
Whittington
Cowan Bridge
Ireby
Selside
Yealand Redmayne
Leighton Hall
Overtown
Masongill
Ingleborough
724
Horton Moor
Newton
Skirwith
White Scar Cave
Simon Fell
Yealand Conyers
Docker
Nether Burrow
Westhouse
New Houses
Pen-y-Ghent
694
Priest Hutton
Tunstall
Thornton in Lonsdale
Warton
Cantsfield
Ingleborough Common
Berwick
Ingleton
Horton in Ribblesdale
Brackenbottom
Old Rectory
Arkholme
Wrayton
Burton in Lonsdale
Capernwray
Moughton Fell
Carnforth
Melling
Cold Cotes
Studfold
Newby Cote
Over Kellet
Gressingham
Wennington
Foredale
Low Bentham
High Bentham
192
Newby
Tatham
Wharfe
Helwith Bridge
Hawksheads
Clapham
Sands
Nether Kellet
Hornby
Austwick
Clapham Sta
Mill Houses
Feizor
Stainforth (NT)
Little Stainforth
Wenning
Mewith Head
Lawkland
Slyne
Halton Green
Halton Park
Claughton
Keasden
Lawkland Green
Caton Green
0 2 4 6 miles
0 2 4 6 8 10 km

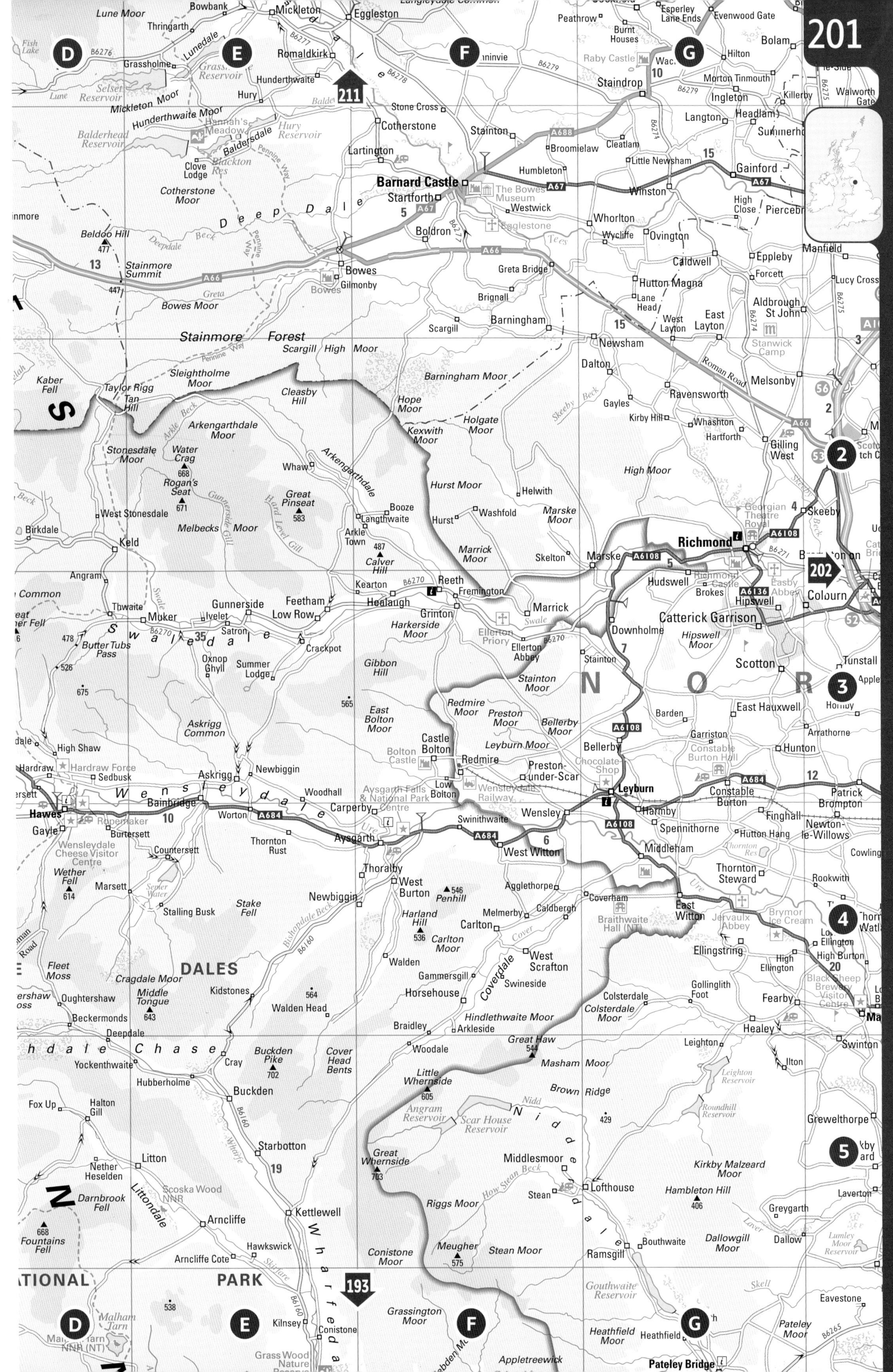
D
E
F
G
211
202
193
2
3
4
5
Lune Moor
Bowbank
Mickleton
Eggleston
Thringarth
Lunedale
Romaldkirk
Grassholme
Grassholme Reservoir
Selset Reservoir
Hunderthwaite
Hury
Mickleton Moor
Hunderthwaite Moor
Hannah's Meadow
Balderhead Reservoir
Baldersdale
Hury Reservoir
Blackton Res
Clove Lodge
Cotherstone Moor
Cotherstone
Lartington
Stone Cross
Stainton
Barnard Castle
The Bowes Museum
Startforth
Westwick
Eglestone
Boldron
Deep Dale
Beldoo Hill
477
Stainmore Summit
447
Bowes
Gilmonby
Bowes Moor
Greta
Greta Bridge
Brignall
Barningham
Scargill
Stainmore Forest
Scargill High Moor
Pennine Way
Kaber Fell
Taylor Rigg
Tan Hill
Sleightholme Moor
Cleasby Hill
Hope Moor
Barningham Moor
Holgate Moor
Kexwith Moor
Arkengarthdale Moor
Arkengarthdale
Stonesdale Moor
Water Crag
668
Rogan's Seat
671
Whaw
Great Pinseat
583
Hurst Moor
Helwith
West Stonesdale
Booze
Langthwaite
Hurst
Washfold
Marske Moor
Birkdale
Melbecks Moor
Arkle Town
487
Calver Hill
Marrick Moor
Skelton
Marske
Keld
Angram
Kearton
Reeth
Fremington
Thwaite
Muker
Ivelet
Gunnerside
Feetham
Low Row
Healaugh
Grinton
Marrick
Swaledale
Butter Tubs Pass
478
526
Satron
Crackpot
Harkerside Moor
Ellerton Priory
Ellerton Abbey
Oxnop Ghyll
Summer Lodge
Gibbon Hill
675
565
Askrigg Common
East Bolton Moor
Redmire Moor
Preston Moor
Bellerby Moor
Stainton Moor
Stainton
High Shaw
Hardraw
Hardraw Force
Sedbusk
Askrigg
Newbiggin
Castle Bolton
Bolton Castle
Redmire
Leyburn Moor
Preston-under-Scar
Chocolate Shop
Leyburn
Wensleydale
Hawes
Gayle
Bainbridge
Woodhall
Aysgarth Falls & National Park Centre
Carperby
Low Bolton
Wensleydale Railway
Wensley
Ropemaker
Burtersett
Worton
Thornton Rust
Aysgarth
Swinithwaite
West Witton
Wensleydale Cheese Visitor Centre
Countersett
Wether Fell
614
Marsett
Semer Water
Stalling Busk
Stake Fell
Thoralby
West Burton
546
Penhill
Agglethorpe
Coverham
Newbiggin
Harland Hill
536
Carlton Moor
Melmerby
Caldbergh
Carlton
Braithwaite Hall (NT)
East Witton
Jervaulx Abbey
Bishopdale Beck
Walden
West Scrafton
Gammersgill
Swineside
Coverdale
Fleet Moss
Cragdale Moor
DALES
Middle Tongue
643
Kidstones
564
Walden Head
Horsehouse
Oughtershaw
Beckermonds
Deepdale
Langstrothdale Chase
Braidley
Arkleside
Hindlethwaite Moor
Great Haw
544
Masham Moor
Yockenthwaite
Buckden Pike
702
Cover Head Bents
Woodale
Cray
Hubberholme
Buckden
Little Whernside
605
Brown Ridge
Fox Up
Halton Gill
Angram Reservoir
Scar House Reservoir
Nidd
Nidderdale
429
Starbotton
Great Whernside
703
Middlesmoor
Litton
Nether Heselden
Littondale
Scoska Wood NNR
Darnbrook Fell
Riggs Moor
How Stean Beck
Stean
Lofthouse
Kettlewell
Arncliffe
Wharfedale
668
Fountains Fell
Hawkswick
Arncliffe Cote
Conistone Moor
Meugher
575
Stean Moor
Ramsgill
NATIONAL PARK
538
Malham Tarn
Malham Tarn NNR (NT)
Kilnsey
Conistone
Grassington Moor
Grass Wood Nature Reserve
Appletreewick
Heathfield Moor
Heathfield
Pateley Bridge
Gouthwaite Reservoir
Peathrow
Esperley Lane Ends
Evenwood Gate
Burnt Houses
Bolam
Raby Castle
Staindrop
Hilton
Morton Tinmouth
Ingleton
Killerby
Walworth Gate
Langton
Headlam
Summerhouse
Cleatlam
Broomielaw
Little Newsham
Gainford
Humbleton
Winston
High Close
Piercebridge
Whorlton
Wycliffe
Ovington
Caldwell
Eppleby
Manfield
Forcett
Lucy Cross
Hutton Magna
Lane Head
West Layton
East Layton
Aldbrough St John
Stanwick Camp
Newsham
Dalton
Roman Road
Melsonby
Ravensworth
Gayles
Kirby Hill
Whashton
Hartforth
Gilling West
Skeeby Beck
High Moor
Georgian Theatre Royal
Skeeby
Richmond
Hudswell
Richmond Castle
Easby Abbey
Brompton on Swale
Brokes
Hipswell
Colburn
Catterick Garrison
Downholme
Hipswell Moor
Scotton
Tunstall
East Hauxwell
Barden
Garriston
Constable Burton Hall
Arrathorne
Hunton
Bellerby
Constable Burton
Patrick Brompton
Harmby
Spennithorne
Finghall
Hutton Hang
Newton-le-Willows
Middleham
Thornton Res
Thornton Steward
Cowling
Rookwith
Brymor Ice Cream
Low Ellington
High Burton
Ellingstring
High Ellington
Black Sheep Brewery Visitor Centre
Gollinglith Foot
Colsterdale
Colsterdale Moor
Fearby
Masham
Healey
Leighton
Swinton
Ilton
Leighton Reservoir
Roundhill Reservoir
Grewelthorpe
Kirkby Malzeard Moor
Hambleton Hill
406
Laverton
Greygarth
Bouthwaite
Dallowgill Moor
Dallow
Lumley Moor Reservoir
Skell
Eavestone
Pateley Moor
A66
A67
A688
A684
A6108
A6136
A1
B6276
B6277
B6278
B6279
B6274
B6275
B6270
B6271
B6160
B6265
NOR

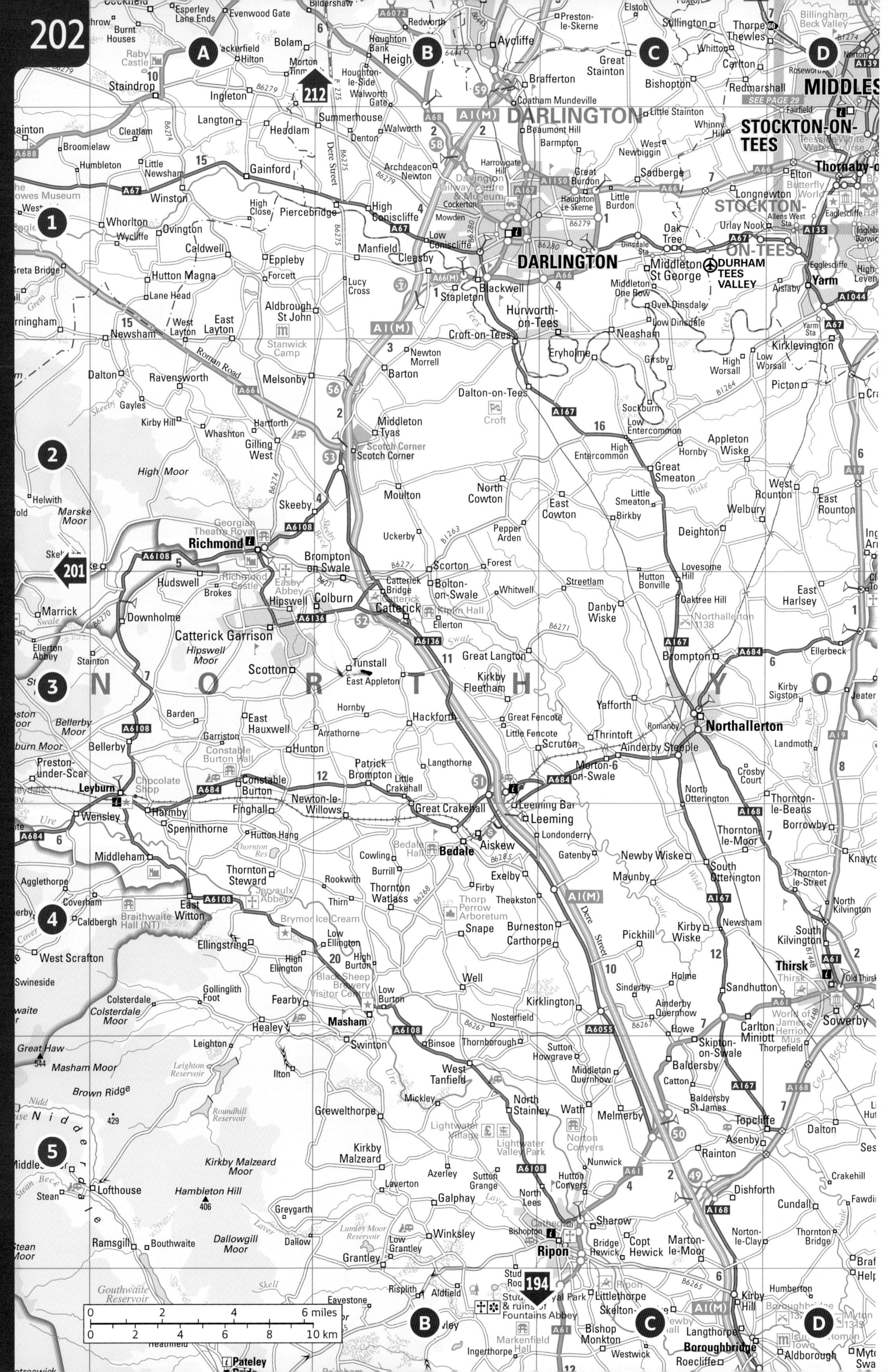
A
B
C
D
1
2
3
4
5
212
201
194
Esperley Lane Ends
Evenwood Gate
Burnt Houses
Raby Castle
Hilton
Bolam
Morton Tinmouth
Houghton Bank
Heighington
Redworth
Aycliffe
Preston-le-Skerne
Stillington
Thorpe Thewles
Billingham Beck Valley
Staindrop
Ingleton
Houghton-le-Side
Walworth Gate
Brafferton
Great Stainton
Bishopton
Carlton
Redmarshall
MIDDLESBROUGH
SEE PAGE 29
Coatham Mundeville
DARLINGTON
Little Stainton
Fairfield
STOCKTON-ON-TEES
Cleatlam
Langton
Summerhouse
Headlam
Walworth
Denton
Beaumont Hill
Barmpton
Whinny Hill
West Newbiggin
Teesside White Water Course
Broomielaw
Humbleton
Little Newsham
Gainford
Archdeacon Newton
Harrowgate Hill
Great Burdon
Sadberge
Elton
Thornaby-on-Tees
Darlington Railway Centre & Museum
Haughton Le Skerne
Little Burdon
Longnewton
Butterfly World
Winston
High Close
Piercebridge
High Coniscliffe
Cockerton
Mowden
STOCKTON-ON-TEES
Urlay Nook
Allens West Sta
Eaglescliffe
Whorlton
Wycliffe
Ovington
Low Coniscliffe
Oak Tree
Caldwell
Manfield
Cleasby
DARLINGTON
Dinsdale Sta
Middleton St George
DURHAM TEES VALLEY
Egglescliffe
Yarm
Greta Bridge
Eppleby
Hutton Magna
Forcett
Lucy Cross
Blackwell
Stapleton
Middleton One Row
Aislaby
Lane Head
Aldbrough St John
Hurworth-on-Tees
Over Dinsdale
Low Dinsdale
Newsham
West Layton
East Layton
Croft-on-Tees
Neasham
Yarm Sta
Kirklevington
Stanwick Camp
Newton Morrell
Eryholme
Girsby
High Worsall
Low Worsall
Dalton
Ravensworth
Roman Road
Melsonby
Barton
Picton
Gayles
Dalton-on-Tees
Croft
Kirby Hill
Whashton
Hartforth
Gilling West
Middleton Tyas
Scotch Corner
Sockburn
Low Entercommon
High Entercommon
Appleton Wiske
Hornby
High Moor
Great Smeaton
Helwith
Marske Moor
Skeeby
Moulton
North Cowton
East Cowton
Little Smeaton
Birkby
West Rounton
East Rounton
Welbury
Georgian Theatre Royal
Richmond
Uckerby
Pepper Arden
Deighton
Brompton-on-Swale
Scorton
Forest
Lovesome Hill
Hudswell
Richmond Castle
Easby Abbey
Bolton-on-Swale
Whitwell
Streetlam
Hutton Bonville
Brokes
Hipswell
Colburn
Catterick Bridge
Catterick
Kiplin Hall
Ellerton
Danby Wiske
Oaktree Hill
Northallerton
East Harlsey
Marrick
Downholme
Catterick Garrison
Hipswell Moor
Ellerton Abbey
Stainton
Scotton
Tunstall
East Appleton
Great Langton
Brompton
Ellerbeck
Kirby Fleetham
Kirby Sigston
N O R T H Y O
Barden
East Hauxwell
Hornby
Hackforth
Great Fencote
Little Fencote
Yafforth
Romanby
Northallerton
Bellerby Moor
Bellerby
Garriston
Arrathorne
Constable Burton Hall
Hunton
Scruton
Thrintoft
Ainderby Steeple
Landmoth
Preston-under-Scar
Chocolate Shop
Constable Burton
Patrick Brompton
Langthorne
Little Crakehall
Morton-on-Swale
Crosby Court
Leyburn
Harmby
Finghall
Newton-le-Willows
Great Crakehall
Leeming Bar
Leeming
North Otterington
Thornton-le-Beans
Wensley
Spennithorne
Hutton Hang
Thornton Res
Bedale Hall
Bedale
Aiskew
Londonderry
Thornton-le-Moor
Borrowby
Middleham
Cowling
Burrill
Gatenby
Newby Wiske
South Otterington
Agglethorpe
Thornton Steward
Rookwith
Exelby
Maunby
Thornton-le-Street
Coverham
Jervaulx Abbey
Thornton Watlass
Firby
Caldbergh
Braithwaite Hall (NT)
East Witton
Thirn
Thorp Perrow Arboretum
Theakston
North Kilvington
Brymor Ice Cream
Snape
Burneston
Carthorpe
Dere Street
Pickhill
Kirby Wiske
Newsham
South Kilvington
West Scrafton
Ellingstring
Low Ellington
High Ellington
High Burton
Thirsk
Swineside
Gollinglith Foot
Black Sheep Brewery Visitor Centre
Well
Sinderby
Holme
Sandhutton
Old Thirsk
Colsterdale
Colsterdale Moor
Fearby
Low Burton
Kirklington
Ainderby Quernhow
Healey
Masham
Nosterfield
Howe
Carlton Miniott
World of James Herriot
Sowerby
Leighton
Swinton
Binsoe
Thornborough
Sutton Howgrave
Skipton-on-Swale
Thorpefield
Great Haw
544
Masham Moor
Leighton Reservoir
Ilton
West Tanfield
Middleton Quernhow
Baldersby
Catton
Brown Ridge
Roundhill Reservoir
Mickley
North Stainley
Wath
Melmerby
Baldersby St James
Topcliffe
Dalton
Nidderdale
429
Grewelthorpe
Lightwater Village
Lightwater Valley Park
Norton Conyers
Asenby
Rainton
Kirkby Malzeard
Kirkby Malzeard Moor
Nunwick
Crakehill
Lofthouse
Stean
Hambleton Hill
406
Laverton
Azerley
Sutton Grange
Hutton Conyers
Dishforth
Cundall
Galphay
North Lees
Greygarth
Lumley Moor Reservoir
Winksley
Sharow
Thornton Bridge
Ramsgill
Bouthwaite
Dallowgill Moor
Dallow
Low Grantley
Bishopton
Cathedral
Ripon
Bridge Hewick
Copt Hewick
Marton-le-Moor
Norton-le-Clay
Grantley
Stud Royal Park
Humberton
Gouthwaite Reservoir
Eavestone
Risplith
Aldfield
Studley Royal & ruins of Fountains Abbey
Littlethorpe
Skelton-on-Ure
Kirby Hill
Boroughbridge
Bishop Monkton
Markenfield Hall
Langthorpe
Ingerthorpe
Westwick
Roecliffe
Aldborough
Pateley Bridge
0 2 4 6 miles
0 2 4 6 8 10 km

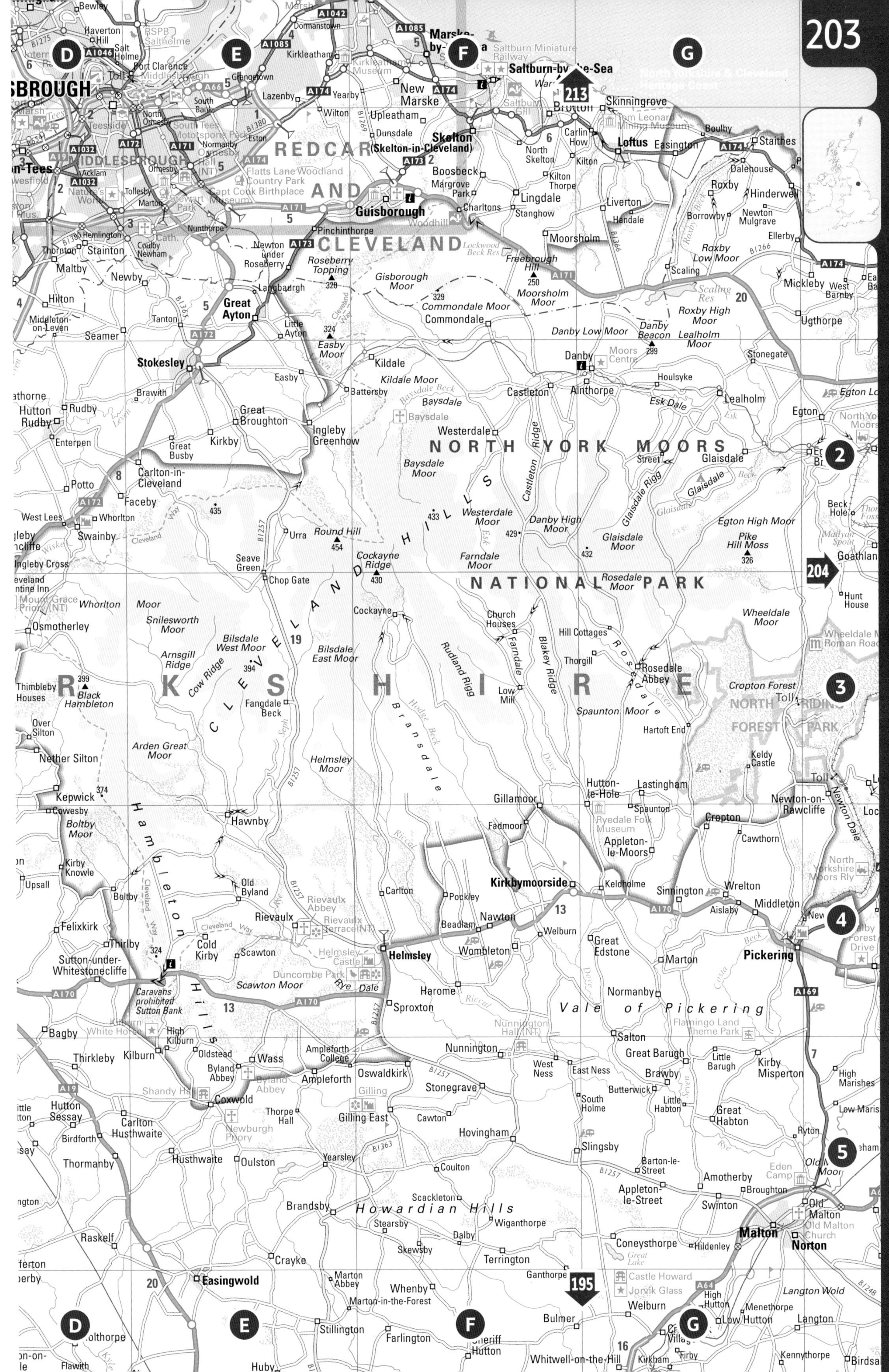
D
E
F
G
Bewley
Haverton Hill
RSPB Saltholme
Port Clarence
Middlesbrough
Grangetown
South Bank
North Ormesby
Teesside
Eston
Normanby
Ormesby
Acklam
MIDDLESBROUGH
Nature's World
Tollesby
Marton
Stewart Park
Capt Cook Birthplace Museum
Nunthorpe
Hemlington
Coulby Newham
Thornton
Stainton
Maltby
Newby
Hilton
Middleton-on-Leven
Seamer
Tanton
Great Ayton
Little Ayton
Stokesley
Dormanstown
Kirkleatham
Kirkleatham Museum
Marske-by-the-Sea
Saltburn Miniature Railway
Saltburn-by-the-Sea
New Marske
Yearby
Lazenby
Wilton
Upleatham
Dunsdale
Skelton (Skelton-in-Cleveland)
Boosbeck
Margrove Park
Charltons
Flatts Lane Woodland Country Park
REDCAR AND CLEVELAND
Guisborough
Woodhill
Pinchinthorpe
Newton under Roseberry
Roseberry Topping
Langbaurgh
Gisborough Moor
Commondale Moor
Commondale
Freebrough Hill
Moorsholm Moor
Moorsholm
Lingdale
Stanghow
North Skelton
Kilton Thorpe
Brotton
Carlin How
Skinningrove
Tom Leonard Mining Museum
Loftus
Easington
Boulby
Staithes
Dalehouse
Roxby
Hinderwell
Newton Mulgrave
Borrowby
Ellerby
Roxby Low Moor
Scaling
Scaling Res
Mickleby
West Barnby
Ugthorpe
Liverton
Handale
North Yorkshire & Cleveland Heritage Coast
213
Danby Low Moor
Danby Beacon
Roxby High Moor
Lealholm Moor
Danby
Moors Centre
Easby Moor
Kildale
Kildale Moor
Easby
Battersby
Baysdale
Castleton
Ainthorpe
Houlsyke
Stonegate
Lealholm
Egton
Esk Dale
Hutton Rudby
Rudby
Brawith
Great Broughton
Ingleby Greenhow
Enterpen
Kirkby
Great Busby
Westerdale
NORTH YORK MOORS NATIONAL PARK
Street
Glaisdale
Glaisdale Rigg
Potto
Carlton-in-Cleveland
Faceby
Whorlton
West Lees
Swainby
Baysdale Moor
CLEVELAND HILLS
Castleton Ridge
Westerdale Moor
Danby High Moor
Glaisdale Moor
Egton High Moor
Beck Hole
Urra
Round Hill
Ingleby Cross
Seave Green
Chop Gate
Cockayne Ridge
Farndale Moor
Rosedale Moor
Pike Hill Moss
Goathland
204
Mount Grace Priory (NT)
Whorlton Moor
Snilesworth Moor
Osmotherley
Bilsdale West Moor
Arnsgill Ridge
Cockayne
Church Houses
Hill Cottages
Hunt House
Wheeldale Moor
Wheeldale Roman Road
Bilsdale East Moor
Rudland Rigg
Farndale
Blakey Ridge
Thorgill
Rosedale Abbey
Rosedale
Cow Ridge
Thimbleby Houses
Black Hambleton
Fangdale Beck
Bransdale
Low Mill
Spaunton Moor
Crofton Forest
NORTH RIDING FOREST PARK
Hartoft End
Over Silton
Nether Silton
Arden Great Moor
Helmsley Moor
Keldy Castle
Kepwick
Cowesby
Boltby Moor
Hambleton Hills
Hawnby
Gillamoor
Hutton-le-Hole
Lastingham
Spaunton
Ryedale Folk Museum
Appleton-le-Moors
Fadmoor
Cropton
Cawthorn
Newton-on-Rawcliffe
Newton Dale
North Yorkshire Moors Rly
Kirby Knowle
Upsall
Boltby
Old Byland
Carlton
Pockley
Kirkbymoorside
Keldholme
Sinnington
Wrelton
Aislaby
Middleton
Pickering
Felixkirk
Rievaulx
Rievaulx Abbey
Rievaulx Terrace (NT)
Beadlam
Nawton
Welburn
Great Edstone
Marton
Thirlby
Cold Kirby
Scawton
Helmsley
Helmsley Castle
Wombleton
Sutton-under-Whitestonecliffe
Duncombe Park
Rye Dale
Harome
Scawton Moor
Caravans prohibited Sutton Bank
Sproxton
Normanby
Vale of Pickering
Flamingo Land Theme Park
Kilburn White Horse
High Kilburn
Bagby
Oldstead
Wass
Ampleforth College
Nunnington Hall (NT)
Nunnington
Salton
Great Barugh
Little Barugh
Kirby Misperton
High Marishes
Thirkleby
Kilburn
Byland Abbey
Ampleforth
Oswaldkirk
Gilling
West Ness
East Ness
Brawby
Shandy Hall
Coxwold
Stonegrave
Butterwick
South Holme
Little Habton
Great Habton
Low Marishes
Hutton Sessay
Carlton Husthwaite
Newburgh Priory
Thorpe Hall
Gilling East
Cawton
Hovingham
Slingsby
Ryton
Birdforth
Husthwaite
Oulston
Yearsley
Coulton
Barton-le-Street
Eden Camp
Amotherby
Old Malton Moor
Thormanby
Appleton-le-Street
Broughton
Swinton
Scackleton
Brandsby
Howardian Hills
Wiganthorpe
Stearsby
Dalby
Coneysthorpe
Hildenley
Malton
Old Malton
Old Malton Church
Norton
Raskelf
Skewsby
Terrington
Great Lake
Crayke
Ganthorpe
195
Castle Howard
Jorvik Glass
Easingwold
Marton Abbey
Whenby
Marton-in-the-Forest
Welburn
High Hutton
Menethorpe
Langton Wold
Langton
Low Hutton
Bulmer
Stillington
Farlington
Sheriff Hutton
Whitwell-on-the-Hill
Crambe
Kirkham
Firby
Kennythorpe
Birdsall
Tholthorpe
Flawith
Huby
Welburn
A1042
A1085
A1046
A66
A174
A172
A171
A1032
A19
A173
B1380
B1365
B1257
B1266
B1275
B1269
B1366
A170
A169
A64
B1363
B1248
Dalby Forest Drive
Egton Low Moor

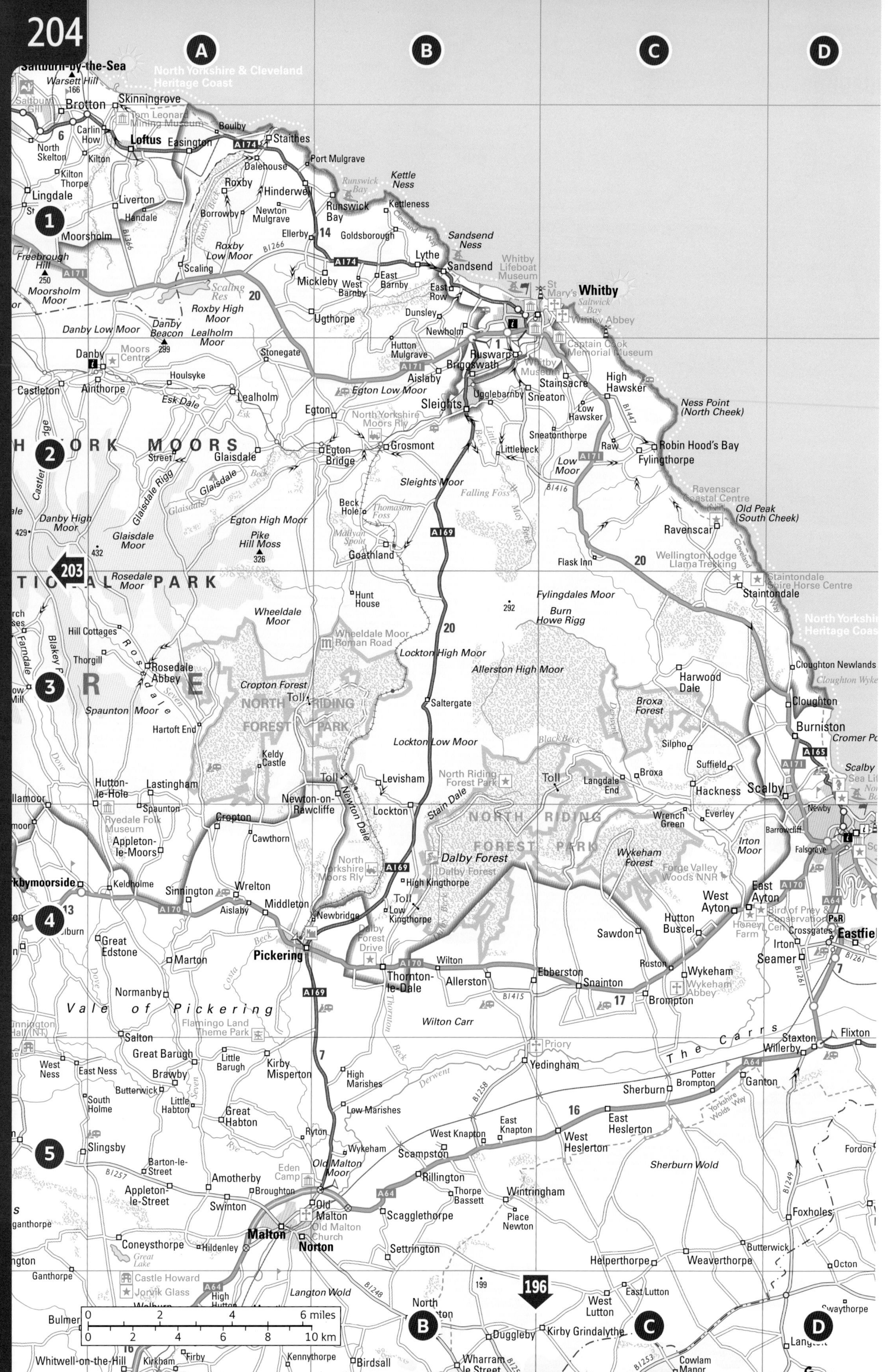

A
B
C
D
1
2
3
4
5
Saltburn-by-the-Sea
Warsett Hill
166
North Yorkshire & Cleveland Heritage Coast
Brotton
Skinningrove
Tom Leonard Mining Museum
Carlin How
Loftus
Easington
Boulby
Staithes
North Skelton
Kilton
Kilton Thorpe
A174
Dalehouse
Port Mulgrave
Lingdale
Liverton
Roxby
Hinderwell
Runswick Bay
Kettle Ness
Kettleness
Handale
Borrowby
Newton Mulgrave
Moorsholm
B1366
Ellerby
14
Goldsborough
Sandsend Ness
Roxby Low Moor
B1266
Lythe
Sandsend
Whitby Lifeboat Museum
Freebrough Hill
250
A171
Scaling
Mickleby
East Barnby
West Barnby
East Row
St Mary's
Whitby
Saltwick Bay
Whitby Abbey
Moorsholm Moor
Scaling Res
20
Roxby High Moor
Ugthorpe
Dunsley
Newholm
Danby Low Moor
Danby Beacon
299
Lealholm Moor
Captain Cook Memorial Museum
Danby
Moors Centre
Stonegate
Hutton Mulgrave
Ruswarp
Briggswath
Whitby Museum
High Hawsker
Castleton
Ainthorpe
Houlsyke
Aislaby
Stainsacre
Lealholm
Esk Dale
Egton Low Moor
Ugglebarnby
Sneaton
Ness Point (North Cheek)
Egton
Sleights
Low Hawsker
North Yorkshire Moors Rly
B1447
Sneatonthorpe
NORTH YORK MOORS
Street
Glaisdale
Egton Bridge
Grosmont
Littlebeck
Raw
Robin Hood's Bay
Fylingthorpe
A171
Low Moor
Glaisdale Rigg
Sleights Moor
B1416
Falling Foss
Ravenscar Coastal Centre (NT)
Old Peak (South Cheek)
Beck Hole
Thomason Foss
Danby High Moor
Egton High Moor
Ravenscar
429
Mallyan Spout
A169
Glaisdale Moor
Pike Hill Moss
432
326
Goathland
Flask Inn
20
Wellington Lodge Llama Trekking
203
Rosedale Moor
NATIONAL PARK
Staintondale Shire Horse Centre
Staintondale
Hunt House
Fylingdales Moor
292
Wheeldale Moor
Burn Howe Rigg
North Yorkshire Heritage Coast
Hill Cottages
Wheeldale Moor Roman Road
20
Rosedale
Lockton High Moor
Cloughton Newlands
Blakey
Thorgill
Rosedale Abbey
Allerston High Moor
Cloughton Wyke
Farndale
Harwood Dale
Cropton Forest
Toll
Saltergate
Cloughton
NORTH RIDING FOREST PARK
Broxa Forest
Spaunton Moor
Seven
Hartoft End
Lockton Low Moor
Black Beck
Burniston
Cromer Point
Silpho
Keldy Castle
Toll
A165
Suffield
Scalby
Levisham
North Riding Forest Park
Toll
Langdale End
Broxa
Hutton-le-Hole
Lastingham
Hackness
Spaunton
Newton-on-Rawcliffe
Lockton
Stain Dale
Newby
Ryedale Folk Museum
Cropton
Newton Dale
Wrench Green
Everley
Cawthorn
Irton Moor
Barrowcliff
Appleton-le-Moors
Dalby Forest
Wykeham Forest
Falsgrave
North Yorkshire Moors Rly
A169
Forge Valley Woods NNR
Kirkbymoorside
Keldholme
Sinnington
Wrelton
High Kingthorpe
West Ayton
East Ayton
A170
13
Aislaby
Middleton
Toll
Low Kingthorpe
Hutton Buscel
Bird of Prey & Conservation Cen
P&R
Great Edstone
Newbridge
Dalby Forest Drive
Sawdon
Honey Farm
Crossgates
Eastfield
Marton
Pickering
Irton
Seamer
A170
Wilton
Ruston
Wykeham
B1261
Thornton-le-Dale
Allerston
Ebberston
Snainton
Wykeham Abbey
Normanby
A169
B1415
17
Brompton
Vale of Pickering
Wilton Carr
Flamingo Land Theme Park
The Carrs
Salton
Priory
Staxton
Flixton
Great Barugh
Little Barugh
Willerby
West Ness
East Ness
Kirby Misperton
7
Yedingham
A64
Brawby
High Marishes
Derwent
Potter Brompton
Ganton
Butterwick
Sherburn
South Holme
Little Habton
B1258
Low Marishes
16
Yorkshire Wolds Way
Great Habton
East Knapton
East Heslerton
Ryton
West Knapton
West Heslerton
Slingsby
Wykeham
Fordon
Scampston
Barton-le-Street
Eden Camp
Old Malton Moor
Sherburn Wold
B1257
Amotherby
Rillington
B1249
Appleton-le-Street
Broughton
Thorpe Bassett
Wintringham
A64
Swinton
Old Malton
Scagglethorpe
Place Newton
Foxholes
Old Malton Church
Malton
Norton
Coneysthorpe
Hildenley
Settrington
Butterwick
Great Lake
Helperthorpe
Weaverthorpe
Octon
Ganthorpe
Castle Howard
Jorvik Glass
A64
Langton Wold
B1248
199
196
East Lutton
High Hutton
West Lutton
Swaythorpe
North Grimston
Bulmer
0 2 4 6 miles
0 2 4 6 8 10 km
Duggleby
Kirby Grindalythe
Kirkham
Firby
Kennythorpe
Birdsall
B1253
Cowlam Manor
Whitwell-on-the-Hill
Wharram le Street

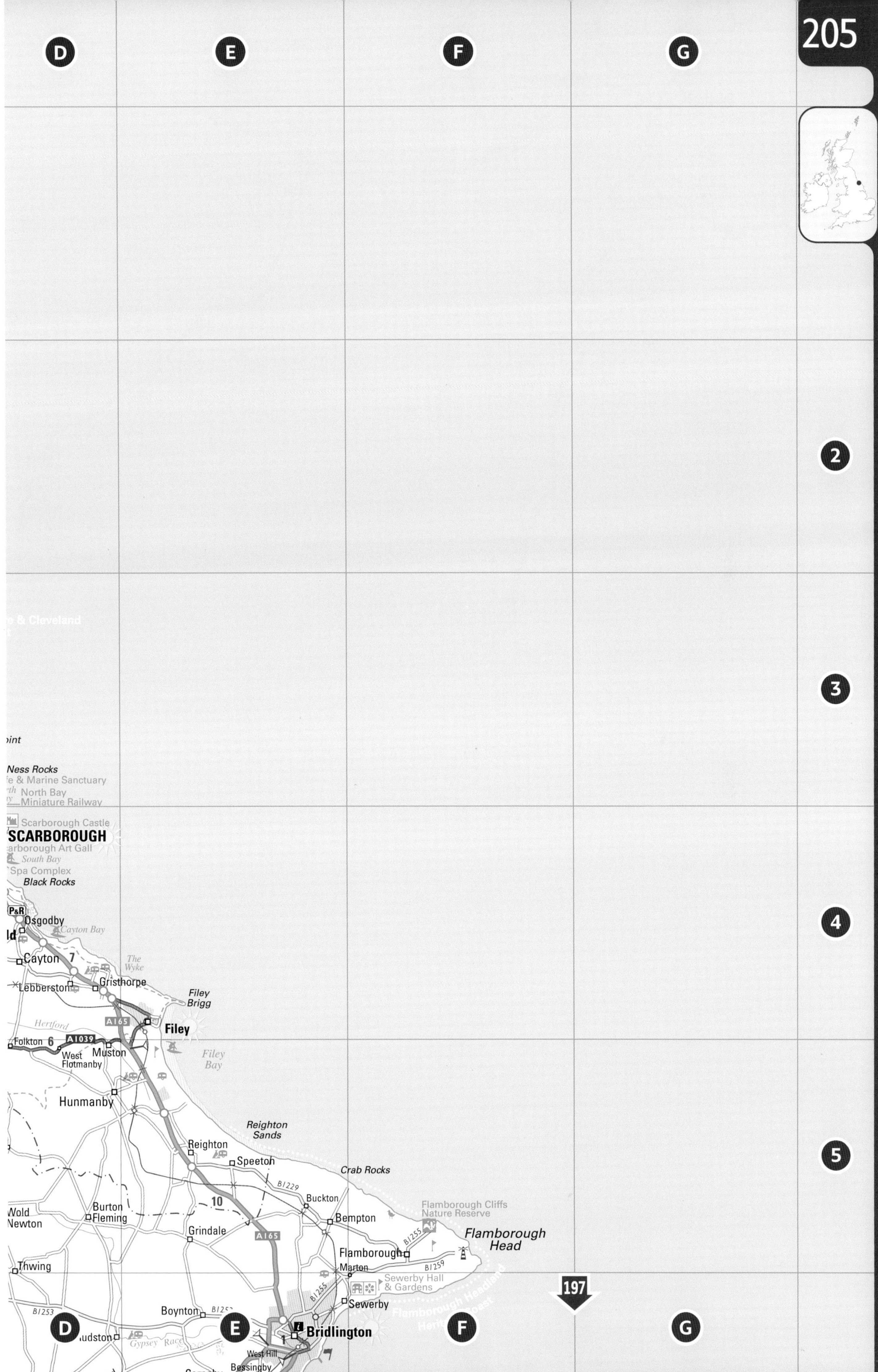

D   E   F   G

2

3

4

5

Scarborough Castle
SCARBOROUGH
Scarborough Art Gall
South Bay
Spa Complex
Black Rocks
P&R
Osgodby
Cayton Bay
Cayton   7
The Wyke
Lebberston
Gristhorpe
Filey Brigg
Hertford
A165
Folkton 6   A1039
Filey
West
Flotmanby   Muston
Filey Bay
Hunmanby
Reighton Sands
Reighton
Speeton
Crab Rocks
B1229
Buckton
Flamborough Cliffs
Nature Reserve
Wold   Burton
Newton   Fleming   10
Grindale   A165
Bempton
B1255
Flamborough
Head
Thwing
Flamborough
Marton
Sewerby Hall
& Gardens
B1253
Boynton   B1253
Sewerby
197
udston   Gypsey Race
Bridlington
West Hill
Carnaby   Bessingby
Hildarthorne

Ness Rocks
e & Marine Sanctuary
North Bay
Miniature Railway

D   E   F   G

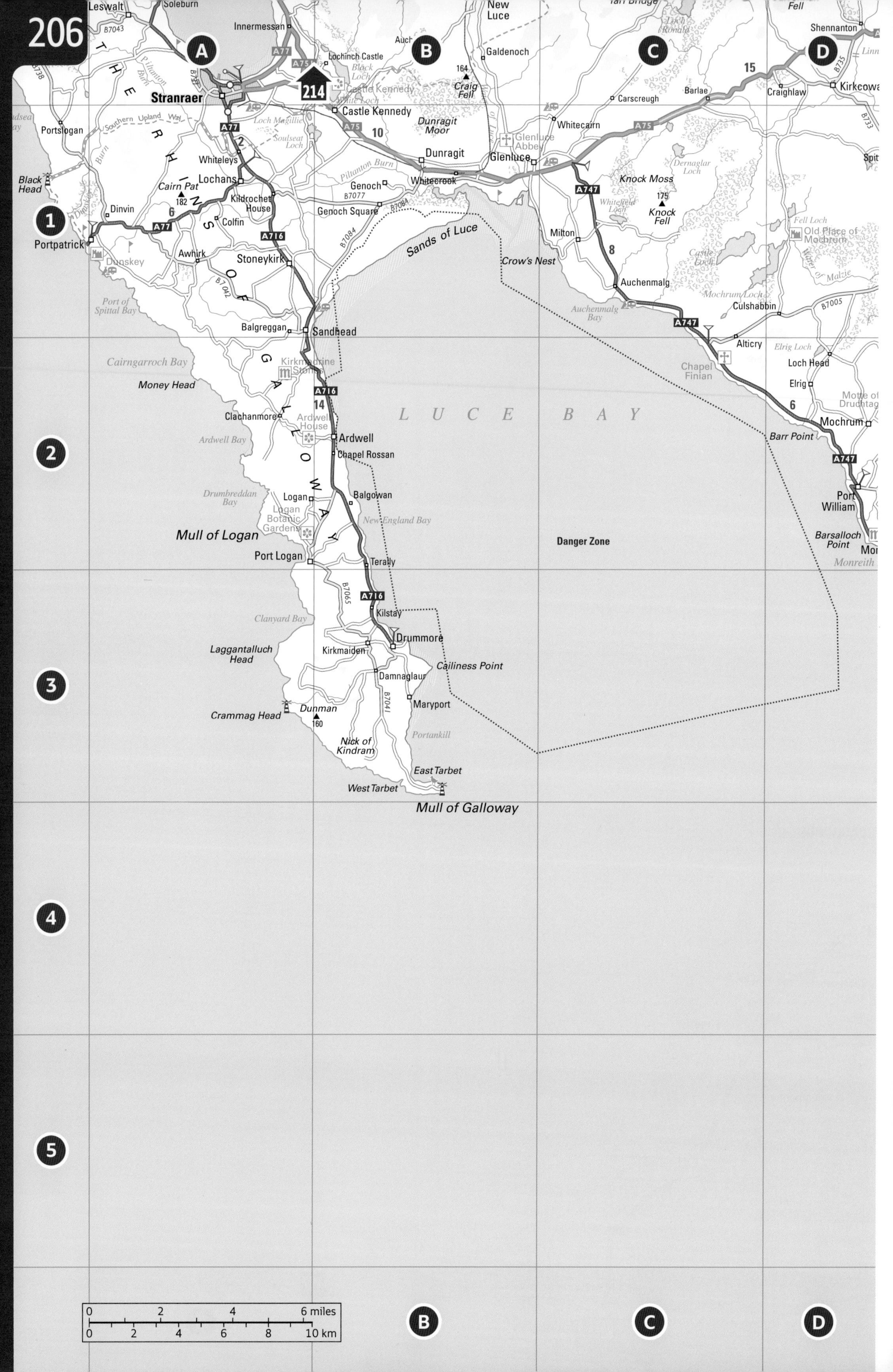
Stranraer
Portpatrick
Portslogan
Black Head
Dinvin
Cairn Pat
Lochans
Whiteleys
Kildrochet House
Colfin
Awhirk
Stoneykirk
Dunskey
Port of Spittal Bay
Balgreggan
Sandhead
Cairngarroch Bay
Money Head
Kirkmadrine Stones
Clachanmore
Ardwell House
Ardwell
Ardwell Bay
Chapel Rossan
Balgowan
Drumbreddan Bay
Logan
Logan Botanic Gardens
Mull of Logan
New England Bay
Port Logan
Terally
Kilstay
Clanyard Bay
Drummore
Laggantalluch Head
Kirkmaiden
Cailiness Point
Damnaglaur
Maryport
Crammag Head
Dunman
Portankill
Nick of Kindram
East Tarbet
West Tarbet
Mull of Galloway
Leswalt
Soleburn
Innermessan
Lochinch Castle
Castle Kennedy
Black Loch
White Loch
Loch Magillie
Soulseat Loch
New Luce
Galdenoch
Craig Fell
Dunragit Moor
Dunragit
Genoch
Genoch Square
Whitecrook
Piltanton Burn
Southern Upland Way
Sands of Luce
Crow's Nest
Glenluce
Glenluce Abbey
Carscreugh
Whitecairn
Barlae
Craighlaw
Kirkcowan
Shennanton
Knock Moss
Knock Fell
Dernaglar Loch
Whitefield Loch
Milton
Castle Loch
Auchenmalg
Auchenmalg Bay
Mochrum Loch
Culshabbin
Old Place of Mochrum
Fell Loch
Alticry
Chapel Finian
Elrig Loch
Loch Head
Elrig
Motte of Druchtag
Mochrum
Barr Point
Port William
Barsalloch Point
Monreith
LUCE BAY
Danger Zone
THE RHINS OF GALLOWAY
A77
A75
A716
A747
B7043
B7042
B7077
B7084
B7065
B7041
B7005
B735
B733
214
A
B
C
D
1
2
3
4
5
0 2 4 6 miles
0 2 4 6 8 10 km

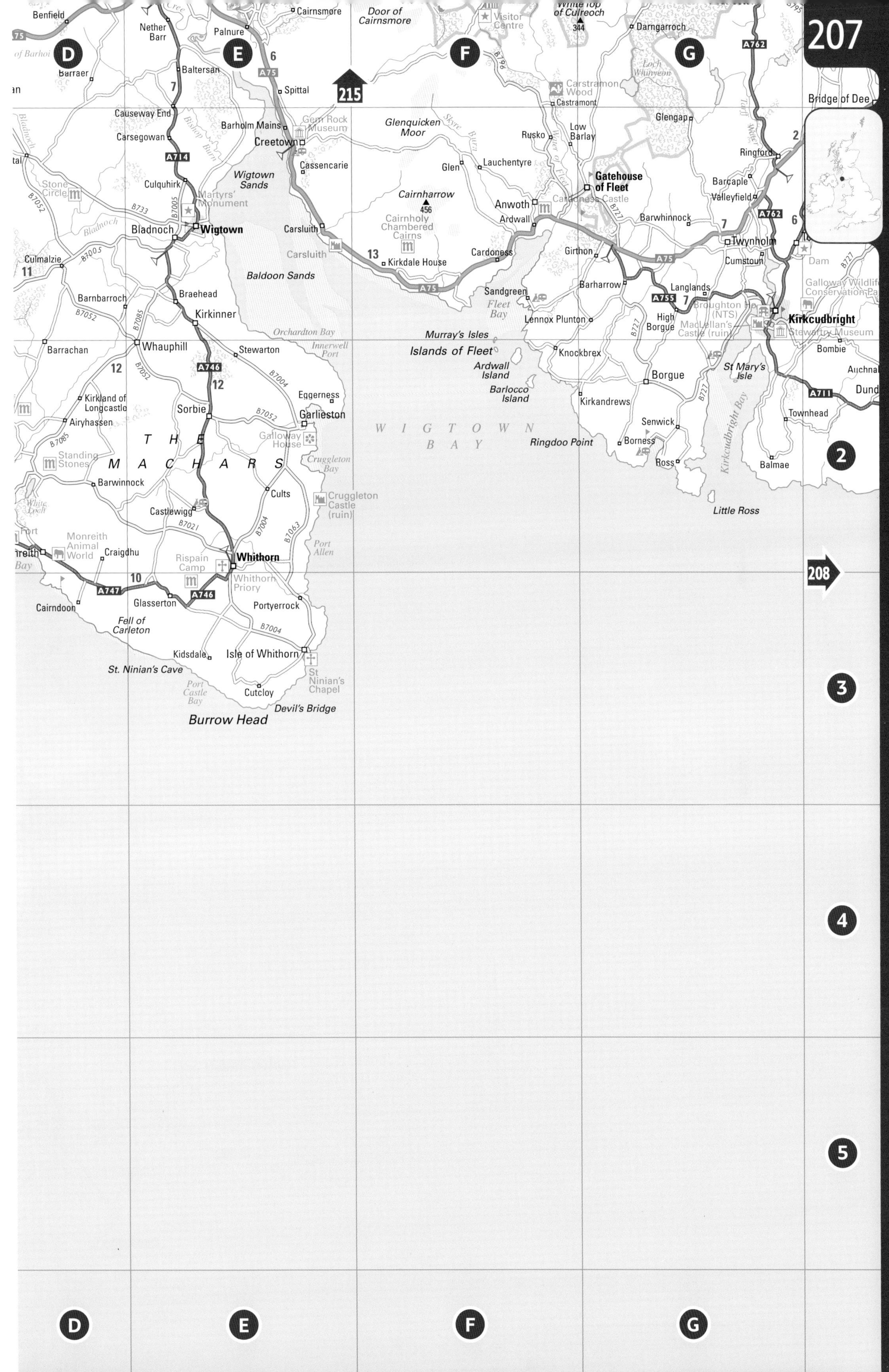
Benfield
Nether Barr
Palnure
Cairnsmore
Door of Cairnsmore
Visitor Centre
White Top of Culreoch
344
Darngarroch
Barraer
Baltersan
Spittal
215
Loch Whinyeon
Carstramon Wood
Castramont
Bridge of Dee
Causeway End
Barholm Mains
Gem Rock Museum
Glenquicken Moor
Rusko
Low Barlay
Glengap
Carsegowan
Creetown
Ringford
Cassencarie
Glen
Lauchentyre
Wigtown Sands
Culquhirk
Gatehouse of Fleet
Barcaple
Stone Circle
Cairnharrow
456
Valleyfield
Martyrs' Monument
Anwoth
Cardoness Castle
Ardwall
Barwhinnock
Bladnoch
Wigtown
Carsluith
Cairnholy Chambered Cairns
Twynholm
Carsluith
Kirkdale House
Cardoness
Girthon
Cumstoun
Dam
Culmalzie
Baldoon Sands
Barharrow
Langlands
Galloway Wildlife Conservation Park
Braehead
Sandgreen
Fleet Bay
Barnbarroch
Broughton Ho
High Borgue
Kirkcudbright
Kirkinner
Lennox Plunton
MacLellan's Castle (ruin)
Stewartry Museum
Orchardton Bay
Murray's Isles
Barrachan
Whauphill
Stewarton
Innerwell Port
Islands of Fleet
Knockbrex
Bombie
Ardwall Island
Borgue
St Mary's Isle
Auchnab
Kirkland of Longcastle
Eggerness
Barlocco Island
Kirkandrews
Dund
Airyhassen
Sorbie
Garlieston
Townhead
Senwick
W I G T O W N B A Y
Galloway House
Ringdoo Point
Borness
Standing Stones
T H E M A C H A R S
Cruggleton Bay
Ross
Balmae
Kirkcudbright Bay
Barwinnock
Cults
Cruggleton Castle (ruin)
Little Ross
White Loch
Castlewigg
Port William
Monreith Animal World
Craigdhu
Port Allen
Monreith Bay
Rispain Camp
Whithorn
208
Whithorn Priory
Cairndoon
Glasserton
Portyerrock
Fell of Carleton
Kidsdale
Isle of Whithorn
St. Ninian's Cave
St Ninian's Chapel
Port Castle Bay
Cutcloy
Devil's Bridge
Burrow Head
D
E
F
G
2
3
4
5

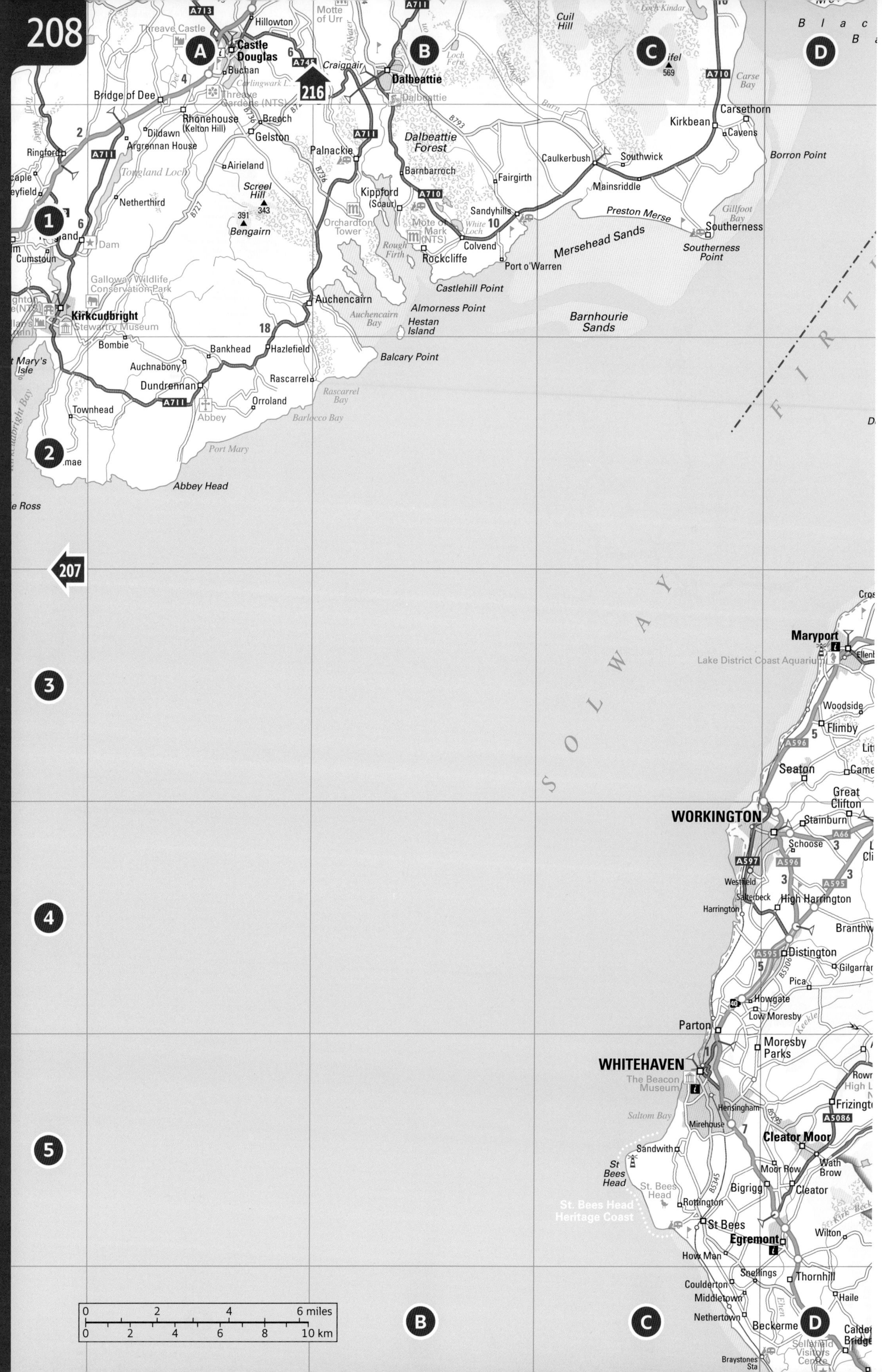
Castle Douglas
Threave Castle
Hillowton
Motte of Urr
Buchan
Bridge of Dee
Threave Gardens (NTS)
Carlingwark L.
Craignair
Dalbeattie
216
Rhonehouse (Kelton Hill)
Breoch
Gelston
Dildawn
Argrennan House
Ringford
Tongland Loch
Airieland
Netherthird
Screel Hill
343
391
Bengairn
Palnackie
Dalbeattie Forest
Barnbarroch
Kippford (Scaur)
Orchardton Tower
Rough Firth
Mote of Mark (NTS)
White Loch
Rockcliffe
Colvend
Sandyhills
Fairgirth
Caulkerbush
Southwick
Mainsriddle
Preston Merse
Mersehead Sands
Port o'Warren
Castlehill Point
Almorness Point
Hestan Island
Auchencairn Bay
Auchencairn
Barnhourie Sands
Balcary Point
Cuil Hill
Criffel
569
Loch Kindar
Carse Bay
Carsethorn
Kirkbean
Cavens
Borron Point
Gillfoot Bay
Southerness
Southerness Point
Dam
Cumstoun
Galloway Wildlife Conservation Park
Kirkcudbright
Stewartry Museum
Bombie
Bankhead
Hazlefield
Auchnabony
Dundrennan
Rascarrel
Rascarrel Bay
Orroland
Abbey
Barlocco Bay
Townhead
Port Mary
Abbey Head
St Mary's Isle
Kirkcudbright Bay
Ross
207
SOLWAY FIRTH
Maryport
Lake District Coast Aquarium
Woodside
Flimby
Seaton
Great Clifton
WORKINGTON
Stainburn
Schoose
Westfield
Salterbeck
Harrington
High Harrington
Distington
Pica
Howgate
Low Moresby
Parton
Moresby Parks
WHITEHAVEN
The Beacon Museum
Saltom Bay
Hensingham
Mirehouse
Cleator Moor
Frizington
Sandwith
St Bees Head
St. Bees Head Heritage Coast
Moor Row
Wath Brow
Bigrigg
Cleator
Rottington
St Bees
Egremont
Wilton
How Man
Thornhill
Snellings
Coulderton
Middletown
Haile
Nethertown
Beckermet
Sellafield Visitors Centre
Braystones Sta
A B C D
1 2 3 4 5
0 2 4 6 miles
0 2 4 6 8 10 km

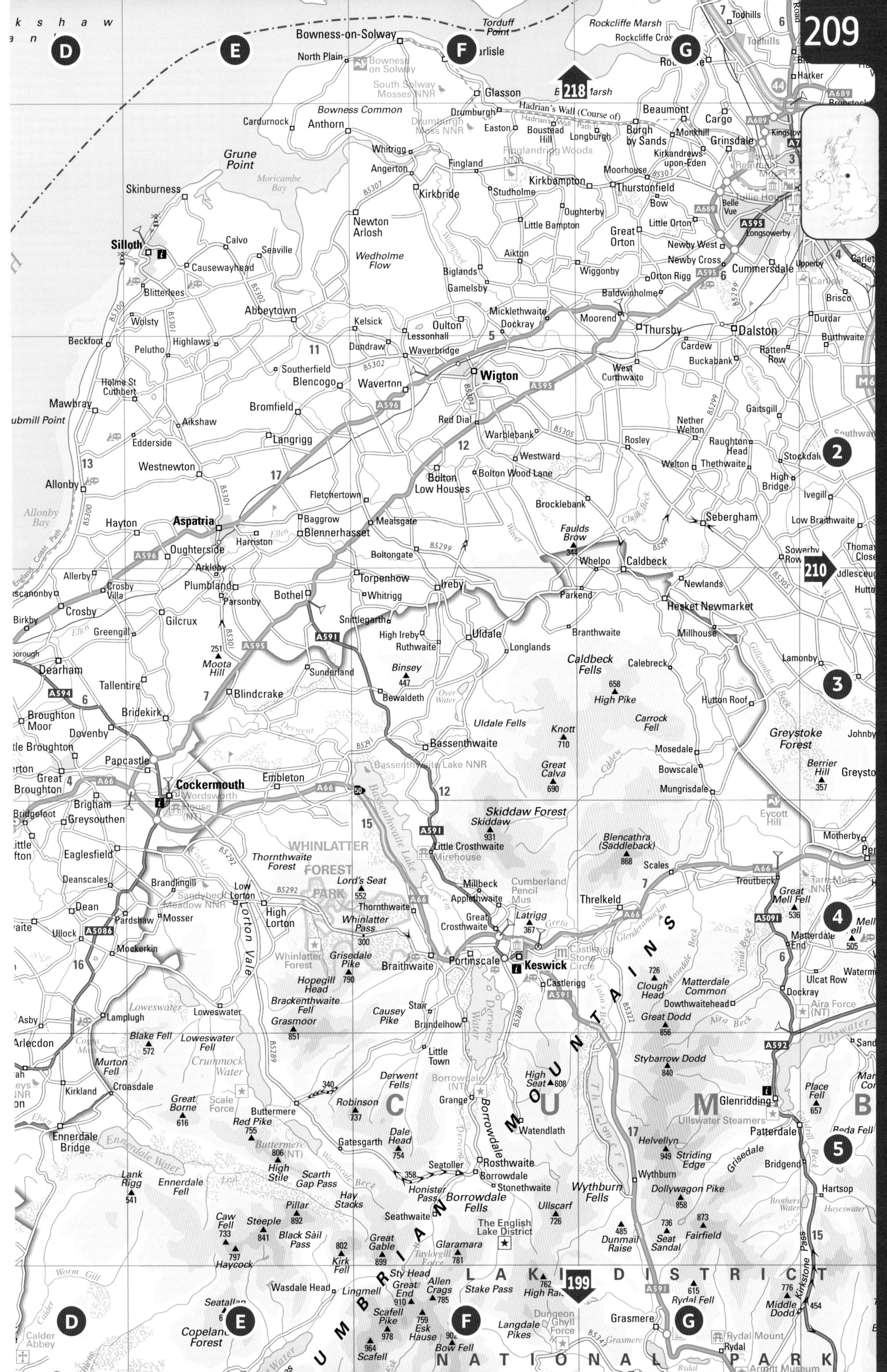
D
E
F
G
Torduff Point
Rockcliffe Marsh
Rockcliffe Cross
Todhills
Harker
Bowness-on-Solway
North Plain
Bowness on Solway
South Solway Mosses NNR
Glasson
218
Drumburgh
Hadrian's Wall (Course of)
Beaumont
Cargo
Bowness Common
Cardurnock
Anthorn
Drumburgh Moss NNR
Easton
Boustead Hill
Longburgh
Burgh by Sands
Monkhill
Grinsdale
Kingstown
Kirkandrews-upon-Eden
Whitrigg
Glandersgill Woods
Grune Point
Angerton
Fingland
Moorhouse
Moricambe Bay
Kirkbampton
Thurstonfield
Skinburness
Kirkbride
Studholme
Bow
Oughterby
Newton Arlosh
Little Bampton
Little Orton
Belle Vue
Great Orton
Longsowerby
Silloth
Calvo
Newby West
Seaville
Wedholme Flow
Aikton
Newby Cross
Causewayhead
Biglands
Wiggonby
Cummersdale
Upperby
Orton Rigg
Blitterlees
Gamelsby
Baldwinholme
Brisco
Abbeytown
Micklethwaite
Moorend
Wolsty
Kelsick
Oulton
Dockray
Thursby
Dalston
Durdar
Beckfoot
Highlaws
Lessonhall
Burthwaite
Pelutho
Dundraw
Waverbridge
Cardew
Ratten Row
Southerfield
Buckabank
Holme St Cuthbert
Blencogo
Waverton
Wigton
West Curthwaite
Mawbray
Bromfield
Red Dial
Gaitsgill
Dubmill Point
Aikshaw
Warblebank
Nether Welton
Langrigg
Rosley
Raughton Head
Edderside
Westward
Stockdalewath
Welton
Thethwaite
Westnewton
Bolton Low Houses
Bolton Wood Lane
High Bridge
Allonby
Fletchertown
Ivegill
Brocklebank
Allonby Bay
Hayton
Aspatria
Baggrow
Mealsgate
Sebergham
Low Braithwaite
Harriston
Blennerhasset
Faulds Brow
344
Oughterside
Boltongate
Sowerby Row
Thomas Close
England Coast Path
Arkleby
Welpo
Caldbeck
210
Allerby
Torpenhow
Newlands
Crosby Villa
Plumbland
Ireby
Parkend
Whitrigg
Bothel
Parsonby
Hesket Newmarket
Crosby
Snittlegarth
Birkby
Gilcrux
Millhouse
Greengill
High Ireby
Branthwaite
Ruthwaite
Uldale
Longlands
251
Moota Hill
Caldbeck Fells
Calebreck
Lamonby
Dearham
Binsey
447
Tallentire
Sunderland
658
High Pike
Blindcrake
Bewaldeth
Over Water
Hutton Roof
Bridekirk
Carrock Fell
Broughton Moor
Uldale Fells
Greystoke Forest
Dovenby
Knott
710
Johnby
Little Broughton
Bassenthwaite
Mosedale
Papcastle
Great Calva
690
Berrier Hill
357
Greystoke
Great Broughton
Embleton
Bassenthwaite Lake NNR
Bowscale
Cockermouth
Wordsworth House (NT)
Mungrisdale
Brigham
Skiddaw Forest
Bridgefoot
Greysouthen
Skiddaw
931
Eycott Hill
Eaglesfield
WHINLATTER FOREST PARK
Thornthwaite Forest
Little Crosthwaite
Mirehouse
Blencathra (Saddleback)
868
Motherby
Scales
Deanscales
Brandlingill
Lord's Seat
552
Millbeck
Cumberland Pencil Mus
Troutbeck
Tarn Moss NNR
Low Lorton
Applethwaite
Threlkeld
Great Mell Fell
536
Dean
Sandybeck Meadow NNR
High Lorton
Thornthwaite
Great Crosthwaite
Latrigg
367
Pardshaw
Mosser
Whinlatter Pass
300
Matterdale End
Mell Fell
505
Ullock
Castlerigg Stone Circle
Mockerkin
Portinscale
Keswick
Whinlatter Forest
Grisedale Pike
790
Braithwaite
Castlerigg
Lorton Vale
Hopegill Head
726
Clough Head
Matterdale Common
Ulcat Row
Brackenthwaite Fell
Stair
Dockray
Dowthwaitehead
Aira Force (NT)
Asby
Lamplugh
Loweswater
Grasmoor
851
Causey Pike
Brandelhow
Great Dodd
856
Arlecdon
Blake Fell
572
Loweswater Fell
Crummock Water
Little Town
Stybarrow Dodd
840
Murton Fell
Derwent Fells
High Seat
608
Kirkland
Croasdale
Borrowdale (NT)
Place Fell
657
Great Borne
616
Scale Force
Buttermere
Robinson
737
Grange
Glenridding
Ullswater Steamers
Ennerdale Bridge
Red Pike
755
Borrowdale
Watendlath
Patterdale
Reda Fell
Ennerdale Water
806
High Stile
Dale Head
754
Helvellyn
949
Striding Edge
Gatesgarth
Seatoller
Rosthwaite
Wythburn
Grisedale
Bridgend
Lank Rigg
541
Ennerdale Fell
Scarth Gap Pass
358
Borrowdale
Stonethwaite
Wythburn Fells
Dollywagon Pike
858
Hartsop
Hay Stacks
Honister Pass
Borrowdale Fells
Brothers Water
Hayeswater
Caw Fell
733
Steeple
841
Pillar
892
Seathwaite
Ullscarf
726
736
873
Black Sail Pass
797
Haycock
802
Kirk Fell
Great Gable
899
Glaramara
781
The English Lake District
485
Dunmail Raise
Seat Sandal
Fairfield
Kirkstone Pass
15
Worm Gill
Sty Head
762
High Raise
199
Wasdale Head
Lingmell
Great End
910
Allen Crags
785
Stake Pass
615
Rydal Fell
776
Middle Dodd
454
Seatallan
Scafell Pike
978
759
Esk Hause
Langdale Pikes
Dungeon Ghyll Force
Grasmere
Rydal Mount
Calder Abbey
Copeland Forest
964
Scafell
902
Bow Fell
Rydal
CUMBRIAN MOUNTAINS
LAKE DISTRICT NATIONAL PARK
A595
A596
A591
A594
A66
A5086
A5091
A592
A689
A7
B5307
B5300
B5301
B5302
B5304
B5305
B5299
B5292
B5289
B5322
B5343
M6
2
3
4
5

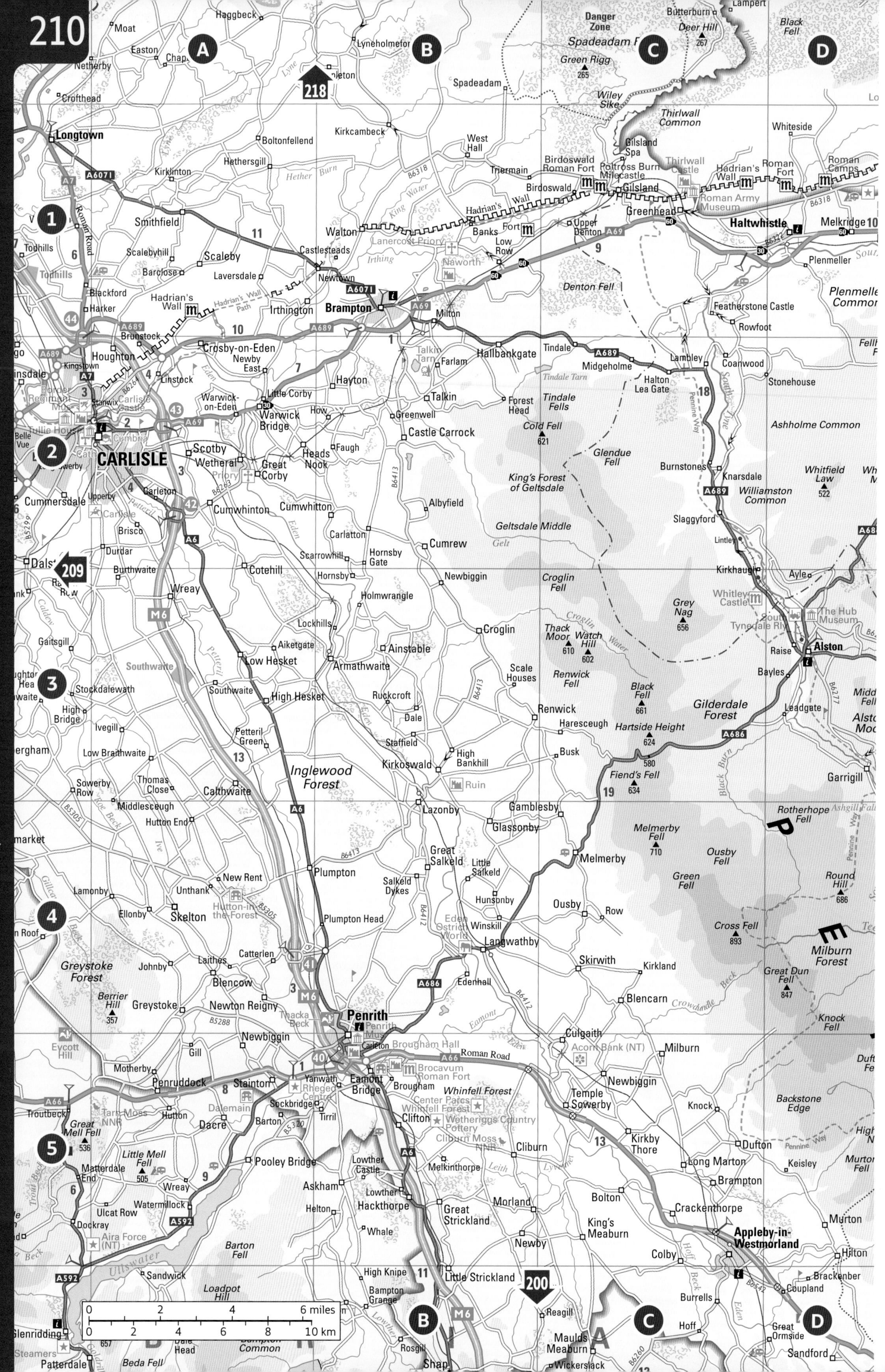
A
B
C
D
1
2
3
4
5
218
209
200
Moat
Haggbeck
Easton
Netherby
Crofthead
Lyneholmeford
Danger Zone
Spadeadam Forest
Green Rigg
265
Butterburn
Deer Hill
267
Lampert
Black Fell
Spadeadam
Wiley Sike
Thirlwall Common
Gilsland Spa
Longtown
Boltonfellend
Kirkcambeck
West Hall
Whiteside
Hethersgill
Hether Burn
Kirklinton
A6071
A7
Roman Road
Triermain
Birdoswald Roman Fort
Poltross Burn Milecastle
Thirlwall Castle
Hadrian's Wall
Roman Fort
Roman Camps
Birdoswald
Gilsland
Roman Army Museum
Greenhead
Haltwhistle
Melkridge
B6318
B6318
King Water
Hadrian's Wall
Smithfield
Walton
Lanercost Priory
Banks
Fort
Upper Denton
A69
Low Row
Todhills
Scaleby
Scalebyhill
Castlesteads
Irthing
Naworth
Plenmeller
Barclose
Laversdale
Newtown
Denton Fell
Plenmeller Common
Blackford
Harker
Hadrian's Wall
Hadrian's Wall Path
Irthington
Brampton
A6071
Milton
Featherstone Castle
Rowfoot
A689
Brunstock
Crosby-on-Eden
Hallbankgate
Tindale
Talkin Tarn
Farlam
Lambley
Coanwood
Houghton
Kingstown
Newby East
Midgeholme
Halton Lea Gate
Stonehouse
Linstock
Hayton
Tindale Tarn
Border Regiment Museum
Stanwix
Carlisle Castle
Little Corby
Warwick-on-Eden
Talkin
Forest Head
Tindale Fells
Pennine Way
Tullie House
Warwick Bridge
How
Greenwell
Castle Carrock
Cold Fell
621
Ashholme Common
Belle Vue
Cumbria
CARLISLE
Scotby
Wetheral
Priory
Great Corby
Heads Nook
Faugh
Glendue Fell
Cummersdale
Upperby
Carleton
B6263
King's Forest of Geltsdale
Burnstones
Knarsdale
Whitfield Law
522
Williamston Common
Carlisle
Cumwhinton
Cumwhitton
Albyfield
Slaggyford
Brisco
Eden
Carlatton
Geltsdale Middle
Durdar
Gelt
Cumrew
Lintley
Scarrowhill
Hornsby Gate
Dalston
Burthwaite
Cotehill
Hornsby
Newbiggin
Croglin Fell
Kirkhaugh
Ayle
Wreay
Holmwrangle
Whitley Castle
Grey Nag
656
The Hub Museum
M6
South Tynedale Rly
Lockhills
Croglin
Thack Moor
610
Watch Hill
602
Croglin Water
Gaitsgill
Aiketgate
Ainstable
Low Hesket
Armathwaite
Alston
Raise
Southwaite
Petteril
Scale Houses
Renwick Fell
Bayles
Stockdalewath
Southwaite
High Hesket
Ruckcroft
Black Fell
661
Gilderdale Forest
B6277
High Bridge
Dale
Renwick
Leadgate
Ivegill
Petteril Green
Harescough
Hartside Height
624
Staffield
A686
Low Braithwaite
13
Busk
580
Inglewood Forest
Kirkoswald
High Bankhill
Fiend's Fell
634
Garrigill
Thomas Close
Sowerby Row
Ruin
Calthwaite
19
Black Burn
Middlesceugh
Hutton End
Lazonby
Gamblesby
Rotherhope Fell
Roe Beck
B5305
Glassonby
Ive
Melmerby Fell
710
Great Salkeld
B6413
Little Salkeld
Melmerby
Ousby Fell
New Rent
Plumpton
Lamonby
Unthank
Hutton-in-the-Forest
Salkeld Dykes
Round Hill
686
Hunsonby
Green Fell
Ousby
Row
Ellonby
Skelton
Plumpton Head
B6412
Eden Ostrich World
Winskill
Cross Fell
893
Langwathby
Milburn Forest
Greystoke Forest
Johnby
Laithes
Catterlen
Skirwith
Kirkland
Blencow
41
A686
Edenhall
Great Dun Fell
847
Berrier Hill
357
Greystoke
Newton Reigny
Blencarn
Crowdundle Beck
Thacka Beck
Penrith
Penrith Museum
B5288
Eamont
Knock Fell
Culgaith
Eycott Hill
Newbiggin
Carleton
Brougham Hall
Roman Road
Acorn Bank (NT)
Milburn
Gill
A66
Motherby
40
Yanwath
Brocavum Roman Fort
Whinfell Forest
Newbiggin
Penruddock
Stainton
Rheged Centre
Eamont Bridge
Brougham
Temple Sowerby
Backstone Edge
Troutbeck
Dalemain
Sockbridge
Center Parcs Whinfell Forest
Knock
Great Mell Fell
536
Tarn Moss NNR
Hutton
Dacre
Barton
Tirril
Clifton
Wetheriggs Country Pottery
Kirkby Thore
B5320
Cliburn Moss NNR
Cliburn
Dufton
Little Mell Fell
505
Pooley Bridge
Lowther Castle
Melkinthorpe
Leith
Lyvennet
Long Marton
Keisley
Matterdale End
Askham
Brampton
Wreay
Lowther
Hackthorpe
Great Strickland
Morland
Bolton
Watermillock
Ulcat Row
Helton
Crackenthorpe
A592
Dockray
Aira Force (NT)
Whale
King's Meaburn
Appleby-in-Westmorland
Murton
Barton Fell
Newby
Colby
Hilton
Ullswater
High Knipe
Little Strickland
Sandwick
Loadpot Hill
Bampton Grange
Reagill
Brackenber
Coupland
Burrells
Hoff
Glenridding
Great Ormside
Rosgill
Maulds Meaburn
Steamers
Patterdale
Beda Fell
Shap
Wickerslack
Sandford
B6260
0 2 4 6 miles
0 2 4 6 8 10 km

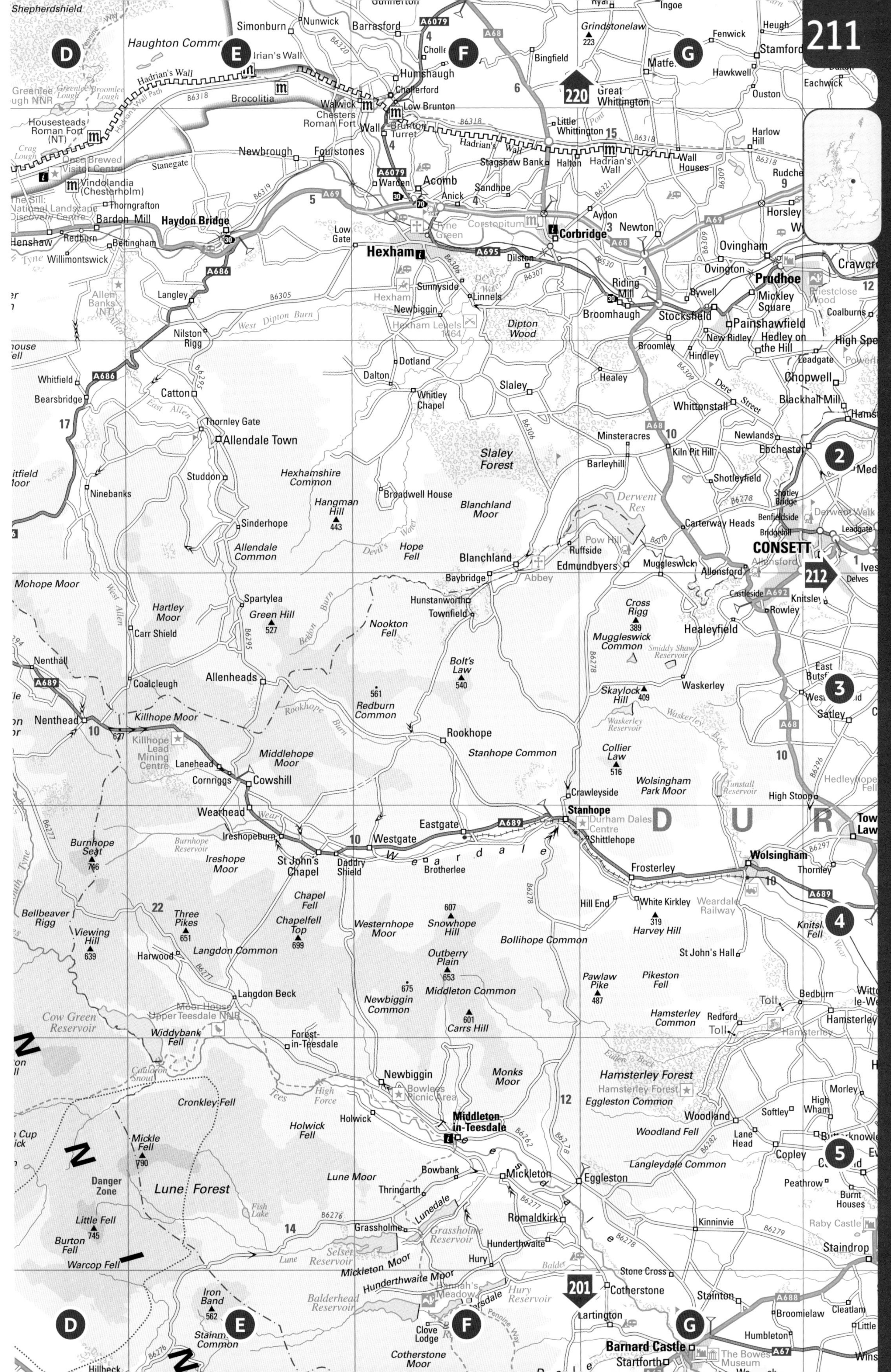
Shepherdshield
Simonburn
Nunwick
Barrasford
Haughton Common
Hadrian's Wall
Humshaugh
Chollerford
Brocolitia
Walwick
Chesters Roman Fort
Low Brunton
Wall
Brunton Turret
Housesteads Roman Fort (NT)
Newbrough
Fourstones
Once Brewed Visitor Centre
Stanegate
Vindolanda (Chesterholm)
The Sill: National Landscape Discovery Centre
Thorngrafton
Bardon Mill
Haydon Bridge
Henshaw
Redburn
Beltingham
Willimontswick
Acomb
Warden
Anick
Sandhoe
Low Gate
Hexham
Tyne Green
Corstopitum
Corbridge
Dilston
Grindstonelaw
Ingoe
Fenwick
Heugh
Stamford
Matfen
Hawkwell
Eachwick
Ouston
Bingfield
Great Whittington
Little Whittington
Stagshaw Bank
Halton
Wall Houses
Harlow Hill
Rudchester
Horsley
Aydon
Newton
Ovingham
Ovington
Prudhoe
Crawcrook
Riding Mill
Broomhaugh
Stocksfield
Bywell
Mickley Square
Priestclose Wood
Coalburns
Painshawfield
New Ridley
Hedley on the Hill
High Spen
Broomley
Hindley
Leadgate
Chopwell
Blackhall Mill
Hamsterley Mill
Langley
Allen Banks (NT)
Nilston Rigg
Sunnyside
Linnels
Newbiggin
Hexham Levels 1464
Dipton Wood
West Dipton Burn
Dotland
Dalton
Slaley
Healey
Whitley Chapel
Whittonstall
Dere Street
Whitfield
Bearsbridge
Catton
Thornley Gate
Allendale Town
Minsteracres
Newlands
Ebchester
Kiln Pit Hill
Barleyhill
Slaley Forest
Hexhamshire Common
Studdon
Ninebanks
Broadwell House
Hangman Hill 443
Blanchland Moor
Shotleyfield
Shotley Bridge
Benfieldside
Derwent Walk
Derwent Res
Carterway Heads
Sinderhope
Allendale Common
Hope Fell
Pow Hill
Ruffside
Leadgate
CONSETT
Blanchland
Abbey
Edmundbyers
Muggleswick
Allensford
Baybridge
Ivesley
Delves
Mohope Moor
Spartylea
Hunstanworth
Townfield
Castleside
Knitsley
Rowley
Hartley Moor
Green Hill 527
Nookton Fell
Cross Rigg 389
Healeyfield
Carr Shield
Muggleswick Common
Smiddy Shaw Reservoir
Nenthall
Bolt's Law 540
Coalcleugh
Allenheads
Waskerley
East Butsfield
Skaylock Hill 409
Nenthead
Killhope Moor
Rookhope
561 Redburn Common
Waskerley Reservoir
Satley
Killhope Lead Mining Centre
Lanehead
Middlehope Moor
Stanhope Common
Collier Law 516
Cornriggs
Cowshill
Wolsingham Park Moor
Crawleyside
Tunstall Reservoir
High Stoop
Hedleyhope Fell
Wearhead
Stanhope
Durham Dales Centre
Eastgate
Shittlehope
DUR
Town Law
Ireshopeburn
Westgate
Burnhope Seat 746
Burnhope Reservoir
Weardale
Wolsingham
Thornley
Ireshope Moor
St John's Chapel
Daddry Shield
Brotherlee
Frosterley
Chapel Fell
Three Pikes 651
607 Snowhope Hill
Hill End
White Kirkley
Weardale Railway
Bellbeaver Rigg
Chapelfell Top 699
Westernhope Moor
319 Harvey Hill
Knitsley Fell
Viewing Hill 639
Harwood
Langdon Common
Bollihope Common
St John's Hall
Outberry Plain 653
Langdon Beck
675
Newbiggin Common
Middleton Common
Pawlaw Pike 487
Pikeston Fell
Bedburn
Witton-le-Wear
Moor House Upper Teesdale NNR
601 Carrs Hill
Hamsterley Common
Redford
Toll
Hamsterley
Cow Green Reservoir
Widdybank Fell
Forest-in-Teesdale
Cauldron Snout
Newbiggin
Monks Moor
Hamsterley Forest
Morley
Bowlees Picnic Area
High Force
Tees
Cronkley Fell
Holwick
Middleton-in-Teesdale
Eggleston Common
High Wham
Softley
Woodland
Holwick Fell
Mickle Fell 790
Woodland Fell
Lane Head
Copley
Danger Zone
Lune Forest
Lune Moor
Bowbank
Mickleton
Eggleston
Langleydale Common
Peathrow
Thringarth
Lunedale
Fish Lake
Burnt Houses
Little Fell 745
Burton Fell
Grassholme
Grassholme Reservoir
Romaldkirk
Kinninvie
Raby Castle
Warcop Fell
Selset Reservoir
Hunderthwaite
Staindrop
Mickleton Moor
Hury
Hunderthwaite Moor
Stone Cross
Cotherstone
Hannah's Meadow
Hury Reservoir
Balderhead Reservoir
Iron Band 562
Stainton
Baldersdale
Pennine Way
Lartington
Broomielaw
Cleatlam
Stainmore Common
Clove Lodge
Barnard Castle
Humbleton
The Bowes Museum
Little
Startforth
Cotherstone Moor
Hillbeck
220
212
201
A68
A69
A695
A686
A689
A692
A6079
A688
A67
B6318
B6319
B6320
B6321
B6305
B6306
B6307
B6309
B6278
B6295
B6296
B6297
B6277
B6276
B6282
B6279
B6262
B6530

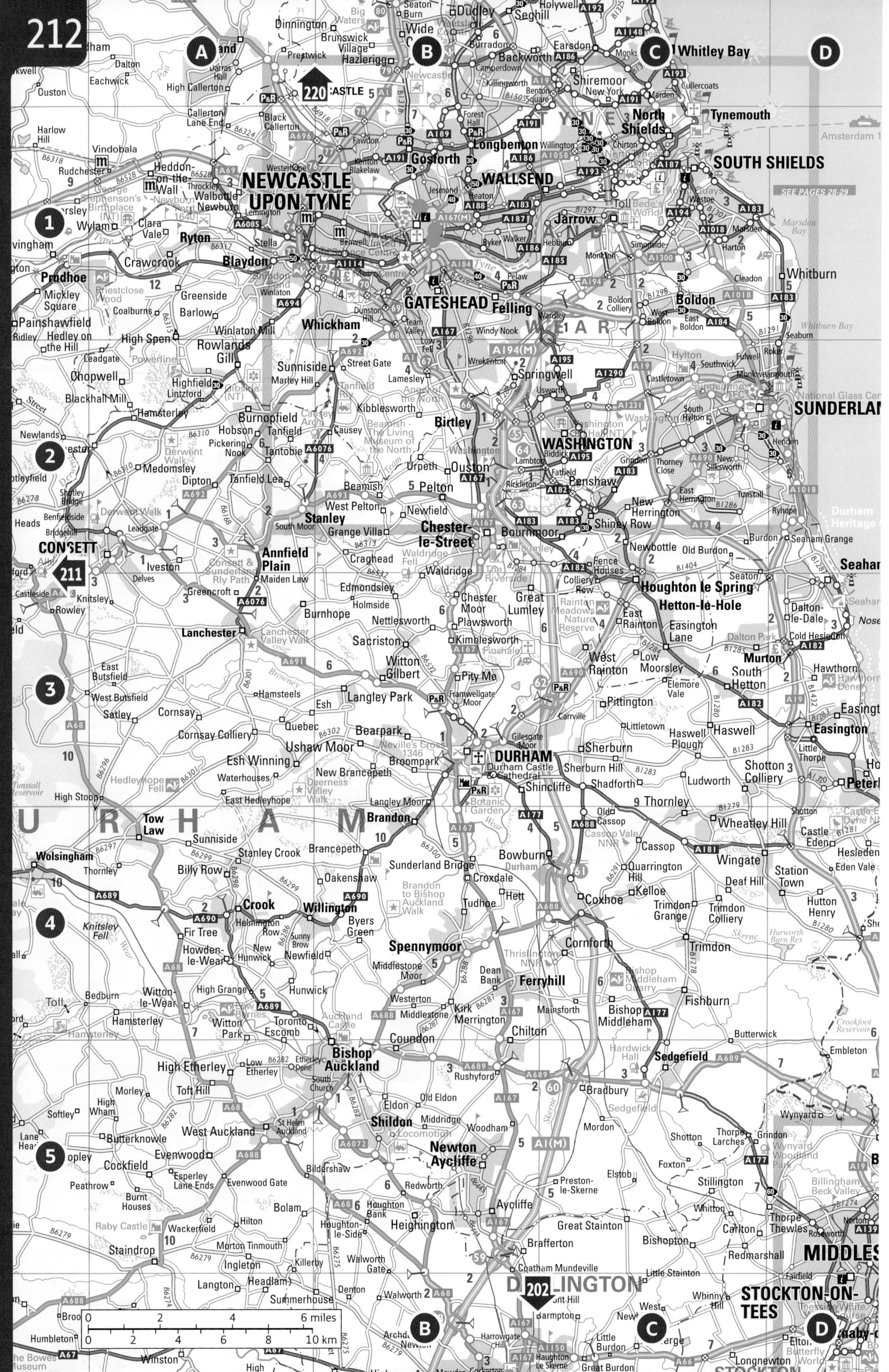
A
B
C
D
1
2
3
4
5
220
211
202
NEWCASTLE UPON TYNE
GATESHEAD
SOUTH SHIELDS
SUNDERLAND
WASHINGTON
DURHAM
WALLSEND
CONSETT
Whitley Bay
Tynemouth
North Shields
Jarrow
Gosforth
Longbenton
Felling
Whickham
Blaydon
Ryton
Prudhoe
Stanley
Chester-le-Street
Birtley
Houghton le Spring
Hetton-le-Hole
Murton
Easington
Peterlee
Lanchester
Tow Law
Crook
Willington
Spennymoor
Ferryhill
Sedgefield
Bishop Auckland
Shildon
Newton Aycliffe
Aycliffe
Heighington
West Auckland
Wolsingham
Staindrop
DARLINGTON
STOCKTON-ON-TEES
MIDDLESBROUGH
Seaham
Boldon
Whitburn
Pelton
Annfield Plain
Sacriston
Langley Park
Ushaw Moor
Esh Winning
Brandon
Bowburn
Coxhoe
Cornforth
Trimdon
Wingate
Shotton Colliery
Fishburn
Chilton
Coundon
Wheatley Hill
Thornley
Sherburn
Shincliffe
Durham Castle & Cathedral
Beamish - The Living Museum of the North
SEE PAGES 28-29
Amsterdam
0 2 4 6 miles
0 2 4 6 8 10 km
A1(M)
A167
A68
A689
A690
A691
A692
A693
A694
A19
A181
A182
A183
A184
A194(M)
A688
A66
A67

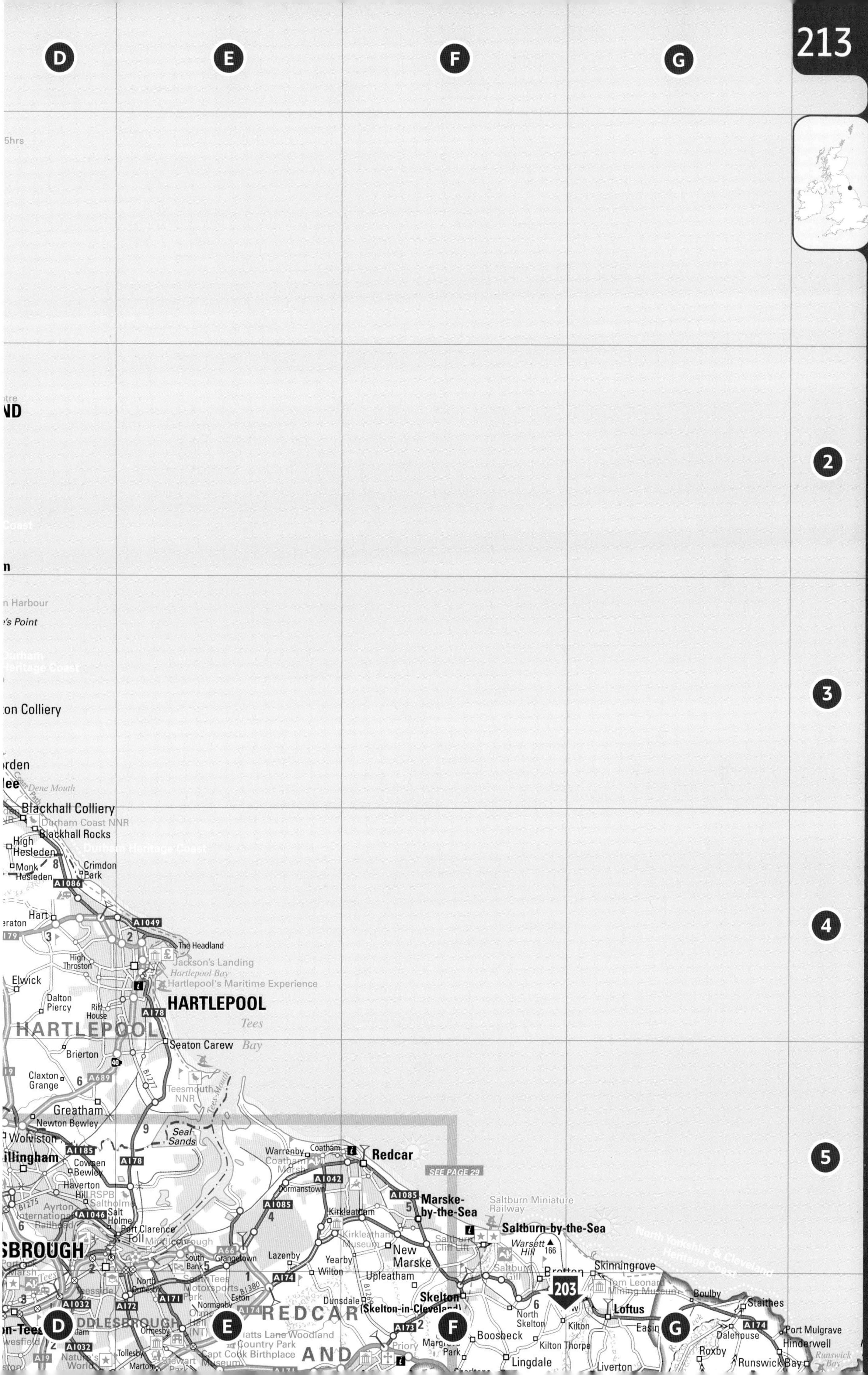

D
E
F
G

2

3

4

5

5hrs

ND

Coast

n

n Harbour

e's Point

Durham
Heritage Coast

on Colliery

rden

ee *Dene Mouth*
Blackhall Colliery
Durham Coast NNR
Blackhall Rocks
High
Hesleden
Monk 8
Hesleden
A1086
Crimdon
Park

Durham Heritage Coast

Hart
eraton
A1049
A179
3
2
The Headland
High
Throston
Jackson's Landing
Hartlepool Bay
Hartlepool's Maritime Experience
Elwick
Dalton
Piercy
Rift
House
A178
HARTLEPOOL
HARTLEPOOL
Tees
Seaton Carew *Bay*
Brierton
40
19
Claxton
Grange
6
A689
B1277
Teesmouth
NNR
Greatham
Newton Bewley
Wolviston
A1185
9
*Seal
Sands*
illingham
A178
Warrenby Coatham
Coatham
Marsh
Redcar

SEE PAGE 29

Cowpen
Bewley
Haverton
Hill RSPB
Saltholm
A1042
Dormanstown
A1085
Marske-
by-the-Sea
5
Saltburn Miniature
Railway
Ayrton
International
Railway
A1046
Salt
Holme
Port Clarence
A66
Kirkleatham
5
i
Saltburn-by-the-Sea
B1275
6
Toll Middlesbrough
Lazenby
Yearby
Kirkleatham
Museum
New
Marske
Saltburn
Cliff Lift
*Warsett
Hill*
166
North Yorkshire & Cleveland
Heritage Coast
SBROUGH
South Bank 5
South Tees
Motorsports
Park
A66
Grangetown
Wilton
Upleatham
Saltburn
Brotton
Skinningrove
Tom Leonard
Mining Museum
Boulby
Staithes
on-Tees
A1032
A172
A171
Normanby
Eston
B1380
A174
Dunsdale
Skelton
(Skelton-in-Cleveland)
6
203
North
Skelton
Kilton
Loftus
Easin
A174
Port Mulgrave
Hinderwell
wesfield
A19
A1032
Natures
World
Ormesby
Tollesby
Marton
atts Lane Woodland
Country Park
Capt Cook Birthplace
Museum
A171
Priory
2
Margrove
Park
Boosbeck
Kilton Thorpe
Lingdale
Liverton
Roxby
Dalehouse
Runswick
Bay

D
E
F
G
REDCAR
AND

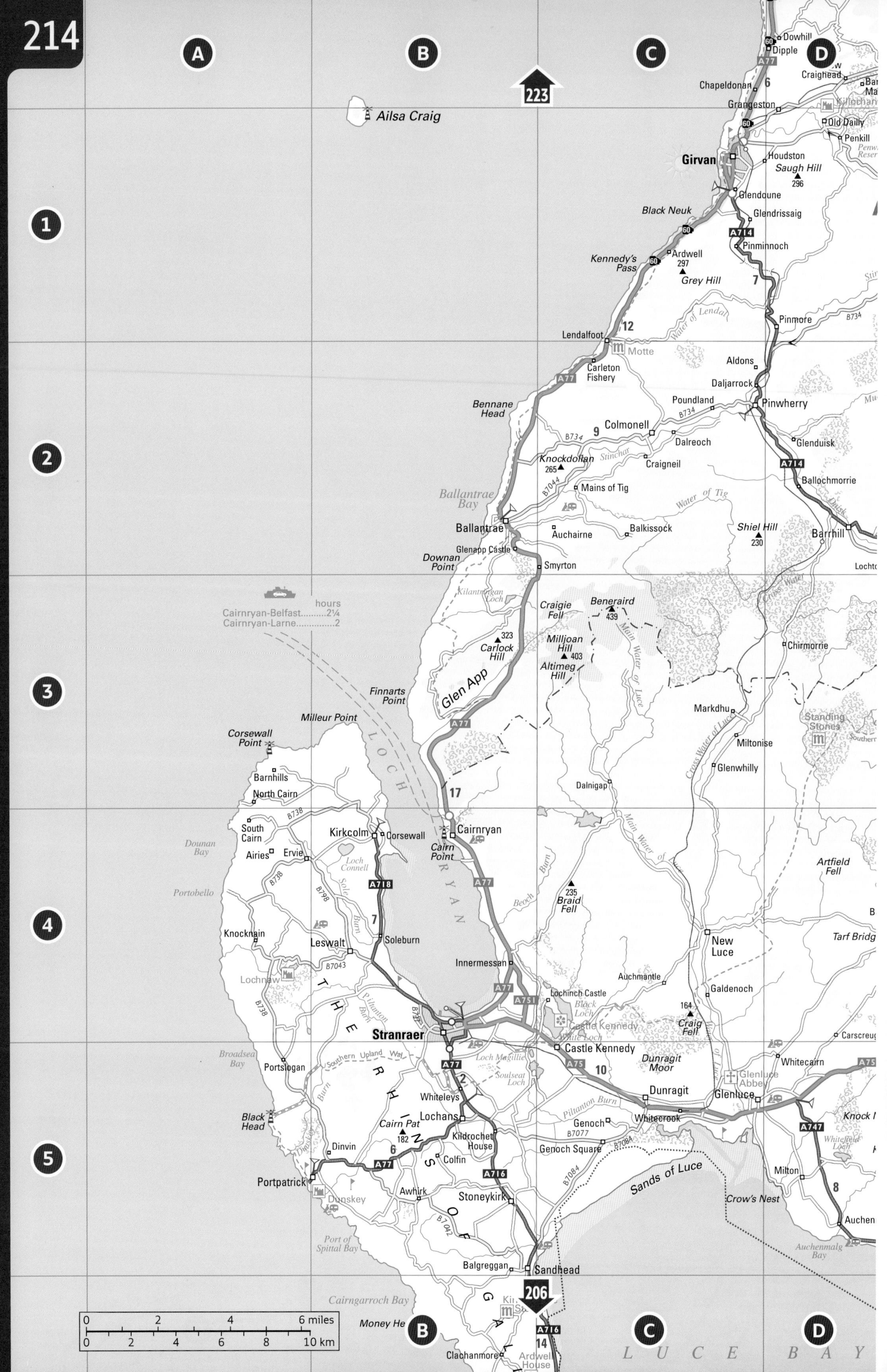

A   B   223   C   D

Ailsa Craig

Dowhill
Dipple
A77   60
Craighead
Chapeldonan
Grangeston   6
Old Daily
Penkill
Pemw
Reser

Girvan
Houdston
Saugh Hill
296

Glendoune
Black Neuk   Glendrissaig
60   A714
Kennedy's   60   Ardwell   Pinminnoch
Pass   297
Grey Hill   7
Pinmore
B73A
Lendalfoot   12
Motte
Aldons
Carleton   Daljarrock
Fishery   Poundland   Pinwherry
Bennane   B734
Head   Colmonell   Dalreoch   Glenduisk
9   B734
Stinchar   A714
Knockdolian   Craigneil   Ballochmorrie
265
B744   Mains of Tig   Shiel Hill   Barrhill
230
Ballantrae   Auchairne   Balkissock   Lochto
Bay
Ballantrae   Smyrton
Glenapp Castle
Downan
Point

Kilantringan
Loch   Craigie   Beneraird   Chirmorrie
Fell   439
Carlock   Milljoan   Standing
323   Hill   Markdhu   Stones
Finnarts   Carlock   403   m
Point   Hill   Altimeg   Miltonise
Milleur Point   Hill   Glenwhilly
Corsewall   Glen App
Point   A77   Dalnigap
Barnhills   17
North Cairn   Cairnryan   Braid   New
South   Kirkcolm   Corsewall   235   Fell   Luce   Tarf Bridg
Cairn   Cairn   Artfield
Airies   Ervie   Point   Auchmantle   Fell
B738   Knocknain   A718   7   Soleburn   A77   Galdenoch
Leswalt   Beoch
B7043   Innermessan   Lochinch Castle   164   Carscreu
Lochnaw   A77   Castle Kennedy   Craig
B738   A751   Fell
Stranraer   A75   10   Dunragit   Whitecairn   A75
Broadsea   Castle Kennedy   Moor   Glenluce
Bay   Portslogan   A77   Loch Magillie   Dunragit   Abbey   A747
Southern Upland Wal   Soulseat   Glenluce
Whiteleys   Loch   Genoch   Whitecrook   Knock
Black   Cairn Pat   2   Lochans   B7077   Milton
Head   182   Kildrocheta   Genoch Square   B7084
6   House   B7084   Crow's Nest   8
Dinvin   A77   Colfin   A716   Auchen
Portpatrick   Awhirk   Sands of Luce   Auchenmalg
Dunskey   Stoneykirk   Bay
B7042
Port of   Balgreggan   Sandhead
Spittal Bay   206

0   2   4   6 miles
0   2   4   6   8   10 km

Cairngarroch Bay   Money He   B   14   C   D
Clachanmore   Ardwell   L U C E   B A Y
House

Cairnryan-Belfast.........2¼   hours
Cairnryan-Larne..............2

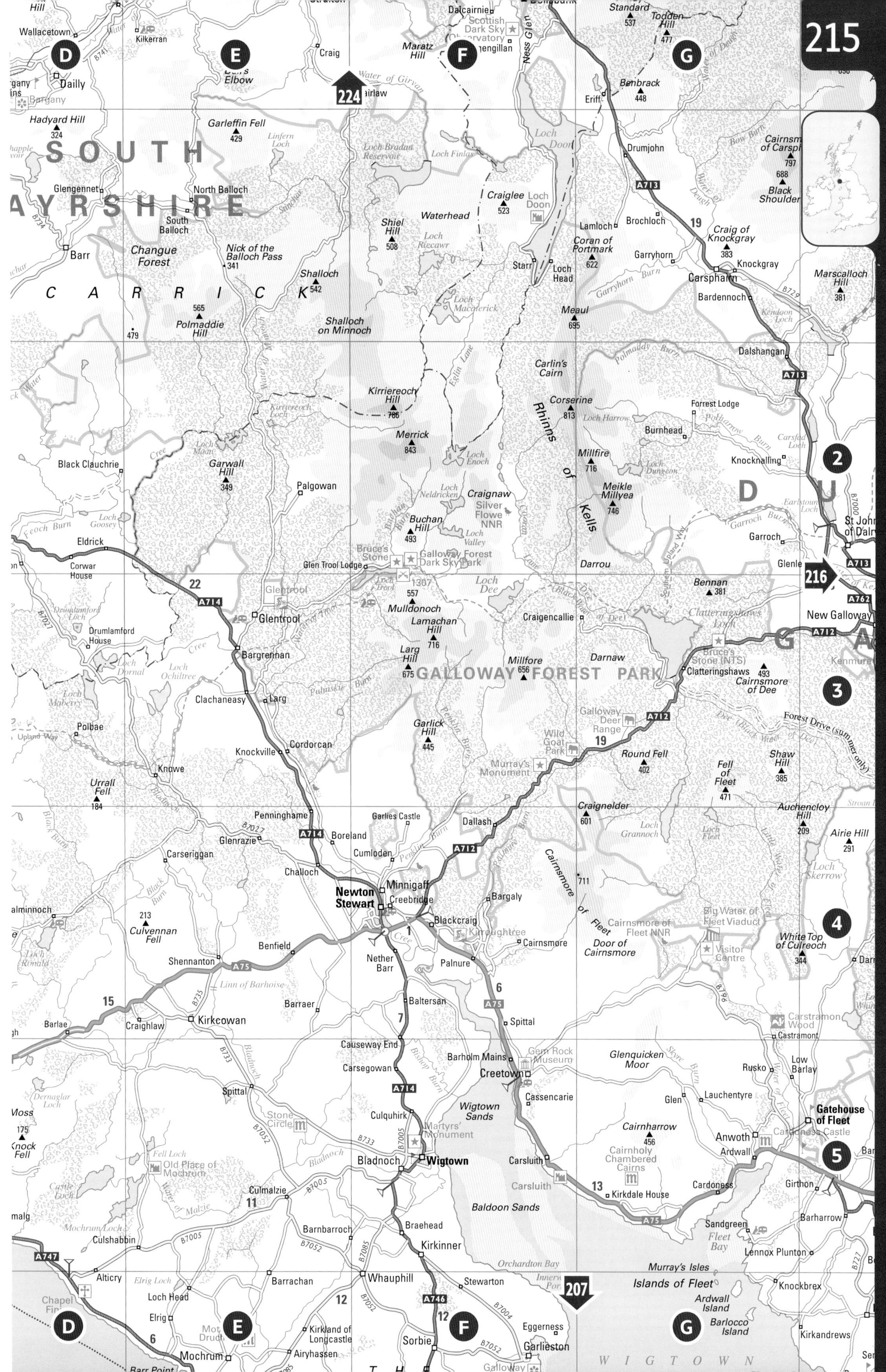
SOUTH AYRSHIRE
CARRICK
GALLOWAY FOREST PARK
Newton Stewart
Wigtown
Creetown
Carsphairn
Gatehouse of Fleet
Glentrool
Barr
Dailly
Kirkcowan
Garlieston
Sorbie
Mochrum
Merrick
843
Corserine
813
Rhinns of Kells
Loch Doon
Loch Dee
Clatteringshaws Loch
Wigtown Sands
Baldoon Sands
Islands of Fleet
Murray's Isles
224
216
207

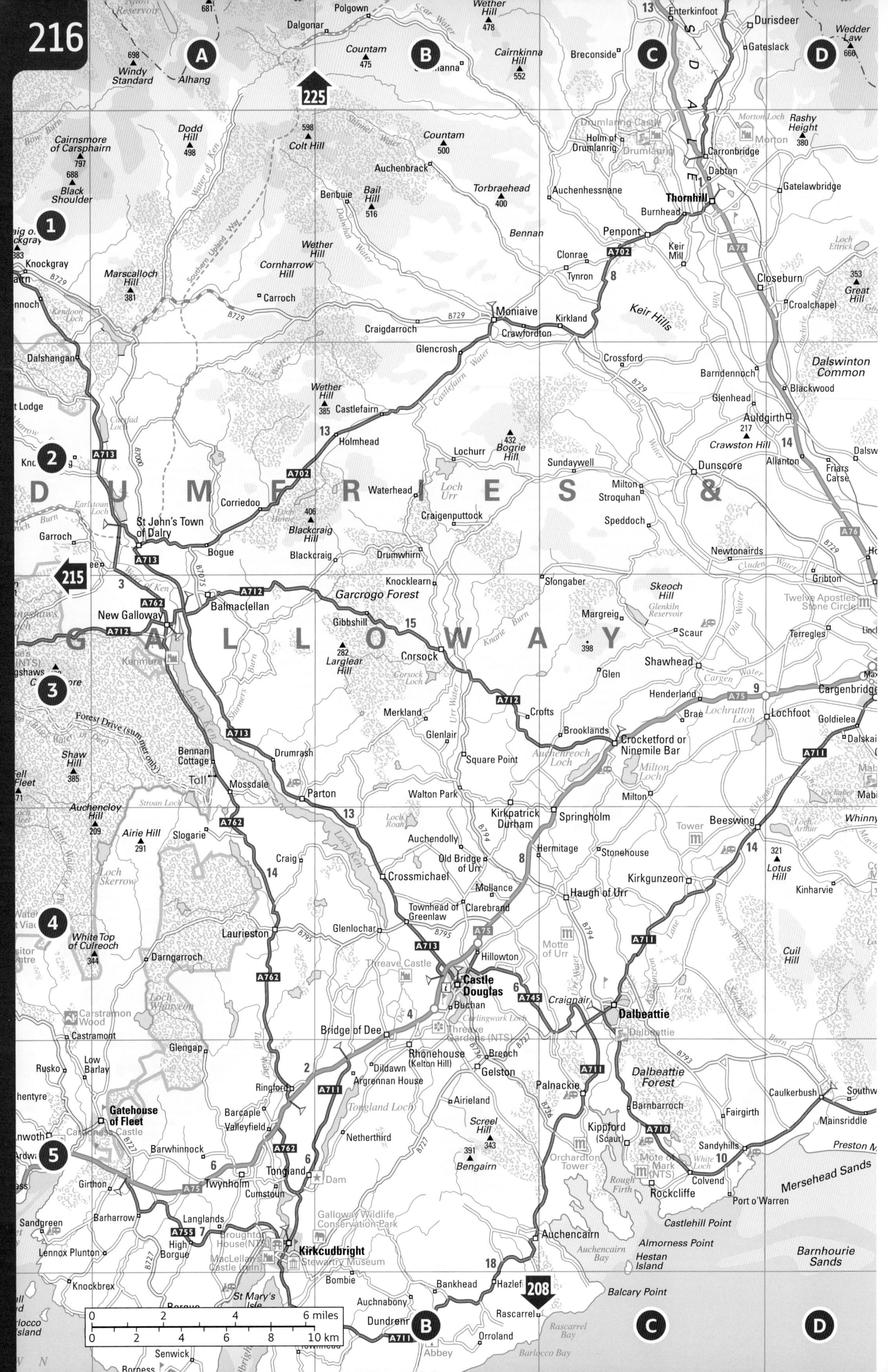
Windy Standard
Alhang
Dalgonar
Polgown
Scar Water
Countam
Wether Hill
Cairnkinna Hill
Breconside
Enterkinfoot
Durisdeer
Gateslack
Wedder Law
225
Cairnsmore of Carsphairn
Black Shoulder
Dodd Hill
Colt Hill
Countam
Auchenbrack
Drumlanrig Castle
Holm of Drumlanrig
Carronbridge
Morton
Rashy Height
Dabton
Thornhill
Gatelawbridge
Benbuie
Bail Hill
Torbraehead
Auchenhessnane
Burnhead
Penpont
Keir Mill
Bennan
Southern Upland Way
Wether Hill
Cornharrow Hill
Knockgray
Marscalloch Hill
Carroch
Clonrae
Tynron
Closeburn
Great Hill
Moniaive
Kirkland
Keir Hills
Croalchapel
Craigdarroch
Crawfordton
Glencrosh
Dalshangan
Crossford
Barndennoch
Dalswinton Common
Blackwood
Glenhead
Wether Hill
Castlefairn
Auldgirth
Holmhead
Bogrie Hill
Crawston Hill
Lochurr
Sundaywell
Dunscore
Allanton
Friars Carse
D U M F R I E S &
Waterhead
Loch Urr
Milton
Stroquhan
Corriedoo
Craigenputtock
Speddoch
Garroch
St John's Town of Dalry
Blackcraig Hill
Bogue
Blackcraig
Drumwhirn
Newtonairds
Cluden Water
215
Knocklearn
Slongaber
Skeoch Hill
Gribton
Garcrogo Forest
Twelve Apostles Stone Circle
Balmaclellan
New Galloway
Glenkiln Reservoir
Margreig
Gibbshill
Scaur
G A L L O W A Y
Terregles
Kenmure
Larglear Hill
Corsock
Shawhead
Glen
Corsock Loch
Cargenbridge
Henderland
Merkland
Crofts
Brae
Lochrutton Loch
Lochfoot
Goldielea
Forest Drive (summer only)
Glenlair
Brooklands
Crocketford or Ninemile Bar
Shaw Hill
Bennan Cottage
Drumrash
Square Point
Auchenreoch Loch
Toll
Mossdale
Milton Loch
Parton
Walton Park
Milton
Auchencloy Hill
Stroan Loch
Kirkpatrick Durham
Springholm
Airie Hill
Slogarie
Loch Roan
Tower
Beeswing
Auchendolly
Loch Ken
Hermitage
Stonehouse
Lotus Hill
Loch Skerrow
Craig
Old Bridge of Urr
Crossmichael
Kirkgunzeon
Kinharvie
Mollance
Haugh of Urr
Townhead of Greenlaw
Clarebrand
White Top of Culreoch
Laurieston
Glenlochar
Motte of Urr
Cuil Hill
Hillowton
Darngarroch
Threave Castle
Castle Douglas
Loch Whinyeon
Craignair
Dalbeattie
Carstramon Wood
Buchan
Carlingwark Loch
Castramont
Bridge of Dee
Threave Gardens (NTS)
Glengap
Rhonehouse (Kelton Hill)
Breoch
Low Barlay
Rusko
Dildawn
Gelston
Dalbeattie Forest
Argrennan House
Palnackie
Ringford
Caulkerbush
Airieland
Barnbarroch
Fairgirth
Tongland Loch
Gatehouse of Fleet
Cardoness Castle
Barcaple
Valleyfield
Screel Hill
Kippford (Scaur)
Mainsriddle
Netherthird
Barwhinnock
Bengairn
Orchardton Tower
Sandyhills
Preston
Mote of Mark (NTS)
White Loch
Tongland
Dam
Twynholm
Cumstoun
Girthon
Rough Firth
Colvend
Mersehead Sands
Rockcliffe
Port o'Warren
Galloway Wildlife Conservation Park
Barharrow
Sandgreen
Langlands
Castlehill Point
Broughton House (NTS)
High Borgue
Kirkcudbright
Auchencairn
Almorness Point
Lennox Plunton
MacLellan's Castle (ruin)
Stewartry Museum
Auchencairn Bay
Hestan Island
Barnhourie Sands
Bombie
Knockbrex
Bankhead
Hazlefield
208
Balcary Point
St Mary's Isle
Auchnabony
Rascarrel
Rascarrel Bay
Dundrennan
Orroland
Abbey
Barlocco Bay
Senwick
0 2 4 6 miles
0 2 4 6 8 10 km
A713
A702
A712
A762
A75
A711
A745
A710
A755
A76
B729
B7000
B7075
B795
B794
B727
B736
B793

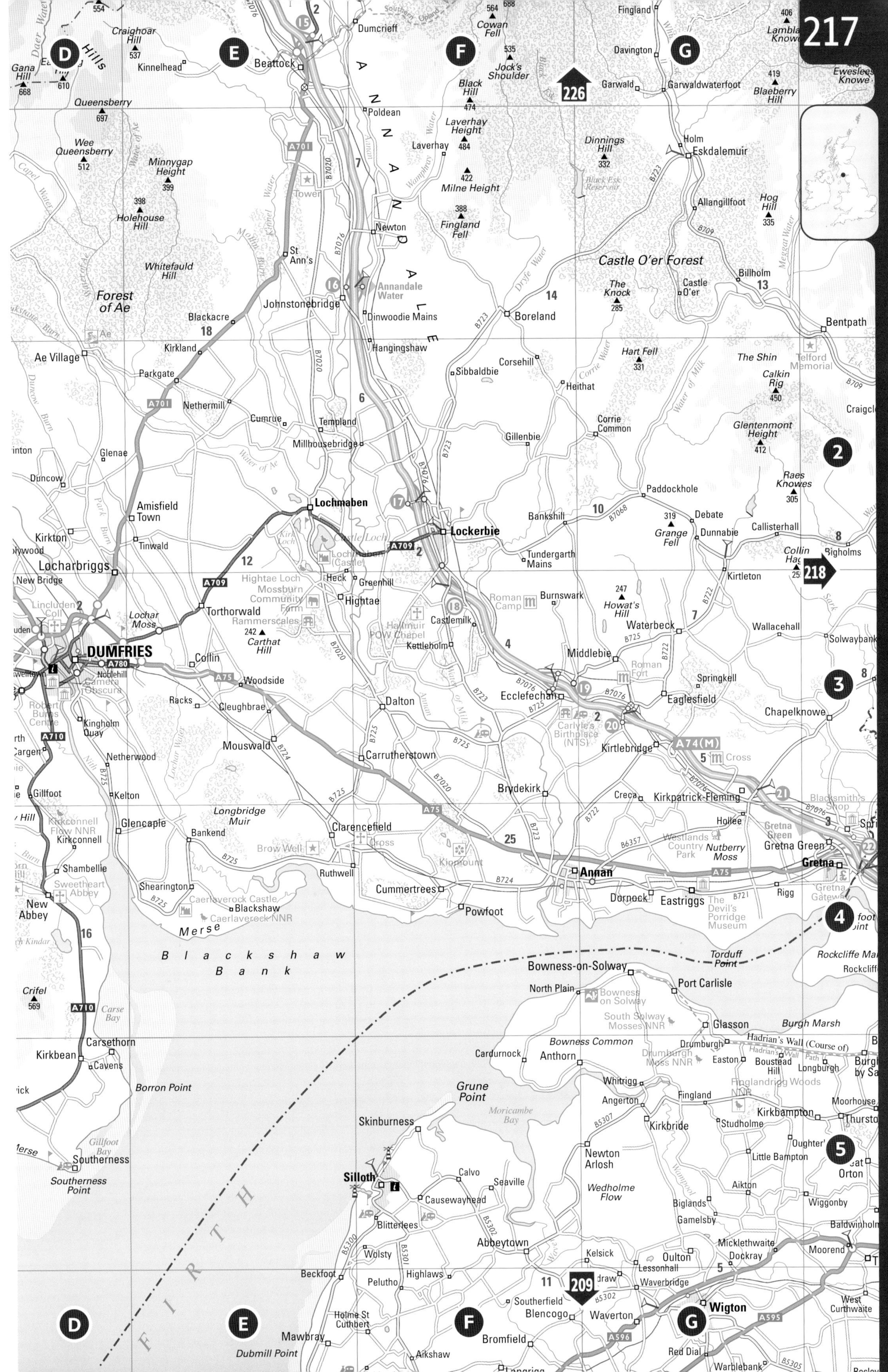
D
E
F
G
Craighoar Hill
537
Gana Hill
668
610
Hills
Kinnelhead
Beattock
Dumcrieff
15
2
564
Cowan Fell
535
Jock's Shoulder
Fingland
Davington
406
Lambla Knowe
Eweslees Knowe
419
Blaeberry Hill
Garwald
Garwaldwaterfoot
226
Queensberry
697
Poldean
A N N A N D A L E
Black Hill
474
Laverhay Height
484
Laverhay
Wee Queensberry
512
Minnygap Height
399
A701
B7020
7
Tower
Dinnings Hill
332
Black Esk Reservoir
Holm
Eskdalemuir
B723
422
Milne Height
398
Holehouse Hill
388
Fingland Fell
Newton
Allangillfoot
Hog Hill
335
B709
St Ann's
B7076
Whitefauld Hill
Castle O'er Forest
Billholm
13
16
Annandale Water
Castle O'er
The Knock
285
Forest of Ae
Johnstonebridge
Dinwoodie Mains
14
Boreland
Blackacre
18
Ae
Hangingshaw
Bentpath
Ae Village
Kirkland
Corsehill
Hart Fell
331
The Shin
Telford Memorial
Sibbaldbie
Calkin Rig
450
Parkgate
Heithat
B709
6
A701
Nethermill
Craigcl
Cumrue
Templand
Corrie Common
Glentenmont Height
412
Gillenbie
Millhousebridge
B723
2
Glenae
Duncow
Paddockhole
Raes Knowes
305
17
Lochmaben
Amisfield Town
10
Bankshill
B7068
319
Grange Fell
Debate
Dunnabie
Callisterhall
8
Kirkton
Tinwald
Lockerbie
Castle Loch
A709
2
Bigholms
Locharbriggs
12
Tundergarth Mains
Collin Hag
218
New Bridge
Hightae Loch
Heck
Greenhill
Kirtleton
A709
Mossburn Community Farm
Hightae
247
Howat's Hill
Burnswark
Roman Camp
Lincluden Coll
Torthorwald
18
Lochar Moss
Rammerscales
Castlemilk
Waterbeck
7
Wallacehall
242
Carthat Hill
Hallmuir POW Chapel
Kettleholm
B725
Solwaybank
4
Middlebie
DUMFRIES
A780
Collin
Noblehill
Roman Fort
Camera Obscura
A75
Woodside
B7076
19
Springkell
8
3
Robert Burns Centre
Racks
Cleughbrae
Ecclefechan
B725
2
Eaglesfield
B7076
Kingholm Quay
Dalton
20
Chapelknowe
A710
Carlyle's Birthplace (NTS)
Mouswald
B724
B725
Kirtlebridge
A74(M)
Netherwood
Carrutherstown
5
Cross
B725
B7020
Brydekirk
B7076
21
Gillfoot
Kelton
B725
Creca
Kirkpatrick-Fleming
Blacksmith's Shop
Longbridge Muir
B722
B7076
Kirkconnell Flow NNR
Glencaple
Clarencefield
A75
Hollee
3
Kirkconnell
Bankend
Cross
25
Gretna Green
Westlands Country Park
Nutberry Moss
Gretna Green
22
Brow Well
B723
B6357
Shambellie
B725
Ruthwell
Kinmount
Annan
Gretna
Sweetheart Abbey
Shearington
A75
New Abbey
Caerlaverock Castle
Blackshaw
Cummertrees
B724
Dornock
Eastriggs
B721
Rigg
Gretna Gateway
Caerlaverock NNR
Powfoot
The Devil's Porridge Museum
16
Merse
4
Blackshaw Bank
Torduff Point
Rockcliffe Ma
Rockcliff
Bowness-on-Solway
Crifel
569
North Plain
Port Carlisle
A710
Carse Bay
Bowness on Solway
South Solway Mosses NNR
Glasson
Burgh Marsh
Carsethorn
Cardurnock
Bowness Common
Drumburgh
Hadrian's Wall (Course of)
Kirkbean
Cavens
Anthorn
Drumburgh Moss NNR
Easton
Boustead Hill
Longburgh
Burgh by Sa
Borron Point
Whitrigg
Finglandrigg Woods NNR
Grune Point
Angerton
Fingland
Moorhouse
Moricambe Bay
B5307
Kirkbampton
Thursto
Skinburness
Kirkbride
Studholme
Gillfoot Bay
Oughterby
5
Southerness
Newton Arlosh
Little Bampton
Orton
Southerness Point
Silloth
Calvo
Seaville
Wedholme Flow
Aikton
Causewayhead
Biglands
Wiggonby
Gamelsby
B5302
Blitterlees
Baldwinholm
Abbeytown
Micklethwaite
Moorend
Wolsty
B5300
B5301
Kelsick
Oulton
Dockray
Lessonhall
5
Beckfoot
Highlaws
11
Waverbridge
Pelutho
209
B5302
Southerfield
Wigton
West Curthwaite
Holme St Cuthbert
Blencogo
Waverton
A595
D
E
F
G
FIRTH
Mawbray
Bromfield
A596
Red Dial
Dubmill Point
Aikshaw
Warblebank
B5305

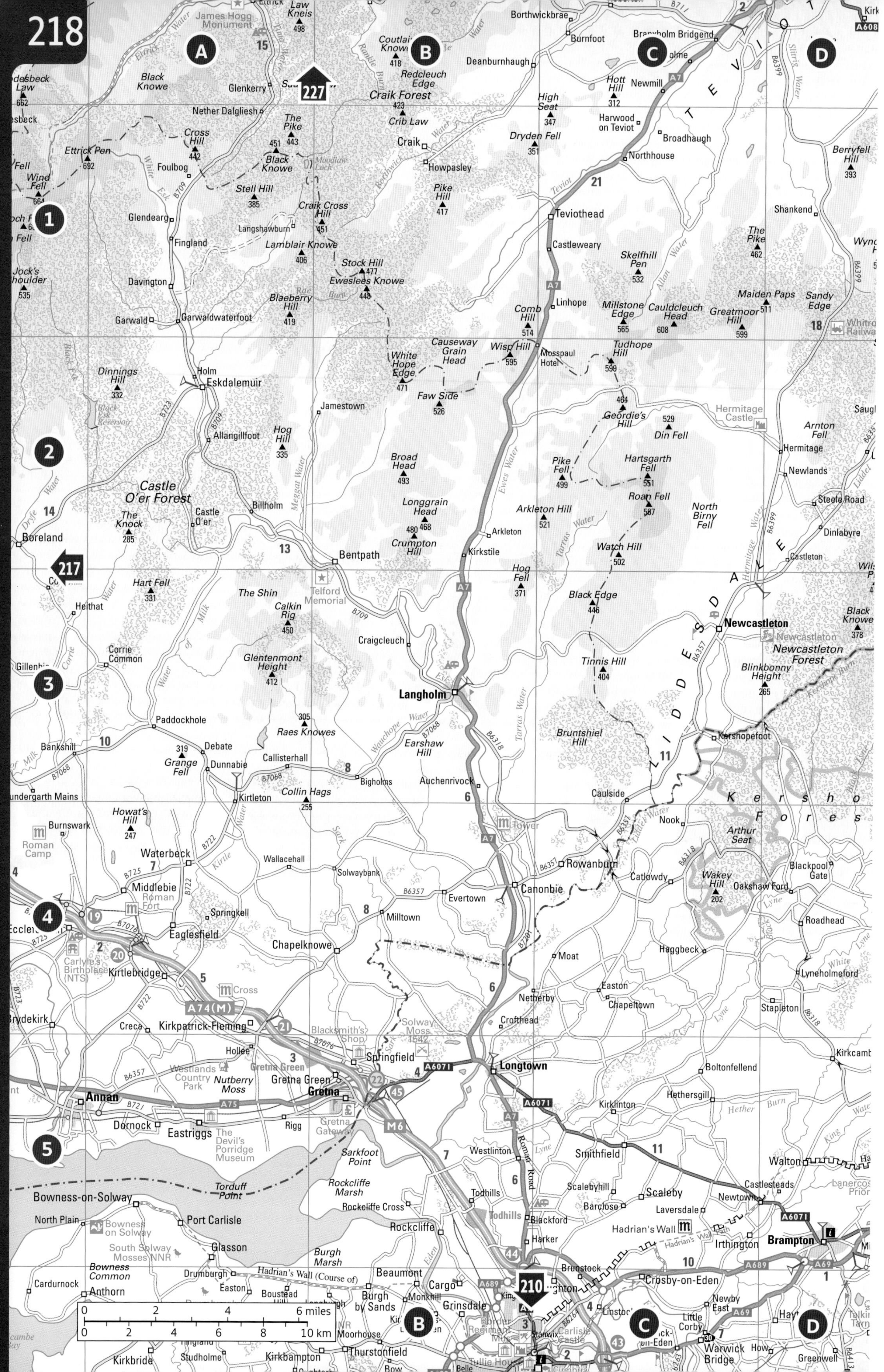
A
B
C
D
1
2
3
4
5
227
217
210
James Hogg Monument
Ettrick
Law Kneis
498
15
Coutlair Knowe
418
Borthwickbrae
Burnfoot
Branxholm Bridgend
Deanburnhaugh
Black Knowe
Glenkerry
Redcleuch Edge
Craik Forest
423
Crib Law
Newmill
Hott Hill
312
High Seat
347
Nether Dalgliesh
The Pike
443
451
Cross Hill
442
Ettrick Pen
692
Harwood on Teviot
Broadhaugh
Craik
Dryden Fell
351
Black Knowe
Moodlaw Loch
Foulbog
Howpasley
Northhouse
Berryfell Hill
393
Wind Fell
664
Stell Hill
385
Pike Hill
417
Teviot
21
B709
Glendearg
Craik Cross Hill
451
Teviothead
Shankend
Langshawburn
Fingland
Lamblair Knowe
406
Castleweary
The Pike
462
Skelfhill Pen
532
Stock Hill
477
Eweslees Knowe
448
Jock's Shoulder
535
Davington
A7
Linhope
Maiden Paps
511
Sandy Edge
Blaeberry Hill
419
Comb Hill
514
Millstone Edge
565
Cauldcleuch Head
608
Greatmoor Hill
599
18
Garwald
Garwaldwaterfoot
Causeway Grain Head
Wisp Hill
595
Mosspaul Hotel
Tudhope Hill
599
Whitrope Railway
White Hope Edge
471
Faw Side
526
Dinnings Hill
332
Holm
Eskdalemuir
Jamestown
464
Geordie's Hill
529
Din Fell
Hermitage Castle
Black Esk Reservoir
B723
Allangillfoot
Hog Hill
335
Arnton Fell
Hermitage
Broad Head
493
Pike Fell
499
Hartsgarth Fell
551
Newlands
Castle O'er Forest
Roan Fell
587
Steele Road
14
The Knock
285
Castle O'er
Billholm
Longgrain Head
468
480
Crumpton Hill
Arkleton Hill
521
North Birny Fell
Dryfe Water
Boreland
13
Bentpath
Arkleton
Kirkstile
Watch Hill
502
Dinlabyre
Castleton
Hart Fell
331
The Shin
Telford Memorial
Hog Fell
371
Black Edge
446
Heithat
Calkin Rig
450
B709
Newcastleton
Black Knowe
378
Craigcleuch
Newcastleton Forest
Corrie Common
Glentenmont Height
412
Tinnis Hill
404
Blinkbonny Height
265
Gillenbie
Langholm
Paddockhole
305
Raes Knowes
Earshaw Hill
Bruntshiel Hill
Kershopefoot
Bankshill
10
319
Debate
Grange Fell
Dunnabie
Callisterhall
8
Bigholms
Auchenrivock
B6318
11
B7068
Undergarth Mains
Kirtleton
Collin Hags
255
6
Caulside
Kershope Forest
Howat's Hill
247
Burnswark
Roman Camp
Tower
Nook
Arthur Seat
Waterbeck
Wallacehall
Rowanburn
Catlowdy
Blackpool Gate
B725
7
Solwaybank
Middlebie
Roman Fort
Evertown
Canonbie
Wakey Hill
202
Oakshaw Ford
B6357
Springkell
Milltown
Roadhead
Ecclefechan
19
Eaglesfield
Chapelknowe
20
Haggbeck
Carlyle's Birthplace (NTS)
Kirtlebridge
Moat
Lyneholmeford
5
Cross
Easton
Netherby
Chapeltown
A74(M)
Stapleton
Brydekirk
Creca
Kirkpatrick-Fleming
21
Crofthead
Blacksmith's Shop
Solway Moss 1542
Hollee
3
Springfield
A6071
Longtown
Kirkcambeck
Westlands Country Park
Nutberry Moss
Gretna Green
Gretna
22
45
Boltonfellend
Annan
A75
B721
Kirklinton
Hethersgill
Hether Burn
Dornock
Eastriggs
The Devil's Porridge Museum
Rigg
Gretna Gateway
M6
Sarkfoot Point
Westlinton
Roman Road
Smithfield
Walton
Torduff Point
Rockcliffe Marsh
Todhills
Scaleby
Castlesteads
Bowness-on-Solway
Port Carlisle
Rockcliffe Cross
Scalebyhill
Barclose
Laversdale
Newtown
A6071
North Plain
Bowness on Solway
Rockcliffe
Todhills
Blackford
Hadrian's Wall
Brampton
Glasson
South Solway Mosses NNR
Harker
Irthington
Burgh Marsh
44
10
A689
A69
Bowness Common
Drumburgh
Hadrian's Wall (Course of)
Beaumont
Brunstock
Cardurnock
Anthorn
Easton
Boustead Hill
Cargo
Crosby-on-Edena
Burgh by Sands
Monkhill
Grinsdale
Newby East
Little Corby
Warwick Bridge
How
Hayton
Greenwell
Moorhouse
Thurstonfield
Stanwix
Carlisle Castle
43
Kirkbride
Studholme
Kirkbampton
0 2 4 6 miles
0 2 4 6 8 10 km

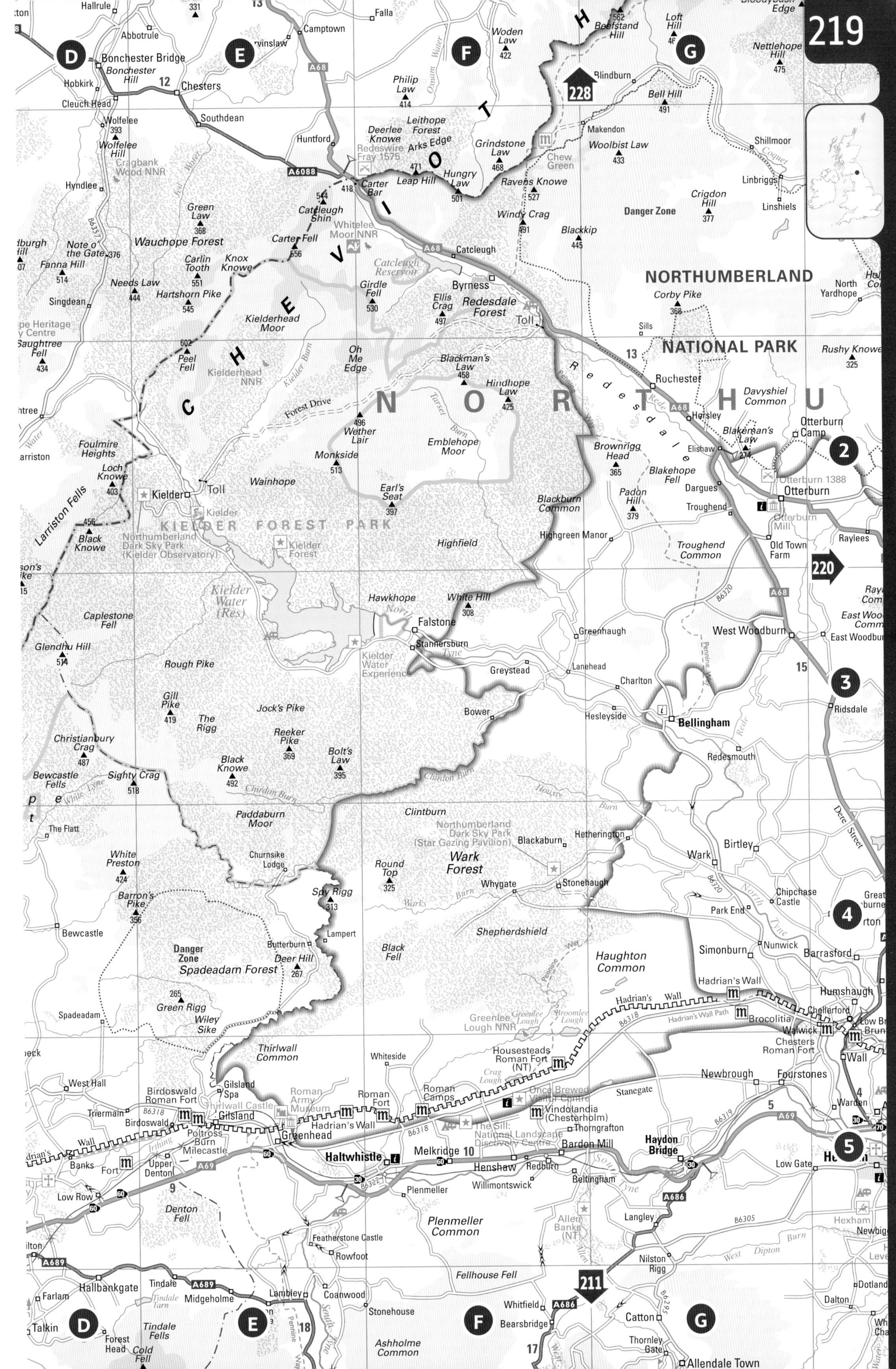

Hallrule
Abbotrule
Bonchester Bridge
Bonchester Hill
Hobkirk
Chesters
Cleuch Head
Southdean
Wolfelee
Wolfelee Hill
Cragbank Wood NNR
Hyndlee
Camptown
Falla
Philip Law
Woden Law
Beefstand Hill
Loft Hill
Nettlehope Hill
Blindburn
Bell Hill
Makendon
Woolbist Law
Shillmoor
Coquet
Linbriggs
Linshiels
Crigdon Hill
Danger Zone
Huntford
Deerlee Knowe
Leithope Forest
Arks Edge
Redeswire Fray 1575
Grindstone Law
Chew Green
Leap Hill
Hungry Law
Ravens Knowe
Carter Bar
Catcleugh Shin
Windy Crag
Blackkip
Whitelee Moor NNR
Carter Fell
Catcleugh
Catcleugh Reservoir
Green Law
Wauchope Forest
Note o' the Gate
Fanna Hill
Carlin Tooth
Knox Knowe
Needs Law
Hartshorn Pike
Singdean
Kielderhead Moor
Girdle Fell
Byrness
Ellis Crag
Redesdale Forest
Toll
NORTHUMBERLAND
NATIONAL PARK
Corby Pike
Sills
North Yardhope
Rushy Knowe
Saughtree Fell
Peel Fell
Kielderhead NNR
Kielder Burn
Oh Me Edge
Blackman's Law
Hindhope Law
Rochester
Davyshiel Common
Redesdale
Rede
Horsley
Otterburn Camp
Blakeman's Law
Elishaw
Forest Drive
Wether Lair
Emblehope Moor
Tarset Burn
Brownrigg Head
Blakehope Fell
Padon Hill
Otterburn 1388
Otterburn
Dargues
Troughend
Otterburn Mill
Foulmire Heights
Loch Knowe
Larriston Fells
Kielder
Monkside
Wainhope
Earl's Seat
Blackburn Common
Highgreen Manor
Raylees
Old Town Farm
Troughend Common
KIELDER FOREST PARK
Black Knowe
Northumberland Dark Sky Park (Kielder Observatory)
Kielder Forest
Highfield
Kielder Water (Res)
Caplestone Fell
Hawkhope
White Hill
Falstone
Stannersburn
Greenhaugh
West Woodburn
East Woodburn
East Wood Common
Glendhu Hill
Kielder Water Experience
Greystead
Lanehead
Charlton
Rough Pike
Gill Pike
Jock's Pike
The Rigg
Bower
Hesleyside
Bellingham
Ridsdale
Christianbury Crag
Reeker Pike
Bolt's Law
Redesmouth
Black Knowe
Bewcastle Fells
Sighty Crag
Chirdon Burn
Houxty
The Flatt
Paddaburn Moor
Clintburn
Northumberland Dark Sky Park (Star Gazing Pavilion)
Blackaburn
Hetherington
Birtley
Dere Street
White Preston
Churnsike Lodge
Round Top
Wark Forest
Wark
Whygate
Stonehaugh
Barron's Pike
Spy Rigg
Warks Burn
Park End
Chipchase Castle
Bewcastle
Lampert
Shepherdshield
Danger Zone
Spadeadam Forest
Butterburn
Deer Hill
Black Fell
Simonburn
Nunwick
Barrasford
Haughton Common
Pennine Way
Green Rigg
Spadeadam
Wiley Sike
Hadrian's Wall
Humshaugh
Chollerford
Brocolitia
Greenlee Lough NNR
Broomlee Lough
Walwick
Chesters Roman Fort
Thirlwall Common
Whiteside
Housesteads Roman Fort (NT)
Crag Lough
West Hall
Birdoswald Roman Fort
Gilsland Spa
Roman Army Museum
Roman Fort
Roman Camps
Once Brewed Visitor Centre
Stanegate
Newbrough
Fourstones
Wall
Triermain
Thirlwall Castle
Vindolanda (Chesterholm)
Birdoswald
Gilsland
Thorngrafton
Warden
Poltross Burn Milecastle
Greenhead
Hadrian's Wall
The Sill: National Landscape Discovery Centre
Haydon Bridge
Banks
Irthing
Upper Denton
Haltwhistle
Melkridge
Bardon Mill
Henshaw
Redburn
Low Gate
Fort
Low Row
Plenmeller
Willimontswick
Beltingham
South Tyne
Denton Fell
Plenmeller Common
Allen Banks (NT)
Langley
Hexham
Featherstone Castle
Rowfoot
Fellhouse Fell
Nilston Rigg
West Dipton Burn
Dotland
Hallbankgate
Farlam
Tindale
Tindale Tarn
Midgeholme
Lambley
Coanwood
Stonehouse
Whitfield
Dalton
Catton
Talkin
Forest Head
Tindale Fells
Cold Fell
Ashholme Common
Bearsbridge
Thornley Gate
Allendale Town
A68
A6088
A69
A689
A686
B6318
B6320
B6319
B6305
B6322
B6295
B6357
228
220
211

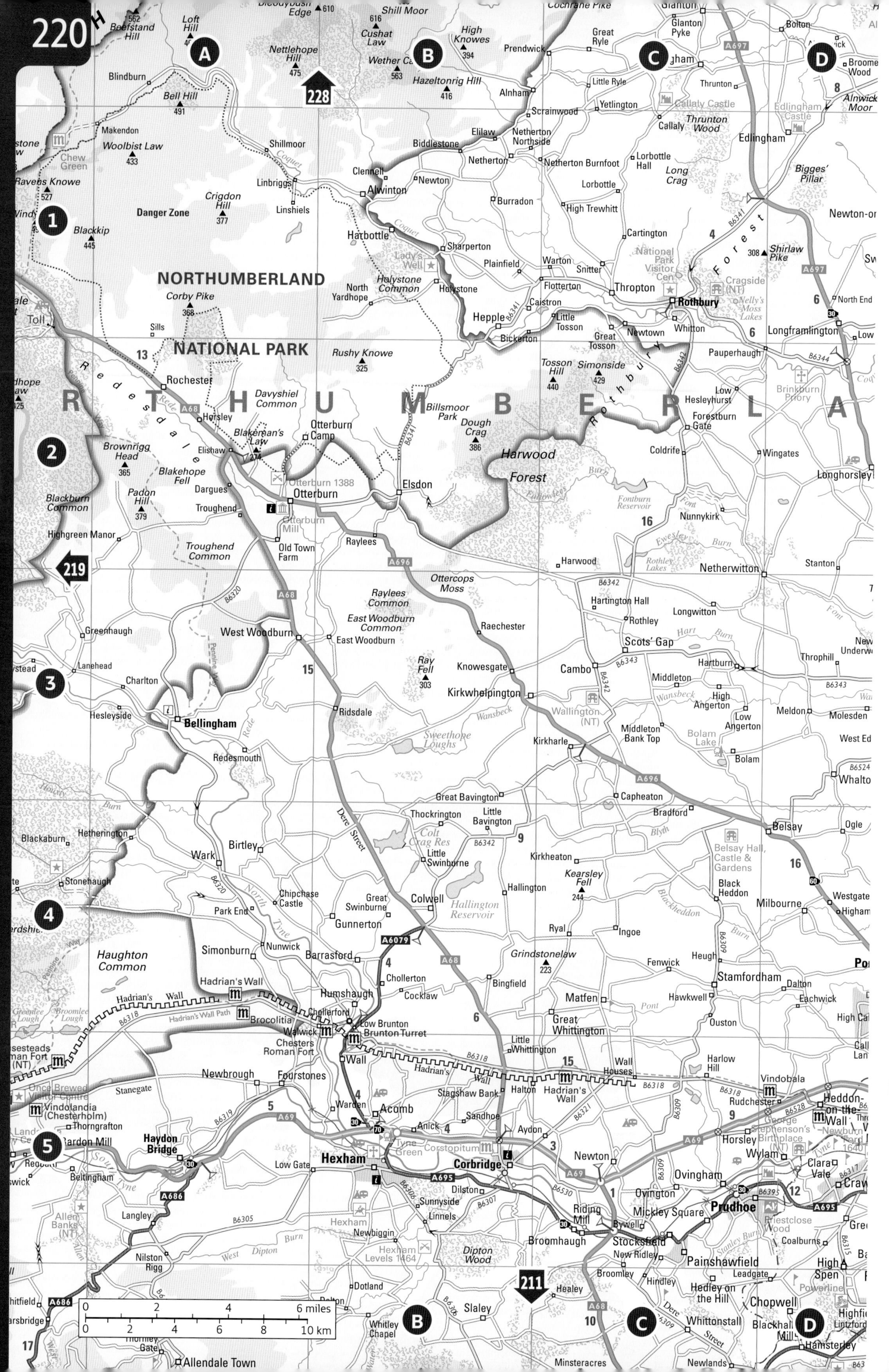
A
B
C
D
1
2
3
4
5
228
219
211
NORTHUMBERLAND
NATIONAL PARK
N O R T H U M B E R L A
Beefstand Hill
Loft Hill
Nettlehope Hill
Cushat Law
Shill Moor
High Knowes
Wether Cairn
Hazeltonrig Hill
Prendwick
Great Ryle
Glanton Pyke
Bolton
Broome Wood
Alnwick Moor
Blindburn
Bell Hill
Alnham
Little Ryle
Thrunton
Yetlington
Callaly Castle
Callaly
Thrunton Wood
Edlingham Castle
Edlingham
Scrainwood
Makendon
Woolbist Law
Chew Green
Shillmoor
Biddlestone
Elilaw
Netherton Northside
Netherton
Netherton Burnfoot
Lorbottle Hall
Lorbottle
Long Crag
Bigges' Pillar
Ravens Knowe
Clennell
Linbriggs
Alwinton
Newton
Burradon
High Trewhitt
Crigdon Hill
Danger Zone
Linshiels
Blackkip
Harbottle
Sharperton
Lady's Well
Cartington
Plainfield
Warton
Snitter
National Park Visitor Centre
Forest
Shirlaw Pike
Newton-on
Holystone Common
North Yardhope
Holystone
Flotterton
Thropton
Rothbury
Cragside (NT)
Nelly's Moss Lakes
North End
Corby Pike
Hepple
Caistron
Little Tosson
Bickerton
Great Tosson
Newtown
Whitton
Longframlington
Toll
Sills
Rushy Knowe
Pauperhaugh
Redesdale
Rochester
Tosson Hill
Simonside
Rothbury
Brinkburn Priory
Davyshiel Common
Billsmoor Park
Low Hesleyhurst
Forestburn Gate
Horsley
Otterburn Camp
Blakeman's Law
Dough Crag
Brownrigg Head
Elishaw
Harwood Forest
Coldrife
Wingates
Blakehope Fell
Otterburn 1388
Elsdon
Longhorsley
Padon Hill
Dargues
Otterburn
Blackburn Common
Troughend
Otterburn Mill
Fontburn Reservoir
Nunnykirk
Highgreen Manor
Raylees
Troughend Common
Old Town Farm
Harwood
Rothley Lakes
Netherwitton
Stanton
Ottercops Moss
Raylees Common
Hartington Hall
Longwitton
Rothley
East Woodburn Common
Raechester
Greenhaugh
West Woodburn
East Woodburn
Scots' Gap
Throphill
Lanehead
Ray Fell
Knowesgate
Cambo
Hartburn
Charlton
Kirkwhelpington
Middleton
High Angerton
Low Angerton
Meldon
Molesden
Hesleyside
Bellingham
Ridsdale
Wallington (NT)
Middleton Bank Top
Bolam Lake
Sweethope Loughs
Kirkharle
Bolam
West Ed
Redesmouth
Whalton
Great Bavington
Capheaton
Bradford
Thockrington
Little Bavington
Belsay
Ogle
Blackaburn
Hetherington
Colt Crag Res
Birtley
Little Swinburne
Kirkheaton
Belsay Hall, Castle & Gardens
Wark
Kearsley Fell
Stonehaugh
Hallington
Black Heddon
Westgate
Chipchase Castle
Great Swinburne
Colwell
Hallington Reservoir
Milbourne
Higham
Park End
Gunnerton
Ryal
Ingoe
Haughton Common
Simonburn
Nunwick
Barrasford
Grindstonelaw
Fenwick
Heugh
Stamfordham
Dalton
Chollerton
Cocklaw
Bingfield
Hadrian's Wall
Humshaugh
Matfen
Hawkwell
Eachwick
Brocolitia
Chollerford
Low Brunton
Walwick
Brunton Turret
Great Whittington
Ouston
Chesters Roman Fort
Little Whittington
Harlow Hill
Housesteads Roman Fort (NT)
Wall
Newbrough
Fourstones
Wall Houses
Vindobala
Once Brewed Visitor Centre
Stanegate
Stagshaw Bank
Halton
Rudchester
Heddon-on-the-Wall
Vindolanda (Chesterholm)
Thorngrafton
Warden
Acomb
Sandhoe
George Stephenson's Birthplace (NT)
Bardon Mill
Haydon Bridge
Anick
Aydon
Horsley
Newburn Ford 1640
Tyne Green
Corstopitum
Newton
Wylam
Clara Vale
Low Gate
Hexham
Corbridge
Ovingham
Beltingham
Dilston
Ovington
Crawcrook
Allen Banks (NT)
Langley
Sunnyside
Riding Mill
Mickley Square
Prudhoe
Hexham Racecourse
Linnels
Bywell
Priestclose Wood
Newbiggin
Broomhaugh
Stocksfield
Coalburns
Nilston Rigg
Hexham Levels 1464
Dipton Wood
New Ridley
Painshawfield
High Spen
Broomley
Leadgate
Dotland
Hindley
Hedley on the Hill
Chopwell
Whitfield
Healey
Slaley
Whittonstall
Blackhall Mill
Highfield
Lintzford
Whitley Chapel
Dere Street
Allendale Town
Hamsterley
Minsteracres
Newlands
0 2 4 6 miles
0 2 4 6 8 10 km

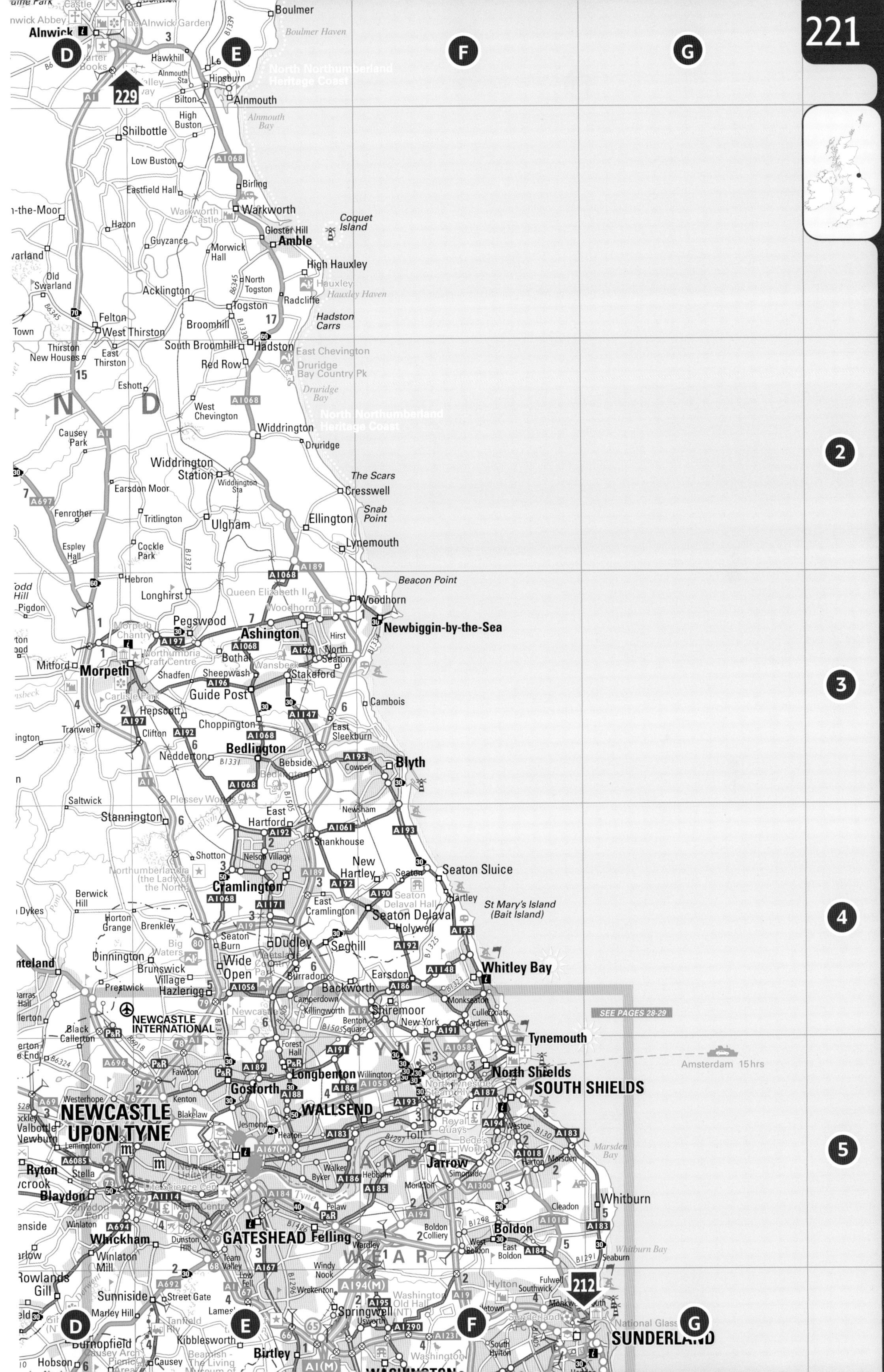
Alnwick
Boulmer
Boulmer Haven
North Northumberland Heritage Coast
Alnmouth
Alnmouth Bay
229
Shilbottle
Warkworth
Coquet Island
Amble
High Hauxley
Hauxley Haven
Hadston Carrs
Hadston
East Chevington
Druridge Bay Country Pk
Druridge Bay
Widdrington
Druridge
The Scars
Cresswell
Snab Point
Ellington
Lynemouth
Beacon Point
Woodhorn
Newbiggin-by-the-Sea
Ashington
Morpeth
Cambois
Bedlington
Blyth
Seaton Sluice
St Mary's Island (Bait Island)
Cramlington
Seaton Delaval
Whitley Bay
SEE PAGES 28-29
Tynemouth
Amsterdam 15hrs
North Shields
SOUTH SHIELDS
NEWCASTLE INTERNATIONAL
NEWCASTLE UPON TYNE
Gosforth
Longbenton
WALLSEND
Jarrow
Marsden Bay
Whitburn
Boldon
GATESHEAD
Felling
Whitburn Bay
Seaburn
212
SUNDERLAND
Washington
Birtley
Whickham
Blaydon
Ryton
D
E
F
G
2
3
4
5

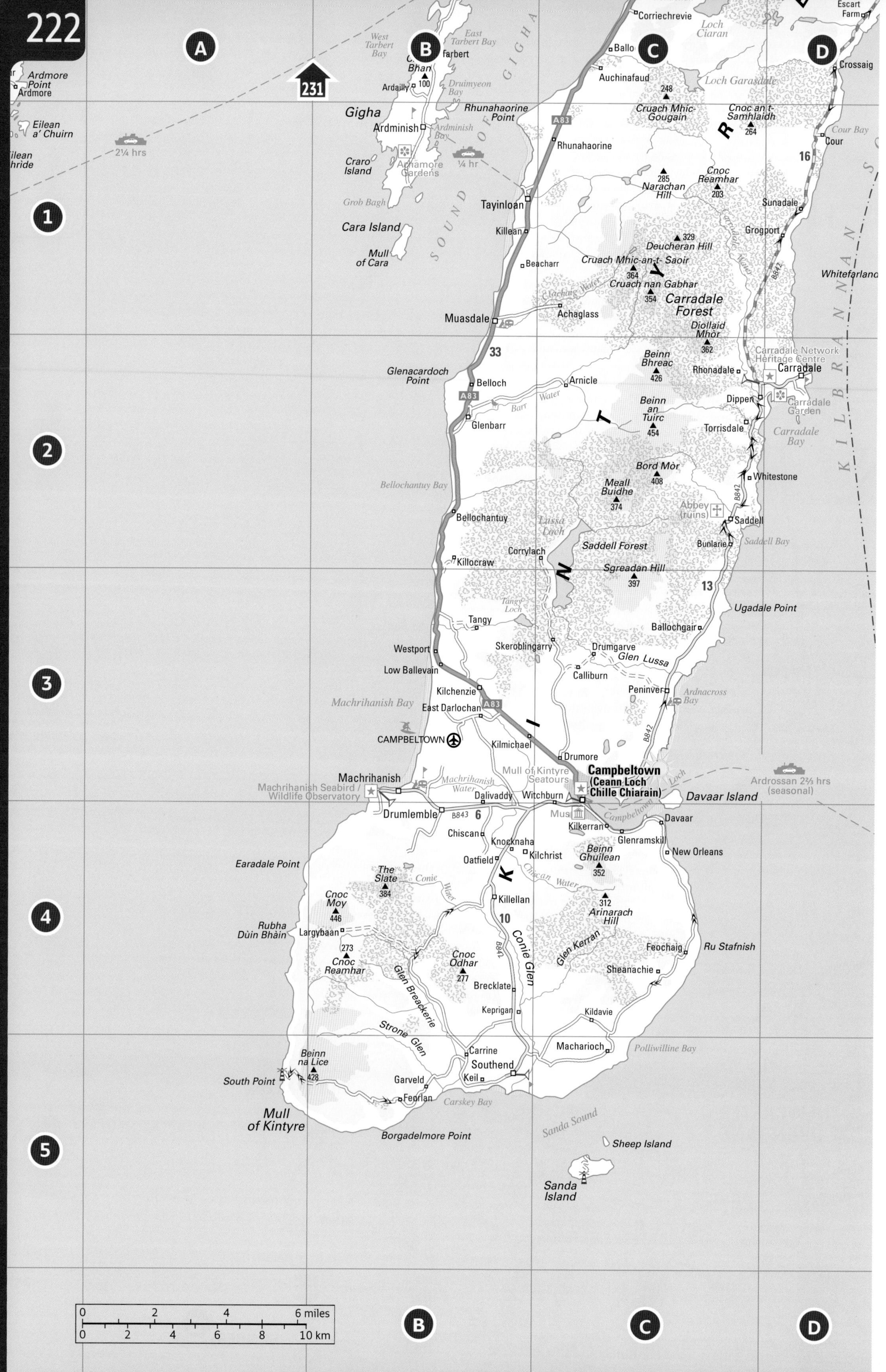

A B C D

231

Ardmore
Point
Ardmore

Eilean
a' Chuirn

Eilean
hride

West
Tarbert
Bay

East
Tarbert
Bay

Tarbert

Bhan

100

Ardailly

Druimyeon
Bay

Rhunahaorine
Point

Gigha

Ardminish

Ardminish
Bay

¼ hr

2¼ hrs

Craro
Island

Achamore
Gardens

Grob Bagh

Tayinloan

Killean

*Mull
of Cara*

Cara Island

Beacharr

Corriechrevie

Ballo

Auchinafaud

Corriechrevie

Loch
Ciaran

Loch Garasdale

248

Cruach Mhic-
Gougain

Escart
Farm

Crossaig

Cnoc an t-
Samhlaidh
264

Cour Bay
Cour

16

Rhunahaorine

285

Narachan
Hill

Cnoc
Reamhar
203

Sunadale

329

Deucheran Hill

Cruach Mhic-an-t-Saoir

Grogport

Whitefarland

364

354

Cruach nan Gabhar

Carradale
Forest

Muasdale

Achaglass

Diollaid
Mhòr

362

Carradale Network
Heritage Centre

Carradale

Glenacardoch
Point

Belloch

Arnicle

Beinn
Bhreac
426

Rhonadale

Dippen

Carradale
Garden

Sound of Gigha

Clachaig Water

Barr Water

Glenbarr

Beinn
an
Tuirc
454

Torrisdale

Carradale
Bay

Kilbrannan Sound

Bellochantuy Bay

Bellochantuy

Bord Mòr
408

Lussa
Loch

Meall
Buidhe
374

Abbey
(ruins)

Saddell

Whitestone

Killocraw

Corrylach

Saddell Forest

Bunlarie

Saddell Bay

Sgreadan Hill
397

13

Tangy

Tangy
Loch

Westport

Skeroblingarry

Drumgarve

Glen Lussa

Ballochgair

Ugadale Point

Low Ballevain

Calliburn

Peninver

Ardnacross
Bay

Machrihanish Bay

Kilchenzie

East Darlochan

A83

CAMPBELTOWN

Kilmichael

Drumore

**Campbeltown
(Ceann Loch
Chille Chiarain)**

Davaar Island

Ardrossan 2⅔ hrs
(seasonal)

Machrihanish

Machrihanish
Water

Mull of Kintyre
Seatours

Dalivaddy

Witchburn

Mus

Davaar

Machrihanish Seabird /
Wildlife Observatory

Drumlemble

B843

6

Chiscan

Knocknaha

Kilchrist

Oatfield

Kilkerran

Glenramskill

New Orleans

Earadale Point

The
Slate
384

Conie

Water

Beinn
Ghuilean
352

Cnoc
Moy
446

Killellan

Chiscan Water

312
Arinarach
Hill

Rubha
Dùin Bhàin

Largybaan

273

10

B842

Glen Kerran

Feochaig

Ru Stafnish

Cnoc
Reamhar

Cnoc
Odhar
277

Glen Breackerie

Brecklate

Conie Glen

Sheanachie

Kildavie

Strone Glen

Keprigan

Macharioch

Polliwilline Bay

Beinn
na Lice
428

Carrine

South Point

Garveld

Keil

Southend

Feorlan

Carskey Bay

**Mull
of Kintyre**

Borgadelmore Point

Sanda Sound

Sheep Island

Sanda
Island

0		2		4		6 miles
0	2	4	6	8		10 km

B C D

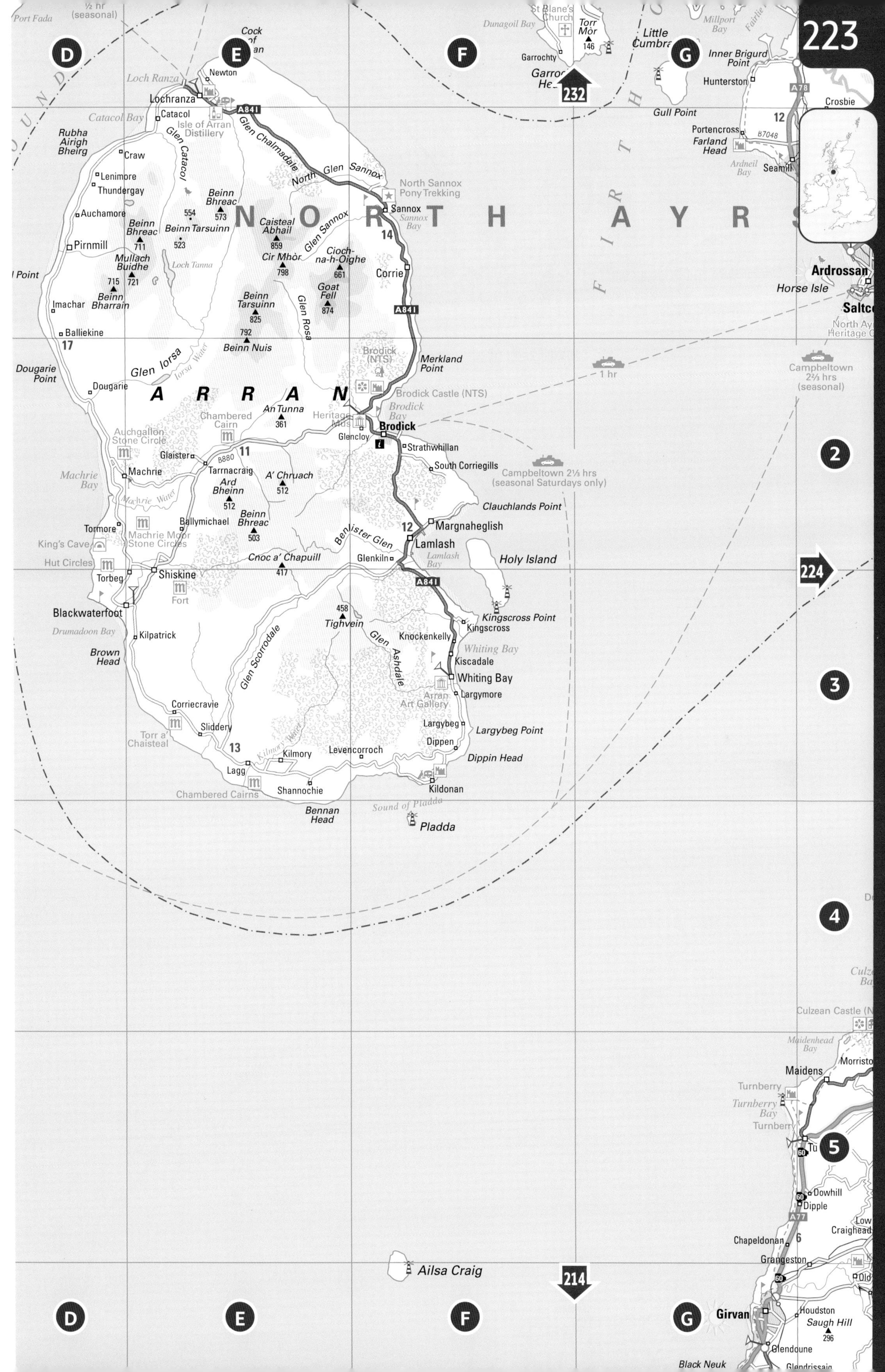

ARRAN
NORTH AYRS
FIRTH
Lochranza
Newton
Catacol
Isle of Arran Distillery
Glen Catacol
Glen Chalmadale
North Glen Sannox
North Sannox Pony Trekking
Sannox
Corrie
Craw
Lenimore
Thundergay
Auchamore
Pirnmill
Imachar
Balliekine
Dougarie
Dougarie Point
Glen Iorsa
Beinn Bhreac
Beinn Tarsuinn
Caisteal Abhail
Cir Mhòr
Cioch-na-h-Oighe
Goat Fell
Beinn Nuis
Glen Rosa
Glen Sannox
Mullach Buidhe
Beinn Bharrain
Loch Tanna
Brodick (NTS)
Brodick Castle (NTS)
Brodick Bay
Brodick
Glencloy
Strathwhillan
South Corriegills
Merkland Point
An Tunna
Chambered Cairn
Auchgallon Stone Circle
Glaister
Machrie
Machrie Bay
Tarrnacraig
Ard Bheinn
A' Chruach
Beinn Bhreac
Ballymichael
Machrie Moor Stone Circles
King's Cave
Tormore
Hut Circles
Torbeg
Shiskine
Fort
Blackwaterfoot
Drumadoon Bay
Kilpatrick
Brown Head
Cnoc a' Chapuill
Benlister Glen
Glenkiln
Lamlash
Lamlash Bay
Margnaheglish
Clauchlands Point
Holy Island
Kingscross Point
Kingscross
Tighvein
Glen Ashdale
Glen Scorrodale
Knockenkelly
Whiting Bay
Kiscadale
Largymore
Arran Art Gallery
Largybeg
Largybeg Point
Dippen
Dippin Head
Kildonan
Levencorroch
Kilmory
Lagg
Shannochie
Sliddery
Corriecravie
Torr a' Chaisteal
Chambered Cairns
Bennan Head
Sound of Pladda
Pladda
Ailsa Craig
Campbeltown 2⅓ hrs (seasonal Saturdays only)
Campbeltown 2⅔ hrs (seasonal)
1 hr
½ hr (seasonal)
Port Fada
Cock of Arran
Loch Ranza
Catacol Bay
Rubha Airigh Bheirg
Garrochty
Dunagoil Bay
St Blane's Church
Torr Mòr
Little Cumbrae
Millport Bay
Inner Brigurd Point
Hunterston
Crosbie
Gull Point
Portencross
Farland Head
Ardneil Bay
Seamill
Ardrossan
Horse Isle
North Ayrshire Heritage C
Culzean Castle
Maidenhead Bay
Maidens
Morriston
Turnberry
Turnberry Bay
Dowhill
Dipple
Craighead
Chapeldonan
Grangeston
Girvan
Houdston
Saugh Hill
Glendoune
Black Neuk
A841
A78
A77
B880
B7048
232
224
214

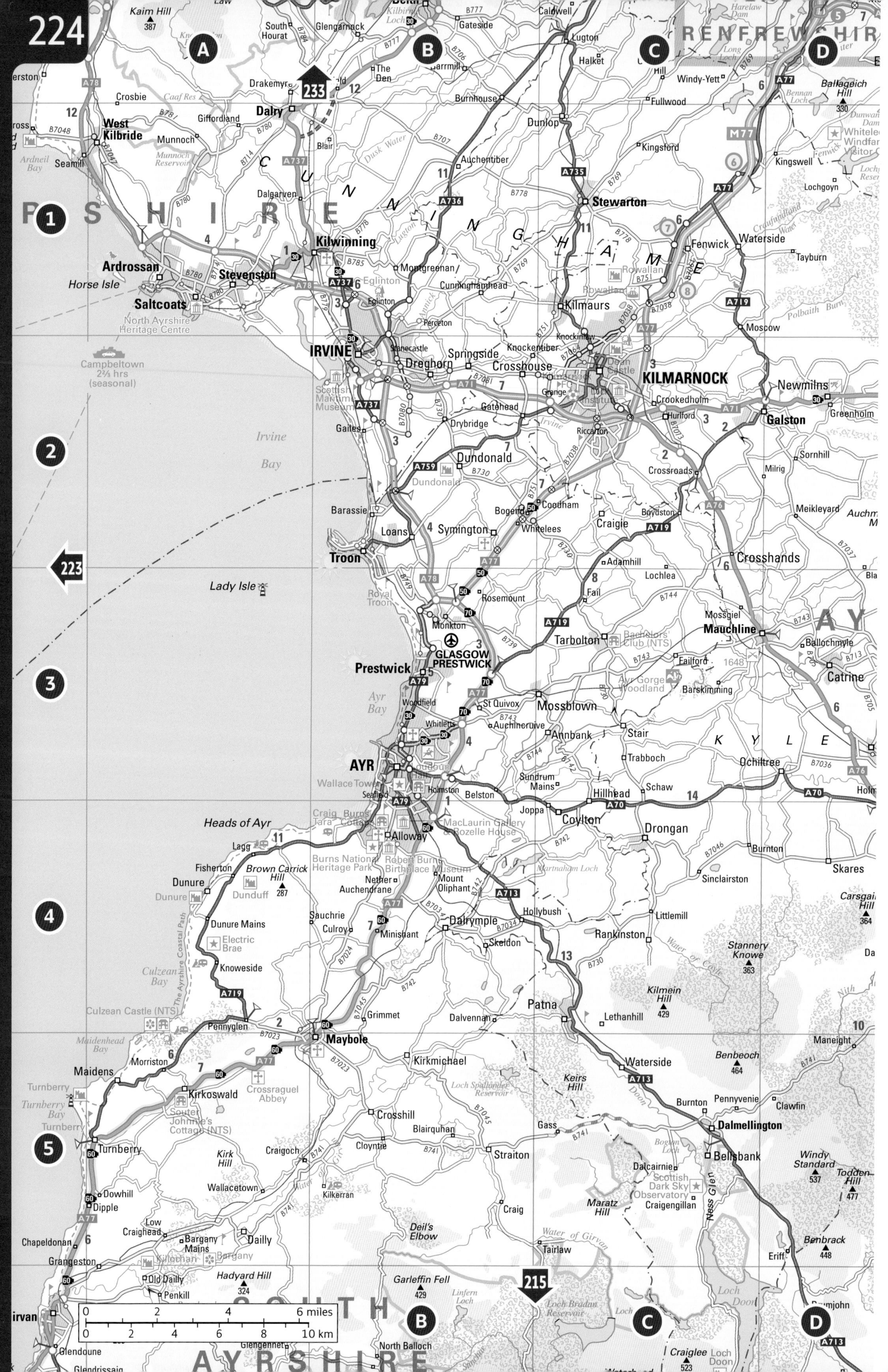

RENFREWSHIRE
AYRSHIRE
CUNNINGHAME
KYLE
SOUTH AYRSHIRE
Kaim Hill
West Kilbride
Seamill
Ardrossan
Saltcoats
Stevenston
Horse Isle
North Ayrshire Heritage Centre
Campbeltown 2⅔ hrs (seasonal)
Dalry
Kilwinning
Irvine
IRVINE
Dreghorn
Springside
Crosshouse
KILMARNOCK
Stewarton
Kilmaurs
Fenwick
Galston
Newmilns
Dundonald
Symington
Troon
Lady Isle
Irvine Bay
Prestwick
GLASGOW PRESTWICK
Mauchline
Tarbolton
Catrine
Mossblown
Annbank
Stair
AYR
Ayr Bay
Heads of Ayr
Alloway
Coylton
Drongan
Ochiltree
Dunure
Electric Brae
Culzean Bay
Culzean Castle (NTS)
Maybole
Maidens
Kirkoswald
Turnberry
Dalrymple
Patna
Waterside
Dalmellington
Bellsbank
Straiton
Crosshill
Dailly
Girvan
Loch Doon
Scottish Dark Sky Observatory
0 2 4 6 miles
0 2 4 6 8 10 km
233
223
215

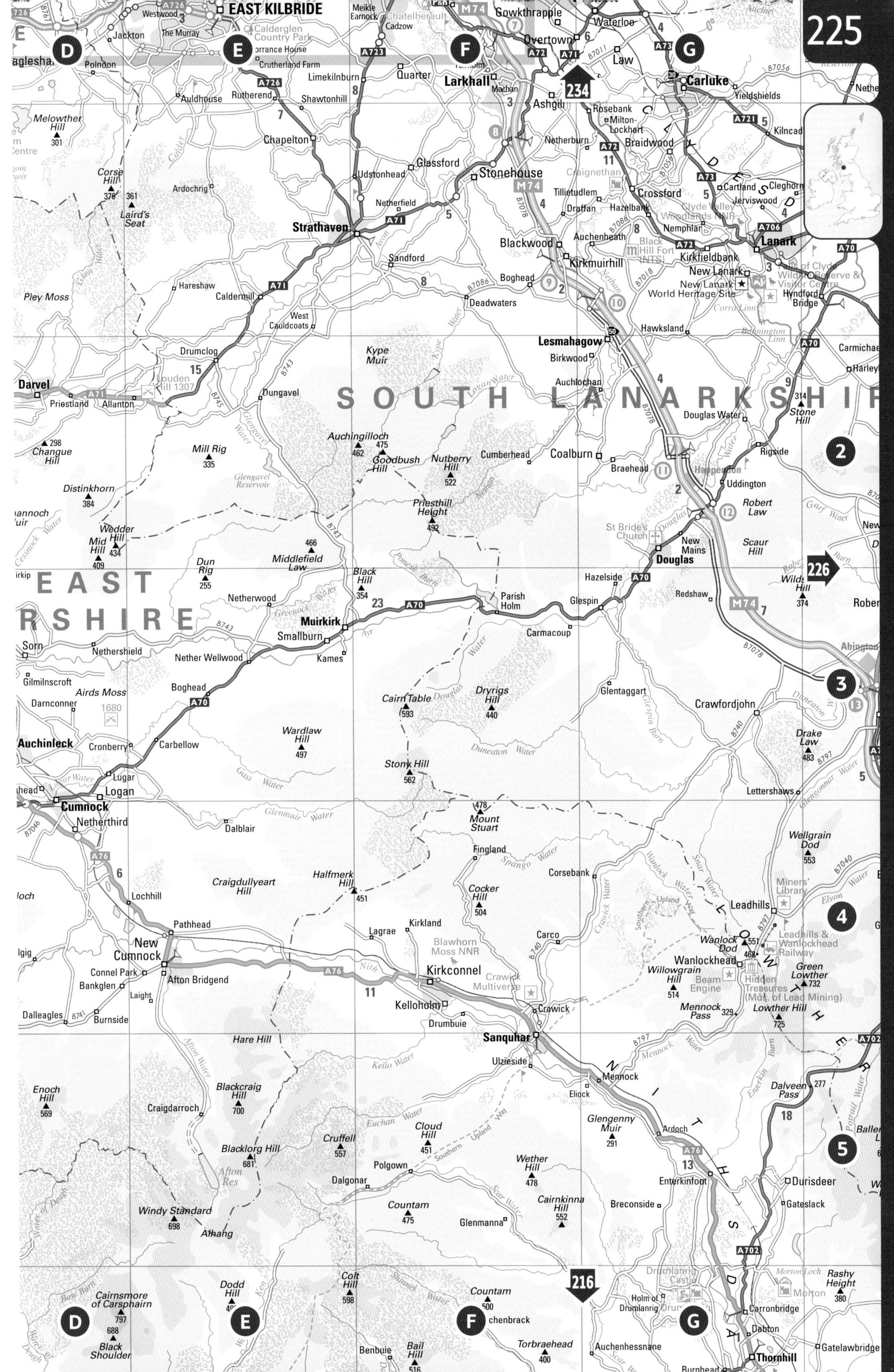
EAST KILBRIDE
SOUTH LANARKSHIRE
EAST AYRSHIRE
Strathaven
Larkhall
Carluke
Lanark
Stonehouse
Lesmahagow
Douglas
Muirkirk
Darvel
Auchinleck
Cumnock
New Cumnock
Kirkconnel
Sanquhar
Leadhills
Wanlockhead
Thornhill
Crawfordjohn
Coalburn
Blackwood
Kirkmuirhill
New Lanark
New Lanark World Heritage Site
Falls of Clyde Wildlife Reserve & Visitor Centre
Clyde Valley Woodlands NNR
Black Hill Fort (NTS)
Craignethan
Drumlanrig Castle
Cairn Table 593
Blawhorn Moss NNR
Museum of Lead Mining
Leadhills & Wanlockhead Railway
Lowther Hill 725
Green Lowther 732
Wanlock Dod 551
Mennock Pass
Dalveen Pass
Cairnsmore of Carsphairn 797
Windy Standard 698
Blacklorg Hill 681
Afton Res
Glengavel Reservoir
Crawick Multiverse
234
216
226
D
E
F
G
2
3
4
5

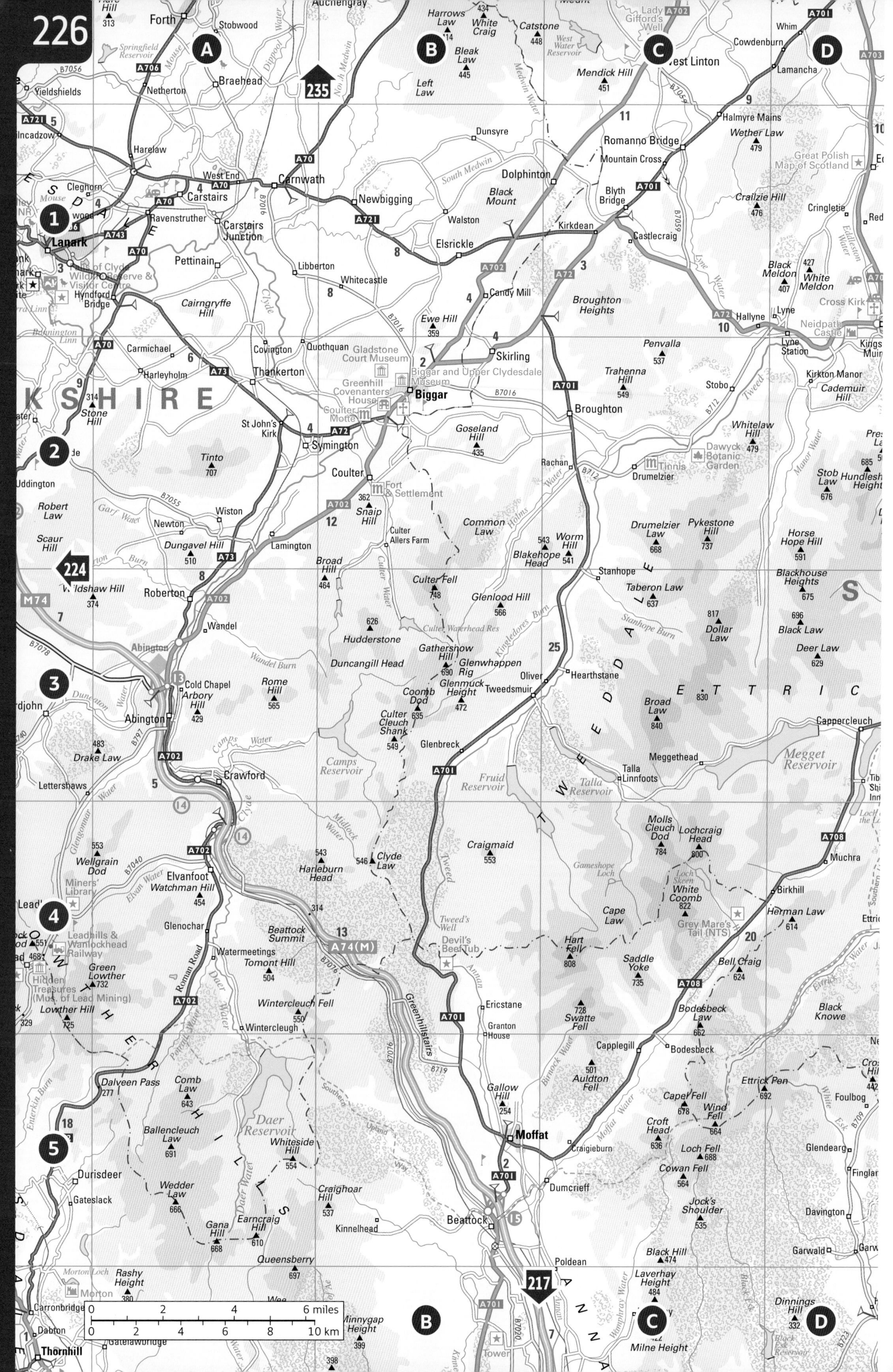
A
B
C
D
1
2
3
4
5
235
224
217
Forth
Stobwood
Springfield Reservoir
Braehead
Netherton
Yieldshields
Harelaw
West End
Carnwath
Cleghorn
Carstairs
Ravenstruther
Carstairs Junction
Lanark
Pettinain
Hyndford Bridge
Cairngryffe Hill
Carmichael
Harleyholm
Covington
Quothquan
Thankerton
Gladstone Court Museum
Biggar and Upper Clydesdale Museum
Greenhill Covenanters' House
Coulter Motte
Biggar
St John's Kirk
Symington
Coulter
Fort & Settlement
Snaip Hill
Tinto
Uddington
Robert Law
Scaur Hill
Wiston
Newton
Dungavel Hill
Lamington
Wildshaw Hill
Roberton
Wandel
Abington
Cold Chapel
Arbory Hill
Rome Hill
Drake Law
Crawford
Lettershaws
Camps Reservoir
Wellgrain Dod
Miners' Library
Elvanfoot
Watchman Hill
Glenochar
Leadhills & Wanlockhead Railway
Hidden Treasures (Mus. of Lead Mining)
Green Lowther
Lowther Hill
Roman Road
Watermeetings
Tomont Hill
Wintercleuch Fell
Wintercleugh
Beattock Summit
Harleburn Head
Dalveen Pass
Comb Law
Ballencleuch Law
Daer Reservoir
Whiteside Hill
Durisdeer
Gateslack
Wedder Law
Gana Hill
Earncraig Hill
Craighoar Hill
Kinnelhead
Queensberry
Rashy Height
Morton Loch
Morton
Carronbridge
Dabton
Thornhill
Gatelawbridge
Minnygap Height
LOWTHER HILLS
Harrows Law
White Craig
Catstone
West Water Reservoir
Bleak Law
Left Law
Mendick Hill
West Linton
Lady Gifford's Well
Dunsyre
Newbigging
Walston
Black Mount
Dolphinton
Elsrickle
Libberton
Whitecastle
Ewe Hill
Candy Mill
Skirling
Romanno Bridge
Mountain Cross
Blyth Bridge
Kirkdean
Castlecraig
Broughton Heights
Broughton
Goseland Hill
Rachan
Common Law
Culter Allers Farm
Broad Hill
Culter Fell
Hudderstone
Culter Waterhead Res
Duncangill Head
Gathersnow Hill
Glenwhappen Rig
Glenmuck Height
Coomb Dod
Culter Cleuch Shank
Tweedsmuir
Oliver
Glenbreck
Fruid Reservoir
Craigmaid
Clyde Law
Tweed's Well
Devil's Beef Tub
Ericstane
Granton House
Gallow Hill
Moffat
Beattock
Dumcrieff
Poldean
Tower
Whim
Cowdenburn
Lamancha
Halmyre Mains
Wether Law
Great Polish Map of Scotland
Crailzie Hill
Cringletie
Black Meldon
White Meldon
Cross Kirk
Hallyne
Lyne
Lyne Station
Neidpath Castle
Penvalla
Trahenna Hill
Stobo
Kirkton Manor
Cademuir Hill
Whitelaw Hill
Dawyck Botanic Garden
Tinnis
Drumelzier
Stob Law
Hundleshope Heights
Drumelzier Law
Pykestone Hill
Worm Hill
Blakehope Head
Horse Hope Hill
Stanhope
Taberon Law
Blackhouse Heights
Glenlood Hill
Dollar Law
Black Law
Deer Law
Hearthstone
Broad Law
Cappercleuch
Meggethead
Megget Reservoir
Talla Linnfoots
Talla Reservoir
Molls Cleuch Dod
Lochcraig Head
Gameshope Loch
Loch Skeen
White Coomb
Grey Mare's Tail (NTS)
Cape Law
Hart Fell
Saddle Yoke
Herman Law
Birkhill
Muchra
Bell Craig
Bodesbeck Law
Bodesbeck
Capplegill
Swatte Fell
Auldton Fell
Black Knowe
Ettrick Pen
Capel Fell
Wind Fell
Croft Head
Craigieburn
Loch Fell
Cowan Fell
Jock's Shoulder
Foulbog
Glendearg
Davington
Garwald
Black Hill
Laverhay Height
Milne Height
Dinnings Hill
Black Esk Reservoir
TWEEDDALE
ETTRICK
ANNANDALE
LANARKSHIRE
Greenhillstairs
0 2 4 6 miles
0 2 4 6 8 10 km

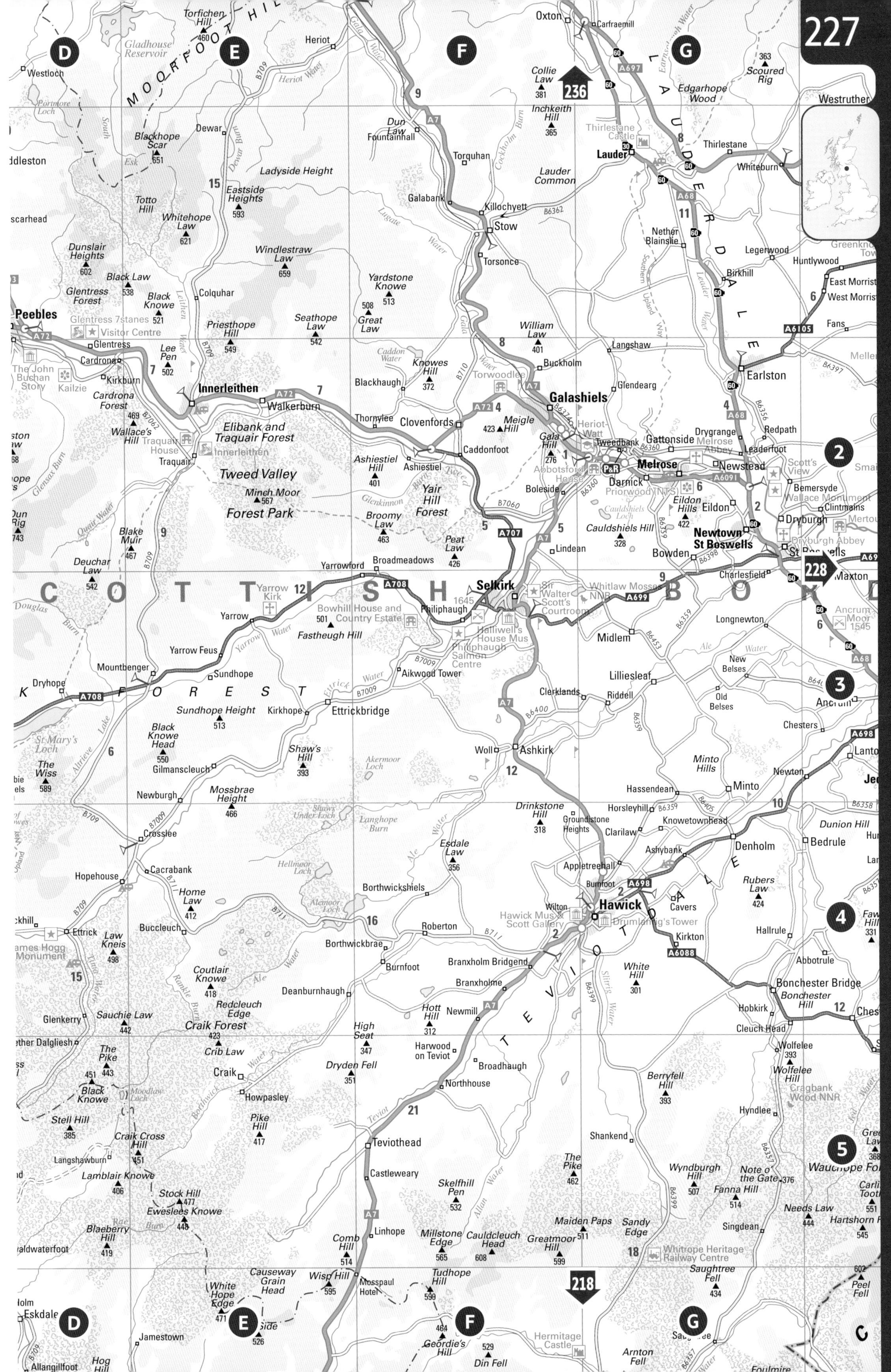

D
E
F
G
Torfichen Hill 460
MOORFOOT HILLS
Gladhouse Reservoir
Heriot
Oxton
Carfraemill
363 Scoured Rig
Westloch
Portmore Loch
Collie Law 381
236
Edgarhope Wood
Westruther
Inchkeith Hill 365
Thirlestane Castle
Thirlestane
Lauder
Whiteburn
Dewar
Blackhope Scar 651
Dun Law
Fountainhall
Torquhan
Lauder Common
Eddleston
Ladyside Height
Eastside Heights 593
Totto Hill
Galabank
Killochyett
Stow
Whitehope Law 621
Nether Blainslie
LAUDERDALE
Eshiels
Torsonce
Legerwood
Huntlywood
Greenknowe Tower
Dunslair Heights 602
Windlestraw Law 659
Birkhill
East Morriston
West Morriston
Glentress Forest
Black Law 538
Black Knowe 521
Colquhar
Yardstone Knowe 513
508 Great Law
Peebles
Glentress 7stanes Visitor Centre
Priesthope Hill 549
Seathope Law 542
William Law 401
Fans
A6105
Langshaw
Glentress
Cardrona
Lee Pen 502
Caddon Water
Knowes Hill 372
Buckholm
Earlston
Mellerstain
The John Buchan Story
Kailzie
Kirkburn
Innerleithen
Walkerburn
Blackhaugh
Torwoodlee
Glendearg
Galashiels
Cardrona Forest
Wallace's Hill
Elibank and Traquair Forest
Thornylee
Clovenfords
Meigle Hill
Heriot-Watt
Drygrange
Redpath
Traquair House
Innerleithen
Traquair
Caddonfoot
Gala Hill 276
Tweedbank
Gattonside
Melrose Abbey
Leaderfoot
Tweed Valley
Ashiestiel Hill 401
Ashiestiel
Abbotsford House
Melrose
Newstead
Scott's View
Minch Moor 567
Yair Hill Forest
Boleside
Darnick
Priorwood (NTS)
Bemersyde
Wallace Monument
Forest Park
Broomy Law 463
Eildon Hills 422
Eildon
Clintmains
Dryburgh
Dryburgh Abbey
Blake Muir 467
Peat Law 426
Lindean
Cauldshields Hill 328
Cauldshields Loch
Newtown St Boswells
St Boswells
Deuchar Law 542
Yarrowford
Broadmeadows
Bowden
Charlesfield
228
Maxton
SCOTTISH BORDERS
Yarrow Kirk
Selkirk
Whitlaw Mosses NNR
Sir Walter Scott's Courtroom
Bowhill House and Country Estate
Philiphaugh
1645
Longnewton
Ancrum Moor 1545
Yarrow
Fastheugh Hill
Halliwell's House Mus
Philiphaugh Salmon Centre
Midlem
Yarrow Feus
New Belses
Mountbenger
Sundhope
Aikwood Tower
Lilliesleaf
Dryhope
ETTRICK FOREST
Clerklands
Riddell
Old Belses
Ancrum
Sundhope Height 513
Kirkhope
Ettrickbridge
Chesters
St Mary's Loch
Black Knowe Head 550
Shaw's Hill 393
Akermoor Loch
Woll
Ashkirk
Lanton
The Wiss 589
Gilmanscleuch
Minto Hills
Newton
Newburgh
Mossbrae Height 466
Hassendean
Minto
Drinkstone Hill 318
Groundistone Heights
Horsleyhill
Knowetownhead
Dunion Hill
Crosslee
Shaws Under Loch
Langhope Burn
Clarilaw
Denholm
Bedrule
Esdale Law 356
Ashybank
Hopehouse
Cacrabank
Hellmoor Loch
Appletreehall
Rubers Law 424
Home Law 412
Borthwickshiels
Burnfoot
Hawick
Cavers
Ettrick
Law Kneis 498
Buccleuch
Alemoor Loch
Robertson
Wilton
Hawick Mus & Scott Gallery
Drumlanrig's Tower
Hallrule
Fawside Hill 331
James Hogg Monument
Borthwickbrae
Kirkton
Abbotrule
Burnfoot
Branxholm Bridgend
Coutlair Knowe 418
Deanburnhaugh
Branxholme
White Hill 301
Bonchester Bridge
Bonchester Hill
Redcleuch Edge
Hobkirk
Glenkerry
Sauchie Law 442
Hott Hill 312
Newmill
Craik Forest
High Seat 347
Cleuch Head
Crib Law
TEVIOTDALE
Harwood on Teviot
Wolfelee 393
The Pike 443
Craik
Dryden Fell 351
Broadhaugh
Wolfelee Hill
Berryfell Hill 393
Black Knowe
Howpasley
Northhouse
Cragbank Wood NNR
Stell Hill 385
Pike Hill 417
Hyndlee
Craik Cross Hill 451
Teviothead
Shankend
Langshawburn
The Pike 462
Wauchope Forest
Lamblair Knowe 406
Castleweary
Skelfhill Pen 532
Wyndburgh Hill 507
Note o' the Gate 376
Carlin Tooth 551
Stock Hill 477
Fanna Hill 514
Eweslees Knowe 448
Needs Law 444
Hartshorn Pike 545
Blaeberry Hill 419
Linhope
Comb Hill 514
Millstone Edge 565
Cauldcleuch Head 608
Greatmoor Hill 599
Maiden Paps 511
Sandy Edge
Singdean
Causeway Grain Head
Wisp Hill 595
Mosspaul Hotel
Tudhope Hill 599
218
Whitrope Heritage Railway Centre
Saughtree Fell 434
Peel Fell 602
White Hope Edge 471
Eskdale
Holm
Jamestown
Geordie's Hill 464
529 Din Fell
Hermitage Castle
Arnton Fell
Allangillfoot
Hog Hill
Foulmire

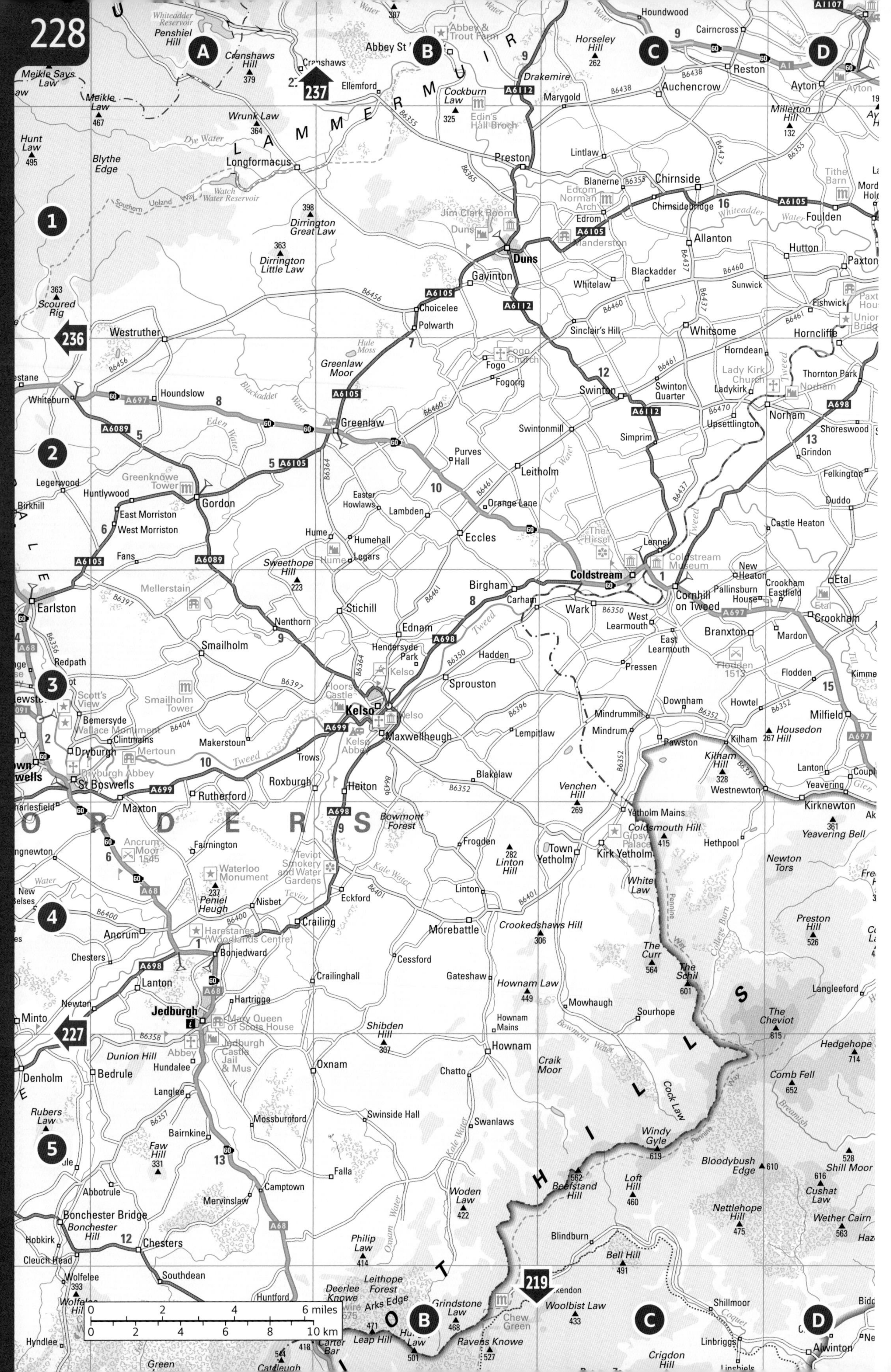

Whiteadder Reservoir
Penshiel Hill
Cranshaws Hill
379
Cranshaws
237
Abbey St Bathans
Abbey & Trout Farm
Ellemford
Houndwood
Horseley Hill
262
Cairncross
Reston
A1107
Ayton
Meikle Says Law
Meikle Law
467
Wrunk Law
364
LAMMERMUIR
Drakemire
A6112
Cockburn Law
325
Edin's Hall Broch
Marygold
B6438
Auchencrow
Millerton Hill
132
Hunt Law
495
Blythe Edge
Dye Water
Longformacus
B6355
Preston
Lintlaw
B6437
Watch Water Reservoir
Southern Upland Way
Blanerne
Chirnside
Edrom
Norman Arch
Tithe Barn
Chirnsidebridge
16
A6105
Whiteadder Water
Fouldens
398
Dirrington Great Law
Jim Clark Room
Duns
Manderston
Allanton
Hutton
363
Dirrington Little Law
Paxton
Blackadder
B6460
Gavinton
Whitelaw
Sunwick
363
Scoured Rig
B6456
Choicelee
A6112
Fishwick
Polwarth
Sinclair's Hill
Whitsome
Horncliffe
236
Westruther
Hule Moss
Fogo Church
Fogo
Fogorig
Horndean
Lady Kirk Church
Ladykirk
Thornton Park
Greenlaw Moor
B6461
Swinton Quarter
Norham
Swinton
Whiteburn
A697
Houndslow
Blackadder Water
A6105
A6112
B6470
Upsettlington
A698
Shoreswood
A6089
Eden Water
Greenlaw
Swintonmill
Simprim
Grindon
Purves Hall
Leitholm
Legerwood
Greenknowe Tower
A6105
Felkington
Birkhill
Huntlywood
Gordon
10
Orange Lane
Leet Water
Easter Howlaws
Lambden
Duddo
East Morriston
West Morriston
Hume
Humehall
Eccles
The Hirsel
Lennel
Castle Heaton
Fans
A6089
Sweethope Hill
223
Legars
Coldstream
Coldstream Museum
New Heaton
Etal
Mellerstain
Birgham
Crookham
Crookham Eastfield
Pallinsburn House
Earlston
B6397
Stichill
Carham
Wark
Cornhill on Tweed
Nenthorn
Ednam
B6350
West Learmouth
Branxton
Crookham
B6356
Smailholm
Hendersyde Park
A698
Tweed
Hadden
East Learmouth
Mardon
Redpath
Kelso
Pressen
Flodden 1513
Flodden
Scott's View
Smailholm Tower
Floors Castle
Sprouston
Downham
Howtel
Milfield
Bemersyde
Wallace Monument
B6404
Kelso Abbey
Mindrummill
B6352
Housedon Hill
267
Clintmains
Makerstoun
Maxwellheugh
Lempitlaw
Mindrum
Dryburgh
Mertoun
Tweed
Trows
Pawston
Kilham
Kilham Hill
328
Lanton
Dryburgh Abbey
Roxburgh
Heiton
Blakelaw
Westnewton
Yeavering
St Boswells
A699
Rutherford
B6352
Venchen Hill
269
Kirknewton
Maxton
BORDERS
Bowmont Forest
Yetholm Mains
Coldsmouth Hill
415
361
Yeavering Bell
Ancrum Moor 1545
Fairnington
Teviot Smokery and Water Gardens
Frogden
282
Linton Hill
Town Yetholm
Kirk Yetholm
Hethpool
Newton Tors
Waterloo Monument
Kale Water
White Law
237
Peniel Heugh
Nisbet
Eckford
Linton
B6401
Preston Hill
526
B6400
Crailing
Morebattle
Crookedshaws Hill
306
Ancrum
Harestanes (Woodlands Centre)
The Curr
564
Chesters
Bonjedward
Cessford
The Schil
601
A698
Lanton
Crailinghall
Gateshaw
Hownam Law
449
Langleeford
Hartrigge
Mowhaugh
Newton
Jedburgh
Mary Queen of Scots House
Hownam Mains
Sourhope
The Cheviot
815
Minto
227
B6358
Shibden Hill
307
Jedburgh Abbey
Jedburgh Castle Jail & Mus
Hownam
Craik Moor
Hedgehope
714
Dunion Hill
Hundalee
Oxnam
Chatto
Comb Fell
652
Denholm
Bedrule
Langlee
Cock Law
Rubers Law
Swinside Hall
Swanlaws
Bairnkine
Mossburnford
Windy Gyle
619
Faw Hill
331
13
Falla
Bloodybush Edge
610
528
Shill Moor
616
Cushat Law
562
Beefstand Hill
Loft Hill
460
Abbotrule
Camptown
Woden Law
422
Nettlehope Hill
475
Wether Cairn
563
Mervinslaw
Bonchester Bridge
Bonchester Hill
Chesters
Blindburn
Hobkirk
12
Philip Law
414
Bell Hill
491
Cleuch Head
Southdean
Wolfelee
393
219
Leithope Forest
Kendon
Huntford
Deerlee Knowe
Arks Edge
Grindstone Law
468
Woolbist Law
433
Shillmoor
Coquet
Chew Green
471
Leap Hill
501
Ravens Knowe
527
Linbriggs
Alwinton
Hyndlee
544
Carter Bar
418
Catcleugh
Crigdon Hill
Linshiels
Green
0 2 4 6 miles
0 2 4 6 8 10 km
A B C D
1 2 3 4 5

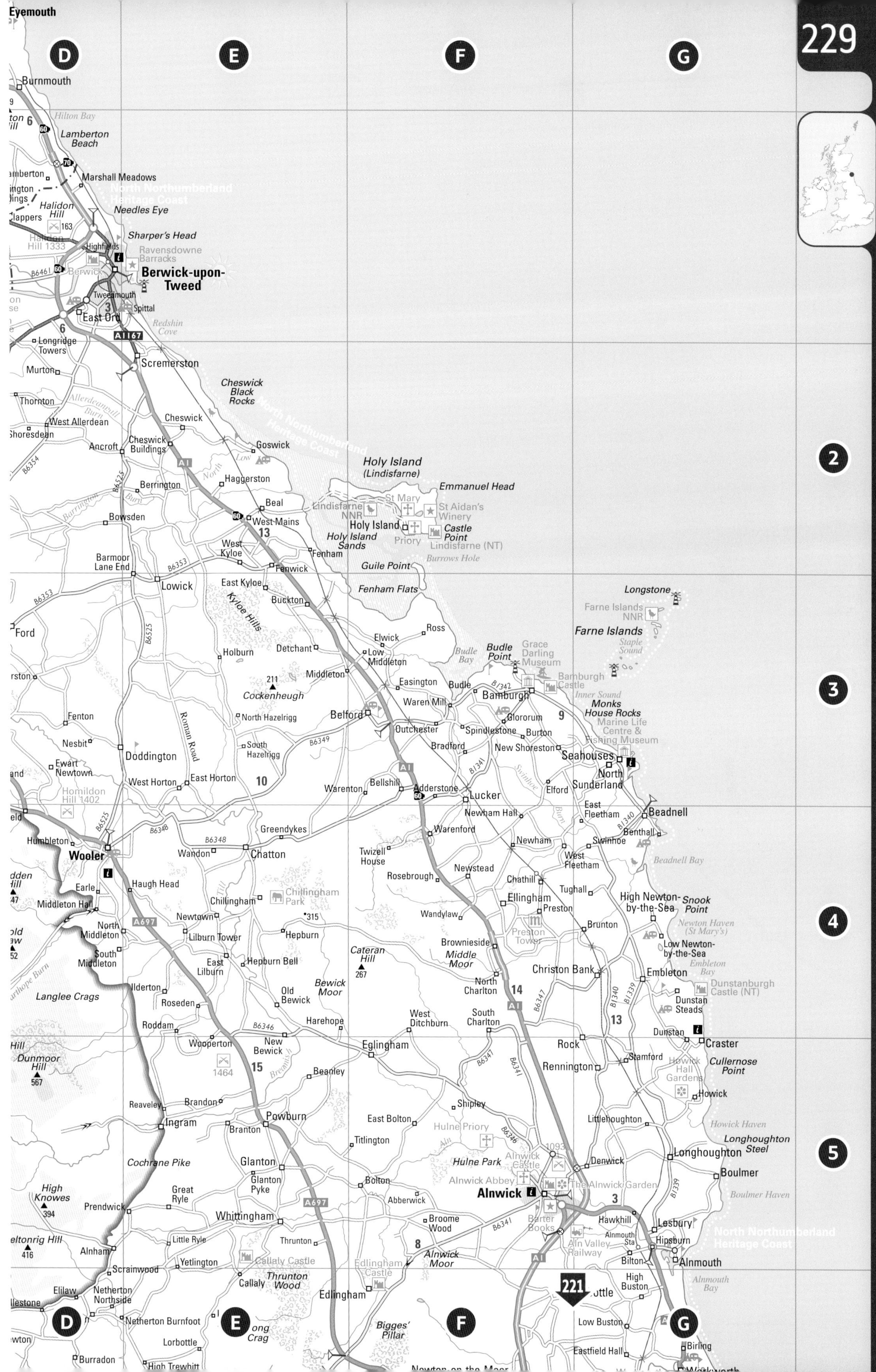
Eyemouth
D
E
F
G
Burnmouth
Hilton Bay
Lamberton Beach
Marshall Meadows
North Northumberland Heritage Coast
Halidon Hill
Needles Eye
163
Sharper's Head
Halidon Hill 1333
Highfields
Ravensdowne Barracks
Berwick
Berwick-upon-Tweed
B6461
Tweedmouth
Spittal
East Ord
Redshin Cove
A1167
Longridge Towers
Scremerston
Murton
Cheswick Black Rocks
Thornton
Allerdean Mill Burn
West Allerdean
Shoresdean
Cheswick
Cheswick Buildings
Ancroft
Goswick
B6354
A1
Low North
Haggerston
Berrington
B6525
Holy Island (Lindisfarne)
Emmanuel Head
St Mary
Lindisfarne NNR
St Aidan's Winery
Beal
Barrington Burn
Bowsden
West Mains
Holy Island
Castle Point
Holy Island Sands
Priory
Lindisfarne (NT)
West Kyloe
Fenham
Burrows Hole
Barmoor Lane End
B6353
Fenwick
Guile Point
Lowick
East Kyloe
Kyloe Hills
Fenham Flats
Buckton
Longstone
Farne Islands NNR
Farne Islands
Ford
Ross
Elwick
Staple Sound
Holburn
Detchant
Low Middleton
Budle Bay
Budle Point
Grace Darling Museum
211
Cockenheugh
Middleton
Easington
Budle
Bamburgh Castle
Bamburgh
B1342
Inner Sound
Waren Mill
Monks House Rocks
Fenton
North Hazelrigg
Belford
Glororum
Marine Life Centre & Fishing Museum
Roman Road
Outchester
Spindlestone
Burton
Nesbit
South Hazelrigg
B6349
Bradford
New Shoreston
Seahouses
Doddington
Ewart Newtown
B1341
North Sunderland
Swinhoe
Homildon Hill 1402
West Horton
East Horton
10
Warenton
Bellshill
Adderstone
Lucker
Elford
East Fleetham
Beadnell
Newham Hall
B1340
Benthall
B6348
Greendykes
Warenford
Humbleton
Wooler
Wandon
Chatton
Newham
Swinhoe
Twizell House
Beadnell Bay
West Fleetham
Newstead
Haugh Head
Rosebrough
Chathill
Earle
Chillingham
Chillingham Park
Tughall
Middleton Hall
Ellingham
High Newton-by-the-Sea
Snook Point
Preston
Newtown
315
Wandylaw
North Middleton
A697
Lilburn Tower
Hepburn
Preston Tower
Brunton
Newton Haven (St Mary's)
Low Newton-by-the-Sea
Brownieside
South Middleton
Cateran Hill
Middle Moor
East Lilburn
Hepburn Bell
267
Christon Bank
Embleton Bay
Embleton
Ilderton
Bewick Moor
North Charlton
14
Dunstanburgh Castle (NT)
Langlee Crags
Old Bewick
B6347
B1340
B1339
Dunstan Steads
Roseden
13
South Charlton
Roddam
Harehope
West Ditchburn
Dunstan
B6346
Craster
Dunmoor Hill
567
Wooperton
New Bewick
Eglingham
Rock
Stamford
Howick Hall Gardens
Cullernose Point
1464
15
Breamish
Rennington
B6341
Beanley
Howick
Reaveley
Brandon
Shipley
Ingram
Powburn
East Bolton
Littlehoughton
Branton
Hulne Priory
Howick Haven
Titlington
Longhoughton Steel
Cochrane Pike
Glanton
1093
Alnwick Castle
Hulne Park
Denwick
Longhoughton
Glanton Pyke
Bolton
Alnwick Abbey
The Alnwick Garden
Boulmer
High Knowes
394
Great Ryle
Alnwick
3
Abberwick
Boulmer Haven
Prendwick
A697
Whittingham
Broome Wood
Barter Books
Hawkhill
Lesbury
Little Ryle
Thrunton
8
Aln Valley Railway
Alnmouth Sta
Hipsburn
Eltonrig Hill
416
Alnham
Callaly Castle
Edlingham Castle
Alnwick Moor
Bilton
Alnmouth
Yetlington
Scrainwood
Thrunton Wood
High Buston
Alnmouth Bay
Netherton Northside
Callaly
Edlingham
221
Elilaw
Netherton Burnfoot
Bigges' Pillar
Low Buston
Lorbottle
Burradon
Eastfield Hall
Birling
High Trewhitt
2
3
4
5

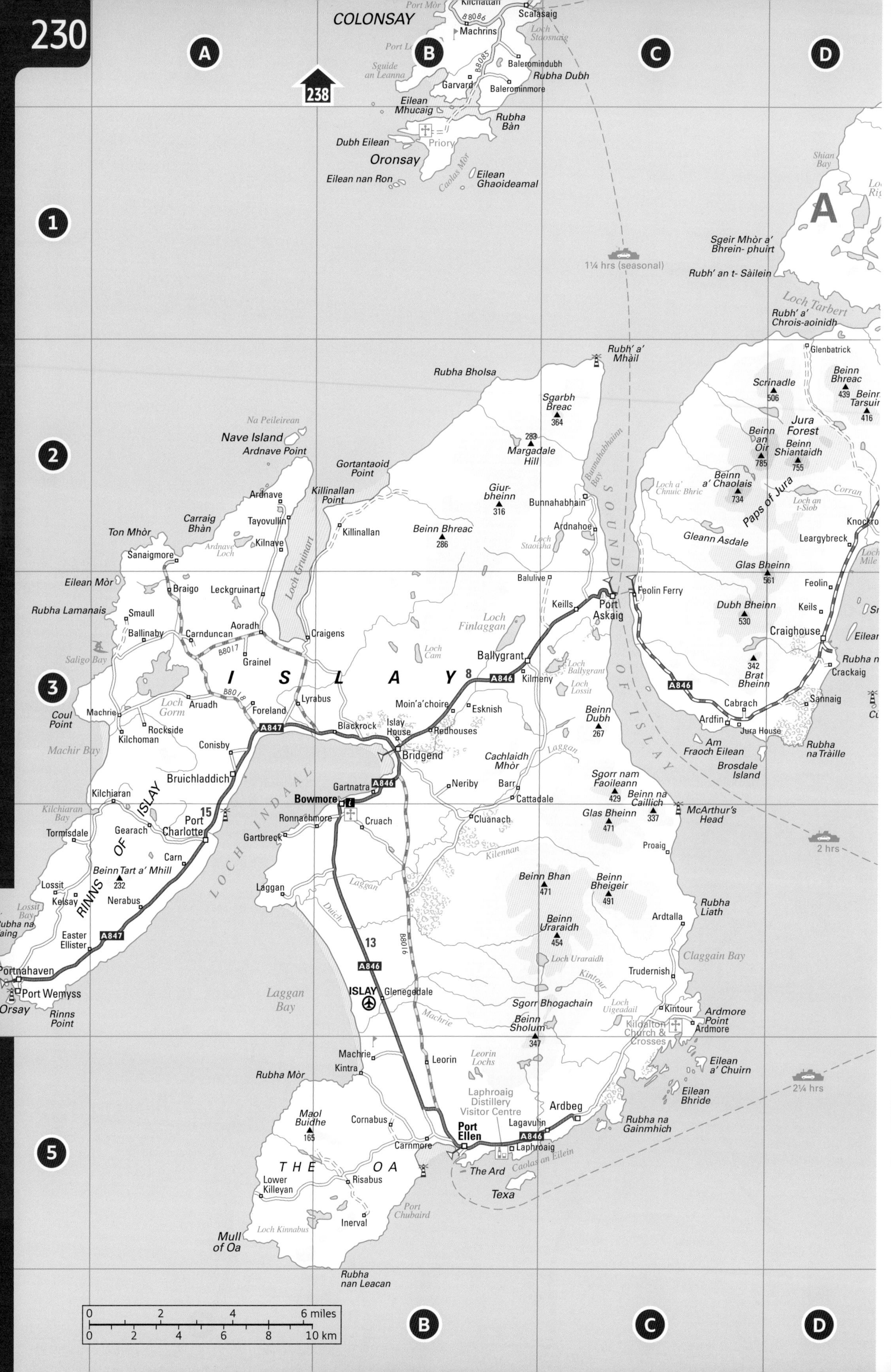

COLONSAY
Scalasaig
Machrins
Balerominduhb
Rubha Dubh
Garvard
Balerominmore
Eilean Mhucaig
Rubha Bàn
Dubh Eilean
Priory
Oronsay
Eilean nan Ron
Eilean Ghaoideamal
238
A
B
C
D
1
2
3
5
1¼ hrs (seasonal)
Sgeir Mhòr a' Bhrein- phuirt
Rubh' an t- Sàilein
Loch Tarbert
Rubh' a' Chrois-aoinidh
Glenbatrick
Scrinadle 506
Beinn Bhreac 439
Jura Forest
Beinn an Oir 785
Beinn Shiantaidh 755
Beinn a' Chaolais 734
Paps of Jura
Gleann Asdale
Leargybreck
Glas Bheinn 561
Feolin
Dubh Bheinn 530
Keils
Craighouse
342 Brat Bheinn
Crackaig
A846
Cabrach
Sannaig
Ardfin
Jura House
Am Fraoch Eilean
Brosdale Island
Rubha na Tràille
Rubh' a' Mhàil
Rubha Bholsa
Sgarbh Breac 364
283 Margadale Hill
Giur-bheinn 316
Bunnahabhain
Beinn Bhreac 286
Ardnahoe
SOUND OF ISLAY
Feolin Ferry
Balulive
Keills
Port Askaig
Loch Finlaggan
Ballygrant
Kilmeny
Nave Island
Ardnave Point
Gortantaoid Point
Killinallan Point
Ardnave
Tayovullin
Carraig Bhàn
Ton Mhòr
Kilnave
Killinallan
Loch Gruinart
Sanaigmore
Eilean Mòr
Braigo
Leckgruinart
Rubha Lamanais
Smaull
Ballinaby
Carnduncan
Aoradh
Craigens
B8017
Grainel
Saligo Bay
ISLAY
Coul Point
Machrie
Loch Gorm
Aruadh
B8018
Foreland
Lyrabus
Moin'a'choire
Esknish
Rockside
Kilchoman
A847
Blackrock
Islay House
Redhouses
Machir Bay
Conisby
Bridgend
Cachlaidh Mhòr
Beinn Dubh 267
Bruichladdich
Neriby
Barr
Sgorr nam Faoileann 429
Beinn na Caillich 337
Kilchiaran
Gartnatra
A846
Bowmore
Cattadale
Glas Bheinn 471
McArthur's Head
Kilchiaran Bay
Port Charlotte
Ronnachmore
Cruach
Cluanach
Tormisdale
Gearach
Gartbreck
Proaig
RINNS OF ISLAY
LOCH INDAAL
Carn
2 hrs
Beinn Tart a' Mhill 232
Lossit
Kelsay
Nerabus
Laggan
Beinn Bhan 471
Beinn Bheigeir 491
Rubha Liath
Ardtalla
Rubha na Faing
Easter Ellister
Beinn Uraraidh 454
B8016
Claggain Bay
Loch Uraraidh
Portnahaven
Trudernish
Port Wemyss
Orsay
Rinns Point
Laggan Bay
ISLAY
Glenegedale
Sgorr Bhogachain
Kintour
Ardmore Point
Ardmore
Beinn Sholum 347
Kildalton Church & Crosses
Machrie
Leorin
Leorin Lochs
Eilean a' Chuirn
Kintra
Rubha Mòr
2¼ hrs
Laphroaig Distillery Visitor Centre
Eilean Bhride
Ardbeg
Maol Buidhe 165
Cornabus
Lagavulin
Rubha na Gainmhich
Port Ellen
Carnmore
Laphroaig
THE OA
The Ard
Caolas an Eilein
Risabus
Lower Killeyan
Texa
Port Chubaird
Inerval
Loch Kinnabus
Mull of Oa
Rubha nan Leacan
0 2 4 6 miles
0 2 4 6 8 10 km

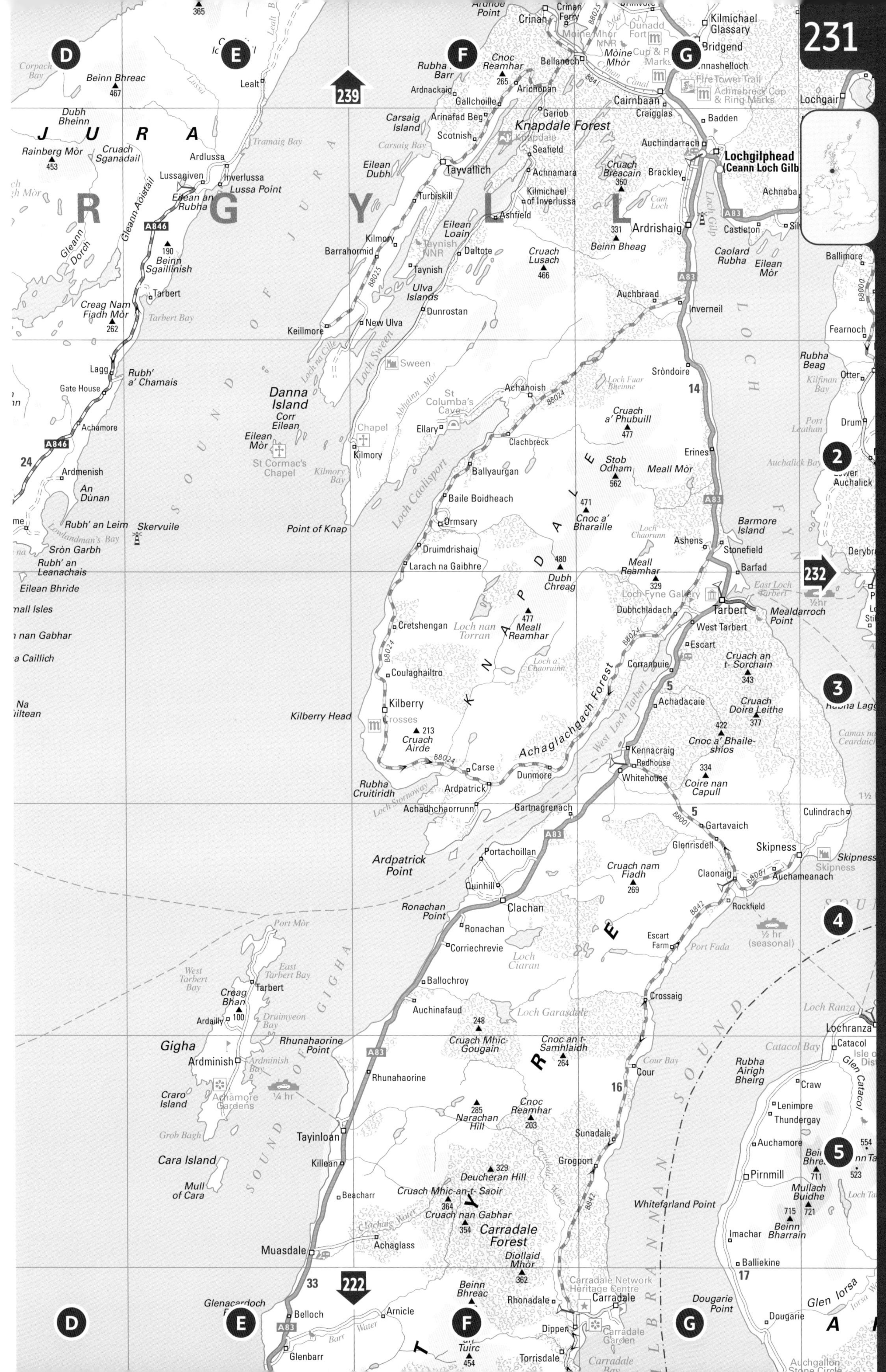

JURA
ARGYLL
KNAPDALE
Crinan
Bellanoch
Kilmichael Glassary
Bridgend
Cairnbaan
Lochgair
Knapdale Forest
Tayvallich
Lochgilphead (Ceann Loch Gilb
Ardrishaig
Lealt
Ardlussa
Inverlussa
Lussa Point
Tarbert
Lagg
Ardmenish
Danna Island
Eilean Mòr
St Cormac's Chapel
Kilmory
Ellary
Achahoish
Ormsary
Point of Knap
Sound of Jura
Loch Fyne
Tarbert
West Tarbert
Kilberry
Kilberry Head
Skipness
Claonaig
Clachan
Ronachan Point
Ardpatrick Point
Gigha
Ardminish
Cara Island
Sound of Gigha
Tayinloan
Muasdale
Carradale
Carradale Forest
Kilbrannan Sound
Lochranza
Dougarie
Pirnmill
Glenbarr
A83
A846
B8024
B8025
B842
B8001
239
222
232

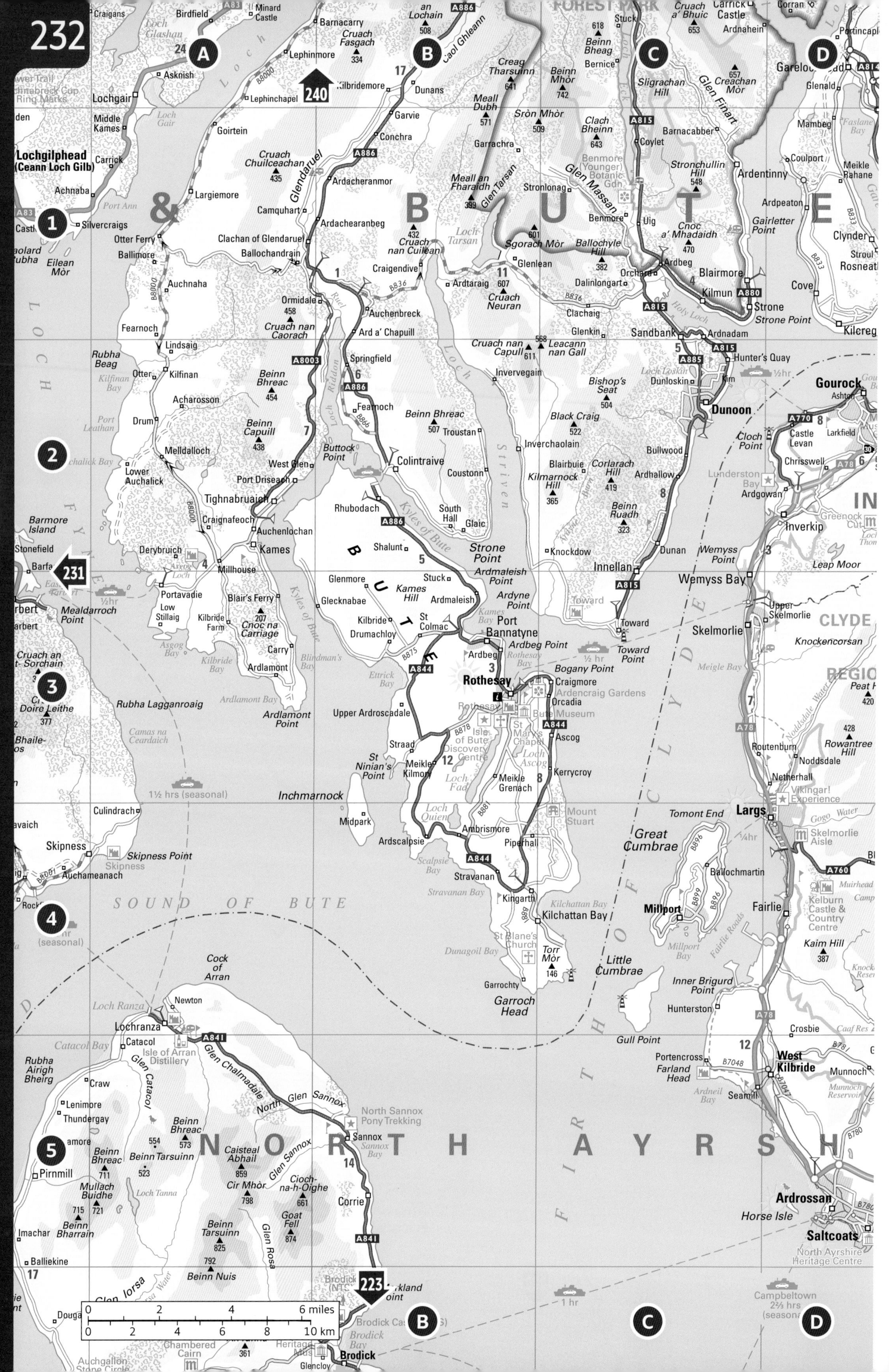

Birdfield
Minard Castle
Loch Glashan
Barnacarry
Cruach Fasgach
334
Lephinmore
Asknish
Lochgair
Loch Gair
Middle Kames
Goirtein
Lephinchapel
240
Kilbridemore
Dunans
Garvie
Conchra
Lochgilphead (Ceann Loch Gilb)
Carrick
Achnaba
Port Ann
Silvercraigs
Largiemore
Cruach Chuilceachan
435
Glendaruel
Ardacheranmor
Camquhart
Ardachearanbeg
Clachan of Glendaruel
Otter Ferry
Ballimore
Ballochandrain
Eilean Mòr
Auchnaha
Ormidale
458
Cruach nan Caorach
Fearnoch
Lindsaig
Rubha Beag
Kilfinan Bay
Otter
Kilfinan
Acharosson
Port Leathan
Drum
Melldalloch
Lower Auchalick
Barmore Island
Stonefield
Barfa
231
Tighnabruaich
Port Driseach
West Glen
Craignafeoch
Auchenlochan
Kames
Derybruich
Millhouse
Portavadie
Mealdarroch Point
Low Stillaig
Kilbride Farm
Blair's Ferry
Cnoc na Carriage
207
Asgog Bay
Kilbride Bay
Carry
Ardlamont
Ardlamont Bay
Ardlamont Point
Cruach an t-Sorchain
Doire Leithe
377
Rubha Lagganroaig
Camas na Ceardaich
1½ hrs (seasonal)
Culindrach
Skipness
Skipness Point
Auchameanach
SOUND OF BUTE
(seasonal)
Inchmarnock
Midpark
an Lochain
508
Caol Ghleann
Creag Tharsuinn
641
Meall Dubh
571
Garrachra
Meall an Fharaidh
399
Glen Tarsan
B U T E
432
Cruach nan Cuilean
Loch Tarsan
Craigendive
Ardtaraig
607
Cruach Neuran
Auchenbreck
Ard a' Chapuill
Springfield
Loch Riddon
Feornoch
Beinn Bhreac
454
Beinn Capuill
438
Beinn Bhreac
507
Troustan
Buttock Point
Colintraive
Coustonn
Rhubodach
Kyles of Bute
South Hall
Glaic
Shalunt
Strone Point
Ardmaleish Point
Glenmore
Stuck
Kames Hill
Ardmaleish
Ardyne Point
Glecknabae
Kilbride
St Colmac
Drumachloy
Port Bannatyne
Kames Bay
Ardbeg Point
Ardbeg
Rothesay Bay
Ettrick Bay
Rothesay
Upper Ardroscadale
Isle of Bute Discovery Centre
Straad
St Ninian's Point
Meikle Kilmory
Loch Fad
Loch Quien
Meikle Grenach
Loch Ascog
Ardscalpsie
Ambrismore
Piperhall
Scalpsie Bay
Stravanan
Stravanan Bay
Kingarth
Kilchattan Bay
St Blane's Church
Dunagoil Bay
Torr Mòr
146
Garrochty
Garroch Head
Craigmore
Ardencraig Gardens
Orcadia
Bute Museum
St Mary's Chapel
Ascog
Kerrycroy
Mount Stuart
Bogany Point
FOREST PARK
Stuck
618
Beinn Bheag
Bernice
Beinn Mhòr
742
Sròn Mhòr
509
Clach Bheinn
643
Benmore (Younger) Botanic Gdn
Glen Massan
Stronlonag
Benmore
601
Sgorach Mòr
Glenlean
Ballochyle Hill
382
Uig
Dalinlongart
Orchard
Ardbeg
Clachaig
Glenkin
Cruach nan Capull
611
568
Leacann nan Gall
Invervegain
Loch Striven
Bishop's Seat
504
Black Craig
522
Inverchaolain
Blairbuie
Corlarach Hill
419
Kilmarnock Hill
365
Beinn Ruadh
323
Knockdow
Innellan
Toward
Toward Point
½ hr
Cruach a' Bhuic
653
Carrick Castle
Ardnahein
Sligrachan Hill
Glen Finart
657
Creachan Mòr
Coylet
Barnacabber
Stronchullin Hill
548
Cnoc a' Mhadaidh
470
Blairmore
Kilmun
Holy Loch
Strone
Strone Point
Sandbank
Ardnadam
Hunter's Quay
Loch Loskin
Dunloskin
Kirn
Dunoon
Bullwood
Ardhallow
Dunan
Corran
Portincaple
Garelochhead
Glenfield
Mambeg
Faslane Bay
Coulport
Meikle Rahane
Ardentinny
Ardpeaton
Gairletter Point
Clynder
Stroul
Rosneath
Cove
Kilcreggan
E
Gourock
Ashton
Cloch Point
Castle Levan
Larkfield
Chrisswell
Lunderston Bay
Ardgowan
Greenock Cut
Inverkip
Wemyss Point
Wemyss Bay
Leap Moor
Upper Skelmorlie
Skelmorlie
CLYDE
Knockencorsan
Meigle Bay
REGION
Peat Hill
420
428
Rowantree Hill
Routenburn
Noddsdale
Netherhall
Vikingar! Experience
Largs
Tomont End
Gogo Water
Skelmorlie Aisle
Great Cumbrae
Ballochmartin
Millport
Millport Bay
Fairlie Roads
Fairlie
Muirhead
Kelburn Castle & Country Centre
Kaim Hill
387
Little Cumbrae
Inner Brigurd Point
Hunterston
Crosbie
Gull Point
Portencross
Farland Head
West Kilbride
Munnoch
Munnoch Reservoir
Ardneil Bay
Seamill
FIRTH OF CLYDE
Ardrossan
Horse Isle
Saltcoats
North Ayrshire Heritage Centre
Campbeltown 2⅔ hrs (seasonal)
1 hr
Cock of Arran
Loch Ranza
Newton
Lochranza
Catacol Bay
Catacol
Isle of Arran Distillery
Glen Catacol
Glen Chalmadale
North Glen Sannox
North Sannox Pony Trekking
Rubha Airigh Bheirg
Craw
Lenimore
Thundergay
Beinn Bhreac
573
554
Caisteal Abhail
859
Sannox
Sannox Bay
Glen Sannox
Pirnmill
Beinn Bhreac
711
Beinn Tarsuinn
523
Loch Tanna
Cir Mhòr
798
Cioch-na-h-Oighe
661
Corrie
Mullach Buidhe
715
721
Beinn Bharrain
Goat Fell
874
Imachar
Beinn Tarsuinn
825
Glen Rosa
Balliekine
792
Beinn Nuis
Glen Iorsa
Dougarie
223
Brodick Castle
Brodick Bay
Brodick
Glencloy
Chambered Cairn
361
Auchgallon Stone Circle
NORTH AYRSHIRE
0 2 4 6 miles
0 2 4 6 8 10 km

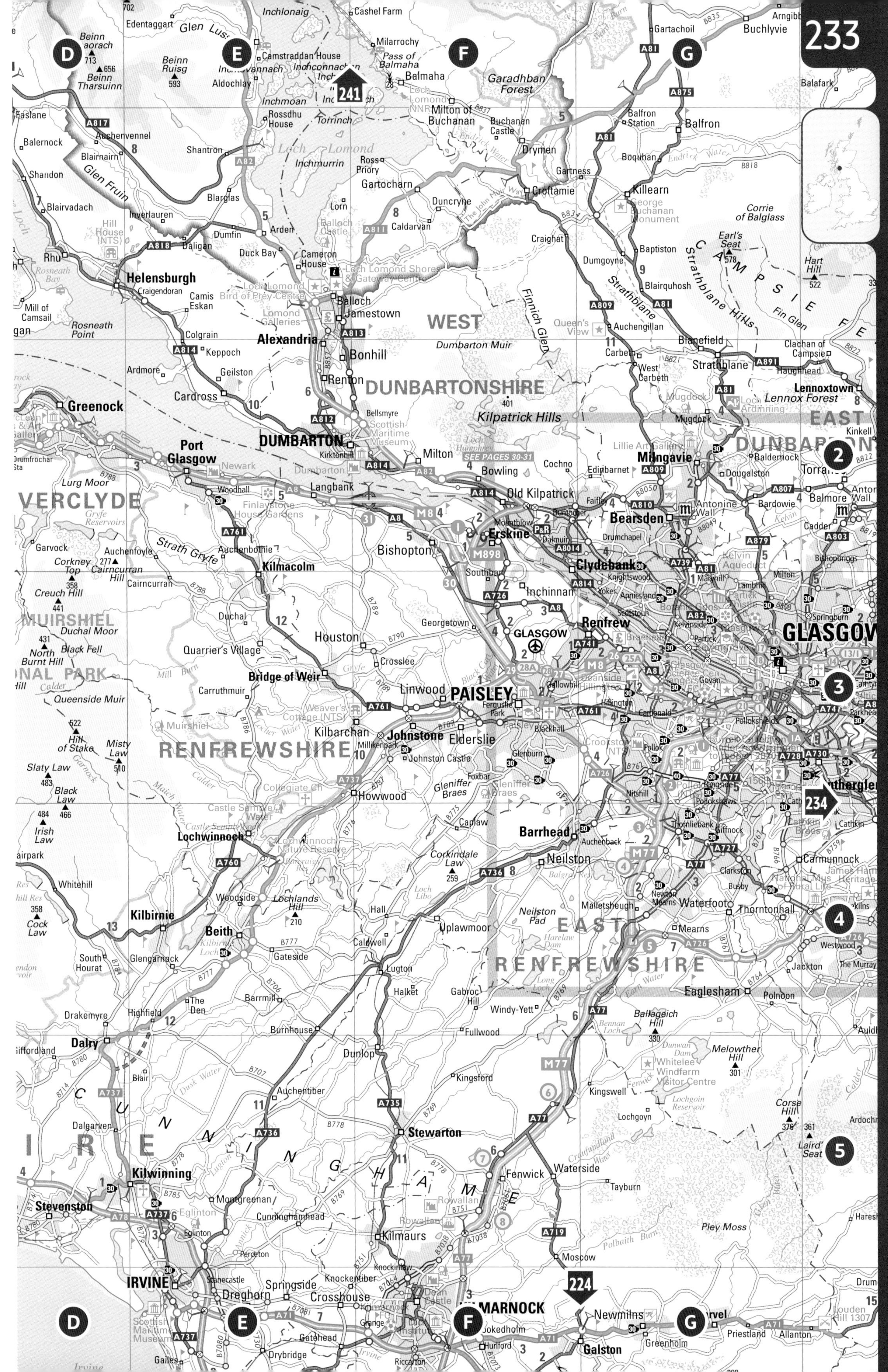
241
234
224
SEE PAGES 30-31
Helensburgh
Greenock
Port Glasgow
DUMBARTON
Alexandria
Balloch
Jamestown
Bonhill
Renton
Cardross
WEST
DUNBARTONSHIRE
EAST
DUNBARTONSHIRE
INVERCLYDE
RENFREWSHIRE
EAST
RENFREWSHIRE
CUNNINGHAME
Kilpatrick Hills
Campsie Fells
Loch Lomond
Drymen
Balfron
Balmaha
Killearn
Strathblane
Blanefield
Milngavie
Bearsden
Clydebank
Erskine
Renfrew
GLASGOW
PAISLEY
Johnstone
Linwood
Elderslie
Kilbarchan
Bridge of Weir
Kilmacolm
Houston
Bishopton
Barrhead
Neilston
Eaglesham
Lochwinnoch
Kilbirnie
Beith
Dalry
Kilwinning
Stevenston
IRVINE
Dreghorn
Crosshouse
Kilmaurs
Stewarton
Dunlop
Fenwick
KILMARNOCK
Newmilns
Galston
Lennoxtown
Kirkintilloch
Torrance
Rutherglen
Waterfoot
Thorntonhall
Newton Mearns
Uplawmoor
Lugton
Howwood
Auchenflower
Whitelee Windfarm Visitor Centre
Loch Lomond Shores & Gateway Centre
Scottish Maritime Museum
Glasgow Airport

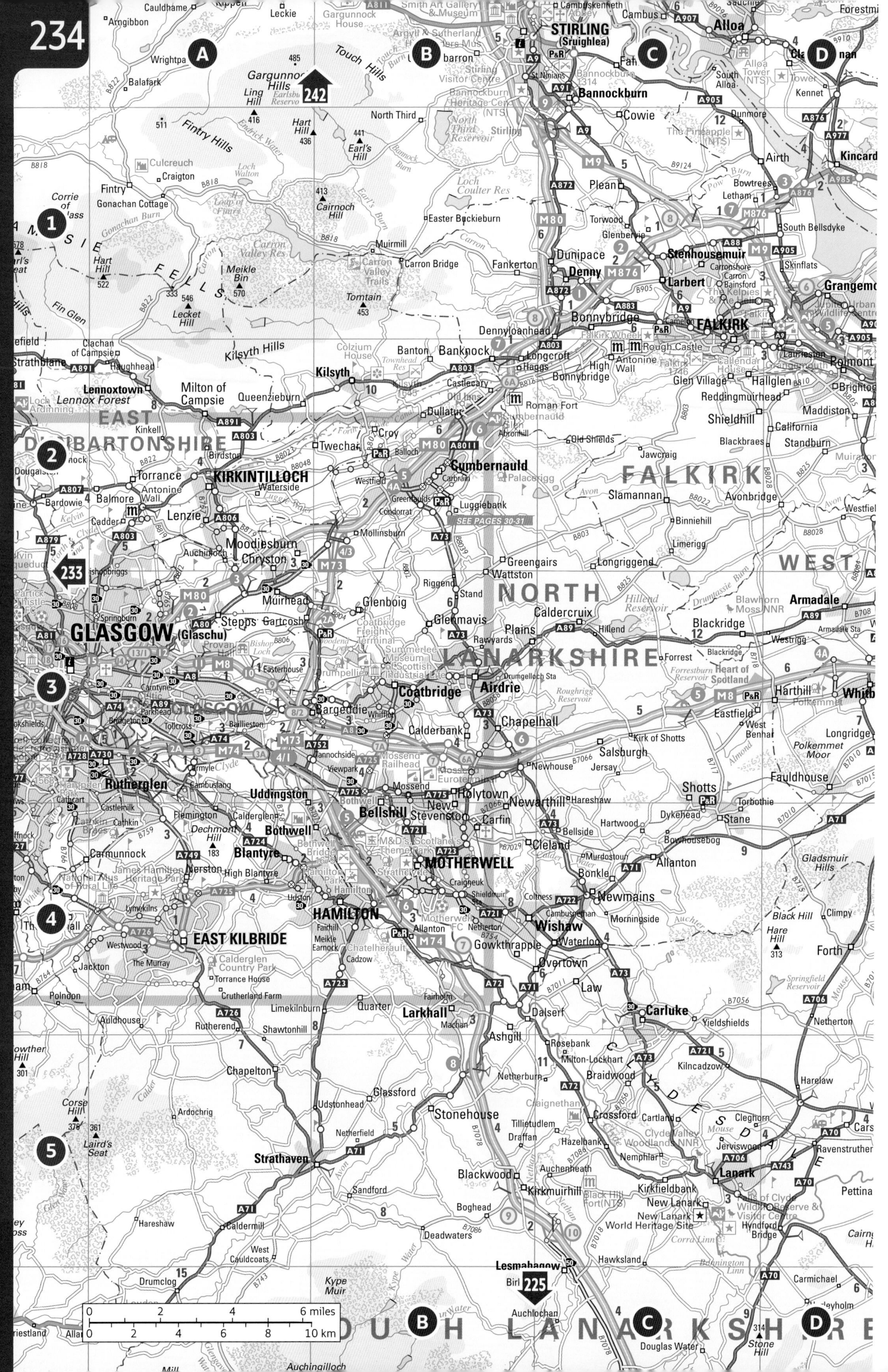
A
B
C
D
1
2
3
4
5
242
233
225
STIRLING (Sruighlea)
Alloa
Cambus
Bannockburn
Bannockburn Heritage Centre (NTS)
Stirling Visitor Centre
Argyll & Sutherland Highlanders Mus
Smith Art Gallery & Museum
Cambuskenneth Abbey
South Alloa
Alloa Tower (NTS)
Kennet
Cowie
Dunmore
The Pineapple (NTS)
Airth
Kincardine
Plean
North Third
North Third Reservoir
Gargunnock Hills
Gargunnock House
Touch Hills
Leckie
Cauldhame
Arngibbon
Wrightpark
Balafark
Fintry Hills
Culcreuch
Craigton
Fintry
Gonachan Cottage
Corrie of Balglass
Loch Walton
Carron Valley Res
Cairnoch Hill
Meikle Bin
Earl's Hill
Hart Hill
Easter Buckieburn
Muirmill
Carron Bridge
Carron Valley Trails
Tomtain
Fankerton
Loch Coulter Res
Torwood
Glenbervie
Dunipace
Denny
Larbert
Stenhousemuir
Carronshore
Bainsford
The Kelpies & The Helix
FALKIRK
Falkirk Wheel
Rough Castle
Grangemouth
Laurieston
Polmont
Brightons
Bonnybridge
Dennyloanhead
Longcroft
Haggs
Banknock
Banton
Colzium House
Kilsyth
Kilsyth Hills
Lecket Hill
Fin Glen
Campsie Fells
Clachan of Campsie
Strathblane
Haughhead
Lennoxtown
Lennox Forest
Milton of Campsie
Queenzieburn
Castlecary
Cumbernauld
Roman Fort
Old Shields
Palacerigg
Condorrat
Luggiebank
SEE PAGES 30-31
Croy
Twechar
Dullatur
EAST DUNBARTONSHIRE
Kirkintilloch
Kinkell
Birdston
Torrance
Balmore
Bardowie
Lenzie
Waterside
Cadder
Moodiesburn
Chryston
Auchinloch
Muirhead
Stepps
Gartcosh
Glenboig
Glenmavis
Riggend
Stand
Greengairs
Wattston
FALKIRK
Slamannan
Avonbridge
Binniehill
Limerigg
Longriggend
Jawcraig
Blackbraes
California
Standburn
Maddiston
Reddingmuirhead
Shieldhill
Hallglen
Glen Village
WEST
Armadale
Blawhorn Moss NNR
Hillend Reservoir
Blackridge
Westrigg
Caldercruix
Plains
Rawyards
Hillend
NORTH LANARKSHIRE
Forrest
Heart of Scotland
Harthill
Whitburn
Eastfield
West Benhar
Longridge
Polkemmet Moor
Fauldhouse
Shotts
Torbothie
Stane
Dykehead
Bowhousebog
Hartwood
Allanton
Gladsmuir Hills
Black Hill
Hare Hill
Forth
Springfield Reservoir
GLASGOW (Glaschu)
Provan Hall
Springburn
Bishopbriggs
Partick
Coatbridge
Airdrie
Drumgelloch Sta
Summerlee Museum of Scottish Industrial Life
Drumpellier
Easterhouse
Carntyne
Parkhead
Tollcross
Baillieston
Bargeddie
Calderbank
Chapelhall
Kirk of Shotts
Salsburgh
Jersay
Newhouse
Holytown
Newarthill
Hareshaw
Carfin
New Stevenston
Mossend
Bellshill
Viewpark
Tannochside
Uddingston
Bothwell
Rutherglen
Cambuslang
Carmyle
Castlemilk
Cathkin
Cathcart
Carmunnock
Flemington
Dechmont Hill
Calderglen
Blantyre
High Blantyre
Nerston
James Hamilton Heritage Park
National Mus of Rural Life
East Kilbride
Lymekilns
Westwood
Jackton
The Murray
Calderglen Country Park
Torrance House
Crutherland Farm
Polnoon
Auldhouse
M&D's Scotland's Theme Park
Strathclyde Park
MOTHERWELL
Craigneuk
Shieldmuir Sta
Cleland
Bellside
Murdostoun
Bonkle
Newmains
Coltness
Cambusnethan
Morningside
Wishaw
Waterloo
Netherton
Gowkthrapple
Overtown
Motherwell FC
HAMILTON
Fairhill
Meikle Earnock
Chatelherault
Cadzow
Allanton
Udston
Larkhall
Fairholm
Quarter
Limekilnburn
Machan
Ashgill
Dalserf
Law
Carluke
Yieldshields
Rosebank
Milton-Lockhart
Braidwood
CLYDESDALE
Kilncadzow
Harelaw
Netherburn
Rutherend
Shawtonhill
Chapelton
Glassford
Udstonhead
Stonehouse
Ardochrig
Corse Hill
Laird's Seat
Strathaven
Netherfield
Sandford
Hareshaw
Caldermill
West Cauldcoats
Drumclog
Kype Muir
Blackwood
Kirkmuirhill
Boghead
Deadwaters
Tillietudlem
Draffan
Hazelbank
Crossford
Cartland
Nemphlar
Clyde Valley Woodlands NNR
Craignethan
Auchenheath
Black Hill Fort (NTS)
Kirkfieldbank
New Lanark
New Lanark World Heritage Site
Lanark
Cleghorn
Jerviswood
Ravenstruther
Carstairs
Pettinain
Falls of Clyde Wildlife Reserve & Visitor Centre
Hyndford Bridge
Corra Linn
Bonnington Linn
Hawksland
Lesmahagow
Birkwood
Auchlochan
Douglas Water
Carmichael
Stone Hill
SOUTH LANARKSHIRE
0 2 4 6 miles
0 2 4 6 8 10 km

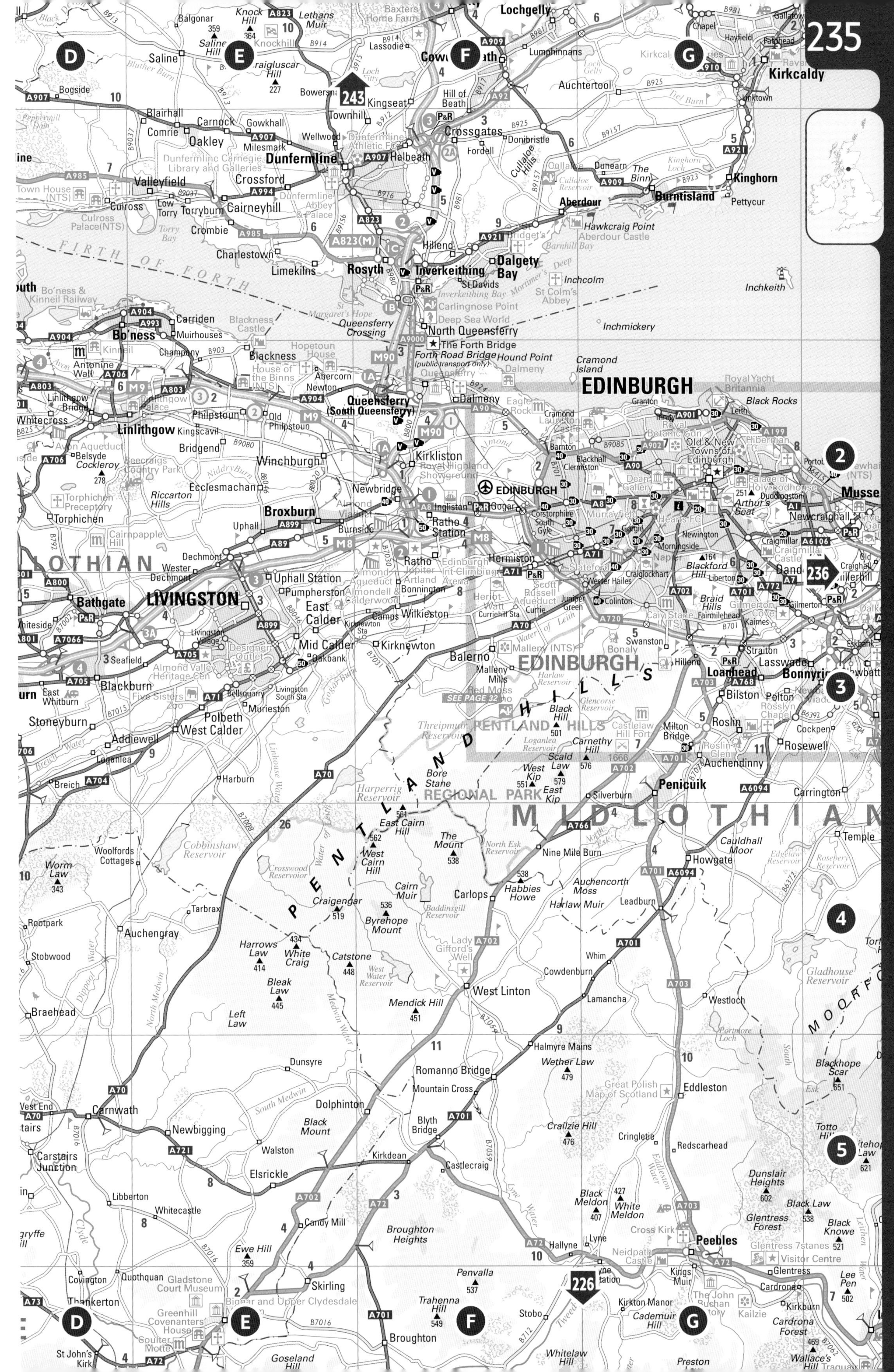

EDINBURGH
LOTHIAN
MIDLOTHIAN
PENTLAND HILLS
PENTLAND HILLS REGIONAL PARK
EDINBURGH HILLS
FIRTH OF FORTH
Dunfermline
Kirkcaldy
Kinghorn
Burntisland
Aberdour
Dalgety Bay
Inverkeithing
Rosyth
Crossgates
Halbeath
Cowdenbeath
Lochgelly
Lumphinnans
Auchtertool
Kingseat
Townhill
Saline
Oakley
Comrie
Carnock
Blairhall
Valleyfield
Culross
Torryburn
Cairneyhill
Crossford
Crombie
Charlestown
Limekilns
North Queensferry
Queensferry (South Queensferry)
Queensferry Crossing
The Forth Bridge
Forth Road Bridge (public transport only)
Inchcolm
Inchkeith
Inchmickery
Cramond Island
Bo'ness
Carriden
Blackness
Linlithgow
Philpstoun
Winchburgh
Kirkliston
Newbridge
Broxburn
Uphall
Ratho
Ratho Station
Livingston
Bathgate
Blackburn
Whitburn
Stoneyburn
Addiewell
Polbeth
West Calder
Mid Calder
East Calder
Kirknewton
Wilkieston
Balerno
Currie
Juniper Green
Colinton
Hermiston
Corstorphine
Leith
Granton
Portobello
Musselburgh
Newcraighall
Dalkeith
Loanhead
Bonnyrigg
Lasswade
Bilston
Roslin
Penicuik
Auchendinny
Rosewell
Carrington
Temple
Howgate
Silverburn
Nine Mile Burn
Carlops
Leadburn
West Linton
Lamancha
Eddleston
Peebles
Romanno Bridge
Mountain Cross
Dolphinton
Blyth Bridge
Carnwath
Newbigging
Walston
Elsrickle
Skirling
Broughton
Biggar and Upper Clydesdale
Libberton
Carstairs Junction
Covington
Thankerton
Auchengray
Tarbrax
Woolfords Cottages
Harburn
Breich
Loganlea
Edinburgh Airport
Arthur's Seat
Royal Yacht Britannia
Old & New Towns of Edinburgh
Royal Botanic Gdn
Palace of Holyroodhouse
Hopetoun House
House of the Binns
Linlithgow Palace
Dalmeny
Lauriston Castle
Malleny (NTS)
Great Polish Map of Scotland
Glentress 7stanes Visitor Centre
Kailzie
Neidpath Castle
Dunfermline Abbey & Palace
Dunfermline Carnegie Library and Galleries
Culross Palace (NTS)
Bo'ness & Kinneil Railway
Deep Sea World
Hawkcraig Point
Aberdour Castle
St Colm's Abbey
243
236
226
SEE PAGE 32

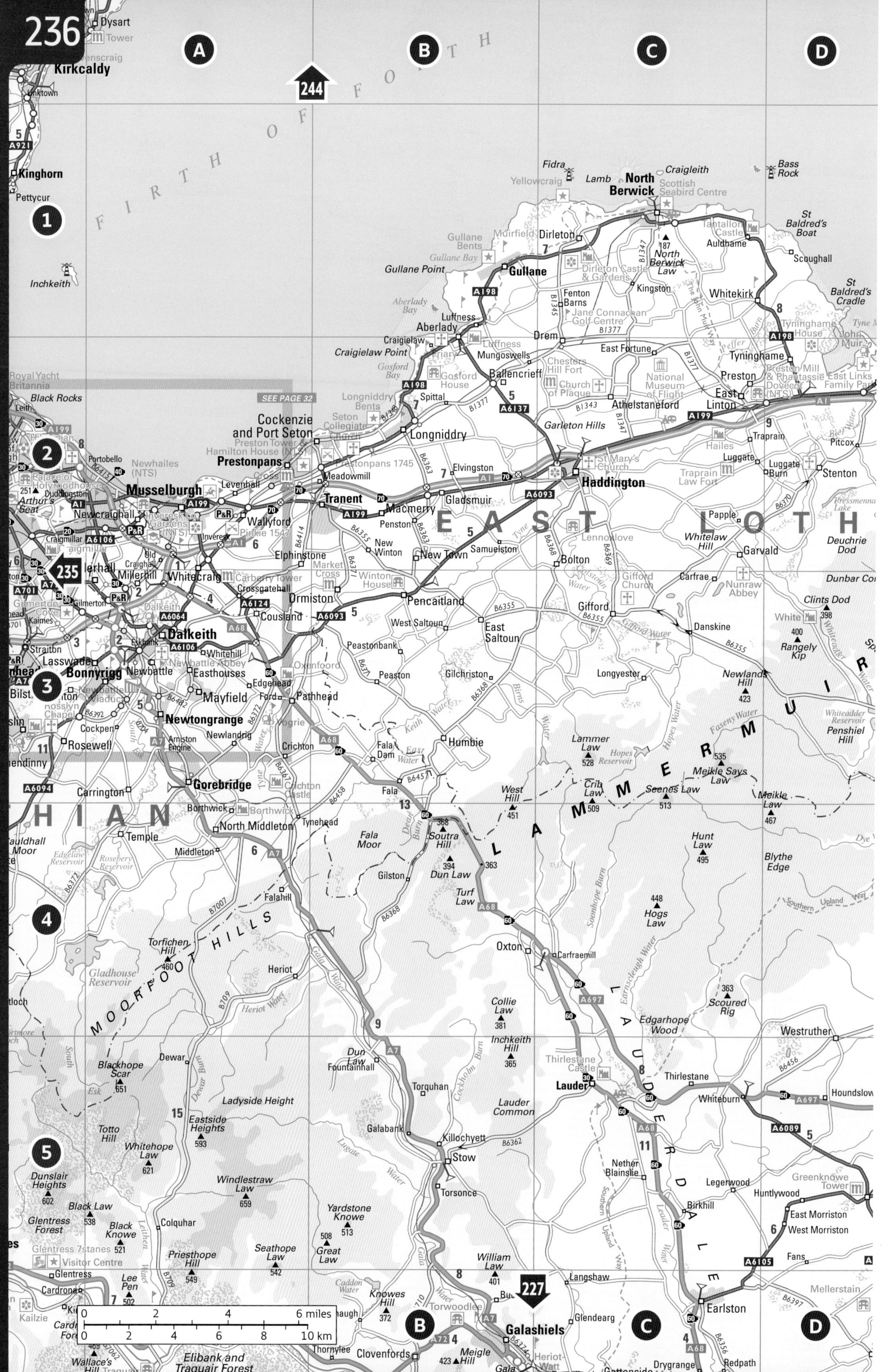
A
B
C
D
1
2
3
4
5
244
FIRTH OF FORTH
Dysart
Tower
Kirkcaldy
Linktown
Kinghorn
Pettycur
Inchkeith
Fidra
Yellowcraig
Lamb
North Berwick
Craigleith
Scottish Seabird Centre
Bass Rock
St Baldred's Boat
Tantallon Castle
Auldhame
Scoughall
St Baldred's Cradle
Muirfield
Dirleton
Gullane Bents
Gullane Bay
Gullane Point
Gullane
North Berwick Law
187
Dirleton Castle & Gardens
Kingston
Whitekirk
Fenton Barns
Jane Connachan Golf Centre
Drem
Aberlady Bay
Luffness
Aberlady
Craigielaw
Craigielaw Point
Gosford Bay
Gosford House
Mungoswells
Chesters Hill Fort
Church of Plaque
East Fortune
National Museum of Flight
Tyninghame
Tyninghame House
John Muir
Preston Mill & Phantassie Doocot (NTS)
East Links Family Park
Preston
East Linton
Ballencrieff
Athelstaneford
Garleton Hills
Royal Yacht Britannia
Black Rocks
Leith
SEE PAGE 32
Longniddry Bents
Spittal
Seton Collegiate Church
Cockenzie and Port Seton
Preston Tower & Hamilton House (NTS)
Longniddry
Prestonpans
Prestonpans 1745
Meadowmill
Elvingston
Traprain
Hailes
Luggate
Luggate Burn
Stenton
Pitcox
St Mary's Church
Haddington
Traprain Law Fort
Portobello
Newhailes (NTS)
Palace of Holyroodhouse
Duddingston
Arthur's Seat
251
Musselburgh
Levenhall
Tranent
Macmerry
Gladsmuir
Newcraighall
Inveresk Lodge Gardens (NTS)
Wallyford
Pinkie 1547
Penston
EAST LOTHIAN
Papple
Pressmennan Lake
Craigmillar
Inveresk
New Winton
New Town
Samuelston
Lennoxlove
Bolton
Whitelaw Hill
Garvald
Deuchrie Dod
Elphinstone
Market Cross
Winton House
Old Craighall
Millerhill
Whitecraig
Carberry Tower
Crossgatehall
Ormiston
Pencaitland
Gifford Church
Carfrae
Nunraw Abbey
Dunbar Common
Clints Dod
398
235
Gilmerton
Kaimes
Dalkeith
Cousland
West Saltoun
East Saltoun
Gifford
Danskine
White
400
Rangely Kip
Straiton
Lasswade
Eskbank
Newbattle Abbey
Peastonbank
Loanhead
Bonnyrigg
Newbattle
Whitehill
Easthouses
Oxenfoord
Peaston
Gilchriston
Longyester
Newlands Hill
423
Bilston
Newbattle Viaduct
Mayfield
Edgehead
Ford
Pathhead
Roslin
Rosslyn Chapel
Cockpen
Newtongrange
Vogrie
Rosewell
Arniston Engine
Newlandrig
Crichton
Humbie
Fala Dam
Lammer Law
528
Hopes Reservoir
Meikle Says Law
535
LAMMERMUIR
Whiteadder Reservoir
Penshiel Hill
Penicuik
Carrington
Gorebridge
Crichton Castle
Fala
West Hill
451
Crib Law
509
Seenes Law
513
Meikle Law
467
LOTHIAN
Borthwick
Borthwick Castle
North Middleton
Tynehead
368
Soutra Hill
Fala Moor
Temple
Middleton
Edgelaw Reservoir
Rosebery Reservoir
394
Dun Law
363
Hunt Law
495
Blythe Edge
Gladhouse Reservoir
Falahill
Gilston
Turf Law
Southern Upland Way
448
Hogs Law
Torfichen Hill
460
MOORFOOT HILLS
Heriot
Oxton
Carfraemill
363
Scoured Rig
Collie Law
381
LAUDERDALE
Edgarhope Wood
Westruther
Blackhope Scar
651
Dewar
Dun Law
Fountainhall
Inchkeith Hill
365
Thirlestane Castle
Lauder
Thirlestane
Whiteburn
Houndslow
Ladyside Height
Torquhan
Lauder Common
Eastside Heights
593
Totto Hill
Whitehope Law
621
Galabank
Killochyett
Stow
Nether Blainslie
Legerwood
Greenknowe Tower
Huntlywood
Dunslair Heights
602
Windlestraw Law
659
Torsonce
Birkhill
East Morriston
West Morriston
Black Law
538
Glentress Forest
Black Knowe
521
Yardstone Knowe
513
508
Great Law
Glentress 7stanes Visitor Centre
Priesthope Hill
549
Seathope Law
542
William Law
401
Fans
Glentress
Cardrona
Lee Pen
502
Caddon Water
Knowes Hill
372
Langshaw
227
Mellerstain
Kailzie
Torwoodlee
Glendearg
Earlston
Galashiels
Clovenfords
Thornylee
Meigle Hill
423
Elibank and Traquair Forest
Wallace's Hill
Traquair
Heriot Watt
Gala
Gattonside
Drygrange
Redpath
0 2 4 6 miles
0 2 4 6 8 10 km

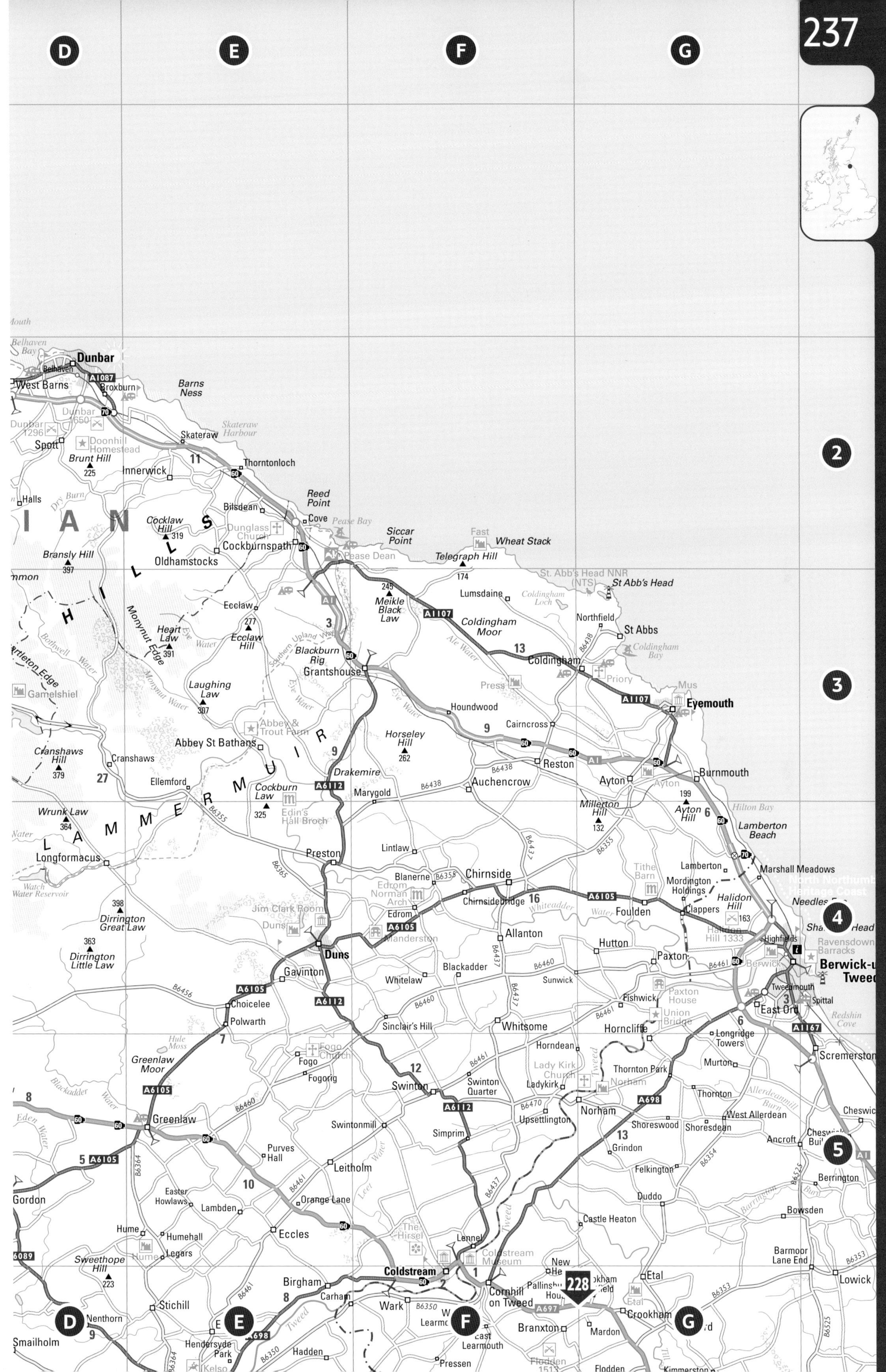

D   E   F   G

2

3

4

5

Dunbar
Belhaven
Belhaven Bay
West Barns
A1087
Broxburn
Dunbar 1650
Dunbar 1296
Spott
Doonhill Homestead
Brunt Hill 225
Skateraw
Barns Ness
Skateraw Harbour
Reed Point
11
Innerwick
Thorntonloch
Bilsdean
Cove
Pease Bay
60
Dunglass Church
Cockburnspath
Siccar Point
Fast
Wheat Stack
Cocklaw Hill 319
Oldhamstocks
Pease Dean
Telegraph Hill
174
St Abb's Head NNR (NTS)
St Abb's Head
Bransly Hill 397
IAN
Ecclaw
245
Meikle Black Law
Lumsdaine
Coldingham Loch
Northfield
St Abbs
Ecclaw Hill 277
A107
Coldingham Moor
13
Coldingham
Coldingham Bay
H
Heart Law 391
3
Blackburn Rig
Ale Water
60
Press
Mus
Eyemouth
Gamelshiel
Monynut Edge
Laughing Law 307
Grantshouse
Houndwood
A107
Cartleton Edge
Bothwell Water
Abbey & Trout Farm
M U I R
Horseley Hill 262
9
Cairncross
60
Reston
A1
60
Burnmouth
Cranshaws Hill 379
Cranshaws
Abbey St Bathans
9
Drakemire
Eye Water
Auchencrow
Ayton
Ayton
Hilton Bay
27
Ellemford
A6112
Marygold
B6438
Millerton Hill 132
199
Ayton Hill
6
60
Lamberton Beach
Wrunk Law 364
Cockburn Law 325
Edin's Hall Broch
Lintlaw
B6355
Tithe Barn
Lamberton
Mordington Holdings
Halidon Hill
Marshall Meadows
Longformacus
Preston
B6355
Blanerne
Chirnside
Edrom Norman Arch
A6105
Whiteadder Water
Foulden
Clappers
Halidon Hill 1333
163
North Northumb Heritage Coast
Needles Eye
Sh Head
Watch Water Reservoir
398
Dirrington Great Law
Jim Clark Room
Duns
Chirnsidebridge
16
Edrom
Allanton
Hutton
Paxton
Highfields
Berwick
Berwick-u Tweed
Ravensdown
363
Dirrington Little Law
Manderston
Duns
Blackadder
B6437
B6460
Sunwick
Fishwick
Paxton House
B6461
Tweedmouth
East Ord
Spittal
Sh Head
Gavinton
A6105
A6112
Whitelaw
Blackadder
Union Bridge
A1167
Redshin Cove
Choicelee
Polwarth
Sinclair's Hill
Whitsome
Horncliffe
Longridge Towers
Murton
Scremerston
7
Hule Moss
Foga Church
Fogo
Horndean
Lady Kirk Church
Ladykirk
Thornton Park
Norham
Thornton
West Allerdean
Greenlaw Moor
A6105
Fogorig
12
Swinton
Swinton Quarter
A698
Shoreswood
Shoresdean
Cheswick Bui
8
Blackadder Water
60
Greenlaw
60
Swintonmill
Simprim
A6112
Upsettlington
13
Grindon
Ancroft
Cheswick
5
A6105
B6364
Purves Hall
Leitholm
B6461
B6470
Norham
Felkington
Berrington
Gordon
10
Easter Howlaws
Lambden
Orange Lane
60
B6437
Duddo
B6354
B6525
Bowsden
6089
Hume
Humehall
Legars
Eccles
Leet Water
The Hirsel
Lennel
Castle Heaton
Barmoor Lane End
Lowick
Sweethope Hill 223
Coldstream Museum
New He
B6353
Stichill
Birgham
Carham
60
Coldstream
1
Cornhill on Tweed
228
okham field
Etal
Nenthorn
9
B6461
Wark
B6350
W Learmo
Pallinsburn Hou
A697
Crookham
rd
Smailholm
Hendersyde Park
698
Tweed
East Learmouth
Branxton
Mardon
Kelso
B6350
Hadden
Pressen
Flodden 1513
Flodden
Kimmerston

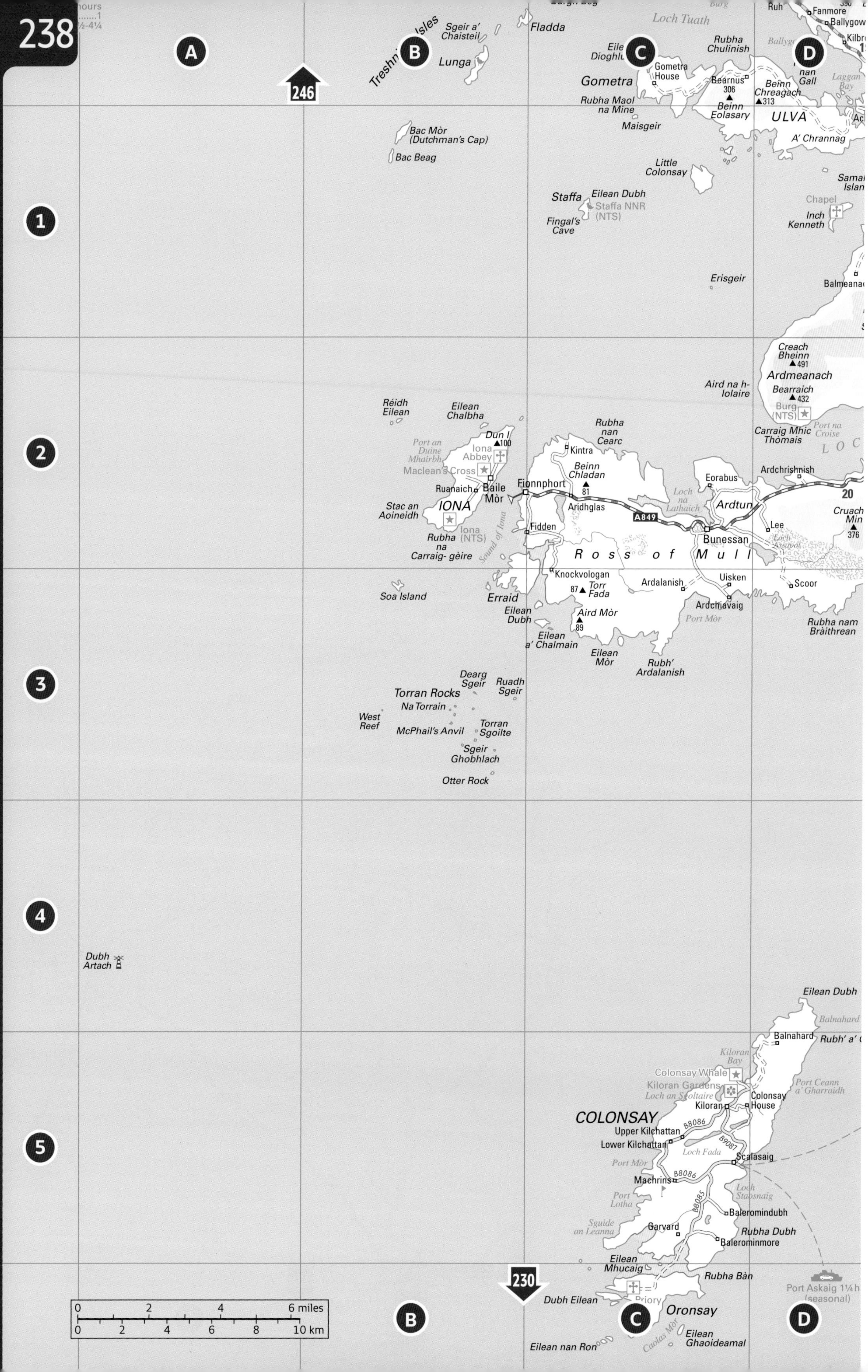

A

B

C

D

1

2

3

4

5

246

230

Treshni_ Isles
Sgeir a' Chaisteil
Lunga
Fladda

Eile Dioghlu
Gometra House
Rubha Chulinish
Ballygow
Kilbr

Ruh Fanmore

Loch Tuath

Burg

nan Gall

Laggan Bay

Gometra
Rubha Maol na Mine
Beinn Chreagach ▲313
Beinn Eolasary
306 ▲
ULVA

Maisgeir

A' Chrannag

Bac Mòr
(Dutchman's Cap)

Bac Beag

Little Colonsay

Sama Islan

Staffa
Eilean Dubh
Staffa NNR (NTS)

Fingal's Cave

Chapel
Inch Kenneth

Erisgeir

Balmeana

Creach Bheinn ▲491
Ardmeanach
Bearraich ▲432
Burg (NTS) ★

Aird na h-Iolaire

Réidh Eilean
Eilean Chalbha
Rubha nan Cearc

Carraig Mhic Thòmais

Port na Croise

LOC

Port an Duine Mhairbh
Dun I ▲100
Iona Abbey
Kintra
Beinn Chladan ▲ 81

Ardchrishnish

20

Maclean's Cross
Ruanaich
Bàile Mòr
Fionnphort
Aridhglas
A849
Ardtun
Eorabus
Loch na Lathaich
Lee
Cruach Min 376

Stac an Aoineidh
IONA ★
Fidden
Ross of Mull
Bunessan
Loch Assapol

Rubha na Carraig-gèire
Iona (NTS)

Sound of Iona

Soa Island
Erraid
Eilean Dubh
Knockvologan
Torr Fada 87 ▲
Ardalanish
Uisken
Scoor

Aird Mòr 89 ▲
Ardchiavaig
Port Mòr
Rubha nam Bràithrean

Eilean a' Chalmain
Eilean Mòr
Rubh' Ardalanish

Dearg Sgeir
Ruadh Sgeir

Torran Rocks
Na Torrain

West Reef
McPhail's Anvil
Torran Sgoilte

Sgeir Ghobhlach

Otter Rock

Dubh Artach

Eilean Dubh
Balnahard

Balnahard
Rubh' a' C

Kiloran Bay

Colonsay Whale ★
Kiloran Gardens
Loch an Stroltaire

Port Ceann a' Gharraidh

Colonsay House

Kiloran

COLONSAY
Upper Kilchattan
Lower Kilchattan
B8086
B9087
Scalasaig

Port Mòr
Loch Fada

B8086
Machrins
B8085
Baleromindubh
Loch Staosnaig

Port Lotha
Garvard
Rubha Dubh
Balerominmore

Sguide an Leanna

Eilean Mhucaig
Rubha Bàn
Port Askaig 1¼h (seasonal)

Dubh Eilean
Priory
Oronsay
Caolas Mòr

Eilean nan Ron
Eilean Ghaoideamal

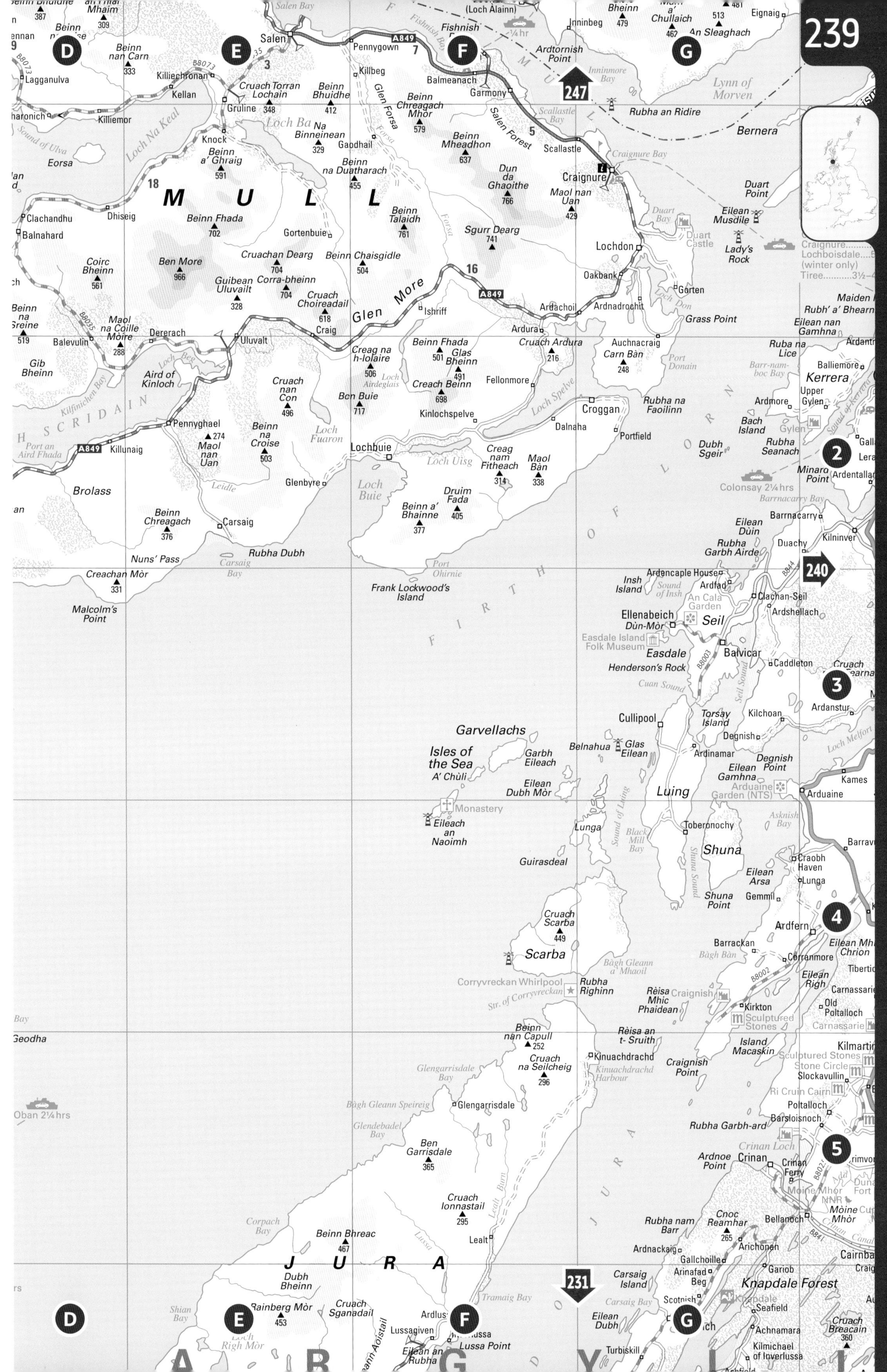

Salen Bay
(Loch Alainn)
Inninbeg
Eignaig
An Sleaghach
Salen
Pennygown
A849
Fishnish
Ardtornish Point
247
Killiechronan
Kellan
Gruline
Cruach Torran Lochain
348
Beinn Bhuidhe
412
Killbeg
Balmeanach
Garmony
Lynn of Morven
Rubha an Ridire
Bernera
Lagganulva
Killiemor
Loch Ba
Na Binneinean
329
Gaodhail
Glen Forsa
Beinn Chreagach Mhòr
579
Salen Forest
Scallastle Bay
Scallastle
Beinn Mheadhon
637
Knock
Beinn a' Ghraig
591
Loch Na Keal
Sound of Ulva
Eorsa
Beinn na Duatharach
455
Craignure Bay
Craignure
Dun da Ghaoithe
766
Maol nan Uan
429
Duart Point
MULL
Clachandhu
Dhiseig
Balnahard
Beinn Fhada
702
Beinn Talaidh
761
Gortenbuie
Sgurr Dearg
741
Duart Bay
Duart Castle
Eilean Musdile
Lady's Rock
Lochdon
Coirc Bheinn
561
Ben More
966
Cruachan Dearg
704
Beinn Chaisgidle
504
Guibean Uluvailt
328
Corra-bheinn
704
Oakbank
Gorten
Glen More
A849
Cruach Choireadail
618
Ishriff
Ardachoil
Ardnadrochit
Loch Don
Grass Point
Beinn na Sreine
519
Maol na Coille Mòire
288
Dererach
Craig
Balevulin
Uluvalt
Ardura
Cruach Ardura
216
Auchnacraig
Carn Bàn
248
Port Donain
Rubh' a' Bhearn
Eilean nan Gamhna
Ruba na Lice
Gib Bheinn
Aird of Kinloch
Loch Beg
Creag na h-Iolaire
506
Beinn Fhada
501
Glas Bheinn
491
Creach Beinn
698
Fellonmore
Balliemore
Kerrera
Upper Gylen
Cruach nan Con
496
Ben Buie
717
Kinlochspelve
Loch Spelve
Croggan
Dalnaha
Rubha na Faoilinn
Ardmore
Bach Island
Gylen
Sound of Kerrera
Pennyghael
274
Maol nan Uan
Beinn na Croise
503
Loch Fuaron
Lochbuie
Portfield
Dubh Sgeir
Rubha Seanach
Killunaig
Brolass
Leidle
Glenbyre
Loch Uisg
Loch Buie
Creag nam Fitheach
314
Maol Bàn
338
Minard Point
Ardentallan
Colonsay 2¼ hrs
Barnacarry Bay
Beinn a' Bhainne
377
Druim Fada
405
Barnacarry
Beinn Chreagach
376
Carsaig
Eilean Dùin
Rubha Garbh Airde
Duachy
Kilninver
Nuns' Pass
Carsaig Bay
Rubha Dubh
Port Ohirnie
Insh Island
Sound of Insh
Ardencaple House
Ardfad
240
Creachan Mòr
331
Frank Lockwood's Island
FIRTH OF LORN
An Cala Garden
Clachan-Seil
Ardshellach
Malcolm's Point
Ellenabeich
Dùn-Mòr
Seil
Easdale Island Folk Museum
Easdale
Balvicar
B8003
Henderson's Rock
Caddleton
Cuan Sound
Seil Sound
Ardanstur
Cullipool
Torsay Island
Kilchoan
Garvellachs
Belnahua
Glas Eilean
Degnish
Isles of the Sea
A' Chùli
Garbh Eileach
Ardinamar
Eilean Gamhna
Degnish Point
Loch Melfort
Eilean Dubh Mòr
Luing
Arduaine Garden (NTS)
Arduaine
Kames
Monastery
Eileach an Naoimh
Lunga
Sound of Luing
Black Mill Bay
Toberonochy
Asknish Bay
Shuna
Shuna Sound
Guirasdeal
Craobh Haven
Eilean Arsa
Lunga
Shuna Point
Gemmil
Barravullin
Cruach Scarba
449
Ardfern
Scarba
Barrackan
Bàgh Bàn
Corranmore
Eilean Mhic Chrion
Bàgh Gleann a' Mhaoil
Corryvreckan Whirlpool
Rubha Righinn
Str. of Corryvreckan
Eilean Righ
B8002
Rèisa Mhic Phaidean
Craignish
Kirkton
Carnassarie
Old Poltalloch
Sculptured Stones
Carnassarie
Beinn nan Capull
252
Rèisa an t-Sruith
Island Macaskin
Geodha
Cruach na Seilcheig
296
Kinuachdrachd
Kinuachdrachd Harbour
Craignish Point
Kilmartin
Sculptured Stones
Stone Circle
Slockavullin
Glengarrisdale Bay
Ri Cruin Cairn
Oban 2¼ hrs
Bàgh Gleann Speireig
Glengarrisdale
Poltalloch
Glendebadel Bay
Rubha Garbh-ard
Barsloisnoch
Ben Garrisdale
365
Crinan Loch
Ardnoe Point
Crinan
Crinan Ferry
B8025
Moine Mhor NNR
Mòine Mhòr
Dunadd Fort
Crinan Canal
Cruach Ionnastail
295
Corpach Bay
Lealt Burn
Rubha nam Barr
Cnoc Reamhar
265
Bellanoch
B841
Beinn Bhreac
467
Lealt
Lussa
Ardnackaig
Arichonan
Cairnbaan
Gallchoille
JURA
Arinafad Beg
Gariob
Craig
Dubh Bheinn
231
Carsaig Island
Knapdale Forest
Tramaig Bay
Carsaig Bay
Knapdale
Scotnish
Seafield
Shian Bay
Rainberg Mòr
453
Cruach Sganadail
Ardlussa
Eilean Dubh
Achnamara
Cruach Breacain
360
Loch Righ Mòr
Lussagiven
Lussa Point
Eilean an Rubha
Turbiskill
Kilmichael of Inverlussa
Craignure
Lochboisdale
(winter only)
Tiree
Maiden

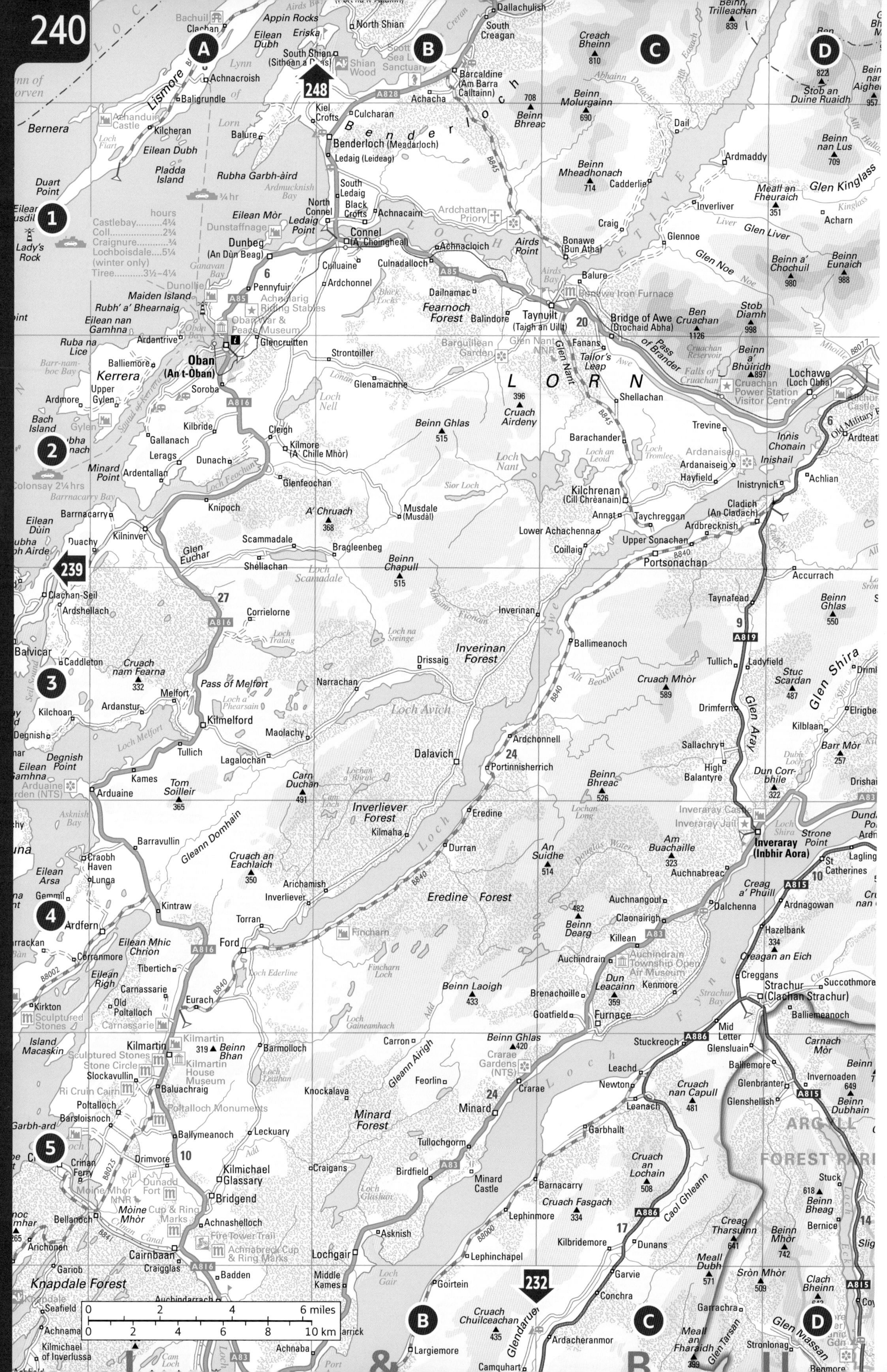
A
B
C
D
1
2
3
4
5
248
239
232
Bachuil
Clachan
Appin Rocks
Eriska
North Shian
Dallachulish
South Creagan
Eilean Dubh
South Shian (Sithean a Phris)
Shian Wood
South Sea Loch Sanctuary
Creach Bheinn
810
Lismore
Achnacroish
Baligrundle
Barcaldine (Am Barra Calltainn)
Achacha
Culcharan
Kiel Crofts
Beinn Molurgainn
690
708
Beinn Bhreac
Bernera
Achanduin Castle
Kilcheran
Eilean Dubh
Lorn
Balure
Benderloch (Meadarloch)
Ledaig (Leideag)
Benderloch
Dail
Ardmaddy
Beinn nan Lus
709
Glen Kinglass
Duart Point
Pladda Island
Rubha Garbh-àird
Ardmucknish Bay
Beinn Mheadhonach
714
Cadderlie
Meall an Fheuraich
351
Inverliver
Acharn
Lady's Rock
Castlebay 4¾
Coll 2¾
Craignure ¾
Lochboisdale 5¼
(winter only)
Tiree 3½–4¼
Eilean Mòr
Dunstaffnage
North Connel
Ledaig Point
South Ledaig
Black Crofts
Achnacairn
Ardchattan Priory
Craig
Glen Liver
Glennoe
Glen Noe
Beinn a' Chochuil
980
Beinn Eunaich
988
Dunbeg (An Dùn Beag)
Connel (A' Choingheal)
Achnacloich
Airds Point
Bonawe (Bun Atha)
Balure
Cuiluaine
Culnadalloch
Ardchonnel
Pennyfuir
Dunollie
Maiden Island
Rubh' a' Bhearnaig
Achnalarig Riding Stables
Dailnamac
Fearnoch Forest
Balindore
Taynuilt (Taigh an Uillt)
Bonawe Iron Furnace
Bridge of Awe (Drochaid Abha)
Ben Cruachan
1126
Stob Diamh
998
Eilean nan Gamhna
Oban War & Peace Museum
Ruba na Lice
Ardantrive
Oban (An t-Òban)
Glencruitten
Strontoiller
Barguillean Garden
Glen Nant NNR
Fanans
Tailor's Leap
Pass of Brander
Beinn a' Bhùiridh
897
Falls of Cruachan
Cruachan Reservoir
Cruachan Power Station Visitor Centre
Lochawe (Loch Obha)
Kerrera
Balliemore
Upper Gylen
Ardmore
Soroba
Glenamachrie
Loch Nell
LORN
396
Cruach Airdeny
Glen Nant
Shellachan
Bach Island
Gylen
Kilbride
Gallanach
Lerags
Dunach
Cleigh
Kilmore (A' Chille Mhòr)
Beinn Ghlas
515
Loch Nant
Barachander
Loch an Leoid
Loch Tromlee
Trevine
Ardanaiseig
Hayfield
Innis Chonain
Inishail
Ardteatle
Old Military Road
Minard Point
Ardentallan
Loch Feochan
Glenfeochan
Colonsay 2¼ hrs
Barnacarry Bay
Sior Loch
Kilchrenan (Cill Chrèanain)
Inistrynich
Achlian
Barrnacarry
Knipoch
A' Chruach
368
Musdale (Musdàl)
Annat
Taychreggan
Cladich (An Cladach)
Eilean Dùin
Duachy
Kilninver
Glen Euchar
Scammadale
Bragleenbeg
Lower Achachenna
Coillaig
Upper Sonachan
Ardbrecknish
Portsonachan
Shellachan
Loch Scamadale
Beinn Chapull
515
Accurrach
Clachan-Seil
Ardshellach
Corrielorne
Inverinan
Taynafead
Beinn Ghlas
550
Loch Tralaig
Loch na Sreinge
Ballimeanoch
Inverinan Forest
Balvicar
Caddleton
Cruach nam Fearna
332
Drissaig
Allt Beochlich
Tullich
Ladyfield
Cruach Mhòr
589
Stuc Scardan
487
Glen Shira
Pass of Melfort
Narrachan
Kilchoan
Ardanstur
Melfort
Loch a' Phearsain
Loch Avich
Drimfern
Glen Aray
Elrigbeg
Kilmelford
Maolachy
Ardchonnell
Kilblaan
Degnish
Loch Melfort
Tullich
Lagalochan
Dalavich
Sallachry
Barr Mòr
257
Degnish Point
Eilean Gamhna
Kames
Tom Soilleir
365
Carn Dùchan
491
Portinnisherrich
Beinn Bhreac
526
High Balantyre
Dun Corr-bhile
322
Arduaine
Arduaine Garden (NTS)
Asknish Bay
Inverliever Forest
Kilmaha
Eredine
Loch Awe
Lochan Long
Inveraray Castle
Inveraray Jail
Inveraray (Inbhir Aora)
Loch Shira
Strone Point
Barravullin
Gleann Domhain
Durran
An Suidhe
514
Am Buachaille
323
Auchnabreac
St Catherines
Craobh Haven
Lunga
Eilean Arsa
Cruach an Eachlaich
350
Arichamish
Inverliever
Eredine Forest
Creag a' Phuill
Ardnagowan
Gemmil
Kintraw
Auchnangoul
Dalchenna
Ardfern
Torran
482
Beinn Dearg
Claonairigh
Hazelbank
334
Fincharn
Killean
Eilean Mhic Chrion
Corranmore
Ford
Auchindrain
Auchindrain Township Open Air Museum
Creagan an Eich
Eilean Righ
Tibertich
Loch Ederline
Fincharn Loch
Creggans
Strachur (Clachan Strachur)
Succothmore
Carnassarie
Beinn Laoigh
433
Brenachoille
Dun Leacainn
359
Kenmore
Strachur Bay
Balliemeanoch
Kirkton
Sculptured Stones
Old Poltalloch
Eurach
Goatfield
Furnace
Loch Fyne
Carnassarie
Loch Gaineamhach
Mid Letter
Glensluain
Carnach Mòr
Island Macaskin
Kilmartin
Kilmartin Sculptured Stones
319
Beinn Bhan
Barmolloch
Carron
Beinn Ghlas
420
Crarae Gardens (NTS)
Stuckreoch
Stone Circle
Kilmartin House Museum
Slockavullin
Gleann Airigh
Feorlin
Leachd
Balliemore
Invernoaden
649
Ri Cruin Cairn
Baluachraig
Knockalava
Crarae
Newton
Glenbranter
Poltalloch
Poltalloch Monuments
Minard
Leanach
Cruach nan Capull
481
Glenshellish
Beinn Dubhain
Barsloisnoch
Ballymeanoch
Leckuary
Minard Forest
Garbhallt
ARGYLL FOREST PARK
Garbh-ard
Drimvore
Kilmichael Glassary
Tullochgorm
Cruach an Lochain
508
Crinan Ferry
Dunadd Fort
Craigans
Birdfield
Minard Castle
Barnacarry
Stuck
618
Beinn Bheag
Mòine Mhór NNR
Bridgend
Loch Glashan
Cruach Fasgach
334
Caol Ghleann
Mòine Mhòr
Cup & Ring Marks
Bellanoch
Achnashelloch
Lephinmore
Creag Tharsuinn
641
Bernice
Crinan Canal
Fire Tower Trail
Achnabreck Cup & Ring Marks
Asknish
Kilbridemore
Dunans
Beinn Mhòr
742
Arichonen
Cairnbaan
Lochgair
Lephinchapel
Loch Eck
Gariob
Craigglas
Badden
Middle Kames
Loch Gair
Goirtein
Garvie
Meall Dubh
571
Sròn Mhòr
509
Clach Bheinn
Knapdale Forest
Auchindarroch
Conchra
Seafield
Achnamara
Cruach Chuilceachan
435
Glendaruel
Garrachra
Glen Massan
Kilmichael of Inverlussa
Achnaba
Largiemore
Ardacheranmor
Meall an Fharaidh
399
Glen Tarsan
Stronlonag
Camquhart
Benmore
0 2 4 6 miles
0 2 4 6 8 10 km
A828
A85
A816
A819
A83
A815
A886
B845
B840
B8077
B8000
B8002
B8025
B841

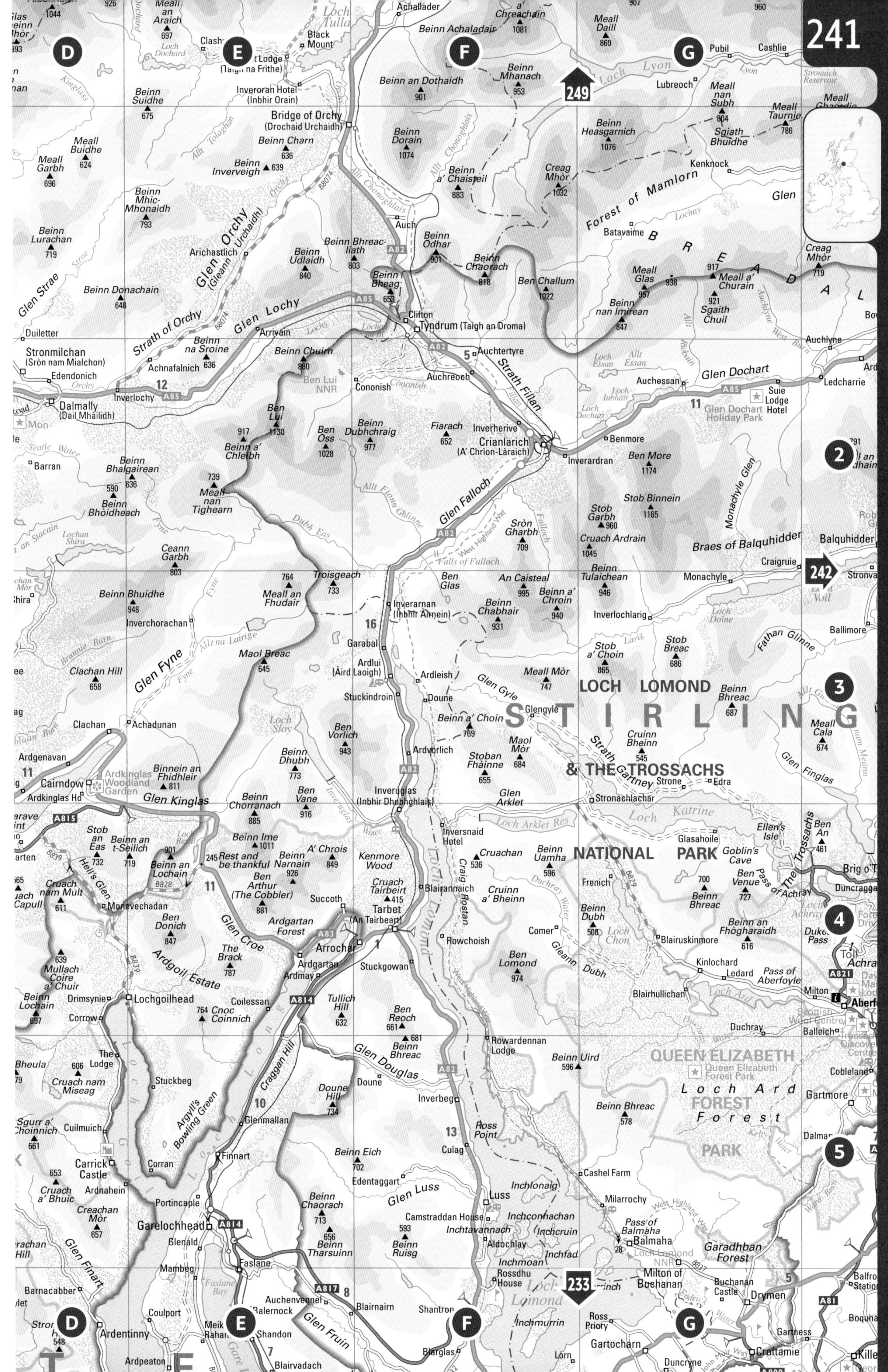

D
E
F
G
249
Loch Tulla
Achallader
Beinn Achaladair
Meall Daill
869
Pubil
Cashlie
Loch Lyon
Stronuich Reservoir
Black Mount
Clashgour
Inveroran Hotel
(Inbhir Orain)
Beinn an Dothaidh
901
Beinn Mhanach
953
Lubreoch
Meall nan Subh
804
Meall Taurnie
786
Beinn Suidhe
675
Bridge of Orchy
(Drochaid Urchaidh)
Beinn Dorain
1074
Beinn Heasgarnich
1076
Sgiath Bhuidhe
Meall Buidhe
624
Beinn Charn
636
Meall Garbh
696
Beinn Inverveigh
639
Beinn a' Chaisteil
883
Creag Mhòr
1032
Kenknock
Beinn Mhic-Mhonaidh
793
Glen Orchy
(Gleann Urchaidh)
Forest of Mamlorn
Glen Lochay
Auch
Batavaime
B R E A D A L
Beinn Lurachan
719
Arichastlich
Beinn Udlaidh
840
Beinn Bhreac-liath
803
Beinn Odhar
901
Beinn Chaorach
818
Meall Glas
957
938
917
Meall a' Churain
921
Sgaith Chuil
Creag Mhòr
719
Glen Strae
Beinn Donachain
648
Beinn Bheag
653
A82
A85
Ben Challum
1022
Beinn nan Imirean
847
Auchlyne
Duiletter
Stronmilchan
(Sròn nam Mialchon)
Edendonich
Strath of Orchy
Glen Lochy
Arrivain
Clifton
Tyndrum (Taigh an Droma)
Auchtertyre
Strath Fillan
Loch Essan
Allt Essan
Glen Dochart
Auchessan
Ledcharrie
Beinn na Sroine
636
Achnafalnich
Beinn Chuirn
880
Ben Lui NNR
Cononish
Auchreoch
Loch Iubhair
Suie Lodge Hotel
Glen Dochart Holiday Park
12
Dalmally
(Dail Mhàilidh)
Inverlochy
Ben Lui
1130
Beinn Dubhchraig
977
Ben Oss
1028
Fiarach
652
Inverherive
Crianlarich
(A' Chrìon-Làraich)
Benmore
Inverardran
Ben More
1174
Barran
Beinn Bhalgairean
636
917
Beinn a' Chleibh
590
Beinn Bhoidheach
739
Meall nan Tighearn
Glen Falloch
Stob Binnein
1165
Stob Garbh
960
Cruach Ardrain
1045
Monachyle Glen
Braes of Balquhidder
Balquhidder
Sròn Gharbh
709
Falls of Falloch
West Highland Way
Craigruie
242
Stronvar
Monachyle
Ceann Garbh
803
764
Troisgeach
733
Meall an Fhudair
Ben Glas
An Caisteal
995
Beinn a' Chroin
940
Beinn Tulaichean
946
Loch Voil
Beinn Bhuidhe
948
Inverarnan
(Inbhir Àirnein)
Beinn Chabhair
931
Inverlochlarig
Loch Doine
Ballimore
Inverchorachan
16
Garabal
Stob a' Choin
865
Stob Breac
686
Fathan Glinne
Maol Breac
645
Ardlui
(Àird Laoigh)
Ardleish
Meall Mòr
747
LOCH LOMOND
Clachan Hill
658
Glen Fyne
Stuckindroin
Doune
Glen Gyle
Beinn Bhreac
687
Glengyle
STIRLING
Achadunan
Clachan
Loch Sloy
Ben Vorlich
943
Beinn a' Choin
769
Maol Mòr
684
Cruinn Bheinn
545
Meall Cala
674
Ardgenavan
Beinn Dubh
773
Ardvorlich
Stoban Fhàinne
655
Strath Gartney
& THE TROSSACHS
Glen Finglas
11
Cairndow
Ardkinglas Woodland Garden
Binnein an Fhidhleir
811
Strone
Edra
Ardkinglas Ho
Glen Kinglas
Beinn Chorranach
885
Ben Vane
916
Inveruglas
(Inbhir Dhubhghlais)
Glen Arklet
Stronachlachar
Loch Katrine
Ellen's Isle
Ben An
461
A815
Stob an Eas
732
Beinn an t-Seilich
719
Beinn Ime
1011
Loch Arklet Res
Inversnaid Hotel
Glasahoile
The Trossachs
901
245
Rest and be thankful
Beinn Narnain
926
A' Chrois
849
Kenmore Wood
Cruachan
536
Beinn Uamha
596
NATIONAL PARK
Goblin's Cave
Brig o' Turk
Hell's Glen
Beinn an Lochain
Ben Arthur
(The Cobbler)
881
Craig Rostan
Frenich
700
Ben Venue
727
Pass of Achray
Duncraggan
Cruach nam Mult
611
B828
11
Succoth
Cruach Tairbeirt
415
Blairannaich
Cruinn a' Bheinn
Beinn Bhreac
Loch Achray
Monevechadan
Glen Croe
Tarbet
(An Tairbeart)
Beinn Dubh
508
Loch Chon
Beinn an Fhògharaidh
616
4
Duke's Pass
Ben Donich
847
Ardgartan Forest
A83
Arrochar
Comer
Blairuskinmore
639
Mullach Coire a' Chuir
The Brack
787
Ardgoil Estate
Ardgartan
Ardmay
Stuckgowan
Rowchoish
Ben Lomond
974
Gleann Dubh
Kinlochard
Ledard
Pass of Aberfoyle
Loch Ard
Milton
Aberfoyle
A821
Beinn Lochain
697
Drimsynie
Lochgoilhead
Corrow
764
Cnoc Coinnich
Coilessan
A814
Tullich Hill
632
Ben Reoch
661
681
Blairhullichan
Duchray
Balleich
Scottish Wool Centre
The Lodge
Beinn Bhreac
Rowardennan Lodge
Beinn Uird
596
QUEEN ELIZABETH
Queen Elizabeth Forest Park
Cobleland
Beinn Bheula
606
Cruach nam Miseag
Stuckbeg
Craggan Hill
Glen Douglas
Doune
Doune Hill
734
Inverbeg
A82
Loch Ard Forest
FOREST
Gartmore
Argyll's Bowling Green
Loch Long
Loch Goil
10
Glenmallan
Beinn Bhreac
578
Sgurr a' Choinnich
661
Cuilmuich
13
Ross Point
Culag
Dalmary
PARK
5
Carrick Castle
Corran
Finnart
Beinn Eich
702
Edentaggart
Cashel Farm
653
Cruach a' Bhuic
Ardnahein
Portincaple
Beinn Chaorach
713
Glen Luss
Luss
Inchlonaig
Milarrochy
Creachan Mòr
657
Garelochhead
A814
656
Beinn Tharsuinn
593
Beinn Ruisg
Camstraddan House
Inchconnachan
Inchtavannach
Inchcruin
Pass of Balmaha
Balmaha
Garadhban Forest
Glen Finart
Glenald
Faslane
Aldochlay
Inchfad
Loch Lomond NNR
Mambeg
Faslane Bay
A817
8
Inchmoan
Rossdhu House
233
Milton of Buchanan
Buchanan Castle
Drymen
Balfron Station
Barnacabber
Auchenvennel
Balernock
Blairnairn
Shantron
Loch Lomond
A81
Coulport
Glen Fruin
Inchmurrin
Ross Priory
Boquhan
548
Ardentinny
Meikle Rahane
Shandon
7
Gartness
Ardpeaton
Blairvadach
Blarglas
Gartochan
Lorn
Duncryne
Croftamie
Killearn
2
3

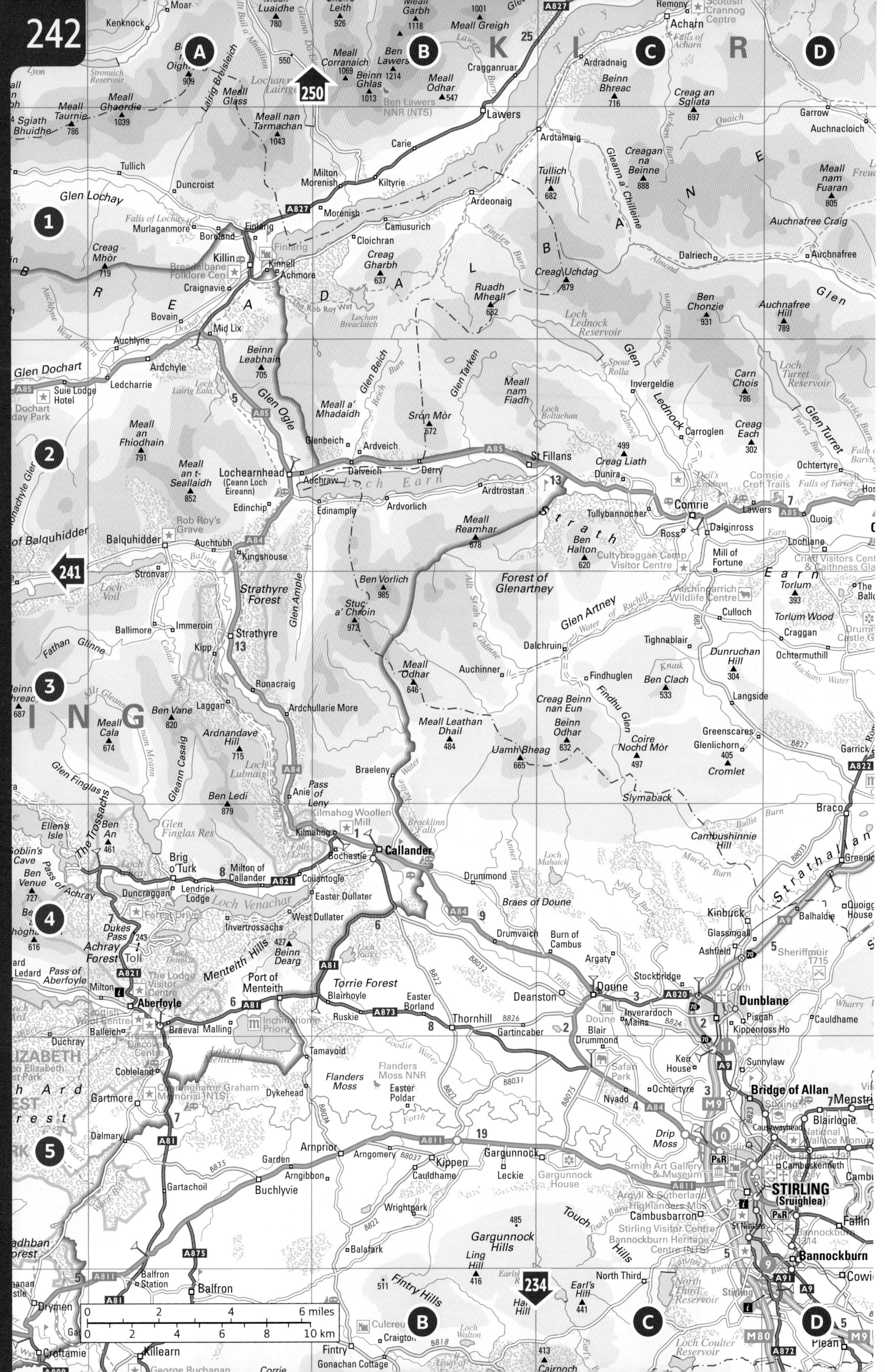

A
B
C
D
1
2
3
4
5
250
241
234
Moar
Kenknock
Luaidhe 780
Leith 926
Meall Garbh 1118
1001
Meall Greigh
A827
Remony
Scottish Crannog Centre
Acharn
Falls of Acharn
K
I
R
25
Lawers
Cragganruar
Ardradnaig
Beinn Bhreac 716
Creag an Sgliata 697
Quaich
Garrow
Auchnacloich
Lairig Breisleich
Stronuich Reservoir
Meall Ghaordie 1039
Meall Taurnie 786
Sgiath Bhuidhe
Meall Glass
Lochan na Lairige
Meall Corranaich 1069
Ben Lawers 1214
Beinn Ghlas 1013
Meall Odhar 547
Ben Lawers NNR (NTS)
Meall nan Tarmachan 1043
Carie
Ardtalnaig
Creagan na Beinne 888
Glenn a' Chilleine
Tullich Hill 682
Meall nam Fuaran 805
Auchnafree Craig
Tullich
Duncroist
Glen Lochay
Milton Morenish
Kiltyrie
A827
Morenish
Ardeonaig
Camusurich
Falls of Lochay
Murlaganmore
Boreland
Finlarig
Cloichran
Killin
Kinnell
Achmore
Breadalbane Folklore Cen
Creag Mhòr 719
Creag Gharbh 637
Finglen Burn
Dalriech
Auchnafree
Almond
Craignavie
The Rob Roy Way
Lochan Breaclaich
Ruadh Mheall 682
Creag Uchdag 879
Ben Chonzie 931
Auchnafree Hill 789
Glen
Bovain
Mid Lix
Auchlyne
Loch Lednock Reservoir
Glen Dochart
Ardchyle
Beinn Leabhain 705
Glen Beich
Glen Tarken
Spout Rolla
Loch Turret Reservoir
Carn Chois 786
A85
Suie Lodge Hotel
Ledcharrie
Lairig Eala
Loch Eala
Glen Ogle
Meall nam Fiadh
Invergeldie
Lednock
Glen Turret
Dochart Holiday Park
Meall a' Mhadaidh
Sròn Mòr 672
Loch Boltachan
Carroglen
Creag Each 302
Meall an Fhiodhain 791
Glenbeich
Ardveich
A85
St Fillans
499
Creag Liath
Ochtertyre
Meall an t-Seallaidh 852
Lochearnhead (Ceann Loch Eireann)
Dalveich
Derry
Auchraw
Loch Earn
Dunira
Deil's Cauldron
Comrie Croft Trails
Falls of Turret
Ardtrostan
13
Comrie
Lawers
A85
7
Quoig
Edinchip
Edinample
Ardvorlich
Meall Reamhar 678
Strath
Tullybannocher
Ross
Dalginross
Earn
Lochlane
Balquhidder
Rob Roy's Grave
Auchtubh
A84
Kingshouse
Ben Halton 620
Cultybraggan Camp Visitor Centre
Mill of Fortune
Crieff Visitors Centre & Caithness Glass
Braes of Balquhidder
Stronvar
Balvag
Loch Voil
Strathyre Forest
Glen Ample
Ben Vorlich 985
Forest of Glenartney
Auchingarrich Wildlife Centre
Earn
Torlum 393
Stuc a' Chroin 972
Glen Artney
Water of Ruchill
Culloch
Torlum Wood
Ballimore
Immeroin
Strathyre
13
Kipp
Fathan Glinne
Calair Burn
Dalchruin
Tighnablair
Craggan
Ochtermuthill
B827
Meall Odhar 646
Auchinner
Allt Srath a' Ghlinne
Findhuglen
Knaik
Ben Clach 533
Dunruchan Hill 304
Machany Water
Runacraig
Langside
Laggan
Ardchullarie More
Ben Vane 820
Meall Cala 674
Glen Finglas
Gleann Casaig
Ardnandave Hill 715
Meall Leathan Dhail 484
Creag Beinn nan Eun
Beinn Odhar 632
Findhu Glen
Coire Nochd Mòr 497
Greenscares
Glenlichorn
405
Cromlet
B827
Garrick
A822
Uamh Bheag 665
Loch Lubnaig
A84
Braeleny
Keltie Water
Slymaback
Anie
Pass of Leny
Ben Ledi 879
Braco
Ellen's Isle
The Trossachs
Ben An 461
Glen Finglas Res
Kilmahog Woollen Mill
Kilmahog
Falls of Leny
Bracklinn Falls
Bullie Burn
Cambushinnie Hill
Strathallan
Greenloaning
Goblin's Cave
Ben Venue 727
Pass of Achray
Loch Achray
Brig o'Turk
Milton of Callander
A821
Bochastle
Callander
Coilantogle
Loch Mahaick
Annet Burn
Drummond
Muckle Burn
B8033
Duncraggan
Lendrick Lodge
Loch Venachar
Easter Dullater
West Dullater
Ardoch Burn
Braes of Doune
Kinbuck
A9
Balhaldie
Quoigs House
Achray Forest
Dukes Pass 243
Forest Drive
Invertrossachs
Menteith Hills
427 Beinn Dearg
A84
9
Drumvaich
Burn of Cambus
Glassingall
Ashfield
Sheriffmuir 1715
Ledard
Pass of Aberfoyle
Toll
A821
The Lodge Visitor Centre
Loch Drunkie
Loch Rusky
Port of Menteith
A81
Torrie Forest
B8032
B822
Argaty
Stockbridge
Teith
Milton
Aberfoyle
A81
Blairhoyle
Easter Borland
Deanston
Doune
A820
Cath
Dunblane
Wharry Burn
Cauldhame
Scottish Wool Centre
Balleich
Braeval
Malling
Inchmahome Priory
Ruskie
A873
Thornhill
B826
Gartincaber
Doune Castle
Inveraddoch Mains
B824
Pisgah
Kippenross Ho
Duchray
Trossachs Discovery Centre
Lake of Menteith
Tamavoid
Goodie Water
Blair Drummond
Elizabeth
Queen Elizabeth Forest Park
Cobleland
Flanders Moss
Flanders Moss NNR
B8031
Safari Park
Keir House
A9
Sunnylaw
Loch Ard Forest
Gartmore
Cunninghame Graham Memorial (NTS)
Dykehead
Easter Poldar
B822
B8075
Nyadd
Ochtertyre
Bridge of Allan
Menstrie
Forth
B8034
A84
M9
B823
Blairlogie
Dalmary
Drip Moss
Causewayhead
National Wallace Monument
A81
Arnprior
A811
19
Gargunnock
Stirling
Cambuskenneth Abbey
B835
Garden
Arngomery
B8037
Kippen
Smith Art Gallery & Museum
Arngibbon
Cauldhame
Leckie
Gargunnock House
A811
Gartachoil
Buchlyvie
STIRLING (Sruighlea)
Argyll & Sutherland Highlanders Mus
Cambusbarron
Wrightpark
Touch Hills
Touch Burn
Fallin
485
Stirling Visitor Centre
Bannockburn Heritage Centre (NTS)
St Ninians
Bannockburn 1314
Bannockburn
B822
Gargunnock Hills
Balafark
Ling Hill 416
A875
Earlsburn Reservoirs
North Third
North Third Reservoir
Cowie
Balfron Station
Balfron
A811
Drymen
A81
Fintry Hills
511
Earl's Hill 441
Hart Hill
Culcreuch
Craigton
Loch Walton
B818
Fintry
Gonachan Cottage
Loup of Fintry
413
Cairnoch
Earl's Burn
Loch Coulter Reservoir
M80
A872
Plean
M9
A91
A9
Killearn
Croftamie
Corrie
Glengoyne
Garth
0 2 4 6 miles
0 2 4 6 8 10 km

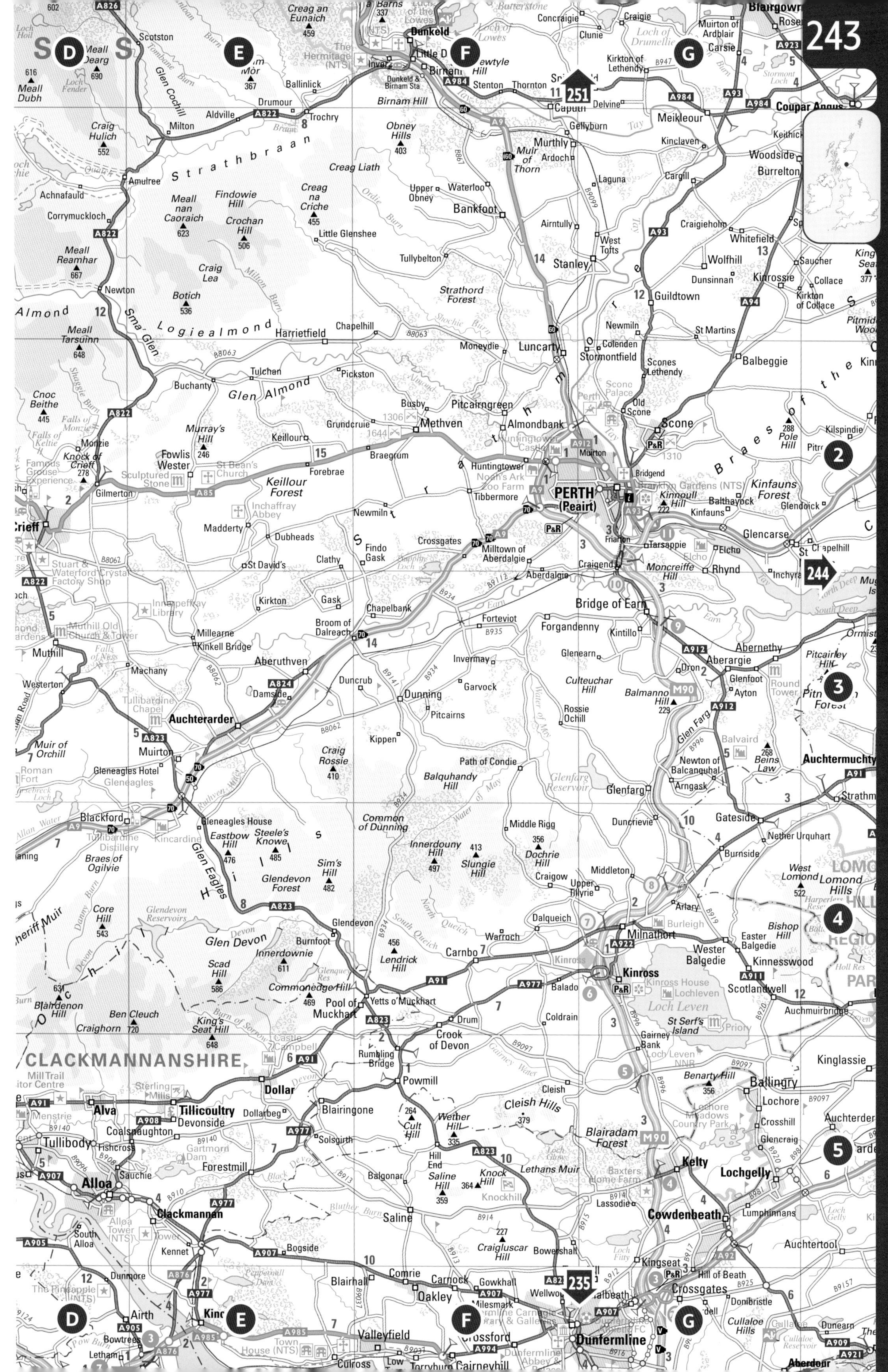
D
E
F
G
251
244
235
2
3
4
5
Dunkeld
Birnam
Little Dunkeld
Inver
Dunkeld & Birnam Sta
The Hermitage (NTS)
Creag an Eunaich
459
Meall Dearg
690
Meall Dubh
616
Scotston
Glen Cochill
Milton
Aldville
Drumour
Trochry
Ballinlick
Birnam Hill
Craig Hulich
552
Amulree
Strathbraan
Achnafauld
Corrymuckloch
Meall nan Caoraich
623
Findowie Hill
Crochan Hill
506
Creag na Criche
455
Creag Liath
Little Glenshee
Obney Hills
403
Upper Obney
Waterloo
Bankfoot
Meall Reamhar
667
Craig Lea
Botich
536
Newton
Sma' Glen
Logiealmond
Almond
Meall Tarsuinn
648
Harrietfield
Chapelhill
Moneydie
Luncarty
Tullybelton
Strathord Forest
Stenton
Thornton
Caputh
Gellyburn
Murthly
Ardoch
Muir of Thorn
Laguna
Airntully
West Tofts
Stanley
Concraigie
Clunie
Craigie
Loch of Drumellie
Blairgowrie
Rosemount
Muirton of Ardblair
Carsie
Kirkton of Lethendy
Delvine
Meikleour
Coupar Angus
Keithick
Kinclaven
Woodside
Burrelton
Cargill
Craigieholm
Whitefield
Wolfhill
Dunsinnan
Saucher
Kinrossie
Collace
Kirkton of Collace
Guildtown
Newmiln
St Martins
Colenden
Stormontfield
Scones Lethendy
Balbeggie
Scone Palace
Old Scone
Scone
Pole Hill
288
Kilspindie
Pitroddie
Braes of the Carse
Kinfauns Forest
Glendoick
Glencarse
St Madoes
Chapelhill
Inchyra
Tulchan
Buchanty
Glen Almond
Pickston
Busby
Pitcairngreen
Almondbank
Methven
Grundcruie
Keillour
Murray's Hill
246
Cnoc Beithe
445
Falls of Monzie
Falls of Keltie
Monzie
Knock of Crieff
278
Famous Grouse Experience
Gilmerton
Crieff
Fowlis Wester
Sculptured Stone
St Bean's Church
Keillour Forest
Forebrae
Braegrum
Huntingtower
Huntingtower Castle
Noah's Ark Zoo Farm
Tibbermore
PERTH (Peairt)
Muirton
Bridgend
Branklyn Gardens (NTS)
Kinnoull Hill
222
Balthayock
Kinfauns
Friarton
Tarsappie
Elcho
Rhynd
Moncreiffe Hill
Craigend
Aberdalgie
Milltown of Aberdalgie
Crossgates
Findo Gask
Newmiln
Inchaffray Abbey
Madderty
Dubheads
St David's
Clathy
Stuart & Waterford Crystal Factory Shop
Innerpeffray Library
Kirkton
Gask
Chapelbank
Broom of Dalreach
Muthill Old Church & Tower
Muthill
Millearne
Kinkell Bridge
Forteviot
Forgandenny
Bridge of Earn
Kintillo
Abernethy
Aberargie
Pitcairley Hill
Round Tower
Pitmedden Forest
Glenfoot
Ayton
Dron
Glenearn
Culteuchar Hill
Balmanno Hill
229
Rossie Ochill
Invermay
Garvock
Aberuthven
Machany
Westerton
Duncrub
Dunning
Pitcairns
Damside
Auchterarder
Tullibardine Chapel
Kippen
Muir of Orchill
Muirton
Roman Fort
Gleneagles Hotel
Gleneagles
Craig Rossie
410
Path of Condie
Balquhandy Hill
Glenfarg Reservoir
Glenfarg
Glen Farg
Balvaird
Beins Law
268
Newton of Balcanquhal
Arngask
Auchtermuchty
Strathmiglo
Blackford
Tullibardine Distillery
Kincardine
Gleneagles House
Eastbow Hill
476
Steele's Knowe
485
Braes of Ogilvie
Common of Dunning
Innerdouny Hill
497
Slungie Hill
413
Middle Rigg
Dochrie Hill
356
Duncrievie
Gateside
Nether Urquhart
Burnside
West Lomond
Lomond Hills
522
Sim's Hill
482
Glendevon Forest
Glen Eagles
Ochil Hills
Craigow
Middleton
Upper Tillyrie
Arlary
Bishop Hill
Easter Balgedie
Wester Balgedie
Kinnesswood
Core Hill
543
Glendevon Reservoirs
Glendevon
Glen Devon
Burnfoot
Innerdownie
611
Lendrick Hill
456
Carnbo
Warroch
Dalqueich
Milnathort
Burleigh
Kinross
Balado
Kinross House
Lochleven
Loch Leven
Scotlandwell
Auchmuirbridge
Scad Hill
586
Commonedge Hill
469
Yetts o' Muckhart
Pool of Muckhart
Blairdenon Hill
631
Ben Cleuch
720
Craighorn
King's Seat Hill
648
Castle Campbell
Drum
Coldrain
St Serf's Island
Priory
Gairney Bank
Loch Leven NNR
Crook of Devon
Rumbling Bridge
CLACKMANNANSHIRE
Mill Trail Visitor Centre
Sterling Mills
Dollar
Powmill
Cleish
Cleish Hills
379
Benarty Hill
356
Ballingry
Lochore
Kinglassie
Lochore Meadows Country Park
Crosshill
Glencraig
Auchterderran
Alva
Menstrie
Tillicoultry
Dollarbeg
Devonside
Blairingone
Cult Hill
264
Wether Hill
335
Blairadam Forest
Coalsnaughton
Tullibody
Fishcross
Gartmorn Dam
Solsgirth
Forestmill
Hill End
Saline Hill
359
Knock Hill
364
Knockhill
Lethans Muir
Baxters Home Farm
Kelty
Lochgelly
Alloa
Sauchie
Balgonar
Lassodie
Cowdenbeath
Lumphinnans
Clackmannan
Alloa Tower (NTS)
Tower
South Alloa
Saline
Craigluscar Hill
227
Bowershall
Kingseat
Auchtertool
Kennet
Bogside
Hill of Beath
Crossgates
Dunmore
The Pineapple (NTS)
Blairhall
Comrie
Carnock
Oakley
Gowkhall
Milesmark
Wellwood
Dunfermline Carnegie Library & Galleries
Dunfermline
Dunfermline Abbey
Donibristle
Cullaloe Hills
Cullaloe Reservoir
Dunearn
Aberdour
Airth
Kincardine
Bowtrees
Letham
Valleyfield
Crossford
Culross
Torryburn
Cairneyhill
Town House (NTS)

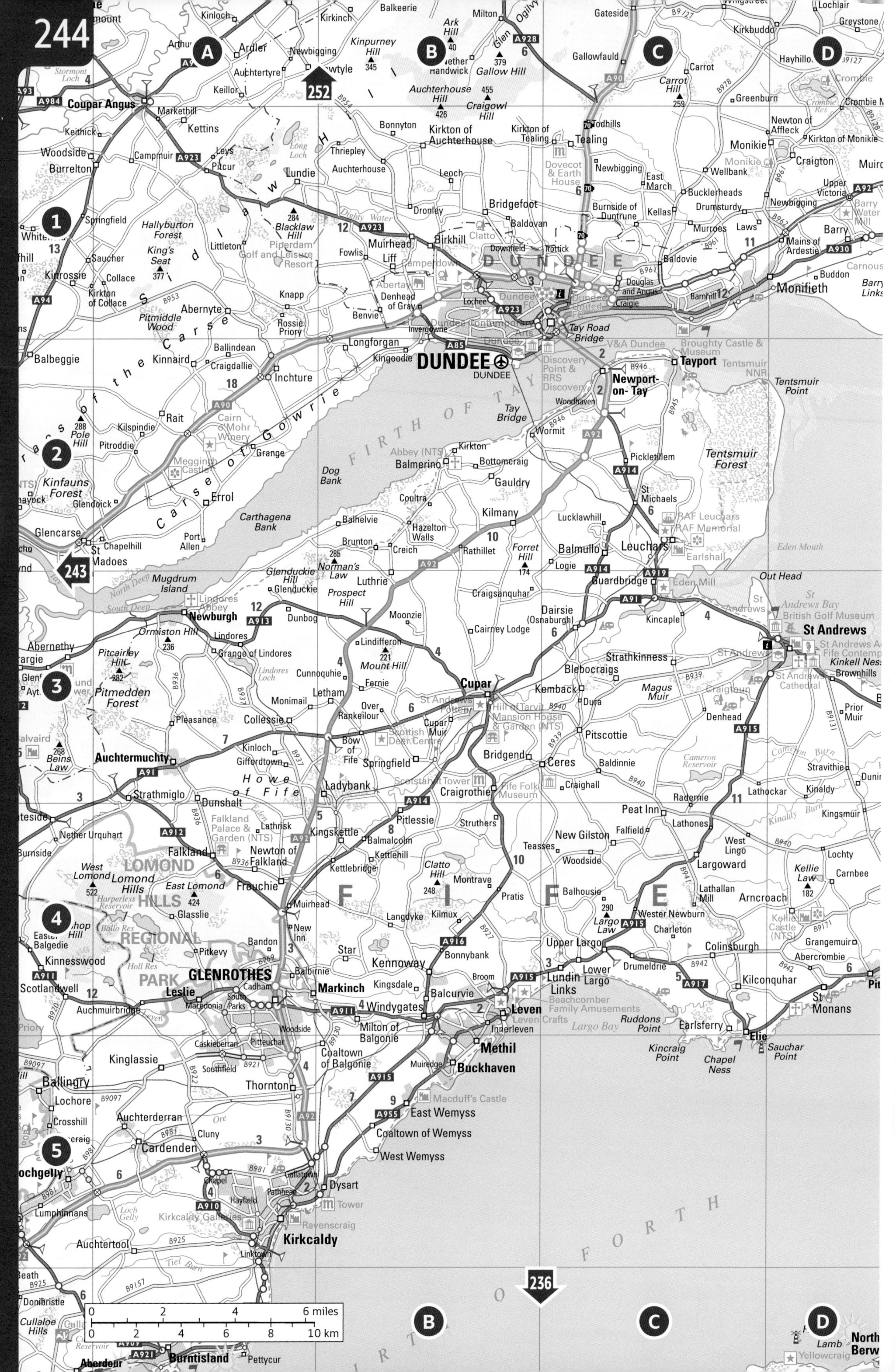
A
B
C
D
252
Kinloch
Kirkinch
Balkeerie
Milton
Gateside
Lochlair
Greystone
Ardler
Newbigging
Kinpurney Hill 345
Ark Hill
Glen Ogilvy
A928
Gallowfauld
Kirkbuddo
Hayhillock
Auchtertyre
Keillor
Nether Handwick
Gallow Hill 379
Carrot
Carrot Hill 259
Crombie
Greenburn
Crombie Res
Stormont Loch
A93
A984
Coupar Angus
Markethill
Kettins
Auchterhouse Hill 426
455
Craigowl Hill
A90
Todhills
Newton of Affleck
Kirkton of Monikie
Keithick
Bonnyton
Kirkton of Auchterhouse
Kirkton of Tealing
Tealing
Monikie
Craigton
Woodside
Campmuir
A923
Leys
Long Loch
Thriepley
Dovecot & Earth House
Newbigging
East March
Wellbank
Burrelton
Pitcur
Lundie
Auchterhouse
Leoch
Bucklerheads
Upper Victoria
A92
Bridgefoot
Burnside of Duntrune
Drumsturdy
Newbigging
Barry Water Mill
1
Springfield
Hallyburton Forest
284
Blacklaw Hill
12
Dighty Water
Dronley
Baldovan
Kellas
Murroes
Laws
Barry
Mains of Ardestie
13
Saucher
King's Seat 377
Littleton
Piperdam Golf and Leisure Resort
Fowlis
Muirhead
Liff
Birkhill
Clatto
Downfield
Rottick
DUNDEE
Baldovie
11
A930
Carnoustie
Kinrossie
Collace
Kirkton of Collace
Camperdown
Douglas and Angus
Buddon
Monifieth
Barry Links
A94
B953
Sidlaw Hills
Abernyte
Knapp
Abertay
Denhead of Gray
Lochee
Dundee FC
Dundee United FC
Craigie
Barnhill
Pitmiddle Wood
Rossie Priory
Benvie
Invergowrie
Dundee Contemporary Arts
Tay Road Bridge
V&A Dundee
Broughty Castle & Museum
Balbeggie
Carse of Gowrie
Kinnaird
Ballindean
Craigdallie
Longforgan
Kingoodie
A85
DUNDEE
Discovery Point & RRS Discovery
Tayport
Tentsmuir NNR
Tentsmuir Point
Inchture
Newport-on-Tay
Woodhaven
18
Braes of the Carse
288 Pole Hill
Rait
Cairn o'Mohr Winery
FIRTH OF TAY
Tay Bridge
Wormit
Kilspindie
2
Pitroddie
Grange
Abbey (NTS)
Kirkton
Balmerino
Bottomcraig
Pickletillem
Tentsmuir Forest
Megginch Castle
Dog Bank
Gauldry
A914
Kinfauns Forest
Glendoick
Errol
Coultra
St Michaels
Kilmany
RAF Leuchars
RAF Memorial
Lucklawhill
Glencarse
Carthagena Bank
Balhelvie
Hazelton Walls
10
Port Allen
St Madoes
Chapelhill
Brunton
Creich
285 Norman's Law
Rathillet
Forret Hill 174
Balmullo
Leuchars
Earlshall
Eden Mouth
243
Logie
A919
Eden Mill
Outhead
Mugdrum Island
North Deep
South Deep
Glenduckie Hill
Glenduckie
Luthrie
Prospect Hill
Craigsanquhar
Guardbridge
A91
St Andrews Bay
British Golf Museum
Lindores Abbey
12
Newburgh
A913
Dunbog
Moonzie
Dairsie (Osnaburgh)
Kincaple
Ormiston Hill
236
Cairney Lodge
6
St Andrews
Abernethy
Lindores
Lindifferon
Mount Hill 221
St Andrews Aquarium
Fife Contemporary
Kinkell Ness
Grange of Lindores
Pitcairlie Hill
282
Lindores Loch
Cunnoquhie
Fernie
Strathkinness
Blebocraigs
St Andrews Cathedral
Brownhills
3
Pitmedden Forest
Cupar
Kemback
Magus Muir
Craigtoun
B939
Monimail
Letham
St Andrews Pottery
Dura
Denhead
Prior Muir
B936
B937
Collessie
Over Rankeilour
Hill of Tarvit Mansion House & Garden (NTS)
B940
Pleasance
Cupar Muir
Pitscottie
Scottish Deer Centre
A915
268 Beins Law
Auchtermuchty
Kinloch
Giffordtown
Bow of Fife
Springfield
Bridgend
Ceres
Baldinnie
Cameron Reservoir
Stravithie
Dunino
Howe of Fife
Scotstarvit Tower
Craighall
A91
3
Strathmiglo
Ladybank
Craigrothie
Fife Folk Museum
Lathockar
Kinaldy
Dunshalt
A914
Radernie
Peat Inn
Kingsmuir
Nether Urquhart
Falkland Palace & Garden (NTS)
Lathrisk
Pitlessie
Struthers
Falfield
Lathones
Burnside
A912
Kingskettle
Balmalcolm
New Gilston
Teasses
West Lingo
Lochty
Falkland
Newton of Falkland
Kettlehill
Woodside
Largoward
West Lomond 522
LOMOND HILLS REGIONAL PARK
East Lomond 424
Kettlebridge
Clatto Hill 248
Montrave
Kellie Law 182
Carnbee
Freuchie
FIFE
Pratis
Balhousie
Lathallan Mill
Arncroach
4
Harperleas Reservoir
Glasslie
Muirhead
290 Largo Law
Wester Newburn
Kellie Castle (NTS)
Bishop Hill
Bishop Res
Kilmux
Langdyke
Charleton
Easter Balgedie
New Inn
Bandon
Pitkevy
Star
Bonnybank
Upper Largo
Colinsburgh
Grangemuir
A911
Kinnesswood
Holl Res
A916
Abercrombie
GLENROTHES
Balbirnie
Kennoway
Broom
Lower Largo
Drumeldrie
6
Leslie
Cadham
Markinch
Kingsdale
Lundin Links
A917
Kilconquhar
Scotlandwell
South Parks
Windygates
Balcurvie
Beachcomber Family Amusements
St Monans
Auchmuirbridge
Maredonia
Leven
Leven Crafts
Largo Bay
Ruddons Point
Earlsferry
Elie
Woodside
Milton of Balgonie
Methil
Innerleven
Caskieberran
Pitteuchar
Coaltown of Balgonie
Kincraig Point
Chapel Ness
Saucher Point
Kinglassie
B921
Southfield
Muiredge
Buckhaven
B9097
B922
Ballingry
Lochore
Thornton
A915
Macduff's Castle
Crosshill
Auchterderran
Ore
East Wemyss
A955
Coaltown of Wemyss
5
Cluny
Cardenden
West Wemyss
Lochgelly
Chapel
Gallatown
Dysart
Pathhead
A910
Hayfield
Tower
Lumphinnans
Loch Gelly
Kirkcaldy Galleries
Ravenscraig
Auchtertool
Kirkcaldy
B925
Tiel Burn
Linktown
FIRTH OF FORTH
B9157
236
Donibristle
0 2 4 6 miles
0 2 4 6 8 10 km
Cullaloe Hills
Cullaloe Reservoir
Aberdour
A921
Burntisland
Pettycur
Lamb
North Berwick
Yellowcraig

Redford
Marywell
A933
Meg's
Craig
St Vigeans
Carmylie
Denhead of
birlot
A92
Carlingheugh
Bay
D
E
F
G
Guynd
B9127
The Deil's Heid
Mill
Arbirlot
Arbroath Abbey
Bonnyton
Easter
Knox
Arbroath
Salmond's Muir
Elliot
A92
6
Drum
Salmond's Muir
2
Panbride
East Haven
Carnoustie

Buddon Ness

253

Bell Rock
(Inchcape)

2

quarium
orary Art & Craft

Buddo Ness
oarhills
Babbet Ness
10
A917
Kingsbarns
Distillery &
Visitor Centre
Kingsbarns
Cambo
Ness
North
Carr
Cambo
Estate
Tullybothy Craigs
Wormiston
Craighead
B940
Fife Ness
Airdrie
B9171
Crail
4
West Ness
Spalefield
A917
Innergellie
Kilrenny
Cellardyke
Anstruther
Scottish Fisheries Museum
tenweem

3

4

North Ness
Isle of May NNR
Isle of May
Chapel
South Ness

5

237

Craigl
D
E
F
G
Bass Rock
ick
Scottish
Seabird
Centre

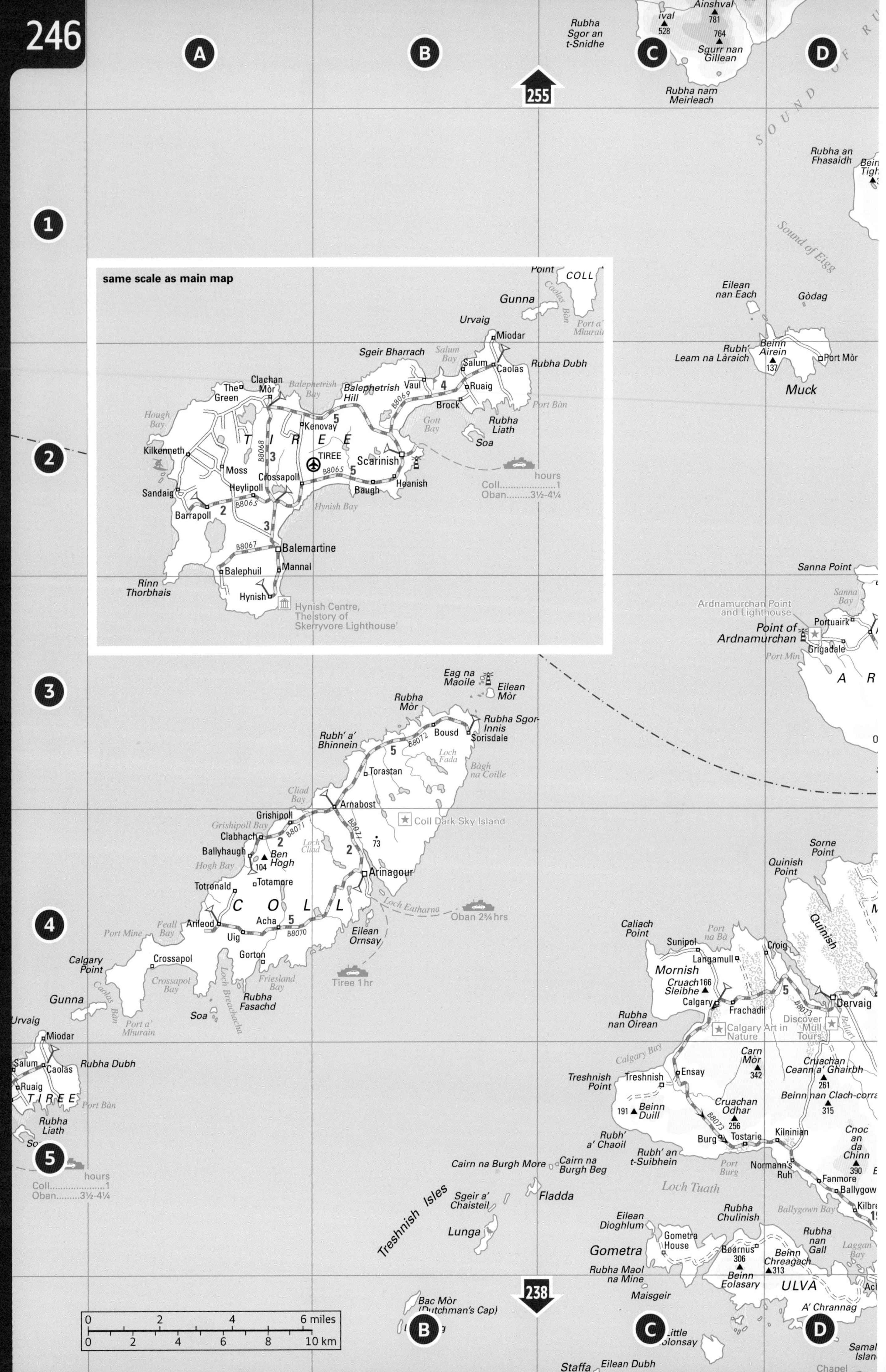

A   B   C   D

255

1

2

same scale as main map

COLL
Point
Gunna
Urvaig
Sgeir Bharrach
Balephetrish
Bay
Balephetrish
Hill
Vaul
Salum
Bay
Miodar
Salum
Caolas
Rubha Dubh
Ruaig
Brock
Rubha
Liath
Port Bàn
Soa
The
Green
Clachan
Mòr
Hough
Bay
Kenovay
5
TIREE
Kilkenneth
B8068
3
Moss
Crossapoll
TIREE
Scarinish
Heylipoll
B8065
5
Baugh
Heanish
Sandaig
Gott
Bay
Barrapoll
2
B8065
3
Hynish Bay
B8067
Balemartine
Mannal
Balephuil
Rinn
Thorbhais
Hynish
Hynish Centre,
'The story of
Skerryvore Lighthouse'

Coll.....................1
Oban...........3½-4¼
hours

Rubha
Sgor an
t-Snidhe
ival
528
Ainshval
781
Sgurr nan
Gillean
764
Rubha nam
Meirleach
SOUND OF RU
Rubha an
Fhasaidh
Beinn
Tigh
Eilean
nan Each
Gòdag
Rubh'
Leam na Làraich
Beinn
Airein
137
Port Mòr
Muck
Sound of Eigg

3

Eag na
Maoile
Eilean
Mòr
Rubha
Mòr
Rubha Sgor-
Innis
Sorisdale
Rubh' a'
Bhinnein
5
B8072
Bousd
Torastan
Loch
Fada
Bàgh
na Coille
Cliad
Bay
Arnabost
Grishipoll
Grishipoll Bay
Clabhach
B8071
2
Loch
Cliad
B8071
Coll Dark Sky Island
Ballyhaugh
Ben
Hogh
104
73
Hogh Bay
Totamore
2
Arinagour
Totronald
COLL
Acha
5
Loch Eatharna
Oban 2¾ hrs
Arileod
Uig
B8070
Gorton
Eilean
Ornsay
Sanna Point
Sanna
Bay
Ardnamurchan Point
and Lighthouse
Point of
Ardnamurchan
Portuairk
Grigadale
Port Min
AR

Sorne
Point
Quinish
Point
Caliach
Point
Port
na Bà
Croig
Quinish
Sunipol
Langamull
Mornish
Cruach
Sleibhe
166
Calgary
Frachadil
5
B8073
Dervaig
Discover
Mull
Tours
Rubha
nan Oirean
Calgary Art in
Nature
Carn
Mòr
342
Cruachan
Ceann a' Ghairbh
261

4

Calgary
Point
Gunna
Urvaig
Miodar
Salum
Ruaig
Caolas
Rubha Dubh
TIREE
Rubha
Liath
So
Port Bàn
Caolas
Bàn
Port a'
Mhurain
Crossapol
Crossapol
Bay
Soa
Loch
Breachacha
Rubha
Fasachd
Friesland
Bay
Feall
Bay
Port Mine
Tiree 1 hr
Treshnish
Point
Treshnish
Ensay
Beinn
Duill
191
256
Cruachan
Odhar
Beinn nan Clach-corra
315
Rubh'
a' Chaoil
Rubh' an
t-Suibhein
Burg
B8073
Tostarie
Kilninian
Normann's
Ruh
Cnoc
an
da Chinn
390
Fanmore
Ballygow
Kilbr
Calgary Bay
Loch Tuath
Ballygown Bay
Laggan
Bay
M

5

hours
Coll.....................1
Oban.........3½-4¼

Cairn na Burgh More
Cairn na
Burgh Beg
Fladda
Treshnish Isles
Sgeir a'
Chaisteil
Lunga
Bac Mòr
(Dutchman's Cap)
238
B
Little
Colonsay
Staffa   Eilean Dubh

Eilean
Dioghlum
Gometra
House
Gometra
Rubha Maol
na Mine
Maisgeir
Bèarnus
306
Beinn
Chreagach
313
Beinn
Eolasary
Rubha
Chulinish
Rubha
nan
Gall
ULVA
A' Chrannag
Samal
Islan
Chapel
C   D

0   2   4   6 miles
0   2   4   6   8   10 km

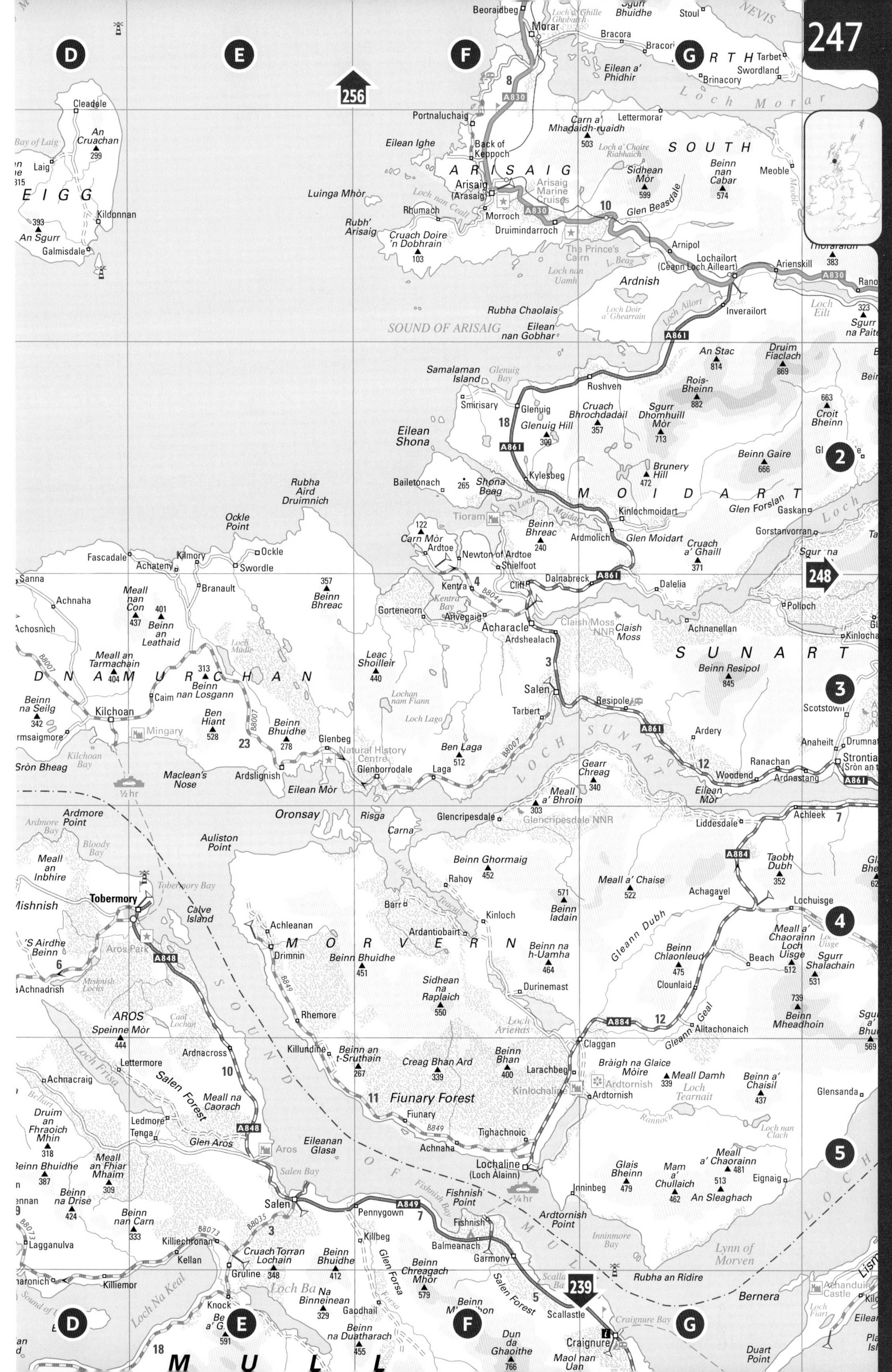
D
E
F
G
256
248
239
Morar
Beoraidbeg
Bracora
Bracorina
NORTH
Tarbet
Swordland
Stoul
Eilean a' Phidhir
Brinacory
Loch Morar
Lettermorar
Carn a' Mhadaidh-ruaidh
503
SOUTH
Beinn nan Cabar
574
Meoble
Sidhean Mòr
599
Glen Beasdale
Cleadale
An Cruachan
299
Bay of Laig
Laig
EIGG
Kildonnan
393
An Sgurr
Galmisdale
Portnaluchaig
Eilean Ighe
Back of Keppoch
ARISAIG
Arisaig (Arasaig)
Arisaig Marine Cruises
Luinga Mhòr
Rhumach
Morroch
Druimindarroch
Rubh' Arisaig
Cruach Doire 'n Dobhrain
103
The Prince's Cairn
Loch nan Uamh
Arnipol
Lochailort (Ceann Loch Ailleart)
Arienskill
Ardnish
Inverailort
Rubha Chaolais
Eilean nan Gobhar
SOUND OF ARISAIG
Loch Eilt
Sgurr na Paite
An Stac
814
Druim Fiaclach
869
Rois-Bheinn
882
Samalaman Island
Glenuig Bay
Roshven
Smirisary
Glenuig
Cruach Bhrochdadail
357
Sgurr Dhomhuill Mòr
713
Croit Bheinn
663
Glenuig Hill
300
Eilean Shona
Beinn Gaire
666
Kylesbeg
Brunery Hill
472
Baileteonach
265
Shona Beag
MOIDART
Rubha Aird Druimnich
Tioram
Kinlochmoidart
Glen Forslan
Gaskan
Ockle Point
122
Carn Mòr
Ardtoe
Beinn Bhreac
240
Ardmolich
Glen Moidart
Gorstanvorran
Cruach a' Ghaill
371
Fascadale
Achateny
Kilmory
Ockle
Swordle
Newton of Ardtoe
Shielfoot
Dalnabreck
Dalelia
Sanna
Branault
357
Beinn Bhreac
Kentra
Kentra Bay
Cliff
Polloch
Achnaha
Meall nan Con
437
401
Beinn an Leathaid
Gorteneorn
Arivegaig
Acharacle
Ardshealach
Claish Moss NNR
Claish Moss
Achnanellan
Achosnich
Loch Mudle
Meall an Tarmachain
404
313
Beinn nan Losgann
ARDNAMURCHAN
Leac Shoilleir
440
SUNART
Beinn Resipol
845
Beinn na Seilg
342
Kilchoan
Caim
Ben Hiant
528
Lochan nam Fiann
Salen
Resipole
Tarbert
Scotstown
Loch Laga
Beinn Bhuidhe
278
Ardery
Mingary
Kilchoan Bay
Sròn Bheag
Glenbeg
Natural History Centre
Ben Laga
512
LOCH SUNART
Anaheilt
Strontian
Maclean's Nose
Ardslignish
Glenborrodale
Laga
Gearr Chreag
340
Ranachan
Woodend
Ardnastang
Eilean Mòr
Meall a' Bhròin
303
Eilean Mòr
½ hr
Ardmore Point
Ardmore Bay
Oronsay
Risga
Carna
Glencripesdale
Glencripesdale NNR
Liddesdale
Achleek
Bloody Bay
Auliston Point
Beinn Ghormaig
452
Taobh Dubh
352
Meall an Inbhire
Rahoy
Meall a' Chaise
522
Achagavel
Tobermory
Tobermory Bay
Mishnish
Calve Island
Barr
Loch Teacuis
571
Beinn Iadain
Lochuisge
Kinloch
Gleann Dubh
Meall a' Chaorainn
Loch Uisge
Achleanan
MORVERN
Ardantiobairt
Drimnin
Beinn Bhuidhe
451
Beinn na h-Uamha
464
Beinn Chlaonleud
475
Beach
Sgurr Shalachain
531
'S Airdhe Beinn
Aros Park
Achnadrish
Mishnish Lochs
Clounlaid
Sidhean na Raplaich
550
Durinemast
739
Beinn Mheadhoin
AROS
Caol Lochan
Rhemore
Loch Arienas
Gleann Geal
Alltachonaich
Speinne Mòr
444
SOUND OF MULL
Claggan
Loch Frisa
Lettermore
Ardnacross
Killundine
Beinn an t-Sruthain
267
Creag Bhan Ard
339
Beinn Bhan
400
Larachbeg
Bràigh na Glaice Mòire
339
Meall Damh
Beinn a' Chaisil
437
Achnacraig
Salen Forest
Kinlochaline
Ardtornish
Loch Tearnait
Glensanda
Druim an Fhraoich Mhin
318
Meall na Caorach
Fiunary Forest
Fiunary
Loch nan Clach
Ledmore
Tenga
Glen Aros
Aros
Eileanan Glasa
Tighachnoic
Achnaha
Meall a' Chaorainn
481
Beinn Bhuidhe
387
Meall an Fhiar Mhaim
309
Salen Bay
Lochaline (Loch Alainn)
Glais Bheinn
479
Mam a' Chullaich
462
513
An Sleaghach
Eignaig
Beinn na Drise
424
Fishnish Point
Inninbeg
Salen
Pennygown
Fishnish Bay
Fishnish
Ardtornish Point
Beinn nan Carn
333
Lagganulva
Killiechronan
Kellan
Cruach Torran Lochain
348
Killbeg
Balmeanach
Inninmore Bay
Lynn of Morven
Gruline
Beinn Bhuidhe
412
Glen Forsa
Beinn Chreagach Mhor
579
Garmony
Scallastle Bay
Rubha an Ridire
Killiemor
Loch Na Keal
Loch Ba
Na Binneinean
329
Gaodhail
Salen Forest
Bernera
Achadun Castle
Loch Fiart
Knock
Craignure Bay
Scallastle
Craignure
Beinn na Duatharach
455
Dun da Ghaoithe
766
Maol nan Uan
Duart Point
591
MULL
¼ hr

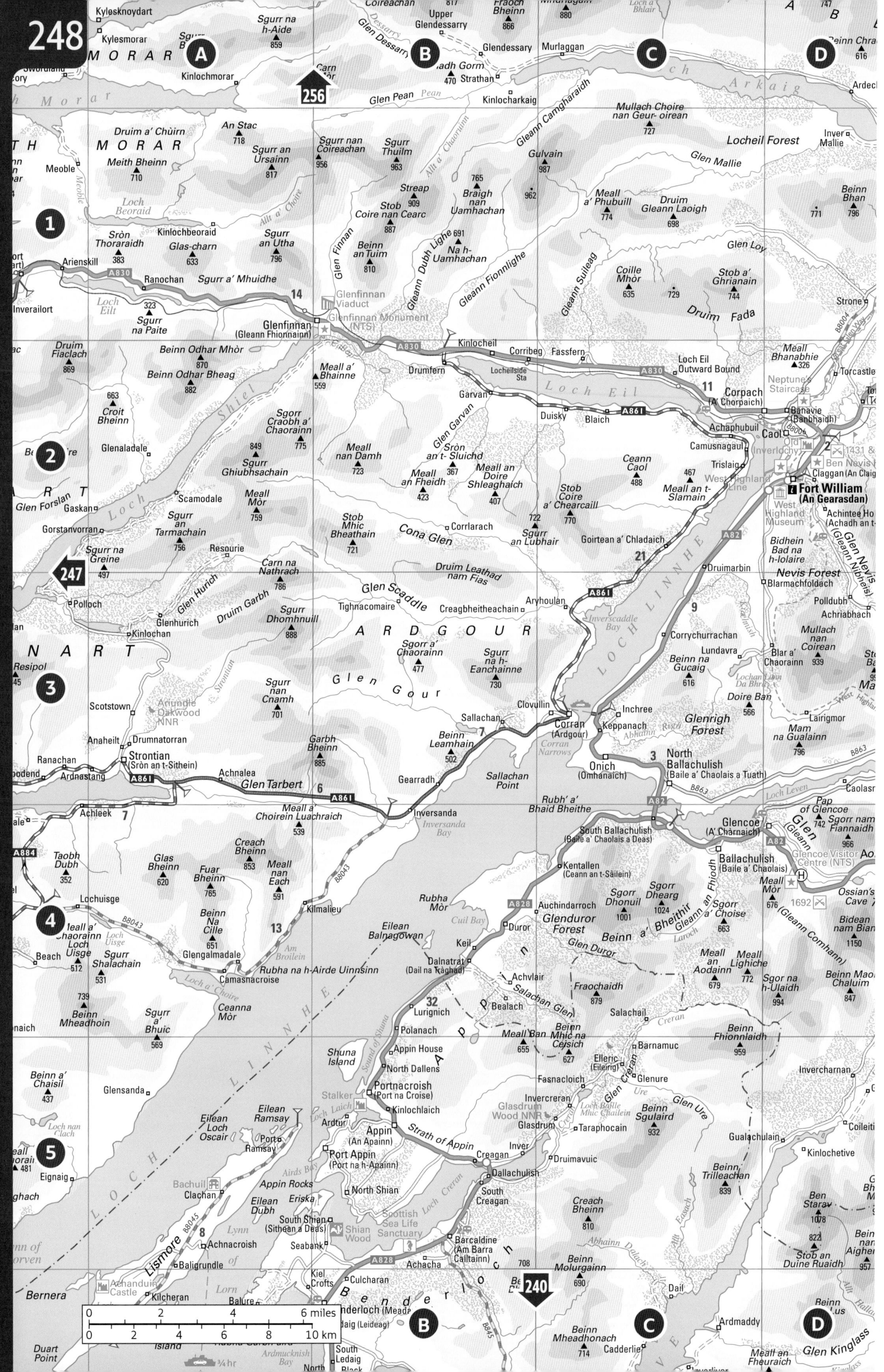

Kylesknoydart
Kylesmorar
M O R A R
Kinlochmorar
Sgurr na h-Aide
859
Upper Glendessarry
Glen Dessarry
Glendessary
Murlaggan
Fraoch Bheinn
866
880
Strathan
470
Kinlocharkaig
Glen Pean
256
Loch Arkaig
Ardechive
Mullach Choire nan Geur-oirean
727
Gleann Camgharaidh
Druim a' Chùirn
An Stac
718
MORAR
Meith Bheinn
710
Meoble
Sgurr an Ursainn
817
Sgurr nan Coireachan
956
Sgurr Thuilm
963
Gulvain
987
962
Locheil Forest
Inver Mallie
Glen Mallie
Loch Beoraid
Streap
909
765
Braigh nan Uamhachan
Stob Coire nan Cearc
887
Meall a' Phubuill
774
Druim Gleann Laoigh
698
Beinn Bhan
796
771
Sròn Thoraraidh
383
Kinlochbeoraid
Glas-charn
633
Sgurr an Utha
796
Beinn an Tuim
810
691
Na h-Uamhachan
Glen Finnan
Gleann Dubh Lighe
Gleann Fionnlighe
Gleann Suileag
Glen Loy
Coille Mhòr
635
729
Stob a' Ghrianain
744
Arienskill
A830
Ranochan
Sgurr a' Mhuidhe
Loch Eilt
323
Sgurr na Paite
Inverailort
14
Glenfinnan Viaduct
Glenfinnan Monument (NTS)
Glenfinnan (Gleann Fhionnainn)
Druim Fada
Strone
Druim Fiaclach
869
Beinn Odhar Mhòr
870
Beinn Odhar Bheag
882
Meall a' Bhainne
559
Kinlocheil
Corribeg
Fassfern
Drumfern
Lochellside Sta
Loch Eil
Loch Eil Outward Bound
Meall Bhanabhie
326
Torcastle
Neptune's Staircase
Garvan
Duisky
Blaich
A861
11
Corpach (A' Chorpaich)
Banavie (Banbhaidh)
Caol
663
Croit Bheinn
Sgorr Craobh a' Chaorainn
775
Meall nan Damh
723
Glen Garvan
Sròn an t-Sluichd
367
Achaphubuil
Camusnagaul
Inverlochy
1431
Ben Nevis
Claggan (An Claigeann)
Glenaladale
849
Sgurr Ghiubhsachain
Meall an Fheidh
423
Meall an Doire Shleaghaich
407
Ceann Caol
488
Trislaig
467
Meall an t-Slamain
West Highland Line
Fort William (An Gearasdan)
West Highland Museum
Achintee House (Achadh an t-Suidhe)
Glen Forslan
Gaskan
Scamodale
Loch Shiel
Meall Mòr
759
Stob Mhic Bheathain
721
Stob Coire a' Chearcaill
770
722
Sgurr an Lubhair
Goirtean a' Chladaich
Gorstanvorran
Sgurr an Tarmachain
756
Corrlarach
Cona Glen
A82
Sgurr na Greine
497
Resourie
Carn na Nathrach
786
Druim Leathad nam Fias
21
Druimarbin
Bidhein Bad na h-Iolaire
Glen Nevis (Gleann Nibheis)
Nevis Forest
Blarmachfoldach
247
Polloch
Glen Hurich
Druim Garbh
Glen Scaddle
Tighnacomaire
Creagbheitheachain
Aryhoulan
Polldubh
Achriabhach
Glenhurich
Kinlochan
Sgurr Dhomhnuill
888
A R D G O U R
Inverscaddle Bay
LOCH LINNHE
9
Mullach nan Coirean
939
N A R T
Resipol
3
Sgorr a' Chaorainn
477
Sgurr na h-Eanchainne
730
Corrychurrachan
Lundavra
Beinn na Gucaig
616
Blar a' Chaorainn
Lochan Lùnn Da Bhra
Glen Gour
Sgurr nan Cnamh
701
Scotstown
Ariundle Oakwood NNR
Strontian
Clovullin
Sallachan
Corran (Ardgour)
Inchree
Keppanach
Glenrigh Forest
Doire Ban
566
Lairigmor
Anaheilt
Drumnatorran
Garbh Bheinn
885
Beinn Leamhain
502
7
Corran Narrows
Onich (Omhanaich)
North Ballachulish (Baile a' Chaolais a Tuath)
Mam na Gualainn
796
B863
Ranachan
Ardnastang
Strontian (Sròn an t-Sìthein)
A861
Achnalea
Glen Tarbert
6
Gearradh
Sallachan Point
3
Caolasnacon
Loch Leven
Achleek
7
Meall a' Choirein Luachraich
539
Inversanda
Inversanda Bay
Rubh' a' Bhaid Bheithe
South Ballachulish (Baile a' Chaolais a Deas)
Glencoe (A' Chàrnaich)
Pap of Glencoe
742
Sgorr nam Fiannaidh
966
A884
Taobh Dubh
352
Glas Bheinn
620
Creach Bheinn
853
Fuar Bheinn
765
Meall nan Each
591
B8043
Kentallen (Ceann an t-Sàilein)
Ballachulish (Baile a' Chaolais)
Glencoe Visitor Centre (NTS)
Lochuisge
4
Meall a' Chaorainn
Loch Uisge
Beinn Na Cille
651
Kilmalieu
Rubha Mòr
A828
Auchindarroch
Sgorr Dhonuil
1001
Sgorr Dhearg
1024
Glen an Fhiodh
Meall Mòr
676
1692
Ossian's Cave
Beach
Sgurr Shalachain
512
531
13
Glengalmadale
Am Broilein
Eilean Balnagowan
Cuil Bay
Duror
Glenduror Forest
Beinn a' Bheithir
Sgorr a' Choise
663
Gleann Comhann
Bidean nam Bian
1150
Rubha na h-Airde Uinnsinn
Camasnacroise
Keil
Dalnatrat (Dail na Tràghad)
Glen Duror
Meall an Aodainn
679
Meall Lighiche
772
Sgor na h-Ulaidh
994
Beinn Maol Chaluim
847
739
Beinn Mheadhoin
Loch a' Choire
Ceanna Mòr
Achvlair
Salachan Glen
Fraochaidh
879
32
Lurignich
Bealach
Salachail
Creran
Sgurr a' Bhuic
569
Polanach
Meall Ban
655
Beinn Mhic na Ceisich
627
Barnamuc
Beinn Fhionnlaidh
959
Shuna Island
Sound of Shuna
Appin House
North Dallens
Elleric (Eileirig)
Glenure
Beinn a' Chaisil
437
Glensanda
Portnacroish (Port na Croise)
Stalker
Fasnacloich
Inverchanan
Eilean Ramsay
Eilean Loch Oscair
Kinlochlaich
Invercreran
Glasdrum Wood NNR
Glasdrum
Glen Creran
Loch Baile Mhic Chailein
Glen Ure
Beinn Sgulaird
932
Ardtur
Appin (An Apainn)
Port
Ramsay
Strath of Appin
Taraphocain
Gualachulain
Coileitir
Loch nan Clach
5
Port Appin (Port na h-Apainn)
Creagan
Inver
Druimavuic
Kinlochetive
481
Eignaig
Airds Bay
Bachuil
Appin Rocks
Eriska
Dallachulish
Beinn Trilleachan
839
Clachan
Eilean Dubh
South Creagan
Creach Bheinn
810
Ben Starav
1078
822
South Shian (Sithean a Deas)
Shian Wood
Scottish Sea Life Sanctuary
Loch Creran
Lynn of Lorn
8
B8045
Achnacroish
Seabank
Barcaldine (Am Barra Calltainn)
Abhainn Dalach
Allt Easach
Stob an Duine Ruaidh
Beinn nan Aighenan
957
Lismore
Baligrundle
Achacha
A828
708
Beinn Molurgainn
690
Achanduin Castle
Bernera
Kilcheran
Kiel Crofts
Culcharan
Benderloch
240
Dail
Beinn Lus
Balure
Benderloch (Meadarloch)
Ledaig (Leideag)
B845
Beinn Mheadhonach
714
Ardmaddy
Cadderlie
Glen Kinglass
Meall an Fheuraich
Duart Point
Ardmucknish Bay
South Ledaig
3/4 hr
0 2 4 6 miles
0 2 4 6 8 10 km
A B C D
1 2 3 4 5

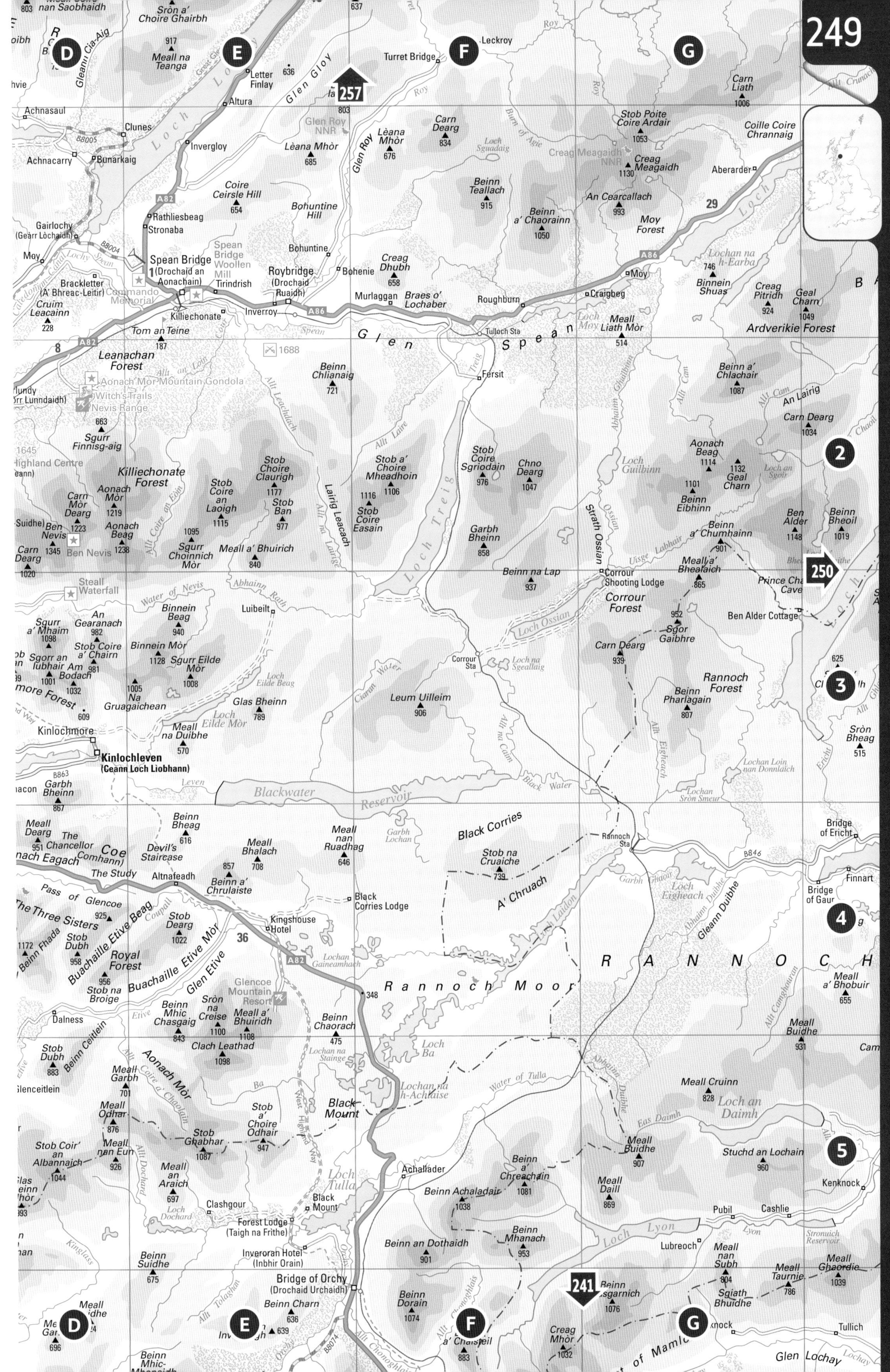

Spean Bridge
Roybridge
Glen Spean
Loch Treig
Corrour Forest
Blackwater Reservoir
Rannoch Moor
RANNOCH
Kinlochleven
Ben Nevis
Loch Ossian
Loch Laggan
Loch Tulla
Bridge of Orchy
Kingshouse Hotel
Loch Lyon
Rannoch Sta
Black Mount
Ardverikie Forest
Creag Meagaidh
257
250
241

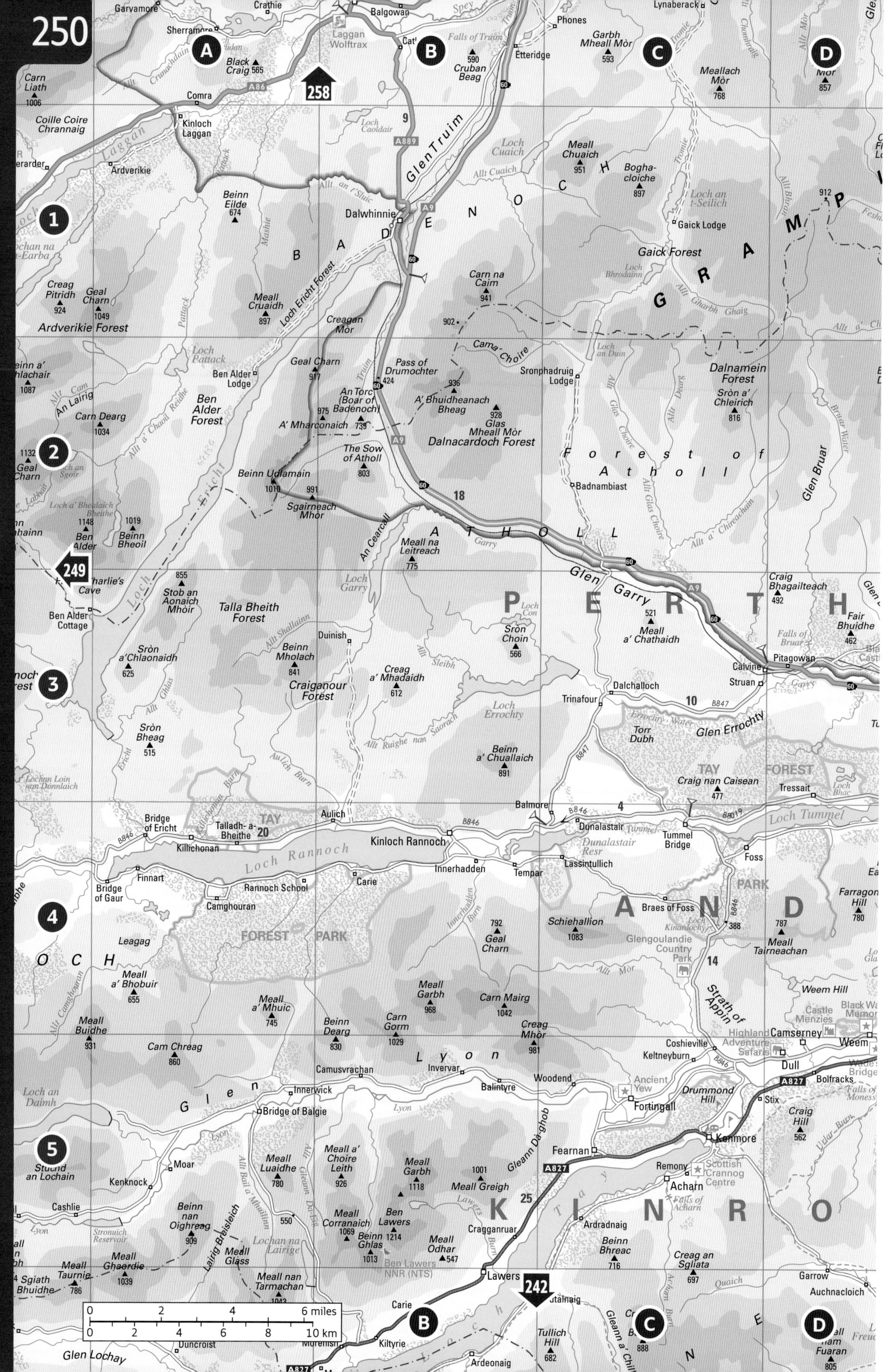

Garvamore
Crathie
Balgowan
Spey
Lynaberack
Sherramore
Laggan Wolftrax
Cat
Falls of Truim
Phones
Garbh Mheall Mòr 593
A
B
C
D
Black Craig 565
590
Cruban Beag
Etteridge
Meallach Mòr 768
Mòr 857
Carn Liath 1006
Comra
A86
258
Coille Coire Chrannaig
Kinloch Laggan
Loch Caoldair
A889
Glen Truim
Loch Cuaich
Meall Chuaich 951
Bogha-cloiche 897
Laggan
Ardverikie
Allt Cuaich
Loch an t-Seilich
912
Beinn Eilde 674
Gaick Lodge
1
Dalwhinnie
A9
B A D E N O C H
G R A M P
Gaick Forest
Loch Bhrodainn
Carn na Caim 941
Creag Pitridh 924
Geal Charn 1049
Meall Cruaidh 897
Loch Ericht Forest
Creagan Mòr
902
Ardverikie Forest
Loch Pattack
Cama-Choire
Loch an Duin
Geal Charn 917
Pass of Drumochter 424
Sronphadruig Lodge
Dalnamein Forest
Ben Alder Lodge
936
Carn Dearg 1034
An Lairig
Ben Alder Forest
An Torc (Boar of Badenoch) 739
975
A' Mharconaich
A' Bhuidheanach Bheag
928
Glas Mheall Mòr
Dalnacardoch Forest
Sròn a' Chleirich 816
2
1132
Geal Charn
The Sow of Atholl 803
Forest of Atholl
Glen Bruar
Bruar Water
Beinn Udlamain 1010
991
Sgairneach Mhòr
Badnambiast
18
Loch a' Bhealaich Bheithe
1148
Ben Alder
1019
Beinn Bheoil
A T H O L L
Meall na Leitreach 775
An Cearcall
Garry
249
Charlie's Cave
855
Stob an Aonaich Mhòir
Loch Garry
Glen Garry
Craig Bhagailteach 492
Ben Alder Cottage
Talla Bheith Forest
P E R T H
Loch Con
521
Meall a' Chathaidh
Fair Bhuidhe 462
Falls of Bruar
Duinish
Sròn Choin 566
Sròn a' Chlaonaidh 625
Beinn Mholach 841
Creag a' Mhadaidh 612
Calvine
Pitagowan
Struan
3
Craiganour Forest
Dalchalloch
Trinafour
10
B847
Loch Errochty
Errochty Water
Glen Errochty
Torr Dubh
Allt Ruighe nan Saorach
Sròn Bheag 515
Beinn a' Chuallaich 891
TAY FOREST
Craig nan Caisean 477
Tressait
Lochan Loin nan Donnlaich
Aulich Burn
Balmore
B846
4
Loch Tummel
Bridge of Ericht
TAY
Aulich
Talladh-a-Bheithe
20
Dunalastair
Tummel Bridge
Killichonan
Kinloch Rannoch
Dunalastair Resr
Foss
Loch Rannoch
Innerhadden
Tempar
Lassintullich
Finnart
Bridge of Gaur
Rannoch School
Carie
PARK
Camghouran
Braes of Foss
A N D
Farragon Hill 780
4
Schiehallion 1083
388
787
Meall Tairneachan
FOREST PARK
792
Geal Charn
Glengoulandie Country Park
Leagag
O C H
14
Meall a' Bhobuir 655
Allt Mòr
Weem Hill
Meall Garbh 968
Carn Mairg 1042
Strath of Appin
Castle Menzies
Meall a' Mhuic 745
Carn Gorm 1029
Creag Mhòr 981
Meall Buidhe 931
Beinn Dearg 830
Highland Adventure Safaris
Camserney
Weem
Cam Chreag 860
Coshieville
Keltneyburn
L y o n
Dull
Camusvrachan
Invervar
Woodend
Ancient Yew
Drummond Hill
A827
Bolfracks
Loch an Daimh
G l e n
Innerwick
Balintyre
Fortingall
Stix
Bridge of Balgie
Craig Hill 562
5
Kenmore
Stuchd an Lochain
Moar
Meall Luaidhe 780
Meall a' Choire Leith 926
Meall Garbh 1118
1001
Meall Greigh
Fearnan
Remony
Scottish Crannog Centre
Kenknock
Acharn
Falls of Acharn
Cashlie
Beinn nan Oighreag 909
550
Meall Corranaich 1069
Ben Lawers 1214
25
K I N R O
Stronuich Reservoir
Lochan na Lairige
Beinn Ghlas 1013
Meall Odhar 547
Cragganruar
Ardradnaig
Beinn Bhreac 716
Meall Ghaordie 1039
Meall Glas
Lairig Breisleich
Ben Lawers NNR (NTS)
Creag an Sgliata 697
Meall Taurnie 786
Sgiath Bhuidhe
Meall nan Tarmachan
Lawers
242
Garrow
Auchnacloich
0 2 4 6 miles
0 2 4 6 8 10 km
Carie
B
C
D
Duncroist
Kiltyrie
Tullich Hill 682
888
Glen Lochay
Ardeonaig
805

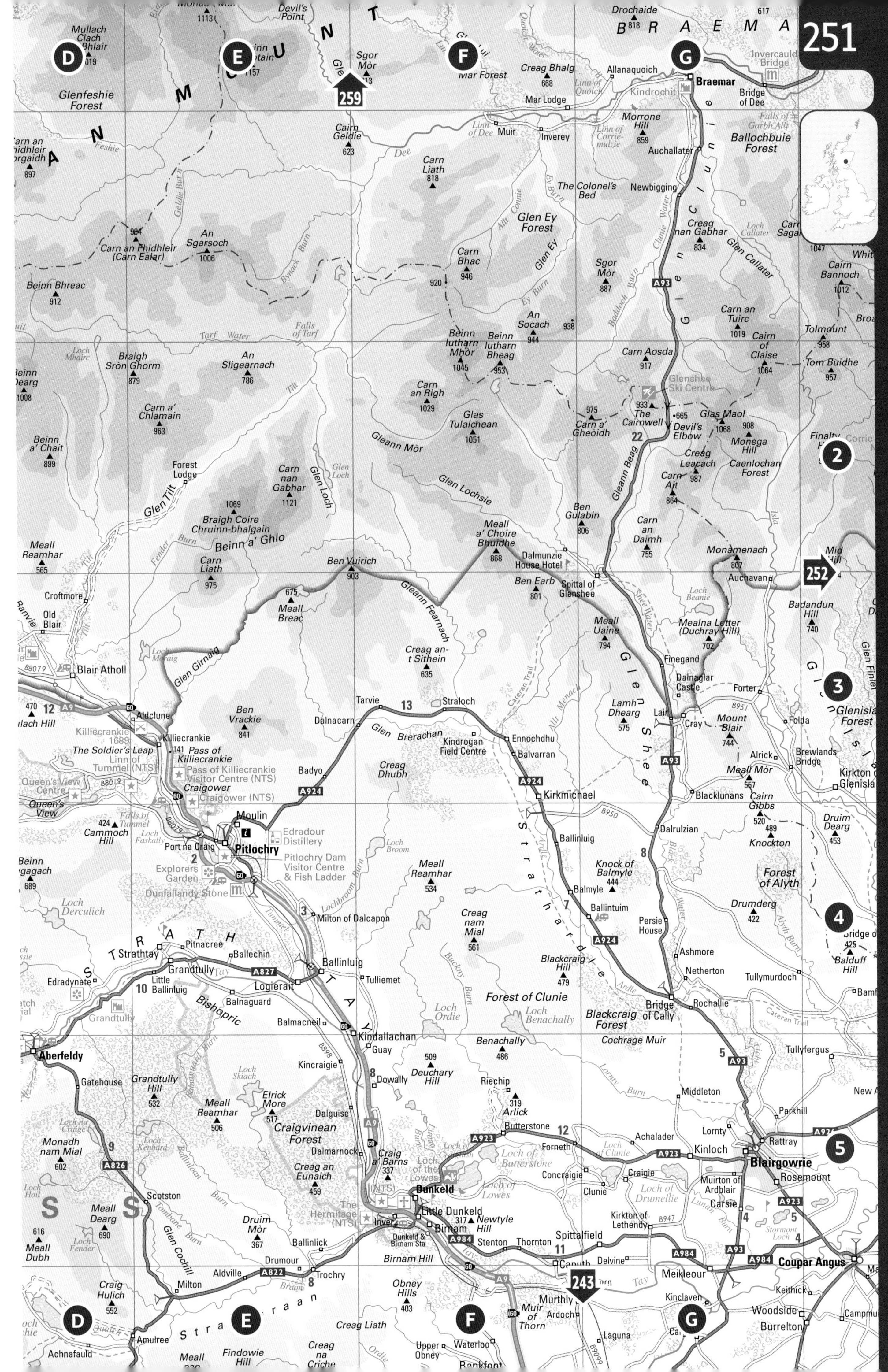
Mullach Clach a' Bhlair
Glenfeshie Forest
Devil's Point
Sgor Mòr
259
Mar Forest
Creag Bhalg
668
Drochaide
818
BRAEMAR
Allanaquoich
Braemar
Kindrochit
Invercauld Bridge
Bridge of Dee
Mar Lodge
Linn of Quoich
Linn of Dee
Muir
Inverey
Linn of Corriemulzie
Morrone Hill
859
Auchallater
Falls of Garbh Allt
Ballochbuie Forest
Cairn Geldie
623
Dee
Feshie
Carn Liath
818
The Colonel's Bed
Newbigging
Carn an Fhidhleir (Carn Ealar)
An Sgarsoch
1006
Geldie Burn
Bynack Burn
Glen Ey Forest
Carn Bhac
946
Glen Ey
Clunie Water
Creag nan Gabhar
834
Loch Callater
Glen Callater
Cairn Bannoch
1012
Beinn Bhreac
912
920
Sgor Mòr
887
A93
Glen Clunie
An Socach
944
938
Ey Burn
Baddoch Burn
Carn an Tuirc
1019
Cairn of Claise
1064
Tolmount
958
Tom Buidhe
957
Tarf Water
Falls of Tarf
Loch Mhairc
Braigh Sròn Ghorm
879
An Sligearnach
786
Beinn Iutharn Mhòr
1045
Beinn Iutharn Bheag
953
Carn Aosda
917
Glenshee Ski Centre
Beinn Dearg
1008
Carn an Righ
1029
Carn a' Chlamain
963
Glas Tulaichean
1051
975
Carn a' Gheòidh
933
The Cairnwell
665
Devil's Elbow
Glas Maol
1068
908
Monega Hill
22
Gleann Mòr
Beinn a' Chait
899
Forest Lodge
Tilt
Carn nan Gabhar
1121
Glen Loch
Glen Lochsie
Creag Leacach
987
Caenlochan Forest
Finalty Hill
Corrie
2
Carn Ait
864
Gleann Beag
Glen Tilt
1069
Braigh Coire Chruinn-bhalgain
Beinn a' Ghlo
Ben Gulabin
806
Carn an Daimh
755
Meall a' Choire Bhuidhe
868
Meall Reamhar
565
Fender Burn
Carn Liath
975
Ben Vuirich
903
Dalmunzie House Hotel
Spittal of Glenshee
Ben Earb
801
Monamenach
807
Auchavan
252
Mid Hill
Croftmore
675
Meall Breac
Gleann Fearnach
Loch Beanie
Badandun Hill
740
Old Blair
Meall Uaine
794
Mealna Letter (Duchray Hill)
702
Loch Moraig
Glen Girnaig
Creag an-t Sithein
635
Glen Shee
Finegand
Dalnaglar Castle
Forter
Glen Isla
3
Blair Atholl
B8079
470
12
A9
Aldclune
Ben Vrackie
841
Tarvie
13
Straloch
Dalnacarn
Glen Brerachan
Kindrogan Field Centre
Ennochdhu
Balvarran
Lamh Dhearg
575
Lair
Cray
Mount Blair
744
B951
Folda
Glenisla Forest
Killiecrankie 1689
Killiecrankie
The Soldier's Leap
141
Pass of Killiecrankie
Linn of Tummel (NTS)
Pass of Killiecrankie Visitor Centre (NTS)
Queen's View Centre
B8019
Craigower
Craigower (NTS)
Badyo
Creag Dhubh
A924
Kirkmichael
Alrick
Brewlands Bridge
Meall Mòr
557
Kirkton of Glenisla
Blacklunans
Cairn Gibbs
520
Queen's View
424
Cammoch Hill
Falls of Tummel
Loch Faskally
Moulin
Edradour Distillery
Pitlochry
Port na Craig
Pitlochry Dam Visitor Centre & Fish Ladder
Explorers Garden
Dunfallandy Stone
Loch Broom
Meall Reamhar
534
B950
Ballinluig
Dalrulzian
489
Knockton
Druim Dearg
453
Beinn Eagagach
689
Loch Derculich
3
Milton of Dalcapon
Lochbroom Burn
Knock of Balmyle
444
Balmyle
8
Forest of Alyth
Ballintuim
Persie House
Drumderg
422
4
Bridge of
425
Balduff Hill
Creag nam Mial
561
Strathardle
Cateran Trail
Ardle
Strathtay
Pitnacree
Ballechin
Grandtully
A827
Tay
Logierait
Ballinluig
Tulliemet
Edradynate
Little Ballinluig
10
Bishopric
Balnaguard
Blackcraig Hill
479
Ashmore
Netherton
Tullymurdoch
Bridge of Cally
Rochallie
Grandtully
Balmacneil
Loch Ordie
Forest of Clunie
Loch Benachally
Blackcraig Forest
Cochrage Muir
Benachally
486
Kindallachan
Guay
Aberfeldy
Gatehouse
Grandtully Hill
532
Loch Skiach
Kincraigie
B898
509
Deuchary Hill
8
Dowally
Riechip
319
Arlick
Middleton
Tullyfergus
5
A93
New Alyth
Meall Reamhar
506
Elrick More
517
Dalguise
Craigvinean Forest
Butterstone
12
Lornty
Parkhill
Achalader
Rattray
Monadh nam Mial
602
A826
Loch Kennard
Dalmarnock
Craig a' Barns
337
A923
Loch of Butterstone
Forneth
Loch of Clunie
Kinloch
Blairgowrie
5
Creag an Eunaich
459
Loch of the Lowes
Dunkeld
Concraigie
Clunie
Craigie
Loch of Drumellie
Muirton of Ardblair
Rosemount
Scotston
Meall Dearg
690
Druim Mòr
367
The Hermitage (NTS)
Inver
Little Dunkeld
Birnam
317
Newtyle Hill
Kirkton of Lethendy
B947
Carsie
616
Meall Dubh
Loch Fender
Glen Cochill
Ballinlick
Dunkeld & Birnam Sta
A984
Stenton
Thornton
Spittalfield
11
Stormont Loch
Drumour
Birnam Hill
Caputh
Delvine
Meikleour
A984
Coupar Angus
Aldville
A822
Trochry
Craig Hulich
552
Milton
Braan
Obney Hills
403
243
Murthly
Kinclaven
Keithick
Woodside
Burrelton
Campmuir
Muir of Thorn
Ardoch
Laguna
B9099
Strathbraan
Creag Liath
Amulree
Achnafauld
Meall
Findowie Hill
Creag na Criche
Upper Obney
Waterloo
Bankfoot
D
E
F
G

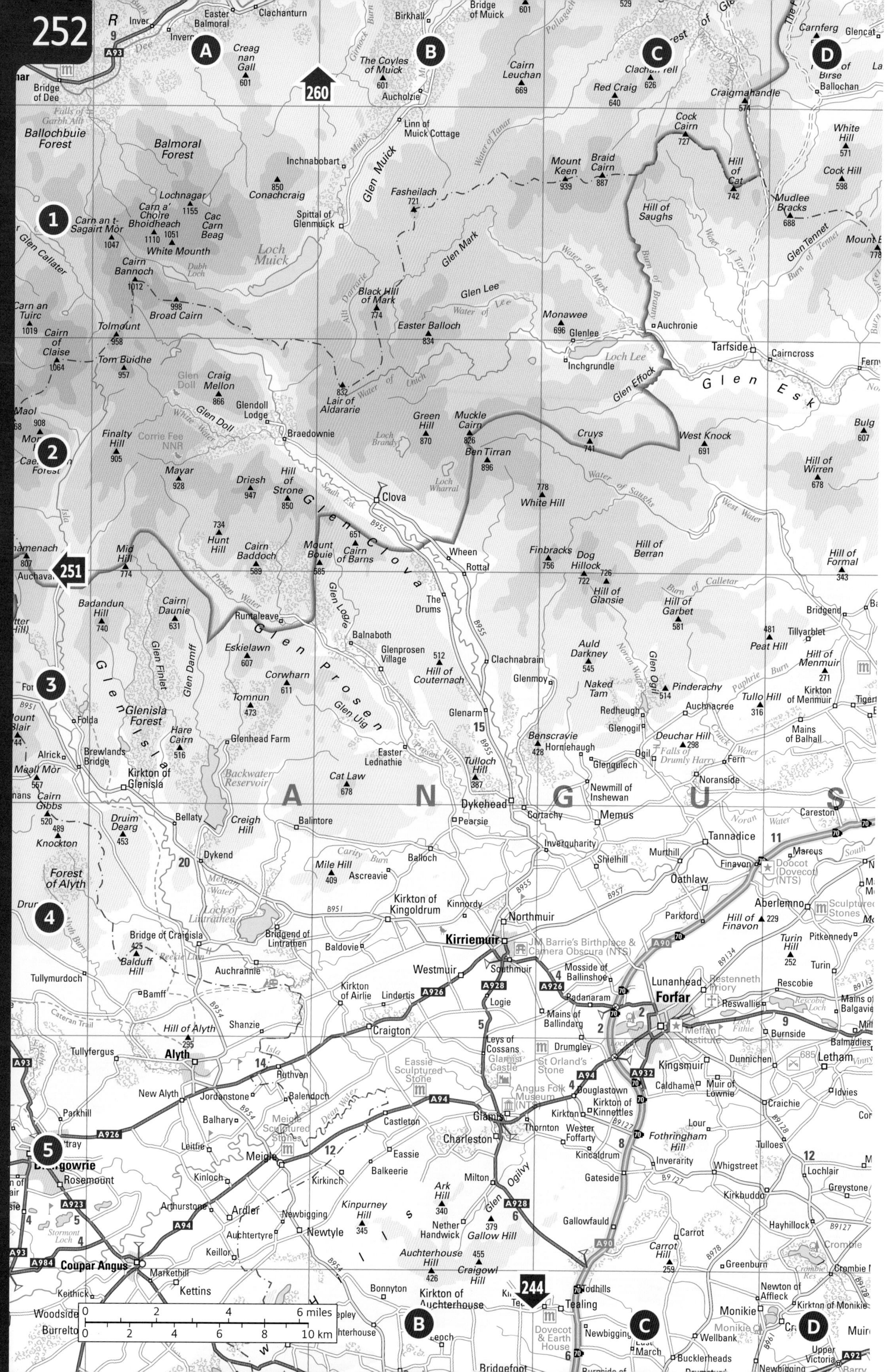
A
B
C
D
1
2
3
4
5
260
251
244
Inver
Easter Balmoral
Clachanturn
Birkhall
Bridge of Muick
Creag nan Gall
601
The Coyles of Muick
Aucholzie
Cairn Leuchan
669
Clachan Yell
626
Red Craig
640
Craigmahandle
574
Carnferg
Glencat
Birse
Ballochan
Bridge of Dee
Ballochbuie Forest
Balmoral Forest
Linn of Muick Cottage
Inchnabobart
Glen Muick
Conachcraig
850
Lochnagar
1155
Carn a' Choire Bhoidheach
1110
Cac Carn Beag
1051
Carn an t-Sagairt Mòr
1047
White Mounth
Glen Callater
Spittal of Glenmuick
Loch Muick
Fasheilach
721
Mount Keen
939
Braid Cairn
887
Cock Cairn
727
Hill of Cat
742
White Hill
571
Cock Hill
598
Mudlee Bracks
688
Hill of Saughs
Glen Tennet
Water of Tanar
Water of Mark
Burn of Branny
Cairn Bannoch
1012
Dubh Loch
998
Broad Cairn
Carn an Tuirc
1019
Cairn of Claise
1064
Tolmount
958
Tom Buidhe
957
Black Hill of Mark
774
Glen Mark
Glen Lee
Water of Lee
Easter Balloch
834
Monawee
696
Glenlee
Auchronie
Loch Lee
Inchgrundle
Tarfside
Cairncross
Glen Esk
Glen Effock
Glen Doll
Craig Mellon
866
Glendoll Lodge
Braedownie
832
Lair of Aldararie
Water of Unich
Green Hill
870
Muckle Cairn
826
Ben Tirran
896
Cruys
741
West Knock
691
Bulg
607
Hill of Wirren
678
Finalty Hill
905
Corrie Fee NNR
White Water
Loch Brandy
Loch Wharral
Mayar
928
Driesh
947
Hill of Strone
850
Clova
South Esk
B955
Glen Clova
778
White Hill
Water of Saughs
West Water
734
Hunt Hill
Cairn Baddoch
589
Mount Bouie
585
651
Cairn of Barns
Wheen
Rottal
Finbracks
756
Dog Hillock
722
726
Hill of Berran
Hill of Formal
343
Mid Hill
774
Auchavan
Prosen Water
Badandun Hill
740
Cairn Daunie
631
Runtaleave
Glen Lodge
The Drums
Hill of Glansie
Burn of Calletar
Hill of Garbet
581
Bridgend
481
Peat Hill
Tillyarblet
Balnaboth
Glen Prosen
Glenprosen Village
512
Hill of Couternach
Clachnabrain
Auld Darkney
545
Hill of Menmuir
271
Eskielawn
607
Corwharn
611
Glen Finlet
Glen Damff
Glen Isla
Glenmoy
Naked Tam
Glen Ogil
514
Pinderachy
Paphrie Burn
Tomnun
473
Glen Uig
Glenarm
15
Redheugh
Auchnacree
Tullo Hill
316
Kirkton of Menmuir
Folda
Glenisla Forest
Hare Cairn
516
Glenhead Farm
Easter Lednathie
Tulloch Hill
387
Benscravie
428
Horniehaugh
Glenogil
Deuchar Hill
298
Falls of Drumly Harry
Ogil
Fern
Glenquiech
Noranside
Mains of Balhall
Alrick
Brewlands Bridge
Kirkton of Glenisla
Backwater Reservoir
Cat Law
678
Newmill of Inshewan
Meall Mòr
Cairn Gibbs
520
489
Knockton
A N G U S
Dykehead
Cortachy
Memus
Careston
Bellaty
Creigh Hill
Balintore
Pearsie
Noran Water
Druim Dearg
453
Dykend
20
Carity Burn
Balloch
Inverquharity
Shielhill
Murthill
Tannadice
11
Finavon
Docoot (Dovecot) (NTS)
Marcus
Forest of Alyth
Mile Hill
409
Ascreavie
Oathlaw
Melgam Water
Loch of Lintrathen
Kirkton of Kingoldrum
Kinnordy
B955
B957
Aberlemno
Sculptured Stones
Parkford
Hill of Finavon
229
Northmuir
B951
Bridge of Craigisla
425
Bridgend of Lintrathen
Baldovie
Kirriemuir
JM Barrie's Birthplace & Camera Obscura (NTS)
Turin Hill
252
Pitkennedy
Balduff Hill
Reekie Linn
Auchrannie
Westmuir
Southmuir
Mosside of Ballinshoe
Lunanhead
Restenneth Priory
Turin
Rescobie
Tullymurdoch
Bamff
Kirkton of Airlie
Lindertis
A926
A928
Logie
Padanaram
Forfar
Reswallie
Rescobie Loch
Mains of Balgavies
Cateran Trail
B954
Shanzie
Mains of Ballindarg
Loch Fithie
Meffan Institute
Burnside
Balmadies
Hill of Alyth
295
Craigton
Leys of Cossans
Glamis Castle
Drumgley
Letham
685
Tullyfergus
Alyth
14
Isla
Ruthven
Eassie Sculptured Stone
St Orland's Stone
Kingsmuir
Dunnichen
A932
A94
Caldhame
Muir of Lownie
Idvies
New Alyth
Jordanstone
Balendoch
Angus Folk Museum (NTS)
Douglastown
Kirkton of Kinnettles
Craichie
Parkhill
Balhary
Meigle Sculptured Stones
Castleton
Glamis
Kirkton
Thornton
Wester Foffarty
Lour
Fothringham Hill
B9128
A926
Leitfie
Meigle
12
Eassie
Charleston
Kincaldrum
Inverarity
Tulloes
Whigstreet
Lochlair
Blairgowrie
Rosemount
Kinloch
Kirkinch
Balkeerie
Milton
Glen Ogilvy
Gateside
B9127
Kirkbuddo
Greystone
A923
Arthurstone
Ardler
Newbigging
Kinpurney Hill
345
Ark Hill
340
Nether Handwick
379
Gallow Hill
Gallowfauld
Hayhillock
Stormont Loch
Auchtertyre
Newtyle
A94
Keillor
Auchterhouse Hill
426
455
Craigowl Hill
A90
Carrot
Carrot Hill
259
B978
Greenburn
Crombie
A984
Coupar Angus
Markethill
Kettins
Bonnyton
Kirkton of Auchterhouse
Todhills
Tealing
Newton of Affleck
Kirkton of Monikie
Keithick
Woodside
Burrelton
Dovecot & Earth House
Newbigging
Monikie
Wellbank
Bucklerheads
East March
Upper Victoria
Bridgefoot
0 2 4 6 miles
0 2 4 6 8 10 km

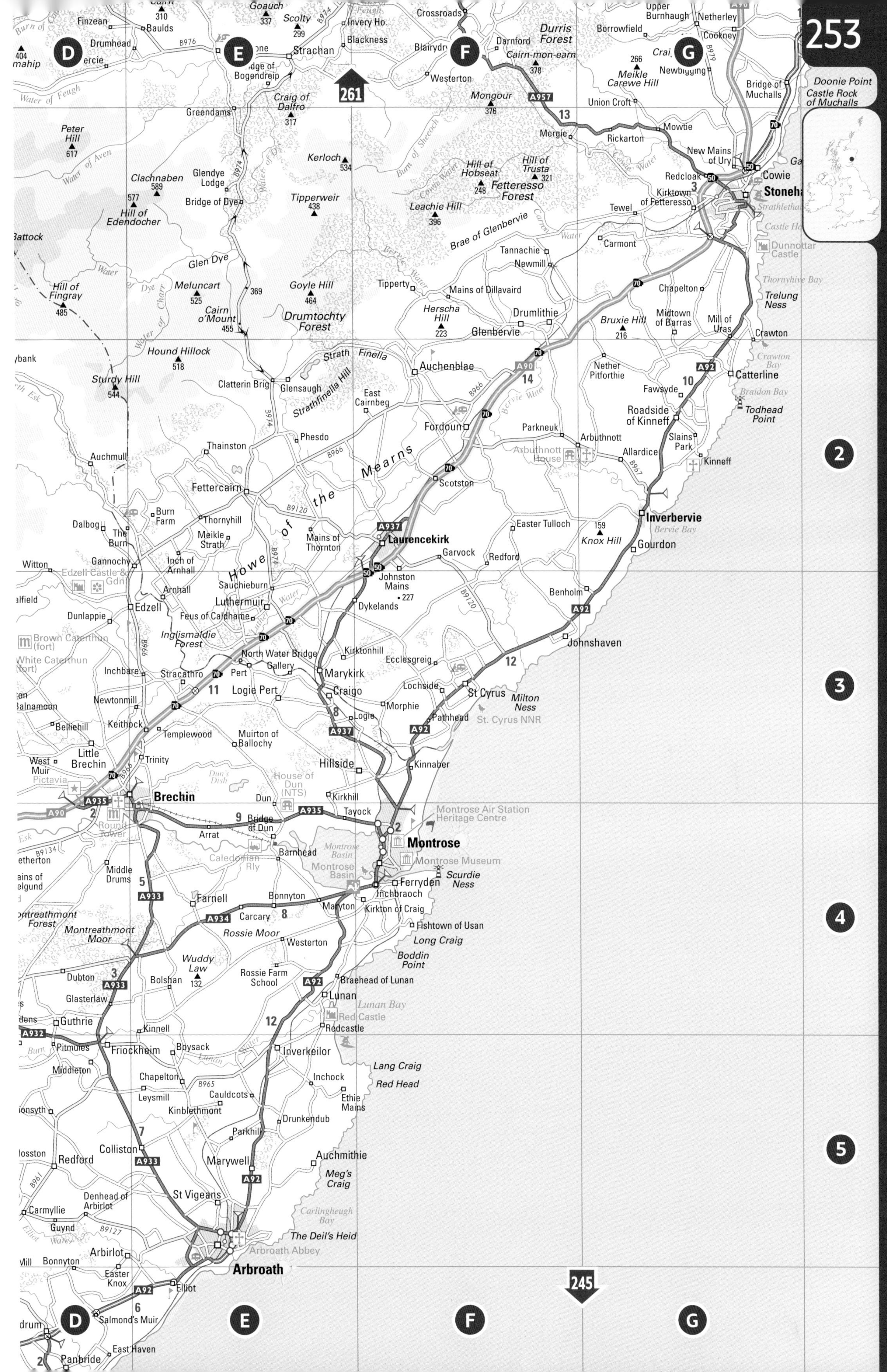
Stonehaven
Laurencekirk
Inverbervie
Montrose
Brechin
Arbroath
Edzell
Fettercairn
Auchenblae
Fordoun
Johnshaven
St Cyrus
Friockheim
Catterline
Howe of the Mearns
Fetteresso Forest
Drumtochty Forest
Durris Forest
Montrose Basin
Lunan Bay
261
245

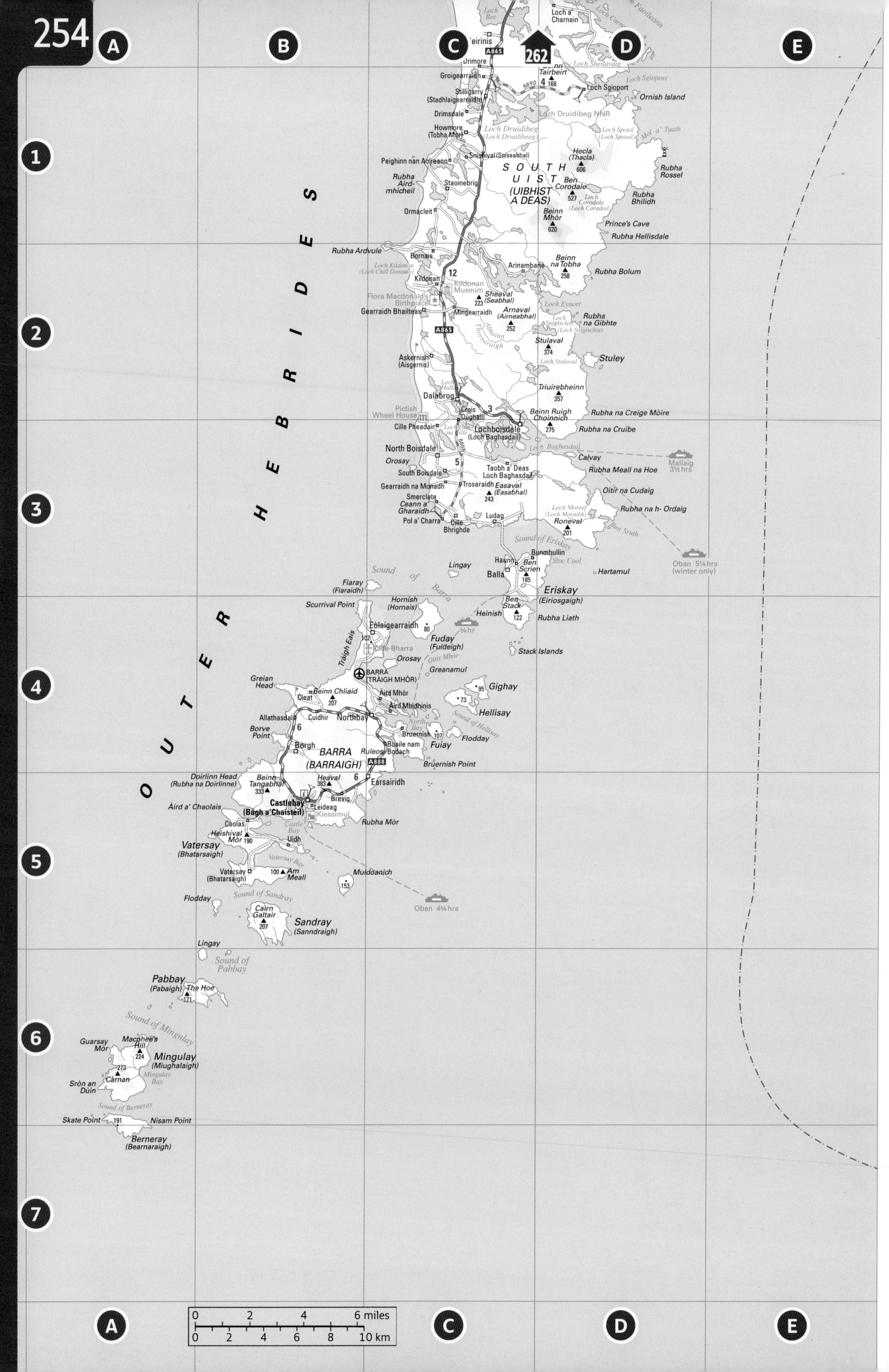
262
OUTER HEBRIDES
SOUTH UIST (UIBHIST A DEAS)
Loch Bee
Loch a Charnain
Eirinis
Drimore
Groigearraidh
Stilligarry (Stadhlaigearraidh)
Drimsdale
Howmore (Tobha Mòr)
Loch Druidibeg (Loch Druidibeag)
Loch Druidibeg NNR
Beinn Tairbeirt
168
Loch Sheilavaig
Loch Sgioport
Ornish Island
Loch Spotal (Loch Spotail)
Mol a' Tuath
Hecla (Thacla)
606
Rubha Rossel
Snishival (Sniseabhal)
Peighinn nan Aoireann
Rubha Aird-mhicheil
Staoinebrig
Ben Corodale
527
Loch Corodale (Loch Coradail)
Rubha Bhilidh
Ormacleit
Beinn Mhòr
620
Prince's Cave
Rubha Hellisdale
Rubha Ardvule
Bornais
Loch Kildonan (Loch Chill Donnain)
Kildonan
Kildonan Museum
Arinambane
Beinn na Tobha
258
Rubha Bolum
Flora Macdonald's Birthplace
Sheaval (Seabhal)
223
Gearraidh Bhailteas
Mingearraidh
Arnaval (Airneabhal)
252
Loch Eynort
Loch Snigiscleit (Loch Snigiscleit)
Rubha na Gibhte
A865
Abhainn Thornaraigh
Stulaval
374
Loch Stulaval
Stuley
Askernish (Aisgernis)
Loch Hallan
Triuirebheinn
357
Dalabrog
Crois Dùghaill
Beinn Ruigh Choinnich
275
Rubha na Creige Mòire
Pictish Wheel House
Cille Pheadair
Loch Dùn na Cille
Lochboisdale (Loch Baghasdail)
Rubha na Cruibe
Loch Baghasdail
North Boisdale
Calvay
Mallaig 3½ hrs
Orosay
Taobh a' Deas Loch Baghasdail
Rubha Meall na Hoe
South Boisdale
B888
Gearraidh na Monadh
Trosaraidh
Easaval (Easabhal)
243
Oitir na Cudaig
Smerclate
Ceann a' Gharaidh
Pol a' Charra
Cille Bhrighde
Ludag
Loch Moreef (Loch Moraibh)
Roneval
201
Rubha na h- Ordaig
Bun Sruth
Sound of Eriskay
Bunmhullin
Sloc Caol
Oban 5¼ hrs (winter only)
Lingay
Haunn
Ben Scrien
185
Balla
Hartamul
Sound of Barra
Fiaray (Fiaraidh)
Eriskay (Eiriosgaigh)
Ben Stack
122
Rubha Liath
Heinish
Scurrival Point
Hornish (Hornais)
80
¼ hr
Eòlaigearraidh
102
Cille-Bharra
Fuday (Fuideigh)
Stack Islands
Traigh Eais
Orosay
Oitir Mhòr
Greanamul
BARRA (TRAIGH MHÒR)
Gighay
95
Greian Head
Beinn Chliaid
207
Aird Mhòr
Cleat
Aird Mhidhinis
73
Hellisay
Allathasdal
Cuidhir
Northbay
North Bay
Sound of Hellisay
Borve Point
Bruernish
107
Flodday
Fuiay
Borgh
Buaile nam Bodach
BARRA (BARRAIGH)
Ruleos
A888
Bruernish Point
Doirlinn Head (Rubha na Doirlinne)
Beinn Tangabhal
333
Heaval
383
Earsairidh
Brevig
Àird a' Chaolais
Castlebay (Bagh a' Chaisteil)
Leideag
Kiessimul
Rubha Mòr
Caolas
Castle Bay
Heishival Mòr
190
Uidh
Vatersay (Bhatarsaigh)
Vatersay Bay
Vatersay (Bhatarsaigh)
100
Am Meall
Muldoanich
153
Oban 4¾ hrs
Flodday
Sound of Sandray
Cairn Galtair
207
Sandray (Sanndraigh)
Lingay
Sound of Pabbay
Pabbay (Pabaigh)
The Hoe
171
Sound of Mingulay
Guarsay Mòr
Macphee's Hill
224
Mingulay (Miughalaigh)
273
Càrnan
Mingulay Bay
Sròn an Dùin
Sound of Berneray
Skate Point
191
Nisam Point
Berneray (Bearnaraigh)
0 2 4 6 miles
0 2 4 6 8 10 km
A B C D E
1 2 3 4 5 6 7

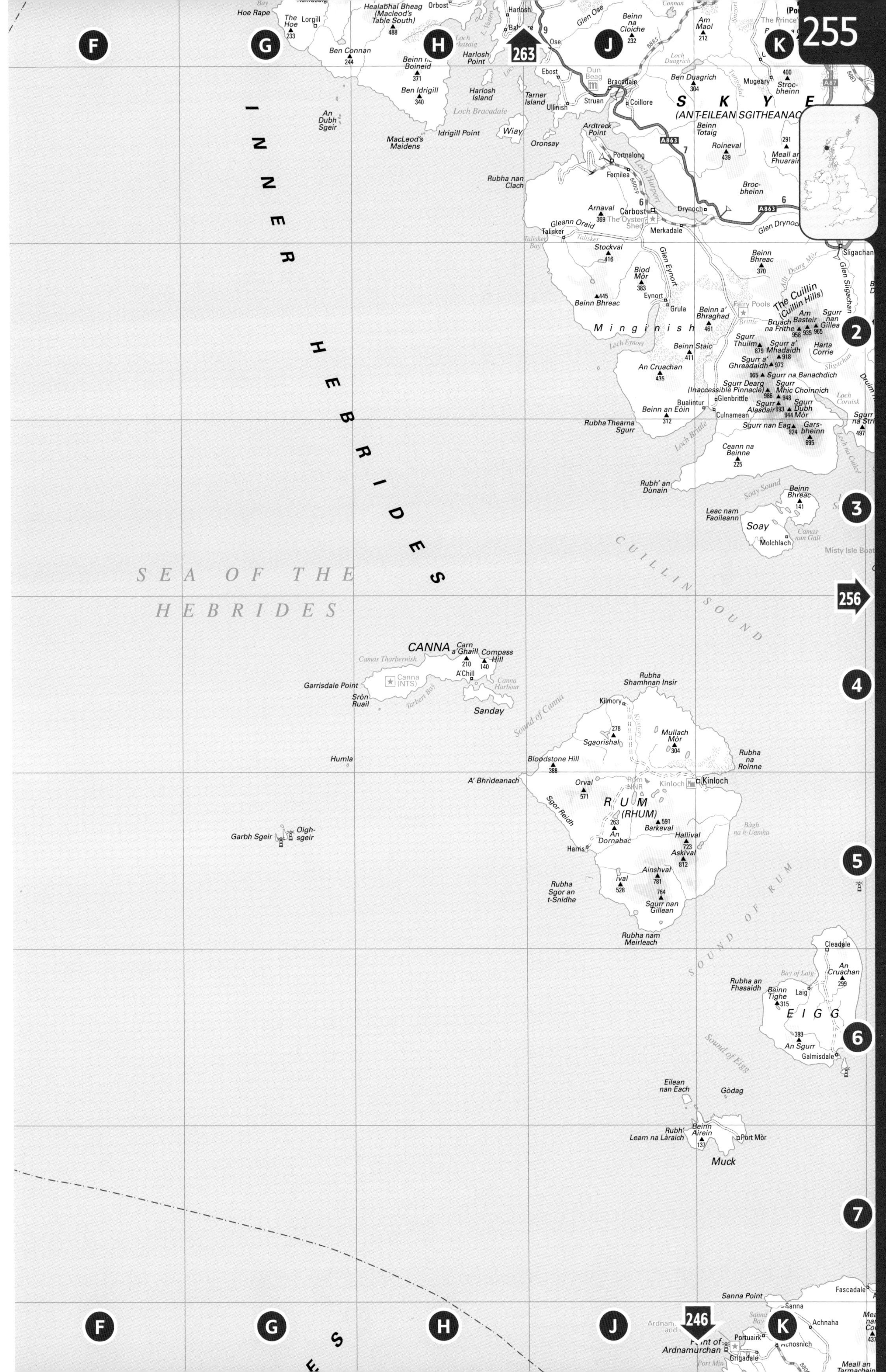
SKYE
(ANT-EILEAN SGITHEANACH)
INNER HEBRIDES
SEA OF THE HEBRIDES
CUILLIN SOUND
SOUND OF RUM
CANNA
Sanday
RUM (RHUM)
EIGG
Muck
Soay
Minginish
The Cuillin (Cuillin Hills)
Hoe Rape
The Hoe
Lorgill
Healabhal Bheag (Macleod's Table South)
Orbost
Harlosh
Ben Connan
Beinn na Boineid
Ben Idrigill
Harlosh Point
Harlosh Island
Loch Bracadale
Idrigill Point
MacLeod's Maidens
An Dubh Sgeir
Tarner Island
Wiay
Oronsay
Ullinish
Ebost
Dun Beag
Bracadale
Struan
Coillore
Glen Ose
Beinn na Cloiche
Am Maol
Ben Duagrich
Mugeary
Stroc-bheinn
Beinn Totaig
Roineval
Meall an Fhuarain
Broc-bheinn
Ardtreck Point
Portnalong
Fernilea
Loch Harport
Rubha nan Clach
Arnaval
Carbost
The Oyster Shed
Drynoch
Glen Drynoch
Gleann Oraid
Talisker
Talisker Bay
Merkadale
Stockval
Biod Mòr
Glen Eynort
Eynort
Beinn Bhreac
Grula
Beinn a' Bhraghad
Fairy Pools
Brittle
Sligachan
Glen Sligachan
Beinn Bhreac
Bruach na Frithe
Am Basteir
Sgurr nan Gillea
Sgurr Thuilm
Sgurr a' Mhadaidh
Harta Corrie
Sgurr a' Ghreadaidh
Sgurr na Banachdich
Sgurr Dearg (Inaccessible Pinnacle)
Sgurr Mhic Choinnich
Glenbrittle
Sgurr Alasdair
Sgurr Dubh Mòr
Loch Coruisk
Loch Eynort
Beinn Staic
An Cruachan
Bualintur
Beinn an Eòin
Culnamean
Sgurr nan Eag
Gars-bheinn
Rubha Thearna Sgurr
Loch Brittle
Ceann na Beinne
Rubh' an Dùnain
Soay Sound
Beinn Bhreac
Leac nam Faoileann
Camas nan Gall
Molchlach
Misty Isle Boat
Carn a' Ghaill
Compass Hill
Camas Tharbernish
Canna (NTS)
A'Chill
Canna Harbour
Garrisdale Point
Sròn Ruail
Tarbert Bay
Sound of Canna
Rubha Shamhnan Insir
Kilmory
Sgaorishal
Mullach Mòr
Humla
Bloodstone Hill
Rubha na Roinne
A' Bhrìdeanach
Orval
Rum NNR
Kinloch
Sgor Reidh
An Dornabac
Barkeval
Hallival
Bàgh na h-Uamha
Askival
Harris
Garbh Sgeir
Oigh-sgeir
Ainshval
Ival
Rubha Sgor an t-Snidhe
Sgurr nan Gillean
Rubha nam Meirleach
Cleadale
Bay of Laig
An Cruachan
Rubha an Fhasaidh
Beinn Tighe
Laig
An Sgurr
Galmisdale
Sound of Eigg
Eilean nan Each
Gòdag
Beinn Airein
Rubh' Leam na Làraich
Port Mòr
Sanna Point
Sanna
Sanna Bay
Fascadale
Achnaha
Portuairk
Achosnich
Point of Ardnamurchan
Grigadale
Port Min
Meall an Tarmachain
A863
A87
B8009
263
256
246
F
G
H
J
K
2
3
4
5
6
7

264
255
247

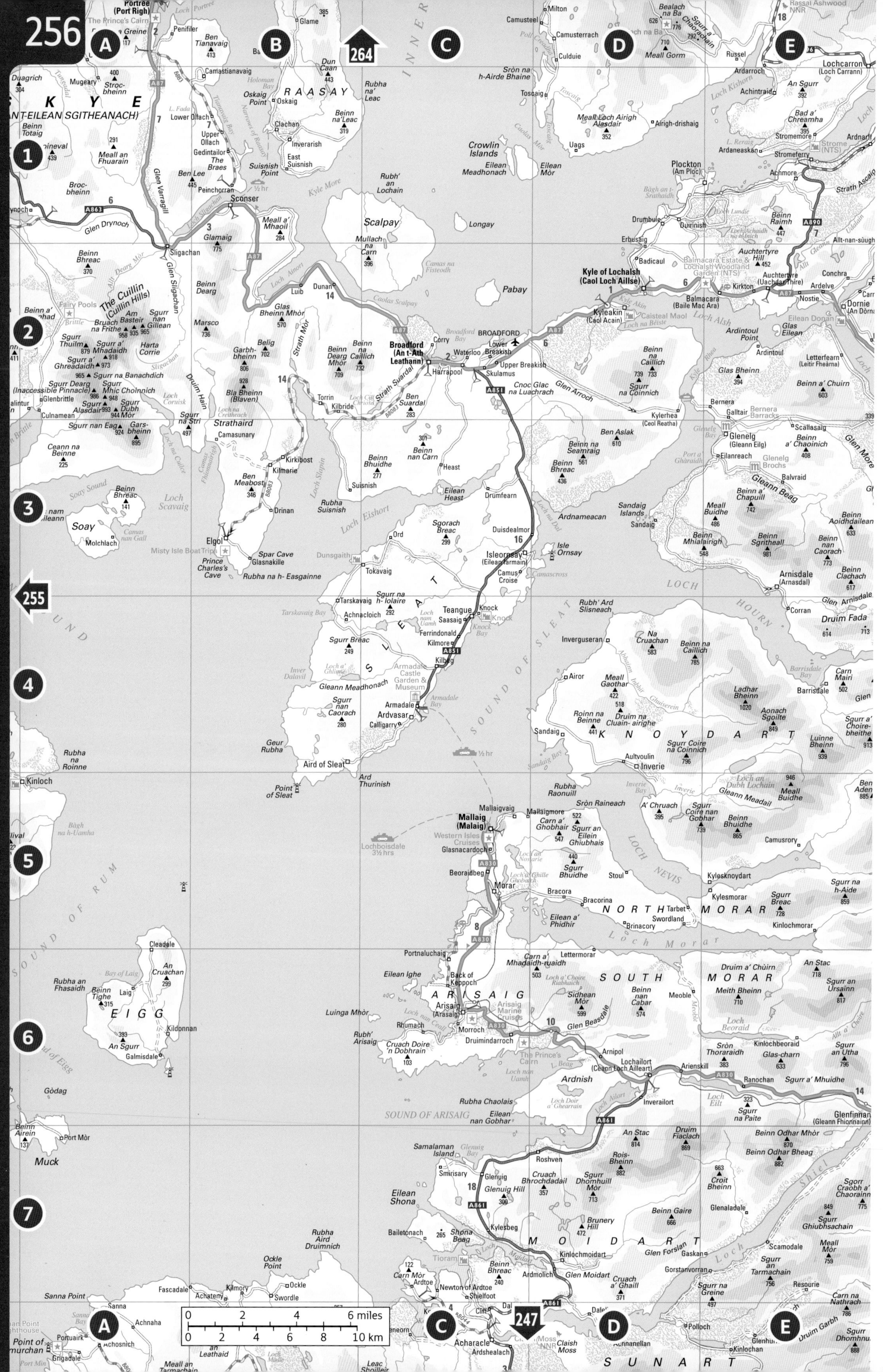
A
B
C
D
E
1
2
3
4
5
6
7
SKYE
(AN T-EILEAN SGITHEANACH)
Portree (Port Righ)
RAASAY
Scalpay
Pabay
Longay
Crowlin Islands
Soay
EIGG
Muck
Plockton (Am Ploc)
Kyle of Lochalsh (Caol Loch Aillse)
Kyleakin (Caol Acain)
Broadford (An t-Ath Leathann)
BROADFORD
Sligachan
Sconser
Elgol
Isleornsay (Eilean Iarmain)
Teangue
Armadale
Ardvasar
Aird of Sleat
Point of Sleat
SLEAT
SOUND OF SLEAT
KNOYDART
Inverie
Mallaig (Malaig)
Morar
NORTH MORAR
SOUTH MORAR
ARISAIG
Arisaig (Arasaig)
SOUND OF ARISAIG
MOIDART
SUNART
Glenelg (Gleann Eilg)
Lochcarron (Loch Carrann)
Dornie (An Dòrn)
Glenfinnan (Gleann Fhionnainn)
Acharacle
Kilchoan
Lochailort (Ceann Loch Ailleart)
Loch Alsh
LOCH HOURN
LOCH NEVIS
Loch Morar
Loch Shiel
Loch Eishort
Loch Scavaig
The Cuillin (Cuillin Hills)
Glen Drynoch
Glen Sligachan
Strathaird
Glen Arroch
Glen Beasdale
Glen Moidart
Sanna Point
Point of Ardnamurchan
Kyle Rhea
Lochboisdale 3½ hrs
½ hr
A87
A863
A851
A830
A861
A890
0 2 4 6 miles
0 2 4 6 8 10 km

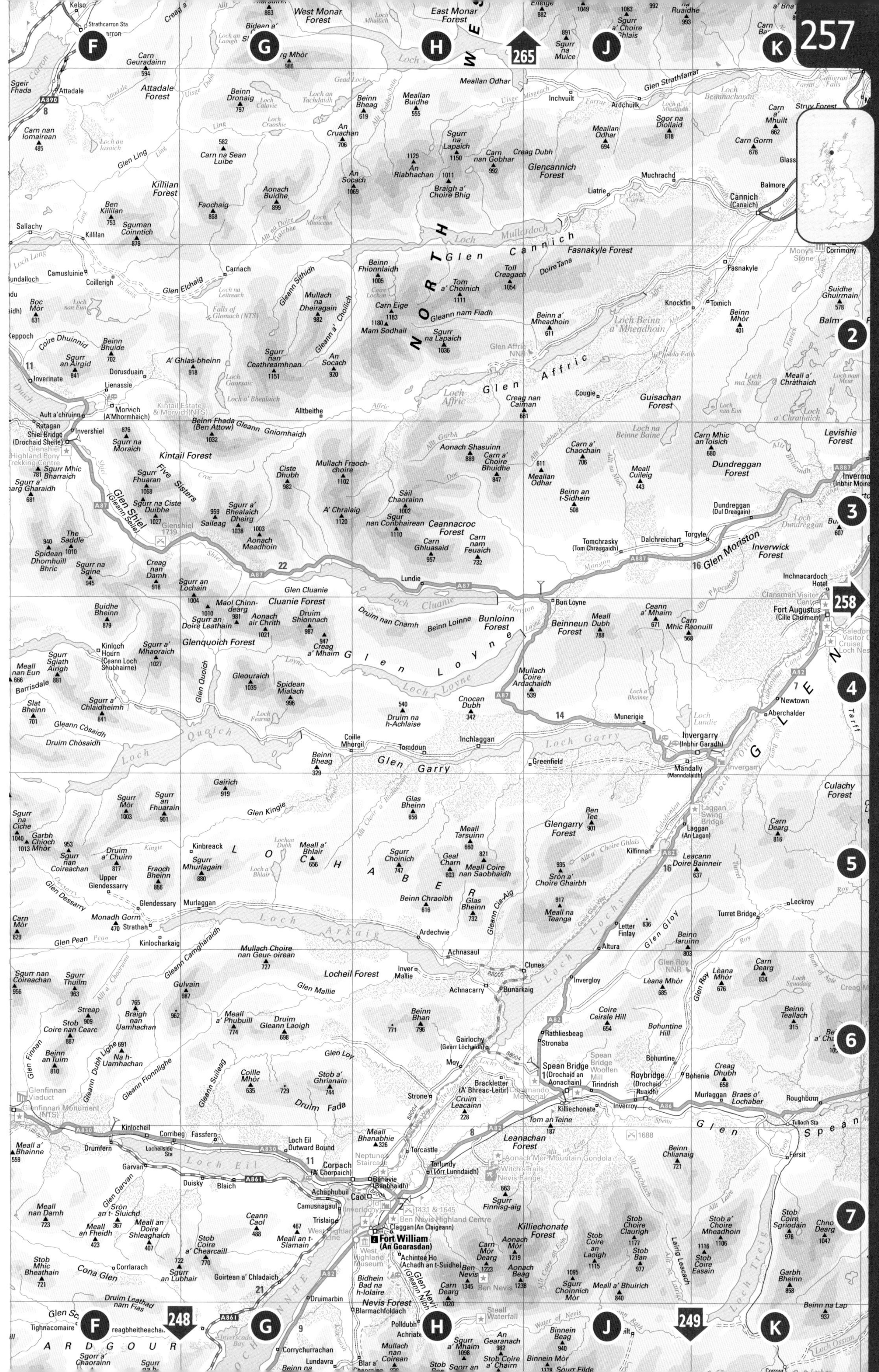
F
G
H
J
K
265
258
248
249
2
3
4
5
6
7
West Monar Forest
East Monar Forest
Strathcarron Sta
Carn Geuradainn
594
Attadale
Attadale Forest
Beinn Dronaig
797
Carn nan Iomairean
485
Glen Ling
Carn na Sean Luibe
Killilan Forest
Faochaig
868
Aonach Buidhe
899
Ben Killilan
753
Sguman Coinntich
879
Sallachy
Killilan
An Cruachan
706
An Socach
1069
Beinn Bheag
619
Meallan Buidhe
555
Meallan Odhar
Sgurr na Lapaich
1150
An Riabhachan
1129
Braigh a' Choire Bhig
1011
Carn nan Gobhar
992
Creag Dubh
Glencannich Forest
Inchvuilt
Glen Strathfarrar
Ardchuilk
Sgor na Diollaid
818
Meallan Odhar
694
Carn a' Mhuilt
662
Carn Gorm
676
Struy Forest
Muchrachd
Liatrie
Cannich (Canaich)
Balmore
Corrimony
Loch Mullardoch
NORTH
Glen Cannich
Fasnakyle Forest
Fasnakyle
Toll Creagach
1054
Tom a' Choinich
1111
Beinn Fhionnlaidh
1005
Carn Eige
1183
Mam Sodhail
1180
Gleann nam Fiadh
Sgurr na Lapaich
1036
Beinn a' Mheadhoin
611
Knockfin
Tomich
Loch Beinn a' Mheadhoin
Beinn Mhòr
401
Suidhe Ghuirmain
578
Carnach
Camusluinie
Coillerigh
Glen Elchaig
Falls of Glomach (NTS)
Mullach na Dheiragain
982
Gleann Sithidh
Boc Mòr
631
Keppoch
Coire Dhuinnid
Beinn Bhuide
702
Sgurr an Airgid
841
A' Ghlas-bheinn
918
Sgurr nan Ceathreamhnan
1151
An Socach
920
Dorusduain
Lienassie
Inverinate
Morvich (A'Mhormhaich)
Kintail Estate & Morvich (NTS)
Alltbeithe
Glen Affric
Loch Affric
Creag nan Calman
661
Cougie
Guisachan Forest
Loch ma Stac
Meall a' Chràthaich
Ault a'chruinn
Ratagan
Shiel Bridge (Drochaid Sheile)
Invershiel
Glenshiel Highland Pony Trekking Centre
876
Sgurr na Moraich
Beinn Fhada (Ben Attow)
1032
Gleann Gniomhaidh
Kintail Forest
Aonach Shasuinn
889
Carn a' Choire Bhuidhe
847
Carn a' Chaochain
706
Loch na Beinne Baine
Carn Mhic an Toisich
680
Levishie Forest
Sgurr Mhic Bharraich
781
Sgurr a' Bhairg Gharaidh
681
Five Sisters
Sgurr Fhuaran
1068
Sgurr na Ciste Duibhe
1027
Glen Shiel (Gleann Seile)
Ciste Dhubh
982
Mullach Fraoch-choire
1102
Meallan Odhar
611
Meall Cuileig
443
Dundreggan Forest
Beinn an t-Sidhein
508
Dundreggan (Dul Dreagain)
Invermoriston (Inbhir Moireasdan)
Sàil Chaorainn
1002
A' Chralaig
1120
Sgurr nan Conbhairean
1110
Ceannacroc Forest
Carn Ghluasaid
957
Carn nam Feuaich
732
Saileag
959
Sgurr a' Bhealaich Dheirg
1038
Aonach Meadhoin
1003
Glenshiel 1719
The Saddle
1010
Spidean Dhomhuill Bhric
940
Sgurr na Sgine
945
Creag nan Damh
918
Tomchrasky (Tom Chrasgaidh)
Dalchreichart
Torgyle
16 Glen Moriston
Inverwick Forest
Loch Dundreggan
Lundie
Loch Cluanie
Glen Cluanie
Cluanie Forest
Sgurr an Lochain
1004
Maol Chinn-dearg
981
1010
Aonach air Chrith
1021
Druim Shionnach
987
Creag a' Mhaim
947
Druim nan Cnamh
Beinn Loinne
Bunloinn Forest
Bun Loyne
Beinneun Forest
Meall Dubh
788
Ceann a' Mhaim
671
Carn Mhic Raonuill
568
Inchnacardoch Hotel
Clansman Visitor Centre
Fort Augustus (Cille Chuimein)
Buidhe Bheinn
879
Kinloch Hourn (Ceann Loch Shubhairne)
Sgurr a' Mhaoraich
1027
Glenquoich Forest
Glen Loyne
Loch Loyne
Sgurr Sgiath Airigh
881
Meall nan Eun
666
Barrisdale
Gleouraich
1035
Spidean Mialach
996
Mullach Coire Ardachaidh
539
Slat Bheinn
701
Sgurr a' Chlaidheimh
841
Glen Quoich
Loch Quoich
Druim na h-Achlaise
540
Cnocan Dubh
342
Munerigie
Loch Lundie
Newtown
Aberchalder
Gleann Còsaidh
Druim Chòsaidh
Coille Mhorgil
Tomdoun
Inchlaggan
Loch Garry
Invergarry (Inbhir Garadh)
Greenfield
Mandally (Manndalaidh)
Beinn Bheag
329
Glen Garry
Gairich
919
Culachy Forest
Sgurr Mòr
1003
Sgurr an Fhuarain
901
Glen Kingie
Glas Bheinn
656
Ben Tee
901
Glengarry Forest
Laggan Swing Bridge
Laggan (An Lagan)
Carn Dearg
816
Sgurr na Ciche
1040
Garbh Chioch Mhòr
1013
Sgurr nan Coireachan
953
Kinbreack
Druim a' Chuirn
817
Sgurr Mhurlagain
880
Meall a' Bhlair
656
LOCHABER
Meall Tarsuinn
660
Sgurr Choinich
747
Geal Charn
803
Meall Coire nan Saobhaidh
821
Kilfinnan
Leacann Doire Bainneir
637
Upper Glendessarry
Fraoch Bheinn
866
Srón a' Choire Ghairbh
935
Glen Dessarry
Glendessary
Murlaggan
Beinn Chraoibh
616
Glas Bheinn
732
Meall na Teanga
917
Turret Bridge
Leckroy
Monadh Gorm
470
Strathan
Carn Mòr
829
Loch Arkaig
Ardechvie
Letter Finlay
Glen Gloy
Beinn Iaruinn
803
Glen Pean
Kinlocharkaig
Mullach Choire nan Geur-oirean
727
Achnasaul
Altura
Glen Roy NNR
Sgurr nan Coireachan
956
Sgurr Thuilm
963
Gleann Camgharaidh
Gulvain
987
Locheil Forest
Inver Mallie
Glen Mallie
Clunes
Achnacarry
Bunarkaig
Invergloy
Lèana Mhòr
685
Lèana Mhòr
676
Carn Dearg
834
Glen Roy
Streap
909
Braigh nan Uamhachan
765
962
Meall a' Phubuill
774
Druim Gleann Laoigh
698
Beinn Bhan
796
771
Coire Ceirsle Hill
654
Rathliesbeag
Stronaba
Bohuntine Hill
Beinn Teallach
915
Stob Coire nan Cearc
887
Beinn an Tuim
810
Glen Finnan
Na h-Uamhachan
691
Gleann Fionnlighe
Gleann Suileag
Coille Mhòr
635
729
Stob a' Ghrianain
744
Glen Loy
Druim Fada
Gairlochy (Gearr Lòchaidh)
Moy
Spean Bridge (Drochaid an Aonachain)
Spean Bridge Woollen Mill
Tirindrish
Bohuntine
Roybridge (Drochaid Ruaidh)
Bohenie
Creag Dhubh
658
Murlaggan
Braes o' Lochaber
Roughburn
Glenfinnan Viaduct
Glenfinnan Monument (NTS)
Strone
Bracklettter (A' Bhreac-Leitir)
Commando Memorial
Cruim Leacainn
228
Killiechonate
Inverroy
Tulloch Sta
Glen Spean
Kinlocheil
Corribeg
Fassfern
Meall a' Bhainne
559
Drumfern
Lochailort Sta
Loch Eil
Loch Eil Outward Bound
Corpach (A' Chorpaich)
Meall Bhanabhie
326
Neptune's Staircase
Banavie (Banbhaidh)
Torcastle
Torlundy (Torr Lunndaidh)
Tom an Teine
187
Leanachan Forest
Aonach Mòr Mountain Gondola
Witch's Trails
Nevis Range
1688
Beinn Chlianaig
721
Fersit
Garvan
Duisky
Blaich
Achaphubuil
Caol
Inverlochy
Glen Garvan
Srón an t-Sluichd
367
Meall nan Damh
723
Meall an Fheidh
423
Meall an Doire Shleaghaich
407
Camusnagaul
Trislaig
Ceann Caol
488
Meall an t-Slamain
467
West Highland Line
1431 & 1645
Ben Nevis Highland Centre
Claggan (An Claigeann)
Fort William (An Gearasdan)
West Highland Museum
Achintee Ho (Achadh an t-Suidhe)
Sgurr Finnisg-aig
663
Killiechonate Forest
Aonach Mòr
1219
Carn Mòr Dearg
1223
Ben Nevis
1345
Aonach Beag
1238
Stob Coire an Laoigh
1115
Stob Choire Claurigh
1177
Stob Ban
977
Lairig Leacach
Stob a' Choire Mheadhoin
1106
Stob Coire Easain
1116
Stob Coire Sgriodain
976
Chno Dearg
1047
Garbh Bheinn
858
Stob Mhic Bheathain
721
Cona Glen
Corrlarach
Stob Coire a' Chearcaill
770
Sgurr an Lubhair
722
Goirtean a' Chladaich
Druim Leathad nam Fias
Druimarbin
Bidhein Bad na h-Iolaire
Glen Nevis (Gleann Nibheis)
Nevis Forest
Blarmachfoldach
Carn Dearg
1020
Sgurr Choinnich Mòr
1095
Meall a' Bhuirich
840
Steall Waterfall
Beinn na Lap
937
Loch Treig
Glen Scaddle
Tighnacomaire
ARDGOUR
Inverscaddle Bay
Corrychurrachan
Polldubh
Achriabhach
Mullach nan Coirean
Sgurr a' Mhaim
1098
An Gearanach
982
Stob Coire a' Chairn
Binnein Beag
940
Binnein Mòr
Loch Ossian

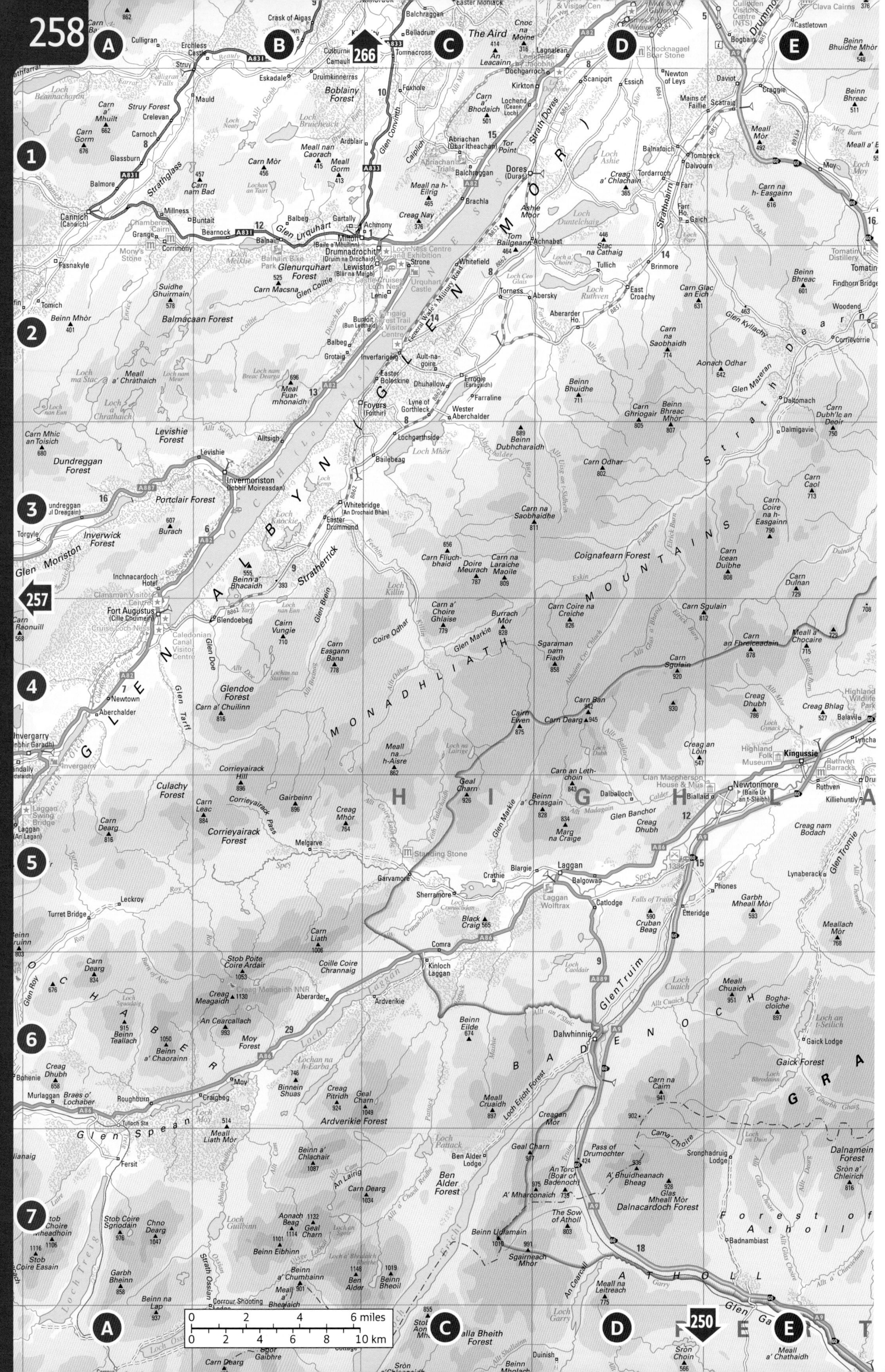

Loch Ness
Fort Augustus
Monadhliath Mountains
Strathglass
Glen Urquhart
Drumnadrochit
Kingussie
Newtonmore
Dalwhinnie
Laggan
Ben Alder Forest
Dalnacardoch Forest
Glen Moriston
Invermoriston
Foyers
Dores
Cannich
Badenoch
Strathdearn
Coignafearn Forest
Corrieyairack Forest
Ardverikie Forest
Forest of Atholl
Loch Ericht Forest
0 2 4 6 miles
0 2 4 6 8 10 km
266
257
250

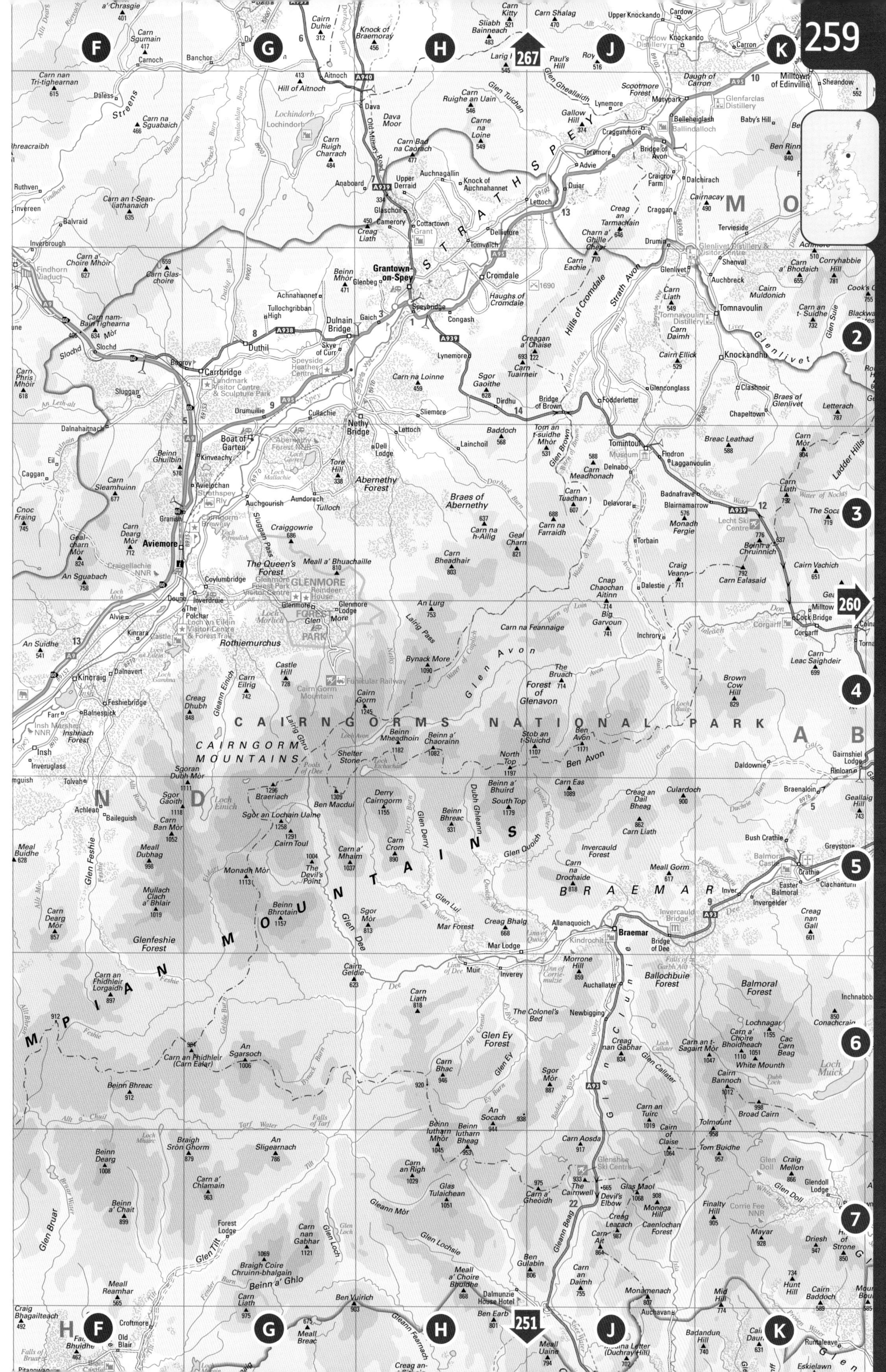

F
G
H
J
K
267
260
251
CAIRNGORMS NATIONAL PARK
CAIRNGORM MOUNTAINS
GRAMPIAN MOUNTAINS
STRATHSPEY
BRAEMAR
MORAY
ABERDEENSHIRE
Grantown-on-Spey
Carrbridge
Aviemore
Boat of Garten
Nethy Bridge
Dulnain Bridge
Duthil
Cromdale
Tomintoul
Braemar
Kincraig
Inverdruie
Coylumbridge
Glenmore
Glenmore Forest Park
Rothiemurchus
Abernethy Forest
The Queen's Forest
Cairn Gorm 1245
Ben Macdui 1309
Braeriach 1296
Cairn Toul 1291
Sgor an Lochain Uaine 1258
Beinn a' Bhuird
Ben Avon 1171
Beinn Mheadhoin 1182
Derry Cairngorm 1155
Beinn Bhrotain 1157
Monadh Mòr 1113
Lochnagar 1155
Glas Maol 1068
Carn an Righ 1029
Beinn Iutharn Mhòr 1045
Bynack More 1090
Glen Feshie
Glenfeshie Forest
Glen Tilt
Glen Bruar
Glen Ey
Glen Dee
Glen Derry
Glen Quoich
Glen Avon
Glen Livet
Glenlivet
Tomnavoulin
Knockandhu
Hills of Cromdale
Strath Avon
Ladder Hills
Lecht Ski Centre
Corgarff
Cock Bridge
Balmoral Castle
Crathie
Invercauld Bridge
Ballochbuie Forest
Balmoral Forest
Loch Muick
White Mounth
Broad Cairn
Glenshee Ski Centre
The Cairnwell
Devil's Elbow
Spittal of Glenshee
Linn of Dee
Inverey
Mar Lodge
Mar Forest
Lairig Ghru
Lairig an Laoigh
Shelter Stone
Loch Avon
Loch Einich
Loch an Eilein
Loch Morlich
Lochindorb
Dava Moor
Dava
Aitnoch
Ballindalloch
Bridge of Avon
Marypark
Knockando
Cardow
Carron
Milltown of Edinvillie
Glenfarclas Distillery
Glenlivet Distillery & Visitor Centre
Tomnavoulin Distillery
Speyside Heather Centre
Landmark Visitor Centre & Sculpture Park
Strathspey Rly
Cairngorm Reindeer House
Loch an Eilein Visitor Centre & Forest Trail
Funicular Railway
Insh Marshes NNR
Craigellachie NNR
Slochd
Findhorn Viaduct
Inverbrough
Sluggan
Ruthven
Streens
Forest of Glenavon
Braes of Abernethy
Braes of Glenlivet
Fodderletter
Bridge of Brown
Lynemore
Gairnshiel Lodge
Inchnabobart
Glendoll Lodge
Corrie Fee NNR
Forest Lodge
Dalmunzie House Hotel
Ben Vuirich
Blair Atholl
Old Blair
Glen Doll

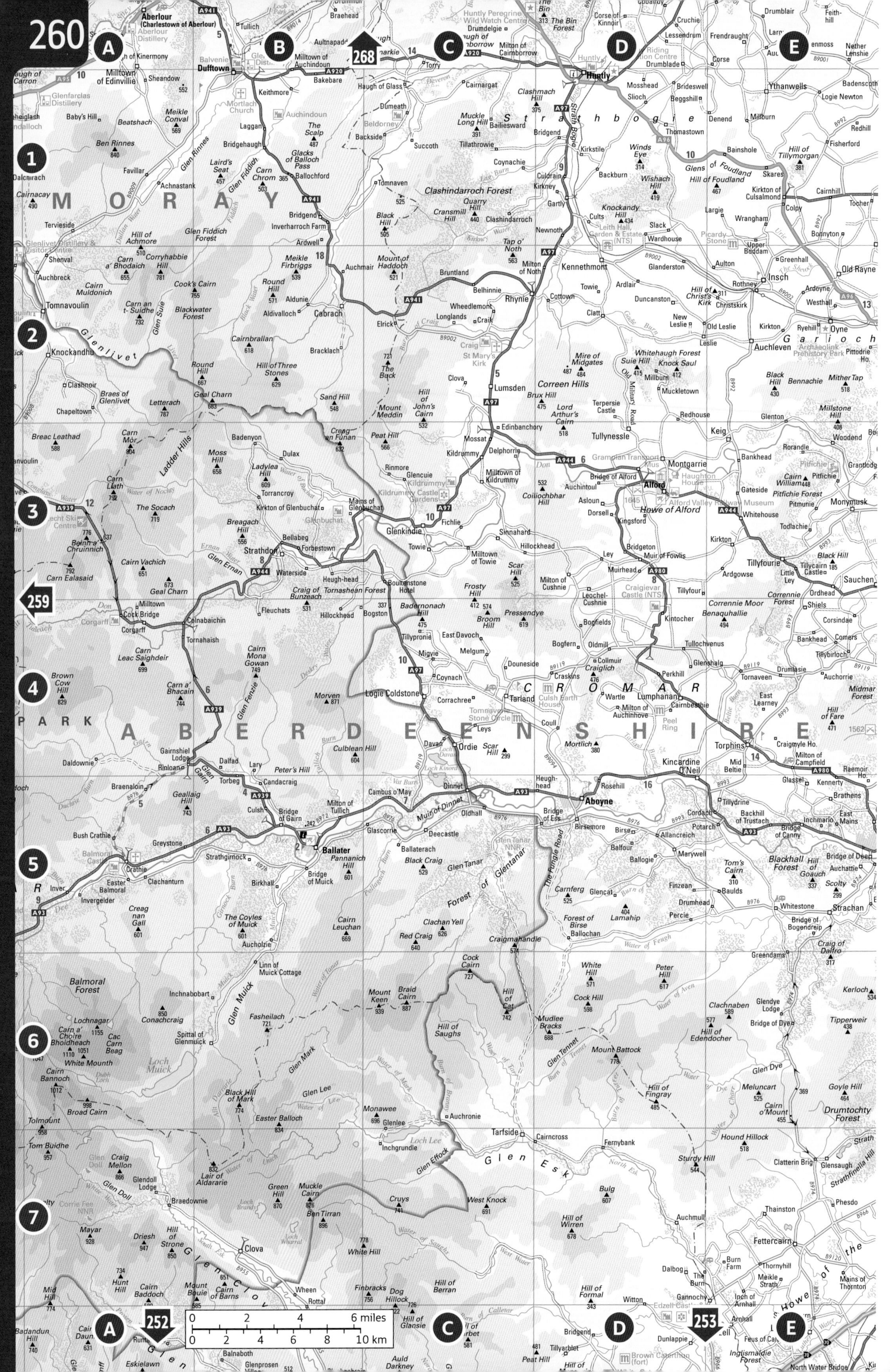

A
B
C
D
E
268
259
252
253
1
2
3
4
5
6
7
0 2 4 6 miles
0 2 4 6 8 10 km
Aberlour (Charlestown of Aberlour)
Aberlour Distillery
Milltown of Edinvillie
Glenfarclas Distillery
Dufftown
Balvenie
Tullich
Braehead
Aultnapadd
Milltown of Auchindoun
Bakebare
Torry
Haugh of Glass
Huntly Peregrine Wild Watch Centre
Drumdelgie
Milton of Cairnborrow
The Bin
The Bin Forest
Corse of Kinnoir
Huntly
Riding Instruction Centre
Cruchie
Lessendrum
Frendraught
Drumblade
Corse
Drumblair
Feith-hill
Nether Lenshie
Sheandow
Keithmore
Mortlach Church
Meikle Conval
Baby's Hill
Beatshach
Ben Rinnes
Auchindoun
Dumeath
Beldorney
Cairnargat
Clashmach Hill
Muckle Long Hill
Bailiesward
Strathbogie
Mosshead
Sliach
Brideswell
Beggshill
Denend
Ythanwells
Logie Newton
Badenscoth
Millburn
Redhill
Thomastown
Laggan
The Scalp
Bridgehaugh
Glacks of Balloch Pass
Backside
Succoth
Tillathrowie
Bridgend
Kirkstile
Winds Eye
Glens of Foudland
Hill of Foudland
Bainshole
Hill of Tillymorgan
Fisherford
Glen Rinnes
Laird's Seat
Carn Chrom
Glen Fiddich
Ballochford
Favillar
Achnastank
Tomnaven
Coynachie
Clashindarroch Forest
Culdrain
Kirkney
Backburn
Wishach Hill
Skares
Kirkton of Culsalmond
Cairnhill
Colpy
Tocher
Dalchirach
Cairnacay
MORAY
Quarry Hill
Cransmill Hill
Clashindarroch
Gartly
Knockandy Hill
Largie
Wrangham
Black Hill
Bridgend
Inverharroch Farm
Tervieside
Hill of Achmore
Glen Fiddich Forest
Ardwell
Newnoth
Cults
Leith Hall, Garden & Estate (NTS)
Slack
Wardhouse
Picardy Stone
Upper Boddam
Bonnyton
Glenlivet Distillery & Visitor Centre
Shenval
Carn a' Bhodaich
Corryhabbie Hill
Meikle Firbriggs
Auchmair
Mount of Haddoch
Tap o' Noth
Milton of Noth
Kennethmont
Glanderston
Aulton
Greenhall
Old Rayne
Auchbreck
Cairn Muldonich
Cook's Cairn
Round Hill
Aldunie
Bruntland
Belhinnie
Rhynie
Towie
Ardlair
Hill of Christ's Kirk
Christskirk
Rothney
Insch
Ardoyne
Westhall
Tomnavoulin
Carn an t-Suidhe
Glen Suie
Blackwater Forest
Aldivalloch
Cabrach
Elrick
Wheedlemont
Longlands
Craik
Cottown
Clatt
Duncanston
New Leslie
Old Leslie
Kirkton
Ryehill
Oyne
Glenlivet
Knockandhu
Cairnbrallan
Bracklach
Craig
St Mary's Kirk
Mire of Midgates
Whitehaugh Forest
Suie Hill
Knock Saul
Millburn
Leslie
Auchleven
Garioch
Archaeolink Prehistoric Park
Pittodrie Ho.
Clashnoir
Braes of Glenlivet
Round Hill
Hill of Three Stones
The Buck
Clova
Lumsden
Correen Hills
Old Military Road
Muckletown
Black Hill
Bennachie
Mither Tap
Chapeltown
Letterach
Geal Charn
Sand Hill
Mount Meddin
Hill of John's Cairn
Brux Hill
Lord Arthur's Cairn
Terpersie Castle
Redhouse
Glenton
Millstone Hill
Woodend
Breac Leathad
Carn Mòr
Badenyon
Creag an Fhuarain
Peat Hill
Edinbanchory
Mossat
Tullynessle
Keig
Rorandle
Ladder Hills
Moss Hill
Dulax
Ladylea Hill
Rinmore
Glencuie
Kildrummy
Delphorrie
Milltown of Kildrummy
Don
Grampian Transport Mus
Montgarrie
Bridge of Alford
Alford
Haughton House
Bankhead
Pitfichie
Cairn William
Pitfichie Forest
Grantlodge
Carn Liath
Water of Nochty
Torrancroy
Kildrummy Castle Gardens
Auchintoul
Coiliochbhar Hill
Alford Valley Railway Museum
Howe of Alford
Gateside
Pitmunie
Monymusk
Lecht Ski Centre
The Socach
Kirkton of Glenbuchat
Mains of Glenbuchat
Glenbuchat
Glenkindie
Fichlie
Asloun
Dorsell
Kingsford
Whitehouse
Todlachie
Beinn a' Chruinnich
Breagach Hill
Bellabeg
Forbestown
Towie
Sinnahard
Hillockhead
Bridgeton
Muir of Fowlis
Kirkton
Cairn Vachich
Strathdon
Glen Ernan
Waterside
Heugh-head
Boultenstone Hotel
Milltown of Towie
Scar Hill
Ley
Muirhead
Tillyfourie
Black Hill
Tillycairn Castle
Little Ley
Carn Ealasaid
Geal Charn
Craig of Bunzeach
Tornashean Forest
Frosty Hill
Milton of Cushnie
Leochel-Cushnie
Craigievar Castle (NTS)
Tillyfour
Corrennie Moor
Corrennie Forest
Sauchen
Ordhead
Milltown
Cock Bridge
Corgarff
Colnabaichin
Fleuchats
Hillockhead
Bogston
Badernonach Hill
Broom Hill
Pressendye
Benaquhallie
Kintocher
Shiels
Corsindae
Tornahaish
Tillypronie
East Davoch
Bogfields
Bankhead
Comers
Tillybirloch
Carn Leac Saighdeir
Cairn Mona Gowan
Migvie
Melgum
Bogfern
Oldmill
Tullochvenus
Glenshalg
Collmuir
Craiglich
Douneside
Craskins
Perkhill
Tornaveen
Drumlasie
Auchorrie
Brown Cow Hill
Carn a' Bhacain
Glen Fenzie
Coynach
Logie Coldstone
Morven
Corrachree
Tarland
CROMAR
Culsh Earth House
Wartle
Milton of Auchinhove
Lumphanan
Cairnbeathie
Peel Ring
East Learney
Midmar Forest
Hill of Fare
PARK
ABERDEENSHIRE
Tomnaverie Stone Circle
Leys
Coull
Davan
Ordie
Scar Hill
Mortlich
Torphins
Craigmyle Ho.
Milton of Campfield
Raemoir Ho.
Daldownie
Gairnshiel Lodge
Culblean Hill
Loch Davan
Loch Kinord
Kincardine O'Neil
Mid Beltie
Dalfad
Lary
Rinloan
Glen Gairn
Peter's Hill
Heugh-head
Rosehill
Glassel
Kennerty
Braenaloin
Torbeg
Candacraig
Cambus o' May
Dinnet
Aboyne
Tillydrine
Brathens
Geallaig Hill
Culsh
Bridge of Gairn
Milton of Tullich
Muir of Dinnet
Oldhall
Bridge of Ess
Birsemore
Birse
Allancreich
Cordach
Potarch
Backhill of Trustach
Bridge of Canny
Inchmarlo
East Mains
Bush Crathie
Greystone
Ballater
Glascorrie
Deecastle
Ballaterach
Glen Tanar NNR
The Fungle Road
Balfour
Marywell
Blackhall Forest
Hill of Goauch
Bridge of Dee
Auchattie
Balmoral Castle
Crathie
Strathgirnock
Pannanich Hill
Black Craig
Glen Tanar
Ballogie
Tom's Cairn
Scolty
Inver
Easter Balmoral
Clachanturn
Birkhall
Bridge of Muick
Forest of Glentanar
Carnferg
Glencat
Finzean
Baulds
Invergelder
Creag nan Gall
The Coyles of Muick
Cairn Leuchan
Clachan Yell
Lamahip
Drumhead
Percie
Whitestone
Strachan
Forest of Birse
Ballochan
Bridge of Bogendreip
Red Craig
Craigmahandle
Water of Feugh
Aucholzie
Craig of Dalfro
Greendams
Linn of Muick Cottage
Cock Cairn
White Hill
Peter Hill
Balmoral Forest
Inchnabobart
Glen Muick
Mount Keen
Braid Cairn
Hill of Cat
Cock Hill
Clachnaben
Glendye Lodge
Kerloch
Conachcraig
Fasheilach
Hill of Saughs
Mudlee Bracks
Bridge of Dye
Tipperweir
Lochnagar
Cac Carn Beag
Carn a' Choire Bhoidheach
Spittal of Glenmuick
Glen Mark
Glen Tennet
Mount Battock
Hill of Edendocher
White Mounth
Loch Muick
Dubh Loch
Cairn Bannoch
Glen Dye
Black Hill of Mark
Glen Lee
Hill of Fingray
Meluncart
Goyle Hill
Broad Cairn
Easter Balloch
Monawee
Glenlee
Auchronie
Cairn o'Mount
Drumtochty Forest
Tolmount
Tom Buidhe
Inchgrundle
Loch Lee
Tarfside
Cairncross
Fernybank
Hound Hillock
Glen Esk
Glen Effock
Sturdy Hill
Clatterin Brig
Glensaugh
Strathfinella Hill
Craig Mellon
Glen Doll
Glendoll Lodge
Lair of Aldararie
Green Hill
Muckle Cairn
Cruys
West Knock
Bulg
Phesdo
Corrie Fee NNR
Braedownie
Ben Tirran
Thainston
Auchmull
Mayar
Driesh
Hill of Strone
Clova
White Hill
Hill of Wirren
Fettercairn
Howe of the Mearns
Hunt Hill
Cairn Baddoch
Mount Blair
Cairn of Barns
Glen Clova
Finbracks
Dog Hillock
Hill of Berran
Dalbog
The Burn
Burn Farm
Thornyhill
Meikle Strath
Mains of Thornton
Mid Hill
Wheen
Rottal
Hill of Glansie
Hill of Formal
Witton
Gannochy
Inch of Arnhall
Edzell Castle
Arnhall
Badandun Hill
Hill of Corbet
Bridgend
Tillyarblet
Dunlappie
Feus of Caldhame
Inglismaldie Forest
Eskielawn
Balnaboth
Glenprosen Village
Auld Darkney
Peat Hill
Brown Caterthun (fort)
North Water Bridge

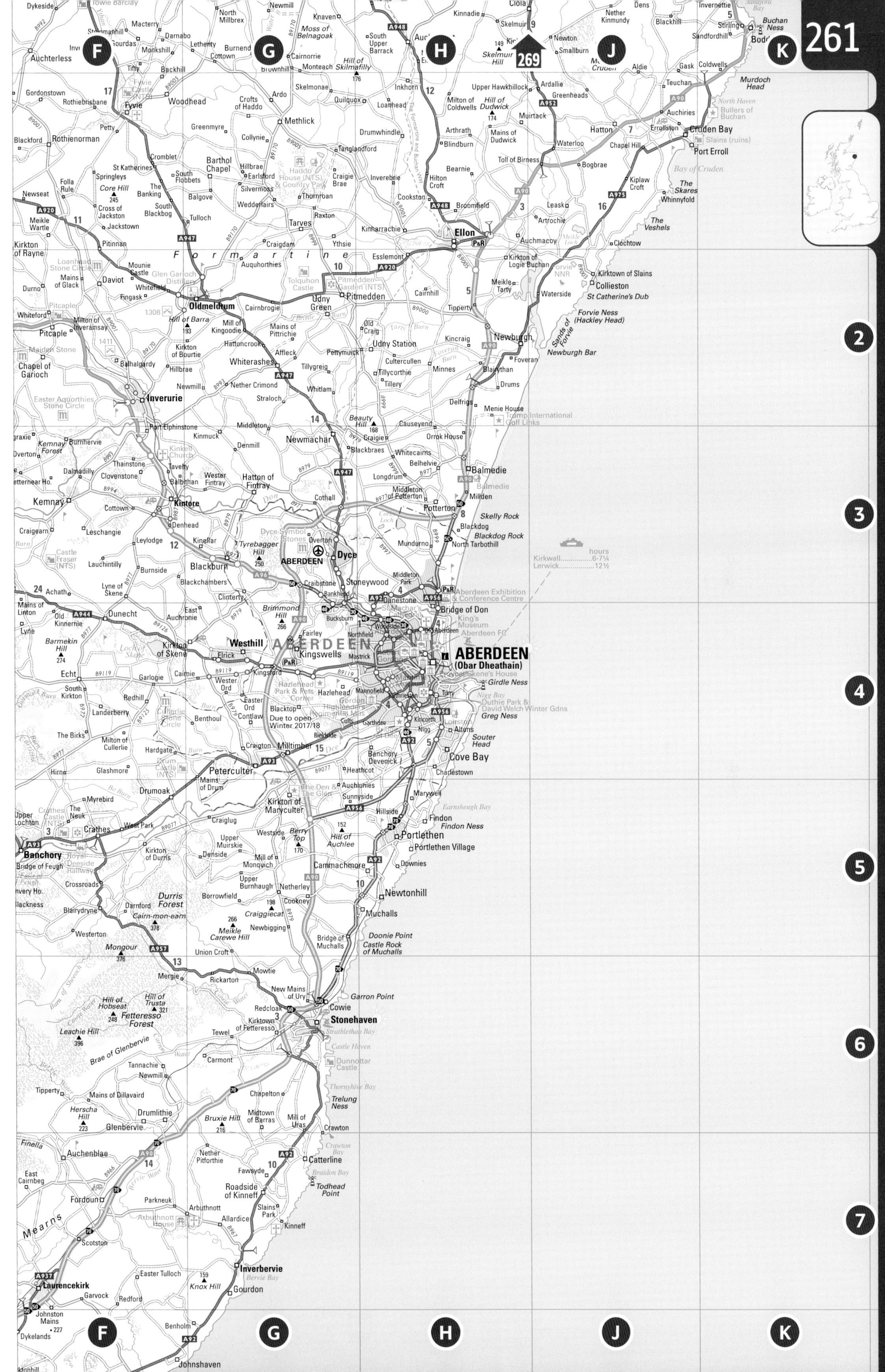
F
G
H
J
K
269
2
3
4
5
6
7
Auchterless
Fyvie
Woodhead
Methlick
Rothienorman
Gordonstown
Rothiebrisbane
Blackford
Barthol Chapel
Haddo House (NTS) & Country Park
Tarves
Ythsie
Ellon
Esslemont
Kinharrachie
Skelmonae
Inkhorn
Auchnagatt
Skelmuir Hill
Newton
Smallburn
Nether Kinmundy
Dens
Blackhill
Invernettie
Stirling
Buchan Ness
Boddam
Sandfordhill
Murdoch Head
Gask
Coldwells
Teuchan
Auchiries
Bullers of Buchan
Hatton
Cruden Bay
Slains (ruins)
Port Erroll
Chapel Hill
Bay of Cruden
Kiplaw Croft
The Skares
Whinnyfold
The Veshels
Bogbrae
Toll of Birness
Waterloo
Milton of Coldwells
Hill of Dudwick
Mains of Dudwick
Arthrath
Blindburn
Bearnie
Hilton Croft
Cookston
Broomfield
Leask
Artrochie
Auchmacoy
Clochtow
Kirkton of Logie Buchan
Kirktown of Slains
Collieston
St Catherine's Dub
Forvie NNR
Waterside
Forvie Ness (Hackley Head)
Sands of Forvie
Newburgh Bar
Newburgh
Foveran
Kincraig
Tipperty
Meikle Tarty
Formartine
Pitmedden
Pitmedden Garden (NTS)
Tolquhon Castle
Udny Green
Udny Station
Oldmeldrum
Glen Garioch Distillery
Daviot
Mains of Glack
Durno
Pitcaple
Whiteford
Chapel of Garioch
Maiden Stone
Inverurie
Easter Aquorthies Stone Circle
Port Elphinstone
Kintore
Kemnay
Kemnay Forest
Hatton of Fintray
Newmachar
Whiterashes
Straloch
Cothall
Balmedie
Potterton
Blackdog
Skelly Rock
Blackdog Rock
North Tarbothill
Belhelvie
Whitecairns
Menie House
Trump International Golf Links
Blairythan
Drums
Delfrigs
Tillycorthie
Cultercullen
Minnes
Dyce
ABERDEEN
Stoneywood
Bucksburn
Blackburn
Tyrebagger Hill
Kirkhill
Kirkwall
Lerwick
hours
Aberdeen Exhibition & Conference Centre
Bridge of Don
King's Museum
Aberdeen FC
ABERDEEN (Obar Dheathain)
Provost Skene's House
Girdle Ness
Nigg Bay
Duthie Park & David Welch Winter Gdns
Greg Ness
Souter Head
Cove Bay
Charlestown
Altens
Westhill
Kingswells
Kirkton of Skene
Elrick
Echt
Dunecht
Westhill
Hazlehead
Milltimber
Peterculter
Drum Castle (NTS)
Drumoak
Crathes
Crathes Castle (NTS)
Banchory
Kirkton of Maryculter
Portlethen
Portlethen Village
Findon
Findon Ness
Earnsheugh Bay
Hill of Auchlee
Cammachmore
Newtonhill
Muchalls
Doonie Point
Castle Rock of Muchalls
Bridge of Muchalls
Durris Forest
Cairn-mon-earn
Meikle Carewe Hill
Netherley
Mongour
Fetteresso Forest
Hill of Trusta
Hill of Hobseat
Leachie Hill
Brae of Glenbervie
Garron Point
Cowie
Stonehaven
Strathlethan Bay
Castle Haven
Dunnottar Castle
Thornyhive Bay
Trelung Ness
Crawton
Crawton Bay
Catterline
Braidon Bay
Todhead Point
Kinneff
Roadside of Kinneff
Arbuthnott
Arbuthnott House
Allardice
Inverbervie
Bervie Bay
Gourdon
Knox Hill
Benholm
Johnshaven
Mearns
Auchenblae
Fordoun
Glenbervie
Drumlithie
Laurencekirk
Garvock
Redford
Johnston Mains
Dykelands
Due to open Winter 2017/18

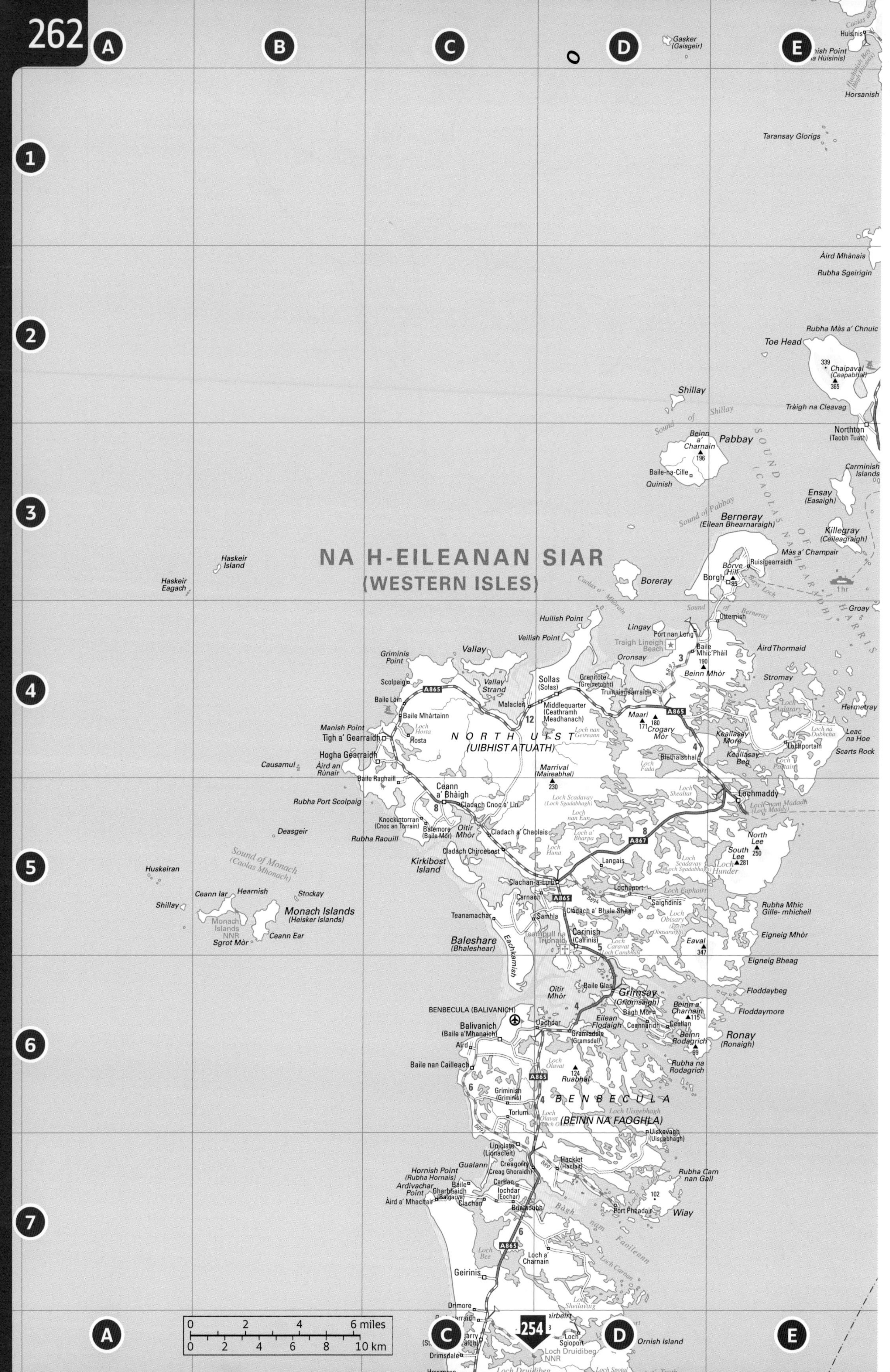

A   B   C   D   E

1

2

3

NA H-EILEANAN SIAR
(WESTERN ISLES)

Haskeir
Island

Haskeir
Eagach

4

5

6

7

Huilish Point

Veilish Point

Griminis
Point

Valley

Valley
Strand

Scolpaig

Baile Lòin

A865

Baile Mhàrtainn

Loch
Hosta

Hosta

Manish Point

Tigh a' Gearraidh

Hogha Gearraidh

Causamul

Àird an
Rùnair

Baile Raghaill

NORTH UIST
(UIBHIST A TUATH)

Rubha Port Scolpaig

Ceann
a' Bhàigh

8

Cladach Cnoc a' Lin

Knocklntorran
(Cnoc an Torrain)

Deasgeir

Baitemore
(Baile Mòr)

Oitir
Mhòr

Cladach a' Chaolais

Rubha Raouill

Cladach Chircebost

Kirkibost
Island

Loch
Huna

Clachan-a-Luib

Carnach

A865

Cladach a' Bhale Shear

Samhla

Teanamachar

Carinish
(Càirinis)

Loch
Caravat
Loch Caruibhidh

5

Teampull na
Trionaid

Baleshare
(Bhaleshear)

Sollas
(Solas)

Malaclen

Middlequarter
(Ceathramh
Meadhanach)

12

Marrival
(Maireabhal)
230

Granitote
(Greinetobht)

Trumaisgearraidh

A865

Maari

Crogary
Mòr

171

Loch nan
Geireann

Loch
Fada

Biathaisbhal

Loch Scadavay
(Loch Sgadabhagh)

Loch
nan Eun

Loch a'
Bharpa

Loch Huna

Langais

A867

8

Loch a'
Bharpa

Locheport

Saighdinis

Loch Obisary
(Loch
Obasaraigh)

Eaval
347

Loch
Skealtar

Loch Scadavay
Loch Sgadabhagh

Loch
Euphoirt

Loch
Hunder

Shillay

Sound
of Shillay

Beinn
a'
Charnain
196

Baile-na-Cille

Quinish

Pabbay

Boreray

Borve
Hill
85

Borgh

Ruisigearraidh

Màs a' Champair

Berneray
(Eilean Bhearnaraigh)

Killegray
(Ceileagraigh)

SOUND OF HARRIS (CAOLAS NA HEARADH)

Groay

Sound
of Berneray

Caolas a' Mhorain

Oronsay

Tràigh Linéigh
Beach

Lingay

Port nan Long

Baile
Mhic'Phàil
190

Beinn Mhòr

3

Beinn
Charnain

Àird Thormaid

Maari
180

A865

Keallasay
More

Keallasay
Beg

4

Lochmaddy

Loch nam Madadh
(Loch Maddy)

North
Lee

South
Lee
250

Loch
Aulasary

Hermetray

Stromay

Leac
na Hoe

Scarts Rock

Lochportain

Loch
Portain

Rubha Mhic
Gille- mhicheil

Eigneig Mhòr

Eigneig Bheag

Gasker
(Gaisgeir)

Huisnis

Taransay Glorigs

Àird Mhànais

Rubha Sgeirigin

Rubha Màs a' Chnuic

Toe Head

339

Chaipaval
(Ceapabhal)
365

Tràigh na Cleavag

Northton
(Taobh Tuath)

Carminish
Islands

Ensay
(Easaigh)

Màs a' Champair

1 hr

Husekeiran

Ceann Iar   Hearnish   Stockay

Shillay

Monach Islands
(Heisker Islands)

Monach
Islands
NNR

Ceann Ear

Sgrot Mòr

Sound of Monach
(Caolas Mhonach)

Baile Glas

Oitìr
Mhòr

Grimsay
(Griomsaigh)

Bàgh Mòr

Eilean
Flodaigh

Ceannaridh

Beinn a'
Charnain
115

Ceallan

Beinn
Rodagrich
99

Rubha na
Rodagrich

Ronay
(Ronaigh)

Floddaybeg

Floddaymore

BENBECULA (BALIVANICH)

Balivanich
(Baile a'Mhanaich)

Aird

Baile nan Cailleach

Griminish
(Griminis)

6

Torlum

Uachdar

4

Gramsdale
(Gramsdal)

A865

Loch
Olavat

Loch
Olavat

Ruabhal
124

BENBECULA
(BEINN NA FAOGHLA)

Loch Uisgebhagh

Uiskevagh
(Uisgebhagh)

Rubha Cam
nan Gall

Liniclate
(Lìonacleit)

Gualann

Creagorry
(Creag Ghoraidh)

Hacklet
(Haclait)

Hornish Point
(Rubha Hornais)

Ardivachar
Point

Baile
Gharbhaidh
Balgarva

Carnan

Iochdar
(Eochar)

102

Wiay

Àird a' Mhachair

Clachan

Bualadubh

6

A865

Port Phèadair

Geirinis

Loch
Bee

Loch a'
Charnain

Loch Carnan

Bàgh nam Faoileann

Drimore

Howmore

254

C   D   E

0   2   4   6 miles
0 2 4 6 8 10 km

Carnach

Loch
Druidibeg
NNR

Loch Druidibeg

Loch Spotal

Ornish Island

Loch
Sgioport

A

C   D   E

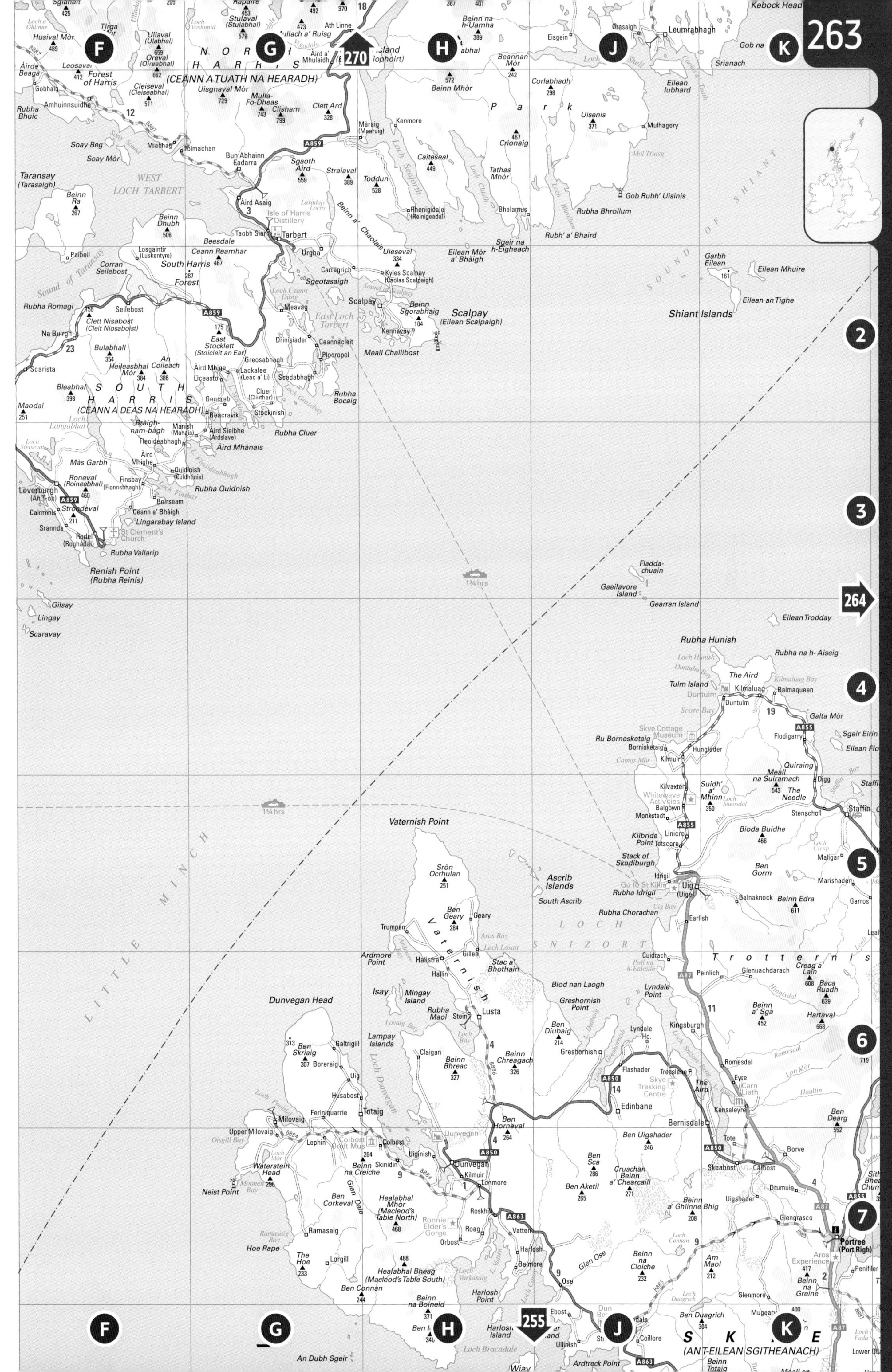

F
G
H
J
K
270
255
264
2
3
4
5
6
7
NORTH HARRIS
(CEANN A TUATH NA HEARADH)
Forest of Harris
Husival Mòr
Tirga Mòr
Ullaval (Ulabhal)
Oreval (Oireabhal)
Stulaval (Stulabhal)
Àirde Beaga
Leosaval
Gobhaig
Cleiseval (Cleiseabhal)
Uisgnaval Mòr
Mulla-Fo-Dheas
Clisham
Clett Ard
Amhuinnsuidhe
Rubha Bhuic
Soay Beg
Soay Mòr
Miabhag
Tolmachan
Bun Abhainn Eadarra
Sgaoth Aird
Straiaval
Toddun
Taransay (Tarasaigh)
WEST LOCH TARBERT
Beinn Ra
Aird Asaig
Isle of Harris Distillery
Beinn Dhubh
Taobh Siar
Tarbert
Urgha
Beesdale
Ceann Reamhar
Losgaintir (Luskentyre)
Paibeil
South Harris Forest
Corran Seilebost
Sound of Taransay
Seilebost
Rubha Romagi
Clett Nisabost (Cleit Niosaboist)
Na Buirgh
Bulabhall
Scarista
Heileasbhal Mòr
An Coileach
East Stocklett (Stoicleit an Ear)
Àird Mhige
Liceasto
Bleabhal
SOUTH HARRIS
(CEANN A DEAS NA HEARADH)
Maodal
Loch Langabhat
Braigh-nam-bagh
Manish (Manais)
Àird Sleibhe (Ardslave)
Fleoideabhagh
Àird Mhànais
Màs Garbh
Àird Mhighe
Quidinish (Cuidhtinis)
Roneval (Roineabhal)
Finsbay (Fionnsbhagh)
Leverburgh (An t-Ob)
Rubha Quidnish
Cairminis
Strondeval
Boirseam
Ceann a' Bhàigh
Lingarabay Island
Srannda
Rodel (Roghadal)
St Clement's Church
Rubha Vallarip
Renish Point (Rubha Reinis)
Gilsay
Lingay
Scaravay
Meavag
Drinisiader
Ceannacleit
Plocropol
Greosabhagh
Lackalee (Leac a' Li)
Scadabhagh
Cluer (Cliuthar)
Stockinish
Beacravik
Geocrab
Rubha Bocaig
Rubha Cluer
East Loch Tarbert
Sgeotasaigh
Scalpay
Carragrich
Kyles Scalpay (Caolas Scalpaigh)
Uieseval
Beinn Sgorabhaig
Kennaway
Scalpay (Eilean Scalpaigh)
Meall Challibost
Beinn na h-Uamha
Beinn Mhòr
Beannan Mòr
Màraig (Maaruig)
Kenmore
Loch Seaforth
Caiteseal
Rhenigidale (Reinigeadal)
Beinn a' Chaolais
Eilean Mòr a' Bhàigh
Sgeir na h-Eigheach
Eisgein
Orasaigh
Leumrabhagh
Kebock Head
Gob na
Srianach
Eilean Iubhard
Corlabhadh
Park
Uisenis
Mulhagery
Crionaig
Tathas Mhòr
Bhalamus
Gob Rubh' Uisinis
Rubha Bhrollum
Rubh' a' Bhaird
SOUND OF SHIANT
Garbh Eilean
Eilean Mhuire
Eilean an Tighe
Shiant Islands
1¼ hrs
Fladda-chuain
Gaeilavore Island
Gearran Island
Eilean Trodday
Rubha Hunish
Rubha na h- Aiseig
The Aird
Kilmaluag
Balmaqueen
Tulm Island
Duntulm
Score Bay
Galta Mòr
Skye Cottage Museum
Ru Bornesketaig
Borniesketaig
Hunglader
Flodigarry
Sgeir Eirin
Eilean Flo
Kilmuir
Camas Mòr
Quiraing
Meall na Suiramach
Digg
Kilvaxter
Suidh' a' Mhinn
Whitewave Activities
Balgown
The Needle
Staffin
Monkstadt
Stenscholl
Bioda Buidhe
Linicro
Kilbride Point
Totscore
Maligar
Stack of Skudiburgh
Ben Gorm
Idrigil
Uig (Uige)
Go to St Kilda
Rubha Idrigil
Balnaknock
Beinn Edra
Marishader
Garros
Ascrib Islands
South Ascrib
Rubha Chorachan
Earlish
Vaternish Point
LITTLE MINCH
Sròn Ocrhulan
Ben Geary
Geary
Trumpan
Vaternish
Aros Bay
Gillen
Loch Losait
LOCH SNIZORT
Cuidrach
Trotternish
Ardmore Point
Halistra
Stac a' Bhothain
Hallin
Poll na h-Ealaidh
Peinlich
Glenuachdarach
Creag a' Lain
Baca Ruadh
Biod nan Laogh
Lyndale Point
Isay
Mingay Island
Greshornish Point
Dunvegan Head
Rubha Maol
Lusta
Stein
Ben Diubaig
Lyndale Ho.
Kingsburgh
Beinn a' Sgà
Hartaval
Lampay Islands
Galtrigill
Ben Skriaig
Boreraig
Claigan
Beinn Bhreac
Beinn Chreagach
Greshornish
Loch Dunvegan
Uig
Husabost
Flashader
Treaslane
Skye Trekking Centre
The Aird
Romesdal
Eyre
Carn Liath
Loch Pooltiel
Milovaig
Feriniquarrie
Totaig
Edinbane
Kensaleyre
Upper Milovaig
Oisgill Bay
Lephin
Colbost Croft Mus
Colbost
Dunvegan
Ben Horneval
Bernisdale
Ben Uigshader
Ben Dearg
Tote
Borve
Waterstein Head
Neist Point
Beinn na Creiche
Skinidin
Uiginish
Dunvegan
Kilmuir
Lonmore
Ben Sca
Cruachan Beinn a' Chearcaill
Skeabost
Carbost
Ben Aketil
Drumuie
Ben Corkeval
Glen Dale
Healabhal Mhòr (Macleod's Table North)
Roskhill
Beinn a' Ghlinne Bhig
Uigshader
Ramasaig
Ramasaig Bay
Hoe Rape
Ronnie Elder's Gorge
Orbost
Roag
Vatten
Glengrasco
Portree (Port Rìgh)
Aros Experience
The Hoe
Lorgill
Healabhal Bheag (Macleod's Table South)
Harlosh
Balmore
Glen Ose
Beinn na Cloiche
Am Maol
Beinn na Greine
Penifiler
Ben Connan
Harlosh Point
Ose
Glenmore
Beinn na Boineid
Ebost
Ben Duagrich
Mugeary
Harlosh Island
Ullinish
Coillore
SKYE
(ANT-EILEAN SGITHEANACH)
An Dubh Sgeir
Loch Bracadale
Wiay
Ardtreck Point
A859
A855
A87
A850
A863
B884
B885
B886
B887

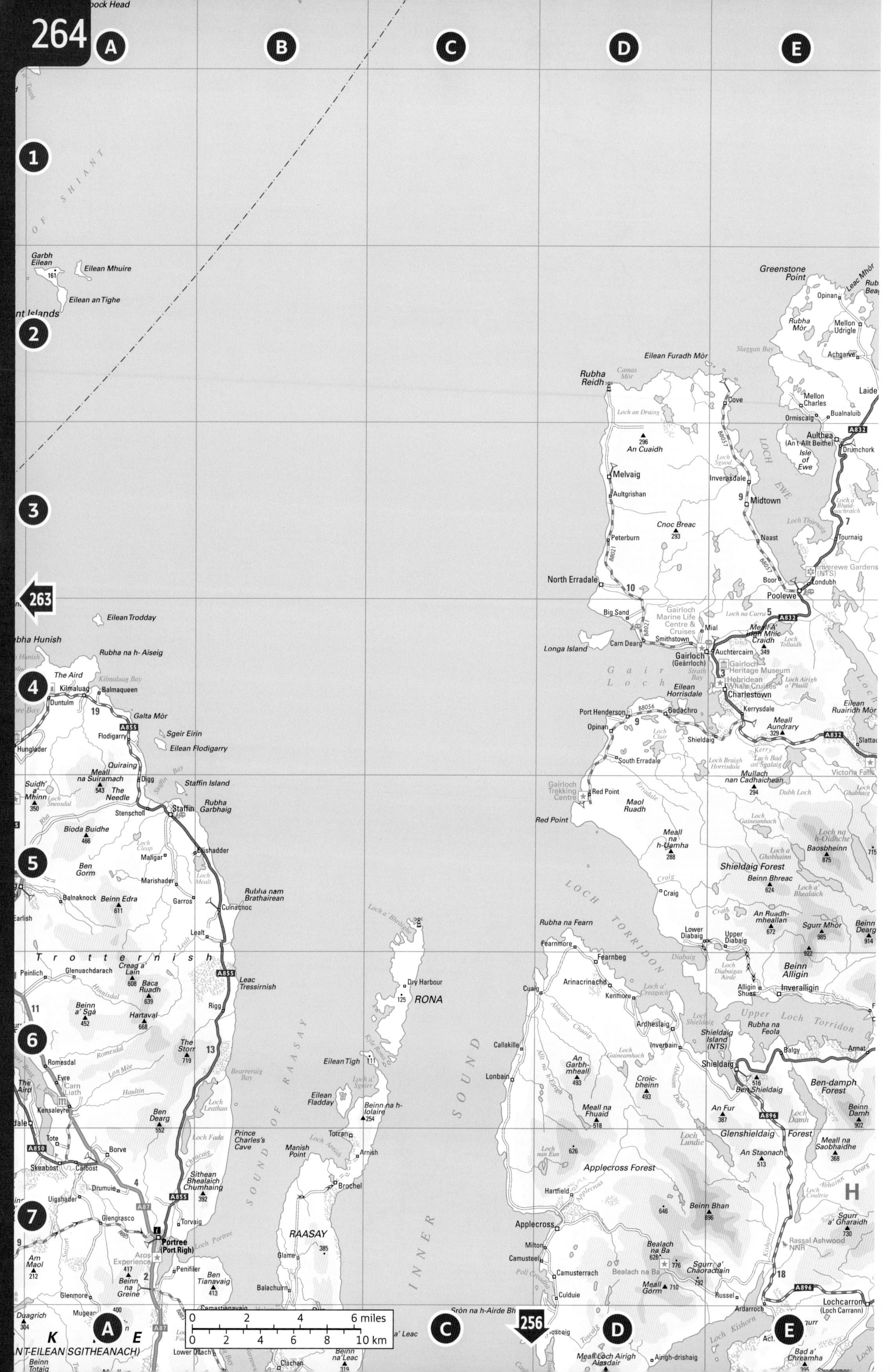

Garbh Eilean
Eilean Mhuire
Eilean an Tighe
Eilean Trodday
Rubha Hunish
Rubha na h- Aiseig
The Aird
Kilmaluag
Balmaqueen
Duntulm
Galta Mòr
Flodigarry
Sgeir Eirin
Eilean Flodigarry
Hunglader
Quiraing
Meall na Suiramach
The Needle
Digg
Staffin Island
Staffin
Rubha Garbhaig
Stenscholl
Bioda Buidhe
Maligar
Ellishadder
Ben Gorm
Marishader
Rubha nam Brathairean
Balnaknock
Beinn Edra
Garros
Culnacnoc
Earlish
Lealt
Trotternish
Peinlich
Glenuachdarach
Creag a' Lain
Baca Ruadh
Leac Tressirnish
Beinn a' Sgà
Hartaval
Rigg
The Storr
Romesdal
Eyre
Carn Liath
Kensaleyre
Ben Dearg
Tote
Borve
Skeabost
Carbost
Drumuie
Sithean Bhealaich Chumhaing
Uigshader
Glengrasco
Torvaig
Portree (Port Righ)
Aros Experience
Am Maol
Beinn na Greine
Penifiler
Ben Tianavaig
Glenmore
Duagrich
Mugeary
Prince Charles's Cave
Manish Point
Torran
Arnish
Brochel
RAASAY
Glame
Balachuirn
Eilean Tigh
Eilean Fladday
Beinn na h-Iolaire
RONA
Dry Harbour
SOUND OF RAASAY
INNER SOUND
Sròn na h-Airde Bh
Greenstone Point
Opinan
Rubha Mòr
Mellon Udrigle
Achgarve
Laide
Eilean Furadh Mòr
Rubha Reidh
Cove
Mellon Charles
Ormiscaig
Bualnaluib
Aultbea (An t-Allt Beithe)
Drumchork
Isle of Ewe
An Cuaidh
Melvaig
Aultgrishan
Inverasdale
Midtown
LOCH EWE
Cnoc Breac
Peterburn
Naast
Tournaig
Inverewe Gardens (NTS)
North Erradale
Boor
Londubh
Poolewe
Big Sand
Gairloch Marine Life Centre & Cruises
Mial
Meall A' Ghiubhais
Longa Island
Carn Dearg
Smithstown
Auchtercairn
Gairloch (Geàrrloch)
Gairloch Heritage Museum
Gair Loch
Hebridean Whale Cruises
Eilean Horrisdale
Charlestown
Port Henderson
Badachro
Kerrysdale
Meall Aundrary
Opinan
Shieldaig
South Erradale
Mullach nan Cadhaichean
Victoria Falls
Gairloch Trekking Centre
Red Point
Maol Ruadh
Red Point
Meall na h-Uamha
Baosbheinn
Shieldaig Forest
Beinn Bhreac
LOCH TORRIDON
Craig
An Ruadh-mheallan
Sgurr Mhòr
Rubha na Fearn
Lower Diabaig
Upper Diabaig
Beinn Dearg
Fearnmore
Fearnbeg
Beinn Alligin
Arinacrinachd
Alligin Shuas
Inveralligin
Cuaig
Kenmore
Upper Loch Torridon
Ardheslaig
Rubha na Feola
Shieldaig Island (NTS)
Callakille
Inverbain
Balgy
Annat
An Garbh-mheall
Shieldaig
Lonbain
Croic-bheinn
Ben Shieldaig
Ben-damph Forest
Meall na Fhuaid
An Fur
Glenshieldaig
Forest
Beinn Damh
Meall na Saobhaidhe
An Staonach
Applecross Forest
Hartfield
Beinn Bhan
Sgurr a' Gharaidh
Applecross
Rassal Ashwood NNR
Milton
Camusteel
Bealach na Ba
Sgurr a' Chaorachain
Camusterrach
Culduie
Meall Gorm
Russel
Ardarroch
Lochcarron (Loch Carrann)
Meall Loch Airigh Alasdair
Airigh-drishaig
Bad a' Chreamha
0 2 4 6 miles
0 2 4 6 8 10 km

263
256

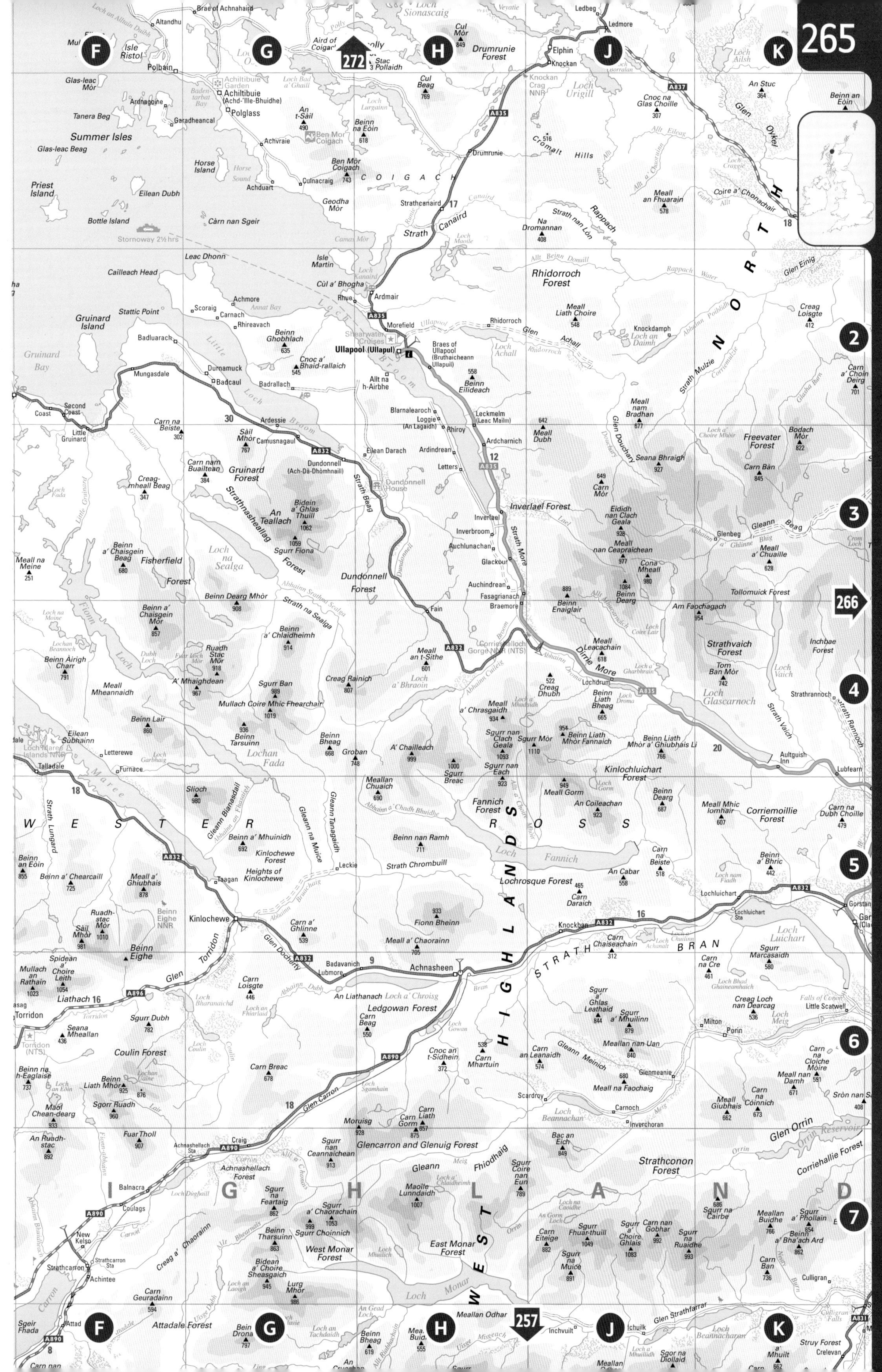

272
257
266
Summer Isles
Achiltibuie
Polglass
Ullapool (Ullapul)
Loch Broom
Little Loch Broom
Gruinard Bay
Gruinard Island
Priest Island
Tanera Beg
Isle Ristol
Isle Martin
Horse Island
Bottle Island
Stornoway 2½ hrs
Coigach
Ben Mòr Coigach
Cul Mòr
Cul Beag
Drumrunie Forest
Elphin
Knockan
Ledmore
Ledbeg
Cromalt Hills
Strath Canaird
Rhidorroch Forest
Glen Achall
Strath Mulzie
Freevater Forest
Inverlael Forest
Strath More
Braemore
Corrieshalloch Gorge NNR (NTS)
Dirrie More
Loch Glascarnoch
Strathvaich Forest
Inchbae Forest
Aultguish Inn
An Teallach
Gruinard Forest
Fisherfield Forest
Dundonnell Forest
Dundonnell
Strath Beag
Loch na Sealga
Loch Maree
Slioch
Kinlochewe
Beinn Eighe
Liathach
Torridon
Glen Torridon
Glen Docherty
Loch Fannich
Fannich Forest
Kinlochluichart Forest
Corriemoillie Forest
Lochrosque Forest
Strath Bran
Achnasheen
Loch a' Chroisg
Ledgowan Forest
Coulin Forest
Glen Carron
Achnashellach
Glencarron and Glenuig Forest
West Monar Forest
East Monar Forest
Loch Monar
Strathconon Forest
Glen Orrin
Corriehallie Forest
Loch Luichart
Lochluichart
Gorstan
Strathcarron
Lochcarron
Attadale Forest
Glen Strathfarrar
Struy Forest
Wester Ross
Highlands
West Highlands
Highland
North
A835
A832
A837
A890
A896
A831

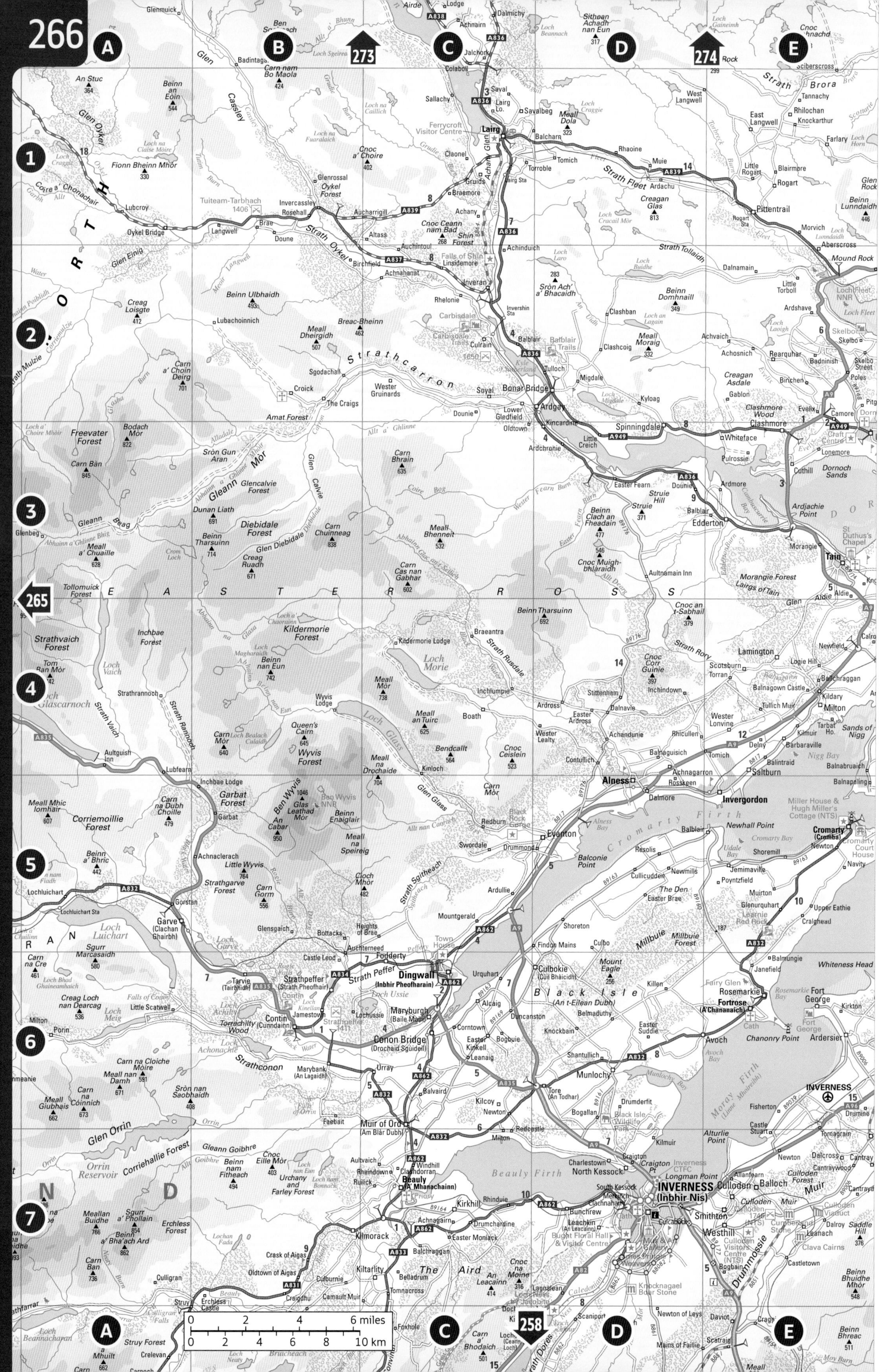
A
B
C
D
E
1
2
3
4
5
6
7
273
274
265
258
Lairg
Strath Oykel
Strathcarron
Bonar Bridge
Ardgay
Spinningdale
Clashmore
Dornoch Sands
Edderton
Tain
E A S T E R R O S S
Loch Morie
Loch Glass
Wyvis Forest
Ben Wyvis
Alness
Invergordon
Cromarty Firth
Cromarty
Evanton
Dingwall
(Inbhir Pheofharain)
Strathpeffer
Contin
Garve
Loch Luichart
Conon Bridge
Maryburgh
Black Isle
(An t-Eilean Dubh)
Fortrose
Rosemarkie
Avoch
Munlochy
Muir of Ord
Beauly
Beauly Firth
North Kessock
INVERNESS
(Inbhir Nis)
Culloden
Moray Firth
Ardersier
Fort George
Kilmorack
The Aird
Orrin Reservoir
Glen Orrin
Strathconon
0 2 4 6 miles
0 2 4 6 8 10 km

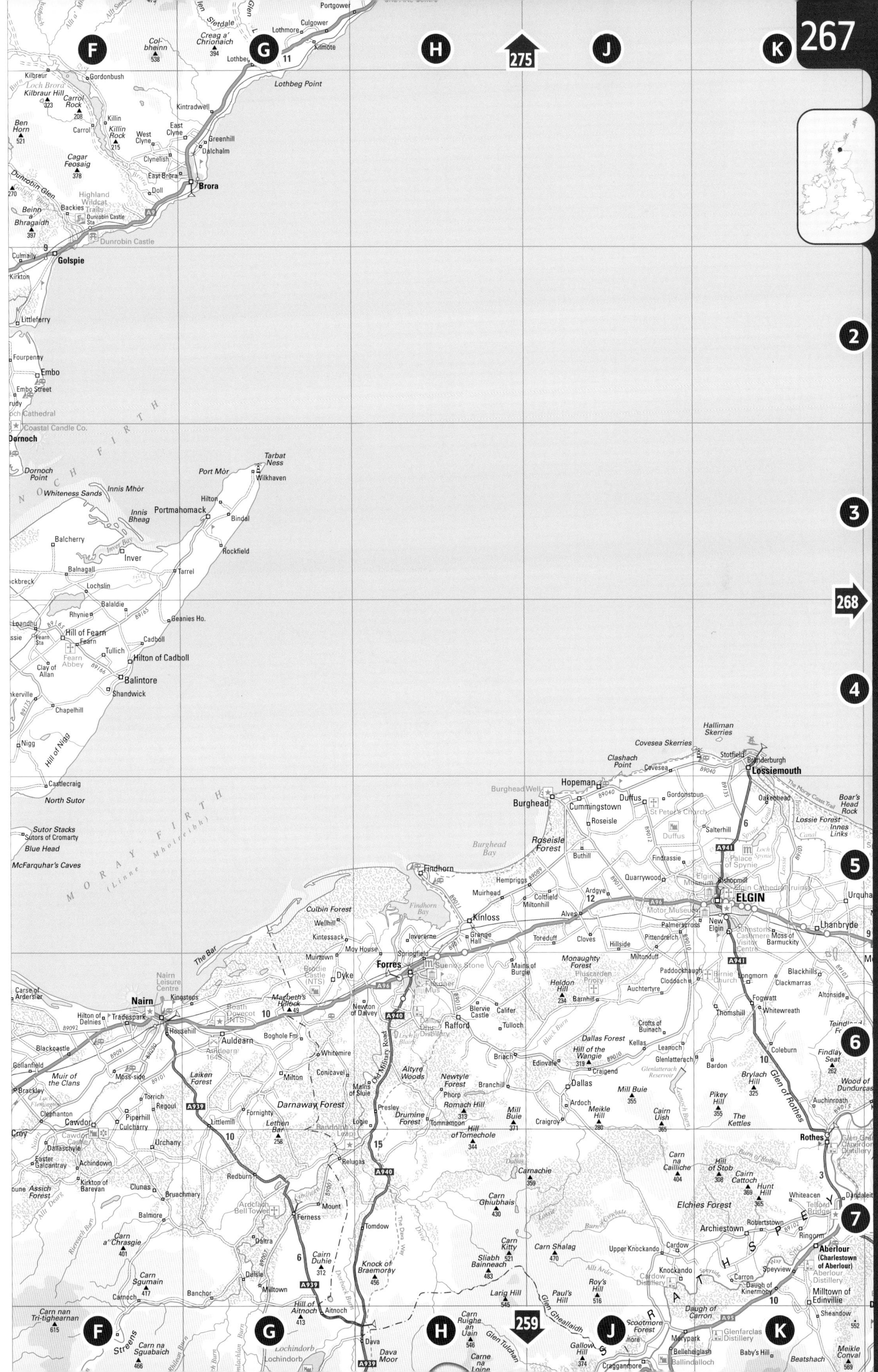
F
G
H
275
J
K
Portgower
Culgower
Lothmore
Kilmote
Creag a' Chrionaich
394
Col-bheinn
538
Lothbeg
Lothbeg Point
Kilbraur
Gordonbush
Loch Brora
Kilbraur Hill
323
Carrol Rock
208
Killin
Carrol
Killin Rock
215
Ben Horn
521
Kintradwell
East Clyne
West Clyne
Greenhill
Dalchalm
Clynelish
Cagar Feosaig
378
East Brora
Doll
Brora
Dunrobin Glen
Highland Wildcat Trails
Backies
Dunrobin Castle Sta
Beinn a' Bhragaidh
397
Dunrobin Castle
Culmaily
Golspie
Kirkton
Littleferry
Fourpenny
Embo
Embo Street
Coastal Candle Co.
Dornoch
Dornoch Point
Whiteness Sands
Innis Mhòr
Innis Bheag
Tarbat Ness
Wilkhaven
Port Mòr
Hilton
Portmahomack
Bindal
Rockfield
Balcherry
Inver
Inver Bay
Balnagall
Tarrel
Lochslin
Rhynie
Balaldie
Beanies Ho.
Hill of Fearn
Fearn
Fearn Abbey
Tullich
Cadboll
Hilton of Cadboll
Clay of Allan
Balintore
Shandwick
Chapelhill
Nigg
Hill of Nigg
Castlecraig
North Sutor
Sutor Stacks
Sutors of Cromarty
Blue Head
McFarquhar's Caves
MORAY FIRTH
(Linne Mhoireibh)
2
3
268
4
5
6
7
Halliman Skerries
Covesea Skerries
Clashach Point
Covesea
Stotfield
Branderburgh
Lossiemouth
Burghead Well
Hopeman
Burghead
Cummingstown
Duffus
Gordonstoun
St Peter's Church
Roseisle
Oakenhead
Boar's Head Rock
Lossie Forest
Innes Links
Salterhill
Roseisle Forest
Burghead Bay
Buthill
Findrassie
Palace of Spynie
Findhorn
Hempriggs
Quarrywood
Bishopmill
Elgin Cathedral (ruins)
Muirhead
Coltfield
Miltonhill
Ardgye
ELGIN
Urquhart
Culbin Forest
Wellhill
Kinloss
Alves
Motor Museum
New Elgin
Lhanbryde
Kintessack
Inverene
Grange Hall
Toreduff
Cloves
Pittendreich
Hillside
Johnstons Cashmere Visitor Centre
Moss of Barmuckity
The Bar
Moy House
Muirtown
Springfield
Forres
Sueno's Stone
Brodie Castle (NTS)
Dyke
Mains of Burgie
Monaughty Forest
Miltonduff
Paddockhaugh
Pluscarden Priory
Birnie Church
Longmorn
Blackhills
Clackmarras
Heldon Hill
234
Barnhill
Auchtertyre
Cloddach
Altonside
Carse of Ardersier
Nairn
Nairn Leisure Centre
Kingsteps
Macbeth's Hillock
Boath Dovecot (NTS)
Newton of Dalvey
Blervie Castle
Califer
Rafford
Tulloch
Fogwatt
Whitewreath
Thornshill
Hilton of Delnies
Tradespark
Househill
Auldearn
Boghole Fm
Crofts of Buinach
Dallas Forest
Kellas
Leanoch
Blackcastle
Whitemire
Briach
Hill of the Wangie
319
Edinvale
Craigend
Glenlatterach
Bardon
Coleburn
Findlay Seat
262
Gollanfield
Muir of the Clans
Moss-side
Laiken Forest
Milton
Conicavel
Altyre Woods
Newtyle Forest
Branchill
Dallas
Mill Buie
355
Brylach Hill
325
Glen of Rothes
Wood of Dundurcas
Brackley
Torrich
Regoul
Mains of Sluie
Phorp
Romach Hill
313
Ardoch
Meikle Hill
280
Cairn Uish
365
Pikey Hill
355
Auchinroath
Clephanton
Piperhill
Littlemill
Fornighty
Darnaway Forest
Presley
Drumine Forest
Tomnamoon
Mill Buie
371
Craigroy
The Kettles
Croy
Cawdor
Cawdor Castle
Culcharry
Lethen Bar
258
Logie
Hill of Tomechole
344
Rothes
Dallaschyle
Urchany
Relugas
Carnachie
359
Carn na Cailliche
404
Hill of Stob
308
Cairn Cattoch
369
Easter Galcantray
Achindown
Redburn
Kirkton of Barevan
Assich Forest
Clunas
Bruachmary
Carn Ghiubhais
430
Hunt Hill
365
Whiteacen
Dandaleith
Ardclach Bell Tower
Ferness
Mount
Balmore
Tomdow
Elchies Forest
Telford Bridge
Archiestown
Robertstown
Ringorm
Carn a' Chrasgie
401
Daltra
Cairn Duhie
312
Knock of Braemoray
456
Carn Kitty
521
Carn Shalag
470
Upper Knockando
Cardow
Aberlour (Charlestown of Aberlour)
Sliabh Bainneach
483
Speyview
Carn Sgumain
417
Dulsie
Knockando
Cardow Distillery
Aberlour Distillery
Carnoch
Banchor
Milltown
Larig Hill
545
Paul's Hill
Roy's Hill
516
Carron
Daugh of Kinermony
Milltown of Edinvillie
Carn nan Tri-tighearnan
615
Hill of Aitnoch
413
Aitnoch
Carn Ruighe an Uain
546
259
Glen Gheallaidh
Daugh of Carron
Scootmore Forest
Sheandow
Streens
Carn na Sguabaich
466
Lochindorb
Dava
Dava Moor
Glen Tulchan
Carne na Loine
Gallow Hill
374
Marypark
Glenfarclas Distillery
Ballindalloch
Baby's Hill
Beatshach
Meikle Conval
569
Craggan more
SPEY
A9
A96
A940
A939
A941
A95
B9040
B9092
B9101

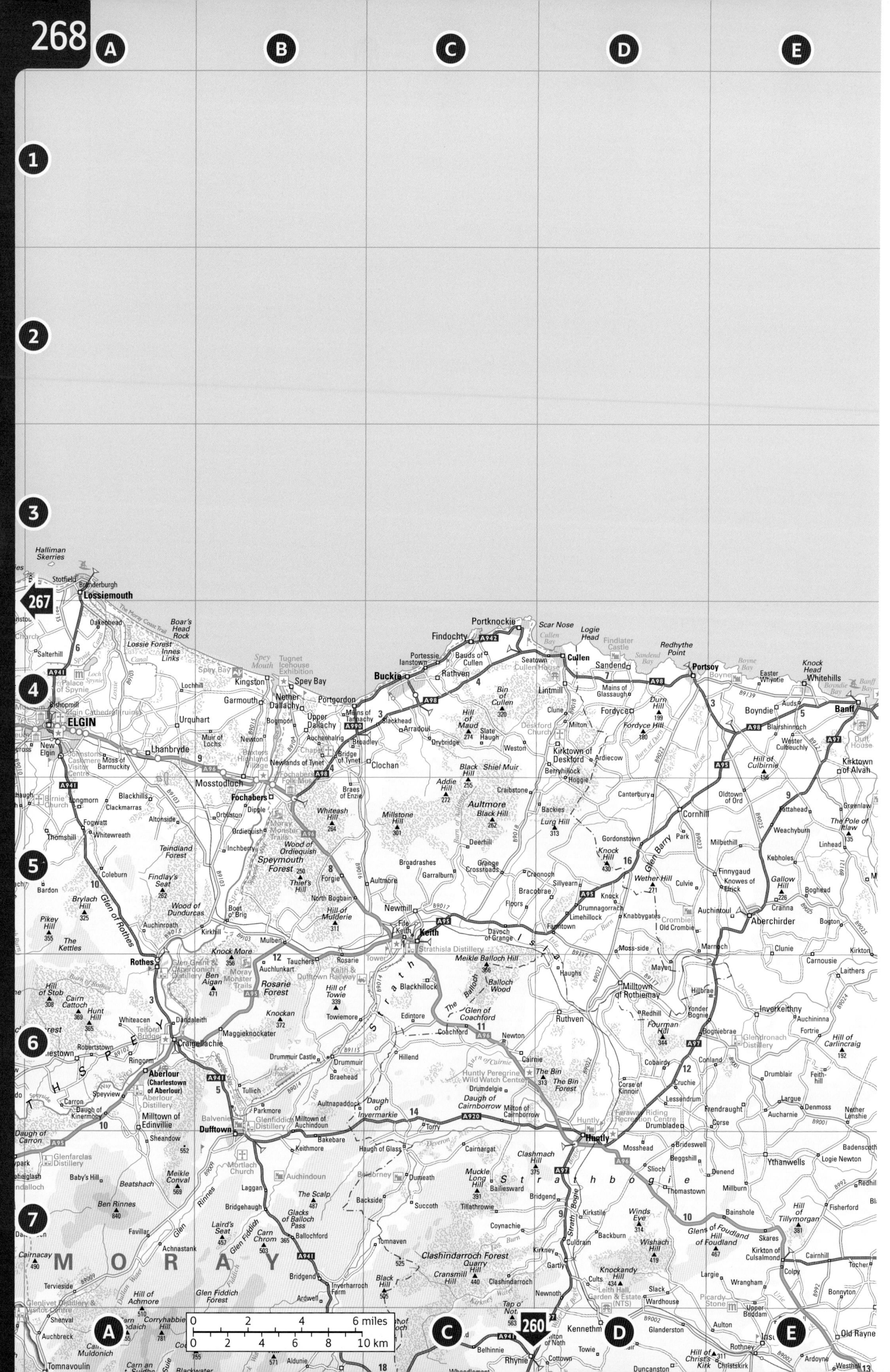
A
B
C
D
E
1
2
3
4
5
6
7
Halliman Skerries
Stotfield
Branderburgh
Lossiemouth
267
Oakenhead
Boar's Head Rock
The Moray Coast Trail
Lossie Forest
Innes Links
Salterhill
Spey Bay
Spey Mouth
Tugnet Icehouse Exhibition
Spey Bay
Kingston
Palace of Spynie
Lochhill
Garmouth
Bishopmill
Elgin Cathedral (ruins)
ELGIN
Urquhart
New Elgin
Johnstons Cashmere Visitor Centre
Moss of Barmuckity
Lhanbryde
Muir of Lochs
Newton
Baxters Highland Village
Newlands of Tynet
Mosstodloch
Fochabers
Fochabers Folk Mus
Longmorn
Blackhills
Clackmarras
Altonside
Orbliston
Dipple
Fogwatt
Whitewreath
Thomshill
Ordiequish
Moray Monster Trails
Inchberry
Teindland Forest
Wood of Ordiequish
Speymouth Forest
Thief's Hill
Coleburn
Findlay's Seat
Bardon
Brylach Hill
Glen of Rothes
Wood of Dundurcas
Pikey Hill
The Kettles
Auchinroath
Kirkhill
Boat o' Brig
Mulben
Knock More
Rothes
Glen Grant & Caperdonich Distillery
Auchlunkart
Tauchers
Rosarie
Ben Aigan
Rosarie Forest
Hill of Stob
Cairn Cattoch
Hunt Hill
Whiteacen
Telford Bridge
Dandaleith
Maggieknockater
Knockan
Craigellachie
Robertstown
Ringorm
Aberlour (Charlestown of Aberlour)
Aberlour Distillery
Speyview
Carron
Daugh of Kinermony
Milltown of Edinvillie
Daugh of Carron
Tullich
Parkmore
Balvenie
Dufftown
Glenfiddich Distillery
Sheandow
Glenfarclas Distillery
Baby's Hill
Beatshach
Meikle Conval
Mortlach Church
Ben Rinnes
Laggan
Bridgehaugh
Favillar
Achnastank
Laird's Seat
Glen Fiddich
Carn Chrom
Cairnacay
MORAY
Tervieside
Hill of Achmore
Glen Fiddich Forest
Glenlivet Distillery & Visitor Centre
Shenval
Corryhabbie Hill
Auchbreck
Tomnavoulin
Findochty
Portknockie
Portessie
Ianstown
Bauds of Cullen
Rathven
Buckie
Portgordon
Nether Dallachy
Upper Dallachy
Bogmoor
Mains of Tannachy
Slackhead
Arradoul
Auchenhalrig
Broadley
Bridge of Tynet
Clochan
Braes of Enzie
Whiteash Hill
Drybridge
Millstone Hill
Addie Hill
Black Hill
Shiel Muir
Aultmore
Broadrashes
Garralburn
Deerhill
Grange Crossroads
Forgie
North Bogbain
Hill of Mulderie
Newmill
Fife Keith
Keith
Strathisla Distillery
Keith & Dufftown Railway
Blackhillock
Hill of Towie
Towiemore
Edintore
Coachford
Glen of Coachford
Balloch Wood
Meikle Balloch Hill
Drummuir Castle
Drummuir
Braehead
Hillend
Aultnapaddock
Daugh of Invermarkie
Milltown of Auchindoun
Torry
Bakebare
Keithmore
Haugh of Glass
Auchindoun
Beldorney
Dumeath
The Scalp
Backside
Glacks of Balloch Pass
Ballochford
Tomnaven
Bridgend
Inverharroch Farm
Black Hill
Ardwell
Scar Nose
Logie Head
Cullen Bay
Findlater Castle
Sandend Bay
Redhythe Point
Seatown
Cullen
Cullen House
Sandend
Mains of Glassaugh
Portsoy
Bin of Cullen
Hill of Maud
Slate Haugh
Lintmill
Clune
Milton
Deskford Church
Durn Hill
Fordyce
Fordyce Hill
Weston
Kirktown of Deskford
Ardiecow
Berryhillock
Hoggie
Craibstone
Canterbury
Aultmore
Black Hill
Backies
Lurg Hill
Gordonstown
Knock Hill
Glen Barry
Cornhill
Park
Crannoch
Sillyearn
Bracobrae
Wether Hill
Culvie
Knock
Floors
Drumnagorrach
Limehillock
Knabbygates
Crombie
Old Crombie
Davoch of Grange
Farmtown
Moss-side
Haughs
Milltown of Rothiemay
Mayen
Redhill
Fourman Hill
Ruthven
Newton
Cairnie
The Bin
The Bin Forest
Huntly Peregrine Wild Watch Centre
Drumdelgie
Daugh of Cairnborrow
Milton of Cairnborrow
Cobairdy
Corse of Kinnoir
Farawa Riding Recreation Centre
Huntly
Drumblade
Cairnargat
Clashmach Hill
Muckle Long Hill
Baillieswards
Strathbogie
Mosshead
Sliach
Tillathrowie
Bridgend
Kirkstile
Winds Eye
Coynachie
Culdrain
Backburn
Wishach Hill
Clashindarroch Forest
Cransmill Hill
Quarry Hill
Clashindarroch
Kirkney
Gartly
Knockandy Hill
Cults
Leith Hall, Garden & Estate (NTS)
Newnoth
Tap o' Noth
Kennethmont
Rhynie
Boyne Bay
Knock Head
Whitehills
Boyne
Easter Whyntie
Boyndie Bay
Banff Bay
Boyndie
Auds
Banff
Blairshinnoch
Wester Culbeuchly
Duff House
Hill of Culbirnie
Kirktown of Alvah
Oldtown of Ord
Fattahead
Greenlaw
The Pole of Itlaw
Milbethill
Weachyburn
Linhead
Kebholes
Finnygaud
Knowes of Elrick
Gallow Hill
Boghead
Auchintoul
Cranna
Aberchirder
Bognie
Marnoch
Clunie
Carnousie
Kirkton
Laithers
Hillbrae
Yonder Bognie
Inverkeithny
Auchininna
Bogniebrae
Glendronach Distillery
Fortrie
Hill of Carlincraig
Conland
Drumblair
Feith-hill
Cruchie
Lessendrum
Frendraught
Largue
Aucharnie
Denmoss
Nether Lenshie
Corse
Brideswell
Beggshill
Denend
Thomastown
Ythanwells
Logie Newton
Badenscoth
Millburn
Bainshole
Hill of Tillymorgan
Fisherford
Glens of Foudland
Hill of Foudland
Skares
Kirkton of Culsalmond
Cairnhill
Colpy
Tocher
Largie
Wrangham
Bonnyton
Slack
Wardhouse
Picardy Stone
Upper Boddam
Glanderston
Aulton
Insch
Old Rayne
Rothney
Hill of Christ's Kirk
Christskirk
Ardoyne
Westhall
Towie
Duncanston
Belhinnie
Cottown
260
0 2 4 6 miles
0 2 4 6 8 10 km

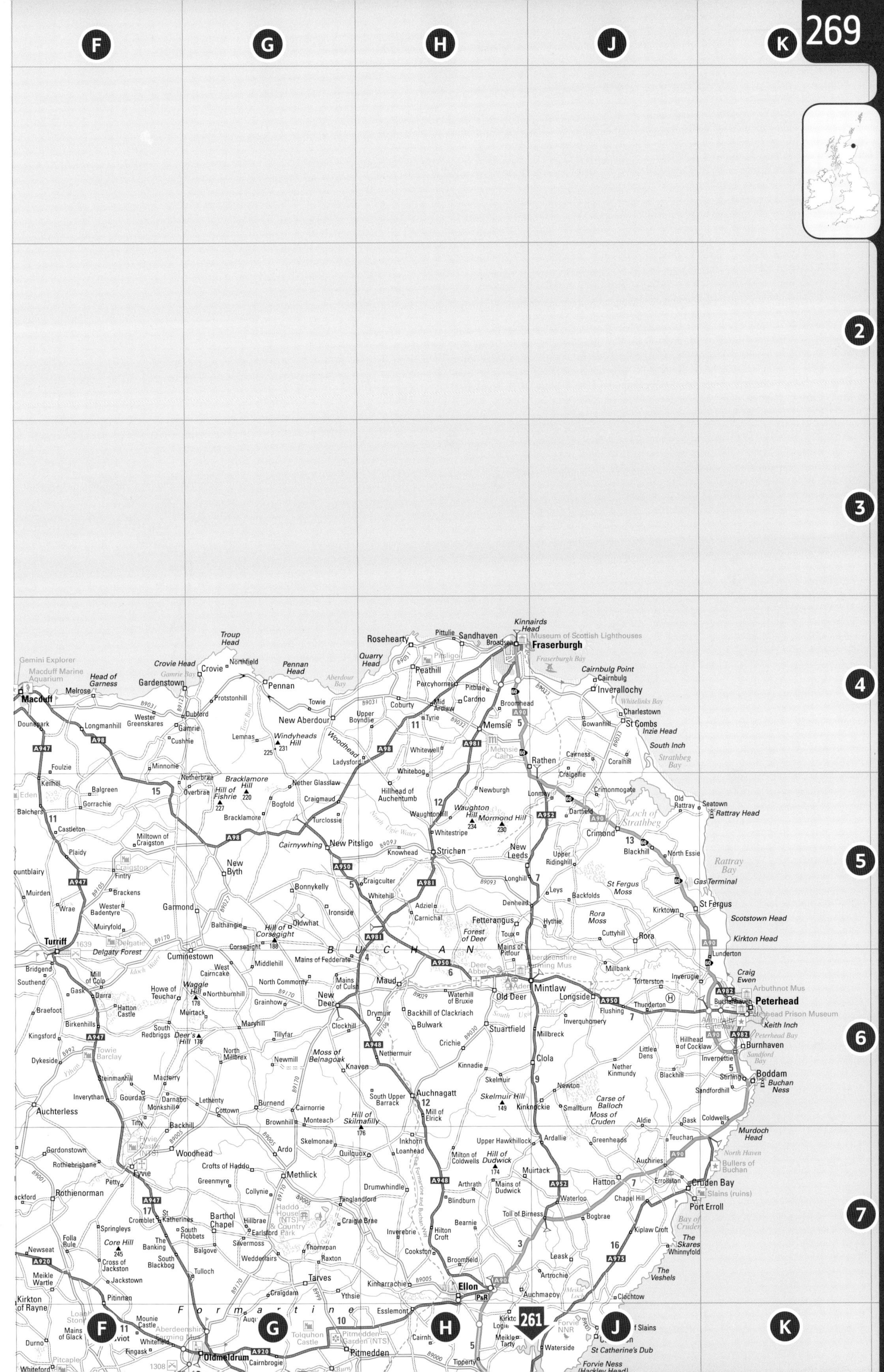
F
G
H
J
K
2
3
4
5
6
7
Kinnairds Head
Museum of Scottish Lighthouses
Fraserburgh
Fraserburgh Bay
Rosehearty
Pittulie
Sandhaven
Broadsea
Troup Head
Quarry Head
Pitsligo
Peathill
Percyhorner
Pitblae
Crovie Head
Crovie
Northfield
Pennan Head
Aberdour Bay
Pennan
Gemini Explorer
Macduff Marine Aquarium
Head of Garness
Gardenstown
Gamrie Bay
Melrose
Macduff
Protstonhill
Dubford
Gamrie
Wester Greenskares
Cushnie
Doune Park
Longmanhill
Towie
Coburty
Mid Ardlaw
Cardno
Broomhead
Upper Boyndlie
New Aberdour
Tyrie
Memsie
Cairnbulg Point
Cairnbulg
Inverallochy
Whitelinks Bay
Charlestown
St Combs
Inzie Head
South Inch
Strathbeg Bay
Gowanhill
Coralhill
Cairness
Rathen
Memsie Cairn
Whitewell
Ladysford
Woodhead
Lemnas
Windyheads Hill
Foulzie
Minnonie
Netherbrae
Overbrae
Hill of Fishrie
Bracklamore Hill
Nether Glasslaw
Whitebog
Hillhead of Auchentumb
Newburgh
Craigellie
Lonmay
Crimonmogate
Dartfield
Loch of Strathbeg
Old Rattray
Seatown
Rattray Head
Keilhill
Balgreen
Gorrachie
Eden
Balchers
Castleton
Bracklamore
Bogfold
Craigmaud
Turclossie
Waughtonhill
Waughton Hill
Mormond Hill
Whitestripe
Crimond
Blackhill
North Essie
Milltown of Craigston
Plaidy
Craigston
Fintry
Brackens
Cairnywhing
New Pitsligo
Knowhead
Strichen
New Leeds
Upper Ridinghill
Rattray Bay
Gas Terminal
New Byth
Craigculter
Whitehill
Longhill
Leys
Backfolds
St Fergus Moss
Muirden
Wrae
Wester Badentyre
Muiryfold
Garmond
Bonnykelly
Ironside
Adziel
Carnichal
Denhead
Hythie
Rora Moss
Kirktown
St Fergus
Scotstown Head
Turriff
Delgatie
Delgaty Forest
Balthangie
Hill of Corsegight
Oldwhat
Corsegight
Fetterangus
Forest of Deer
Toux
Cuttyhill
Rora
Kirkton Head
Cuminestown
B U C H A N
Mains of Pitfour
Aberdeenshire Farming Mus
Lunderton
Bridgend
Southend
Mill of Colp
Gask
Darra
West Cairncake
Middlehill
Mains of Fedderate
Deer Abbey
Aden
Millbank
Inverugie
Craig Ewen
Arbuthnot Mus
Howe of Teuchar
Waggle Hill
Northburnhill
North Commonty
Mains of Culsh
Maud
Mintlaw
Longside
Torterston
Thunderton
Buchanhaven
Peterhead
Peterhead Prison Museum
Braefoot
Hatton Castle
Birkenhills
Muirtack
Grainhow
New Deer
Drymuir
Waterhill of Bruxie
Backhill of Clackriach
Old Deer
South Ugie Water
Flushing
Inverquhomery
Admiralty Gateway
Keith Inch
Kingsford
South Redbriggs
Deer's Hill
Maryhill
Clockhill
Bulwark
Stuartfield
Millbreck
Hillhead of Cocklaw
Peterhead Bay
Burnhaven
Towie Barclay
Tillyfar
Crichie
Little Dens
Sandford Bay
Dykeside
North Millbrex
Newmill
Moss of Belnagoak
Nethermuir
Knaven
Kinnadie
Clola
Nether Kinmundy
Blackhill
Invernettie
Stirling
Boddam
Buchan Ness
Steinmanhill
Mackerry
Inverythan
Gourdas
Darnabo
Lethenty
Burnend
South Upper Barrack
Auchnagatt
Skelmuir
Skelmuir Hill
Newton
Carse of Balloch
Sandfordhill
Monkshill
Cairnorrie
Mill of Elrick
Auchterless
Tifty
Cottown
Brownhill
Monteach
Hill of Skilmafilly
Kinknockie
Smallburn
Moss of Cruden
Aldie
Gask
Coldwells
Backhill
Fyvie Castle
Woodhead
Skelmonae
Inkhorn
Ardallie
Greenheads
Teuchan
Murdoch Head
Gordonstown
Ardo
Quilquox
Loanhead
Upper Hawkhillock
North Haven
Rothiebrisbane
Crofts of Haddo
Methlick
Milton of Coldwells
Hill of Dudwick
Auchiries
Bullers of Buchan
Petty
Fyvie
Greenmyre
Drumwhindle
Muirtack
Hatton
Erroll
Cruden Bay
Collynie
Arthrath
Mains of Dudwick
Slains (ruins)
Rothienorman
Haddo House (NTS) & Country Park
Tanglandford
Blindburn
Waterloo
Chapel Hill
Port Erroll
Crombiet
St Katherines
Barthol Chapel
Hillbrae
Earlsford
Craigie Brae
Toll of Birness
Bogbrae
Bay of Cruden
Springleys
South Flobbets
Inverebrie
Hilton Croft
Bearnie
Kiplaw Croft
The Skares
Folla Rule
Core Hill
The Banking
Silvermoss
Thornroan
Cookston
Whinnyfold
Newseat
Cross of Jackston
South Blackbog
Balgove
Wedderlairs
Raxton
Broomfield
Leask
Meikle Wartle
Jackstown
Tulloch
Tarves
Kinharrachie
Artrochie
The Veshels
Pitinnan
Craigdam
Yithsie
Ellon
Auchmacoy
Meikle Loch
Clochtow
Kirkton of Rayne
Loanend Stone
Mains of Glack
Mounie Castle
Aberdeenshire Farming Mus
Formartine
Auquharney
Esslemont
Kirkton Logie
Forvie NNR
Collieston
Slains
Durno
Whiteford
Fingask
Oldmeldrum
Tolquhon Castle
Pitmedden Garden (NTS)
Cairnbrogie
Pitmedden
Cairnhill
Meikle Tarty
Waterside
St Catherine's Dub
Tipperty
Forvie Ness
Pitcaple
261
A98
A947
A981
A950
A948
A952
A90
A982
A975
A920
B9031
B9032
B9033
B9093
B9027
B9029
B9030
B9170
B9005
B9000
B9105
B9001
B992
B9106
B9999
B9043

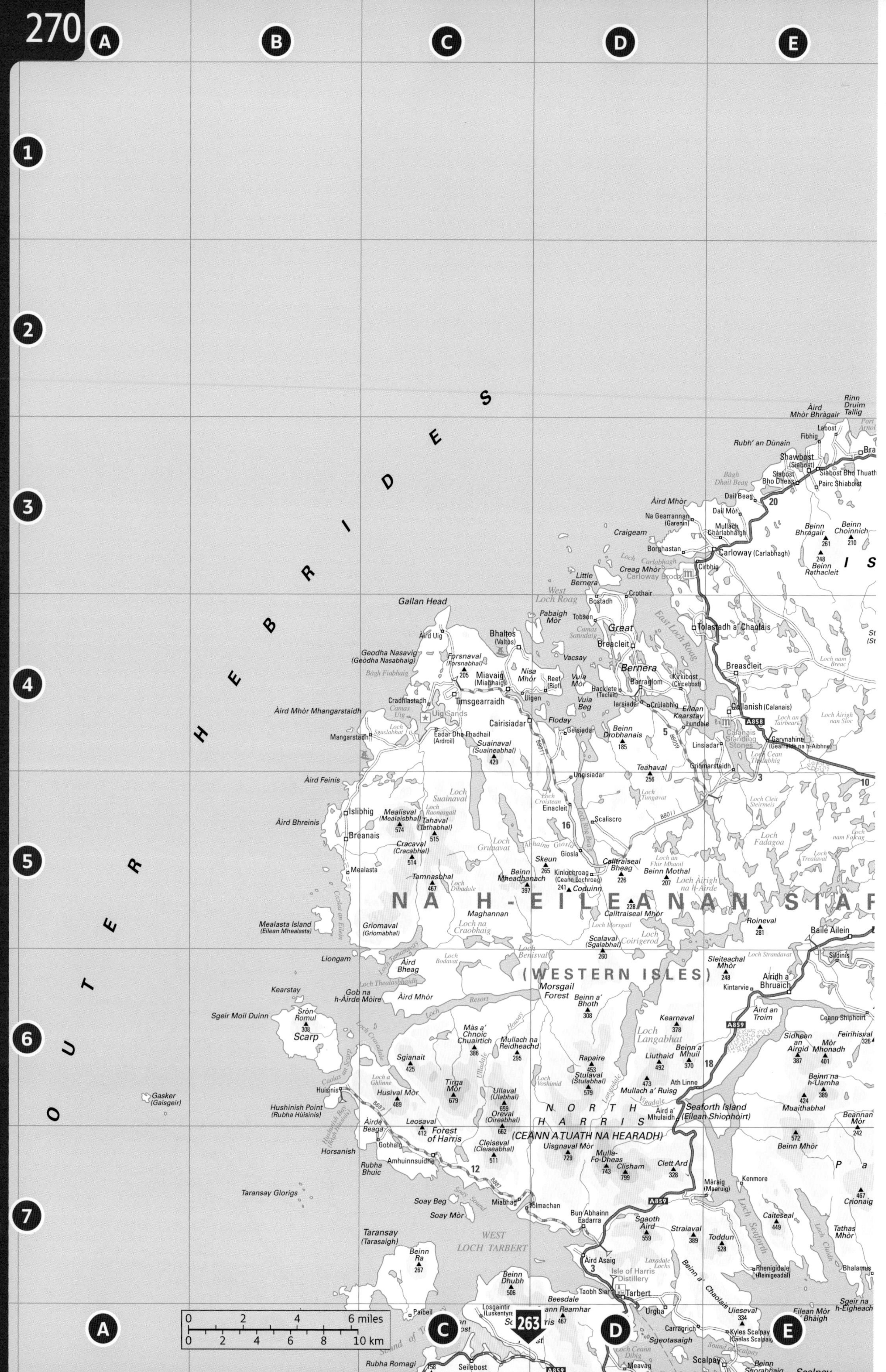
A
B
C
D
E
1
2
3
4
5
6
7
OUTER HEBRIDES
NA H-EILEANAN SIAR
(WESTERN ISLES)
NORTH HARRIS
(CEANN A TUATH NA HEARADH)
Àird Mhòr Bhràgair
Rinn Druim Tallig
Labost
Fibhig
Rubh' an Dùnain
Shawbost (Siabost)
Siabost Bho Dheas
Siabost Bho Thuath
Pairc Shiaboist
Bàgh Dhail Beag
Dail Beag
Àird Mhòr
Dail Mòr
Na Gearrannan (Garenin)
Mullach Chàrlabhaigh
Craigeam
Borghastan
Carloway (Carlabhagh)
Beinn Bhragair 261
Beinn Choinnich 210
Beinn Rathacleit 248
Loch Carlabhagh
Creag Mhòr
Carloway Broch
Cirbhig
Little Bernera
Crothair
West Loch Roag
Bostadh
Gallan Head
Pabaigh Mòr
Tobson
Camas Sanndaig
Great Bernera
Tolastadh a' Chaolais
East Loch Roag
Àird Uig
Bhaltos (Valtos)
Breacleit
Geodha Nasavig (Geòdha Nasabhaig)
Forsnaval (Forsnabhal) 205
Vacsay
Breascleit
Bàgh Fiabhaig
Miavaig (Miabhaig)
Nisa Mhòr
Reef (Rìof)
Vuia Mòr
Hacklete (Tacleit)
Barraglom
Kirkibost (Circebost)
Cradhlastadh
Camas Uig
Timsgearraidh
Uigen
Vuia Beg
Iarsiadar
Crùlabhig
Callanish (Calanais)
Àird Mhòr Mhangarstaidh
Uig Sands
Cairisiadar
Floday
Eilean Kearstay
Lundale
A858
Loch Sgaslabhat
Mangarstadh
Eadar Dha Fhadhail (Ardroil)
Geisiadar
Beinn Drobhanais 185
Calanais Standing Stones
Garynahine (Gearraidh na h-Aibhne)
Suainaval (Suaineabhal) 429
Linsiadar
Loch Cean Thulabhig
Teahaval 256
Griomarstaidh
Àird Feinis
Ungisiadar
Loch Suainaval
Loch Croistean
Einacleit
Loch Tungavat
Loch Cleit Steirmeis
Islibhig
Mealisval (Mealaisbhal) 574
Loch Raonasgail
Tahaval (Tathabhal) 515
Scaliscro
Àird Bhreinis
Breanais
Loch Grunavat
Giosla
Loch Fadagoa
Cracaval (Cracabhal) 514
Skeun 265
Calltraiseal Bheag 226
Beinn Mothal 207
Mealasta
Tamnasbhal 467
Beinn Mheadhanach 397
Kinlochroag (Ceann Lochroag)
Coduinn 241
Loch Àirigh na h-Àirde
Loch Dibadale
Calltraiseal Mhòr 228
Maghannan
Loch na Craobhaig
Mealasta Island (Eilean Mhealasta)
Griomaval (Griomabhal)
Loch Morsgail
Roineval 281
Scalaval (Sgalabhal) 260
Loch Coirigerod
Baile Ailein
Liongam
Loch Bodavat
Loch Benisval
Sleiteachal Mhòr 248
Sildinis
Àird Bheag
Morsgail Forest
Àirigh a Bhruaich
Kintarvie
Kearstay
Gob na h-Àirde Mòire
Àird Mhòr
Beinn a' Bhoth 308
Àird an Troim
Sgeir Moil Duinn
Sròn Romul 308
Scarp
Kearnaval 378
Ceann Shìphoirt
Màs a' Chnoic Chuairtich 386
Mullach na Reidheachd 295
Loch Langabhat
Sidhean an Airgid 387
Mòr Mhonadh 401
Feirihisval 326
Sgianait 425
Beinn a' Mhuil 370
Liuthaid 492
Rapaire 453
Caolas an Scarp
Stulaval (Stulabhal) 579
Mullach a' Ruisg 473
Ath Linne
Beinn na h-Uamha 389
Huisinis
Husival Mòr 489
Tirga Mòr 679
Ullaval (Ulabhal) 659
Gasker (Gaisgeir)
Hushinish Point (Rubha Hùisinis)
Oreval (Oireabhal) 662
Àird a' Mhulaidh
Seaforth Island (Eilean Shìophoirt)
Muaithabhal 424
Àirde Beaga
Leosaval 412
Forest of Harris
Uisgnaval Mòr 729
Beannan Mòr 242
Gobhaig
Cleiseval (Cleiseabhal) 511
Beinn Mhòr 572
Horsanish
Amhuinnsuidhe
Mulla-Fo-Dheas 743
Clisham 799
Clett Ard 328
Rubha Bhuic
Màraig (Maaruig)
Kenmore
Taransay Glorigs
Soay Beg
Soay Mòr
Miabhag
Tolmachan
A859
Crionaig 467
Bun Abhainn Eadarra
Sgaoth Àird 559
Straiaval 389
Caiteseal 449
Taransay (Tarasaigh)
WEST LOCH TARBERT
Toddun 528
Loch Seaforth
Tathas Mhòr
Beinn Ra 267
Àird Asaig
Isle of Harris Distillery
Rhenigidale (Reinigeadal)
Bhalamus
Beinn Dhubh 506
Taobh Siar
Tarbert
Beinn a' Chaolais
Sgeir na h-Eigheach
Beesdale
Paibeil
Losgaintir (Luskentyre)
Ceann Reamhar 487
Urgha
Uieseval 334
Eilean Mòr Bhàigh
263
Carragrich
Kyles Scalpay (Caolas Scalpaigh)
Sgeotasaigh
Rubha Romagi
Seilebost
Loch Ceann Dibig
Scalpay
Meavaig
Beinn Sgorabhaig
0 2 4 6 miles
0 2 4 6 8 10 km

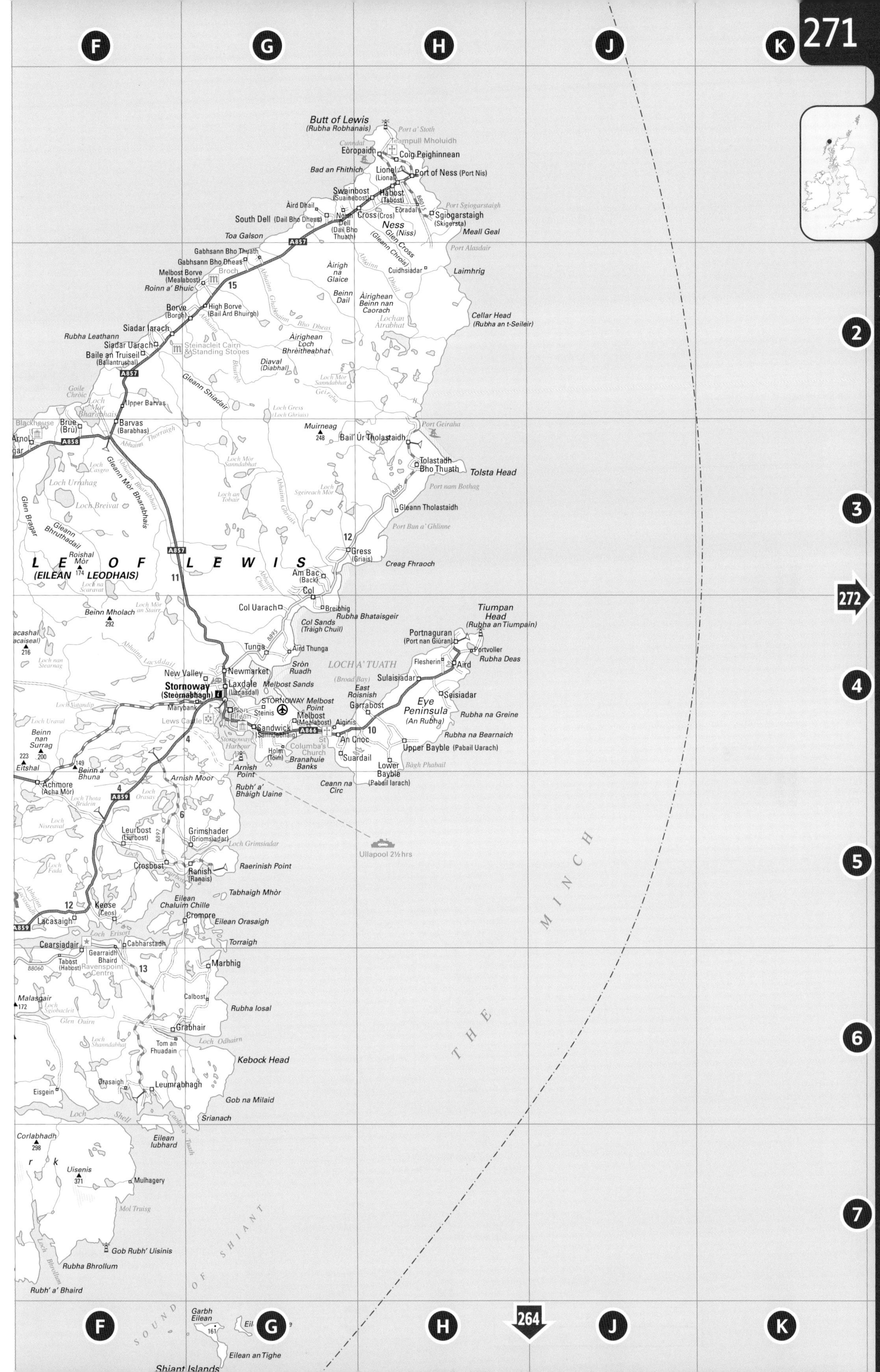

Butt of Lewis
(Rubha Robhanais)
Port a' Stoth
Teampull Mholuidh
Eòropaidh
Coig Peighinnean
Lionel
(Lional)
Port of Ness (Port Nis)
Bad an Fhithich
Swainbost
(Suainebost)
Habost
(Tàbost)
Àird Dhail
North
Cross (Cros)
Eòradal
Port Sgiogarstaigh
South Dell (Dail Bho Dheas)
Dell
(Dail Bho
Thuath)
Ness
(Niss)
Sgiogarstaigh
(Skigersta)
Toa Galson
Meall Geal
Gabhsann Bho Thuath
Port Alasdair
Gabhsann Bho Dheas
Broch
Àirigh
na
Glaice
Cuidhsiàdar
Laimhrig
Melbost Borve
(Mealabost)
Àirighean
Beinn nan
Caorach
Roinn a' Bhuic
Beinn
Dail
Cellar Head
(Rubha an t-Seileir)
Borve
(Borgh)
High Borve
(Bail Àrd Bhuirgh)
15
Lochan
Atrabhat
Siadar Iarach
Rubha Leathann
Siadar Uarach
Àirighean
Loch
Bhrèitheabhat
Baile an Truiseil
(Ballantrushal)
A857
Steinacleit Cairn
& Standing Stones
Diaval
(Diabhal)
Loch Mòr
Sanndabhat
Goile
Chròic
Gleann Shiadair
Upper Barvas
Loch Mòr
Bharabhais
Loch Gress
(Loch Ghrias)
Blackhouse
Brue
(Brù)
Barvas
(Barabhas)
Muirneag
248
Bail' Ùr Tholastaidh
Port Geiraha
Arnol
A858
Loch Urrahag
Loch Breivat
Loch Mòr
Sanndabhat
Tolastadh
Bho Thuath
Tolsta Head
Glen Bragar
Gleann
Bhruthadail
Roishal
Mòr
174
Loch an
Tobair
Loch
Sgeireach Mòr
Port nam Bothag
L E   O F   L E W I S
(EILEAN   LEODHAIS)
Gleann Tholastaidh
11
Port Bun a' Ghlinne
Loch na Scaravat
12
Gress
(Griais)
Creag Fhraoch
Beinn Mholach
292
Am Bac
(Back)
Col
acashal
acaiseal)
216
Col Uarach
Breibhig
Rubha Bhataisgeir
Tiumpan
Head
(Rubha an Tiumpain)
Loch nan
Stearnag
Col Sands
(Tràigh Chuil)
Portnaguran
(Port nan Giùran)
Loch Uraval
Tunga
Àird Thunga
LOCH A' TUATH
(Broad Bay)
Flesherin
Portvoller
Rubha Deas
New Valley
Newmarket
Sròn
Ruadh
Melbost Sands
Sulaisiadar
Aird
Beinn
nan
Surrag
Stornoway
(Steòrnabhagh)
Laxdale
(Lacasdal)
East
Roinnish
Garrabost
Seisiadar
Rubha na Greine
223   200
Marybank
STORNOWAY
Steinis
Melbost
Point
Melbost
(Mealabost)
Eye
Peninsula
(An Rubha)
Rubha na Bearnaich
149
Eitshal
Beinn a'
Bhuna
Lews Castle
Sandwick
(Sanndabhaig)
Aiginis
10
An Cnoc
Achmore
(Acha Mòr)
A859
Stornoway
Harbour
Holm
(Tòim)
Columba's
Church
Upper Bayble (Pabail Uarach)
Suardail
Arnish Moor
Arnish
Point
Branahuie
Banks
Lower
Bayble
(Pabail Iarach)
Bàgh Phabail
6
Rubh' a'
Bhàigh Uaine
Ceann na
Circ
Leurbost
(Liurbost)
Grimshader
(Griomsiadar)
Ullapool 2½ hrs
Loch Grimsiadar
Crosbost
Raerinish Point
Loch
Fada
Ranish
(Ranais)
Tabhaigh Mhòr
12
Keose
(Ceos)
Eilean
Chaluim Chille
Lacasaigh
Cromore
Eilean Orasaigh
Cearsiadair
Cabharstadh
Torraigh
88060
Gearraidh
Bhaird
Ravenspoint
Centre
Marbhig
Tabost (Habost)
13
Malasgair
172
Calbost
Rubha Iosal
Glen Ouirn
Grabhair
Tom an
Fhuadain
Loch Odhairn
Kebock Head
Eisgein
Orasaigh
Leumrabhagh
Gob na Milaid
Srianach
Corlabhadh
298
Eilean
Iubhard
r   k
Uisenis
371
Mulhagery
Mol Truisg
THE   MINCH
Gob Rubh' Uisinis
Rubha Bhrollum
Rubh' a' Bhaird

272
264

SOUND   OF   SHIANT
Garbh
Eilean
161
Eil
Eilean an Tighe
Shiant Islands

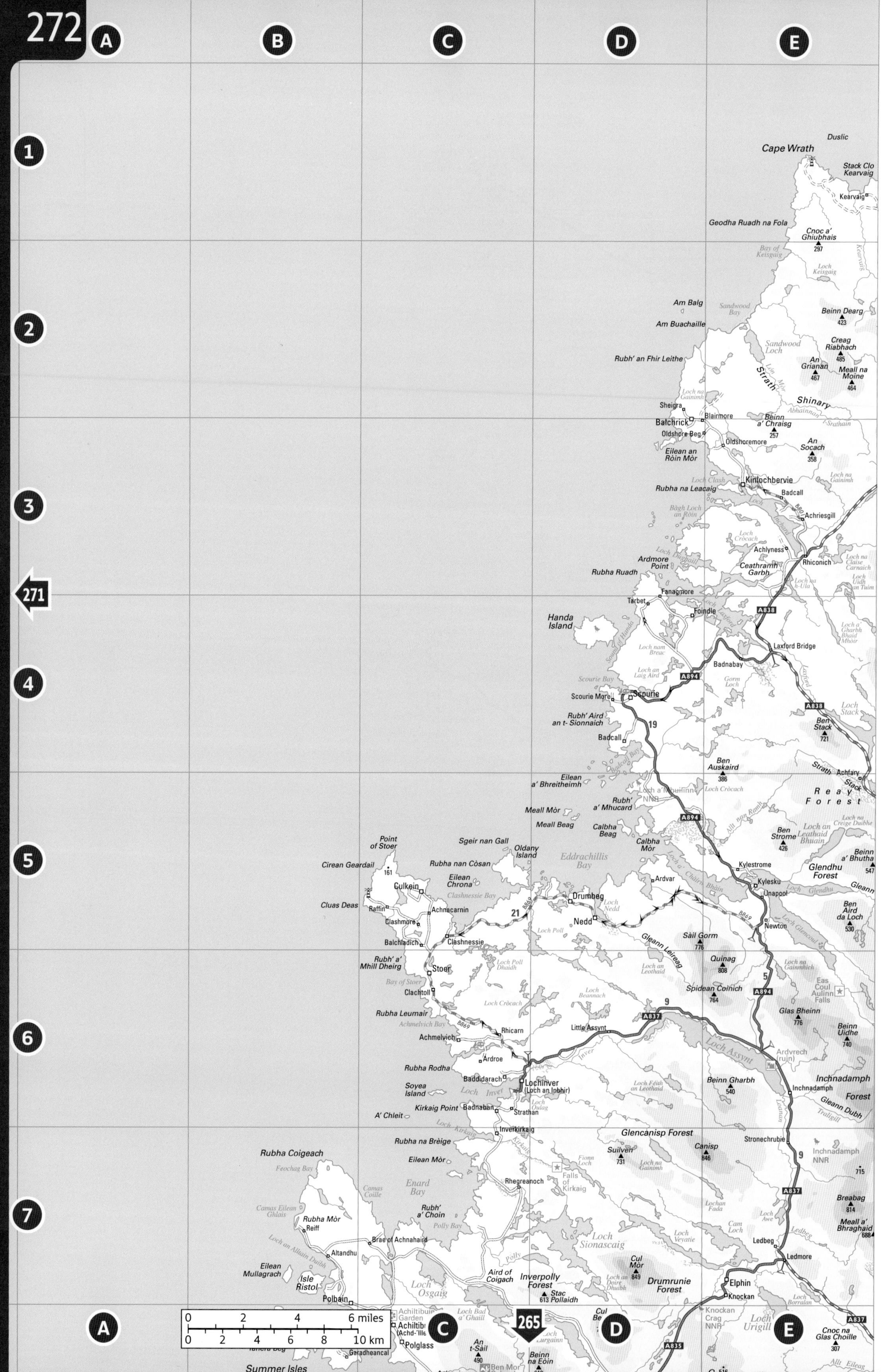

A B C D E

1

2

3

271

4

5

6

7

Duslic
Cape Wrath
Stack Clo
Kearvaig
Kearvaig

Geodha Ruadh na Fola
Cnoc a'
Ghiubhais
297

Bay of
Keisgaig
Loch
Keisgaig

Am Balg
Sandwood
Bay
Beinn Dearg
423

Am Buachaille
Sandwood
Loch
Creag
Riabhach
485

Rubh' an Fhir Leithe
An
Grianan
467
Meall na
Moine
464

Strath
Shinary

Sheigra
Blairmore
Beinn
a' Chraisg
257

Balchrick
Oldshore Beg
Oldshoremore
An
Socach
558

Eilean an
Ròin Mòr
Kinlochbervie

Rubha na Leacaig
Badcall

Achriesgill

Bàgh Loch
an Ròin
Loch
Cròcach

Ardmore
Point
Achlyness
Rhiconich

Rubha Ruadh
Ceathramh
Garbh

Fanagmore

Tarbet
Foindle
A838

Handa
Island
Laxford Bridge

Loch nam
Breac
Badnabay

Scourie Bay
A894
Gorm
Loch

Scourie More
Scourie
Ben
Stack
721

Loch an
Laig Aird
A838
Loch
Stack

Rubh' Aird
an t- Sionnaich
19

Badcall
Ben
Auskaird
386
Loch Cròcach
Strath
Achfary
Stack

Eilean
a' Bhreitheimh
Reay
Forest

Meall Mòr
Rubh'
a' Mhucard
NNR
Ben
Strome
426
Loch an
Leathaid
Bhuain

Meall Beag
Calbha
Beag

Point
of Stoer
Sgeir nan Gall
Oldany
Island
Calbha
Mòr
A894
Beinn
a' Bhutha
547

Cìrean Geardail
161
Rubha nan Còsan
Eddrachillis
Bay
Kylestrome
Glendhu
Forest

Culkein
Eilean
Chrona
Kylesku
Gleann

Cluas Deas
Clashnessie Bay
Ardvar
Unapool
Ben
Aird
da Loch
530

Raffin
Achnacarnin
B869
Drumbeg
Loch
Nedd
Newton

Clashmore
21
Nedd
Sàil Gorm
776

Balchladich
Clashnessie
Loch Poll
Gleann Leireag
Quinag
808
Loch na
Gainimh

Rubh' a'
Mhill Dheirg
Stoer
Loch Poll
Dhaidh
Spidean Coinich
764
A894
5
Eas
Coul
Aulinn
Falls

Clachtoll
Bay of Stoer
Loch
Beannach
9
Glas Bheinn
776

Rubha Leumair
Loch Cròcach
Little Assynt
A837
Beinn
Uidhe
740

Achmelvich Bay
B869
Rhicarn

Achmelvich
Ardroe
Loch
Inver
Ardvreck
(ruin)

Rubha Rodha
Baddidarach
Lochinver
(Loch an Inbhir)
Beinn Gharbh
540
Inchnadamph
Forest

Soyea
Island
Badnabàn
Loch Fèith
an Leothaid
Inchnadamph
Gleann
Dubh

Kirkaig Point
Strathan
Traligill

A' Chleit
Loch Kirkaig
Inverkirkaig
Glencanisp Forest
Stronechrubie
9
Inchnadamph
NNR

Rubha Coigeach
Rubha na Brèige
Rhegreanoch
Suilven
731
Canisp
846
715

Feochag Bay
Eilean Mòr
Fionn
Loch
Falls
of
Kirkaig
A837
Breabag
814

Enard
Bay
Meall a'
Bhraghaid
688

Camus
Coille
Rubh'
a' Choin
Polly Bay
Loch
Sionascaig
Lochan
Fada
Ledbeg
Ledmore

Camas Eilean
Ghlais
Rubha Mòr
Reiff
Cul
Mòr
849
Cam
Loch

Altandhu
Brae of Achnahaird
Polly
Loch
Veyatie
Ledmore

Eilean
Mullagrach
Isle
Ristol
Aird of
Coigach
Inverpolly
Forest
Stac
613 Pollaidh
Drumrunie
Forest
Elphin

Polbain
Loch
Osgaig
Cul
Be
Knockan
Loch
Borralan
A837

A C 265 D E

Achiltibuie
Garden
An
t-Sàil
490
Knockan
Crag
NNR
Cnoc na
Glas Choille
307

Achiltibuie
(Achd-'Ille
Polglass
Loch Bad
a' Ghaill
Loch na
Gainimh
Beinn
na Eòin
618
Loch
Urigill
A835

0 2 4 6 miles
0 2 4 6 8 10 km

Summer Isles
Garadheancal
Ben Mòr
G. 516

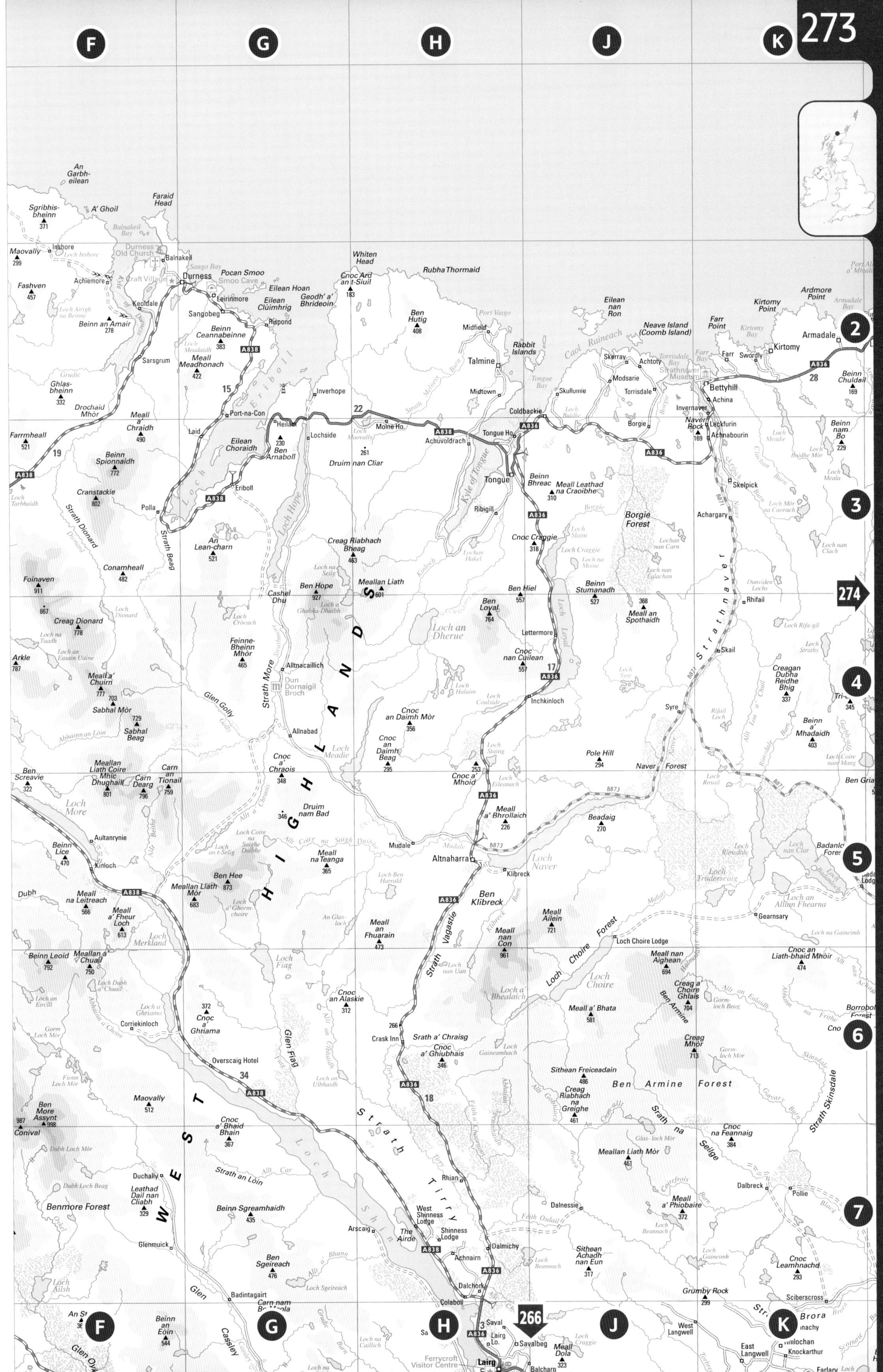
F
G
H
J
K
An Garbh-eilean
Faraid Head
Sgribhis-bheinn 371
A' Ghoil
Balnakeil Bay
Maovally 299
Inshore
Loch Inshore
Durness Old Church
Balnakeil
Sango Bay
Durness
Pocan Smoo
Smoo Cave
Whiten Head
Cnoc Ard an t-Siuil 183
Rubha Thormaid
Fashven 457
Achiemore
Craft Village
Leirinmore
Eilean Hoan
Geodh' a' Bhrideoin
Eilean Clùimhrig
Keoldale
Sangobeg
Rispond
Beinn an Amair 278
Beinn Ceannabeinne 383
Ben Hutig 408
Port Vasgo
Midfield
Eilean nan Ron
Neave Island (Coomb Island)
Farr Point
Kirtomy Point
Ardmore Point
Armadale Bay
Armadale
Kirtomy
Swordly
Farr
Rabbit Islands
Talmine
Caol Raineach
Skerray
Achtoty
Torrisdale Bay
Strathnaver Museum
Modsarie
Torrisdale
Bettyhill
Achina
Beinn Chuldail 169
Sarsgrum
Meall Meadhonach 422
Ghlas-bheinn 332
Drochaid Mhòr
Inverhope
Midtown
Skullomie
Invernaver
Naver Rock 169
Leckfurin
Achnabourin
Meall a' Chraidh 490
Port-na-Con
Heilam
Lochside
Moine Ho.
Coldbackie
Tongue Ho.
Borgie
Beinn nam Bo 229
Farrmheall 521
Laid
Eilean Choraidh
Ben Arnaboll 230
Druim nan Cliar
261
Achuvoldrach
Beinn Spionnaidh 772
Tongue
Beinn Bhreac
Meall Leathad na Craoibhe 310
Skelpick
Cranstackie 802
Eriboll
Polla
Ribigill
Kyle of Tongue
Loch Eriboll
Loch Hope
Achargary
Strath Dionard
Strath Beag
An Lean-charn 521
Creag Riabhach Bheag 463
Cnoc Craggie 318
Borgie Forest
Conamheall 482
Foinaven 911
Ben Hope 927
Meallan Liath 601
Ben Hiel 557
Ben Stumanadh 527
Meall an Spothaidh 368
Rhifail
Cashel Dhu
867
Creag Dionard 778
Ben Loyal 764
Loch an Dherue
Lettermore
Loch Loyal
Feinne-Bheinn Mhòr 465
Cnoc nan Cuilean 557
Skail
Arkle 787
Strathnaver
Creagan Dubha Reidhe Bhig 337
Meall a' Chuirn 777
703
Alltnacaillich
Dun Dornaigil Broch
Strath More
Sabhal Mòr
Glen Golly
Inchkinloch
Syre
Tri-a 345
729
Sabhal Beag
Cnoc an Daimh Mòr 356
Beinn a' Mhadaidh 403
Allnabad
Cnoc an Daimh Beag 295
Pole Hill 294
Loch Meadie
Naver Forest
Meallan Liath Coire Mhic Dhughaill 801
Carn Dearg 796
Carn an Tionail 759
Cnoc a' Chraois 348
253
Cnoc a' Mhoid
Ben Screavie 322
Ben Griam
Loch More
Druim nam Bad
346
Meall a' Bhrollaich 226
Beadaig 270
Aultanrynie
Beinn Lice 470
Mudale
Altnaharra
Loch Naver
Badanloch Forest
Meall na Teanga 365
Kinloch
Klibreck
Ben Hee 873
Meallan Liath Mòr 683
Meall na Leitreach 566
Ben Klibreck
Meall Ailein 721
Loch Coire nan Eun
Gearnsary
Meall a' Fheur Loch 613
Loch Merkland
Meall an Fhuarain 473
Meall nan Con 961
Loch Choire Forest
Loch Choire Lodge
Beinn Leoid 792
Meallan a' Chuail 750
Loch Fiag
Strath Vagastie
Meall nan Aighean 694
Cnoc an Liath-bhaid Mhòir 474
Loch Choire
Creag a' Choire Ghlais 704
Ben Armine
Cnoc an Alaskie 312
372
Cnoc a' Ghriama
Meall a' Bhata 581
Corriekinloch
266
Crask Inn
Strath a' Chraisg
Cnoc a' Ghiubhais 346
Glen Fiag
Creag Mhòr 713
Overscaig Hotel
Sithean Freiceadain 486
Ben Armine Forest
Strath Skinsdale
Maovally 512
Creag Riabhach na Greighe 461
Ben More Assynt 998
987
Conival
Dubh Loch Mòr
Cnoc a' Bhaid Bhain 367
Strath Tirry
Strath na Seilge
Cnoc na Feannaig 384
WEST HIGHLANDS
Loch Shin
Meallan Liath Mòr 461
Duchally
Strath an Lòin
Rhian
Dalbreck
Pollie
Dubh Loch Beag
Leathad Dail nan Cliabh 329
Benmore Forest
Beinn Sgreamhaidh 435
West Shinness Lodge
Shinness Lodge
Dalnessie
Meall a' Phiobaire 372
Arscaig
The Airde
Glenmuick
Dalmichy
Sithean Achadh nan Eun 317
Achnairn
Ben Sgeireach 476
Cnoc Leamhnachd 293
Loch Ailsh
Dalchork
Grumby Rock 299
Glen Cassley
Badintagairt
Colaboll
Sciberscross
Beinn an Eoin 544
Saval
Lairg Lo.
Savalbeg
West Langwell
Brora
East Langwell
Meall Dola 323
Ferrycroft Visitor Centre
Lairg
Balcharn
Knockarthur
A838
A836
B871
B873
15
17
18
19
22
28
34
2
3
4
5
6
7
274
266

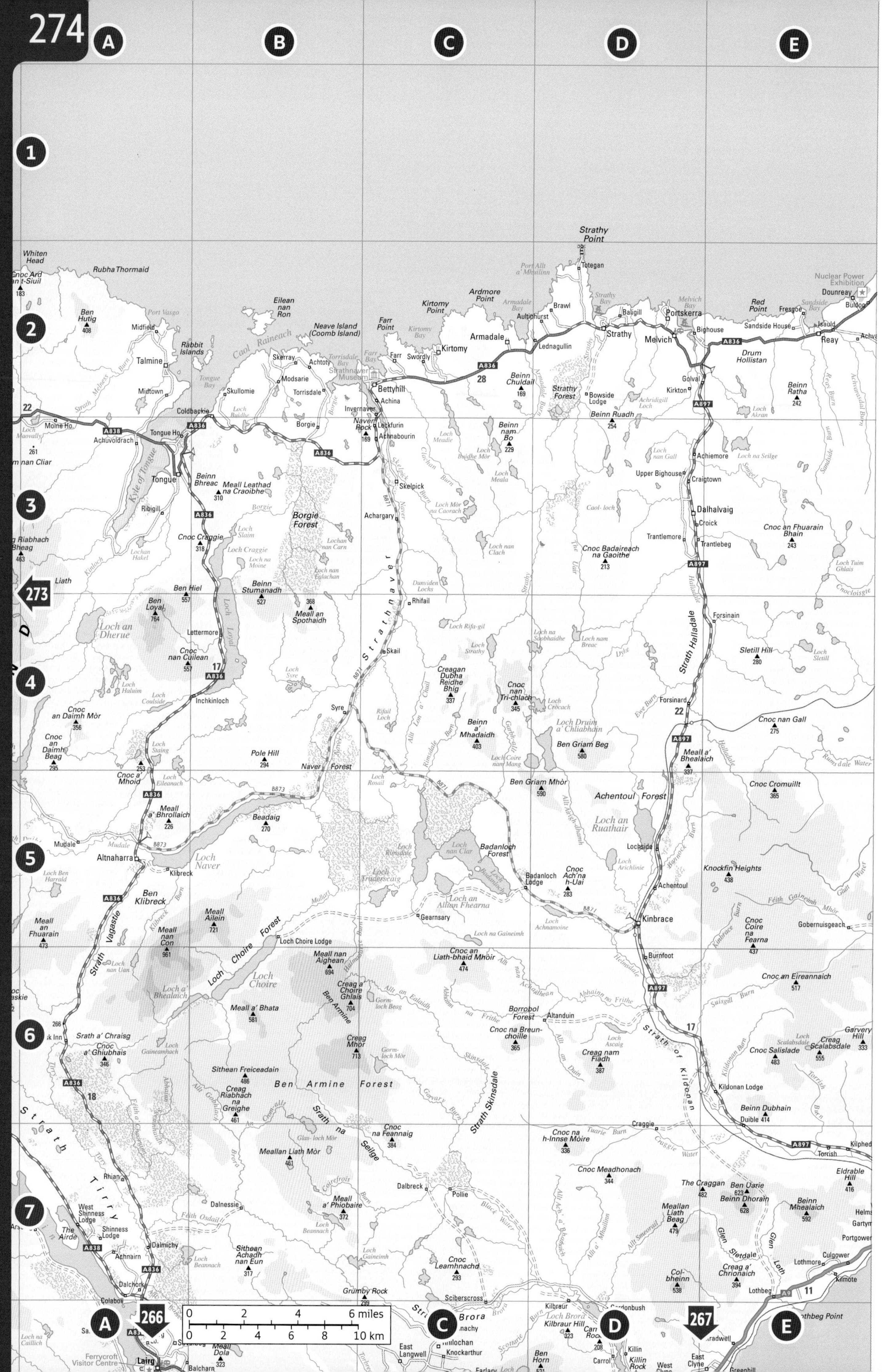
A
B
C
D
E
1
2
3
4
5
6
7
Strathy Point
Whiten Head
Rubha Thormaid
Eilean nan Ron
Kirtomy Point
Ardmore Point
Neave Island (Coomb Island)
Farr Point
Caol Raineach
Rabbit Islands
Talmine
Midfield
Ben Hutig
Tongue
Bettyhill
Armadale
Kirtomy
Strathy
Melvich
Portskerra
Reay
Dounreay
Nuclear Power Exhibition
Red Point
Fresgoe
Sandside House
Bighouse
Drum Hollistan
Strathnaver Museum
Skerray
Borgie
Coldbackie
Tongue Ho.
Moine Ho.
Achuvoldrach
Kyle of Tongue
Borgie Forest
Beinn Stumanadh
Ben Loyal
Loch Loyal
Loch an Dherue
Lettermore
Cnoc nan Cuilean
Inchkinloch
Strathnaver
Skelpick
Achargary
Rhifail
Skail
Syre
Naver Forest
Pole Hill
Loch Naver
Altnaharra
Mudale
Klibreck
Ben Klibreck
Strath Vagastie
Loch Choire Forest
Loch Choire Lodge
Loch Choire
Meall nan Con
Ben Armine
Ben Armine Forest
Strath na Seilge
Strath Skinsdale
Loch Badanloch
Badanloch Forest
Badanloch Lodge
Loch nan Clar
Loch an Ruathair
Achentoul Forest
Kinbrace
Strath of Kildonan
Strath Halladale
Forsinard
Forsinain
Dalhalvaig
Achiemore
Craigtown
Trantlemore
Trantlebeg
Croick
Kirkton
Golval
Sletill Hill
Knockfin Heights
Ben Griam Mhòr
Ben Griam Beg
Cnoc Badaireach na Gaoithe
Beinn Ruadh
Strathy Forest
Gearnsary
Borrobol Forest
Altanduin
Kildonan Lodge
Burnfoot
Achentoul
Lochside
Creag nam Fiadh
Cnoc Salislade
Creag Scalabsdale
Ben Uarie
Beinn Dhorain
The Craggan
Beinn Mhealaich
Glen Loth
Lothbeg
Lothbeg Point
Kilphedir
Torrish
Eldrable Hill
Portgower
Lothmore
Culgower
Kilmote
Craggie
Dalbreck
Pollie
Scibercross
Grumby Rock
Dalnessie
Strath Tirry
Rhian
Dalmichy
Achnairn
Dalchork
Colaboll
Shinness Lodge
West Shinness Lodge
The Airde
Lairg
Ferrycroft Visitor Centre
Balcharn
East Langwell
Knockarthur
Brora
Kilbraur
Loch Brora
Carrol
Killin
East Clyne
Gardonbush
A836
A838
A897
B871
B873
A9
0 2 4 6 miles
0 2 4 6 8 10 km
273
266
267

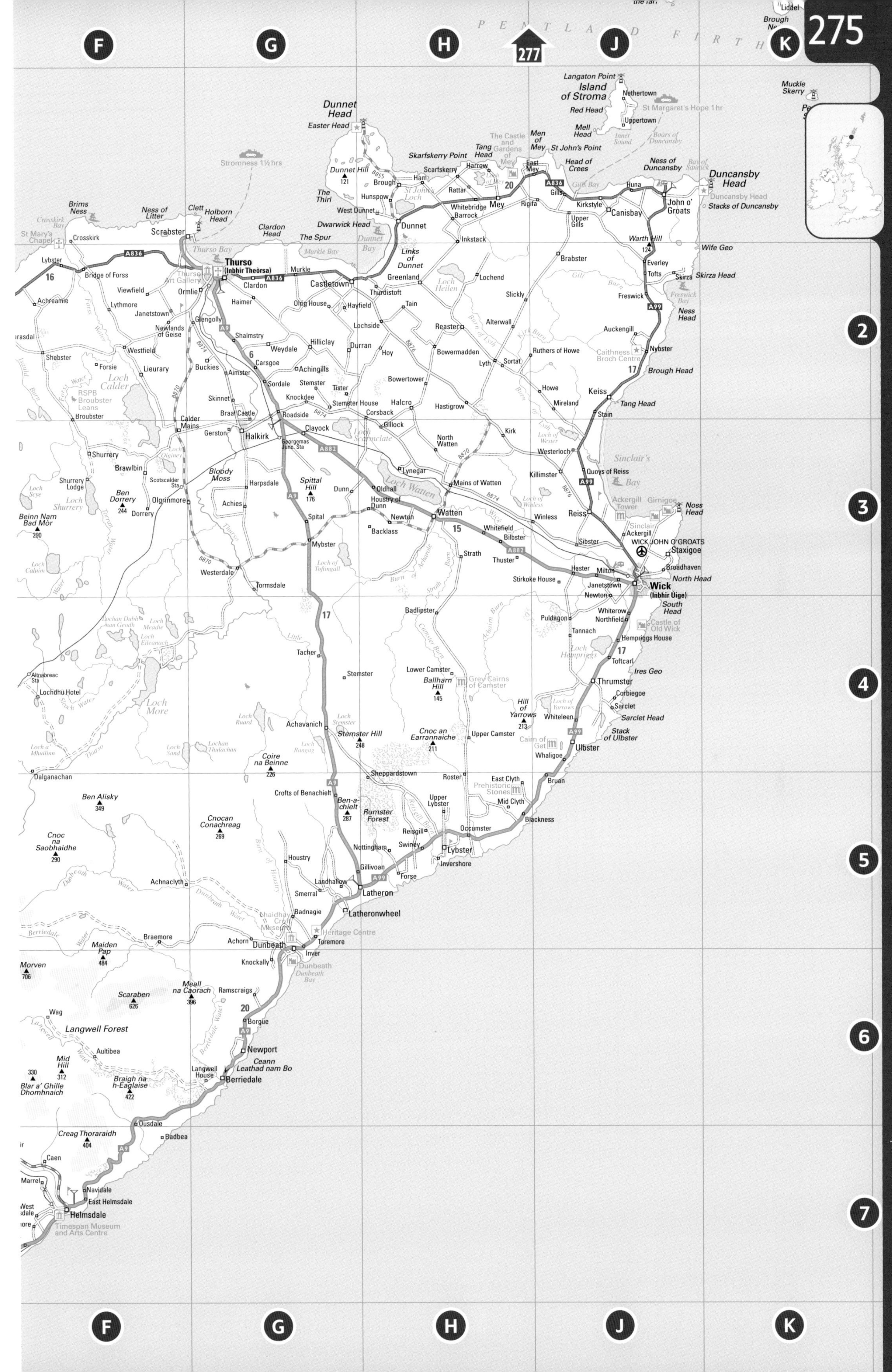
F
G
H
J
K
277
PENTLAND FIRTH
Liddel
Brough Ness
Muckle Skerry
Langaton Point
Island of Stroma
Nethertown
Red Head
Uppertown
St Margaret's Hope 1hr
Mell Head
Inner Sound
Boars of Duncansby
Dunnet Head
Easter Head
The Castle and Gardens of Mey
Men of Mey
St John's Point
Tang Head
Skarfskerry Point
Head of Crees
Ness of Duncansby
Bay of Sannick
Duncansby Head
Duncansby Head
Stacks of Duncansby
Stromness 1½ hrs
Dunnet Hill
121
Scarfskerry
Harrow
East Mey
A836
Gills Bay
Huna
Ham
Brough
St John's Loch
Rattar
20
Gills
Kirkstyle
John o' Groats
The Thirl
Hunspow
Whitebridge
Mey
Rigifa
Canisbay
Barrock
West Dunnet
Upper Gills
Dwarwick Head
Dunnet
Inkstack
Warth Hill
124
Wife Geo
Brims Ness
Ness of Litter
Clett
Holborn Head
Clardon Head
The Spur
Dunnet Bay
Crosskirk Bay
Scrabster
Links of Dunnet
Brabster
Everley
St Mary's Chapel
Crosskirk
Thurso Bay
Murkle Bay
Tofts
Skirza
Skirza Head
Lybster
Thurso (Inbhir Theòrsa)
Murkle
Loch Heilen
Lochend
A836
Greenland
Castletown
Thurdistoft
Freswick
16
Bridge of Forss
Thurso Art Gallery
Clardon
Slickly
Freswick Bay
Viewfield
Ormlie
Haimer
Olrig House
Hayfield
Tain
A99
Achreamie
Lythmore
Janetstown
Glengolly
Ness Head
Lochside
Reaster
Alterwall
Newlands of Geise
Shalmstry
Hilliclay
Auckengill
Westfield
Durran
Weydale
Bowermadden
Ruthers of Howe
Nybster
Shebster
6
Carsgoe
Hoy
Caithness Broch Centre
Forsie
Loch Calder
Lieurary
Buckies
Aimster
Achingills
Lyth
Sortat
17
Brough Head
Sordale
Stemster
Bowertower
RSPB Broubster Leans
Tister
Howe
Keiss
Skinnet
Knockdee
Stemster House
Halcro
Mireland
Broubster
Braal Castle
Roadside
Corsback
Hastigrow
Tang Head
Calder Mains
Stain
Clayock
Gillock
Gerston
Halkirk
Loch Scarmclate
North Watten
Kirk
Georgemas Junc. Sta
A882
Westerloch
Shurrery
Sinclair's Bay
Brawlbin
Bloody Moss
Lynegar
Quoys of Reiss
Scotscalder Sta
Harpsdale
Spittal Hill
176
Oldhall
Killimster
Shurrery Lodge
Loch Watten
Mains of Watten
A99
Ben Dorrery
244
Olgrimmore
Dunn
Houstry of Dunn
B874
Loch Shurrery
Achies
Ackergill Tower
Girnigoe
Noss Head
Beinn Nam Bad Mòr
290
Dorrery
Spital
Watten
Winless
Reiss
Newton
15
Whitefield
Sinclair
Ackergill
Backlass
Bilbster
Mybster
Sibster
WICK JOHN O'GROATS
Staxigoe
Strath
Thuster
Broadhaven
Westerdale
Loch of Toftingall
Haster
Milton
North Head
Tormsdale
Stirkoke House
Janetstown
Wick (Inbhir Ùige)
Newton
South Head
Badlipster
Whiterow
17
Northfield
Pulldagon
Castle of Old Wick
Tannach
Hempriggs House
Loch Hempriggs
17
Toftcarl
Tacher
Ires Geo
Altnabreac Sta
Stemster
Lower Camster
Grey Cairns of Camster
Ballharn Hill
145
Thrumster
Lochdhu Hotel
Loch More
Corbiegoe
Hill of Yarrows
213
Sarclet
Sarclet Head
Whiteleen
Achavanich
Loch Stemster
Stemster Hill
248
Cnoc an Earrannaiche
211
Upper Camster
Stack of Ulbster
Cairn of Get
Ulbster
Loch Sand
Loch Rangag
Coire na Beinne
226
Whaligoe
Dalganachan
Sheppardstown
Roster
East Clyth
Bruan
Ben Alisky
349
Crofts of Benachielt
Prehistoric Stones
Ben-a-chielt
287
Rumster Forest
Upper Lybster
Mid Clyth
Blackness
Cnocan Conachreag
269
Occumster
Cnoc na Saobhaidhe
290
Reisgill
Nottingham
Swiney
Lybster
Houstry
Gillivoan
Invershore
A99
Achnaclyth
Landhallow
Forse
Smerral
Latheron
Badnagie
Latheronwheel
Laidhay Croft Museum
Heritage Centre
Braemore
Achorn
Dunbeath
Toremore
Maiden Pap
484
Inver
Morven
706
Knockally
Dunbeath
Dunbeath Bay
Scaraben
626
Meall na Caorach
396
Ramscraigs
20
Wag
Borgue
Langwell Forest
A9
Newport
Aultibea
Ceann Leathad nam Bo
Mid Hill
312
Langwell House
Berriedale
330
Blar a' Ghille Dhomhnaich
Braigh na h-Eaglaise
422
Ousdale
Badbea
Creag Thoraraidh
404
A9
Caen
Marrel
Navidale
East Helmsdale
Helmsdale
Timespan Museum and Arts Centre
2
3
4
5
6
7
F
G
H
J
K

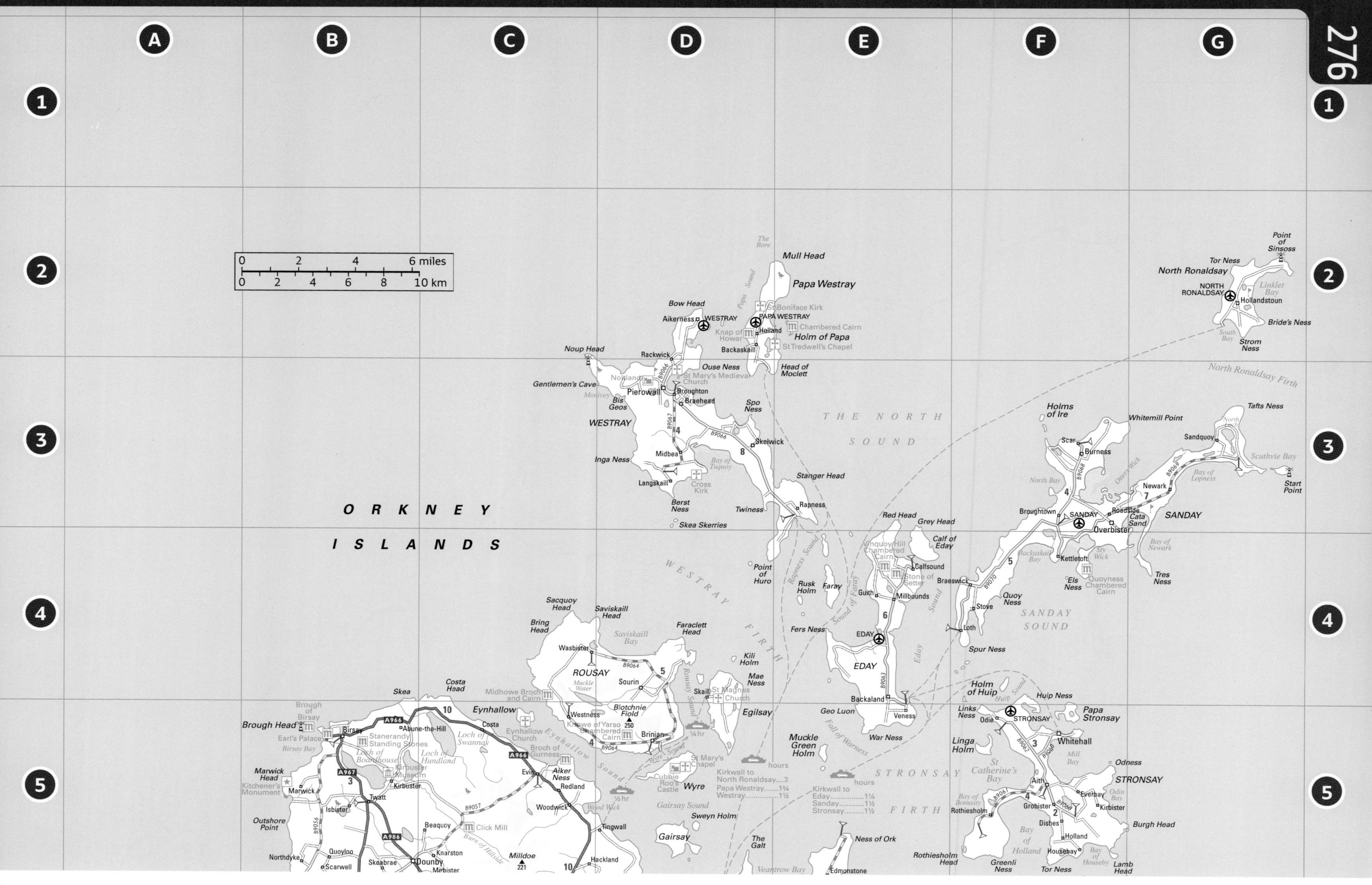
ORKNEY ISLANDS
North Ronaldsay
NORTH RONALDSAY
Hollandstoun
Point of Sinsoss
Tor Ness
Linklet Bay
Bride's Ness
South Bay
Strom Ness
North Ronaldsay Firth
Tafts Ness
Sandquoy
Scuthvie Bay
Start Point
Bay of Lopness
Whitemill Point
Holms of Ire
Scar
Burness
North Bay
Otters Wick
Newark
SANDAY
Broughtown
Roadside
Cata Sand
Overbister
Bay of Newark
Tres Ness
Backaskaill Bay
Kettletoft
Sty Wick
Els Ness
Quoyness Chambered Cairn
Quoy Ness
Stove
Loth
SANDAY SOUND
Spur Ness
Mull Head
Papa Westray
The Bore
Papa Sound
St Boniface Kirk
PAPA WESTRAY
Holland
Chambered Cairn
Knap of Howar
Holm of Papa
Backaskaill
St Tredwell's Chapel
Head of Moclett
Bow Head
Aikerness
WESTRAY
Noup Head
Rackwick
Ouse Ness
Noltland
St Mary's Medieval Church
Gentlemen's Cave
Pierowall
Broughton
Braehead
Bis Geos
Spo Ness
WESTRAY
Skelwick
Midbea
Inga Ness
Bay of Tuquoy
Langskaill
Cross Kirk
Berst Ness
Skea Skerries
Twiness
Rapness
Stanger Head
THE NORTH SOUND
Red Head
Grey Head
Calf of Eday
Vinquoy Hill Chambered Cairn
Calfsound
Stone of Setter
Braeswick
Guith
Millbounds
Point of Huro
Rusk Holm
Faray
Rapness Sound
Sound of Faray
Fers Ness
EDAY
Backaland
Veness
War Ness
Geo Luon
Fall of Warness
Muckle Green Holm
WESTRAY FIRTH
Kili Holm
Mae Ness
Skaill
St Magnus Church
Egilsay
Sacquoy Head
Saviskaill Head
Bring Head
Saviskaill Bay
Faraclett Head
Wasbister
ROUSAY
Muckle Water
Sourin
Rousay Sound
Midhowe Broch and Cairn
Westness
Blotchnie Fiold
250
Knowe of Yarso Chambered Cairn
Brinian
Wyre Sound
St Mary's Chapel
Cubbie Roo's Castle
Wyre
Gairsay Sound
Sweyn Holm
Gairsay
The Galt
Veantrow Bay
Ness of Ork
Edmonstone
Kirkwall to North Ronaldsay....3 Papa Westray.......1¾ Westray...............1½ hours
Kirkwall to Eday...............1¼ Sanday............1½ Stronsay..........1½ hours
¼ hr
½ hr
STRONSAY FIRTH
Holm of Huip
Huip Sound
Huip Ness
Links Ness
Odie
STRONSAY
Papa Stronsay
Whitehall
Linga Holm
Mill Bay
St Catherine's Bay
Odness
STRONSAY
Aith
Everbay
Odin Bay
Bay of Bomasty
Rothiesholm
Grobister
Kirbister
Dishes
Burgh Head
Holland
Bay of Holland
Housebay
Bay of Houseby
Rothiesholm Head
Greenli Ness
Tor Ness
Lamb Head
Skea
Costa Head
Eynhallow
Costa
Loch of Swannay
Eynhallow Church
Eynhallow Sound
Broch of Gurness
Aiker Ness
Evie
Redland
Woodwick
Wood Wick
Tingwall
Hackland
Milldoe
221
Click Mill
Burn of Hillside
Brough of Birsay
Brough Head
Birsay
Abune-the-Hill
Earl's Palace
Birsay Bay
Stanerandy Standing Stones
Loch of Boardhouse
Loch of Hundland
Kirbuster Museum
Kirbuster
Marwick Head
Kitchener's Monument
Marwick
Isbister
Twatt
Beaquoy
Outshore Point
Quoyloo
Northdyke
Scarwell
Skeabrae
Dounby
Knarston
Mirbister
A966
A967
A986
B9056
B9057
B9063
B9064
B9066
B9067
B9068
B9069
B9070
0 2 4 6 miles
0 2 4 6 8 10 km

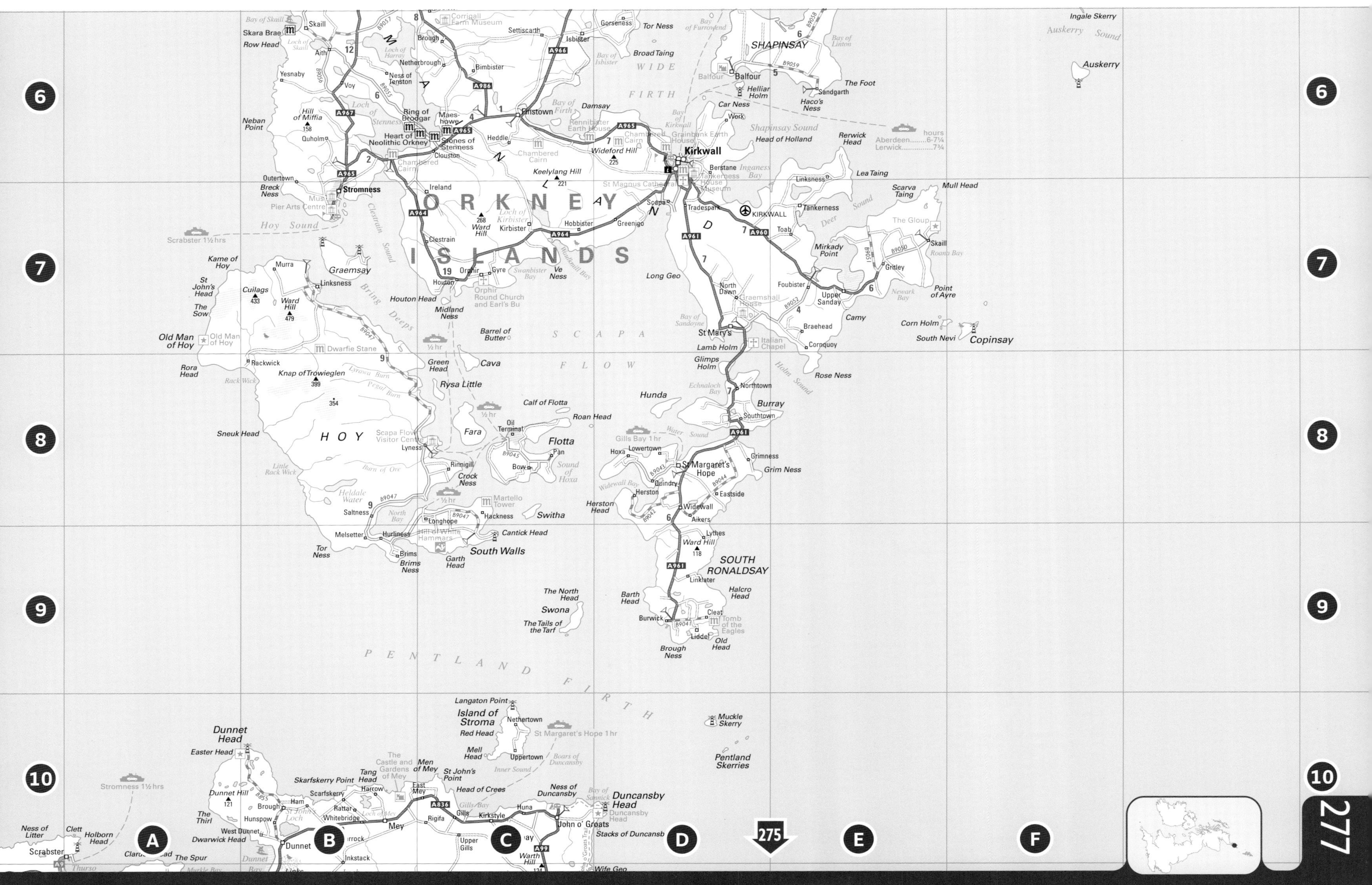
ORKNEY ISLANDS
MAINLAND
Kirkwall
Stromness
Finstown
SHAPINSAY
Balfour
Helliar Holm
Haco's Ness
The Foot
Sandgarth
Auskerry
Ingale Skerry
Auskerry Sound
Tor Ness
Broad Taing
WIDE FIRTH
Damsay
Gorseness
Isbister
Settiscarth
Bimbister
Netherbrough
Brough
Corrigall Farm Museum
Skaill
Skara Brae
Bay of Skaill
Row Head
Aith
Yesnaby
Voy
Ness of Tenston
Ring of Brodgar
Maeshowe
Heart of Neolithic Orkney
Stones of Stenness
Clouston
Heddle
Hill of Miffia
Quholm
Neban Point
Outertown
Breck Ness
Pier Arts Centre
Hoy Sound
Scrabster 1½ hrs
Ireland
Keelylang Hill
Wideford Hill
Car Ness
Work
Shapinsay Sound
Head of Holland
Rerwick Head
Aberdeen 6-7¼ hours
Lerwick 7¾
Berstane
Inganess Bay
St Magnus Cathedral
Tradespark
KIRKWALL
Tankerness
Linksness
Lea Taing
Scarva Taing
Mull Head
The Gloup
Skaill
Deer Sound
Toab
Mirkady Point
Gritley
Foubister
Upper Sanday
Point of Ayre
Corn Holm
South Nevi
Copinsay
Camy
Braehead
Corquoy
Rose Ness
Holm Sound
Italian Chapel
Graemshall House
North Dawn
St Mary's
Lamb Holm
Glimps Holm
Bay of Sandoyne
Long Geo
Scapa
Greenigo
Hobbister
Kirbister
Clestrain
Ward Hill
Orphir
Gyre
Orphir Round Church and Earl's Bu
Swanbister Bay
Ve Ness
Houton
Houton Head
Midland Ness
Clestrain Sound
Graemsay
Kame of Hoy
St John's Head
The Sow
Murra
Linksness
Cuilags
Ward Hill
Old Man of Hoy
Rora Head
Rackwick
Dwarfie Stane
Knap of Trowieglen
Bring Deeps
HOY
Sneuk Head
Green Head
Cava
Rysa Little
Barrel of Butter
SCAPA FLOW
Calf of Flotta
Roan Head
Fara
Oil Terminal
Flotta
Pan
Bow
Sound of Hoxa
Scapa Flow Visitor Centre
Lyness
Rinnigill
Crock Ness
Martello Tower
Hackness
Switha
Heldale Water
Saltness
North Bay
Longhope
Melsetter
Hurliness
Hill of White Hammars
Cantick Head
South Walls
Brims
Brims Ness
Garth Head
Tor Ness
Hunda
Burray
Northtown
Southtown
Echnaloch Bay
Water Sound
Gills Bay 1 hr
Hoxa
Lowertown
St Margaret's Hope
Grimness
Grim Ness
Widewall Bay
Herston
Herston Head
Eastside
Widewall
Aikers
Lythes
Ward Hill
SOUTH RONALDSAY
Linklater
Halcro Head
Barth Head
Burwick
Cleat
Tomb of the Eagles
Liddel
Old Head
Brough Ness
The North Head
Swona
The Tails of the Tarf
PENTLAND FIRTH
Muckle Skerry
Pentland Skerries
Langaton Point
Island of Stroma
Nethertown
Red Head
Mell Head
Uppertown
St Margaret's Hope 1 hr
Boars of Duncansby
Inner Sound
Dunnet Head
Easter Head
Dunnet Hill
The Thirl
Dwarwick Head
West Dunnet
Hunspow
Brough
Ham
Scarfskerry
Skarfskerry Point
Tang Head
Harrow
The Castle and Gardens of Mey
Men of Mey
East Mey
St John's Point
Head of Crees
Rattar
Whitebridge
Mey
Rigifa
Gills
Gills Bay
Kirkstyle
Huna
Ness of Duncansby
Duncansby Head
John o' Groats
Stacks of Duncansby
Upper Gills
Warth Hill
Wife Geo
Inkstack
Dunnet
Stromness 1½ hrs
Ness of Litter
Clett
Holborn Head
Scrabster
The Spur
Thurso
275
A B C D E F
6 7 8 9 10

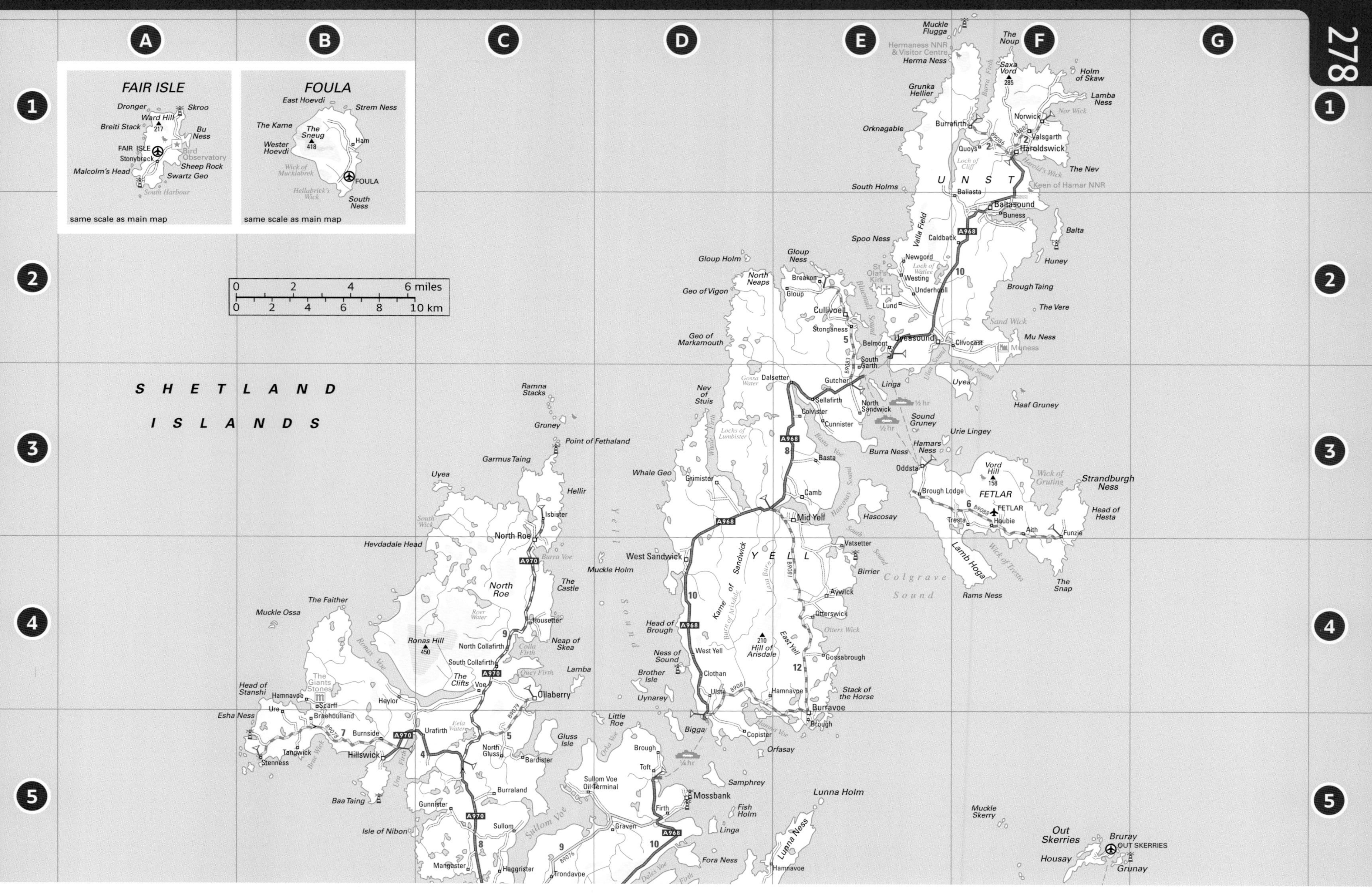

FOULA

East Hoevdi
St</br>
The Kame
The Sneug
418
Wester Hoevdi
Ham
Strem Ness
FOULA
South Ness
Hellabrick's Wick
Wick of Mucklaberg

same scale as main map

FAIR ISLE

Dronger
Skroo
Bu Ness
Ward Hill
217
Breiti Stack
Stonybreck
Bird Observatory
Sheep Rock
Swartz Geo
FAIR ISLE
Malcolm's Head
South Harbour

same scale as main map

6 miles
10 km

SHETLAND
ISLANDS

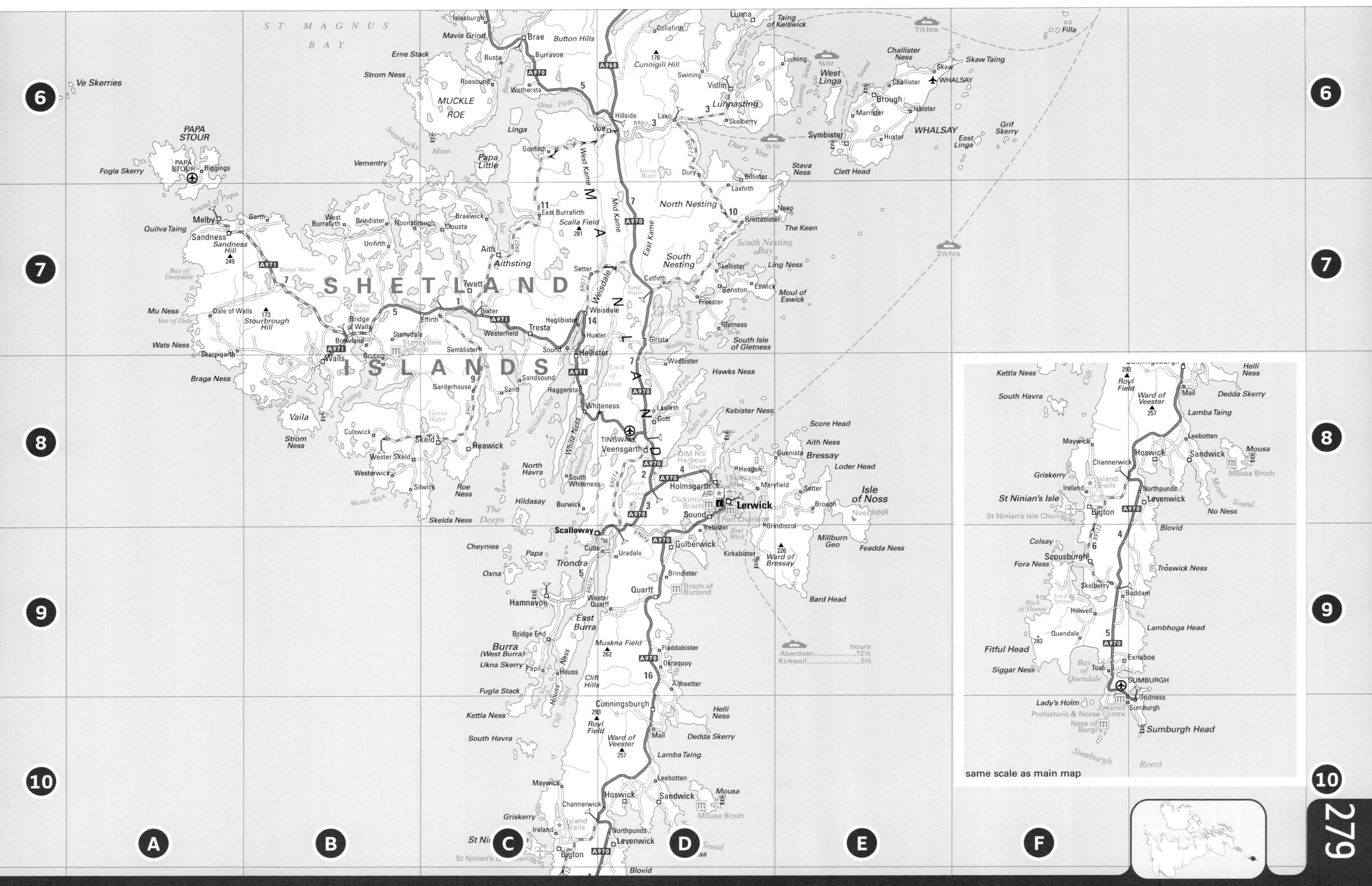
SHETLAND ISLANDS
MAINLAND
St Magnus Bay
Papa Stour
Muckle Roe
Whalsay
West Linga
Bressay
Isle of Noss
Lerwick
Scalloway
Trondra
Burra (West Burra)
East Burra
Vaila
Walls
Voe
Brae
Aith
Weisdale
Tingwall
North Nesting
South Nesting
Lunnasting
Symbister
Sandness
Melby
Dale of Walls
Skeld
Reawick
Sandwick
Hoswick
Levenwick
Cunningsburgh
Quarff
Gulberwick
Mousa
St Ninian's Isle
Bigton
Fitful Head
Sumburgh Head
Sumburgh
Aberdeen hours 12½
Kirkwall 5½
same scale as main map

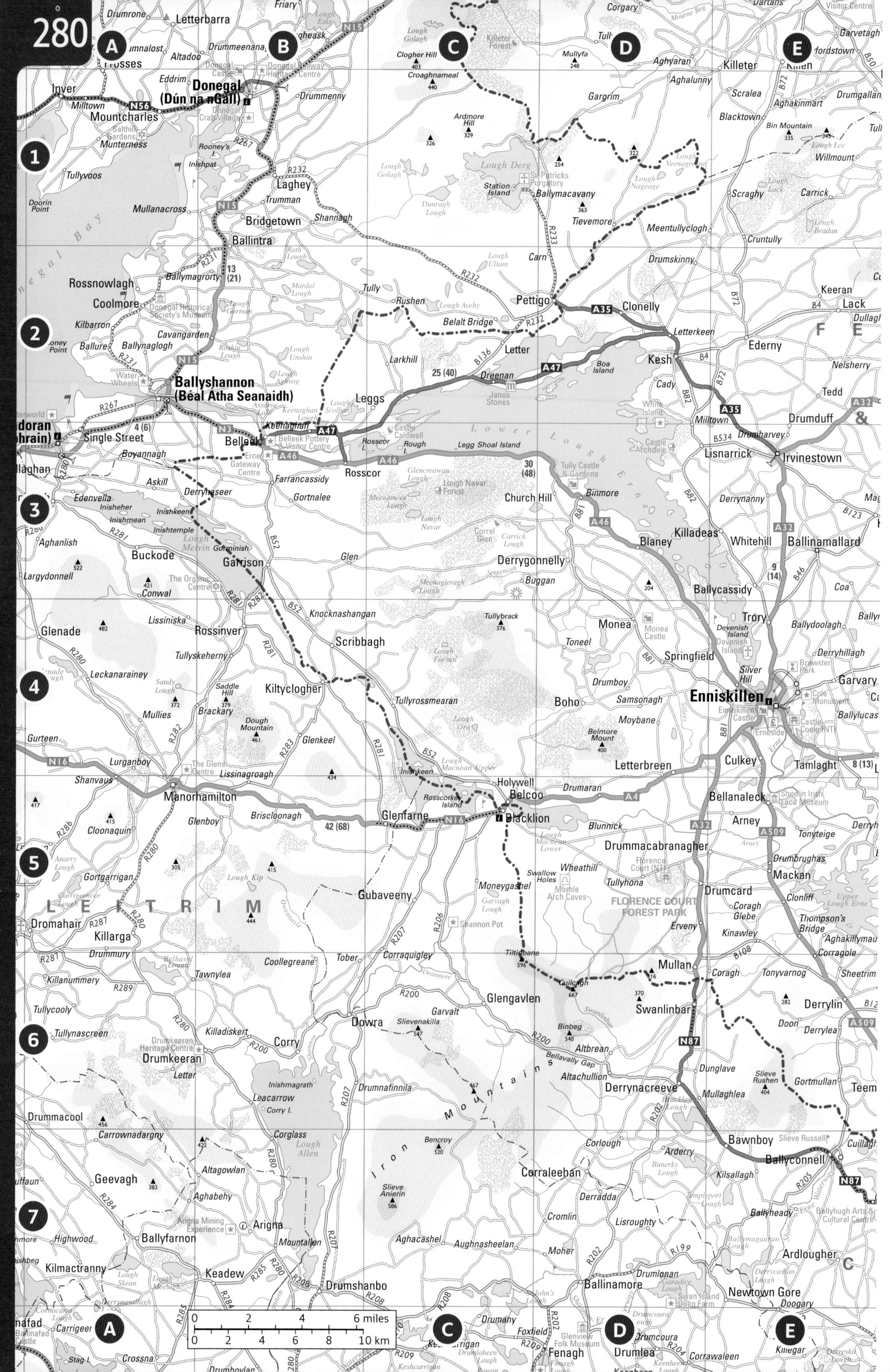

A
B
C
D
E
1
2
3
4
5
6
7
Drumrone
Letterbarra
Friary
Lough Eske
Frosses
Altadoo
Drummeenana
Lough Golagh
Clogher Hill
Croaghnameal
Killeter Forest
Corgary
Mullyfa
Aghyaran
Killeter
Aghalunny
Inver
Milltown
Mountcharles
Eddrim
Donegal
(Dún na nGall)
Donegal Castle
Donegal Railway Heritage Centre
Donegal Craft Village
Drummenny
Salthill Gardens
Munterness
Rooney's I.
Inishpat
Tullyvoos
Doorin Point
Mullanacross
Laghey
Trumman
Bridgetown
Shannagh
Ballintra
Ardmore Hill
Lough Derg
St Patrick's Purgatory
Station Island
Ballymacavany
Lough Nageage
Tievemore
Gargrim
Scralea
Blacktown
Aghakinmart
Drumgallan
Bin Mountain
Willmount
Scraghy
Carrick
Lough Bradan
Meentullyclogh
Cruntully
Drumskinny
Carn
Lough Ultam
Dunragh Lough
Rath Lough
Ballymagrorty
Rossnowlagh
Coolmore
Donegal Historical Society's Museum
Mardal Lough
Tully
Rushen
Lough Avehy
Pettigo
Belalt Bridge
Clonelly
Keeran
Lack
Dullagh
Kilbarron
Cavangarden
Ballure
Ballynaglogh
Lough Unshin
Larkhill
Letter
Letterkeen
Kesh
Ederny
Nelsherry
Dreenan
Boa Island
Cady
Tedd
Water Wheels
Ballyshannon
(Béal Átha Seanaidh)
Leggs
Janus Stones
White Island
Milltown
Drumduff
Lough Scolban
Assaroe Lake
Keenaghan Lough
Keenaghan
Castle Caldwell
Lower Lough Erne
Drumharvey
Single Street
Belleek
Belleek Pottery & Visitor Centre
Rosscor
Rough I.
Legg Shoal Island
Castle Archdale
Lisnarrick
Irvinestown
Boyannagh
Erne Gateway Centre
Farrancassidy
Rosscor
Glencreawan Lough
Lough Navar Forest
Tully Castle & Gardens
Church Hill
Binmore
Derrynanny
Askill
Derryhaseer
Gortnalee
Meenameen Lough
Lough Navar
Edenvella
Inisheher
Inishmean
Inishkeen
Inishtemple
Lough Melvin
Gorminish
Garrison
Aghanlish
Buckode
Correl Glen
Carrick Lough
Killadeas
Whitehill
Ballinamallard
Largydonnell
Conwal
The Organic Centre
Glen
Derrygonnelly
Buggan
Blaney
Meenaglerah Lough
Ballycassidy
Coa
Glenade
Lissiniska
Rossinver
Knocknashangan
Tullybrack
Monea
Monea Castle
Trory
Ballydoolagh
Scribbagh
Devenish Island
Toneel
Springfield
Derryhillagh
Tullyskeherny
Lough Formal
Leckanarainey
Sandy Lough
Saddle Hill
Brackary
Kiltyclogher
Tullyrossmearan
Drumboy
Silver Hill
Brewster Park
Garvary
Enniskillen
Enniskillen Castle
Cole Monument
Boho
Samsonagh
Moybane
Castle Coole (NT)
Ballylucas
Mullies
Dough Mountain
Lough Ora
Glenkeel
Belmore Mount
Erneside
Gurteen
Lurganboy
The Glens Centre
Lough Macnean Upper
Letterbreen
Culkey
Tamlaght
Shanvaus
Lissinagroagh
Inishkeen
Holywell
Belcoo
Drumaran
Bellanaleck
Sheelin Irish Lace Museum
Manorhamilton
Rosscorkey Island
Glenboy
Briscloonagh
Glenfarne
Blacklion
Blunnick
Arney
Tonyteige
Cloonaquin
Lough Macnean Lower
Drummacabranagher
Drumbrughas
Mackan
Anarry Lough
Gortgarrigan
Lough Kip
Swallow Holes
Wheathill
Florence Court (NT)
Marble Arch Caves
Tullyhona
Moneygashel
Drumcard
Clonliff
Upper Lough Erne
Gubaveeny
Garvagh Lough
FLORENCE COURT FOREST PARK
Coragh Glebe
LEITRIM
Dromahair
Killarga
Shannon Pot
Erveny
Thompson's Bridge
Kinawley
Aghakillymaud
Drummury
Tober
Corraquigley
Coollegreane
Belhavel Lough
Tiltinbane
Cuilcagh
Mullan
Coragh
Tonyvarnog
Sheetrim
Corragole
Tawnylea
Killanummery
Glengavlen
Swanlinbar
Derrylin
Tullycooly
Garvalt
Dowra
Slievenakilla
Binbeg
Doon
Derrylea
Killadiskert
Corry
Tullynascreen
Drumkeeran Heritage Centre
Drumkeeran
Letter
Altbrean
Bellavally Gap
Iron Mountains
Altachullion
Inishmagrath
Leacarrow
Corry I.
Drumnafinnila
Dunglave
Derrynacreeve
Mullaghlea
Slieve Rushen
Gortmullan
Teem
Drummacool
Carrownadargny
Corglass
Lough Allen
Bencroy
Corlough
Brackley Lough
Bawnboy
Arderry
Slieve Russell
Cuilagh
Geevagh
Altagowlan
Slieve Anierin
Corraleehan
Bunerky Lough
Kilsallagh
Ballyconnell
Aghabehy
Derradda
Templeport Lough
Arigna Mining Experience
Arigna
Cromlin
Lisroughty
Ballyheady
Ballyhugh Arts & Cultural Centre
Highwood
Ballyfarnon
Mountallen
Aghacashel
Aughnasheelan
Moher
Ballymagauran Lough
Ardlougher
Kilmactranny
Lough Skean
Lough Meelagh
Keadew
Drumshanbo
Ballinamore
Drumlonan
Garadice Lough
Swan Island Open Farm
Newtown Gore
Doogary
Derrycassan Lough
Carrigeen
Drumany
Foxfield
Glenview Folk Museum
Drumcoura Lough
Drumlea
Drumcoura
Corrawaleen
Killegar
Fenagh
Keshcarrigan
Crossna
Stag I.
0 2 4 6 miles
0 2 4 6 8 10 km

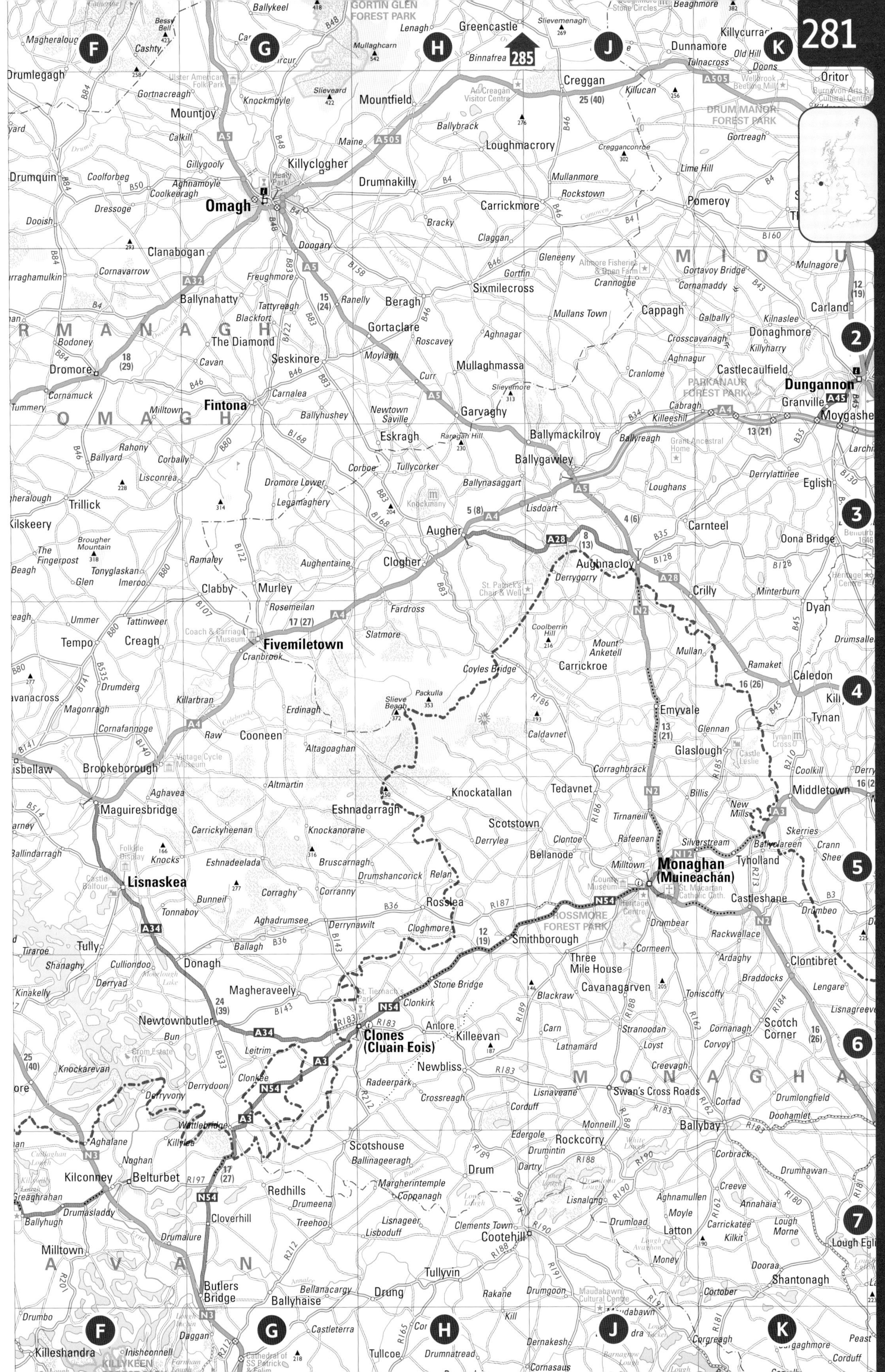
285
Omagh
Mountjoy
Killyclogher
Mountfield
Greencastle
Creggan
Dunnamore
Killycurragh
Oritor
GORTIN GLEN FOREST PARK
DRUM MANOR FOREST PARK
Loughmacrory
Drumnakilly
Carrickmore
Pomeroy
Drumquin
Dromore
Fintona
Seskinore
The Diamond
Ballynahatty
Clanabogan
Beragh
Gortaclare
Sixmilecross
Cappagh
Donaghmore
Carland
Castlecaulfield
Dungannon
Granville
Moygashel
PARKANAUR FOREST PARK
Garvaghy
Ballymackilroy
Ballygawley
Eskragh
Augher
Clogher
Aughnacloy
Carnteel
Eglish
Crilly
Oona Bridge
Trillick
Clabby
Murley
Fivemiletown
Tempo
Creagh
Emyvale
Glaslough
Caledon
Tynan
Middletown
Brookeborough
Maguiresbridge
Lisnaskea
Cooneen
Knockatallan
Scotstown
Tedavnet
Monaghan (Muineachán)
Rosslea
Smithborough
Castleshane
Clontibret
Donagh
Newtownbutler
Clones (Cluain Eois)
Newbliss
Scotch Corner
Ballybay
Rockcorry
Cootehill
Belturbet
Redhills
Butlers Bridge
Ballyhaise
Killeshandra
Drung
Tullyvin
Shantonagh
Lough Egish
Carrickmacross
F
G
H
J
K
2
3
4
5
6
7
FERMANAGH
OMAGH
MID ULSTER
MONAGHAN
CAVAN
A5
A505
A32
A4
A28
A34
A3
N2
N54
N12
N3
A45

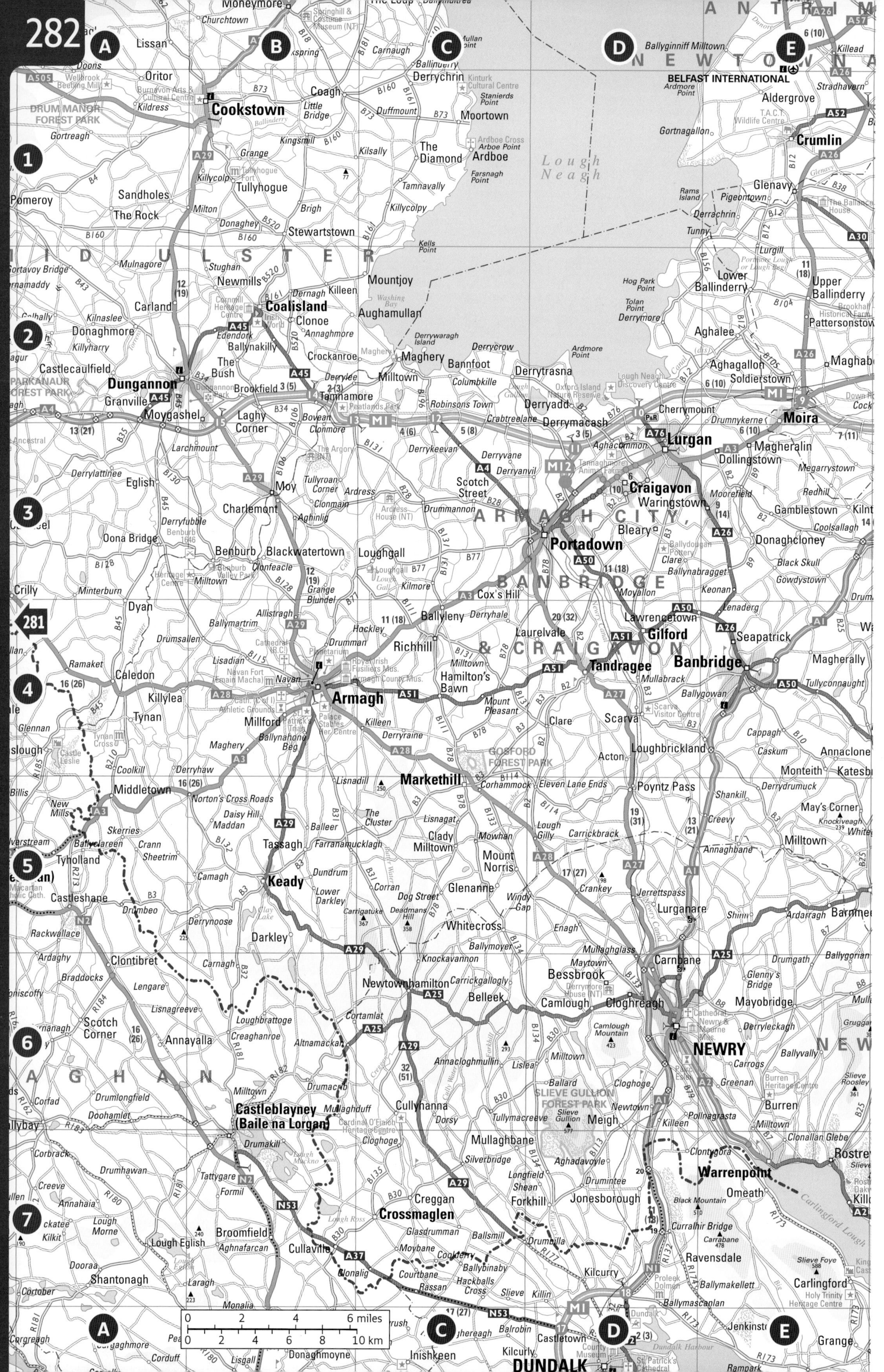
Moneymore
Churchtown
Springhill & Costume Museum (NT)
Lissan
Oritor
Wellbrook Beetling Mill
Burnavon Arts & Cultural Centre
Kildress
DRUM MANOR FOREST PARK
Cookstown
Coagh
Little Bridge
Kingsmill
Duffmount
Carnaugh
Ballinderry
Derrychrin
Kinturk Cultural Centre
Stanierds Point
Moortown
The Diamond
Ardboe Cross
Arboe Point
Ardboe
Farsnagh Point
Lough Neagh
Ballyginniff Milltown
ANTRIM
NEWTOWNABBEY
BELFAST INTERNATIONAL
Ardmore Point
Aldergrove
Stradhavern
Killead
T.A.C.T. Wildlife Centre
Gortnagallon
Crumlin
Glenavy
Rams Island
Pigeontown
Derrachrin
Tunny
The Ballance House
Gortreagh
Grange
Tullyhogue Fort
Killycolp
Tullyhogue
Kilsally
Tamnavally
Killycolpy
Sandholes
Pomeroy
The Rock
Milton
Donaghey
Brigh
Stewartstown
Kells Point
MID ULSTER
Mulnagore
Stughan
Gortavoy Bridge
Newmills
Cornmill Heritage Centre
Carland
Coalisland
Irish World
Dernagh
Killeen
Mountjoy
Washing Bay
Aughamullan
Clonoe
Annaghmore
Crockanroe
Maghery
Derrywaragh Island
Derrycrow
Ardmore Point
Hog Park Point
Tolan Point
Derrymore
Lower Ballinderry
Upper Ballinderry
Portmore Lough or Lough Beg
Lurgill
Brookhall Historical Farm
Pattersonstown
Aghalee
Aghagallon
Soldierstown
Maghaberry
Kilnaslee
Donaghmore
Killyharry
Edendork
Ballynakilly
The Bush
Castlecaulfield
PARKANAUR FOREST PARK
Dungannon
Dungannon Park
Granville
Brookfield
Moygashel
Laghy Corner
Tamnamore
Derrylee
Milltown
Bannfoot
Columbkille
Derrytrasna
Lough Neagh Discovery Centre
Oxford Island Nature Reserve
Robinsons Town
Peatlands Park
Bovean
Clonmore
Derryadd
Derrymacash
Crabtreelane
Cherrymount
Drumnykerne
Moira
Lurgan
Aghacommon
Tannaghmore Animal Farm
Magheralin
Dollingstown
Megarrystown
Larchmount
The Argory (NT)
Derrykeevan
Derryvane
Derryvanil
Scotch Street
Craigavon
Waringstown
Moorefield
Redhill
Gamblestown
Ancestral
Derrylattinee
Eglish
Moy
Tullyroan Corner
Ardress
Ardress House (NT)
Clonmain
Drummannon
Charlemont
Aghinlig
ARMAGH CITY, BANBRIDGE & CRAIGAVON
Portadown
Bleary
Coolsallagh
Donaghcloney
Derryfubble
Benburb 1646
Oona Bridge
Benburb
Blackwatertown
Loughgall
Clonfeacle
Benburb Valley Park
Heritage Centre
Milltown
Ballydougan Pottery
Clare
Ballynabragget
Black Skull
Gowdystown
Crilly
Minterburn
Grange Blundel
Kilmore
Cox's Hill
Moyallon
Keonan
Dyan
Allistragh
Ballymartrim
Ballyleny
Derryhale
Laurelvale
Lawrencetown
Lenaderg
Gilford
Seapatrick
Banbridge
Magherally
Tullyconnaught
Drumsallen
Hockley
Drumman
Richhill
Planetarium
Royal Irish Fusiliers Mus.
Armagh County Mus.
Cathedral (R.C.)
Milltown
Hamilton's Bawn
Tandragee
Mullabrack
Ballygowan
Ramaket
Lisadian
Navan Fort (Emain Macha)
Navan
Caledon
Killylea
Armagh
Cath. (C of I)
Athletic Grounds
Palace Stables Her. Centre
Mount Pleasant
Clare
Scarva
Scarva Visitor Centre
Tynan
Glennan
Millford
Killeen
Derryraine
Ballynahone Beg
Tynan Cross
Castle Leslie
Maghery
GOSFORD FOREST PARK
Acton
Loughbrickland
Cappagh
Caskum
Annaclone
Coolkill
Derryhaw
Lisnadill
Markethill
Corhammock
Eleven Lane Ends
Poyntz Pass
Monteith
Derrydrumuck
Middletown
Norton's Cross Roads
Daisy Hill
Maddan
Shankill
May's Corner
Knockiveagh
New Mills
Billis
Skerries
The Cluster
Lisnagat
Clady Milltown
Mowhan
Lough Gilly
Carrickbrack
Creevy
Milltown
Ballyclareen
Tyholland
Crann
Sheetrim
Tassagh
Farranamucklagh
Balleer
Mount Norris
Annaghbane
Camagh
Keady
Dundrum
Lower Darkley
Corran
Dog Street
Glenanne
Windy Gap
Crankey
Jerrettspass
Lurganare
Macartan Catholic Cath.
Castleshane
Drumbeo
Derrynoose
Carrigatuke
Deadmans Hill
Whitecross
Enagh
Shinn
Ardarragh
Barnmeen
Rackwallace
Darkley
Clay Lake
Ballymoyer
Knockavannon
Mullaghglass
Carnbane
Drumgath
Ballygorian
Ardaghy
Clontibret
Carnagh
Maytown
Bessbrook
Glenny's Bridge
Braddocks
Lengare
Newtownhamilton
Carrickgallogly
Belleek
Derrymore House (NT)
Camlough
Cloghreagh
Mayobridge
Lisnagreeve
Loughbrattoge
Cortamlat
Camlough Mountain
Cathedral
Newry & Mourne Mus.
Derryleckagh
Scotch Corner
Annayalla
Creaghanroe
Altnamackan
NEWRY
Ballyvally
NEW
Annacloghmullin
Lislea
Milltown
Carrogs
Greenan
Burren Heritage Centre
Roosley
MONAGHAN
Milltown
Drumacrib
Cullyhanna
Ballard
Cloghoge
Corfad
Drumlongfield
SLIEVE GULLION FOREST PARK
Newtown
Burren
Doohamlet
Castleblayney (Baile na Lorgan)
Mullaghduff
Cardinal O'Fiaich Heritage Centre
Dorsy
Tullymacreeve
Slieve Gullion
Meigh
Killeen
Pollnagrasta
Milltown
Clonallan Glebe
Rostrevor
Drumakill
Cloghoge
Lough Muckno
Mullaghbane
Clontygora
Corbrack
Drumhawan
Silverbridge
Longfield
Aghadavoyle
Warrenpoint
Tattygare
Formil
Shean
Drumintee
Forkhill
Jonesborough
Black Mountain
Omeath
Creeve
Annahaia
Creggan
Lough Ross
Crossmaglen
Curralhir Bridge
Carrabane
Lough Morne
Kilkit
Broomfield
Glasdrumman
Ballsmill
Drumbilla
Carlingford Lough
Lough Eglish
Aghnafarcan
Cullaville
Moybane
Coolderry
Ballybinaby
Ravensdale
Slieve Foye
Dooraa
Shantonagh
Laragh
Clonalig
Courtbane
Rassan
Hackballs Cross
Kilcurry
Proleek Dolmen
Ballymakellett
Carlingford
Holy Trinity Heritage Centre
Cortober
Monalia
Slieve
Killin
Dundalk
Ballymascanlan
Balrobin
Castletown
County Museum
Jenkinstown
Grange
Corgreagh
Carrickmacross
Corduff
Lisgall
Donaghmoyne
Inishkeen
Kilcurly
DUNDALK
Dundalk Harbour
St Patrick's Cathedral
Rampark
0 2 4 6 miles
0 2 4 6 8 10 km
281

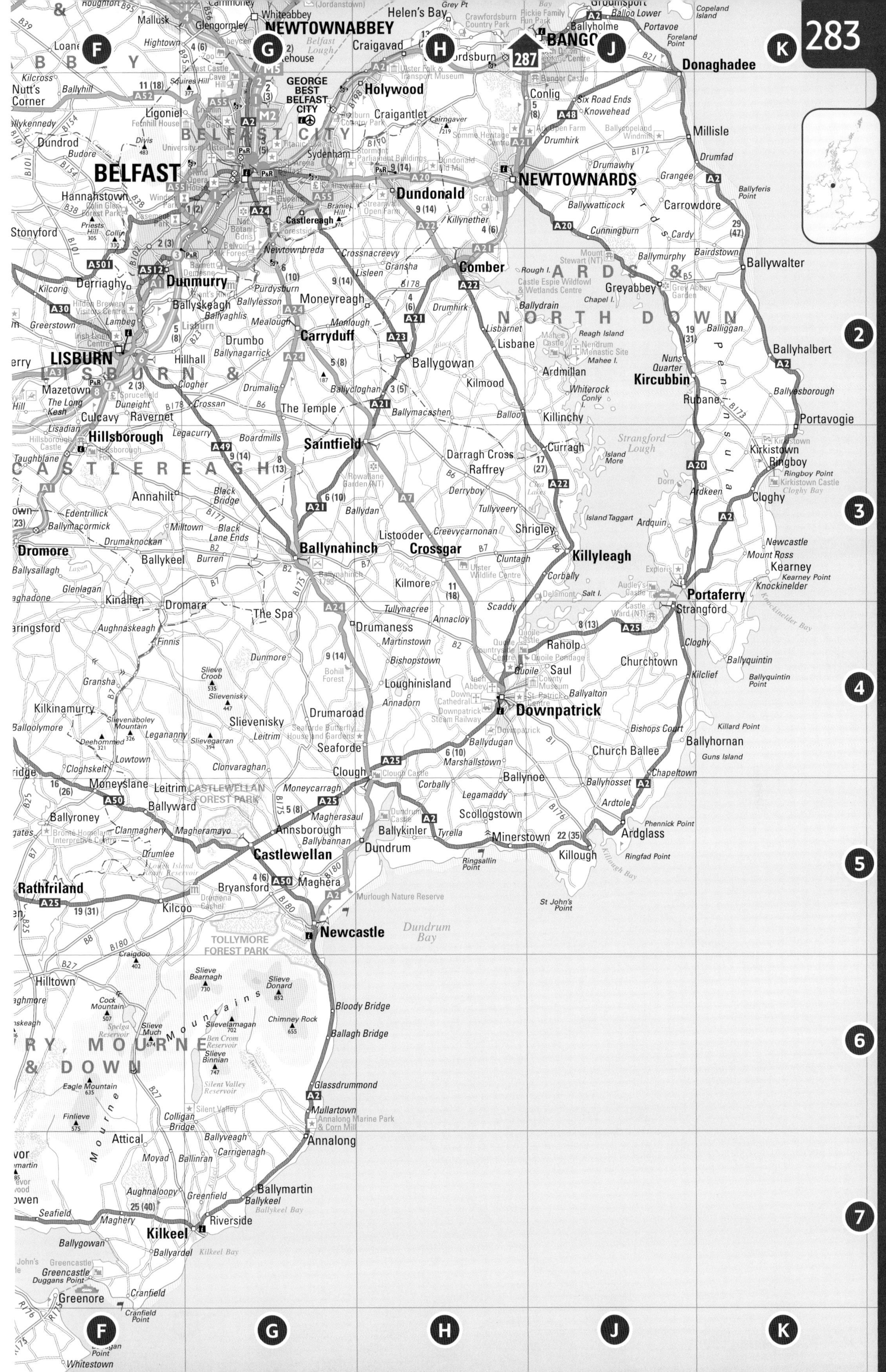
F
G
H
J
K
2
3
4
5
6
7
NEWTOWNABBEY
Whiteabbey
Helen's Bay
Grey Pt
Crawfordsburn Country Park
BANGOR
287
Groomsport
Balloo Lower
Ballyholme
Portavoe
Copeland Island
Foreland Point
Donaghadee
Mallusk
Glengormley
Loanends
Hightown
Craigavad
Holywood
GEORGE BEST BELFAST CITY
Kilcross
Nutt's Corner
Ballyhill
Ligoniel
Fernhill House
BELFAST CITY
Craigantlet
Cairngaver
Conlig
Six Road Ends
Knowehead
Millisle
Dundrod
Budore
Divis
Sydenham
Somme Heritage Centre
Drumhirk
Ballycopeland Windmill
Drumfad
BELFAST
Dundonald
NEWTOWNARDS
Drumawhy
Grangee
Hannahstown
Colin Glen Forest Park
Carrowdore
Ballyferis Point
Priests Hill
Collin
Castlereagh
Killynether
Ballywatticock
Stonyford
Cunningburn
Cardy
Newtownbreda
Crossnacreevy
Gransha
Mount Stewart (NT)
Ballymurphy
Bairdstown
Ballywalter
Kilcorig
Derriaghy
Dunmurry
Lisleen
Comber
Rough I.
ARDS & NORTH DOWN
Greyabbey
Grey Abbey Gardens
Castle Espie Wildfowl & Wetlands Centre
Chapel I.
Hilden Brewery Visitors Centre
Ballyskeagh
Purdysburn
Ballylesson
Moneyreagh
Ballydrain
Greenstown
Lambeg
Mealough
Monlough
Drumhirk
Irish Linen Centre
Carryduff
Lisbarnet
Reagh Island
Balligan
Ballyhalbert
LISBURN
Drumbo
Ballynagarrick
Lisbane
Mahee Castle
Nendrum Monastic Site
Mahee I.
Nuns Quarter
Kircubbin
Hillhall
Ballygowan
Ardmillan
LISBURN & CASTLEREAGH
Mazetown
Clogher
Drumalig
Ballycloghan
Kilmood
Whiterock
Conly I.
Rubane
Ballyesborough
The Long Kesh
Duneight
Crossan
The Temple
Ballymacashen
Balloo
Killinchy
Portavogie
Culcavy
Ravernet
Lisadian
Hillsborough
Legacurry
Boardmills
Saintfield
Strangford Lough
Curragh
Kirkistown
Ringboy
Ringboy Point
Kirkistown Castle
Cloghy Bay
Taughblane
Darragh Cross
Raffrey
Island More
Rowallane Garden (NT)
Derryboy
Dorn
Ardkeen
Cloghy
Annahilt
Black Bridge
Ballydan
Tullyveery
Edentrillick
Ballymacormick
Milltown
Black Lane Ends
Creevycarnonan
Shrigley
Island Taggart
Ardquin
Drumaknockan
Listooder
Newcastle
Mount Ross
Kearney
Kearney Point
Knockinelder
Dromore
Ballykeel
Burren
Ballynahinch
Crossgar
Cluntagh
Killyleagh
Ballysallagh
Glenlagan
Kilmore
Corbally
Exploris
Audley's Castle
Portaferry
Strangford
Kinallen
Dromara
Ballynahinch 1798
Delamont
Salt I.
Castle Ward (NT)
Knockinelder Bay
Tullynacree
Scaddy
Aughnaskeagh
The Spa
Annacloy
Drumaness
Raholp
Cloghy
Finnis
Martinstown
Quoile Castle
Quoile Pondage
Churchtown
Ballyquintin
Dunmore
Bishopstown
Saul
Kilclief
Ballyquintin Point
Slieve Croob
Bohill Forest
Quoile
Inch Abbey
Down County Museum
Gransha
Slievenisky
Loughinisland
Ballyalton
St Patrick Centre
Kilkinamurry
Annadorn
Down Cathedral
Downpatrick
Downpatrick Steam Railway
Slievenaboley Mountain
Drumaroad
Killard Point
Balloolymore
Slievenisky
Seaforde Butterfly House and Gardens
Bishops Court
Leganany
Leitrim
Deehommed
Slievegarran
Dunpatrick
Ballydugan
Ballyhornan
Lowtown
Seaforde
Marshallstown
Church Ballee
Guns Island
Cloghskelt
Clonvaraghan
Clough
Clough Castle
Ballynoe
Chapeltown
Moneyslane
Leitrim
CASTLEWELLAN FOREST PARK
Moneycarragh
Corbally
Legamaddy
Ballyhosset
Ardtole
Ballyward
Magherasaul
Dundrum Castle
Scollogstown
Ballyroney
Clanmaghery
Magheramayo
Annsborough
Ballybannan
Ballykinler
Tyrella
Phennick Point
Ardglass
Brontë Homeland Interpretive Centre
Minerstown
Killough
Drumlee
Castlewellan
Dundrum
Ringsallin Point
Ringfad Point
Killough Bay
Rathfriland
Bryansford
Maghera
Murlough Nature Reserve
Kilcoo
Drumena Cashel
St John's Point
TOLLYMORE FOREST PARK
Newcastle
Dundrum Bay
Craigdoo
Hilltown
Slieve Bearnagh
Slieve Donard
Cock Mountain
Bloody Bridge
Chimney Rock
Spelga Reservoir
Slieve Muck
Slievelamagan
Ballagh Bridge
Ben Crom Reservoir
Slieve Binnian
MOURNE & DOWN
Mourne Mountains
Eagle Mountain
Silent Valley Reservoir
Glassdrummond
Finlieve
Silent Valley
Colligan Bridge
Mullartown
Annalong Marine Park & Corn Mill
Attical
Ballyveagh
Annalong
Carrigenagh
Moyad
Ballinran
Aughnaloopy
Greenfield
Ballymartin
Ballykeel
Ballykeel Bay
Seafield
Maghery
Riverside
Kilkeel
Ballygowan
Ballyardel
Kilkeel Bay
Greencastle
Greencastle
Duggans Point
Cranfield
Greenore
Cranfield Point
Whitestown

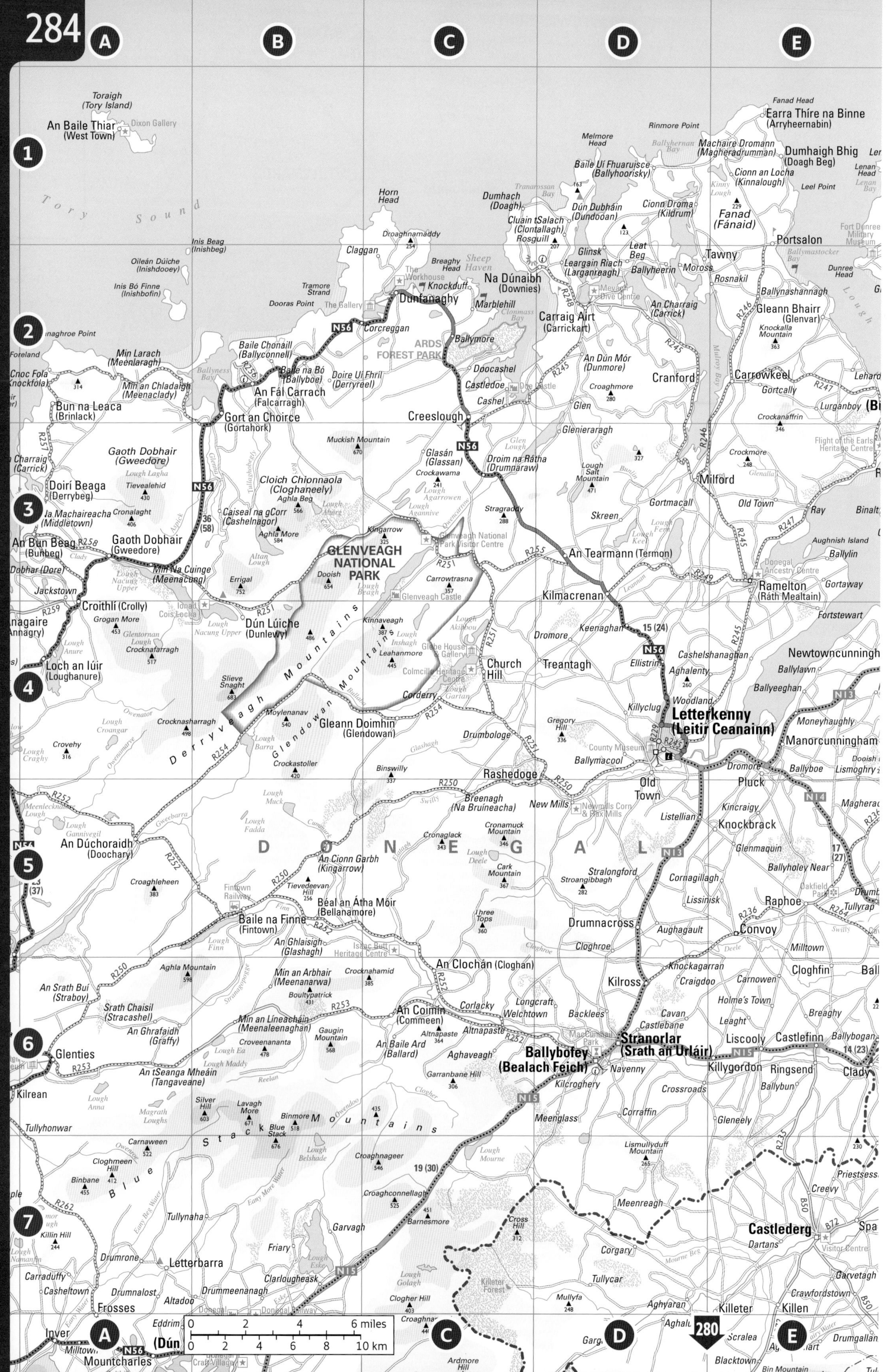
A
B
C
D
E
1
2
3
4
5
6
7
Toraigh
(Tory Island)
An Baile Thiar
(West Town)
Dixon Gallery
Tory Sound
Inis Beag
(Inishbeg)
Oileán Dúiche
(Inishdooey)
Inis Bó Finne
(Inishbofin)
Tramore Strand
Dooras Point
Horn Head
Droaghnamaddy
Claggan
The Workhouse
Knockduff
Breaghy Head
Sheep Haven
Na Dúnaibh
(Downies)
Marblehill
The Gallery
Dunfanaghy
Corcreggan
N56
ARDS FOREST PARK
Ballymore
Doocashel
Castledoe
Doe Castle
Cashel
Creeslough
Baile Chonaill
(Ballyconnell)
Baile na Bó
(Ballyboe)
Doire Uí Fhríl
(Derryreel)
An Fál Carrach
(Falcarragh)
Gort an Choirce
(Gortahork)
Min Larach
(Meenlaragh)
Mín an Chladaigh
(Meenaclady)
Cnoc Fola
(Knockfola)
Bun na Leaca
(Brinlack)
Gaoth Dobhair
(Gweedore)
Doirí Beaga
(Derrybeg)
Na Machaireacha
(Middletown)
An Bun Beag
(Bunbeg)
Gaoth Dobhair
(Gweedore)
Cloich Chionnaola
(Cloghaneely)
Caiseal na gCorr
(Cashelnagor)
Muckish Mountain
Errigal
Min Na Cuinge
(Meenacung)
Croithlí (Crolly)
Dún Lúiche
(Dunlewy)
Loch an Iúir
(Loughanure)
GLENVEAGH NATIONAL PARK
Kingarrow
Glenveagh National Park Visitor Centre
Glenveagh Castle
Derryveagh Mountains
Glendowan Mountains
Glebe House & Gallery
Colmcille Heritage Centre
Church Hill
Corderry
Gleann Doimhin
(Glendowan)
Crockastoller
Binswilly
Glasán
(Glassan)
Crockawama
Droim na Rátha
(Drumnaraw)
Stragraddy
An Tearmann (Termon)
Kilmacrenan
Keenaghan
Dromore
Treantagh
Drumbologe
Rashedoge
Breenagh
(Na Bruíneacha)
New Mills
Newmills Corn & Flax Mills
DONEGAL
An Dúchoraidh
(Doochary)
An Cionn Garbh
(Kingarrow)
Béal an Átha Móir
(Bellanamore)
Baile na Finne
(Fintown)
Fintown Railway
An Ghlaisigh
(Glashagh)
Isaac Butt Heritage Centre
An Clochán (Cloghan)
An Coimín
(Commeen)
Corlacky
Welchtown
Altnapaste
Aghaveagh
Ballybofey
(Bealach Feich)
Stranorlar
(Srath an Urláir)
Kilcroghery
Navenny
N15
An Srath Buí
(Straboy)
Srath Chaisil
(Stracashel)
Glenties
Kilrean
Tullyhonwar
Blue Stack Mountains
Lavagh More
Binmore
Blue Stack
Silver Hill
Croaghnageer
Croaghconnellagh
Barnesmore
Garvagh
Friary
Lough Eske
Clarlougheask
Drummeenanagh
Letterbarra
Drumrone
Tullynaha
Carraduffy
Casheltown
Frosses
Drumnalost
Altadoo
Eddrim
Inver
Milltown
Mountcharles
Killin Hill
Cloghmeen Hill
Binbane
Carnaween
Meenglass
Corraffin
Lismullyduff Mountain
Meenreagh
Cross Hill
Corgary
Tullycar
Mullyfa
Killeter Forest
Aghyaran
Killeter
Castlederg
Dartans
Visitor Centre
Garvetagh
Crawfordstown
Killen
Scralea
Blacktown
Drumgallan
Bin Mountain
Ardmore Hill
Clogher Hill
280
19 (30)
Dunmore
Dúmhach
(Doagh)
Melmore Head
Baile Uí Fhuaruisce
(Ballyhoorisky)
Dún Dubháin
(Dundooan)
Cluain tSalach
(Clontallagh)
Rosguill
Glinsk
Leargain Riach
(Larganreagh)
Leat Beg
Ballyheerin
Mevagh Dive Centre
Carraig Airt
(Carrickart)
An Dún Mór
(Dunmore)
Croaghmore
Glen
Glenieraragh
Cranford
Cionn Droma
(Kildrum)
Tawny
Moross
Rosnakil
An Charraig
(Carrick)
Fanad
(Fánaid)
Rinmore Point
Fanad Head
Earra Thíre na Binne
(Arryheernabin)
Machaire Dromann
(Magheradrumman)
Dumhaigh Bhig
(Doagh Beg)
Cionn an Locha
(Kinnalough)
Leel Point
Portsalon
Ballynashannagh
Gleann Bhairr
(Glenvar)
Knockalla Mountain
Carrowkeel
Gortcally
Lurganboy
Crockanaffrin
Crockmore
Mulroy Bay
Milford
Gortmacall
Old Town
Ray
Skreen
Ramelton
(Ráth Mealtain)
Donegal Ancestry Centre
Aughnish Island
Ballylin
Gortaway
Fortstewart
Flight of the Earls Heritage Centre
Fort Dunree Military Museum
Dunree Head
Cashelshanaghan
Aghalenty
Ellistrin
Woodland
Killyclug
Letterkenny
(Leitir Ceanainn)
County Museum
Ballymacool
Gregory Hill
Old Town
Listellian
15 (24)
N13
N14
Newtowncunningham
Ballylawn
Ballyeeghan
Moneyhaughly
Manorcunningham
Dromore
Pluck
Ballyboe
Lismoghry
Kincraigy
Knockbrack
Glenmaquin
Ballyholey Near
Oakfield Park
Raphoe
Tullyrap
Convoy
Milltown
Cloghfin
Carnowen
Holme's Town
Breaghy
Leaght
Liscooly
Castlefinn
Ballybogan
Killygordon
Ringsend
Clady
Ballybun
Gleneely
Crossroads
Priestsessagh
Creevy
Cavan
Castlebane
Backlees
Kilross
Knockagarran
Craigdoo
Cloghroe
Drumnacross
Aughagault
Lissinisk
Cornagillagh
Stralongford
Stroangibbagh
Three Tops
Cronamuck Mountain
Cark Mountain
Cronaglack
Tievedeevan Hill
Croaghleheen
Aghla Mountain
Mín an Arbhair
(Meenanarwa)
Crocknahamid
Boultypatrick
Mín an Lineacháin
(Meenaleenaghan)
Croveenananta
Gaugin Mountain
An Ghrafaidh
(Graffy)
An tSeanga Mheáin
(Tangaveane)
An Baile Ard
(Ballard)
Garranbane Hill
Longcraft
MacCumhaill Park
Crocknasharragh
Slieve Snaght
Crovehy
Moylenanav
Kinnaveagh
Leahanmore
Carrowtrasna
Dooish
Aghla Beg
Aghla More
Tievealehid
Cronalaght
Grogan More
Crocknafarragh
Lough Salt Mountain
Horn Head
0 2 4 6 miles
0 2 4 6 8 10 km

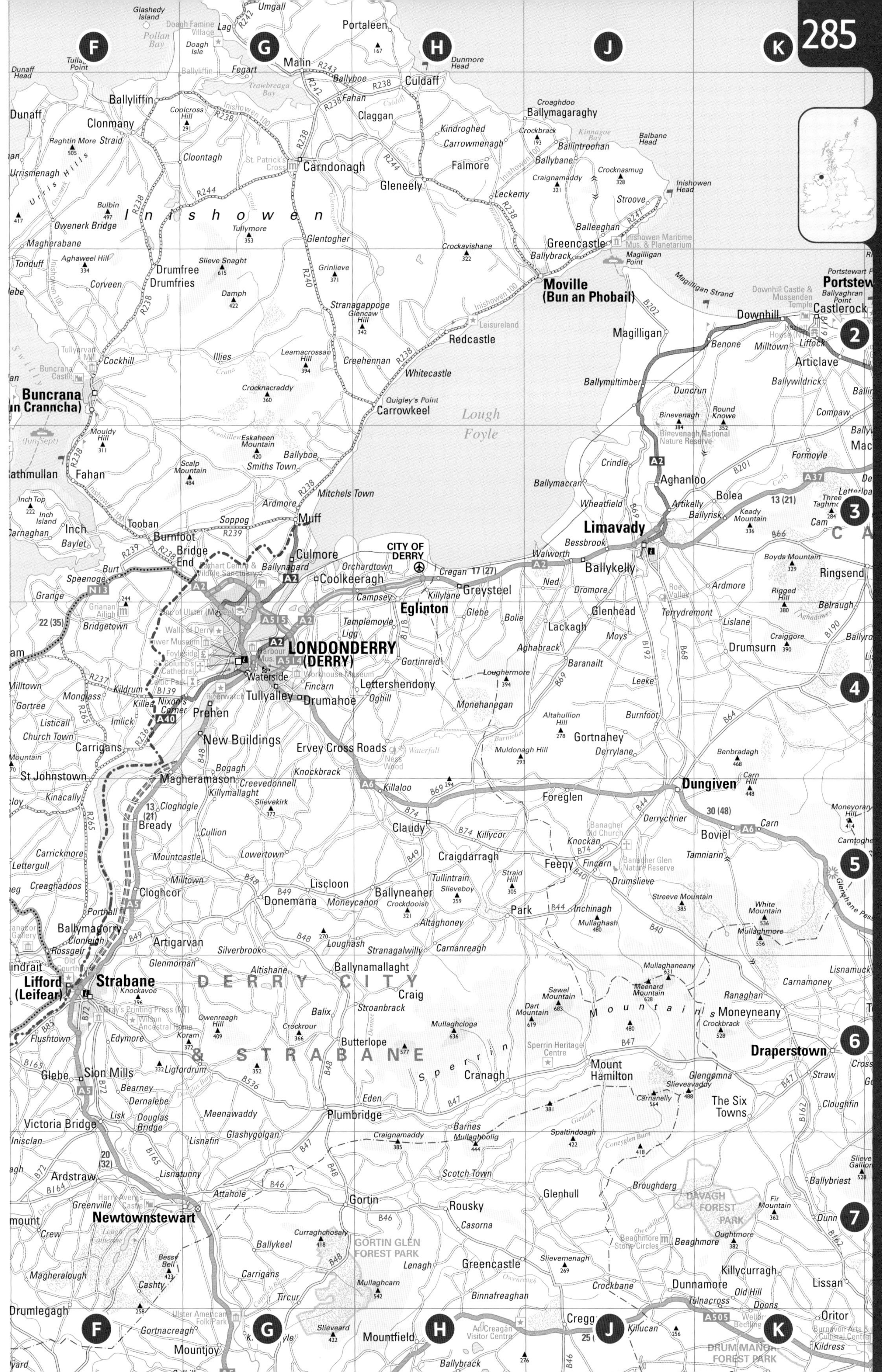
F
G
H
J
K
2
3
4
5
6
7
Glashedy Island
Pollan Bay
Doagh Famine Village
Doagh Isle
Lag
Umgall
Portaleen
Malin
Dunmore Head
Tullagh Point
Dunaff Head
Ballyliffin
Fegart
Trawbreaga Bay
Ballyboe
Fahan
Culdaff
Dunaff
Ballyliffin
Coolcross Hill
Clonmany
Claggan
Croaghdoo
Ballymagaraghy
Raghtin More
Straid
Kindroghed
Carrowmenagh
Crockbrack
Kinnagoe Bay
Ballintroohan
Balbane Head
Urris Hills
Urrismenagh
Cloontagh
St. Patrick's Cross
Carndonagh
Falmore
Ballybane
Craignamaddy
Crocknasmug
Gleneely
Leckemy
Inishowen Head
Stroove
Bulbin
Inishowen
Owenerk Bridge
Tullymore
Magherabane
Glentogher
Balleeghan
Greencastle
Inishowen Maritime Mus. & Planetarium
Aghaweel Hill
Slieve Snaght
Crockavishane
Ballybrack
Magilligan Point
Tonduff
Drumfree
Drumfries
Grinlieve
Corveen
Moville
(Bun an Phobail)
Magilligan Strand
Portstewart
Damph
Downhill Castle & Mussenden Temple
Ballyaghran Point
Castlerock
Stranagappoge
Glencaw Hill
Leisureland
Downhill
Hezlett House (NT)
Liffock
Magilligan
Redcastle
Benone
Milltown
Tullyarvan Mill
Illies
Leamacrossan Hill
Creehennan
Whitecastle
Articlave
Cockhill
Buncrana Castle
Buncrana
(Bun Crannacha)
Crocknacraddy
Ballymultimber
Ballywildrick
Duncrun
Quigley's Point
Carrowkeel
Lough Foyle
Binevenagh
Round Knowe
Compaw
Binevenagh National Nature Reserve
Mouldy Hill
Eskaheen Mountain
Ballyboe
Smiths Town
Crindle
Formoyle
Rathmullan
Fahan
Scalp Mountain
Aghanloo
Ballymacran
Mitchels Town
Inch Top
Inch Island
Inch
Ardmore
Wheatfield
Artikelly
Bolea
Ballyrisk
Keady Mountain
Three Taghmo
Cam
Tooban
Burnfoot
Soppog
Muff
Limavady
Carnaghan
Baylet
Bridge End
Culmore
CITY OF DERRY
Bessbrook
Boyds Mountain
Ringsend
Burt
Speenoge
Ballynagard
Orchardtown
Cregan
Walworth
Ballykelly
Grange
Coolkeeragh
Greysteel
Ned
Dromore
Ardmore
Grianan Ailigh
Campsey
Killylane
Roe Valley
Rigged Hill
Belraugh
Bridgetown
Eglinton
Glebe
Bolie
Glenhead
Terrydremont
Lislane
Walls of Derry
Tower Museum
Templemoyle
Ligg
Lackagh
Moys
Drumsurn
Craiggore
LONDONDERRY
(DERRY)
Aghabrack
Foyleside
St Columb's Cathedral
Gortinreid
Baranailt
Milltown
Kildrum
Waterside
Workhouse Museum
Loughermore
Leeke
Monglass
Killea
Nixon's Corner
Tullyalley
Fincarn
Lettershendony
Gortree
Prehen
Drumahoe
Oghill
Monehanegan
Burnfoot
Imlick
Altahullion Hill
Listicall
Gortnahey
Church Town
Carrigans
New Buildings
Ervey Cross Roads
Waterfall
Ness Wood
Muldonagh Hill
Derrylane
Benbradagh
St Johnstown
Bogagh
Knockbrack
Magheramason
Creevedonnell
Killaloo
Dungiven
Carn Hill
Kinacally
Killymallaght
Foreglen
Cloghogle
Slievekirk
Derrychrier
Moneyoran Hill
Bready
Claudy
Banagher Old Church
Carn
Cullion
Killycor
Knockan
Boviel
Carrickmore
Lettergull
Mountcastle
Lowertown
Craigdarragh
Feeny
Fincarn
Banagher Glen Nature Reserve
Tamniarin
Milltown
Tullintrain
Straid Hill
Creaghadoos
Cloghcor
Liscloon
Ballyneaner
Slieveboy
Drumslieve
Streeve Mountain
Donemana
Moneycanon
Crockdooish
Park
Inchinagh
Porthall
Altaghoney
Mullaghash
White Mountain
Ballymagorry
Clonleigh
Artigarvan
Loughash
Mullaghmore
Rossgeir
Silverbrook
Stranagalwilly
Carnanreagh
Glenmornan
Altishane
Ballynamallaght
Mullaghaneany
Lifford
(Leifear)
Strabane
DERRY CITY & STRABANE
Craig
Meenard Mountain
Sawel Mountain
Lisnamuck
Carnamoney
Knockavoe
Stroanbrack
Dart Mountain
Ranaghan
Gray's Printing Press (NT)
Wilson Ancestral Home
Balix
Sperrin Mountains
Moneyneany
Crockbrack
Owenreagh Hill
Crockrour
Mullaghcloga
Flushtown
Edymore
Koram
Butterlope
Sperrin Heritage Centre
Draperstown
Glebe
Sion Mills
Ligfordrum
Mount Hamilton
Glengomna
Slieveavaddy
Bearney
Cranagh
Dernalebe
Eden
Carnanelly
The Six Towns
Cloughfin
Victoria Bridge
Lisk
Douglas Bridge
Meenawaddy
Plumbridge
Barnes
Mullaghbolig
Craignamaddy
Spaltindoagh
Slieve Gallion
Iniscan
Lisnafin
Glashygolgan
Coneyglen Burn
Ardstraw
Lisnatunny
Scotch Town
Ballybriest
Harry Avery's Castle
Attahole
Gortin
Rousky
Glenhull
Broughderg
Davagh Forest Park
Fir Mountain
Greenville
Newtownstewart
Casorna
Dunn
Crew
Curraghchosaly
Gortin Glen Forest Park
Beaghmore Stone Circles
Beaghmore
Oughtmore
Ballykeel
Lenagh
Greencastle
Slievemenagh
Bessy Bell
Killycurragh
Magheralough
Carrigans
Crockbane
Dunnamore
Lissan
Cashty
Mullaghcarn
Binnafreaghan
Old Hill
Tulnacross
Drumlegagh
Tircur
Doons
Oritor
Ulster American Folk Park
Cregg
A505
Wellbrook Beetling
Burnavon Arts & Cultural Centre
Gortnacreagh
Slieveard
Mountfield
An Creagán Visitor Centre
Killucan
Kildress
Drum Manor Forest Park
Mountjoy
Ballybrack
R238
R242
R243
R244
R239
R240
R237
R236
R265
R241
A2
A37
A6
A5
A40
A515
A514
N13
B202
B201
B66
B69
B68
B192
B64
B190
B118
B139
B48
B49
B74
B40
B44
B47
B72
B85
B165
B164
B536
B46
B162
B119
Inishowen 100
17 (27)
13 (21)
22 (35)
30 (48)
20 (32)

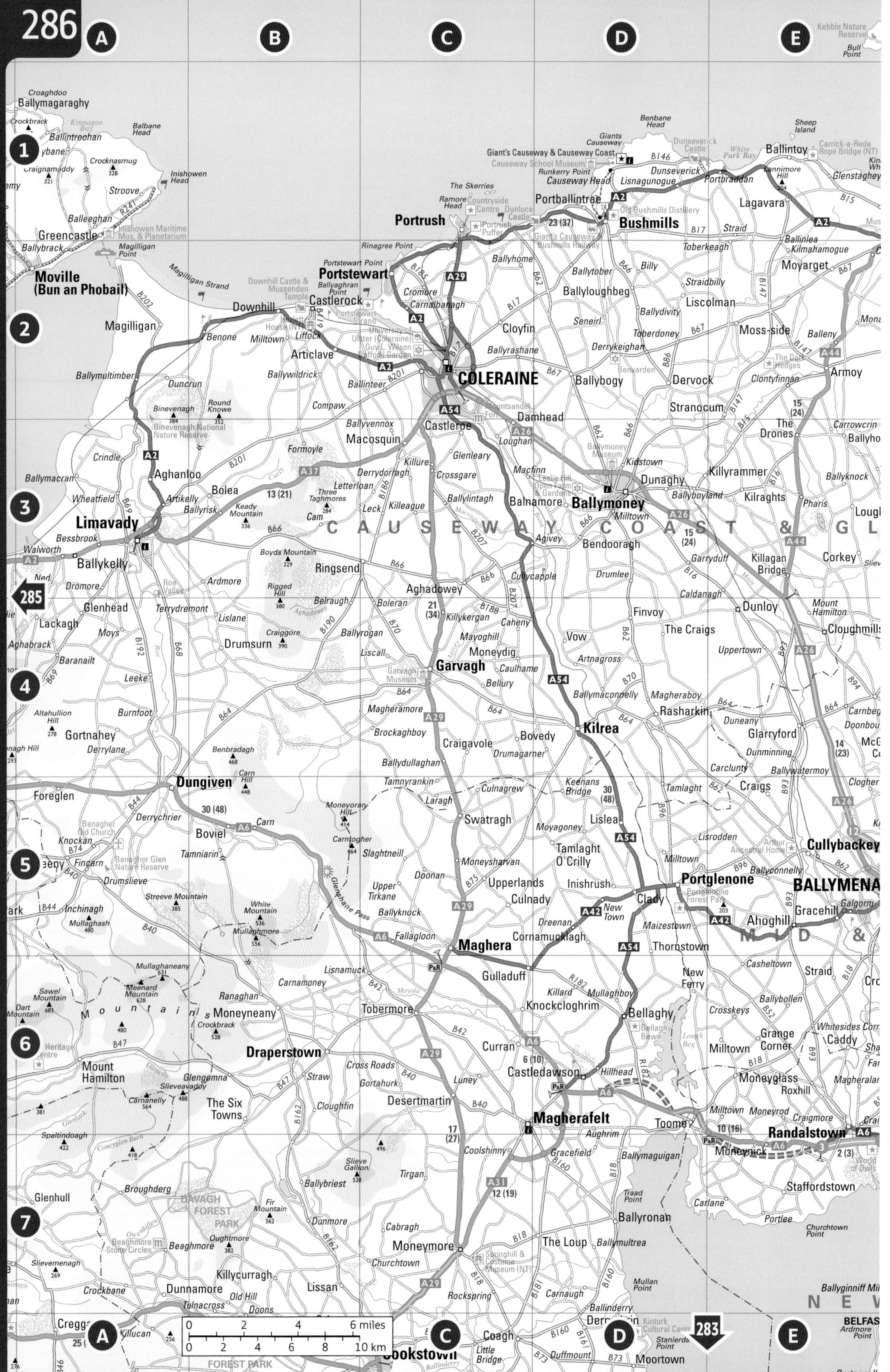
A
B
C
D
E
1
2
3
4
5
6
7
285
283
Croaghdoo
Ballymagaraghy
Crockbrack
Kinnagoe Bay
Balbane Head
Ballintroohan
Craignamaddy
Crocknasmug
Inishowen Head
Stroove
Balleeghan
Greencastle
Inishowen Maritime Mus. & Planetarium
Ballybrack
Magilligan Point
Moville
(Bun an Phobail)
Magilligan Strand
Magilligan
Downhill
Benone
Milltown
Liffock
Castlerock
Downhill Castle & Mussenden Temple
Portstewart Point
Ballyaghran Point
Portstewart
Portstewart Strand
Rinagree Point
Portrush
Ramore Head
Countryside Centre
Dunluce Castle
Portrush Puffer
The Skerries
Giants Causeway
Giant's Causeway & Causeway Coast
Causeway School Museum
Runkerry Point
Causeway Head
Benbane Head
Dunseverick Castle
Dunseverick
Lisnagunogue
Portballintrae
Bushmills
Old Bushmills Distillery
Giant's Causeway & Bushmills Railway
White Park Bay
Portbraddan
Ballintoy
Carrick-a-Rede Rope Bridge (NT)
Sheep Island
Kebble Nature Reserve
Bull Point
Lannimore Hill
Glenstaghey
Lagavara
Straid
Toberkeagh
Ballinlea
Kilmahamogue
Moyarget
Ballyhome
Ballytober
Billy
Straidbilly
Ballyloughbeg
Liscolman
Cromore
Carnalbanagh
Ballydivity
Seneirl
Toberdoney
Moss-side
Balleny
Cloyfin
Derrykeighan
Benvarden
The Dark Hedges
Armoy
University of Ulster (Coleraine)
Guy L. Wilson Daffodil Garden
Articlave
Ballyrashane
COLERAINE
Ballybogy
Dervock
Clontyfinnan
Ballymultimber
Duncrun
Ballywildrick
Ballinteer
Compaw
Mountsandel Fort
Damhead
Stranocum
Binevenagh
Round Knowe
Binevenagh National Nature Reserve
Ballyvennox
Macosquin
Castleroe
Loughan
The Drones
Carrowcrin
Crindle
Formoyle
Killure
Glenleary
Ballymoney Museum
Kidstown
Ballymacran
Aghanloo
Derrydorragh
Crossgare
Macfinn
Killyrammer
Ballyknock
Bolea
Letterloan
Leslie Hill Open Farm & Gardens
Dunaghy
Wheatfield
Artikelly
Ballyrisk
Three Taghmores
Leck
Killeague
Ballylintagh
Balnamore
Ballymoney
Ballyboyland
Kilraghts
Limavady
Keady Mountain
Cam
Milltown
Phairis
CAUSEWAY COAST & GL
Bessbrook
Walworth
Ballykelly
Agivey
Bendooragh
Boyds Mountain
Ringsend
Garryduff
Killagan Bridge
Corkey
Ned
Dromore
Roe Valley
Ardmore
Aghadowey
Cullycapple
Drumlee
Caldanagh
Glenhead
Rigged Hill
Belraugh
Boleran
Killykergan
Finvoy
Dunloy
Mount Hamilton
Lackagh
Terrydremont
Lislane
Caheny
The Craigs
Cloughmills
Moys
Drumsurn
Craiggore
Ballyrogan
Mayoghill
Vow
Aghabrack
Baranailt
Liscall
Moneydig
Artnagross
Uppertown
Garvagh Museum
Garvagh
Caulhame
Leeke
Bellury
Ballymaconnelly
Magheraboy
Rasharkin
Altahullion Hill
Burnfoot
Magheramore
Kilrea
Duneany
Gortnahey
Derrylane
Brockaghboy
Craigavole
Bovedy
Glarryford
Benbradagh
Drumagarner
Dunminning
Ballydullaghan
Carclunty
Ballywatermoy
Carn Hill
Tamnyrankin
Keenans Bridge
Craigs
Dungiven
Foreglen
Culnagrew
Tamlaght
Clogher
Laragh
Lislea
Derrychrier
Moneyoran Hill
Swatragh
Moyagoney
Banagher Old Church
Boviel
Carn
Lisrodden
Knockan
Carntogher
Slaghtneill
Tamlaght O'Crilly
Milltown
Arthur Ancestral Home
Cullybackey
Fincarn
Tamniarin
Moneysharvan
Banagher Glen Nature Reserve
Doonan
Ballyconnelly
Drumslieve
Upperlands
Inishrush
Portglenone
Portglenone Forest Park
BALLYMENA
Upper Tirkane
Culnady
Clady
Streeve Mountain
Glenshane Pass
New Town
Inchinagh
White Mountain
Ballyknock
Dreenan
Maizestown
Gracehill
Galgorm
Mullaghash
Mullaghmore
Fallagloon
Cornamucklagh
Ahoghill
MID &
Maghera
Thornstown
Mullaghaneany
Lisnamuck
Gulladuff
Casheltown
Straid
Meenard Mountain
Sawel Mountain
Carnamoney
Moyola
New Ferry
Killard
Mullaghboy
Ballybollen
Dart Mountain
Mountains
Ranaghan
Moneyneany
Tobermore
Knockcloghrim
Crossreys
Bellaghy
Bellaghy Bawn
Whitesides Corner
Caddy
Crockbrack
Curran
Lough Beg
Grange Corner
Milltown
Heritage Centre
Draperstown
Mount Hamilton
Glengomna
Slieveavaddy
Straw
Cross Roads
Gortahurk
Luney
Castledawson
Hillhead
Moneyglass
Roxhill
Magheralane
Carnanelly
The Six Towns
Cloughfin
Desertmartin
Milltown
Moneyrod
Craigmore
Toome
Randalstown
Magherafelt
Aughrim
Spaltindoagh
Coneyglen Burn
Slieve Gallion
Coolshinny
Gracefield
Ballymaguigan
Moneynick
World of Owls
Tirgan
Ballybriest
Broughderg
Davagh Forest Park
Fir Mountain
Glenhull
Traad Point
Carlane
Staffordstown
Ballyronan
Portlee
Churchtown Point
Beaghmore Stone Circles
Beaghmore
Oughtmore
Dunmore
Cabragh
Moneymore
The Loup
Ballymultrea
Slievemenagh
Churchtown
Springhill & Costume Museum (NT)
Killycurragh
Mullan Point
Crockbane
Dunnamore
Lissan
Old Hill
Rockspring
Carnaugh
Ballyginniff Mill
Tulnacross
Doons
Ballinderry
Derrychrin
NEW
Kinturk Cultural Centre
Stanierds Point
BELFAST
Ardmore Point
Creggan
Killucan
0 2 4 6 miles
0 2 4 6 8 10 km
Coagh
Cookstown
Little Bridge
Duffmount
Moortown
Forest Park
Gortnagallon
A2
A29
A26
A44
A37
A54
A6
A42
A31
B146
B17
B15
B67
B66
B62
B185
B119
B201
B202
B69
B192
B68
B70
B186
B190
B207
B188
B64
B16
B93
B94
B44
B74
B40
B47
B75
B42
B182
B18
B162
B160
B161
B73
B52
B96
B147
B86
B241
B46
23 (37)
13 (21)
21 (34)
15 (24)
14 (23)
30 (48)
6 (10)
17 (27)
12 (19)
10 (16)
2 (3)
25
P&R

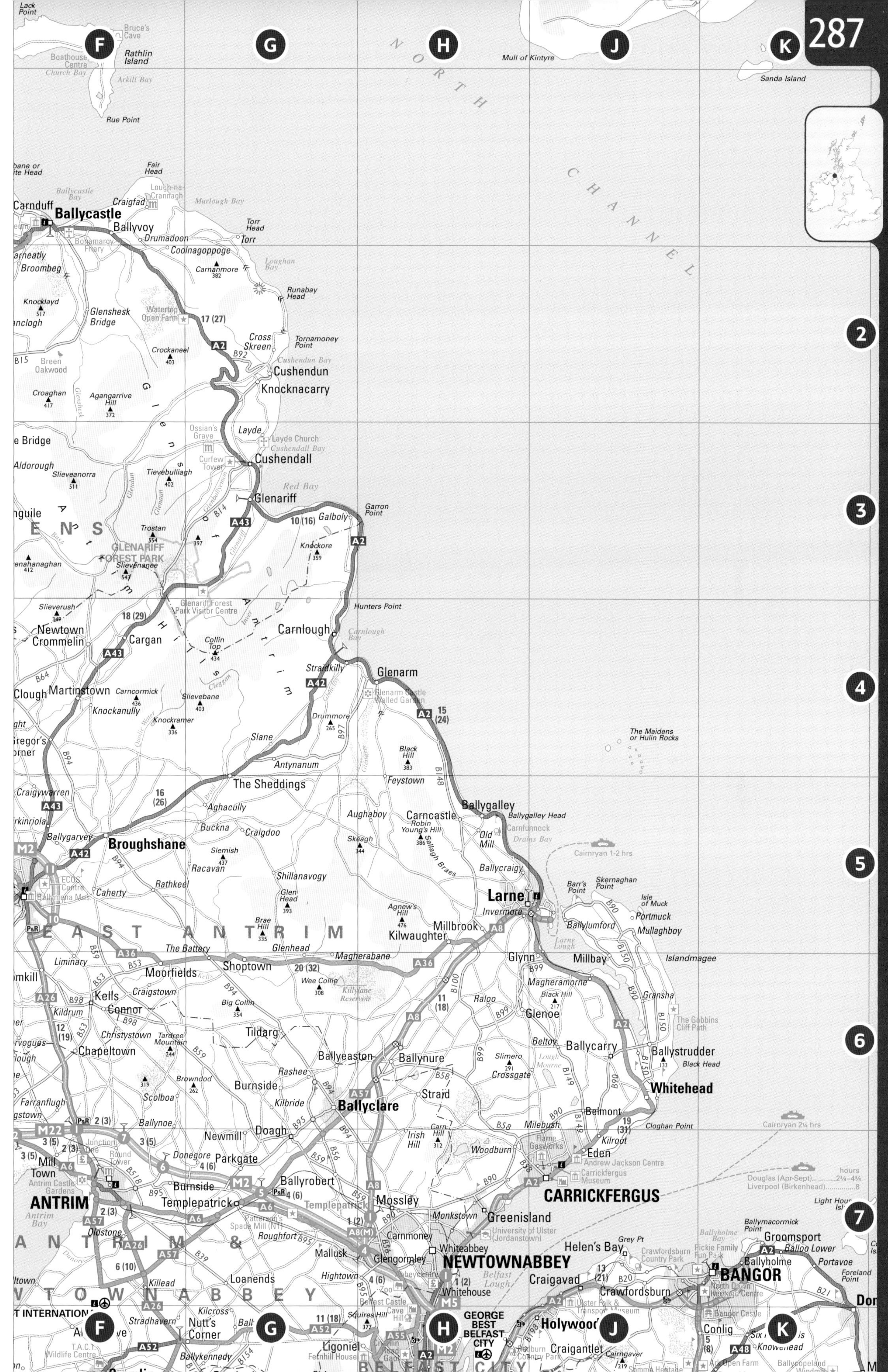

Place, place of interest and World Heritage Site names are followed by a **page number** and a grid reference in black type. The feature can be found on the map somewhere within the grid square shown.

Where two or more places have the same name the abbreviated *county* or *unitary authority* names are shown to distinguish between them.
A list of these abbreviated names appears below.

A selection of the most popular places of interest are shown within the index in blue type. Their postcode information is supplied after the county / unitary authority names to aid integration with satnav systems.

Sites with World Heritage Status are shown within the index in maroon type.

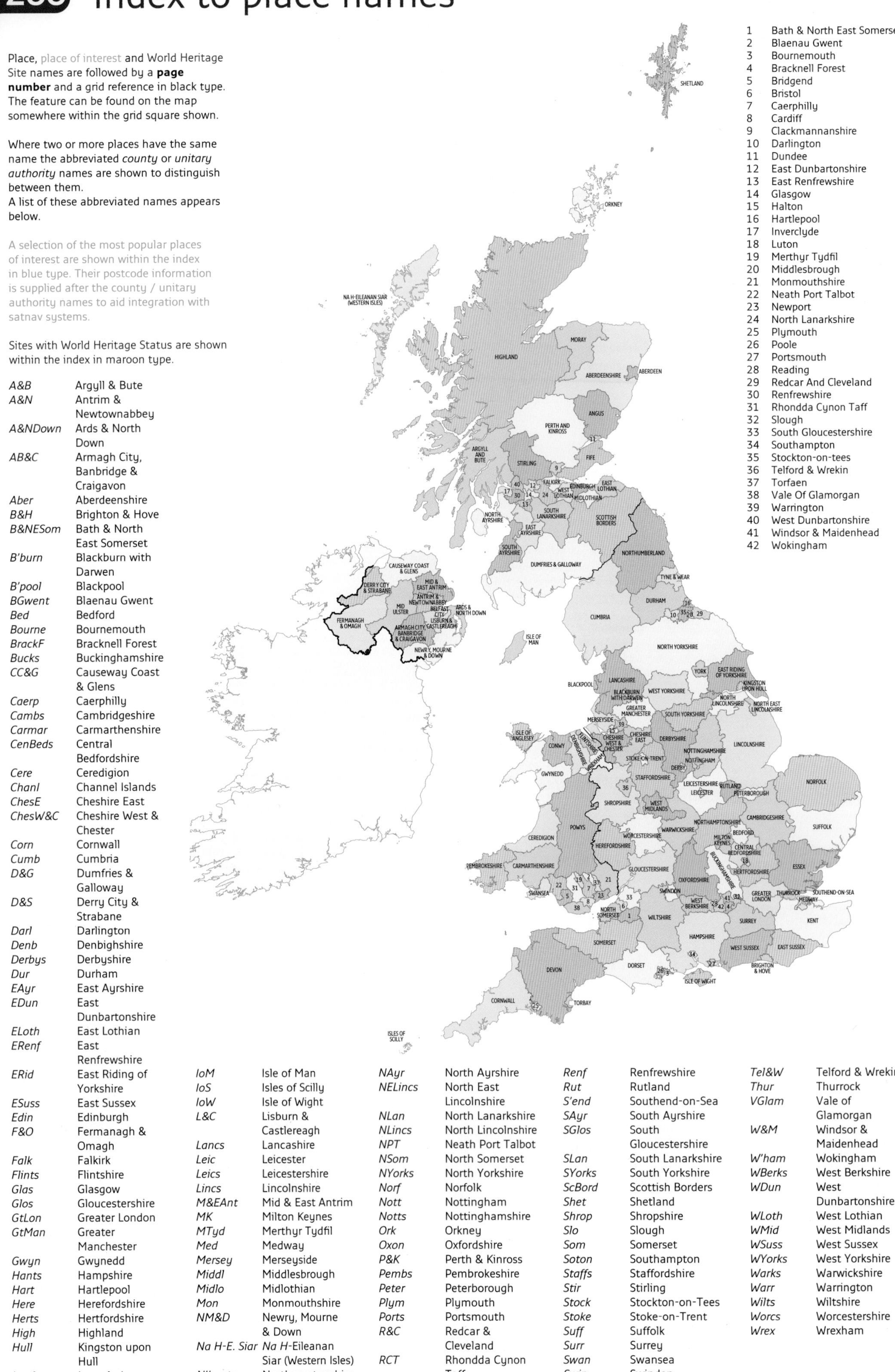

A&B	Argyll & Bute
A&N	Antrim & Newtownabbey
A&NDown	Ards & North Down
AB&C	Armagh City, Banbridge & Craigavon
Aber	Aberdeenshire
B&H	Brighton & Hove
B&NESom	Bath & North East Somerset
B'burn	Blackburn with Darwen
B'pool	Blackpool
BGwent	Blaenau Gwent
Bed	Bedford
Bourne	Bournemouth
BrackF	Bracknell Forest
Bucks	Buckinghamshire
CC&G	Causeway Coast & Glens
Caerp	Caerphilly
Cambs	Cambridgeshire
Carmar	Carmarthenshire
CenBeds	Central Bedfordshire
Cere	Ceredigion
Chanl	Channel Islands
ChesE	Cheshire East
ChesW&C	Cheshire West & Chester
Corn	Cornwall
Cumb	Cumbria
D&G	Dumfries & Galloway
D&S	Derry City & Strabane
Darl	Darlington
Denb	Denbighshire
Derbys	Derbyshire
Dur	Durham
EAyr	East Ayrshire
EDun	East Dunbartonshire
ELoth	East Lothian
ERenf	East Renfrewshire
ERid	East Riding of Yorkshire
ESuss	East Sussex
Edin	Edinburgh
F&O	Fermanagh & Omagh
Falk	Falkirk
Flints	Flintshire
Glas	Glasgow
Glos	Gloucestershire
GtLon	Greater London
GtMan	Greater Manchester
Gwyn	Gwynedd
Hants	Hampshire
Hart	Hartlepool
Here	Herefordshire
Herts	Hertfordshire
High	Highland
Hull	Kingston upon Hull
Invcly	Inverclyde
IoA	Isle of Anglesey

IoM	Isle of Man
IoS	Isles of Scilly
IoW	Isle of Wight
L&C	Lisburn & Castlereagh
Lancs	Lancashire
Leic	Leicester
Leics	Leicestershire
Lincs	Lincolnshire
M&EAnt	Mid & East Antrim
MK	Milton Keynes
MTyd	Merthyr Tydfil
Med	Medway
Mersey	Merseyside
Middl	Middlesbrough
Midlo	Midlothian
Mon	Monmouthshire
NM&D	Newry, Mourne & Down
Na H-E. Siar	Na H-Eileanan Siar (Western Isles)
N'hants	Northamptonshire
N'umb	Northumberland

NAyr	North Ayrshire
NELincs	North East Lincolnshire
NLan	North Lanarkshire
NLincs	North Lincolnshire
NPT	Neath Port Talbot
NSom	North Somerset
NYorks	North Yorkshire
Norf	Norfolk
Nott	Nottingham
Notts	Nottinghamshire
Ork	Orkney
Oxon	Oxfordshire
P&K	Perth & Kinross
Pembs	Pembrokeshire
Peter	Peterborough
Plym	Plymouth
Ports	Portsmouth
R&C	Redcar & Cleveland
RCT	Rhondda Cynon Taff
Read	Reading

Renf	Renfrewshire
Rut	Rutland
S'end	Southend-on-Sea
SAyr	South Ayrshire
SGlos	South Gloucestershire
SLan	South Lanarkshire
SYorks	South Yorkshire
ScBord	Scottish Borders
Shet	Shetland
Shrop	Shropshire
Slo	Slough
Som	Somerset
Soton	Southampton
Staffs	Staffordshire
Stir	Stirling
Stock	Stockton-on-Tees
Stoke	Stoke-on-Trent
Suff	Suffolk
Surr	Surrey
Swan	Swansea
Swin	Swindon
T&W	Tyne & Wear

Tel&W	Telford & Wrekin
Thur	Thurrock
VGlam	Vale of Glamorgan
W&M	Windsor & Maidenhead
W'ham	Wokingham
WBerks	West Berkshire
WDun	West Dunbartonshire
WLoth	West Lothian
WMid	West Midlands
WSuss	West Sussex
WYorks	West Yorkshire
Warks	Warwickshire
Warr	Warrington
Wilts	Wiltshire
Worcs	Worcestershire
Wrex	Wrexham

1	Bath & North East Somerset
2	Blaenau Gwent
3	Bournemouth
4	Bracknell Forest
5	Bridgend
6	Bristol
7	Caerphilly
8	Cardiff
9	Clackmannanshire
10	Darlington
11	Dundee
12	East Dunbartonshire
13	East Renfrewshire
14	Glasgow
15	Halton
16	Hartlepool
17	Inverclyde
18	Luton
19	Merthyr Tydfil
20	Middlesbrough
21	Monmouthshire
22	Neath Port Talbot
23	Newport
24	North Lanarkshire
25	Plymouth
26	Poole
27	Portsmouth
28	Reading
29	Redcar And Cleveland
30	Renfrewshire
31	Rhondda Cynon Taff
32	Slough
33	South Gloucestershire
34	Southampton
35	Stockton-on-tees
36	Telford & Wrekin
37	Torfaen
38	Vale Of Glamorgan
39	Warrington
40	West Dunbartonshire
41	Windsor & Maidenhead
42	Wokingham

Balgowan D&G 206 B2
Balgowan High 258 D5
Balgown 263 J5
Balgreen 269 F5
Balgreggan 214 B5
Balgy 264 E6
Balhaldie 242 D4
Balhalgardy 261 F2
Balham 136 B5
Balhary 252 A5
Balhelvie 244 B2
Balhousie 244 C4
Baliasta 278 F2
Baligill 274 D2
Baligrundle 248 A5
Balindore 240 B1
Balintore Angus 252 A4
Balintore High 267 F4
Balintraid 266 E4
Balintyre 250 B5
Balivanich (Baile a'Mhanaich) 262 C6
Balix 285 G6
Balkeerie 252 B5
Balkholme 195 G5
Balkissock 214 C2
Ball 170 A5
Ball Haye Green 171 G2
Ball Hill 119 F1
Balla 254 C3
Ballabeg 190 A4
Ballacannell 190 C3
Ballacarnane Beg 190 A3
Ballachulish (Baile a' Chaolais) 248 C4
Balladoole 190 A5
Ballafesson 190 A4
Ballagh 281 G5
Ballagh Bridge 283 G6
Ballagyr 190 A3
Ballajora 190 C2
Ballakilpheric 190 A4
Ballamodha 190 A4
Ballantrae 214 B2
Ballard 282 D6
Ballards Gore 138 C3
Ballasalla IoM 190 A4
Ballasalla IoM 190 B2
Ballater 260 B5
Ballaterach 260 C5
Ballaugh 190 B2
Ballaveare 190 B4
Ballchraggan 266 E4
Ballechin 251 E4
Balleer 282 B5
Balleich 242 A4
Ballencrieff 236 B2
Balleny 286 E2
Ballidon 172 D2
Balliekine 231 G5
Balliemeanoch 240 D4
Balliemore A&B 240 D5
Balliemore A&B 240 A2
Ballig 190 A3
Balliggan 283 K2
Ballimeanoch 240 C3
Ballimore A&B 232 A1
Ballimore Stir 242 A3
Ballinaby 230 A3
Ballinamallard 280 E3
Ballindarragh 281 F5
Ballindean 244 A2
Ballinderry 286 D7
Ballingdon 151 G3
Ballinger Common 135 E2
Ballingham 145 E4
Ballingry 243 G5
Ballinlea 286 E2
Ballinlick 251 E5
Ballinluig P&K 251 E4
Ballinluig P&K 251 F4
Ballinran 283 G7
Ballinteer 286 C2
Ballintoy 286 E1
Ballintuim 251 G4
Balloch Angus 252 B4
Balloch High 266 E7
Balloch NLan 234 B2
Balloch WDun 233 E1
Ballochan 260 D5
Ballochandrain 232 A1
Ballochford 260 B1
Ballochgair 222 C3
Ballochmartin 232 C4
Ballochmorrie 214 D2
Ballochmyle 224 D3
Ballochroy 231 F4
Ballogie 260 D5
Balloo 283 H2
Balloo Lower 287 K7
Balloolymore 282 E4
Balls Cross 121 E5
Balls Green Essex 152 B5
Ball's Green Glos 132 A3
Balls Hill 158 B3
Ballsmill 282 C7
Ballyaghlis 283 G2
Ballyalton 283 J4
Ballyard 281 F3
Ballyardel 283 F7
Ballyaurgan 231 F2
Ballybannan 283 G5
Ballybogy 286 D2
Ballybollen 286 E6
Ballyboyland 286 D3
Ballybrack 281 H1
Ballybriest 286 B7
Ballycarry 287 J6
Ballycassidy 280 E3
Ballycastle 287 F1
Ballyclare 287 G6
Ballycloghan 283 H2
Ballyconnelly 286 E5
Ballycraigy 287 H5
Ballydan 283 H3
Ballydivity 286 D2
Ballydoolagh 280 E4
Ballydrain 283 H2
Ballydugan 283 H4
Ballydullaghan 286 C4
Ballyeaston 287 G6
Ballyesborough 283 K2
Ballygalley 287 H5
Ballygarvey 287 F5
Ballygawley 281 J3
Ballyginniff Milltown 287 F7
Ballygorian 282 E6
Ballygowan A&NDown 283 H2
Ballygowan AB&C 282 E4
Ballygowan NM&D 283 F7
Ballygown 246 D5
Ballygrant 230 B3
Ballyhalbert 283 K2
Ballyhaugh 246 A4
Ballyhill 283 F1
Ballyhoe Bridge 286 E3
Ballyholme 287 K7
Ballyhome 286 C2
Ballyhornan 283 J4
Ballyhosset 283 J5
Ballyhushey 281 G2
Ballykeel F&O 285 G7
Ballykeel L&C 283 F3
Ballykeel NM&D 283 G7
Ballykelly 285 J3
Ballykennedy 283 F1
Ballykinler 283 H5
Ballyknock CC&G 286 E3
Ballyknock Mid Ulster 286 C5
Ballyleny 282 C4
Ballylesson 283 G2
Ballylintagh 286 C3
Ballyloughbeg 286 D2
Ballylucas 280 E4
Ballylumford 287 J5
Ballymacashen 283 H2
Ballymackilroy 281 J3
Ballymaconnelly 286 D4
Ballymacormick 283 F3
Ballymacran 285 J3
Ballymagorry 285 F5
Ballymaguigan 286 D7
Ballymartin NM&D 283 G7
Ballymartrim AB&C 282 B4
Ballymeanoch 240 A5
Ballymena 287 F5
Ballymichael 223 E2
Ballymoney 286 D3
Ballymoyer 282 C5
Ballymultimber 285 J2
Ballymultrea 286 D7
Ballymurphy 283 J2
Ballynabragget 282 E3
Ballynagard 285 G3
Ballynagarrick 283 G2
Ballynahatty 281 G2
Ballynahinch 283 G3
Ballynahone Beg 282 B4
Ballynakilly 282 B2
Ballynamallaght 285 G6
Ballynasaggart 281 H3
Ballyneaner 285 H5
Ballynoe A&N 287 F6
Ballynoe NM&D 283 H5
Ballynure 287 H6
Ballyquintin 283 K4
Ballyrashane 286 C2
Ballyreagh F&O 281 F4
Ballyreagh Mid Ulster 281 J3
Ballyrisk 286 B3
Ballyrobert 287 G7
Ballyrogan 286 C4
Ballyronan 286 D7
Ballyroney 283 F5
Ballysallagh 283 F3
Ballyskeagh 283 F2
Ballystrudder 287 J6
Ballytober 286 D2
Ballyvally 282 E6
Ballyveagh 283 G7
Ballyvennox 286 C3
Ballyvoy 287 F1
Ballywalter 283 K2
Ballyward 283 F5
Ballywatermoy 286 E5
Ballywatticock 283 J1
Ballywildrick 286 B2
Balmacara (Baile Mac Ara) 256 E2
Balmaclellan 216 A3
Balmacneil 251 E4
Balmadies 253 D5
Balmae 207 G2
Balmaha 241 G5
Balmalcolm 244 B4
Balmaqueen 263 K4
Balmeanach A&B 247 F5
Balmeanach A&B 238 D1
Balmedie 261 H3
Balmedie Country Park Aber AB23 8XG 261 H3
Balmer Heath 170 B4
Balmerino 244 B2
Balmerlawn 106 C2
Balminnoch 215 D4
Balmore EDun 234 A2
Balmore High 267 F7
Balmore High 257 K1
Balmore High 263 H7
Balmore P&K 250 C4
Balmullo 244 C2
Balmungie 266 E6
Balmyle 251 F4
Balnaboth 252 B3
Balnabruaich 266 E4
Balnacra 265 F7
Balnafoich 258 D1
Balnagall 267 F3
Balnagown Castle 266 E4
Balnaguard 251 E4
Balnaguisich 266 D4
Balnahard A&B 238 D5
Balnahard A&B 239 D1
Balnain 258 B1
Balnakeil 273 F2
Balnaknock 263 K5
Balnamoon 252 D3
Balnamore 286 D3
Balnapaling 266 E5
Balnespick 259 F4
Balquhidder 242 A2
Balsall 159 E5
Balsall Common 159 E5
Balsall Heath 158 C4
Balscote 147 F3
Balsham 151 D2
Baltasound 278 F2
Balterley 171 E2
Balterley Heath 171 E2
Baltersan 215 F4
Balthangie 269 G5
Balthayock 243 G2
Baltonsborough 116 C4
Baluachraig 240 A5
Balulive 230 C3
Balure A&B 240 C1
Balure A&B 240 A1
Balvaird 266 C6
Balvarran 251 F3
Balvicar 239 G3
Balvraid High 256 E3
Balvraid High 259 F1
Bamber Bridge 192 B5
Bamber's Green 151 D5
Bamburgh 229 F3
Bamburgh Castle N'umb NE69 7DF 229 F3
Bamff 252 A4
Bamford Derbys 185 G4
Bamford GtMan 184 C1
Bampton Cumb 199 G1
Bampton Devon 114 C5
Bampton Oxon 133 F2
Bampton Grange 199 G1
Banavie (Banbhaidh) 248 D2
Banbridge 282 E4
Banbury 147 G3
Banbury Museum Oxon OX16 2PQ 147 G4
Bancffosfelen 128 A1
Banchor 267 G7
Banchory 261 F5
Banchory Devenick 261 H4
Bancycapel 128 A1
Bancyfelin 127 G1
Bancyffordd 142 A4
Bandon 244 A4
Bandrake Head 199 E4
Banff 268 E4
Bangor A&NDown 287 K7
Bangor Gwyn 181 D5
Bangor-on-Dee (Bangor-is-y-coed) 170 A3
Bangor's Green 183 E2
Banham 164 B3
Banham Zoo Norf NR16 2HE 164 B3
Bank 106 B2
Bank End 198 C4
Bank Newton 193 F2
Bank Street 145 F1
Bank Top Lancs 183 G2
Bank Top WYorks 194 A5
Bankend 217 E4
Bankfoot 243 F1
Bankglen 225 D4
Bankhead Aber 260 E3
Bankhead Aber 260 E4
Bankhead Aberdeen 261 G3
Bankhead D&G 208 A2
Bankland 116 A5
Banknock 234 B2
Banks Cumb 210 B1
Banks Lancs 191 G5
Bankshill 217 F2
Bannfoot 282 C2
Banningham 178 D3
Bannister Green 151 E5
Bannockburn 242 D5
Banstead 122 B3
Bantam Grove 194 B5
Bantham 100 C3
Banton 234 B2
Banwell 116 A2
Banwen Pyrddin 129 E2
Banyard's Green 165 E4
Bapchild 124 B2
Baptiston 233 G1
Bapton 118 A4
Bar End 119 F5
Bar Hill 150 B1
Bar Hill Fort (Frontiers of the Roman Empire) EDun 31 G1
Barachander 240 C2
Baranailt 285 J4
Barassie 224 B2
Barbaraville 266 E4
Barber Booth 185 F4
Barber Green 199 E4
Barber's Moor 183 F1
Barbican Arts & Conference Centre GtLon EC2Y 8DS 45 J1
Barbon 200 B4
Barbridge 170 D2
Barbrook 114 A3
Barby 160 A5
Barcaldine (Am Barra Calltainn) 248 B5
Barcaple 216 A5
Barcheston 147 E4
Barclose 210 A1
Barcombe 109 G2
Barcombe Cross 109 G2
Barden 202 A3
Barden Park 123 E4
Bardennoch 215 G1
Bardfield End Green 151 E4
Bardfield Saling 151 E5
Bardister 278 C5
Bardney 175 G1
Bardon Leics 159 G1
Bardon Moray 267 K6
Bardon Mill 211 D1
Bardowie 233 G2
Bardsea 199 D5
Bardsey 194 C3
Bardsey Island (Ynys Enlli) 166 A5
Bardwell 164 A4
Bare 192 A1
Barewood 144 C2
Barfad 231 G3
Barford Norf 178 C5
Barford Warks 147 E1
Barford St. John 147 G4
Barford St. Martin 118 B4
Barford St. Michael 147 G4
Barfrestone 125 E3
Bargaly 215 F4
Bargany Mains 224 A5
Bargeddie 234 A3
Bargoed 130 A3
Bargrennan 215 E3
Barham Cambs 161 G5
Barham Kent 125 E3
Barham Suff 152 C2
Barharrow 216 A5
Barholm 161 F1
Barholm Mains 215 F5
Barkby 160 B2
Barkby Thorpe 160 B2
Barkers Green 170 C5
Barkestone-le-Vale 174 C4
Barkham 120 C1
Barking GtLon 136 D4
Barking Suff 152 B2
Barking Tye 152 B2
Barkisland 193 G5
Barkston 175 E3
Barkston Ash 195 D4
Barkway 150 B4
Barlae 215 D4
Barland 144 B1
Barlaston 171 F4
Barlavington 108 B2
Barlborough 186 B5
Barlby 195 F4
Barlestone 159 G2
Barley Herts 150 B4
Barley Lancs 193 E3
Barley Green 164 D4
Barleycroft End 150 C5
Barleyhill 211 G2
Barleythorpe 160 D2
Barling 138 C4
Barlings 188 A5
Barlow Derbys 186 A5
Barlow NYorks 195 F5
Barlow T&W 212 A1
Barmby Moor 195 G3
Barmby on the Marsh 195 F5
Barmer 177 G4
Barmolloch 240 A5
Barmoor Lane End 229 E3
Barmouth (Abermaw) 154 C1
Barmpton 202 C1
Barmston 197 D2
Barnaby Green 165 F4
Barnacabber 232 C1
Barnacarry 240 B5
Barnack 161 F2
Barnacle 159 F4
Barnamuc 248 C5
Barnard Castle 201 F1
Barnard Gate 133 G1
Barnardiston 151 F3
Barnard's Green 145 G3
Barnbarroch D&G 215 E5
Barnbarroch D&G 216 C5
Barnburgh 186 B2
Barnby 165 F3
Barnby Dun 186 D2
Barnby in the Willows 175 D2
Barnby Moor 187 D4
Barndennoch 216 C2
Barne Barton 100 A2
Barnehurst 137 E5
Barnes D&S 285 H6
Barnes GtLon 136 B5
Barnes Street 123 F4
Barnet 136 B3
Barnet Gate 136 B3
Barnetby le Wold 188 A2
Barney 178 A2
Barnham Suff 163 G5
Barnham WSuss 108 B3
Barnham Broom 178 B5
Barnhead 253 E4
Barnhill ChesW&C 170 B2
Barnhill Dundee 244 C1
Barnhill Moray 267 J6
Barnhills 214 A3
Barningham Dur 201 F1
Barningham Suff 164 A4
Barningham Green 178 C2
Barnmeen 282 E5
Barnoldby le Beck 188 C2
Barnoldswick 193 E3
Barns Green 121 G5
Barnsdale Bar 186 C1
Barnsley Glos 132 C2
Barnsley SYorks 186 A2
Barnsole 125 E3
Barnstaple 113 F2
Barnston Essex 137 F1
Barnston Mersey 183 D4
Barnstone 174 C4
Barnt Green 158 C5
Barnton ChesW&C 184 A5
Barnton Edin 235 F2
Barnwell All Saints 161 F4
Barnwell Country Park N'hants PE8 5PB 161 F4
Barnwell St. Andrew 161 F4
Barnwood 132 A1
Barons' Cross 145 D2
Barr A&B 230 B3
Barr High 247 F4
Barr SAyr 215 D1
Barr Som 115 E5
Barr Hall 151 F4
Barra (Barraigh) 254 B4
Barra (Tràigh Mhòr) Airport 254 B4
Barrachan 207 D2
Barrackan 239 G4
Barraer 215 E4
Barraglom 270 D4
Barrahormid 231 F1
Barran 241 D2
Barrapoll 246 A2
Barrasford 220 B4
Barravullin 240 A4
Barregarrow 190 B3
Barrets Green 170 C2
Barrhead 233 F4
Barrhill 214 D2
Barrington Cambs 150 B3
Barrington Som 103 G1
Barripper 94 D3
Barrisdale 256 E4
Barrmill 233 E4
Barrnacarry 240 A2
Barrock 275 H1
Barrow Glos 146 A5
Barrow Lancs 192 D4
Barrow Rut 161 D1
Barrow Shrop 157 F2
Barrow Som 117 E4
Barrow Som 116 C3
Barrow Suff 151 F1
Barrow Gurney 116 C1
Barrow Hann 196 C5
Barrow Haven 196 C5
Barrow Hill 186 B5
Barrow Nook 183 F2
Barrow Street 117 F4
Barrow upon Humber 196 C5
Barrow upon Soar 160 A1
Barrow upon Trent 173 E5
Barroway Drove 163 D2
Barrowby 175 D4
Barrowcliff 204 D4
Barrowden 161 E2
Barrowford 193 E4
Barrow-in-Furness 191 F1
Barrows Green 199 G4
Barry Angus 244 D1
Barry VGlam 115 E1
Barry Island Pleasure Park VGlam CF62 5TR 115 E1
Barsby 160 B1
Barsham 165 E3
Barskimming 224 C3
Barsloisnoch 240 A5
Barston 159 E5
Barter Books, Alnwick N'umb NE66 2NP 229 F5
Bartestree 145 E3
Barthol Chapel 261 G1
Bartholomew Green 151 F5
Barthomley 171 E2
Bartley 106 C1
Bartley Green 158 C4
Bartlow 151 D3
Barton Cambs 150 C2
Barton ChesW&C 170 B2
Barton Cumb 210 A5
Barton Glos 146 C5
Barton Lancs 192 B4
Barton Lancs 183 E2
Barton NYorks 202 B2
Barton Oxon 134 A2
Barton Torbay 101 F1
Barton Warks 146 D2
Barton Bendish 163 F2
Barton End 132 A3
Barton Green 159 D1
Barton Hartshorn 148 B4
Barton Hill 195 G1
Barton in Fabis 173 G4
Barton in the Beans 159 F2
Barton Mills 163 F5
Barton on Sea 106 B3
Barton St. David 116 C4
Barton Seagrave 161 D5
Barton Stacey 119 F3
Barton Town 113 G1
Barton Turf 179 E3
Bartongate 147 G5
Barton-le-Clay 149 F4
Barton-le-Street 203 G5
Barton-le-Willows 195 G1
Barton-on-the-Heath 147 E4
Barton-under-Needwood 159 D1
Barton-upon-Humber 196 C5
Barvas (Barabhas) 271 F3
Barway 162 D5
Barwell 159 G3
Barwhinnock 216 A5
Barwick Herts 136 C1
Barwick Som 104 B1
Barwick in Elmet 194 C4
Barwinnock 207 D2
Baschurch 170 B5
Bascote 147 G1
Base Green 152 B1
Basford Green 171 G2
Bashall Eaves 192 C3
Bashall Town 192 D3
Bashley 106 B3
Basildon Essex 137 G4
Basildon WBerks 134 B5
Basingstoke 120 B2
Baslow 185 G5
Bason Bridge 116 A3
Bassaleg 130 B4
Bassenthwaite 209 F3
Basset's Cross 113 F5
Bassett 106 D1
Bassingbourn 150 B3
Bassingfield 174 B4
Bassingham 175 E1
Bassingthorpe 175 E5
Basta 278 E3
Baston 161 G1
Bastonford 146 A2
Bastwick 179 F4
Batavaime 241 G1
Batch 116 A2
Batchley 146 C1
Batchworth 135 F3
Batchworth Heath 135 F3
Batcombe Dorset 104 C2
Batcombe Som 117 D4
Bate Heath 184 A5
Bath 117 E1
Bath Abbey B&NESom BA1 1LT 63 Bath
Bathampton 117 E1
Bathealton 115 D5
Batheaston 117 E1
Bathford 117 E1
Bathgate 235 D3
Bathley 174 C2
Bathpool Corn 97 G2
Bathpool Som 115 F5
Bathway 116 C2
Batley 194 B5
Batsford 147 D4
Batson 100 D4
Battersby 203 E2
Battersea 136 B5
Battersea Cats & Dogs Home GtLon SW8 4AA 13 A5
Battersea Park Children's Zoo GtLon SW11 4NJ 13 A5
Battisborough Cross 100 C3
Battisford 152 B2
Battisford Tye 152 B2
Battle ESuss 110 C2
Battle Powys 143 G4
Battle Abbey ESuss TN33 0AD 110 C2
Battledown 146 B5
Battlefield 157 E1
Battlesbridge 137 G3
Battlesden 149 E5
Battlesea Green 164 D4
Battleton 114 C5
Battlies Green 152 A1
Battramsley 106 C3
Batt's Corner 120 D3
Bauds of Cullen 268 C4
Baugh 246 B2
Baughton 146 A3
Baughurst 119 G1
Baulds 260 E5
Baulking 133 F3
Baumber 188 C5
Baunton 132 C2
Baveney Wood 157 F5
Baverstock 118 B4
Bawburgh 178 C5
Bawdeswell 178 B3
Bawdrip 116 A4
Bawdsey 153 E3
Bawdsey Manor 153 E4
Bawsey 163 E1
Bawtry 187 D3
Baxenden 193 D5
Baxterley 159 E3
Baxter's Green 151 F2
Baxters Highland Village Moray IV32 7LD 268 B4
Baxters Home Farm Fife KY4 0JR 243 G5
Bay 117 F5
Baybridge 211 F3
Baycliff 199 D5
Baydon 133 E5
Bayford Herts 136 C2
Bayford Som 117 E5
Bayfordbury 136 C1
Bayham Abbey 123 F5
Bayles 210 D3
Baylham 152 C2
Baynards Green 148 A5
Baysham 145 E5
Bayston Hill 157 D2
Bayswater 136 B4
Baythorn End 151 F3
Bayton 157 F5
Bayworth 134 A2
Beach High 247 G4
Beach SGlos 131 G5
Beachampton 148 C4
Beachamwell 163 F2
Beacharr 231 E5
Beachley 131 E3
Beacon Devon 103 E2
Beacon Devon 103 F2
Beacon Fell Country Park Lancs PR3 2NL 192 B3
Beacon Hill Dorset 105 F3
Beacon Hill Essex 138 B1
Beacon Hill Surr 121 D4
Beacon Hill Country Park Leics LE12 8SR 17 A2
Beacon Park, Up Holland Lancs WN8 7RU 183 G2
Beacon's Bottom 134 C3
Beaconsfield 135 E3
Beacravik 263 G2
Beadlam 203 F4
Beadlow 149 G4
Beadnell 229 G4
Beaford 113 F4
Beagh 280 E3
Beaghmore 285 J7
Beaghmore Stone Circles Mid Ulster BT80 9PA 285 J7
Beal N'umb 229 E2
Beal NYorks 195 E5
Bealach 248 B4
Beale Park WBerks RG8 9NH 134 B5
Bealsmill 99 D3
Beambridge 170 D2
Beamhurst 172 B4
Beaminster 104 A2
Beamish 212 B3
Beamish - The Living Museum of the North Dur DH9 0RG 29 A1
Beamsley 193 G2
Bean 137 E5
Beanacre 118 A1
Beanley 229 E5
Beaquoy 276 C5
Beardon 99 F2
Beardwood 192 C5
Beare 102 C2
Beare Green 121 G3
Bearley 147 D1
Bearney 285 F6
Bearnie 261 H1
Bearnock 258 B1
Bearnus 246 C5
Bearpark 212 B3
Bearsbridge 211 D2
Bearsden 233 G2
Bearsted 123 G3
Bearstone 171 E4
Bearwood Poole 105 G3
Bearwood WMid 158 C4
Beatles Story Mersey L3 4AD 42 B5
Beattock 226 B5
Beauchamp Roding 137 E1
Beauchief 186 A4
Beaudesert 147 D1
Beaufort 130 A1
Beaulieu 106 C2
Beaulieu: National Motor Museum, Abbey & Palace House Hants SO42 7ZN 4 A5
Beauly (A' Mhanachainn) 266 C7
Beaumaris (Biwmares) 181 E5
Beaumaris Castle (Castles & Town Walls of King Edward in Gwynedd) Gwyn LL58 8AP 181 E5
Beaumont Chanl 100 C5
Beaumont Cumb 209 G1
Beaumont Essex 152 C5
Beaumont Hill 202 B1
Beaumont Leys 160 A2
Beausale 159 E5
Beauvale 173 F3
Beauworth 119 G5
Beaver Green 124 B4
Beaworthy 99 E1
Beazley End 151 F5
Bebington 183 E4
Bebside 221 E3
Beccles 165 F2
Beccles Heliport 165 F3
Becconsall 192 A5
Beck Foot 200 B3
Beck Hole 204 B2
Beck Row 163 E5
Beck Side Cumb 198 D4
Beck Side Cumb 199 E4
Beckbury 157 G2
Beckenham 122 C2
Beckering 188 B4
Beckermet 198 B2
Beckermonds 201 D4
Beckett End 163 F3
Beckfoot Cumb 198 C2
Beckfoot Cumb 209 D2
Beckford 146 B4
Beckhampton 118 B1
Beckingham Lincs 175 D2
Beckingham Notts 187 E4
Beckington 117 F2
Beckley ESuss 111 D1
Beckley Oxon 134 A1
Beck's Green 165 E3
Beckside 200 B4
Beckton 136 D4
Beckwithshaw 194 B2
Becontree 137 D4
Bedale 202 B4
Bedburn 211 G4
Bedchester 105 E1
Beddau 129 G4
Beddgelert 167 E3
Beddingham 109 G3
Beddington 122 B2
Beddington Corner 122 B2
Bedfield 152 D1
Bedfield Little Green 152 D1
Bedford 149 F3
Bedgebury Cross 123 G5
Bedgrove 134 D1
Bedham 121 F5
Bedhampton 107 G2
Bedingfield 152 C1
Bedingfield Green 152 C1
Bedingfield Street 152 C1
Bedingham Green 165 D2
Bedlam Lancs 193 D5
Bedlam NYorks 194 B1
Bedlar's Green 150 D5
Bedlington 221 E3
Bedlinog 129 G2
Bedminster 131 E5
Bedmond 135 F2
Bednall 158 B1
Bedol 182 D5
Bedrule 228 A5
Bedstone 156 C5
Bedwas 130 A4
Bedwell 150 A5
Bedwellty 130 A2
Bedworth 159 F4
Bedworth Woodlands 159 F4
Beeby 160 B2
Beech Hants 120 B4
Beech Staffs 171 F4
Beech Hill 120 B1
Beechingstoke 118 B2
Beechwood 183 G4
Beecraigs Country Park WLoth EH49 6PL 235 D2
Beedon 133 G5
Beeford 196 D2
Beeley 173 D1
Beelsby 188 C2
Beenham 119 G1
Beeny 98 B1
Beer 103 F4
Beer Hackett 104 C1
Beercrocombe 116 A5
Beesands 101 E3
Beesby Lincs 189 E4
Beesby NELincs 188 C3
Beeson 101 E3
Beeston CenBeds 149 G3
Beeston ChesW&C 170 C2
Beeston Norf 178 A4
Beeston Notts 173 G4
Beeston WYorks 194 B4
Beeston Regis 178 C1
Beeston St. Lawrence 179 E3
Beeswing 216 C4
Beetham Cumb 199 F5
Beetham Som 103 F1
Beetley 178 A4
Beffcote 158 A1
Began 130 B4
Begbroke 133 G1
Begdale 162 C2
Begelly 127 E2
Beggar's Bush 144 B1
Beggearn Huish 114 D4
Beggshill 260 D1
Beguildy (Bugeildy) 156 A5
Beighton Norf 179 E5
Beighton SYorks 186 B4
Beili-glas 130 C2
Beith 233 E4
Bekesbourne 125 D3
Bekonscot Model Village Bucks HP9 2PL 135 E3
Belaugh 179 D4
Belbroughton 158 B5
Belchalwell 105 D2
Belchalwell Street 105 D2
Belchamp Otten 151 G3
Belchamp St. Paul 151 F3

299

Easter Ardross 266 D4
Easter Balgedie 243 G4
Easter Balmoral 259 K5
Easter Boleskine 258 C2
Easter Borland 242 B4
Easter Brae 266 D5
Easter Buckieburn 234 B1
Easter Compton 131 E4
Easter Drummond 258 B3
Easter Dullater 242 B4
Easter Ellister 230 A4
Easter Fearn 266 D3
Easter Galcantray 267 F7
Easter Howlaws 237 E5
Easter Kinkell 266 C6
Easter Knox 253 D5
Easter Lednathie 252 B3
Easter Moniack 266 C7
Easter Ord 261 G4
Easter Poldar 242 B5
Easter Skeld (Skeld) 279 C8
Easter Suddie 266 D6
Easter Tulloch 253 F2
Easter Whyntie 268 E4
Eastergate 108 B3
Easterhouse 234 A3
Easterton 118 B2
Easterton Sands 118 B2
Eastertown 116 A2
Eastfield Bristol 131 E5
Eastfield NLan 234 C3
Eastfield NYorks 204 D4
Eastfield Hall 221 E1
Eastgate Dur 211 F4
Eastgate Lincs 161 G1
Eastgate Norf 178 C3
Easthall 150 A5
Eastham Mersey 183 E4
Eastham Worcs 145 F1
Easthampstead 121 D1
Easthampton 144 D1
Easthaugh 178 B4
Eastheath 120 D1
Easthope 157 E3
Easthorpe Essex 152 A5
Easthorpe Leics 174 D4
Easthorpe Notts 174 C2
Easthouses 236 A3
Eastington Devon 102 A2
Eastington Glos 132 D1
Eastington Glos 131 G2
Eastleach Martin 133 E2
Eastleach Turville 133 E2
Eastleigh Devon 113 E3
Eastleigh Hants 106 D1
Eastling 124 B3
Eastmoor Derbys 186 A5
Eastmoor Norf 163 F2
Eastnor 145 G4
Eastoft 187 F1
Eastoke 107 G3
Easton Cambs 161 G5
Easton Cumb 218 C4
Easton Cumb 209 F1
Easton Devon 102 A4
Easton Dorset 104 C5
Easton Hants 119 G4
Easton IoW 106 C4
Easton Lincs 175 E5
Easton Norf 178 C4
Easton Som 116 C3
Easton Suff 153 D2
Easton Wilts 132 A5
Easton Grey 132 A4
Easton Maudit 149 D2
Easton on the Hill 161 F2
Easton Royal 118 D1
Easton-in-Gordano 131 E5
Eastrea 162 A3
Eastriggs 218 A5
Eastrington 195 G4
Eastry 125 F3
Eastside 277 D8
East-the-Water 113 E3
Eastville 131 F5
Eastwell 174 C5
Eastwick 136 D1
Eastwood Notts 173 F3
Eastwood S'end 138 B4
Eastwood SYorks 186 B3
Eastwood WYorks 193 F5
Eastwood End 162 C3
Eathorpe 147 F1
Eaton ChesE 171 F1
Eaton ChesW&C 170 C1
Eaton Leics 174 C5
Eaton Norf 178 D5
Eaton Norf 177 E4
Eaton Notts 187 E5
Eaton Oxon 133 G2
Eaton Shrop 157 E3
Eaton Shrop 156 C4
Eaton Bishop 144 D4
Eaton Bray 149 E5
Eaton Constantine 157 F2
Eaton Ford 149 G2
Eaton Hall 170 B1
Eaton Hastings 133 E3
Eaton Socon 149 G2
Eaton upon Tern 171 D5
Eaves Green 159 E4
Eavestone 194 B1
Ebberston 204 B4
Ebbesborne Wake 118 A5
Ebbw Vale
(Glyn Ebwy) 130 A2
Ebchester 212 A2
Ebdon 116 A1
Ebford 102 C4
Ebley 132 A2
Ebnal 170 B3
Ebost 255 J1
Ebrington 147 D3
Ebsworthy Town 99 F1
Ecchinswell 119 F2
Ecclaw 237 E3
Ecclefechan 217 F3
Eccles GtMan 184 B3
Eccles Kent 123 G2
Eccles ScBord 237 E5
Eccles Green 144 C3
Eccles Road 164 B2
Ecclesfield 186 A3
Ecclesgreig 253 F3
Eccleshall 171 F5
Eccleshill 194 A4
Ecclesmachan 235 E2
Eccles-on-Sea 179 F3
Eccleston
ChesW&C 170 B1
Eccleston Lancs 183 G1
Eccleston Mersey 183 F3
Eccup 194 B3
Echt 261 F4
Eckford 228 B4
Eckington Derbys 186 B5
Eckington Worcs 146 B3
Ecton N'hants 148 D1
Ecton Staffs 172 B2
Edale 185 F4
Eday 276 E4
Eday Airfield 276 E4
Edburton 109 E2
Edderside 209 E2
Edderton 266 E3
Eddington 119 E1
Eddleston 235 G5
Eden D&S 285 H6
Eden M&EAnt 287 J7
Eden Camp NYorks
YO17 6RT 204 B5
Eden Park 122 C2
Eden Project Corn
PL24 2SG 97 E4
Eden Vale 212 D4
Edenbridge 122 D4
Edendonich 241 D2
Edendork 282 B2
Edenfield 184 B1
Edenhall 210 B4
Edenham 175 F5
Edensor 185 G5
Edentaggart 241 F5
Edenthorpe 186 D2
Edentrillick 283 F3
Edern 166 B4
Ederny 280 E2
Edgarley 116 C4
Edgbaston 158 C4
Edgcote 148 A3
Edgcott Bucks 148 B5
Edgcott Som 114 B4
Edgcumbe 95 E3
Edge Glos 132 A2
Edge Shrop 156 C2
Edge End 131 E1
Edge Green
ChesW&C 170 B2
Edge Green GtMan 183 G3
Edge Green Norf 164 B3
Edgebolton 170 C5
Edgefield 178 B2
Edgehead 236 A3
Edgeley 170 C3
Edgerley 156 C1
Edgerton 185 F1
Edgeworth 132 B2
Edginswell 101 E1
Edgmond 157 G1
Edgmond Marsh 171 E5
Edgton 156 C4
Edgware 136 B3
Edgworth 184 B1
Edinample 242 B2
Edinbanchory 260 C3
Edinbane 263 J6
Edinbarnet 233 G2
Edinburgh 235 G2
Edinburgh Airport 235 F2
Edinburgh Castle Edin
EH1 2NG 37 E4
Edinburgh Zoo Edin
EH12 6TS 32 B2
Edinchip 242 A2
Edingale 159 E1
Edingley 174 B2
Edingthorpe 179 E2
Edingthorpe Green 179 E2
Edington Som 116 A4
Edington Wilts 118 A2
Edintore 268 C6
Edinvale 267 J6
Edistone 112 C3
Edith Weston 161 E2
Edithmead 116 A3
Edlaston 172 C3
Edlesborough 135 E1
Edlingham 220 D1
Edlington 188 C5
Edmondsham 105 G1
Edmondsley 212 B3
Edmondstown 129 G3
Edmondthorpe 161 D1
Edmonstone 276 E5
Edmonton Corn 97 D2
Edmonton GtLon 136 C3
Edmundbyers 211 G2
Ednam 228 B3
Ednaston 172 D3
Edney Common 137 F2
Edra 241 G3
Edradynate 251 D4
Edrom 237 F4
Edstaston 170 C4
Edstone 147 D1
Edvin Loach 145 F2
Edwalton 173 G4
Edwardstone 152 A3
Edwardsville 129 G3
Edwinsford 142 C4
Edwinstowe 174 B1
Edworth 150 A3
Edwyn Ralph 145 F2
Edymore 285 F6
Edzell 253 E3
Efail Isaf 129 G4
Efail-fâch 129 D3
Efailnewydd 166 C4
Efailwen 141 E5
Efenechtyd 169 E2
Effingham 121 G2
Effirth 279 C7
Efflinch 159 D1
Efford 102 B2
Egbury 119 F2
Egdean 121 E5
Egdon 146 B2
Egerton GtMan 184 B1
Egerton Kent 124 B4
Egerton Forstal 124 A4
Egerton Green 170 C2
Egg Buckland 100 A2
Eggborough 195 E5
Eggerness 207 E2
Eggesford Barton 113 G4
Eggington 149 E5
Egginton 173 D5
Egglescliffe 202 D1
Eggleston 211 F5
Egham 135 F5
Egham Wick 135 E5
Egilsay 276 D5
Egleton 161 D2
Eglingham 229 F5
Eglinton D&S 285 H3
Eglinton NAyr 233 E5
Eglish 282 A3
Egloshayle 97 E2
Egloskerry 97 G1
Eglwys Cross 170 B3
Eglwys Fach 154 C3
Eglwys Nunydd 129 E4
Eglwysbach 181 G5
Eglwys-Brewis 114 D1
Eglwyswrw 141 E4
Egmanton 174 C1
Egmere 178 A2
Egremont 208 D5
Egton 204 B2
Egton Bridge 204 B2
Egypt 119 F3
Eigg 247 D1
Eight Ash Green 152 A5
Eignaig 247 G5
Eil 259 F3
Eilanreach 256 E3
Eildon 227 G2
Eilean Darach 265 H3
Eilean Donan Castle High
IV40 8DX 256 E2
Eilean Shona 247 F2
Einacleit 270 D5
Eisgein 271 F6
Eisingrug 167 F4
Eisteddfa Gurig 155 D4
Elan Valley Visitor Centre
Powys LD6 5HP 143 F1
Elan Village 143 F1
Elberton 131 F4
Elborough 116 A2
Elburton 100 B2
Elcho 243 G2
Elcombe 132 D4
Elder Street 151 D4
Eldernell 162 B3
Eldersfield 145 G4
Elderslie 233 F3
Eldon 212 B5
Eldrick 215 D2
Eldroth 193 D1
Eldwick 194 A3
Elemore Vale 212 C3
Eleven Lane Ends 282 D5
Elford N'umb 229 F3
Elford Staffs 159 D1
Elford Closes 162 D5
Elgin 267 K5
Elgol 256 B3
Elham 125 D4
Elie 244 C4
Elilaw 220 B1
Elim 180 B4
Eling Hants 106 C1
Eling WBerks 134 A5
Eling Tide Mill Hants
SO40 9HF 4 A3
Eliock 225 G5
Elishaw 220 A2
Elkesley 187 D5
Elkington 160 B5
Elkstone 132 B1
Elland 194 A5
Elland Upper Edge
194 A5
Ellary 231 F2
Ellastone 172 C3
Ellbridge 100 A1
Ellel 192 A2
Ellemford 237 E3
Ellenabeich 239 G3
Ellenborough 208 D3
Ellenhall 171 F5
Ellen's Green 121 F4
Ellerbeck 202 D3
Ellerby 203 G1
Ellerdine 170 D5
Ellerdine Heath 170 D5
Elleric (Eileirig) 248 C5
Ellerker 196 B5
Ellerton ERid 195 G3
Ellerton NYorks 202 B3
Ellerton Shrop 171 E5
Ellerton Abbey 201 F3
Ellesborough 134 D2
Ellesmere 170 A4
Ellesmere Park 184 B3
Ellesmere Port 183 F5
Ellingham Hants 106 A2
Ellingham N'umb 229 F4
Ellingham Norf 165 E2
Ellingstring 202 A4
Ellington Cambs 161 G5
Ellington N'umb 221 E2
Ellington Thorpe 161 G5
Elliot 245 E1
Elliot's Green 117 E3
Ellisfield 120 B3
Ellishadder 263 K5
Ellistown 159 G1
Ellon 261 H1
Ellonby 210 A4
Ellough 165 F3
Ellough Moor 165 F3
Elloughton 196 B5
Ellwood 131 E2
Elm 162 C2
Elm Park 137 E4
Elmbridge 146 B1
Elmdon Essex 150 C4
Elmdon WMid 159 D4
Elmdon Heath 159 D4
Elmers End 122 C2
Elmer's Green 183 F2
Elmesthorpe 159 G3
Elmhurst 158 D1
Elmley Castle 146 B3
Elmley Lovett 146 A1
Elmore 131 G1
Elmore Back 131 G1
Elmscott 112 C3
Elmsett 152 B3
Elmstead Essex 152 B5
Elmstead GtLon 136 D5
Elmstead Market 152 B5
Elmstone 125 E2
Elmstone
Hardwicke 146 B5
Elmswell ERid 196 B2
Elmswell Suff 152 A1
Elmton 186 C5
Elphin 272 E7
Elphinstone 236 A2
Elrick Aber 261 G4
Elrick Moray 260 C2
Elrig 206 D2
Elrigbeag 240 D3
Elsdon 220 B2
Elsecar 186 A2
Elsecar Heritage Centre
SYorks S74 8HJ 186 A3
Elsenham 150 D5
Elsfield 134 A1
Elsham 188 A1
Elsing 178 B4
Elslack 193 F3
Elson Hants 107 F2
Elson Shrop 170 A4
Elsrickle 235 E5
Elstead 121 E3
Elsted 108 A2
Elsthorpe 175 F5
Elstob 212 C5
Elston Lancs 192 B4
Elston Notts 174 C3
Elstone 113 G4
Elstow 149 F3
Elstree 136 A3
Elstronwick 197 E4
Elswick 192 A4
Elsworth 150 B1
Elterwater 199 E2
Eltham 136 D5
Eltisley 150 A2
Elton Cambs 161 F3
Elton ChesW&C 183 F5
Elton Derbys 172 D1
Elton Glos 131 G1
Elton GtMan 184 B1
Elton Here 157 D5
Elton Notts 174 C4
Elton Stock 202 D1
Elton Green 183 F5
Elvanfoot 226 A4
Elvaston 173 F4
Elvaston Castle Country Park
Derbys DE72 3EP 18 C4
Elveden 163 G5
Elvingston 236 B2
Elvington Kent 125 E3
Elvington York 195 G3
Elwick Hart 213 D4
Elwick N'umb 229 F3
Elworth 171 E1
Elworthy 115 D4
Ely Cambs 162 D5
Ely Cardiff 130 A5
Emberton 149 D3
Emberton Country Park
MK MK46 5FJ 149 D2
Embleton Cumb 209 E3
Embleton Hart 212 D5
Embleton N'umb 229 G4
Embo 267 F2
Embo Street 267 F2
Emborough 116 D2
Embsay 193 G2
Embsay Steam Railway
NYorks
BD23 6AF 193 G2
Emerson Park 137 E4
Emery Down 106 B2
Emley 185 G1
Emmington 134 C2
Emneth 162 C2
Emneth Hungate 162 D2
Empingham 161 E2
Empshott 120 C4
Empshott Green 120 C4
Emsworth 107 G2
Enagh 282 D5
Enborne 119 F1
Enborne Row 119 F1
Enchmarsh 157 E3
Enderby 160 A3
Endmoor 199 G4
Endon 171 G2
Endon Bank 171 G2
Enfield 136 C3
Enfield Wash 136 C3
Enford 118 C2
Engine Common 131 F4
Englefield 134 B5
Englefield Green 135 E5
Englesea-brook 171 E2
English Bicknor 131 E1
English Frankton 170 B5
Englishcombe 117 E1
Enham Alamein 119 E3
Enmore 115 F4
Ennerdale Bridge 209 D5
Enniscaven 97 D4
Enniskillen 280 E4
Enniskillen Castle
F&O BT74 7ER 280 E4
Ennochdhu 251 F3
Ensay 246 C5
Ensdon 156 D1
Ensis 113 F3
Enson 171 G5
Enstone 147 F5
Enterkinfoot 225 G5
Enterpen 203 D2
Enton Green 121 E3
Enville 158 A4
Eòlaigearraidh 254 C4
Eorabus 238 C2
Eòrodal 271 H1
Eòropaidh 271 H1
Epney 131 G1
Epperstone 174 B3
Epping 137 D2
Epping Green
Essex 136 D2
Epping Green
Herts 136 B2
Epping Upland 136 D2
Eppleby 202 A1
Eppleworth 196 C4
Epsom 122 B2
Epwell 147 F3
Epworth 187 E2
Epworth Turbary 187 E2
Erbistock 170 A3
Erbusaig 256 D2
Erchless Castle 266 B7
Erdinagh 281 G4
Erdington 158 D3
Eredine 240 B4
Eriboll 273 G3
Ericstane 226 B4
Eridge Green 123 E5
Eriff 224 D5
Erines 231 G2
Erisey Barton 95 E5
Eriskay
(Eiriosgaigh) 254 C3
Eriswell 163 F5
Erith 137 E5
Erlestoke 118 A2
Ermington 100 C2
Ernesettle 100 A1
Erpingham 178 C2
Erringden Grange 193 F5
Errogie (Earagaidh) 258 C2
Errol 244 A2
Errollston 261 J1
Erskine 233 F2
Erveny 280 D5
Ervey Cross Roads 285 H4
Ervie 214 A4
Erwarton 152 D4
Erwood 143 G3
Eryholme 202 C2
Eryrys 169 F2
Escart 231 G3
Escart Farm 231 G4
Escomb 212 A5
Escrick 195 F3
Esgair 141 G5
Esgairgeiliog 155 D2
Esgyryn 181 G5
Esh 212 A3
Esh Winning 212 A3
Esher 121 G1
Eshnadarragh 281 H5
Eshnadeelada 281 G5
Eshott 221 E2
Eshton 193 F2
Eskadale 258 B1
Eskbank 236 A3
Eskdale Green 198 C2
Eskdalemuir 218 A2
Eskham 189 D3
Esknish 230 B3
Eskragh 281 H3
Esperley Lane Ends 212 A5
Espley Hall 221 D2
Esprick 192 A4
Essendine 161 F1
Essendon 136 B2
Essich 258 D1
Essington 158 B2
Esslemont 261 H2
Eston 203 E1
Eswick 279 D7
Etal 228 D3
Etchilhampton 118 B1
Etchingham 110 C1
Etchinghill Kent 125 D5
Etchinghill Staffs 158 C1
Etherdwick Grange 197 E4
Etherley Dene 212 A5
Etherow Country Park
GtMan SK6 5JQ 25 H5
Ethie Mains 253 E5
Eton 135 E5
Eton Wick 135 E5
Etteridge 258 D5
Ettiley Heath 171 E1
Ettington 147 E3
Etton ERid 196 B3
Etton Peter 161 G2
Ettrick 227 D4
Ettrickbridge 227 E3
Ettrickhill 227 D4
Etwall 173 D4
Eudon George 157 F4
Eurach 240 A4
Eureka! Museum for
Children WYorks
HX1 2NE 26 B4
Euston 163 G5
Euxton 183 G1
Evanstown 129 F4
Evanton 266 D5
Evedon 175 F3
Evelix 266 E2
Evenjobb 144 B1
Evenley 148 A4
Evenlode 147 E5
Evenwood 212 A5
Evenwood Gate 212 A5
Everbay 276 F5
Evercreech 116 D4
Everdon 148 A2
Everingham 196 A3
Everleigh 118 D2
Everley High 275 J2
Everley NYorks 204 C4
Eversholt 149 E4
Evershot 104 B2
Eversley 120 C1
Eversley Cross 120 C1
Everthorpe 196 B4
Everton CenBeds 150 A2
Everton Hants 106 B3
Everton Mersey 183 E3
Everton Notts 187 D3
Evertown 218 B4
Eves Corner 138 C3
Evesbatch 145 F3
Evesham 146 C3
Evesham Country Park
Shopping & Garden
Centre Worcs
WR11 4TP 146 C3
Evie 276 C5
Evington 160 B2
Ewart Newtown 229 D3
Ewden Village 185 G3
Ewell 122 B2
Ewell Minnis 125 E4
Ewelme 134 B3
Ewen 132 C3
Ewenny 129 F5
Ewerby 175 G3
Ewerby Thorpe 175 G3
Ewhurst 121 F3
Ewhurst Green
ESuss 110 C1
Ewhurst Green
Surr 121 F4
Ewloe 170 A1
Ewloe Green 169 F1
Ewood 192 C5
Ewood Bridge 193 D5
Eworthy 99 E1
Ewshot 120 D3
Ewyas Harold 144 C5
Exbourne 113 G5
Exbury 106 D2
Exbury Gardens Hants
SO45 1AZ 4 B6
Exceat 110 A4
Exebridge 114 C5
Exelby 202 B4
Exeter 102 C3
Exeter Cathedral Devon
EX1 1HS 72 Exeter
Exeter International
Airport 102 C3
Exford 114 B4
Exfords Green 157 D2
Exhall Warks 146 D2
Exhall Warks 159 F4
Exlade Street 134 B4
Exminster 102 C4
Exmoor International Dark
Sky Reserve Devon/Som.
114 A3
Exmouth 102 D4
Exnaboe 279 F9
Exning 151 E1
Explore-At-Bristol
BS1 5DB 66 Bristol
Exton Devon 102 C4
Exton Hants 120 B5
Exton Rut 161 E1
Exton Som 114 C4
Exwick 102 C3
Eyam 185 G5
Eydon 148 A3
Eye Here 145 D1
Eye Peter 162 A2
Eye Suff 164 C4
Eye Green 162 A2
Eyemouth 237 G3
Eyeworth 150 A3
Eyhorne Street 124 A3
Eyke 153 E2
Eynesbury 149 G2
Eynort 255 J2
Eynsford 123 E2
Eynsham 133 G2
Eype 104 A3
Eyre 263 K6
Eythorne 125 E4
Eyton Here 145 D1
Eyton Shrop 156 C4
Eyton on Severn 157 E2
Eyton upon the Weald
Moors 157 F1
Eywood 144 C2

F
Faccombe 119 E2
Faceby 203 D2
Fachwen 167 E1
Facit 184 C1
Faddiley 170 C2
Fadmoor 203 F4
Faebait 266 B6
Faifley 233 G2
Fail 224 C3
Failand 131 E5
Failford 224 C3
Failsworth 184 C2
Fain 265 H4
Fair Isle 278 A1
Fair Isle Airstrip 278 A1
Fair Oak Devon 102 D1
Fair Oak Hants 107 D1
Fair Oak Hants 119 G1
Fair Oak Green 120 B1
Fairbourne 154 C1
Fairburn 195 D5
Fairfield Derbys 185 E5
Fairfield GtMan 184 D3
Fairfield Kent 111 E1
Fairfield Mersey 183 D4
Fairfield Stock 202 D1
Fairfield Worcs 158 B5
Fairfield Halls, Croydon
GtLon CR9 1DG 122 C2
Fairford 132 D2
Fairgirth 216 C5
Fairhaven 191 G5
Fairhill 234 B4
Fairholm 234 B4
Fairlands Valley Park Herts
SG2 0BL 150 A5
Fairley 261 G4
Fairlie 232 D4
Fairlight 111 D2
Fairlight Cove 111 D2
Fairmile Devon 103 D3
Fairmile Surr 121 G1
Fairmilehead 235 G3
Fairnington 228 A4
Fairoak 171 E4
Fairseat 123 F2
Fairstead 137 G1
Fairwarp 109 G1
Fairwater 130 A5
Fairy Cross 113 E3
Fairyhill 128 A3
Fakenham 178 A3
Fakenham Magna 164 A4
Fala 236 B3
Fala Dam 236 B3
Falahill 236 A4
Faldingworth 188 A4
Falfield Fife 244 C4
Falfield SGlos 131 F3
Falin-Wnda 141 G3
Falkenham 153 D4
Falkirk 234 C2
Falkirk Wheel Falk
FK1 4RS 234 C1
Falkland 244 A4
Falla 228 B5
Fallgate 173 E1
Fallagloon 286 C5
Fallin 242 D5
Falmer 109 F3
Falmouth 95 F3
Falsgrave 204 D4
Falstone 219 F3
Famous Grouse Experience,
Glenturret Distillery
P&K PH7 4HA 243 D2
Fanagmore 272 D4
Fanans 240 C2
Fancott 149 F5
Fangdale Beck 203 E3
Fangfoss 195 G2
Fankerton 234 B1
Fanmore 246 D5
Fanner's Green 137 F1
Fans 236 D5
Fantasy Island Lincs
PE25 1RH 177 D1
Far Cotton 148 C2
Far Forest 157 G5
Far Gearstones 200 C4
Far Green 131 G2
Far Moor 183 G2
Far Oakridge 132 B2
Far Royds 194 B4
Far Sawrey 199 E3
Farcet 162 A3
Farden 157 E5
Fardross 281 H4
Fareham 107 E2
Farewell 158 C1
Farforth 188 D5
Faringdon 133 E3
Farington 192 B5
Farlam 210 B2
Farlary 266 E1
Farleigh NSom 116 C1
Farleigh Surr 122 C2
Farleigh Hungerford 117 F2
Farleigh Wallop 120 B3
Farlesthorpe 189 E5
Farleton Cumb 199 G4
Farleton Lancs 192 B1
Farley Derbys 173 D1
Farley Shrop 156 C2
Farley Staffs 172 B3
Farley Wilts 118 D5
Farley Green Suff 151 F2
Farley Green Surr 121 F3
Farley Hill 120 C1
Farleys End 131 G1
Farlington 195 F1
Farlough 286 E6
Farlow 157 F4
Farm Town 159 F1
Farmborough 117 D1
Farmcote 146 C5
Farmington 132 D1
Farmoor 133 G2
Farmtown 268 D5
Farnborough
GtLon 122 D2
Farnborough
Hants 121 D2
Farnborough
Warks 147 G3
Farnborough
WBerks 133 G4
Farnborough Street 121 D2
Farncombe 121 E3
Farndish 149 E1
Farndon ChesW&C 170 B2
Farndon Notts 174 C2
Farne Islands 229 G3
Farnell 253 E4
Farnham Dorset 105 F1
Farnham Essex 150 C5
Farnham NYorks 194 C1
Farnham Suff 153 E1
Farnham Surr 120 D3
Farnham Common 135 E4
Farnham Green 150 C5
Farnham Royal 135 E4
Farningham 123 E2
Farnley NYorks 194 B3
Farnley WYorks 194 B4
Farnley Tyas 185 F1
Farnsfield 174 B2
Farnworth GtMan 184 B2
Farnworth Halton 183 G4
Farr High 274 C2
Farr High 258 D1
Farr High 259 F4
Farr House 258 D1
Farraline 258 C2
Farranamucklagh 282 B5
Farrancassidy 280 B3
Farranflugh 287 F6
Farringdon 102 D3
Farrington Gurney 116 D2
Farsley 194 B4
Farthing Corner 124 A2
Farthing Green 124 A4
Farthinghoe 148 A4
Farthingstone 148 B2
Farthorpe 188 C5
Fartown 185 F1
Farway 103 E3
Fasag 264 E6
Fasagrianach 265 H3
Fascadale 247 E2
Fashion Museum B&NESom
BA1 2QH 117 E1
Faslane 232 D1
Fasnacloich 248 C5
Fasnakyle 257 K2
Fassfern 248 C2
Fatfield 212 C2
Fattahead 268 E5
Faugh 210 B2
Fauldhouse 234 D3
Faulkbourne 137 G1
Faulkland 117 E2
Fauls 170 C4
Faulston 118 B5
Faversham 124 C2
Favillar 259 K1
Fawdington 202 D5
Fawdon 212 B1
Fawfieldhead 172 B1
Fawkham Green 123 E2
Fawler 133 F1
Fawley Bucks 134 C4
Fawley Hants 107 D2
Fawley WBerks 133 F4
Fawley Chapel 145 E5
Fawsyde 253 G2
Faxfleet 196 A5
Faxton 160 C5
Faygate 122 B5
Fazakerley 183 E3
Fazeley 159 E2

Fearby 202 A4
Fearn 267 F4
Fearnan 250 C5
Fearnbeg 264 D6
Fearnhead 184 A3
Fearnmore 264 D5
Fearnoch A&B 232 B2
Fearnoch A&B 232 A1
Featherstone Staffs 158 B2
Featherstone WYorks 194 D5
Featherstone Castle 210 C1
Feckenham 146 C1
Feeny 285 J5
Feering 151 G5
Feetham 201 E3
Feith-hill 268 E6
Feizor 193 D1
Felbridge 122 C5
Felbrigg 178 D2
Felcourt 122 C4
Felden 135 F2
Felhampton 156 D4
Felindre Carmar 142 D5
Felindre Carmar 142 B5
Felindre Carmar 141 G4
Felindre Carmar 142 C4
Felindre Cere 142 B2
Felindre Powys 156 A4
Felindre Powys 144 A5
Felindre Swan 128 C2
Felinfach Cere 142 B2
Felinfach Powys 143 G4
Felinfoel 128 B2
Felingwmisaf 142 B5
Felingwmuchaf 142 B5
Felixkirk 203 D4
Felixstowe 153 E4
Felixstowe Ferry 153 E4
Felkington 237 G5
Felldownhead 99 D2
Felling 212 B1
Fellonmore 239 F2
Felmersham 149 E2
Felmingham 179 D3
Felpham 108 B4
Felsham 152 A2
Felsted 151 E5
Feltham 136 A5
Felthamhill 136 A5
Felthorpe 178 C4
Felton Here 145 E3
Felton N'umb 221 D1
Felton NSom 116 C1
Felton Butler 156 C1
Feltwell 163 F3
Fen Ditton 150 C1
Fen Drayton 150 B1
Fen End 159 E5
Fen Street Norf 164 A2
Fen Street Norf 164 B4
Fen Street Suff 164 A4
Fen Street Suff 152 C1
Fenay Bridge 185 F1
Fence 193 E4
Fence Houses 212 C2
Fencott 134 A1
Fendike Corner 176 C1
Fenham 229 E2
Fenhouses 176 A3
Feniscowles 192 C5
Feniton 103 E3
Fenn Street 137 G5
Fenni-fach 143 G5
Fenny Bentley 172 C2
Fenny Bridges 103 E3
Fenny Compton 147 G2
Fenny Drayton 159 F3
Fenny Stratford 149 D4
Fenrother 221 D2
Fenstanton 150 B1
Fenton Cambs 162 B5
Fenton Lincs 187 F5
Fenton Lincs 175 D2
Fenton N'umb 229 D3
Fenton Notts 187 E4
Fenton Stoke 171 F3
Fenton Barns 236 C1
Fenwick EAyr 233 F5
Fenwick N'umb 220 C4
Fenwick N'umb 229 E2
Fenwick SYorks 186 C1
Feochaig 222 C4
Feock 95 F3
Feolin 230 D3
Feolin Ferry 230 C3
Feorlan 222 B5
Feorlin 240 B5
Ferens Art Gallery HU1 3RA 76 Kingston upon Hull
Ferguslie Park 233 F3
Feriniquarrie 263 G6
Fern 252 C3
Ferndale 129 F3
Ferndown 105 G2
Ferness 267 G7
Fernham 133 E3
Fernhill Heath 146 A2
Fernhurst 121 D5
Fernie 244 B3
Fernilea 255 J1
Fernilee 185 E5
Fernybank 252 D2
Ferrensby 194 C1
Ferrers Centre for Arts & Crafts Leics LE65 1RU 173 E5
Ferrindonald 256 C4
Ferring 108 C3
Ferry Hill 162 B4
Ferrybridge 195 D5
Ferryden 253 F4
Ferryhill 212 B4
Ferryside (Glanyferi) 127 G1
Fersfield 164 B3
Fersit 249 F2
Ferwig 141 E3
Feshiebridge 259 F4
Festival Park BGwent NP23 8FP 130 A2
Fetcham 121 G2
Fetlar 278 F3
Fetlar Airport 278 F3
Fetterangus 269 H5
Fettercairn 253 E2
Fetternear House 261 F3
Feus of Caldhame 253 E3
Fewcott 148 A5
Fewston 194 A2
Feystown 287 H5
Ffairfach 142 C5
Ffair-Rhos 142 D1
Ffaldybrenin 142 C3
Ffarmers 142 C3
Ffawyddog 130 B1
Ffestiniog (Llan Ffestiniog) 168 A3
Ffestiniog Railway Gwyn LL49 9NF 167 F3
Ffordd-las Denb 169 E1
Ffordd-las Powys 144 B4
Fforest 128 B2
Fforest-fach 128 C3
Ffostrasol 141 G3
Ffos-y-ffin 142 A1
Ffridd Uchaf 167 E2
Ffrith Denb 182 B4
Ffrith Flints 169 F2
Ffrwdgrech 143 G5
Ffynnon 127 G1
Ffynnongroyw 182 C4
Fibhig 270 E3
Fichlie 260 C3
Fidden 238 C2
Fiddington Glos 146 B4
Fiddington Som 115 F3
Fiddleford 105 E1
Fiddler's Green Glos 146 B5
Fiddler's Green Here 145 E4
Fiddler's Green Norf 163 G1
Fiddler's Green Norf 164 B2
Fiddlers Hamlet 137 D2
Field 172 B4
Field Broughton 199 E4
Field Dalling 178 B2
Field Head 159 G2
Fife Keith 268 C5
Fifehead Magdalen 117 E5
Fifehead Neville 105 D1
Fifehead St. Quintin 105 D1
Fifield Oxon 133 E1
Fifield W&M 135 E5
Fifield Bavant 118 B5
Figheldean 118 C3
Filby 179 F4
Filey 205 E4
Filgrave 149 D3
Filham 100 C2
Filkins 133 E2
Filleigh Devon 113 G3
Filleigh Devon 102 A1
Fillingham 187 G4
Fillongley 159 E4
Filmore Hill 120 B5
Filton 131 F5
Fimber 196 A1
Finavon 252 C4
Fincairn CC&G 285 J5
Fincarn D&S 285 G4
Fincham 163 E2
Finchampstead 120 C1
Finchdean 107 G1
Finchingfield 151 E4
Finchley 136 B3
Findern 173 E4
Findhorn 267 H5
Findhorn Bridge 259 F2
Findhuglen 242 C3
Findo Gask 243 F2
Findochty 268 C4
Findon Aber 261 H5
Findon WSuss 108 D3
Findon Mains 266 D5
Findon Valley 108 D3
Findrassie 267 J5
Findron 259 J3
Finedon 161 E5
Finegand 251 G3
Fingal Street 164 D4
Fingask 261 F2
Fingerpost 157 G5
Fingest 134 C3
Finghall 202 A4
Fingland Cumb 209 F1
Fingland D&G 226 D5
Fingland D&G 225 F4
Finglesham 125 F3
Fingringhoe 152 B5
Finkle Street 186 A3
Finlarig 242 A1
Finmere 148 B4
Finnart A&B 241 E5
Finnart P&K 250 A4
Finney Hill 159 G1
Finningham 152 B1
Finningley 187 D3
Finnis 283 F4
Finnygaud 268 E5
Finsbay (Fionnsbhagh) 263 F3
Finsbury 136 C4
Finstall 158 B5
Finsthwaite 199 E4
Finstock 133 F1
Finstown 277 C6
Fintona 281 G2
Fintry Aber 269 F5
Fintry Stir 234 A1
Finvoy 286 D4
Finwood 147 D1
Finzean 260 D5
Fionnphort 238 B2
Fir Tree 212 A4
Firbank 200 B3
Firbeck 186 C4
Firby NYorks 202 B4
Firby NYorks 195 G1
Firgrove 184 D1
Firs Lane 184 A2
Firsby 176 C1
Firsdown 118 D4
Firth 278 D5
Fishbourne IoW 107 E3
Fishbourne WSuss 108 A3
Fishburn 212 C4
Fishcross 243 E5
Fisherford 260 E1
Fishers Farm Park WSuss RH14 0EG 121 F5
Fisher's Pond 119 F5
Fisher's Row 192 A3
Fishersgate 109 E3
Fisherstreet 121 E4
Fisherton High 266 E6
Fisherton SAyr 224 A4
Fisherton de la Mere 118 A4
Fishguard (Abergwaun) 140 C4
Fishlake 187 D1
Fishleigh Barton 113 F3
Fishley 179 F4
Fishnish 247 F5
Fishpond Bottom 103 G3
Fishponds 131 F5
Fishpool 184 C2
Fishtoft 176 B3
Fishtoft Drove 176 B3
Fishtown of Usan 253 F4
Fishwick 237 G4
Fiskerton Lincs 188 A5
Fiskerton Notts 174 C2
Fitling 197 E4
Fittleton 118 C3
Fittleworth 108 C2
Fitton End 162 C1
Fitz 156 D1
Fitzhead 115 E5
Fitzroy 115 E5
Fitzwilliam 186 B1
Fitzwilliam Museum Cambs CB2 1RB 66 Cambridge
Fiunary 247 F5
Five Acres 131 E1
Five Ash Down 109 G1
Five Ashes 110 A1
Five Bridges 145 F3
Five Houses 106 D4
Five Lanes 130 D3
Five Oak Green 123 F4
Five Oaks Chanl 100 C5
Five Oaks WSuss 121 F5
Five Roads 128 A2
Five Turnings 156 B5
Five Wents 124 A3
Fivehead 116 A5
Fivelanes 97 G1
Fivemiletown 281 G4
Flack's Green 137 G1
Flackwell Heath 135 D4
Fladbury 146 B3
Fladdabister 279 D9
Flagg 172 C1
Flambards Experience, The Corn TR13 0QA 95 D4
Flamborough 205 F5
Flamborough Cliffs Nature Reserve ERid YO15 1BJ 205 F5
Flamingo Land Theme Park NYorks YO17 6UX 203 G4
Flamingo Park, Hastings ESuss TN34 3AR 110 D3
Flamstead 135 F1
Flamstead End 136 C2
Flansham 108 B3
Flanshaw 194 C5
Flasby 193 F2
Flash 172 B1
Flashader 263 J6
Flask Inn 204 C2
Flatts Lane Woodland Country Park R&C TS6 0NN 29 D4
Flaunden 135 F2
Flawborough 174 C3
Flawith 195 D1
Flax Bourton 116 C1
Flax Moss 193 D5
Flaxby 194 C2
Flaxholme 173 E3
Flaxlands 164 C2
Flaxley 131 F1
Flaxpool 115 E4
Flaxton 195 F1
Fleckney 160 B3
Flecknoe 148 A1
Fledborough 187 F5
Fleet Hants 120 D2
Fleet Hants 107 G2
Fleet Lincs 176 B5
Fleet Air Arm Museum Som BA22 8HT 116 C5
Fleet Hargate 176 B5
Fleetville 136 A2
Fleetwood 191 G3
Fleggburgh (Burgh St. Margaret) 179 F4
Flemingston 129 G5
Flemington 234 A4
Flempton 151 G1
Fleoideabhagh 263 F3
Flesherin 271 H4
Fletchersbridge 97 F3
Fletchertown 209 F2
Fletching 109 G1
Fleuchats 260 B4
Fleur-de-lis 130 A3
Flexbury 112 C5
Flexford 121 E2
Flimby 208 D3
Flimwell 123 G5
Flint (Y Fflint) 182 D5
Flint Cross 150 C3
Flint Mountain 182 D5
Flintham 174 C3
Flinton 197 E4
Flint's Green 159 E4
Flishinghurst 123 G5
Flitcham 177 F5
Flitholme 200 C1
Flitton 149 F4
Flitwick 149 F4
Flixborough 187 F1
Flixton GtMan 184 B3
Flixton NYorks 204 D5
Flixton Suff 165 E3
Flockton 185 G1
Flockton Green 185 G1
Flodden 228 D3
Flodigarry 263 K4
Flood's Ferry 162 B3
Flookburgh 199 E5
Floors 268 C5
Flordon 164 C2
Flore 148 B1
Florence Court (NT) F&O BT92 1DB 280 D5
Flotta 277 C8
Flotterton 220 C1
Flowton 152 B3
Flushdyke 194 B5
Flushing Aber 269 J6
Flushing Corn 95 F3
Flushing Corn 95 E4
Flushtown 285 F6
Fluxton 103 D3
Flyford Flavell 146 B2
Foals Green 165 D4
Fobbing 137 G4
Fochabers 268 B5
Fochriw 130 A2
Fockerby 187 F1
Fodderletter 259 J2
Fodderty 266 C6
Foddington 116 C5
Foel 155 F1
Foelgastell 128 B1
Foggathorpe 195 G4
Fogo 237 E5
Fogorig 237 E5
Fogwatt 267 K6
Foindle 272 D4
Folda 251 G3
Fole 172 B4
Foleshill 159 F4
Folke 104 C1
Folkestone 125 E5
Folkingham 175 F4
Folkington 110 A3
Folksworth 161 G4
Folkton 205 D5
Folla Rule 261 F1
Follifoot 194 C2
Folly Dorset 104 D2
Folly Pembs 140 C5
Folly Farm, Begelly Pembs SA68 0XA 127 E2
Folly Gate 99 F1
Fonmon 115 D1
Fonthill Bishop 118 A4
Fonthill Gifford 118 A4
Fontmell Magna 105 E1
Fontmell Parva 105 E1
Fontwell 108 B3
Font-y-gary 115 D1
Foolow 185 F5
Footherley 158 D2
Foots Cray 137 D5
Forbestown 260 B3
Force Forge 199 E3
Force Green 122 D3
Forcett 202 A1
Forches Cross 102 A2
Ford A&B 240 A4
Ford Bucks 134 C2
Ford Devon 100 C2
Ford Devon 113 E3
Ford Devon 101 D3
Ford Glos 146 C5
Ford Mersey 183 E3
Ford Midlo 236 A3
Ford N'umb 229 D3
Ford Pembs 140 C5
Ford Plym 100 A2
Ford Shrop 156 D1
Ford Som 115 D5
Ford Staffs 172 B2
Ford Wilts 132 A5
Ford WSuss 108 B3
Ford End 137 F1
Ford Green 192 A3
Ford Heath 156 D1
Ford Street 103 E1
Forda 99 F1
Fordbridge 159 D4
Fordcombe 123 E4
Fordell 235 F1
Forden (Ffordun) 156 B2
Forder Green 101 D1
Fordgate 116 A4
Fordham Cambs 163 E5
Fordham Essex 152 A5
Fordham Norf 163 E3
Fordham Abbey 151 E1
Fordham Heath 152 A5
Fordhouses 158 B2
Fordingbridge 106 A1
Fordon 205 D5
Fordoun 253 F2
Ford's Green 152 B1
Fordstreet 152 A5
Fordwells 133 F1
Fordwich 125 D3
Fordyce 268 D4
Forebrae 243 E2
Forebridge 171 G5
Foredale 193 E1
Foreglen 285 J5
Foreland 230 A3
Foremark 173 E5
Foremark Reservoir Derbys DE65 6EG 173 E5
Forest 202 B2
Forest Coal Pit 144 B5
Forest Gate 136 D4
Forest Green 121 G3
Forest Hall Cumb 199 G2
Forest Hall T&W 212 B1
Forest Head 210 B2
Forest Hill GtLon 136 C5
Forest Hill Oxon 134 A2
Forest Lane Head 194 C2
Forest Lodge (Taigh na Frithe) A&B 249 E5
Forest Lodge P&K 251 E2
Forest Row 122 D5
Forest Side 107 D4
Forest Town 173 G1
Forestburn Gate 220 C2
Forest-in-Teesdale 211 E5
Forestmill 243 E5
Forestside 107 G1
Forfar 252 C4
Forfar Loch Country Park Angus DD8 1BT 252 C4
Forgandenny 243 F3
Forge 155 D3
Forgie 268 B5
Forhill 158 C5
Forkhill 282 D7
Formby 183 D2
Formoyle 286 B3
Forncett End 164 C2
Forncett St. Mary 164 C2
Forncett St. Peter 164 C2
Forneth 251 F5
Fornham All Saints 151 G1
Fornham St. Martin 151 G1
Fornighty 267 G6
Forres 267 H6
Forrest 234 C3
Forrest Lodge 215 G2
Forsbrook 171 G3
Forse 275 H5
Forsie 275 F2
Forsinain 274 E4
Forsinard 274 D4
Forston 104 C3
Fort Augustus (Cille Chuimein) 257 K4
Fort Fun, Eastbourne ESuss BN22 7LQ 110 B3
Fort George 266 E6
Fort William (An Gearasdan) 248 D2
Forter 251 G3
Forteviot 243 F3
Forth 234 D4
Forthampton 146 A4
Fortingall 250 C5
Fortis Green 136 B4
Forton Hants 119 F3
Forton Lancs 192 A2
Forton Shrop 156 D1
Forton Som 103 G2
Forton Staffs 171 E5
Fortrie 268 E6
Fortrose (A'Chananaich) 266 E6
Fortuneswell 104 C5
Forty Green 135 E3
Forty Hill 136 C3
Forward Green 152 B2
Fosbury 119 E2
Foscot 147 E5
Fosdyke 176 B4
Foss 250 C4
Foss Cross 132 C2
Fossdale 201 D3
Fossebridge 132 C1
Foster Street 137 D2
Fosterhouses 186 D1
Foster's Booth 148 B2
Foston Derbys 172 C4
Foston Leics 160 B3
Foston Lincs 175 D3
Foston NYorks 195 F1
Foston on the Wolds 196 D2
Fotherby 188 D3
Fotheringhay 161 F3
Foubister 277 E7
Foul Mile 110 B2
Foula 278 B1
Foula Airstrip 278 B1
Foulbog 226 D5
Foulden Norf 163 F3
Foulden ScBord 237 G4
Foulness Island 138 D3
Foulridge 193 E3
Foulsham 178 B3
Foulstone 199 G4
Foulzie 269 F4
Fountainhall 236 B5
Four Ashes Staffs 158 B2
Four Ashes Staffs 158 A4
Four Ashes Suff 164 A4
Four Crosses Denb 168 D3
Four Crosses Powys 156 B1
Four Crosses Powys 155 G2
Four Crosses Staffs 158 B2
Four Elms 123 D4
Four Forks 115 F4
Four Gotes 162 C1
Four Lane Ends B'burn 192 C5
Four Lane Ends ChesW&C 170 C1
Four Lane Ends York 195 F2
Four Lanes 95 D3
Four Marks 120 B4
Four Mile Bridge 180 A5
Four Oaks ESuss 111 D1
Four Oaks Glos 145 F5
Four Oaks WMid 159 E4
Four Oaks WMid 158 D3
Four Oaks Park 158 D3
Four Roads 128 A2
Four Throws 110 C1
Fourlane Ends 173 E2
Fourlanes End 171 F2
Fourpenny 267 F2
Fourstones 211 E1
Fovant 118 B5
Foveran 261 H2
Fowey 97 F4
Fowlis 244 B1
Fowlis Wester 243 E2
Fowlmere 150 C3
Fownhope 145 E4
Fox Hatch 137 E3
Fox Lane 121 D2
Fox Street 152 B5
Fox Up 201 D5
Foxbar 233 F3
Foxcombe Hill 133 G2
Foxcote Glos 132 C1
Foxcote Som 117 E2
Foxdale 190 A4
Foxearth 151 G3
Foxfield 198 D4
Foxham 132 B5
Foxhole Corn 97 D4
Foxhole High 258 C1
Foxholes 204 D5
Foxhunt Green 110 A2
Foxley Here 144 D3
Foxley N'hants 148 B2
Foxley Norf 178 B3
Foxley Wilts 132 A4
Foxt 172 B3
Foxton Cambs 150 C3
Foxton Dur 212 C5
Foxton Leics 160 B3
Foxton Locks Leics LE16 7RA 160 B4
Foxwist Green 170 D1
Foy 145 E5
Foyers (Foithir) 258 B2
Frachadil 246 C4
Fraddam 94 C3
Fraddon 96 D4
Fradley 159 D1
Fradswell 171 G4
Fraisthorpe 197 D1
Framfield 109 G1
Framingham Earl 179 D5
Framingham Pigot 179 D5
Framlingham 153 D1
Frampton Dorset 104 C3
Frampton Lincs 176 B4
Frampton Cotterell 131 F4
Frampton Mansell 132 B2
Frampton on Severn 131 G2
Frampton West End 176 A3
Framsden 152 D2
Framwellgate Moor 212 B3
France Lynch 132 B2
Frances Green 192 C4
Franche 158 A5
Frandley 184 A5
Frankby 182 D4
Frankfort 179 E3
Frankley 158 B4
Franksbridge 144 A2
Frankton 159 G5
Frant 123 E5
Fraserburgh 269 H4
Frating 152 B5
Fratton 107 F2
Freasley 159 E3
Freathy 99 D5
Freckenham 163 E5
Freckleton 192 A5
Freeby 174 D5
Freefolk 119 F3
Freehay 172 B3
Freeland 133 G1
Freester 279 D7
Freethorpe 179 F5
Freethorpe Common 179 F5
Freiston 176 B3
Freiston Shore 176 B3
Fremington Devon 113 F2
Fremington NYorks 201 F3
French Brothers Cruises W&M SL4 5JH 135 E5
Frenchay 131 F5
Frenchbeer 99 G2
Frendraught 268 E6
Frenich 241 G4
Frensham 120 D3
Fresgoe 274 E2
Freshbrook 132 D4
Freshfield 183 D2
Freshford 117 E2
Freshwater 106 C4
Freshwater Bay 106 C4
Freshwater East 126 D3
Fressingfield 165 D4
Freston 152 C4
Freswick 275 J2
Fretherne 131 G2
Frettenham 178 D4
Freuchie 244 A4
Freughmore 281 G2
Freystrop Cross 126 C1
Friars, The, Aylesford Kent ME20 7BX 123 G3
Friars Carse 216 D2
Friar's Gate 123 D5
Friarton 243 G2
Friday Bridge 162 C2
Friday Street ESuss 110 B3
Friday Street Suff 152 D2
Friday Street Suff 153 E2
Friday Street Surr 121 G3
Fridaythorpe 196 A2
Friern Barnet 136 B3
Friesthorpe 188 A4
Frieston 175 E3
Frieth 134 C3
Frilford 133 G3
Frilsham 134 A5
Frimley 121 D2
Frimley Green 121 D2
Frindsbury 123 G2
Fring 177 F4
Fringford 148 B5
Friningham 124 A3
Frinsted 124 A3
Frinton-on-Sea 139 F1
Friockheim 253 D5
Friog 154 C1
Frisby on the Wreake 160 B1
Friskney 176 C2
Friskney Eaudyke 176 C2
Friston ESuss 110 A4
Friston Suff 153 F1
Fritchley 173 E2
Frith 124 B3
Frith Bank 176 B3
Frith Common 145 F1
Fritham 106 B1
Frithelstock 113 E4
Frithelstock Stone 113 E4
Frithville 176 B2
Frittenden 124 A4
Frittiscombe 101 E3
Fritton Norf 164 D2
Fritton Norf 179 F5
Fritwell 148 A5
Frizinghall 194 A4
Frizington 208 D5
Frocester 131 G2
Frochas 156 B2
Frodesley 157 E2
Frodesley Lane 157 E2
Frodingham 187 F1
Frodsham 183 G5
Frog End 150 C2
Frog Pool 145 G1
Frogden 228 B4
Froggatt 185 G5
Froghall 172 B3
Frogham 106 A1
Frogland Cross 131 F4
Frogmore Devon 101 D3
Frogmore Hants 120 D2
Frogmore Herts 136 A2
Frogwell 98 D4
Frolesworth 160 A3
Frome 117 E3
Frome Market 117 F2
Frome St. Quintin 104 B2
Frome Whitfield 104 C3
Fromes Hill 145 F3
Fron Gwyn 166 C4
Fron Powys 156 B2
Fron Powys 143 G1
Fron Powys 156 A3
Fron Isaf 169 F4
Froncysyllte 169 F3
Fron-goch 168 C4
Frostenden 165 F3
Frosterley 211 G4
Froxfield 119 E1
Froxfield Green 120 C5
Fruitmarket Gallery Edin EH1 1DF 37 G4
Fryerning 137 F2
Fugglestone St. Peter 118 C4
Fulbeck 175 E2
Fulbourn 150 D2
Fulbrook 133 E1
Fulflood 119 F5
Fulford Som 115 F5
Fulford Staffs 171 G4
Fulford York 195 F3
Fulham 136 B5
Fulking 109 E2
Full Sutton 195 G2
Fullaford 113 G2
Fuller Street 137 G1
Fuller's Moor 170 B2
Fullerton 119 E4
Fulletby 188 C5
Fullwood 233 F4
Fulmer 135 F4
Fulmodeston 178 A2
Fulnetby 188 B5
Fulready 147 E3
Fulstone 185 F2
Fulstow 188 D3
Fulwell Oxon 147 F5
Fulwell T&W 212 C2
Fulwood Lancs 192 B4
Fulwood SYorks 186 A4
Fun Farm, Spalding Lincs PE12 6JU 176 A5
Fundenhall 164 C2
Fundenhall Street 164 C2
Funtington 108 A3
Funtley 107 E2
Funzie 278 F3
Furley 103 F2
Furnace A&B 240 C4
Furnace Carmar 128 B2
Furnace Cere 154 C3
Furnace High 265 F4
Furnace End 159 E3
Furner's Green 109 G1
Furness Vale 185 E4
Furneux Pelham 150 C5
Furnham 103 G2
Further Quarter 124 A5
Furtho 148 C3
Furze Green 164 D3
Furze Platt 135 D4
Furzehill Devon 114 A3
Furzehill Dorset 105 G2
Furzeley Corner 107 F1
Furzey Lodge 106 C2
Furzley 106 B1
Fyfett 103 F1
Fyfield Essex 137 E2
Fyfield Glos 133 E2
Fyfield Hants 119 D3
Fyfield Oxon 133 G3
Fyfield Wilts 118 C1
Fyfield Wilts 118 C1
Fylingthorpe 204 C2
Fyning 120 D5
Fyvie 261 F1

G

Gabalfa 130 A5
Gabhsann Bho Dheas 271 G2
Gabhsann Bho Thuath 271 G2
Gablon 266 E2
Gabroc Hill 233 F4
Gaddesby 160 B1
Gaddesden Row 135 F1
Gadebridge 135 F2
Gadshill 137 G5
Gaer Newport 130 B4
Gaer Powys 144 A5
Gaer-fawr 130 D3
Gaerllwyd 130 D3
Gaerwen 180 C5
Gagingwell 147 G5
Gaich High 259 H2
Gaich High 258 D1
Gaick Lodge 250 C1
Gailes 224 B2
Gailey 158 B1
Gainford 202 A1
Gainsborough 187 F3
Gainsford End 151 F4
Gairloch (Geàrrloch) 264 D4
Gairlochy (Geàrr Lòchaidh) 249 D1
Gairney Bank 243 G5
Gairnshiel Lodge 259 K4
Gaitsgill 209 G2
Galabank 236 B5
Galashiels 227 F2
Galbally 281 K2
Galboly 287 G3
Galdenoch 214 C4
Gale 184 D1
Galgate 192 A2
Galgorm 286 E5
Galhampton 116 D5
Gallanach 240 A2

Gra - Ham

Grange *Mid Ulster* **282** B1
Grange *P&K* **244** A2
Grange Blundel **282** B3
Grange Corner **286** E6
Grange Crossroads **268** C5
Grange de Lings **187** G5
Grange Hall **267** H5
Grange Hill **136** D3
Grange Moor **185** G1
Grange of Lindores **244** A3
Grange Villa **212** B2
Grangee **283** J1
Grangemill **172** D2
Grangemouth **234** D1
Grangemuir **244** D4
Grange-over-Sands **199** F5
Grangeston **214** D1
Grangetown *Cardiff* **130** A5
Grangetown *R&C* **213** E5
Granish **259** G3
Gransha *AB&C* **283** F4
Gransha *L&C* **283** H2
Gransha *M&EAnt* **287** J6
Gransmoor **196** D2
Granston **140** B4
Grantchester **150** C2
Grantham **175** E4
Grantley **202** B5
Grantlodge **261** F3
Granton **235** G2
Granton House **226** B5
Grantown-on-Spey **259** H2
Grantsfield **145** E1
Grantshouse **237** F3
Granville **282** A2
Grappenhall **184** A4
Grasby **188** A2
Grasmere **199** E2
Grass Green **151** F4
Grasscroft **185** D2
Grassendale **183** E4
Grassgarth **199** F3
Grassholme **211** F5
Grassington **193** G1
Grassmoor **173** F1
Grassthorpe **174** C1
Grateley **119** D3
Gratwich **172** B4
Gravel Hill **135** F3
Graveley *Cambs* **150** A1
Graveley *Herts* **150** A5
Gravelly Hill **158** D3
Gravels **156** C2
Graven **278** D5
Graveney **124** C2
Gravesend **137** F5
Grayingham **187** G3
Grayrigg **199** G3
Grays **137** F5
Grayshott **121** D4
Grayswood **121** E4
Grazeley **120** B1
Greasbrough **186** B3
Greasby **183** D4
Great Aberystwyth Camera Obscura *Cere* SY23 2DN **154** B4
Great Abington **150** D3
Great Addington **161** E5
Great Alne **146** D2
Great Altcar **183** E2
Great Amwell **136** C1
Great Asby **200** B1
Great Ashfield **152** A1
Great Ayton **203** E1
Great Baddow **137** G2
Great Bardfield **151** E4
Great Barford **149** G2
Great Barr **158** C3
Great Barrington **133** E1
Great Barrow **170** B1
Great Barton **151** G1
Great Barugh **203** G5
Great Bavington **220** B3
Great Bealings **152** D3
Great Bedwyn **119** D1
Great Bentley **152** C5
Great Bernera **270** D4
Great Billing **148** D1
Great Bircham **177** F4
Great Blakenham **152** C2
Great Bolas **170** D5
Great Bookham **121** G2
Great Bourton **147** G3
Great Bowden **160** C4
Great Bradley **151** E2
Great Braxted **138** B1
Great Bricett **152** B2
Great Brickhill **149** E4
Great Bridgeford **171** F5
Great Brington **148** B1
Great Bromley **152** B5
Great Broughton *Cumb* **209** D3
Great Broughton *NYorks* **203** E2
Great Buckland **123** F2
Great Budworth **184** A5
Great Burdon **202** C1
Great Burstead **137** F3
Great Busby **203** E2
Great Cambourne **150** B2
Great Canfield **137** E1
Great Canney **138** B2
Great Carlton **189** E4
Great Casterton **161** F2
Great Chalfield **117** F1
Great Chart **124** B4
Great Chatwell **157** G1
Great Chell **171** F2
Great Chesterford **150** D3
Great Cheverell **118** A2
Great Chishill **150** C4
Great Clacton **139** E1
Great Clifton **208** D4
Great Coates **188** C2
Great Comberton **146** B3
Great Corby **210** A2
Great Cornard **151** G3
Great Cowden **197** E3
Great Coxwell **133** E3
Great Crakehall **202** B4
Great Cransley **160** D5
Great Cressingham **163** G2
Great Crosby **183** E2
Great Crosthwaite **209** F4
Great Cubley **172** C4
Great Cumbrae **232** C4
Great Dalby **160** C1
Great Doddington **149** D1
Great Doward **131** E1
Great Dunham **163** G1
Great Dunmow **151** E5
Great Dunford **118** C4
Great Easton *Essex* **151** E5
Great Easton *Leics* **160** D3
Great Eccleston **192** A3
Great Edstone **203** G4
Great Ellingham **164** B2
Great Elm **117** E3
Great Eversden **150** B2
Great Fencote **202** B3
Great Finborough **152** B2
Great Fransham **163** G1
Great Gaddesden **135** F1
Great Gidding **161** G4
Great Givendale **196** A2
Great Glemham **153** E1
Great Glen **160** B3
Great Gonerby **175** D4
Great Gransden **150** A2
Great Green *Cambs* **150** A3
Great Green *Norf* **165** D3
Great Green *Suff* **152** A2
Great Green *Suff* **164** C4
Great Green *Suff* **164** B4
Great Habton **203** G5
Great Hale **175** G3
Great Hall *Hants* SO23 8UJ **89** Winchester
Great Hallingbury **137** E1
Great Hampden **134** D2
Great Harrowden **161** D5
Great Harwood **192** D4
Great Haseley **134** B2
Great Hatfield **197** D3
Great Haywood **172** B5
Great Heath **159** F4
Great Heck **195** E5
Great Henny **151** G4
Great Hinton **118** A2
Great Hockham **164** A2
Great Holland **139** F1
Great Horkesley **152** A4
Great Hormead **150** C4
Great Horton **194** A4
Great Horwood **148** C4
Great Houghton *N'hants* **148** C2
Great Houghton *SYorks* **186** B2
Great Hucklow **185** F5
Great Kelk **196** D2
Great Kimble **134** D2
Great Kingshill **135** D3
Great Langton **202** B3
Great Leighs **137** G1
Great Limber **188** B2
Great Linford **148** D3
Great Livermere **163** G5
Great Longstone **185** G5
Great Lumley **212** B3
Great Lyth **157** D2
Great Malvern **145** G3
Great Maplestead **151** G4
Great Marton **191** G4
Great Massingham **177** F5
Great Melton **178** C5
Great Milton **134** B2
Great Missenden **135** D2
Great Mitton **192** D4
Great Mongeham **125** F3
Great Moulton **164** C2
Great Munden **150** B5
Great Musgrave **200** C1
Great Ness **156** D1
Great Notley **151** F5
Great Nurcot **114** C4
Great Oak **130** C2
Great Oakley *Essex* **152** C5
Great Oakley *N'hants* **161** D4
Great Offley **149** G5
Great Orme Tramway *Conwy* LL30 2HG **181** F4
Great Ormside **200** C1
Great Orton **209** G1
Great Ouseburn **194** D1
Great Oxendon **160** C4
Great Oxney Green **137** F2
Great Palgrave **163** G1
Great Parndon **136** D2
Great Paxton **150** A1
Great Plumpton **191** G4
Great Plumstead **179** E5
Great Ponton **175** E4
Great Potheridge **113** F4
Great Preston **194** C5
Great Purston **148** A4
Great Raveley **162** A4
Great Rissington **133** D1
Great Rollright **147** F4
Great Ryburgh **178** A3
Great Ryle **229** E5
Great Ryton **157** D2
Great St. Mary's Church *Cambs* CB2 3PQ **66** Cambridge
Great Saling **151** F5
Great Salkeld **210** B4
Great Sampford **151** E4
Great Sankey **183** G4
Great Saredon **158** B2
Great Saxham **151** F1
Great Shefford **133** F5
Great Shelford **150** C2
Great Smeaton **202** C2
Great Snoring **178** A2
Great Somerford **132** B4
Great Stainton **212** C5
Great Stambridge **138** C3
Great Staughton **149** G1
Great Steeping **176** C1
Great Stonar **125** F3
Great Strickland **210** B5
Great Stukeley **162** A5
Great Sturton **188** C5
Great Sutton *ChesW&C* **183** E5
Great Sutton *Shrop* **157** E4
Great Swinburne **220** B4
Great Tew **147** F5
Great Tey **151** G5
Great Thorness **107** D3
Great Thurlow **151** E3
Great Torr **100** C3
Great Torrington **113** E4
Great Tosson **220** C1
Great Totham *Essex* **138** B1
Great Totham *Essex* **138** B1
Great Tows **188** C3
Great Urswick **199** D5
Great Wakering **138** C4
Great Waldingfield **152** A3
Great Walsingham **178** A2
Great Waltham **137** F1
Great Warley **137** E3
Great Washbourne **146** B4
Great Weeke **102** A4
Great Welnetham **151** G2
Great Wenham **152** B4
Great Whittington **220** C4
Great Wigborough **138** C1
Great Wigsell **110** C1
Great Wilbraham **150** D2
Great Wilne **173** F4
Great Wishford **118** B4
Great Witcombe **132** B1
Great Witley **145** G1
Great Wolford **147** E4
Great Wratting **151** E3
Great Wymondley **150** A5
Great Wyrley **158** B2
Great Wytheford **157** E1
Great Yarmouth **179** G5
Great Yeldham **151** F4
Greatford **161** F1
Greatgate **172** B3
Greatham *Hants* **120** C4
Greatham *Hart* **213** D5
Greatham *WSuss* **108** C2
Greatness **123** E3
Greatstone-on-Sea **111** F1
Greatworth **148** A3
Green **169** D1
Green Cross **121** D4
Green End *Bed* **149** G2
Green End *Bucks* **149** E4
Green End *Cambs* **162** A5
Green End *Cambs* **162** B5
Green End *Herts* **150** B5
Green End *Herts* **150** B4
Green End *Warks* **159** E4
Green Hammerton **195** D2
Green Hill **132** C4
Green Lane **146** C1
Green Moor **185** G3
Green Ore **116** C2
Green Quarter **199** F2
Green Street *ESuss* **110** C2
Green Street *Herts* **136** A3
Green Street *Herts* **150** C5
Green Street *Worcs* **146** A3
Green Street *WSuss* **121** G5
Green Street Green *GtLon* **123** D2
Green Street Green *Kent* **137** E5
Green Tye **136** D1
Greenan **282** E6
Greenburn **252** C5
Greencastle *F&O* **285** H7
Greencastle *NM&D* **283** F7
Greencroft **212** A3
Greendams **253** E1
Greendykes **229** E4
Greenend **147** F5
Greenfaulds **234** B2
Greenfield *CenBeds* **149** F4
Greenfield (Maes-Glas) *Flints* **182** C5
Greenfield *GtMan* **185** E2
Greenfield *High* **257** J4
Greenfield *Lincs* **189** E5
Greenfield *NM&D* **283** G7
Greenfield *Oxon* **134** C3
Greenford **136** A4
Greengairs **234** B2
Greengates **194** A4
Greengill **209** E3
Greenhalgh **192** A4
Greenhall **260** E2
Greenham **119** F1
Greenhaugh **219** F3
Greenhead **210** C1
Greenheads **261** J1
Greenheys **184** B2
Greenhill *D&G* **217** F3
Greenhill *GtLon* **136** A4
Greenhill *High* **267** G1
Greenhill *SYorks* **186** A4
Greenhithe **137** E5
Greenholm **224** D2
Greenholme **199** G2
Greenhow Hill **194** A1
Greenigo **277** D7
Greenisland **287** H7
Greenland **275** H2
Greenlands **134** C4
Greenlaw *Aber* **268** E5
Greenlaw *ScBord* **237** E5
Greenloaning **242** D4
Greenmeadow **130** B3
Greenmoor Hill **134** B4
Greenmount **184** B1
Greenmyre **261** G1
Greenock **233** D2
Greenodd **199** E4
Greens Norton **148** B3
Greenscares **242** C3
Greenside *T&W* **212** A1
Greenside *WYorks* **185** F1
Greenstead **152** B5
Greenstead Green **151** G5
Greensted **137** E2
Greensted Green **137** E2
Greenville **285** F7
Greenway *Pembs* **141** D4
Greenway *Som* **116** A5
Greenwell **210** B2
Greenwich **136** C5
Greenwood Forest Park, Y Felinheli *Gwyn* LL56 4QN **167** E1
Greerstown **283** F2
Greet **146** C4
Greete **157** E5
Greetham *Lincs* **188** D5
Greetham *Rut* **161** E1
Greetland **193** G5
Gregson Lane **192** B5
Greinton **116** B4
Grenaby **190** A4
Grendon *N'hants* **149** D1
Grendon *Warks* **159** E3
Grendon Common **159** E3
Grendon Green **145** E2
Grendon Underwood **148** B5
Grenitote (Greinetobht) **262** D4
Grenofen **99** E3
Grenoside **186** A3
Greosabhagh **263** G2
Gresford **170** A2
Gresham **178** C2
Greshornish **263** J6
Gress (Griais) **271** G3
Gressenhall **178** A4
Gressingham **192** B1
Greta Bridge **201** F1
Gretna **218** B5
Gretna Green **218** B5
Gretton *Glos* **146** C4
Gretton *N'hants* **161** E3
Gretton *Shrop* **157** E3
Grewelthorpe **202** B5
Greyabbey **283** J2
Greygarth **202** A5
Greylake **116** A4
Greys Green **134** C4
Greysouthen **209** D4
Greystead **219** F3
Greysteel **285** H3
Greystoke **210** A4
Greystone *Aber* **259** K5
Greystone *Angus* **252** D5
Greystone *Lancs* **193** E3
Greystones **186** A4
Greywell **120** C2
Gribthorpe **195** G4
Gribton **216** D2
Griff **159** F4
Griffithstown **130** B3
Grigadale **246** D3
Grigghall **199** F3
Grimeford Village **184** A1
Grimesthorpe **186** A3
Grimethorpe **186** B2
Griminish (Griminis) **262** C6
Grimister **278** D3
Grimley **146** A1
Grimmet **224** B4
Grimness **277** D8
Grimoldby **189** D4
Grimpo **170** A5
Grimsargh **192** B4
Grimsay (Griomsaigh) **262** D6
Grimsbury **147** G3
Grimsby **188** C2
Grimscote **148** B2
Grimscott **112** C5
Grimshader (Griomsiadar) **271** G5
Grimsthorpe **175** F5
Grimston *ERid* **197** E4
Grimston *Leics* **174** B5
Grimston *Norf* **177** F5
Grimstone **104** C3
Grimstone End **152** A1
Grindale **205** E5
Grindiscol **279** D9
Grindle **157** G2
Grindleford **185** G5
Grindleton **193** D3
Grindley **172** B5
Grindley Brook **170** C3
Grindlow **185** F5
Grindon *N'umb* **237** G5
Grindon *Staffs* **172** B2
Grindon *Stock* **212** C5
Grindon *T&W* **212** C2
Gringley on the Hill **187** E3
Grinsdale **209** G1
Grinshill **170** C5
Grinton **201** F3
Griomarstaidh **270** E4
Grisdale **200** C3
Grishipoll **246** A4
Gristhorpe **205** D4
Griston **164** A2
Gritley **277** E7
Grittenham **132** C4
Grittleton **132** A5
Grizebeck **198** D4
Grizedale **199** E3
Grizedale Forest Park *Cumb* LA22 0QJ **199** E3
Grobister **276** F5
Groby **160** A2
Groes **168** D1
Groes-faen **129** G4
Groesffordd **166** B4
Groesffordd Marli **182** B5
Groeslon *Gwyn* **167** D2
Groeslon *Gwyn* **167** E1
Groes-lwyd **156** B1
Groes-wen **130** A4
Grogport **231** G5
Groigearraidh **254** C1
Gromford **153** E2
Gronant **182** B4
Groombridge **123** E5
Groombridge Place Gardens *Kent* TN3 9QG **123** E5
Groomsport **287** K7
Grosmont *Mon* **144** D5
Grosmont *NYorks* **204** B2
Grotaig **258** B2
Groton **152** A3
Groundistone Heights **227** F4
Grouville **100** C5
Grove *Bucks* **149** E5
Grove *Dorset* **104** C5
Grove *Kent* **125** E2
Grove *Notts* **187** E5
Grove *Oxon* **133** G3
Grove End **124** A2
Grove Green **123** G3
Grove Park **136** D5
Grove Town **195** D5
Grovehill **135** F2
Grovesend *SGlos* **131** F4
Grovesend *Swan* **128** B2
Gruids **266** C1
Grula **255** J2
Gruline **247** E5
Grumbla **94** B4
Grundcruie **243** F2
Grundisburgh **152** D2
Gruting **279** B8
Grutness **279** G10
Gualachulain **248** D5
Guardbridge **244** C3
Guarlford **146** A3
Guay **251** F5
Gubbergill **198** B3
Gubblecote **135** E1
Guernsey **101** F5
Guernsey Airport **101** E5
Guestling Green **111** D2
Guestling Thorn **111** D2
Guestwick **178** B3
Guestwick Green **178** B3
Guide **192** D5
Guide Post **221** E3
Guilden Down **156** C4
Guilden Morden **150** A3
Guilden Sutton **170** B1
Guildford **121** E3
Guildford House Gallery *Surr* GU1 3AJ **74** Guildford
Guildtown **243** G1
Guilsborough **160** B5
Guilsfield (Cegidfa) **156** B1
Guilthwaite **186** B4
Guisborough **203** F1
Guiseley **194** A3
Guist **178** B3
Guith **276** E4
Guiting Power **146** C5
Gulberwick **279** D9
Gulladuff **286** C6
Gullane **236** B1
Gullane Bents *ELoth* EH31 2AZ **236** B1
Gulval **94** B3
Gulworthy **99** E3
Gumfreston **127** E2
Gumley **160** B3
Gunby *Lincs* **175** E5
Gunby *Lincs* **176** C1
Gundleton **120** B4
Gunn **113** G2
Gunnersbury **136** A5
Gunnerside **201** E3
Gunnerton **220** B4
Gunness **187** F1
Gunnislake **99** E3
Gunnista **279** E8
Gunnister **278** C5
Gunstone **158** A2
Gunter's Bridge **121** E5
Gunthorpe *Norf* **178** B2
Gunthorpe *Notts* **174** B3
Gunthorpe *Rut* **161** D2
Gunville **107** D4
Gunwalloe **95** D4
Gupworthy **114** C4
Gurnard **107** D3
Gurnett **184** D5
Gurney Slade **116** D3
Gurnos *MTyd* **129** G2
Gurnos *Powys* **129** D2
Gushmere **124** C3
Gussage All Saints **105** G1
Gussage St. Andrew **105** F1
Gussage St. Michael **105** F1
Guston **125** F4
Gutcher **278** E3
Guthram Gowt **175** G5
Guthrie **253** D4
Guyhirn **162** B2
Guynd **253** D5
Guy's Head **176** C5
Guy's Marsh **117** F5
Guyzance **221** E1
Gwaelod-y-garth **130** A4
Gwaenysgor **182** B4
Gwaithla **144** B2
Gwalchmai **180** B5
Gwastad **140** D5
Gwastadnant **167** F2
Gwaun-Cae-Gurwen **128** D1
Gwaynynog **168** D1
Gwbert **141** E3
Gweek **95** E4
Gwehelog **130** C2
Gwenddwr **143** G3
Gwendreath **95** E5
Gwennap **96** B5
Gwennap Mining District (Cornwall & West Devon Mining Landscape) *Corn* **96** B5
Gwenter **95** E5
Gwernaffield **169** F1
Gwernesney **130** D2
Gwernogle **142** B4
Gwernymynydd **169** F1
Gwern-y-Steeple **129** G5
Gwersyllt **170** A2
Gwespyr **182** C4
Gwinear **94** C3
Gwithian **94** C2
Gwredog **180** C4
Gwrhay **130** A3
Gwyddelwern **169** D3
Gwyddgrug **142** A4
Gwynfryn **169** F2
Gwystre **143** G1
Gwytherin **168** B1
Gyfelia **170** A3
Gyre **277** C7
Gyrn Goch **166** D3

H

H.M.S. Belfast *GtLon* SE1 2JH **12** C4
H.M.S. Victory PO1 3PX **82** Portsmouth
H.M.S. Warrior PO1 3QX **82** Portsmouth
Habberley **156** C2
Habin **120** D5
Habost (Tabost) **271** F6
Habrough **188** B1
Haccombe **102** B5
Hacconby **175** G5
Haceby **175** F4
Hacheston **153** E2
Hackbridge **122** B2
Hackenthorpe **186** B4
Hackford **178** B5
Hackforth **202** B3
Hackland **276** C5
Hacklet (Haclait) **262** D7
Hacklete (Tacleit) **270** D4
Hackleton **148** D2
Hacklinge **125** F3
Hackness *NYorks* **204** C3
Hackness *Ork* **277** C8
Hackney **136** C4
Hackthorn **187** G4
Hackthorpe **210** B5
Hacton **137** E4
Hadden **228** B3
Haddenham *Bucks* **134** C2
Haddenham *Cambs* **162** C5
Haddington *ELoth* **236** C2
Haddington *Lincs* **175** E1
Haddiscoe **165** F2
Haddo Country Park *Aber* AB41 7EQ **261** G1
Haddon **161** G3
Hade Edge **185** F2
Hademore **159** D2
Hadfield **185** E3
Hadham Cross **136** D1
Hadham Ford **150** C5
Hadleigh *Essex* **138** B4
Hadleigh *Suff* **152** B3
Hadleigh Castle Country Park *Essex* SS7 2PP **138** B4
Hadleigh Farm *Essex* SS7 2AP **138** B4
Hadleigh Heath **152** A3
Hadley *Tel&W* **157** F1
Hadley *Worcs* **146** A1
Hadley End **172** C5
Hadley Wood **136** B3
Hadlow **123** F4
Hadlow Down **110** A1
Hadnall **170** C5
Hadrian's Wall (Frontiers of the Roman Empire) *Cumb/N'umb* **210** C1 & **211** G1
Hadspen **117** D4
Hadstock **151** D3
Hadston **221** E2
Hadzor **146** B1
Haffenden Quarter **124** A4
Hafod Bridge **142** C4
Hafod-Dinbych **168** B2
Hafodunos **168** B1
Hafodyrynys **130** B3
Haggate **193** E4
Haggbeck **218** C4
Haggersta **279** C8
Haggerston *GtLon* **136** C4
Haggerston *N'umb* **229** E2
Haggrister **278** C5
Haggs **234** B2
Hagley *Here* **145** E3
Hagley *Worcs* **158** B4
Hagnaby *Lincs* **176** B1
Hagnaby *Lincs* **189** E5
Hague Bar **185** D4
Hagworthingham **176** B1
Haigh **184** A2
Haigh Hall Country Park *GtMan* WN2 1PE **183** G2
Haighton Green **192** B4
Hail Weston **149** G1
Haile **198** B2
Hailes **146** C4
Hailey *Herts* **136** C1
Hailey *Oxon* **134** B4
Hailey *Oxon* **133** F1
Hailsham **110** A3
Haimer **275** G2
Hainault **137** D3
Hainault Forest Country Park *Essex* IG7 4QN **137** D3
Haine **125** F2
Hainford **178** D4
Hainton **188** B4
Haisthorpe **196** D1
Hakin **126** B2
Halam **174** B2
Halbeath **235** F1
Halberton **102** D1
Halcro **275** H2
Hale *Cumb* **199** G5
Hale *GtMan* **184** B4
Hale *Halton* **183** F4
Hale *Hants* **106** A1
Hale *Surr* **120** D3
Hale Bank **183** F4
Hale Barns **184** B4
Hale Nook **191** G3
Hale Street **123** F4
Hales *Norf* **165** E2
Hales *Staffs* **171** E4
Hales Green **172** C3
Hales Place **124** D3
Halesgate **176** B5
Halesowen **158** B4
Halesworth **165** E4
Halewood **183** F4
Half Way Inn **102** D3
Halford *Devon* **102** B5
Halford *Shrop* **156** D4
Halford *Warks* **147** E3
Halfpenny **199** G4
Halfpenny Green **158** A3
Halfway *Carmar* **142** C4
Halfway *Carmar* **128** B2
Halfway *Powys* **143** E4
Halfway *SYorks* **186** B4
Halfway *WBerks* **119** F1
Halfway Bridge **121** E5
Halfway House **156** C1
Halfway Houses *Kent* **124** B1
Halfway Houses *Lincs* **175** D1
Halghton Mill **170** B3
Halifax **193** G5
Halistra **263** H6
Halket **233** F4
Halkirk **275** G3
Halkyn **182** D5
Hall **233** F4
Hall Cross **192** A5
Hall Dunnerdale **198** D3
Hall Green *ChesE* **171** F2
Hall Green *Lancs* **192** A5
Hall Green *WMid* **158** D4
Hall Grove **136** B1
Hall of the Forest **156** B4
Halland **110** A2
Hallaton **160** C3
Hallatrow **116** D2
Hallbankgate **210** B2
Hallen **131** E4
Hallfield Gate **173** E2
Hallglen **234** C2
Hallin **263** H6
Halling **123** G2
Hallington *Lincs* **188** D4
Hallington *N'umb* **220** B4
Halliwell **184** A1
Halloughton **174** B2
Hallow **146** A2
Hallow Heath **146** A2
Hallrule **227** G4
Halls **237** D2
Halls Green *Essex* **136** D2
Hall's Green *Herts* **150** A5
Hallsands **101** E4
Hallthwaites **198** C4
Hallwood Green **145** F4
Hallworthy **97** F1
Hallyne **235** F5
Halmer End **171** E3
Halmond's Frome **145** F3
Halmore **131** F2
Halmyre Mains **235** F5
Halnaker **108** B3
Halsall **183** E1
Halse *N'hants* **148** A3
Halse *Som* **115** E5
Halsetown **94** C3
Halsham **197** E5
Halsinger **113** F2
Halstead *Essex* **151** G4
Halstead *Kent* **123** D2
Halstead *Leics* **160** C2
Halstock **104** B2
Halsway **115** E4
Haltemprice Farm **196** C4
Haltham **176** A1
Haltoft End **176** B3
Halton *Bucks* **135** D1
Halton *Halton* **183** G4
Halton *Lancs* **192** B1
Halton *N'umb* **211** F1
Halton *Wrex* **170** A4
Halton East **193** G2
Halton Gill **201** D5
Halton Green **192** B1
Halton Holegate **176** C1
Halton Lea Gate **210** C2
Halton Park **192** B1
Halton West **193** E2
Haltwhistle **210** D1
Halvergate **179** F5
Halwell **101** D2
Halwill **99** E1
Halwill Junction **99** E1
Ham *Devon* **103** F2
Ham *Glos* **131** F3
Ham *Glos* **146** B5
Ham *GtLon* **136** A5
Ham *High* **275** H1
Ham *Kent* **125** F3
Ham *Plym* **100** A2
Ham *Shet* **278** B1
Ham *Som* **115** F5
Ham *Som* **103** F1
Ham *Wilts* **119** E1
Ham Common **117** F5
Ham Green *Here* **145** G3
Ham Green *Kent* **124** A2
Ham Green *Kent* **111** D1
Ham Green *NSom* **131** E5
Ham Green *Worcs* **146** C1
Ham Hill **123** F2
Ham Hill Country Park *Som* TA14 6RW **104** A1
Ham Street **116** C4
Hambleden **134** C4
Hambledon *Hants* **107** F1
Hambledon *Surr* **121** E4
Hamble-le-Rice **107** D2
Hambleton *Lancs* **191** G3
Hambleton *NYorks* **195** E4
Hambridge **116** A5
Hambrook *SGlos* **131** F5
Hambrook *WSuss* **107** G2
Hameringham **176** B1
Hamerton **161** G5
Hamilton **234** B4
Hamilton's Bawn **282** C4
Hamlet *Devon* **103** E3
Hamlet *Dorset* **104** B2
Hammer **121** D4
Hammerpot **108** C3
Hammersmith **136** B5
Hammersmith Apollo *GtLon* W6 9QH **11** E5
Hammerwich **158** C2
Hammerwood **122** D5
Hammond Street **136** C2
Hammoon **105** E1
Hamnavoe *Shet* **279** C9
Hamnavoe *Shet* **278** D4
Hamnavoe *Shet* **278** B4
Hamnavoe *Shet* **278** D5
Hamnish Clifford **145** E2
Hamp **115** F4
Hampden Park **110** B3
Hampden Park Stadium *Glas* G42 9BA **30** D4
Hamperden End **151** D4
Hampnett **132** D1
Hampole **186** C2
Hampreston **105** G3
Hampstead **136** B4
Hampstead Norreys **134** A5
Hampsthwaite **194** B2
Hampton *Devon* **103** F3
Hampton *GtLon* **121** G1
Hampton *Kent* **125** D2
Hampton *Peter* **161** G3
Hampton *Shrop* **157** G4
Hampton *Swin* **133** D3
Hampton *Worcs* **146** C3

Hampton Bishop 145 E4
Hampton Court Palace & Garden GtLon KT8 9AU 11 B8
Hampton Fields 132 A3
Hampton Heath 170 B3
Hampton in Arden 159 E4
Hampton Loade 157 G4
Hampton Lovett 146 A1
Hampton Lucy 147 E2
Hampton on the Hill 147 E1
Hampton Poyle 134 A1
Hampton Wick 121 G1
Hamptworth 106 B1
Hamsey 109 G2
Hamstall Ridware 158 D1
Hamstead 106 C3
Hamstead Marshall 119 F1
Hamsteels 212 A3
Hamsterley Dur 212 A4
Hamsterley Dur 212 A2
Hamsterley Forest Dur DL13 3NL 211 G5
Hamstreet 124 C5
Hamworthy 105 F3
Hanbury Staffs 172 C5
Hanbury Worcs 146 B1
Hanbury Woodend 172 C5
Hanby 175 F4
Hanchurch 171 F3
Handa Island 272 D4
Handale 203 G1
Handbridge 170 B1
Handcross 122 B5
Handforth 184 C4
Handley ChesW&C 170 B2
Handley Derbys 173 E1
Handley Green 137 F2
Handsacre 158 C1
Handside 136 B1
Handsworth SYorks 186 B4
Handsworth WMid 158 C3
Handwoodbank 156 D1
Handy Cross 135 D3
Hanford Dorset 105 E1
Hanford Stoke 171 F3
Hanging Bridge 172 C3
Hanging Houghton 160 C5
Hanging Langford 118 B4
Hangingshaw 217 F2
Hanham 131 F5
Hankelow 171 D3
Hankerton 132 B3
Hankham 110 B3
Hanley 171 F3
Hanley Castle 146 A3
Hanley Child 145 F1
Hanley Swan 146 A3
Hanley William 145 F1
Hanlith 193 F1
Hanmer 170 B4
Hannah 189 E5
Hannahstown 283 F1
Hannington Hants 119 G2
Hannington N'hants 160 D5
Hannington Swin 133 D3
Hannington Wick 133 D3
Hanslope 148 D3
Hanthorpe 175 F5
Hanwell GtLon 136 A4
Hanwell Oxon 147 G3
Hanwood 156 D2
Hanworth GtLon 136 A5
Hanworth Norf 178 C2
Happisburgh 179 E2
Happisburgh Common 179 E3
Hapsford 183 F5
Hapton Lancs 193 D4
Hapton Norf 164 C2
Harberton 101 D2
Harbertonford 101 D2
Harbledown 124 D3
Harborne 158 C4
Harborough Magna 159 G5
Harbottle 220 B1
Harbour Park Amusements, Littlehampton WSuss BN17 5LL 108 C3
Harbourneford 100 D1
Harbridge 106 A1
Harbridge Green 106 A1
Harburn 235 E3
Harbury 147 F2
Harby Leics 174 C4
Harby Notts 187 F5
Harcombe 103 E3
Harcombe Bottom 103 G3
Harden WMid 158 C2
Harden WYorks 193 G4
Hardendale 199 G1
Hardenhuish 132 B5
Hardgate Aber 261 F4
Hardgate NYorks 194 B1
Hardham 108 C2
Hardhorn 191 G4
Hardingham 178 B5
Hardingstone 148 C2
Hardington 117 E2
Hardington Mandeville 104 B1
Hardington Marsh 104 B2
Hardington Moor 104 B1
Hardley 106 D2
Hardley Street 179 E5
Hardmead 149 E3
Hardraw 201 D3
Hardstoft 173 F1
Hardway Hants 107 F2
Hardway Som 117 E4
Hardwick Bucks 134 D1
Hardwick Cambs 150 B2
Hardwick Lincs 187 F5
Hardwick N'hants 149 D1
Hardwick Norf 164 D2
Hardwick Oxon 133 F2
Hardwick Oxon 148 A5
Hardwick SYorks 186 B4
Hardwick WMid 158 C3
Hardwick Hall Derbys S44 5QJ 173 F1
Hardwick Hall Country Park, Sedgefield Dur TS21 2EH 212 C5
Hardwick Village 186 D5
Hardwicke Glos 146 B5
Hardwicke Glos 131 G1
Hardwicke Here 144 B3
Hardy's Green 152 A5
Hare Green 152 B5
Hare Hatch 134 D5
Hare Street Herts 150 B5
Hare Street Herts 150 B5
Hareby 176 B1
Harecroft 193 G4
Hareden 192 C2
Harefield 135 F3
Harehill 172 C4
Harehills 194 C4
Harehope 229 E4
Harelaw 234 D5
Hareplain 124 A5
Haresceugh 210 C3
Harescombe 132 A1
Haresfield 132 A1
Hareshaw NLan 234 C3
Hareshaw SLan 234 A5
Harestock 119 F4
Harewood 194 C3
Harewood End 145 E5
Harewood House WYorks LS17 9LG 194 C3
Harford Devon 100 C2
Harford Devon 102 B3
Hargate 164 C2
Hargatewall 185 F5
Hargrave ChesW&C 170 B1
Hargrave N'hants 161 F5
Hargrave Suff 151 F2
Hargrave Green 151 F2
Harker 218 B5
Harkstead 152 C4
Harlaston 159 E1
Harlaxton 175 D4
Harle Syke 193 E4
Harlech 167 E4
Harlech Castle (Castles & Town Walls of King Edward in Gwynedd) Gwyn LL46 2YH 167 E4
Harlequin 174 B4
Harlescott 157 E1
Harlesden 136 B4
Harleston Devon 101 D3
Harleston Norf 164 D3
Harleston Suff 152 B1
Harlestone 148 C1
Harley Shrop 157 E2
Harley SYorks 186 A3
Harleyholm 226 A2
Harlington CenBeds 149 F4
Harlington GtLon 135 F5
Harlosh 263 H7
Harlow 136 D2
Harlow Hill 211 G1
Harlthorpe 195 G4
Harlton 150 B2
Harlyn 96 C2
Harman's Cross 105 F4
Harmby 202 A4
Harmer Green 136 B1
Harmer Hill 170 B5
Harmondsworth 135 F5
Harmston 175 E1
Harnage 157 E2
Harnham 118 C5
Harnhill 132 C2
Harold Hill 137 E3
Harold Park 137 E3
Harold Wood 137 E3
Haroldston West 126 B1
Haroldswick 278 F1
Harome 203 F4
Harpenden 136 A1
Harpford 103 D3
Harpham 196 C1
Harpley Norf 177 F5
Harpley Worcs 145 F1
Harpole 148 B1
Harprigg 200 B4
Harpsdale 275 G3
Harpsden 134 C4
Harpswell 187 G4
Harpur Hill 185 E5
Harpurhey 184 C2
Harracott 113 F3
Harrapool 256 C2
Harrietfield 243 E2
Harrietsham 124 A3
Harringay 136 C4
Harrington Cumb 208 C4
Harrington Lincs 189 D5
Harrington N'hants 160 C5
Harringworth 161 E3
Harris 255 J5
Harris Green 164 D2
Harris Museum & Art Gallery, Preston Lancs PR1 2PP 192 B5
Harriseahead 171 F2
Harriston 209 E2
Harrogate 194 C2
Harrogate International Centre NYorks HG1 5LA 74 Harrogate
Harrold 149 E2
Harrold-Odell Country Park Bed MK43 7DS 149 E2
Harrop Fold 192 D3
Harrow GtLon 136 A4
Harrow High 275 H1
Harrow Green 151 G2
Harrow Museum GtLon HA2 6PX 10 B1
Harrow on the Hill 136 A4
Harrow Weald 136 A3
Harrowbarrow 99 E3
Harrowden 149 F3
Harrowgate Hill 202 B1
Harry Stoke 131 F5
Harston Cambs 150 C2
Harston Leics 174 D4
Harswell 196 A3
Hart 213 D4
Hartburn 220 C3
Hartest 151 G2
Hartfield ESuss 123 D5
Hartfield High 264 D7
Hartford Cambs 162 A5
Hartford ChesW&C 184 A5
Hartford Som 114 C5
Hartford End 137 F1
Hartfordbridge 120 C2
Hartforth 202 A2
Hartgrove 105 E1
Harthill ChesW&C 170 C2
Harthill NLan 234 D3
Harthill SYorks 186 B4
Hartington 172 C1
Hartington Hall 220 C3
Hartland 112 C3
Hartland Quay 112 C3
Hartlebury 158 A5
Hartlepool 213 E4
Hartlepool's Maritime Experience Hart TS24 0XZ 213 E4
Hartley Cumb 200 C2
Hartley Kent 123 F2
Hartley Kent 123 G5
Hartley N'umb 221 F4
Hartley Green 171 G5
Hartley Mauditt 120 C4
Hartley Wespall 120 B2
Hartley Wintney 120 C2
Hartlington 193 G1
Hartlip 124 A2
Hartoft End 203 G3
Harton NYorks 195 G1
Harton Shrop 157 D4
Harton T&W 212 C1
Hartpury 146 A5
Hartrigge 228 A4
Hartshead 194 A5
Hartshill 159 F3
Hartsholme Country Park Lincs LN6 0EY 175 E1
Hartshorne 173 E5
Hartsop 199 F1
Hartwell Bucks 134 C1
Hartwell ESuss 123 D5
Hartwell N'hants 148 C2
Hartwith 194 B1
Hartwood 234 C4
Harvel 123 F2
Harvington Worcs 146 C3
Harvington Worcs 158 A5
Harwell Notts 187 D3
Harwell Oxon 133 G4
Harwich 152 D4
Harwood Dur 211 E4
Harwood GtMan 184 B1
Harwood N'umb 220 C2
Harwood Dale 204 C3
Harwood on Teviot 227 F5
Harworth 186 D3
Hasbury 158 B4
Hascombe 121 F3
Haselbech 160 C5
Haselbury Plucknett 104 A1
Haseley 147 E1
Haseley Knob 159 E5
Haselor 146 D2
Hasfield 146 A5
Hasguard 126 B2
Haskayne 183 E2
Hasketon 153 D2
Hasland 173 E1
Hasland Green 173 E1
Haslemere 121 E4
Haslingden 193 D5
Haslingden Grane 193 D5
Haslingfield 150 C2
Haslington 171 E2
Hassall 171 E2
Hassall Green 171 E2
Hassell Street 124 C4
Hassendean 227 G3
Hassingham 179 E5
Hassocks 109 F2
Hassop 185 G5
Haster 275 J3
Hasthorpe 176 C1
Hastigrow 275 H2
Hastingleigh 124 C4
Hastings ESuss 110 D3
Hastings Som 103 G1
Hastings Fishermen's Museum ESuss TN34 3DW 75 Hastings
Hastingwood 137 D2
Hastoe 135 E2
Haswell 212 C3
Haswell Plough 212 C3
Hatch CenBeds 149 G3
Hatch Hants 120 B2
Hatch Beauchamp 116 A5
Hatch End 136 A3
Hatch Green 103 G1
Hatching Green 136 A1
Hatchmere 183 G5
Hatcliffe 188 C2
Hatfield Here 145 E2
Hatfield Herts 136 B2
Hatfield SYorks 187 D2
Hatfield Broad Oak 137 E1
Hatfield Heath 137 E1
Hatfield House Herts AL9 5NF 136 B2
Hatfield Peverel 137 G1
Hatfield Woodhouse 187 D2
Hatford 133 F3
Hatherden 119 E2
Hatherleigh 113 F5
Hathern 173 F5
Hatherop 133 D2
Hathersage 185 G4
Hathersage Booths 185 G4
Hathershaw 184 D2
Hatherton ChesE 171 D3
Hatherton Staffs 158 B1
Hatley St. George 150 A2
Hatt 99 D4
Hattingley 120 B4
Hatton Aber 261 J1
Hatton Derbys 172 D5
Hatton GtLon 136 A5
Hatton Lincs 188 B5
Hatton Shrop 157 D3
Hatton Warks 147 E1
Hatton Warr 183 G4
Hatton Castle 269 F6
Hatton Country World Warks CV35 8XA 147 E1
Hatton Heath 170 B1
Hatton of Fintray 261 G3
Hattoncrook 261 G2
Haugh 189 E5
Haugh Head 229 E4
Haugh of Glass 260 C1
Haugh of Urr 216 C4
Haugham 188 D4
Haughhead 234 A2
Haughley 152 B1
Haughley Green 152 B1
Haughley New Street 152 B1
Haughs 268 D6
Haughton ChesE 170 C2
Haughton Notts 187 D5
Haughton Powys 156 C1
Haughton Shrop 157 F3
Haughton Shrop 157 E1
Haughton Shrop 170 A5
Haughton Staffs 171 F5
Haughton Green 184 D3
Haughton Le Skerne 202 C1
Haultwick 150 B5
Haunn 254 C3
Haunton 159 E1
Hauxton 150 C2
Havannah 171 F1
Havant 107 G2
Haven 144 D2
Havenstreet 107 E3
Havercroft 186 A1
Haverfordwest (Hwlffordd) 126 C1
Haverhill 151 E3
Haverigg 198 C5
Havering Park 137 D3
Havering-atte-Bower 137 E3
Haversham 148 D3
Haverthwaite 199 E4
Haverton Hill 213 D5
Haviker Street 123 G4
Havyat 116 C4
Hawarden (Penarlâg) 170 A1
Hawbridge 146 B3
Hawbush Green 151 F5
Hawcoat 198 D5
Hawes 201 D4
Hawe's Green 164 D2
Hawick 227 G4
Hawkchurch 103 G2
Hawkedon 151 F2
Hawkenbury Kent 123 E5
Hawkenbury Kent 124 A4
Hawkeridge 117 F2
Hawkerland 103 D4
Hawkes End 159 E4
Hawkesbury 131 G4
Hawkesbury Upton 131 G4
Hawkhill 229 G5
Hawkhurst 123 G5
Hawkinge 125 E4
Hawkley 120 C5
Hawkridge 114 B4
Hawkshead 199 E3
Hawkshead Hill 199 E3
Hawksheads 192 A1
Hawksland 234 C5
Hawkswick 201 E5
Hawksworth Notts 174 C3
Hawksworth WYorks 194 A3
Hawksworth WYorks 194 B4
Hawkwell Essex 138 B3
Hawkwell N'umb 220 C4
Hawley Hants 121 D2
Hawley Kent 137 E5
Hawley's Corner 122 D3
Hawling 146 C5
Hawnby 203 E4
Haworth 193 G4
Hawstead 151 G2
Hawstead Green 151 G2
Hawthorn Dur 212 D3
Hawthorn Hants 120 B4
Hawthorn RCT 129 G4
Hawthorn Wilts 117 F1
Hawthorn Hill BrackF 135 D5
Hawthorn Hill Lincs 176 A2
Hawthorpe 175 F5
Hawton 174 C2
Haxby 195 F2
Haxey 187 E2
Haxted 122 D4
Haxton 118 C3
Hay Green 162 D1
Hay Mills 158 D4
Hay Street 150 B5
Haydock 183 G3
Haydon Dorset 104 C1
Haydon Swin 132 D4
Haydon Bridge 211 E1
Haydon Wick 132 D4
Hayes GtLon 135 F4
Hayes GtLon 122 D2
Hayes End 135 F4
Hayfield A&B 240 C2
Hayfield Derbys 185 E4
Hayfield Fife 244 A5
Hayfield High 275 G2
Haygrove 115 F4
Hayhillock 252 D5
Hayle 94 C3
Hayling Island 107 G2
Haymoor Green 171 D2
Hayne 102 C1
Haynes 149 G3
Haynes Church End 149 F3
Haynes West End 149 F3
Hay-on-Wye (Y Gelli Gandryll) 144 B3
Hayscastle 140 B5
Hayscastle Cross 140 C5
Hayton Cumb 210 B2
Hayton Cumb 209 E2
Hayton ERid 196 A3
Hayton Notts 187 E4
Hayton's Bent 157 E4
Haytor Vale 102 A5
Haytown 113 D4
Hayward Gallery GtLon SE1 8XZ 45 F4
Haywards Heath 109 F1
Haywood Oaks 174 B2
Hazel End 150 C5
Hazel Grove 184 D4
Hazel Street 123 F5
Hazelbank A&B 240 C4
Hazelbank SLan 234 C5
Hazelbury Bryan 104 D2
Hazeleigh 138 B2
Hazeley 120 C2
Hazelhurst 184 B1
Hazelside 225 G3
Hazelslack 199 F5
Hazelslade 158 C1
Hazelton Walls 244 B2
Hazelwood Derbys 173 E3
Hazelwood GtLon 122 D2
Hazlefield 208 A2
Hazlehead Aber 261 G4
Hazlehead SYorks 185 F2
Hazlemere 135 D3
Hazlerigg 221 E4
Hazleton 132 C1
Hazon 221 D1
Heacham 177 E4
Head Bridge 113 G4
Headbourne Worthy 119 F4
Headcorn 124 A4
Headingley 194 B4
Headington 134 A2
Headlam 202 A1
Headless Cross 146 C1
Headley Hants 120 D4
Headley Hants 119 G1
Headley Surr 122 B3
Headley Down 120 D4
Headley Heath 158 C5
Headon 187 E5
Heads Nook 210 A2
Heady Hill 184 C1
Heage 173 E2
Healaugh NYorks 201 F3
Healaugh NYorks 195 E3
Heald Green 184 C4
Heale Devon 113 G1
Heale Som 116 A5
Healey Lancs 184 C1
Healey N'umb 211 G2
Healey NYorks 202 A4
Healey WYorks 194 B5
Healeyfield 211 G3
Healey's Cornish Cyder Farm Corn TR4 9LW 96 B4
Healing 188 C1
Heamoor 94 B3
Heaning 199 F3
Heanish 246 B2
Heanor 173 F3
Heanton Punchardon 113 F2
Heanton Satchville 113 F4
Heap Bridge 184 C1
Heapey 192 C5
Heapham 187 F4
Hearn 120 D4
Heart of Neolithic Orkney Ork 277 C6
Heart of the Country Centre Staffs WS14 9QR 158 D2
Hearthstane 226 C3
Heasley Mill 114 A4
Heast 256 C3
Heath Cardiff 130 A4
Heath Derbys 173 F1
Heath WYorks 186 A1
Heath & Reach 149 E5
Heath End Derbys 173 E5
Heath End Hants 119 G1
Heath End Hants 119 F1
Heath End Surr 120 D3
Heath Hayes 158 C1
Heath Hill 157 G1
Heath House 116 B3
Heath Town 158 B3
Heathbrook 170 D5
Heathcot 261 G4
Heathcote Derbys 172 C1
Heathcote Shrop 171 D5
Heathencote 148 C3
Heather 159 F1
Heatherton Activity Park Pembs SA70 8RJ 127 D2
Heathfield Devon 102 B5
Heathfield ESuss 110 A1
Heathfield NYorks 194 A1
Heathfield Som 115 E5
Heathrow Airport 135 F5
Heathton 158 A3
Heatley 184 B4
Heaton Lancs 192 A1
Heaton Staffs 171 G1
Heaton T&W 212 B1
Heaton WYorks 194 A4
Heaton Moor 184 C3
Heaton Park GtMan M25 2SW 25 E2
Heaton's Bridge 183 F1
Heaverham 123 E3
Heaviley 184 D4
Heavitree 102 C3
Hebburn 212 C1
Hebden 193 G1
Hebden Bridge 193 F5
Hebden Green 170 D1
Hebing End 150 B5
Hebron Carmar 141 E5
Hebron N'umb 221 D3
Heck 217 E2
Heckfield 120 C1
Heckfield Green 164 C4
Heckfordbridge 152 A5
Heckingham 165 E2
Heckington 175 G3
Heckmondwike 194 B5
Heddington 118 A1
Heddle 277 C6
Heddon-on-the-Wall 212 A1
Hedenham 165 E2
Hedge End 107 D1
Hedgerley 135 E4
Hedging 116 A5
Hedley on the Hill 211 G2
Hednesford 158 C1
Hedon 197 D5
Hedsor 135 E4
Heeley 186 A4
Heglibister 279 C7
Heighington Darl 212 B5
Heighington Lincs 175 F1
Heightington 157 G5
Heights of Brae 266 C5
Heilam 273 G3
Heisker Islands (Monach Islands) 262 B5
Heithat 217 F2
Heiton 228 B3
Hele Devon 113 F1
Hele Devon 102 C2
Hele Devon 98 D1
Hele Devon 102 A5
Hele Som 115 E5
Hele Torbay 101 F1
Hele Bridge 113 F5
Hele Lane 102 A1
Helebridge 112 C5
Helen's Bay 287 J7
Helensburgh 233 D1
Helford 95 E4
Helhoughton 177 G5
Helions Bumpstead 151 E3
Hell Corner 119 E1
Hellaby 186 C3
Helland Corn 97 E2
Helland Som 116 A5
Hellandbridge 97 E2
Hellesdon 178 D4
Hellidon 148 A2
Hellifield 193 E2
Hellingly 110 A2
Hellington 179 E5
Hellister 279 C8
Helmdon 148 A3
Helmingham 152 C2
Helmington Row 212 A4
Helmsdale 275 F7
Helmshore 193 D5
Helmsley 203 F4
Helperby 194 D1
Helperthorpe 204 C5
Helpringham 175 G3
Helpston 161 G2
Helsby 183 F5
Helsey 189 F5
Helston 95 D4
Helstone 97 E1
Helton 210 B5
Helwith 201 F2
Helwith Bridge 193 E1
Hem 156 B2
Hemborough Post 101 E2
Hemel Hempstead 135 F2
Hemerdon 100 B2
Hemingbrough 195 F4
Hemingby 188 C5
Hemingfield 186 A2
Hemingford Abbots 162 A5
Hemingford Grey 162 A5
Hemingstone 152 C2
Hemington Leics 173 F5
Hemington N'hants 161 F4
Hemington Som 117 E2
Hemley 153 D3
Hemlington 203 D1
Hemp Green 153 E1
Hempholme 196 C2
Hempnall 164 D2
Hempnall Green 164 D2
Hempriggs 267 J5
Hempriggs House 275 J4
Hempstead Essex 151 E4
Hempstead Med 123 G2
Hempstead Norf 179 F3
Hempstead Norf 178 C2
Hempsted 132 A1
Hempton Norf 178 A3
Hempton Oxon 147 G4
Hemsby 179 F4
Hemswell 187 G3
Hemswell Cliff 187 G4
Hemsworth 186 B1
Hemyock 103 E1
Henbury Bristol 131 E5
Henbury ChesE 184 C5
Henderland 216 C3
Hendersyde Park 228 B3
Hendham 100 D2
Hendon GtLon 136 B4
Hendon T&W 212 C2
Hendraburnick 97 F1
Hendre Bridgend 129 F4
Hendre Gwyn 166 C4
Hendreforgan 129 F4
Hendy 128 B2
Heneglwys 180 C5
Henfield SGlos 131 F5
Henfield WSuss 109 E2
Henford 99 D1
Hengherst 124 B5
Hengoed Caerp 130 A3
Hengoed Powys 144 B2
Hengoed Shrop 169 F4
Hengrave 151 G1
Henham 150 D5
Heniarth 156 A2
Henlade 115 F5
Henley Dorset 104 C2
Henley Shrop 157 E5
Henley Som 116 B4
Henley Som 104 A2
Henley Suff 152 C2
Henley WSuss 121 D5
Henley Corner 116 B4
Henley Park 121 E2
Henley-in-Arden 147 D1
Henley-on-Thames 134 C4
Henley's Down 110 C2
Henllan Carmar 141 G3
Henllan Denb 168 D1
Henllan Amgoed 141 E5
Henllys 130 B3
Henlow 149 G4
Hennock 102 B4
Henny Street 151 G4
Henryd 181 F5
Henry's Moat 140 D5
Hensall 195 E5
Henshaw 211 D1
Hensingham 208 C5
Henstead 165 F3
Hensting 119 F5
Henstridge 104 D1
Henstridge Ash 104 D1
Henstridge Bowden 117 D5
Henstridge Marsh 117 E5
Henton Oxon 134 C2
Henton Som 116 B3
Henwood 97 G2
Heogan 279 D8
Heol Senni 143 F5
Heolgerrig 129 G2
Heol-y-Cyw 129 F4
Hepburn 229 E4
Hepburn Bell 229 E4
Hepple 220 B1
Hepscott 221 E3
Hepthorne Lane 173 F1
Heptonstall 193 F5
Hepworth Suff 164 A4
Hepworth WYorks 185 F2
Hepworth South Common 164 A4
Herbrandston 126 B2
Hereford 145 E3
Hereford Cathedral Here HR1 2NG 75 Hereford
Heriot 236 A4
Heritage Motor Centre, Gaydon Warks CV35 0BJ 147 F2
Herm 101 G5
Hermiston 235 F2
Hermitage D&G 216 B4
Hermitage Dorset 104 C2
Hermitage ScBord 218 D2
Hermitage WBerks 134 A5
Hermitage WSuss 107 G2
Hermitage Green 184 A3
Hermon Carmar 141 G4
Hermon IoA 166 C1
Hermon Pembs 141 F4
Herne 125 D2
Herne Bay 125 D2
Herne Common 125 D2
Herne Pound 123 F3
Herner 113 F3
Hernhill 124 C2
Herodsfoot 97 G3
Herongate 137 F3
Heron's Ghyll 109 G1
Heronsgate 135 F3
Herriard 120 B3
Herringfleet 165 F2
Herring's Green 149 F3
Herringswell 151 F1
Herringthorpe 186 B3
Hersden 125 D2
Hersham Corn 112 C5
Hersham Surr 121 G1
Herstmonceux 110 B2
Herston 277 D8
Hertford 136 C1
Hertford Heath 136 C1
Hertingfordbury 136 C1
Hesket Newmarket 209 G3
Hesketh Bank 192 A5
Hesketh Lane 192 C3
Heskin Green 183 G1
Hesleden 212 D4
Hesleyside 220 A3
Heslington 195 F2
Hessay 195 E2
Hessenford 98 D5
Hessett 152 A1
Hessle 196 C5
Hest Bank 192 A1
Hester's Way 146 B5
Hestley Green 152 C1
Heston 136 A5
Heswall 183 D4
Hethe 148 A5
Hethelpit Cross 145 G5
Hetherington 220 A4
Hethersett 178 C5
Hethersgill 210 A1
Hethpool 228 C4
Hett 212 B4
Hetton 193 F2
Hetton-le-Hole 212 C3
Heugh 220 C4
Heugh-head Aber 260 B3
Heugh-head Aber 260 D5
Heveningham 165 E4
Hever 123 D4
Hever Castle & Gardens Kent TN8 7NG 123 D4
Heversham 199 F4
Hevingham 178 C3
Hewas Water 97 D5
Hewell Grange 146 C1
Hewell Lane 146 C1
Hewelsfield 131 E2
Hewelsfield Common 131 E2
Hewish NSom 116 B1
Hewish Som 104 A2
Hewood 103 G2
Heworth 195 F2
Hewton 99 F1
Hexham 211 F1
Hexham Abbey N'umb NE46 3NB 211 F1
Hextable 137 E5
Hexthorpe 186 C2
Hexton 149 G4
Hexworthy 99 G3
Hey 193 E3
Hey Houses 191 G5
Heybridge Essex 137 F3
Heybridge Essex 138 B2
Heybridge Basin 138 B2
Heybrook Bay 100 A3
Heydon Cambs 150 C3
Heydon Norf 178 C3
Heydour 175 F4
Heylipoll 246 A2
Heylor 278 B4
Heyop 156 B5
Heysham 192 A1
Heyshaw 194 A1
Heyshott 108 A2
Heyside 184 D2
Heytesbury 118 A3
Heythrop 147 F5
Heywood GtMan 184 C1
Heywood Wilts 117 F2
Hibaldstow 187 G2
Hibb's Green 151 G2
Hickleton 186 B2

Hickling Norf 179 F3
Hickling Notts 174 B5
Hickling Green 179 F3
Hickling Heath 179 F3
Hickstead 109 E1
Hidcote Bartrim 147 D3
Hidcote Boyce 147 D3
Hidcote Manor Garden Glos GL55 6LR 147 D3
High Ackworth 186 B1
High Angerton 220 C3
High Balantyre 240 C3
High Bankhill 210 B3
High Beach 136 D3
High Bentham (Higher Bentham) 192 C1
High Bickington 113 F3
High Birkwith 200 C5
High Blantyre 234 A4
High Bonnybridge 234 C2
High Borgue 216 A5
High Borve (Bail Àrd Bhuirgh) 271 G2
High Bradfield 185 G3
High Bradley 193 G3
High Bransholme 196 D4
High Bray 113 G2
High Bridge 209 G2
High Brooms 123 E4
High Bullen 113 F3
High Burton 202 B4
High Buston 221 E1
High Callerton 221 D4
High Casterton 200 B5
High Catton 195 G2
High Close 202 A1
High Cogges 133 F2
High Common 164 C3
High Coniscliffe 202 B1
High Crompton 184 D2
High Cross Hants 120 C5
High Cross Herts 136 C1
High Cross WSuss 109 E2
High Easter 137 F1
High Ellington 202 A4
High Entercommon 202 C2
High Ercall 157 E1
High Etherley 212 A5
High Ferry 176 B3
High Flatts 185 G2
High Garrett 151 F5
High Gate 193 F5
High Grange 212 A4
High Green Norf 178 C5
High Green Norf 178 A4
High Green Norf 178 A5
High Green Suff 151 G1
High Green SYorks 186 A3
High Green Worcs 146 A3
High Halden 124 A5
High Halstow 137 G5
High Ham 116 B4
High Harrington 208 D4
High Harrogate 194 C2
High Hatton 170 D5
High Hauxley 221 E1
High Hawsker 204 C2
High Heath Shrop 171 D5
High Heath WMid 158 C2
High Hesket 210 A3
High Hesleden 213 D4
High Hoyland 185 G1
High Hunsley 196 B4
High Hurstwood 109 G1
High Hutton 195 G1
High Ireby 209 F3
High Kelling 178 B2
High Kilburn 203 E5
High Kingthorpe 204 B4
High Knipe 199 G1
High Lane Derbys 173 F3
High Lane GtMan 185 D4
High Lane Worcs 145 F1
High Laver 137 E2
High Legh 184 B4
High Leven 203 D1
High Littleton 116 D2
High Lodge Forest Centre Suff IP27 0AF 163 G4
High Lorton 209 E4
High Marishes 204 B5
High Marnham 187 F5
High Melton 186 C2
High Moor 186 B4
High Moorland Visitor Centre, Princetown Devon PL20 6QF 99 F3
High Newton 199 F4
High Newton-by-the-Sea 229 G4
High Nibthwaite 199 D3
High Offley 171 E5
High Ongar 137 E2
High Onn 158 A1
High Park Corner 152 B5
High Roding 137 F1
High Shaw 201 D3
High Spen 212 A1
High Stoop 212 A3
High Street Corn 97 D4
High Street Kent 123 G5
High Street Suff 153 F2
High Street Suff 165 E3
High Street Suff 165 F4
High Street Suff 151 G3
High Street Green 152 B2
High Throston 213 D4
High Town 158 B1
High Toynton 176 A1
High Trewhitt 220 C1
High Wham 212 A5
High Wigsell 110 C1
High Woods Country Park Essex CO4 5JR 152 B5
High Woolaston 131 E3
High Worsall 202 C2
High Wray 199 E3
High Wych 137 D1
High Wycombe 135 D3
Higham Derbys 173 E2
Higham Kent 137 G5
Higham Lancs 193 E4
Higham Suff 151 F1
Higham Suff 152 B4
Higham SYorks 186 A2
Higham Dykes 220 D4
Higham Ferrers 149 E1
Higham Gobian 149 G4
Higham on the Hill 159 F3
Higham Wood 123 F4
Highampton 113 E5
Highams Park 136 C3
Highbridge Hants 119 F5
Highbridge Som 116 A3
Highbrook 122 C5
Highburton 185 F1
Highbury 117 D3
Highclere 119 F1
Highcliffe 106 B3
Higher Alham 117 D3
Higher Ansty 105 D2
Higher Ashton 102 B4
Higher Ballam 191 G4
Higher Bentham (High Bentham) 192 C1
Higher Blackley 184 C2
Higher Brixham 101 F2
Higher Cheriton 103 E2
Higher Combe 114 C4
Higher Folds 184 A2
Higher Gabwell 101 F1
Higher Green 184 B3
Higher Halstock Leigh 104 B2
Higher Kingcombe 104 B3
Higher Kinnerton 170 A1
Higher Muddiford 113 F2
Higher Nyland 117 E5
Higher Prestacott 99 D1
Higher Standen 193 D3
Higher Tale 103 D2
Higher Thrushgill 192 C1
Higher Town Corn 97 E3
Higher Town IoS 96 B1
Higher Walreddon 99 E3
Higher Walton Lancs 192 B5
Higher Walton Warr 183 G4
Higher Wambrook 103 F2
Higher Whatcombe 105 E2
Higher Wheelton 192 C5
Higher Whiteleigh 98 C1
Higher Whitley 184 A4
Higher Wincham 184 A5
Higher Woodhill 184 B1
Higher Woodsford 105 D4
Higher Wraxall 104 B2
Higher Wych 170 B3
Highfield ERid 195 G4
Highfield NAyr 233 E4
Highfield Oxon 148 A5
Highfield SYorks 186 A4
Highfield T&W 212 A2
Highfields Cambs 150 B2
Highfields N'umb 237 G4
Highgate ESuss 122 D5
Highgate GtLon 136 B4
Highgreen Manor 220 A2
Highlane ChesE 171 F1
Highlane Derbys 186 B4
Highlaws 209 E2
Highleadon 145 G5
Highleigh Devon 114 C5
Highleigh WSuss 108 A4
Highley 157 G4
Highmead 142 B3
Highmoor Cross 134 B4
Highmoor Hill 131 D4
Highnam 131 G1
Highstead 125 E2
Highsted 124 B2
Highstreet 124 C2
Highstreet Green Essex 151 F4
Highstreet Green Surr 121 E4
Hightae 217 E3
Highter's Heath 158 C5
Hightown A&N 287 H7
Hightown Hants 106 A2
Hightown Mersey 183 D2
Hightown Green 152 A2
Highway 132 C5
Highweek 102 B5
Highwood 145 F1
Highwood Hill 136 B3
Highworth 133 E3
Hilborough 163 G2
Hilcote 173 F2
Hilcott 118 C2
Hilden Park 123 E4
Hildenborough 123 E4
Hildenley 203 G5
Hildersham 150 D3
Hilderstone 171 G4
Hilderthorpe 197 D1
Hilfield 104 C2
Hilgay 163 E3
Hill SGlos 131 F3
Hill Warks 147 G1
Hill Worcs 146 B3
Hill Brow 120 C5
Hill Chorlton 171 E4
Hill Common 179 F3
Hill Cottages 203 G3
Hill Croome 146 A3
Hill Deverill 117 F3
Hill Dyke 176 B3
Hill End Dur 211 G4
Hill End Fife 243 F5
Hill End Glos 146 A4
Hill End GtLon 135 F3
Hill End NYorks 193 G2
Hill Green 150 C4
Hill Head 107 E2
Hill Houses 157 F5
Hill Mountain 126 C2
Hill of Beath 235 F1
Hill of Fearn 267 F4
Hill Ridware 158 C1
Hill Row 162 C5
Hill Side 185 F1
Hill Street 106 C1
Hill Top Hants 106 D2
Hill Top SYorks 186 B3
Hill Top SYorks 185 G4
Hill View 105 F3
Hill Wootton 147 F1
Hillam 195 E5
Hillbeck 200 C1
Hillberry 190 B4
Hillborough 125 E2
Hillbrae Aber 268 E6
Hillbrae Aber 261 F2
Hillbrae Aber 261 G1
Hillbutts 105 F2
Hillclifflane 173 D3
Hillend Aber 268 C6
Hillend Fife 235 F1
Hillend Midlo 235 G3
Hillend NLan 234 C3
Hillend Swan 128 A3
Hillend Green 145 G5
Hillersland 131 E1
Hillesden 148 B5
Hillesley 131 G4
Hillfarrance 115 E5
Hillfoot End 149 G4
Hillhall 283 F2
Hillhead Devon 101 F2
Hillhead Mid Ulster 286 D6
Hillhead SAyr 224 C3
Hillhead of Auchentumb 269 H5
Hillhead of Cocklaw 269 J6
Hilliard's Cross 159 D1
Hilliclay 275 G2
Hillingdon 135 F4
Hillington Glas 233 G3
Hillington Norf 177 F5
Hillmorton 160 A5
Hillockhead Aber 260 B4
Hillockhead Aber 260 C3
Hillowton 216 B4
Hillpound 107 E1
Hill's End 149 E4
Hills Town 173 F1
Hillsborough L&C 283 F3
Hillsborough SYorks 186 A3
Hillsborough Castle L&C BT26 6AG 283 F3
Hillsford Bridge 114 A3
Hillside Aber 261 H5
Hillside Angus 253 F3
Hillside Moray 267 J5
Hillside Shet 279 D6
Hillside Worcs 145 G1
Hillswick 278 B5
Hilltown 283 F6
Hillway 107 F4
Hillwell 279 F9
Hillyfields 106 C1
Hilmarton 132 C5
Hilperton 117 F2
Hilsea 107 F2
Hilston 197 E4
Hilton Cambs 150 A1
Hilton Cumb 210 D5
Hilton Derbys 172 D4
Hilton Dorset 105 D2
Hilton Dur 212 A5
Hilton High 267 G3
Hilton Shrop 157 G3
Hilton Staffs 158 C2
Hilton Stock 203 D1
Hilton Croft 261 H1
Hilton of Cadboll 267 F4
Hilton of Delnies 267 F6
Himbleton 146 B2
Himley 158 A3
Himley Hall & Park WMid DY3 4DF 14 A2
Hincaster 199 G4
Hinchley Wood 121 G1
Hinckley 159 G3
Hinderclay 164 B4
Hinderton 183 E5
Hinderwell 203 G1
Hindford 170 A4
Hindhead 121 D4
Hindley GtMan 184 A2
Hindley N'umb 211 G2
Hindley Green 184 A2
Hindlip 146 A2
Hindolveston 178 B3
Hindon Som 114 C3
Hindon Wilts 118 A4
Hindringham 178 A2
Hingham 178 B5
Hinksford 158 A4
Hinstock 171 D5
Hintlesham 152 B3
Hinton Glos 131 F2
Hinton Hants 106 B3
Hinton Here 144 C4
Hinton N'hants 148 A2
Hinton SGlos 131 G5
Hinton Shrop 156 D2
Hinton Admiral 106 B3
Hinton Ampner 119 G5
Hinton Blewett 116 C2
Hinton Charterhouse 117 E2
Hinton Martell 105 G2
Hinton on the Green 146 C3
Hinton Parva Dorset 105 F2
Hinton Parva Swin 133 E4
Hinton St. George 104 A1
Hinton St. Mary 105 D1
Hinton Waldrist 133 F3
Hinton-in-the-Hedges 148 A4
Hints Shrop 157 F5
Hints Staffs 159 D2
Hinwick 149 E1
Hinxhill 124 C4
Hinxton 150 C3
Hinxworth 150 A3
Hipperholme 194 A5
Hipsburn 229 G5
Hipswell 202 A3
Hirn 261 F4
Hirnant 169 D5
Hirst 221 E3
Hirst Courtney 195 F5
Hirwaen 169 E1
Hirwaun 129 F2
Hiscott 113 F3
Histon 150 C1
Hitcham Bucks 135 E4
Hitcham Suff 152 A2
Hitchin 149 G5
Hither Green 136 C5
Hittisleigh 102 A3
Hittisleigh Barton 102 A3
Hive 196 A4
Hixon 172 B5
Hoaden 125 E3
Hoaldalbert 144 C5
Hoar Cross 172 C5
Hoar Park Craft Centre Warks CV10 0QU 159 E3
Hoarwithy 145 E5
Hoath 125 E2
Hobarris 156 C5
Hobbister 277 C7
Hobbles Green 151 F2
Hobbs Cross 137 D3
Hobbs Lots Bridge 162 B2
Hobkirk 227 G4
Hobland Hall 179 G5
Hobson 212 A2
Hoby 160 B1
Hockerill 150 C5
Hockering 178 B4
Hockerton 174 C2
Hockley AB&C 282 C4
Hockley Essex 138 B3
Hockley Heath 159 D5
Hockliffe 149 E5
Hockwold cum Wilton 163 F4
Hockworthy 102 D1
Hoddesdon 136 C2
Hoddlesden 192 D5
Hodgehill 171 F1
Hodgeston 126 D3
Hodnet 170 D5
Hodnetheath 170 D5
Hodsoll Street 123 F2
Hodson 133 D4
Hodthorpe 186 C5
Hoe 178 A4
Hoe Gate 107 F1
Hoff 200 B1
Hoffleet Stow 176 A4
Hoggard's Green 151 G2
Hoggeston 148 D5
Hoggie 268 D5
Hoggrill's End 159 E3
Hogha Gearraidh 262 C4
Hoghton 192 C5
Hognaston 172 D2
Hogsthorpe 189 F5
Holbeach 176 B5
Holbeach Bank 176 B5
Holbeach Clough 176 B5
Holbeach Drove 162 B1
Holbeach Hurn 176 B5
Holbeach St. Johns 162 B1
Holbeach St. Marks 176 B4
Holbeach St. Matthew 176 C4
Holbeck 186 C5
Holbeck Woodhouse 186 C5
Holberrow Green 146 C2
Holbeton 100 C2
Holborough 123 G2
Holbrook Derbys 173 E3
Holbrook Suff 152 C4
Holbrooks 159 F4
Holburn 229 E3
Holbury 106 D2
Holcombe Devon 102 C5
Holcombe GtMan 184 B1
Holcombe Som 117 D3
Holcombe Burnell Barton 102 B3
Holcombe Rogus 103 D1
Holcot 148 C1
Holden 193 D3
Holden Gate 193 E5
Holdenby 148 B1
Holdenhurst 106 A3
Holder's Green 151 E5
Holders Hill 136 B4
Holdgate 157 E4
Holdingham 175 F3
Holditch 103 G2
Hole 103 E1
Hole Park 124 A5
Holehouse 185 E3
Hole-in-the-Wall 145 F5
Holford 115 E3
Holgate 195 E2
Holker 199 E5
Holkham 177 G3
Hollacombe Devon 113 D5
Hollacombe Devon 102 B2
Hollacombe Town 113 G4
Holland Ork 276 D2
Holland Ork 276 F5
Holland Surr 122 D3
Holland Fen 176 A3
Holland-on-Sea 139 E1
Hollandstoun 276 G2
Hollee 218 A5
Hollesley 153 E3
Hollicombe 101 F1
Hollingbourne 124 A3
Hollingbury 109 F3
Hollingrove 110 B1
Hollington Derbys 172 D4
Hollington ESuss 110 C2
Hollington Staffs 172 B4
Hollingworth 185 E3
Hollins 186 A5
Hollins Green 184 A3
Hollins Lane 192 A2
Hollinsclough 172 B1
Hollinwood GtMan 184 D2
Hollinwood Shrop 170 C4
Hollocombe 113 G4
Hollow Meadows 185 G4
Holloway 173 E2
Hollowell 160 B5
Holly Bush 170 B3
Holly End 162 C2
Holly Green 134 C2
Hollybush Caerp 130 A2
Hollybush EAyr 224 B4
Hollybush Worcs 145 G4
Hollyhurst 170 C3
Hollym 197 F5
Hollywater 120 D4
Hollywood 158 C5
Holm D&G 218 A2
Holm (Tolm) Na H-E. Siar 271 G4
Holm of Drumlanrig 216 C1
Holmbridge 185 F2
Holmbury St. Mary 121 G3
Holmbush 122 B5
Holme Cambs 161 G4
Holme Cumb 199 G5
Holme NLincs 187 G2
Holme Notts 174 D2
Holme NYorks 202 C4
Holme WYorks 185 F2
Holme Chapel 193 E5
Holme Hale 163 G2
Holme Lacy 145 E4
Holme Marsh 144 C2
Holme next the Sea 177 F3
Holme on the Wolds 196 B3
Holme Pierrepont 174 B4
Holme St. Cuthbert 209 E2
Holme-on-Spalding-Moor 196 A4
Holmer 145 E3
Holmer Green 135 E3
Holmes 183 F1
Holmes Chapel 171 E1
Holme's Hill 110 A2
Holmesfield 186 A5
Holmeswood 183 F1
Holmewood 173 F1
Holmfield 193 G5
Holmfirth 185 F2
Holmhead D&G 216 B2
Holmhead EAyr 225 D3
Holmpton 197 F5
Holmrook 198 B2
Holmsgarth 279 D8
Holmside 212 B3
Holmsleigh Green 103 F2
Holmston 224 B3
Holmwrangle 210 B3
Holne 100 D1
Holnest 104 C2
Holnicote 114 C3
Holsworthy 112 D5
Holsworthy Beacon 113 D5
Holt Dorset 105 G2
Holt Norf 178 B2
Holt Wilts 117 F1
Holt Worcs 146 A1
Holt Wrex 170 B2
Holt End Hants 120 B4
Holt End Worcs 146 C1
Holt Fleet 146 A1
Holt Heath Dorset 105 G2
Holt Heath Worcs 146 A1
Holt Wood 105 G2
Holtby 195 F2
Holton Oxon 134 B2
Holton Som 117 D5
Holton Suff 165 F4
Holton cum Beckering 188 B4
Holton Heath 105 F3
Holton le Clay 188 C2
Holton le Moor 188 A3
Holton St. Mary 152 B4
Holtspur 135 E4
Holtye 123 D5
Holtye Common 123 D5
Holway 115 F5
Holwell Dorset 104 C1
Holwell Herts 149 G4
Holwell Leics 174 C5
Holwell Oxon 133 E2
Holwell Som 117 E3
Holwick 211 F5
Holworth 105 D4
Holy Cross 158 B5
Holy Island IoA 180 A5
Holy Island (Lindisfarne) N'umb 229 F2
Holy Trinity Church, Skipton NYorks BD23 1NJ 193 F2
Holy Trinity Church, Stratford-upon-Avon Warks CV37 6BG 85 Stratford-upon-Avon
Holybourne 120 C3
Holyfield 136 C2
Holyhead (Caergybi) 180 A4
Holymoorside 173 E1
Holyport 135 D5
Holystone 220 B1
Holytown 234 B3
Holywell Cambs 162 B5
Holywell Corn 96 B4
Holywell Dorset 104 B2
Holywell ESuss 110 B4
Holywell F&O 280 C5
Holywell (Treffynnon) Flints 182 C5
Holywell N'umb 221 F4
Holywell Bay Fun Park Corn TR8 5PW 96 B4
Holywell Green 185 E1
Holywell Lake 115 E5
Holywell Row 163 F5
Holywood A&NDown 283 H1
Holywood D&G 216 D2
Hom Green 145 E5
Homer 157 F2
Homersfield 165 D3
Homington 118 C5
Honey Hill 124 D2
Honey Street 118 C1
Honey Tye 152 A4
Honeyborough 126 C2
Honeybourne 146 D3
Honeychurch 113 G5
Honicknowle 100 A2
Honiley 159 E5
Honing 179 E3
Honingham 178 C4
Honington Lincs 175 E3
Honington Suff 164 A4
Honington Warks 147 E3
Honiton 103 E2
Honkley 170 A2
Honley 185 F1
Hoo Med 137 G5
Hoo Suff 153 D2
Hoo Green 184 B4
Hoo Meavy 100 B1
Hood Green 186 A2
Hood Hill 186 A3
Hooe ESuss 110 B3
Hooe Plym 100 B2
Hooe Common 110 B2
Hook Cambs 162 C3
Hook ERid 195 G5
Hook GtLon 121 G1
Hook Hants 120 C2
Hook Hants 107 E2
Hook Pembs 126 C1
Hook Wilts 132 C4
Hook Green Kent 123 F5
Hook Green Kent 123 F2
Hook Green Kent 137 F5
Hook Green Kent 137 E5
Hook Norton 147 F4
Hook-a-Gate 157 D2
Hooke 104 B2
Hookgate 171 E4
Hookway 102 B3
Hookwood 122 B4
Hoole 170 B1
Hooley 122 B3
Hoop 131 E2
Hooton 183 E5
Hooton Levitt 186 C3
Hooton Pagnell 186 B2
Hooton Roberts 186 B3
Hop Farm, The Kent TN12 6PY 123 F4
Hop Pocket, The Here WR6 5BT 145 F3
Hop Pole 161 G1
Hopcrofts Holt 147 G5
Hope Derbys 185 F4
Hope Devon 100 C4
Hope Flints 170 A2
Hope Powys 156 B2
Hope Shrop 156 C2
Hope Staffs 172 C2
Hope Bagot 157 E5
Hope Bowdler 157 D3
Hope End Green 151 D5
Hope Mansell 131 F1
Hope under Dinmore 145 E2
Hopehouse 227 D4
Hopeman 267 J5
Hope's Green 137 G4
Hopesay 156 C4
Hopkinstown 129 G3
Hopley's Green 144 C2
Hopperton 194 D2
Hopsford 159 G4
Hopstone 157 G3
Hopton Derbys 173 D2
Hopton Norf 165 G2
Hopton Shrop 170 C5
Hopton Shrop 170 A5
Hopton Staffs 171 G5
Hopton Suff 164 A4
Hopton Cangeford 157 E4
Hopton Castle 156 C5
Hopton Wafers 157 F5
Hoptonheath 156 C5
Hopwas 159 D2
Hopwood 158 C5
Horam 110 A2
Horbling 175 G4
Horbury 185 G1
Horden 212 D3
Horderley 156 D4
Hordle 106 B3
Hordley 170 A4
Horeb Carmar 128 A2
Horeb Cere 141 G3
Horeb Flints 169 F2
Horfield 131 E5
Horham 164 D4
Horkesley Heath 152 A5
Horkstow 187 G1
Horley Oxon 147 G3
Horley Surr 122 B4
Horn Hill 135 F3
Hornblotton 116 C4
Hornblotton Green 116 C4
Hornby Lancs 192 B1
Hornby NYorks 202 B3
Hornby NYorks 202 C2
Horncastle 176 A1
Hornchurch 137 E4
Horncliffe 237 G5
Horndean Hants 107 G1
Horndean ScBord 237 G5
Horndon 99 F2
Horndon on the Hill 137 F4
Horne 122 C4
Horne Row 137 G2
Horner 114 B3
Horniehaugh 252 C3
Horniman Museum GtLon SE23 3PQ 13 C7
Horning 179 E4
Horninghold 160 D3
Horninglow 172 D5
Horningsea 150 C1
Horningsham 117 F3
Horningtoft 178 A3
Horningtops 97 G3
Horns Cross Devon 113 D3
Horns Cross ESuss 110 D1
Horns Green 123 D3
Hornsbury 103 G1
Hornsby 210 B3
Hornsby Gate 210 B2
Hornsea 197 E3
Hornsea Freeport ERid HU18 1UT 197 E3
Hornsey 136 C4
Hornton 147 F3
Horrabridge 100 B1
Horridge 102 A5
Horringer 151 G1
Horrocks Fold 184 B1
Horse Bridge 171 G2
Horsebridge Devon 99 E3
Horsebridge Hants 119 E4
Horsebrook 158 A1
Horsecastle 116 B1
Horsehay 157 F2
Horseheath 151 E3
Horsehouse 201 F4
Horsell 121 E2
Horseman's Green 170 B3
Horsenden 134 C2
Horseshoe Green 123 D4
Horseway 162 C4
Horsey 179 F3
Horsey Corner 179 F3
Horsford 178 C4
Horsforth 194 B4
Horsham Worcs 145 G2
Horsham WSuss 121 G4
Horsham St. Faith 178 D4
Horsington Lincs 175 G1
Horsington Som 117 E5
Horsington Marsh 117 E5
Horsley Derbys 173 E3
Horsley Glos 132 A3
Horsley N'umb 211 G1
Horsley N'umb 220 A2
Horsley Cross 152 C5
Horsley Woodhouse 173 E3
Horsleycross Street 152 C5
Horsleygate 186 A5
Horsleyhill 227 G4
Horsmonden 123 F4
Horspath 134 A2
Horstead 179 D4
Horsted Keynes 109 F1
Horton Bucks 135 E1
Horton Dorset 105 G2
Horton Lancs 193 E2
Horton N'hants 148 D2
Horton SGlos 131 G4
Horton Shrop 170 B5
Horton Som 103 G1
Horton Staffs 171 G2
Horton Swan 128 A4
Horton Tel&W 157 F1
Horton W&M 135 F5
Horton Wilts 118 B1
Horton Cross 103 G1
Horton Grange 221 E4
Horton Green 170 B3
Horton Heath 107 D1
Horton in Ribblesdale 200 D5
Horton Inn 105 G2
Horton Kirby 123 E2
Horton Park Farm Surr KT19 8PT 121 G1
Horton-cum-Studley 134 B1
Horwich 184 A1
Horwich End 185 E4
Horwood 113 F3
Hoscar 183 F1
Hose 174 C5
Hoses 198 D3
Hosh 243 D2
Hosta 262 C4
Hoswick 279 D10
Hotham 196 A4
Hothfield 124 B4
Hoton 173 G5
Houbie 278 F3
Houdston 214 C1
Hough 171 E2
Hough Green 183 F4
Hougham 175 D3
Hough-on-the-Hill 175 E3
Houghton Cambs 162 A5
Houghton Cumb 210 A2
Houghton Devon 100 C3
Houghton Hants 119 E4
Houghton Pembs 126 C2
Houghton WSuss 108 C2
Houghton Bank 212 B5
Houghton Conquest 149 F3
Houghton le Spring 212 C3
Houghton on the Hill 160 B2
Houghton Regis 149 F5
Houghton St. Giles 178 A2
Houghton-le-Side 212 B5
Houlsyke 203 G2
Hound 107 D2
Hound Green 120 C2
Houndslow 236 D5
Houndsmoor 115 E5
Houndwood 237 F3
Hounsdown 106 C1
Hounslow 136 A5
House of Marbles & Teign Valley Glass Devon TQ13 9DS 102 B5
Housebay 276 F5
Househill 267 F6
Houses Hill 185 F1
Housesteads Roman Fort (Frontiers of the Roman Empire) N'umb NE47 6NN 211 D1
Housetter 278 C4
Housham Tye 137 E1
Houss 279 C9
Houston 233 F3
Houstry 275 G5
Houstry of Dunn 275 H3
Houton 277 C7
Hove 109 E3
Hove Edge 194 A5
Hoveringham 174 B3
Hoveton 179 E4
Hovingham 203 F5
How 210 B2
How Caple 145 F4
How End 149 F3
How Green 123 D4
How Man 208 C5
Howbrook 186 A3
Howden 195 G5
Howden Clough 194 B5
Howden-le-Wear 212 A4
Howe Cumb 199 F4
Howe High 275 J2
Howe Norf 165 D2
Howe NYorks 202 C4
Howe Green 137 G2
Howe of Teuchar 269 F6
Howe Street Essex 137 F1
Howe Street Essex 151 E4
Howegreen 138 B2
Howell 175 G3
Howey 143 G2
Howgate Cumb 208 C4
Howgate Midlo 235 G4
Howgill Lancs 193 E3
Howgill NYorks 193 G2
Howick 229 G5
Howle 171 D5
Howle Hill 145 F5
Howlett End 151 D4
Howletts Wild Animal Park Kent CT4 5EL 125 D3
Howley 103 F2
Howmore (Tobha Mòr) 254 C1
Hownam 228 B5
Hownam Mains 228 B4
Howpasley 227 E5
Howsham NLincs 188 A2
Howsham NYorks 195 G1
Howt Green 124 A2

Kettleburgh 153 D1
Kettlehill 244 B4
Kettleholm 217 F3
Kettleness 204 B1
Kettleshulme 185 D5
Kettlesing 194 B2
Kettlesing Bottom 194 B2
Kettlesing Head 194 B2
Kettlestone 178 A2
Kettlethorpe 187 F5
Kettletoft 276 F4
Kettlewell 201 E5
Ketton 161 E2
Kevingtown 123 D2
Kew 136 A5
Kewstoke 116 A1
Kexbrough 186 A2
Kexby Lincs 187 F4
Kexby York 195 G2
Key Green 171 F1
Keyham 160 B2
Keyhaven 106 C3
Keyingham 197 E5
Keymer 109 F2
Keynsham 117 D1
Key's Toft 176 C2
Keysoe 149 F1
Keysoe Row 149 F1
Keyston 161 F5
Keyworth 174 B4
Kibblesworth 212 B2
Kibworth
Beauchamp 160 B3
Kibworth Harcourt 160 B3
Kidbrooke 136 D5
Kiddemore Green 158 A2
Kidderminster 158 A5
Kiddington 147 G5
Kidlington 133 G1
Kidmore End 134 B5
Kidnal 170 B3
Kidsdale 207 E3
Kidsgrove 171 F2
Kidstones 201 E4
Kidstown 286 D3
Kidwelly (Cydweli) 128 A2
Kiel Crofts 240 A1
Kielder 219 E2
Kielder Forest N'umb
NE48 1ER 219 E2
Kielder Water N'umb
NE48 1BX 219 F3
Kilbarchan 233 F3
Kilbeg 256 C4
Kilberry 231 F3
Kilbirnie 233 E4
Kilblaan 240 D3
Kilbraur 274 D7
Kilbrennan 246 D5
Kilbride A&B 240 A2
Kilbride A&B 232 B3
Kilbride A&N 287 G6
Kilbride High 256 B2
Kilbride Farm 232 A3
Kilbridemore 240 C5
Kilburn Derbys 173 E3
Kilburn GtLon 136 B4
Kilburn NYorks 203 E5
Kilby 160 B3
Kilchattan Bay 232 C4
Kilchenzie 222 B3
Kilcheran 240 A1
Kilchiaran 230 A3
Kilchoan A&B 239 G3
Kilchoan High 247 D3
Kilchoman 230 A3
Kilchrenan
(Cill Chrèanain) 240 C2
Kilchrist 222 B4
Kilclief 283 J4
Kilcoo 283 F5
Kilconquhar 244 C4
Kilcorig 283 F2
Kilcot 145 F5
Kilcoy 266 C6
Kilcreggan 232 D1
Kilcross 283 F1
Kildale 203 F2
Kildary 266 E4
Kildavie 222 C4
Kildermorie Lodge 266 C4
Kildonan NAyr 223 F3
Kildonan Na H-E. Siar
254 C2
Kildonan Lodge 274 E6
Kildonnan 247 D1
Kildress 282 A1
Kildrochet House 214 B5
Kildrum 287 F6
Kildrummy 260 C3
Kildwick 193 G3
Kilfinan 232 A2
Kilfinnan 257 J5
Kilgetty 127 E2
Kilgwrrwg Common 131 D3
Kilham ERid 196 C1
Kilham N'umb 228 C3
Kilkeel 283 G7
Kilkenneth 246 A2
Kilkenny 132 C1
Kilkerran A&B 222 C4
Kilkerran SAyr 224 B5
Kilkhampton 112 C4
Kilkinamurry 283 F4
Killadeas 280 E3
Killagan Bridge 286 E3
Killaloo 285 H5
Killamarsh 186 B4
Killarbran 281 G4
Killard 286 D6
Killay 128 C3
Killbeg 247 F5
Killead 287 F7
Killeague 286 C3
Killean A&B 231 E5
Killean A&B 240 C4
Killearn 233 G1
Killeen AB&C 282 C4
Killeen Mid Ulster 282 B2
Killeen NM&D 282 D6
Killeeshil 281 J3
Killellan 222 B4
Killen D&S 284 E7
Killen High 266 D6
Killerby 212 A5
Killerton 102 C2
Killerton Devon
EX5 3LE 102 C2
Killeter 284 E7
Killichonan 250 A4
Killiechonate 249 E1
Killiechronan 247 E5
Killiecrankie 251 E3
Killiehuntly 258 E5
Killiemor 239 D1
Killilan 257 F1
Killimster 275 J3
Killin High 267 F1
Killin Stir 242 A1
Killinallan 230 B2
Killinchy 283 J2
Killinghall 194 B2
Killington Cumb 200 B4
Killington Devon 113 G1
Killingworth 221 E4
Killochyett 236 B5
Killocraw 222 B2
Killough 283 J5
Killowen 282 E7
Killucan 281 J1
Killunaig 239 D2
Killundine 247 E5
Killure 286 C3
Killyclogher 281 G1
Killycolp 282 B1
Killycolpy 282 C1
Killycor 285 H5
Killycurragh 286 B7
Killyharry 281 K2
Killykergan 286 C4
Killylane 285 H3
Killylea AB&C 282 A4
Killyleagh 283 J3
Killymallaght 285 G5
Killynether 283 H1
Killyrammer 286 D3
Kilmacolm 233 E3
Kilmaha 240 B4
Kilmahamogue 286 E2
Kilmahog 242 B4
Kilmalieu 248 A4
Kilmaluag 263 K4
Kilmany 244 B2
Kilmarie 256 B3
Kilmarnock 224 C2
Kilmartin 240 A5
Kilmaurs 233 F5
Kilmelford 240 A3
Kilmeny 230 B3
Kilmersdon 117 D2
Kilmeston 119 G5
Kilmichael 222 B3
Kilmichael
Glassary 240 A5
Kilmichael of
Inverlussa 231 F1
Kilmington Devon 103 F3
Kilmington Wilts 117 E4
Kilmington
Common 117 E4
Kilmood 283 H2
Kilmorack 266 B7
Kilmore (A' Chille Mhòr)
A&B 240 A2
Kilmore AB&C 282 C3
Kilmore High 256 C4
Kilmore NM&D 283 H3
Kilmory A&B 231 F1
Kilmory A&B 231 F2
Kilmory High 255 J4
Kilmory High 247 E2
Kilmory NAyr 223 E3
Kilmote 274 E7
Kilmuir High 263 H7
Kilmuir High 266 D7
Kilmuir High 266 E4
Kilmuir High 263 J4
Kilmun 232 C1
Kilmux 244 B4
Kiln Green Here 131 F1
Kiln Green W'ham
134 D5
Kiln Pit Hill 211 G2
Kilnaslee 281 K2
Kilnave 230 A2
Kilncadzow 234 C5
Kilndown 123 G5
Kilnhurst 186 B3
Kilninian 246 D5
Kilninver 240 A2
Kilnsea 189 E1
Kilnsey 193 F1
Kilntown 282 E3
Kilnwick 196 B3
Kilnwick Percy 196 A2
Kiloran 238 C5
Kilpatrick 223 E3
Kilpeck 144 D4
Kilphedir 274 E7
Kilpin 195 G5
Kilpin Pike 195 G5
Kilraghts 286 E3
Kilrea 286 D4
Kilrenny 245 D4
Kilroot 287 J7
Kilsally 282 B1
Kilsby 160 A5
Kilskeery 280 E3
Kilspindie 244 A2
Kilstay 206 B3
Kilsyth 234 B2
Kiltarlity 266 C7
Kilton Notts 186 C5
Kilton R&C 203 F1
Kilton Som 115 E3
Kilton Thorpe 203 F1
Kiltyrie 242 B1
Kilvaxter 263 J5
Kilve 115 E3
Kilverstone 163 G4
Kilvington 174 D3
Kilwaughter 287 H5
Kilwinning 233 E5
Kimberley Norf 178 B5
Kimberley Notts 173 G3
Kimberworth 186 B3
Kimble Wick 134 D2
Kimblesworth 212 B3
Kimbolton Cambs 149 F1
Kimbolton Here 145 E1
Kimbridge 119 E5
Kimcote 160 A4
Kimmeridge 105 F5
Kimmerston 229 D3
Kimpton Hants 119 D3
Kimpton Herts 136 A1
Kinakelly 281 F6
Kinaldy 244 D3
Kinallen 283 F4
Kinawley 280 E5
Kinblethmont 253 E5
Kinbrace 274 D5
Kinbreack 257 G5
Kinbuck 242 C4
Kincaldrum 252 C5
Kincaple 244 C3
Kincardine Fife 234 D1
Kincardine High 266 D3
Kincardine O'Neil 260 D5
Kinclaven 243 G1
Kincorth 261 H4
Kincraig Aber 261 H2
Kincraig High 259 F4
Kincraigie 251 E5
Kindallachan 251 E4
Kindrogan Field
Centre 251 F3
Kinellar 261 G3
Kineton Glos 146 C5
Kineton Warks 147 F2
Kineton Green 158 D4
Kinfauns 243 G2
King Sterndale 185 E5
Kingarth 232 B4
Kingcoed 130 D2
Kingerby 188 A3
Kingham 147 E5
Kingholm Quay 217 D3
Kinghorn 235 G1
Kinglassie 244 A5
Kingoodie 244 B2
King's Acre 145 D3
King's Bank 111 D1
King's Bromley 158 D1
Kings Caple 145 E5
King's Cliffe 161 F3
King's College Chapel,
Cambridge Cambs
CB2 1ST 150 C2
King's Coughton 146 C2
King's Green 145 G4
King's Heath 158 C4
Kings Hill Kent 123 F3
King's Hill Warks 159 F5
King's Hill WMid 158 B3
Kings Langley 135 F2
King's Lynn 177 E5
King's Meaburn 210 C5
Kings Mills 101 E5
King's Moss 183 G2
Kings Muir 227 D2
King's Newnham 159 G5
King's Newton 173 E5
King's Norton Leics 160 B2
King's Norton
WMid 158 C5
Kings Nympton 113 G4
King's Pyon 144 D2
Kings Ripton 162 A5
King's Somborne 119 E4
King's Stag 104 D1
King's Stanley 132 A2
King's Sutton 147 G4
King's Tamerton 100 A2
King's Walden 149 G5
Kings Worthy 119 F4
Kingsand 100 A2
Kingsbarns 245 D3
Kingsbridge Devon 100 D3
Kingsbridge Som 114 C4
Kingsburgh 263 J6
Kingsbury GtLon 136 A4
Kingsbury Warks 159 E3
Kingsbury Episcopi 116 B5
Kingsbury Water Park
Warks B76 0DY 159 E3
Kingscavil 235 E2
Kingsclere 119 G2
Kingscote 132 A3
Kingscott 113 F4
Kingscross 223 F3
Kingsdale 244 B4
Kingsdon 116 C5
Kingsdown Kent 125 F4
Kingsdown Swin 133 D4
Kingsdown Wilts 117 F1
Kingseat 243 G5
Kingsey 134 C2
Kingsfold Pembs 126 C3
Kingsfold WSuss 121 G4
Kingsford Aber 269 F6
Kingsford Aber 260 D3
Kingsford
Aberdeen 261 G4
Kingsford EAyr 233 F5
Kingsford Worcs 158 A4
Kingsgate 125 F1
Kingshall Street 152 A1
Kingsheanton 113 F2
Kingshouse 242 A2
Kingshouse Hotel 249 E4
Kingshurst 159 D4
Kingskerswell 101 E1
Kingskettle 244 B4
Kingsland Here 144 D1
Kingsland IoA 180 A4
Kingsley ChesW&C 183 G5
Kingsley Hants 120 C4
Kingsley Staffs 172 B3
Kingsley Green 121 D4
Kingsley Holt 172 B3
Kingslow 157 G3
Kingsmill 282 B1
Kingsmoor 136 D2
Kingsmuir Angus 252 C5
Kingsmuir Fife 244 D4
Kingsnorth 124 C5
Kingsnorth Power
Station 124 A1
Kingstanding 158 C3
Kingsteignton 102 B5
Kingsteps 267 G6
Kingsthorne 145 D4
Kingsthorpe 148 C1
Kingston Cambs 150 B2
Kingston Corn 99 D3
Kingston Devon 100 C3
Kingston Devon 103 D4
Kingston Dorset 104 D2
Kingston Dorset 105 F5
Kingston ELoth 236 C1
Kingston GtMan 184 D3
Kingston Hants 106 A2
Kingston IoW 107 D4
Kingston Kent 125 D3
Kingston MK 149 E4
Kingston Moray 268 B4
Kingston WSuss 108 C3
Kingston Bagpuize 133 G3
Kingston Blount 134 C3
Kingston by Sea 109 E3
Kingston Deverill 117 F4
Kingston Gorse 108 C3
Kingston Lacy Dorset
BH21 4EA 3 A1
Kingston Lisle 133 F4
Kingston Maurward 104 D3
Kingston near
Lewes 109 F3
Kingston on Soar 173 G5
Kingston Russell 104 B3
Kingston St. Mary 115 F5
Kingston Seymour 116 B1
Kingston Stert 134 C2
Kingston upon Hull 196 D5
Kingston upon
Thames 121 G1
Kingston Warren 133 F4
Kingstone Here 144 D4
Kingstone Here 145 F5
Kingstone Som 103 G1
Kingstone Staffs 172 B5
Kingstone Winslow 133 E4
Kingstown 209 G1
Kingswear 101 E2
Kingswell 233 G5
Kingswells 261 G4
Kingswinford 158 A4
Kingswood Bucks 134 B1
Kingswood Glos 131 G3
Kingswood Here 144 B2
Kingswood Kent 124 A3
Kingswood Powys 156 B2
Kingswood SGlos 131 F5
Kingswood Som 115 E4
Kingswood Surr 122 B3
Kingswood Warks 159 D5
Kingthorpe 188 B5
Kington Here 144 B2
Kington Worcs 146 B2
Kington Langley 132 B5
Kington Magna 117 E5
Kington St. Michael 132 B5
Kingussie 258 E4
Kingweston 116 C4
Kinharrachie 261 H1
Kinharvie 216 D4
Kinkell 234 A2
Kinkell Bridge 243 E3
Kinknockie 269 J6
Kinlet 157 G4
Kinloch Fife 244 A3
Kinloch High 273 F5
Kinloch High 247 F4
Kinloch High 255 K5
Kinloch High 266 C4
Kinloch P&K 252 A5
Kinloch P&K 251 G5
Kinloch Hourn (Ceann Loch
Shubhairne) 257 F4
Kinloch Laggan 250 A1
Kinloch Rannoch 250 B4
Kinlochan 248 A3
Kinlochard 241 G4
Kinlocharkaig 257 F5
Kinlochbeoraid 248 A1
Kinlochbervie 272 E3
Kinlocheil 248 B2
Kinlochetive 248 D5
Kinlochewe 265 G5
Kinlochlaich 248 B5
Kinlochleven (Ceann Loch
Liobhann) 249 D3
Kinlochmoidart 247 G2
Kinlochmorar 256 E5
Kinlochmore 249 D3
Kinlochroag (Ceann
Lochroag) 270 D5
Kinlochspelve 239 F2
Kinloss 267 H5
Kinmel Bay
(Bae Cinmel) 182 A4
Kinmuck 261 G3
Kinnaber 253 F3
Kinnadie 269 H6
Kinnaird 244 A2
Kinneff 253 G2
Kinnelhead 226 B5
Kinnell Angus 253 E4
Kinnell Stir 242 A1
Kinnerley 170 A5
Kinnersley Here 144 C3
Kinnersley Worcs 146 A3
Kinnerton 144 B1
Kinnerton Green 170 A1
Kinnesswood 243 G4
Kinninvie 211 G5
Kinnordy 252 B4
Kinoulton 174 B4
Kinrara 259 F4
Kinross 243 G4
Kinrossie 243 G1
Kinsbourne Green 136 A1
Kinsham Here 144 C1
Kinsham Worcs 146 B4
Kinsley 186 B1
Kinson 105 G3
Kintarvie 270 E6
Kintbury 119 E1
Kintessack 267 G5
Kintillo 243 G3
Kintocher 260 D4
Kinton Here 156 D5
Kinton Shrop 156 C1
Kintore 261 F3
Kintour 230 C4
Kintra A&B 230 B5
Kintra A&B 238 C2
Kintradwell 267 G1
Kintraw 240 A4
Kinuachdrachd 239 G5
Kinveachy 259 G3
Kinver 158 A4
Kinwarton 146 D2
Kiplaw Croft 261 J1
Kipp 242 A3
Kippax 194 D4
Kippen P&K 243 F3
Kippen Stir 242 B5
Kippenross House 242 C4
Kippford (Scaur) 216 C5
Kipping's Cross 123 F4
Kippington 123 E3
Kirbister Ork 277 C7
Kirbister Ork 276 F5
Kirbuster 276 B5
Kirby Bedon 179 D5
Kirby Bellars 160 C1
Kirby Cane 165 E2
Kirby Corner 159 E5
Kirby Cross 152 D5
Kirby Fields 160 A2
Kirby Green 165 E2
Kirby Grindalythe 196 B1
Kirby Hill NYorks 202 A2
Kirby Hill NYorks 194 C1
Kirby Knowle 203 D4
Kirby le Soken 152 D5
Kirby Misperton 203 G5
Kirby Muxloe 160 A2
Kirby Row 165 E2
Kirby Sigston 202 D3
Kirby Underdale 196 A2
Kirby Wiske 202 C4
Kircubbin 283 J2
Kirdford 121 F5
Kirk 275 H3
Kirk Bramwith 186 D1
Kirk Deighton 194 C2
Kirk Ella 196 C5
Kirk Hallam 173 F3
Kirk Hammerton 195 D2
Kirk Ireton 173 D2
Kirk Langley 173 D4
Kirk Merrington 212 B4
Kirk Michael 190 B2
Kirk of Shotts 234 C3
Kirk Sandall 186 D2
Kirk Smeaton 186 C1
Kirk Yetholm 228 C4
Kirkabister 279 D9
Kirkandrews 207 G2
Kirkandrews-upon-
Eden 209 G1
Kirkbampton 209 G1
Kirkbean 217 D5
Kirkbride 209 F1
Kirkbuddo 252 D5
Kirkburn ERid 196 B2
Kirkburn ScBord 227 D2
Kirkburton 185 F1
Kirkby Lincs 188 A3
Kirkby Mersey 183 F3
Kirkby NYorks 203 E2
Kirkby Fleetham 202 B3
Kirkby Green 175 F2
Kirkby in Ashfield 173 F2
Kirkby la Thorpe 175 F3
Kirkby Lonsdale 200 B5
Kirkby Malham 193 E1
Kirkby Mallory 159 G2
Kirkby Malzeard 202 B5
Kirkby on Bain 176 A1
Kirkby Overblow 194 C3
Kirkby Stephen 200 C2
Kirkby Thore 210 C5
Kirkby Underwood 175 F5
Kirkby Wharfe 195 E3
Kirkby Woodhouse 173 F2
Kirkby-in-Furness 198 D4
Kirkbymoorside 203 F4
Kirkcaldy 244 A5
Kirkcambeck 210 B1
Kirkcolm 214 B4
Kirkconnel 225 F4
Kirkconnell 217 D4
Kirkcowan 215 E4
Kirkcudbright 216 A5
Kirkdale House 215 G5
Kirkdean 235 F5
Kirkfieldbank 234 C5
Kirkgunzeon 216 C4
Kirkham Lancs 192 A4
Kirkham NYorks 195 G1
Kirkhamgate 194 C5
Kirkharle 220 C3
Kirkhaugh 210 C3
Kirkheaton N'umb 220 C4
Kirkheaton WYorks 185 F1
Kirkhill Angus 253 E3
Kirkhill High 266 C7
Kirkhill Moray 268 B5
Kirkhope 227 E3
Kirkibost High 256 B3
Kirkibost (Circebost)
Na H-E. Siar 270 D4
Kirkinch 252 B5
Kirkinner 215 F5
Kirkinriola 287 F5
Kirkintilloch 234 A2
Kirkistown 283 K3
Kirkland Cumb 210 C4
Kirkland Cumb 209 D5
Kirkland D&G 216 C1
Kirkland D&G 225 F4
Kirkland D&G 217 E2
Kirkland of
Longcastle 207 D2
Kirkleatham 213 E5
Kirklevington 202 D1
Kirkley 165 G2
Kirklington Notts 174 B2
Kirklington NYorks 202 C4
Kirklinton 210 A1
Kirkliston 235 F2
Kirkmaiden 206 B3
Kirkmichael P&K 251 F3
Kirkmichael SAyr 224 B5
Kirkmuirhill 234 B5
Kirknewton N'umb 228 D3
Kirknewton WLoth 235 F3
Kirkney 260 D1
Kirkoswald Cumb 210 B3
Kirkoswald SAyr 224 A5
Kirkpatrick Durham 216 B3
Kirkpatrick-Fleming 218 A4
Kirksanton 198 C4
Kirkstall 194 B4
Kirkstead 175 G1
Kirkstile Aber 260 D1
Kirkstile D&G 218 B2
Kirkstyle 275 J1
Kirkthorpe 194 C5
Kirkton A&B 239 G4
Kirkton Aber 260 E2
Kirkton Aber 268 E5
Kirkton Aber 260 E3
Kirkton Angus 252 C5
Kirkton D&G 217 D2
Kirkton Fife 244 B2
Kirkton High 258 D1
Kirkton High 266 E2
Kirkton High 266 E6
Kirkton High 274 D2
Kirkton High 256 E2
Kirkton P&K 243 E3
Kirkton ScBord 227 G4
Kirkton Manor 226 D2
Kirkton of Airlie 252 B4
Kirkton of
Auchterhouse 244 B1
Kirkton of Barevan 267 F7
Kirkton of Bourtie 261 G2
Kirkton of Collace 243 G1
Kirkton of Craig 253 F4
Kirkton of
Culsalmond 260 E1
Kirkton of Durris 261 F5
Kirkton of
Glenbuchat 260 B3
Kirkton of Glenisla 252 A3
Kirkton of
Kingoldrum 252 B4
Kirkton of Kinnettles
252 C5
Kirkton of Lethendy 251 G5
Kirkton of Logie
Buchan 261 H2
Kirkton of
Maryculter 261 G5
Kirkton of Menmuir 252 D3
Kirkton of Monikie 244 D1
Kirkton of Rayne 260 E1
Kirkton of Skene 261 G4
Kirkton of Tealing 244 C1
Kirktonhill Aber 253 E3
Kirktonhill WDun 233 E2
Kirktown 269 J5
Kirktown of Alvah 268 E4
Kirktown of
Deskford 268 D4
Kirktown of
Fetteresso 253 G1
Kirktown of Slains 261 J2
Kirkwall 277 D6
Kirkwall Airport 277 D7
Kirkwhelpington 220 B3
Kirmington 188 B1
Kirmond le Mire 188 B3
Kirn 232 C2
Kirriemuir 252 B4
Kirstead Green 165 D2
Kirtlebridge 218 A4
Kirtleton 218 A3
Kirtling 151 E2
Kirtling Green 151 E2
Kirtlington 134 A1
Kirtomy 274 C2
Kirton Lincs 176 B4
Kirton Notts 174 B1
Kirton Suff 153 D4
Kirton End 176 A3
Kirton Holme 176 A3
Kirton in Lindsey 187 G3
Kiscadale 223 F3
Kislingbury 148 B2
Kismeldon Bridge 113 D4
Kit Hill Country Park
Corn PL17 8AX 99 D3
Kites Hardwick 147 G1
Kitley 100 B2
Kittisford 115 D5
Kittisford Barton 115 D5
Kittle 128 B4
Kitt's End 136 B3
Kitt's Green 159 D4
Kitwood 120 B4
Kivernoll 145 D4
Kiveton Park 186 B4
Klibreck 273 H5
Knabbygates 268 D5
Knaith 187 F4
Knaith Park 187 F4
Knap Corner 117 F5
Knaphill 121 E2
Knaplock 114 B4
Knapp P&K 244 A1
Knapp Som 116 A5
Knapthorpe 174 C2
Knaptoft 160 B4
Knapton Norf 179 E2
Knapton York 195 E2
Knapton Green 144 D2
Knapwell 150 B1
Knaresborough 194 C2
Knarsdale 210 C2
Knarston 276 C5
Knaven 269 G6
Knayton 202 D4
Knebworth 150 A5
Knebworth House Herts
SG3 6PY 150 A5
Knedlington 195 G5
Kneesall 174 C1
Kneesworth 150 B3
Kneeton 174 C3
Knelston 128 A4
Knenhall 171 G4
Knettishall 164 A3
Knettishall Heath Country
Park Suff
IP22 2TQ 164 A3
Knightacott 113 G2
Knightcote 147 G2
Knightley 171 F5
Knightley Dale 171 F5
Knighton Devon 100 B3
Knighton Dorset 104 C1
Knighton Leic 160 A2
Knighton Poole 105 G3
Knighton (Tref-y-clawdd)
Powys 156 B5
Knighton Som 115 E3
Knighton Staffs 171 E5
Knighton Staffs 171 E3
Knighton Wilts 133 E5
Knighton on Teme
157 F5
Knightswood 233 G3
Knightwick 145 G2
Knill 144 B1
Knipoch 240 A2
Knipton 174 D4
Knitsley 212 A3
Kniveton 172 D2
Knock A&B 239 E1
Knock Cumb 210 C5
Knock High 256 C4
Knock Moray 268 D5
Knock of
Auchnahannet 259 H1
Knockalava 240 B5
Knockally 275 G6
Knockaloe Moar 190 A3
Knockan CC&G 285 J5
Knockan High 272 E7
Knockandhu 259 K2
Knockando 267 J7
Knockanorane 281 G5
Knockanully 287 F4
Knockarevan 281 F6
Knockarthur 266 E1
Knockavannon 282 C6
Knockbain 266 D6
Knockban 265 J5
Knockbrack D&S 285 G4
Knockbreck 266 E3
Knockbrex 207 F2
Knockcloghrim 286 C6
Knockdamph 265 J2
Knockdee 275 G2
Knockdow 232 C2
Knockdown 132 A4
Knockenkelly 223 F3
Knockentiber 224 B2
Knockfin 257 K2
Knockgray 215 G1
Knockholt 123 D3
Knockholt Pound 123 D3
Knockin 170 A5
Knockinelder 283 K3
Knockinlaw 224 C2
Knockintorran (Cnoc an
Torrain) 262 C5
Knocklearn 216 B3
Knockmany Passage Grave
Mid Ulster BT76 0XJ
281 H3
Knockmill 123 E2
Knockmoyle 281 G1
Knocknacarry 287 G2
Knocknaha 222 B4
Knocknain 214 A4
Knocknalling 215 G2
Knocknashangan 280 B4
Knockrome 231 D2
Knocks 281 F5
Knocksharry 190 A3
Knockville 215 E3
Knockvologan 238 C3
Knodishall 153 F1
Knodishall
Common 153 F1
Knodishall Green 153 F1
Knole 116 B5
Knolls Green 184 C5
Knolton 170 A4
Knook 118 A3
Knossington 160 D2
Knott End-on-Sea 191 G3
Knotting 149 F1
Knotting Green 149 F1
Knottingley 195 E5
Knotts 193 D2
Knotty Green 135 E3
Knowbury 157 E5
Knowe 215 E3
Knowehead 283 J1
Knowes of Elrick 268 E5
Knowesgate 220 B3
Knoweside 224 A4
Knowetownhead 227 G4
Knowhead 269 H5
Knowl Green 151 F3
Knowl Hill 134 D5
Knowl Wall 171 F4
Knowle Bristol 131 F5
Knowle Devon 102 A2
Knowle Devon 113 E2
Knowle Devon 103 D4
Knowle Shrop 157 E5
Knowle Som 114 C3
Knowle WMid 159 D5
Knowle Cross 102 D3
Knowle Green 192 C4
Knowle Hall 116 A3
Knowle St. Giles 103 G1
Knowlton Dorset 105 G1
Knowlton Kent 125 E3
Knowsley 183 F3
Knowsley Safari Park
Mersey L34 4AN 23 E2
Knowstone 114 B5
Knox Bridge 123 G4
Knucklas (Cnwclas)
156 B5
Knutsford 184 B5
Knypersley 171 F2
Krumlin 185 E1
Kuggar 95 E5
Kyle of Lochalsh (Caol
Loch Aillse) 256 D2
Kyleakin
(Caol Acain) 256 D2
Kylerhea
(Ceol Reatha) 256 D2
Kyles Scalpay (Caolas
Scalpaigh) 263 H2
Kylesbeg 247 F2
Kylesknoydart 256 E5
Kylesku 272 E5
Kylesmorar 256 E5
Kylestrome 272 E5
Kyloag 266 D2
Kynaston 170 A5
Kynnersley 157 F1
Kyre Park 145 F1

L
Labost 270 E3
Lacasaigh 271 F5
Lace Market Centre
NG1 1HF
80 Nottingham
Laceby 188 C2
Lacey Green 134 D2
Lach Dennis 184 B5
Lack 280 E2
Lackagh 285 J4
Lackalee
(Leac a' Li) 263 G2
Lackford 163 F5
Lacock 118 A1
Ladbroke 147 G2
Laddingford 123 F4
Lade Bank 176 B2

Ladies Hill **192** A3
Ladock **96** C4
Lady Hall **198** C4
Lady Lever Art Gallery *Mersey* CH62 5EQ **22** B4
Ladybank **244** B3
Ladycross **98** D2
Ladyfield **240** C3
Ladykirk **237** F5
Ladysford **269** H4
Ladywood **146** A1
Laga **247** F3
Lagalochan **240** A3
Lagavara **286** E1
Lagavulin **230** C5
Lagg *A&B* **231** D2
Lagg *NAyr* **223** E3
Lagg *SAyr* **224** A4
Laggan *A&B* **230** A4
Laggan (An Lagan) *High* **257** J5
Laggan *High* **258** D5
Laggan *Moray* **260** B1
Laggan *Stir* **242** A3
Lagganulva **247** D5
Lagganvoulin **259** J3
Laghy Corner **282** B2
Laglingarten **240** D4
Lagnalean **266** D7
Lagrae **225** F4
Laguna **243** G1
Laid **273** G3
Laide **265** F2
Laig **247** D1
Laight **225** E4
Lainchoil **259** H3
Laindon **137** F4
Laing Art Gallery *T&W* NE1 8AG **79** Newcastle upon Tyne
Lair **251** G3
Lairg **266** C1
Lairg Lodge **266** C1
Lairigmor **248** D3
Laisterdyke **194** A4
Laithers **268** E6
Laithes **210** A4
Lake *Devon* **113** F2
Lake *Devon* **100** B1
Lake *IoW* **107** E4
Lake *Wilts* **118** C4
Lake District Visitor Centre at Brockhole *Cumb* LA23 1LJ **199** E2
Lakenham **178** D5
Lakenheath **163** F4
Lakes Aquarium *Cumb* LA12 8AS **199** E4
Lakes End **162** D3
Lakes Glass Centre, Ulverston *Cumb* LA12 7LY **199** D5
Lakeside *Cumb* **199** E4
Lakeside *Thur* **137** E5
Lakeside & Haverthwaite Railway *Cumb* LA12 8AL **199** E4
Laleham **121** F1
Laleston **129** E5
Lamancha **235** G4
Lamarsh **151** G4
Lamas **178** D3
Lamb Corner **152** B4
Lamb Roe **192** D4
Lambden **237** E5
Lambeg **283** F2
Lamberhurst **123** F5
Lamberhurst Quarter **123** F5
Lamberton **237** G4
Lambfell Moar **190** A3
Lambley *N'umb* **210** C2
Lambley *Notts* **174** B3
Lambourn **133** F5
Lambourn Woodlands **133** F5
Lambourne End **137** D3
Lambs Green **122** B5
Lambston **126** C1
Lambton **212** B2
Lamellion **97** G3
Lamerton **99** E3
Lamesley **212** B2
Lamington *High* **266** E4
Lamington *SLan* **226** A2
Lamlash **223** F2
Lamloch **215** G1
Lamonby **210** A4
Lamorna **94** B4
Lamorran **96** C5
Lampert **219** E4
Lampeter (Llanbedr Pont Steffan) **142** B3
Lampeter Velfrey **127** E1
Lamphey **126** D2
Lamplugh **209** D4
Lamport **160** C5
Lamyatt **117** D4
Lana *Devon* **98** D1
Lana *Devon* **112** D5
Lanark **234** C5
Lanarth **95** E4
Lancaster **192** A1
Lancaster Leisure Park *Lancs* LA1 3LA **192** A1
Lancaster Priory *Lancs* LA1 1YZ **192** A1
Lanchester **212** A3
Lancing **109** D3
Landbeach **150** C1
Landcross **113** E3
Landerberry **261** F4
Landewednack **95** E5
Landford **106** B1
Landhallow **275** G5
Landican **183** D4
Landimore **128** A3
Landkey **113** F2
Landmoth **202** D3
Landore **128** C3
Landrake **99** D4
Land's End *Corn* TR19 7AA **94** A4
Land's End Airport **94** A4
Landscove **101** D1
Landshipping **126** D1
Landulph **100** A1
Landwade **151** E1
Landywood **158** B2
Lane Bottom **193** E4
Lane End *Bucks* **134** D3
Lane End *Cumb* **198** C3
Lane End *Derbys* **173** F1
Lane End *Dorset* **105** E3
Lane End *Hants* **119** G5
Lane End *Here* **131** F1
Lane End *Kent* **137** E5
Lane End *Wilts* **117** F3
Lane Ends *Derbys* **172** D4
Lane Ends *GtMan* **185** D3
Lane Ends *Lancs* **193** D4
Lane Ends *NYorks* **193** F3
Lane Green **158** A2
Lane Head *Dur* **202** A1
Lane Head *Dur* **211** G5
Lane Head *GtMan* **184** A3
Lane Head *WYorks* **185** F2
Lane Heads **192** A4
Lane Side **193** D5
Laneast **97** G1
Lane-end **97** E3
Laneham **187** F5
Lanehead *Dur* **211** E3
Lanehead *N'umb* **219** F3
Lanesend **127** D2
Lanesfield **158** B3
Laneshawbridge **193** F3
Langais **262** D5
Langamull **246** C4
Langar **174** C4
Langbank **233** E2
Langbar **193** G2
Langbaurgh **203** E1
Langcliffe **193** E1
Langdale End **204** C3
Langdon *Corn* **98** C1
Langdon *Corn* **98** D2
Langdon Beck **211** E4
Langdon Hills **137** F4
Langdon Hills Country Park *Essex* SS17 9NH **137** F4
Langdon House **102** C5
Langdyke **244** B4
Langford *CenBeds* **149** G3
Langford *Essex* **138** B2
Langford *Notts* **174** D2
Langford *Oxon* **133** E2
Langford Budville **115** E5
Langham *Essex* **152** B4
Langham *Norf* **178** B1
Langham *Rut* **160** D1
Langham *Suff* **152** A1
Langham Moor **152** B4
Langho **192** C4
Langholm **218** B3
Langland **128** C4
Langlands **216** A5
Langlee **228** A5
Langleeford **228** D4
Langley *ChesE* **184** D5
Langley *Derbys* **173** F3
Langley *Essex* **150** C4
Langley *Glos* **146** C5
Langley *GtMan* **184** C2
Langley *Hants* **106** D2
Langley *Herts* **150** A5
Langley *Kent* **123** G3
Langley *N'umb* **211** E1
Langley *Oxon* **133** F1
Langley *Slo* **135** F5
Langley *Som* **115** D5
Langley *Warks* **147** D1
Langley *WSuss* **120** D5
Langley Burrell **132** B5
Langley Corner **135** F4
Langley Green *Derbys* **173** D4
Langley Green *Warks* **147** E1
Langley Green *WSuss* **122** B5
Langley Heath **124** A3
Langley Marsh **115** D5
Langley Mill **173** F3
Langley Moor **212** B3
Langley Park **212** B3
Langley Park *Bucks* SL3 6DW **135** F4
Langley Street **179** E5
Langney **110** B3
Langold **186** C4
Langore **97** G1
Langport **116** B5
Langrick **176** A3
Langrick Bridge **176** A3
Langridge *B&NESom* **117** E1
Langridge *Devon* **113** F3
Langridgeford **113** F3
Langrigg **209** E2
Langrish **120** C5
Langsett **185** G2
Langshaw **227** G2
Langshawburn **227** D5
Langside *Glas* **233** G3
Langside *P&K* **242** C3
Langskaill **276** D3
Langstone *Hants* **107** G2
Langstone *Newport* **130** C3
Langthorne **202** B3
Langthorpe **194** C1
Langthwaite **201** F2
Langtoft *ERid* **196** C1
Langtoft *Lincs* **161** G1
Langton *Dur* **202** A1
Langton *Lincs* **189** D5
Langton *Lincs* **176** A1
Langton *NYorks* **195** G1
Langton by Wragby **188** B5
Langton Green *Kent* **123** E5
Langton Green *Suff* **164** C4
Langton Herring **104** C4
Langton Long Blandford **105** E2
Langton Matravers **105** F5
Langtree **113** E4
Langtree Week **113** E4
Langwathby **210** B4
Langwell **266** B1
Langwell House **275** G6
Langwith **186** C5
Langworth **188** A5
Lanhydrock *Corn* PL30 5AD **97** E3
Lanivet **97** E3
Lank **97** E2
Lanlivery **97** E4
Lanner **96** B5
Lanoy **97** G2
Lanreath **97** F4
Lansallos **97** F4
Lansdown **117** E1
Lanteglos **97** E1
Lanteglos Highway **97** F4
Lanton *N'umb* **228** D3
Lanton *ScBord* **228** A4
Lanvean **96** C3
Lapford **102** A2
Laphroaig **230** B5
Lapley **158** A1
Lapworth **159** D5
Larach na Gaibhre **231** F2
Larachbeg **247** F5
Laragh **286** C5
Larbert **234** C1
Larbreck **192** A3
Larchmount **282** B3
Larden Green **170** C2
Larg **215** E3
Largie **260** E1
Largiemore **232** A1
Largoward **244** C4
Largs **232** D4
Largue **268** E6
Largybaan **222** B4
Largybeg **223** F3
Largymore **223** F3
Lark Hall **151** D2
Larkfield **232** D2
Larkhall **234** B4
Larkhill *F&O* **280** C2
Larkhill *Wilts* **118** C3
Larklands **173** F3
Larling **164** A3
Larne **287** H5
Larriston **218** D2
Lartington **201** F1
Lary **260** B4
Lasborough **132** A3
Lasham **120** B3
Lashbrook **113** E5
Lashenden **124** A4
Lassington **145** G5
Lassintullich **250** C4
Lassodie **243** G5
Lasswade **236** A3
Lastingham **203** G3
Latchford **184** A4
Latchingdon **138** B2
Latchley **99** E3
Lately Common **184** A3
Lathallan Mill **244** C4
Lathbury **149** D3
Latheron **275** G5
Latheronwheel **275** G5
Lathockar **244** C3
Lathones **244** C4
Lathrisk **244** A4
Latimer **135** F3
Latteridge **131** F4
Lattiford **117** D5
Latton **132** C3
Lauchentyre **215** G5
Lauchintilly **261** F3
Lauder **236** C5
Laugharne (Lacharn) **127** G1
Laughterton **187** F5
Laughton *ESuss* **110** A2
Laughton *Leics* **160** B4
Laughton *Lincs* **175** F4
Laughton *Lincs* **187** F3
Laughton en le Morthen **186** C4
Launcells **112** C5
Launcells Cross **112** C5
Launceston **98** D2
Launde Abbey **160** C2
Launton **148** B5
Laurelvale **282** D4
Laurencekirk **253** F2
Laurieston *D&G* **216** A4
Laurieston *Falk* **234** D2
Lavendon **149** E2
Lavenham **152** A3
Laverhay **217** F1
Lavernock **115** E1
Laversdale **210** A1
Laverstock **118** C4
Laverstoke **119** F3
Laverton *Glos* **146** C4
Laverton *NYorks* **202** B5
Laverton *Som* **117** E2
Lavister **170** A2
Law **234** C4
Lawers *P&K* **242** C2
Lawers *P&K* **242** B1
Lawford *Essex* **152** B4
Lawford *Som* **115** E4
Lawhitton **99** D2
Lawkland **193** D1
Lawkland Green **193** D1
Lawley **157** F2
Lawnhead **171** F5
Lawrence Weston **131** E5
Lawrencetown **282** D4
Lawrenny **126** D2
Laws **244** C1
Lawshall **151** G2
Lawshall Green **151** G2
Lawton **144** D2
Laxdale (Lacasdal) **271** G4
Laxey **190** C3
Laxfield **165** D4
Laxfirth *Shet* **279** D7
Laxfirth *Shet* **279** D8
Laxford Bridge **272** E4
Laxo **279** D6
Laxton *ERid* **195** G5
Laxton *N'hants* **161** E3
Laxton *Notts* **174** C1
Laycock **193** G3
Layde **287** G3
Layer Breton **138** C1
Layer de la Haye **138** C1
Layer Marney **138** C1
Layham **152** B3
Laymore **103** G2
Layter's Green **135** E3
Laytham **195** G4
Layton **191** G4
Lazenby **213** E5
Lazonby **210** B4
Lea *Derbys* **173** E2
Lea *Here* **145** F5
Lea *Lincs* **187** F4
Lea *Shrop* **156** C4
Lea *Shrop* **156** D2
Lea *Wilts* **132** B4
Lea Bridge **173** E2
Lea Green **145** F1
Lea Marston **159** E3
Lea Town **192** A4
Lea Yeat **200** C4
Leachd **240** C5
Leachkin (An Leacainn) **266** D7
Leadburn **235** G4
Leaden Roding **137** E1
Leadenham **175** E2
Leaderfoot **227** G2
Leadgate *Cumb* **210** D3
Leadgate *Dur* **212** A2
Leadgate *N'umb* **212** A2
Leadhills **225** G4
Leadingcross Green **124** A3
Leafield **133** F1
Leagrave **149** F5
Leake Commonside **176** B2
Leake Hurn's End **176** C3
Lealands **110** A2
Lealholm **203** G2
Lealt *A&B* **239** F5
Lealt *High* **264** B5
Leam **185** G5
Leamington Hastings **147** G1
Leamington Spa **147** F1
Leamington Spa Art Gallery & Museum *Warks* CV32 4AA **16** B6
Leamoor Common **156** D4
Leanach *A&B* **240** C5
Leanach *High* **266** E7
Leanaig **266** C6
Leanoch **267** J6
Leargybreck **230** D2
Leasgill **199** F4
Leasingham **175** F3
Leask **261** J1
Leason **128** A3
Leasowe **183** D3
Leat **98** D2
Leatherhead **121** G2
Leathley **194** B3
Leaton *Shrop* **157** D1
Leaton *Tel&W* **157** F1
Leaveland **124** C3
Leavenheath **152** A4
Leavening **195** G1
Leaves Green **122** D2
Leavesden Green **136** A2
Lebberston **205** D4
Lechlade-on-Thames **133** E3
Leck *CC&G* **286** C3
Leck *Lancs* **200** B5
Leckford **119** E4
Leckfurin **274** C3
Leckgruinart **230** A3
Leckhampstead *Bucks* **148** C4
Leckhampstead *WBerks* **133** G5
Leckhampstead Thicket **133** G5
Leckhampton **132** B1
Leckie *High* **265** G5
Leckie *Stir* **242** B5
Leckmelm (Leac Mailm) **265** H3
Leckroy **257** K5
Leckuary **240** A5
Leckwith **130** A5
Leconfield **196** C3
Ledaig (Leideag) **240** B1
Ledard **241** G4
Ledbeg **272** E7
Ledburn **149** D5
Ledbury **145** G4
Ledcharrie **242** A2
Ledgemoor **144** D2
Ledicot **144** D1
Ledmore *A&B* **247** E5
Ledmore *High* **272** E7
Lednagullin **274** D2
Ledsham *ChesW&C* **183** E5
Ledsham *WYorks* **195** D5
Ledston **194** D5
Ledstone **100** D3
Ledwell **147** G5
Lee *A&B* **238** D2
Lee *Devon* **113** E1
Lee *Hants* **106** C1
Lee *Lancs* **192** B2
Lee *Shrop* **170** B4
Lee Brockhurst **170** C5
Lee Chapel **137** F4
Lee Clump **135** E2
Lee Mill Bridge **100** B2
Lee Moor **100** B1
Lee Valley Park *Essex* EN9 1XQ **136** C2
Leebotten **279** D10
Leebotwood **157** D3
Leece **191** F1
Leeds *Kent* **124** A3
Leeds *WYorks* **194** B4
Leeds Art Gallery *WYorks* LS1 3AA **40** E3
Leeds Bradford International Airport **194** B3
Leeds Castle & Gardens *Kent* ME17 1PL **124** A3
Leedstown **94** D3
Leegomery **157** F1
Leek **171** G2
Leek Wootton **147** E1
Leekbrook **171** G2
Leeke **285** J4
Leeming *NYorks* **202** B4
Leeming *WYorks* **193** G4
Leeming Bar **202** B4
Lee-on-the-Solent **107** E2
Lees *Derbys* **173** D4
Lees *GtMan* **185** D2
Leeswood **169** F2
Leftwich **184** A5
Legacurry **283** F3
Legamaddy **283** H5
Legamaghery **281** G3
Legananny **283** F4
Legars **237** E5
Legbourne **189** D4
Legerwood **236** C5
Leggs **280** C2
Legoland Windsor *W&M* SL4 4AY **135** E5
Legsby **188** B4
Leicester **160** A2
Leicester Forest East **160** A2
Leideag **254** B5
Leigh *Dorset* **104** C2
Leigh *Dorset* **105** G3
Leigh *GtMan* **184** A2
Leigh *Kent* **123** E4
Leigh *Shrop* **156** C2
Leigh *Surr* **122** B4
Leigh *Wilts* **132** C3
Leigh *Worcs* **145** G2
Leigh Beck **138** B4
Leigh Common **117** E5
Leigh Delamere **132** A5
Leigh Green **124** B5
Leigh Park **107** G2
Leigh Sinton **145** G2
Leigh upon Mendip **117** D3
Leigh Woods **131** E5
Leigham **100** B2
Leighland Chapel **114** D4
Leigh-on-Sea **138** B4
Leighterton **132** A3
Leighton *NYorks* **202** A5
Leighton (Tre'r Llai) *Powys* **156** B2
Leighton *Shrop* **157** F2
Leighton *Som* **117** E3
Leighton Bromswold **161** G5
Leighton Buzzard **149** E5
Leinthall Earls **144** D1
Leinthall Starkes **144** D1
Leintwardine **156** D5
Leire **160** A4
Leirinmore **273** G2
Leiston **153** F1
Leitfie **252** A5
Leith **235** G2
Leitholm **237** E5
Leitrim *F&O* **281** G6
Leitrim *NM&D* **283** G4
Leitrim *NM&D* **283** G5
Lelant **94** C3
Lelley **197** E4
Lemington **212** A1
Lemnas **269** G4
Lempitlaw **228** B3
Lemsford **136** B1
Lenaderg **282** E4
Lenagh **285** H7
Lenchwick **146** C3
Lendalfoot **214** C1
Lendrick Lodge **242** A4
Lenham **124** A3
Lenham Heath **124** B4
Lenie **258** C2
Lenimore **231** G5
Lennel **237** F5
Lennox Plunton **216** A5
Lennoxtown **234** A2
Lent Rise **135** E4
Lenton *Lincs* **175** F4
Lenton *Nott* **173** G4
Lenton Abbey **173** G4
Lenwade **178** B4
Lenzie **234** A2
Leoch **244** B1
Leochel-Cushnie **260** D3
Leominster **145** D2
Leonard Stanley **132** A2
Leorin **230** B5
Lepe **106** D3
Lephin **263** G7
Lephinchapel **240** B5
Lephinmore **240** B5
Leppington **195** G1
Lepton **185** G1
Lerags **240** A2
Lerryn **97** F4
Lerwick **279** D8
Lesbury **229** G5
Leschangie **261** F3
Leslie *Aber* **260** D2
Leslie *Fife* **244** A4
Lesmahagow **225** G2
Lesnewth **98** B1
Lessendrum **268** D6
Lessingham **179** E3
Lessness Heath **137** D5
Lessonhall **209** F1
Leswalt **214** B4
Letchmore Heath **136** A3
Letchworth Garden City **150** A4
Letcombe Bassett **133** F4
Letcombe Regis **133** F4
Letham *Angus* **252** D5
Letham *Falk* **234** C1
Letham *Fife* **244** B3
Lethanhill **224** C4
Lethenty **269** G6
Letheringham **153** D2
Letheringsett **178** B2
Lettaford **102** A4
Letter **280** C2
Letter Finlay **257** J5
Letterbreen **280** D4
Letterewe **265** F4
Letterfearn (Leitir Fheàrna) **256** E2
Letterkeen **280** D2
Letterloan **286** C3
Lettermorar **247** G1
Lettermore *A&B* **247** D5
Lettermore *High* **273** J4
Letters **265** H3
Lettershaws **225** G3
Lettershendony **285** H4
Letterston **140** C5
Lettoch *High* **259** H3
Lettoch *High* **259** J1
Letton *Here* **156** C5
Letton *Here* **144** C3
Letty Green **136** B1
Letwell **186** C4
Leuchars **244** C2
Leumrabhagh **271** F6
Leurbost (Liurbost) **271** F5
Leusdon **102** A5
Levedale **158** A1
Level's Green **150** C5
Leven *ERid* **196** D3
Leven *Fife* **244** B4
Levencorroch **223** F3
Levenhall **236** A2
Levens **199** F4
Levens Green **150** B5
Levenshulme **184** C3
Levenwick **279** D10
Leverburgh (An T-Òb) **263** F3
Leverington **162** C1
Leverstock Green **135** F2
Leverton **176** B3
Leverton Lucasgate **176** C3
Leverton Outgate **176** C3
Levington **152** D4
Levisham **204** B3
Levishie **258** B3
Lew **133** F2
Lewannick **97** G1
Lewcombe **104** B2
Lewdown **99** E2
Lewes **109** G2
Leweston **140** C5
Lewisham **136** C5
Lewiston (Blàr na Maigh) **258** C2
Lewistown **129** F4
Lewknor **134** C3
Leworthy **113** G2
Lewson Street **124** B2
Lewth **192** A4
Lewtrenchard **99** E2
Ley *Aber* **260** D3
Ley *Corn* **97** F3
Ley Green **149** G5
Leybourne **123** F3
Leyburn **202** A3
Leyland **192** B5
Leylodge **261** F3
Leymoor **185** F1
Leys *Aber* **269** J5
Leys *Aber* **260** C4
Leys *P&K* **244** A1
Leys of Cossans **252** B5
Leysdown-on-Sea **124** C1
Leysmill **253** E5
Leysters **145** E1
Leyton **136** C4
Leytonstone **136** C4
Lezant **98** D3
Lezerea **95** D3
Lhanbryde **267** K5
Liatrie **257** J1
Libanus **143** F5
Libberton **235** D5
Libbery **146** B2
Liberton **235** G3
Liceasto **263** G2
Lichfield **158** D2
Lichfield Cathedral *Staffs* WS13 7LD **158** D2
Lickey **158** B5
Lickey End **158** B5
Lickey Hills Country Park *Worcs* B45 8ER **14** C6
Lickfold **121** E5
Liddaton Green **99** E2
Liddel **277** D9
Liddesdale **247** G4
Liddington **133** E4
Lidgate *Derbys* **186** A5
Lidgate *Suff* **151** F2
Lidgett **174** B1
Lidlington **149** E4
Lidsey **108** B3
Lidsing **123** G2
Lidstone **147** F5
Lienassie **257** F2
Lieurary **275** F2
Liff **244** B1
Liffock **286** B2
Lifton **99** D2
Liftondown **99** D2
Ligfordrum **285** G6
Ligg **285** G4
Lightcliffe **194** A5
Lighthorne **147** F2
Lighthorne Heath **147** F2
Lighthouse, The, Glasgow *Glas* G1 3NU **39** F4
Lighthouse, The - Poole's Centre for the Arts *Poole* BH15 1UG **3** B4
Lightwater **121** E1
Lightwater Valley Park *NYorks* HG4 3HT **202** B5
Lightwood **171** G3
Lightwood Green *ChesE* **170** D3
Lightwood Green *Wrex* **170** A3
Ligoniel **283** G1
Lilbourne **160** A5
Lilburn Tower **229** E4
Lillesdon **116** A5
Lilleshall **157** G1
Lilley *Herts* **149** G5
Lilley *WBerks* **133** G5
Lilliesleaf **227** G3
Lilling Green **195** F1
Lillingstone Dayrell **148** C4
Lillingstone Lovell **148** C3
Lillington *Dorset* **104** C1
Lillington *Warks* **147** F1
Lilliput **105** G4
Lilly **113** F2
Lilstock **115** E3
Lilyhurst **157** G1
Limavady **285** J3
Limbury **149** F5
Lime Hill **281** J1
Lime Side **184** D2
Limefield **184** C1
Limehillock **268** D5
Limehurst **184** D2
Limekilnburn **234** B4
Limekilns **235** E1
Limerigg **234** C2
Limerstone **106** D4
Liminary **287** F6
Limington **116** C5
Limpenhoe **179** E5
Limpley Stoke **117** E1
Limpsfield **122** D3
Limpsfield Chart **122** D3
Linacre Reservoirs *Derbys* S42 7JW **186** A5
Linbriggs **220** A1
Linby **173** G2
Linchmere **121** D4
Lincluden **217** D3
Lincoln **187** G5
Lincoln Castle *Lincs* LN1 3AA **77** Lincoln
Lincoln Cathedral *Lincs* LN2 1PL **77** Lincoln
Lincomb **146** A1
Lincombe *Devon* **100** D2
Lincombe *Devon* **100** D3
Lindal in Furness **199** D5
Lindale **199** F4
Lindean **227** F2
Lindertis **252** B4
Lindfield **109** F1
Lindford **120** D4
Lindifferon **244** B3
Lindisfarne (Holy Island) **229** F2
Lindley **194** B3
Lindores **244** A3
Lindow End **184** C5
Lindridge **145** F1
Lindsaig **232** A2
Lindsell **151** E5
Lindsey **152** A3
Lindsey Tye **152** A3
Linfitts **185** D2
Linford *Hants* **106** A2
Linford *Thur* **137** F5
Linford Wood **148** D3
Lingague **190** A4
Lingards Wood **185** E1
Lingdale **203** F1
Lingen **144** C1
Lingfield **122** C4
Lingley Green **183** G4
Lingwood **179** E5
Linhead **268** E5
Linhope **227** F5
Liniclate (Lionacleit) **262** C7
Linicro **263** J5
Linkend **146** A4
Linkenholt **119** E2
Linkhill **110** D1
Linkinhorne **98** D3
Linklater **277** D9
Linksness *Ork* **277** B7
Linksness *Ork* **277** E6
Linktown **244** A5
Linley *Shrop* **156** C3
Linley *Shrop* **157** F3
Linley Green **145** F2
Linlithgow **235** E2
Linlithgow Bridge **235** D2
Linn of Muick Cottage **252** B1
Linnels **211** F1
Linney **126** B3
Linshiels **220** A1
Linsiadar **270** E4
Linsidemore **266** C2
Linslade **149** E5
Linstead Parva **165** E4
Linstock **210** A2
Linthwaite **185** F1
Lintlaw **237** F4
Lintmill **268** D4
Linton *Cambs* **151** D3
Linton *Derbys* **159** E1
Linton *Here* **145** F5
Linton *Kent* **123** G3
Linton *NYorks* **193** F1
Linton *ScBord* **228** B4
Linton *WYorks* **194** C3
Linton-on-Ouse **195** D1
Lintzford **212** A2
Linwood *Hants* **106** A2
Linwood *Lincs* **188** B4
Linwood *Renf* **233** F3
Lionel (Lional) **271** H1
Liphook **120** D4
Lipley **171** E4
Lisadian *AB&C* **282** B4
Lisadian *L&C* **283** F3
Lisbane **283** H2
Lisbarnet **283** H2
Lisbellaw **281** F4
Lisburn **283** F2
Liscall **286** C4
Liscard **183** E3
Liscloon **285** G5
Liscolman **286** D2
Liscombe **114** B4
Lisconrea **281** F3
Lisdoart **281** J3
Lisk **285** F6
Liskeard **97** G3
Lislane **286** B4
Lislea *Mid Ulster* **286** D5
Lislea *NM&D* **282** D6
Lisleen **283** H2
L'Islet **101** F4
Lismore **240** A1
Lisnadill **282** B5
Lisnafin **285** G7
Lisnagat **282** C5
Lisnagunogue **286** D1
Lisnamuck **286** C6
Lisnarick **280** D3
Lisnaskea **281** F5
Lisnatunny **285** F7
Lisrodden **286** D5
Liss **120** C5
Liss Forest **120** C5
Lissan **286** B7
Lissett **196** D2
Lissington **188** B4
Liston **151** G3
Listooder **283** H3
Lisvane **130** A4
Liswerry **130** C4
Litcham **163** G1
Litchborough **148** B2
Litchfield **119** F2
Litherland **183** E3
Litlington *Cambs* **150** B3
Litlington *ESuss* **110** A3

Mallusk 287 G7
Mallwyd 155 E1
Malmesbury 132 B4
Malmsmead 114 A3
Malpas ChesW&C 170 B3
Malpas Corn 96 C5
Malpas Newport 130 C3
Maltby Lincs 188 D4
Maltby Stock 203 D1
Maltby SYorks 186 C3
Maltby le Marsh 189 E4
Malting End 151 F2
Malting Green 138 C1
Maltman's Hill 124 A4
Malton 203 G5
Malvern Link 145 G3
Malvern Wells 145 G3
Mambeg 232 D1
Mamble 157 F5
Mamhead 102 C4
Mamhilad 130 C2
Manaccan 95 E4
Manadon 100 A2
Manafon 156 A2
Manaton 102 A4
Manby 189 D4
Mancetter 159 F3
Manchester 184 C3
Manchester Airport 184 C4
Manchester Apollo GtMan M12 6AP 47 H6
Manchester Art Gallery GtMan M2 3JL 47 E4
Manchester Central GtMan M2 3GX 46 D5
Manchester Craft & Design Centre GtMan M4 5JD 47 F3
Manchester Museum GtMan M13 9PL 47 F7
Manchester United Museum & Stadium Tour Centre GtMan M16 0RA 24 D3
Mancot Royal 170 A1
Mandally (Manndalaidh) 257 J4
Manea 162 C4
Maneight 224 D5
Manfield 202 B1
Mangarstadh 270 C4
Mangaster 278 C5
Mangerton 104 A3
Mangotsfield 131 F5
Mangrove Green 149 G5
Manish (Manais) 263 G3
Mankinholes 193 F5
Manley 183 G5
Manmoel 130 A2
Mannal 246 A2
Manningford Abbots 118 C2
Manningford Bohune 118 C2
Manningford Bruce 118 C2
Manningham 194 A4
Mannings Amusement Park Suff IP11 2DW 153 D4
Mannings Heath 109 E1
Mannington 105 G2
Manningtree 152 C4
Mannofield 261 H4
Manor Farm Country Park Hants SO30 2ER 4 D3
Manor Park 135 E4
Manorbier 127 D3
Manorbier Newton 126 D2
Manordeifi 141 F3
Manordeilo 142 C5
Manorowen 140 C4
Mansell Gamage 144 C3
Mansell Lacy 144 D3
Mansergh 200 B4
Mansfield 173 G1
Mansfield Woodhouse 173 G1
Manson Green 178 B5
Mansriggs 199 D4
Manston Dorset 105 E1
Manston Kent 125 F2
Manston WYorks 194 C4
Manswood 105 F2
Manthorpe Lincs 161 F1
Manthorpe Lincs 175 E4
Manton NLincs 187 G2
Manton Notts 186 C5
Manton Rut 161 D2
Manton Wilts 118 C1
Manuden 150 C5
Manwood Green 137 E1
Maolachy 240 A3
Maperton 117 D5
Maple Cross 135 F3
Maplebeck 174 C1
Mapledurham 134 B5
Mapledurwell 120 B2
Maplehurst 121 G5
Maplescombe 123 E2
Mapleton 172 C3
Mapperley Derbys 173 F3
Mapperley Notts 173 G3
Mapperton Dorset 104 B3
Mapperton Dorset 105 F3
Mappleborough Green 146 C1
Mappleton 197 E3
Mapplewell 186 A2
Mappowder 104 D2
Mar Lodge 259 H5
Màraig (Maaruig) 270 E7
Marazion 94 C3
Marbhig 271 G6
Marbury 170 C3
Marbury Country Park ChesW&C CW9 6AT 184 A5
March 162 C3
Marcham 133 G3
Marchamley 170 C5
Marchamley Wood 170 C4
Marchington 172 C4
Marchington Woodlands 172 C5
Marchwiel 170 A3
Marchwood 106 C1
Marcross 114 C1
Marcus 252 D4
Marden Here 145 E3
Marden Kent 123 G4
Marden T&W 221 F4
Marden Wilts 118 B2
Marden Ash 137 E2
Marden Beech 123 G4
Marden Thorn 123 G4
Marden's Hill 123 D5
Mardon 228 D3
Mardy 130 C1
Mare Green 116 A5
Marefield 160 C2
Mareham le Fen 176 A1
Mareham on the Hill 176 A1
Maresfield 109 G1
Marfleet 196 D4
Marford 170 A2
Margam 129 D4
Margam Country Park NPT SA13 2TJ 129 E4
Margaret Marsh 105 E1
Margaret Roding 137 E1
Margaretting 137 F2
Margaretting Tye 137 F2
Margate 125 F1
Margnaheglish 223 F2
Margreig 216 C3
Margrove Park 203 F1
Marham 163 F2
Marhamchurch 112 C5
Marholm 161 G2
Marian Cwm 182 B5
Mariandyrys 181 E4
Marian-glas 180 D4
Mariansleigh 114 A5
Marine Town 124 B1
Marishader 263 K5
Maristow House 100 A1
Maritime Greenwich GtLon SE10 9NF 13 D5
Mark 116 A3
Mark Causeway 116 A3
Mark Cross 123 E5
Markbeech 123 D4
Markby 189 E5
Markdhu 214 C3
Markeaton 173 E4
Markeaton Park Craft Village Derby DE22 3BG 18 A3
Market Bosworth 159 G2
Market Bosworth Country Park Leics CV13 0LP 159 G2
Market Deeping 161 G1
Market Drayton 171 D4
Market Harborough 160 C4
Market Lavington 118 B2
Market Overton 161 D1
Market Rasen 188 B4
Market Stainton 188 C5
Market Street 179 D3
Market Warsop 173 G1
Market Weighton 196 A3
Market Weston 164 A4
Markethill P&K 244 A1
Markethill AB&C 282 C5
Markfield 159 G1
Markham 130 A2
Markham Moor 187 E5
Markinch 244 A4
Markington 194 B1
Marks Gate 137 D3
Marks Tey 152 A5
Marksbury 117 D1
Markwell 99 D5
Markyate 135 F1
Marl Bank 145 G3
Marland 184 C1
Marlborough 118 C1
Marlbrook 158 B5
Marlcliff 146 C2
Marldon 101 E1
Marle Green 110 A2
Marlesford 153 E2
Marley Green 170 C3
Marley Hill 212 B2
Marlingford 178 C5
Marloes 126 A2
Marlow Bucks 135 D4
Marlow Here 156 D5
Marlpit Hill 122 D4
Marlpool 173 F3
Marnhull 105 D1
Marnoch 268 D5
Marple 185 D4
Marple Bridge 185 D4
Marr 186 C2
Marrel 275 F7
Marrick 201 F3
Marrister 279 E6
Marros 127 F2
Marsden T&W 212 C1
Marsden WYorks 185 E1
Marsett 201 E4
Marsh 103 F1
Marsh Baldon 134 A3
Marsh Benham 119 F1
Marsh Farm Country Park Essex CM3 5WP 138 B3
Marsh Gibbon 148 B5
Marsh Green Devon 102 D3
Marsh Green GtMan 183 G2
Marsh Green Kent 122 D4
Marsh Green Tel&W 157 F1
Marsh Lane 186 B5
Marsh Street 114 C3
Marshall Meadows 237 G4
Marshallstown 283 H4
Marshalsea 103 G2
Marshalswick 136 A2
Marsham 178 C3
Marshaw 192 B2
Marshborough 125 F3
Marshbrook 156 D4
Marshchapel 189 D3
Marshfield Newport 130 B4
Marshfield SGlos 131 G5
Marshgate 98 B1
Marshland St. James 162 D2
Marshside 183 E1
Marshwood 103 G3
Marske 202 A2
Marske-by-the-Sea 213 F5
Marsland Green 184 A3
Marston ChesW&C 184 A5
Marston Here 144 C2
Marston Lincs 175 D3
Marston Oxon 134 A2
Marston Staffs 171 G5
Marston Staffs 158 A1
Marston Warks 159 E3
Marston Wilts 118 A2
Marston Doles 147 G2
Marston Green 159 D4
Marston Magna 116 C5
Marston Meysey 132 D3
Marston Montgomery 172 C4
Marston Moretaine 149 E3
Marston on Dove 172 D5
Marston St. Lawrence 148 A3
Marston Stannett 145 E2
Marston Trussell 160 B4
Marston Vale Millennium Country Park CenBeds MK43 0PR 149 F3
Marstow 131 E1
Marsworth 135 E1
Marten 119 D1
Marthall 184 B5
Martham 179 F4
Martin Hants 105 G1
Martin Lincs 175 G2
Martin Lincs 176 A1
Martin Drove End 118 B5
Martin Hussingtree 146 A1
Martin Mere Lancs L40 0TA 183 F1
Martinhoe 113 G1
Martinscroft 184 A4
Martinstown Dorset 104 C4
Martinstown M&EAnt 287 F4
Martinstown NM&D 283 H4
Martlesham 152 D3
Martlesham Heath 152 D3
Martletwy 126 D1
Martley 145 G1
Martock 104 A1
Marton ChesE 171 F1
Marton Cumb 198 D5
Marton ERid 197 D4
Marton ERid 197 E1
Marton Lincs 187 F4
Marton Middl 203 E1
Marton NYorks 194 D1
Marton NYorks 203 G4
Marton Shrop 156 B2
Marton Shrop 170 B5
Marton Warks 147 G1
Marton Abbey 195 E1
Marton-in-the-Forest 195 E1
Marton-le-Moor 202 C5
Martyr Worthy 119 G4
Martyr's Green 121 F2
Marwell Zoo Hants SO21 1JH 4 D1
Marwick 276 B5
Marwood 113 F2
Mary Rose PO1 3LX 82 Portsmouth
Mary Tavy 99 F3
Marybank (An Lagaidh) High 266 B6
Marybank Na H-E. Siar 271 G4
Maryburgh (Baile Mairi) 266 C6
Maryfield Corn 100 A2
Maryfield Shet 279 D8
Marygold 237 F4
Maryhill Aber 269 G6
Maryhill Glas 233 G3
Marykirk 253 E3
Marylebone GtLon 136 B4
Marylebone GtMan 183 G2
Marypark 259 J1
Maryport Cumb 208 D3
Maryport D&G 206 B3
Marystow 99 E2
Maryton 253 E4
Marywell Aber 261 H5
Marywell Aber 260 D5
Marywell Angus 253 E5
Masham 202 B4
Mashbury 137 F1
Masongill 200 B5
Mastin Moor 186 B5
Mastrick 261 H4
Matchborough 146 C1
Matching 137 E1
Matching Green 137 E1
Matching Tye 137 E1
Matfen 220 C4
Matfield 123 F4
Mathern 131 E3
Mathon 145 G3
Mathry 140 B4
Matlaske 178 C2
Matlock 173 E1
Matlock Bank 173 E1
Matlock Bath 173 D2
Matson 132 A1
Matterdale End 209 G4
Mattersey 187 D4
Mattersey Thorpe 187 D4
Mattingley 120 C2
Mattishall 178 B4
Mattishall Burgh 178 B4
Mauchline 224 C3
Maud 269 H6
Maufant 100 C5
Maugersbury 147 D5
Maughold 190 C2
Mauld 257 K1
Maulden 149 F4
Maulds Meaburn 200 B1
Maunby 202 C4
Maund Bryan 145 E2
Maundown 115 D5
Mautby 179 F4
Mavesyn Ridware 158 C1
Mavis Enderby 176 B1
Maw Green 171 E2
Mawbray 209 D2
Mawdesley 183 F1
Mawdlam 129 E4
Mawgan 95 E4
Mawgan Porth 96 C3
Mawla 96 B5
Mawnan 95 E4
Mawnan Smith 95 E4
Mawsley 160 D5
Mawthorpe 189 E5
Maxey 161 G2
Maxstoke 159 E4
Maxted Street 124 D4
Maxton Kent 125 F4
Maxton ScBord 228 A3
Maxwellheugh 228 B3
Maxwelltown 217 D3
Maxworthy 98 C1
May Hill 145 G5
Mayals 128 C3
Maybole 224 B5
Maybury 121 F2
Mayen 268 D6
Mayfair 136 B4
Mayfield ESuss 110 A1
Mayfield Midlo 236 A3
Mayfield Staffs 172 C3
Mayford 121 E2
Mayland 138 C2
Maylandsea 138 C2
Maynard's Green 110 A2
Maybridge 282 E6
Mayoghill 286 C4
Maypole IoS 96 B1
Maypole Kent 125 D2
Maypole Mon 131 D1
Maypole Green Essex 152 A5
Maypole Green Norf 165 F2
Maypole Green Suff 153 D1
Maypole Green Suff 152 A2
May's Corner 282 E5
May's Green NSom 116 A1
Mays Green Oxon 134 C4
Maytown 282 D6
Maywick 279 C10
Mazetown 283 F2
McGregor's Corner 287 F4
Mead 112 C4
Mead End 118 B5
Meadgate 117 D2
Meadle 134 D2
Meadow Green 145 G2
Meadowhall 186 A3
Meadowmill 236 B2
Meadowtown 156 C2
Meadwell 99 E2
Meaford 171 F4
Meal Bank 199 G3
Mealasta 270 B5
Mealough 283 G2
Meals 189 E3
Mealsgate 209 F2
Meanley 192 D3
Meanwood 194 B4
Mearbeck 193 E1
Meare 116 B3
Meare Green 115 F5
Mearns 233 G4
Mears Ashby 148 D1
Measham 159 F1
Meathop 199 F4
Meavag Na H-E. Siar 263 G2
Meavy 100 B1
Medbourne 160 D3
Meddon 112 C4
Meden Vale 173 G1
Medlar 192 A4
Medmenham 134 D4
Medomsley 212 A2
Medstead 120 B4
Meenawaddy 285 G6
Meentullyclogh 280 D1
Meer Common 144 C2
Meer End 159 E5
Meerbrook 171 G1
Meesden 150 C4
Meeson 171 D5
Meeth 113 F5
Meeting House Hill 179 E3
Megarrystown 282 E3
Meggethead 226 C3
Meidrim 141 F5
Meifod Denb 168 D2
Meifod Powys 156 A1
Meigh 282 D6
Meigle 252 A5
Meikle Earnock 234 B4
Meikle Grenach 232 B3
Meikle Kilmory 232 B3
Meikle Rahane 232 D1
Meikle Strath 253 E2
Meikle Tarty 261 H2
Meikle Wartle 261 F1
Meikleour 243 G1
Meikleyard 224 D2
Meinciau 128 A1
Meir 171 G3
Meirheath 171 G3
Melbost (Mealabost) 271 G4
Melbost Borve (Mealabost) 271 G2
Melbourn 150 B3
Melbourne Derbys 173 E5
Melbourne ERid 195 G3
Melbury 113 D4
Melbury Abbas 105 E1
Melbury Bubb 104 B2
Melbury Osmond 104 B2
Melbury Sampford 104 B2
Melby 279 A7
Melchbourne 149 F1
Melcombe Bingham 105 D2
Melcombe Regis 104 C4
Meldon Devon 99 F1
Meldon N'umb 220 D3
Meldreth 150 B3
Meledor 96 D4
Melfort 240 A3
Melgarve 258 B5
Melgum 260 C4
Meliden (Gallt Melyd) 182 B4
Melincourt 129 E2
Melin-y-coed 168 B1
Melin-y-ddol 155 G2
Melin-y-grug 155 G2
Melin-y-Wig 168 D3
Melkinthorpe 210 B5
Melkridge 210 D1
Melksham 118 A1
Melksham Forest 118 A1
Melldalloch 232 A2
Melling Lancs 199 G5
Melling Mersey 183 E2
Melling Mount 183 F2
Mellis 164 B4
Mellon Charles 264 E2
Mellon Udrigle 264 E2
Mellor GtMan 185 D4
Mellor Lancs 192 C4
Mellor Brook 192 C4
Mells 117 E3
Melmerby Cumb 210 C4
Melmerby NYorks 201 F4
Melmerby NYorks 202 C5
Melplash 104 A3
Melrose Aber 269 F4
Melrose ScBord 227 G2
Melsetter 277 B9
Melsonby 202 A2
Meltham 185 E1
Melton ERid 196 B5
Melton Suff 153 D2
Melton Constable 178 B2
Melton Mowbray 160 C1
Melton Ross 188 A1
Meltonby 195 G2
Melvaig 264 D3
Melverley 156 C1
Melverley Green 156 C1
Melvich 274 D2
Membury 103 F2
Memsie 269 H4
Memus 252 C4
Menabilly 97 E4
Menai Bridge (Porthaethwy) 181 D5
Mendham 165 D3
Mendlesham 152 C1
Mendlesham Green 152 B1
Menethorpe 195 G1
Menheniot 97 G3
Menie House 261 H2
Menithwood 145 G1
Mennock 225 G5
Menston 194 A3
Menstrie 242 D5
Mentmore 135 E1
Meoble 247 G1
Meole Brace 157 D1
Meon 107 E2
Meonstoke 107 F1
Meopham 123 F2
Meopham Green 123 F2
Mepal 162 C4
Meppershall 149 G4
Merbach 144 C3
Mercaston 173 D3
Mere ChesE 184 B4
Mere Wilts 117 F4
Mere Brow 183 F1
Mere Green 158 D3
Mere Heath 184 A5
Mereclough 193 E4
Mereside 191 G4
Meretown 171 E5
Mereworth 123 F3
Mergie 253 F1
Meriden 159 E4
Merkadale 255 J1
Merkinch 266 D7
Merkland 216 B3
Merley 105 G3
Merlin's Bridge 126 C1
Merridge 115 F4
Merrifield 101 E3
Merrington 170 B5
Merrion 126 C3
Merriott 104 A1
Merrivale 99 F3
Merrow 121 F2
Merry Hill Herts 136 A3
Merry Hill WMid 158 B4
Merry Hill WMid 158 A3
Merrymeet 97 G3
Mersea Island 138 D1
Mersey Ferries Mersey CH44 6QY 42 A4
Merseyside Maritime Museum Mersey L3 4AQ 42 B5
Mersham 124 C5
Merstham 122 B3
Merston 108 A3
Merstone 107 E4
Merther 96 C5
Merthyr 141 G5
Merthyr Cynog 143 F4
Merthyr Dyfan 115 E1
Merthyr Mawr 129 E5
Merthyr Tydfil 129 G2
Merthyr Vale 129 G3
Merton Devon 113 F4
Merton Norf 164 A2
Merton Oxon 134 A1
Mervinslaw 228 A5
Meshaw 102 A1
Messing 138 C1
Messingham 187 F2
Metcombe 103 D3
Metfield 165 D3
Metherell 100 A1
Metheringham 175 F1
Methil 244 B5
Methlem 166 A4
Methley 194 C5
Methley Junction 194 C5
Methlick 261 G1
Methven 243 F2
Methwold 163 F3
Methwold Hythe 163 F3
MetroCentre 212 B1
Mettingham 165 E3
Metton 178 C2
Mevagissey 97 E5
Mewith Head 192 D1
Mexborough 186 B3
Mey 275 H1
Meysey Hampton 132 D2
Miabhag Na H-E. Siar 270 C7
Mial 264 D4
Miavaig (Miabhaig) 270 C4
Michaelchurch 145 E5
Michaelchurch Escley 144 C4
Michaelchurch-on-Arrow 144 B2
Michaelston-le-Pit 130 A5
Michaelston-super-Ely 130 A5
Michaelston-y-Fedw 130 B4
Michaelstow 97 E2
Michelcombe 100 C1
Micheldever 119 G4
Michelmersh 119 E5
Mickfield 152 C1
Mickle Trafford 170 B1
Micklebring 186 C3
Mickleby 204 B1
Micklefield 194 D4
Micklefield Green 135 F3
Mickleham 121 G2
Micklehurst 185 D2
Mickleover 173 E4
Micklethwaite Cumb 209 F1
Micklethwaite WYorks 193 G3
Mickleton Dur 211 F5
Mickleton Glos 147 D3
Mickletown 194 C5
Mickley Derbys 186 A5
Mickley NYorks 202 B5
Mickley Green 151 G2
Mickley Square 211 G1
Mid Ardlaw 269 H4
Mid Beltie 260 E4
Mid Calder 235 E3
Mid Clyth 275 H5
Mid Hants Railway Hants SO24 9JG 120 B4
Mid Lambrook 104 A1
Mid Lavant 108 A3
Mid Letter 240 C4
Mid Lix 242 A1
Mid Mossdale 200 D3
Mid Yell 278 E3
Midbea 276 D3
Middle Assendon 134 C4
Middle Aston 147 G5
Middle Barton 147 G5
Middle Bickenhill 159 E4
Middle Bockhampton 106 A3
Middle Claydon 148 C5
Middle Drift 97 F3
Middle Drums 253 D4
Middle Duntisbourne 132 B2
Middle Handley 186 B5
Middle Harling 164 A3
Middle Kames 232 A1
Middle Littleton 146 C3
Middle Maes-coed 144 C4
Middle Marwood 113 F2
Middle Mill 140 B5
Middle Quarter 124 A5
Middle Rasen 188 A4
Middle Rigg 243 F4
Middle Salter 192 C1
Middle Sontley 170 A3
Middle Stoford 115 E5
Middle Taphouse 97 F3
Middle Town 96 B1
Middle Tysoe 147 F3
Middle Wallop 119 D4
Middle Winterslow 118 D4
Middle Woodford 118 C4
Middlebie 218 A4
Middlecliff 186 B2
Middlecott 113 E5
Middleham 202 A4
Middlehill Aber 269 G6
Middlehill Corn 97 G3
Middlehope 157 E4
Middlemarsh 104 C2
Middlemoor 99 E3
Middlequarter (Ceathramh Meadhanach) 262 D4
Middlesbrough 213 D5
Middlesceugh 210 A3
Middleshaw 199 G4
Middlesmoor 201 F5
Middlestone 212 B4
Middlestone Moor 212 B4
Middlestown 185 G1
Middleton Aber 261 G3
Middleton Angus 253 D5
Middleton Cumb 200 B4
Middleton Derbys 173 D2
Middleton Derbys 172 C1
Middleton Essex 151 G3
Middleton GtMan 184 C2
Middleton Hants 119 F3
Middleton Here 145 E1
Middleton Lancs 192 A2
Middleton Midlo 236 A4
Middleton N'hants 160 D4
Middleton N'umb 220 C3
Middleton N'umb 229 E3
Middleton Norf 163 E1
Middleton NYorks 203 G4
Middleton P&K 243 G4
Middleton P&K 251 G5
Middleton Shrop 156 B3
Middleton Shrop 157 E5
Middleton Shrop 170 A5
Middleton Suff 153 F1
Middleton Swan 128 A4
Middleton Warks 159 D3
Middleton WYorks 194 A3
Middleton WYorks 194 C5
Middleton Baggot 157 F3
Middleton Bank Top 220 C3
Middleton Cheney 147 G3
Middleton Green 171 G4
Middleton Hall 229 D4
Middleton Moor 153 F1
Middleton of Potterton 261 H3
Middleton on the Hill 145 E1
Middleton One Row 202 C1
Middleton Park 261 H3
Middleton Priors 157 F4
Middleton Quernhow 202 C5
Middleton St. George 202 C1
Middleton Scriven 157 F4
Middleton Stoney 148 A5
Middleton Tyas 202 B2
Middleton-in-Teesdale 211 F5
Middleton-on-Leven 203 D1
Middleton-on-Sea 108 B3
Middleton-on-the-Wolds 196 B3
Middletown AB&C 282 A5
Middletown Cumb 198 A2
Middletown Powys 156 C1
Middlewich 171 E1
Middlewood ChesE 184 D4
Middlewood SYorks 186 A3
Middlewood Green 152 B1
Middlezoy 116 A4
Middridge 212 B5
Midfield 273 H2
Midford 117 E1
Midge Hall 192 B5
Midgeholme 210 C2
Midgham 119 G1
Midgley WYorks 185 G1
Midgley WYorks 193 G5
Midhopestones 185 G3
Midhurst 121 D5
Midland Railway Centre Derbys DE5 3QZ 173 F2
Midlem 227 G3
Midloe Grange 149 G1
Midpark 232 B4
Midsomer Norton 117 D2
Midthorpe 188 C5
Midtown High 273 H2
Midtown High 264 E3
Midtown of Barras 253 G1
Midville 176 B2
Midway 173 E5
Migdale 266 D2
Migvie 260 C4
Milarrochy 241 G5
Milber 102 B5
Milbethill 268 E5
Milborne Port 104 C1
Milborne St. Andrew 105 D3
Milborne Wick 117 D5
Milbourne N'umb 220 D4
Milbourne Wilts 132 B4
Milburn 210 C5
Milbury Heath 131 F3
Milcombe 147 G4
Milden 152 A3
Mildenhall Suff 163 F5
Mildenhall Wilts 118 D1
Mile Elm 118 A1
Mile End Essex 152 A5
Mile End Glos 131 E1
Mile End Park GtLon E3 4HL 12 D4
Mile Oak 123 F4
Mile Town 124 B1
Milebrook 156 C5
Milebush Kent 123 G4
Milebush M&EAnt 287 J7
Mileham 178 A4
Miles Green 171 F3
Miles Hope 145 E1
Milesmark 235 E1
Miles's Green 119 G1
Milfield 228 D3
Milford Derbys 173 E3
Milford Devon 112 C3
Milford Shrop 170 B5
Milford Staffs 171 G5
Milford Surr 121 E3
Milford Haven (Aberdaugleddau) 126 B2
Milford on Sea 106 B3
Milkwall 131 E2
Milky Way Adventure Park Devon EX39 5RY 112 D3
Mill Bank 193 G5
Mill Brow 185 D4
Mill End Bucks 134 C4
Mill End Cambs 151 E2
Mill End Herts 150 B4
Mill End Green 151 E5
Mill Green Cambs 151 E3
Mill Green Essex 137 F2
Mill Green Herts 136 B2
Mill Green Norf 164 C3
Mill Green Shrop 171 D5
Mill Green Staffs 172 B5
Mill Green Suff 153 E1
Mill Green Suff 152 C2
Mill Green Suff 152 A2
Mill Green WMid 158 C2
Mill Hill B'burn 192 C5
Mill Hill Cambs 150 A2
Mill Hill GtLon 136 B3
Mill Houses 192 C1
Mill Lane 120 C2
Mill of Camsail 233 D1
Mill of Colp 269 F6
Mill of Elrick 269 H6
Mill of Fortune 242 C2
Mill of Kingoodie 261 G2
Mill of Monquich 261 G5
Mill of Uras 253 G1
Mill Side 199 F4
Mill Street Kent 123 F3
Mill Street Norf 178 B4
Mill Town 287 F7
Milland 120 D5
Millbank 269 J6
Millbay 288 J6
Millbeck 209 F4
Millbounds 276 E4
Millbreck 269 J6
Millbridge 120 D3
Millbrook CenBeds 149 F4
Millbrook Corn 100 A2
Millbrook Devon 103 G3
Millbrook M&EAnt 287 H5
Millbrook Soton 106 C1
Millburn Aber 260 D2
Millburn Aber 260 E1
Millcombe 101 E3
Millcorner 110 D1
Milldale 172 C2
Millden 261 H3
Milldens 252 D4

313

Nash Here 144 C1
Nash Newport 130 C4
Nash Shrop 157 F5
Nash VGlam 129 F5
Nash Street 123 F2
Nassington 161 F3
Nasty 150 B5
Nateby Cumb 200 C2
Nateby Lancs 192 A3
Nately Scures 120 C2
National Agricultural Centre, Stoneleigh Warks CV8 2LZ 16 B5
National Army Museum GtLon SW3 4HT 13 A5
National Botanic Garden of Wales Carmar SA32 8HG 128 B1
National Botanic Gardens Belfast City BT7 1LP 283 G1
National Coal Mining Museum for England WYorks WF4 4RH 27 F6
National Exhibition Centre WMid B40 1NT 15 H4
National Fishing Heritage Centre, Grimsby NELincs DN31 1UZ 188 C2
National Gallery GtLon WC2N 5DN 44 D4
National Gallery of Scotland Edin EH2 2EL 37 F4
National Indoor Arena, Birmingham WMid B1 2AA 34 D4
National Marine Aquarium PL4 0LF 81 Plymouth
National Maritime Museum Cornwall Corn TR11 3QY 95 F3
National Maritime Museum, Greenwich GtLon SE10 9NF 13 D5
National Media Museum WYorks BD1 1NQ 65 Bradford
National Memorial Arboretum, Alrewas Staffs DE13 7AR 159 D1
National Motorcycle Museum, Solihull WMid B92 0EJ 159 E4
National Museum Cardiff CF10 3NP 67 Cardiff
National Museum of Scotland Edin EH1 1JF 37 G5
National Portrait Gallery GtLon WC2H 0HE 44 D4
National Railway Museum YO26 4XJ 90 York
National Sea Life Centre, Birmingham WMid B1 2JB 34 D4
National Seal Sanctuary Corn TR12 6UG 95 E4
National Slate Museum, Llanberis Gwyn LL55 4TY 167 E2
National Space Centre, Leicester Leic LE4 5NS 17 C4
National Wallace Monument Stir FK9 5LF 242 D5
National War Museum, Edinburgh Edin EH1 2NG 37 E4
National Waterfront Museum SA1 3RD 86 Swansea
National Wildflower Centre, Liverpool Mersey L16 3NA 22 D3
Natland 199 G4
Natural History Museum at Tring Herts HP23 6AP 135 E1
Natural History Museum, London GtLon SW7 5BD 11 F5
Natureland Seal Sanctuary Lincs PE25 1DB 177 D1
Naughton 152 B3
Naunton Glos 146 D5
Naunton Worcs 146 A4
Naunton Beauchamp 146 B2
Navan 282 B4
Navan Fort AB&C BT60 4LD 282 B4
Navenby 175 E2
Navestock 137 E3
Navestock Side 137 E3
Navidale 275 F7
Navity 266 E5
Nawton 203 F4
Nayland 152 A4
Nazeing 136 D2
Neacroft 106 A3
Neal's Green 159 F4
Neap 279 E7
Neap House 187 F1
Near Sawrey 199 E3
Nearton End 148 D5
Neasden 136 B4
Neasham 202 C1
Neat Enstone 147 F5
Neath (Castell-nedd) 129 D3
Neatham 120 C3
Neatishead 179 E3
Nebo Cere 142 B1
Nebo Conwy 168 B2
Nebo Gwyn 167 D2
Nebo IoA 180 C3
Necton 163 G2
Ned 285 J3
Nedd 272 D5
Nedderton 221 E3
Nedging 152 A3
Nedging Tye 152 B3
Needham 164 D3
Needham Lake Suff IP6 8NU 152 B2
Needham Market 152 B2
Needham Street 151 F1
Needingworth 162 B5
Needles Pleasure Park IoW PO39 0JD 106 C4
Needwood 172 C5
Neen Savage 157 F5
Neen Sollars 157 F5
Neenton 157 F4
Nefyn 166 C3
Neighbourne 116 D3
Neilston 233 F4
Neithrop 147 G3
Nelsherry 280 E2
Nelson Caerp 130 A3
Nelson Lancs 193 E4
Nelson Village 221 E4
Nemphlar 234 C5
Nempnett Thrubwell 116 C1
Nenthall 211 D3
Nenthead 211 D3
Nenthorn 228 A3
Neopardy 102 A3
Nerabus 230 A4
Nercwys 169 F1
Neriby 230 B3
Nerston 234 A4
Nesbit 229 D3
Nesfield 193 G3
Ness 183 E5
Ness Botanic Gardens ChesW&C CH64 4AY 183 E5
Ness of Tenston 277 B6
Nesscliffe 156 C1
Neston ChesW&C 183 D5
Neston Wilts 117 F1
Nether Alderley 184 C5
Nether Auchendrane 224 B4
Nether Barr 215 F4
Nether Blainslie 236 C5
Nether Broughton 174 B5
Nether Burrow 200 B5
Nether Cerne 104 C3
Nether Compton 104 B1
Nether Crimond 261 G2
Nether Dalgliesh 227 D5
Nether Dallachy 268 B4
Nether Edge 186 A4
Nether End 185 G5
Nether Exe 102 C3
Nether Glasslaw 269 G5
Nether Handwick 252 B5
Nether Haugh 186 B3
Nether Heage 173 E2
Nether Heselden 201 D5
Nether Heyford 148 B2
Nether Kellet 192 B1
Nether Kinmundy 269 J6
Nether Langwith 186 C5
Nether Lenshie 268 E6
Nether Loads 173 E1
Nether Moor 173 E1
Nether Padley 185 G5
Nether Pitforthie 253 G2
Nether Poppleton 195 E2
Nether Silton 203 D3
Nether Skyborry 156 B5
Nether Stowey 115 E4
Nether Urquhart 243 G4
Nether Wallop 119 E4
Nether Wasdale 198 C2
Nether Wellwood 225 E3
Nether Welton 209 G2
Nether Westcote 147 E5
Nether Whitacre 159 E3
Nether Winchendon (Lower Winchendon) 134 C1
Nether Worton 147 G5
Netheravon 118 C3
Netherbrae 269 F5
Netherbrough 277 C6
Netherburn 234 C5
Netherbury 104 A3
Netherby Cumb 218 B4
Netherby NYorks 194 C3
Nethercott 147 G5
Netherfield ESuss 110 C2
Netherfield Notts 174 B3
Netherfield SLan 234 B5
Netherhall 232 D3
Netherhampton 118 C5
Netherhay 104 A2
Netherland Green 172 C4
Netherley 261 G5
Nethermill 217 E2
Nethermuir 269 H6
Netherseal 159 E1
Nethershield 225 D3
Netherstreet 118 A1
Netherthird D&G 216 B5
Netherthird EAyr 225 D4
Netherthong 185 F2
Netherthorpe 186 C4
Netherton Angus 252 D4
Netherton ChesW&C 183 G5
Netherton Devon 102 B5
Netherton Hants 119 E2
Netherton Mersey 183 E2
Netherton N'umb 220 B1
Netherton NLan 234 B4
Netherton Oxon 133 G2
Netherton P&K 251 G4
Netherton SLan 234 D4
Netherton WMid 158 B4
Netherton Worcs 146 B3
Netherton WYorks 185 G1
Netherton WYorks 185 F1
Netherton Burnfoot 220 B1
Netherton Northside 220 B1
Nethertown Cumb 198 A2
Nethertown Ork 275 J1
Nethertown Staffs 158 D1
Netherwitton 220 D2
Netherwood D&G 217 D3
Netherwood EAyr 225 E3
Nethy Bridge 259 H2
Netley Abbey 107 D2
Netley Marsh 106 C1
Nettlebed 134 B4
Nettlebridge 116 D3
Nettlecombe Dorset 104 B3
Nettlecombe IoW 107 E5
Nettlecombe Som 115 D4
Nettleden 135 F1
Nettleham 188 A5
Nettlestead Kent 123 F3
Nettlestead Suff 152 B3
Nettlestead Green 123 F3
Nettlestone 107 F3
Nettlesworth 212 B3
Nettleton Lincs 188 B2
Nettleton Wilts 132 A5
Nettleton Hill 185 E1
Netton Devon 100 B3
Netton Wilts 118 C4
Neuadd Cere 142 A2
Neuadd IoA 180 B3
Neuadd Powys 143 F3
Nevendon 137 G3
Nevern 141 D4
Nevill Holt 160 D3
New Abbey 217 D4
New Aberdour 269 G4
New Addington 122 C2
New Alresford 119 G4
New Alyth 252 A5
New Arley 159 E3
New Arram 196 C3
New Ash Green 123 F2
New Balderton 174 D2
New Barn 123 F2
New Belses 227 G3
New Bewick 229 E4
New Bolingbroke 176 B2
New Boultham 187 G5
New Bradwell 148 D3
New Brancepeth 212 B3
New Bridge D&G 216 D3
New Bridge Devon 102 A5
New Brighton Flints 169 F1
New Brighton Hants 107 G2
New Brighton Mersey 183 E3
New Brighton Wrex 169 F2
New Brighton WYorks 194 B5
New Brinsley 173 F2
New Broughton 170 A2
New Buckenham 164 B2
New Buildings 285 G4
New Byth 269 G5
New Cheriton 119 G5
New Cross Cere 154 C5
New Cross GtLon 136 C5
New Cumnock 225 E4
New Deer 269 G6
New Duston 148 C1
New Earswick 195 F2
New Edlington 186 C3
New Elgin 267 K5
New Ellerby 197 D4
New Eltham 136 D5
New End 146 C1
New England 161 G2
New Farnley 194 B4
New Ferry Mersey 183 E4
New Ferry M&EAnt 286 D6
New Galloway 216 A3
New Gilston 244 C4
New Greens 136 A2
New Grimsby 96 A1
New Hartley 221 F4
New Haw 121 F1
New Heaton 228 C3
New Hedges 127 E2
New Herrington 212 C2
New Hinksey 134 A2
New Holland 196 C5
New Houghton Derbys 173 G1
New Houghton Norf 177 F5
New Houses 200 D5
New Hunwick 212 A4
New Hutton 199 G3
New Hythe 123 G3
New Inn Carmar 142 A4
New Inn Fife 244 A4
New Inn Mon 131 D2
New Inn Torfaen 130 B3
New Invention Shrop 156 B5
New Invention WMid 158 B2
New Kelso 265 F7
New Lanark 234 C5
New Lanark SLan ML11 9DB 234 C5
New Lane 183 F1
New Lane End 184 A3
New Leake 176 C2
New Leeds 269 H5
New Leslie 260 D2
New Lodge 186 A2
New Longton 192 B5
New Luce 214 C4
New Mains 225 G2
New Mains of Ury 253 G1
New Malden 122 B2
New Marske 213 F5
New Marton 170 A4
New Mill Corn 94 B3
New Mill Herts 135 E1
New Mill WYorks 185 F2
New Mill End 136 A1
New Mills Corn 96 C4
New Mills Derbys 185 E4
New Mills Glos 131 F2
New Mills Mon 131 E2
New Mills (Y Felin Newydd) Powys 155 G2
New Milton 106 B3
New Mistley 152 C4
New Moat 141 D5
New Ollerton 174 B1
New Orleans 222 C4
New Oscott 158 C3
New Palace & Adventureland, New Brighton Mersey CH45 2JX 22 A2
New Park Corn 97 F1
New Park NYorks 194 B2
New Pitsligo 269 G5
New Polzeath 96 D2
New Quay (Ceinewydd) 141 G1
New Rackheath 179 D4
New Radnor (Maesyfed) 144 B1
New Rent 210 A4
New Ridley 211 G1
New Road Side 193 F3
New Romney 111 F1
New Rossington 186 D3
New Row Cere 154 D5
New Row Lancs 192 C4
New Sawley 173 F4
New Shoreston 229 F3
New Silksworth 212 C2
New Stevenston 234 B4
New Swannington 159 G1
New Totley 186 A5
New Town CenBeds 149 G3
New Town Cere 141 E3
New Town Dorset 105 F1
New Town Dorset 105 F2
New Town ELoth 236 B2
New Town ESuss 109 G1
New Town Glos 146 C4
New Town Mid Ulster 286 D5
New Tredegar 130 A2
New Tupton 173 E1
New Ulva 231 F1
New Valley 271 G4
New Village 186 C2
New Walk Museum & Art Gallery LE1 7EA 77 Leicester
New Walsoken 162 C2
New Waltham 188 C2
New Walton Pier Essex CO14 8ES 153 D5
New Winton 236 B2
New World 162 B3
New Yatt 133 F1
New York Lincs 176 A2
New York T&W 221 F4
Newall 194 B3
Newark Ork 276 G3
Newark Peter 162 A2
Newark Castle, Newark-on-Trent Notts NG24 1BG 174 C2
Newark-on-Trent 174 D2
Newarthill 234 B4
Newball 188 A5
Newbarn 125 D5
Newbarns 198 D5
Newbattle 236 A3
Newbiggin Cumb 210 A5
Newbiggin Cumb 210 C5
Newbiggin Cumb 210 B3
Newbiggin Cumb 191 F1
Newbiggin Cumb 198 B3
Newbiggin Dur 211 F5
Newbiggin N'umb 211 F1
Newbiggin NYorks 201 F4
Newbiggin NYorks 201 E3
Newbiggin-by-the-Sea 221 F3
Newbigging Aber 261 G5
Newbigging Aber 251 G1
Newbigging Angus 244 C1
Newbigging Angus 244 C1
Newbigging Angus 252 A5
Newbigging SLan 235 E5
Newbiggin-on-Lune 200 C2
Newbold Derbys 186 A5
Newbold Leics 159 G1
Newbold on Avon 159 G5
Newbold on Stour 147 E3
Newbold Pacey 147 E2
Newbold Verdon 159 G2
Newborough (Niwbwrch) IoA 166 D1
Newborough Peter 162 A2
Newborough Staffs 172 C5
Newbottle N'hants 148 A4
Newbottle T&W 212 C2
Newbourne 153 D3
Newbridge (Cefn Bychan) Caerp 130 B3
Newbridge Corn 94 B3
Newbridge Corn 98 D4
Newbridge Edin 235 F2
Newbridge ESuss 123 D5
Newbridge Hants 106 B1
Newbridge IoW 106 D4
Newbridge NYorks 204 B4
Newbridge Oxon 133 G2
Newbridge Pembs 140 C4
Newbridge Wrex 169 F3
Newbridge Green 146 A4
Newbridge on Wye 143 G2
Newbridge-on-Usk 130 C3
Newbrough 211 E1
Newbuildings 102 A2
Newburgh Aber 269 H5
Newburgh Aber 261 H2
Newburgh Fife 244 A3
Newburgh Lancs 183 F1
Newburgh ScBord 227 E3
Newburn 212 A1
Newbury Som 117 D2
Newbury WBerks 119 F1
Newbury Wilts 117 F3
Newbury Park 136 D4
Newby Cumb 210 B5
Newby Lancs 193 E3
Newby NYorks 203 E1
Newby NYorks 192 D1
Newby NYorks 204 D4
Newby Bridge 199 E4
Newby Cote 200 C5
Newby Cross 209 G1
Newby East 210 A2
Newby Hall NYorks HG4 5AE 194 C1
Newby West 209 G1
Newby Wiske 202 C4
Newcastle A&NDown 283 K3
Newcastle Bridgend 129 E5
Newcastle Mon 130 D1
Newcastle NM&D 283 G5
Newcastle Shrop 156 B4
Newcastle Emlyn (Castell Newydd Emlyn) 141 G3
Newcastle International Airport 221 D4
Newcastle upon Tyne 212 B1
Newcastleton 218 C3
Newcastle-under-Lyme 171 F3
Newchapel Pembs 141 F4
Newchapel Staffs 171 F2
Newchapel Surr 122 C4
Newchurch Carmar 141 G5
Newchurch IoW 107 E4
Newchurch Kent 124 C5
Newchurch Lancs 193 E5
Newchurch Lancs 193 E4
Newchurch Mon 131 D3
Newchurch Powys 144 B2
Newchurch Staffs 172 C5
Newcott 103 F2
Newcraighall 236 A2
Newdigate 121 G3
Newell Green 135 D5
Newenden 110 D1
Newent 145 G5
Newerne 131 F2
Newfield Dur 212 B4
Newfield Dur 212 B2
Newfield High 266 E4
Newfound 119 G2
Newgale 140 B5
Newgate 178 B1
Newgate Street 136 C2
Newgord 278 E2
Newhall ChesE 170 D3
Newhall Derbys 173 D5
Newham 229 F4
Newham Hall 229 F4
Newhaven 109 G3
Newhey 184 D1
Newholm 204 B1
Newhouse 234 B3
Newick 109 G1
Newingreen 124 D5
Newington Edin 235 G2
Newington Kent 125 D5
Newington Kent 124 A2
Newington Notts 187 D3
Newington Oxon 134 B3
Newington Bagpath 132 A3
Newland Cumb 199 E5
Newland Glos 131 E2
Newland Hull 196 C4
Newland NYorks 195 F5
Newland Oxon 133 F1
Newland Worcs 145 G3
Newlandrig 236 A3
Newlands Cumb 209 G3
Newlands Essex 138 B4
Newlands N'umb 211 G2
Newlands ScBord 218 D2
Newland's Corner 121 F3
Newlands of Geise 275 F2
Newlands of Tynet 268 B4
Newlyn 94 B4
Newmachar 261 G3
Newmains 234 C4
Newman's End 137 E1
Newman's Green 151 G3
Newmarket Suff 151 E1
Newmarket Na H-E. Siar 271 G4
Newmill A&N 287 G7
Newmill Aber 253 F1
Newmill Aber 269 G6
Newmill Aber 261 G2
Newmill Moray 268 C5
Newmill ScBord 227 F4
Newmill of Inshewan 252 C3
Newmillerdam 186 A1
Newmillerdam Country Park WYorks WF2 6QP 27 H6
Newmills High 266 D5
Newmills Mid Ulster 282 B2
Newmiln P&K 243 G1
Newmiln P&K 243 F2
Newmilns 224 D2
Newney Green 137 F2
Newnham Glos 131 F1
Newnham Hants 120 C2
Newnham Herts 150 A4
Newnham Kent 124 B3
Newnham N'hants 148 A2
Newnham Bridge 145 F1
Newnham Paddox 159 G4
Newnoth 260 D1
Newport Corn 98 D2
Newport Devon 113 F2
Newport ERid 196 A4
Newport Essex 150 D4
Newport Glos 131 F3
Newport High 275 G6
Newport IoW 107 E4
Newport (Casnewydd) Newport 130 C4
Newport Norf 179 G4
Newport (Trefdraeth) Pembs 141 D4
Newport Som 116 A5
Newport Tel&W 157 G1
Newport Pagnell 149 D3
Newport-on-Tay 244 C2
Newpound Common 121 F5
Newquay 96 C3
Newquay Zoo Corn TR7 2LZ 96 C3
Newry 282 D6
Newsbank 171 F1
Newseat 261 F1
Newsells 150 B4
Newsham Lancs 192 B4
Newsham N'umb 221 E4
Newsham NYorks 202 A1
Newsham NYorks 202 C4
Newsholme ERid 195 G5
Newsholme Lancs 193 E2
Newsome 185 F1
Newstead N'umb 229 F4
Newstead Notts 173 G2
Newstead ScBord 227 G2
Newstead Abbey Notts NG15 8NA 173 G2
Newthorpe Notts 173 F3
Newthorpe NYorks 195 D4
Newtoft 188 A4
Newton A&B 240 C5
Newton Aber 268 C6
Newton Aber 269 J6
Newton Bridgend 129 E5
Newton Cambs 150 C3
Newton Cardiff 130 B5
Newton ChesW&C 170 C2
Newton ChesW&C 183 G5
Newton Cumb 198 D5
Newton D&G 217 F1
Newton Derbys 173 F2
Newton GtMan 185 D3
Newton Here 144 C1
Newton Here 145 E2
Newton Here 144 C4
Newton High 275 J3
Newton High 266 E7
Newton High 275 H3
Newton High 272 E5
Newton High 266 C6
Newton High 266 E5
Newton Lancs 192 C2
Newton Lancs 199 G5
Newton Lancs 191 G4
Newton Lincs 175 F4
Newton Moray 268 B4
Newton N'hants 161 D4
Newton N'umb 211 G1
Newton N'umb 220 B1
Newton NAyr 232 A4
Newton Norf 163 G1
Newton Notts 174 B3
Newton P&K 243 D1
Newton Pembs 140 B5
Newton Pembs 126 C2
Newton ScBord 228 A4
Newton SGlos 131 F3
Newton Shrop 170 B4
Newton SLan 226 A2
Newton Som 115 E4
Newton Staffs 172 B5
Newton Suff 152 A3
Newton Swan 128 C4
Newton Warks 160 A5
Newton Wilts 118 D5
Newton WLoth 235 E2
Newton WYorks 194 D5
Newton Abbot 102 B5
Newton Arlosh 209 F1
Newton Aycliffe 212 B5
Newton Bewley 213 D5
Newton Blossomville 149 E2
Newton Bromswold 149 E1
Newton Burgoland 159 F2
Newton by Toft 188 A4
Newton Ferrers 100 B3
Newton Flotman 164 D2
Newton Green 131 E3
Newton Harcourt 160 B3
Newton Kyme 195 D3
Newton Longville 148 D4
Newton Mearns 233 G4
Newton Morrell NYorks 202 B2
Newton Morrell Oxon 148 B5
Newton Mountain 126 C2
Newton Mulgrave 203 G1
Newton of Affleck 244 C1
Newton of Ardtoe 247 F2
Newton of Balcanquhal 243 G3
Newton of Dalvey 267 H6
Newton of Falkland 244 A4
Newton of Leys 258 D1
Newton on the Hill 170 B5
Newton on Trent 187 F5
Newton Poppleford 103 D4
Newton Purcell 148 B4
Newton Regis 159 E2
Newton Reigny 210 A4
Newton St. Cyres 102 B3
Newton St. Faith 178 D4
Newton St. Loe 117 E1
Newton St. Petrock 113 E4
Newton Solney 173 D5
Newton Stacey 119 F3
Newton Stewart 215 F4
Newton Tony 118 D3
Newton Tracey 113 F3
Newton under Roseberry 203 E1
Newton Underwood 221 D3
Newton upon Derwent 195 G3
Newton Valence 120 C4
Newton with Scales 192 A4
Newtonairds 216 C2
Newtongrange 236 A3
Newtonhill 261 H5
Newton-in-the-Isle 162 C1
Newton-le-Willows Mersey 183 G3
Newton-le-Willows NYorks 202 B4
Newtonmill 253 E3
Newtonmore (Baile Ùr an t-Slèibh) 258 E5
Newton-on-Ouse 195 E2
Newton-on-Rawcliffe 204 B3
Newton-on-the-Moor 221 D1
Newtown Bucks 135 E2
Newtown ChesW&C 170 C2
Newtown Corn 97 G2
Newtown Corn 94 C4
Newtown Cumb 210 B1
Newtown Derbys 185 D4
Newtown Devon 114 A5
Newtown Devon 103 D3
Newtown Dorset 104 A2
Newtown Glos 131 F2
Newtown GtMan 183 G2
Newtown GtMan 184 B2
Newtown Hants 107 F1
Newtown Hants 119 F1
Newtown Hants 106 B1
Newtown Hants 119 E5
Newtown Hants 107 E1
Newtown Here 145 F3
Newtown Here 145 D2
Newtown High 257 K4
Newtown IoM 190 B4
Newtown IoW 106 D3
Newtown NM&D 282 D6
Newtown N'umb 220 C1
Newtown N'umb 229 E4
Newtown Oxon 134 C4
Newtown (Y Drenewydd) Powys 156 A3
Newtown RCT 129 G3
Newtown Shrop 170 B4
Newtown Som 115 F4
Newtown Som 103 F1
Newtown Staffs 171 G1
Newtown Staffs 172 B1
Newtown Staffs 158 B2
Newtown Wilts 118 A5
Newtown Wilts 119 E1
Newtown Crommelin 287 F4
Newtown Linford 160 A2
Newtown St. Boswells 227 G2
Newtown Saville 281 H3
Newtown Unthank 159 G2
Newtownabbey 287 H7
Newtownards 283 H1
Newtownbreda 283 G1
Newtownbutler 281 G6
Newtownhamilton 282 C6
Newtown-in-Saint-Martin 95 E4
Newtownstewart 285 G7
Newtyle 252 A5
Newyears Green 135 F4
Neyland 126 C2
Nibley Glos 131 F2
Nibley SGlos 131 F4
Nibley Green 131 G3
Nicholashayne 103 E1
Nicholaston 128 B4
Nidd 194 C1
Nigg Aberdeen 261 H4
Nigg High 267 F4
Nightcott 114 B5
Nilig 168 D2
Nilston Rigg 211 E1
Nimlet 131 G5
Nine Ashes 137 E2
Nine Elms 132 D4
Nine Mile Burn 235 F4
Ninebanks 211 D2
Ninemile Bar (Crocketford) 216 C3
Nineveh 145 F1
Ninfield 110 C2
Ningwood 106 D4
Nisbet 228 A4
Niton 107 E5
Nitshill 233 G3
Nixon's Corner 285 G4
Nizels 123 E3
No Man's Heath ChesW&C 170 C3
No Man's Heath Warks 159 E2
No Man's Land 97 G4
Noah's Ark 123 E3
Noak Hill 137 E3
Noblehill 217 D3
Noblethorpe 185 G2
Nobottle 148 B1
Nocton 175 F1
Noddsdale 232 D3
Nogdam End 179 E5
Noke 134 A1
Nolton 126 B1
Nolton Haven 126 B1
Nomansland Devon 102 B1
Nomansland Wilts 106 B1
Noneley 170 B5
Nonington 125 E3
Nook Cumb 218 C4
Nook Cumb 199 G4
Noonsbrough 279 B7
Noranside 252 C3
Norbreck 191 G3
Norbury ChesE 170 C3
Norbury Derbys 172 C3
Norbury GtLon 136 C5
Norbury Shrop 156 C3
Norbury Staffs 171 E5
Norbury Common 170 C3
Norbury Junction 171 E5
Norchard 127 D3
Norcott Brook 184 A4
Nordelph 163 D2
Norden Dorset 105 F4
Norden GtMan 184 C1
Nordley 157 F3
Norfolk Lavender, Heacham Norf PE31 7JE 177 E4
Norham 237 G5
Norland Town 193 G5
Norley 183 G5
Norleywood 106 C3
Norlington 109 G2
Norman Cross 161 G3
Normanby NLincs 187 F1
Normanby NYorks 203 G4
Normanby R&C 203 E1
Normanby by Stow 187 F4
Normanby Hall Country Park NLincs DN15 9HU 187 F1
Normanby le Wold 188 B3
Normanby-by-Spital 188 A4
Normandy 121 E2
Normann's Ruh 246 D5
Norman's Bay 110 B3
Norman's Green 103 D2
Normanston 165 G2
Normanton Derby 173 E4
Normanton Leics 174 D3
Normanton Lincs 175 E3
Normanton Notts 174 C2
Normanton Rut 161 E2
Normanton WYorks 194 C5
Normanton le Heath 159 F1
Normanton on Soar 173 G5
Normanton on Trent 174 C1
Normanton-on-the-Wolds 174 B4

317

Scaur (Kippford) D&G 216 C5
Scaur D&G 216 C3
Scawby 187 G2
Scawby Brook 187 G2
Scawton 203 E4
Scayne's Hill 109 F1
Scethrog 144 A5
Schaw 224 C3
Scholar Green 171 F2
Scholes SYorks 186 A3
Scholes WYorks 194 C4
Scholes WYorks 185 F2
Scholes WYorks 194 A5
School Green 170 D1
School House 103 G2
Schoose 208 D4
Sciberscross 266 E1
Science Museum GtLon SW7 2DD 11 F5
Scilly Isles (Isles of Scilly) 96 B1
Scissett 185 G1
Scleddau 140 C4
Sco Ruston 179 D3
Scofton 186 D4
Scolboa 287 F6
Scole 164 C4
Scollogstown 283 H5
Scolpaig 262 C4
Scone 243 G2
Scones Lethendy 243 G2
Sconser 256 B1
Scoor 238 D3
Scopwick 175 F2
Scoraig 265 G2
Scorborough 196 C3
Scorrier 96 B5
Scorriton 100 D1
Scorton Lancs 192 B3
Scorton NYorks 202 B2
Scot Hay 171 E3
Scotby 210 A2
Scotch Corner 202 B2
Scotch Street 282 C3
Scotch Town 285 H7
Scotch Whisky Heritage Centre Edin EH1 2NE 37 F4
Scotforth 192 A2
Scothern 188 A5
Scotland 175 F4
Scotland End 147 F4
Scotland Street 152 A4
Scotland Street School Museum of Education Glas G5 8QB 38 C6
Scotlandwell 243 G4
Scotnish 231 F1
Scots' Gap 220 C3
Scotsburn 266 E4
Scotston Aber 253 F2
Scotston P&K 251 E5
Scotstoun 233 G3
Scotstown 248 A3
Scott Willoughby 175 F4
Scotter 187 F2
Scotterthorpe 187 F2
Scottish Exhibition & Conference Centre (S.E.C.C.) Glas G3 8YW 38 B4
Scottish National Gallery of Modern Art Edin EH4 3DR 36 B4
Scottish National Portrait Gallery Edin EH2 1JD 37 F3
Scottish Parliament Edin EH99 1SP 37 H4
Scottish Seabird Centre, North Berwick ELoth EH39 4SS 236 C1
Scottish Wool Centre, Aberfoyle Stir FK8 3UQ 242 A4
Scottlethorpe 175 F5
Scotton Lincs 187 F3
Scotton NYorks 202 A3
Scotton NYorks 194 C2
Scottow 179 D3
Scoughall 236 D1
Scoulton 178 A5
Scounslow Green 172 B5
Scourie 272 D4
Scourie More 272 D4
Scousburgh 279 F9
Scouthead 185 D2
Scrabster 275 G1
Scrafield 176 B1
Scraghy 280 E1
Scrainwood 220 B1
Scralea 280 E1
Scrane End 176 B3
Scraptoft 160 B2
Scratby 179 G4
Scrayingham 195 G2
Scredington 175 F3
Scremby 176 C1
Scremerston 229 E2
Screveton 174 C3
Scribbagh 280 B4
Scriven 194 C2
Scronkey 192 A3
Scrooby 187 D3
Scropton 172 C4
Scrub Hill 176 A2
Scruton 202 C3
Sculthorpe 177 G4
Scunthorpe 187 F1
Sculage 128 A4
Sea 103 G1
Sea Life Centre, Blackpool FY1 5AA 64 Blackpool
Sea Life Centre, Brighton B&H BN2 1TB 65 Brighton
Sea Life Centre, Great Yarmouth Norf NR30 3AH 179 G5
Sea Life London Aquarium GtLon SE1 7PD 45 F5
Sea Life Sanctuary, Hunstanton Norf PE36 5BH 177 E3
Sea Mills 131 E5
Sea Palling 179 F3
Seabank 248 B5
Seaborough 104 A2
Seaburn 212 D1
Seacombe 183 E3
Seacroft Lincs 177 D1
Seacroft WYorks 194 C4
Seadyke 176 B4
Seafield A&B 231 F1
Seafield NM&D 283 F7
Seafield SAyr 224 B3
Seafield WLoth 235 E3
Seaford 109 G4
Seaforde 283 H4
Seaforth 183 E3
Seagrave 160 B1
Seagry Heath 132 B4
Seaham 212 D3
Seaham Grange 212 D2
Seahouses 229 G3
Seal 123 E3
Sealand 170 A1
Seale 121 D3
Sea-Life Adventure, Southend-on-Sea S'end SS1 2ER 138 B4
Sealyham 140 C5
Seamer NYorks 203 D1
Seamer NYorks 204 D4
Seamill 232 C5
Seapatrick 282 E4
SeaQuarium, Rhyl Denb LL18 3AF 182 B4
Searby 188 A2
Seasalter 124 C2
Seascale 198 B2
Seathorne 177 D1
Seathwaite Cumb 209 F5
Seathwaite Cumb 198 D3
Seatle 199 E4
Seatoller 209 F5
Seaton Corn 98 D5
Seaton Cumb 208 D3
Seaton Devon 103 F3
Seaton Dur 212 C2
Seaton ERid 197 D3
Seaton N'umb 221 F4
Seaton Rut 161 E3
Seaton Burn 221 E4
Seaton Carew 213 E5
Seaton Delaval 221 F4
Seaton Junction 103 F3
Seaton Ross 195 G3
Seaton Sluice 221 F4
Seaton Tramway Devon EX12 2NQ 103 F3
Seatown Aber 269 J5
Seatown Dorset 104 A3
Seatown Moray 268 D4
Seave Green 203 E2
Seaview 107 F3
Seaville 209 E1
Seavington St. Mary 104 A1
Seavington St. Michael 104 A1
Seawick 139 E1
Sebastopol 130 B3
Sebergham 209 G2
Seckington 159 E2
Second Coast 265 F2
Sedbergh 200 B3
Sedbury 131 E3
Sedbusk 201 D3
Seddington 149 G3
Sedgeberrow 146 C4
Sedgebrook 175 D4
Sedgefield 212 C5
Sedgeford 177 F4
Sedgehill 117 F5
Sedgemere 159 E5
Sedgley 158 B3
Sedgwick 199 G4
Sedlescombe 110 C2
Sedlescombe Street 110 C2
Seend 118 A1
Seend Cleeve 118 A1
Seer Green 135 E3
Seething 165 E2
Sefton 183 E2
Seghill 221 E4
Seifton 157 D4
Seighford 171 F5
Seil 239 G3
Seilebost 263 F2
Seion 167 E1
Seisdon 158 A3
Seisiadar 271 H4
Seized! Revenue & Customs Uncovered Mersey L3 4AQ 42 B5
Selattyn 169 F4
Selborne 120 C4
Selby 195 F4
Selham 121 E5
Selhurst 122 C2
Selkirk 227 F3
Sellack 145 E5
Sellafield 198 B2
Sellafield Visitors Centre Cumb CA20 1PG 198 B2
Sellafirth 278 E3
Sellindge 124 D5
Selling 124 C3
Sells Green 118 A1
Selly Oak 158 C4
Selmeston 110 A3
Selsdon 122 C2
Selsey 108 A4
Selsfield Common 122 C5
Selside Cumb 199 G3
Selside NYorks 200 C5
Selsley 132 A2
Selstead 125 E4
Selston 173 F2
Selworthy 114 C3
Semblister 279 C7
Semer 152 A3
Semington 117 F1
Semley 117 F5
Send 121 F2
Send Marsh 121 F2
Seneirl 286 D2
Senghenydd 130 A3
Sennen 94 A4
Sennen Cove 94 A4
Sennybridge 143 F5
Senwick 207 G2
Sequer's Bridge 100 C2
Serlby 186 D4
Serpentine Gallery GtLon W2 3XA 11 F5
Serrington 118 B4
Seskinore 281 G2
Sessay 203 D5
Setchey 163 E1
Setley 106 C2
Setter Shet 279 E8
Setter Shet 279 C7
Settiscarth 277 C6
Settle 193 E1
Settrington 204 B5
Seven Ash 115 E4
Seven Bridges 132 D3
Seven Kings 137 D4
Seven Sisters 129 E2
Seven Springs 132 B1
Sevenhampton Glos 146 C5
Sevenhampton Swin 133 E3
Sevenoaks 123 E3
Sevenoaks Weald 123 E3
Severn Beach 131 E4
Severn Stoke 146 A3
Severn Valley Railway Shrop DY12 1BG 157 G4
Sevick End 149 F2
Sevington 124 C4
Sewards End 151 D4
Sewardstone 136 C3
Sewerby 197 D1
Sewerby Hall & Gardens ERid YO15 1EA 197 E1
Seworgan 95 E3
Sewstern 175 D5
Seymour Villas 113 E1
Sezincote 147 D4
Sgiogarstaigh (Skigersta) 271 H1
Sgodachail 266 B2
Shabbington 134 B2
Shackerley 158 A2
Shackerstone 159 F2
Shackleford 121 E3
Shadfen 221 E3
Shadforth 212 C3
Shadingfield 165 F3
Shadoxhurst 124 B5
Shadsworth 192 D5
Shadwell Norf 164 A3
Shadwell WYorks 194 C3
Shaftenhoe End 150 C4
Shaftesbury 117 F5
Shafton 186 A1
Shakespeare's Birthplace Warks CV37 6QW 85 Stratford-upon-Avon
Shakespeare's Globe Theatre GtLon SE1 9DT 45 J4
Shalbourne 119 E1
Shalcombe 106 C4
Shalden 120 B3
Shalden Green 120 C3
Shaldon 102 C5
Shalfleet 106 D4
Shalford Essex 151 F5
Shalford Surr 121 F3
Shalford Green 151 F5
Shallowford Devon 114 A3
Shallowford Staffs 171 F5
Shalmsford Street 124 C3
Shalmstry 275 G2
Shalstone 148 B4
Shalunt 232 B2
Shambellie 217 D4
Shamley Green 121 F3
Shanaghy 281 F6
Shandon 233 D1
Shandwick 267 F4
Shangton 160 C3
Shankend 227 G5
Shankhouse 221 E4
Shanklin 107 E4
Shanklin Chine IoW PO37 6BW 107 E4
Shannochie 223 E3
Shantron 233 E1
Shantullich 266 D6
Shanzie 252 A4
Shap 199 G1
Shapinsay 277 E6
Shapwick Dorset 105 F2
Shapwick Som 116 B4
Sharcott 118 C2
Shard End 159 D4
Shardlow 173 F4
Shareshill 158 B2
Sharlston 186 A1
Sharlston Common 186 A1
Sharnal Street 137 G5
Sharnbrook 149 E2
Sharneyford 193 E5
Sharnford 159 G3
Sharnhill Green 104 D2
Sharow 202 C5
Sharp Street 179 E3
Sharpenhoe 149 F4
Sharperton 220 B1
Sharpham House 101 E2
Sharpness 131 F2
Sharpthorne 122 C5
Sharrington 178 B2
Sharvogues 287 F6
Shatterford 157 G4
Shatterling 125 E3
Shaugh Prior 100 B1
Shave Cross 104 A3
Shavington 171 E2
Shaw GtMan 184 D2
Shaw Swin 132 D4
Shaw WBerks 119 F1
Shaw Wilts 117 F1
Shaw Green Herts 150 A4
Shaw Green NYorks 194 B2
Shaw Mills 194 B1
Shaw Side 184 D2
Shawbost (Siabost) 270 E3
Shawbury 170 C5
Shawell 160 A4
Shawfield GtMan 184 C1
Shawfield Staffs 172 B1
Shawford 119 F5
Shawforth 193 E5
Shawhead 216 C3
Shawtonhill 234 A5
Shean 282 D7
Sheanachie 222 C4
Sheandow 259 K1
Shearington 217 E4
Shearsby 160 B3
Shebbear 113 E5
Shebdon 171 E5
Shebster 275 F2
Shedfield 107 E1
Sheen 172 C1
Sheepridge 185 F1
Sheepscombe 132 A1
Sheepstor 100 B1
Sheepwash Devon 113 E5
Sheepwash N'umb 221 E3
Sheepway 131 D5
Sheepy Magna 159 F2
Sheepy Parva 159 F2
Sheering 137 E1
Sheerness 124 B1
Sheet 120 C5
Sheetrim AB&C 282 A5
Sheetrim F&O 280 E6
Sheffield 186 A4
Sheffield Botanic Gardens SYorks S10 2LN 21 B3
Sheffield Bottom 120 B1
Sheffield Green 109 G1
Sheffield Park Garden ESuss TN22 3QX 109 G1
Shefford 149 G4
Shefford Woodlands 133 F5
Sheigra 272 D2
Sheinton 157 F2
Shelderton 156 D5
Sheldon Derbys 172 C1
Sheldon Devon 103 E2
Sheldon WMid 158 D4
Sheldwich 124 C3
Sheldwich Lees 124 C3
Shelf Bridgend 129 F4
Shelf WYorks 194 A5
Shelfanger 164 C3
Shelfield Warks 146 D1
Shelfield WMid 158 C2
Shelfield Green 146 D1
Shelford 174 B3
Shellachan A&B 240 A2
Shellachan A&B 240 C2
Shellbrook 159 F1
Shellbrook Hill 170 A3
Shelley Essex 137 E2
Shelley Suff 152 B4
Shelley WYorks 185 G1
Shellingford 133 F3
Shellow Bowells 137 F2
Shelsley Beauchamp 145 G1
Shelsley Walsh 145 G1
Shelswell 148 B4
Shelthorpe 160 A1
Shelton Bed 149 F1
Shelton Norf 164 D2
Shelton Notts 174 C3
Shelton Shrop 157 D1
Shelve 156 C3
Shelwick 145 E3
Shelwick Green 145 E3
Shenfield 137 F3
Shenington 147 F3
Shenley 136 A2
Shenley Brook End 148 D4
Shenley Church End 148 D4
Shenleybury 136 A2
Shenmore 144 C4
Shennanton 215 E4
Shenstone Staffs 158 D2
Shenstone Worcs 158 A5
Shenstone Woodend 158 D2
Shenton 159 F2
Shenval 259 K2
Shepeau Stow 162 B1
Shephall 150 A5
Shepherd's Bush 136 B5
Shepherd's Green 134 C4
Shepherd's Patch 131 G2
Shepherdswell (Sibertswold) 125 E4
Shepley 185 F2
Sheppardstown 275 H5
Shepperdine 131 F3
Shepperton 121 F1
Shepreth 150 B3
Shepreth Wildlife Park Cambs SG8 6PZ 150 B3
Shepshed 159 G1
Shepton Beauchamp 104 A1
Shepton Mallet 116 D3
Shepton Montague 117 D4
Shepway 123 G3
Sheraton 212 D4
Sherborne Dorset 104 C1
Sherborne Glos 133 D1
Sherborne St. John 120 B2
Sherbourne 147 E1
Sherbourne Street 152 A3
Sherburn Dur 212 C3
Sherburn NYorks 204 C5
Sherburn Hill 212 C3
Sherburn in Elmet 195 D4
Shere 121 F3
Shereford 177 G5
Sherfield English 119 D5
Sherfield on oddon 120 B2
Sherford Devon 101 D3
Sherford Som 115 F5
Sheriff Hutton 195 F1
Sheriffhales 157 G1
Sheringham 178 C1
Sheringham Park Norf NR26 8TL 178 C1
Sherington 149 D3
Shernal Green 146 B1
Shernborne 177 F4
Sherramore 258 C5
Sherrington 118 A4
Sherston 132 A4
Sherwood 173 G3
Sherwood Forest Country Park Notts NG21 9HN 174 B1
Sherwood Forest Fun Park Notts NG21 9QA 174 B1
Sherwood Green 113 F3
Sherwood Pines Forest Park Notts NG21 9JL 174 B1
Shetland Islands 279 B7
Shevington 183 G2
Shevington Moor 183 G1
Sheviock 99 D5
Shide 107 E4
Shiel Bridge (Drochaid Sheile) 257 F3
Shieldaig High 264 E6
Shieldaig High 264 E4
Shieldhill 234 C2
Shielfoot 247 F2
Shielhill 252 C4
Shiels 260 E4
Shifford 133 F2
Shifnal 157 G2
Shilbottle 221 D1
Shildon 212 B5
Shillanavogy 287 G5
Shillingford Devon 114 C5
Shillingford Oxon 134 A3
Shillingford Abbot 102 C4
Shillingford St. George 102 C4
Shillingstone 105 E1
Shillington 149 G4
Shillmoor 220 A1
Shilstone 113 F5
Shilton Oxon 133 E2
Shilton Warks 159 G4
Shimpling Norf 164 C3
Shimpling Suff 151 G2
Shimpling Street 151 G2
Shincliffe 212 B3
Shiney Row 212 C2
Shinfield 120 C1
Shingay 150 B3
Shingham 163 F2
Shingle Street 153 E3
Shinn 282 E5
Shinness Lodge 273 H7
Shipbourne 123 E3
Shipbrookhill 184 A5
Shipdham 178 A5
Shipham 116 B2
Shiphay 101 E1
Shiplake 134 C5
Shiplake Row 134 C5
Shipley N'umb 229 F5
Shipley Shrop 158 A3
Shipley WSuss 121 G5
Shipley WYorks 194 A4
Shipley Bridge Devon 100 C1
Shipley Bridge Surr 122 C4
Shipley Common 173 F3
Shipley Country Park Derbys DE75 7GX 18 D2
Shipmeadow 165 E2
Shippea Hill 163 E4
Shippon 133 G3
Shipston on Stour 147 E3
Shipton Glos 132 C1
Shipton NYorks 195 E2
Shipton Shrop 157 E3
Shipton Bellinger 118 D3
Shipton Gorge 104 A3
Shipton Green 108 A3
Shipton Moyne 132 A4
Shipton Oliffe 132 C1
Shipton Solers 132 C1
Shipton-on-Cherwell 133 G1
Shiptonthorpe 196 A3
Shipton-under-Wychwood 133 E1
Shira 241 D3
Shirburn 134 B3
Shirdley Hill 183 E1
Shire Hall Gallery, Stafford Staffs ST16 2LD 171 G5
Shire Oak 158 C2
Shirebrook 173 G1
Shirecliffe 186 A3
Shiregreen 186 A3
Shirehampton 131 E5
Shiremoor 221 F4
Shirenewton 131 D3
Shireoaks 186 C4
Shirl Heath 144 D2
Shirland 173 E2
Shirley Derbys 172 D3
Shirley GtLon 122 C2
Shirley Hants 106 A3
Shirley Soton 106 D1
Shirley WMid 158 D5
Shirley Heath 158 D5
Shirley Warren 106 C1
Shirleywich 171 G5
Shirrell Heath 107 E1
Shirwell 113 F2
Shirwell Cross 113 F2
Shiskine 223 E3
Shittlehope 211 G4
Shobdon 144 C1
Shobley 106 A2
Shobrooke 102 B2
Shocklach 170 B3
Shocklach Green 170 B3
Shoeburyness 138 C4
Sholden 125 F3
Sholing 107 D1
Shoot Hill 156 D1
Shooter's Hill 136 D5
Shop Corn 96 C2
Shop Corn 112 C4
Shop Corner 152 D4
Shopnoller 115 E4
Shoptown 287 G6
Shore 184 D1
Shoreditch 136 C4
Shoreham 123 E2
Shoreham-by-Sea 109 E3
Shoremill 266 E5
Shoresdean 237 G5
Shoreswood 237 G5
Shoreton 266 D5
Shorley 119 G5
Shorncote 132 C3
Shorne 137 F5
Shorne Ridgeway 137 F5
Short Cross 156 B2
Short Green 164 B3
Short Heath Derbys 159 F1
Short Heath WMid 158 C3
Shortacombe 99 F2
Shortbridge 109 G1
Shortfield Common 120 D3
Shortgate 109 G2
Shortgrove 150 D4
Shorthampton 147 F5
Shortlands 122 C2
Shortlanesend 96 C5
Shorton 101 E1
Shorwell 107 D4
Shoscombe 117 E2
Shotatton 170 A5
Shotesham 164 D2
Shotgate 137 G3
Shotley N'hants 161 E3
Shotley Suff 152 D4
Shotley Bridge 211 G2
Shotley Gate 152 D4
Shotleyfield 211 G2
Shottenden 124 C3
Shottermill 121 D4
Shottery 147 D2
Shotteswell 147 G3
Shottisham 153 E3
Shottle 173 E2
Shottlegate 173 E3
Shotton Dur 212 D4
Shotton Dur 212 C5
Shotton Flints 170 A1
Shotton N'umb 221 E4
Shotton Colliery 212 C3
Shotts 234 C3
Shotwick 183 E5
Shouldham 163 E2
Shouldham Thorpe 163 E2
Shoulton 146 A2
Shover's Green 123 F5
Shrawardine 156 C1
Shrawley 146 A1
Shreding Green 135 F4
Shrewley 147 E1
Shrewsbury 157 D1
Shrewton 118 B3
Shri Venkateswara (Balaji) Temple of the United Kingdom WMid B69 3DU 14 C3
Shrigley 283 J3
Shrine of Our Lady of Walsingham (Anglican) Norf NR22 6EF 178 A2
Shripney 108 B3
Shrivenham 133 E4
Shropham 164 A2
Shroton (Iwerne Courtney) 105 E1
Shrub End 152 A5
Shucknall 145 E3
Shudy Camps 151 E3
Shugborough Estate Staffs ST17 0XB 171 G5
Shurdington 132 B1
Shurlock Row 134 D5
Shurnock 146 C1
Shurrery 275 F3
Shurrery Lodge 275 F3
Shurton 115 F3
Shustoke 159 E3
Shut Heath 171 F5
Shute Devon 103 F3
Shute Devon 102 B2
Shutford 147 F3
Shuthonger 146 A4
Shutlanger 148 C3
Shutt Green 158 A2
Shuttington 159 E2
Shuttlewood 186 B5
Shuttleworth 184 B1
Siabost Bho Dheas 270 E3
Siabost Bho Thuath 270 E3
Siadar Iarach 271 F2
Siadar Uarach 271 F2
Sibbaldbie 217 F2
Sibbertoft 160 B4
Sibdon Carwood 156 D4
Sibertswold (Shepherdswell) 125 E4
Sibford Ferris 147 F4
Sibford Gower 147 F4
Sible Hedingham 151 F4
Sibley's Green 151 E5
Sibsey 176 B2
Sibson Cambs 161 F3
Sibson Leics 159 F2
Sibster 275 J3
Sibthorpe 174 C3
Sibton 153 E1
Sibton Green 165 E4
Sicklesmere 151 G1
Sicklinghall 194 C3
Sidbury Devon 103 E3
Sidbury Shrop 157 F4
Sidcot 116 B2
Sidcup 137 D5
Siddal 194 A5
Siddington ChesE 184 C5
Siddington Glos 132 C3
Sidemoor 158 B5
Sidestrand 179 D2
Sidford 103 E3
Sidlesham 108 A4
Sidley 110 C3
Sidlow 122 B4
Sidmouth 103 E4
Sigford 102 A5
Sigglesthorne 197 D3
Sigingstone 129 F5
Signet 133 E1
Silbury Hill (Stonehenge, Avebury & Associated Sites) Wilts SN8 1QH 118 C1
Silchester 120 B1
Sildinis 270 E6
Sileby 160 B1
Silecroft 198 C4
Silent Valley NM&D BT33 0HU 283 G6
Silfield 164 C2
Silian 142 B2
Silk Willoughby 175 F3
Silkstead 119 F5
Silkstone 185 G2
Silkstone Common 185 G2
Sill Field 199 G4
Silloth 209 E1
Sills 220 A1
Sillyearn 268 D5
Silpho 204 C3
Silsden 193 G3
Silsoe 149 F4
Silver End CenBeds 149 G3
Silver End Essex 151 G5
Silver Green 165 D2
Silver Hill 280 E4
Silver Street Kent 124 A2
Silver Street Som 116 C4
Silverbridge 282 C7
Silverbrook 285 G5
Silverburn 235 G3
Silvercraigs 231 G1
Silverdale Lancs 199 F5
Silverdale Staffs 171 F3
Silvergate 178 C3
Silverhill 110 C2
Silverlace Green 153 E2
Silverley's Green 165 D4
Silvermoss 261 G1
Silverstone 148 B3
Silverton 102 C2
Silvington 157 F5
Silwick 279 B8
Simister 184 C2
Simmondley 185 E3
Simonburn 220 A4
Simonsbath 114 A4
Simonside 212 C1
Simonstone Bridgend 129 F4
Simonstone Lancs 193 D4
Simprim 237 F5
Simpson 149 D4
Sinclair's Hill 237 F4
Sinclairston 224 C4
Sinderby 202 C4
Sinderhope 211 E2
Sindlesham 120 C1
Sinfin 173 E4
Singdean 227 G5
Singleton Lancs 191 G4
Singleton WSuss 108 A2
Singlewell 137 F5
Singret 170 A2
Sinkhurst Green 124 A4
Sinnahard 260 C3
Sinnington 203 G4
Sion Mills 285 F6
Sinton Green 146 A1
Sipson 135 F5
Sirhowy 130 A1
Sirhowy Valley Country Park Caerp NP11 7BD 130 A3
Sisland 165 E2
Sissinghurst 123 G5
Sissinghurst Castle Garden Kent TN17 2AB 124 A5
Siston 131 F5
Sithney 94 D4
Sittingbourne 124 B2
Six Ashes 157 G4
Six Hills 174 B5
Six Mile Bottom 151 D2
Six Road Ends 283 J1
Six Roads End 172 C5
Sixhills 188 B4
Sixmile 124 D4
Sixmilecross 281 H2
Sixpenny Handley 105 G1
Sizewell 153 F1
Skail 274 C4
Skaill Ork 277 B6
Skaill Ork 277 E7
Skaill Ork 276 D4
Skara Brae (Heart of Neolithic Orkney) Ork KW16 3LR 277 B6
Skares Aber 260 E1
Skares EAyr 224 D4
Skarpigarth 279 A7
Skateraw 237 E2
Skaw 279 E6
Skeabost 263 K7
Skeabrae 276 B5
Skeeby 202 B2
Skeffington 160 C2
Skeffling 189 D1
Skegby 173 G1
Skegness 177 D1
Skegness Water Leisure Park Lincs PE25 1JF 177 D1
Skelberry Shet 279 F9
Skelberry Shet 279 D6
Skelbo 266 E2
Skelbo Street 266 E2
Skelbrooke 186 C1
Skeld (Easter Skeld) 279 C8
Skeldon 224 B4
Skeldyke 176 B4
Skellingthorpe 187 G5
Skellister 279 D7
Skellow 186 C1
Skelmanthorpe 185 G1
Skelmersdale 183 F2
Skelmonae 261 G1
Skelmorlie 232 C3
Skelmuir 269 H6
Skelpick 274 C3
Skelton Cumb 210 A4
Skelton ERid 195 G5
Skelton NYorks 201 F2
Skelton (Skelton-in-Cleveland) R&C 203 F1
Skelton York 195 E2
Skelton-in-Cleveland (Skelton) 203 F1
Skelton-on-Ure 194 C1
Skelwick 276 D3
Skelwith Bridge 199 E2
Skendleby 176 C1
Skendleby Psalter 189 E5
Skenfrith 145 D5
Skerne 196 C2
Skeroblingarry 222 C3
Skerray 273 J2
Skerries 282 A5
Skerton 192 A1
Sketchley 159 G3
Sketty 128 C3
Skewen 128 D3

Statham 184 A4
Stathe 116 A5
Stathern 174 C4
Station Town 212 D4
Staughton Green 149 G1
Staughton Highway 149 G1
Staunton Glos 131 E1
Staunton Glos 145 G5
Staunton Harold Hall 173 E5
Staunton Harold Reservoir Derbys DE73 8DN 173 E5
Staunton in the Vale 174 D3
Staunton on Arrow 144 C1
Staunton on Wye 144 C3
Staveley Cumb 199 F3
Staveley Derbys 186 B5
Staveley NYorks 194 C1
Staveley-in-Cartmel 199 E4
Staverton Devon 101 D1
Staverton Glos 146 A5
Staverton N'hants 148 A1
Staverton Wilts 117 F1
Staverton Bridge 146 A5
Stawell 116 A4
Stawley 115 D5
Staxigoe 275 J3
Staxton 204 D5
Staylittle (Penffordd-las) 155 E3
Staynall 191 G3
Staythorpe 174 C2
Stean 201 F5
Steane 148 A4
Stearsby 203 F5
Steart 115 F3
Stebbing 151 E5
Stebbing Green 151 E5
Stechford 158 D4
Stedham 121 D5
Steel Cross 123 E5
Steel Green 198 C5
Steele Road 218 D2
Steen's Bridge 145 E2
Steep 120 C5
Steep Marsh 120 C5
Steeple Dorset 105 F4
Steeple Essex 138 C2
Steeple Ashton 118 A2
Steeple Aston 147 G5
Steeple Barton 147 G5
Steeple Bumpstead 151 E3
Steeple Claydon 148 B5
Steeple Gidding 161 G4
Steeple Langford 118 B4
Steeple Morden 150 A3
Steeraway 157 F2
Steeton 193 G3
Stein 263 H6
Steinis 271 G4
Steinmanhill 269 F6
Stella 212 A1
Stelling Minnis 124 D4
Stembridge 116 B5
Stemster High 275 G2
Stemster High 275 G4
Stemster House 275 G2
Stenalees 97 E4
Stenhill 103 D1
Stenhousemuir 234 C1
Stenigot 188 C4
Stenness 278 B5
Stenscholl 263 K5
Stenson 173 E5
Stenton ELoth 236 D2
Stenton P&K 251 F5
Stepaside Pembs 127 E2
Stepaside Powys 155 G4
Stepney 136 C4
Steppingley 149 F4
Stepps 234 A3
Sternfield 153 E1
Sterridge 113 F1
Stert 118 B2
Stetchworth 151 E2
Stevenage 150 A5
Stevenston 233 D5
Steventon Hants 119 G3
Steventon Oxon 133 G3
Steventon End 151 E3
Stevington 149 E2
Stewart Park, Middlesbrough Middl TS7 8AR 29 C4
Stewartby 149 F3
Stewarton D&G 207 E2
Stewarton EAyr 233 F5
Stewartstown 282 B1
Stewkley 149 D5
Stewley 103 G1
Stewton 189 D4
Steyning 109 D2
Steynton 126 C2
Stibb 112 C4
Stibb Cross 113 E4
Stibb Green 118 D1
Stibbard 178 A3
Stibbington 161 F3
Stichill 228 B3
Sticker 97 D4
Stickford 176 B1
Sticklepath Devon 99 G1
Sticklepath Som 103 G1
Stickling Green 150 C4
Stickney 176 B2
Stiff Street 124 A2
Stiffkey 178 A1
Stifford's Bridge 145 G3
Stileway 116 B3
Stilligarry (Stadhlaigearraidh) 254 C1
Stillingfleet 195 E3
Stillington NYorks 195 E1
Stillington Stock 212 C5
Stilton 161 G4
Stinchcombe 131 G3
Stinsford 104 D3
Stirchley Tel&W 157 G2
Stirchley WMid 158 C4
Stirkoke House 275 J3
Stirling Aber 269 K6
Stirling (Sruighlea) Stir 242 C5
Stirling Castle Stir FK8 1EJ 242 C5
Stirling Visitor Centre Stir FK8 1EH 242 C5
Stirton 193 F2
Stisted 151 G5
Stitchcombe 118 D1
Stithians 95 E3
Stittenham 266 D4
Stivichall 159 F5
Stix 250 C5
Stixwould 175 G1
Stoak 183 F5
Stobo 226 C2
Stoborough 105 F4
Stoborough Green 105 F4
Stobwood 235 D4
Stock 137 F3
Stock Green 146 B2
Stock Lane 133 E5
Stock Wood 146 C2
Stockbridge Hants 119 E4
Stockbridge Stir 242 C4
Stockbridge WSuss 108 A3
Stockbury 124 A2
Stockcross 119 F1
Stockdale 95 E3
Stockdalewath 209 G2
Stockerston 160 D3
Stockgrove Country Park CenBeds LU7 0BA 149 E5
Stocking Green Essex 151 D4
Stocking Green MK 148 D3
Stocking Pelham 150 C5
Stockingford 159 F3
Stockinish 263 G2
Stockland Cardiff 130 A5
Stockland Devon 103 F2
Stockland Bristol 115 F3
Stockleigh English 102 B2
Stockleigh Pomeroy 102 B2
Stockley 118 B1
Stocklinch 103 G1
Stockport 184 C3
Stocksbridge 185 G3
Stocksfield 211 G1
Stockton Here 145 E1
Stockton Norf 165 E2
Stockton Shrop 157 G3
Stockton Shrop 156 B2
Stockton Tel&W 157 G1
Stockton Warks 147 G1
Stockton Wilts 118 A4
Stockton Heath 184 A4
Stockton on Teme 145 G1
Stockton on the Forest 195 F2
Stockton-on-Tees 202 D1
Stockwell 132 B1
Stockwell Heath 172 B5
Stockwood Bristol 116 D1
Stockwood Dorset 104 B2
Stodday 192 A2
Stodmarsh 125 E2
Stody 178 B2
Stoer 272 C6
Stoford Som 104 B1
Stoford Wilts 118 B4
Stogumber 115 D4
Stogursey 115 F3
Stoke Devon 112 C3
Stoke Hants 119 F2
Stoke Hants 107 G2
Stoke Med 124 A1
Stoke Plym 100 A2
Stoke WMid 159 F5
Stoke Abbott 104 A2
Stoke Albany 160 D4
Stoke Ash 164 C4
Stoke Bardolph 174 B3
Stoke Bishop 131 E5
Stoke Bliss 145 F1
Stoke Bruerne 148 C2
Stoke by Clare 151 F3
Stoke Canon 102 C3
Stoke Charity 119 F4
Stoke Climsland 99 D3
Stoke D'Abernon 121 G2
Stoke Doyle 161 F4
Stoke Dry 161 D3
Stoke Edith 145 F3
Stoke Farthing 118 B5
Stoke Ferry 163 F3
Stoke Fleming 101 E3
Stoke Gabriel 101 E2
Stoke Gifford 131 F5
Stoke Golding 159 F3
Stoke Goldington 148 D3
Stoke Green 135 E4
Stoke Hammond 149 D5
Stoke Heath Shrop 171 D5
Stoke Heath Worcs 146 B1
Stoke Holy Cross 178 D5
Stoke Lacy 145 F3
Stoke Lyne 148 A5
Stoke Mandeville 134 D1
Stoke Newington 136 C4
Stoke on Tern 170 D5
Stoke Orchard 146 B5
Stoke Pero 114 B3
Stoke Poges 135 E4
Stoke Pound 146 B1
Stoke Prior Here 145 E2
Stoke Prior Worcs 146 B1
Stoke Rivers 113 G2
Stoke Rochford 175 E5
Stoke Row 134 B4
Stoke St. Gregory 116 A5
Stoke St. Mary 115 F5
Stoke St. Michael 117 D3
Stoke St. Milborough 157 E4
Stoke sub Hamdon 104 A1
Stoke Talmage 134 B3
Stoke Trister 117 E5
Stoke Villice 116 C1
Stoke Wake 105 D2
Stoke-by-Nayland 152 A4
Stokeford 105 E4
Stokeham 187 E5
Stokeinteignhead 102 C5
Stokenchurch 134 C3
Stokenham 101 E3
Stoke-on-Trent 171 F3
Stokesay 156 D4
Stokesby 179 F4
Stokesley 203 E2
Stolford 115 F3
Ston Easton 116 D2
Stonar Cut 125 F2
Stondon Massey 137 E2
Stone Bucks 134 C1
Stone Glos 131 F3
Stone Kent 137 E5
Stone Kent 111 E1
Stone Som 116 C4
Stone Staffs 171 G4
Stone SYorks 186 C4
Stone Worcs 158 A5
Stone Allerton 116 B2
Stone Cross Dur 201 F1
Stone Cross ESuss 110 B3
Stone Cross ESuss 110 A1
Stone Cross Kent 124 C5
Stone Cross Kent 123 E5
Stone House 200 C4
Stone Street Kent 123 E3
Stone Street Suff 165 E3
Stone Street Suff 152 A4
Stonea 162 C3
Stonebridge ESuss 110 A1
Stonebridge NSom 116 A2
Stonebridge Warks 159 E4
Stonebroom 173 F2
Stonecross Green 151 G2
Stonefield A&B 231 G2
Stonefield Staffs 171 G4
Stonegate ESuss 110 B1
Stonegate NYorks 203 G2
Stonegrave 203 F5
Stonehaugh 219 F4
Stonehaven 253 G1
Stonehenge (Stonehenge, Avebury & Associated Sites) Wilts SP4 7DE 118 C3
Stonehill 121 E1
Stonehouse ChesW&C 183 G5
Stonehouse D&G 216 C4
Stonehouse Glos 132 A2
Stonehouse N'umb 210 C2
Stonehouse Plym 100 A2
Stonehouse SLan 234 B5
Stoneleigh Surr 122 B2
Stoneleigh Warks 159 F5
Stoneley Green 170 D2
Stonely 149 G1
Stoner Hill 120 C5
Stones 193 F5
Stones Green 152 C5
Stones of Stenness (Heart of Neolithic Orkney) Ork KW16 3JZ 277 C6
Stonesby 174 D5
Stonesfield 133 F1
Stonestreet Green 124 C5
Stonethwaite 209 F5
Stoney Cross 106 B1
Stoney Middleton 185 G5
Stoney Stanton 159 G3
Stoney Stoke 117 E4
Stoney Stratton 117 D4
Stoney Stretton 156 C2
Stoneyburn 235 D3
Stoneyford 103 D4
Stoneygate 160 B2
Stoneyhills 138 C3
Stoneykirk 214 B5
Stoneywood 261 G3
Stonganess 278 E2
Stonham Aspal 152 C2
Stonham Barns Suff IP14 6AT 152 C2
Stonnall 158 C2
Stonor 134 C4
Stonton Wyville 160 C3
Stony Houghton 173 F1
Stony Stratford 148 C3
Stonybreck 278 A1
Stonyford 283 F1
Stoodleigh Devon 102 C1
Stoodleigh Devon 113 G2
Stopham 108 C2
Stopsley 149 G5
Stoptide 96 D2
Storeton 183 E4
Stormontfield 243 G2
Stornoway (Steòrnabhagh) 271 G4
Stornoway Airport 271 G4
Storridge 145 G3
Storrington 108 C2
Storrs 185 G4
Storth 199 F4
Storwood 195 G3
Stotfield 267 K4
Stotfold 150 A4
Stottesdon 157 F4
Stoughton Leics 160 B2
Stoughton Surr 121 E2
Stoughton WSuss 107 G1
Stoughton Cross 116 B3
Stoul 256 D5
Stoulton 146 B3
Stour Provost 117 E5
Stour Row 117 F5
Stourbridge 158 A4
Stourhead Wilts BA12 6QD 117 E4
Stourpaine 105 E2
Stourport-on-Severn 158 A5
Stourton Staffs 158 A4
Stourton Warks 147 E4
Stourton Wilts 117 E4
Stourton Caundle 104 D1
Stove 276 F4
Stoven 165 F3
Stow Lincs 187 F4
Stow ScBord 236 B5
Stow Bardolph 163 E2
Stow Bedon 164 A2
Stow cum Quy 150 D1
Stow Longa 161 G5
Stow Maries 138 B3
Stow Pasture 187 F4
Stowbridge 163 D2
Stowe Glos 131 E2
Stowe Shrop 156 C5
Stowe Staffs 158 D1
Stowe Landscape Gardens Bucks MK18 5DQ 148 B4
Stowe-by-Chartley 172 B5
Stowehill 148 B2
Stowell Glos 132 C1
Stowell Som 117 D5
Stowey 116 C2
Stowford Devon 99 E2
Stowford Devon 113 G3
Stowford Devon 103 E4
Stowlangtoft 152 A1
Stowmarket 152 B2
Stow-on-the-Wold 147 D5
Stowting 124 D4
Stowupland 152 B2
Straad 232 B3
Strabane 285 F6
Stracathro 253 E3
Strachan 260 E5
Strachur (Clachan Strachur) 240 C4
Stradbroke 164 D4
Stradhavern 282 E1
Stradishall 151 F2
Stradsett 163 E2
Stragglethorpe 175 E2
Straid A&N 287 H6
Straid CC&G 286 E1
Straid M&EAnt 286 E6
Straidbilly 286 D2
Straidkilly 287 G4
Straight Soley 133 F5
Straiton Edin 235 G3
Straiton SAyr 224 B5
Straloch Aber 261 G2
Straloch P&K 251 F3
Stramshall 172 B4
Stranagalwilly 285 H5
Strands 198 C4
Strang 190 B4
Strangford Here 145 E5
Strangford NM&D 283 J4
Stranocum 286 E2
Stranraer 214 B4
Strata Florida 142 D1
Stratfield Mortimer 120 B1
Stratfield Saye 120 B1
Stratfield Turgis 120 B2
Stratford CenBeds 149 G3
Stratford Glos 146 A4
Stratford GtLon 136 C4
Stratford St. Andrew 153 E2
Stratford St. Mary 152 B4
Stratford sub Castle 118 C4
Stratford Tony 118 B5
Stratford-upon-Avon 147 E2
Stratford-upon-Avon Butterfly Farm Warks CV37 7LS 85 Stratford-upon-Avon
Strath 275 H3
Strathan High 272 C6
Strathan High 257 F5
Strathaven 234 B5
Strathblane 233 G2
Strathcanaird 265 H1
Strathcarron 265 F7
Strathclyde Country Park NLan ML1 3ED 31 G5
Strathdon 260 B3
Strathgirnock 260 B5
Strathkinness 244 C3
Strathmiglo 244 A3
Strathpeffer (Strath Pheofhair) 266 B6
Strathrannoch 265 K4
Strathtay 251 E4
Strathwhillan 223 F2
Strathy 274 D2
Strathyre 242 A3
Stratton Corn 112 C5
Stratton Dorset 104 C3
Stratton Glos 132 C2
Stratton Audley 148 B5
Stratton Hall 152 D4
Stratton St. Margaret 133 D4
Stratton St. Michael 164 D2
Stratton Strawless 178 D3
Stratton-on-the-Fosse 117 D2
Stravanan 232 B4
Stravithie 244 D3
Straw 286 B6
Strawberry Hill 136 A5
Stream 115 D4
Streat 109 F2
Streatham 136 B5
Streatham Ice and Leisure Centre GtLon SW16 6HX 13 B7
Streatham Vale 136 B5
Streatley CenBeds 149 F5
Streatley WBerks 134 A4
Street Devon 103 E4
Street Lancs 192 B2
Street NYorks 203 G2
Street Som 116 B4
Street Som 103 G2
Street Ashton 159 G4
Street Dinas 170 A4
Street End 108 A4
Street Gate 212 B2
Street Houses 195 E3
Street Lane 173 E3
Street on the Fosse 116 D4
Streethay 158 D1
Streethouse 194 C5
Streetlam 202 C3
Streetly 158 C3
Streetly End 151 E3
Strefford 156 D4
Strelley 173 G3
Strensall 195 F1
Strensham 146 B3
Stretcholt 115 F3
Strete 101 E3
Stretford GtMan 184 B3
Stretford Here 144 D2
Stretford Here 145 E2
Strethall 150 C4
Stretham 162 D5
Strettington 108 A3
Stretton ChesW&C 170 B2
Stretton Derbys 173 E1
Stretton Rut 161 E1
Stretton Staffs 158 A1
Stretton Staffs 173 D5
Stretton Warr 184 A4
Stretton en le Field 159 F1
Stretton Grandison 145 F3
Stretton Heath 156 C1
Stretton Sugwas 145 D3
Stretton under Fosse 159 G4
Stretton Westwood 157 E3
Stretton-on-Dunsmore 159 G5
Stretton-on-Fosse 147 E4
Stribers 199 E4
Strichen 269 H5
Strines 185 D4
Strinesdale Countryside Area GtMan OL4 2JJ 25 H1
Stringston 115 E3
Strixton 149 E1
Stroanbrack 285 H6
Stroat 131 E3
Stromeferry 256 E1
Stromemore 256 E1
Stromness 277 B7
Stronaba 249 E1
Stronachlachar 241 G3
Strone A&B 232 C1
Strone High 258 C2
Strone High 248 D1
Strone Stir 241 G3
Stronechrubie 272 E7
Stronlonag 232 C1
Stronmilchan (Sròn nam Mialchon) 241 D2
Stronsay 276 F5
Stronsay Airfield 276 F5
Strontian (Sròn an t-Sithein) 248 A3
Strontoiller 240 B2
Stronvar 242 A2
Strood 123 G2
Strood Green Surr 122 B4
Strood Green WSuss 121 F5
Strood Green WSuss 121 G4
Stroquhan 216 C2
Stroud Glos 132 A2
Stroud Hants 120 C5
Stroud Common 121 F3
Stroud Green Essex 138 B3
Stroud Green Glos 132 A2
Stroude 121 F1
Stroul 232 D1
Stroxton 175 E4
Struan High 255 J1
Struan P&K 250 C3
Strubby Lincs 189 E4
Strubby Lincs 188 B5
Strumpshaw 179 E5
Struthers 244 B4
Struy 258 B1
Stryd y Facsen 180 B4
Stryt-cae-rhedyn 169 F1
Stryt-issa 169 F3
Stuart & Waterford Crystal Factory Shop, Crieff P&K PH7 4HQ 243 D2
Stuart Line Cruises, Exmouth Devon EX8 1EJ 102 D4
Stuartfield 269 H6
Stub Place 198 B3
Stubber's Green 158 C2
Stubbington 107 E2
Stubbins 184 B1
Stubbs Green 165 E2
Stubhampton 105 F1
Stubley 186 A5
Stubshaw Cross 183 G2
Stubton 175 D3
Stuck A&B 232 B3
Stuck A&B 240 D5
Stuckbeg 241 E5
Stuckgowan 241 F4
Stuckindroin 241 F3
Stuckreoch 240 C5
Stuckton 106 A1
Stud Green 135 D5
Studdon 211 E2
Studfold 200 D5
Studham 135 F1
Studholme 209 F1
Studland 105 G4
Studland & Godlingston Heath NNR Dorset BH19 3AX 105 G4
Studley Warks 146 C1
Studley Wilts 132 B5
Studley Common 146 C1
Studley Green 134 C3
Studley Roger 202 B5
Studley Royal Park & Ruins of Fountains Abbey NYorks HG4 3DY 194 B1
Stuggadhoo 190 B4
Stughan 282 B2
Stump Cross Essex 150 D3
Stump Cross Lancs 192 B4
Stuntney 163 D5
Stunts Green 110 B2
Sturbridge 171 F4
Sturgate 187 F4
Sturmer 151 E3
Sturminster Common 105 D1
Sturminster Marshall 105 F2
Sturminster Newton 105 D1
Sturry 125 D2
Sturton by Stow 187 F4
Sturton le Steeple 187 E4
Stuston 164 C4
Stutton NYorks 195 D3
Stutton Suff 152 C4
Styal 184 C4
Styrrup 186 D3
Suardail 271 G4
Succoth A&B 241 E4
Succoth Aber 260 C1
Succothmore 240 D4
Suckley 145 G2
Suckley Green 145 G2
Suckley Knowl 145 G2
Sudborough 161 E4
Sudbourne 153 F2
Sudbrook Lincs 175 E3
Sudbrook Mon 131 E4
Sudbrooke 188 A5
Sudbury Derbys 172 C4
Sudbury GtLon 136 A4
Sudbury Suff 151 G3
Sudbury Hall Derbys DE6 5HT 172 C4
Sudden 184 C1
Sudgrove 132 B2
Suffield Norf 178 D2
Suffield NYorks 204 C3
Sugarloaf 124 B5
Sugnall 171 E4
Sugwas Pool 145 D3
Suie Lodge Hotel 241 G2
Suisnish 256 B3
Sulaisiadar 271 H4
Sulby IoM 190 B2
Sulby IoM 190 B4
Sulgrave 148 A3
Sulham 134 B5
Sulhamstead 120 B1
Sullington 108 C2
Sullom 278 C5
Sullom Voe Oil Terminal 278 C5
Sully 115 E1
Sumburgh 279 F10
Sumburgh Airport 279 F9
Summer Bridge 194 B1
Summer Isles 265 F1
Summer Lodge 201 E3
Summercourt 96 C4
Summerfield Norf 177 F4
Summerfield Worcs 158 A5
Summerhill 170 A2
Summerhouse 202 B1
Summerlands 199 G4
Summerleaze 130 D4
Summertown 134 A2
Summit 184 D1
Sun Green 185 D3
Sunadale 231 G5
Sunbiggin 200 B2
Sunbury-on-Thames 121 G1
Sundaywell 216 C2
Sunderland Cumb 209 E3
Sunderland Lancs 192 A2
Sunderland T&W 212 C2
Sunderland Bridge 212 B4
Sunderland Museum & Winter Gardens T&W SR1 1PP 86 Sunderland
Sundhope 227 E3
Sundon Park 149 F5
Sundown Adventure Land Notts DN22 0HX 187 E5
Sundridge 123 D3
Sundrum Mains 224 C3
Sunhill 132 D2
Sunipol 246 C4
Sunk Island 188 C1
Sunningdale 121 E1
Sunninghill 121 E1
Sunningwell 133 G2
Sunniside Dur 212 A4
Sunniside T&W 212 B2
Sunny Bank 199 D3
Sunny Brow 212 A4
Sunnylaw 242 C5
Sunnyside Aber 261 G5
Sunnyside N'umb 211 F1
Sunnyside SYorks 186 B3
Sunnyside WSuss 122 C5
Sunton 118 D2
Sunwick 237 F4
Surbiton 121 G1
Surfleet 176 A5
Surfleet Seas End 176 A5
Surlingham 179 E5
Sustead 178 C2
Susworth 187 F2
Sutcombe 112 D4
Sutcombemill 112 D4
Suton 164 B2
Sutors of Cromarty 267 F5
Sutterby 189 D5
Sutterton 176 A4
Sutton Cambs 162 C5
Sutton CenBeds 150 A3
Sutton Devon 102 A2
Sutton Devon 100 D3
Sutton GtLon 122 B2
Sutton Kent 125 F4
Sutton Lincs 175 D2
Sutton Norf 179 E3
Sutton Notts 174 C4
Sutton Notts 187 D4
Sutton Oxon 133 G2
Sutton Pembs 126 C1
Sutton Peter 161 F3
Sutton Shrop 157 G4
Sutton Shrop 171 D4
Sutton Shrop 157 E1
Sutton Shrop 170 A5
Sutton Staffs 171 E5
Sutton Suff 153 E3
Sutton SYorks 186 C1
Sutton WSuss 108 B2
Sutton Abinger 121 G3
Sutton at Hone 137 E5
Sutton Bank National Park Centre NYorks YO7 2EH 203 E4
Sutton Bassett 160 C4
Sutton Benger 132 B5
Sutton Bingham 104 B1
Sutton Bonington 173 G5
Sutton Bridge 176 C5
Sutton Cheney 159 G2
Sutton Coldfield 158 D3
Sutton Courtenay 134 A3
Sutton Crosses 176 C5
Sutton Grange 202 B5
Sutton Green Oxon 133 G2
Sutton Green Surr 121 F2
Sutton Green Wrex 170 B3
Sutton Holms 105 G2
Sutton Howgrave 202 C5
Sutton in Ashfield 173 F2
Sutton in the Elms 160 A3
Sutton Ings 196 D4
Sutton Lane Ends 184 D5
Sutton le Marsh 189 F4
Sutton Leach 183 G3
Sutton Maddock 157 G2
Sutton Mallet 116 A4
Sutton Mandeville 118 A5
Sutton Montis 116 D5
Sutton on Sea 189 F4
Sutton on the Hill 172 D4
Sutton on Trent 174 C1
Sutton Poyntz 104 D4
Sutton St. Edmund 162 B1
Sutton St. James 162 C1
Sutton St. Nicholas 145 E3
Sutton Scarsdale 173 F1
Sutton Scotney 119 F4
Sutton upon Derwent 195 G3
Sutton Valence 124 A4
Sutton Veny 117 F3
Sutton Waldron 105 E1
Sutton Weaver 183 G5
Sutton Wick B&NESom 116 C2
Sutton Wick Oxon 133 G3
Sutton-in-Craven 193 G3
Sutton-on-Hull 196 D4
Sutton-on-the-Forest 195 E1
Sutton-under-Brailes 147 F4
Sutton-under-Whitestonecliffe 203 D4
Swaby 189 D5
Swadlincote 159 F1
Swaffham 163 G2
Swaffham Bulbeck 151 D1
Swaffham Prior 151 D1
Swafield 179 D2
Swainbost (Suainebost) 271 H1
Swainby 203 D2
Swainshill 145 D3
Swainsthorpe 178 D5
Swainswick 117 E1
Swalcliffe 147 F4
Swalecliffe 124 D2
Swallow 188 B2
Swallow Beck 175 E1
Swallow Falls Conwy LL24 0DW 168 A2
Swallowcliffe 118 A5
Swallowfield 120 C1
Swallows Cross 137 F3
Swampton 119 F2
Swan Green ChesW&C 184 B5
Swan Green Suff 165 D4
Swan Street 151 G5
Swanage 105 G5
Swanage Railway Dorset BH19 1HB 105 G5
Swanbach 171 D3
Swanbourne 148 D5
Swanbridge 115 E1
Swancote 157 G3
Swanland 196 B5
Swanlaws 228 B5
Swanley 123 E2
Swanley Village 123 E2
Swanmore Hants 107 E1
Swanmore IoW 107 E3
Swannington Leics 159 G1
Swannington Norf 178 C4
Swanscombe 137 F5
Swansea (Abertawe) 128 C3
Swansea Museum SA1 1SN 86 Swansea
Swanston 235 G3
Swanton Abbot 179 D3
Swanton Morley 178 B4
Swanton Novers 178 B2
Swanton Street 124 A3
Swanwick Derbys 173 F2
Swanwick Hants 107 E2
Swanwick Green 170 C3
Swarby 175 F3
Swardeston 178 D5
Swarkestone 173 E5
Swarland 221 D1
Swarraton 119 G4
Swarthmoor 199 D5
Swaton 175 G4
Swatragh 286 C5
Swavesey 150 B1
Sway 106 B3
Swayfield 175 E5
Swaythling 106 D1
Swaythorpe 196 C1
Sweetham 102 B3
Sweethay 115 F5
Sweetshouse 97 E3
Sweffling 153 E1
Swell 116 A5
Swepstone 159 F1
Swerford 147 F4
Swettenham 171 F1
Swffryd 130 B3
Swift's Green 124 A4
Swiftsden 110 C1
Swilland 152 C2
Swillington 194 C4
Swimbridge 113 G3
Swimbridge Newland 113 F2
Swinbrook 133 E1
Swincliffe 194 B2
Swincombe 113 G1
Swinden 193 E2
Swinderby 175 D1
Swindon Staffs 158 A3
Swindon Swin 133 D4
Swindon Village 146 B5
Swine 196 D4
Swinefleet 195 G5
Swineford 117 D1
Swineshead Bed 149 F1
Swineshead Lincs 176 A3
Swineshead Bridge 176 A3
Swineside 201 F4
Swiney 275 H5
Swinford Leics 160 A5
Swinford Oxon 133 G2
Swingate 173 G3
Swingfield Minnis 125 E4
Swingleton Green 152 A3
Swinhoe 229 G4
Swinhope 188 C3
Swining 279 D6
Swinithwaite 201 F4
Swinscoe 172 C3
Swinside Hall 228 B5
Swinstead 175 F5
Swinton GtMan 184 B2
Swinton NYorks 203 G5
Swinton NYorks 202 B5
Swinton ScBord 237 F5
Swinton SYorks 186 B3
Swinton Quarter 237 F5
Swintonmill 237 F5

Tilstock 170 C4
Tilston 170 B2
Tilstone Fearnall 170 C1
Tilsworth 149 E5
Tilton on the Hill 160 C2
Tiltups End 132 A3
Timberland 175 G2
Timberland Dales 175 G1
Timbersbrook 171 F1
Timberscombe 114 C3
Timble 194 A2
Timewell 114 C5
Timperley 184 B4
Timsbury B&NESom 117 D2
Timsbury Hants 119 E5
Timsgearraidh 270 C4
Timworth 151 G1
Timworth Green 151 G1
Tincleton 105 D3
Tindale 210 C2
Tindon End 151 E4
Tingewick 148 B4
Tingley 194 B5
Tingrith 149 F4
Tingwall 276 D5
Tingwall (Lerwick) Airport 279 D8
Tinhay 99 D2
Tinney 98 C1
Tinshill 194 B4
Tinsley 186 B3
Tinsley Green 122 B5
Tintagel 97 E1
Tintagel Castle Corn PL34 0HE 97 E1
Tintern Parva 131 E2
Tintinhull 104 A1
Tintwistle 185 E3
Tinwald 217 E2
Tinwell 161 F2
Tippacott 114 A3
Tipperty Aber 253 F1
Tipperty Aber 261 H2
Tipps End 162 C3
Tiptoe 106 B3
Tipton 158 B3
Tipton St. John 103 D3
Tiptree 138 B1
Tiptree Heath 138 B1
Tiptree Museum Essex CO5 0RF 138 C1
Tirabad 143 E3
Tiraroe 281 F6
Tircur 285 G7
Tiree 246 A2
Tiree Airport 246 B2
Tirgan 286 C7
Tirindrish 249 E1
Tirley 146 A5
Tirphil 130 A2
Tirril 210 B5
Tir-y-dail 128 C1
Tisbury 118 A5
Tisman's Common 121 F4
Tissington 172 C2
Tister 275 G2
Titanic Trail Belfast City BT1 5GB 283 G1
Titchberry 112 C3
Titchfield 107 E2
Titchmarsh 161 F5
Titchwell 177 F3
Titchwell Marsh Norf PE31 8BB 177 F3
Tithby 174 B4
Titley 144 C1
Titlington 229 F5
Titmore Green 150 A5
Titsey 122 D3
Titson 112 C5
Tittensor 171 F4
Tittesworth Reservoir & Visitor Centre Staffs ST13 8TQ 171 G2
Tittleshall 177 G5
Tiverton ChesW&C 170 C1
Tiverton Devon 102 C1
Tivetshall St. Margaret 164 C3
Tivetshall St. Mary 164 C3
Tivington 114 C3
Tixall 171 G5
Tixover 161 E2
Toab Ork 277 E7
Toab Shet 279 F9
Toberdoney 286 D2
Toberkeagh 286 E2
Tobermore 286 C6
Tobermory 247 E4
Toberonochy 239 G4
Tobson 270 D4
Tocher 260 E1
Tockenham 132 C5
Tockenham Wick 132 C4
Tockholes 192 C5
Tockington 131 F4
Tockwith 195 D2
Todber 117 E5
Toddington CenBeds 149 F5
Toddington Glos 146 C4
Todenham 147 E4
Todhills Angus 244 C1
Todhills Cumb 218 B5
Todlachie 260 E3
Todmorden 193 F5
Todwick 186 B4
Toft Cambs 150 B2
Toft Lincs 161 F1
Toft Shet 278 D5
Toft Hill 212 A5
Toft Monks 165 F2
Toft next Newton 188 A4
Toftcarl 275 J4
Toftrees 177 G5
Tofts 275 J2
Toftwood 178 A4
Togston 221 E1
Tokavaig 256 C3
Tokers Green 134 B5
Tolastadh a' Chaolais 270 D4
Tolastadh Bho Thuath 271 H3
Tolastadh Ur 271 H3
Toll Bar 186 C2
Toll of Birness 261 J1
Tolland 115 E4
Tollard Farnham 105 F1
Tollard Royal 105 F1
Tollcross 234 A3
Toller Down Gate 104 B2
Toller Fratrum 104 B3
Toller Porcorum 104 B3
Toller Whelme 104 B2
Tollerton Notts 174 B4
Tollerton NYorks 195 E1
Tollesbury 138 C1
Tollesby 203 E1
Tolleshunt D'Arcy 138 C1
Tolleshunt Knights 138 C1
Tolleshunt Major 138 B1
Tolmachan 270 C7
Tolpuddle 105 D3
Tolvah 259 F5
Tolworth 121 G1
Tom an Fhuadain 271 F6
Tomatin 259 F2
Tombreck 258 D1
Tomchrasky (Tom Chrasgaidh) 257 J3
Tomdoun 257 H4
Tomdow 267 H7
Tomich High 257 K2
Tomich High 266 E4
Tomich High 266 D1
Tomintoul 259 J3
Tomnacross 266 C7
Tomnamoon 267 H6
Tomnaven 260 C1
Tomnavoulin 259 K2
Tomvaich 259 H1
Ton Pentre 129 F3
Tonbridge 123 E4
Tondu 129 E4
Tonedale 115 E5
Toneel 280 D4
Tonfanau 154 B2
Tong Kent 124 A4
Tong Shrop 157 G2
Tong WYorks 194 B4
Tong Norton 157 G2
Tong Street 194 A4
Tonge 173 F5
Tongham 121 D3
Tongland 216 A5
Tongue 273 H3
Tongue House 273 H3
Tongwynlais 130 A4
Tonmawr 129 E3
Tonna 129 D3
Tonnaboy 281 F5
Tonwell 136 C1
Tonyglaskan 281 F3
Tonypandy 129 F3
Tonyrefail 129 G4
Tonyteige 280 E5
Tonyvarnog 280 E6
Toome 286 D6
Toot Baldon 134 A2
Toot Hill 137 E2
Toothill Hants 106 C1
Toothill Swin 132 D4
Tooting Graveney 136 B5
Top End 149 F1
Top of Hebers 184 C2
Topcliffe 202 D5
Topcroft 165 D2
Topcroft Street 165 D2
Toppesfield 151 F4
Toppings 184 B1
Toprow 164 C2
Topsham 102 C4
Topsham Bridge 100 D2
Torastan 246 B3
Torbain 259 J3
Torbeg Aber 260 B5
Torbeg NAyr 223 E3
Torbothie 234 C4
Torbryan 101 E1
Torcastle 248 D2
Torcross 101 E3
Tordarroch 258 D1
Tore (An Todhar) 266 D6
Toreduff 267 J5
Toremore High 259 J1
Toremore High 275 G5
Torfrey 97 F4
Torgyle 257 K3
Torksey 187 F5
Torlum 262 C6
Torlundy (Tòrr Lunndaidh) 248 D2
Tormarton 131 G5
Tormisdale 230 A4
Tormore 223 D2
Tormsdale 275 G3
Tornagrain 266 E6
Tornahaish 259 K4
Tornaveen 260 E4
Torness 258 C2
Toronto 212 A4
Torpenhow 209 F3
Torphichen 235 D2
Torphins 260 E4
Torpoint 100 A2
Torquay 101 F1
Torquhan 236 B5
Torr CC&G 287 G1
Torr Devon 100 B2
Torran A&B 240 A4
Torran High 266 E4
Torran High 264 B7
Torrance 234 A2
Torrance House 234 A4
Torrancroy 260 B3
Torre Som 114 D3
Torre Torbay 101 F1
Torrich 267 F6
Torridon 264 E6
Torrin 256 B2
Torrisdale A&B 222 C2
Torrisdale High 273 J2
Torrish 274 E7
Torrisholme 192 A1
Torroble 266 C1
Torry Aber 268 C6
Torry Aberdeen 261 H4
Torryburn 235 E1
Torsonce 236 B5
Torterston 269 J6
Torthorwald 217 E3
Tortington 108 B3
Torton 158 A5
Tortworth 131 G3
Torvaig 263 K7
Torver 199 D3
Torwood 234 C1
Torworth 187 D4
Tosberry 112 C3
Toscaig 256 D1
Toseland 150 A1
Tosside 193 D2
Tostarie 246 C5
Tostock 152 A1
Totaig 263 G6
Totamore 246 A4
Tote 263 K7
Tote Hill 121 D5
Totegan 274 D2
Totford 119 G4
Totham Hill 138 B1
Tothill 189 E4
Totland 106 C4
Totley 186 A5
Totnes 101 E1
Toton 173 G4
Totronald 246 A4
Totscore 263 J5
Tottenham 136 C3
Tottenhill 163 E1
Tottenhill Row 163 E1
Totteridge Bucks 135 D3
Totteridge GtLon 136 B3
Totternhoe 149 E5
Tottington GtMan 184 B1
Tottington Norf 163 G3
Totton 106 C1
Toulton 115 E4
Tournaig 264 E3
Toux 269 H5
Tovil 123 G3
Tow Law 212 A4
Towan Cross 96 B5
Toward 232 C3
Towcester 148 B3
Towednack 94 B3
Tower Bridge Exhibition GtLon SE1 2UP 12 C4
Tower End 163 E1
Tower of London GtLon EC3N 4AB 12 C4
Towersey 134 C2
Towie Aber 269 G4
Towie Aber 260 D2
Towie Aber 260 C3
Towiemore 268 B6
Town End Cambs 162 C3
Town End Cumb 199 F4
Town End Mersey 183 F4
Town Green Lancs 183 F2
Town Green Norf 179 E4
Town of Lowton 184 A3
Town Row 123 E5
Town Street 163 F4
Town Yetholm 228 C4
Towneley Hall Art Gallery & Museum Lancs BB11 3RQ 193 E4
Townfield 211 F3
Townhead D&G 207 G2
Townhead SYorks 185 F2
Townhead of Greenlaw 216 B4
Townhill Fife 235 F1
Townhill Swan 128 C3
Towns End 119 G2
Towns Green 170 D1
Townshend 94 C3
Towthorpe ERid 196 B1
Towthorpe York 195 F2
Towton 195 D4
Towyn 182 A5
Toynton All Saints 176 B1
Toynton Fen Side 176 B1
Toynton St. Peter 176 C1
Toy's Hill 123 D3
Trabboch 224 C3
Traboe 95 E4
Tradespark High 267 F6
Tradespark Ork 277 D7
Trafford Centre 184 B3
Trafford Park 184 B3
Trago Mills, Newton Abbot Devon TQ12 6JD 102 B5
Trallong 143 F5
Trallwn 128 C3
Tram Inn 145 D4
Tranent 236 B2
Tranmere 183 E4
Trantlebeg 274 D3
Trantlemore 274 D3
Tranwell 221 D3
Trap 128 C1
Trap Street 171 F1
Traprain 236 C2
Trap's Green 146 D1
Traquair 227 E2
Trawden 193 F4
Trawscoed (Crosswood) 154 C5
Trawsfynydd 168 A4
Trealaw 129 G3
Treales 192 A4
Trearddur 180 A5
Treaslane 263 J6
Tre-Aubrey 129 G5
Trebah Garden Corn TR11 5JZ 95 E4
Trebanog 129 G3
Trebanos 128 D2
Trebarrow 98 C1
Trebartha 97 G2
Trebarvah 95 E3
Trebarwith 97 E1
Trebeath 97 G1
Trebetherick 96 D2
Trebister 279 D9
Tre-boeth 128 C3
Treborough 114 D4
Trebudannon 96 C3
Trebullett 98 D3
Treburley 98 D3
Treburrick 96 C2
Trebyan 97 E3
Trecastle 143 E5
Trecott 113 G5
Trecrogo 98 D2
Trecwn 140 C4
Trecynon 129 F2
Tredaule 97 G1
Tredavoe 94 B4
Treddiog 140 B5
Tredegar 130 A2
Tredington Glos 146 B5
Tredington Warks 147 E3
Tredinnick Corn 96 D3
Tredinnick Corn 97 G4
Tredogan 115 D1
Tredomen 144 A4
Tredrissi 141 D3
Tredunnock 130 C3
Tredustan 144 A4
Tredworth 132 A1
Treen Corn 94 A4
Treen Corn 94 B3
Treesmill 97 E4
Treeton 186 B4
Trefasser 140 B4
Trefdraeth 180 C5
Trefecca 144 A4
Trefechan 129 G2
Trefeglwys 155 F3
Trefenter 142 C1
Treffgarne 140 C5
Treffynnon 140 B5
Trefgarn Owen 140 B5
Trefil 130 A1
Trefilan 142 B2
Trefin 140 B4
Treflach 169 F5
Trefnanney 156 B1
Trefnant 182 B5
Trefonen 169 F5
Trefor Gwyn 166 C3
Trefor IoA 180 B4
Treforest 129 G4
Treforest Industrial Estate 130 A4
Trefriw 168 A1
Tregadillett 97 G1
Tregaian 180 C5
Tregare 130 D1
Tregarland 97 G4
Tregarne 95 E4
Tregaron 142 C2
Tregarth 167 F1
Tregaswith 96 C3
Tregavethan 96 B5
Tregear 96 C4
Tregeare 97 G1
Tregeiriog 169 E4
Tregele 180 B3
Tregidden 95 E4
Tregiskey 97 E5
Treglemais 140 B5
Tregolds 96 C2
Tregole 98 B1
Tregonetha 97 D3
Tregonning & Gwinear Mining Districts (Cornwall & West Devon Mining Landscape) Corn 94 C3
Tregony 96 D5
Tregoodwell 97 F1
Tregoss 97 D3
Tregowris 95 E4
Tregoyd 144 A4
Tregrehan Mills 97 E4
Tre-groes 142 A3
Treguff 129 G5
Tregullon 97 E3
Tregunnon 97 G1
Tregurrian 96 C3
Tregynon 155 G3
Trehafod 129 G3
Trehan 100 A2
Treharris 129 G3
Treherbert 129 F3
Tre-hill 129 G5
Trekenner 98 D3
Treknow 97 E1
Trelan 95 E5
Trelash 98 B1
Trelassick 96 C4
Trelawnyd 182 B5
Trelech 141 F4
Treleddyd-fawr 140 A5
Trelewis 130 A3
Treligga 97 E1
Trelights 97 D2
Trelill 97 E2
Trelissick 95 F3
Trelissick Corn TR3 6QL 95 F3
Trellech 131 E2
Trelleck Grange 131 D2
Trelogan 182 C4
Trelowla 97 G4
Trelystan 156 B2
Tremadog 167 E3
Tremail 97 F1
Tremain 141 F3
Tremaine 97 G1
Tremar 97 G3
Trematon 99 D5
Tremeirchion 182 B5
Tremethick Cross 94 B3
Tremore 97 E3
Trenance Corn 96 C3
Trenance Corn 96 D2
Trenarren 97 E5
Trench Tel&W 157 F1
Trench Wrex 170 A4
Trencreek 96 C3
Trenear 95 D3
Treneglos 97 G1
Trenewan 97 F4
Trengune 98 B1
Trent 104 B1
Trent Port 187 F4
Trent Vale 171 F3
Trentham 171 F3
Trentishoe 113 G1
Trenwheal 94 D3
Treoes 129 F5
Treorchy 129 F3
Treowen 130 B3
Trequite 97 E2
Tre'r-ddol 154 C3
Trerhyngyll 129 G5
Tre-Rhys 141 E3
Trerulefoot 98 D5
Tresaith 141 F2
Tresco 96 A1
Trescott 158 A3
Trescowe 94 C3
Tresean 96 B4
Tresham 131 G3
Treshnish 246 C5
Tresillian 96 C5
Tresinney 97 F1
Tresinwen 140 B3
Treskinnick Cross 98 C1
Treslea 97 F3
Tresmeer 97 G1
Tresowes Green 94 D4
Tresparrett 98 B1
Tresparrett Posts 98 B1
Tressait 250 D3
Tresta Shet 278 F3
Tresta Shet 279 C7
Treswell 187 E5
Trethewey 94 A4
Trethomas 130 A4
Trethurgy 97 E4
Tretio 140 A5
Tretire 145 E5
Tretower 144 A5
Treuddyn 169 F2
Trevadlock 97 G2
Trevalga 98 A1
Trevalyn 170 A2
Trevanson 97 D2
Trevarnon 94 C3
Trevarrack 94 B3
Trevarren 96 D3
Trevarrian 96 C3
Trevarrick 97 D5
Tre-vaughan Carmar 141 G5
Trevaughan Carmar 127 E1
Treveighan 97 E2
Trevellas 96 B4
Trevelmond 97 G3
Trevenen 95 D4
Treverva 95 E3
Trevescan 94 A4
Trevethin 130 B2
Trevigro 98 D4
Trevine 240 C2
Treviscoe 96 D4
Trevivian 97 F1
Trevone 96 C2
Trevor 169 F3
Trewalder 97 E1
Trewarmett 97 E1
Trewarthenick 96 D5
Trewassa 97 F1
Trewellard 94 A3
Trewen Corn 97 G1
Trewen Here 131 E1
Trewennack 95 D4
Trewent 126 D3
Trewern 156 B1
Trewethern 97 E2
Trewidland 97 G4
Trewilym 141 E3
Trewint Corn 98 B1
Trewint Corn 97 G1
Trewithian 95 F3
Trewoon 97 D4
Treworga 96 C5
Treworlas 95 F3
Trewornan 97 D2
Treworthal 95 F3
Tre-wyn 144 C5
Treyarnon 96 C2
Treyford 108 A2
Trezaise 97 D4
Triangle 193 G5
Trickett's Cross 105 G2
Triermain 210 B1
Trillick 281 F3
Trimdon 212 C4
Trimdon Colliery 212 C4
Trimdon Grange 212 C4
Trimingham 179 D2
Trimley Lower Street 153 D4
Trimley St. Martin 153 D4
Trimley St. Mary 153 D4
Trimpley 157 G5
Trimsaran 128 A2
Trimstone 113 E1
Trinafour 250 C3
Trinant 130 B3
Tring 135 E1
Trinity Angus 253 E3
Trinity Chanl 100 C5
Trinity Edin 235 G2
Trisant 154 D5
Triscombe Som 114 C4
Triscombe Som 115 E4
Trislaig 248 C2
Trispen 96 C4
Tritlington 221 E2
Trochry 243 E1
Troedyraur 141 G3
Troedyrhiw 129 G2
Trofarth 181 G5
Trondavoe 278 C5
Troon Corn 95 D3
Troon SAyr 224 B2
Tropical Butterfly House, Wildlife & Falconry Centre SYorks S25 4EQ 21 F3
Tropical World, Roundhay WYorks LS8 2ER 27 G1
Trory 280 E4
Trosaraidh 254 C3
Troston 163 G5
Troswell 98 C1
Trottick 244 C1
Trottiscliffe 123 F2
Trotton 120 D5
Trough Gate 193 E5
Troughend 220 A2
Troustan 232 B2
Troutbeck Cumb 199 F2
Troutbeck Cumb 209 G4
Troutbeck Bridge 199 F2
Trow Green 131 E2
Troway 186 A5
Trowbridge Cardiff 130 B4
Trowbridge Wilts 117 F2
Trowell 173 F4
Trowle Common 117 F2
Trowley Bottom 135 F1
Trows 228 A3
Trowse Newton 178 D5
Troy 194 B4
Trudernish 230 C4
Trudoxhill 117 E3
Trull 115 F5
Trumaisgearraidh 262 D4
Trumpan 263 H5
Trumpet 145 F4
Trumpington 150 C2
Trumps Green 121 E1
Trunch 179 D2
Trunnah 191 G3
Truro 96 C5
Truro Cathedral Corn TR1 2AF 96 C5
Truscott 98 D2
Trusham 102 B4
Trusley 173 D4
Trusthorpe 189 F4
Truthan 96 C4
Trysull 158 A3
Tubney 133 G3
Tuckenhay 101 E2
Tuckhill 157 G4
Tuckingmill 96 A5
Tuddenham Suff 152 C3
Tuddenham Suff 163 F5
Tudeley 123 F4
Tudeley Hale 123 F4
Tudhoe 212 B4
Tudweiliog 166 B4
Tuesley 121 E3
Tuffley 132 A1
Tufton Hants 119 F3
Tufton Pembs 140 D5
Tugby 160 C2
Tugford 157 E4
Tughall 229 G4
Tulchan 243 E2
Tulleys Farm WSuss RH10 4PE 122 C5
Tullibardine Distillery P&K PH4 1QG 243 E4
Tullibody 243 D5
Tullich A&B 240 C3
Tullich A&B 240 A3
Tullich High 267 F4
Tullich High 258 D2
Tullich Moray 268 B6
Tullich Stir 242 A1
Tullich Muir 266 E4
Tullie House Museum & Art Gallery Cumb CA3 8TP 68 Carlisle
Tulliemet 251 F4
Tullintrain 285 H5
Tulloch Aber 261 G1
Tulloch High 266 D2
Tulloch Moray 267 H6
Tullochgorm 240 B5
Tullochgribban High 259 G2
Tullochvenus 260 D4
Tulloes 252 D5
Tully F&O 281 F5
Tullyalley 285 G4
Tullyard 281 F1
Tullybannocher 242 C2
Tullybelton 243 F1
Tullycar 284 D7
Tullyconnaught 282 E4
Tullycorker 281 H3
Tullyfergus 252 A5
Tullyhogue 282 B1
Tullyhogue Fort Mid Ulster BT80 8UB 282 B1
Tullyhona 280 D5
Tullymacreeve 282 C6
Tullymurdoch 251 G4
Tullynacree 283 H4
Tullynessle 260 D3
Tullyroan Corner 282 B3
Tullyrossmearan 280 C4
Tullyveery 283 H3
Tulnacross 286 B7
Tulse Hill 136 C5
Tumble (Y Tymbl) 128 B1
Tumby 176 A2
Tumby Woodside 176 A2
Tummel Bridge 250 C4
Tummery 280 E2
Tunbridge Wells 123 E5
Tundergarth Mains 217 F2
Tunga 271 G4
Tungate 179 D3
Tunley 117 D2
Tunny 282 E1
Tunstall ERid 197 F4
Tunstall Kent 124 A2
Tunstall Lancs 200 B5
Tunstall Norf 179 F5
Tunstall NYorks 202 B3
Tunstall Stoke 171 F2
Tunstall Suff 153 E2
Tunstall T&W 212 C2
Tunstead GtMan 185 E2
Tunstead Norf 179 E3
Tunstead Milton 185 E4
Tunworth 120 B3
Tupholme 175 G1
Tupsley 145 E4
Tupton 173 E1
Tur Langton 160 C3
Turbiskill 231 F1
Turclossie 269 G5
Turgis Green 120 B2
Turin 252 D4
Turkdean 132 D1
Turleigh 117 F1
Turn 184 C1
Turnastone 144 C4
Turnberry 224 A5
Turnchapel 100 A2
Turnditch 173 D3
Turner's Green 147 D1
Turners Hill 122 C5
Turners Puddle 105 E3
Turnford 136 C2
Turnworth 105 E2
Turret Bridge 257 K5
Turriff 269 F6
Turton Bottoms 184 B1
Turvey 149 E2
Turville 134 C3
Turville Heath 134 C3
Turweston 148 B4
Tutankhamun Exhibition, Dorchester Dorset DT1 1UW 104 C3
Tutbury 172 D5
Tutbury Castle Staffs DE13 9JF 172 D5
Tutnall 158 B5
Tutshill 131 E3
Tuttington 178 D3
Tutts Clump 134 A5
Tutwell 99 D3
Tuxford 187 E5
Twatt Ork 276 B5
Twatt Shet 279 C7
Twechar 234 B2
Tweedbank 227 G2
Tweedmouth 237 G4
Tweedsmuir 226 B3
Twelve Oaks 110 B1
Twelveheads 96 B5
Twemlow Green 171 E1
Twenty 175 G5
Twickenham 136 A5
Twigworth 146 A5
Twineham 109 E1
Twineham Green 109 E1
Twinhoe 117 E2
Twinstead 151 G4
Twiss Green 184 A3
Twiston 193 E3
Twitchen Devon 114 A4
Twitchen Shrop 156 C5
Twitton 123 E3
Twizell House 229 F4
Two Bridges Devon 99 G3
Two Bridges Glos 131 F2
Two Dales 173 D1
Two Gates 159 E2
Two Mills 183 E5
Twycross 159 F2
Twycross Zoo Leics CV9 3PX 159 F2
Twyford Bucks 148 B5
Twyford Derbys 173 E5
Twyford Dorset 105 E1
Twyford Hants 119 F5
Twyford Leics 160 C1
Twyford Norf 178 B3
Twyford Oxon 147 G4
Twyford W'ham 134 C5
Twyford Common 145 E4
Twyn Shôn-Ifan 130 A3
Twynholm 216 A5
Twyning 146 A4
Twynllanan 143 D5
Twyn-yr-odyn 130 A5
Twyn-y-Sheriff 130 D2
Twywell 161 E5
Ty Croes 180 B5
Tyberton 144 C4
Tycroes 128 C1
Tycrwyn 156 A1
Tydd Gote 162 C1
Tydd St. Giles 162 C1
Tydd St. Mary 162 C1
Tye Common 137 F3
Tye Green Essex 151 F5
Tye Green Essex 150 D5
Tye Green Essex 137 F1
Tye Green Essex 136 D2
Tyersal 194 A4
Ty-hen 166 A4
Tyldesley 184 A2
Tyle-garw 129 G4
Tyler Hill 124 D2
Tylers Green Bucks 135 E3
Tyler's Green Essex 137 E2
Tylorstown 129 G3
Tylwch 155 F5
Ty-Mawr Conwy 168 C3
Ty-mawr Denb 169 E3
Tynan 282 A4
Ty-nant Conwy 168 C3
Ty-nant Gwyn 168 C5
Tyndrum (Taigh an Droma) 241 F1
Tyne Green Country Park N'umb NE46 3RY 211 F1
Tyneham 105 E4
Tynehead 236 A4
Tynemouth 212 C1
Tynewydd 129 F3
Tyninghame 236 D2
Tynron 216 C1
Tyntesfield 131 E5
Tyn-y-cefn 169 D3
Ty'n-y-coedcae 130 A4
Tyn-y-cwm 155 E4
Tyn-y-ffridd 169 E4
Ty'n-y-garn 129 E4
Tyn-y-gongl 180 D4
Tynygraig Cere 142 C1
Tyn-y-graig Powys 143 G3
Ty'n-y-groes 181 F5
Tyrella 283 H5
Tyrie 269 H4
Tyringham 149 D3
Tyseley 158 D4
Tythegston 129 E5
Tytherington ChesE 184 D5
Tytherington SGlos 131 F4
Tytherington Som 117 E3
Tytherington Wilts 118 A3
Tytherton Lucas 132 B5
Tyttenhanger 136 A2
Ty-uchaf 168 C5
Tywardreath 97 E4
Tywardreath Highway 97 E4
Tywyn 154 B2

U

Uachdar 262 D6
Uags 256 D1
Ubberley 171 G3
Ubbeston Green 165 E4
Ubley 116 C2
Uckerby 202 B2
Uckfield 109 G1
Uckinghall 146 A4
Uckington 146 B5
Uddingston 234 A3
Uddington 225 G2
Udimore 111 D2
Udley 116 B1
Udny Green 261 G2
Udny Station 261 H2
Udston 234 B4
Udstonhead 234 B5
Uffcott 132 D5
Uffculme 103 D1
Uffington Lincs 161 F2
Uffington Oxon 133 F4
Uffington Shrop 157 E1
Ufford Peter 161 F2
Ufford Suff 153 D2
Ufton 147 F1
Ufton Green 120 B1
Ufton Nervet 120 B1
Ugborough 100 C2
Ugford 118 B4
Uggeshall 165 F3
Ugglebarnby 204 B2
Ugley 150 D5

Watton Norf 178 A5
Watton at Stone 136 C1
Watton Green 178 A5
Watton's Green 137 E3
Wattston 234 B3
Wattstown 129 G3
Wattsville 130 B3
Waughtonhill 269 H5
Waun Fawr 154 C4
Waun y Clyn 128 A2
Waunarlwydd 128 C3
Waunclunda 142 C4
Waunfawr 167 E2
Waun-Lwyd 130 A2
Wavendon 149 E4
Waverbridge 209 F2
Waverton ChesW&C 170 B1
Waverton Cumb 209 F2
Wavertree 183 E4
Wawne 196 C4
Waxham 179 F3
Waxholme 197 F5
Way Gill 193 F1
Way Village 102 B1
Way Wick 116 A1
Wayford 104 A2
Waytown 104 A3
Weachyburn 268 E5
Weacombe 115 E3
Weald 133 F2
Weald & Downland Open Air Museum WSuss PO18 0EU 108 A2
Weald Country Park Essex CM14 5QS 137 E3
Wealdstone 136 A3
Weardley 194 B3
Weare 116 B2
Weare Giffard 113 E3
Wearhead 211 E4
Wearne 116 B5
Weasenham All Saints 177 G5
Weasenham St. Peter 177 G5
Weathercote 200 C5
Weatheroak Hill 158 C5
Weaverham 184 A5
Weaverthorpe 204 C5
Webheath 146 C1
Webton 144 D4
Wedderlairs 261 G1
Weddington 159 F3
Wedhampton 118 B2
Wedmore 116 B3
Wednesbury 158 B3
Wednesfield 158 B3
Weedon 134 D1
Weedon Bec 148 B2
Weedon Lois 148 B3
Weeford 158 D2
Week Devon 102 A1
Week Devon 101 D1
Week Som 114 C4
Week Orchard 112 C5
Week St. Mary 98 C1
Weeke 119 F4
Weekley 161 D4
Weel 196 C4
Weeley 152 C5
Weeley Heath 152 C5
Weem 250 D4
Weeping Cross 171 G5
Weethley 146 C2
Weeting 163 F4
Weeton ERid 197 F5
Weeton Lancs 191 G4
Weeton NYorks 194 B3
Weetwood 194 B4
Weir Essex 138 B4
Weir Lancs 193 E5
Weir Quay 100 A1
Weirbrook 170 A5
Weisdale 279 C7
Welbeck Abbey 186 C5
Welborne 178 B5
Welbourn 175 E2
Welburn NYorks 195 G1
Welburn NYorks 203 F4
Welbury 202 C2
Welby 175 E4
Welches Dam 162 C4
Welcombe 112 C4
Weldon 161 E4
Welford N'hants 160 B4
Welford WBerks 133 G5
Welford-on-Avon 146 D2
Welham Leics 160 C3
Welham Notts 187 E4
Welham Green 136 B2
Well Hants 120 C3
Well Lincs 189 E5
Well NYorks 202 B4
Well End Bucks 135 D4
Well End Herts 136 B3
Well Hill 123 D2
Well Street 123 F3
Well Town 102 C2
Welland 145 G3
Wellbank 244 C1
Wellesbourne 147 E2
Wellhill 267 G5
Wellhouse WBerks 134 A5
Wellhouse WYorks 185 E1
Welling 137 D5
Wellingborough 149 D1
Wellingham 177 G5
Wellingore 175 E2
Wellington Cumb 198 B2
Wellington Here 145 D3
Wellington Som 115 E5
Wellington Tel&W 157 F1
Wellington Heath 145 G3
Wellington Marsh 145 D3
Wellow B&NESom 117 E2
Wellow IoW 106 C4
Wellow Notts 174 B1
Wells 116 C3
Wells Cathedral Som BA5 2UE 116 C3
Wells Green 158 D4
Wellsborough 159 F2
Wells-next-the-Sea 178 A1
Wellstyle Green 137 F1
Wellwood 235 E1
Welney 162 D3
Welsh Bicknor 131 E1
Welsh End 170 C4
Welsh Frankton 170 A4
Welsh Hook 140 C5
Welsh Mountain Zoo Conwy LL28 5UY 181 G5
Welsh Newton 131 D1
Welsh St. Donats 129 G5
Welshampton 170 B4
Welshpool (Y Trallwng) 156 B2
Welton B&NESom 117 D2
Welton Cumb 209 G2
Welton ERid 196 B5
Welton Lincs 188 A4
Welton N'hants 148 A1
Welton le Marsh 176 C1
Welton le Wold 188 C4
Welwick 197 F5
Welwyn 136 B1
Welwyn Garden City 136 B1
Wem 170 C5
Wembdon 115 F4
Wembley 136 A4
Wembley GtLon HA9 0WS 10 C3
Wembley Park 136 A4
Wembury 100 B3
Wembworthy 113 G4
Wemyss Bay 232 C3
Wenallt Cere 154 C5
Wenallt Gwyn 168 C3
Wendens Ambo 150 D4
Wendlebury 134 A1
Wendling 178 A4
Wendover 135 D2
Wendover Dean 135 D2
Wendron 95 D3
Wendron Mining District (Cornwall & West Devon Mining Landscape) Corn 95 D3
Wendy 150 B3
Wenfordbridge 97 E2
Wenhaston 165 F4
Wenlli 168 B1
Wennington Cambs 162 A5
Wennington GtLon 137 E4
Wennington Lancs 200 B5
Wensley Derbys 173 D1
Wensley NYorks 201 F4
Wensleydale Cheese Visitor Centre, Hawes NYorks DL8 3RN 201 D4
Wentbridge 186 B1
Wentnor 156 C3
Wentworth Cambs 162 C5
Wentworth SYorks 186 A3
Wenvoe 130 A5
Weobley 144 C2
Weobley Marsh 144 D2
Weoley Castle 158 C4
Wepham 108 C3
Wepre 169 F1
Wepre Country Park Flints CH5 4HL 169 F1
Wereham 163 E2
Wergs 158 A2
Wern Gwyn 167 E4
Wern Powys 156 B1
Wern Powys 130 A1
Wern Shrop 169 F4
Wernffrwd 128 B3
Wern-olau 128 B3
Wernrheolydd 130 C1
Wern-y-cwrt 130 C2
Werrington Corn 98 D2
Werrington Peter 161 G2
Werrington Staffs 171 G3
Wervil Grange 141 G2
Wervin 183 F5
Wesham 192 A4
Wessington 173 E2
West Aberthaw 114 D1
West Acre 163 F1
West Acton 136 A4
West Allerdean 237 G5
West Alvington 100 D3
West Amesbury 118 C3
West Anstey 114 B5
West Ashby 188 C5
West Ashford 113 F2
West Ashling 108 A3
West Ashton 117 F2
West Auckland 212 A5
West Ayton 204 C4
West Bagborough 115 E4
West Barkwith 188 B4
West Barnby 204 B1
West Barns 237 D2
West Barsham 178 A2
West Bay 104 A3
West Beckham 178 C2
West Benhar 234 C3
West Bergholt 152 A5
West Bexington 104 B4
West Bilney 163 F1
West Blatchington 109 E3
West Boldon 212 C1
West Bourton 117 E5
West Bowling 194 A4
West Brabourne 124 C4
West Bradford 192 D3
West Bradley 116 C4
West Bretton 185 G1
West Bridgford 173 G4
West Bromwich 158 C3
West Buckland Devon 113 G2
West Buckland Som 115 E5
West Burrafirth 279 B7
West Burton NYorks 201 F4
West Burton WSuss 108 B2
West Butsfield 211 G3
West Butterwick 187 F2
West Byfleet 121 F1
West Cairncake 269 G6
West Caister 179 G4
West Calder 235 E3
West Camel 116 C5
West Carbeth 233 G2
West Carr Houses 187 E2
West Cauldcoats 234 A5
West Chaldon 105 D4
West Challow 133 F4
West Charleton 101 D3
West Chevington 221 E2
West Chiltington 108 C2
West Chiltington Common 108 C2
West Chinnock 104 A1
West Chisenbury 118 C2
West Clandon 121 F2
West Cliffe 125 F4
West Clyne 267 F1
West Coker 104 B1
West Compton Dorset 104 B3
West Compton Som 116 C3
West Cowick 195 F5
West Cross 128 C4
West Crudwell 132 B3
West Curry 98 C1
West Curthwaite 209 G2
West Dean Wilts 119 D5
West Dean WSuss 108 A2
West Deeping 161 G2
West Derby 183 E3
West Dereham 163 E2
West Ditchburn 229 F4
West Down 113 F1
West Drayton GtLon 135 F5
West Drayton Notts 187 E5
West Dullater 242 A4
West Dunnet 275 H1
West Edington 221 D3
West Ella 196 C5
West End Bed 149 E2
West End BrackF 135 D5
West End Caerp 130 B3
West End Cambs 162 C3
West End ERid 196 C1
West End Hants 107 D1
West End Herts 136 B2
West End Kent 125 D2
West End Lancs 192 A1
West End Lincs 189 D3
West End Norf 179 F4
West End Norf 178 A5
West End NSom 116 B1
West End NYorks 194 A2
West End Oxon 133 G2
West End Oxon 134 A4
West End SLan 235 D5
West End Suff 165 F3
West End Surr 121 G1
West End Surr 121 E1
West End Wilts 132 B5
West End Wilts 118 A5
West End Wilts 118 A5
West End Green 120 B1
West Farleigh 123 G3
West Farndon 148 A2
West Felton 170 A5
West Firle 109 G3
West Fleetham 229 F4
West Flotmanby 205 D5
West Garforth 194 C4
West Ginge 133 G4
West Glen 232 A2
West Grafton 118 D1
West Green GtLon 136 C4
West Green Hants 120 C2
West Grimstead 118 D5
West Grinstead 121 G5
West Haddlesey 195 E5
West Haddon 160 B5
West Hagbourne 134 A4
West Hagley 158 B4
West Hall 210 B1
West Hallam 173 F3
West Halton 196 B5
West Ham 136 C4
West Handley 186 A5
West Hanney 133 G3
West Hanningfield 137 G3
West Hardwick 186 B1
West Harnham 118 C5
West Harptree 116 C2
West Harrow 136 A4
West Harting 120 C5
West Hatch Som 115 F5
West Hatch Wilts 118 A5
West Head 163 D2
West Heath ChesE 171 F1
West Heath GtLon 137 D5
West Heath Hants 121 D2
West Heath Hants 119 G2
West Heath WMid 158 C5
West Helmsdale 275 F7
West Hendon 136 B4
West Hendred 133 G4
West Heslerton 204 C5
West Hewish 116 A1
West Hill Devon 103 D3
West Hill ERid 197 D1
West Hill NSom 131 D5
West Hoathly 122 C5
West Holme 105 E4
West Horndon 137 F4
West Horrington 116 C3
West Horsley 121 F2
West Horton 229 E3
West Hougham 125 E5
West Howe 105 G3
West Howetown 114 C4
West Huntspill 116 A3
West Hyde 135 F3
West Hythe 124 D5
West Ilsley 133 G4
West Itchenor 107 G2
West Keal 176 B1
West Kennett 118 C1
West Kennett Long Barrow (Stonehenge, Avebury & Associated Sites) Wilts SN8 1QH 118 C1
West Kilbride 232 D5
West Kingsdown 123 E2
West Kington 132 A5
West Kington Wick 132 A5
West Kirby 182 D4
West Knapton 204 B5
West Knighton 104 D4
West Knoyle 117 F4
West Kyloe 229 E2
West Lambrook 104 A1
West Langdon 125 F4
West Langwell 266 D1
West Lavington Wilts 118 B2
West Lavington WSuss 121 D5
West Layton 202 A2
West Leake 173 G5
West Learmouth 228 C3
West Lees 203 D2
West Leigh Devon 113 G5
West Leigh Devon 101 D2
West Leigh Som 115 E4
West Leith 135 E1
West Lexham 163 G1
West Lilling 195 F1
West Lingo 244 C4
West Linton 235 F4
West Liss 120 C5
West Littleton 131 G5
West Lockinge 133 G4
West Looe 97 G4
West Lulworth 105 E4
West Lutton 196 B1
West Lydford 116 C4
West Lyn 114 A3
West Lyng 116 A5
West Lynn 163 E1
West Mains 229 E2
West Malling 123 F3
West Malvern 145 G3
West Marden 107 G1
West Markham 187 E5
West Marsh 188 C2
West Marton 193 E2
West Melbury 117 F5
West Melton 186 B2
West Meon 120 B5
West Meon Hut 120 B5
West Mersea 138 D1
West Midland Safari Park & Leisure Park Worcs DY12 1LF 158 A5
West Milton 104 A3
West Minster 124 B1
West Molesey 121 G1
West Monkton 115 F5
West Moors 105 G2
West Morden 105 F3
West Morriston 236 D5
West Morton 193 G3
West Mostard 200 C3
West Mudford 116 C5
West Muir 253 D3
West Ness 203 F5
West Newbiggin 202 C1
West Newton ERid 197 D4
West Newton Norf 177 E5
West Norwood 136 C5
West Ogwell 101 E1
West Orchard 105 E1
West Overton 118 C1
West Panson 98 D1
West Park Aber 261 F5
West Park Mersey 183 G3
West Parley 105 G3
West Peckham 123 F3
West Pelton 212 B2
West Pennard 116 C4
West Pentire 96 B3
West Perry 149 G1
West Porlock 114 B3
West Prawle 101 D4
West Preston 108 C3
West Pulham 104 D2
West Putford 113 D4
West Quantoxhead 115 E3
West Raddon 102 B2
West Rainton 212 C3
West Rasen 188 A4
West Raynham 177 G5
West Retford 187 D4
West Rounton 202 D2
West Row 163 E5
West Rudham 177 G5
West Runton 178 C1
West Saltoun 236 B3
West Sandford 102 B2
West Sandwick 278 D4
West Scrafton 201 F4
West Shepton 116 D3
West Shinness Lodge 273 H7
West Somerset Railway Som TA24 5BG 115 E4
West Somerton 179 F4
West Stafford 104 D4
West Stockwith 187 E3
West Stoke 108 A3
West Stonesdale 201 D2
West Stoughton 116 B3
West Stour 117 E5
West Stourmouth 125 E2
West Stow 163 G5
West Stow Country Park Suff IP28 6HG 163 F5
West Stowell 118 C1
West Stratton 119 G3
West Street Kent 124 B3
West Street Med 137 G5
West Street Suff 164 A4
West Tanfield 202 B5
West Taphouse 97 F3
West Tarbert 231 G3
West Tarring 108 D3
West Thirston 221 D1
West Thorney 107 G2
West Thurrock 137 E5
West Tilbury 137 F5
West Tisted 120 B5
West Tofts Norf 163 G3
West Tofts P&K 243 G1
West Torrington 188 B4
West Town B&NESom 116 C1
West Town Hants 107 G3
West Town NSom 116 B1
West Town Som 116 C4
West Tytherley 119 D5
West Walton 162 C1
West Wellow 106 B1
West Wembury 100 B3
West Wemyss 244 B5
West Wick 116 A1
West Wickham Cambs 151 E3
West Wickham GtLon 122 C2
West Williamston 126 D2
West Winch 163 E1
West Winterslow 118 D4
West Wittering 107 G3
West Witton 201 F4
West Woodburn 220 A3
West Woodhay 119 E1
West Woodlands 117 E3
West Worldham 120 C4
West Worlington 102 A1
West Worthing 108 D3
West Wratting 151 E2
West Wycombe 134 D3
West Yatton 132 A5
West Yell 278 D4
West Youlstone 112 C4
Westbere 125 D2
Westborough 174 D3
Westbourne Bourne 105 G3
Westbourne WSuss 107 G2
Westbourne Green 136 B4
Westbrook Kent 125 F1
Westbrook WBerks 133 G5
Westbrook Wilts 118 A1
Westbury Bucks 148 B4
Westbury Shrop 156 C2
Westbury Wilts 117 F2
Westbury Leigh 117 F2
Westbury on Trym 131 E5
Westbury-on-Severn 131 G1
Westbury-sub-Mendip 116 C3
Westby Lancs 191 G4
Westby Lincs 175 E5
Westcliff-on-Sea 138 B4
Westcombe 117 D4
Westcot 133 F4
Westcott Bucks 134 C1
Westcott Devon 102 D2
Westcott Surr 121 G3
Westcott Barton 147 G5
Westcourt 118 D1
Westcroft 148 D4
Westdean 110 A4
Westdowns 97 E1
Westend Town 131 G5
Wester Aberchalder 258 C2
Wester Badentyre 269 F5
Wester Balgedie 243 G4
Wester Culbeuchly 268 E4
Wester Dechmont 235 E2
Wester Fintray 261 G3
Wester Foffarty 252 C5
Wester Greenskares 269 F4
Wester Gruinards 266 C2
Wester Hailes 235 G3
Wester Lealty 266 D4
Wester Lonvine 266 E4
Wester Newburn 244 C4
Wester Ord 261 G4
Wester Quarff 279 D9
Wester Skeld 279 B8
Westerdale High 275 G3
Westerdale NYorks 203 F2
Westerfield Shet 279 C7
Westerfield Suff 152 C3
Westergate 108 B3
Westerham 122 D3
Westerhope 212 A1
Westerleigh 131 F5
Westerloch 275 J3
Westerton Aber 261 F5
Westerton Angus 253 E4
Westerton Dur 212 B4
Westerton P&K 243 D3
Westerwick 279 B8
Westfield Cumb 208 C4
Westfield ESuss 110 D2
Westfield High 275 F2
Westfield NLan 234 B2
Westfield Norf 178 A5
Westfield WLoth 234 D2
Westfield WYorks 194 B5
Westfield Sole 123 G2
Westgate Dur 211 F4
Westgate N'umb 220 D4
Westgate NLincs 187 E2
Westgate Norf 178 A1
Westgate Hill 194 B5
Westgate on Sea 125 F1
Westhall Aber 260 E2
Westhall Suff 165 F3
Westham Dorset 104 C5
Westham ESuss 110 B3
Westham Som 116 B3
Westhampnett 108 A3
Westhay Devon 103 G2
Westhay Som 116 B3
Westhead 183 F2
Westhide 145 E3
Westhill Aber 261 G4
Westhill High 266 E7
Westhope Here 145 D2
Westhope Shrop 157 D4
Westhorp 148 A2
Westhorpe Lincs 176 A4
Westhorpe Notts 174 B2
Westhorpe Suff 152 B1
Westhoughton 184 A2
Westhouse 200 B5
Westhouses 173 F2
Westhumble 121 G2
Westing 278 E2
Westlake 100 C2
Westlands 171 F3
Westlea 132 D4
Westleigh Devon 113 E3
Westleigh Devon 103 D1
Westleigh GtMan 184 A2
Westleton 153 F1
Westley Shrop 156 C2
Westley Suff 151 G1
Westley Heights 137 F4
Westley Waterless 151 E2
Westlington 134 C1
Westlinton 218 B5
Westloch 235 G4
Westmancote 146 B4
Westmarsh 125 E2
Westmeston 109 F2
Westmill 150 B5
Westminster 136 B5
Westminster Abbey (Palace of Westminster & Westminster Abbey inc. St Margaret's Church) GtLon SW1P 3PA 44 E6
Westminster Abbey - Chapter House & Pyx Chamber GtLon SW1P 3PA 44 E6
Westminster Cathedral GtLon SW1P 2QW 44 C7
Westmuir 252 B4
Westness 276 C5
Westnewton Cumb 209 E2
Westnewton N'umb 228 D3
Westoe 212 C1
Weston B&NESom 117 E1
Weston ChesE 171 E2
Weston Devon 103 E4
Weston Devon 103 E2
Weston Dorset 104 C5
Weston Halton 183 G4
Weston Hants 120 C5
Weston Here 144 C2
Weston Herts 150 A4
Weston Lincs 176 A5
Weston Moray 268 C4
Weston N'hants 148 A3
Weston Notts 174 C1
Weston NYorks 194 A3
Weston Shrop 170 C5
Weston Shrop 157 E3
Weston Shrop 156 C5
Weston Soton 107 D1
Weston Staffs 171 G5
Weston WBerks 133 G5
Weston Bampfylde 116 D5
Weston Beggard 145 E3
Weston by Welland 160 C3
Weston Colville 151 E2
Weston Corbett 120 B3
Weston Coyney 171 G3
Weston Favell 148 C1
Weston Green Cambs 151 E2
Weston Green Norf 178 C4
Weston Heath 157 G1
Weston Hills 176 A5
Weston in Arden 159 F4
Weston Jones 171 E5
Weston Longville 178 C4
Weston Lullingfields 170 B5
Weston Park Staffs TF11 8LE 158 A1
Weston Patrick 120 B3
Weston Point 183 F4
Weston Rhyn 169 F4
Weston Subedge 146 D3
Weston Town 117 E3
Weston Turville 135 D1
Weston under Penyard 145 F5
Weston under Wetherley 147 F1
Weston Underwood Derbys 173 D3
Weston Underwood MK 149 D3
Westonbirt 132 A4
Westonbirt - The National Arboretum Glos GL8 8QS 132 A4
Westoning 149 F4
Weston-in-Gordano 131 D5
Weston-on-Avon 147 D2
Weston-on-the-Green 134 A1
Weston-on-Trent 173 F5
Weston-super-Mare 116 A1
Weston-under-Lizard 158 A1
Westonzoyland 116 A4
Westow 195 G1
Westpoint Arena, Clyst St. Mary Devon EX5 1DJ 102 C3
Westport A&B 222 B3
Westport Som 116 A5
Westra 130 A5
Westray 276 D3
Westray Airfield 276 D2
Westridge Green 134 A5
Westrigg 234 D3
Westruther 236 D5
Westry 162 B3
Westside 261 G5
Westvale 183 F3
Westville 173 G3
Westward 209 F2
Westward Ho! 113 E3
Westwell Kent 124 B4
Westwell Oxon 133 E2
Westwell Leacon 124 B4
Westwick Cambs 150 C1
Westwick Dur 201 F1
Westwick Norf 179 D3
Westwick NYorks 194 C1
Westwood Devon 102 D3
Westwood Peter 161 G3
Westwood SLan 234 A4
Westwood Wilts 117 F2
Westwood Heath 159 E5
Westwoodside 187 E3
Wetham Green 124 A2
Wetheral 210 A2
Wetherby 194 D3
Wetherden 152 B1
Wetherden Upper Town 152 B1
Wetheringsett 152 C1
Wethersfield 151 F4
Wethersta 279 C6
Wetherup Street 152 C1
Wetley Abbey 171 G3
Wetley Rocks 171 G3
Wettenhall 170 D1
Wettenhall Green 170 D1
Wetton 172 C2
Wetwang 196 B2
Wetwood 171 E4
Wexcombe 119 D2
Wexham Street 135 E4
Weybourne Norf 178 C1
Weybourne Surr 121 D3
Weybread 164 D3
Weybread Street 165 D4
Weybridge 121 F1
Weycroft 103 G2
Weydale 275 G2
Weyhill 119 E3
Weymouth 104 C5
Weymouth Sea Life Adventure Park & Marine Sanctuary Dorset DT4 7SX 104 C4
Whaddon Bucks 148 D4
Whaddon Cambs 150 B3
Whaddon Glos 132 A1
Whaddon Glos 146 B5
Whaddon Wilts 118 C5
Whaddon Wilts 117 F1
Whaddon Gap 150 B3
Whale 210 B5
Whaley 186 C5
Whaley Bridge 185 E4
Whaley Thorns 186 C5
Whaligoe 275 J4
Whalley 192 D4
Whalsay 279 E6
Whalsay Airport 279 E6
Whalton 220 D3
Wham 193 D1
Whaplode 176 B5
Whaplode Drove 162 B1
Whaplode St. Catherine 162 B1
Wharfe 193 D1
Wharles 192 A4
Wharley End 149 E3
Wharncliffe Side 185 G3
Wharram le Street 196 A1
Wharram Percy 196 A1
Wharton ChesW&C 171 D1
Wharton Here 145 E2
Whashton 202 A2
Whatcote 147 F3
Whateley 159 E3
Whatfield 152 B3
Whatley 117 E3
Whatlington 110 C2
Whatsole Street 124 D4
Whatstandwell 173 E2
Whatton 174 C4
Whauphill 207 E2
Whaw 201 E2
Wheal Peevor (Cornwall & West Devon Mining Landscape) Corn 95 E2
Wheatacre 165 F2
Wheatcroft 173 E2
Wheatenhurst 131 G2
Wheatfield CC&G 285 J3
Wheatfield Oxon 134 B3
Wheathampstead 136 A1
Wheathill F&O 280 D5
Wheathill Shrop 157 F4
Wheathill Som 116 C4
Wheatley Hants 120 C4
Wheatley Oxon 134 B2
Wheatley WYorks 193 G5
Wheatley Hill 212 C4
Wheatley Lane 193 E4
Wheatley Park 186 C2
Wheaton Aston 158 A1
Wheddon Cross 114 C4
Wheedlemont 260 C2
Wheelerstreet 121 E3
Wheelock 171 E2
Wheelock Heath 171 E2
Wheelton 192 C5
Wheen 252 B2
Wheldale 195 D5
Wheldrake 195 F3
Whelford 133 D3
Whelley 183 G2
Whelpley Hill 135 E2
Whelpo 209 G3
Whelston 182 D5
Whenby 195 F1
Whepstead 151 G2
Wherstead 152 C3
Wherwell 119 E3
Wheston 185 F5
Whetley Cross 104 A2
Whetsted 123 F4
Whetstone GtLon 136 B3
Whetstone Leics 160 A3
Whicham 198 C4
Whichford 147 F4
Whickham 212 B1
Whiddon 113 E5
Whiddon Down 99 G1
Whifflet 234 B3
Whigstreet 252 C5
Whilton 148 B1
Whim 235 G4
Whimble 112 D5
Whimple 102 D3
Whimpwell Green 179 E3
Whin Lane End 191 G3
Whinburgh 178 B5
Whinlatter Forest Cumb CA12 5TW 209 E4
Whinny Hill 202 C1
Whinnyfold 261 J1
Whippingham 107 E3
Whipsnade 135 F1
Whipsnade Zoo CenBeds LU6 2LF 135 F1
Whipton 102 C3
Whirlow 186 A4
Whisby 175 E1
Whissendine 160 D1
Whissonsett 178 A3
Whisterfield 184 C5
Whistley Green 134 C5
Whiston Mersey 183 F3
Whiston N'hants 148 D1
Whiston Staffs 172 B3
Whiston Staffs 158 A1
Whiston SYorks 186 B3
Whiston Cross 157 G2
Whiston Eaves 172 B3
Whitacre Fields 159 E3
Whitacre Heath 159 E3
Whitbeck 198 C4
Whitbourne 145 G2
Whitburn T&W 212 D1
Whitburn WLoth 234 D3
Whitby ChesW&C 183 E5
Whitby NYorks 204 B1
Whitby Abbey NYorks YO22 4JT 204 C1
Whitby Lifeboat Museum NYorks YO21 3PU 204 B1
Whitbyheath 183 E5
Whitchurch B&NESom 116 D1
Whitchurch Bucks 148 D5
Whitchurch Cardiff 130 A4
Whitchurch Devon 99 E3
Whitchurch Hants 119 F3
Whitchurch Here 131 E1
Whitchurch Pembs 140 A5
Whitchurch Shrop 170 C3
Whitchurch Warks 147 E3
Whitchurch Canonicorum 103 G3
Whitchurch Hill 134 B5
Whitchurch-on-Thames 134 B5
Whitcombe 104 D4
Whitcott Keysett 156 B4
White Ball 103 D1
White Colne 151 G5
White Coppice 184 A1
White Cross Corn 96 C4
White Cross Devon 102 D3
White Cross Here 145 D3
White Cross Wilts 117 E4

White Cube GtLon N1 6PB 12 C4
White End 146 A5
White Hill 117 F4
White Houses 187 E5
White Kirkley 211 G4
White Lackington 104 D3
White Ladies Aston 146 B2
White Lund 192 A1
White Mill 142 A5
White Moor 173 E3
White Notley 137 G1
White Ox Mead 117 E2
White Pit 189 D5
White Post Farm Centre, Farnsfield Notts NG22 8HL 174 B2
White Rocks 144 D5
White Roding 137 E1
White Waltham 134 D5
Whiteabbey 287 H7
Whiteacen 267 K7
Whiteash Green 151 F4
Whitebirk 192 D5
Whitebog 269 H5
Whitebridge High 275 H1
Whitebridge (An Drochaid Bhàn) High 258 B3
Whitebrook 131 E2
Whiteburn 236 C5
Whitecairn 214 D5
Whitecairns 261 H3
Whitecastle 235 E5
Whitechapel 192 B3
Whitechurch 141 E4
Whitecote 194 B4
Whitecraig 236 A2
Whitecroft 131 F2
Whitecrook 214 C5
Whitecross Corn 94 C3
Whitecross Corn 97 D2
Whitecross Dorset 104 A3
Whitecross Falk 235 D2
Whitecross NM&D 282 C5
Whiteface 266 E3
Whitefield Aber 261 F2
Whitefield Devon 114 A4
Whitefield Dorset 105 F3
Whitefield GtMan 184 C2
Whitefield High 258 C2
Whitefield High 275 H3
Whitefield P&K 243 G1
Whiteford 261 F2
Whitegate 170 D1
Whitegates 283 F5
Whitehall Devon 103 E1
Whitehall Hants 120 C2
Whitehall Ork 276 F5
Whitehall WSuss 121 G5
Whitehaven 208 C5
Whitehead 287 J6
Whitehill Aber 269 H5
Whitehill F&O 280 E3
Whitehill Hants 120 C4
Whitehill Kent 124 B3
Whitehill Midlo 236 A3
Whitehill NAyr 233 D4
Whitehills 268 E4
Whitehouse A&B 231 G3
Whitehouse A&N 287 H7
Whitehouse Aber 260 E3
Whitehouse Common 158 D3
Whitekirk 236 C1
Whitelackington 103 G1
Whitelaw 237 F4
Whiteleen 275 J4
Whitelees 224 B2
Whiteley 107 E2
Whiteley Bank 107 E4
Whiteley Green 184 D5
Whiteley Village 121 F1
Whiteleys 214 B5
Whitemans Green 109 F1
Whitemire 267 G6
Whitemoor 97 D4
Whiteness 279 C8
Whiteoak Green 133 F1
Whiteparish 118 D5
Whiterashes 261 G2
Whiterock 283 J2
Whiterow 275 J4
Whiteshill 132 A2
Whiteside N'umb 210 D1
Whiteside WLoth 235 D3
Whitesides Corner 286 E6
Whitesmith 110 A2
Whitestaunton 103 F1
Whitestone A&B 222 C2
Whitestone Aber 260 E5
Whitestone Devon 102 B3
Whitestreet Green 152 A4
Whitestripe 269 H5
Whiteway 132 B1
Whitewell Aber 269 H4
Whitewell Lancs 192 C3
Whitewell Wrex 170 B3
Whiteworks 99 G3
Whitewreath 267 K6
Whitfield Here 144 D4
Whitfield Kent 125 F4
Whitfield N'hants 148 B4
Whitfield N'umb 211 D2
Whitfield SGlos 131 F3
Whitford Devon 103 F3
Whitford (Chwitffordd) Flints 182 C5
Whitgift 196 A5
Whitgreave 171 F5
Whithorn 207 E2
Whiting Bay 223 F3
Whitkirk 194 C4
Whitlam 261 G2
Whitland (Hendy-Gwyn) 127 F1
Whitland Abbey 127 F1
Whitleigh 100 A1
Whitletts 224 B3
Whitley NYorks 195 E5
Whitley Read 120 C1
Whitley Wilts 117 F1
Whitley WMid 159 F5
Whitley Bay 221 F4
Whitley Chapel 211 F2
Whitley Heath 171 F5
Whitley Lower 185 G1
Whitley Row 123 D3
Whitlock's End 158 D5
Whitminster 131 G2
Whitmore Dorset 105 G2
Whitmore Staffs 171 F3
Whitnage 102 D1
Whitnash 147 F1
Whitnell 115 F3
Whitney-on-Wye 144 B3
Whitrigg Cumb 209 F1
Whitrigg Cumb 209 F3
Whitsbury 106 A1
Whitsome 237 F4
Whitson 130 C4
Whitstable 124 D2
Whitstone 98 C1
Whittingham 229 E5
Whittingslow 156 D4
Whittington Derbys 186 A5
Whittington Glos 146 C5
Whittington Lancs 200 B5
Whittington Norf 163 F3
Whittington Shrop 170 A4
Whittington Staffs 158 A4
Whittington Staffs 159 D2
Whittington Worcs 146 A2
Whittlebury 148 B3
Whittle-le-Woods 192 B5
Whittlesey 162 A3
Whittlesford 150 C3
Whittlestone Head 184 B1
Whitton GtLon 136 A5
Whitton N'umb 220 C1
Whitton NLincs 196 B5
Whitton Powys 144 B1
Whitton Shrop 157 E5
Whitton Stock 212 C5
Whitton Suff 152 C3
Whittonditch 133 E5
Whittonstall 211 G2
Whitway 119 F2
Whitwell Derbys 186 C5
Whitwell Herts 149 G5
Whitwell IoW 107 E5
Whitwell NYorks 202 B3
Whitwell Rut 161 E2
Whitwell Street 178 C3
Whitwell-on-the-Hill 195 G1
Whitwick 159 G1
Whitwood 194 D5
Whitworth 184 C1
Whitworth Art Gallery, Manchester GtMan M15 6ER 25 E4
Whixall 170 C4
Whixley 194 D2
Whorlton Dur 202 A1
Whorlton NYorks 203 D2
Whygate 219 F4
Whyle 145 E1
Whyteleafe 122 C3
Wibdon 131 E3
Wibsey 194 A4
Wibtoft 159 G4
Wichenford 145 G1
Wichling 124 B3
Wick Bourne 106 A3
Wick Devon 103 E2
Wick (Inbhir Ùige) High 275 J3
Wick SGlos 131 G5
Wick Som 115 F3
Wick Som 116 C4
Wick VGlam 129 F5
Wick Wilts 118 C5
Wick Worcs 146 B3
Wick WSuss 108 C3
Wick John O'Groats Airport 275 J3
Wick Hill Kent 124 A4
Wick Hill W'ham 120 C1
Wick St. Lawrence 116 A1
Wicken Cambs 163 D5
Wicken N'hants 148 C4
Wicken Bonhunt 150 C4
Wickenby 188 A4
Wicker Street Green 152 A3
Wickersiack 200 B1
Wickersley 186 B3
Wicketwood Hill 174 B3
Wickford 137 G3
Wickham Hants 107 E1
Wickham WBerks 133 F5
Wickham Bishops 138 B1
Wickham Heath 119 F1
Wickham Market 153 E2
Wickham St. Paul 151 G4
Wickham Skeith 152 B1
Wickham Street Suff 151 F2
Wickham Street Suff 152 B1
Wickhambreaux 125 E3
Wickhambrook 151 F2
Wickhamford 146 C3
Wickhampton 179 F5
Wicklewood 178 B5
Wickmere 178 C2
Wicksteed Park N'hants NN15 6NJ 161 D5
Wickstreet 110 A3
Wickwar 131 G4
Widcombe 117 E1
Widdington 150 D4
Widdop 193 F4
Widdrington 221 E2
Widdrington Station 221 E2
Wide Open 221 E4
Widecombe in the Moor 102 A5
Widegates 97 G4
Widemouth Bay 112 C5
Widewall 277 D8
Widford Essex 137 F2
Widford Herts 136 D1
Widford Oxon 133 E1
Widgham Green 151 E2
Widmer End 135 D3
Widmerpool 174 B5
Widnes 183 G4
Widworthy 103 F3
Wigan 183 G2
Wigan Pier GtMan WN3 4EU 183 G2
Wiganthorpe 203 F5
Wigborough 104 A1
Wiggaton 103 E3
Wiggenhall St. Germans 163 D1
Wiggenhall St. Mary Magdalen 163 D1
Wiggenhall St. Mary the Virgin 163 D1
Wiggenhall St. Peter 163 E1
Wiggens Green 151 E3
Wigginton Herts 135 E1
Wigginton Oxon 147 F4
Wigginton Shrop 170 A4
Wigginton Staffs 159 E2
Wigginton York 195 F2
Wigglesworth 193 E2
Wiggonby 209 G1
Wiggonholt 108 C2
Wighill 195 D3
Wighton 178 A2
Wightwizzle 185 G3
Wigley 106 C1
Wigmore Here 144 D1
Wigmore Med 124 A2
Wigsley 187 F5
Wigsthorpe 161 F4
Wigston 160 B3
Wigston Parva 159 G4
Wigthorpe 186 C4
Wigtoft 176 A4
Wigton 209 F2
Wigtown 215 F5
Wike 194 C3
Wilbarston 160 D4
Wilberfoss 195 G2
Wilburton 162 C5
Wilby N'hants 149 D1
Wilby Norf 164 B2
Wilby Suff 164 D4
Wilcot 118 C1
Wilcott 156 C1
Wilcrick 130 D4
Wilday Green 186 A5
Wildboarclough 171 G1
Wilde Street 163 F5
Wilden Bed 149 F2
Wilden Worcs 158 A5
Wildhern 119 E2
Wildhill 136 B2
Wildmoor 158 B5
Wildsworth 187 F3
Wilford 173 G4
Wilkesley 170 D3
Wilkhaven 267 G3
Wilkieston 235 F3
Wilksby 176 A1
Willand Devon 102 D1
Willand Som 103 E1
Willaston ChesE 171 D2
Willaston ChesW&C 183 E5
Willaston Shrop 170 C4
Willen 149 D3
Willen Lakeside Park MK MK15 9HQ 9 D2
Willenhall WMid 158 B3
Willenhall WMid 159 F5
Willerby ERid 196 C5
Willerby NYorks 204 D5
Willersey 146 D4
Willersley 144 C3
Willesborough 124 C4
Willesborough Lees 124 C4
Willesden 136 B4
Willesleigh 113 F2
Willesley 132 A4
Willett 115 E4
Willey Shrop 157 F3
Willey Warks 159 G4
Willey Green 121 E2
William's Green 152 A3
Williamscot 147 G3
Williamson Park, Lancaster Lancs LA1 1UX 192 A1
Williamthorpe 173 F1
Willian 150 A4
Willimontswick 211 D1
Willingale 137 E2
Willingdon 110 A3
Willingham 162 C5
Willingham by Stow 187 F4
Willingham Green 151 E2
Willington Bed 149 G2
Willington Derbys 173 D5
Willington Dur 212 A4
Willington Kent 123 G3
Willington T&W 212 C1
Willington Warks 147 E4
Willington Corner 170 C1
Willisham 152 B2
Willitoft 195 G4
Williton 115 D3
Willmount 280 E1
Willoughbridge 171 E3
Willoughby Lincs 189 E5
Willoughby Warks 148 A1
Willoughby Waterleys 160 A3
Willoughby-on-the-Wolds 174 B5
Willoughton 187 G3
Willow Green 184 A5
Willows Farm Village Herts AL2 1BB 136 A2
Willows Green 137 G1
Willsbridge 131 F5
Willslock 172 B4
Willsworthy 99 F2
Willtown 116 A5
Wilmcote 147 D2
Wilmington B&NESom 117 D1
Wilmington Devon 103 F2
Wilmington ESuss 110 A3
Wilmington Kent 137 E5
Wilmslow 184 C4
Wilnecote 159 E2
Wilney Green 164 B3
Wilpshire 192 C4
Wilsden 193 G4
Wilsford Lincs 175 F3
Wilsford Wilts 118 C4
Wilsford Wilts 118 C2
Wilsham 114 A3
Wilshaw 185 F2
Wilsill 194 A1
Wilsley Green 123 G5
Wilsley Pound 123 G5
Wilson 173 F5
Wilstead 149 F3
Wilsthorpe ERid 197 D1
Wilsthorpe Lincs 161 F1
Wilstone 135 E1
Wilton Cumb 208 D5
Wilton Here 145 E5
Wilton NYorks 204 B4
Wilton R&C 203 E1
Wilton ScBord 227 F4
Wilton Wilts 119 D1
Wilton Wilts 118 B4
Wilton House Wilts SP2 0BJ 118 B4
Wiltown 103 E1
Wimbish 151 D4
Wimbish Green 151 E4
Wimblebury 158 C1
Wimbledon 136 B5
Wimbledon All England Lawn Tennis & Croquet Club GtLon SW19 5AG 11 E7
Wimblington 162 C3
Wimborne Minster 105 G2
Wimborne Minster Dorset BH21 1HT 3 B2
Wimborne St. Giles 105 G1
Wimbotsham 163 E2
Wimpole 150 B2
Wimpole Home Farm Cambs SG8 0BW 150 B3
Wimpole Lodge 150 B3
Wimpstone 147 E3
Wincanton 117 E5
Winceby 176 B1
Wincham 184 A5
Winchburgh 235 E2
Winchcombe 146 C5
Winchelsea 111 E2
Winchelsea Beach 111 E2
Winchester 119 F5
Winchester Cathedral Hants SO23 9LS 89 Winchester
Winchet Hill 123 G4
Winchfield 120 C2
Winchmore Hill Bucks 135 E3
Winchmore Hill GtLon 136 C3
Wincle 171 G1
Wincobank 186 A3
Windermere 199 F3
Windermere Lake Cruises Cumb LA12 8AS 199 E3
Winderton 147 F3
Windhill 266 C7
Windle Hill 183 E5
Windlehurst 185 D4
Windlesham 121 E1
Windley 173 E3
Windmill 185 F5
Windmill Hill ESuss 110 B2
Windmill Hill Som 103 G1
Windmill Hill Worcs 146 B3
Windmill Hill (Stonehenge, Avebury & Associated Sites) Wilts SN4 9NW 132 C5
Windrush 133 D1
Windsor 135 E5
Windsor Castle W&M SL4 1NJ 89 Windsor
Windsor Green 151 G2
Windy Gap 282 D5
Windy Nook 212 B1
Windygates 244 B4
Windy-Yett 233 F4
Wineham 109 E1
Winestead 197 E5
Winewall 193 F4
Winfarthing 164 C3
Winford IoW 107 E4
Winford NSom 116 C1
Winforton 144 B3
Winfrith Newburgh 105 E4
Wing Bucks 149 D5
Wing Rut 161 D2
Wingate 212 C4
Wingates GtMan 184 A2
Wingates N'umb 220 C2
Wingerworth 173 E1
Wingfield CenBeds 149 F5
Wingfield Suff 164 D4
Wingfield Wilts 117 F2
Wingfield Green 164 D4
Wingham 125 E3
Wingham Well 125 E3
Wingmore 125 D4
Wingrave 135 D1
Winkburn 174 C2
Winkfield 135 E5
Winkfield Row 135 D5
Winkhill 172 B2
Winkleigh 113 G5
Winksley 202 B5
Winkton 106 A3
Winlaton 212 A1
Winlaton Mill 212 A1
Winless 275 J3
Winmarleigh 192 A3
Winnard's Perch 96 D3
Winnersh 134 C5
Winnington 184 A5
Winscombe 116 B2
Winsford ChesW&C 171 D1
Winsford Som 114 C4
Winsham Devon 113 E2
Winsham Som 103 G2
Winshill 173 D5
Winsh-wen 128 C3
Winskill 210 B4
Winslade 120 B3
Winsley 117 F1
Winslow 148 C5
Winson 132 C2
Winsor 106 C1
Winster Cumb 199 F3
Winster Derbys 172 D1
Winston Dur 202 A1
Winston Suff 152 C1
Winston Green 152 C1
Winstone 132 B2
Winswell 113 E4
Winter Gardens FY1 1HW 64 Blackpool
Winter Gardens NSom BS23 1AJ 88 Weston-super-Mare
Winterborne Came 104 D4
Winterborne Clenston 105 E2
Winterborne Herrington 104 C4
Winterborne Houghton 105 E2
Winterborne Kingston 105 E3
Winterborne Monkton 104 C4
Winterborne Stickland 105 E2
Winterborne Whitechurch 105 E2
Winterborne Zelston 105 E3
Winterbourne SGlos 131 F4
Winterbourne WBerks 133 G5
Winterbourne Abbas 104 C3
Winterbourne Bassett 132 D5
Winterbourne Dauntsey 118 C4
Winterbourne Earls 118 C4
Winterbourne Gunner 118 C4
Winterbourne Monkton 132 D5
Winterbourne Steepleton 104 C4
Winterbourne Stoke 118 B3
Winterbrook 134 B4
Winterburn 193 F2
Wintercleugh 226 A4
Winteringham 196 B5
Winterley 171 E2
Wintersett 186 A1
Wintershill 107 E1
Winterslow 118 D4
Winterton 187 G1
Winterton-on-Sea 179 F4
Winthorpe Lincs 177 D1
Winthorpe Notts 174 D2
Winton Bourne 105 G3
Winton Cumb 200 C1
Wintringham 204 B5
Winwick Cambs 161 G4
Winwick N'hants 160 B5
Winwick Warr 184 A3
Wirksworth 173 D2
Wirksworth Moor 173 E2
Wirral Country Park Mersey CH61 0HN 182 D4
Wirswall 170 C3
Wisbech 162 C2
Wisbech St. Mary 162 C2
Wisborough Green 121 F5
Wiseton 187 E4
Wishaw NLan 234 B4
Wishaw Warks 159 D3
Wisley 121 F2
Wispington 188 C5
Wissett 165 E4
Wissington 152 A4
Wistanstow 156 D4
Wistanswick 171 D5
Wistaston 171 D2
Wiston Pembs 126 D1
Wiston SLan 226 A2
Wiston WSuss 108 D2
Wistow Cambs 162 A4
Wistow NYorks 195 E4
Wiswell 192 D4
Witcham 162 C5
Witchampton 105 F2
Witchburn 222 C3
Witchford 162 D5
Witcombe 116 B5
Witham 138 B1
Witham Friary 117 E3
Witham on the Hill 161 F1
Withcall 188 C4
Withcote 160 C2
Withdean 109 F3
Witherenden Hill 110 B1
Witherhurst 110 B1
Witheridge 102 B1
Witherley 159 F3
Withern 189 E4
Withernsea 197 F5
Withernwick 197 D3
Withersdale Street 165 D3
Withersfield 151 E3
Witherslack 199 F4
Witherslack Hall 199 F4
Withiel 97 D3
Withiel Florey 114 C4
Withielgoose 97 E3
Withington Glos 132 C1
Withington GtMan 184 C3
Withington Here 145 E3
Withington Shrop 157 E1
Withington Staffs 172 B4
Withington Green 184 C5
Withington Marsh 145 E3
Withleigh 102 C1
Withnell 192 C5
Withnell Fold 192 C5
Withybrook Som 117 D3
Withybrook Warks 159 G4
Withycombe 114 D3
Withycombe Raleigh 102 D4
Withyham 123 D5
Withypool 114 B4
Witley 121 E4
Witnesham 152 C2
Witney 133 F2
Wittering 161 F2
Wittersham 111 D1
Witton Angus 253 D2
Witton Norf 179 E5
Witton Worcs 146 A1
Witton Bridge 179 E2
Witton Gilbert 212 B3
Witton Park 212 A4
Witton-le-Wear 212 A4
Wiveliscombe 115 D5
Wivelsfield 109 F1
Wivelsfield Green 109 F2
Wivenhoe 152 B5
Wiveton 178 B1
Wix 152 C5
Wixford 146 C2
Wixhill 170 C5
Wixoe 151 F3
Woburn 149 E4
Woburn Safari Park CenBeds MK17 9QN 9 F3
Woburn Sands 149 E4
Wokefield Park 120 B1
Woking 121 F2
Wokingham 120 D1
Wolborough 102 B5
Wold Newton ERid 204 D5
Wold Newton NELincs 188 C3
Woldingham 122 C3
Wolds Village, Bainton ERid YO25 9EF 196 B2
Wolfelee 227 G5
Wolferlow 145 F1
Wolferton 177 E5
Wolfhampcote 148 A1
Wolfhill 243 G1
Wolfpits 144 B2
Wolf's Castle 140 C5
Wolfsdale 140 C5
Woll 227 F3
Wollaston N'hants 149 E1
Wollaston Shrop 156 C1
Wollaston WMid 158 A4
Wollaton 173 G4
Wollerton 170 D5
Wollescote 158 B4
Wolsingham 211 G4
Wolston 159 G5
Wolsty 209 E1
Wolvercote 134 A2
Wolverhampton 158 B3
Wolverhampton Art Gallery WMid WV1 1DU 14 A1
Wolverley Shrop 170 B4
Wolverley Worcs 158 A5
Wolvers Hill 116 A1
Wolverton Hants 119 G2
Wolverton MK 148 D3
Wolverton Warks 147 E1
Wolverton Wilts 117 E4
Wolverton Common 119 G2
Wolvesnewton 131 D3
Wolvey 159 G4
Wolvey Heath 159 G4
Wolviston 213 D5
Womaston 144 B1
Wombleton 203 F4
Wombourne 158 A3
Wombwell 186 A2
Womenswold 125 E3
Womersley 186 C1
Wonastow 131 D1
Wonersh 121 F3
Wonford 102 C3
Wonson 99 G2
Wonston 119 F4
Wooburn 135 E4
Wooburn Green 135 E4
Wood Bevington 146 C2
Wood Burcote 148 B3
Wood Dalling 178 B3
Wood Eaton 158 A1
Wood End Bed 149 F3
Wood End Bed 149 F1
Wood End Bucks 148 C4
Wood End Herts 150 B5
Wood End Warks 159 E3
Wood End Warks 158 D5
Wood End Warks 159 E4
Wood End WMid 158 B2
Wood Enderby 176 A1
Wood Green GtLon 136 C3
Wood Green Norf 164 D2
Wood Green Animal Shelter, Godmanchester Cambs PE29 2NH 150 A1
Wood Lane 170 B4
Wood Norton 178 B3
Wood Seats 186 A3
Wood Stanway 146 C4
Wood Street 179 E3
Wood Street Village 121 E2
Woodacott 113 D5
Woodale 201 F5
Woodall 186 B4
Woodbastwick 179 E4
Woodbeck 187 E5
Woodborough Notts 174 B3
Woodborough Wilts 118 C2
Woodbridge Devon 103 E3
Woodbridge Dorset 104 D1
Woodbridge Suff 153 D3
Woodburn 287 H7
Woodbury Devon 102 D4
Woodbury Som 116 C3
Woodbury Salterton 102 D4
Woodchester 132 A2
Woodchurch Kent 124 B5
Woodchurch Mersey 183 D4
Woodcombe 114 C3
Woodcote Oxon 134 B4
Woodcote Tel&W 157 G1
Woodcote Green 158 B5
Woodcott 119 F2
Woodcroft 131 E3
Woodcutts 105 F1
Woodditton 151 E2
Woodeaton 134 A1
Woodend Aber 260 E3
Woodend Cumb 198 C3
Woodend High 258 E2
Woodend High 247 G3
Woodend N'hants 148 B3
Woodend P&K 250 C5
Woodend WSuss 108 A3
Woodend Green 151 D5
Woodfalls 118 C5
Woodfield Oxon 148 A5
Woodfield SAyr 224 B3
Woodfoot 200 B1
Woodford Corn 112 C4
Woodford Devon 101 D2
Woodford Glos 131 F3
Woodford GtLon 136 D3
Woodford GtMan 184 C4
Woodford N'hants 161 E5
Woodford Som 115 D4
Woodford Bridge 136 D3
Woodford Green 136 D3
Woodford Halse 148 A2
Woodgate Devon 103 E1
Woodgate Norf 178 B4
Woodgate WMid 158 B4
Woodgate Worcs 146 B1
Woodgate WSuss 108 B3
Woodgreen 106 A1
Woodhall Invcly 233 E2
Woodhall NYorks 201 E3
Woodhall Hills 194 A4
Woodhall Spa 175 G1
Woodham Bucks 134 B1
Woodham Dur 212 B5
Woodham Surr 121 F1
Woodham Ferrers 137 G3
Woodham Mortimer 138 B2
Woodham Walter 138 B2
Woodhaven 244 C2
Woodhead Aber 261 F1
Woodhead Staffs 172 B3
Woodhenge (Stonehenge, Avebury & Associated Sites) Wilts SP4 7AR 118 C3
Woodhey 183 E4
Woodhey Green 170 C2
Woodhill Shrop 157 G4
Woodhill Som 116 A5
Woodhorn 221 E3
Woodhouse Cumb 199 G4
Woodhouse Leics 160 A1
Woodhouse SYorks 186 B4
Woodhouse WYorks 194 B4
Woodhouse WYorks 194 C5
Woodhouse WYorks 194 A5
Woodhouse Down 131 F4
Woodhouse Eaves 160 A1
Woodhouse Green 171 G1
Woodhouses GtMan 184 C2
Woodhouses Staffs 159 D1
Woodhouses Staffs 158 C2
Woodhuish 101 F2
Woodhurst 162 B5
Woodingdean 109 F3
Woodington 119 E5
Woodland Devon 101 D1
Woodland Dur 211 G5
Woodland Kent 124 D4
Woodland Head 102 A3
Woodlands Dorset 105 G2
Woodlands Hants 106 C1
Woodlands NYorks 194 C2
Woodlands Shrop 157 G4
Woodlands Som 115 E3
Woodlands Leisure Park, Dartmouth Devon TQ9 7DQ 101 E2
Woodlands Park 135 D5
Woodlands St. Mary 133 F5
Woodlane 172 C5
Woodleigh 100 D3
Woodlesford 194 C5
Woodley GtMan 184 D3
Woodley W'ham 134 C5
Woodmancote Glos 132 C2
Woodmancote Glos 146 B5
Woodmancote Glos 131 G3
Woodmancote WSuss 109 E2
Woodmancote WSuss 107 G2
Woodmancott 119 G3
Woodmansey 196 C4
Woodmansterne 122 B3
Woodmanton 102 D4
Woodmill 172 C5
Woodminton 118 B5
Woodmoor 156 B2
Woodnesborough 125 F3
Woodnewton 161 F3
Woodperry 134 A1
Woodplumpton 192 B4
Woodrising 178 A5
Woodrow 105 D1
Wood's Corner 110 B2
Woods Eaves 144 B3
Wood's Green 123 F5
Woodseaves Shrop 171 D4
Woodseaves Staffs 171 E5
Woodsend 133 E5
Woodsetts 186 C4
Woodsford 105 D3
Woodside Aberdeen 261 H4
Woodside BrackF 135 E5
Woodside CenBeds 135 F1
Woodside Cumb 208 D3
Woodside D&G 217 E3
Woodside Fife 244 C4
Woodside Fife 244 A4
Woodside GtLon 122 C2
Woodside Hants 106 C3
Woodside Herts 136 B2
Woodside NAyr 233 E4
Woodside P&K 243 G1
Woodside Shrop 156 C4
Woodside WMid 158 B4
Woodside Animal Farm & Leisure Park CenBeds LU1 4DG 135 F1
Woodside Green 124 B3
Woodstock Oxon 133 G1
Woodstock Pembs 140 D5
Woodthorpe Derbys 186 B5
Woodthorpe Leics 160 A1
Woodthorpe Lincs 189 E4
Woodthorpe SYorks 186 A4
Woodthorpe York 195 E3
Woodton 165 D2
Woodtown 113 E3
Woodvale 183 E1
Woodville 159 F1
Woodwall Green 171 E4
Woodwalton 162 A4
Woodwick 276 C5
Woodworth Green 170 C2
Woodyates 105 G1
Woofferton 145 E1
Wookey 116 C3
Wookey Hole 116 C3
Wookey Hole Caves & Papermill Som BA5 1BB 116 C3
Wool 105 E4
Woolacombe 113 E1
Woolage Green 125 E4
Woolage Village 125 E3
Woolaston 131 E2
Woolaston Slade 131 E2
Woolavington 116 A3
Woolbeding 121 D5
Woolcotts 114 C4
Wooldale 185 F2
Wooler 229 D4
Woolfardisworthy Devon 102 B2
Woolfardisworthy Devon 112 D3
Woolfold 184 B1
Woolfords Cottages 235 E4
Woolgarston 105 F4
Woolgreaves 186 A1
Woolhampton 119 G1
Woolhope 145 F4
Woolland 105 D2
Woollard 116 D1
Woollaton 113 E4
Woollensbrook 136 C2
Woolley B&NESom 117 E1
Woolley Cambs 161 G5
Woolley Corn 112 C4
Woolley Derbys 173 E1
Woolley WYorks 186 A1
Woolley Green W&M 135 D5
Woolley Green Wilts 117 F1
Woolmer Green 136 B1
Woolmere Green 146 B1